The Advertising Age

Encyclopedia of Advertising

THE **AdvertisingAge**

Encyclopedia of Advertising

VOLUME 2

F–O

Editors
JOHN MCDONOUGH AND THE MUSEUM OF
BROADCAST COMMUNICATIONS

KAREN EGOLF, ADVERTISING AGE

Illustration Editor
JACQUELINE V. REID
HARTMAN CENTER FOR SALES, ADVERTISING, AND
MARKETING HISTORY OF DUKE UNIVERSITY

FITZROY DEARBORN
An Imprint of the Taylor & Francis Group
New York · London

Published in 2003 by
Fitzroy Dearborn
An imprint of the Taylor and Francis Group
29 West 35th Street
New York, NY 10001

Published in Great Britain by
Fitzroy Dearborn
An imprint of the Taylor and Francis Group
11 New Fetter Lane
London EC4P 4EE

10   9   8   7   6   5   4   3   2   1

British Library and Library of Congress Cataloguing-in-Publication Data are available.

ISBN 1-57958-172-2

First published in the USA and UK 2003

Typeset by Andrea Rosenberg
Printed by Edwards Brothers, Ann Arbor, Michigan
Cover design by Peter Aristedes, Chicago Advertising and Design, Chicago, Illinois

Front cover illustrations: *Maidenform,* courtesy of Maidenform, Inc., all rights reserved. *Ford Motor Company,* courtesy of Ford Motor Company. *Pepsi-Cola,* courtesy of the Pepsi-Cola Company. *Uneeda Biscuit,* courtesy of Kraft Foods Holdings, Inc. *Motorola,* courtesy of Motorola Archives © 2000 Motorola, Inc. *Nokia;* NOKIA and "8890" are registered trademarks of NOKIA Corporation or its affiliates; © 2000 NOKIA Mobile Phones, Inc.; all rights reserved. *C.F. Hathaway Shirt Company,* courtesy of Hathaway, Waterville, Maine. *War Production Coordinating Committee* (Rosie the Riveter). *Breck Shampoo,* courtesy of The Dial Corporation and Cybill Shepherd. *A&P,* courtesy of The Great Atlantic & Pacific Tea Company, Inc.

Back cover illustrations: *U.S. Forest Service* (Smokey Bear). *Rowlands' Macassar Oil. WorkRite* radio sets. *French parasol ad,* ca. 1715. *Mendoza Fur Dyeing Works, Inc. Firestone Tires,* courtesy of Bridgestone/Firestone, Inc. *Ohrbach's. The Pullman Company.*

CONTENTS

LIST OF ENTRIES

F

Fallon Worldwide

(Fallon McElligott)

Founded in Minneapolis, Minnesota, as Fallon McElligott Rice by Patrick Fallon, Tom McElligott, Nancy Rice, Fred Senn, and Irv Fish, 1981; acquired by Scali, McCabe, Sloves, 1986; repurchased by employees of Fallon McElligott, 1993; opened first branch office, Fallon McElligott Berlin, with partner Andy Berlin in New York City, 1995; opened first overseas office in London, England, 1997; purchased by Publicis Group and renamed Fallon Worldwide, 2000.

Major Clients
BMW of North America
Lee Jeans
McDonald's Corporation
Miller Brewing Company
Nordstrom
John Nuveen & Company
Prudential Insurance Company of America
Ralston Purina Company
Rolling Stone magazine
Starbucks Coffee Company
United Air Lines
Wall Street Journal

Fallon McElligott Rice, as it was initially called, was formed when Patrick Fallon and writer Tom McElligott, who had met while freelancing in Minneapolis, Minnesota, asked art director Nancy Rice and two other partners, Fred Senn and Irv Fish, to join them in opening an advertising agency. The principals developed seven core values, beliefs to which the agency still adheres: the power of creativity, the dignity of the individual, "family" as a business model, seeing risk-taking as a friend, success as a business imperative, the importance of remaining humble, and the necessity of having fun. Every morning the computers at Fallon McElligott greet employees with the agency's mission statement:

"To be the premier agency in the world producing extraordinary, effective work for a short list of blue-chip clients."

During its first year, Fallon McElligott Rice captured high-profile advertising awards for work that it created for its small roster of clients, which ranged from a local bait shop to the Episcopal Church of North America. Along with other "renegade" regional shops such as Wieden & Kennedy, Inc., in Portland, Oregon, and the Martin Agency in Richmond, Virginia, Fallon McElligott was one of several shops at the center of a renaissance in advertising creativity in the 1980s. At the same time, it put Minneapolis on the map as a hotbed of innovative advertising.

In 1982 Fallon landed the account of US West, one of the regional telephone companies created by the breakup of AT&T. In 1984, after winning six Clios and six gold medals at the One Show, Fallon was named "Agency of the Year" by *Advertising Age*. Annual billings reached $30.2 million.

In 1984 the agency acquired Duffy Design, headed by artist Joe Duffy, a studio that specializes in corporate identity, logo work, and product and package design. As of 2001 it had offices in Minneapolis, New York City, and London, England, with 690 full-time employees. Duffy Design has completed graphics assignments for such advertisers as BMW, Coca-Cola, Colgate-Palmolive, McDonald's, Nikon, Nordstrom, and the Rainforest Café.

In 1985 Fallon nabbed its first major national account, the venerable and conservative *Wall Street Journal*, surprising established agencies. There were growing pains—that same year founding partner Rice resigned and opened Rice & Rice Advertising with her husband, Nick—but more national accounts, including that of Federal Express, soon followed. Also in 1985 Fallon was hired by *Rolling Stone* to improve the magazine's image and make it attractive to media buyers. By 1985 the agency's billings had grown to $80 million, raising its ranking among U.S. agencies from 165th to 79th, according to *Advertising Age*.

In one of the most acclaimed advertising campaigns of the 1980s, the agency developed the "Perception. Reality." theme, which effectively repositioned *Rolling Stone* as a magazine that was popular not only among ex-hippies but also among "yuppies." One memorable ad showed a Volkswagen van decorated with "flower-power" decals under the "Perception" headline, followed on the next page by a sports car under the headline "Reality." Fallon placed these ads in industry publications such as *Advertising Age, Adweek,* and *Marketing and Media Decisions.* With a relatively small budget (approximately $500,000, including production costs), and the use of only one medium, Fallon altered not only media buyers' perceptions of *Rolling Stone* but also their actual purchasing behavior with respect to the magazine. From 1985 to 1991, advertising pages in the magazine increased 58 percent, and the publication now competes successfully with more traditional male-oriented magazines such as *GQ* and *Esquire.* Advertising revenues increased more than 200 percent over the same period. In addition to winning Clios and gold medals in the One Show, "Perception. Reality." was selected by the board of directors of the One Club as one of the best print campaigns of the 1980s.

By 1986 the agency had grown to 100 employees and $100 million in billings. Such dramatic growth did not go unnoticed. Several large shops soon expressed interest in acquiring the agency. In 1986 the partners sold an 80 percent interest in the agency to Scali, McCabe, Sloves. McElligott observed that because Scali had paid a substantial amount of money for its share in Fallon, he believed the focus of the agency had shifted from generating risk-taking, effective, creative advertising to meeting "bottom line" objectives.

Between 1987 and 1989 Fallon acquired additional blue-chip clients, including Lee Jeans, Porsche, and Timex. Its work for Lee Jeans once again demonstrated Fallon's belief that truly creative advertising begins on the strategic rather than the executional level—that is, all creative tactics must grow logically from a predetermined marketing business plan. After some focused qualitative research, Fallon discovered that women try on an average of 16 pairs of jeans before finding ones that fit. This research, coupled with the fact that women have a more emotional connection with their jeans than men do, led the agency to recommend that Lee position itself more as a brand for women. Under the slogan, "The brand that fits," Fallon created award-winning print ads with such headlines as, "Our jeans solve two major problems. Inhaling and Exhaling." Television commercials soon followed, and Fallon injected its special brand of humor into these executions. One commercial featured a woman taking so long to try on jeans before a blind date that her roommate has time to fall in love with and marry the date. Two years after "The brand that fits" campaign began, Lee's market share had risen 20 percent, while Levi's had dropped 17 percent. As this positioning began to grow stale in the late 1990s, Fallon repositioned Lee as a sexier, hipper choice for women—and placed ads with the new "Cut to be noticed" theme in such publications as *Vogue.*

In 1988 frustrated that, in his view, the agency was watering down its creative efforts to please difficult clients such as Federal Express, McElligott broke his contract with the agency, a move that required him to take a year off from working in advertising.

Although there was speculation about whether Fallon could maintain its edge without McElligott at the creative helm, in 1989 Fallon not only landed the Jim Beam account but also captured 14 Clio awards, the most the agency had ever won in a single year.

According to the agency's official history, Fallon fell into a slump from 1990 to 1991. It lost its bid for the MasterCard account, a failure that it described as the "mother of all wake-up calls." To revitalize itself, the agency made a slew of new hires in 1992, including Bill Westbrook, who became president and creative director. Undoubtedly the single most motivating act the agency performed was its repurchase from Scali by the agency's own employees for $14.6 million ($10 million in cash). Billings were flat at $125 million.

Driven by the need to succeed, Fallon posted a banner year in 1994. It acquired new clients that would have been the envy of any large national agency. These included Coca-Cola, McDonald's, Ameritech, and BMW. Prudential Insurance Company of America followed in 1995 and became the agency's biggest account.

Fallon's history with Prudential encapsulated the agency's new approach to doing business. Simply put, it expected a great deal of latitude in developing and executing advertising for its clients. As Bill Bernbach had done in the 1960s, Fallon all but insisted that its clients follow the creative recommendations made by the agency. Fallon developed a campaign for Prudential that was built around the slogan, "Be your own rock," a derivation of the "Piece of the rock" positioning that had been the mainstay of Prudential's advertising for many years. After Fallon had developed an innovative follow-up campaign, the agency's biggest supporter at Prudential was removed during an executive "housecleaning." Although Fallon lost a great deal of revenue in the short term, the agency chose to resign the account in 1996 rather than allow itself to be transformed from a partner with Prudential to a mere vendor. Patrick Fallon has stated that the decision to resign the Prudential account was one of the most painful of his career, because he was so proud of the work the agency had created for the client.

By 1995 the agency boasted 200 employees and $200 million in billings. That year it opened its first branch office, Fallon McElligott Berlin, with partner Andy Berlin in New York City. The partnership did not work out, however, and Berlin bought out the branch office after two years. Fallon McElligott launched a new branch office in New York (called, simply, Fallon McElligott) in November 1997, which currently handles the advertising for ABC Sports, MTV Networks, Conseco, the Georgia Pacific paper company, and *Time* magazine. Also in 1997 McDonald's awarded Fallon the assignment to create a campaign for the Arch Deluxe, a sandwich positioned to appeal to adults. To stress the fact that the sandwich was designed for sophisticated taste buds, Fallon created a campaign that depicted children literally turning up their noses at the new menu item. The campaign generated controversy in the advertising community. Critics argued that it damaged the brand equity McDonald's had created with children and that depicting the food as undesirable was too risky. While McDonald's was initially pleased with sales of the sandwich, the

Perception.

Reality.

You no longer have to barbeque your underwear to assert your equality. For a new generation of female Rolling Stone readers, it's possible to be a feminist without giving up femininity. If your target market is women 18 to 34, your media plan will catch fire in the pages of Rolling Stone.

Rolling Stone

Fallon McElligott's "Perception. Reality." campaign helped persuade advertisers that *Rolling Stone* magazine had replaced its hippie-era readership with a more sophisticated audience.

campaign was short-lived, and Fallon chose to resign the account in 1997.

In 1996 Fallon and its clients won several awards that demonstrated the success and profitability of its advertising creativity. For instance, the American Marketing Association awarded Ralston Purina, a Fallon client since 1990, the Grand Effie, the highest award for advertising effectiveness. In 1997 both *Advertising Age* and *Adweek* named Fallon "Advertising Agency of the Year." No doubt one of the contributing factors to this honor was United Air Lines' decision to award Fallon its $100 million domestic account. Fallon has admitted that the agency "had no business pitching" the United account, as Fallon had only limited airline experience (a short relationship with Northwest Airlines). Nevertheless, United Air Lines tapped Fallon as its new agency, ending a relationship with the Leo Burnett Company that had lasted more than 30 years. Despite its inexperience in the airline category, Fallon's first campaign for United won an Effie, an award that recognizes not just creativity but also effectiveness. The work for United was also awarded the Media Plan of the Year award (budget of $25 million or more) by *Mediaweek* magazine, because

United registered a 50 percent jump in ad awareness, even as it was outspent by three competitors.

In 1997 Fallon also began its controversial advertising campaign for Miller Lite. The overarching premise was that a fictional genius named "Dick" was responsible for the bizarre ads for the brand. In fact, two Swedish advertising men, Linus Karlsson and Paul Malmstrom, recruited from Stockholm, originated the campaign. Fallon's assignment to revitalize the flagging sales of Miller Lite, which had lost one-third of its market share to Bud Light from 1990 to 1997, was no small task. The agency developed a campaign that included some standard fare for beer commercials, such as women in bikinis and talking animals, but these elements were filtered through "Dick's" bizarre perspective on life. For instance, one commercial featured a man who steps onto a road clothed only from the waist up, with a Miller Lite cap covering his bottom. In another, a woman discovers true love with an aluminum robot, and in yet another spot a giant beaver pursues a group of people in the woods. Within two years, more than 50 versions of the "Dick" campaign had been created, with many people at the agency contributing ideas, and while the ads prompted criticism and controversy in the advertising trade press, many Hollywood directors were eager to be involved in the series. Although reviews of the campaign were mixed, the work enabled Fallon to practice its belief in "brand stewardship," or the nurturing of a personality and image for a brand over time. In 1999, however, Miller dismissed Fallon and reassigned Lite to Ogilvy & Mather Wordlwide.

By 1998 Fallon had grown to $500 million in billings and more than 500 employees. Four highly visible new clients—Nordstrom, Qualcomm, John Nuveen & Company, and Starbucks Coffee Company—were added to the roster. Fallon's new interactive company, Revolv, won the most awards in the interactive design competition sponsored by the One Show. Moreover, Fallon's first international office opened in London, with Lee Jeans Europe and BBC's Radio 1 in hand.

The awards that Fallon has captured include a Grand AME for Most Effective Campaign Worldwide, three gold Lions at the Cannes (France) International Advertising Festival, 20 Clio awards in 1998, and 23 awards in the *Print Regional Design* annual of that year. Fallon's work has also received commendation in the British Design and Art Direction annual and the American Institute of Graphic Artists annual. In 1996 Fallon also received the Ogilvy award for most effective use of research.

In February 2000 Fallon (renamed Fallon Worldwide) was acquired by the Publicis Group. The agency had worldwide gross income in 2000 of $99.6 million, up 10.5 percent from its 1999 gross. It operated three domestic offices (Minneapolis, New York City, and Los Angeles, California) and one European office (London), as well as subsidiaries Duffy Design and Fallon Interactive. In *Advertising Age*'s 2000 list of U.S. agency brands ranked by gross income, Fallon was 30th (U.S. gross income of $93.1 million, up 7.6 percent from 1999, on U.S. billings of $965.6 million).

Fallon has been candid about its belief that its creatively driven approach to advertising is not for everyone. The agency's loyalty to its own creative output, and its unwillingness to water down its executions, have contributed to its decision to resign major accounts and, possibly, to its inability to secure others. Nonetheless, Fallon has, in its short life, helped many clients achieve spectacular successes in the marketplace.

CELE C. OTNES

See also color plate in this volume

Further Reading

Advertising's Ten Best of the Decade, 1980–1990, New York: One Club for Art and Copy, 1990

Arndorfer, James B., "Miller Freshens Creative for Lite, Genuine Draft," *Advertising Age* (6 April 1998)

Hume, Scott, "Y&R, Fallon Split United Account," *Adweek* (Eastern Edition) (21 October 1996)

Ind, Nicholas, *Great Advertising Campaigns*, Lincolnwood, Illinois: NTC Business Books, and London: Kogan Page, 1993

Martin, Ellen Rooney, "National Agency of the Year: Fallon McElligott," *Adweek* (Eastern Edition) (7 April 1997)

Melcher, Richard A., "Hot Shop in the Heartland," *Business Week* (13 January 1997)

Minsky, Laurence, and Emily Thornton Calvo, *How to Succeed in Advertising When All You Have Is Talent*, Lincolnwood, Illinois: NTC Business Books, 1994, 2nd edition, 1997

"1996 Media All-Stars," *Adweek* (9 December 1996)

Parpis, Eleftheria, "Of Beer and Brain Candy," *Adweek* (Eastern Edition) (16 March 1998)

Sellers, Patricia, "Leo Burnett: Undone by an Upstart," *Fortune* 135, no. 10 (May 1997)

Fashion and Apparel

Perhaps no segment in advertising more closely reflects the social trends of its time than apparel advertising. Whether encouraging women to don pants or helping men to decipher dress codes for "casual Friday," apparel ads almost immediately echo changes in social mores and attitudes.

The connection between fashion advertising and social history stems from fashion's function. Fashion advertising creates an image and a mood for a brand, whether it represents all-American style (Tommy Hilfiger) or spare sexuality (Calvin Klein). It seeks to connect with the personality of the consumer or the image the consumer wants to project to the world.

Apparel advertising and promotion rely strongly on retailer feedback and cooperation. Most fashion marketers run co-op ads—that is, they share the cost of the advertising with the retailers that carry their products in exchange for a retailer presence in the ad. They also sponsor various events and promotions and use point-of-purchase materials to lure the consumer to their products once inside the store.

In-store shops—apparel companies' best promotional tool at point of purchase—often feature trunk shows (for designer labels) or fashion videos (common among both designer and lower-priced lines). In the 1990s, as both department store sales and the influence of large retailers declined, co-op spending and the size of in-store shops became bones of contention between retailers and suppliers.

The advent of shop-at-home channels, such as QVC in the 1980s, made possible direct-response television marketing of fashion items. Designer Diane Von Furstenberg was one of the first clothiers to go on the air, selling a selection of her wrap dresses on QVC in 1992. The Internet added yet another dimension to the

My friend, Joe Holmes, is now a horse

JOE always said when he died he'd like to become a horse.

One day Joe died.

Early this May I saw a horse that looked like Joe drawing a milk wagon.

I sneaked up to him and whispered, "Is it you, Joe?"

He said, "Yes, and am I happy!" I said, "Why?"

He said, "I am now wearing a comfortable collar for the first time in my life. My shirt collars always used to shrink and murder me. In fact, one choked me to death. That is why I died!"

"Goodness, Joe," I exclaimed, "Why didn't you tell me about your shirts sooner? I would have told you about Arrow shirts. *They never shrink*. Not even the oxfords."

"G'wan," said Joe. "Oxford's the worst shrinker of all!"

"Maybe," I replied, "but not *Gordon*, the Arrow oxford. I know. I'm wearing one. It's Sanforized-shrink-proof. Besides, it's cool. Besides, this creamy shade I chose is the newest shirt color, *bamboo*."

"Swell," said Joe. "My boss needs a shirt like that. I'll tell him about Gordon. Maybe he'll give me an extra quart of oats. And, gosh, do I love oats!"

If it hasn't an Arrow Label it isn't an Arrow Shirt

ARROW SHIRTS
Sanforized Shrunk — a new shirt free if one ever shrinks
Made by CLUETT, PEABODY & CO., INC.

A 1938 Arrow advertisement is representative of the campaign famous for its creative use of humor to emphasize the unique features of the garment maker's shirts.
Cluett, Peabody & Co., Inc.

channel conflict between clothing companies and retailers. Most companies now have Web sites that can be merely an on-line version of the line's "look book"—the catalog of its styles and items for a particular season—or a full-fledged on-line shop and community with content aimed at the target audience for the brand.

A Look Back

While tailors and dressmakers have plied their trade for centuries, the modern apparel industry—and its advertising—did not begin to develop until the late 19th century. The invention of the sewing machine in 1845 made possible the creation of an apparel industry, as machine-produced clothes began to replace homemade items in consumers' wardrobes. Early ready-to-wear apparel was aimed at low-income consumers who could not afford to hire dressmakers. It was advertised mainly with store signs and "trade cards," featuring pictures and the shop's address. It was not until the turn of the 20th century that the term "store-bought clothes" lost some of its derogatory connotation.

It was shortly after the debut of the sewing machine that the California gold rush of 1848 led to the creation of what at the start of the 21st century was the largest apparel advertising account in the United States, Levi Strauss & Company. The company's namesake founder arrived in California, along with a supply of fabrics, to sew tents for miners but found a better use for the material making work pants. In the 1920s, responding to complaints that the rivets in its jeans scratched furniture, Levi's engaged in its first brand advertising, promoting covered rivets. In 1930 it hired San Francisco, California, ad agency Leon Livingston, which became Honig-Cooper after World War II and would later be acquired by Foote, Cone & Belding. The 67-year pairing—one of the longest in the industry—produced ads that vowed jeans "go on" or sang the "501 blues" until the jeans account moved in 1998 to TBWA/Chiat/Day, of Playa del Rey, California.

Helping the fledgling apparel industry, retailers first pushed mass-produced clothing onto racks and into newspaper ads, with big-city department stores leading the way. John Wanamaker, a Philadelphia, Pennsylvania, dry-goods merchant, brought about many early innovations in retail and apparel advertising while promoting his department store. Wanamaker's was the first major retailer to place page ads and the first to hire a full-time copywriter.

While Wanamaker refused to advertise on Sundays, based on his religious beliefs, he pioneered concepts such as fixed prices and money-back guarantees. He promoted those innovations in ads that departed from the simple agate type traditionally used for newspaper ads of the time. In 1879 his store ran the first front-page ad, delivering daily messages about the store in story form with drawings illustrating its wares. In 1890 Wanamaker hired John E. Powers as the first full-time department store copywriter to direct his advertising efforts. Powers enforced Wanamaker's marketing philosophy and brought a new style to advertising. Wanamaker's, which began as a men's clothing shop, later expanded into women's and children's apparel. Wanamaker was the first merchant to put his label on clothing and advertise the better service and higher quality of his apparel stores. His ads were narratives weaving in clothing features and styles, an ancestor of 21st century retailers such as the J. Peterman Company.

While women have come to be considered the main targets for apparel advertising, it was men's shoes and clothing brands that first broke ground in the segment. New England shoemaker William L. Douglas, billed as "The Three-Dollar Shoe Man," was the first to advertise a small line of mass-produced men's shoes in the late 1800s. His Brockton, Massachusetts, factory began its newspaper advertising with a $10,000 ad account with Boston, Massachusetts, agency S.R. Niles. The account, which concentrated on newspaper ads in rural weeklies to boost mail-order sales, grew to $175,000 in annual spending by 1894.

Another footwear company, Red Cross Shoes, was partly responsible for the development of marketing research. Stanley Resor, then president of the J. Walter Thompson Company, sought to figure out national retail distribution patterns for his client to help manage the account. He commissioned a study that listed retailers by state and by category, a structure that became the basis of modern market research.

Some menswear advertisers from the turn of the last century remain today. Hart, Schaffner & Marx, later known as Hartmarx, began national advertising in 1890, and Joseph & Feiss, later owned by Phillips-Van Heusen, launched ads in 1901 to promote what it called "clothescraft clothes" and told retailers the ads would drive customers to their stores—a predecessor of today's retail co-op ads.

Arrow Shirts pioneered the use of humor in advertising in 1932 with a series of ads from Young & Rubicam (Y&R). Each ad used a humorous anecdote to tout a different shirt feature. The best-known execution used reincarnation as the setup to promote Arrow's shrink-proof shirts. "My friend, Joe Holmes, is now a horse," a narrator said. A horse pulling a milk wagon happily agreed: "I am now wearing a comfortable collar for the first time in my life."

World War II presented an opportunity for U.S. designers and apparel brands. With Parisian fashions out of the reach of U.S. consumers in wartime, Lord & Taylor President Dorothy Shaver led U.S. retailers by being the first to promote clothing by U.S. designers and feature their names in advertising. This broke the French monopoly on fashion and led to the rise of a generation of U.S. designers such as Geoffrey Beene, Bill Blass, and Halston.

Icons and Images

In the first half of the century, apparel advertising was mostly practical and utilitarian, focusing on product benefits. Even Arrow's whimsical campaign mainly touted the shrink-proof fabric of its shirts. With the arrival of television and new photographic technologies, advertising became more visual and image-oriented. Photography replaced illustration, and models and celebrities began their rise to fashion icon status.

In the years after the war, legendary advertising man David Ogilvy established his agency—then known as Hewitt, Ogilvy, Benson and Mather, Inc.—and himself as innovators with an unusual image campaign, "The man in the Hathaway shirt." The idea grew out of Ogilvy's memory of one of his schoolmasters. Inspired by images of Ernest Hemingway and William Faulkner, the ads featured an urbane, eyepatch-wearing gentleman—nicknamed "The Baron"—engaged in thoroughly upper-crust pursuits. The campaign first appeared in 1951 in *The New Yorker* and ran four years, during which the Hathaway Man hunted big game, conducted orchestras, and painted pictures. For more than 30 years, the baron remained the icon of the Hathaway brand, and the campaign is hailed as a milestone in "aspirational" image advertising.

Image was everything in the 1960s, when the Great Lakes Mink Association (GLMA) hired Trahey Advertising to create a campaign to sell its extra-dark mink furs. Agency President Jane Trahey, one of the first women to run her own agency, took the group's acronym and created the glitzy Blackglama brand. Trahey and Vice President–Marketing Director Peter Rogers created the tag line, "What becomes a legend most?" Through her own personal contacts, Trahey enlisted stars such as Bette Davis, Carol Channing, Barbra Streisand, and Lauren Bacall. The celebrities were photographed by Richard Avedon; their only compensation for appearing in the campaign was the photo and a fur coat. The spare ads themselves each featured only three elements: a photo, the "What becomes a legend . . ." tag line, and the Blackglama name. The personalities pictured were considered so legendary that identifying them was unnecessary. The campaign broke in 1968 and ran for almost three decades. Rogers continued the campaign after Trahey exited the agency business in the 1970s at his own agency, Peter Rogers Group. It marked a significant milestone in celebrity advertising (a trend that would return with a vengeance in the 1990s). Broadway performer Tommy Tune appeared in the last ad of the campaign, which ran in 1996.

Fashion as Lifestyle

The 1980s saw the rise of the star designer and fashion-as-lifestyle marketing best represented by American designers such as Ralph Lauren, Calvin Klein, and Tommy Hilfiger. Lifestyles and image were to become the hallmarks of Ralph Lauren, who began his rise in the 1970s with a collection of ties made from upholstery fabrics. His company, Polo Ralph Lauren, pioneered the concept of the "lifestyle brand" in fashion, creating an all-over image, from clothing and fragrance to housewares. In the 1980s Wells, Rich, Greene, Inc., and Kurtz & Tarlow (later Tarlow Advertising) created ads that made the Polo brand synonymous with an upscale, preppy elegance perfectly in tune with the ethos of the times.

The designer-jeans craze of the late 1970s was a prime example of the power of advertising to turn a utilitarian commodity such as blue jeans into a fashion statement by branding it as such. While apparel companies had previously relied on retailers to push product on their shoppers, advertisers now pulled customers into the stores with large campaigns and spot TV ads. Two campaigns were icons of the era: the 1978 Jordache Jeans effort and Calvin Klein's 1980 jeans ads featuring Brooke Shields.

Jordache spent most of its $250,000 ad budget in 1978 on TV buys to air its "Jordache Look" spot. The commercial, with its catchy "You've got the look" jingle, projected a fun, sexy, fashionable image that took Jordache from an unknown quantity to a brand with $130 million in sales and a $9 million advertising budget by 1980. The spot proved to be such a cultural artifact that when Jordache decided to capitalize on the return of 1980s retro fashions in 2000, it went right back to the original ad. The spot, created in-house by Howard Goldstein, aired in October 2000 to relaunch the Jordache Jeans line.

But it was Calvin Klein who pushed apparel advertising to its limits—or, in the opinion of some, beyond. His 1980 campaign featured a teenage Brooke Shields suggestively asking the camera, "Want to know what comes between me and my Calvins? Nothing." It was only the first of many efforts from the designer to be condemned as exploitative, but it made both Shields and Calvin Klein Jeans household words.

Nearly every Calvin Klein campaign since 1980 has raised hackles among media watchdogs. His in-house agency, CRK Advertising, which handled the Brooke Shields effort, was forced to pull a 1995 jeans campaign after complaints that the TV ads too closely resembled outtakes from pornographic films. CRK was forced to cancel a 1999 spring campaign to promote the launch of a line of children's underwear after children's rights groups condemned photographer Mario Testino's black-and-white photographs of scantily attired boys as "kiddie porn." A billboard in New York City's Times Square was taken down the day it was due to be unveiled, and planned print ads and TV spots were canceled.

Not all lifestyle advertising to emerge from the 1980s, however, was suggestive or status driven. Marketers such as Kenneth Cole Productions and United Colors of Benetton made often-controversial social statements with their advertising—at a cost. Cole's print and outdoor ads, created largely in-house, have taken stands on divisive issues such as gun control, abortion rights, and domestic violence. In 1985 Cole was one of the first designers to draw attention to AIDS with an ad that featured a shoelace in the shape of an AIDS-awareness lapel ribbon. On a lighter note, a 1986 ad following the fall of Philippine President Ferdinand Marcos poked fun at his wife's acquisitive ways: "Imelda Marcos bought 2,700 pairs of shoes. She could've at least had the courtesy to buy a pair of ours," the copy read.

Benetton also started with humor, but its socially conscious advertising took a turn in the late 1990s that would end in lawsuits and retailer discord. In 1972 Benetton, then a small Italian company selling colorful knits to the youth market, hired Milan shop Eldorado to create a poster campaign. Ten years later, Benetton began working with a photographer from Eldorado, Oliviero Toscani, who later became Benetton's creative director.

Under Toscani's watch, Benetton's advertising during the 1980s increasingly evolved from shots of racially diverse models into issue-oriented messages. By the 1990s Benetton's advertising had become even more controversial and often did not feature any of the company's products, focusing instead on shocking images such as a priest kissing a nun or a black woman breast-feeding a white

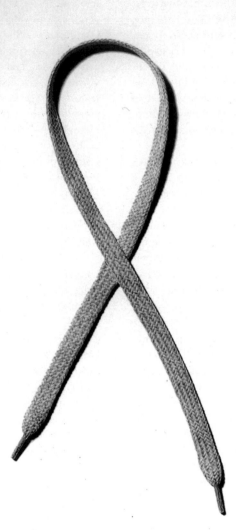

"AIDS can't be fought on a shoestring budget."
-Kenneth Cole

On December 1, World AIDS Day, 40% of all purchases at Kenneth Cole Stores will be donated to
AmFAR, (The American Foundation for AIDS Research). For a store location call 1-800-KEN COLE

NEW YORK   AMSTERDAM   ASPEN   LOS ANGELES   TROY   SAN FRANCISCO   ATLANTA   DALLAS

In the 1980s designer Kenneth Cole was among those using advertising to promote awareness of AIDS.
Courtesy Kenneth Cole Productions.

baby. According to Benetton's Web site, Toscani defended his images, saying, "I am not here to sell pullovers but to promote an image." Company founder Luciano Benetton supported him, arguing, "The purpose of advertising is not to sell more. It's to do with institutional publicity, whose aim is to communicate the company's values."

The ads initially succeeded in raising the brand's profile, but eventually began to cause costly rifts with consumers and retailers. In 1995 Benetton was sued by German retailers, which said the ads sabotaged their sales efforts. Things came to a head in February 2000, when Benetton launched a series of ads featuring death-row prison inmates. Within weeks of the first ads, Benetton was hit by a lawsuit from the state of Missouri, which claimed Toscani and his colleagues lied to state officials to gain access to the inmates. Sears, Roebuck & Company ended a joint venture to sell a private-label line, Benetton USA, after victims' rights groups picketed a Texas Sears store. In May 2000 Toscani stepped down, saying he wished to devote more time to his other projects. Benetton's creative responsibility fell to Fabrica, a creative laboratory he founded in 1994 backed by Benetton.

Reinvention of Retail

In an ironic twist, retail-based advertisers pumped new life into the apparel segment in the 1990s. Even as designers and fashion brands launched their own flagship stores and department stores' influence on fashion trends declined, some large retailers turned to fashion to reinvent themselves. Sears, for example, which had pioneered direct-mail merchandising of fashion products in the late 1800s, turned to TV to promote its "softer side." The 1992 campaign, from Young & Rubicam, focused on the retailer's fashion offerings to refocus an image better known for household appliances.

Some of the more successful apparel brands in the 1990s were retailers in disguise. Companies such as The Gap, Abercrombie & Fitch, and Victoria's Secret succeeded by combining a strong fashion sense with creative branding and savvy merchandising.

The Gap, which had begun in 1969 as a retailer of inexpensive Levi's jeans, reinvented itself in the 1980s as a sportswear shop via advertising. The company branded its wares as quality essentials of fashionable wardrobes with ads that gave T-shirts and

A 1991 Benetton ad featured the kind of controversial image that became synonymous with the brand.
Concept: O Toscani. Courtesy of United Colors of Benetton.

khakis an aura of classic elegance. Its 1988 campaign, "Individuals of Style," featured celebrities such as Arthur Ashe and Miles Davis modeling simple white shirts and turtlenecks, all shot by renowned photographers such as Annie Liebowitz and Herb Ritts. In 1994 Gap revived khaki sales with its "Who wears khakis?" effort that featured art and style icons such as Gene Kelly in vintage shots. Gap's campaigns, created in-house, have continued to break ground, including its popular "Khakis Swing" spot from 1999.

The Gap's parent company took over Banana Republic in 1983 and repositioned it in the early 1990s. Banana Republic went from a retailer of safari-style clothing and travel accessories to a more upscale version of The Gap, with sleek, sophisticated clothes. That positioning was backed with ads that reinforced the classic, fashionable brand image, usually done in-house.

Old Navy, Gap's kid brother launched in 1994, went for a more youthful, playful image in both its products and its advertising. It promoted itself with a series of kitschy ads using celebrities such as Morgan Fairchild, Joan Collins, and the cast of the 1970s sitcom *The Jeffersons* in campy tongue-in-cheek spots that mentioned merchandise such as polar fleece vests or Hawaiian shirts.

Abercrombie & Fitch (A&F) took a slightly different route to fashionable status from outdated preppy retailer. A series of suggestive ads from Shahid & Company featured campus streakers and nude and nearly nude couples, culminating with the spring 2001 campaign, which featured nude men and clothed women. Each successive campaign encountered further opposition, particularly to the content of A&F's catalog. The magazine-style publication was condemned in some markets, and some municipalities banned its sale to minors because of its suggestive content, which in the past included an article on sex tips from a porn star and a list of drinking games. The ads got as much attention as the clothes but succeeded in making the brand popular with teens, who were not put off by their parents' protestations about the ads' content.

The market for retail-based apparel brands is not limited to U.S. companies, however. Sweden's Hennes & Mauritz (H&M), sometimes called "the Ikea of fashion," made a splash in the U.S. market in 2000 with a flagship store on New York City's Fifth Avenue selling cut-price fashion. The opening was backed by a print and outdoor ad campaign in the New York market featuring independent film celebrities such as actress Chloe Sevigny.

H&M was among the latest advertisers to climb on the fashion/celebrity bandwagon. In a return to the "What becomes a legend most?" era, celebrities replaced supermodels on the covers of fashion magazines and in advertising campaigns at the turn of the new century. Actress Gwyneth Paltrow pitched handbags for Christian Dior, and the Rolling Stones appeared in ads for Tommy Hilfiger.

Nor was celebrity marketing limited to designer brands. Mass-market retailers also used star power to improve their apparel sales by launching brands tied to celebrities such as TV host Kathie Lee Gifford, who lent her name to a clothes brand from Wal-Mart Stores and her face to its advertising.

Global Market

As with most other social and artistic trends, fashion had also become a global affair by the end of the 20th century. Some small distinctions remain, however. In Arab countries, fashion advertising has drawn fire from devout Muslims for flaunting Islamic rules. In Mexico, billboards advertising the introduction of the Wonderbra in 1996 were covered up after complaints about the revealing cleavage shot and the suggestive ad copy. Local church leaders complained about the decline of sexual and family values, blaming TV, movies, and ads such as the Wonderbra billboards.

But more secular matters can also account for cultural differences in advertising. The Chinese market, which had been closed to Western-style marketing during the years of the Cultural Revolution, only experienced branding again in the1980s. In 1986 the J. Walter Thompson Company (JWT) reintroduced the brand concept with an ad campaign for the International Wool Secretariat. The marketer's three-pointed Woolmark logo was one of the first corporate symbols introduced in the Chinese market and quickly gained wide recognition in the land of the Mao suit. According to subsequent market research studies, the Woolmark logo had more customer recognition in the market than the Coca-Cola trademark in the two years after the JWT campaign broke.

With the growth of multinational fashion conglomerates such as LVMH Moet Hennesy Louis Vuitton and worldwide expansion of fashion retailers such as H&M and The Gap, regional differences in fashion and fashion marketing are becoming as rare as a national costume. LVMH, a French luxury-goods holding company that is the parent company to brands such as Givenchy and Louis Vuitton, has reached far and wide from its European base. It markets heavily in the United States and Asia, often with the same high-fashion ads created for the French market. Conversely, Tommy Hilfiger and Ralph Lauren have established flagship stores in Europe's major capitals. While fashionistas in New York City parade in head-to-toe Gucci, their counterparts in France are just as likely to be outfitted in full Calvin Klein. And they are probably looking at identical fashion ads.

MERCEDES M. CARDONA

See also Benetton; Fruit of the Loom; C.F. Hathaway Shirt Company; Intimate Apparel; Levi Strauss & Company; Wanamaker, John

Further Reading

DePaola, Helena, and Carol Stewart Mueller, *Marketing Today's Fashion*, Englewood Cliffs, New Jersey: Prentice-Hall, 1980; 3rd edition, by Mueller and Eleanor Lewit Smiley, Englewood Cliffs, New Jersey: Prentice Hall Education, Career, and Technology, 1995
Diamond, Jay, and Ellen Diamond, *The World of Fashion*, San Diego, California: Harcourt Brace Jovanovich, 1990; 2nd edition, New York: Fairchild, 1997
Diamond, Jay, and Ellen Diamond, *Fashion Advertising and Promotion*, New York: Fairchild, 1999

Drake, Mary Frances, Janice Harrison Spoone, and Herbert Greenwald, *Retail Fashion Promotion and Advertising,* New York: Macmillan, and Toronto: Macmillan Canada, 1992

Fox, Stephen R., *The Mirror Makers: A History of American Advertising and Its Creators,* New York: Morrow, 1984

Harris, Neil, *Cultural Excursions: Marketing Appetites and Cultural Tastes in Modern America,* Chicago: University of Chicago Press, 1990

Jarnow, Jeannette, and Beatrice Judelle, *Inside the Fashion Business,* New York: Wiley, 1965; 6th edition, by Jarnow and

Kitty G. Dickerson, Upper Saddle River, New Jersey: Merrill, 1997

Lears, Jackson, *Fables of Abundance: A Cultural History of Advertising in America,* New York: BasicBooks, 1994

Phillips, Pamela M., Ellye Bloom, and John D. Mattingly, *Fashion Sales Promotion: The Selling behind the Selling,* New York: Wiley, 1985

Winters, Peggy Fincher, et al., *What Works in Fashion Advertising: Interpreting the Strategic Thinking behind the Advertising and Communications of Fashion Producers and Retailers,* New York: Retail Reporting, 1996

Fast Food. *See* Restaurants/Fast Food

FCB Worldwide. *See* Foote, Cone & Belding

FedEx Corporation

(Federal Express Corporation)

Principal Agencies

Ally & Gargano, Inc. (later Ally Gargano/MCA Advertising, Ltd.)
Fallon McElligott Rice
BBDO Worldwide, Inc.

In 1965 Frederick W. Smith, an undergraduate at Yale University, New Haven, Connecticut, wrote a term paper about the inadequacy of the routing systems being used by most airfreight companies; he suggested that there was a pressing need for a system designed to handle shipments of time-sensitive items such as blood, medicines, computer parts, and electronics. The paper failed to get an A, but Smith—the future chairman, president, and chief executive officer of FedEx Corporation—knew that he had a great idea. After serving briefly in the military, he bought the controlling interest in Arkansas Aviation Sales of Little Rock in 1969. As a new manager, Smith saw firsthand the frustrations inherent in trying to deliver packages and other airfreight in one or two days. Looking for a better distribution system, he came up with the idea of Federal Express. The company was incorporated on 18 June 1971. Promising on-time delivery with service in 25 cities, company officials launched 14 small aircraft from Memphis (Tennessee) International Airport, shipping 186 packages the first night in operation, 17 April 1973.

The use of the word *Federal* in the name carried connotations of patriotism and helped to attract public attention and promote name recognition. Memphis became the company's worldwide headquarters because it was the geographic center of the original delivery area, offered good weather, and had a cooperative airport authority. Federal Express did not show a profit until July 1975, but customers increasingly came to rely on the company to transport high-priority goods. The business took off in 1977 when the air cargo industry was deregulated, and the company invested in larger aircraft. By the year 2000, the fleet had 662 planes, including Boeing 727s, MD-11s, Airbus A310s and A300s, and Cessnas.

Painted white and adorned with the familiar purple and orange logo, the trucks, planes, and drop-off locations of FedEx Express (as the company is known today) became ubiquitous in the 1990s. In the 2001 fiscal year FedEx Corporation (of which FedEx Express is a part, along with FedEx Ground, FedEx Freight,

FedEx Custom Critical, and FedEx Trade Networks) earned $20 billion. With more than 218,000 employees worldwide and service to 211 countries, the company boasts regional headquarters for operations in Asia (Hong Kong), Europe (Brussels), Canada (Toronto), and Latin America (Miami, Florida).

Over the years FedEx's advertising campaigns have reflected the stages of the company's development. The early ads were done in house. Ally & Gargano was the company's first agency, winning the account in 1973. Carl Ally and Amil Gargano nearly turned the account down but changed their minds after talking to Smith for 15 minutes. In 1974, with an advertising budget of $150,000, the first Federal Express commercial aired in six markets. Concentrating on the aircraft fleet, the theme was "Federal Express—A whole new airline for packages only." In the year following the campaign's introduction, the number of overnight packages shipped via FedEx rose from 3,000 to 11,400. (Package volume reached one million in November 1988.) In 1975 the Clio Award-winning 30-second spot "America, you've got a new airline," aired for four weeks in New York City; Los Angeles, California; Chicago, Illinois; and Atlanta, Georgia. Federal Express then expanded its advertising efforts into other cities, including Philadelphia, Pennsylvania; Boston, Massachusetts; San Francisco, California; Detroit, Michigan; Dallas, Texas; and Cleveland, Ohio. A network deal was under consideration in 1975; that year John Malmo Advertising handled FedEx's sales promotion and direct mail advertising.

In 1979 the agency created the highly successful tag line, "When it absolutely, positively has to be there overnight." FedEx targeted its competitor, Emery Air Freight, and decided to do research to see who was better. It filled 47 packages with sand and shipped them by both FedEx and Emery. The result was turned into a 1980 print ad with the caption, "If you're using Emery, you'd better not let your boss see these figures."

Also in the late 1970s FedEx took a new approach: using humor in television ads. In 1979 Ally & Gargano developed an ad called "Pass it On," in which the company president and employees at all levels blame each other for a package not arriving on time. Previous ads had always targeted middle- and senior management only. In October 1981 FedEx began airing 60-second spots on televised National Football League games. At the time, the industry felt that making fun of customers was inappropriate, and ad executives feared that people would remember the jokes but not the product. When executives at Ally & Gargano saw fast-talking actor John Moschitta on the television show *That's Incredible!*, however, the agency convinced FedEx to defy conventional wisdom. Trying to convey both the get-it-done-yesterday pace of business and the speed with which Federal Express delivers packages, the "Fast-Paced World" (also known as "Fast Talker") spot cast Moschitta as a senior manager frantically arranging meetings and tracking packages. The commercial entertained viewers and made them laugh while reflecting the universal anxiety about being overwhelmed with work. The ad ignored the traditional selling method of listing the virtues of a product, and the ad industry loved it. "Fast-Paced World" and other commercials in the campaign won Effies, Clios, One Show awards, and

The 1982 "Fast Talker" commercial made its point about the pace of modern business in a wry manner and gave Federal Express name recognition that extended far beyond the business world.
©1982-1997 *Federal Express Corporation. All Rights Reserved.*

New York Art Directors Awards. "Fast-Paced World" also earned a place in the book *The 100 Best TV Commercials and Why They Worked*, and in 1999 *Advertising Age* ranked it 11th in its list of

BBDO's award-winning 1997 outdoor campaign transformed ordinary package-handling stickers into humorous recommendations for FedEx services

the 100 greatest ad campaigns of the 20th century. Later commercials in the series featured the travails of mail clerks, administrative assistants, and other office professionals. Much of the credit for the quirky style of the commercials goes to the unique touch of director Joe Sedelmaier.

In 1984 FedEx began its international expansion, offering service to Asia and Europe. In Europe the company battled its chief competitor, DHL, for market share, while facing such obstacles as flight contract negotiations and delays in ad launches. The company also struggled because many potential European clients did not know about the successful track record of FedEx in the United States. Because television advertising was not as prevalent in Europe as in the United States, the company could not use commercials to establish itself as a household name in the new market. Instead, it relied on its reputation with office employees to sell the service. Airfreight service to Japan began in 1988.

FedEx initially used a London, England-based agency, GRC International, to handle its European ads but later moved to McCann-Erickson, viewed as a truly international agency. FedEx subsequently has used a variety of shops for its international accounts, including HDM and, beginning in 1990, BBDO.

In the United States, the Federal Express/Ally & Gargano relationship diminished. The agency created more than 80 commercials during its association with the courier, billing $20 million–$25 million to make FedEx a household name. By 1985, however, the formula was growing stale, and the jokes did not seem as funny as they once had. Furthermore, the agency, now called Ally Gargano/MCA Advertising, Ltd., was losing money and experiencing a high turnover rate. Hoping to present a more serious image, FedEx hired another agency, Fallon McElligott Rice, to handle the ZapMail account. Introduced in 1984, ZapMail was a new electronic document transmission service that moved high-quality, plain-paper copies of documents in two hours or less. The new venture posted operating losses of $317 million because of high equipment costs, technological problems, and competition from fax machines, and the $10 million *Star Trek*–centered campaign from Fallon was scrapped when ZapMail was discontinued in 1987.

Nonetheless, Fallon won the entire FedEx account later in 1985. An agency known for putting humor into commercials, its early ads for FedEx provoked smiles but also conveyed serious messages with the tag line "If it's important, send it Federal Express." By 1988 the humor returned to FedEx ads in a series of 11 zany "Reminders" spots, produced by Coppos Films, which showed office workers joining together to complete a project.

By 1990 FedEx was splitting its business between Fallon and BBDO Worldwide, with the latter company handling international accounts. As domestic sales dropped, Fallon remained the agency of record but most of the accounts shifted to BBDO. One of BBDO's European campaigns, "The best way to ship it over there," was modified to "The best way to ship it over here" for the U.S. market. BBDO won the account based on presentation and creativity.

In 1996, at the direction of FedEx, BBDO created the company's first global ad campaign, featuring ads that depicted the company as a global force in the shipping business. The ads featured a spinning globe and the tag line, "The way the world works." Five 30-second commercials and one 60-second spot allowed viewers to travel from New York to Austria, and from Istanbul to Bangkok. Actress Linda Hunt read the voice-overs: "How did such ordinary people come by such extraordinary powers? Believe it or not, all it took was the wave of a wand." The series of ads, which took almost a year to produce, depicted business owners around the world—from a publisher in Wales to a dressmaker in Milan—using FedEx as their primary courier. This campaign was a departure for FedEx, which had previously customized its international advertising.

FedEx actively promotes many sports, sponsoring the FedEx Championship Auto Racing, USA Basketball, and the FedEx St. Jude Classic golf tournament. The company also sponsors the annual FedEx Orange Bowl between two of the top collegiate football teams in the United States. In November 1999 the company became the title sponsor of the Washington Redskins Stadium/FedExField. In its 1999 "We want the cup!" spot, a careless courier service accidentally switches the National Hockey League Stanley Cup trophy with a sack of coffee; in the next two scenes a Latin American villager uses the Stanley Cup as a fruit bowl, and 20,000 hockey fans are dumbfounded by the sack of coffee. Similar scenarios were enacted in subsequent ads, continuing to feature the humor that has long been the FedEx trademark. The FedEx campaign in 2000 carried the tag line, "Be absolutely sure," and featured characteristic humor in its ad series, which tested the reliability of the competition. Ads for 2001 retained the humor but focused on the various FedEx services, using the tag line, "Don't worry: there's a FedEx for that."

CARRIE SMOOT

Further Reading

Berry, Leonard L., "Cultivating Service Brand Equity," *Academy of Marketing Science* 28 (Winter 2000)

Cooper, Ann, "Frenetic Funnyman: Patrick Kelly Won't Stop at Ads in Fervent Desire to Make You Laugh," *Advertising Age* (16 May 1985)

Fox, Stephen R., *The Mirror Makers: A History of American Advertising and Its Creators,* New York: Morrow, 1984

Garcia, Shelly, "Federal Express' New World View: Delivery Company Breaks Global Ad Campaign Created by BBDO," *Adweek Eastern Edition* (16 September, 1996)

Kanner, Bernice, *The 100 Best TV Commercials and Why They Worked,* New York: Times Business, 1999

Mason, Richard O., et al., "Absolutely Positively Operations Research: The Federal Express Story," *Interfaces* 27, no. 2 (March–April 1997)

Seiden, Hank, *Advertising Pure and Simple: The New Edition,* New York: AMACON, 1976

Wetherbe, James C., *The World on Time: The 11 Management Principles That Made FedEx an Overnight Sensation,* Santa Monica, California: Knowledge Exchange, 1996

Fee System

The labor-based fee system is one of two basic methods advertising agencies use to bill their clients. The other is the media commission system. Under the fee system, an advertising agency bills for compensation based on the precise number of employee hours worked on behalf of the client. In much the same way that many professional service providers—such as lawyers, accountants, and architects—charge for their services, the agency charges the advertiser for the specific services rendered. The advertiser pays for exactly what it receives from the agency—no more, no less. (Under the media commission system, on the other hand, the agency keeps 15 percent of the gross ad rate set by the medium running an ad.)

The media commission system was the dominant form of advertising agency compensation until the late 1950s, when fees began to gain popularity. The fee system, however, has a long history, having been used since the early years of the 20th century by agencies whose accounts were either very labor intensive or generated insufficient media commissions to compensate the agency adequately—or both. Moreover, agencies handling clients that required multiple advertisements, usually in small-circulation trade publications and professional journals reaching a specialized audience, have long used the fee system as their billing method.

The fee method of compensation has both advantages and disadvantages. Its strength lies in the direct correlation of agency service costs with the number of service hours provided by the agency. In addition, fee compensation arrangements provide the advertiser with detailed knowledge of and control over the actual cost of agency service. On the other hand, the fee method tends to be complex and difficult to administer, requiring elaborate record keeping and continuous dialogue between advertiser and agency regarding detailed costs and work hours required (estimated and real) to provide satisfactory service to the advertiser. In addition, when using the fee method, the advertiser often intrudes into the realm of its agency's management and accounting practices. The routine discussion of agency costs and their components may tempt a client to impose its own accounting precepts and management standards upon the agency, steering both advertiser and agency away from advertising and toward accounting and managerial definitions, practices, and issues.

Ironically, the advertiser may, in the process, preempt the managerial prerogatives of the agency that it hired precisely for its management expertise.

Although a wide variety of fee compensation systems are in use, no two are alike. The basic labor-based fee is composed of five common elements. The first is direct labor cost—that is, the salaries of the agency personnel working on the advertiser's account. Ad agency employees typically work on more than one account at a time, therefore, direct labor costs are usually expressed as hourly rates. Agency employees generally keep detailed records of the number of hours spent working on individual accounts; the hourly rate is then used to convert hours worked into direct labor cost. The second component of most fee-based systems is employee benefit costs, which correlate with direct labor costs. These include payroll taxes such as FICA and unemployment taxes, and employee benefit plans such as health, life, and long-term disability insurance. Third are overhead costs, which include the costs of occupancy of an office (rent, heat, light, power, cleaning, and trash removal), communications, security, and the costs of agency personnel such as receptionists, accounting personnel, human resources, and agency management, which cannot be charged directly to specific client accounts. The fourth and fifth factors, respectively, are agency out-of-pocket costs associated with servicing the account and the agency's profit.

Several questions must be asked when developing a labor-based fee structure. Is the direct labor cost purely salary, or does it also include the cost of taxes and benefits that follow salaries? How is the agency's overhead allocated among its accounts, and what constitutes an excessive level of agency overhead? How many hours make up an employee work year? How are hourly direct labor costs adjusted when an employee works hours in excess of the defined work year? How are agency costs allocated to a client's multiple brands? What is a fair agency profit?

Beginning around 1960, with only about 5 percent of advertisers using fee compensation, a minority of industry leaders began arguing for a more general adoption of the fee system. This was partially the result of a consent decree at the time, which ended the monopoly ad agencies had enjoyed on media purchases at discounted prices. When media became available to all buyers at a net discounted price, some felt the commission system would be impractical. Among the most prominent was David Ogilvy, whose agency won the large Shell account in 1961 on a fee basis. It triggered an ongoing and sometime bitter controversy in an industry still committed to commissions and convinced that Ogilvy was either a fool or a publicity seeker.

By the 1980s and 1990s, however, the fee system had made significant gains. According to figures from the U.S. Association of National Advertisers, nearly a third of American agencies were using some version of fee compensation by 1985, and by 2000 the segment had shot up to 68 percent.

In the late 20th century the trend was clear in the United States. Regardless of the difficulties of conceptualizing and administering labor-based fees, an increasing proportion of advertisers preferred this system. Accordingly, most agencies were flexible, as long as they earned a reasonable profit. In the 1990s such leading ad executives as Peter Georgescu of Young & Rubicam, Inc., and Keith Reinhard at DDB Worldwide, Inc., were vigorous advocates for the fee system, providing that it includes a built-in profit margin and added incentive compensation.

WILLIAM M. WEILBACHER

Further Reading

Beals, David, and Robert H. Lundin, *Trends in Agency Compensation,* New York: Association of National Advertisers, 2001

Jones, Charles B., *Agency Compensation: A Guidebook,* New York: Association of National Advertisers, 1989

Weilbacher, William M., *Choosing and Working with Your Advertising Agency,* Lincolnwood, Illinois: NTC Business Books, 1991

Feminine Hygiene and Intimacy Products

Advertisements for feminine hygiene products have long been a subject of public comment and consternation; in fact, they are often cited by consumers as among their least favorite ads. Products that have been advertised under the category of "intimacy" and "feminine hygiene" include sanitary napkins, tampons, panty liners, deodorant sprays and douches, and condoms and other birth control-related items.

Early Hygiene Products

In the late 1800s disposable cloth towels to be worn during menstruation were introduced as a product category marketed to middle- and upper-class women. (Prior to that time, even the wealthiest women had made their own menstrual supplies from yard goods.) As Shelley M. Park recounts in her 1996 essay for *Journal of Popular Culture,* the fact that "Canfield disposable sanitary towels were sold by the dozen, as a specialty item alongside bustles, dress shields, corset hose supporters and prefabricated children's diapers, indicated that the target consumer was not the washerwoman." Park also quotes an 1892 English ad suggesting that Southall's sanitary towels were especially suited for "Ladies traveling by land or sea, visiting, or away from home," a reference to upper-class women's practice of making a journey in order to "convalesce" from the "periodic wound."

During World War I Ernest Mahler, a Kimberly-Clark Corporation chemist, developed cellucotton, a wood-based substitute for surgical cotton. Red Cross nurses stationed in France discovered that cellucotton worked extremely well as a sanitary napkin. Following the war, Kimberly-Clark decided to market Kotex as its first consumer product through a separate subsidiary—the International Cellucotton Products Company—in order to avoid public embarrassment of having the Kimberly-Clark name associated with such a product. Under the direction of Albert Lasker, the advertising agency of Lord & Thomas took over the Kotex account in 1924 from Wallace C. Meyer, account manager at Charles F.W. Nichols Company (and later at the J. Walter Thompson Company [JWT]). Bearing the medical symbol of the red cross, Kotex napkins were advertised as "a wonderful sanitary absorbent which science perfected for the use of our men and Allied soldiers wounded in France." Many women in the 1920s and 1930s continued to use traditional methods of making their own sanitary supplies, but in the United States maternity nurses, along with advertising agencies, fostered women's confidence in disposable napkins and tampons. Most of the early advertisements emphasized Kotex's status as "scientific" and endorsed by medical professionals.

"Feminine Hygiene": Euphemism for Birth Control

In the late 1800s and early 1900s, the practice of birth control was rarely discussed publicly, being deemed beyond the bounds of good taste. In the United States, the Comstock Law of 1873 banned "obscene" materials from the mails, making it illegal to sell or advertise products that were explicitly labeled contraceptives or otherwise referred directly to sex. Despite the law, sales of contraceptives were brisk. Manufacturers often had to resort to euphemisms and code language to mask the products' purpose while still allowing the savvy consumer to understand the advertisers' claims. Patent medicine advertisements in popular magazines offered women the necessary elements to concoct a contraceptive douche or obtain "female monthly pills" to "regulate" their cycles.

The term *feminine hygiene* was created around 1924 by the makers of Zonite and Lysol, two popular household disinfectants that were also used as contraceptive douches. Under the banner of "feminine" or "marital" hygiene, these products could be purchased in the United States in the 1920s and 1930s in department stores, through Sears, Roebuck & Company catalogs, and in drugstores.

At that time, exaggerated and fraudulent claims were a regular part of the advertising ploys used to attract consumers to contraceptives (as well as to many medicines). Margaret Sanger, a noted advocate of family planning, wanted to make reliable birth control more readily available to women, and she sought to limit fraudulent advertisements in the United States. She advocated an amendment to the Comstock Law that would allow companies to advertise birth control to doctors. This proposal was an attempt to win support from the American Medical Association (AMA) and to legitimize birth control in the minds of consumers by replacing

Today women know more . .

about feminine hygiene

A HIGHER standard of cleanliness and hygiene is the rule among the modern women surrounding you on every side. There is a more general recognition also among physicians and nurses of the benefits of feminine hygiene.

This is the age of antiseptics, and a great deal of the credit is due to *Zonite*. For this famous product that came out of the World War has taken the antiseptic idea completely *out of the poison class*.

Zonite is non-poisonous, non-caustic —safe to use on the body and safe to have in the house, even with little children around. Yet Zonite is actually stronger, far stronger, in its effect than *carbolic acid itself* in any dilution you would dare use on the body.

Get Zonite at any drugstore in the U. S. A. or Canada; in bottles, 30c, 60c, and $1.00. Also send coupon below for small-sized booklet full of feminine hygiene information. Zonite Products Corporation, Chrysler Building, New York, N. Y.

Use Zonite Ointment for burns, abrasions, sunburn or skin irritations. Also as an effective deodorant in greaseless cream form. Large tube 50c.

In bottles: 30c, 60c, $1   In both U. S. A. and Canada

ZONITE PRODUCTS CORPORATION   LH-08
Chrysler Building, New York, N. Y.
Please send me free copy of the Zonite booklet or booklets
checked below.
☐ The Newer Knowledge of Feminine Hygiene
☐ Use of Antiseptics in the Home
Name:..
            (Please print name)
Address..
City....................................State...............
            (In Canada: 165 Dufferin St., Toronto)

After years of using coded language to discuss "taboo" subjects, marketers such as Zonite began using the term *feminine hygiene*.

the inaccurate or veiled claims of advertisers with more reliable products backed up by the authoritative scientific discourse of doctors. Although publicly critical of advertisers, Sanger and others privately acknowledged that commercial interests had done much to promote the cause of birth control through advertising.

A 1930 court decision in a trademark infringement suit over Trojan condoms (*Youngs Rubber Corporation, Inc., v. C.I. Lee & Co.*) recognized the trademark rights of Youngs Rubber Corporation, Inc., to the Trojan product. Although selling a product as a contraceptive device was illegal in the United States under the Comstock Law, the ruling noted that birth control devices could nonetheless be used for "lawful purposes" other than contraception, and therefore such products could be legally advertised and sold as noncontraceptive devices or remedies. This ruling meant that companies could market their birth control products as long as the advertisements and marketing did not refer to those products' benefits as contraceptives. Taking advantage of this legal loophole, more than 400 companies were competing in the female contraceptive market by 1938. Advertising campaigns were launched for such products as jellies, foaming tablets, suppositories, and douches.

These ads often played upon women's fears of pregnancy, suggesting that fear itself might destroy the spontaneity and delights of the conjugal bed. A Lysol ad from the 1930s used a photo of a grim reaper–like figure posed between a husband and wife, suggesting that apprehensions about unwanted pregnancies might spell the death of the marriage. The copy stated, "The nervous fears of a wife, her natural reluctance to be frank about such a delicate subject . . . a husband's puzzled resentment. These are the rocks on which thousands of marriages crash." Advertisers knew that consumers could decode claims such as "the product is a true germicide" or "it remains effective in the presence of organic matter (mucous, serum, etc.) when many products *don't* work."

Such indirect appeals did not violate the letter of the law, but the melodramatic overstatements and bogus claims of these ads provoked criticism from both advocates and opponents of birth control. It was not until 1936 that U.S. law began permitting physicians to distribute birth control information. In 1945 the AMA helped to kill consumer advertising for contraception in the United States by stipulating that contraceptive manufacturers restrict their advertising solely to the medical community.

From "Periodic Wound" to "Problem Day"

Until the 1930s Western doctors treated the female menstrual cycle as a disability and advised menstruating women to refrain from participating in rigorous physical activity. To some degree, advertisements for sanitary hygiene products countered this view. In a 1937 issue of *Ladies' Home Journal,* advertisements from JWT depicting women wearing tennis togs, golfing outfits, or other fashionable clothing bore captions reading, "For extra comfort on active summer days, demand Kotex." The three main product benefits touted in these campaigns were "Can't chafe," "Can't fail," and "Can't show," addressing women's concerns about comfort and their fears that blood stains or embarrassing bulges might ruin sleek fashions. Among the most blatant of the pitches implying that women needed to worry about other people discovering that they were menstruating was one for Quest, a deodorizing powder to be used along with Kotex, which suggested, "They don't talk behind her back!" In the 1930s manufacturers developed napkins with flat, pressed ends to address the concern (routinely evoked in ad copy) that pads might show under formfitting clothing.

Tampons, which had been improvised by women around the world from vegetable or cloth fibers since ancient Egyptian times, became a commercial product in 1936 with the introduction of Tampax tampons to the U.S. market in a series of print ads. Tampax Sales Corporation, chartered on 2 January 1934, originally sold its product using direct sales to department and dry goods stores and pharmacies. In 1936 Tampax Incorporated was formed and launched a series of advertisements beginning with a campaign in New York newspapers, followed by a magazine campaign in the *American Weekly* magazine insert for newspapers. Small, discreet black-and-white ads began appearing in the back sections of women's magazines. Headlines suggested that women could demonstrate their modernity by using the product: "I confess I was prejudiced . . . at first the Tampax idea seemed too revolutionary, too novel," ran the headline for one Tampax ad. Another ad, "Tampax is a challenge to all women," suggested that because Tampax departed "so much from 'the usual' it had made itself into a test of open-mindedness." Even grandmothers could show that they were "young and flexible in spirit" through the use of the product (the copywriter failing to recognize that women of a certain age would have no such need). Ads for competing brands of tampons centered on price comparisons or design superiority and featured photos of the actual tampons. Kimberly-Clark's Kotex product line marketed a competing tampon product through a magazine campaign created by JWT, using small black-and-white ads. Tampax, however, dominated the market.

With the advent of World War II, new norms of femininity arose in the United States. As women were expected to replace men sent off to war in the workplace, the medical approach to menstruation as a kind of disability came to seem inappropriate: if menstruation was viewed as a health problem, then female workers might use their periods as a reason to avoid the regimented schedules of wartime factories. Advertisers of feminine hygiene products thus revised their appeals to help the war effort. Women were encouraged with problem-solution ads: "I don't want to be an absentee, but what's a girl to do?" and "Do's and don'ts every woman absentee should know." The copy suggested that a number of absentees were "women who miss 1 to 3 days of work each month, frequently on 'problem days.'" Kotex offered a booklet ("That Day Is Here Again!") written by "problem day specialists—the Kotex people," which offered tips to keep women working, playing, shopping, and tending children during their monthly periods. Moddess, a competing product marketed by Johnson & Johnson, relied less upon patriotic calls as a part of its advertising campaigns.

From the earliest days of the marketing of sanitary products, advertisers recognized the importance of reaching pubescent

"I'll do a lot for love, but I'm not ready to die for it."

"I never thought having an intimate relationship with someone could be a matter of life or death. But with everything I hear about AIDS these days, I'm more than uncomfortable. I'm afraid."

AIDS isn't just a gay disease, it's everybody's disease.

And everybody who gets it dies.

AIDS is transmitted from one sexual partner to another, often by a mate who has contracted the disease without even knowing it.

But what we find so alarming about this terrible disease is that people are doing so little to try to prevent it.

Especially since the Surgeon General recently stated, "The best protection against infection right now, barring abstinence, is use of a condom."

It's for this reason that we at LifeStyles® say that the proper use of a LifeStyles Brand Condom can greatly reduce the chances of you or your partner contracting AIDS.

Because a LifeStyles condom acts as a shield that helps prevent the transfer of the AIDS virus. So the likelihood of getting this disease is dramatically diminished. And LifeStyles Brand Condoms, when properly used, help prevent other sexually transmitted diseases like herpes and gonorrhea.

LifeStyles condoms are manufactured by Ansell International, America's largest manufacturers of condoms. Tinton Falls, NJ 07724. © Ansell, Inc. 1987.

Emphasizing the role of condoms in disease prevention, a 1987 print ad for LifeStyles condoms minced no words.
Copyright Ansell Healthcare, Inc. 1987.

females as potential first-time consumers, and they relied upon advertising campaigns aimed at mothers and/or daughters on the subject of the "facts of life." Most such ads included a coupon or an address to order a booklet explaining the physiological changes affecting the adolescent girl. Mothers were encouraged to overcome the social taboo against frank discussions of menstruation and provide their daughters with sound information. A 1925 ad headline suggested that "Every mother should tell her daughter this," while a headline from the 1930s showed a teen with her mother on a bobsled and then telling her friends, "My mom's a modern." In 1949 Kotex sponsored a "public service" ad in *Ladies' Home Journal* asking mothers, "Do you scare her to death?" The ad warned mothers not to share "some of the bogey ideas you picked up when you were a teen-ager" but rather to send away for a booklet or arrange for the school to borrow a film produced by Kotex to explain menarche to girls. "A girl's first experience with menstruation can and does condition her for life," the ad cautioned mothers. "And you're to blame if she develops complexes, imaginary ailments and a twisted personality!"

Following their stint as war workers, middle-class American women were encouraged through the media and social pressure to return to their domestic role, and advertising for feminine hygiene products conformed to the normative image of the contented suburban homemaker. Ads from the 1950s suggested that American women could not use their periods as excuses for avoiding responsibilities such as tending the home, cooking, caring for children, playing hostess, or serving their working husbands; instead, women were expected to carry on with appointed tasks while managing the inconveniences of menstruation. A 1956 Modess campaign featured full-page color photos of serene models wearing stunning ball gowns. The simple tag line, "Modess because . . ." left the unmentionable subject unmentioned. During the war years, ads for Kotex had been less reliant than those for Modess on prevailing stereotypes of femininity. Following the war, however, Kotex too based its ads on appeals to femininity. A series of two-page color ads in *Ladies' Home Journal* for Kotex in 1956 featured illustrations of two women, or a woman with her teen daughter, promoting the comfort of the product: "New and softest ever. New Kotex with Wondersoft covering." Photos or illustrations of the product box appeared in the ads but not the product itself. Although the earliest Tampax ads had contained an educational component and occasionally had included an illustration—as opposed to a photograph—even these visual representations of the actual product faded from advertising once women had been educated as to the function of the tampon. Marketers relied instead upon lifestyle ads with a small photo of the product box.

In the 1950s Tampax developed a series of quarter-page black-and-white ads emphasizing the virtues of the product, especially in the summer: "Everything is twice as tiring in hot weather. . . . Why add to your problems at 'problem times'?" For years Tampax placed similar ads in general circulation magazines, such as *Look*, at the onset of summer when women were more apt to be swimming, playing sports, or wearing shorts or other revealing clothes.

By the 1960s Kotex was advertising that its napkins were "proportioned," and the company offered a selection of four styles of pads. Tampax revamped its packaging ideas and promoted a removable cellophane wrapper that enabled consumers to keep their tampons in a decorative and discretely unlabeled box. Also included in the package was a purse-size plastic container that held two tampons. The advertising showed the box and container and suggested, "A beautiful new way to keep a secret." An ad for New Confidets sanitary napkins conveyed the new shape of its product, while continuing the accepted advertising practice of not actually showing the product, by inserting a small sketch of the tapered napkin within the copy. "It's shaped to follow the lines of your body, wide in front and slim in back. It's new from Scott—a sanitary napkin that really fits." A color photo of a blonde in a white sweater and clingy white stretch slacks attested to the confidence with which women could wear the product. Indeed, models wearing white apparel became common in 1960s and 1970s ads for sanitary products, emphasizing security and effectiveness. Summertime ads for Tampax showed an underwater photo of a woman clad in a white bathing suit.

You've Come a Long Way, Baby

By the 1970s douches were a major feminine hygiene product line. In 1974 Zonite, marketed by Zonite Products Corporation, an early pioneer in the advertising of douches, capitalized on the knowledge that vaginal secretions were part of the normal functioning of women's bodies to promote its product as an "internal deodorizer" for women to combat the "tiny period" that "your body has every day." "Usually occurring about every 12 hours, this discharge can be triggered by exercise, excitement, or simply a busy day . . . many women feel nature's cleansing needs help!" The company also introduced a capsule suppository form of the douche with a name worthy of a science fiction story: Zonitors. A new product, Summer's Eve, offered a "quick effective way to douche." Its color ads included a photo of a premixed douche bottle with its applicator in front of the product box and a sprig of greenery. Cunningham & Walsh handled the early advertising for the product and produced North America's first television commercial for a douche. Ads for Norforms suppositories (like Summer's Eve, a product of the C.B. Fleet Company, Inc.) admonished women that "feminine odor starts on the inside." A color photo featured a picture of a flower ("freshness where you need it, when you need it") and a feminine hand holding a single suppository between the thumb and forefinger to demonstrate the product's small size.

In the 1970s the benefits of freshness were also promised by a new entry into the tampon category, Playtex deodorant tampons. "This fresh scent helps reduce doubt about intimate odor," the copy announced. More and more frequently, tampons and douches, and not simply their packaging, were depicted in the ads. The 1970s also saw the introduction of Johnson & Johnson's Stayfree Mini-pad. "Why wear more than you have to?" the ad copy asked. The ads suggested that women might need the pad

Pro-Higiene and then purchased the company, acquiring the third-ranking Brazilian brand Ela and extending its position in disposable diapers and sanitary pads in Chile, Argentina, Paraguay, Uruguay, and Bolivia under the Babysan and Ladysan brands. P&G also acquired Higie Bras, giving the company three additional established Brazilian pad brands: Livre Atual, Mulher Atual, and Lady Care. P&G acquired Chilean company Empresas CMPC and purchased all outstanding shares of Productos Sanitarios SA Chile and Prosan SA Argentina. Also seeking to compete in South America, Kimberly-Clark Argentina S.A. combined operations with Argentine absorbent-products supplier Descartables Argentinos, which manufactured the third-most-popular brand of feminine care products in Argentina. The Spanish company Arbora S.A. partnered with Tambrands and later entered into a joint venture with P&G in 1990. Johnson & Johnson held a 60 percent share of the feminine protection category in Latin America by 1998. Alliances and joint ventures also became commonplace throughout Europe and Asia.

Acceptance of advertising for sanitary products in Europe and elsewhere has been slightly slower than in the United States. In the United Kingdom, the Independent Television Commission (ITC) first permitted televised ads for sanitary products in 1986; subsequently, the commission restricted the ad content and the hours during which the ads could run. In 1992 the ITC received complaints about the propriety of a Saatchi & Saatchi campaign for Johnson & Johnson's Vespre Silhouette sanitary towels, which demonstrated the product's absorbency and secure fastening rather than relying upon lifestyle campaigns used by competing brands. Print ads in the United Kingdom, however, routinely showed products and even resorted to humor. One ad from the 1980s, for Dr. White's Contour Applicator Tampons, featured illustrations of a tube-shaped tampon next to Dr. White's conical applicator; the copy read, "If men were shaped like tampons, the human race would have died out by now."

Johnson & Johnson launched the feminine protection pad Slinea to Latin American countries with a McCann-Erickson Publicidade television ad centering on the absorbent "flockgel" used in the ultra-thin napkin. The ad suggested that flockgel was a new technology comparable to a computer microchip. In one Brazilian ad, a young woman using a laptop computer presented both developments as parallel technologies that reduced the size of things while increasing efficiency: "Try it. I don't know how I could have lived without it until yesterday." She concludes, "For me there is nothing older than yesterday." The spot ends with the tagline, "Sempre Livre Slinea. For today's women, tomorrow's protection." The 1997 Slinea campaign for Brazil, Colombia, Argentina, and Venezuela concentrated on television commercials, particularly on MTV.

In India the first TV ads for sanitary products featured sari-wearing mothers instructing their daughters in the use of these modern conveniences. Indian television advertisements in the 1990s usually featured lifestyle ads showing urban teenage girls or young adult women in Western dress moving freely about the city with their female friends. Six new brands were launched in India between 1992 and 1996, bringing the total to 20, produced by four companies. In 1998 Johnson & Johnson India Ltd. held almost half the sanitary napkin market in India, and older brands still accounted for a 90 percent share of the market. However, new brands and brand extensions were the most rapidly growing sector of the Indian market.

In Japan, Sofy, a feminine hygiene product marketed by Unicharm, dominated the market. The Sofy account was initially handled by Hakuhodo, the nation's second-largest agency, which produced spots in which the well-known actress Misako Tanaka described the product's features. In 1997 Unicharm moved the business to JWT Japan and charged the agency with developing a stronger brand image that could be extended throughout Asia. Although both the Japanese and U.S. agencies used computer animation to demonstrate the napkin's design features, the JWT campaign employed a girl-next-door character who emphasized how the product made her feel: "I don't know why, but I feel secure—it's that kind of feeling, isn't it?" Unicharm also manufactured and marketed its sanitary protection products in Indonesia, Thailand, and China.

Advertising for "global" brands is often developed by an agency in the country where a company is based and then distributed to various international markets, and, at times, such ads bear the cultural imprimatur of the geographic locale of the home office. Advertisers based in the United States, hoping to make inroads in the highly developed domestic market, have begun using stronger, bolder advertising claims that might not be as appropriate for some other cultures. A $60 million Tampax campaign from Foote, Cone & Belding, New York (FCB), that aired on broadcast and cable TV in the United States in 1997 addressed women's concerns about toxic shock syndrome. The commercials showed ethnically diverse tampon users under the headline, "Some thoughts on 'Should I sleep with it . . . or not?'" The headline for a print ad for Tampax, also from FCB, aimed at U.S. teens concerned about tampon use plainly stated, "You want me to put that . . . where?"

Global ads for these same products attempted both to convey a unifying theme and to make adjustments to suit local cultures and languages. The Tampax campaign in international markets was as bold as that used in the United States, but ads were customized to reflect local mores. A 1997 Brazilian ad reassured young women, "Of course you're not going to lose your virginity [by using tampons] . . . that will happen in a much more romantic way." In China, where pads were still preferred to tampons, ads employed young women who stated that Tampax "fits my body . . . Can't feel it at all . . . compared to what I am used to, it's more comfortable." All ads in the global campaign used the umbrella theme "Tambrands. Women know."

Cultivating the Teen Market

In the 1990s education programs continued to play a prime role in the promotion of the feminine hygiene market around the world, extending a practice begun in the United States in which manufacturers provided literature, product samples, and even films on puberty to schools. Companies such as Sancella participated in school programs in the United Kingdom, Australia, and New Zealand. Sancella Bodyform's Bodyclocks resource pack of information for students was provided free to teachers and school nurses in the United Kingdom and was used by about 80 percent of British secondary and middle schools. Sancella also gave sample packs of both sanitary towels and liners to British school girls. The campaign was supported by a major public relations campaign aimed at teen consumers. Sancella invested £6 million to advertise its teen-centered Bodyform line on TV and in print. In Mexico, P&G used a self-esteem videotape and distributed samples in 1998 to generate brand awareness for its feminine hygiene products in schools.

Advertisers have also embraced the latest technology for advertising and marketing—the Internet. Tampax created a Web site to provide information to women and girls who might be reluctant to discuss sanitary hygiene products with one another. The site features information on toxic shock syndrome, instructions on how to insert a tampon, inspirational stories of women athletes, music selections, chat rooms for girls of different ages, and a page where teens can submit poetry and fiction.

L. CLARE BRATTEN

See also Johnson & Johnson; Kimberly-Clark Corporation

Further Reading

Farrell-Beck, Jane, and Laura Klosterman Kidd, "The Roles of Health Professionals in the Development and Dissemination of Women's Sanitary Products, 1880–1940," *Journal of the History of Medicine and Allied Sciences* 51, no. 3 (1996)

"The Four Ps of Growth Marketing: Feminine Hygiene," *Business Today* 100, no. 6 (November 1997)

Haddad, Clare, "Wings and Things: The U.K. Feminine Hygiene Market," *Nonwovens Industry* 23, no. 10 (October 1992)

"Kao Commercial to Invest 300m Baht," *Business Day* (Thailand) (17 July 1998)

Kennard, Margot Elizabeth, "The Corporation in the Classroom: The Struggles over Meanings of Menstrual Education in Sponsored Films, 1947–1983," Ph.D. diss., University of Wisconsin at Madison, 1989

Kilburn, David, "Copying from the Masters," *Adweek* (Eastern edition) (17 August 1998)

"Libra Hearts Sanitary Pads with Wings: Regular, Super," *International Product Alert* 14, no. 9 (5 May 1997)

"Libra Invisible Ultra Thin Sanitary Pads: Regular Wings, Regular without Wings, Super Wings, without Wings," *International Product Alert* 15, no. 8 (20 April 1998)

Museum of Menstruation and Women's Health Web site <www.mum.org>

Park, Jaclyn H., "McCann-Erickson Approaches 'Today's Woman' for J&J Slinea," *Advertising Age International Supplement* (5 October 1998)

Park, Shelley M., "From Sanitation to Liberation? The Modern and Postmodern Marketing of Menstrual Products," *Journal of Popular Culture* 5, no. 30 (Fall 1996)

Picardie, Ruth, "In Here: Wooaah for Wings: How Can I Possibly Choose between Super, Super Plus, Ultra Plus, Ultra Super, Ultra Super Plus, Not to Mention Normal and Ultra Normal?" *The Independent* (London) (15 July 1995)

"Real Cool Customers," *Chemist and Druggist* 22, no. 6081 (12 April 1997)

Riessman, Catherine Kohler, "Women and Medicalization: A New Perspective," *Social Policy* 14, no. 1 (1983)

Rigg, Cynthia, "The Condom Quandary: After the Hype Subsides, What Will Retailers Do?" *Crain's New York Business* 2 (March 1987)

"SCA Hygiene's Bodyform Invisible Ultra Towel Gets UKPd2.5 mil TV Ad Campaign," *Community Pharmacy* 41 (October 1998)

"Securing a Lead," *Financial Express: NA* (27 January 1998)

"Si, Si for Me," *Promo* 10, no. 111 (September 1997)

Spurgeon, Anne M., "Marketing the Unmentionable: Wallace Meyer and the Introduction of Kotex," *Maryland Historian* 19, no. 1 (1988)

"Tailored to Teen Market," *Community Pharmacy* 53 (May 1997)

Tanenbaum, Leora, "Red Alert: Health Hazards of Tampons," *Vegetarian Times* (December 1998)

Tone, Andrea, "Contraceptive Consumers: Gender and the Political Economy of Birth Control in the 1930s," *Journal of Social History* 29, no. 3 (1996)

Vertinsky, Patricia, "Exercise, Physical Capability, and the Eternally Wounded Woman in Late Nineteenth-Century North America," *Journal of Sport History* 14, no. 1 (1987)

Feminism, Impact of

The impact of feminism in advertising began in the United States early in the 20th century. The "New Woman," who came of age around the turn of the century, rejected the "separate spheres" ideology of the Victorian era, the belief that women should occupy private rather than public space. The New Woman—largely identified in the press as white, educated, urban, and middle class—embraced the ideals of modernity over those of tradition; she actively entered public life by giving speeches for women's suffrage, protesting tenement housing, and working towards other reforms associated with the Progressive Era of the early 1900s.

The New Woman was also, significantly, a consumer. It was in their role as consumers, in fact, that women were permitted and even encouraged to enter the public arena. Technical innovations in the 19th century had spurred tremendous industrial growth; increased consumption was thus necessary to maintain a sound economy. And as branded products replaced commodities in the marketplace, it became increasingly necessary to advertise the differences, real or imagined, between products in a given category. Because women were the primary purchasing agents for their households, they became the logical targets of such advertising.

Although advertisers and feminists had different goals, neither group had anything to gain by keeping women secluded in their homes. For different reasons, then, each embraced the image of the public, modern woman.

Advertising's use of the emancipated woman to promote sales became especially pronounced in the 1920s, when a boom in the production of leisure goods and laborsaving items necessitated changes in advertising strategies. Ads began to put less emphasis on the objective value of the product and instead based appeals more on what historian Roland Marchand has termed "the personal sell." Because advertisers were often promoting nonessential products, demand had to be created and nurtured. Advertisers played on consumers' individual fears and desires, especially their desire for leisure and glamour. In this context, appealing to women's desires for personal pleasure or freedom from convention was a particularly useful strategy and ads frequently appropriated feminist rhetoric and practices to make their products more appealing to women.

An example of this strategy, which historian Stuart Ewen has termed "commercialized feminism," is a 1929 campaign by the American Tobacco Industry (ATI) to encourage women to smoke in public, a societal taboo for "nice" women. The ATI's campaign manager, Edward Bernays, felt that by associating cigarettes with women's equality, he might be able to shatter that taboo. Referring to cigarettes as "torches of freedom," Bernays enlisted a recognized feminist named Ruth Hale to lead a group of cigarette-smoking women down New York City's Fifth Avenue in the Easter Parade, and referred to the walk as a "protest against women's inequality." The event was widely publicized across the country. While ads based on tactics similar to these were fairly plentiful in the 1920s, ads portraying "career women" were not. Although ads often linked products to progressive rhetoric, most advertisers still preferred to emphasize a woman's role within the family. For example, to sell vacuum cleaners, ads promised women "freedom" from household drudgery. From the 1920s through the 1950s the woman as housekeeper remained the preeminent image of women in advertising.

The importance of women as consumers had another effect on the advertising industry in the early part of the century: more women were hired in the advertising business. A "woman's viewpoint" was considered essential and, as a result, agencies hired more women than ever before. While most were in assistant posi-

tions or segregated into "women's only" departments and were not paid as much as men, the accepted presence of women in the industry reflected society's changing attitudes regarding women in public life. This change, however, must be viewed as the result of both feminist activism and the needs of a consumption-based economy.

The rebirth of feminism in the 1960s found feminists and advertisers much more in conflict with each other than they had been in the 1920s. As Ewen has shown, in the 1920s consumption was seen as a relief from a "chronically oppressive industrial situation." For the next 30 years, advertisers targeting women responded to what they believed to be the lifestyle and aspirations of the typical homemaker. Reality and imagery had a mutually reinforcing effect within the larger consumer culture, but the imagery offered by advertisers did little to accommodate or acknowledge the emergence of new aspirations among some women, who sought choices outside their perceived role as domestic consumers. By the 1960s second-wave feminists perceived advertising as one of the primary means by which society pressured women to fit into idealized roles as wives and mothers. Betty Friedan's 1963 book *The Feminine Mystique*, largely credited with sounding the alarm of second-wave feminism, included a detailed, blistering critique of women's images in advertising. Friedan's influence, along with the passage of the 1963 Equal Pay Act (which mandated that all workers, regardless of sex, receive equal pay for equal work) and the Civil Rights Act of 1964, whose Title VII prohibited discrimination in employment based on sex, forced society to reevaluate the status of women in the workplace and drew attention to their representation in the media. The advertising industry, especially, noted the popularity of Friedan's critique and debated its response to the book.

It was not until the late 1960s and early 1970s, however, that feminists began to actively organize protests against advertisers. These protests were at first concentrated in the United States, which influenced advertising in most Western cultures and was the most advertising-saturated society in the world. Feminists in the United States first attacked discrimination against women in help-wanted ads and their representation in several specific advertising campaigns. As a result of protests and lawsuits in which women proved that classified ads were not providing them equal access to work, help-wanted advertising was changed throughout the United States and Canada. No longer were there separate listings labeled "Men" and "Women."

This victory encouraged other protests, such as the one against National Airline's 1971 "Fly me" campaign, which required stewardesses to wear buttons bearing the slogans "Fly me" and "We make you feel good all over." The National Organization for Women (NOW) worked together with Stewardesses for Women's Rights in protest against the ads. They picketed the ad agency that created the ads as well as National Airlines ticket offices. (One of their signs read: "Haven't you heard, I'm not a bird.") The groups ran television commercials showing how the ads failed to reflect the reality of a stewardess's primary function as the enforcer of safety regulations. While the protests generated a great deal of

Charlie

Charlie's a gorgeous,
sexy-young smell.
(Concentrated!)
And full of surprises.
Just like you.
If you haven't met Charlie yet,
what are you waiting for?

A most original fragrance. By REVLON

Concentrated Cologne Spray/Concentrated Cologne/Concentrated Perfume Spray

Targeting the emerging feminist market in 1973, this ad for Revlon's Charlie perfume was among the first to show a businesswoman ready to take on the corporate world.
Courtesy of Revlon Consumer Products Corporation.

publicity, the ads did not stop and were even imitated by other airlines.

Other protests, such as NOW's campaign against widely advertised feminine hygiene sprays, which were suspected of being be physically harmful and implied that women were "smelly" and "dirty," were more successful. NOW's protests spurred an investigation of these products by the Federal Trade Commission (FTC) that concluded that vaginal sprays had no hygienic value and were indeed dangerous. Advertising of these products largely ceased as a result.

Throughout the 1970s feminist groups worked to draw the public's attention to sexual stereotypes in advertising and to change them through protests, product boycotts, letter-writing campaigns, and lawsuits. Feminist groups met with advertisers to point out sexist ads and encourage companies to adopt new guidelines. These meetings were widely covered in both the advertising and mainstream media. While feminists were sometimes successful in their protests against specific ad campaigns, they were not able to achieve their ultimate goal of government regulation. Both the Federal Communications Commission (FCC) and the FTC rejected arguments by feminists that stereotypes of women in advertising violated the FCC's "Fairness Doctrine" (which requires that television stations provide fair coverage of controversial issues) or the FTC's mandate against unfair or false advertising. The First Amendment's prohibition against media censorship made such regulation unlikely in any case, and the deregulation policies of the 1980s effectively ended this strategy.

Feminists worked instead to encourage the industry to self-regulate sexism in advertising. This avenue was somewhat more successful. In 1975 the National Advertising Review Board (NARB), an industry self-regulation organization that deals with truth and accuracy in advertising, released a report titled *Advertising and Women,* confirming the existence of sexist advertising and criticizing the industry for reinforcing dated stereotypes of men and women. The NARB proceeded to offer advertisers guidelines for revising images of women to conform to the realities of a changed society. While this report was much publicized, the NARB has no binding power on the industry so the direct effects of the report are uncertain.

What clearly had changed by the mid-1970s, however, was the amount of attention the industry itself paid to images of women in advertising. Industry journals from the period repeatedly cite the marketing changes advertisers felt they needed to make to appeal to the "new woman" of the 1970s and thus maintain their profits. Companies such as Procter & Gamble, which usually only broadcast commercials to women during the day, began buying time on nightly news programs to reach working women. Industry magazines began to report on revamped approaches to advertising that included more images of working women. Studies of women's representation in the media in academic and industry journals proliferated during the mid-1970s, putting more pressure on the industry to make changes. Jean Kilbourne's influential 1976 film *Killing Us Softly* assessed the industry's sexism in particularly devastating and detailed ways that produced widespread

industry response. (The film was updated in 1987 as *Still Killing Us Softly* and again in 2000 as *Killing Us Softly 3.*)

Both print and television ads from 1970s and early 1980s began to reflect the impact of feminism. Some ads from the 1970s portrayed women in nontraditional roles, such as jockeys and airline pilots. A popular Clairol Loving Care ad featured a woman over 40, a rare presence on television, who announced proudly in the final scene: "I'm 40, I've got a new job, and I've only just begun." In addition, ads increasingly featured husbands fixing dinner for their working wives or taking care of children, and ads for convenience foods began to target the working woman who did not have time to cook. One particularly popular and successful campaign was Revlon's 1970s ads for Charlie perfume, which featured model Shelley Hack as a confident, assertive young woman who very much identified herself with the feminist movement.

As the feminist challenge to cultural norms became more politicized, agencies spent hours discussing and debating the subtleties of various situations and the messages they might be sending. An early 1970s commercial for RC Cola, for example, showed a young man and a woman riding on a motorcycle. Writers, art directors, and account people at Leo Burnett, the RC agency, had long discussions over whether the woman should be driving or sitting behind the man as a passenger. Some of the younger women at the agency argued that the woman should be driving by herself. In the final commercial she was a passenger.

The presence of women in the advertising business also changed because of the women's movement. As historian Linda Lazier-Smith has suggested, advertising experienced a "feminization at both university and industry levels" in the 1970s and 1980s. The numbers of women in advertising nearly tripled from 1973 to 1986. Women finally received equal pay with men at starting levels, although men continued to occupy most upper-level and management jobs. In addition, women began to dominate communications fields in universities. Since 1977 the majority of students enrolled in journalism and mass communication courses have been female. Although men still outnumber women in terms of faculty, there has been tremendous growth in the number of articles and books devoted to the representation of women in academic journals, a trend that reflects the presence of women and women's concerns among students and faculty.

Feminist activism against sexist advertising has occurred worldwide since the 1970s. Feminist groups in Western Europe, Japan, Australia, and India (among other countries) held protests similar to those held in the United States in the 1970s and early 1980s. Feminist groups boycotted products, met with advertisers, and worked hard to create awareness of the issue within their own specific cultural contexts. Feminists worldwide worked together to form their own media organizations to fight sexism, most notably in Europe, North America, and Australia. The United Nations (UN) devoted a great deal of attention to the subject and has produced several reports on the representation of women in the media since the early 1970s. In 1980 the United Nations Educational, Scientific, and Cultural Organization (UNESCO) published a detailed report, *Women in the Media,* which confirmed an earlier finding that women in advertising worldwide were mostly portrayed as housewives or glamour girls. The 1980 report emphasized the importance of this problem, calling images of women in advertising "among the main obstacles to eliminating discrimination against women and to preserving traditional sex-role attitudes and behaviors." Data from a questionnaire distributed by the UN in 1985 showed that while some changes had been made in terms of women's employment and representation in advertising worldwide, there was still a long way to go.

Feminist global activism regarding this issue has resulted in both government regulation and self-regulation of sexist imagery in some countries, although the effectiveness of these regulations is often difficult to determine. At present, the Scandinavian countries, Canada, and the United Kingdom have developed the strongest regulatory codes regarding the sexist portrayals of women in the media. Self-regulation in advertising is well developed in still only a small number of countries (ranging from 20 to 40 in recent years), however, and generally much more is done about "indecent" as opposed to sexist advertising. Religious beliefs, for example, are more influential in determining advertising restrictions in most of these countries, although a 1991 report in the *Journal of Advertising* cited the importance of the feminist movement in "reducing some sex stereotypes in advertisements worldwide."

What became most clear in the 1990s in terms of global advertising was the growing influence of transnational corporations, based largely in the United States and Western Europe, on media around the world. In such a context, both Western feminism and Western patriarchy were seen as a threat to women in Third World countries, whose class and cultural positions are very different from those of the middle-class white woman who has been the dominant image of Western feminism. The same solutions are not applicable to women in areas where Western feminist ideals threaten established social practices and where profound poverty is the most pressing concern. In response, feminists in the 1990s (especially socialist feminists) paid more attention to the complex situations of poor and Third World women. Although feminist media organizations remain active, many feminists have shifted their focus from issues of women's representation in advertising worldwide to those of labor exploitation within a global corporate economy.

Within the United States, feminists have also taken a more oppositional position regarding advertisers since the 1980s. The mid-to-late 1980s were widely perceived by feminists as one of backlash against feminism in both politics and the media. Susan Faludi's influential book *Backlash* (1991) documented how advertising began to shift away from images of the liberated woman in the 1980s to reflect the more conservative politics of the time. Women were portrayed as more insecure and dependent on men, while listening fearfully to their "biological clocks," a social phenomenon that was a direct consequence of the postponed choices made possible by the feminist movement. Faludi notes, for example, that in 1982 the Charlie perfume campaign replaced the liberated woman model with one who wanted a husband and family.

Several studies of women's images in advertising from this period would seem to confirm Faludi's position. Lazier-Smith's

influential 1986 study found ads to be more sexist in the mid-to-late 1980s than they had been in the early 1970s, a position that Kilbourne's *Still Killing Us Softly* confirmed. The most recent major study, in 1993, also supports this view; researchers writing in *Journalism Quarterly* concluded that, although women have gained ground in being portrayed as more autonomous and less home-centered since the 1970s, they are also more frequently shown in decorative roles. Reflecting the ads of the 1920s, these studies show that advertising in the 1980s and 1990s encouraged women's pursuit of personal pleasure and physical perfection rather than explicitly feminist goals. Instead of women's "liberation" or their support of other women, ads stressed a woman's self-improvement through commodity purchases. These ads also emphasized class identity over gender identity. Certain advertisers responded to feminism in the 1980s by changing marketing strategies and targeting certain groups of women consumers, specifically those with substantial disposable income.

While feminists have continued to monitor women's representation in advertising, advertisers and feminists are no longer trying to work together. In her study, Lazier-Smith argued that advertising's representation of women's roles suggests that the industry does not reflect society's demographics so well as it reflects the traditional balance of power. Later studies have also made the case that advertising reflects values rather than social realities. In terms of employment in the business of advertising, women have not advanced as quickly as some feminist activists once predicted or would have liked. And feminists who hoped that having women in key positions of power and influence within the industry would help promote a feminist agenda regarding the portrayal of women in advertising have been largely disappointed. While there have been women executives within advertising, as the careers of Rochelle Lazarus at Ogilvy & Mather and Charlotte Beers at J. Walter Thompson attest, they are successful because of their ability to set effective marketing strategies and manage for long-term growth. A feminist commitment may not directly hinder an employee's ascent into the executive ranks, but market success and perceived dominant social values take precedence.

Consequently, some feminists have been frustrated in their efforts to change the advertising industry from within according to their vision. Linda Busby and Greg Leichty's 1993 study concluded that the goals of feminists and advertisers are incompatible and, perhaps, even directly opposed. The story of *Ms.* magazine is a case in point. The publication, founded in 1972, was originally supported by advertisers such as airlines and life insurance companies that did not sell traditional "women's products." As *Ms.* entered the 1980s, however, its editors found it increasingly difficult to obtain advertising and were forced to accept ads for more traditional women's products. In her famous 1991 essay "Sex, Lies and Advertising," *Ms.* founder Gloria Steinem recounted her exhaustive struggle to obtain advertising from companies that did not want their products associated with "feminist" women, although the largely young, educated, and middle-class readers of *Ms.* were a valuable demographic group. Steinem concluded that making money alone was not of utmost importance to advertisers; to them, patriarchy "is also a bottom line." In 1991 *Ms.* became an ad-free, subscriber-supported publication.

Feminism's impact on advertising can be felt most in society's increased awareness of sexism in advertising, an awareness continually encouraged by feminist scholars, journalists, advertisers, and activists. There are currently many Internet sites devoted to the representation of women, and a large number of international women's organizations that continue both to monitor women's representation and to resist increasing global domination by a small number of corporations in which women have very little power.

ALLISON MCCRACKEN

See also Women: Careers in Advertising; Women: Representations in Advertising; *and color plate in this volume*

Further Reading

Bartos, Rena, *The Moving Target: What Every Marketer Should Know about Women,* New York: Free Press, 1982

Boddewyn, Jean, "Controlling Sex and Decency in Advertising around the World," *Journal of Advertising* 20, no. 4 (December 1991)

Busby, Linda, and Greg Leichty, "Feminism and Advertising in Traditional and Non-Traditional Women's Magazines, 1950s–1980s," *Journalism Quarterly* 70, no. 2 (1993)

Courtney, Alice, and Thomas Whipple, *Sex Stereotyping in Advertising,* Lexington, Massachusetts: Lexington Books, 1983

Ewen, Stuart, *Captains of Consciousness: Advertising and the Social Roots of the Consumer Culture,* New York: McGraw-Hill, 1976

Faludi, Susan, *Backlash: The Undeclared War against American Women,* New York: Crown, 1991; as *Backlash: The Undeclared War against Women,* London: Chatto and Windus, 1992

Lazier-Smith, Linda, "A New 'Genderation' of Images for Women," in *Women in Mass Communication: Challenging Gender Values,* edited by Pamela J. Creedon, Newbury Park, California: Sage, 1989

Marchand, Roland, *Advertising the American Dream: Making Way for Modernity, 1920–1940,* Berkeley: University of California Press, 1985

Ohmann, Richard, *Selling Culture: Magazines, Markets, and Class at the Turn of the Century,* New York and London: Verso, 1996

Steeves, H. Leslie, "Gender and Mass Communication in a Global Context," in *Women in Mass Communication: Challenging Gender Values,* edited by Pamela Creedon, Newbury Park, California: Sage, 1989

Steinem, Gloria, *Moving beyond Words,* New York: Simon and Schuster, and London: Bloomsbury, 1994

FHV

(FHV/BBDO)

Founded by Giep Franzen, Nico Hey, and Martin Veltman, in Amstelveen, The Netherlands, 1962; sold 30 percent share to U.S. agency Batten Barton Durstine & Osborn and changed name to FHV/BBDO, 1970; won "Print Campaign of the Century," "Advertising Personality of the Century," and "Agency of the Century" awards from the Dutch branch of the International Association of Advertisers, 2000.

Major Clients
Albert Heijn
Foot Locker Europe
Grolsch
Henkel
Mars, Inc.
Pepsi-Cola International
PTT Post
Rabobank

Sara Lee Corporation/Douwe Egberts & Pickwick
Schiphol Group

FHV, which was renamed FHV/BBDO when it became part of the BBDO family in 1970, was founded in November 1962 by marketing director Giep Franzen, art director Nico Hey, and copywriter Martin Veltman. The company is one of the largest advertising agencies in The Netherlands, both in billings and staff size, and is headed by three co-chief executive officers: Walter Amerika, creative managing director; Jacques Kuyf, account managing director; and Andy Mosmans, managing director of research and development.

Over the last four decades of the 20th century, the agency, based in Amstelveen, The Netherlands, evolved from an advertising agency into a creative marketing agency. It offers strategic branding, in-store concept creation, and other marketing services, as well as media buying and planning and creative advertising execution.

From its start in the early 1960s, FHV's mandate has been to combine creativity with sound marketing principles. FHV/BBDO is known for its long-standing client relationships; some of its clients having been with the agency for nearly 40 years. Douwe Egberts & Pickwick (coffee, tea, and tobacco brands acquired by Sara Lee Corporation) has worked with the agency since 1964; Henkel, a marketer of household cleaners and body-care products, since 1968; Pepsi-Cola International since 1973; baby-care marketer Zwitsal and Artis, the Amsterdam Zoo, since 1978; supermarket chain Albert Heijn, since 1980; PTT Post, The Netherlands' Royal Mail, since 1986; and Grolsch beer, since 1989.

In 1970 Batten Barton Durstine & Osborn (BBDO), then the world's sixth-largest agency, began a wave of international expansion, purchasing minority stakes in independent agencies around the world. Its first such alliance was with FHV, in which it acquired a 30 percent interest that year. The expansion continued through the 1980s, as BBDO acquired minority stakes in such agencies as Australia's Clemenger, the United Kingdom's Abbott Mead Vickers, New Zealand's Colenso, Germany's Team, and Argentina's Ratto.

By the time BBDO took an ownership share in FHV and renamed it FHV/BBDO, the Dutch shop was already one of the largest ad agencies in The Netherlands, a position it retained into the 21st century. The agency, with billings of $7.68 million in 1969, had and continues to have a client base comprised of both Dutch and international advertisers. It shared two accounts with BBDO prior to the purchase: Henkel, for which FHV handled Vernel fabric softener and Fleuril and Fakt detergents, and Gillette Company, for which it was responsible for the Right Guard, Dippity Do, Tempo Pen, Paper-Mate, and Braun brands. Some of FHV's other clients at the time were Amsterdam-Rotterdam (Amro) Bank, Heineken's Amstel beer, Koninklijke Brinkers' Wajang margarine, Hero soft drinks, Organon pharmaceuticals, and Centra Z, a grocery chain.

In the 1970s FHV/BBDO gained a reputation for award-winning creative work. One notable FHV/BBDO campaign was for Douwe Egberts's Drum cigarette tobacco in 1975. In one commercial set on a train, a couple rolls their own cigarettes as havoc reigns around them. Indians attack the train and a flaming arrow pierces an apple on the head of a child in the couple's compartment as the child reads a book about William Tell; the man then uses the flame to light his cigarette. The spot ran in movie theaters and was intended to make roll-your-own tobacco acceptable socially. It gained attention in the media and among consumers and won several advertising awards.

In 1981 FHV/BBDO expanded its offerings to a full range of integrated communications services, becoming one of the first full-service advertising agencies in The Netherlands. That expansion continued, and by 1997 FHV/BBDO had transformed itself into what it called a creative marketing agency, covering an entire range of marketing and communications services, including advertising.

By the mid-1990s, FHV/BBDO was the third-largest agency in The Netherlands, according to the United Kingdom's *Campaign*

FHV created this striking campaign for Artis Zoo in Amsterdam, The Netherlands, using images created by various Dutch artists and photographers.

magazine, with $19.7 million in gross income placing it after Ogilvy & Mather ($23.3 million) and PPGH/JWT ($21.6 million) in the rankings. FHV/BBDO's work during this period included the Dutch launch of a new, clear, caffeine- and preservative-free soft drink from Pepsi-Cola International called 7-Up Ice Cola, which combined the tastes of 7-Up and Pepsi. The effort included TV and extensive sampling.

Other clients during the mid- and late 1990s included Dutch financial institution Rabobank, which retained FHV/BBDO in 1997, and longtime client Zwitsal, for which it oversaw the launch of a new children's toiletries line under the Zwitsal brand, including styling gel, shower gel, bath foam, shampoo, and soap, supporting it with TV, cinema, and women's magazine advertising.

By 2000 FHV/BBDO was one of the largest European offices of BBDO. It continued to expand its services and reorganized as FHV Group in 2000; FHV Group is part of BBDO Nederland, along with Bennis Porter Novelli and other agencies. According to

Advertising Age, BBDO Nederland, Amstelveen, ranked number three among BBDO units in Europe in 2000. Euronext, a European stock exchange formed through the merger of the Amsterdam Exchange, the Paris Bourse, and the Brussels Exchange, retained FHV/BBDO and its BBDO sibling companies in Belgium and France as its agencies of record in 2000.

XPAT.net, owned by the Amsterdam-based Expatriate Information Network, also tapped FHV/BBDO for a corporate identity campaign as well as the launch of a Web site providing news, information, and advertising for expatriates living in Europe. Other international and Dutch clients as of the first years of the 21st century included confectionery company Mars, Inc., for which FHV/BBDO handled M&M's and Snickers; Hunkemöller, a European chain of women's apparel and lingerie shops; Greenery International, a marketing group for fruit and vegetable growers; Maastricht, The Netherlands–based Libertel telecommunications company; Schiphol Group, the organization that operates the Amsterdam airport; dairy marketer Campina Melkunie; and Foot Locker Europe.

FHV/BBDO's work has won creative accolades throughout its history. The Dutch chapter of the International Advertising Association named an FHV/BBDO campaign for the Albert Heijn supermarket chain The Netherlands' "Print Campaign of the Century." It also chose FHV/BBDO as the "Agency of the Century" and its cofounder Giep Franzen as "Advertising Personality of the Century."

KAREN RAUGUST

Further Reading

"BBDO Sets Pact with Dutch Shop," *Advertising Age* (1 June 1970)

"Drum Promoting Roll-Your-Own via Dutch Theater Ad," *Advertising Age* (1 December 1975)

Reed, David, "A Tale of Two Cities: Netherlands," *Campaign* (15 July 1994)

"7UP Ice Cola Launches," *Euromarketing* 8 (14 February 1995)

Wentz, Laurel, "BBDO Victor in '95 Creative Awards Derby," *Advertising Age International Supplement* (June 1996)

Fiat Panda

Principal Agencies
(in house staff)
D'Arcy Masius Benton & Bowles
Barbella Gagliardi Saffirio
Barbella Gagliardi Saffirio DMB&B

Fiat, founded in Turin, Italy, in 1899, is one of the world's biggest industrial groups, operating in 62 countries via 888 companies, which employ about 242,000 people, including more than 95,000 employees outside of Italy. Fiat operates 211 production facilities (94 outside of Italy) and 126 research and development centers (41 outside of Italy). Almost 40 percent of Fiat's products are manufactured outside of Italy, while sales outside of Italy account for 62 percent of Fiat's sales.

Fiat Group companies are organized into ten operating sectors: automobiles, commercial vehicles, agricultural and construction equipment, metallurgical products, components, production systems, aviation, rolling stock and railway systems, publishing and communications, and insurance. According to the company's mission statement, Fiat "is an Italian industrial group with a strong international presence. Operating primarily in the automotive industry and related services, it is also a major player in other manufacturing activities."

In the early 1980s, continuing its tradition of introducing small cars (*venture utilitarie*) into the market, Fiat launched the Panda, named for the animal used as the logo of the World Wildlife Fund.

The Panda represented the first time that Fiat had entrusted the design of a mass-production model to a designer outside the Fiat Group, Giorgetto Giugiaro, the founder of Ital Design. The car was innovative, both in its general design and because of the new systems used in its production.

Initially, the advertising campaign (television and press) for the Panda was handled by Fiat's house agency, which traced its origins to Fiat's press and propaganda department created in the 1940s by Gino Pestelli. In this first campaign, the Panda was defined as "a great small car," notable both for its roomy passenger compartment and spacious trunk. The car was also advertised as "the small car that changes the concept of a small car." In 1982 a new version of the car, the Super, was displayed at the automobile show in Paris. At the same time, a new slogan was introduced, "Panda, the freedom car." A 4x4 version of the Panda appeared in 1983.

In the first advertising campaign, the ads invoked an unusual visual reference, using two different models of athletic shoes to represent the new cars. Athletic shoes were just then emerging in popular culture as symbols of free time, casual style, and comfort, and the images of the shoes suggested that the Panda, too, was associated with such pursuits.

In 1983 Fiat turned for the first time to the agency D'Arcy Masius Benton & Bowles (DMB&B), under the direction of Gavino Sanna, one of the best-known Italian creative executives, for a new campaign for Panda. This campaign was built around the slogans "The unbelievable world of Panda" and "The fantas-

An acclaimed Italian ad for the Fiat Panda said of the car, "If it didn't exist, it would have to be invented."
Courtesy of Fiat.

tic possibilities of Panda." The campaign focused on the car's versatility and several of the strengths of the product.

At the 1984 auto show in Turin, Fiat introduced the full line of Panda products, stressing the style and "charm" of the latest version of the car, the New College Panda. In January 1986, another new Panda, the Supernova, appeared. This car was first produced with a gasoline engine; a diesel oil version soon followed. The Supernova also incorporated a number of changes in overall design and in the interior of the car. The campaign for the Supernova line was created by the agency Barbella Gagliardi Saffirio (BGS), which had worked in a limited capacity with Fiat since the early 1980s. The ads exploited the name "Supernova," making use of associations between the car and astronomical images and figures of speech. The innovative nature of this latest addition to the product line was suggested by the claim "Panda, you have come a long way."

Between 1987 and 1990 Fiat introduced 13 new versions of the Panda. Each model had a particular image in the advertising campaigns by BGS. The Panda Young, introduced in 1987, for example, was advertised as an economical choice, showing "the importance of being a Fiat car" and representing the "unbeat-

able" Panda. Advertisements for the Sergio Tacchini Panda (launched in 1989), by contrast, were aimed at presumably sophisticated consumers and took advantage of the fact that the brand name Sergio Tacchini was well known in the world of tennis; the ads capitalized on the sports reference in the slogan "Set and jet set." Advertisements for the Trekking model suggested that the vehicle was capable of handling any driving situation or problem, from traffic jams to parking to the open road.

In another notable Panda advertising endeavor, Fiat sponsored a series of caravans in a campaign entitled, "Panda on the most difficult roads of the world." The "Panda in China" caravan, for example, started from Venice and followed the journey to the Far East made by Marco Polo. Between 1989 and 1991 Fiat also used a television and print campaign for Panda organized around the slogan "If it didn't exist, you'd have to invent it." No new campaign was created for the Panda for several years. Ads continued to run, but they retained the slogan, "If it didn't exist, it would have to be invented."

In 1998 Fiat relaunched the Panda line with an ad campaign created by the agency Barbella Gagliardi Saffirio DMB&B, which had been formed in 1996 by the merger of the two previous agencies handling the Panda ads. (Prior to the merger, both agencies had worked for Fiat at the same time, each dealing with its own models.) This campaign reaffirmed the established image of Panda as a product characterized by "easy access" and a "nice price." The campaign stressed the extraordinarily low price of the car (less than 10 million lire, or just less than $5,000) and appealed to a youthful market. In 1998 more than 119,000 cars were sold, a figure that rose to more than 121,000 in 1999. Ad spending for 1998 was 2.8 billion lire (about $1.5 million).

EDOARDO T. BRIOSCHI

Film. *See* Motion Pictures [Advertising of]; Motion Pictures, Television, and Literature, Representations of Advertising in

Financial Services

Financial services is a comprehensive term describing financial products related to retail and commercial banking, securities underwriting, brokerage and trust services, and insurance products. These services are provided to individual and commercial customers by banks, insurance companies, investment firms, and brokerage houses. The history of financial services advertising mirrors the evolution of the industry itself, reflecting the regulatory and demographic changes and advances in technology.

Early History

The first financial advertisements were sponsored by banks and insurance companies. They appeared in newspapers and resembled classified ads—lines of text with no image. Retail banks regularly advertised their locations, hours of operation, and savings deposits interest rates, and they promoted mortgage lending and bond sales. The ads frequently listed the names of the bank's president and secretary. Occasionally an advertiser would have a one-column illustration. The Globe Insurance Company, by reason of a single-column cut image of its trademark positioned at the top of the page, was a dominant advertiser in New York City papers in the early 19th century. The Mutual Insurance Company of New York was also one of the first to use illustrations in its advertising. An ad for the company in 1818 displayed an eagle beneath a banner with the word "protection" in bold capital letters across the top and advised readers to insure against loss or damage by fire. However, images did not regularly appear in financial advertisements until later in the century.

In 1896 the Prudential Insurance Company introduced its famous Rock of Gibraltar logo featuring the rock and an image of its home office. The company's slogan was embedded in the logo, announcing that "The Prudential has the strength of Gibraltar." The famous rock has appeared regularly in Prudential advertising for more than 100 years.

By the early 1900s bank advertisements promoted their locations along with other desirable features—accuracy in bookkeeping, signature checking, quality service—to attract customers. In 1907 the Schenectady (New York) Savings Bank took out a ten-page advertisement displaying the account number and balance of each of its 22,235 savings accounts. This allowed customers to reconcile their passbooks with the bank's recorded balance without making a visit. The ad was such a success that the bank distributed a circular to other institutions describing its efforts.

In 1906 the three leading companies in the insurance industry, Mutual Life, Equitable Life, and New York Life, were the subject of a scandal that involved company insiders milking corporations for the financial benefit of others. Following a public inquiry and corrective measures, Mutual Life Insurance sought to rehabilitate its image by conducting a national advertising campaign. The campaign cost approximately $100,000; ad copy proclaimed "The great difference in life insurance companies" and assured readers that "new management has been installed."

In the 1920s the Metropolitan Life Insurance Company launched an innovative series of ads promoting public health. Rather than using fear of illness to spur sales, the ad campaigns offered health tips, encouraged parents to take their children to the doctor for regular checkups, and urged people to learn about artificial respiration (today called cardiopulmonary resuscitation, or CPR). In 1925 one ad ran in *National Geographic* with the headline, "The toll of water." It explained how 6,000 Americans drowned each year and educated the public on the prevention of accidental drowning. Other companies continued to use scare methods to lure policy buyers, such as playing upon the loss of a spouse to spur life insurance sales. Fire insurance firms used ads showing houses in flames; one such ad carried the headline, "Stick 'em up, Santa Claus," followed by the warning, "It will be a good plan to apply for insurance . . . the very day you receive your Christmas jewels." Prudential pointed out to parents-to-be that the possibility of twins was greater than one would think, "One in eighty-nine, in fact."

At the same time, bank advertisements focused on making banks and bank managers more accessible to the public. Ads depicted bank managers as friendly people willing to assist potential clients and promoted the benefits of regular savings plans. In 1913 ads for the Mechanics Bank of New Haven, Connecticut, touted its courteous service and an "open office policy" for customers. In 1927 the Bowery Savings Bank encouraged potential clients to "Come in and talk over your financial problems."

Regulation and the Crash of 1929

The stock market crash of 1929 and the Great Depression ushered in an era of regulation of banks, insurance companies, and financial companies, including laws governing how they could advertise their services. Institutional advertisements that conveyed information about stock offerings, bond sales, mutual funds, and other financial services were subjected to tight government restrictions to end "blue sky" offerings—improbable claims of fabulous investment returns.

The U.S. Securities and Exchange Commission (SEC) now required "tombstone" ads, named for the black borders that usually appear around the text-oriented design. The rules regarding tombstone ads strictly limited their content to prescribed financial data and general company descriptions, leaving out product names and photographs of products. When stocks or bonds were sold and a prospectus was required, SEC rules imposed the requirement for tombstone advertising to prevent companies from making wild claims that could mislead potential investors.

Tombstones, found only in financial publications, are intended to attract potential investors who are sufficiently interested in the advertised offering to request a prospectus. As the sale must be made by prospectus, the ads may not include performance or performance-related information. They are limited to simply identifying the existence of the offering and the availability of a prospectus. Sales-oriented promotional language is forbidden. Although some advertisers introduced colored borders and company logos, and restrictions were relaxed for mutual fund advertising, these regulations remained largely in effect at the start of the 21st century.

Throughout the 1930s the public remained wary of the stock market, insurance companies, and banks. A Roper public opinion survey, conducted in 1939, revealed a high degree of distrust, lack of interest, and misunderstanding of the financial markets among consumers. Despite this negative public perception, financial advertisers looked beyond the difficulties of the Great Depression and employed educational and motivational themes in their ads.

Banks and investment companies worked with ad agencies ranging from the major shops that handled ordinary consumer products (J. Walter Thompson Company [JWT], Batten Barton Durstine & Osborn, McCann-Erickson) to agencies that specialized in financial marketing. Among the most important were Doremus & Company and Albert Frank-Guenther Law, Inc. Each of these agencies handled so many different clients in banking and investments that the normal rules of client conflict did not apply to these specialist agencies.

The Union Central Life Insurance Company, whose advertising was handled by JWT, ran ads appealing to fathers who wanted better lives for their sons. One ad headline read, "The lonely uphill struggle . . . You would like to save your boy," and suggested that "boys braving the handicap of lack of education" would have a more difficult future than "college men." An ad by Penn Mutual Insurance Company from the N.W. Ayer & Son, Inc., carried the headline, "The boy deserves his turn," and similarly suggested that uneducated youth would face a more difficult future than their educated peers.

However, one investment banker saw an opportunity in the consumer's distrust. In 1940 Charlie Merrill came up with a blueprint for a new company that would cater to a mass of investors as a "department store of finance" and would bring "Wall Street to Main Street." The company, Merrill Lynch, E.A. Pierce & Cassat, introduced itself to the public by running national advertisements. The first ad, from Albert Frank-Guenther Law, consisted of a "Statement of Our Basic Policy" and touted the company's nine principles of operation. The first principle read, "The interests of our customers must come first." The ad received considerable attention, and by the end of the year, the company had increased its customer accounts by more than 20 percent.

In the 1950s Merrill Lynch, Pierce, Fenner & Beane, as it was then known, used advertising to expand its reach and attract new customers. One advertisement (also from Albert Frank-Guenther Law) that appeared in the *New York Times* contained 6,540 words—the most ever used on a single page. The headline read, "What everybody ought to know . . . about this stock and bond business." The ad featured "plain talk" about investing that explained the business of Wall Street to average consumers. An offer for an information booklet generated 10,000 responses.

With a traditional emphasis on personal selling, financial services advertising created general awareness and provided field support for agents and brokers. However, much advertising was confined to selected print media, including newspapers and magazines. In the 1970s competition among Wall Street brokerages was fierce. In response, Merrill Lynch broke from the pages of business and financial journals and took its advertising into U.S. living rooms through television. During the 1970 World Series, the company launched a television campaign, later supported by print media, that took its department store of finance directly to Main Street investors. Its memorable campaign featured a herd of bulls thundering across a beach. The narrator proclaimed, "Merrill Lynch is bullish on America."

Following Merrill Lynch's lead, E.F. Hutton also launched a memorable campaign created by Benton & Bowles that same year. The company wanted to build on its image as a stable institution providing quality investment advice. Its goal was simple: to get customers to listen when its account executives called. One

Merrill Lynch is bullish on America.

We hold no brief with those who take a dim view of America. At Merrill Lynch, we are bullish on America. Now and for the long haul.

Here are some key indicators from the reports of our own economic analysts:

• By the end of this year, America's economy should top $1.1 trillion—highest in our nation's history.

• In 1972, U.S. corporations expect to spend $89 billion for plants and equipment—up 9% from this year's indicated total. On top of that, $21 billion will go into research and development.

• Industrial production should climb at a rate of 5 to 6 percent per year during the 1972-1974 period.

• Consumer purchases of goods and services are expected to increase at a rate of 4.7 percent through 1974. Spending for durables will be sharply up.

Those are just a few figures from our economists (we'll be glad to send our current business outlook on request).

We see other favorable signs, some within our own offices—and we have 197 of them throughout the U.S. This year, Merrill Lynch will welcome about 400,000 new customers. Approximately 35 percent of those people will be making the first investment of their lives in the securities market. *They* must be bullish on America.

A matter of attitude.

Any long-range view of America's future must, of course, be tempered by the realities of today's problems.

And economic projections—no matter how exhaustive—do not suggest how those problems will be solved.

Will they be solved?

That is a matter of attitude rather than facts. Of spirit rather than statistics.

We are businessmen, not sociological seers, but we have been a part of America's economic life for a long time. And we are consciously aware of a force in this country that is more easily felt than defined. It is part energy, part imagination, part pride. Call it American know-how—call it American instinct—call it what you will, *it gets things done*. And it is alive and thriving.

Let others count this country out, if they wish.

At Merrill Lynch, we are bullish on America.

Merrill Lynch, Pierce, Fenner & Smith Inc

A 1972 ad used a memorable slogan and a herd of stampeding bulls to promote Merrill Lynch's services in a fiercely competitive market.

television ad featured two well-appointed ladies discussing investments at a garden party. When one mentions that her broker is E.F. Hutton, a hush immediately falls over the party, and the guests turn their heads to hear what she has to say. The voice-over then delivers the tag line: "When E.F. Hutton talks, people listen."

Rise of Credit Cards

The postwar economic boom of the 1950s gave rise to mass consumerism in the United States. Credit cards offered consumers a convenient method of paying for goods and services. The first charge card, the Diners' Club card, was introduced in 1950. It was followed eight years later by the American Express Card and the BankAmericard. Master Charge, later known as MasterCard, would arrive in 1966. As the fledgling cards worked to build their merchant networks, a battle for consumers was brewing.

In 1975 American Express launched its popular campaign to promote consumer acceptance of its American Express Card. The company's "Do you know me?" campaign, from agency Ogilvy & Mather, consisted of television ads featuring high achievers whose names were better known than their faces. While the average person might not recognize the spokesperson, the card extended to them the status they deserved. The ad campaign ran for 11 years and incorporated such personalities as track-and-field star Jesse Owens, bandleader Benny Goodman, author Stephen King, and violinist Itzhak Perlman. The commercials ran concurrently with another American Express campaign promoting traveler's checks, which had been launched a year earlier. The notable ads featured the actor Karl Malden, who, for 21 years, was heard admonishing travelers, "Don't leave home without them."

Competition among bankcard issuers remained fierce as banks of all sizes entered the business. In 1977 BankAmericard was relaunched as Visa, with a heavy print and radio advertising campaign aimed at younger consumers. The new moniker provided greater name recognition worldwide because it was pronounced the same in every language.

Citibank launched an aggressive television advertising campaign promoting the uniqueness of its Visa and MasterCard credit cards, which offered cardholders "Citidollars" earned on all their purchases with the card and other exclusive benefits. In 1985 the smaller Savings Bank of Baltimore (Maryland) increased its cardholder base by 12,000 through an advertising campaign launched in the city's Sunday paper. The ad contained a complete credit application for the no-fee credit cards with no minimum balance required. By the mid-1980s, credit card companies were among the top three financial service advertisers behind insurance firms and banks.

Deregulation

The financial services industry would remain a highly segmented field until the push for deregulation in the 1970s. In 1975 the U.S. Congress passed legislation that eliminated restrictions on brokerage houses and thrift institutions, promoting competition in all financial services industries. With fewer restrictions and changes in federal tax laws, companies could provide an array of products that they had previously been prohibited from offering. Mergers in the financial sector became so frequent that some customers were often confused about their own brokerage firm or bank's name.

Wall Street firms also recognized that many investors had difficulty distinguishing among them and turned to advertising to more clearly delineate their identities. They frequently employed TV ads to present a positive image of the company. Advertising of specific products or services was limited to radio and print.

Dean Witter Reynolds, formed in 1978 after a merger, turned to television and radio advertising to build awareness and to capitalize on its strength in regional markets. The initial campaign featured happy Dean Witter customers who had just received good news from their broker. The ads used the theme line, "You look like you just heard from Dean Witter," implying that working with Dean Witter brought wealth and relief from worry.

Shearson Loeb Rhoades, which became the second largest Wall Street firm after a series of mergers, also rolled out a major campaign in 1979 to communicate its new identity. In each 30-second TV spot, a Shearson broker challenged a speaker who spouted a platitude such as, "A penny saved is a penny earned." Each time, the broker explained why the old saying was nonsense in the current economic environment. "With today's inflation, a penny might do better in a Shearson-managed investment program," the broker suggests. Each commercial ended with the tag line, "When the question is money . . . the answer is Shearson."

Although Smith Barney was one of the smallest among Wall Street advertisers, its 1979 campaign from Ogilvy & Mather was among the most enduring. The firm hired as its spokesman actor John Houseman, who had recently played the role of a tyrannical Harvard law professor with deep integrity who embodied the old-fashioned values of hard work and intellectual rigor. TV spots featured the actor in various Wall Street situations declaring, "Smith Barney. They make money the old-fashioned way. They *earn* it."

Consumer demographics were drastically changing too. Baby boomers, the largest and wealthiest generation in U.S. history, had come of age. Women had entered the workforce in great numbers. Two-income families had more disposable income than traditional families with a single breadwinner. Growing numbers of families were moving to the suburbs in search of a better quality of life. Financial service advertising reflected these changes.

In 1975 PaineWebber moved to create broader awareness of the firm in the upscale consumer market. The company initiated its "Thank you, PaineWebber" campaign, which showed scenes of people celebrating a child's graduation from college, admiring a new fur coat, or lounging poolside, along with the tag line implying that PaineWebber deserved the credit.

While financial institutions primarily marketed themselves to men, many realized that they could not overlook the business opportunity created by the 2 million women entering the workforce annually. Headlines in traditional women's magazines such as *Vogue*, *Harper's Bazaar*, and *Working Woman* appealed directly to this burgeoning market. One Chemical Bank ad claimed, "What this country needs is more women in business." Another from

New York Life suggested that "A family with dual incomes needs to protect both." Oppenheimer Investor Services asked, "Heard the one about the woman who made a fortune? . . ."

Deregulation also gave rise to advertising by direct-to-consumer mutual funds and discount brokerages that had previously been hampered by government restrictions. One mutual fund company, Fidelity Investments, relied heavily on advertising as it switched from a broker distribution system to direct-to-consumer distribution in the 1970s. It frequently advertised in newspapers and magazines and emphasized the performance of its funds. Its later ads featured the company's highly successful Magellan fund and its manager Peter Lynch, who, through the firm's TV commercials, was to become one of the most recognizable faces on Wall Street.

Charles Schwab & Company was the first discount brokerage to advertise nationally. The company discovered early on that having a real name and face appealed to many independent investors. The practice began in 1975, when Charles Schwab paid the *San Francisco Examiner* $1.50 for a black-and-white file photo of himself next to a stack of order files. The photo appeared in the fledgling company's first newspaper ad, a small box promising new customers a free Kodak Hawk-Eye camera for opening an account. Throughout the 1980s Schwab remained a fixture in most of the company's ads, concluding his TV spots with the tag line: "You'll like our low commissions, our convenience, and our quality service. That's a promise."

Friendly Companies

During the 1980s large financial service companies faced pressure from consumers to become more friendly and empathetic. In 1985 Metropolitan Life departed from the typical insurance advertisement that attempted either to scare consumers or to show images of reliability. Its campaign featured the characters from the popular "Peanuts" comic strip as insurance salespeople. The approach stressed reliability but also conveyed warmth and humor. Each of the ads ended with the tag line, "Get Met. It Pays."

Advertisements for the John Hancock Mutual Life Insurance Company suggested that the company understood real people and their needs. In 1985 the 124-year-old life insurer was under siege from banks and brokers. The company had expanded its services to compete but needed to let the world know what it offered. Hancock's "Real life, real answers" campaign featured emotional dramas that combined reality with sentimentality. There was no sales pitch, and the company name was used only at the end of the ad. The campaign ran for ten years and was credited with sharp increases in sales.

After the stock market crash of 1987, many major investment houses changed their advertising to messages of reassurance about market conditions. Merrill Lynch & Company continued to run ads using the symbol of the bull to portray strength and stability. In one commercial, a storm sweeps through a farmyard. But the barn and its weathervane, which carries the familiar image of a bull, are left unscathed.

Other firms changed their ads to acknowledge that customers prized service and relationships over discovering how to make money quickly. They moved away from touting market know-how to pitching an eagerness to take a personal interest in each customer's situation. PaineWebber dropped its long-running "Thank you, PaineWebber" campaign in favor of new ads that told stories about PaineWebber brokers who were farsighted on behalf of clients. In one ad a daughter discovered that her newly widowed mother would not have to sell the house to pay the bills because her father worked out an investment plan years earlier that provided a steady income to his wife. "How did your broker know?" the ad ends. "He asked," is the reply. The ad closed with the line, "PaineWebber . . . We invest in relationships."

Automation and E-Trading

Improvements in technology became increasingly important to financial services companies as consumers demanded faster service and greater convenience. The introduction of automated teller machines (ATMs) in the early 1980s afforded bank customers the ease and convenience of electronic banking using a bank or credit card. Advertising was used to educate wary consumers about the new machines. Print ads for the AmeriTrust bank promoted its ATMs as a "Bank-in-a-Box" and detailed the available transactions, including dispensing cash, making deposits, and transferring money. For convenience-minded customers, the ads noted that the bank's "Fast Cashier" was available "All around the clock. All around town." Advertisements for FirstBank also promoted speed and convenience. One print ad touted the ATM as a "Wait reducing machine," while another noted that "It won't smile and say hello. But at three in the morning, neither would our tellers."

Breakthroughs in communications technology and the advent of the Internet eliminated distance as an obstacle to doing business with financial institutions. These advances gave rise to on-line brokerages such as E*trade and Ameritrade and provided new outlets for traditional brokerages. E*Trade Group, Inc., one of the first brokers to put stock trading on-line, took an aggressive approach in its advertising. In page ads in financial publications such as the *Wall Street Journal* and *Barron's,* the company announced what it believed to be the effects of technology on traditional investing. The copy read, "Your broker is now obsolete." E*Trade subsequently dropped the ads at the request of the National Association of Securities Dealers. The company also used television commercials to demonstrate the democratizing power of on-line investing. In one TV spot, a basketball player misfires on a slam dunk and bangs his head into a pole. He blames his shoes, throws them into the trash, and uses E*Trade to sell his stock in the fictitious shoe company.

Technological advances and regulatory reforms continue to transform the landscape of the financial services industry. Accordingly, financial services advertising will continue to reflect those changes, along with changes in consumers' attitudes toward the market, the industry, and their own finances. As such, the ads will

The popular "Peanuts" cartoon characters helped Metropolitan Life present a corporate image of warmth and reliability.
Peanuts © United Feature Syndicate, Inc. Courtesy of Metlife.

likely educate, encourage, and entertain investors, current and potential, as they have for more than 100 years.

PATRICK O'NEIL

See also Insurance

Further Reading

"Brokers Taking New Approach in '90s Advertising," *Marketing News* (10 June 1991)

Elliot, Stuart, "Wall St. Ads Taking Detour On Wary Path," *New York Times* (19 April 2000)

"Financial Advertising," *Madison Avenue* (December 1977)

"Financial Advertising to Women," *Madison Avenue* (November 1980)

Germain, Richard, *Dollars Through the Doors: A Pre-1930 History of Bank Marketing in America*, Westport, Connecticut: Greenwood Press, 1996

Hunt, Margaret, "Wall Street: Bullish toward Broadcast," *Madison Avenue* (November 1980)

Perez, Robert C., *Marketing Financial Services*, New York: Praeger, 1983

Pratt, Tom, "Whatever Happened to the Great Street Ad Campaigns?" *The Investment Dealers' Digest* (28 June 1993)

Presbrey, Frank, *The History and Development of Advertising*, Garden City, New York: Doubleday, Doran, 1929

Zenoff, David B., *Marketing Financial Services*, Cambridge, Massachusetts: Ballinger, 1989

Firestone Tire & Rubber Company

Principal Agencies

Sweeney & James Company

Grey Advertising Agency, Inc.

Campbell-Ewald Company, Inc.

J. Walter Thompson Company

Thomas Murray & Austin Chaney, Inc. (later Murray & Chaney-Ketchum)

Batten Barton Durstine & Osborn, Inc.

TBWA Chiat/Day

Harvey S. Firestone started the Firestone Tire & Rubber Company in 1900 in Akron, Ohio, the home of the U.S. rubber industry. With the automobile in development, Firestone quickly recognized the limitations of a business dedicated to producing tires for horse-drawn carriages. In 1905 Firestone convinced Henry Ford to put Firestone tires on the $500 Ford automobiles that would soon be coming off the assembly line. It was the first step for a small tire company that would become a global giant in the industry.

Firestone Tire & Rubber, through its agency of many years, Sweeney & James, was an early and loyal sponsor of network radio programming and would go on to become one of television's first advertisers. The Firestone Company sponsored a prestigious music program on the NBC radio network for nearly 30 years. It began in 1928 as the *Firestone Hour,* with show tunes and popular music. When the name was changed to the *Voice of Firestone* in 1937 the musical selections turned increasingly to the classical repertoire, and there were frequent appearances by guest vocalists from the Metropolitan Opera.

In the late 1930s the Monday night show was at the height of its popularity, drawing seven to eight million listeners weekly. It

continued on NBC in its traditional 8:30 P.M. time slot throughout the 1940s and began simulcasting live on NBC television in 1949. In the 1950s, as the audience for the television show dwindled, NBC was unhappy with the effect of those ratings on the programs before and after the valuable 8:30 to 9:00 prime-time slot. By offering classical and semi-classical concerts with well-known singers and musicians, the *Voice of Firestone* triggered a debate that continues today: the importance of high-rating mass audience shows versus that of culturally and intellectually significant programming that appeals to a smaller audience. The network proposed rescheduling the TV show while keeping the radio show at its regular time. Firestone refused.

NBC canceled both the radio and TV broadcasts of the *Voice of Firestone* in June 1954. One week later both programs appeared on the ABC network in their traditional time slot. The radio show was dropped in June 1957. After a brief summer hiatus, the TV show continued for two years until it was canceled in June 1959.

Public complaints were vociferous and included a joint resolution opposing the move by the National Education Association and the National Congress of Parents and Teachers. All three television networks offered Firestone time slots outside of prime time, but the company declined. The show was brought back to ABC in the fall of 1962 on Sunday nights, but despite all efforts, the audience never grew to more than 2.5 million viewers. The final performance took place in June 1963.

But even before it televised the *Voice of Firestone,* the company had made its mark as one of the first TV network sponsors. A little remembered documentary series, *Voice of Firestone Televues,* began airing in 1943 on the New York City station owned and operated by NBC. It included documentaries on a variety of subjects, including football, vocational guidance, and farming. NBC began providing the show to stations in Philadelphia, Pennsylvania, and Schenectady, New York, in 1944. *Televues* ended in January 1947.

In 1972 the Federal Trade Commission (FTC) ruled that Firestone's ads had falsely implied its tires were "safe under all conditions of use." The company was ordered to cease and desist making such claims unless scientifically substantiated. Firestone appealed the ruling unsuccessfully in late 1973. In 1976 the company learned what happens to those who ignore FTC cease-and-desist orders. Firestone was required to develop a $750,000 print and TV consumer education campaign focusing on tire safety. The TV spots began airing in April 1977, and print ads followed in June.

Then in July the National Highway Traffic Safety Administration issued notification that the Firestone 500 steel-belted radial tire had a "safety-related defect" and called upon the company to voluntarily recall the tires. Firestone initially balked, but after negotiating a waiver of penalties that could have reached $800,000, the company agreed to recall and replace millions of Firestone 500 tires. It was the largest recall in the history of the tire industry to that point (estimated at between 7.5 and 10 million tires).

Following the disastrous 1970s, Firestone brought in its first president from outside the company in 1980. John J. Nevin faced the challenge of repairing the damaged credibility of the 80-year-old company that was also suffering from a dramatically reduced cash flow. Nevin quickly made headlines as he cut 27,000 jobs, eliminated quarterly dividends, cut tire inventories, shut down seven North American tire plants, and sold the Plastics Division. The dramatic measures returned Firestone to profitability and allowed the company to focus on restoring its image.

In the spring of 1981 Batten Barton Durstine & Osborn (BBDO) introduced an innovative and costly ($10 million) TV ad campaign for Firestone. Departing from the traditional tire-on-the-road commercial, BBDO turned to humor. The new ads featured a fictional tire designer, George Peabody, who was frustrated by his assignment to create a better tire than the Firestone 721. The three TV spots all carried the tag line, "It's one tough tire to top."

They aired in prime time on the networks and during sports events and late-night programming; the latter was a new approach for tire advertising

The Bridgestone Tire Company of Japan bought Firestone in 1988 for $2.6 billion, and in 1989 Bridgestone USA and Firestone Tire and Rubber merged, forming Bridgestone/Firestone. In 2000 Firestone Tires used by Ford on its Explorer sports utility vehicles were shown to have a history of tread separation that resulted in fatal car accidents. The dimensions of the problem quickly escalated from crisis to scandal when it was revealed that the manufacturer had knowledge of the problem. Six-point-five million Firestone tires on Explorers were recalled, and relations between Ford and Bridgestone/Firestone were irreparably damaged as each blamed the other's product for the accidents. Late in 2001 Firestone reached a $41.5 million settlement with authorities from 53 U.S. states and territories. The settlement required the tire company to cooperate with the continuing investigation of Ford to determine what and when the auto manufacturer knew about tire performance problems on the Explorer. There were 271 fatalities linked to accidents caused by the defective tires and more than 800 serious injuries.

SANDRA L. ELLIS

See also color plate in this volume

Further Reading

Cohen, Stanley, "ANA Seeks to Intervene in FTC 'Corrective Ad' Case," *Advertising Age* (7 December 1970)

"Firestone's Voice Silenced by NBC," *New York Times* (15 May 1954)

"FTC Rules Firestone Ads Deceptive," *Advertising Age* (9 October 1972)

"Sparring Begins in Firestone Ad Case," *Advertising Age* (15 March 1971)

United States Congress, House Committee on Interstate and Foreign Commerce, Subcommittee on Oversight and Investigations, *Safety of Firestone Steel-belted Radial 500 Tires: Hearings . . .*, Washington, D.C.: United States Government Printing Office, 1978

Foote, Cone & Belding

(FCB Worldwide)

Founded as successor agency to Lord & Thomas, 1943; became first major U.S. ad agency to make a public offering of its stock, 1963; Foote, Cone & Belding (FCB) Communications set up as holding company, 1980s; entered into partnership with Publicis in Paris, France, and set up joint venture called Publicis-FCB, 1988; Foote, Cone & Belding Communications reorganized and became True North Communications, 1992, with FCB Advertising as the largest of True North's many units; True North acquired by Interpublic Group of Companies, 2001.

Major Clients

American Tobacco Company (Lucky Strike, Pall Mall)
Armour-Dial, Inc.
Clairol, Inc.
Coors Brewing Company
Ford Motor Company (Edsel)
Hall Bros. (Hallmark Cards)
S.C. Johnson & Son
Kimberly-Clark Corporation
Kraft General Foods
Levi Strauss & Company
Mazda Motors of America
Nabisco
Paper-Mate, Inc.
Sears, Roebuck & Company
Toni Company
Hiram Walker, Inc.
Zenith

On 4 January 1943 Foote, Cone & Belding (FCB) opened for business as the successor agency to the venerable Lord & Thomas (L&T). It was basically the same agency it had been the week before, with the same offices, furniture, accounts, and people. The only changes were the agency's name and the departure of Albert Lasker, who had built L&T and had been one of the founding figures of advertising. Late in 1942 he had decided to retire from the agency he had owned since 1910. He retired the L&T name as well. He handed all the company's assets over to the men who ran its three offices: Emerson Foote (New York City); Fairfax Cone (Chicago, Illinois); and Don Belding (Los Angeles, California). They promptly renamed the company Foote, Cone & Belding and incorporated on 31 December 1942.

Formative Years

The new partners raised $100,000 to start operations. Each took slightly less than a third of the stock. The balance went to the agency treasurer, who invested $4,000. Total agency billings at the time of the changeover were approximately $23.5 million. In one of his final acts as head of L&T, Lasker had recommended to all his clients that they continue with the reorganized agency, yet there was some question as to whether they would. All doubt was eased when American Tobacco, its largest client, announced that it would stay with FCB.

After a short time at Leon Livingston Advertising in San Francisco, California, and a failed attempt at running his own company (Yoemans & Foote), Foote had been hired by the J. Stirling Getchell agency to work on the Chrysler account. He joined L&T in 1938 as an account executive on Lucky Strike and proved himself to be a skilled handler of American Tobacco's dictatorial chief, George Washington Hill. He rose quickly and became general manager of the New York City office by 1941.

Cone had joined L&T in 1929 but left in the mid-1930s for the Getchell agency to work on DeSoto and Plymouth, both part of the agency's Chrysler business. He returned in 1936 and worked on the Southern Pacific Railroad account in L&T's San Francisco office. After a brief tenure in New York City, he went to Chicago in April 1942 and was named manager in October. Belding began as a nonpaid office boy in 1923 at the L&T Los Angeles office; he became general manager in 1938 with the move of Don Francisco to New York City.

In some ways the trio's position in 1943 resembled Lasker's position when he took over L&T. Lasker had neither founded the company nor taken over a struggling enterprise. He came into what was already one of the leading ad agencies in the United States. Forty years later Foote, Cone, and Belding did the same; only the scale had changed. But while L&T had reached maturity in 1904, advertising had not. Lasker, therefore, had the luxury of shaping function to form. By 1943 the new partners inherited not only a mature company but a mature industry, leaving them with two main jobs: first, to move away from the cult of Lasker's personality and institutionalize what he had built to run in perpetuity; and second, to keep the agency growing at the rate of the economy or better. FCB ended its first year with billings estimated by *Advertising Age* to be $27.5 million.

At the same time, there was a war going on. The United States was throwing 40 percent of its gross national product (GNP) at Germany and Japan, and for the duration FCB pushed conservation over consumption on everything from tires to toothpaste. The War Advertising Council began organizing agencies to undertake public service campaigns for appropriate causes, including U.S. savings bonds, Red Cross disaster relief, and timber conservation. In service to the latter cause, FCB created Smokey Bear for the U.S. Forest Service.

Hall Bros., maker of Hallmark greeting cards, was added to the agency roster in 1944 and would become another client on which FCB would make a profound and lasting impression. By the beginning of 1945, FCB ranked fifth among U.S. agencies.

FCB emerged from the war to face an unexpected irony for an ad agency. It had spent so many years crafting durable images for others, it had never stopped to think of its own image. In the spring of 1946 it got its first look at itself. During Frederic Wakeman's years at FCB as an account executive on Lucky Strike, he had seen everything and forgotten nothing. It all came out with a sexy and sharp satiric edge in his best-selling novel *The Hucksters* (1946). In 1947 Metro-Goldwyn-Mayer (MGM) turned it into the juiciest movie ever made about advertising.

Although soap replaced cigarettes in Wakeman's book, and critics discreetly did not mention names, the key players behind the tissue-paper-thin fiction were obvious to those in the advertising field. In the film, Sidney Greenstreet's Evan Llewellyn Evans turned the real-life George Washington Hill into Madison Avenue's answer to Citizen Kane. Adolphe Menjou played the part of the smart, opportunistic but frazzled agency chief whose opposite number was Emerson Foote. Said Foote: "I couldn't impersonate Menjou any better than he impersonated me." Clark Gable played the hero Victor Norman, a Rhett Butler of the boardroom with the guts to quit it all at the end. Wakeman viewed advertising as a submissive, fear-driven business, powerless to assert a will of

The memorable jingle created by Foote, Cone & Belding in 1956 helped make Pepsodent a leading toothpaste in that decade. *Courtesy of Unilever.*

its own. Ironically, however, in 1948 FCB would prove him wrong in one of the boldest and most courageous assertions of independence in the history of advertising.

Four months after *The Hucksters* was published, tobacco mogul Hill died. There then began a fierce, internecine battle for control of American Tobacco and, particularly, control of its advertising. On one side was Vincent Riggio, successor to Hill as president and an advocate of more "restrained" marketing policies. On the other was ad manager George Washington Hill, Jr., who was committed to continued production of the ads everybody loved to hate.

FCB was not affected at first. The agency's American Tobacco business grew by approximately $5.5 million in 1946–47 when the client shifted radio production work for Lucky Strike and Pall Mall from Ruthrauff & Ryan (R&R) to FCB. R&R had produced the popular Jack Benny radio show and other programs for the company. The only other agencies in the picture were N.W. Ayer & Son, which worked on television, and M.H. Hackett, Inc., which handled $500,000 in Herbert Tareyton business, a new brand that year. By the beginning of 1948 FCB controlled nearly $12 million in American Tobacco business, making it the largest account in advertising.

Tobacco Tensions

In the 18 months following the death of Hill, Sr., however, Hill, Jr., came into increasing conflict with Riggio over advertising issues. On 18 March 1948 he resigned, and six days later Foote announced that FCB would cease all work on the account as soon as the company selected a new agency. Foote had consulted with his partners. If they wished to retain American Tobacco he would understand—but he would resign. The choice was to resign the account.

The issues involved a long-standing combination of advertising principles and personal loyalties. The agency's relationship with American Tobacco went back to 1925. Foote and Hill, Jr., began assuming leadership in the late 1930s and continued to increase sales based on what the younger Hill called "principles and procedures long established in the company and essential to effective advertising." But after the death of the elder Hill, there was the feeling that their autonomy was being increasingly undermined by Riggio, who had joined American Tobacco in 1905 and come to the top through sales. The assignment of Herbert Tareyton cigarettes to the Hackett agency was a case in point. Hackett was Riggio's son-in-law. The resignation of Hill came when tensions with Reggio exceeded the limits of "respectful disagreement," placing FCB in an untenable position. Many felt that the agency merely anticipated the inevitable, at least as long as Hill's ally Foote was in the picture and acted first.

A startled industry blinked in disbelief, and 150 FCB staffers delayed buying their first television set. Never before had an agency amputated a quarter of its gross billings on principle, albeit a widely criticized one. FCB's New York City billings were halved, and American Tobacco stock dropped six points. American Tobacco wasted no time in naming a successor. Within two weeks Batten Barton Durstine & Osborne had Lucky Strike, and Sullivan, Stauffer, Colwell & Bayles was awarded the Pall Mall account.

Although American Tobacco under the Hills had earned a reputation for a raucous, hard-sell style of advertising, no one could deny that its ads had been effective. The trade press stood by FCB and even considered the action evidence of principle in a business better known for its opportunities. "Thoughtful advertising men cannot help applaud the action," *Advertising Age* editorialized, "which many think strikes a significant blow for the good of advertising [and] should help lend stature to the entire business." The agency bravely announced that it would not cut personnel. And by the good grace of timely new business and the launch of the Kleenex pocket pack, the Toni home permanent, and Dial deodorant soap, billings held even at year's end ($52.5 million), and FCB had slipped only one notch in the *Advertising Age* annual agency rankings.

In October 1950 Foote left FCB after several medical leaves, cashing in his estimated $1 million in stock. In 1951 he joined McCann-Erickson, where he remained for 13 years. He finally quit the smoking habit in 1959, and when McCann took on a tobacco account, he stated, "I will never have anything to do with any agency which promotes the sale of cigarettes." With that, he left and formed his own agency, Emerson Foote, Inc., which merged in 1967 with Bozell & Jacobs. Foote also became a force in the American Cancer Society. He died in 1992 at 85, the last survivor of the original FCB partnership.

Notable Campaigns

Pepsodent, which had come to L&T in 1918 and shot to national prominence in the early days of radio, left FCB in October 1951 for McCann-Erickson. During the 33 years it had been with L&T and FCB, it became so successful that Lever Brothers acquired it along with Pepsodent President Charles Luckman, who went on to head Lever. After four years at McCann, however, Pepsodent returned to FCB in 1955.

Belding, who had been the original account manager on the Sunkist business in the L&T days, retired in 1957 to become a consultant; he died in 1969. As the lone surviving partner, Cone presided over another 13 years of growth, enjoying the visibility and status of a socially conscious community leader. He was the last of the founding icons to run the agency. He became widely known to the public as an advocate of ethics in advertising. He almost never smiled, and only his secretary could read his handwriting. "His staff formed a wall around him as they would a king," said illustrator Don Pegler, who came to FCB in 1962 and became famous drawing Raid bugs. "Once I drew a cartoon of him and they were too shocked and afraid to show it to him."

Many of the agency's most noble hours bore the Hallmark imprint. Since the days of radio's *Hallmark Playhouse*, the marketing mantra FCB created had been, "When you care enough to send the very best." Hallmark founder Joyce Hall took it seriously and made it a point of honor that the quality of the product be matched by the quality of the advertising and the programming it

supported. Thus in the 1950s, *The Hallmark Hall of Fame* became the critics' favorite TV show, and Hall became the first sponsor elected to the Broadcasting Hall of Fame. For more than 20 years FCB operated a special production department devoted to the Hallmark television programs, which became the last major vestige of network programming totally controlled and produced by a single sponsor and agency. Hallmark was the kind of client about which agencies dream. If the elder Hill had represented one approach to advertising, then Hall defined its antithesis.

Other notable campaigns that came out of FCB during this period were the introduction of Paper-Mate ballpoint pens as well as work for Zenith, Contac cold tablets, Fritos, True Cigarettes, and Falstaff Beer. One of the agency's landmark campaigns came together in 1956 when a young copywriter named Shirley Polykoff was assigned to the Clairol account, a hair-care company that was preparing to introduce the first simple hair coloring system that women could use in the home. Polykoff went to the heart of every woman's concern about hair dye—discretion—with the line, "Does she or doesn't she?" Men were quick to see a sly double entendre, but women knew precisely what it meant and made the product a huge success. Other Clairol/Polykoff lines included: "The closer he gets, the better you look," and "Is it true blondes have more fun?"

In 1957 the Ford Motor Company launched the Edsel. FCB won the $12 million in Ford business, beating out rival Leo Burnett. It resulted in a break-even venture for FCB but a $350 million disaster for Ford. When asked what was wrong with the Edsel, Cone succinctly replied, "Almost everything." He, along with several FCB executives, was stuck with one of the failed models in his garage for years. It "was designed to an intellectual formula . . . a product of pure research." Thereafter the word *Edsel* entered the language as a synonym for failure.

Going Public—and Global

FCB entered the 1960s ranking tenth among the top ten U.S. agencies. Men in the agency still wore suits, never sport coats. Women wore skirts of a certain length. Memos outlined dress codes. Every employee received a complete physical and personality test before being hired. Copy and art departments were still on separate floors. As FCB marked its 20th year in 1963, billings hovered at $150 million, only one of the partners remained, and stock had been spread among approximately 100 employees. Cone's generation was passing; younger management wanted equity and a market for it.

Going public was in the air at several agencies. Papert, Koenig, Lois, a small, $6 million agency, had become the first to offer stock to the public in May 1962. At FCB, Chairman Robert Carney was pushing for a similar move. In August 1963 the company, then America's eighth-largest shop, became the first of the major agencies to make a public offering: 500,000 shares representing 40 percent of the company went on the block at $15.50 a share. It was a triumph for many FCB executives, who had bought their shares nine months earlier for $4.75. Within a year, the price climbed to $18.25. More important, as a result of the public offering, a major agency opened its books to public scrutiny for the first time; it made fascinating reading. Salaries were revealed: Carney earned $100,000 a year; Cone, $95,000; chairman-to-be Arthur Schultz, $47,500. Perks included a chauffeur and limousine, an imperial practice that lasted until the 1980s.

In 1971 FCB Los Angeles introduced the Mazda into the United States, a Japanese car with the world's first rotary engine. It was extremely quiet but not fuel efficient. When the oil crisis caused gasoline prices to double in 1973, sales plummeted, forcing the automaker to convert the car to a conventional power source.

Also in the 1970s the largest U.S. agencies continued to expand their global billings. FCB ranked fifth in domestic volume at $234 million in 1973 but failed to make the top ten in worldwide billings. The agency began a more aggressive international expansion program that brought it into alliances with agencies in Europe, South Africa, and Australia. By 1982 its international rank rose to ninth on billings of $1.2 billion. Further acquisition boosted that figure to $1.8 billion in 1984.

It was the billings growth that would be the most impressive. To put it into perspective, in the 30 years (1912–42) that Lasker owned Lord & Thomas, billings rose from $6 million to nearly $24 million, or 400 percent, which seemed enormous at the time. In the first 20 years of FCB, the numbers went from $24 million to $150 million, or 600 percent. After 30 years as a public company FCB went from $150 million to $6 billion, a leap of 4,000 percent. A global network of 180 offices in 46 countries fueled this growth, in addition to the growth of such long-term clients as Kimberly-Clark (1923), Levi Strauss (1930), Kraft (1954), and S.C. Johnson & Son, Inc. (1953). Its association with Sunkist, which the agency won in 1907 and continued to hold in 2001, is believed to be the longest unbroken agency-client relationship in U.S. advertising history.

Although billings grew and creative performance was high, earnings were sluggish. *Advertising Age* had named the company "Agency of the Year" in 1986. The New York office, which had been called "the runt of the litter" by *New York Magazine,* acquired considerable substance when FCB Chairman Norman Brown merged it with Leber Katz Partners (LKP).

LKP had become an acquisition target in the mid-1980s when FCB needed to strengthen its New York City presence. By the time LKP was acquired it ranked 36th among U.S. agencies. With the acquisition, FCB increased its gross billings by approximately $290 million. Lester Leber, who had been at Grey Advertising since starting his career in 1940, had formed Leber Advertising in 1952. Hollander & Son furs was the agency's first account. On 2 January 1954 Leber joined with Stanley Katz to form Leber & Katz. As a minor Manhattan agency serving such small but prestigious clients as Dunhill of London, it attracted little attention in its early years, breaking the $1 million mark in billings by 1958. In 1961 Grey Creative Director Onofrio Paccione joined the agency, and the agency name became Leber, Katz & Paccione. With Onanfrio as a one-third partner, the agency acquired a considerable creative reputation for graphics and photography, which were his specialty. Billings reached $23 billion on the strength of

OUR MOST SHAMEFUL WASTE!

Remember– Only you can PREVENT FOREST FIRES!

Foote, Cone & Belding's public service ad campaign for the U.S. Forest Service gave the American public one of its most enduring spokescharacters, Smokey Bear.

business from such companies as Ford, R.J. Reynolds (Vantage), Revlon (Pub cologne), and Diner's Club. After Paccione's departure in 1970, Seagram's became a major account and helped lift the agency volume to $150 million and its gross income to $19.6 million by 1980.

Brown also worked to put FCB in a commanding international position. He had seen the United States surrender consumer electronics to Japan; he did not want to see it cede advertising to the British. In 1987 the company opened the FCB Center in which to house its Chicago headquarters. It also created Foote, Cone & Belding Communications as a holding company for its various assets.

Although FCB sold off its public relations unit, Golin/Harris, early in 1989, it had already announced the previous May an agreement in principle to form an alliance with Publicis, France's number-one agency. The deal created the world's sixth-largest ad group. Arrangements were consummated several months later, giving FCB 26 percent equity in Publicis, as well as access to a client base that included Nestlé, Renault, and Shell. Publicis, under Maurice Levy, took a 51 percent stake in the new joint company,

Publicis-FCB. During one year it contributed 80 percent to the parent company's earnings. On that note of triumph, Brown retired in 1991. However, what had been a triumph for Brown would soon become trouble for his successor, Bruce Mason. Mason, who had been the only FCB board member to vote against the Publicis partnership, called for an audit, and Levy refused. Slights and insults mounted, followed by a deepening mutual suspicion. In October 1993, Publicis bought Groupe FCA, the French owner of Bloom Advertising, a U.S. agency in competition with FCB. In December 1994 FCB created a new holding company, True North Communications, with the intention of becoming a major multinational player. In February 1995 Mason announced that one of its strategies would be to seek majority control of Publicis-FCB. Levy immediately announced that Publicis would leave the partnership.

After more than a year of bitter negotiations, the parties agreed in principle on terms of separation in March 1996. The bitterness was almost equaled within True North itself. In June Mason was challenged by his own board, narrowly surviving when S.C. Johnson & Son, one of the agency's most valued clients, let it be known that if he went, so would Johnson. Mason remained but was removed from further dealings with Publicis. In January 1997, Publicis-FCB, the joint venture still generating 40 percent of True North's earnings, was dissolved, and True North began building its own European group.

With only the final details of the dissolution to be worked out, suddenly outright warfare erupted. In July 1997 True North said it would buy Bozell Jacobs Kenyon & Eckhardt (BJK&E), the holding company made up of Bozell & Jacobs and the former Kenyon & Eckhardt. The new entity, which would combine domestic billings of $8.2 billion (True North) and $2.5 billion (BJK&E), threatened to overshadow Publicis as well as reduce its stake in True North from 18.5 percent to 11 percent. In November Publicis answered with a hostile tender offer of $28 a share ($269 million) for True North. S.C. Johnson and other clients said pointedly that they would not work with Levy. But Publicis pressed forward, as much to undercut the pending $440 million BJK&E deal as to acquire the company.

Events moved quickly in December 1997. True North stalled Publicis by suing in federal court. Publicis countersued, and the court order was lifted. Finally, on 17 December a Delaware court ended the Publicis bid, and two weeks later True North shareholders voted to acquire the agencies of BJK&E. Bozell Worldwide continued operations under the new parent, True North, which passed the $12 billion mark in combined worldwide billings. The deal also brought Temerlin McClain, Poppe-Tyson, and 14 other Bozell units into True North Communications. FCB and Bozell Worldwide continued to function as independent agency operations within the True North family.

On 19 March 2001 it was announced that True North would be acquired for $2.1 billion by the Interpublic Group of Compa-

nies, the holding company that owned McCann-Erickson, the principal agency for Coca-Cola. The acquisition proved disruptive to FCB, which had major billings from Quaker Oats Company and several Quaker subsidiaries, including Gatorade, Aquafina, and Tropicana. But because Quaker was a unit of PepsiCo, Inc., the latter regarded FCB's purchase by Interpublic as presenting a direct conflict with its arch rival Coca-Cola. In September 2001 PepsiCo pulled $350 million–$400 million in Quaker business from FCB. To help compensate for the loss, Coca-Cola moved Dasani, Powerade, and Minute Maid to FCB, effective 90 days after the departure of the Pepsi brands, according to the standard agency-client contract. But PepsiCo, fearing that FCB employees familiar with its business might compromise confidentialities, sued to block FCB from taking any Coca-Cola business for two years. It was a move that startled not only FCB but the ad industry generally, where it was widely accepted practice for agencies to seek to replace lost business with new accounts in the same product category. In November 2001 the suit was settled privately under terms that permitted FCB to assume the Coca-Cola business 90 days after the withdrawal of the Pepsi-Quaker brands. Further, a dozen FCB staff members were barred from working on the Coke products until 1 June 2002.

JOHN MCDONOUGH

Further Reading

Belding, Don, *Five Talks on Advertising: Speaking from Practical Experience in 35 Years in Advertising,* New York: Foote Cone and Belding, 1960

Cone, Fairfax, *With All Its Faults: A Candid Account of Forty Years in Advertising,* Boston: Little Brown, 1969

Cone, Fairfax, *The Blue Streak: Some Observations, Mostly about Advertising,* Chicago: Crain, 1973

"Delaware Court Stops Publicis," *Wall Street Journal* (17 December 1997)

"Duel of True North and Publicis Get Uglier," *Wall Street Journal* (4 December 1997)

"End of Lord and Thomas Stirs Entire Advertising World," *Advertising Age* (4 January 1943)

"FCB to Sell 500,000 Shares," *Advertising Age* (19 August 1963)

Melcher, Richard, and Gail Edmundson, "A Marriage Made in Hell," *Business Week* (22 December 1997)

O'Toole, John E., *Making Ads: Some of the Things Foote, Cone, and Belding Knows for Sure about What Should Go into, and Stay out of, a Magazine or Newspaper Advertisement,* New York: Foot Cone and Belding, 1976

"The Pencils Are Busily Engaged," *Advertising Age* (2 September 1963)

"Publicis Heads for the Hills," *Wall Street Journal* (11 December 1997)

"Text of Foote, Cone, and Belding Stock Prospectus," *Advertising Age* (9 September 1963)

Ford Motor Company

Principal Agencies

N.W. Ayer & Son
Maxon, Inc.
J. Walter Thompson Company
Kenyon & Eckhardt, Inc.
Young & Rubicam, Inc.
Ogilvy & Mather, Inc.

At the beginning of the 20th century, the Ford Motor Company adopted the slogan, "1906 will be a Ford year." In the nearly 100 years since then, when it comes to advertising, virtually every year has been a Ford year. Nonetheless, Ford has endured some major public relations crises, has switched agencies frequently, and has had to cope with the often-difficult personalities of chief executive officers.

At age 16, Henry Ford moved to Detroit, Michigan, and became an apprentice in a machine shop in 1879. Despite his father's attempts to lure him back to the family farming business, Ford had an intuitive understanding of machinery that left him discontent with the life of a farmer. In the late 1800s, while Ford was tinkering with engines, German auto pioneers Gottlieb Daimler and Karl Benz developed the self-propelled gasoline vehicle. In 1893 the first American-built horseless carriage was taken for a drive in Springfield, Massachusetts. Despite his later claims, there is little proof that Ford had designed or built a self-propelled gasoline vehicle by 1892.

In 1893, the year Edsel Bryant, Ford's only child, was born, Ford became chief engineer at Edison Illuminating Company in Detroit. Three years later, Ford saw the first car on the streets of Detroit. Around this time, he completed what he referred to as a "quadricycle," a vehicle that presented few real improvements over then-current technology. Nonetheless, he was inspired to continue experimenting and in 1899 produced an operable car. On 30 November 1901, after his first attempt at a motor company failed the year before, he formed the Henry Ford Company. Ford and his backers soon fell into dissent, however, and Ford resigned on 10 March 1902. The company was renamed the Cadillac Motor Car Company.

Agency Relationships

Undaunted, the next year Ford launched Ford Motor Company, of which he was vice president and general manager, with responsibilities for design, engineering, and production. The first Ford car, the Model A, debuted five weeks later, in June 1903. Ford had two advertising agencies of record at that time: Chas. H. Fuller and O.J. Mulford Advertising Company. From 1904 through 1908, Ford managed its advertising internally. In 1905, Ford, touting its status as a well-established carmaker, rolled out the slogan, "Don't experiment: just buy a Ford."

The first circulars announcing the introduction of the Model T—"Model T Touring Car. $850.00. High Priced Quality in a Low Priced Car"—were mailed to dealerships in March 1908. The car was designed for rural America and quickly became hugely popular. Some Ford dealers were concerned about the aggressive advertising strategy. One wrote to Ford warning that the result of the circular would be to "flood the factory with orders," and another locked the publicity piece in a drawer to prevent potential buyers from inundating him with requests.

After handling ads in-house for several years, Ford bounced around from agency to agency for several more. The J. Walter Thompson Company became Ford's agency in 1910, to be replaced in 1912 by Glen Buck. The MacManus Company (which would produce "The Penalty of Leadership" ad for Cadillac in 1915) took over the account in 1914—the year Henry Ford announced his famous profit-sharing promotion. An ad for the Ford Coupelet proclaimed, "Buyers of this car will share in profits if we sell at retail 300,000 new Ford cars between August, 1914, and August, 1915." In 1916, Powers, Alexander & Jenkins took over the Ford account and managed it for two years.

From 1917 to 1923, Ford discontinued its paid advertising for products, except for its tractors and the Lincoln (which Ford acquired in January 1922, less than two years after its introduction by Henry Leland and its swift fall into bankruptcy); individual dealers provided their own advertising. In 1923 two new agencies were signed: Long-Costello, Inc., for Ford and the Brotherton Company for Lincoln. A 1923 Ford ad, which has been described as classy and low-pressure, depicted a doctor making a house call; the headline read, "Dependable as the doctor himself."

By this time, Ford had forced out the minority shareholders in his namesake company and was well on his way to wielding complete control over his domain. While he was apparently not terribly concerned that his drive to dispense with skilled labor through the assembly line might dehumanize workers, turnover was starting to become a problem. So on 5 January 1914, all eligible workers at Ford began to receive a basic wage of $5 per day—enough to enable them to purchase the goods they produced.

In 1925 McKinney, Marsh & Cushing, Inc., took over the account from Brotherton. Two years later N.W. Ayer & Son took over the accounts of Ford and Lincoln and managed the account until 1939. During the Depression years, the company lost money—$125 million from 1931 to 1933.

In 1940 McCann-Erickson, Inc., became the agency of record for Ford cars, and Maxon, Inc., signed on as the agency for Mercury, which Edsel Ford had championed as Ford's answer to General Motors' Buick when it was introduced in November 1938. The Lincoln account also went to Maxon. In 1941 McCann-Erickson began managing Ford's institutional advertising. In March of the next year, McCann-Erickson was terminated, and Maxon was removed from the Lincoln account in July. As those agencies were terminated, J. Walter Thompson Company (JWT) took over the accounts without an agreement. JWT has remained a major agency for Ford ever since, in an often-rocky relationship.

Ford's Leadership

By the 1930s founder Henry Ford was becoming increasingly erratic. A fierce anti-Semite, he had spent more money in the early 1920s distributing copies of *The Protocols of the Elders of Zion,* a tract that purported to lay out plans for the Jewish takeover of Western Christian institutions, than he had on Ford advertising. Ford's investment in network radio in the 1930s was mainly the *Ford Sunday Evening Hour,* a program of classical music and inspirational talks reflecting Ford's views of the world—although without the anti-Semitism.

During World War II, Ford, an isolationist, balked at making aircraft engines for British planes. This led to accusations that he was a Nazi sympathizer. By the time the United States entered the war in 1941, the Ford facility at Willow Run, Michigan, had begun producing the B-24 Liberator bomber. The company ceased civilian car production in 1942 and did not resume it until July 1945.

With Maxon's termination from the account in February 1943, JWT took over all Ford advertising. It held that position for two years, until Kenyon & Eckhardt, Inc. (K&E), began managing the institutional advertising, including Ford's advertising on Dinah Shore's television program in the 1950s.

In 1943 Edsel died, and Henry Ford, despite several serious strokes, once again assumed the presidency he had resigned in 1918 in favor of Edsel. An ongoing internal struggle for power at Ford was not resolved until Edsel's son, Henry Ford II, convinced his grandfather to resign in September 1945 and cemented Ford family control again. That year, the Ford Motor Company, which had manufactured 60 percent of the cars purchased in the United States in 1917, saw its share slip to 20 percent. Henry Ford died on 7 April 1947.

The 1940s

The death of Ford and the end of the war allowed the company to move aggressively to reestablish its name. Suddenly Ford was a significant presence on radio, with JWT putting the company into sponsorship of more contemporary shows such as *Philip Marlowe, A Date with Judy,* and *A Man Called X,* and of star vehicles for Bob Crosby, Dinah Shore, and, most famously, Fred Allen.

In March 1948, K&E opened offices in Kansas City, Missouri; San Francisco, California; and Washington, D.C, to better manage Lincoln-Mercury dealer accounts. It also put Lincoln-Mercury on television in *Toast of the Town,* a variety show hosted by columnist Ed Sullivan. Irving W. De Ridder and John J. Wiley, who had previously worked on the Lincoln-Mercury account at JWT, were put in charge of the Kansas City and San Francisco offices, respectively. JWT and K&E would remain Ford's only advertising agencies of record until 1954, when Ford signed Young & Rubicam (Y&R) to the Lincoln division. But the business returned to K&E in 1958.

When Lincoln and Mercury announced an intensive ad campaign in 1949 to back the addition of the Hydramatic automatic transmission to Lincolns and Lincoln Cosmopolitans in July 1949, the campaign consisted of ads in *The New Yorker, Newsweek,* the *Saturday Evening Post,* and *Time.* Ads also appeared in 1,300 newspapers, and radio spots were used extensively. In a departure, Ford also advertised the Hydramatic on its *Ford Radio Theater.* General Motors Corporation (GM) had actually developed the Hydramatic, which enabled drivers to drive without shifting gears. When Benson Ford, vice president of Ford and general manager of the Lincoln-Mercury division and one of Edsel's sons, emphasized that the system was backed by millions of miles of operation, he was referring to miles put on by drivers of competitors' products—GM's Oldsmobiles, Pontiacs, and Cadillacs.

The next year, John W. Shaw Advertising sued Ford and JWT for $450,000, alleging the defendants copied and used ideas for an ad campaign that Shaw presented to Ford. At the time in question, John Shaw was board chairman of Shaw-LeVally, Inc., an agency that had dissolved in 1947. According to the complaint, Shaw made an advertising presentation to Ford officials at company headquarters in Dearborn, Michigan, in December 1945. The presentation—which included copy, pictorial layouts, and explanatory material—was geared toward a complete campaign, including the idea for an illustration of a pair of hands on a Ford steering wheel and the slogan, "Get the feel of the wheel." Ford rejected the presentation the next month, but, according to the complaint, from April through December 1949 Ford used a series of ads "substantially similar, and in some respects identical, to said advertising plan or scheme and said proposed advertising material." The crux of the suit was the phrase "Take the wheel—try the feel of the Ford," and variations. The suit alleged that Ford had spent approximately $3 million on the campaign and that the ads had succeeded in boosting Ford sales. Shaw sued for $450,000, or its usual 15 percent commission on the $3 million. The complaint against JWT charged that agency representatives saw the Shaw material and appropriated it. While the complaint claimed that K&E placed some of the advertising, the agency was not named in the suit.

That same year, Dearborn Motors Corporation, the national marketing organization for Ford tractors, launched a series of community programs to promote American agriculture. The program included a new 40-minute Technicolor film, "Waves of Green." The movie, which was expected to be seen by 3,000 to 4,000 farmers during the six months of the program, took two years and $150,000 to create. Meldrum & Fewsmith, Inc., Cleveland, handled the effort.

Focus on Speed

To introduce its 1952 cars and trucks, Ford took virtually an all-media approach, using spread insertions in 54 newspapers in 42 cities, full-page ads in 6,050 newspapers in 5,400 cities, spots on more than 1,128 radio and 30 television stations, a live presentation on Ford's NBC television show *Ford Festival,* and 13,000 outdoor posters. The campaign that followed up the February 1

HIGH PRICED QUALITY
IN A LOW PRICED CAR

The Ford Four Cylinder, Twenty Horse Power, Five Passenger Touring Car $850.00 Fob. Detroit

THE one real automobile value among all the "season sensation" announcements is the big, roomy, powerful five-passenger touring car at the hitherto unheard of price of $850.00. A car that possesses at least equal value with any "1909" car announced, and at the same time sells for several hundred dollars less than the lowest of the rest.

Compare the following features of the new Ford car with those of any higher priced car offered and see if you can justify in your own mind the additional expenditure that buying any other car involves.

The model T is a 4 cyl. 20 h. p. five passenger family car. Vanadium steel, the finest and costliest steel manufactured, is used throughout the entire car. Unit power plant with magneto an integral part of same,—4 cylinders in one block, water jacketed cylinder head removable, offering easy access to all working parts of engine. 3 bearing crank shaft, cam shaft with 8 cams integral,—silent planetary transmission of new design, splash system of lubrication, —control on left side, all forward speeds by foot lever,—double system of braking,—shaft drive through only one universal joint to Ford system of final drive, patented in all countries. 100' wheel base, 56" tread, 30" wheels, 3" tires front, 3½" rear, where the wear is greatest. Gasoline capacity, 10 gallons,—225 to 250 miles supply,—long, clean-cut lines throughout, handsomely finished and you have the specifications of the real automobile value of this year and next and a couple more thereafter.

Vanadium steel is used throughout the entire car wherever strength is necessary. The axles, shafts, connecting rods, springs, gears, brackets, etc., are all of Vanadium steel,—each from a separate formula and all especially heat treated in our own plant and from our own analyses. We defy anyone to break a Ford Vanadium steel part with any test or strain less than 50% greater than is required to put any other special automobile steel entirely out of business.

The weight of the car is only 1,200 lbs.—brought about by scientific construction and the use of Vanadium steel. Not an ounce of necessary weight sacrificed, not an ounce of dead weight in the car.

That is one of the reasons the Ford car will run more miles for less money than any other touring car manufactured.

We make no apologies for the price,—any car now selling up to several hundred dollars more could, if built from Ford design, in the Ford factory, by Ford methods, and in Ford quantities, be sold at the Ford Price if the makers were satisfied with the Ford profit per car.

Your guarantee that this car is all we claim—and our claims are broad—is in the reputation of Henry Ford, who never designed or built a failure, and in the reputation of the Ford Motor Company, who have built $20,000,000 worth of successful cars of Ford design in the same factory, with the same organization and system, and bearing the same imprint that the Model T is manufactured under. It's the guarantee of works as well as words.

Delivery began October 1st, orders filled in rotation. Cars can be seen at all branch stores; get a demonstration if you are near by, if not, wire your order either for immediate shipment or definite future delivery.

FURTHER details in catalogue, which is yours for the asking.

Ford Motor Company

263 Piquette Avenue
Detroit

BRANCHES: { New York, Boston, Philadelphia, Buffalo, Cleveland, Chicago, St. Louis, Kansas City, Denver, Seattle. Paris, France. London, England. Canadian Trade:—Ford Motor Company of Canada, Ltd. Walkerville, Ont. Branch, Toronto.

This 1908 ad introduced the Model T and launched a revolution. With the Model T, the automobile became part of American public life.
Courtesy of Ford Motor Company.

introduction date of the new models included full-color magazine ads, Sunday comic sections, and ads in 5,250 newspapers in some 5,000 cities. Ford dealers followed the introduction with ads in 6,100 newspapers.

During this period, the industry was coming under fire for building faster cars. Certain executives at Ford and other carmakers blamed salesmen and advertisers for stimulating demand for faster and more powerful passenger cars. Industry engineers claimed that they had long resisted building more power and speed into cars. But the demand was there, and in order to remain competitive, Ford felt obliged to offer what the public wanted. The 1953 Lincoln-Mercury had a 205-horsepower engine, the highest offered by the industry. The blatant focus on speed continued until the mid-1950s, when U.S. automakers agreed to a resolution backing away from it—an agreement Henry Ford II broke in June 1962, when he informed the Automobile Manufacturers Association that Ford would no longer abide by it.

As Ford began to prepare for its 50th anniversary, the company realized it needed an image makeover to counter some perceptions about its founder. Sidney Olson, a K&E copywriter with a background as a newspaper editor, public relations man, and Hollywood screenwriter, spent weeks foraging through Ford archives looking for material that would help prove Henry Ford I was not an ogre. After several false starts, Olson developed the idea of an institutional campaign dubbed "The American road." The first phase of the campaign began with newspaper advertising in November 1951 to establish the phrase before it could be co-opted. It debuted in other media the following month. The first phase contrasted the American road "before and after" the development of the car. The second built a platform for the 50th anniversary, which was launched in June 1953, and the third focused on a forward look for Ford.

Phase two involved a $500,000, two-hour, two-network celebration titled "The American Road" that ran simultaneously on CBS and NBC on 15 June 1953. Time charges for the telecast, handled by K&E, came to $210,000. More than half of all television viewers watched "The American Road," which ran without any traditional commercials. To promote the event, Ford bought newspaper ads in more than 100 cities on June 14 and June 15. Leland Hayward produced the show, and Oscar Hammerstein and Edward R. Murrow provided commentary. Among the other stars involved were the singers Ethel Merman and Mary Martin, who performed a duet so riveting that Decca Records rushed a long-playing disc of the live performance into stores within days of the show.

During these years, Henry Ford II had been striving to return the company to its glory days. He muscled aside his brothers Benson and William. By the year of the company's 50th anniversary, Ford had surpassed Chrysler in sales and introduced the legendary Thunderbird. Henry Ford II did this in part through his hiring of the "whiz kids," college graduates who knew nothing about car making but had learned a great deal about management during the war. They included Charles "Tex" Thornton, Jack Reith, George Moore, Ed Lundy, Ben Mills, Arjay Miller, and Robert McNamara, who went on to serve as U.S. secretary of defense in the 1960s.

Debacle

While responsible for some of the greatest campaigns in American history, Ford was also responsible for one of the most fantastic marketing catastrophes: the rollout of its Edsel division. Ford decided to introduce a new division of mid-priced vehicles in the 1950s. Longtime rival GM had three classes. Chevrolet and Pontiac offered low-priced models; Oldsmobiles and Buicks were pitched as mid-priced alternatives; and Cadillac served as the top of the line. But Ford customers had only two choices: inexpensive Fords and high-priced Lincolns. Henry Ford II and Ernest Breech, Ford's chairman, spearheaded an effort to fill the void in 1952.

Ford enlisted Foote, Cone & Belding (FCB) to develop a brand for its "E" (experimental) division, slated for release in 1956, the year the company went public. Finding a name for the vehicle was an ordeal. After gathering more than 18,000 suggested names, the list was whittled down to 16. The final determination was put before Ford's executive committee on 8 November 1956. Henry Ford II was absent that day, and Breech chaired the meeting. According to legend, Breech surveyed the committee and said, "Why don't we just call it the Edsel!" The car line of the future, slated to roll off the production line in 1957, was to bear the name of Henry Ford's only son. Although it was a name that newspapers had suggested for the new Ford division a year earlier, the idea met with fierce resistance from company executives and even members of the Ford family. C. Gayle Warnock, newly appointed as the Edsel division's public relations director, wrote in a company memo, "We have just lost 200,000 sales."

Despite the misgivings, plans to launch the Edsel shifted into high gear. After $250 million in development costs, the first Edsel models, with their instantly recognizable horse-collar grilles and push-button gear selectors, rolled off the production lines in 1957. Edsels were first put on public display in September of that year. But of the more than 2.5 million Americans who saw the vehicles, few viewed them as anything other than higher-priced versions of other manufacturers' cars.

Already in a frenzy promoting the Edsel line, Ford ratcheted up its marketing even further. On 13 October 1957, Ford booked an hour-long slot on CBS in place of the wildly popular *Ed Sullivan Show*, enlisting Bing Crosby, Frank Sinatra, Louis Armstrong, and Rosemary Clooney to turn the Edsel introduction into a national event.

Preliminary plans called for 200,000 Edsel sales in 1957. Only 63,107 drove off showroom floors. In December 1958 Ford moved Edsel from FCB to K&E, while shifting the Lincoln and Continental accounts from K&E to FCB. In October 1959 the automaker dropped the model completely. The company stopped production of the Edsel in 1959. It was regarded as an unmitigated failure after sales of only 110,847 units (in 1959 alone, 156,640 Mercury units were sold). Explanations for the Edsel's failure varied. Some said it was a victim of an economic recession; others said poor quality control played a factor. Poor styling was also cited, as was the choice of name.

Following the Edsel disaster, Ford's agencies were winnowed down to two for the main auto divisions: JWT, managing the

Ford division, and K&E, which handled the newly merged Lincoln-Mercury (formerly Lincoln-Edsel-Mercury) and institutional divisions.

In 1959 Ford was the nation's fourth-largest advertiser, with advertising expenditures of $92.2 million, an increase over the $87.9 million of the previous year. Newspapers represented the greatest expenditure, $19.7 million. Network television garnered $12 million, while $10.7 million was spent on magazine ads, $7.3 million on spot radio advertising, $5.4 million on outdoor advertising, $4.4 million on spot television advertising, and $1.9 million on farm publications. The increase in advertising paid off: Ford sales climbed to $5.4 billion in 1959, a 30 percent increase over 1958.

In October 1959 Ford introduced its new Falcon in a 20-page advertising section in the *New York Times*. The supplement, which was handled by Ford and Sawyer-Ferguson-Walker Company's Detroit office (which represented the *Times* in Detroit), strove for a patina of editorial integrity. Much of the editorial content was written by independent writers who, after visiting Ford, submitted copy that was to be used "as is" or not at all.

In 1960 Ford and JWT launched the first hour-long Spanish-language television "special" to Latin American viewers. The program, *La Hora Estelar* ("The Star Hour") introduced Ford's 1960 line in Puerto Rico, Venezuela, Peru, Panama, El Salvador, Guatemala, and Cuba. The show, featuring Latin American singing star Lucho Gatica and 12 production numbers, was hailed as a significant breakthrough in markets where it aired. It cost approximately $75,000 to produce the program in Mexico—a bargain, considering such a production in New York would have cost nearly four times as much.

To introduce Ford's new economy car, the Comet, in 1961, K&E launched a three-sided campaign. The theme, "Fine car styling at a compact car price," emphasized the Comet's price, styling, and features. As outlined by R.J. Fisher, advertising and sales promotion manager of the Lincoln-Mercury division, the campaign included a multimillion-dollar advertising schedule, using newspapers, magazines (including color spreads in *Life* and *Look*), television (including spots on the *Leonard Bernstein Show* and Ford *Startime* series), radio, outdoor signs, and direct mail; pre-introductory invitations offering selected prospects advance information on the Comet; and a "sweepstakes" in which 50 Comets were given away in drawings and ten were given away in skills contests. Despite this publicity, it took three years before Mercury turned the corner in sales of the Comet.

Ford bought a business that would become its Autolite division in the spring of 1961. Initially, the outside world was confused about what exactly Ford had paid $28 million for, besides the Autolite trade name and distribution—a good source of original equipment spark plugs and batteries. By September, six months after the purchase, Ford had expanded the product line. Batten Barton Durstine & Osborn (which handled the account before its spin-off to Ford, when it was still known as Electric Autolite Company), acquired the account and managed it until 1968. Autolite was introduced with a color page in *Life* in September. An eight-page color insert broke that September in automotive

trade books. Autolite also sponsored a new adventure series on ABC that fall, *Straightaway,* and participated in American Football League broadcasts on the network. A point-of-sale program supplemented the fall ads. The program, which offered a $2 model racecar kit, was designed to encourage car owners to visit service stations and garages for an "Autolite performance checkup."

After the introduction of the T Bird in 1955, Ford had developed a reputation for sturdy, economical cars. That changed in 1964 when, under the prodding of Lee Iacocca, then vice president and general manager, Ford Division introduced the Mustang. Iacocca, who eventually became president of the company, butted heads with Ford. Fired by Henry Ford II in 1978 (Ford allegedly told him, "I just don't like you"), Iacocca went on to head Chrysler.

The Mustang was, by at least one estimate, the car that made Ford young again. JWT managed the account. The campaign began with a focus on price. However, several months after the rollout, an engine change added more power to the car, rendering all national price advertising obsolete. That led to the "Walter Mitty" approach, which resulted in one of the best commercials of 1964, according to *Advertising Age* columnist Harry W. McMahan. "Have you heard about Henry Foster?" asks a gossipy old lady, as quiet Henry emerges from his antique shop with his lunch bag. "Something's happened to Henry," the voiceover says, as Henry ditches his derby hat for a sporty plaid hat and his glasses for racing goggles. "A Mustang's happened to Henry," says a younger, more seductive voice, as Henry drives off in his new Mustang. In a closing shot, a herd of wild horses gallops across the screen. The next year, Ford launched a $1 million-plus campaign to back the Mustang GT.

Agency Realignments

Rumors that Ford was shopping its accounts—like those that had wended their way through the grapevine during the early 1960s—flared again in 1966. Doyle Dane Bernbach, FCB, and Ogilvy & Mather, Inc. (O&M), would supposedly benefit from JWT's loss of accounts. In fact, K&E found itself relieved of Ford's corporate account, said to be worth $20 million, and Grey Advertising was the beneficiary. K&E's loss in February came at the time a new marketing team was put in place at Ford, including E.F. ("Gar") Laux as vice president of marketing of Ford Motor; John J. Morrissey, director of advertising and sales promotion; and Iacocca, then vice president of the car and truck group. Ford executives explained that they wanted to keep corporate advertising with an agency that did not manage any individual products, and K&E retained the Lincoln-Mercury account, along with 19 dealer accounts, the British Ford line, and Ford Motor Credit Company.

The appointment gave Grey a foothold into the exclusive auto market, along with $10 million in billings. One advantage Grey had was a strong overseas presence, which interested Ford officials greatly. Ford was also increasing its television advertising, which Grey oversaw.

For the 1969 model year, Ford doubled the number of network spots it purchased in the fall of 1968. That year Ford spent $90.3 million in advertising, making it the ninth-largest advertiser in the United States. The success of the company's line of compact cars, particularly the Maverick and subcompact Pinto, slowed Ford profits, since the smaller cars provided relatively less revenue. The company's slogan became, "We listen better." In one of the company's periodic shake-ups, Robert J. Fisher, ad manager of the Lincoln-Mercury division, was sent back to the Ford division. W. Paul Tippett, Jr. moved to Lincoln-Mercury.

Grey did eventually benefit from JWT's loss. In July 1971 Ford pulled its small-car advertising—Pinto, Mustang, and Maverick—from JWT and gave the account, with spending of between $17 million and $20 million, to Grey. According to Henry Ford II, JWT got the slap on the wrist (it still maintained the bulk of Ford division billings) because the agency had become overly ambitious and its work was not up to Ford's standards. Following the move, JWT transferred approximately 20 percent of its personnel out of the Detroit office, which at the time had some 300 people.

During this period, the Federal Trade Commission (FTC) launched its "data bank" program, under which the advertisers for Ford and six other carmakers were required to provide backup information to support factual claims in specific ads. The documents, with any trade secrets removed, were to be made public, a move spurred by consumer advocate Ralph Nader. Ford statements that required documentation included claims that the LTD was more than 700 percent quieter and that the Pinto needed only half the oil changes of the leading import.

The 1970s were a difficult time for U.S. carmakers, with the energy crisis in full swing and major inroads being made by foreign carmakers' brands. In response, Ford, like the other automakers, shifted its emphasis to smaller cars. In 1974 Ford converted its Wayne, Michigan, plant from full-size car production to small-car production in 51 days. Mavericks and Mustangs were among the cars that benefited from an ad strategy switch that called for doubling the number of small cars built from 1 million in 1972 to 2 million in 1974. That fall, Ford (along with rival Volkswagen) gave in to FTC demands and started including fuel-efficiency claims in its ads.

Overseas Expansion

During this time, Ford was expanding overseas. Ford Lio Ho Motor Company, Ltd., was established in 1972 as a joint venture in Chung Li, near Taipei, Taiwan, five years after the establishment of Ford of Europe. In 1973 Ford Motor Company renewed operations in Spain with the incorporation of Ford España S.A. and the opening of a sales office in Madrid. In 1976 the company launched a car assembly and manufacturing complex near Valencia.

In 1975 Ford set out with its biggest June advertising budget ever to promote three new small cars that could get 34 miles per gallon. Rather than wait until the traditional beginning of the model year, the subcompact Pinto, Mustang II, and Mercury Bobcat were introduced in a $15 million campaign with a heavy advertising emphasis on fuel-efficiency. The campaign began with three weeks of television spots, followed by three weeks of radio, and then a return to television. In one ad a Germanic actor announces, "We have dominated the world in fuel economy"; next, a Japanese-looking actor proclaims, "Honorable domination is over." While a voiceover describes the miles-per-gallon numbers of the Fords, the actors speak in their native languages, while subtitles translate: "I didn't know that." Also in 1975 Ford terminated its accounts with Grey, deciding that, with JWT and K&E, it had too many agencies. After losing the Ford business, Grey closed its Detroit office.

Ford ran into image problems when it was forced to recall more than 1 million Pintos from the 1971 to 1976 model years because the cars had a tendency to explode during minor accidents. The Pinto had also had a perception problem in Brazil—the word meant "tiny male genitals" in Portuguese slang, and the company had to replace all the Pinto nameplates in Brazil with a new name, "Corcel."

The success of the Mustang had made Lee Iacocca a star, not only at Ford but throughout the industry. He had also developed a very close personal friendship with K&E president Leo Kelmenson, who had come to K&E in 1967 from Norman, Craig & Kummel. When Ford fired Iacocca 1978, he did not have to look far for a new job. He quickly moved over to a demoralized Chrysler Corporation and set about reconstructing it. If the product line could not be immediately changed, he decided, the advertising could be. So he dismissed Y&R and Chrysler's other agencies and, in the largest account shift in history to that point, consolidated the company's $125 million budget at K&E. On 1 March 1979, Kelmenson sent a hand-delivered note to Henry Ford unceremoniously resigning the $75 million Lincoln-Mercury account. Ford moved Lincoln-Mercury back to Y&R.

In March 1980 the company made a major departure by naming a nonfamily member to run the company for the first time. Company President-Chief Executive Officer Philip Caldwell was named chairman, and Henry Ford II retired as a company officer, though he remained on the board of directors. He died in September 1987.

During the 1980s and 1990s Ford continued its international expansion. In 1986 the company acquired a portion of the equity in Korean automaker Kia Motors Corporation. In 1987 the company bought 75 percent of Aston Martin Lagonda, purchasing the remaining shares in 1994. In February 1990 Ford acquired Jaguar. (Founded in 1922 by William Lyons and William Walmsley, Jaguar had begun as the Swallow Sidecar Company.) Nearly a decade later, in March 1999, Ford acquired Volvo Cars.

As the international business grew, Ford began to whittle down its agencies to three primary shops worldwide in 1987 to 1988—O&M, Y&R, and JWT. In July 1987 O&M picked up the Ford parts and services division from Y&R, its first account for the company in the United States. O&M had already succeeded JWT on Ford cars in nine European countries. The agency switch, following JWT's acquisition by the British-based holding company the WPP Group, again raised the specter that the nearly half-century-old relationship between Ford and JWT was on the rocks.

INTRODUCING THE NEW WORLD CAR FORD ESCORT

ENGINEERING TEAMS FROM AMERICA AND OVERSEAS JOIN FORCES TO CREATE A NEW CAR WITH BETTER IDEAS FROM AROUND THE WORLD

Top engineers drawn from the worldwide resources of Ford Motor Company teamed up to create Escort. They pooled their expertise...compared, tested, evaluated, experimented—to come up with better ideas.

The result: a high-mileage car built in America to take on the world. Escort will be made in America for American drivers...with other models built and sold overseas.

HIGH MILEAGE THROUGH ADVANCED TECHNOLOGY

Escort has higher gas mileage ratings than subcompacts such as VW Rabbit, Honda Accord, Toyota Corolla hatchback—yet Escort has more room—in fact, Escort has the room of a compact (based on EPA Volume Index).

30 EPA EST MPG*   **44** EST HWY*

*Applicable only to sedans without power steering or A/C. For comparison. Your mileage may differ depending on speed, distance, weather. Actual hwy mileage and Calif. ratings lower. Excludes diesels.

ONE OF THE MOST POWER-EFFICIENT ENGINES AVAILABLE IN AMERICA

Escort's new-design compound valve hemispherical head (CVH)

engine gives you high mileage plus power for freeway driving.

FRONT-WHEEL DRIVE AND FOUR-WHEEL INDEPENDENT SUSPENSION

Escort comes with front-wheel drive...four-wheel fully independent suspension...rack-and-pinion steering...stabilizer bar...new all-season steel-belted radials, and other road-control features.

DRIVE A WORLD CAR

Whether you buy or lease, see your Ford Dealer now to order your Escort...3-door Hatchback, 4-door Liftgate...or even a Squire wagon option. And remember to ask about Ford's Extended Service Plan.

Escort Liftgate...4-doors and wagon room when you need it.

BUILT TO TAKE ON THE WORLD

FORD ESCORT

FORD DIVISION Ⓕⓞⓡⓓ

In the late 1970s Ford began rethinking what a car could—or should—be. The result, the Escort, became the best-selling automobile of the 1980s.
Courtesy of Ford Motor Company.

Those rumors subsided slightly when JWT won Ford Lio Ho Motor in Taiwan, beating out O&M. In 1988 O&M had approximately $150 million in Ford billings in the United States and Europe, JWT had more than $300 million in billings in 12 countries, and Y&R had more than $200 million in billings, with advertising in four countries and direct marketing in nine.

Another Image Crisis

The mid-1990s was also a time of global marketing focus. The Ford Division's major vehicle launches included introductions of the newly designed 1996 Taurus in a blitz estimated at $100 million. In January 1996 the division launched its 1997 F-150 pickup during Super Bowl XXX with what it said was the most expensive truck campaign—estimated at $70 million—in its history.

In 1997 Ford again sought to consolidate its massive advertising. The company brought U.S. media buying for all brands and corporate advertising to a new subsidiary of JWT, Ford Motor Media. Based in Detroit, Ford Motor Media handled $1.1 billion in media buying for Ford, Lincoln, Mercury, Mazda, and Jaguar, as well as Ford customer service. Billings included $600 million from JWT's Ford Division client, $245 million from Y&R for the Lincoln-Mercury division, $240 million from FCB for Mazda, and $30 million from O&M Worldwide Jaguar. (Ford had acquired a 25 percent stake in Mazda in 1979 and upped that percentage to 33.4 percent in 1996. Ford continued to hold a 33.4 percent stake in Mazda as of 2001.)

In 1999, for the first time since Henry II retired, a member of the Ford family again held a top leadership position at the company. William Clay Ford, Jr., a great-grandson of Henry Ford, was elected chairman by the board of directors, effective 1 January 1999. At the same time, the board also elected Ford Automotive Operations President Jacques Nasser president-chief executive officer. The changes coincided with the retirement of Alexander Trotman, who had served as chairman, CEO, and president during his 43 years of service to Ford.

William Clay Ford, Jr., soon found himself dealing with Ford's worst image crisis since the Pinto. Tires manufactured by Bridgestone/Firestone for its hugely popular Explorer began to disintegrate, causing the tire-and-vehicle combination to be blamed for some fatalities. Ford began a massive and, in some views, belated recall. To announce the action, Ford ran commercials in which Nasser sought to reassure Ford customers: "I want all of our owners to know that there are two things that we never take lightly: your safety and your trust." In May 2001 Bridgestone ended its nearly century-old relationship with Ford, after Ford's continued criticism of the company's tires. On 30 October 2001 William

Ford took over the title of CEO following Nasser's retirement. Nasser had come under criticism for Ford's handling of the Bridgestone/Firestone situation.

DEREK DATTNER AND AMY I.S. DATTNER

See also color plate in this volume

Further Reading

Clymer, Floyd, *Henry's Wonderful Model T, 1908–1927*, New York: McGraw Hill, 1955

Edwards, Cliff, "Ford's Edsel Drives Pack of Marketing Misses," *Chicago Tribune* (13 June 1999)

"Ford Begins Ad Drive for New Autolite Division," *Advertising Age* (28 September 1961)

"Ford Picks Grey for Corporate Ad Account," *Advertising Age* (30 June 1966)

"Ford's $500,000 TV Birthday Party Wins Raves from Television Critics," *Advertising Age* (16 June 1953)

"FTC Calls on 7 Auto Makers to Document Their Ad Claims," *Advertising Age* (14 July 1971)

Garfield, Bob, "Nasser Spot Lacks Star Quality, but Gets Tire Message Across," *Advertising Age* (28 August 2000)

Gray, Ralph, "New Ford Campaign vs. Imports—Biggest Third-Quarter Drive," *Advertising Age* (16 June 1975)

"High Speeds of Autos Blamed by Some on Admen," *Advertising Age* (22 October 1952)

"John W. Shaw Sues Ford, JWT for $450,000," *Advertising Age* (27 March 1950)

"JWT Didn't Do a Good Job: Ford," *Advertising Age* (11 May 1972)

"JWT Gets Huge Ford Media Plum," *Advertising Age* (23 April 1997)

"K&E Opens Three Offices to Handle Lincoln-Mercury," *Advertising Age* (22 March 1948)

"K&E's Sid Olson's First Ad Copy Was Ford's 'American Road' Series," *Advertising Age* (27 May 1953)

"Lincoln-Mercury Gets Hydra-Matic of General Motors," *Advertising Age* (4 July 1949)

"Lincoln-Mercury Introduces Comet via Major Campaign," *Advertising Age* (16 March 1960)

McMahan, Harry W., "Mustang Kicks Up Its Heels for Ford: 'Mitty' Top Commercial of the Year," *Advertising Age* (16 November 1964)

Quinn, Hugh, "Ford to Relieve K&E of Corporate Account," *Advertising Age* (25 February 1966)

Serafin, Raymond, "Ford Sticks to JWT," *Advertising Age* (2 May 1988)

Forsman & Bodenfors

Founded by Staffan Forsman, Sven-Olof Bodenfors, Mikko Timonen, and Jonas Enghage, 1986; added Volvo Car Company as a client, 1990; voted "Agency of the Year" by the Association of Swedish Advertisers, 1991; named lead agency for Ikea, 1998; created new unit, Forsman & Bodenfors International, 1999.

Major Clients

Arla (dairy and other foods)
Coca-Cola
Ikea
Libero (sanitary products)
Libresse (female sanitary products)
Volvo Car Company

Even by the high creative standards of Sweden's thriving advertising industry, Forsman & Bodenfors (F&B) stands out. Despite early skepticism, the agency has proved that it is possible to operate a top Swedish agency outside the capital city, Stockholm. F&B was founded in October 1986 by Staffan Forsman, Sven-Olof Bodenfors (later managing director), art director Mikko Timonen, and copywriter Jonas Enghage in the southwest coastal city of Göteborg, an unheard-of move at the time. At the beginning of 2001, F&B remained an independent agency, with shares owned by 13 key people in the company; it is one of a handful of indigenous ad agencies still in Swedish hands, the majority having allied with multinational agencies since the 1970s.

F&B's goal when it opened was, as stated in its motto, to create "advertising with heart and soul"; the four founders planned to create a reputable agency that focused on inventive ideas and concepts while competing with the top agencies in Sweden and internationally. The new agency underwent rapid expansion in 1988. It began actively recruiting new talent—including account director Anders Härneman and copywriter Björn Engström—from rival agency Hall & Cederquist. The burst of growth coincided with the agency's winning the *Göteborgs-Posten* national newspaper account, Sweden's second-biggest broadsheet.

By 1989 the agency had taken steps to establish itself as a shop that focused on ideas and the needs of the consumer. It confirmed its capacity to secure well-known Swedish brand-name household products, including Kalles Kaviar, a fish-paste sandwich spread; Semper's products; Frödinge Ostkaka (Swedish cheesecake); Pucko chocolate milk; and Falcon, for a relaunch of its Porla mineral water brand.

Success in domestic and international advertising competitions included a Golden Egg Award for the agency's 1989 Frödinge Ostkaka campaign, which was pivotal in reviving consumer popularity for a product that had appeared to be failing. Sales rose by 9 percent following the campaign.

The early 1990s saw a boom in the number of terrestrial and satellite-based commercial TV channels entering the Swedish market. To increase its expertise in this area, F&B recruited U.K.-based film specialist Mark Whitehouse from the J. Walter Thompson Company, London, England. In 1990 F&B began working with the Volvo Car Company, one of a few Swedish brand names with instant brand recognition among consumers worldwide. F&B's first assignment for Volvo was to market the company's 240 model, followed by the 440/460 model and allied work. The agency made the industry sit up and take notice when it was named the lead agency for Volvo's Nordic account.

The agency continued to turn out cutting-edge creative work for its other clients, Semper (which launched a brand of crêpes), Falcon (which launched Bavarian beer), and Abba (a marketer of fish balls and herring). By the end of 1990, F&B had won the "Rookie of the Year" award sponsored by the business magazine *Veckans Affärers*. F&B also made headlines for a different reason in 1991 when it questioned the advertising role of Volvo's new Nordic organization, a dispute that resulted in F&B retiring as Volvo's main agency to be replaced by Partners, Gothenburg; still, the agency continued to concentrate on the launch of the Volvo 850.

Despite the problems with Volvo, spirits within F&B were high. In 1991 F&B was voted "Agency of the Year" by the Association of Swedish Advertisers. It was the first time the award was given to an agency outside Stockholm. The mood rose further when F&B won a Silver Egg award, the Swedish counterpart of the U.S. Clio, for its Porla campaign. That effort went on to reach the finals in the London International, Eurobest, and New York Festivals competitions.

The agency acquired more high-profile clients in 1992, including the pan-European women's fashion retailer Lindex, the largest domestic retailer of women's wear in Sweden. F&B handled image, advertising, and packaging for Lindex's retail outlets, in what represented the agency's single biggest assignment at that time. By year-end 1992, and after six years in business, F&B had 22 full-time staff as well as billings of $5 million and revenue of $3.3 million.

In 1994 Volvo tapped F&B as agency for Volvo Cars Sweden, an assignment that included responsibility for advertising new car models. In November of that year the business magazine *Månadens Affärers* voted F&B the number-one agency in Sweden in its annual ranking of agencies, with F&B coming in first in creativity as well as in marketing and communications expertise.

One of F&B's hallmarks has been its ability to create ad campaigns that are controversial but informative regarding important social issues in Sweden. The agency's 1995 campaign for client En Rökfri Generation (A Non-Smoking Generation) provoked intense public debate. The campaign, which used headlines such as "Raped by a Prince" and "Murdered by a Prince," stirred debate outside Sweden, where Copenhagen, Denmark-based Prince remains a leader among Nordic cigarette brand marketers. No other ad campaign in Sweden has received so much media attention.

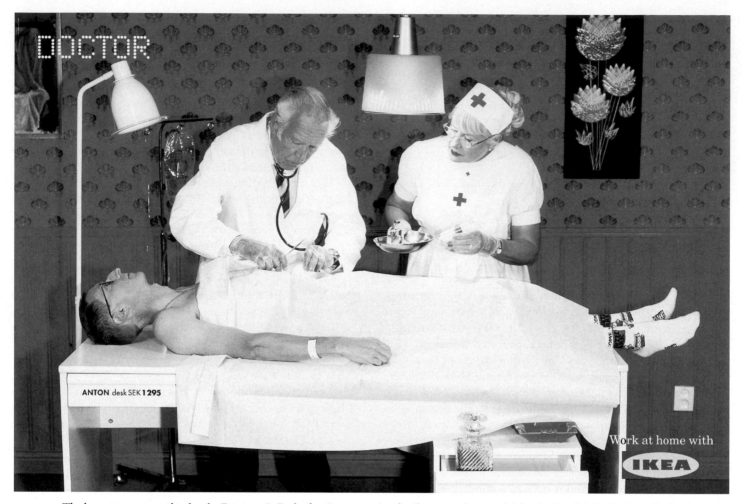

The humorous approach taken by Forsman & Bodenfors in a campaign for Ikea proved successful for the Swedish furniture marketer.

F&B was named agency for Ikea, the multinational furnishings merchandiser, in 1997. In 1998 F&B's campaigns were a critical factor in reversing declining sales for Ikea products in the company's home market of Sweden. The campaigns were successful in achieving four key goals: focusing consumer attention on what was new about Ikea's designs; converting the Ikea brand into a badge of pride; getting consumers more interested in buying by highlighting design; and targeting young people, age 20 to 35, with or without children, who shopped occasionally at Ikea.

In 1997 F&B won its first global assignment with the coveted Libero sanitary products account. Concepts and designs were created by F&B in Sweden and adapted for Libero's markets worldwide. By year's end, F&B's client list included some of the country's most prestigious accounts. Also in 1997 it formed a tactical communications unit, Force F&B. In addition, in 1997—and for the fifth consecutive year—F&B was named Sweden's best agency in *Månadens Affärers*'s prestigious annual ranking. The agency went on to win multiple awards at the International Advertising Festival in Cannes, France, in 1998. In the Press & Poster category the agency received one gold (for Göteborgs-posten), one silver (for the Salvation Army), and one bronze Lion (for Semper).

In film, three of five nominated F&B contributions won awards: "The Teacher" and "Golf" for Volvo won gold and silver, respectively, and an ePostgirot film won a silver. F&B was the only Swedish award winner in film at Cannes that year.

F&B began 1999 by winning SCA Hygiene Products' pan-European advertising account for its feminine personal care brands Bodyform, Libresse, Nana, and Nuvenia; it had competed for the account with several London-based agencies, including Abbot Mead Vickers/BBDO, Bartle Bogle Hegarty, and Lowe Howard-Spink, among others. Hot on the heels of this success, F&B's relationship with Volvo took a new twist when the auto group restructured its global marketing strategy and extended F&B's responsibilities. F&B now found itself handling the carmaker's worldwide marketing communications jointly with New York City agency Messner Vetere Berger McNamee Schmetterer/ Euro RSCG.

In response to unprecedented growth in cross-border assignments, F&B in April 1999 formed a new company, Forsman & Bodenfors International (FBI), to handle and coordinate the agency's growing international work. Tim Ellis, formerly of Goodby, Silverstein & Partners, Inc., and Hall & Cederquist/

Forsman & Bodenfors's campaigns for Volvo, launched in 1990, spanned Europe and the decade.
Courtesy of Volvo.

Y&R, was named to head FBI as European account managing director.

In 2000 F&B resigned as lead agency for the prestigious Volvo European assignment, catching Sweden's advertising industry completely by surprise. Given that Volvo was F&B's biggest account, the action represented a bold move by the agency, which decided that the assignment did not conform with its principles and, more seriously, had begun to tear at the agency's core values and culture. F&B's dropping of Sweden's arguably most prestigious account was widely discussed within the industry internationally. From F&B's viewpoint, the account had become overly politicized and was more about pushing the advertising through

Volvo's newly structured organization than about the quality of the work. Evidence that the breakup was friendly came later in the year when F&B agreed to accept the lead agency role for Volvo's pan-Nordic account.

Also in 2000, F&B won the pan-Nordic account to launch If, a newly formed property and casualty (P&C) insurance company jointly owned by Skandia of Sweden and Storebrand in Norway. The company was the Nordic region's largest P&C insurance company and was number eight in Europe. With the shifts in accounts, F&B's revenue reached $21 million in 2000.

GERARD O'DWYER

France

Historians credit the first French advertisement to the journalist Théophraste Renaudot, whose newspaper, the *Gazette,* printed classified advertisements in 1633. Yet despite this early start, the history of French advertising was to be one of "catching up," first with Great Britain and then with the United States. By the end of the 20th century, however, France had become one of the world's largest advertising nations, with two of its ad agencies, Havas and Publicis, among the world's six largest in terms of gross income.

Two hundred years after Renaudot French advertising consisted mostly of classified advertisements. Significant development of the industry began only in the 1830s with the rise of the French press aimed at the middle classes. France's second innovator in advertising was another man of the press, Émile de Girardin. In the 1830s Girardin became the first to link the price of advertising space to the verified circulation of the newspaper itself. As his newspapers became more successful, Girardin lowered their subscription rates while increasing their advertising rates. His papers also accepted new types of classified advertisements: ads for medicines and financial solicitations. Still, the advertisements themselves remained simple in style and format using no engravings or pictures and relying on brief text to sell the products. This approach reflected Girardin's opinion that "the advertisement must be frank, simple, and concise."

Press and Posters

As the newspaper became more established another innovation came in the 1840s with the Société Générale des Annonces (SGA, or General Society for Advertising). The SGA paid a fixed amount for advertising space in French newspapers and then sold that space to those wishing to advertise. Within the next decade, the organization established more than 200 offices in Paris alone (though most were small businesses that simply took orders for the SGA) and began to develop offices in other French cities. By the 1850s, the SGA suffered financial turmoil and was taken over by Havas, France's leading press agency, for the next two decades. Havas and the SGA separated in 1879, but the families that controlled the two organizations remained closely tied. Havas would eventually take over the SGA again in 1920. While beneficial and convenient for the press, this brokering of space eventually hampered innovation and change in the advertising industry overall. Agence Havas would dominate the sale of advertising space until World War II.

The French press experienced a second wave of development in the first decades of the Third Republic (1870–1940). Cheaper newsprint, faster means of production, increased literacy, and larger urban populations all aided in promoting newspaper circulation. By World War I, for example, the *Petit Parisien* had a circulation of more than 1 million.

Increased circulation, however, did not lead to a corresponding increase in advertising. The reason was a rivalry between classified advertising and two other media that arose just before the turn of the 20th century: the catalog and the poster. The modern department store was born in France with the Bon Marché in 1852, and other stores quickly opened in Paris thereafter. These establishments spent little on advertisements in newspapers, relying instead on catalogs. By 1900 these catalogs were as large as 200 pages, and some even had color illustrations. Bon Marché and other large department stores were spending 2 percent of their revenues on catalog advertising, roughly comparable to the spending by U.S. retailers Sears, Roebuck & Company and Marshall Field & Company. The largest catalog of all, though, was produced by La Manufacture Française d'Armes et de Cycles de Saint-Étienne (maker of guns, hunting equipment, and bicycles). Its 1910 catalog was about 1,200 pages in length and was distributed to more than 600,000 subscribers. The success and scope of these catalog made makers of advertisements seek other media such as the poster.

The poster (*l'affiche*) is France's best claim to advertising fame, not surprising considering the country's artistic tradition. Black-and-white posters had been used in the 17th century, and color appeared the next century. By the 19th century, most posters advertised bookstores and the latest novels. Lithography revolutionized the production of posters in France, becoming a common technique by the 1850s. Replacing the simple textual posters of the past, lithography allowed painted designs and inspired new creativity in advertising. Jules Chéret and his studio were the best example of this new advertising form that usually depicted a young woman with a brief slogan or the name of the institution being advertised, such as the Folies-Bergères.

Following the success of Chéret and his studio, other artists came to the advertising poster at the turn of the century. They included men such as Edouard Manet, Alfons Mucha, Pierre Bonnard, and, most famously, Henri de Toulouse-Lautrec. It was estimated that by 1900, poster advertising was responsible for one-fourth of all French advertising revenue. Not only did the artists sign their posters, so too did the agencies that commissioned them, starting a tradition that continues to the present in which the agency name appears on the border of the ad. Historians credit poster advertising with the spread of the bicycle in France, the beginnings of tourism, and the success of the "entertainment" industry in Paris. Posters remain a vital force in French advertising. A higher percentage is spent on posters in France than in any other Western nation.

Arrested Development

Despite the developments of a popular press and a successful poster industry by 1914, French advertising trailed behind that of Great Britain and the United States, two nations to which French agencies constantly looked for models and sought to emulate. While numbers for this period are not entirely reliable, estimates indicate that Britain spent six times more on advertising than France in 1900.

This 1715 example of poster advertising, traditionally an important advertising medium in France, touted a recent innovation—the folding parasol.

The French lagged for several reasons. First, France, with only half the per capita income of either Great Britain or the United States, was not yet a nation of mass consumption. A majority of its citizens still lived in rural areas and made many of the items they needed. Second, France had few large companies with nationwide name recognition: the country was still a collection of regional markets with few brand-name products. Small retailers distrusted advertising, feeling that it undercut their relationship with their customers.

Third, and most important, many French people resisted or distrusted advertising for cultural reasons. Businesses often refused to advertise because it was widely believed that a "respectable" business had no need to advertise. Most French advertisements at this time were for "quack" pharmaceuticals. Many French businesses were headed by engineers who were more interested in company organization and production than in sales figures. These men felt that the product should speak for itself and not have to rely on advertising. Bribery and scandal tarnished the French press (especially the financial press) during the Third Republic, greatly reducing the public's trust. As a result, newspapers, in an attempt to win back the public, buried advertising at the back of their editions. French intellectuals and writers insisted that advertising was "wasteful" and a deterrent to the economy. Furthermore, advertising represented "Americanization" of France and a way of life inimical to French culture. As a result, French advertising was only poorly developed by the time of World War I.

Pre–World War II Period

From 1918 to 1945, France entered a new phase of development. While still trailing its Anglo-American counterparts, French advertising did become more dynamic as a result of innovation by manufacturers, the media, and the ad industry itself. One example of the former was the case of the automobile maker Citroën in the 1920s. Like Henry Ford, André Citroën wanted to democratize the automobile: advertising would increase sales, which would necessitate increased production and enable economies of scale, thereby lowering prices. Citroën sponsored spectacles such as a 1924 caravan of Citroën cars across Africa and correspondingly smaller caravans through France, which were publicized in newspapers and magazines. The most visible Citroën promotion was the 1925 lighting of the Eiffel Tower with the word "Citroën," readable from some 20 miles away. By 1930 Citroën was spending ten times as much on advertising as its rival, Peugeot, and was France's largest single advertiser and producer of automobiles. Unfortunately, the Great Depression ruined Citroën, the firm eventually being rescued by the tire manufacturer Michelin. As a result, Citroën did not advertise in the press again for 30 years.

The French press continued to expand in the years between the wars. Circulation increased, not only in Paris but also especially in the regional press, where circulation and advertising receipts more than doubled. Paris's evening paper, *L'Intransigeant*, was the first French newspaper to blend advertising with editorial copy and to allot regular spaces in the newspaper for advertisements in the 1920s. *L'Intransigeant*'s evening rival in the 1930s, *Paris-Soir*, became the most successful of all French papers. Its publisher, Jean Provoust, admired the Anglo-American press and advertising and wished to implement some of their styles in France. He thus committed his publications to improve the state of advertising in France. He placed all of the classified advertisements in one section and dispersed all other ads (many using photographs instead of drawings) throughout the paper. *Paris-Soir* also rejected misleading advertisements for patent medicines and ads that made dubious financial claims. Because of Provoust's actions, the advertisements that remained were able to avoid the stain of guilt by association.

French magazines were also innovators in this period, using shiny paper, color covers, photographs, and illustrations. *L'Illustration* was the best example of the type of magazine that blended news, current events, travel, and cultural developments. Advertisements filled more than 20 percent of the magazine (still a much lower percentage than similar American or British publications). *L'Illustration* had a limited circulation due to its bourgeois tone. It found a rival in the late 1930s in Provoust's *Match* (the precursor to *Paris-Match*). Provoust changed *Match* from a sports weekly to a news weekly full of photo illustrations, not unlike the recently introduced *Life* in the United States. *Match* continued the same editorial policy toward misleading advertisements. Unlike *L'Illustration*, *Match* pleased advertisers by placing advertisements throughout the magazine rather than relegating them to the back pages.

The most successful of these French magazines, however, were those aimed at women, especially fashion magazines such as *Vogue*, *Marie-Claire*, and *Femina*. In these magazines, advertisers finally came to recognize the importance of female consumers. *Le Petit Echo de la Mode* enjoyed the highest circulation of any French magazine between the wars with more than 1 million readers. The French historian Marc Martin credits this magazine with transforming Grey Poupon mustard, Tobler chocolates, and Ovalmaltine drink mix into French national brand names. While a national magazine, *Le Petit Echo de la Mode* offered regional editions that allowed advertisers to customize their campaigns according to the market.

Emerging Media: Movies and Radio

Two new media emerged in the 1920s with great potential for advertising: movies and radio. The first movie advertisements of the 1920s were painted slides shown before the films and during intermissions. Later, cartoons replaced these slides and then, in the 1930s with the arrival of sound, actors in one- or two-minute films. Colgate, L'Oréal, Philips, and La Vache qui rit (Laughing Cow, a brand of cheese) were among the early users of this medium. The Great Depression reduced movie attendance and limited the success of movie advertising, which was estimated to be less than one percent of all advertising spending. But radio advertising would far surpass movie advertising and would indeed disturb the established print media.

Regular radio broadcasting first appeared in France in 1921 with a transmitter on the Eiffel Tower. The French government regarded radio as a vital national service, and by 1926 only 11 of the nation's 29 radio stations remained in private hands. After 1926, the government would not allow any new private stations. Radio coverage was further limited by short broadcasting days and a small transmission radius. Furthermore, the government forbade public stations to use advertising. Radio seemed to be a lost medium for advertisers. However, several entrepreneurs entered the private radio industry in the 1930s and revolutionized its use in France.

One of these entrepreneurs was Marcel Bleustein-Blanchet of Publicis. As a competitor to the ad agency Havas, Publicis, founded in 1926, was seeking new clients and recognized the underdevelopment of radio advertising. At first, Publicis acted as a broker for airtime for private radio stations initially in the Paris area and then for several regional stations. In 1935 the agency bought a then small Parisian radio station and renamed it Radio-Cité. Through innovation and experimentation, offering live entertainment, the first broadcast news in France, and quiz shows, Radio-Cité became France's most profitable radio station. Other radio stations emulated Radio-Cité's success. Advertisers with substantial budgets (radio advertisements were relatively costly when compared with print) flocked to radio. Products such as Monsavon and Persil soaps, the apéritif Byrrh, and the drug Quintonine began to reach not only a regional audience but also a national one with their new slogans and jingles, which were often reinforced by print ads. Advertisers came to promote special radio programs such as *Le Kiosque à musique Persil* sponsored by Lever Brothers. The print industry felt so threatened by radio, particularly radio news, that it pressured radio broadcasters to limit their news broadcasts in time and scope. While radio before the war brought in only four percent of all advertising spending, it clearly had become a force for change in French advertising.

Professionalism and Industry Growth

The advertising industry itself made some steps towards regulation and professionalization during this period, though greater steps would not take place until after 1945. A number of professional advertising organizations existed at the turn of the century. However, not until the 1930s would these organizations consolidate under one large umbrella group, the Fédération Française de la Publicité (FFP). The FFP was a weak regulatory force, watching over 22 different smaller advertising groups. As a result it had only slight powers of regulation and surveillance over an industry whose individual members prided themselves on their independence.

Another movement toward professionalization came with the rise of advertising trade journals, the most notable being *Vendre* (which started in 1923). *Vendre* preached the comprehensive advertising campaign to its audience, something that French advertisers rarely tried: they mostly offered a string of single, unrelated ads in various media according to the whims and connections of the agency. *Vendre* focused on the merits of American advertising methods. But while the journal emphasized American techniques, it also placed those techniques within a French context. Like Provoust, *Vendre* stressed the ethical side of the profession, advocating a "truth in advertising" campaign.

The period between the wars also saw the establishment of many longstanding French advertising agencies such as Dam, Dupuy, Elvinger, Jep et Carré, de Plas, and Publicis. While these agencies prospered, the largest had only one-tenth the advertising billings of giant Havas. The main focus of Havas was still the brokerage of advertising space, but in the 1930s the firm turned to creating advertisements. Havas developed a network of subsidiaries throughout France that gave the agency a competitive advantage over its smaller rivals. Not only could the agency produce advertisements, it could place them for its clients. Beyond Havas and its rivals, France had hundreds of one-person agencies that remained fiercely independent and resisted the consolidation process that was simultaneously occurring in Great Britain and the United States. As a result, the advertising industry was pyramid shaped: one large agency at the top, a few medium-sized ones in the middle, and a myriad of smaller agencies below. Foreign agencies in France primarily concentrated on advertising for their

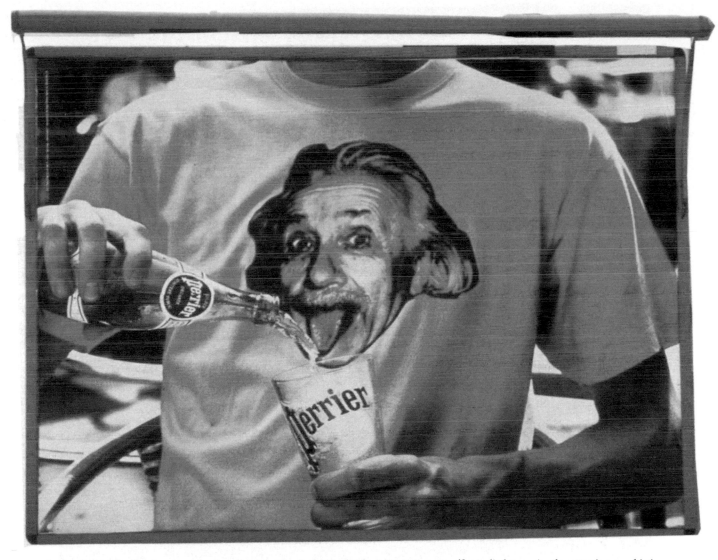

An outdoor ad for Perrier mineral water, produced by Ogilvy & Mather's Paris, France, office, relied on a simple, arresting graphic image.

national clients, as French advertisers preferred to stay with French firms. Thus, the J. Walter Thompson Company, a leading U.S. agency, had prosperous London and Berlin offices, but the Parisian office struggled through the 1930s.

By 1940 French advertising showed potential in several areas, but the Great Depression had limited extensive growth. From the consumer market standpoint, France remained much less developed than its Anglo-American counterparts. Because of radio, movies, and national magazines, a single market was forming, albeit slowly. During the Nazi occupation and under the Vichy government (1940–44), French advertising entered a near hibernation as the French media shrank under Nazi supervision. The Vichy government forbade the advertising of alcohol and also began to regulate the promotion of pharmaceuticals, two items that had been mainstays of advertising. With shortages and rationing, businesses had little to advertise. Only after 1945 did French advertising catch up with its rivals.

Postwar Years

The postwar advertising industry built upon the foundation laid in the 1930s. A true mass market was born, the media continued to innovate, the public and the business community came to accept advertising more readily, and agencies professionalized and expanded. As a result, advertising in this third phase, from 1945 to the beginning of the 21st century, became an integral part of the French economy.

France, like West Germany, accomplished an economic "miracle" from the 1940s through the 1970s. While U.S. Marshall Plan aid was crucial, indigenous French efforts and economic planning helped rebuild a shattered economy. As per capita income increased, so did discretionary spending. By 1970, at least half of French households owned consumer goods such as televisions, radios, washing machines, and refrigerators, whereas in 1950 only radios had been owned by more than five percent of households.

Henri de Toulouse-Lautrec, one of France's most prominent poster artists, popularized the poster as an advertising medium while raising it to an art form in its own right.
TOULOUSE-LAUTREC, Henri de. Divan Japonais (Japanese Settee). 1893. Lithograph, printed in color, composition: 31 5/8 x 23 7/8" (80.3 x 60.7 cm). The Museum of Modern Art, New York. Abby Aldrich Rockefeller Fund. Photograph © 2001 The Museum of Modern Art, New York.

Most importantly, automobile ownership rapidly increased after the war, from around 10 percent in 1945 to 55 percent by 1970. Household spending increased dramatically in other areas as well, especially spending on hygiene/health products, food, and clothing. Advertisers now had a mass market in which to operate. While intermittent recession and high unemployment bedeviled France from 1973 on, advertising revenues generally increased.

Economic and political changes caused the transformation of the French media. Radio, which had been so important during the 1930s, was lost as the French government nationalized all stations and forbade advertising. Once French advertisers could no longer advertise on French stations they moved to border radio stations, the most notable being in Luxembourg and Monaco.

Television, the most prized medium of all, remained elusive for advertisers until 1968. As with radio, the French government controlled France's few television channels and had no intention of allowing advertisements. French agencies chafed at their inability to use this medium and envied American agencies with their large television advertising accounts. Lobbying by agency pressure groups finally resulted in limited advertising being allowed in 1968 (the first advertisement being a Publicis spot for Boursin cheese). Not until the 1980s, with further government deregulation of television and the first private channels, did television advertising far surpass print advertising in terms of spending. The French government allowed more channels in 1986 and also allowed French public television stations to advertise 12 minutes per hour. Finally, by 1997, French TV was completely privatized. Despite these concessions, French advertisers still spent much less per capita on television (and all advertising combined) than did their U.S. counterparts, but they at last had access to this most important medium.

The print media remained clearly important in the postwar advertising world. Newspapers underwent increasing consolidation, and many smaller papers disappeared. Newspapers improved technically, especially during the 1950s, with better reproduction techniques, inks, and paper, making them more attractive to advertisers. Despite these advances, circulation did not increase as much as had been hoped. Instead, newspapers faced increasing competition from newly created periodicals and magazines. *Marie-France* (1945), *Elle* (1945), *Paris-Match* (1950), *Séléction du Reader's Digest* (1950), *L'Express* (1953), and *Le Point* (1972) were some of the leaders in circulation and advertising revenue. Glossy paper, color photographs, and nationwide circulation made these publications the first choice for national advertising campaigns. By the late 1950s, the periodical press received more advertising revenue than all newspapers combined. A growing economy, an increased supply of consumer goods, and improved nationwide distribution of those products finally led to a national market for France.

As this larger market formed, French hostility to advertising gradually eroded. Marketers came to recognize advertising's ability to enlarge their market share. Many businesses hired account managers to act as liaisons with advertising agencies. This attitude was not yet universal, as French ad executive Claude Marcus noted in 1960: "Still today, for many French businesses, advertis-

From 1925 to the mid-1930s Citroën's illuminated sign on the Eiffel Tower dominated the Paris skyline.
Courtesy of Citroën.

ing is a mysterious and incomprehensible phenomenon which can ruin those who have the weakness to become addicted to it." Many marketers continued to resist advertising, preferring to rely on their products' reputation. But the French public in general began to distrust advertising less and to enjoy it more. Postwar advertising focused on visual imagery rather than text and used humor and wit as often as possible. These new attitudes coincided with better-quality advertising, the regulation of quack remedies, and the movement toward a youth culture that was more accepting of advertising than earlier generations had been. Starting in the 1980s Paris hosted an all-night celebration (*la nuit des publivores*) of the best advertisements of the year. By the 1990s the festival had a French tour opening in the country's major cities each February.

While public opinion became more favorable, internal changes were occurring in the advertising industry. The structure of the industry changed in 1945 when the French government nationalized Havas and stripped the company of its news service. While Havas was in turmoil, other agencies, such as Publicis, found themselves better able to compete with the wounded giant in the immediate postwar period. Many of the larger agencies rushed to

Americanize their techniques after the war, some French agencies sending younger executives to visit Madison Avenue and return with American ideas that they could modify according to French taste and tradition. French advertising did not become necessarily "Americanized" as a result of this process but it was clear that both countries were experiencing a similar type of socioeconomic development, with France some 10-20 years behind. Examples of increasing professionalization came with the introduction of American-inspired institutions in France such as ETMAR, the first market research company (1948), the Centre d'Étude des Supports Publicité (CESP, 1956), a media planning firm, and L'Institut de Recherches et d'Études Publicitaires (IREP), which collected, documented, and analyzed French national advertising spending (1958). These institutions gave French agencies and advertisers a better sense of the market, how advertising revenues were dispersed, and where to spend them. Larger agencies followed by establishing their own similar internal departments from the 1950s on.

Other American-based ideas came to France in the 1950s with the work of Ernest Dichter. Dichter, a Viennese-trained psychologist, established a successful market consultant firm in the United States in 1946. His research distilled consumers' purchasing motives to two basic factors: sex and security. Rather than conduct expensive market surveys, Dichter preferred interviewing consumers to discover unconscious purchase decisions. Many French agencies saw Dichter's ideas as a way to cut research costs while producing a clearer picture of consumer wants. Despite these U.S. imports, French advertising maintained some native cultural characteristics. Posters remained an important complement to most advertising campaigns. Sexuality and nudity appeared in ways that shocked American viewers but were commonplace to the French. More often than not ads showed women in the traditional roles of housewife and mother.

Some ideas were not American inspired. France led the way in the application of semiotics to advertising in the 1960s. Semiotics, the study of the function of signs and symbols in language, had many of its early proponents, such as Roland Barthes, in France. Agencies saw the importance of semiotics in advertising as an additional powerful tool in crafting advertisements. Publicis briefly associated with Barthes in 1964 for its Renault campaign. Barthes suggested the use of the letter "R" and a number for the name of upcoming models.

With increasing professionalization, French advertising had need of a better educated work force. With more sophisticated techniques being used, agencies increasingly found it necessary to hire college-educated workers. Agencies became respected businesses in postwar France and now could recruit from the country's finest educational institutions, something the industry had rarely been able to do before.

Agencies still belonged to professional associations, the most notable being the FFP (which became the Fédération Nationale de la Publicité in 1975). However, the FFP represented the interests of smaller agencies. The larger French agencies, notably Publicis and Havas, along with 18 other large agencies, formed the Compagnie d'Agences de Publicité (CAP) in 1964 to represent their interests. Besides being an industry lobbying group, CAP pushed for the right to advertise on French television (still state controlled). CAP was also seen by many as an "anti-Yankee" organization that impeded the influx of American advertising agencies into France. Whether or not CAP did try to do so, the evidence shows that American agencies had a difficult time penetrating the French advertising market. Even by the 1990s U.S. firms accounted for only 30 percent of French advertising spending, far lower than American influence in any other European country.

End-of-the-Century Issues

The government maintained an intrusive influence in French advertising, enacting a series of new regulations in the 1990s. The 1991 Evin Law (Loi Evin) forbade most tobacco and alcohol advertising. In 1992, as part of an anticorruption campaign, the French government passed the Sapin Law (Loi Sapin), which targeted media brokers. These brokers had been acting as wholesalers, buying vast quantities of discounted advertising space and then selling that space to advertisers, reducing (or hiding) their discounts. The Sapin Law required that the media make public their rates and that media buyers become direct agents for their clients rather than brokers for space. The 1994 Toubon Law (Loi Toubon), initiated to protect French language and culture, required that all advertising be done in French. For example, Nike's slogan, "Just Do It" would become "Ta vie est à toi," (Your life is yours). The combination of these laws caused uproar in the industry: one French advertising executive said jokingly, "The good thing about the Toubon Law is that it makes it impossible for [politicians] to come up with anything more stupid. More stupid doesn't exist." Economically, many agencies suffered, losing both revenues and profits in France. These laws encouraged France's largest agencies to look abroad for new and less regulated markets.

Havas (and its most important subsidiary, Euro RSCG) and Publicis, by acquisition and development, became important players in the international advertising market in the late 1990s. According to *Advertising Age*'s survey of world agencies, in 2000 Havas was the fifth-largest and Publicis the sixth-largest agency in the world in terms of gross income. The two also ranked first and second in European advertising. Beyond these two agencies, the third great player in the French advertising world was Carat-Espace, a media buyer. Carat-Espace rapidly became France's largest space broker in the 1980s, surpassing the buying subsidiaries of Havas and Publicis, and by the 1990s became Europe's largest space-buying agency with intentions to expand further its U.S. operations. The success of these three agencies and their multinational networks proved that the French advertising/media world had indeed "caught up" with its Anglo-American counterparts. In March 2002 Publicis acquired Bcom3 Group, forming the fourth-largest communications group in the world.

CLARK HULTQUIST

Further Reading

Bleustein-Blanchet, Marcel, *The Rage to Persuade: Memoirs of a French Advertising Man*, translated by Jean Bodewyn, New York: Chelsea House, 1982

Boutelier, Denis, and Dilip Subramanian, *Le Grand Bluff: Pouvoir et argent dans la publicité*, Paris: Denoël, 1990

Crumley, Bruce, "France's Restrictive New Laws Create Headaches for Ad Industry," *Advertising Age* (4 July 1994)

Kuisel, Richard, *Seducing the French: The Dilemma of Americanization*, Berkeley: University of California Press, 1993

Martin, Marc, *Trois siècles de publicité en France*, Paris: Odile Jacob, 1992

Pope, Daniel, "French Advertising Men and the American 'Promised Land,'" *Historical Reflections/Réflexions historiques* 5, no. 1 (1978)

Freberg, Stan 1926–

U.S. Advertising Copywriter

No one label fits Stan Freberg, but "the father of the funny commercial" seems a fitting epithet. The renowned advertising copywriter has received many more tributes, including Grammy and Clio awards, silver Lions at the Cannes (France) International Advertising Festival, a star on the Hollywood Walk of Fame, and election to the Advertising Hall of Fame at the Museum.

As the creator of radio comedy shows and a recording artist, Freberg had already made a name for himself when Howard Luck Gossage persuaded him to start writing commercials in 1956. In 1957 Gossage and Freberg, along with a third partner, J. Joseph Weiner, formed Weiner & Gossage, setting up shop in the original San Francisco Firehouse No. 1.

During the second half of the 20th century, Freberg delivered many memorable campaigns and set the standard for humor in advertising. His accounts included Chun King, Jeno's Pizza, Sunsweet prunes ("Today the pits, tomorrow the wrinkles"), and Encyclopaedia Britannica, Inc. Some of this work has been preserved at the Center for Advertising History at the National Museum of American History in Washington, D.C.

But comedy was Freberg's first love. He was born in 1926 in Pasadena, California, the only son of a Baptist minister. A self-described lonely child, he spent long hours listening to Fred Allen and Jack Benny on the radio and loved to perform comedy routines for his pet rabbits. Soon after graduating from high school in 1944, he was supplying voices for Warner Bros. Looney Tunes cartoons. At Warner Bros. he joined the ranks of Mel Blanc, Arthur Q. Bryan, and others providing the speaking voices for many of the studio's classic productions. He was also the voice of the beaver in Walt Disney's *Lady and the Tramp* in 1955 and appeared on-camera in several movies, including *Callaway Went Thataway* and *It's a Mad Mad Mad Mad World*. But it was in 1950 that Freberg emerged as a comedy recording artist with a Capitol record called "John and Marsha." He went on to parody many of the cultural trends of the day with a satiric version of the song "On Top of Old Smokey" in 1951, a send-up of crooner

Johnny Ray's overwrought ballad "Cry" in 1952, and even a parody of the infamous U.S. Senator Joseph McCarthy called "Point of Order." Probably his most successful comic record was a satiric version of the police show *Dragnet*. In the summer of 1957 Freberg and his stock company of performers (which included Peter Leeds, June Foray, Daws Butler, and the Billy May big band) starred in radio's final attempt to present a full-scale, weekly comedy variety show, *The Stan Freberg Show*. It ran for 13 weeks, and carrying on in the tradition of Fred Allen, took deadly satiric aim at the advertising business.

Freberg's philosophy of advertising goes beyond simply being funny. He creates commercials that entertain the audience while solving problems for the client. A memorable example is his campaign for Kaiser Aluminum, which addressed the dearth of retail outlets carrying the company's aluminum foil because its competitor, Reynolds Metal Company, had a lock on the market. Freberg's ads introduced a fictional Kaiser salesman who could sell the product to mean old grocers. After the campaign, Kaiser won 43,000 new retail outlets. The radio commercial presented a parody of "Little Red Riding Hood" within a parody of the soap opera format, in which the father told his daughter of "the big bad wolf" who hogged all the shelf space in grocery stores for his aluminum foil.

Freberg sees the core of advertising as salesmanship and honesty and these as the keys to success. That emphasis on honesty is illustrated by an excerpt from his book, *It Only Hurts When I Laugh,* in which he relates his experience in the 1970s with the Chun King chow mein account and his interaction with the company's president and founder, Jeno Paulucci. Freberg told Paulucci publicly that Chun King's current campaign was among the worst advertising he had ever seen. He then created advertising for the product that stood out for its honesty: it told listeners that 95 percent of the people in the United States had never eaten Chun King chow mein. When Paulucci rejected the spot and asked for a new one, Freberg stuck with his convictions. It paid off: product sales grew 25 percent nationally within three months after the radio spot aired in the mid-1960s.

Freberg has said that he was sidetracked into the advertising business from a successful career as a radio and television satirist because he disliked the way most advertisers attempted to communicate with him as a consumer. "I went into it not as a trained marketing person but as an outraged consumer, yelling at my car radio and my television set from morning to night." He did not suppress his outrage. In 1959 he recorded "Green Chritma" ("Deck the halls with advertising . . ."), a parody of Charles Dickens's *A Christmas Carol,* in which he cast Scrooge as the head of a major ad agency and Bob Cratchit as an account executive. The routine was so anticommercial that Capitol Records almost refused to release it.

Freberg tapped into his mistrust by using the industry's cynicism in his ads; an underlying message in many of his ads is that commercials are usually dumb. He attributes this failing to the fact that those who create commercials believe that their own tastes are different from those of the audience. In *It Only Hurts When I Laugh,* he wrote:

> If you don't like an ad, why should anybody else? . . . We're all consumers. . . . That's why I always create commercials for myself first of all. I am the consumer I know best. If I

think it's a great commercial, I figure the rest of the people might think so too. I haven't been wrong so far.

NANCY DIETZ

Biography
Born in Los Angeles, California, 7 August 1926; produced first comedy record, 1950; joined Howard Luck Gossage and J. Joseph Weiner to form Weiner & Gossage, San Francisco, in 1957; established his own company, Freberg, Ltd., in Beverly Hills, California, 1958.

Selected Publications
It Only Hurts When I Laugh, 1988
"Freewheeling Freberg," *Advertising Age* (12 September 1988)
"Freberg Tries Hand at Biting Satire," *Advertising Age* (28 August 1989)

Further Reading
Garfield, Bob, "Freberg: Humor's No Laughing Matter," *Advertising Age* (20 January 1992)
McDonough, John, "Stan Freberg: Curmudgeon of Consequence," *Wall Street Journal* (20 August 1996)

Freeman, Cliff 1941–

U.S. Advertising Copywriter

In the advertising world, the name Cliff Freeman is as synonymous with results as it is with humor. For the consumers who experience his campaigns, his style is pure entertainment. He has given advertising the Mounds and Almond Joy jingle, "Sometimes you feel like a nut"; the celebrated Wendy's "Where's the beef?" commercials; and the toga-clad Little Caesar with his "Pizza! Pizza!" tag line. Freeman's forte is turning underdog brands around with his fresh, quirky advertising and maddening competitors by doing it for millions of dollars less than they themselves pay for original, creative work.

Over the course of his career, Freeman has won nearly every major advertising industry award multiple times, including 97 Clios, 34 One Show awards, 41 Lions from the Cannes (France) International Advertising Festival, and six "Best Campaign of the Year" honors for five different clients. After establishing a reputation for effective work at other agencies, Freeman founded his New York City advertising agency, Cliff Freeman & Partners, in 1987 as part of Saatchi & Saatchi. It became independent in 1999. The agency has created several multiple-award winning campaigns under Freeman's creative direction.

Freeman was born in Vicksburg, Mississippi, on 14 February 1941 and was raised in St. Petersburg, Florida. His first experience with advertising revealed a natural instinct when he won first prize for a campaign he created for a high school journalism convention. Freeman went on to Florida State University in Tallahassee, Florida, where he received a degree in advertising and public relations. Over summers during college, he would pick a city to work in and move there.

One particular summer in Atlanta, Georgia, selling encyclopedias door to door taught Freeman a valuable lesson. "I knew that I had five seconds to make those people like me and hear what I had to say," Freeman has said. His basic advertising philosophy is no different—get the audience's attention immediately, entertain them at a high level throughout, and in the end offer them a simple sales proposition. Freeman's goal has been to make his audience adore his client, and he finds that they do so when commercials leave them happy.

Freeman got his start in advertising at a small shop in Atlanta called Liller Neal in 1967; 18 months later he joined McCann-Erickson, where he worked for two years. In 1971 he moved to

New York City to work as a copywriter at Dancer, Fitzgerald, Sample (DFS), a then-sizable company that was later dissolved within the Saatchi & Saatchi advertising organization in 1987. It was at DFS in 1973 that Freeman first penned the memorable jingle for the Mars brand candy bars Mounds and Almond Joy. "Sometimes you feel like a nut" swept the country seemingly overnight, despite modest media expenditure. Freeman was promoted to creative director at DFS after 12 years with the agency.

Although Freeman worked with a small and highly creative team that developed other successful campaigns, few came close to the success and notoriety of the campaign for Wendy's Old Fashioned Hamburgers. Wendy's came to DFS in 1983 with little to lose. A distant third behind McDonald's and Burger King, it was barely mentioned in the big "burger wars," but Freeman was determined to show that Wendy's had a product that was superior in beef content to the Big Mac and the Whopper.

First aired in January 1984, the Wendy's spots made this claim using three elderly ladies who carefully inspected a burger at a counter modeled after those of Wendy's competition. Dumbfounded by the burger's tiny size, one woman—Clara Peller, who became an ad icon—looked up at the camera and demanded, "Where's the beef?" Freeman developed the concept and script; Joe Sedelmaier directed the spot and cast the under-five-foot, 83-year old Peller.

The commercial's brash humor was unlike anything seen before. Although Wendy's executives threatened to pull the campaign a week before it aired, Freeman stood by the spot. The campaign, which also featured less-remembered elderly men in a similar scenario and Freeman's personal favorite, a tongue-in-cheek Russian fashion show, was credited with boosting Wendy's sales by 31 percent and its profits by 24 percent and with making the chain into a major competitor in the burger wars.

The "Where's the beef?" commercial became the top pick in *USA Today*'s TV Commercial Hall of Fame, which judged classics from the 1960s to 1999. In 1984, U.S. presidential candidate Walter Mondale, in debating the substance of proposals presented by his Democratic primary opponent, Gary Hart, demanded, "Where's the beef?" demonstrating the extent to which the line had entered the national lexicon.

The success of the Wendy's campaign piqued the interest of restaurant executive Mike Ilitch of Little Caesars Pizza. Lagging well behind Pizza Hut and Domino's Pizza in sales, with little national exposure, Little Caesars needed to be bold and aggressive, which was just Freeman's style. In 1987 the marketer gave Freeman the $40 million account provided he set up his own advertising unit within Saatchi & Saatchi, which was already marketing a restaurant chain. As a result, Freeman founded Cliff Freeman & Partners along with two other former DFS creative executives, Arthur Bijou and Pete Regan, and began work for the agency's first client.

The United States was in a recession, so the goal for the Little Caesars campaign was to address and entertain families while offering them a product of great value and convenience. Freeman created a likable cartoon character who wore a Roman toga and appeared at the end of wildly funny commercials that told stories

Cliff Freeman.
Courtesy of Cliff Freeman.

to which regular people could relate. Freeman himself spoke the "Pizza! Pizza!" mantra for the Little Caesar character in the spots. "Two great pizzas for one low price" was exactly what American families were looking for.

By the end of 1987 Little Caesars was a national chain with restaurants in every state. By 1992, after the continued success of commercials such as "Conga," which showed a family, including a poodle, dancing in a conga line around their living room, the restaurant had grown from 900 stores to 4,600. According to a 1992 *Wall Street Journal* survey, Little Caesars had became the most popular and recognized brand in the country, even while it was being outspent ten-fold in advertising by its competitors.

Cliff Freeman & Partners continued to market the Little Caesars brand for 11 years, creating more than 100 commercial spots for the company. Although his agency had created solid campaigns for other big name clients such as Staples office supply stores and Pep Boys auto parts stores, Freeman had come to be known by many in the industry as "the Little Caesars shop."

In February 1998 Freeman resigned the pizza account; Little Caesars had begun to lose its national grip and subsequently began to look for advertising that was more product oriented. "They were asking us to do less than our best work," Freeman told a *Shoot* magazine reporter in a 1998 interview, "We don't create mediocre advertising." Some believed the agency could not survive without its signature account, but Cliff Freeman & Partners quickly attracted new accounts. In 1999 Freeman's agency won more industry awards than any other agency or agency network worldwide for its outrageous work for Outpost.com, Fox Sports Network, and Hollywood Video.

In October 1999 Freeman used these victories to buy his independence from Saatchi & Saatchi. In his new shop he chose to prioritize creativity over rapid global growth, taking only accounts for which he felt the agency could do its best work. Freeman still preferred brands that were trying to make a play against the front-runners, but his cutting-edge style also attracted the attention of the Coca-Cola Company in 2000 to do work for its Coke Classic brand (the agency had already done some spots for the marketer's Fanta and Cherry Coke). Freeman chose broad and all-encompassing themes that many could relate to, although the ads retained a comedic sensibility. For example, "Hiccup," an ad his agency created in Bangkok, Thailand, for Fanta, shows that hiccups are a universal problem.

Freeman, known as an envelope-pusher, acknowledged that clients are often nervous about working with the agency. Looking to the 21st century, the agency augumented its creative and research departments, seeking new and different ideas and a better understanding of its target audiences. In 2001 the agency had 100 employees and more than $400 million in annual billings.

To Freeman, a commercial that viewers mute or flip past with the remote control represents wasted money. But if he knows the secret to getting consumers' attention, why have not all advertisers adopted his technique? Freemen blames timidity. "It just seems to be a part of human nature that a few things will be great and most things will be ordinary," he has said. "I think a lot of people are afraid to be original."

MEGAN CASSADA

Biography

Born in Vicksburg, Mississippi, 14 February 1941; started in advertising in Atlanta, Georgia, before moving to Dancer, Fitzgerald, Sample, New York City, in 1971; founded Cliff Freeman & Partners within Saatchi & Saatchi, 1987; left Saatchi & Saatchi to set up an independent shop, 1999.

Further Reading

"Best Spots of the 1990s," Adweek (20 March 2000)

Cliff Freeman and Partners <www.clifffreeman.com>

Dill, Mallorre, "The Clios Twisted Comedy Puts Cliff Freeman over the Top," Adweek (24 May 1999)

Hume, Scott, "Cliff Freeman on Entertainment As a Marketing Tool," Restaurants and Institutions (1 September 2000)

Kim, Hank, and Greg Farrell, "Top 20 Ad Campaigns," Adweek (9 November 1998)

Linnett, Richard, "Special Report: Shoot's 1998 Agency of the Year," Shoot (11 December 1998)

Linnett, Richard, "Cliff Dwellers," Advertising Age (22 May 2000)

Newman, Judith, "Cliff Notes," Creativity (December/January 2000)

Parpis, Eliftheria, "A Gallery of Winners," Adweek (7 June 1999)

Vedehra, Dave, "Little Caesars' Humorous Ads Take Big Slice of Awareness over Long Haul," Advertising Age (8 January 1996)

Wells, Melanie, "Top Ads Tickled, Tugged at Heart," USA Today (22 March 1999)

"Witty Winners Reign; Panel's Favorite Ads Found Both Artistic, Commercial Success," USA Today (22 March 1999)

French, Neil 1944–

British Advertising Executive

An expatriate English copywriter with an eclectic background, Neil French is widely regarded as the man who taught Asian ad agencies how to do great print advertising. "He woke up Asian advertising to what creativity could be," said Michael Fromowitz, a Canadian art director who was also instrumental in building the creative reputations of various Asian ad agencies, including the Ball Partnership and Batey Ads. "In the role of a guru, he excels," said Jim Aitchison, former creative director of Batey Ads in Singapore.

Given his roundabout approach to the industry, such sentiments might have been hard to predict. French was born on 9 September 1944 in Birmingham, England. After being expelled from school at the age of 16, he worked as a debt collector and sold encyclopedias door-to-door. He landed his first job in advertising at the age of 18, joining a Birmingham agency called Ster-

ling Advertising. He initially worked as a studio assistant before being promoted, after less than two years, to the position of account executive.

Within a year French left the agency to briefly work for his client, a motorcycle manufacturer. When the company folded shortly thereafter, he took off for Spain, where he spent two years in a Hemingway-like search for adventure. He dabbled in bullfighting, sang in nightclubs, and waited on tables.

When he returned to England, French went back to the agency business, where he worked as an account executive at a small Birmingham agency before moving to London and making the transition to the creative side of advertising, initially as a writer, then as an art director. In 1970 he became a partner in his own agency, Blacker Hyde Associates, during which time he also claims to have run a discotheque and a concert hall and managed a rock band. The agency folded in 1978, a move that wiped him out financially as he had personally guaranteed the agency's credit line with its bank. He briefly joined a London agency called Clements Frankis Powell before his first, short-lived job in Asia: he took over—for three days in 1980—as creative director of Batey Ads in Singapore.

French returned to London and freelanced before accepting the post of creative director of Holmes Knight Richie, a newly formed agency. He returned to Singapore in 1983, recruited by Michael Ball, then an executive with Ogilvy & Mather in Asia, to become creative director of its office there.

In 1986 he took over as creative director of Batey Ads, then moved six months later to the Ball Partnership, working again for Michael Ball. By now French had begun working his way up the corporate hierarchy, eventually being named vice chairman of the agency, which in time was acquired by London-based WCRS.

French left Ball in 1994 and spent a year freelancing and directing TV commercials before returning to Ogilvy as regional creative director for Asia/Pacific in 1995. In 1998 the agency reformed its global creative council, and French was named worldwide creative director by Shelley Lazarus, Ogilvy's chief executive officer.

French had long been considered a regional advertising star whose reputation was known to certain members of the creative community outside Asia. His rise to the post of regional creative director for Ogilvy, however, and his subsequent elevation to worldwide creative director put him squarely in the global creative spotlight.

French's success in Asia resulted from a combination of many factors, but timing played an important part, Aitchison said. The ad industry in the region was in its infancy, and French was able to train a cadre of young Asians in his approach, resulting in a reputation not only as a star in his own right but also as a teacher and mentor.

The style popularized by French is typically a minimalist visual approach, one that reflects both an elegance in layout and an economy of graphic elements. The text, which reflects French's fondness for long copy, is written in a literate, sophisticated, and impertinent tone. Often, the copy reflects French's own clipped style of speaking. Further, the print work that blossomed under French's creative direction was always meticulously crafted, with attention to everything from typography and letterspacing to photography, retouching, and engraving.

One of French's claims to fame, in addition to a notorious ability to ruffle the corporate feathers of both his agency bosses and his clients, was his penchant for creating controversial ad campaigns. He did this twice in the early 1990s in Singapore, both times running ads in local newspapers that resulted in considerable media coverage and outright condemnation—results that often delighted French, for whom there was no such thing as bad press as long as his name was spelled correctly. One of these campaigns has become legendary in the ad business. Retained by the Singapore *Straits Times* to produce a campaign that demonstrated the power of newspaper advertising to move beer consumers,

Neil French.
Courtesy of Neil French. Photo by Hanchew Studios.

French created a fictitious brand dubbed "XO" beer that was notable for its high alcohol content. He then created a series of humorous ads extolling this quality and ran them in the newspaper. As a result, Singapore bars were besieged with requests for the brand, which did not exist. In typical Neil French fashion, he had registered the name of the beer in his own name and profited nicely when, as a follow-up to its hoax, the newspaper actually brewed a few hundred cases of the stuff and quickly sold them.

French has posted many of his award-winning print ads on his Web site (www.neilfrench.com), where they are accompanied by his own remarks about the ads and the circumstances behind their creation. Among these are works for Borders, Beck's beer, Chivas Regal, and Parker pens.

ANTHONY VAGNONI

Biography

Born in Birmingham, England, 9 September 1944; got first ad agency job at age 18 at Sterling Advertising, 1962; became partner in his own agency, Blacker Hyde Associates, 1970; Blacker Hyde Associates folded, 1978; named creative director of Singapore office of Ogilvy & Mather, 1983; named creative director, Batey Ads, 1986; six months later, moved to Ball Partnership, where he was eventually named vice chairman; left Ball in 1994; returned to Ogilvy as regional creative director for Asia/Pacific, 1995; named worldwide creative director of Ogilvy, 1998.

Further Reading

Neil French <www.neilfrench.com>

Fruit of the Loom

Principal Agencies

Grey Advertising Agency, Inc.
Leo Burnett Company, Ltd. (Canada)
Warwick Baker O'Neill

Fruit of the Loom is one of the oldest and largest producers of underwear, active wear, and casual wear in the United States. Founded in 1851 in Warwick, Rhode Island, as a single textile mill, B.B. & R. Knight, Inc., it adopted the name Fruit of the Loom in 1856. Fruit of the Loom was acquired by Farley, Inc., in 1985 and became a publicly held company in 1987. Today it is one of the world's largest manufacturers of cotton garments, producing more than 1 billion every year. It sells its products under a number of brand names, including Fruit of the Loom, BVD, Screen Stars, Best, Munsingwear, Wilson, and Gitano. The company distributes its products through more than 10,000 retailers, including all major discount chains and mass merchandisers. It also sells to many department, specialty, drug, and variety stores as well as national chains, supermarkets, and sports-specialty stores. Although most of its sales are in the Unites States, the company also markets its products in Europe, Canada, Japan, Taiwan, Korea, and Mexico.

The brand mark for Fruit of the Loom—the cluster of grapes, gooseberries, and an apple—is one of the oldest and best-recognized trademarks in the United States. It was first registered in August 1871, just one year after Congress passed the first trademark law. Knight Mills, developer of the trade name Fruit of the Loom, was one of the first firms to affix printed labels to its bolts of cloth. The manufacturer quickly noticed that its labeled muslin was the first to sell. The early labels were based on pictures painted by a young artist identified only as "Miss Skeel." The first of her paintings used under the Fruit of the Loom banner featured a lone apple. It was not long before the drawings were expanded to include grapes, pears, and cherries. These drawings evolved into the familiar trademark now recognized by shoppers around the world. Fruit of the Loom also used brand characters as centerpieces of its advertising. It was not until 1975, however, that the popular "Fruit of the Loom Guys" were developed. It was their role to emphasize the quality and comfort of Fruit of the Loom's men's underwear.

The company attributes much of its success to its strategy of low-cost manufacturing, accomplished through offshore operations that keep the costs of cutting, sewing, and finishing low. It also places considerable emphasis on its marketing programs, ranging from conventional advertising to sports and music-festival sponsorships. These programs have built brand equity and customer loyalty. All promotion campaigns focus on a single theme: the quality and consistency of the products. Fruit of the Loom also has been highly innovative in leveraging its relationships with suppliers and retailers—for example, helping them set up Web sites using Fruit of the Loom electronic catalog tools and inventory management software.

The one-time market leader fell on hard times in the 1990s, however. Fruit of the Loom's troubles began in 1993 when it added too much manufacturing capacity. The company then cut back on production just as consumer spending rebounded. In 1995 it posted operating losses and was forced to close 13 of its U.S.-based manufacturing facilities. In 1998 *Fortune* magazine ranked Fruit of the Loom lowest in the apparel industry, and the company dropped to fifth place in terms of market share. In an attempt to reduce its tax burden and become more competitive with designers such as Calvin Klein and Tommy Hilfiger, Fruit of the Loom moved its headquarters to the Cayman Islands in 1998. In addition to cutting costs, the company has placed a renewed emphasis on advertising and marketing to help bolster its position.

Given the company's long history as an American manufacturer and marketer and its long relationship with the Grey Advertising Agency, Inc., dating to the 1930s, it is somewhat surprising that one of its most successful advertising campaigns, the award-winning "Clothesline" campaign, was developed by the Leo Burnett Company's Canadian branch in Toronto. In 1996 the "Clothesline" campaign helped Burnett win the title of global agency of the year at the New York Festivals TV Advertising Awards. The campaign also won the "Billi Award," given by the Canadian Outdoor Advertising Association of Canada, and the *Strategy* magazine "Advertiser of the Year 1966" award.

There were six commercials in the campaign. Each spot showed women's panties bobbing along a clothesline. Viewers first saw a series of colorful, novelty underwear, some with tassels, animal prints, and lace, but all clearly uncomfortable to wear. These items were followed by a single pair of white, 100 percent cotton Fruit of the Loom briefs accompanied by the tag line, "Fruit of the Loom. Really, really comfortable underwear." In another spot the clothesline advanced showing the viewer four pairs of thong underwear. The song "Stuck in the Middle with You" played loudly as the underwear moved along the clothesline. Finally, a pair of Fruit of the Loom underwear appeared as the female voice-over noted, "With more material in the seat, our underwear always stays comfortably in place. Sorry guys."

Burnett knew it had to develop a high-impact campaign to create awareness of Fruit of the Loom and its products in Canada. Although Fruit of the Loom was a well-known brand in the United States, it was new to Canadians. Since the products were to be sold through self-service, mass-merchandising outlets, the agency recognized that creating brand awareness was key—consumers would have to be familiar with the brand name before they would seek out and buy the product. The agency chose TV as the medium most likely to reach consumers quickly. Research showed that people who shopped at mass merchandisers watched a lot of TV. Burnett placed ads during programs—mainly movies and sitcoms—that appealed to discount shoppers. The television campaign was supported by mass transit and shopping mall poster advertising.

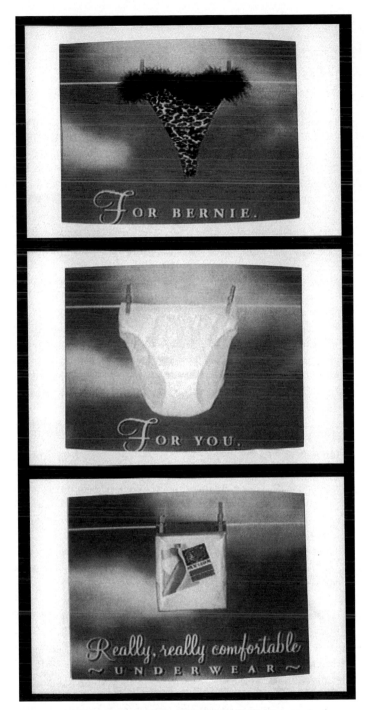

In a 1996 commercial from the acclaimed "Clothesline" campaign, comfortable, practical Fruit of the Loom underwear was contrasted with an uncomfortable-looking "exotic" undergarment.
Courtesy of John W. Shivel, VP Advertising, Fruit of the Loom, Inc.

The target audience for the campaign was value-conscious women in the 18- to 49-year-old age group who shop in mass merchandise outlets. The campaign had a unique selling proposition, namely, that what men want in women's underwear and what women want in women's underwear are two completely different things. Market research had shown that most women in the target group had underwear given to them by men that they had never worn. The women were reluctant to wear these items because they just were not comfortable or practical. Moreover, the women's reactions to traditional print and television underwear commercials were not positive. Emily Bain, account supervisor at Burnett, noted, "We had heard from these women time and time again that they hated seeing models dancing around the television screen in skimpy underwear . . . because . . . those ads are for men, not women."

Surveys conducted after the initial ads aired showed that they scored in the top 1 percent using day-after recall measures. In a subsequent study women shoppers at U.S. and Canadian shopping malls were stopped and asked to compare ads created in the United States with the Canadian-made "Clothesline" series. The latter scored much higher. Even more important were "purchase-intent" scores. Twenty-three percent of those who saw the Canadian commercials said they would buy Fruit of the Loom underwear instead of their current brand. But only 9 percent said they would switch brands after seeing the American-made ads. The results were so convincing that Fruit of the Loom began running the Canadian ads in the United States. In 1993 the company moved its account from Grey Advertising to Burnett to consolidate its North American and European advertising.

In October 1997 Burnett resigned the account, stating that although the agency was very proud of the work it had done, it no longer saw eye-to-eye with the client on the evolution of the advertising strategy. Fruit of the Loom decided to drop the product-focused "Clothesline" approach and move toward more image-based advertising. In 1998 it hired Warwick Baker O'Neill of New York City as its agency. Fruit of the Loom increased ad spending by 30 percent to 40 percent for a total budget of $33 million. The increased spending on advertising was accompanied by greater use of end-of-aisle displays and the creation of "stores-within-stores" to improve merchandising.

At the outset of the 21st century, the company was repositioning itself as an apparel company rather than an underwear company. Over half its sales were in apparel. Thus, in addition to heavy ad spending on its Fruit of the Loom brands, the firm also invested substantial funds to build its BVD and Gitano brands to make them more relevant to young, fashion-conscious buyers.

PEGGY CUNNINGHAM

Further Reading

Fruit of the Loom, "Fruit of the Loom/Evolution of the Logo" <www.fruit.com/static/company/history_logo/index.cfm>
Smith, Barbara, "Brand Building through TV Advertising: Humour Wears Well for Fruit of the Loom," *Strategy: The Canadian Marketing Report* (5 February 1996)
Weimer, De'Ann, "A Killing in the Caymans?" *Business Week* (11 May 1998)

Fuller & Smith & Ross, Inc.

Formed as Fuller & Smith, 1907; merged with F.J. Ross Agency to become Fuller & Smith & Ross, Inc., 1930; merged into Creamer Colarossi Basford, 1976.

Major Clients
Aluminum Company of America (Alcoa)
McGraw-Edison Company
McGraw-Hill Publishing Company, Inc.
Owens-Corning Fiberglass Corporation
Pennzoil Company
Westinghouse Electric and Manufacturing Company

Fuller & Smith & Ross, Inc. (FSR), emerged in the late 1930s and 1940s as one of the leading ad agencies specializing in industrial and business-to-business advertising, generally ranking among the top 20 to 25 U.S. agencies in terms of billings. FSR was organized in Cleveland, Ohio, in 1907 as Fuller & Smith. The agency was born with a single account generating $50 a month in fees. Little is know about the founders. Fuller retired within a year of founding the agency, and Harry Smith left to take a position with the Erickson Company, predecessor to McCann-Erickson, Inc., in 1909. The company was run for the next 19 years by its senior management, which chose to retain the name. The agency emphasized the importance of research in the development of advertising. In 1916 the Westinghouse Electric Corporation assigned some work to the agency just as radio production for World War I was driving Westinghouse growth. Four years later, in 1920, Westinghouse acquired Edwin Armstrong's patent for the superheterodyne circuit, a critical element of radio voice amplification and an asset that would soon bring the company into the patent alliance that formed the basis of the Radio Corporation of America (RCA). The Westinghouse account would become a mainstay of FSR for the next 44 years.

Another factor in the agency's growth was the leadership of Allen Billingsley, who joined the company in 1923 as an account executive on Westinghouse and became Fuller & Smith president in 1928. He was eager to expand out of Cleveland and get a foothold in New York City.

Meanwhile, Frederick Jeffery Ross was establishing himself in the New York City advertising world. Born in 1879 in Toronto, Canada, Ross moved to New York City in 1898 and became a U.S. citizen in 1903. He founded the F.J. Ross Advertising Agency in 1920. In 1929 Billingsley first approached Ross about creating a Cleveland-New York City combination, and in 1930 the two agencies merged to form Fuller & Smith & Ross, Inc. Ross remained in New York City as chairman, but the real authority was in Cleveland, where Billingsley served as president. In 1938 Ross retired, returning to Canada to take Canadian citizenship once again; he died on 10 December 1957 at the age of 78. Billingsley continued to run the agency from Cleveland, while John E.

Wiley, who joined in 1932, assumed the chairmanship in New York City in 1938, serving until 1950.

Under Billingsley, FSR achieved its greatest growth, moving from billings of nearly $2.5 million in 1929 to $41 million in 1954. In 1947 it ranked number 15 among U.S. agencies, according to *Advertising Age*, the highest relative position it would achieve. Between 1944 and 1954 Billings nearly quadrupled from $11 million to $41 million. FSR lost the Westinghouse account briefly to Henri, Hurst & McDonald in 1929, then recovered it in 1930. But FSR handled only print media for Westinghouse. When television arrived, the company used McCann-Erickson to oversee the production of *Studio One* and establish Betty Furness as the spokeswoman for the company's appliance line, while Ketchum, MacLeod & Grove, Inc. (KMG), handled special events such as Westinghouse's political convention sponsorships on the Columbia Broadcasting System (CBS) in 1952 (which launched Walter Cronkite), 1956, and 1960.

Meanwhile, FSR was involved in television with client Alcoa, which sponsored Edward R. Murrow's CBS series, *See It Now*. Many regarded Alcoa's association with the program as a courageous one, since Murrow often tackled controversial topics, none more so than a devastating portrait of Senator Joseph R. McCarthy in March 1954. The agency also produced a short-lived weekly radio series for Alcoa in 1944 to 1945 called *Miss Hatti* starring Ethel Barrymore.

On 8 October 1954 Billingsley died suddenly of a heart attack. But he had built a management structure that would carry the agency forward. Robert Allen, who had replaced Wiley as head of the New York City office in 1950, though without the chairman title, assumed the presidency, and FSR's headquarters moved to New York City.

Then in March 1955, after 39 years with FSR, the print portion of Westinghouse Electric Corporation's consumer business went to McCann-Erickson, a loss of about $4 million. Five years later, in 1960, the remaining trade portion of the business, about $1 million, moved to KMG, ending a 44-year relationship.

In 1957 Allen opened a 90-person office in Pittsburgh, Pennsylvania, to serve Alcoa and the remaining industrial portions of the Westinghouse business, plus three other accounts. By now FSR had offices in Cleveland; New York City; Chicago, Illinois; San Francisco, California; and one overseas outpost in London, England. Also in 1957, FSR absorbed the New York City–based Robert W. Orr Agency after Orr lost the $4 million Andrew Jergens business. In January 1961 FSR formed Fuller & Smith & Ross International, allying the agency with 70 others in 58 countries.

In 1958 FSR created one of the great classics of business-to-business advertising for the McGraw-Hill Publishing Company. The print ad pictured an executive in a bow tie hunched forward in a swivel chair and scowling into the camera. It was an image that represented every salesman's worst nightmare when making a cold sales call. The copy read: "I don't know you. I don't know your company. I don't know your company's product. I don't know what your company stands for. I don't know your company's customers. I don't know your company's record. I don't know your company's reputation. Now, what was it you wanted to sell me?" The ad was conceived by FSR Account Executive Gilbert Morris, who initially posed for the picture to convey the kind of look he wanted in the final ad. His forbidding image fit so perfectly, though, he ended up using himself in his own ad. His face became one of the most familiar in all of industrial advertising and was hung on the walls of agencies and publishers for decades. The ad was widely reprinted in advertising textbooks as well. In 1999 *Advertising Age*'s *Business Marketing* named it the best business-to-business ad of the 20th century. Morris had begun his career in 1925 at Rickard & Company, later absorbed into Marsteller, Inc., and joined FSR in 1945. He retired in 1962 and died in April 1963. But his face still loomed large nearly half a century later.

FSR took pride in the fact that it was one of 17 agencies ranked AAA-1 by Dun & Bradstreet. The agency continued a modest growth curve in the 1960s. In June 1960 it acquired Stomberger, LaVene, McKinzie, of Los Angeles, California. Early in the decade it won Lestoil Products' Lestoil brand cleaner, Air France, Remington Rand Corporation's Univac Division, Renault, Inc., and the presidential campaign for Senator Barry Goldwater.

But none turned into long-term relationships. Arthur Durham succeeded Allen as chairman in 1965, with FSR billings nearing $59 million. But in 1972 billings had dropped to $45.6 million, and by 1975 to about half what they had been a decade before, or about $31.2 million.

FSR began searching for a partner. Merger discussions moved to an advanced stage with Conahay & Lyon, Inc., and de Garmo, Inc., both in New York City, but collapsed with FSR's loss of the $7 million AMF, Inc., account in November 1975. Finally, in April 1976, FSR became the lesser partner in a merger with New York City–based Creamer, Colarossi, Basford, Inc., creating a $50 million company with about 60 percent devoted to industrial accounts. The 1976 merger ended the life of FSR as an independent company. The initials lingered for two years in the new name, Creamer/FSR, but were dropped in 1978 when the company became simply Creamer, Inc., thus retiring one of the oldest names in U.S. advertising.

JOHN McDONOUGH

Further Reading

"F&S&R Finds a Partner; Creamer Merger Set," *Advertising Age* (19 April 1976)
"A Lesson in Contrasts," *Advertising Age* (25 October 1954)

G

Gallup Research

The name *Gallup* is usually associated with political polling, but in addition to his work in this area, George Gallup also had a long and distinguished career in advertising. Beginning with his research as a graduate student during the 1920s, through his 15-year career at Young & Rubicam, Inc. (Y&R), to his work at Gallup & Robinson in the 1950s and 1960s, Gallup developed innovative methods for studying consumer reactions and changed the way advertisers looked at newspapers, magazines, radio, and movies.

Gallup was born in Jefferson, Iowa, on 18 November 1901 and earned undergraduate and graduate degrees at the University of Iowa. As an undergraduate he edited the campus newspaper, *The Daily Iowan*, and became interested in finding out which features people read most often. At that time researchers believed they could ask customers what they read in the paper and receive truthful answers. Gallup challenged this conventional wisdom, arguing that people might not admit their real interests. For his doctoral dissertation, Gallup proposed a different approach in which interviewers visited people at their homes and asked them to point out, page by page, everything they had read in a given issue of the paper, from articles and editorials to advertisements and cartoons.

The results of his research astonished everyone. Earlier studies had shown that people read foreign news, business columns, and political reports—or so they said. Gallup found, however, that more people read the comics than the lead front-page story and that the picture page was the next most attractive feature. Men and women displayed different interests: women read the obituaries and stories dealing with people's lives, while men favored the weather report and the sports page. Department store ads were also more popular with women than were articles dealing with political events.

After he finished his Ph.D. in psychology in 1928, Gallup taught journalism at Drake University and carried out additional reader recognition studies for the *Des Moines Register and Tribune*, the *St. Louis Post-Dispatch*, and the *Cleveland Plain Dealer*. These studies provided further evidence of the popularity of comic strips and drew the attention of trade publications such as *Advertising & Selling* and *Printers' Ink*. In March 1931 newspaper publisher William Randolph Hearst decided to make the comics section of his Sunday papers available for advertising. To persuade advertisers to buy space there, he and his sales manager, Hawley Turner, cited Gallup's finding that more people read that section of the paper than any other.

Several months later, General Foods and its advertising agency, Y&R, decided to try comic-strip advertising for Grape Nuts cereal, whose sales had been declining. The agency designed ads in a comic-strip style that featured characters named Egbert Energy and Suburban Joe, who touted the cereal's benefits to their friends. The ads used humor and suspense to wrap the commercial message in a soft sell. Within two months, Grape Nuts shipments reached their highest level in eight years. One year later 43 other papers announced that they would accept advertising in their comics sections. By the late 1930s annual expenditures on comic strip advertising had jumped from less than $1,000 to $16.5 million. Marketing textbooks published during this time cited Gallup's research as the primary motivation for this major shift in advertising strategy.

In July 1931 Gallup left Iowa to become professor of journalism and advertising at Northwestern University in Evanston, Illinois. During the summer of 1931 he used the method developed in his newspaper work to carry out a study of magazine readership. Interviewers in six cities throughout the United States visited 15,000 homes to ask what people had read in each of four magazines: the *Saturday Evening Post*, *Liberty*, *Literary Digest*, and *Collier's*. Results indicated that more people read *Liberty* than any of the other publications. A follow-up study one year later focused on the advertisements in these magazines. Gallup evaluated which ads attracted the most attention, according to the emotions they appealed to, their use of headlines and illustrations, and the kind of product they promoted. Again, differences between men and women became apparent. While both males and females responded to ads that employed sex appeal as an attraction, men favored ads that stressed product quality, while women noticed those that appealed to their vanity. Women preferred illustrations that showed people using a product, whereas men liked drawings of the product itself.

As part of his research, Gallup also surveyed hundreds of advertising executives to see what kinds of strategies appealed to them. He found that what worked with advertisers did not work with the public—and vice versa. Ads that stressed a product's efficiency and low price ranked high with executives but carried much less weight with the public. Gallup argued that advertising executives could not rely on their own instincts; instead they needed to use empirical research as a guide to public preferences.

On the basis of this work, Y&R hired Gallup to be its director of research in 1932. Under his leadership the agency established its first copy research department to study the quality of its ads and devise ways to improve them. Like other agencies during the Depression, Y&R believed that empirical research would yield more insight into the customers' desires. And if the agency could prove that its advertising worked, business executives might be more willing to spend money on marketing.

At Y&R Gallup and his staff analyzed the components of an ad down to the smallest unit to determine which features attracted customers' interest. Drawing on the theories of Walter Dill Scott, a pioneer in the psychology of advertising, Gallup held that ads appealed to readers on a sensory level rather than a logical one. An ad's color, size, shape, and position on a page could influence a reader's response and induce a desire to buy. Gallup and his staff found evidence to support the common belief that ads "above the fold" of the newspaper attracted more attention than those below it. They also determined that ads placed on the right-hand page of a newspaper did not attract enough attention to warrant paying the higher cost of that popular position. The research department also studied the impact of various layout designs. Gallup suggested that instead of presenting advertising copy in blocks of text that required close reading, copywriters should break the blocks into smaller units and use asterisks, italics, and boldface to highlight important ideas. Designers also began using more white space to break up the monolithic appearance of the copy. Within five years smaller blocks of text became the industry standard.

These manipulations of the visual appearance of an ad were designed to overcome readers' mental inertia and lure them into reading a sales pitch before they realized they were doing so. Gallup and his staff also developed other techniques for gaining attention. As a result of his research, Y&R's copywriters began using drawings and photographic sequences to attract attention. Another strategy developed at this time was the presentation of a dramatic scenario designed to encourage reader identification. The agency's ads for Packard, for example, featured a drawing of a young boy sitting on a fence and gazing at the car. The caption read, "When he grows up, that's what he wants." The ad created a detailed visual image that encouraged readers to fantasize for a moment that they owned the car and could fulfill a childhood dream.

As he had in his earlier newspaper work, Gallup also measured what percentage of an ad people read and whether they just noticed it or actually read part or all of it. As these studies accumulated, the agency began to compile "noting and reading" scores for ads of comparable size. Researchers used these tables to compare new ads with those of proven success and to measure Y&R's work against that of other agencies. These statistics provided proof of the agency's success in selling. In 1937, for exam-

George Gallup, founder and former chairman of the research and opinion polling company that still bears his name, was inducted into the Advertising Hall of Fame in 1977.

ple, Gallup demonstrated that Y&R's page magazine ads had an average readership of 14 percent, compared to only 9 percent for ads produced by other agencies. Knowing how many people read an ad enabled Gallup to calculate a cost per thousand readers and to determine which strategies were most cost-effective for clients.

In addition to his work in print media, Gallup also carried out studies relating to Y&R's work on radio. The agency's clients sponsored more minutes of nighttime network radio from 1936 through 1943 than anyone else, and Y&R won several industry awards for creative advertising. In keeping with Gallup's idea that ads should lure consumers into a commercial before they knew what was happening, Y&R promoted the use of commercials that were integrated with the regular content of the program. On *The Jell-O Program Starring Jack Benny*, for example, Benny might introduce a commercial segment with the greeting, "Jell-O again, Jack Benny here." The pun on "hello" and "Jell-O" was meant to blur the boundaries between the sales pitch and the comedy portions of the show.

Gallup also changed the way ratings were determined during the 1930s. Archibald Crossley had begun regular and continuous studies of radio audiences at the request of the Association of National Advertisers in 1933. Crossley used the telephone recall method, in which interviewers phoned people and asked them to recall what programs they had been listening to the night before.

Because this method asked listeners to remember what they had done in the past, it was considered unreliable. Gallup introduced the "telephone coincidental method," in which interviewers asked people what programs they were listening to at the moment that they called. Y&R used the coincidental method in all of its radio research during the 1930s and 1940s, and other rating services eventually adopted Gallup's approach, including the Hooperatings begun by Claude Hooper, which were the forerunner of today's Nielsen's.

In 1939, while he continued to work at Y&R, Gallup established a separate company, the Audience Research Institute (ARI), to carry out studies for Hollywood film producers. To supervise day-to-day activities he hired David Ogilvy, who had recently arrived in New York City from England. Over the next several years they conducted studies for RKO Radio Pictures, Samuel Goldwyn, David O. Selznick, and Walt Disney. As he had with his print and radio research, Gallup attempted to isolate the specific elements of a film that made viewers want to see it, such as titles, stories, and casts. ARI found that the public wanted to see Fred Astaire reunited with Ginger Rogers (he was), and predicted (incorrectly) that Lucille Ball would not have many fans. After World War II, ARI developed methods to track the impact of film advertising. The company conducted surveys that asked viewers if they had heard of a particular title or story, and those who said yes were said to have been "penetrated" by the film's advertising or publicity. The measure of so-called publicity penetration enabled producers to track the impact of ad campaigns and time the release of films accordingly. Selznick held off releasing *Duel in the Sun* until ARI indicated that most viewers had heard of it. The Walt Disney studio used ARI's research to plan campaigns that carefully coordinated radio and print ads with the release of sound tracks and merchandise. ARI also used measures of publicity penetration to forecast box office returns. The institute found that at least 30 percent of U.S. filmgoers had to have heard of a film before it was released or profits would suffer.

By 1947 Gallup's activities outside of Y&R—his political polls and the Audience Research Institute—were taking up more and more of his attention, and he decided to resign from the agency to pursue these other interests. In August 1948 he and Claude Robinson, the former head of the Opinion Research Corporation who had also worked on Gallup's political surveys, formed Gallup & Robinson. At this new agency the two partners introduced a new method of advertising research they called "Impact," which was designed to determine whether people absorbed the sales message of an ad when they saw it. At Y&R Gallup and his staff had measured whether people read an ad message; with Impact, advertisers could learn not only whether consumers read an ad but also if they felt a desire to buy the product.

The Impact method used a special magazine that was designed to look like an actual publication. Advertisers could test ads under circumstances that approximated normal reading conditions, while controlling the position of an ad on a page and its placement relative to editorial material and competing ads. They could also use more than one format for an ad to compare the effectiveness of different sales strategies. Researchers visited people at their homes to give them copies of the magazine, then returned a few weeks later to question them about what they remembered. Using so-called aided recall procedures, interviewers determined whether readers could remember an ad's content when given the advertiser's name and product. With this information they were able to determine which ads succeeded in communicating the desired message and to make recommendations to their clients about which sales strategies worked. Gallup & Robinson worked with many corporate clients, including Chrysler, General Electric, Firestone, Goodrich, Kellogg, and Westinghouse. Later the agency expanded its research to cover weekly and monthly magazines such as *Life* and *McCall's*, and in the 1950s it began to study television ads as well.

But just because people remembered a sales message did not mean that they acted on it. In the late 1950s Gallup & Robinson sought to carry the Impact method one step further: they sought to understand the process that led consumers to go out and purchase an advertised product. Through a new method, "Activation" research, Gallup & Robinson worked backwards from the point of purchase to determine how advertising had influenced consumers' behavior. With the Activation approach, researchers started by finding people who had purchased the product they were studying and asked them to recount the events leading up to their decision to buy. Through carefully structured interviews, researchers were able to pinpoint when a sales message had prompted a purchase. Gallup & Robinson found that it was easiest for people to recall the steps leading to a purchase in two circumstances: buying a product for the first time and switching from one brand to another. In some product categories nearly half of all purchases could be traced back to advertising.

The Impact and Activation research methods pioneered by Gallup in the 1950s and 1960s represented the continuation of interests that distinguished his advertising career. First and foremost, Gallup believed that consumers were intelligent people who were interested in learning about new products that met their needs. Advertising could serve as a means of communication between seller and buyer by showing the merits and unique benefits of a particular product. He was opposed to gimmicks or arty visual effects, believing that people did not need to be entertained by ads but wanted to learn about a product. At the same time Gallup recognized that although people were rational beings, they were also motivated by subconscious needs and desires. Much of his work was devoted to trying to access this hidden level of the mind to learn how advertisers could suggest that their products satisfied consumers' inner needs.

Above all, Gallup's research exemplified an intelligent and systematic approach to advertising. In his academic work and studies for Y&R and in his own agency, he sought empirical evidence that a particular advertising strategy worked or that a given quality in an ad gained readers' attention. His creative, thoughtful, and scientific approach to advertising gained the respect of his colleagues and continues to be associated with the name *Gallup* today.

SUSAN OHMER

Further Reading

"Ads in Funnies," *Time* (13 June 1932)

Blumberg, Raoul, and Carroll Rheinstrom, "How Advertising Techniques Are Rated by Gallup Survey," *Printers' Ink* (24 May 1932)

Burton, Philip Ward, *Which Ad Pulled Best?* New York: Decker, 1969; 8th edition, by Burton and Scott C. Purvis, Lincolnwood, Illinois: NTC Business Books, 1996

Gallup, George, "A Scientific Method for Determining Reader Interest," *Journalism Quarterly* 8, no. 1 (March 1930)

Gallup, George, "What Do Newspaper Readers Read?" *Advertising and Selling* (31 March 1932)

Gallup, George, "Measuring Advertising's Sales Effectiveness: The Problem and the Prognosis," in *Marketing Research: A*

Management Overview, edited by Evelyn Konrad and Rodney Erickson, New York: American Management Association, 1966

"The Gallup Method of Advertising Research," *Advertising and Selling* (16 March 1932)

"Gallup Survey Paves the Way for Stronger Copy," *Advertising Age* (30 January 1932)

"Gallup Unveils New Copy Research Method," *Editor and Publisher* (16 August 1947)

"George Gallup Looks at Tomorrow's Customer," *Nation's Business* 52 (March 1964)

"How Good Is an Ad, Really?" *Business Week* (28 July 1951)

"Research," *Tide* 6 (March 1932)

General Electric Company

Principal Agencies

Batten Barton Durstine & Osborn

Maxon, Inc.

N.W. Ayer

General Electric (GE) has often been credited as being one of the best-run companies in the world. *Fortune* magazine has named it the World's Most Admired Company (1998, 1999), America's Most Admired Company (1998, 1999), and America's Greatest Wealth Creator (1998, 1999). The consistent rise of its stock prices through the years and the overall positive reports of the media confirm its strong reputation. In 1997 it became the first company to achieve a market value more than $200 billion (reaching more than $412 billion as of mid-November 2001).

General Electric is a multifaceted technology, services, and manufacturing company. It has 11 units, including aircraft engines; appliances (encompassing the Monogram, Profile Performance, Profile, GE, and Hotpoint brands); capital services (a wholly owned diversified financial services subsidiary); industrial systems (circuit breakers, transformers, and switchboards); information services (business-to-business electronic commerce solutions); lighting; medical systems (computed tomography scanners, x-ray equipment, magnetic resonance imaging systems, and nuclear medicine cameras); the National Broadcasting Corporation (NBC, which includes holdings in MSNBC, the History Channel, Cnet, iVillage, Xoom.com, and other media outlets); plastics (including GE Silicones, GE Superabrasives, GE Electromaterials, GE Specialty Chemicals, and Polymerland); power systems (gas, steam, and hydroelectric turbines and generators); and transportation systems (diesel freight locomotives). As of November 2001, the company had a presence in more than 100 countries

and employed more than 300,000 people, more than half of whom worked in the United States.

GE's consumer advertising reflects the company's strength and solidity and provides an important window into its history. In the often fickle business of advertising, GE's accounts have remained remarkably stable. And for a corporation with a reputation for conservatism, GE has also been remarkably innovative in its advertising.

Building Demand

The General Electric Company was formed in 1892 with the merger of Edison General Electric Company (created by Thomas A. Edison in 1878) and the Thomson-Houston Company. When the Dow Jones Industrial Index was formed in 1896, GE was included in the company list and is the only one of the original companies still on the index.

The newly formed GE understood that its success depended on convincing consumers of their need for electricity—not an easy accomplishment since many potential customers did not really know what electricity was. Early on, therefore, GE recognized that its advertising needed both to sell products and to educate the public. An ad from 1899 illustrates this: "Electricity lights our city. Electricity runs our streetcars. Electricity causes wagons without horses to go. Electricity permits us to talk great distances. Electricity will do our cooking and heating. Electricity will soon do everything." And so it did. GE convinced consumers that they needed this new invention by using ads to explain its benefits in practical terms.

GE also understood from the start that traditional advertising alone could not sell the new technology. The company recognized the importance of a full-scale marketing approach. For example,

General Electric was at the forefront of home entertainment in 1939.
Courtesy of General Electric.

at the Chicago World's Fair of 1893, GE secured a major presence by sponsoring an exhibit that included the world's largest direct-current generator, with 2,000 horsepower. GE also gained tremendous publicity at the fair with its Intramural Railway—an electric elevated railroad that circled the fairgrounds—and its futuristic motor-driven sidewalk.

This 1945 ad, which appeared in a youth periodical, highlighted General Electric's ongoing search for products that would improve daily life. *Courtesy of General Electric.*

For the next 100 years, even after customers had come to take electricity for granted, much of GE's advertising focused on the introduction of new products—products that would fill a need the consumer did not even know existed. For example, an advertisement that introduced the electric iron in 1905 read, "An introduction to a modern household and its demonstrator." A 1908 ad introduced the vacuum cleaner as the "Invincible electric renovator." Another ad from 1908 urged customers to "Ask your Electric Light Company about this new lamp tomorrow morning. Find out why it is economical. Learn how you can have Electricity Light at one half of the old cost. When you have these new facts you will plan to use Electricity immediately."

In the early years of advertising, GE was willing to go out on a creative limb to try to help potential customers understand new products. A 1909 ad compared the wonder of the lightbulb to Ahura Mazda, the Persian god of light. (GE actually marketed some of its bulbs under the brand name "Mazda," so this analogy was not quite as strange as it might sound today.)

During the next decade, GE invested heavily in research and development, which paid off handsomely with better products for consumers. In 1909 chemist Irving Langmuir joined GE's research laboratory, and by 1913 Langmuir and his colleagues had developed a lightbulb that lasted three times as long as its predecessor. Once again, GE pronounced the good news via advertising, boasting, "Use 3 lights at the old cost of one."

In 1913 the company gave away calendars that used elaborate and innovative photographic techniques to highlight GE's lightbulbs. In 1919 it mounted a trade show with an extravagant Chinese theme; in 1926 it sponsored a float in the Illinois Central Electrification Pageant, featuring women relaxing in a pastoral setting with GE products strewn at their feet.

General Electric emerged in the 1920s as the dominant manufacturer in the electric lamp (i.e., lightbulb) market, but the company still had to invest in advertising to convince the public of the role that electricity was destined to occupy. A series of ads in the early 1920s illustrates this point. The copy from one ad reads, "Your boy . . . the radio, the electric locomotive and the electric ship will have shortened his distances . . . a different world it's going to be—and a better one!"

GE's preeminence in this market did not come without controversy. One reason the company was able to command the electric light market was because it established the Incandescent Lamp Manufacturers Association (ILMA) in 1897, which allowed GE to fix prices and control the market. Executives realized, though, that price fixing would hold only for so long.

In addition, although GE had a rather large advertising budget (nearly $2 million in 1922), it had not established a solid base of consumer loyalty to the GE name. The company sold products under a variety of brand names, such as Mazda electric bulbs and Hotpoint appliances. It was time for a more aggressive—and cohesive—advertising strategy.

Creating an Enduring Image

GE decided to ask for outside help and solicited agencies to pitch the account. Advertising executive Bruce Barton argued that reputation and repetition go hand in hand and won the account for Barton, Durstine & Osborn in 1922. Barton developed GE's first agency-inspired image campaign with the slogan "A symbol of service, The initials of a friend" to build awareness and goodwill for the company and its logo. Barton insisted that all GE ads prominently display the logo. The logo emerged in advertisements as early as 1907 but had not been used in all of GE's ads. The GE logo remains one of the most highly recognizable company symbols. The logo is so closely connected with the company that insiders affectionately call it the "meatball" (because of its rounded shape), and employees expressed their discontent when the company's housewares division was sold to Black & Decker (B&D) in 1984 with the understanding that B&D could use the GE logo for three years.

The relationship between GE and BDO, which became Batten Barton Durstine & Osborn (BBDO) in 1928 after a merger with the George Batten Company, was mutually beneficial. Within just a few years GE's entire advertising account was housed at BBDO, where the majority of it has remained ever since. (Other agencies such as McCann-Erickson and Cole & Weber have parts of GE's business; however, the stalwart has always been BBDO.) GE gained from BBDO's long-term strategy, which emphasized creativity, stability, consistency, variety, and market saturation. The agency, too, benefited from such a stable and lucrative account.

GE's advertising agency was able to give the company stability and consistency but also variety and market saturation. For example, there is evidence of at least three campaigns running simultaneously during 1924–25. The campaigns, "Developing an electrical consciousness," "Make your house a home," and "Any woman can," were designed to appeal differently to submarkets within GE's larger consumer market.

With the help of BBDO (and the ILMA) GE was able to quickly enter and dominate the refrigeration market between 1927 and 1930. GE spent millions to market the new appliance. With GE's new commitment to the prominence of its logo, beginning in 1926, it even etched the logo on its lightbulbs. During the 1920s GE advertising appeared in all of the top consumer magazines, including the *Saturday Evening Post* and *Cosmopolitan*. The audience was clearly the housewife, and GE's ads helped to redefine the role of homemaker—with the help of GE products, of course—from drudge to family caretaker. The copy of one ad from this era read, "This is the test of a successful mother—she puts things first. She does not give to sweeping the time that belongs to her children."

During the Depression GE continued to take an aggressive approach to advertising and continued its educational strategy, developing a campaign to educate the public on the excitement of lightbulbs. GE saturated newspapers and radio with a campaign called "Science of seeing." It helped Americans understand that electricity had even more uses than they had previously thought. GE even coined a new term, "bulbsnatcher," to define someone who removed a bulb from one socket to put into another. The word quickly caught on, and soon consumers understood that the way to eliminate the "bulbsnatcher" was to purchase more lightbulbs—GE bulbs, of course.

GE's advertising during the Depression demonstrated the company's insight into developing creative and timely strategies. By the 1930s GE had a product line that included electric mixers, clothes washers, dishwashers, air conditioners, and food disposers—products that a family with an unemployed breadwinner could not justify adding to its budget. GE's advertising slogan during this time was "More goods for more people at less cost," a slogan that captured both the poverty of the times as well as hopes for future prosperity.

During the 1930s GE took innovative steps to expand its advertising to include other industries that would benefit from improved lighting technology. A two-page spread ad placed in the *Saturday Evening Post* in 1939 illustrates this. The ad introduces GE's new sealed-beam headlight system. The subhead reads: "Brought about through the united efforts of the automobile manufacturers, the makers of headlighting equipment and safety and state authorities." The only prominent logo in the ad, however, is the ubiquitous GE symbol.

As the country was emerging from the Depression, engineering became the answer to all problems. At the GE Pavilion during the New York World's Fair of 1939 GE displayed many new and prospective products. Advertising during this time reflected the optimism pervasive at the World's Fair. One ad claimed, "General Electric scientists and engineers, by applying electricity to the machines of industry, have been responsible for much of this progress. Their efforts today are creating not only more goods for more people at less cost, but also more and better jobs at higher wages."

GE remained a minor presence in network radio. For much of the 1930s it did not even rank among the top 100 advertisers. And by 1939 it ranked only 53rd with a budget of $367,000. Toward the end of the 1930s, GE assigned its electronics department advertising to Maxon, Inc., which would handle GE television and radio receivers as well as the Hotpoint division into the 1950s. After the Depression GE looked to Barton once again to boost the company's image. This time, it was necessary to convince frugal Americans to use more electric power, provided by GE. BBDO's new campaign was built around the slogan "Better light for better sight."

General Electric played a significant role during World War II. The company provided much of the technology that helped to fuel the war effort. For the first time GE faced the predicament of having to convince consumers not to use its products—but to remember them again after the war. It chose to emphasize patriotism: "When victory was won, you may expect even better GE electric servants."

After the war, pent-up consumer demand for appliances and other electrical products gave GE the opportunity to capture a major segment of an expanding market. Consumers were ready to buy, and GE was ready to supply the demand. GE's new slogan, "You can put your confidence in General Electric," helped convince consumers to purchase GE's new automatic clothes washers and combination refrigerator/freezers. The slogan appeared in ads as late as 1953.

GE THEATER

Running Out

Jenny grew up knowing only her father.
Her father spent 12 years trying to forget her mother.
Now Jenny's mother is back.

Starring Deborah Raffin and Tony Bill · CBS-TV
Wednesday, January 26 · Check local listings for the time.

WE BRING
GOOD THINGS
TO LIFE.

GENERAL **GE** ELECTRIC

General Electric was an active sponsor of family-oriented television programs, including this 1983 made-for-TV movie.
Courtesy of General Electric.

GE on TV

GE was one of the first companies to recognize the potential of television as an advertising medium. In 1948 BBDO produced the TV show *Carnival* for GE. In 1953 the Music Corporation of America (MCA), once a major band-booking agency that after the war had expanded into TV production with its Revue Productions, approached Ben Duffy at BBDO with a proposal for GE. Eager to expand its production volume, MCA sold BBDO on an anthology series called the *General Electric Theater* to be hosted by actor Ronald Reagan. The program went on the Columbia Broadcasting Service (CBS) in February 1953 and continued until 1962, by which time Reagan's association with GE as spokesperson was widely known. The ad slogan carrying GE through the postwar boom aptly read, "Progress is our most important product." The slogan was actually the pay-off line from the introduction of the program: "In engineering, in research, in manufacturing skill, in the values that bring a better, more satisfying life, at General Electric, progress is our most important product."

Reagan and his wife, Nancy, served as the consummate electricity-consuming couple. GE provided the Reagans with every imaginable electrical gadget for their home (including a dishwasher with a built-in garbage disposal), and posed the couple in ads with captions such as: "Ronald and Nancy Reagan, circa 1954, relax in the living room of their GE all-electric home."

With the success of the *General Electric Theater* and the earlier World's Fair sponsorships, GE explored other integrated marketing approaches as well. In 1959 GE took over a radio program called *College Bowl* and moved it to television where it was renamed *The GE College Bowl*. Allen Ludden and later Robert Earle hosted the show from 1959 to 1970. College teams competed for scholarships.

Still Lighting the Way

Legendary Chairman and Chief Executive Officer Jack Welch pursued innovative advertising approaches in the 1970s. He decided that consumer products ought to be developed according to the demands of customers, so he used advertisements that asked customers to help him develop GE products. The company continued to explore nontraditional advertising to promote its products. For example, on 27 June 1976 GE sponsored the CBS special presentation *The Bolshoi Ballet: Romeo & Juliet* to commemorate the Bolshoi's 200th year.

In 1979 GE inaugurated the slogan "We bring good things to life," still in use at the beginning of 2001. This slogan was developed during a time when GE's appliance division was suffering. In some controversial management decisions in the 1980s, GE invested heavily in computerization and factory automation. Critics felt it was too much, too soon, and indeed this proved to be so. While earnings were high ($2 billion in 1983), profits from sales increased marginally. To jump start the company Welch sold off 118 businesses by 1983 and used the revenue to invest in products designed to enhance manufacturing. One such product was a computerized control device for use in automating factories. The device was introduced before the software had been debugged, and although it was advertised heavily ("Stop waiting and start automating"), the experiment was doomed. During this decade, GE also increased its corporate advertising budget and placed more emphasis on GE as a brand.

The company did not stop consumer advertising during the 1980s, but a significant shift occurred when GE focused on music and images to appeal to the new "boom box" market. The prime market for these portable stereos was the 14-to-22-year-old. Richard Cotello, GE manager of marketing and communications for consumer products during the 1980s, argued that it was important to develop "edgy" commercials that would help adolescents realize that General Electric was more than a manufacturer of refrigerators or dishwashers.

At the end of the 20th century, GE's advertising continued to play a significant role in educating consumers about new technologies, and the company remained willing to invest significant money in advertising. It spent more than $12 million to advertise during the 1992 Summer Olympics. In the year 2000 it launched a BBDO-inspired ad campaign for the Advantium oven, a high-end oven that cooks with halogen bulbs. GE budgeted $50 million for the print, TV, and Internet advertising campaign, with supportive sales promotion (requiring retailers to set up in-store product demonstrations) to convince consumers that these ovens were the wave of the future. Nonetheless, GE remained relatively conservative in its advertising expenditures compared to other large companies. Although it typically ranks as one of the top three companies in market value (depending on stock market fluctuation), as of 1999 it ranked 43rd in total U.S. advertising expenditures, at $613 million.

GE was poised for further growth in the 21st century. The company's long-term commitment to BBDO and its tremendous brand recognition remained intact as of 2000. Of course, not everything that General Electric touched turned to gold. The 2001 European Commission's decision to block GE's acquisition of Honeywell is a good example. However, GE's stock has remained relatively stable through the retirement of legend Jack Welch as well as the recession that began early in the new century. Jeffrey R. Immelt, GE's ninth CEO in more than 100 years of GE history, appears likely to continue on the path that Welch laid out. GE's advertising also continues to provide innovation coupled to stability. The campaign for the GE Reveal light bulb is a good example; the advertising combines new themes ("The bulb that uncovers pure, true light") with the decades-old tag line, "We bring good things to life."

CAROL J. PARDUN

Further Reading

Crainer, Stuart, *Business the Jack Welch Way: Ten Secrets of the World's Greatest Turnaround King,* New York: Amacom, 1999

Hammond, John Winthrop, *Men and Volts: The Story of General Electric,* New York: Lippincott, 1941

Keating, Paul W., *Lamps for a Brighter America: A History of the General Electric Lamp Business*, New York: McGraw Hill, 1954

Nye, David E., *Image Worlds: Corporate Identities at General Electric, 1890–1930*, Cambridge, Massachusetts: MIT Press, 1985

General Foods Corporation

Principal Agencies

Young & Rubicam, Inc.
Benton and Bowles, Inc. (later D'Arcy Masius Benton & Bowles)
Foote, Cone & Belding
Ogilvy, Benson & Mather (later Ogilvy & Mather)
Doyle Dane Bernbach
Grey Advertising Agency, Inc.
HCM/Chicago
Ted Bates & Company, Inc.

What was to become General Foods Corporation had its origins in several small companies. Each was started by a food industry pioneer who developed a groundbreaking product, or products, and expanded his operation with entrepreneurial zeal:

- In 1895 inventor Charles William Post created a coffee substitute he called Postum. Two years later he introduced Post Grape Nuts, one of the earliest ready-to-eat breakfast cereals. Another cereal, Post Toasties, arrived on the grocery scene in 1904.
- Joel Cheek of Nashville, Tennessee, developed a coffee in the 1890s that helped make that city's Maxwell House Hotel famous. One story, perhaps apocryphal, holds that President Theodore Roosevelt, while visiting Andrew Jackson's home, the Hermitage, in 1907, pronounced the hotel's coffee "Good to the last drop!" thereby conferring upon Maxwell House coffee the honorific that would become its slogan for decades.
- In 1899 Orator Francis Woodward of LeRoy, New York, owner of a food processing company, bought the Jell-O business from its inventor, Pearl Wait, for $450 and built a market that a decade later made his dessert a household name that generated annual sales of $1 million.
- In 1903 a German coffee merchant, Ludwig Roselius, gave his research laboratory a shipment of coffee that had been submerged in seawater. Scientific analysis of these water-soaked beans led to the discovery of a method for removing caffeine. As a result, Roselius introduced a new coffee in France, calling it Sanka because it was "sans caffeine."
- Mail-order merchant Edwin Perkins had a problem trying to ship "Fruit Smack," a bottled syrup, because glass containers were fragile and costly to mail. He dehydrated the concentrated drink, sold it in paper packets, and renamed it Kool-Aid.
- Clarence Birdseye, on a visit to Labrador in 1914, noticed that fish caught by the Eskimos froze instantly and retained its texture and flavor when thawed. Realizing the commercial possibilities, he began to experiment with the fast freezing of various foods.
- P.J. Towle, a St. Paul, Minnesota, grocer, blended syrup from sugar cane and maple syrup. He then packaged the product in small cans, a new concept, and marketed it in stores across the United States as Log Cabin syrup.

In the meantime, Post had continued to expand his cereal and coffee substitute business at the Postum Cereal Company in Battle Creek, Michigan, in the process becoming a major competitor of crosstown rival Kellogg Company. Post died in May 1914. His daughter, Marjorie Merriwether Post, inherited the company, launching a period of expansion that would lead to the creation of General Foods.

Having often accompanied her father on business trips, Marjorie Post was well acquainted with the company's operations. In 1919 she asked a friend, New York lawyer C.M. Chester, to join the company. A year later she married E.F. Hutton, who ran a New York investment company, and he also came aboard.

In 1922 the Postum Cereal Company went public; Post's husband became chairman and Chester, president. She continued in a key policy-making role, however, as the company began its expansion. (She and Hutton were divorced in 1935, at which time he resigned as chairman. Chester became chairman, a position he would hold until 1943.)

Between 1925 and 1929 the Postum Cereal Company (which changed its name to the Postum Company in 1927) acquired the companies making Jell-O gelatin, Maxwell House coffee, Swans Down cake flour, Minute tapioca, Baker's chocolate and coconut, Calumet baking powder, and Log Cabin syrup, as well as Clarence Birdseye's frozen-food process. By acquiring the Birdseye operation, Postum also inherited the Birdseye corporate name, General Foods Company. Soon after the Birdseye acquisition in 1929, the Postum Company became General Foods Corporation (GF). Three years later, Sanka coffee was added to its product roster via acquisition.

The first major advertising agency to work with General Foods was the then newly formed Young & Rubicam, Inc. (Y&R),

which had been in business just over a year when it got the pre-GF Postum account. The 1924 ad that solidified the agency-client bond was headlined "Why men crack. . . ." Written by agency partner Raymond Rubicam and Lew Greene and appearing in the *Saturday Evening Post,* it touched on the negative aspects of caffeine and extolled the virtues of Postum. This ad, honored by Julian Watson in his book *The 100 Greatest Advertisements,* resulted in Y&R's getting more work from GF in the ensuing years, including the accounts of Jell-O, Sanka coffee, Calumet baking powder, and several of the Post cereals.

The acquisition of the Birdseye frozen-food process launched General Foods into a revolutionary area, as the company set out to introduce frozen foods to the public. Selecting Springfield, Massachusetts, as its first market, GF saturated the community with advertising aimed at educating consumers. Home economists demonstrated how to defrost and cook frozen foods. The company also developed portable machinery that was shipped to growing areas so that food could be frozen immediately after harvesting. Sales and acceptance came slowly, however, and Birds Eye (now two words) lost $17 million before turning a profit in 1941.

Early Radio and TV Advertising

General Foods had entered radio in the late 1920s with a popular show sponsored by Maxwell House. But General Foods and Y&R jumped into the radio arena in a big way on 14 October 1934 with a comedy-variety show starring Jack Benny and sponsored by Jell-O. Although the comedian had been on the air for more than two years for three different sponsors, he had yet to find a breakthrough format. With Jell-O, he quickly caught on. GF spent $7,500 a week for production and network costs; after three months, Jell-O sales had increased to the point that the company declared the gamble a success. And the comic proved a fine pitchman, working the sponsor's name into the script both at the program's opening ("Jell-O again. This is Jack Benny") and in subtle ways throughout the show. In 1937 GF signed Benny to a three-year, $1 million contract. GF remained with Benny through June 1944, substituting Grape Nuts for Jell-O for the last two years. Y&R also produced a successful radio show starring singer Kate Smith for GF's Calumet baking powder.

By 1937 the company was spending $1.4 million in magazine advertising and $2.8 million in radio advertising, which made it the second-largest radio advertiser in the United States (after Procter & Gamble Company, with $4.5 million). GF maintained its high profile in radio until the medium's network decline in the 1950s. Among the long list of programs it sponsored were *The Breakfast Club, My Favorite Husband, Juvenile Jury,* and many of the leading soap operas of the era, including *Our Gal Sunday, The Romance of Helen Trent, When a Girl Marries, Portia Faces Life,* and *Young Doctor Malone.* There was also *Burns and Allen* for Maxwell House and, from 1939 to 1951, *The Aldrich Family* for Jell-O.

Chester retired as GF chairman in 1943 and was succeeded by Clarence Francis, who had joined the Postum Company in sales in 1924 and had worked his way up through a succession of jobs

In 1931, to promote its Calumet brand baking powder, General Foods published *The Calumet Baking Book,* the back cover of which is shown here.
CALUMET and JELL-O are registered trademarks of Kraft Foods Holdings, Inc.

with Postum and General Foods. During and well beyond Francis's 11-year tenure as chairman, the company continued its acquisition mode. Additions included Gaines dog foods (1943), Bird's Custard Powder (1947), Kool-Aid (1953), W. Atlee Burpee garden products (1970), Oscar Mayer & Company meat products (1981), and Entenmann's bakery products (1982).

In 1929 General Foods's advertising was split between Y&R and Benton and Bowles, Inc., the latter agency handling, at various times, Log Cabin syrup, Maxwell House coffee, and those Post cereals not on the Y&R roster. Over the years, the introduction of new products and extensions of existing product lines necessitated more advertising agencies. Foote, Cone & Belding was added in 1949 to handle some Postum products and, later, several Post cereals and Calumet baking powder. Ogilvy, Benson & Mather (for Maxwell House), Grey Advertising Agency, Inc.

(Kool-Aid), and Doyle Dane Bernbach (Gaines Meal) were brought aboard in the 1960s, and Ted Bates & Company, Inc. (Log Cabin, Maxim, Good Seasons salad dressing), and HCM/Chicago (Oscar Mayer) were added in the 1980s.

In 1954 the company marked two milestones: its 25th anniversary as General Foods and the corporate headquarters' move from its longtime New York City home to suburban White Plains, in Westchester County, New York. The anniversary was celebrated on March 28 with a TV extravaganza—a 90-minute comedy-variety show that ran on all three major networks. Headliners included Groucho Marx, and Mary Martin and Ezio Pinza, who reprised their duet "Some Enchanted Evening" from the hit Broadway musical of the day, *South Pacific*. Commercials for Birds Eye, Swans Down, Jell-O, Maxwell House, Sanka, and other GF products were sprinkled through the show.

Also in 1954 Francis turned over the management reins to Austin Igleheart, the new chairman, and Charles Mortimer, who became president. Mortimer, who would himself be named chairman in 1959, had a particularly fitting background to be overseer of a company that was consistently among the largest U.S. advertisers. Before joining Postum Company as assistant advertising manager in 1928, Mortimer spent four years at the George Batten Company, a predecessor to ad agency giant Batten Barton Durstine & Osborn (BBDO), where he worked on the Sanka account. On becoming chairman of GF, Mortimer continued Igleheart's practice of telling stockholders how much the company spent annually for advertising.

A fervent advocate of advertising, Mortimer devoted one-third of his address to stockholders to the subject at the 1959 annual meeting. *Advertising Age* ran his comments in an issue and also offered the text to readers in reprint form. An excerpt read,

> Advertising is necessary if the business and the profits are to continue to show healthy rates of growth so we can continue to pay dividends. . . . One thing our long experience has taught us is that the surest way to overspend on advertising is not to spend enough to do a job properly. It's like buying a ticket three-quarters of the way to Europe. You have spent some money, but you do not arrive.

During Mortimer's years in the executive suite as well as those of his successors, GF was invariably among the top national advertisers in *Advertising Age*'s annual rankings. In 1956 the company was the fourth-largest advertiser, with expenditures of $77.7 million. In the 1958–59 fiscal year the company reached $96 million in ad spending.

In 1965 Mortimer retired and was replaced by C.W. "Tex" Cook. Throughout the 1960s and 1970s, the company continued to be an advertising leader, finishing in third or fourth place, usually behind Procter & Gamble Company (P&G); Sears, Roebuck & Company; and sometimes General Motors Corporation. (In one year, 1979, the company was number two, trailing only P&G.)

As had been the case with radio, GF was a major user of television. In 1972 the company ranked sixth among TV advertisers, with its upfront money spread over 38 nighttime network shows, including *Marcus Welby, M.D.; Ironside; Sanford and Son; Wonderful World of Disney*, and comedy shows starring Bill Cosby, Bob Newhart, and Carol Burnett. The company also used numerous star presenters in TV spots for its products, including Arlene Francis and Doris Day for Gaines dog food, Robert Young for Sanka coffee, and Cosby for Jell-O.

The Contentious 1970s

In 1973 James L. Ferguson replaced Cook as chief executive officer. Like Mortimer, Ferguson came from an ad agency background, having worked on the account side at Lennen & Newell before joining GF, where his climb up the corporate ladder included marketing posts on Birds Eye and Jell-O. Ferguson would remain head of the company until its takeover by Philip Morris Companies in 1985.

In June 1974 the company announced the completion of a management reorganization. Responsibility for strategy moved to upper management whereas operating responsibility was moved down "into the hands of the people on the firing line who are best equipped to handle it." As part of the reorganization, all GF products were assigned to one of three categories: businesses with great growth potential (e.g., decaffeinated coffee and pet foods); businesses operating in relatively mature markets where further growth was expected to be modest (e.g., Jell-O); businesses with little opportunity for either market growth or technical leadership (e.g., Swans Down cake mixes and Calumet baking powder).

In January 1972 the Federal Trade Commission brought a "shared monopoly" antitrust suit against the "Big Three" cereal makers. The suit claimed that the companies had maintained a concentrated, noncompetitive market structure through brand proliferation, product differentiation, and trademark promotion, backed by intensive and steadily increasing levels of advertising and by control of supermarket shelf space. Three new companies were to have been carved out of Kellogg and one each out of General Foods and General Mills. However, the suit was thrown out in the fall of 1981 after Ronald Reagan's election as president.

In another court case, the Committee on Children's Television filed a $260 million class-action suit in California against General Foods; its ad agency, Benton & Bowles; and Safeway Stores, claiming that GF's presweetened cereal products and their supporting commercials caused "lasting poor nutrition habits and tooth decay in millions of children." (Safeway was included in the suit because the plaintiff held that these cereal products should be shelved in the store's candy department.) This suit, too, was thrown out.

Natural cereals began appearing on grocery shelves in the 1970s. In 1973 noted naturalist Euell Gibbons appeared in commercials for GF's Grape Nuts, praising its natural ingredients. But because the cereal was fortified with vitamins and minerals, the company and agency Benton & Bowles were careful not to label the cereal "natural." Then in 1975, the company introduced C.W. Post cereal. Formulated like the natural cereals, it was not truly

This 1952 billboard won top honors from the Art Directors Club for its light-hearted reference to the benefits of Jell-O for those trying to lose weight. *CALUMET and JELL-O are registered trademarks of Kraft Foods Holdings, Inc.*

natural because it, like Grape Nuts, was fortified with vitamins and iron.

While General Foods struggled with various aspects of its cereal business, another of the company's product areas—coffee—was thriving. As late as the mid-1970s, estimates gave GF a staggering 49.5 percent of the total U.S. coffee market. Of this, the Maxwell House line accounted for 24.5 percent; Sanka, 11.1 percent; Maxim, 5.3 percent; Freeze-dried Sanka, 3.1 percent; Yuban, 2 percent; and Max-Pax and Brim combined, 3.5 percent. During this period, coffees accounted for approximately 40 percent of the company's revenue.

GF's hegemony in the coffee realm was threatened, however, by Procter & Gamble. In the 1960s, P&G had purchased J.A. Folger Company of San Francisco, California, and Kansas City, Missouri, which sold its coffees primarily in the Midwest and West. Using its marketing muscle, P&G gradually expanded Folger's, introducing it into the populous eastern markets and precipitating a "coffee war" between the giant marketers.

By January 1973, Folger's was estimated to have about 20 percent of the $1 billion regular (non-instant) coffee market, to Maxwell House's 24 percent. Also in 1973, GF countered P&G's introduction of Folger's ground roast coffee in Philadelphia by reintroducing its own ground roast, Horizon, which was rolled out initially in Pennsylvania's Scranton/Wilkes-Barre market.

The two marketers also went head-to-head with TV spokeswomen. For ten years, Folger's had been running TV spots featuring "Mrs. Olson," an all-knowing, Scandinavian-accented busybody who counseled wives that a key to a happier marriage was serving Folger's to their husbands. In 1971 GF's Maxwell House introduced "Cora," a character similar to Mrs. Olson, played by veteran actress Margaret Hamilton, perhaps best-known for her role as the wicked witch in the film *The Wizard of*

Oz. The Maxwell House spots, from Ogilvy & Mather, were strikingly similar to those for Folger's, from Cunningham & Walsh.

In 1976 the Federal Trade Commission (FTC) issued a complaint against GF, charging it had attempted to monopolize the coffee market in the eastern United States. The FTC complaint alleged that GF had sold Maxwell House below cost or at "unreasonably low prices" and used extensive promotion and advertising in an attempt to eliminate competition. The FTC sought to ban price discriminations and sales below cost and to limit advertising spending. GF responded that it was competing with a larger rival (P&G) and would continue to do so. The charges were dismissed in April 1984, with the FTC commissioners saying they couldn't find any prospect of injury from the events described by its staff. The FTC commissioners also said that competition in the coffee market is "healthy and virtually invulnerable to the assaults of any one firm."

All through the 1970s, the "coffee war" continued to rage, as Folger's gained a foothold in the eastern markets and steadily ate into Maxwell House's market share. To underscore P&G's commitment to its brand, Folger's led all other company products in ad spending in 1979 at $33 million. And the spending paid off. At decade's end, Folger's had a 27.3 percent share in the regular coffee segment to Maxwell House's 22.3 percent. However, General Foods still held a hefty 39.5 percent share of the overall grocery coffee market, and the addition of GF's Sanka, Brim, and Yuban brands gave the company a 31.5 percent share of regular coffees. The company also held a 47.5 percent share of the instant coffee segment, with Maxwell House alone holding 23.4 percent.

Another segment where GF had been consistently strong was moist dog foods. In 1979, the company's Gaines line of products dominated moist sales with 60 percent of the market. In the dry dog food segment, however, GF held just 10.8 percent with Gravy Train, Cycle, and Gaines meal. The company ranked only sixth in the canned dog food sector.

Reverses and Acquisition

In early 1982 the company got out of the fast-food business, selling the Burger Chef chain to Hardees Food Systems for $44 million. GF had acquired Burger Chef in 1968 and the experience had not been pleasant, as the chain had consistently lost money. Shortly before the sale, Burger Chef ranked number 16 in the category, with slightly more than 2 percent of the market.

General Foods entered the 1980s as the third-largest national advertiser, but its ranking declined steadily and its ad expenditures remained generally flat in what would be its final years as a corporate entity. One reason for the lack of advertising growth was the reduction—sometimes as much as 50 percent a year—in ad support for the pet foods division, as rumors swirled in the early 1980s that GF would divest itself of this unit. That shoe dropped in 1984, when Gaines was sold to Anderson, Clayton & Company, a Houston, Texas-based food company, for an after-tax gain to GF of $59.8 million.

By 1984 another rumor was afoot: that General Foods would be taken over by Philip Morris. In that period of megamergers (R.J. Reynolds Industries had recently acquired Nabisco Brands), this would be the biggest yet. On 1 November 1985, Philip Morris acquired GF for $5.67 billion, the largest merger up to that time outside the oil industry. The combination brought together two operations that the previous year had total worldwide sales of $22.8 billion and a combined advertising budget of $1.02 billion.

In its final year of independent operations, General Foods was the 12th-ranked U.S. advertiser, with ad expenditures of $450 million, up from $397 million the previous year. Maxwell House coffee held an 18.9 percent share of the ground market and 22.5 percent of the instant business. Other GF market shares at the time of the company's acquisition included: Kool-Aid, 65 percent of the $800 million powdered beverage market; Tang, 8 percent in the orange/breakfast beverages category; and Grape Nuts, 3.3 percent, and Post Raisin Bran, 2.9 percent, respectively, in the ready-to-eat cereal category. The cereal figures were particularly disappointing. GF had struggled as the number-three player in the $4 billion cold cereal market, and at the time of the company's acquisition, only Grape-Nuts (number 9) and Post Raisin Bran (number 10) were among the top 17 brands.

After the Philip Morris takeover, the General Foods name lingered for a decade. First, a General Foods unit was an arm of Philip Morris. After Philip Morris acquired Kraft, Inc., in 1988, a Kraft General Foods subsidiary was created in 1989. This lasted until January 1995, when the unit was renamed simply Kraft Foods. General Foods had ceased to exist, first in fact and then in name.

ROBERT GOLDSBOROUGH

Postum, Post, Grape-Nuts, Toasties, Maxwell House, Jell-O, Sanka, Kool-Aid, Minute, Baker's, Calumet, Bird's, Good Seasons, Oscar Mayer, Maxim, and Yuban are registered trademarks of Kraft Foods Holdings, Inc.

Further Reading

Ferguson, James L., *General Foods Corporation: A Chronicle of Consumer Satisfaction,* New York: Newcomen Society of the United States, 1985

Fox, Stephen R., *The Mirror Makers: A History of American Advertising and Its Creators,* New York: Morrow, 1984

"FTC Rejects Coffee Anti-Trust Charges against General Foods," *Dow Jones News Service* (27 April 1984)

"General Foods Largest User of Radio Nets," *Advertising Age* (18 July 1938)

"GF Revamp Strategy: Growth through Efficiency," *Advertising Age* (3 June 1974)

International Directory of Company Histories, vol. 2, *Electrical and Electronics—Food Services and Retailers,* edited by Lisa Mirabile, London and Chicago: St. James Press, 1990

Watkins, Julian Lewis, *The 100 Greatest Advertisements: Who Wrote Them and What They Did,* New York: Moore, 1949; 2nd revised edition, New York: Dover, 1959

General Mills

Principal Agencies
Bozell Worldwide
Dancer, Fitzgerald, Sample
DDB Chicago
Saatchi & Saatchi Advertising
Campbell Mithun Esty
Casanova Pendrill Publicidad

Cadwallader C. Washburn formed the Minneapolis Milling Company in Minneapolis, Minnesota, in 1856 as a lessor of power rights to mill operators along the Mississippi River. He built the company's first proprietary flour mill—the largest such structure west of Buffalo, New York—in 1866. Although his mill cost a then-startling $100,000 and his early efforts were dubbed "Washburn's Folly," this marked the beginning of what would eventually become General Mills.

In 1874 Washburn built an even larger mill, called the "A" mill, which was the site of a devastating flour dust explosion four years later that also wiped out five nearby structures and half of the milling capacity of Minneapolis. Washburn constructed a new mill with state-of-the-art machinery—in an industry first, he replaced grinding stones with automatic steel rollers—and ended up producing a higher-quality flour.

Washburn began to sell midwestern spring-wheat flour across the nation. Skeptics said demand would never meet that for winter wheat, a crop that resulted in a whiter flour but could not be grown in the upper Midwest because of the cold weather. Washburn proved them wrong. Both in appearance and baking properties, flour made from his spring wheat rivaled and even surpassed that made from winter wheat.

In 1877 Washburn partnered with John Crosby to form a new company, which became the Washburn Crosby Company in 1879. In 1880 the two men brought their flour to the first Millers' International Exhibition, where they won the gold, silver, and bronze medals. The new Washburn Crosby Company capitalized on the awards by naming its product Gold Medal flour. Some years later, in 1893, the company was responsible for an industry first when it built a "testing room" for employees to prepare foods made with Gold Medal flour. The testing room allowed the company to assure quality under all types of commercial and residential baking conditions.

In 1921 the company introduced what would become one of its best-known icons, Betty Crocker. Two years later, the Gold Medal brand entered the packaged goods sector with Softasilk cake flour, followed by Wheaties in 1924. In 1928 Washburn Crosby led a merger of 27 regional mills around the country, resulting in the formation of General Mills; the new company immediately became the largest milling operation in the world and, despite the fact that its first years coincided with the depths of the Depression, it continued to expand through product introductions and memorable advertising campaigns. In fact, General Mills was one of the few companies to significantly expand its advertising expenditures during the early 1930s.

Among the products General Mills introduced in the next decades were Bisquick baking mix, launched in 1931; Corn Kix, the company's first puffed ready-to-eat cereal, 1937; Cheerioats, the first puffed oat cereal, 1941 (renamed Cheerios in 1945); and the first Betty Crocker–branded cake mix, GingerCake, 1947, which was followed by PartyCake and Devil's Food Cake mixes in 1949. (The first Betty Crocker product was a soup mix, introduced in 1941.)

During and after World War II, General Mills capitalized on its expertise in designing machinery for food processing and translated it to the war effort by manufacturing torpedo indicators for the Navy and, in the 1950s, developing the black box used in airplanes. (The first Betty Crocker appliance, an iron, was introduced in 1946.) After the war, the company went back to expanding its product line. During the 1950s and 1960s—a period of growth in the cereal industry, with the number of brands doubling to about 100—General Mills introduced several new cereals, including its first presweetened variety, Jets (1953), the

Every day--more women buy this "Kitchen-tested" flour
than any other brand in the world

And a simple test in your store will prove to you that Gold Medal Flour is a real business builder.

THE test merely means placing a sack of Gold Medal "Kitchen-tested" Flour where your customers can see it.

Grocers all over the country have told us that this preference for Gold Medal Flour is so strong that by consistent display of this flour they have not only increased their flour business but have greatly reduced the number of brands carried. In fact, many stores report that all customers are being satisfied with a single brand —Gold Medal.

Gold Medal "Kitchen-tested" Flour literally sells itself. Women prefer it —they will go far out of their way for it—because they feel certain that it assures successful baking. Last year

Eventually
Why Not Now?

over 300,000 women took the time to write us about their experiences with this flour.

Back of this interest, their preference for Gold Medal "Kitchen-tested" Flour, are the largest advertising campaigns ever put back of a brand of flour. Right now, the circulation of Gold Medal advertising equals half the total families in the country, and our radio broadcasting covers the entire nation.

Try the Gold Medal Plan of letting your customers know you carry this "Kitchen-tested" Flour. Your flour sales will show an immediate increase, and so will the sales of dozens of other items. Flour customers are better-than-average grocery buyers—and the average family spends over $600 a year on groceries. Test the Gold Medal Plan for a week and prove that it is one of the easiest and surest methods of going after this more profitable class of trade.

GOLD MEDAL FLOUR
~Kitchen-tested

WASHBURN CROSBY COMPANY, Dept. 346. General Offices: Minneapolis, Minn.

Mills at: Minneapolis   Buffalo   Chicago   Kansas City   Louisville   Great Falls   Kalispell   Ogden

The phrases "Kitchen-tested" and "Eventually . . . Why not now?" were both used in this 1928 Gold Medal Flour advertisement. The "Eventually" campaign was launched in 1907 and ran for more than two decades, while the "kitchen-tested" claim was displayed on Gold Medal packaging into the 1990s.
Courtesy of the General Mills Archives.

multicolored Trix (1954), Cocoa Puffs (1958), and nutritional offering Total (1961). In 1959 General Mills launched instant mashed potatoes, which later were marketed under the name Potato Buds. The 1950s also marked a period of international expansion.

The 1960s represented a period of diversification for General Mills, which moved into all sorts of industries having nothing to do with food. It purchased several toy companies—including Kenner in 1967, Parker Brothers in 1968, and Rainbow Crafts, which made Play-Doh, in 1965—to become the world's largest toymaker. It also bought apparel and accessory marketers, including Monet Jewelry, Eddie Bauer, Inc., Izod Lacoste, Ship 'n Shore, Talbots, and Foot-Joy Shoes. At the same time, the company closed half of its flour mills and sold off unprofitable lines such as electronics. By 1978 toys accounted for $483.3 million in sales, or one-third of total revenue.

Also in the 1960s, the company moved into snack foods, including Bugles, introduced in 1966. The launch of Hamburger Helper in 1970 represented the beginning of a new packaged foods category, consisting of prepared food mixes to which the customer added meat. General Mills took over the marketing of Yoplait yogurt from French dairy cooperative Sodima in 1977 and introduced it to the United States; it added the Colombo brand to its yogurt business in 1993 after the purchase of the brand from Bongrain S.A. The company's microwave popcorn brand, Pop Secret, was launched in 1985.

From 1950 to 1985, General Mills had acquired 86 companies in nonfood industries. But, of those purchased before 1975, almost three-quarters had been spun off within five years. During the 1980s, General Mills sold most of its nonfood businesses, cumulatively representing 25 percent of sales. In 1995 the company spun off its Olive Garden and Red Lobster restaurant chains, developed in 1982 and purchased in 1970, respectively, into Darden Corporation, ending the company's divestiture activity and allowing it to focus on its core business of consumer foods.

Meanwhile, General Mills boosted its international operations, forming Cereal Partners Worldwide as a European joint venture with Nestlé in 1989 and establishing Snack Ventures Europe, a joint venture with PepsiCo, in 1993.

Advertising Pioneer

From its early days as the Washburn Crosby Company, the marketer developed a reputation for its advertising and merchandising techniques. When it introduced spring wheat to the southern United States in the 1880s, it hired door-to-door canvassers, distributed pamphlets, and purchased advertisements in St. Louis, Missouri, newspapers. In 1884 Washburn Crosby became one of the first millers to advertise to the trade, running an ad in the publication *Northwestern Miller*. Traditionally, most companies in the industry had sent out calendars and similar premiums rather than reaching their customers through advertising.

In 1893 Washburn Crosby spent $10,000 on advertising, including its first consumer ad, a one-inch item in the *Ladies' Home Journal*. The latter seemed like overspending in the eyes of the company's competitors and to some within the company, who believed that trade advertising was more effective than consumer advertising in this category. The *Ladies' Home Journal* insertion—handled in-house—touted the fact that two bakers at the Chicago World's Fair that year used only Gold Medal flour and included an offer of a free souvenir booklet.

The next year, the company spent a then-huge $220,000 on advertising. In the next decades, media used included billboards with the slogan "Eventually—why not now?" This phrase debuted in 1907 after a company executive received a long, text-heavy ad about the benefits of Gold Medal flour from one of his copywriters. Each paragraph began with the word "Eventually. . . . " The executive edited the copy until all that was left was one word, "Eventually," to which he added the second clause.

The slogan became a widely used catchphrase throughout the nation. It backfired, however, when the company's hometown competitor, Pillsbury—as of 2001 a part of the General Mills family—latched onto it. Pillsbury had a mill directly across the Mississippi River from the Washburn Crosby mill, where there was a large "Eventually—why not now?" sign. Pillsbury put up its own billboard across the river with the answer: "Because Pillsbury's best." (Pillsbury continues to use the slogan "Pillsbury's best" on its flour.)

Singing the Praises of Wheaties

In the early 1920s, per-capita flour consumption was declining. Washburn Crosby countered this trend with a newspaper and billboard campaign developed in-house in 1923, which told consumers to "Eat more wheat" and explained the health benefits of the grain. The company's long association with the Blackett-Sample-Hummert (B-S-H) ad agency also began at this time. B-S-H also turned the focus of the Gold Medal advertising toward a more results-oriented approach. It added the words "Kitchen-tested" or the initials GMKT (Gold Medal kitchen-tested) to its flour bags and stressed in advertising how well baked-goods turned out when created with Gold Medal flour. That remained the philosophy of the newly merged General Mills after 1928; its executives believed that advertising and merchandising that showed consumers specifically what the products could do for them were key to the company's success.

The growth of the Wheaties brand after the formation of General Mills was a testament to the power of advertising. Washburn Crosby had purchased a failing Minneapolis radio station in 1924 and renamed it WCCO, hoping to use it to get the company's advertising messages out to a wide audience. In 1926 it created a radio campaign for Wheaties—thought to represent the first advertising jingle—featuring a male singing group, the Wheaties Quartet. On Christmas Eve, the quartet's half-hour show premiered, during which they sang ballads and other tunes, as well as the Wheaties jingle: "Have you tried Wheaties? / They're whole wheat with all of the bran. / Won't you try Wheaties? / For wheat is the best food of man." The jingle was created by Earl Gammon, station manager at WCCO.

By 1929 Wheaties still had not gained strong national distribution, sales were falling across the country, and General Mills considered discontinuing the brand. But in the Minneapolis-St. Paul area, where the Wheaties Quartet was singing the praises of Wheaties, sales were rising. The company decided to expand the campaign across the country and the quartet, now called the Gold Medal Fast Freight, went national on the CBS Radio network. Sales of Wheaties began to rise, and the quartet's program remained on the air until 1932.

In 1930 General Mills decided to promote the Wheaties brand directly to children, sponsoring a radio program featuring Skippy, an adventurous boy who got into a lot of trouble. Skippy was based on a newspaper comic strip by Percy Crosby. This approach differed from previous Wheaties advertising, which targeted adults in publications such as the *Saturday Evening Post* via slogans such as "Gay as a French confection" and "Eat whole wheat this alluring way."

As part of its sponsorship, General Mills started one of the first children's radio clubs, the Skippy Secret Service Society. Listeners joined by sending in box tops, spurring 20 percent sales growth in

Wheaties, from 1.25 million cases in 1931 to 1932 to 1.5 million in 1932 to 1933. The brand's tie-in with the show was supported by print ads that targeted mothers with slogans such as "No more arguments at breakfast."

Eventually, Skippy was dropped and replaced with the General Mills- and B-S-H-produced *Jack Armstrong, All-American Boy,* a radio show that ran for 18 years from 1933 to 1951. In one of the first episodes, the script mentioned a "shooting plane," a replica of which was offered at the end of the program for a box top and ten cents. So many people sent in orders that it took almost six months for store shelves to be fully stocked with Wheaties again. Similarly, more than 1.2 million listeners sent in box tops for a Jack Armstrong "Hike-O-Meter."

B-S-H and its successor agency in 1943, Dancer, Fitzgerald, Sample, would make General Mills one of the most prolific radio advertisers of the 1930s and 1940s. For the most part, the company's radio sponsorships targeted housewives and young children. However, in 1938 B-S-H, which had managed the radio effort for the Republican presidential bid of Alfred M. Landon in 1936, decided that General Mills should sponsor a prestigious news program and chose H.V. Kaltenborn on CBS. Kaltenborn achieved great distinction with his reporting of the Munich crisis in October 1938 and felt he was entitled to offer an editorial viewpoint in his news analyses. The agency and General Mills promised him complete freedom in his comments. But the civil war in Spain, in which communist-supported loyalists fought Nazi-sponsored fascists, was a controversy the company did not want to be associated with. When a General Mills executive intervened and told Kaltenborn to stop his pro-loyalist commentaries, the newsman refused, causing B-S-H to cancel the General Mills contract after 13 weeks.

General Mills decided to go after the men's market by tying in with local baseball games. It first sponsored broadcasts of the Minneapolis Millers, a minor league team, and soon became involved with 95 teams on 67 radio stations. As part of its Millers sponsorship, it had the right to paint an advertisement on the grandstand at the Millers' field, Nicollet Park, and Knox Reeves, then with Blackett-Sample-Hummert, coined the slogan "Breakfast of champions." Reeves launched his own agency in Minneapolis in 1935, and Knox Reeves Advertising, Inc., would share the General Mills business with B-S-H and other agencies for years to come until its acquisition in 1975 by Bozell & Jacobs (B&J). (Among the assets that B&J acquired in the takeover was Reeves president David Bell, who would later become chief executive officer of True North Communications, the B&J holding company after its merger with Foote, Cone & Belding.) Though the *Jack Armstrong* series was launched by B-S-H, Knox Reeves took over the program and the Wheaties brand by the late 1930s, handling much of the sports-related advertising that supported the "Breakfast of champions" theme. (The company also used the Westco Advertising Agency, of San Francisco, California, for special Pacific Coast regional radio.) General Mills went on to hire athletes such as Babe Ruth and Johnny Weissmuller to appear in advertisements. During the 1939 Major League Baseball All-Star Game, 46 of the 51 All-Stars were Wheaties endorsers.

Sales grew quickly, and by 1941 the brand accounted for 12 percent of the cereal market. Wheaties got some unanticipated publicity when two nonendorsing athletes—one of whom was baseball great Lou Gehrig—said on the air, during radio broadcasts sponsored by Wheaties competitors, that they started their day with a bowl of Wheaties.

In the late 1940s, the cost of baseball sponsorship became prohibitive, so General Mills decided to focus its efforts for Wheaties on TV commercials featuring athlete testimonials. But the spots got lost among the growing commercial clutter, and sales dropped. General Mills moved away from sports altogether and began to target children, associating the brand, as well as several other brands, with the Walt Disney Company. (It also offered many children's promotional premiums.) This campaign proved successful with elementary school children, but the repositioning caused the loss of the male customers Wheaties had long relied on. Overall, sales dropped 10 percent in one year. In 1956 General Mills tried to rectify the situation by returning the brand to its "Breakfast of champions" theme.

In 1958 Wheaties hired Bob Richards, a double gold medalist in Olympic pole vaulting, to endorse the cereal and become its full-time spokesman. Richards went to sales meetings and conventions, launched a fitness campaign for children, wrote self-help books with other athletes, and offered exercise tips on the backs of boxes until his retirement in 1970.

Later in the 1970s, Wheaties aired a campaign consisting of a humorous take-off of its famous slogan, showing athletes such as Johnny Bench stumbling around on the playing field until a voice-over noted, "Hey, John, you didn't have your Wheaties. . . ." In 1980 the brand switched agencies to DDB Needham, which came up with the "Eaties for Wheaties" campaign, featuring copy such as, "Before he whistles pass incompleties, he gets the eaties for his Wheaties." That effort was replaced in 1984 with one starring gymnast Mary Lou Retton that featured the slogan, "Now go tell your mama what the big boys eat!" In the late 1980s, the brand started a long-running campaign, "Better eat your Wheaties," starring sports celebrities such as Michael Jordan.

Birth of Betty Crocker

As Wheaties was rising in fame, General Mills also had been strengthening its Gold Medal brand through advertising and promotions. In the 1920s Washburn Crosby representatives went out into the community, convincing church and civic groups to sell Gold Medal flour at their events in return for a commission and giving demonstrations through its regional Washburn Crosby Cooking School. In 1921 the company ran a magazine ad that contained a puzzle; if consumers finished the puzzle correctly and sent it in, they would receive a pincushion shaped like a sack of Gold Medal flour. The contest generated 30,000 responses, many of which included questions from customers on topics such as how to make a cherry pie or an apple dumpling. Washburn Crosby's policy was to answer every letter personally, but it was not set up to respond to this many or to fulfill the unexpectedly high number of premium requests. The company quickly gathered

The Betty Crocker character was created in 1921 to answer consumers' cooking questions. Many cookbooks have since been published under the Betty Crocker name, including this 1956 Bisquick cookbook.
Courtesy of the General Mills Archives.

recipes from its employees so it could respond to the questions. It decided to sign them with a friendly-sounding woman's name and came up with the fictional Betty Crocker, whose signature was chosen from submissions by female employees.

Betty Crocker's writing style and values reflected those of the company, and she served as a valuable public persona. Actresses representing Betty Crocker ran regional cooking schools and then, starting in 1924, regional radio programs. Soon, *The Betty Crocker Cooking School of the Air,* the country's first radio cooking show, was broadcast nationally over NBC and later CBS, by way of Washburn Crosby's WCCO studios. Listeners enrolled in the school by sending for recipe cards and completed the course by mailing in progress reports. They received their diplomas in ceremonies broadcast over the radio.

In 1925 the company included its first Betty Crocker recipes in sacks of Gold Medal flour, along with coupons for an oak recipe box. In 1931 coupons included in flour sacks were redeemable for free Oneida silverware in exclusive Betty Crocker patterns such as Friendship and Medality. While Betty's name was used throughout the 1930s and 1940s to market products under the Gold Medal brand, Betty Crocker was not used as a brand name until 1941, when it appeared on soup mix.

The first official portrait of Betty Crocker was painted by New York artist Neysa McMein in 1936 and appeared in print ads for Gold Medal flour soon after. The character first appeared on packaging in 1937, when her portrait was featured on Softasilk cake flour. Betty Crocker has since gone through eight incarnations, including one in 1996, in honor of her 75th birthday; that image was composed of photos of 75 women of different ethnicities, morphed by computer into a single portrait.

Although many recipe pamphlets and booklets had been published earlier, the first hardcover Betty Crocker cookbook, *Betty Crocker's Picture Cookbook,* was published in 1950, with almost 1 million copies printed; a 50th anniversary edition was published in 2000. The company has released many Betty Crocker cookbooks since 1950, often to support specific initiatives. For example, when popular opinion turned against bread because it was perceived as a fattening food, General Mills released a Betty Crocker cookbook stressing the nutritional value of bread and including many recipes.

B-S-H and its successor agency, Dancer, Fitzgerald, Sample, continued to handle the Betty Crocker brand until General Mills moved it to Batten Barton Durstine & Osborn in 1955, then to Needham, Louis & Brorby in 1962, where it remained through the 1970s. Betty moved from radio to television in the 1950s, making guest appearances where she taught celebrities such as George Burns and Gracie Allen to cook. She also oversaw a competition, *The Betty Crocker Search for the All-American Home maker of Tomorrow,* which ran from 1955 to 1977, and had several television programs, including *Betty Crocker Star Matinee* and *Bride and Groom,* where Betty interviewed newlyweds back from their honeymoon and taught the brides how to prepare foods for their husbands.

The Betty Crocker umbrella brand has come to cover a plethora of food products, as well as licensed goods such as household electronics and bakeware. One of the products that has come under Betty Crocker's auspices is Bisquick, introduced in 1931. The baking mix initially used the slogan "Makes anybody a perfect biscuit maker." Customers quickly discovered how versatile the product was, however, leading General Mills to reposition the brand to emphasize this characteristic with slogans such as "Bisquick, bride's best bet," "Stop baking risk, use Bisquick," and "A world of baking in a box."

Much of Bisquick's marketing over the years was in response to grassroots movements started by its customers. In the 1960s, it was Bisquick users who came up with one of the product's best-known uses, Impossible Pie, in which all the ingredients are mixed together and poured into a pie tin; while baking, the pie forms its own crust. The first such recipe, Impossible Coconut Pie, spread by word of mouth until eventually it appeared on Bisquick packaging; customers came up with other versions that have since been featured on the yellow box. From 1981 to 1985, Bisquick operated a Recipe Club to allow customers to trade the recipes they had invented using Bisquick.

Breakfast Brands

Another of General Mills' flagship brands was launched in 1941 with the introduction of Cheerioats. In its early years, agency Blackett used the slogan "Makes delicious munching," thought to represent the first time a cereal had been positioned as a snack food. (The company still uses this positioning, touting the product as a baby's first solid snack food.) In 1943 General Mills supplied Cheerioats to the military in ten-ounce "Yank packs," using the slogan "He's feeling his Cheerioats." Other advertising vehicles during the early 1940s including comic books and adult-targeted publications such as the *Saturday Evening Post* and *Look.* A spokescharacter, Cheeri O'Leary, the Cheerioats Girl, offered up celebrity tidbits in support of the brand.

During World War II advertisements for Cheerioats featured Cheeri O'Leary the Cheerioats Girl and the "He's feeling his Cheerioats!" slogan. The cereal's name was changed to "Cheerios" two years after this ad ran. *Courtesy of the General Mills Archives.*

In 1945 General Mills' competitor Quaker Oats objected to the former's use of the word *oats* in its name, claiming it held exclusive commercial rights to that term for its own oatmeal. As a result, General Mills changed Cheerioats' name to Cheerios.

Starting in 1947, Cheerios tied in with *The Lone Ranger* radio show, which Kix had been sponsoring since 1941. The popular program created demand for Lone Ranger premiums and for the Cheerios box tops needed to order them. Sometimes the premiums were printed on the box; 11 million children pestered their parents to buy Cheerios boxes with Lone Ranger masks and 2 million sent for a paper that served as the base of a Lone Ranger frontier town consisting of 79 buildings cut from different Cheerios boxes. Similar demand followed for Lone Ranger pedometers, badges, signed photos, and flashlight pistols. General Mills also promoted other brands on the show; a Kix cereal offer generated 6 million responses, one of the most successful children's tie-ins ever at that time. When *The Lone Ranger* moved to TV, so did General Mills' sponsorship.

General Mills also used many other television programs to support its cereals throughout the 1950s. It sponsored *Captain Midnight* on behalf of Kix starting in 1954, and created a fictional character, Major Jet, to support Sugar Jets. Major Jet, who appeared in both live-action and animated form, was a test pilot. His popularity was such that he inspired more than 6 million children to buy Major Jet magic goggles at toy stores, not to mention other premiums and licensed products.

In 1958 a virtually unknown animator, Jay Ward, was pitching a show called *Rocky and His Friends,* just as General Mills was looking for an entertainment vehicle to raise the profile of Cheerios. General Mills bought all the rights to Ward's characters Rocky and Bullwinkle, and the series debuted in 1959 on ABC, later moving to NBC. The program's opening sequence featured puppets of the characters, which worked in plugs for cereals including Cocoa Puffs, Trix, and Wheat Hearts, as well as Cheerios. By 1967 General Mills owned 350 half hours of *Rocky and His Friends* and a later incarnation, *The Bullwinkle Show,* which it syndicated across the country, and had become the second-biggest cereal marketer in the United States, surpassing General Foods' Post brands. Much of its increase in sales and share was credited to *Rocky and His Friends.*

While General Mills borrowed equity from existing entertainers and characters—over the years, Cheerios alone employed William Bendix, Claudette Colbert, Veronica Lake, Fred MacMurray, the Harlem Globetrotters, Bo Jackson, the Muppets, Care Bears, Mr. Ed, Dick Tracy, the characters from *Star Trek: The Next Generation,* and Underdog, among many others—the company also created its own advertising characters, including the Cheerios Kid.

General Mills moved all its cereal brands except Wheaties to the Dancer, Fitzgerald, Sample agency in 1959, hoping to improve its competitive situation; at the time it was third in the cereal market after the Kellogg Company and General Foods Corporation's Post brands. Dancer developed the "Big G" logotype, still used on General Mills packaging in the 21st century, as a means of branding all the cereals with a cohesive image, promoting the effort with the slogan, "The Big G Stands for Goodness." The agency also created the Cheerios Kid and his friend, Sue, with their slogan "Big G, Little O, Go with Cheerios." The characters were used in advertising for two decades. Another mascot, in the late 1970s, was Cheeriodle, a yodeling stick figure.

The Trix Rabbit first appeared, in puppet form, on *Rocky and His Friends, Captain Kangaroo,* and other General Mills–sponsored programs. The puppet's image first appeared on a box of Trix in 1960, the same year the character debuted in animation. His original sales pitch was, "I'm a rabbit and rabbits are supposed to like carrots. But I hate carrots. I like Trix." Soon afterward, Dancer, Fitzgerald, Sample came up with the slogan, "Silly rabbit, Trix are for kids."

In 1963 Sonny the Cuckoo Bird ("Cuckoo for Cocoa Puffs") first went on the air, helping raise sales for that brand by more than $4 million in six months. He was followed by Lucky the Leprechaun, with his phrase, "'Tis lucky to catch a leprechaun / But of course, nobody can / Catch me and you catch me Lucky Charms." Meanwhile, Cheerios marked an advertising first during the 1960s when Dancer, Fitzgerald, Sample developed an ad for the brand set to the Simon & Garfunkel tune "Feelin' Groovy," showing a white youngster and a black youngster playing basketball together. The spot is thought to represent the debut of an African-American in a primary role in a commercial.

Not all General Mills' advertising has been widely praised. Ads for Total cereal, for example, have been criticized for their nutritional claims since the product's 1961 introduction. In positioning itself as a low-calorie, high-vitamin and -mineral alternative, Total has long used comparative advertising, matching up the nutritional content of one bowl of Total to multiple bowls of competing brands. Some of these comparisons have led competitors and consumer groups to accuse the brand of false and misleading advertising. In response to a 1975 challenge from Quaker on behalf of its 100% Natural cereal, and to ABC-TV's reluctance to air the ad in question, Total remade one commercial to limit its claims.

In 1977 General Mills entered the yogurt market by purchasing the U.S. rights to Yoplait, which had been launched in France by Sodima in 1964. The advertising and promotional campaign—which included sponsorship of bike races and hot-air balloons—emphasized the product's French heritage. Television ads featured celebrities such as Loretta Swit and Jack Klugman tasting the product and rendering the verdict, *"Yoplait est fantastique!"* Because few Americans had ever tried yogurt—by 1985, only 30 percent had tasted it—sampling was a big part of the campaign. Several line extensions were introduced in the 1980s, but sales slumped as General Mills cut back on consumer TV advertising, focusing instead on trade promotions and associated discounting. The marketer turned back to television in 1991, emphasizing the product's appeal to everyday women with the slogan, "Yoplait. Do it for you." Yoplait's agency was DDB Chicago.

In the 1980s General Mills started appealing to Hispanic and African-African consumers with targeted marketing efforts, hiring advertising and promotional agencies with expertise in this market. One Honey Nut Cheerios commercial targeting African-Americans in the Chicago, Illinois, area in the 1990s increased sales for the brand more than 50 percent among that demographic group.

In the 1990s "cereal wars" among the major manufacturers were reflected in an abundance of couponing efforts, leading to higher everyday prices. Economically, this was not a sound strategy; for every 50 cents saved by the consumer, the cost to the manufacturer was estimated at 75 cents. In 1994 General Mills was the first cereal company to cut back couponing efforts, thus saving costs of coupon distribution, handling, and redemption. It also cut prices on some of its cereals by 30 to 70 cents per box in the hope of gaining market share by increasing value.

As of the early 21st century, General Mills and Kellogg were virtually tied in share of the U.S. cereal market, with both maintaining just more than a 31 percent share. General Mills' growth in this area is due to its consistent rollout of new (and unique) cereal brands and its higher average price per box. Meanwhile, Gold Medal flour was the number-one flour brand, while the company's yogurt business (including Yoplait, Go-Gurt, and Colombo) was number two after Dannon. General Mills divisions included Betty Crocker Products, Big G, General Mills Consumer Foods Division, and Yoplait USA.

As of 2000—when company sales surpassed $7.5 billion— General Mills spent $555.6 million on advertising, with 36 percent of that devoted to spot television, 30 percent to network television, 6 percent to cable television, 3 percent to consumer magazines, and the remainder to daily newspapers, network radio, newspaper-distributed magazines, outdoor advertising, spot radio, and other channels.

General Mills' life-long history of acquisitions continued during the late 1990s and early 2000s. A few examples from this period include Chex snacks and cereals from Ralcorp Holdings (1997); Lloyd's Barbeque, a leading producer of refrigerated convenience foods including ready-to-warm barbecue meals (1999), and Small Planet Foods, an organic marketer whose brands include Muir Glen and Cascadian Farms (2000).

Most notably, in July 2000 General Mills announced plans to acquire Pillsbury, its longtime competitor in milling and consumer foods, from Diageo. The deal, which was finalized in late 2001 after long scrutiny by the U.S. government over potential monopoly issues, brought consumer brands such as Pillsbury, Old El Paso, Häagen-Dazs, Progresso, Totino's, and Green Giant into the General Mills fold and nearly doubled its sales to more than $13 billion. General Mills promises to be even more of a force in advertising in the coming years, as two of the leading food company advertisers come together.

KAREN RAUGUST

See also color plate in this volume

Further Reading

Bruce, Scott, and Bill Crawford, *Cerealizing America: The Unsweetened Story of American Breakfast Cereal,* Boston: Faber and Faber, 1995

Campbell, Hannah, *Why Did They Name It . . . ?* New York: Fleet, 1964

Enrico, Dottie, "Top 10 Advertising Icons," *Advertising Age* (29 March 1999)

Gray, James, *Business without Boundary: The Story of General Mills,* Minneapolis: University of Minnesota Press, 1954

Jorgensen, Janice, editor, *Encyclopedia of Consumer Brands,* 3 vols., Detroit, Michigan, and London: St. James Press, 1994; see especially vols. 1 and 2

Kennedy, Gerald S., *Minutes and Moments in the Life of General Mills,* Minneapolis, Minnesota: Kennedy, 1971

Marks-Kerst, "Betty Crocker: Marketing the Modern Woman," *Hennepin History* 58, no. 2 (Spring 1999)

Merrill, Ann, "General Mills Buys Pillsbury for $10 Billion," *Star Tribune* (Minneapolis) (17 July 2000)

Pederson, Jay P., editor, *International Directory of Company Histories,* vol. 38, Detroit, Michigan: St. James Press, 2001

Rawlings, Edwin W., and Edwin B. Stone, *Born to Fly: The Story of General Edwin Rawlings,* Minneapolis, Minnesota: Great Way, 1987

Thompson, Stephanie, "Food Marketers' Power Struggle Feeds Mergers," *Advertising Age* (17 July 2000)

General Motors Corporation

Principal Agencies

MacManus, John & Adams (later D'Arcy Masius Benton & Bowles)
Campbell-Ewald Company, Inc.
Barton, Durstine & Osborn (later Batten Barton Durstine & Osborn)
J. Walter Thompson Company
D.P. Brother & Company (later Leo Burnett USA)
Arthur Kudner, Inc.

McCann-Erickson, Inc. (later McCann-Erickson Worldwide)
Hal Riney & Partners (later Publicis & Hal Riney)

General Motors Corporation (GM), the leading advertiser in the United States at the close of the 20th century, was not only one of the country's top advertisers throughout the century but also one of the few with long-standing agency relationships, some going back to the Detroit, Michigan-based company's earliest days.

The General Motors Company was created on 16 September 1908 by William C. Durant, a former buggy maker and owner of the Buick Motor Company in Flint, Michigan, who realized that an auto manufacturer with only one car line stood little chance of long-term survival. (Of the 1,500 automobile manufacturers established by 1925, only 44 remained in business in 1927; that number was reduced to 15 by the start of the Great Depression in 1929.) Within 18 months of the company's founding, Durant had brought together about 25 carmakers and suppliers under the GM umbrella. In addition to Buick, the new company included Olds Motor Vehicle Company, maker of Oldsmobile; Oakland Motor Car Company, renamed the Pontiac Motor Company, after its popular brand, in 1932; Cadillac Motor Car Company; and Rapid Motor Vehicle Company, a truck manufacturer that helped form the GMC Truck division.

By 1910 Durant had overextended the company, and in September of that year, he was forced out. He then talked to racecar driver Louis Chevrolet about designing a new car, and on 3 November 1911 opened the Chevrolet Motor Company. The automaker adopted its famous bow-tie logo in 1914; company legend claims it was inspired by a piece of wallpaper that Durant had torn from a Paris, France, hotel room in 1908 and carried around in his wallet until he found a use for it. In 1916, with Chevrolet holding 54.5 percent of GM's outstanding shares, Durant returned to GM and became president. The company under Durant and Chairman Pierre S. du Pont was incorporated that year, becoming the General Motors Corporation. In 1918 GM bought Chevrolet's operating assets and another company owned by Durant, United Motors Corporation. United Motors had been formed through the acquisition of five parts-and-accessories manufacturers, including Dayton Engineering Laboratories Company (later Delco), led by Charles F. Kettering, and Hyatt Roller Bearing Company, under Alfred P. Sloan, who became president of United Motors.

"The Penalty of Leadership"

Early advertising for GM cars, like that of its competitors, emphasized mechanical information and prices. The earliest Oldsmobile ads had headlines such as "The passing of the horse" and "Boarding a horse costs $180, gasoline only $35." Cadillac in 1908 introduced what would become its longtime tag line, "Standard of the world"; Buick in 1911 launched "When better automobiles are built, Buick will build them."

One ad that appeared at the time was unlike other contemporary auto advertising, and it came to be considered among the best car ads ever created. It ran in the *Saturday Evening Post* on 2 January 1915 under the headline, "The penalty of leadership." Theodore F. MacManus of the ad agency MacManus, John & Adams, Inc., wrote the ad as a response to rivals' attacks on the new V-8 engine from Cadillac, which, according to advertising historian Stephen Fox in *The Mirror Makers,* had exhibited some problems. The ad, ranked number 49 on *Advertising Age*'s list of the 100 best ad campaigns of the 20th century, read, in part:

In every field of human endeavor, he that is first must perpetually live in the white light of publicity. Whether the leadership be vested in a man or in a manufactured product, emulation and envy are ever at work. . . . When a man's work becomes a standard for the whole world, it also becomes a target for the shafts of the envious few. . . . That which is good or great makes itself known, no matter how loud the clamor of denial. That which deserves to live—lives.

The MacManus agency was the forerunner to D'Arcy Masius Benton & Bowles, which in 2001 still handled the Cadillac account as well as that of Pontiac, its sibling line. (In addition to writing enduring copy, MacManus set an example for a young editor working on Cadillac's house organ—Leo Burnett.) The ad's only tie to the automaker was the Cadillac name at the bottom of the page.

After World War I, GM geared up its mass-production capabilities and introduced a new financing plan designed to boost sales of its vehicles. At a time when consumers found it almost impossible to obtain bank financing to purchase an automobile, GM formed the General Motors Acceptance Corporation to allow people to pay for its new automobiles in installments. With the help of the plan, the company sold almost 2 million vehicles in 1920.

The company was expanding in other areas as well. It followed the lead of Durant, who in 1916 had invested in a company called Guardian Frigerator, which was developing an electric icebox; in 1919 GM bought all outstanding shares of the company, by then called the Frigidaire Corporation. It also acquired a 60 percent interest in the Fisher Body Company (completing the buy in 1926) and in 1920 introduced its new export division.

GM also was undergoing changes in management. Despite rapid growth, the automaker was experiencing financial problems, which were worsened by a slump in the U.S. economy. As a result, Durant resigned in November 1920 and du Pont added the title of president. (During this period, E.I. du Pont de Nemours & Company bought more than a quarter of GM's stock; the company, controlled by the du Pont family, remained GM's largest shareholder until 1961, when it was forced to divest its holdings after the U.S. Supreme Court ruled that its ownership of 23 percent of GM's stock violated the Clayton Antitrust Act.) In 1923 Sloan was named president, a post he held until 1937, when he took over as chairman until his retirement in 1956. Among his early moves, Sloan set GM's long-term strategy by clearly defining each car company's role, giving each company distinctive price and style directives that were designed to stop internecine competition—"A car for every purse and purpose," as he said in GM's 1924 annual report.

"Body by Fisher"

In 1922 GM hired Barton, Durstine & Osborn, forerunner to Batten Barton Durstine & Osborn, Inc. (BBDO), to create a public-

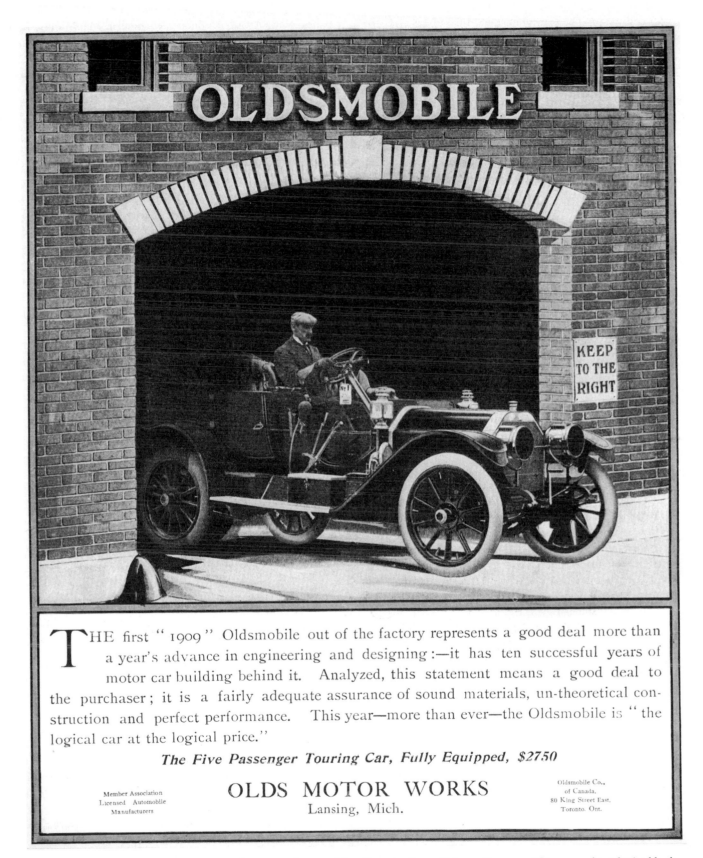

THE first "1909" Oldsmobile out of the factory represents a good deal more than a year's advance in engineering and designing:—it has ten successful years of motor car building behind it. Analyzed, this statement means a good deal to the purchaser; it is a fairly adequate assurance of sound materials, un-theoretical construction and perfect performance. This year—more than ever—the Oldsmobile is "the logical car at the logical price."

The Five Passenger Touring Car, Fully Equipped, $2750

Member Association
Licensed Automobile
Manufacturers

OLDS MOTOR WORKS
Lansing, Mich.

Oldsmobile Co.,
of Canada.
80 King Street East,
Toronto. Ont.

Olds Motor Works was one of the first manufacturers to be consolidated into the General Motors Company. This 1909 ad emphasized both the technical know-how and the experience of the Olds factory.
© *General Motors Corp. Used with permission of GM Media Archives.*

awareness campaign. The Campbell-Ewald Company, Inc., of Detroit, Michigan, which started its relationship with GM in 1916, handled other advertising. By the mid-1920s the automaker's ads, once devoted to mechanical details, had been revamped and now emphasized styling and performance. The new advertising appealed to the eye, and the copy was quick and succinct. Breakthroughs in the use of color and design in both advertising and automobile manufacturing occurred at an accelerated pace between 1924 and 1928. GM, in cooperation with DuPont, developed Duco synthetic lacquers and began introducing color choices for its autos, with impressive results. The company also employed Fisher Body, and its print ads boasted, "Equipped with body by Fisher."

In 1927 the company became the first automaker to create its own styling department, the General Motors Art and Colour Section, headed by Harley Earl. The first car that unit handled was Cadillac's LaSalle, which was designed as a bridge between GM's Buick and Cadillac marques. The smaller, stylish LaSalle was advertised as a "companion car to Cadillac."

Throughout the 1920s, GM also expanded outside the United States and Canada, where in 1919 it had established General Motors of Canada, Ltd. Its global ventures through that decade included the purchase of Vauxhall Motors, Ltd., in Britain, in 1924; establishing operations in Australia, New Zealand, and Japan in 1926; and buying Germany's Adam Opel AG in 1929. In 1927 the company entered into an agreement with the J. Walter Thompson Company (JWT), promising the advertising agency its account anywhere outside the United States where JWT established an office after GM established a production operation. By 1930 the agency had offices on six continents.

At the end of the 1920s, GM began to promote the notion of the two-car family. Its ads empathized with the "marooned" wife who was denied her own personal car. "A car for her, too" was "becoming a necessity," insisted Chevrolet in 1928, while another ad depicted a woman driving a shiny green hardtop up a hill, under the Chevy logo and the headline, "Effortless driving." At the bottom of the ad is a closer view of the driver, wearing a necklace that matches the color of the car.

By the end of 1929, Cadillac had introduced its 16-cylinder model, the Series 452, with prices ranging from $5,350 to $9,700. Chevrolet, by comparison, started at $495 and was consistently the best-selling car in the United States. It had topped the Ford Motor Company's Ford brand in sales for the first time in 1927, selling 1 million more cars than Ford, and, according to GM, remained the top-selling U.S. auto brand for all but four of the next 55 years.

With the Great Depression, car manufacturing dropped by 75 percent, but GM, like its rivals, continued to advertise. Oldsmobile hired Detroit's D.P. Brother & Company, Inc., in the early 1930s, beginning a relationship that would last until the mid-1960s; the agency was bought by the Leo Burnett Company, which continued the relationship through the end of the century. By the mid-1930s GM had built a roster of shops that would remain with the carmaker for decades. In addition to Brother, ad agencies included BBDO (handling institutional advertising); Campbell-Ewald (Chevrolet); Arthur Kudner, Inc. (Buick); MacManus, John & Adams (Cadillac and Pontiac); and JWT (international).

During the Depression, U.S. automakers got some indirect aid from the federal government. In 1931, in an effort to boost the economy, the government called for automakers to introduce their new vehicles at the same time, in the fall, to create a unified selling season for new cars. During the 1930s, as car sales dropped, the government began pouring money into public works projects to get people back to work; among its projects was the U.S. highway system. By the time the Depression ended, the country had more and better roads than ever before, and consumers, who had come to view the automobile not only as a necessity but also a cheap way to travel, were eager to buy new cars.

With the beginning of another world war in Europe and Asia, the government of Germany seized control of GM's Adam Opel AG in 1940, and the following year GM Japan ceased operation. U.S. automakers, ordered by their government to cut back on the use of chrome, replaced it with painted surfaces on what were referred to as "blackout models." Pontiac may have been the last U.S. automaker to create a new car during this period, building its final "blackout model" on 10 February 1942. After that, GM switched its entire production operation to support the war effort. It delivered $12.3 billion in war materials to the U.S. armed forces, including airplanes, airplane engines and parts, trucks, tanks, guns, and shells—and a Series 75 Cadillac that served as General Douglas MacArthur's staff car.

Following the war, U.S. car manufacturing boomed, spurred by postwar prosperity and a pent-up demand for new cars. There were two main automotive advertising themes during this period, according to Charles Goodrum and Helen Dalrymple in *Advertising in America: The First 200 Years*: each new model had to be "dramatically different" from the previous year's, and car owners had to be convinced that the old model was not good enough. At the same time, cars were now touted as "personal expressions of the owner" and often seen as representative of the owner's personal power or even sexual prowess.

"See the USA in Your Chevrolet"

In 1948 Cadillac became the first car to sport fins on its fenders, modeled after the Lockheed P-38 fighter plane. Others soon followed suit, adding more power and more chrome with each model year. In 1949 Cadillac introduced the Coupe de Ville, its first hardtop, and in 1953 launched the Eldorado, touted as the first postwar custom luxury car and priced at $7,750.

Oldsmobile in 1948 introduced the 135-horsepower "Rocket" V-8 engine while designing its cars with a body that was sleeker and lower to the ground. Ads from longtime agency D.P. Brother played up the new "Rocket era," with slogans such as, "Make a date with a 'Rocket 8,'" "There's more than a touch of tomorrow in the Rockets of today," and "Presenting a new way of going places in the Rocket age . . . Oldsmobility!"

Chevrolet also had new postwar offerings, the Fleetline "fastback" and the Styleline "bustleback." In 1953 it became the first

U.S. car company to offer a mass-produced car with a fiberglass body—the Corvette. The automaker followed up in 1954 with what would become one of the best-known jingles ever written: "See the USA in Your Chevrolet." Chevrolet, working with Campbell-Ewald, sponsored *The Dinah Shore Show* for ten years through the early 1960s, with the star singing the carmaker's theme song on the TV program each week.

Pontiac even got an unexpected plug when the Ricardos and the Mertzes hopped into a Pontiac Star Chief convertible and in 1955, over the course of several episodes of the popular television series *I Love Lucy*, drove it cross country to California. Its success was short lived, however; by 1957, after a series of fairly conservative models, Pontiac came under pressure either to create an image for itself or fold. Initial changes included dropping its trademark silver streaks as well as its Indian head hood ornament. But a bigger change came with the 1959 models when Pontiac introduced what came to be known as the "wide track," thanks to MacManus, John & Adams. The car, with the widest base in the industry, was broad, low, and sported a lot less chrome than other models. (The term was revived in 1997, in ads that claimed, "Wider is better.")

During the 1950s, GM returned to the use of events and touring exhibits, including the Motorama, a star-filled entertainment and product touring show that opened in New York City's Waldorf-Astoria Hotel in 1953 and included an hour-long TV broadcast on the NBC network; it reopened its Parade of Progress, a traveling educational exhibit started in 1936 but suspended during the war.

The company also was getting good press. In 1953, during U.S. Senate hearings on his nomination for Secretary of Defense, GM President Charles E. Wilson was asked about possible conflicts of interest. He replied, "I cannot conceive of one, because for years I thought that what was good for our country was good for General Motors, and vice versa."

By 1957, however, the auto industry was feeling the effects of a downturn in the U.S. economy, and car sales slowed. In December Buick severed its long relationship with the Kudner agency and hired McCann-Erickson, Inc., which ended its 12-year relationship with Chrysler Corporation to take the $24 million account; McCann had handled GM's Opel since the company bought the operation in 1929. Several months later, GMC Truck & Coach Division and Frigidaire also dropped Kudner, which retained some GM business, including its $10 million institutional account; its ties to GM continued until 1965. While GM remained the top U.S. advertiser, its ad spending dropped through the end of the decade. In 1959 GM was the country's largest advertiser, spending $155 million, as estimated by *Advertising Age*, but its spending was down from $170 million in 1955, and its share of the new car market had slipped to 42.1 percent, its lowest since 1949.

As the 1960s began, car manufacturers began offering smaller, "compact" cars made in the United States as an alternative to foreign imports, which had captured a small share of the U.S. market. GM introduced three smaller cars in the United States—the Buick Special, the Oldsmobile F-85, and the Pontiac Tempest—

joining the Opel, imported from its German operation but marketed in the United States by Buick.

While small cars were beginning to be popular with U.S. consumers, the market had not lost its taste for power. In 1964 Pontiac introduced the LeMans GTO—Gran Turismo Omologato. Described as a dragster with sports car handling, the GTO was the first of the era's muscle cars. Within two years, it became one of the hottest cars on the market and remained popular until the early 1970s.

In the mid- to late-1960s, American car owners began to tire of the gas-guzzling, glitzy behemoths; carmakers began toning down their designs, moving toward sleeker, more rounded profiles. Chevrolet's Caprice, for example, featured a "dramatic, flowing style" when it was launched in 1965, according to the company. At the same time, Chevrolet captured younger drivers with the 1966 debut of the Camaro for model year 1967; the car proved so popular that it accounted for 10 percent of Chevrolet's 2.2 million unit sales for 1967. In 1969 the carmaker also opened a new category with the introduction of the four-wheel-drive Blazer, the first sport-utility vehicle.

While Camaro and Blazer were luring new customers to GM, Buick had gained a reputation for being solid and respectable, but unexciting. Working with McCann-Erickson, Buick responded by trying to jazz up its models, renaming the low-end Buick Series 40 as the "Special." Series 60 became the Century Series 80, while the Series 90 "Roadmaster" line was tagged the "Limited." Ads reflected Buick's effort to heat up its image, with headlines such as, "Hot? It's a ball of fire!" and "The day of the 1,000 mile-an-hour stock car is here." The cars turned into "great-powered, trigger-quick, light-handling" machines.

"Baseball, Hot Dogs, Apple Pie, and Chevrolet"

By the early- to mid-1970s U.S. automakers were feeling the heat from Japanese and German imports, due in large part to the country's first fuel shortage in 1973, which drove up the price of gas. The smaller foreign cars got considerable advertising mileage out of their fuel efficiency, especially compared to the gas-guzzlers Detroit was famous for producing.

To counter this, with an emphasis on patriotism, Chevrolet launched one of its most popular commercials ever in 1975, from Campbell-Ewald. Senior copywriter Jim Hartzell wanted to make the connection between Chevy and Americana, so he contacted composer and singer Ed Lubanski to write a song tying the two together. While the commercial showed shots of baseball games, hot dogs, and apple pie intermixed with past and present Chevys, a male voice belts out in country style:

> In the years I been livin' lots of things have surely changed.
> Lots of things have come and gone, some even came back again.
> But through all the many changes, some things are for sure.
> And you know that's a mighty fine feelin', kinda makes you feel secure.

'Cause I love baseball, hot dogs, apple pie, and Chevrolet.
Baseball, hot dogs, apple pie, and Chevrolet.
They go together in the good ol' U.S.A.
Baseball, hot dogs, apple pie, and Chevrolet.

Through the second half of that decade, GM focused on downsizing and reengineering its products to meet government-mandated fuel efficiency standards. It backed the restyled cars in corporate ads that touted engineering changes and pushed the idea that the cars were smaller outside but bigger, or at least as big, inside. The individual auto lines ran themes such as Chevrolet's "Now, that's more like it"; Oldsmobile's "efficient family car" for the Delta 88 and luxury "with no sacrifice or compromise" for the 98 Regency; and Pontiac's "redesigned, resized, remarkable."

But coming off a second fuel crisis in 1979, the company found itself facing even harder times. In 1980 GM saw its first loss since 1921, with earnings dropping from $2.9 billion in 1979 to a loss of $762.5 million in 1980; it also dropped to sixth among U.S. advertisers, with spending of $316 million. The "Big Three" U.S. automakers were plagued by a depressed, import-flooded market. To counter the tough economic conditions, GM began to offer a series of rebates—first to clear out its remaining 1979 models, then to push 1980 models with a campaign themed, "Let's get America rolling." Overall, GM's divisions were pushing fuel efficiency and economy, with messages such as "More Pontiac excitement to the gallon," tailored to fit in with Pontiac's overall "We build excitement" effort.

In 1983, in an effort to address the automaker's revenue outlook, GM Chairman Roger Smith reorganized the company into big- and small-car groups as sales rebounded after four years of declines. GM also announced a joint venture with the Toyota Motor Corporation to produce a Toyota-designed subcompact car at one of GM's manufacturing plants; the project resulted in the Chevy Nova, which was rolled out regionally starting in 1985 with a Campbell-Ewald effort themed, "The best of both worlds." The automaker also implemented an import strategy with its partially owned partners Isuzu Motors, Ltd., and Suzuki Motors Corporation; that partnership, with the addition of Toyota, produced the Geo, launched in 1988 and promoted nationally in 1989 with the theme, "Get to know Geo," from Lintas:Campbell-Ewald.

The automaker followed up with a massive acquisition effort that began in 1984 with the purchase of Dallas, Texas–based Electronic Data Systems (EDS) for $2.5 billion and ended in December 1985 with the purchase of Hughes Aircraft Company, in an effort to gain access to new technology as well as diversify into revenue sources separate from the cyclical auto industry. It also formed the GM Media Council to examine its ad agency relationships and to increase the effectiveness of its advertising efforts. Among the group's first acts were reducing agency compensation from the then-standard 15 percent commission level and consolidating GM's TV and magazine buying negotiations corporate-wide, which allowed the automaker to push the media for lower rates and other concessions.

In 1985 the company announced it was creating a new subsidiary, Saturn Corporation. The unit was designed to act as an "experimental laboratory" for trying out new manufacturing, marketing, and management techniques, while making GM competitive with Japanese automakers, whose small, fuel-efficient models were increasingly popular with U.S. consumers.

"Heartbeat of America"

In 1986, amid all this planning, GM's earnings slumped below those of Ford for the first time in 62 years. GM, the fifth-largest U.S. advertiser that year at $839 million, saw its operating profits drop 15.6 percent from 1985 to $3.1 billion. At the same time, its share of the new-car market dropped for the second year in a row to 41 percent.

That same year, Chevrolet broke the "Heartbeat of America" campaign, another ad effort destined for a long life; it was created by Campbell-Ewald and Crushing Enterprises of New York City, which produced the music. At the same time, Buick abandoned its 30-year-old theme ("Wouldn't you rather have a Buick?") in exchange for "Buick. Where better really matters," from McCann-Erickson. Two years later, GM's troubled Oldsmobile division came out with, "Not your father's Oldsmobile"; while the tag line proved to have sticking power with the public, Olds dropped it by the 1990 model year following criticism that it was patronizing to the division's older customers.

The 1990s looked like the decade when GM finally would turn its fortunes around. In April 1990 the automaker signed a three-year, $750 million agreement with NBC giving it access to top-rated prime-time shows and sports programming in what the broadcast network called the largest commitment ever made by an advertiser in the history of television. That fall, the first two models from Saturn were introduced, with a prelaunch teaser campaign themed, "A different kind of company. A different kind of car," via Hal Riney & Partners, of San Francisco, California. But in 1991 GM endured what up until that time was the worst reversal suffered by any U.S. corporation, posting a loss of $7.09 billion. Its 1991 share of the U.S. vehicle market was 35 percent, down from 45.7 percent in 1980. In response, the company announced plans to close 21 U.S. and Canadian production facilities by 1995 and to cut 74,000 jobs.

In 1992 the company underwent a major reorganization as the result of a boardroom coup, establishing two operating units—North American Operations, based in Warren, Michigan, and General Motors International Operations, based in Zürich, Switzerland. As a result, GM spent the decade rebuilding and reshaping its marketing programs. In 1992 it introduced its own branded credit card, backing the launch with $70 million in promotions and advertising. By the end of the decade, it had 15 million cardholders, which provided a sizable database for the carmaker's promotional programs.

It also expanded its use of sports sponsorships. In 1997 GM signed a ten-year, $1 billion sponsorship deal with the U.S. Olympic Committee, making it the exclusive auto advertiser on U.S. broadcast television coverage and the official domestic car and

VELMA WILLARSON wanted something that could fly down the highway with a fifty-pound load of birdseed.

Ask any rosebreasted grosbeak or nuthatch around Winchester, Wisconsin, and they'll tell you about Velma. She feeds them and hundreds of other wild birds out of the goodness of her 76-year-old heart. They'll tell you how they used to watch her struggling to lift big bags of birdseed out of the back of her old sport coupe.

But no more.

Now Velma's got a brand new Saturn. It not only has a roomy, convenient trunk, but back seats that fold down. Meaning, to everyone's benefit, an increased birdseed-per-trip efficiency.

They'll also tell you that Velma's new Saturn is just about as aerodynamic as anything that rolls on the ground can get.

In fact, the only thing they don't seem to like that much is how quiet the Saturn is. When Velma had her old car, they could hear the sound of lunch coming for miles.

But now, she has to honk.

A DIFFERENT KIND OF COMPANY. A DIFFERENT KIND OF CAR.
If you'd like to know more about Saturn, and our new sedans and coupe, please call us at 1-800-522-5000.

©1991 Saturn Corporation. Velma Willarson is pictured with a 1992 Saturn SC.

This early 1990s ad campaign for Saturn, General Motors' newest automotive line, took a personal approach to marketing by building products and corporate identity around real-life situations and real customers.
Courtesy of Saturn Corporation.

truck sponsor of the U.S. Olympic Team through 2008. And in 1999 Buick signed golf pro Tiger Woods to a $20 million–$25 million, five-year endorsement deal with the idea of appealing to a younger, 30-to-40-year-old crowd while giving the line more personality.

GM was also active on-line. In 1996 it launched a Web site to promote its product lines and services, and in 1999 it created a new business group, e-GM, to oversee its e-commerce and Internet marketing initiatives.

The automaker made several organizational changes through the decade as well. In 1995 GM's board, including former Procter & Gamble Corporation chairman John Smale, brought brand management to the company, forcing GM to deal with every vehicle line as a brand. As a result, the automaker broke with Detroit tradition and started hiring brand managers from outside the car industry. In 1996 it merged Pontiac and GMC, naming the combined unit the Pontiac-GMC division. And in 1998 it underwent further restructuring, replacing its North American sales and marketing operations with a single sales, service, and parts system with responsibility for oversight of five U.S. regions.

In its biggest move, however, GM at the end of 1999 announced it was phasing out Oldsmobile. The company's oldest line was no longer able to compete, and many critics blamed that failure on a lack of differentiation from its sibling Buick line. In fact, Oldsmobile had held an account review earlier in the decade, but chose to remain at Burnett. By 2000 GM also was struggling with Cadillac, which had been the top-selling luxury car in the United States from 1950 to 1998 before dropping to sixth place behind Lexus, BMW, Mercedes-Benz, and others. In 2001 GM was spending $4 billion to overhaul the line, building a $560 million Cadillac factory, redesigning the vehicle, and restyling its ads in an effort to shed its stodgy image and instead draw younger, more affluent buyers.

As the 20th century ended, GM was the largest advertiser in the United States, spending more than $4 billion in 1999, according to *Advertising Age*, and holding 28.3 percent of the market. In addition to Cadillac, Buick, Pontiac, Chevrolet, and Saturn, it also owned the Hummer and Saab brands. It sold Frigidaire in 1979 and split off EDS in 1996, but gained Hughes Electronics Corporation, with its popular DirecTV service. In its workings with its ad agencies, GM in 1994 moved from a commissions structure to a fees-plus-incentive system. Still, its agency roster for its oldest brands was almost identical to its lineup in the 1950s: Campbell-Ewald, Warren, Michigan, for Chevrolet; McCann-Erickson Worldwide, Troy, Michigan, for Buick; and D'Arcy Masius Benton & Bowles, Troy, the latest incarnation of the original MacManus, John & Adams, for Cadillac and Pontiac. It added Lowe Lintas & Partners, New York City, for GMC; Publicis & Hal Riney, San Francisco, for Saturn; Modernista! Boston, Massachusetts, for Hummer; and the Martin Agency, Richmond, Virginia, for Saab.

In 2000 the company held the largest account review in history, for its $2.6 billion U.S. media planning account. Bcom3 Group's Starcom MediaVest Group emerged the winner, while the Interpublic Group of Companies' GM MediaWorks retained media-buying responsibilities.

SHARON KISSANE

See also color plate in this volume

Further Reading

About Buick <www.buick.com/home/aboutbuick/history.html>

Bernstein, Marty, "Underpowered," Automotive News.com (15 January 2001) <www.autonews.com/html/main/amarketer/underpowered1115.htm>

"Buick Is McCann's Second GM Auto," *Advertising Age* (17 February 1958)

Cadillac: Privileges and Traditions: Heritage <www.cadillac.com/tradition/hrtge_dec.htm>

The Cadillac Story <www.home.planet.nl/~nagte017/Cadillactext001.html>

"Campbell-Ewald Adds GM Motorama Account," *Advertising Age* (31 March 1958)

Chevy History <www.lubberscars.com/chevy/chevy_history.htm>

Cruising Chevrolet History <www.chevrolet.com/history/index.htm>

The Encyclopedia of Oldsmobile, "Oldsmobile Ad Slogans," <www.worldzone.net/auto/olds/adslogans.html>

Fox, Stephen R., *The Mirror Makers: A History of American Advertising and Its Creators,* New York: Morrow, 1984

General Motors History <www.gm.com/company/corp_info/history>

GM Extreme <www.gmextreme.com/funstuff/history/index.shtml>

Goodrum, Charles A., and Helen Dalrymple, *Advertising in America: The First 200 Years,* New York: Abrams, 1990

Halliday, Jean, "GM Rejiggers As Guarascio Exits," *Advertising Age* (20 March 2000)

"Highlights of General Motors' Olympic Sponsorship Program," *Associated Press Newswires* (11 May 1999)

Linnett, Richard, and Jean Halliday, "GM Rolls Out $2.6 Billion Media Review," *Advertising Age* (26 June 2000)

Meyers, William, *The Image-Makers: Power and Persuasion on Madison Avenue,* New York: Times Books, 1984; as *The Image-Makers: Secrets of Successful Advertising,* London: Macmillan, 1984

Naughton, Keith, "Fixing Cadillac," *Newsweek* (28 May 2001)

Pontiac History <www.pontiac75.com/history.html>

"The Resor Years," *J. Walter Thompson News* (February 1984)

Sloan, Alfred P., Jr., *My Years with General Motors,* edited by John McDonald, Garden City, New York: Doubleday, and London: Pan Books, 1963

Strauss, Gary, and Bruce Horovits, "Can Tiger Drive Young Buyers to Buick?" *Chicago Sun-Times* (26 December 1999)

"350,000 Attend GM's Big Motorama," *Advertising Age* (26 January 1953)

Geritol

Principal Agencies
Edward Kletter Associates
Parkson Advertising
Grey Advertising
Creative Advertising Solutions

Geritol liquid tonic first appeared in 1950, marketed by the privately held Serutan Company as "a remedy for those who felt tired because of iron poor blood." Serutan—which used the tag line "Nature's spelled backwards"—was formed in 1935 and introduced Geritol iron tablets with vitamins in 1952. The brand would remain the number-one iron and vitamin supplement until 1979.

Franklin Bruck Advertising initially handled advertising for Serutan, until Edward Kletter Associates was formed in December 1952 and became the agency for many of Serutan's products. In 1953 Serutan changed its name to Pharmaceuticals, Inc.

Television saw many advertisers sponsoring entire shows in the 1950s, and Geritol marketing embraced both the medium and its most popular format of the time: the quiz show. The ad budget for Pharmaceuticals, Inc., would be enough to place it among the top-20 television ad spenders during the height of quiz show popularity in the mid- to late 1950s. Shows such as *Twenty-One, The Lawrence Welk Show,* and *To Tell the Truth,* with Ralph Bellamy touting Geritol's ability to prevent iron poor blood, were among many programs sponsored by Pharmaceuticals, Inc., but the quiz

This 1972 Geritol ad was part of a successful campaign featuring celebrities who used the product.
The trademark GERITOL® and associated copyrights are the intellectual property of GlaxoSmithKline.

"My wife is incredible."

"The way she takes care of the kids, the house, a job and me—it's incredible. And look at her. She looks better than any of her friends. And they're all about the same age."

Aren't those nice words for a woman to hear? But to be able to get all of those compliments, you have to take care of yourself.

You should eat right, get plenty of rest, exercise. And to make sure you get enough iron and vitamins, take Geritol every morning.

Geritol has more than twice the iron of ordinary supplements. Plus seven vitamins.

Take care of yourself. Take Geritol.

In a Geritol print and television campaign from the early 1970s, proud husbands boasted about their youthful, energetic wives.
The trademark GERITOL® and associated copyrights are the intellectual property of GlaxoSmithKline.

show scandals of the late 1950s soured this marketing approach for sponsors.

In 1960 Pharmaceuticals, Inc., changed its name to that of a subsidiary purchased in 1957: J.B. Williams Company. Coinciding with that purchase, the company created Parkson Advertising as a new house agency. Edward Kletter briefly became president of the new Parkson Advertising before moving on to the position of director of advertising with J.B. Williams Company, a position he held at the time of the quiz show scandals.

The 1960s were not without controversy for Geritol. The Federal Trade Commission (FTC) charged J.B. Williams Company with deceptive advertising in 1963. The FTC maintained that the "tired blood" campaign carried out by Parkson Advertising could mislead people suffering from fatigue due to disorders more serious than iron deficiency. In 1967 the Sixth Circuit Court of Appeals in Cincinnati, Ohio, upheld the FTC's decision, which required J.B. Williams to make affirmative disclosures in its advertising stating that most people who had the symptoms described were not suffering from iron deficiency anemia and would receive no benefit from Geritol. Geritol was reformulated that year to include seven vitamins in addition to the iron.

In 1971 Parkson Advertising created the memorable television campaign featuring contented, middle-aged couples, at the end of which spots the husband quips, "My wife, I think I'll keep her." That same year, Nabisco Company acquired J.B. Williams.

The FTC and J.B. Williams Company reached a final settlement in 1976, with Williams agreeing to pay $280,000 in fines. This was the largest settlement that had ever been collected by the FTC in a false advertising case, although the case was settled without a trial and therefore concluded without J.B. Williams admitting any violation of law in its advertising.

By that time the Geritol campaign was using the theme, "Make every day count. Do what you really want to do," and positioning the product as part of an overall program for maintaining health. Later that year the theme switched to "Look who's using Geritol," and depicted married couples of varying ages. Despite the troubles with the FTC, Geritol still dominated the $25 million tonic market, accounting for 90 percent of the market. J.B. Williams Company spent more than $15 million on advertising in 1976.

In the early 1980s ads by Parkson featured tennis star Evonne Goolagong taking Geritol to enhance her on-court performance. Kletter retired from Parkson in 1981, and Beecham Products acquired the Geritol brand from Nabisco in 1982. Grey Advertising took over advertising from Parkson at the time of the acquisition.

In 1983 Beecham introduced "New, Improved Geritol" with nine vitamins and minerals in addition to the iron. The shift away from the brand's identity as an iron supplement continued the following year when Beecham introduced "Geritol Complete" with iron plus 29 vitamins and minerals. The "Best years" campaign depicted married couples on the anniversary of a watershed event in their lives feeling as youthful and vital as they had 20 years earlier, promoting Geritol as a multivitamin that could help people experience the best years of their lives.

After a number of years without advertising, Geritol turned to Grey again in 1994. The new ads focused on the beta-carotene content of Geritol and emphasized what is not in the product—added sugar, lactose, or artificial sweeteners. The featured tag line was "Complete for what's in it. Special for what's not." Geritol switched agencies to Creative Advertising Solutions in 1999 and spent approximately $2.5 million on advertising that year, according to Competitive Media Reporting.

MARK SCHUMANN

Further Reading

Anderson, Kent, *Television Fraud: The History and Implications of the Quiz Show Scandals,* Westport, Connecticut, and London: Greenwood, 1978

Stone, Joseph, and Tim Yohn, *Prime-time and Misdemeanors: Investigating the 1950's TV Quiz Scandal: A D.A.'s Account,* New Brunswick, New Jersey: Rutgers University Press, 1992

Germany

Although advertising existed in Germany long before the industrial age, it was in the early to mid-19th century that political, economic, and social changes set the scene for the emergence of a modern consumer market. With a modernized state and society in view, Prussian ministers initiated a number of reforms at the beginning of the 19th century, among them the abolition of the traditional guild system. Thus, from 1810 onward freedom of trade was gradually extended to include all producers and all German states. Production became oriented less toward a specific customer and more toward an anonymous market in which producers had to find customers for their goods and compete with other producers. Advertising in the press, the most effective way of drawing the public's attention to one's products, soon reflected this more competitive marketplace, employing eye-catching illustrations, headlines in bold type, a variety of typestyles, and borders that set ads off from other text. In addition, posters were used more widely than before, especially after the introduction of the Litfass-Säule, an advertising board in the form of a pillar set up in busy streets and squares.

Origins and History

Following the changes brought about by the revolution in 1848–49, the press and advertisements in newspapers were freed from censorship. The state monopoly on advertising in newspapers had been abolished in Prussia in 1846, and freedom of the press was established throughout Germany in 1874. With new segments of the population involved in public affairs, these developments dramatically increased the demand for information. In addition, developments such as the invention of telegraphy opened up new forms of communication. Thus it was that political revolution was accompanied by a revolution in communications. In the second half of the 19th century people lived in a rapidly changing world that was becoming increasingly complex, giving them a powerful incentive to keep up with the changes that were taking place.

By the 1870s German industry had entered the era of mass production. The importance of advertising increased in the period after the unification of Germany in 1871 as the number of new companies soared in a short-lived upswing in the economy. But advertising became even more important in the years of economic depression that followed. As Germany experienced its first massive depression, advertising became an integral part of companies' sales policies, and it was at this time that companies first developed publicity departments.

Rise of Consumer Economy

As the population of Germany rose from 41 million in 1871 to nearly 68 million by 1914, the proportion of people living in cities increased dramatically. In 1871 two-thirds of Germans lived in rural areas, but by 1910 only 40 percent did so. The number of towns with more than 5,000 inhabitants more than doubled. In addition, average incomes rose slowly but steadily, so that more and more families could afford goods beyond the bare necessities. At first, companies catered to the middle-class demand for luxury goods by expanding the range of their products. In the process, advertising, which itself had expanded to magazines, was used to show customers what was available in an increasingly diverse market. When competition intensified, however, advertising had to struggle harder to catch people's attention. It was then that the first protests against what was called the "swindle and dirt" of advertising were voiced.

By the end of the 19th century, consumerism had become a part of economic and social life. To consume was not only socially acceptable, it was also a means of creating social distinction as well as a form of leisure activity. The concept of "needs" had been broadened to include the dictates of rapidly changing fashions and fads. Further, advertising was no longer restricted to appeals to the upper classes. Another dramatic change was the development of the proprietary article, when, beginning in 1894, the name of a product could be registered with the Imperial Patent Office and thus protected by law. Food, clothing, cosmetics, and tobacco were among the first products to be branded. The number of products registered at the Patent Office every year grew astronomically, with three times as many in 1913 as in 1894. Hermann Muthesius's Deutscher Werkbund was established in Munich in 1907 to create branded fashion articles. At the same time chain stores and luxurious department stores such as Wertheim in Berlin, established in 1896, as well as mail-order selling, revolutionized the retail business. Producers and retailers alike turned to advertising, and as a consequence, the practice of advertising entered into a new phase. Advertising began to concentrate on the individuality of brands and discovered new means of getting its messages across through the use of signs—roadside billboards and advertisements on buildings, trams, and buses.

Not everyone hailed the presence of this new eye-catching advertising. Protests led to federal and state legislation, which, like the laws against unfair competition (1896; amended in 1909), restricted the scope of advertising. But the overall tendency was one of expansion. Even before the first decade of the 20th century had come to an end, resistance to advertising had ebbed.

Although World War I brought a dramatic decline in commercial advertising, it made politicians and government officials see the business in new ways. They recognized the potential of advertising for propaganda and used it accordingly both during and after the war. This was a time when advertising in a broad sense, embracing the political and ideological as well as the commercial, truly became a mass phenomenon.

The elements of a modern consumer market developed quickly, beginning in 1925, when regulations on reparations payments and financial aid from the United States helped the German economy recover from its postwar depression and inflation. Advertising became a field of scientific research, with advertisers turning to the science of psychology to optimize the effectiveness of their campaigns. Marketing departments came to concentrate on their companies' proprietary goods, and advertising agencies, most of them branches of U.S. shops boosting the concept of full service, began to spread in Germany. Market research was initiated in the 1930s. At the same time, German society after the war lost many of the distinctions that had dominated life during the Wilhelmine period, increasing people's desire to enhance their social status through consumption. While the average income of working-class or lower-middle-class families remained below the prewar levels well into the 1930s, more people had time and at least a bit of money to spend on leisure activities. On the whole, however, the advertising industry failed to convince the working classes—or its intellectual critics—of the idea that the needs of modern man could be satisfied by consumption.

East and West

A modern consumer market that integrated all classes of society developed only in the Federal Republic of Germany (West Germany) from the 1950s onward. With the slogan "Prosperity for all," Ludwig Erhard, the minister of trade and commerce, popularized the concept of a "social market economy," which turned out to be one of the strongest foundations for democracy in West Germany. Mass production underwent an accelerated process of rationalization so that the people of West Germany, as in Western Europe generally, had access to a number and variety of goods and services without parallel. Protectionist regulations were repealed, and producer cartels lost at least some of their power, so that goods and services became more accessible. An increasingly competitive home and world market led to a gradual reduction in prices.

While the average number of work hours was high in the first years after the war, it fell in the long run. The average income rose twice as fast in the 1950s as it had in the previous 150 years. At the same time, the conception of work and leisure began to change, as time spent away from work acquired a new importance to West Germans. After the inflation of the 1920s, a worldwide depression in the 1930s that once again drastically reduced the standard of living, and another world war, ordinary people finally seemed to be getting a share of what the wealthy had always been able to enjoy. The ability to afford consumer goods such as furniture, appliances, fashionable clothing, and even a motor scooter and later a small car was seen as providing access to a better life. Instead of making a political commitment or a sacrifice in the

Innovative German artist Lucian Bernhard designed many advertising posters, including this 1909 example for Kaffee Hag.

present for some future ideal, the majority of West Germans opted for a retreat into private life. All of these factors helped to smooth the way for the development of a modern consumer society.

In the part of Germany occupied by Soviet forces after World War II, however, life took a different turn. With the creation of the German Democratic Republic (East Germany) along socialist principles in 1949, the eastern part came to have a rigidly planned economy, although some aspects of a retail market were retained. With economic development under strict state control and an ensuing concentration on heavy industry, the production of consumer goods for the home market was neglected, producing conditions that were conspicuously different from those in West Germany. Hence, consumption and advertising played a far different role in East Germany. Consumers' purchasing power remained low, and many consumer goods remained in short supply. Nonetheless, East Germans had their own branded articles and used promotional campaigns to market them. Even though the overall situation differed from that of West Germany, the style of East German advertising in the 1950s followed much the same

lines. The advertising industry in East Germany gradually declined, however, as some of its activities were directed toward the promotion of goods difficult to sell or of those intended for foreign markets. Further, advertisers not employed by the two major state agencies, Deutsche Werbe-und Anzeigengesellschaft (DEWAG) and Interwerbung, were forced to spend much of their effort in search of printing capacities.

Development of Ad Agencies

The first German advertising agencies were created in various states in the mid-19th century. At the time they primarily bought columns of space from newspapers to resell to advertisers or companies. The first agency of this type was that of Ferdinand Haasenstein, established in 1855 in Altona; three years later, it became Haasenstein & Vogler.

From 1863 onward the agency set up branches throughout the country and abroad. What was most important to Haasenstein & Vogler and to similar agencies was the promotion of the available space. The content and layouts of ads were under the control of the advertisers, although agencies might offer advice on these matters.

It was Rudolf Mosse who changed this arrangement. From the start his agency, the Annoncen-Expedition Rudolf Mosse, which was established in 1867, combined the sale of space with other services. Mosse was one of the first in German advertising to realize the importance of layout. His clients could turn to a catalog of nearly 2,000 borders and plates or could even have the layout done for them. On the whole, however, at the end of the 19th century German advertising remained far behind in the services offered, particularly when compared to agencies in the United States. Nonetheless, Mosse's agency continued to expand and added new fields of activity when he became a newspaper publisher himself in the early 1870s. By the end of World War I the Mosse Group controlled the advertising space of more than 100 newspapers. This evoked criticism, especially from those who disagreed with Mosse's liberal stance, from nationalist circles, and from tycoons of heavy industry in the Ruhr such as Gustav Krupp von Bohlen und Halbach, August and later Fritz Thyssen, and Hugo Stinnes. In order to foster the interests of these tycooons, in 1914 Alfred Hugenberg created the Auslandsgesellschaft mbH, renamed Allgemeine Anzeigen GmbH in 1917. This combination agency and newspaper publishing group rose to be a powerful competitor of the Mosse Group. Thus, even before the rise to power of National Socialism in the 1930s, political as well as economic motives had their place in the German advertising industry.

In the first decades of the 20th century German advertising agencies sought to give their work a more distinctly national character. They succeeded, especially in the field of poster design. In contrast to American practices, since the 19th century German posters had been designed in accordance with dominant artistic styles. Many of them were designed by artists who worked for the printer Hollerbaum & Schmidt in Berlin. Lucian Bernhard, thought to have created the style of poster that uses a graphical representation of the product against a single-color background, was one of the most prominent. After his emigration to the United States in 1925, he called attention to this so-called German style, in contrast to the American preference for photographs and the presentation of an idea instead of a single object.

Another endeavor to foster an indigenous style was launched by the Werkstatt für neue deutsche Wortkunst (workshop to create a new style in German writing and speech), created in 1912 by Hans Weidenmueller. He advocated a distinct German advertising language and an industry strong enough to ward off the influence of American advertising. Yet the project was unsuccessful in the long run, as was the massive intervention of state ideology into the field of advertising in Germany after 1933. The Nazis wanted to fully control the ad industry and contain its influence. Thus, for example, advertising was banned from radio broadcasts in 1936. Not only the institutions and methods but also the contents of advertising were to be made German, a policy that did not prevent earlier campaigns from being continued, the promotion of Coca-Cola among them.

Even after World War II, the call for a distinctly indigenous advertising continued to be raised. Some advertisers in West Germany tried to revive the style of the late 1920s and early 1930s. As late as 1956 the organization Bund Deutscher Werbeberater und Werbeleiter espoused the idea when it called for a combination of what was seen as German meticulousness with the American capacity to simplify and to concentrate on the essential. Proposals and campaigns such as these were a rearguard action, however, and the West German advertising industry came to follow the American model closely.

Although advertising agencies in the modern sense had appeared in Germany after 1925, there were only a few full-service agencies in 1945. This situation began to change markedly when, after 1949, international agencies set up branches in West Germany. Most of them were American or British shops, for example, McCann-Erickson, Lintas, the J. Walter Thompson Company (JWT), and Young & Rubicam, Inc. (Y&R), with management and creative work controlled by people from abroad. In addition, some of the German advertisers of the prewar years reopened their agencies or launched new ones. Hanns W. Brose started an agency in Frankfurt in 1947, and 11 years later it employed more than 200 people in Frankfurt, Hamburg, and Cologne. Hubert Strauf followed suit with Die Werbe in Essen. The slogan he created for a Coca-Cola campaign, "Mach mal Pause—trink Coca-Cola" ("Have a break—drink Coca-Cola"), became a popular catchphrase and a symbol of the reconstruction era. In 1954 Hubert Troost established the shop that became Troost Campbell-Ewald in the 1970s. Wolfgang Vorwerk, Vilim Vasata, Günter Gahren, and Jürgen Scholz began with Agency Team (later Batten Barton Durstine & Osborn [BBDO]) and Scholz & Friends. Other new agencies included R.W. Eggert and Zernisch, both in Düsseldorf, and Markenwerbung International in Hamburg. The American influence remained overwhelming, however, as many newly created agencies were simply branches of U.S. agencies or mergers. Two prominent examples were Ogilvy & Mather and Doyle Dane Bernbach (DDB) in Düsseldorf, which at the time was the major German center of the industry. In one respect, however, DDB was an exception. Whereas most U.S. agencies followed their American clients abroad, DDB went to Germany in 1961 specifically to serve a German client, Volkswagen. At first, agencies in Germany not only designed campaigns but also advised clients in the marketing of products; this changed, however, in the 1970s as more companies created their own marketing departments.

Role of Advertising in West Germany

After the return to a market economy in West Germany in 1948, advertising was used to inform consumers that merchandise was available again and in a quality they had come to appreciate in peacetime. Until the end of the 1950s printed advertisements used rhymes to suggest familiarity and high quality. Advertising in the 1950s was undeniably conventional and conservative and dominated by traditional gender roles restricting women to home and hearth. There also was an emphasis on factual information. By the end of the decade, however, the nature of advertising began to shift from the provision of information about a product or service to the creation of an image. Fritz Bühler's poster designs for Peter Stuyvesant, created for the Heumann Werbegesellschaft agency from 1958 onward, appealed to contemporary Germans' longing for foreign travel and greater mobility—"Der Duft der grossen weiten Welt" ("The scent of the great wide world"). Often a connection was made to a particular lifestyle, and more and more advertisements appealed to customers' emotions. Actors began to be hired to promote products; Luxor soap, shortened to Lux in 1957, was the first product to be so marketed in Germany in 1951 ads by JWT. German advertising copied practices already common in the United States, including commercials for television beginning in 1956. Television ads had their critics, but these found fault not with particular practices but with the introduction of commercials in general.

Although American agencies continued to dominate, by the 1960s signs of a distinctly German voice could be detected. Advertising professionals such as Michael Schirner and Walter Lürzer, who had begun their careers in U.S. agencies, made German advertising more imaginative and witty, as well as more intelligent. Bill Bernbach of DDB opened the floodgates to a wave of creativity that swept away much of the conventionality of the previous decade. In 1964 DDB introduced a fictional person, known as the "Tchibo expert," into the campaign for Tchibo coffee. The DDB campaigns for Volkswagen became especially well known for their creativity. A 1968 commercial, for example, showed a Volkswagen that drove toward the viewer, passed, and vanished into the distance, accompanied by the text, "Der VW-Käfer. Er läuft und läuft und läuft. . . ." ("The Beetle. It runs and runs and runs. . . ."). The ad refrained from giving a technical description or from talking about the assets of the car but instead simply visualized its message in a catchy way. Agency Team invented a bear to market Puschkin vodka, playing on the paradox of putting a distance between the consumer and the product. Thus, a new variety of humor made its way into German advertising. It was a highly innovative approach at the time, and it did not return until the 1980s.

At the end of the 1960s the reputation of advertisers began to decline. Consumerism was attacked as wasteful, and advertising got into the line of fire as an instrument used to create false ideas and needs. Inflation, the oil crisis of 1973–74, and high interest and unemployment rates operated as a check on people's inclinations to consume. Companies reacted by substantially reducing their marketing budgets, and in the mid-1970s the West German advertising industry tumbled into a major crisis. Hegemann, the fifth-largest agency in 1970, had to dismiss a quarter of its 280 employees, and Dorland, the 12th-largest, let 40 percent of its workforce go. Other agencies had to close down completely or merge with larger ones. Nonetheless, a few—for example, Troost, Eggert, and Agency Team—managed to expand. Some even managed successful start-ups during the crisis. Lürzer and Michael Conrad, for example, set up an agency of their own in 1975. All in all, it was the American agencies that profited from the situation, as they were able to extend their share of the West German

industry, which by the beginning of the decade had become the second-largest advertising market in the world. As far as basic assumptions were concerned, however, during this time German advertisers and smaller agencies were finally successful in asserting their view that consumers should be perceived as being intelligent, responsible, and self-determining.

The mergers of the 1970s were part of the growing trend toward globalization. Since that time markets, products, consumer behavior, and advertising have continued to become more and more global, hence standardized and uniform among countries. Large agencies came to operate on a worldwide basis, and by 1990 only one agency, Springer & Jacoby, among the 15 largest in the country, was still solely under German control. A further change has been that advertising agencies have come to concentrate almost solely on advertising proper, while marketers themselves devise marketing strategies, and the media interact with separate agencies that serve as mediators between the media and the agencies and marketers.

In the 1970s print advertising was still the trendsetter, still the most creative medium, in Germany. During this period Y&R launched imaginative campaigns for brands and products such as Milka chocolate, MM Sekt, Camel cigarettes, and Chiquita bananas. Troost invested Fa soap, made by Henkel but later marketed by Procter & Gamble Company, with an image that conveyed youthfulness and vitality. It was this campaign that introduced the image of a nude woman into German advertising, an innovation that made the agency known throughout West Germany. A distinctly German voice also came from Gerstner, Gredinger, Kutter (GGK), a Swiss agency that opened an agency in Düsseldorf. Schirner and Wolf Rogowsky, who worked for the agency, gave its advertising an original style. Schirner claimed that advertising was a contemporary form of art, and he tried to put his belief into practice in his posters. He looked for the gist of a product or a service and then made this the central message of the campaigns, whether for IBM, Pfanni foods, Jägermeister, or Creme 21 cosmetics. In their promotions for Fiat automobiles, Bosch, Braun electrical equipment, and the BfG bank, Lürzer and Conrad also proved that advertising need not be dull and authoritative but could be witty, playful, and buoyant as well.

Another new development resulted from a change in the political and social climate in West Germany in the 1970s. Oil companies, car manufacturers, and nuclear power companies were among those that began to take up elements of the debate about pollution, and they showed their commitment to the cause by addressing the problem in their lines of business. With this new form of advocacy advertising, business was following signs of the times, since commitment to the environment through "green marketing," as it was called, had become an important issue to the German public at large.

By the 1980s West German society had firmly settled in as an affluent one. The market neared saturation, and consumers were segmented into a number of separate cultures, in which they no longer consumed to satisfy a need but to live up to an image or a lifestyle. Advertising took up the challenge by presenting campaigns that integrated a growing number of products into a particular way of life. Both visuals and text emphasized humor and entertainment, and thus "advotainment" made its appearance. The advertising industry also went beyond the commercial and political when it devised campaigns against drug abuse, AIDS, and later xenophobia. This so-called social advertising was a new kind of communication.

The number and quality of television commercials underwent significant changes when private channels were authorized in 1984, a development that revolutionized the West German media landscape. The television commercial came to supersede the print ad as the most imaginative, and the aesthetic qualities of the presentation and music became essential in appealing to viewers' emotions.

Contemporary Advertising

In the 1990s the options open to individuals in a democratic society multiplied to an amazing degree. The decade began, of course, with a momentous change in Germany's political situation. The reunification of the two German states in 1990 required a single German identity, but there had, in fact, been two separate societies for more than 40 years. A new system shared by all 80 million Germans did not yet exist. It was not clear which of the two different views of consumerism would survive and come to dominate. After an initial period of transition in the early 1990s, the former East Germans discovered that some of the planned economy's branded articles symbolized part of an identity they wanted to preserve. Brands such as Rotkäppchen-Sekt, Club cigarettes, Club Cola (the text of an advertisement in the early 1990s read, "Hurra, ich lebe noch!"— "Hurrah, I am still alive!"), or Florena cosmetics made it into the new market economy, not least because of campaigns launched by imaginative advertising agencies. Tapping a feeling that was termed "ostalgia," (a pun meaning "nostalgia for the East") a harking back to some aspects of the 40 years under socialism, which now seemed acceptable, even attractive, was an effective strategy in the marketing of such products, at least in the eastern part of the country.

The German advertising industry has prepared itself to meet the challenge of thinking big and operating globally. Dresden has become a headquarters city for new advertising agencies. It was predicted, however, that Berlin would develop into the major center of advertising in Germany since, as the capital of a unified government, it reflected many of the trends in German society. One such trend was the introduction of provocative poster advertisements. Whereas in the 1970s advertisers operated with understatement, in the 1990s they made lavish use of elements that stunned, confused, and even irritated their audience. For example,

Horst Wackerbarth's takeoff on Leonardo da Vinci's the *Last Supper* for Otto Kern, done in 1994, attracted criticism from clerics and various self-appointed custodians of good taste. In addition, a type of sincerity entered advertising directed toward the younger generation of consumers, an echo of campaigns of the 1970s that accepted customers as intelligent and self-determined beings. Since that time this assumption has acquired an even broader basis as advertising directed at women has made it the starting point of campaigns. While advertisements in the 1980s did away with differences between the sexes, in the 1990s ads often showed women playing an active role and men a passive one. The range of roles advertisements assigned to women had multiplied greatly, just as had the positions they could take in society at large.

By the turn of the 21st century nearly half a million people were employed in the German advertising industry, and it did more than 50 billion deutsche marks (about $27 billion) worth of business every year. The Internet was beginning to provide a new medium for the advertising industry, although when compared to that in the United States, on-line advertising in Germany was in its infancy. As the media have multiplied, so have the forms and contents of advertising. Strategies and campaigns ever more stunning and imaginative seemed to be needed to attract the attention of consumers who no longer fit the concept of easily defined target groups and whose everyday life was flooded with advertising. The number of commercials broadcast on TV has soared from nearly 405,000 in 1991 to 2,452,000 in 2000, an indication of further growth in the phenomenon of German advertising and its industry in the future.

ANGELA SCHWARZ

Further Reading

Bäumler, Susanne, editor, *Die Kunst zu werben: Das Jahrhundert der Reklame*, Cologne, Germany: DuMont, 1996

Kellner, Joachim, Ulrich Kurth, and Werner Lippert, editors, *1945 bis 1995: 50 Jahre Werbung in Deutschland*, Ingelheim, Germany: Westermann, 1995

Kriegeskorte, Michael, *Werbung in Deutschland, 1945–1965: Die Nachkriegszeit im Spiegel ihrer Anzeigen*, Cologne, Germany: DuMont, 1992

Reinhardt, Dirk, *Von der Reklame zum Marketing: Geschichte der Wirtschaftswerbung in Deutschland*, Berlin: Akademie Verlag, 1993

Schirner, Michael, *Werbung ist Kunst*, Munich: Klinkhardt und Biermann, 1988

Schmidt, Siegfried J., "Werbung," in *Mediengeschichte der Bundesrepublik Deutschland*, edited by Jürgen Wilke, Cologne, Germany: Böhlau, 1999

J. Stirling Getchell, Inc.

Founded in 1931; built reputation on work for Plymouth; became known as an early user of competitive advertising; agency style favored photography in layouts; among the largest U.S. agencies by late 1930s; Getchell died, 1940; agency closed, 1942.

Major Clients

De Soto Motor Corporation
Kelly-Springfield Tire Company
Plymouth Motor Corporation
Schenley Distillers
Socony-Vacuum Oil Company

Possessed of a forceful personality and driven to succeed, J. Stirling Getchell is credited with changing the face of advertising in his time. "Is it fresh? Is it different?" This was invariably his test for any new idea in advertising. His bold style, use of realistic photos, and tabloid-type format were crucial ingredients in creating his attention-grabbing (some critics of the time merely said "ugly") ads.

Getchell was raised in the suburbs of New York City, the son of a silk salesman and a teacher. A case of rheumatic fever when he was about 11 years old left him with a weakened heart but a strong will; he sought to miss out on nothing in life. Always restless, he ran away at the age of 17 to join General John J. Pershing's troops in fighting Pancho Villa in Mexico. The following year he enlisted and served overseas when the United States entered World War I. He returned to the United States in 1919, bringing with him an English wife.

Breaking into Advertising

Getchell held a dozen different jobs in advertising over as many years. Not content to occupy himself with copywriting and layout alone, he sought to absorb all aspects of the business. Although he was hired as a writer, Getchell's primary focus was on layout and design. Throughout his brief career, the visual message of ads was of the utmost importance to him. He wanted to create advertising that spoke to the customer immediately. One of his first ad successes promoted a dealer campaign for a tire company. A picture of a pair of shoes was featured under the headline "Can you fill these shoes?"

After he left his first agency, Getchell worked for a variety of agencies in Philadelphia, Pennsylvania; Toledo, Ohio; and Detroit, Michigan, as well as New York City. He landed his first job at a major agency, Lord & Thomas (L&T) in 1924, where he was hired to write copy for the Studebaker auto company. He was hired for the job by bringing in a book of ad samples, not of his own work, but of celebrated ads by Bruce Barton, Helen Lansdowne Resor, and Raymond Rubicam, among others. He claimed he could write similar ads for L&T's clients, a bit of bravado that he may have believed, even if the agency at first did not.

One of his better-known campaigns was written while he worked for the Batten Agency, which had acquired the Colgate Rapid Shave Cream account on a trial basis a few months before Getchell was hired. The staff was hard at work trying to come up with a bold idea and hoping that if they were successful, they might be given the entire Colgate account. Finally Getchell brought in his idea: a set of "microphotographs" along with a sleek layout for a half-page ad. The headline was set in Bodoni, then a new style of type just coming into fashion for advertising. It read, "How small-bubble lather soaks your beard soft," followed by the subhead: "And gives you the closest, smoothest shave you've ever had." Before-and-after diagrams were included as illustrations, identified as being simulated from actual microphotographs taken in the laboratory. The copy announced that Colgate Rapid Shave Cream brought the proper quantity of bubbles down to the skin line, allowing the water to soften the beard for the smoothest, most comfortable shave possible.

The fact that the microphotographs were done using soft, fine-tooth combs rather than hair did not diminish the ad's effectiveness. The combs were dunked in the lather for a few minutes—about the time it would take to lather up for a shave—and then pulled out, put between sheets of glass, and photographed. When Colgate's chief chemist was told how the photos were made, he said, "By golly, I'd never have thought of that. It's the perfect way to show how soap lowers the surface tension of water so it can penetrate into small spaces and get them thoroughly wet." Not surprisingly, the Batten Agency won the Colgate account.

Another of Getchell's well-known campaigns was written while he was at the J. Walter Thompson Company (JWT). A "terrifying" driver himself, according to some, Getchell started the Silvertown Safety League for the B.F. Goodrich Company's Silvertown Tires. This was a safe-driving initiative that eventually enrolled more than 2.5 million people. He sent a fleet of 15 cars to tour the country, with photographers in tow to cover the news.

Fledgling Agency

Before long, Lennen & Mitchell hired Getchell away from JWT; his secretary, Helen Boyd, and favorite art director, Jack Tarleton, were hired as well. Within a year, the three decided to begin their own company. In 1931, in the midst of the Great Depression, J. Stirling Getchell opened its doors. "We figured we couldn't start at a better time," Getchell said. "Things can't get any worse than they are." Beginning without any accounts, the agency worked for fees that first year for clients such as Chesterfield, Vick's, General Tire, and Lydia Pinkham.

Orrin Kilbourn was hired as a third partner. His contacts at Chrysler Corporation brought in the De Soto automobile division of Chrysler as the agency's first major account. Among other jobs, the fledgling agency was asked to introduce the 1932 Plymouth, another Chrysler nameplate. Ford Motor Company and Chevrolet did not take the Plymouth as serious competition until Getch-

Small bubble lather
works at the "skin-line"

... a closer, smoother shave that lasts longer

If you could only *see* how small bubble lather works. In a jiffy, a peppy little army of bubbles works its way right through the toughest whiskers down to the *base* of every hair. There it softens each whisker right where the razor works.

The minute you lather up with Colgate's two things happen; first, the soap in the lather breaks up the oil film that covers each hair. Second, billions of tiny, moisture-laden bubbles seep down through your beard...crowd around each whisker ...soak it soft with water right at the *skin-line*. The result of this Colgate

small-bubble action is a closer, smoother, longer lasting shave.

FREE!
Colgate's After-Shave
A new lotion. Refreshing ... invigorating...delightful...the perfect shave finale. Trial bottle free, with your sample of Rapid Shave Cream, if you mail coupon NOW.

ORDINARY LATHER
This lather-picture (greatly magnified) of ordinary shaving cream shows how large, air-filled bubbles fail to get down to the base of the beard; and how they hold air, instead of water, against the whiskers.

COLGATE LATHER
This picture of Colgate Lather (same magnification) shows how myriads of tiny bubbles hold water, not air, in direct contact with the *base of the beard*. This softens every whisker right where the razor works.

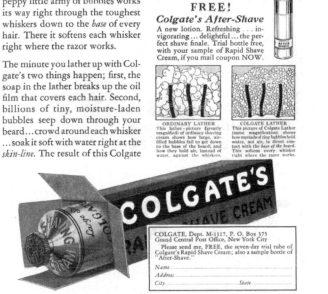

COLGATE, Dept. M-1117, P. O. Box 375
Grand Central Post Office, New York City
Please send me, FREE, the seven-day trial tube of Colgate's Rapid Shave Cream; also a sample bottle of "After-Shave."

Name
Address
City   State

While working at the Batten agency, J. Stirling Getchell created the concept of "microphotographs." A variant, using drawings, is seen in this 1931 ad for Colgate's Rapid Shave Cream.
Courtesy of Colgate-Palmolive Company.

ell's landmark "Look at all three!" ad, which depicted Walter Chrysler leaning over the hood of a Plymouth. The copy featured Chrysler himself giving the technical reasons why the Plymouth was superior to its competitors. Plymouth's share of the low-priced car market rose from 16 percent in 1932 to 24 percent in 1933, its sales leapt 218 percent, and the Getchell Agency won the entire Plymouth account. "Plymouth sets the pace for all three," declared a subsequent campaign, building on the success of the first. It was one of the first major accounts to invite direct comparison with its competition, however oblique. "The low-priced three" became a euphemism for Ford-Chevrolet-Plymouth.

Other memorable campaigns included the "Expect to be stared at" theme for De Soto, as well as the ads for the newly introduced airflow model, "A new kind of car that bores a hole through the air." During the early days Getchell wrote a classic for Lydia Pinkham's vegetable compound that featured a woman speaking to her husband: "I'm sorry . . . not tonight!" (Although the Pinkham family did not uniformly approve, the company made a profit of $400,000 after the ad appeared in 1931. In 1930 it had lost $260,000.)

The success of the Plymouth campaigns opened doors for the agency. New accounts included Socony-Vacuum Oil Company, Mobil Gas and Oil, Airtemp, Devoe and Reynolds, Kelly-Springfield Tire, Mayflower Stations, Sobol Brothers Service Stations, Illinois Meat Company, and Schenley Distillers. J. Stirling Getchell, Inc., was, at one point, one of the ten largest agencies in the nation, with 200 employees and branches in Detroit, Michigan; Chicago, Illinois; Kansas City, Missouri; and Los Angeles, California.

Hallmark Style

Getchell's ads were highly recognizable. He is credited with being the first to use photographs extensively in advertising. In fact, photos became the central focus of the agency's ads. Typeface and headlines were chosen to complement the images. As Getchell said, "We believe people want realism today. Events portrayed as they happen. Products as they really are. Human interest. People. Places. Told in simple photographs that the eye can read and the mind can understand." Loud headlines, attention-getting layouts, and photographs were the hallmarks of the Getchell style.

J. Stirling Getchell, Inc., developed what was probably the most extensive collection of photographs at the time. Getchell compiled thousands of images, all sorted and cross-referenced, ready to be pulled for use as the need arose. While most agencies considered photos to be an inexpensive alternative to artists' drawings, Getchell used them for their clarity, realism, and boldness. And under Getchell's direction they were not inexpensive, either—he may have used a single shot out of ten rolls of film. In addition to hiring the best photographers available, Getchell himself also took many pictures, littering the ground with tabs from his Speed Graphic. He said, "Film is the cheapest thing in this whole operation . . . one lucky shot is worth clicking that camera 100 times." Getchell finally set up Camerart, a photographic subsidiary, to provide access to all the photos the agency would need.

His philosophy was that "an ad is a piece of visual thinking—you can't separate copy and art." His agency functioned under what might be called a creative group system, in which artists and writers worked together to produce an ad or campaign. This was unheard of in those days, when copywriters usually wrote an ad and then handed it off to the art department for illustration. From time to time Getchell called "format meetings," in which all writers and artists met to brainstorm new ideas for existing accounts. During these meetings, artists had to write their own headlines and subheads, while copywriters were required to produce rough layouts.

Although Getchell was always looking for a fresh new idea, he also recognized that the qualities of an ad had to spring from the product if the advertising were to work—that is, ads had to produce sales and not merely be recognized as "good ads" by the industry. He believed that modern ads tried too hard to be clever or to have some gimmick, rather than focusing on the product.

Getchell continued his breakneck pace, forcing his staff into the same sort of tempo. He did not understand why people wanted to go home when they could work around the clock; not surprisingly, turnover at the agency was high. He slowed his pace slightly after his second marriage in 1936, leaving the office at 7:00 P.M. But four years later, in December 1940, he died of a streptococcal infection, possibly related to his decaying teeth. In less than a decade, and during the Depression, Getchell had built an agency with billings of $10 million. He brought the art of photography into advertising, and he changed the way ads were made and the way they looked. Two years after his death at the age of 41, the Getchell agency closed its doors, evidence of the company's dependence on the personality of its founder.

BARBARA KNOLL

Further Reading

Adams, Taylor, "Memories of Admen Past: Close Shave, but Stirling Getchell Charms Colgate with 'Small-Bubble-Lather,'" *Advertising Age* (22 July 1974)

"Exclusivity Is Key to Exciting Ads, Says Spencer, Retiring from Gardner," *Advertising Age* (21 April 1969)

Fox, Stephen R., *The Mirror Makers: A History of American Advertising and Its Creators,* New York: Morrow, 1984

Getchell, J. Stirling, "Creative Credo of Stirling Getchell: The Speech That He Never Made," *Advertising Age* (18 March 1968)

Harris, King, "How Stirling Getchell Chased Walter Chrysler—And Hired a Mail Boy," *Advertising Age* (31 July 1967)

Mayer, Martin, *Madison Avenue, U.S.A.,* New York: Harper, 1958

Gevalia Kaffe

Principal Agency
Young & Rubicam, Inc.

The marketing of Gevalia coffee was one of the most unusual and original advertising successes of the 1980s. It began in 1980 when General Foods Corporation asked Young & Rubicam, Inc. (Y&R), to market its products made outside the United States. Some years earlier General Foods had bought Sweden's largest coffee company, Victor Th. Engwall & Co. KB, which marketed Gevalia, Sweden's best-selling brand of coffee. Y&R was offered the unusual assignment of marketing a premium coffee from a country that had never grown a coffee bean.

The problems faced by Jerry Shereshewsky of Y&R and Bill MacClarence of General Foods were formidable. Gevalia was unknown in the United States; it was not packaged as whole beans, the form preferred in the gourmet market. And although research had shown that there was a market for a super premium coffee among young upscale U.S. consumers, Swedish-made Gevalia cost three times as much as popular supermarket brands. Supermarket sales were therefore impossible, and sales through gourmet and specialty shops too difficult.

The solution Shereshewsky and MacClarence adopted was novel: they would sell Gevalia only on a direct mail subscription basis. Because coffee, unlike books and magazines, is not a "collectible" or a "replaceable," nor is it a service like the telephone, Gevalia marketing was termed "automatic replenishment." Gevalia customers would receive a constant supply of superior coffee on subscription.

Not only was the marketing strategy different, the Gevalia advertising theme was also unique. Gevalia was not marketed as luxurious, stylish, fashionable, or self-indulgent. Instead Y&R relied heavily on the work of the long-dead Swedish founder of Gevalia, Victor Engwall, whose obsession had been to develop "the perfect cup of coffee." Its advertising copy read, "The master roasters of Gevalia earnestly believe that they make the finest cof-

GEVALIA® KAFFE
FINE   COFFEES   OF   EUROPE

Call **1·800·GEVALIA** (1-800-438-2542) toll free, 24 hours, 7 days
You can also order at **www.gevalia.com**

Victor Engwall's quest for the "perfect cup of coffee," begun in 1853, led to a successful and popular direct-mail business supplying gourmet coffees to consumers around the world.
GEVALIA is a registered trademark of Kraft Foods Holdings, Inc.

fee in the world." This message seemed effective in attracting customers, but a better slogan proved to be, "The magnificent obsession that produced the coffee favored by kings."

Subscribers to the basic delivery plan received four half-pound packages every six weeks. The quantity or kind of coffee could be changed any time, and the order could be charged to a credit card. Marketing backup included toll-free hot lines so that subscribers could tell General Foods to speed up or slow down their coffee deliveries or suspend them if they were away on a trip.

The Gevalia Kaffe Import Service provided a "loyalty" contract, and the increased sales per customer provided substantial profits. Brand loyalty was reinforced by a series of special offers of Gevalia cups in Swedish porcelain and Gevalia coffee containers complete with the brand logo. Y&R's direct marketing techniques thus succeeded in transforming a product into a service. Although the product itself continued to compete with other similar products—as books do, for example, when offered by a "book club"—the ongoing nature of the service provided a competitive advantage.

Packaged goods have long been the product category that is most resistant to direct marketing; in the case of Gevalia, however, Y&R was able to devise a direct marketing solution that overcame the market's traditional resistance.

ANDREW QUICKE

Gevalia is a registered trademark of Kraft Foods Holdings, Inc.

Geyer, Cornell & Newell, Inc.

Founded as the Geyer Company in Dayton, Ohio, 1911; bought the Paul L. Cornell Company, New York City, 1933; changed name to Geyer, Cornell & Newell, Inc., with the addition of partner H.W. "Hike" Newell, 1935; renamed Geyer, Newell & Ganger, with promotion of Robert Ganger to vice president, 1945; name changed to Geyer Advertising when Newell left, 1952; merged with Morey, Humm & Warwick, becoming Geyer, Morey, Madden & Ballard, Inc., to reflect President Sam Ballard and new Vice Chairman Edward Madden, 1959; renamed Geyer, Morey, Ballard, Inc., when Madden left, 1962; renamed Geyer-Oswald, 1967; absorbed by Lennen & Newell, 1970.

Major Clients
American Home Products, Inc.
Nash-Kelvinator Corporation (later American Motors Corporation)
Sinclair Oil Corporation
E.R. Squibb & Sons

While Geyer, Cornell & Newell, Inc., was known by many names over its 60-year history, the Geyer name was the one constant in each of the shop's incarnations. Through mergers and management changes it was rechristened perhaps more times than any other major U.S. advertising agency. Despite its own changes, the agency managed to maintain a number of stable client relationships, including those with Black Flag, which became part of American Home Products, and Nash-Kelvinator Corporation, which evolved into American Motors Corporation.

The original Geyer Company was founded in Dayton, Ohio, in 1911 by Charles J. Geyer and his son, Bertram Birch Geyer (known as "Pat" because he was born on St. Patrick's Day in 1891). In 1915 Geyer began acquiring significant business from electrical and industrial clients, which led in the 1920s to the Delco Light and the Frigidaire Division of General Motors Corporation (GM) accounts. (Pat Geyer reportedly invented the modern ice cube tray and sold it to GM for $1.)

But Geyer Advertising, as it was then called in the 1920s, was eager to set up shop in New York City. In 1933 it bought the Paul L. Cornell Company there and two years later became Geyer, Cornell & Newell, Inc. "Newell" was H.W. "Hike" Newell, who became a member of the partnership in 1935 (not the C.D. Newell of Newell-Emmett). Cornell left soon after for a second career in Connecticut politics, but his name remained on the door for some years.

In 1935 the agency moved its headquarters to 745 Fifth Avenue, New York City, though it maintained an office in Dayton. That September, it also opened an office in Detroit, Michigan, to handle the Nash Motors Division of Nash-Kelvinator, maker of Nash and LaFayette automobile brands. During this period, the agency was primarily a print shop, although it handled network radio for Nash. The latter sponsored *Professor Quiz* in the 1937–

1938 season and the *Andrews Sisters Show* in 1944, while another Geyer client, E.R. Squibb & Sons, in 1943 sponsored *Calling America with Robert Trout*; Trout had been the cohost of *Professor Quiz*.

With the United States's entry into World War II in 1941, Nash-Kelvinator, like many other advertisers during the war years, kept its brand prominent through ads about its war materials production. In 1944 the agency's billings soared 50 percent to an estimated $8 million, much of it due to Nash's wartime ads in addition to new business from the Continental Oil Company and the Army Air Force account. Work for Calvert Distillers Corporation and Eureka Vacuum Cleaner also helped boost the agency's billings. That same year Geyer, Cornell & Newell bought the New York City office of Tracy-Locke Company, Inc., which helped it surpass the $10 million mark in 1946 and climb into the ranks of America's top ad agencies.

Meanwhile, Robert M. Ganger, who had been with the agency since 1935, worked his way into upper management as a vice president at the company, which in 1945 became Geyer, Newell & Ganger. He had played a key role in winning business from the P. Lorillard Company, which awarded the agency its new Embassy cigarette account in 1947. (In March 1950, Ganger joined Lorillard and rose to become its president.)

A significant rupture occurred on 1 June 1952 when "Hike" Newell, after a failed merger attempt with Lennen & Mitchell, Inc. (L&M), left Geyer to join L&M, which then became Lennen & Newell (Mitchell had died in 1932). The move created great turmoil, costing Geyer not only the services of Newell but also those of seven vice presidents and 15 other staff members, as well as the P. Lorillard business—all followed Newell to L&M. For 1951 *Advertising Age* ranked Geyer number 24 among U.S. agencies, L&M, 30; a year later the new Lennen & Newell ranked number 24, and Geyer Advertising, the new name as of September 1952, was pushed to number 28. Newell died in 1955.

In September 1952 Geyer acquired the remnants of W. Earle Bothwell, Inc., which had been in business for 19 years, in a secret transaction that resulted in a civil conspiracy suit that was settled out of court in 1953.

Geyer's billings held steady in the low-$20 million range through most of the 1950s. In 1956 Pat Geyer sold 50 percent of his equity to a group of 40 employees that included Sam Ballard, an executive vice president who succeeded Geyer as president (although Geyer's name remained on the masthead). In 1957 Emerson Foote, one of the founders of Foote, Cone & Belding, Inc., and subsequently an executive vice president at McCann-Erickson, Inc., made what at the time was described as "a substantial investment" in Geyer and became chairman; however, he left after seven months.

On 1 January 1959 Ballard engineered another Geyer merger, this time with Morey, Humm & Warwick. Its largest client was Sinclair Oil Corporation; Geyer's was American Motors, the successor to the Nash Motor Division of Nash-Kelvinator. It seemed like a good mix, and the combined agency was called Geyer, Morey, Madden & Ballard, Inc. (GMMB). Edward Madden, who resigned from Keyes, Madden & Jones Advertising to become vice chairman of the new Geyer configuration, provided the fourth element of the name.

GMMB was launched with $30 million in billings, acquiring another $2 million in billings from B.T. Babbitt, Inc. A fifth merger, this time with the Caples Company of Chicago, Illinois, in December 1960, contributed more assets to GMMB. Within two years of the 1959 merger, billings hit $42 million. Madden left in 1960, and the company was rechristened Geyer, Morey, Ballard, Inc., in May 1962. Ballard died in 1963 during a period of healthy growth for the agency.

Geyer ranked number 26 among U.S. agencies in 1965 on billings of $58.6 million, but 1965 was also a watershed year for the agency in other ways. The company resigned American Motors' $15 million account, and lost Kelvinator and Lehn & Fink Products Corporation. In October the agency shuttered its original office in Dayton. In November George Oswald, who had joined Geyer in 1960, became its president. The following year, GMMB acquired Maxon, Inc., an agency located in Detroit, Michigan.

In October 1967 the agency underwent yet another name change, becoming Geyer-Oswald. *Advertising Age* estimated its billings for 1967 and 1968 in the mid-$30 million range, well below the mid-$50 million billings levels the agency claimed in both years. In 1969 it acquired Feeley & Wheeler, Inc., a small New York City industrial agency, but its volume continued to decline. Finally in March 1970 Geyer-Oswald was acquired by Lennen & Newell, Inc. That merger ended the nearly 60-year history of the Geyer name in advertising.

But Lennen & Newell, which billed $160 million in 1970 and dropped to about $30 million in 1971, was badly overextended. In April 1972 the 56-year-old agency went into bankruptcy, with nearly $11 million in debt, and closed its doors.

JOHN MCDONOUGH

Further Reading

"Geyer, Morey Agencies Merge; Madden Joins," *Advertising Age* (15 December 1958)

"Much Guessing about Lennen & Newell," *Advertising Age* (2 June 1952)

"Out-of-Court Settlement Hushes Suit over Geyer-Bothwell Agency Merger," *Advertising Age* (18 January 1954)

Gillette Company

Principal Agencies
Ruthrauff & Ryan, Inc.
Maxon, Inc.
Benton & Bowles, Inc.
Batten Barton Durstine & Osborn (later BBDO Worldwide)

Founded in Boston, Massachusetts, as the American Safety Razor Company in 1901 by King Camp Gillette, the company known as the Gillette Safety Razor Company from 1904 to 1952 and the Gillette Company from 1952 to the present has been an advertising innovator since its inception. Gillette manufactured the first safety razor in 1903, and since that time, the company has been one of the world's leading producers of shaving equipment for both men and women. Gillette has remained steadfastly independent since its inception; it has diversified over time into toiletries, batteries, oral-care products, stationery, and electronics, while strengthening its global market share in the razor and blade business by supporting product innovations with massive advertising campaigns.

King Gillette was born in 1855. His father was an inventor of no great portfolio, and his mother, Fanny Lemira, was the author of *The White House Cook Book*, one of the most successful cook-

books of its time. In 1876 Gillette became a salesman, while dabbling in inventions on the side. Almost 20 years later, while working at the Baltimore Crown Cork & Seal Company, he struggled to shave one morning with a dull straight razor and hit on the idea of a lifetime. Stirred by his insight, he wrote to his wife, "I've got it; our fortune is made!" It would be eight years of trial and error before his prediction materialized. Gillette founded the American Safety Razor Company on 28 September 1901, and a group of investors set out to raise $5,000 by selling 10,000 shares of stock in 20 blocks of 500 shares each. Another 10,000 shares were held by the company, and Gillette himself retained another 17,400 shares. By 1903 machines were finally built capable of producing Gillette's design, but only 51 sets of razors and blades were made.

Once production began in earnest, sales took off. The blades—20 per package, wrapped in green paper with Gillette's visage on the top—sold for $1, and the razor itself cost $5. By the end of 1904, the year in which Gillette finally received a U.S. patent for the safety razor, the company had churned out more than 90,000 razors and 120,000 blades. Sales expanded both domestically and overseas, with Gillette opening a sales office in London, England, a manufacturing plant in Paris, France, a blade factory in Canada, a distribution network in Germany, and by 1906 a sales operation in Mexico. Thanks to Gillette's easily recognizable face and signature adorning every package, the company established one of the first brands known worldwide.

For the "Civilized Man"

Early Gillette advertisements targeted men exclusively; they appeared principally in newspapers and general circulation magazines and stressed the civilizing power of shaving. "The country's future is written in the faces of young men," one blurb from 1910 declared, continuing, "The Gillette is a builder of regular habits. Own a Gillette—be a master of your time—shave in three minutes." Another ad from the same year indicated that Gillette's razors separated independent, civilized men from brutes and effeminate males:

> Woman is the great civilizer. If it were not for her, man would revert to whiskers and carry a club. . . . She admires the clean, healthy skin of a man who uses a Gillette. She does not approve the ladylike massage-finish of the tonsorial artist. . . . There is something fine and wholesome about the Gillette shave. It does not reek of violet water and pomades. . . . It gives a healthy look that suggests the outdoor rather than the indoor man.

Not surprisingly many early ads criticized barbers—who posed a threat to the popularity of home shaving—but such combative advertisements disappeared when the company enticed barbers into selling Gillette products by giving them a percentage of each home kit they sold.

Gillette began attempting to create a profitable women's market in 1915, with an extensive national advertising campaign promoting the Milady Decollette as the "safest and most sanitary method of acquiring a smooth underarm"; the campaign proved only marginally successful.

The company weathered the loss of European sales offices and factories during World War I through its early targeting of the U.S. military market: since 1910 Gillette had asserted that it was a "godsend to a sailor" and equated clean-shaven cheeks with manly military discipline. The company's patriotism was evident in 1917 advertisements asserting that "every man in khaki" ought to have a Gillette kit. The U.S. military reinforced this message: although at first it required American troops to supply their own shaving equipment, in 1918 the military began issuing every soldier a Gillette shaving kit. Military largesse helped Gillette sales rise from 1.1 million razors in 1917 to 3.5 million razors and 32 million blades in 1918.

When the war ended, millions of U.S. servicemen returned home to advertisements that suggested that a Gillette shave was a symbol of civilization and a universal imprimatur of masculinity: "There are some things that all big-brained, red-blooded men agree on. And the Gillette Safety Razor is one of them. Twenty million men of all breeds, all classes, in every country on earth are using Gillettes every day of their lives and liking them," asserted one 1920 ad. Gillette also continued its efforts to reach the women's market during the Roaring Twenties, unveiling the slightly undersized Bobby Gillette razor in 1924 and highlighting its utility for keeping necks and underarms shorn; once again, the campaign to reach women met with only limited success.

Gillette became one of the first major U.S. corporations to exploit commercial network radio broadcasting. Every Friday night on NBC, beginning in 1929, listeners could tune in to music by the Gillette Blades Orchestra, the melodious voices of the Gay Young Blades, accompanied by a pair of pianists called the Original Double Blades, and a five-minute sports summary by famed announcer Graham McNamee. But a costly merger with the Auto-Strop Razor Company, completed in 1930, combined with the onset of the Great Depression to cut into Gillette's advertising budget, and the NBC broadcasts did not last long into the 1930s.

In the midst of this temporary decline, Gillette, who had remained active through the history of the company, became ill; he died on 13 July 1932 at the age of 77. The New York City agency Ruthrauff & Ryan brought the company back into radio in the mid-1930s with the *Gillette Original Community Sing* with Wendall Hall, Milton Berle, and the Happiness Boys.

Although Gillette's market share and profits declined during the Depression, many American men proved unwilling to forego their daily shave. Despite the proliferation of cheap imitations of Gillette products and the increased tendency of consumers to use blades more than once, enough consumers remained loyal to Gillette that it remained profitable during the 1930s. Social consciousness campaigns akin to Listerine's "halitosis" advertisements sought to convince consumers that Gillette's shaving kits were a necessity. Playing on the widespread fear of joblessness, a 1931 print ad implied that poor grooming contributed to unemployment: "He's careless about shaving—frequently leaves a repulsive growth of stubble on his face. Can he expect an employer to overlook this fault?"

The blade maker's honesty might also have impressed some Depression-era consumers. When Gillette rushed inferior blades to the market in 1930, resulting in customer complaints, company president Gerard B. Lambert authorized a 1932 ad that admitted Gillette's error. The bold headline stated simply, "We made a mistake." The same ad also announced the company's first major product and marketing innovation in 30 years: the Gillette Blue Super-Blade, later renamed the Blue Blade. The color of the blade helped convince customers that this product was distinct from its familiar steel predecessor, although the assertion that these higher-quality blades warranted a higher price tag did not initially go over well with consumers. After the failure of reasoned appeals stressing that the new blades actually lowered the cost per shave, Gillette advertisements returned to scare tactics, again playing on economic fears by asserting that a close shave was the difference between prosperity and poverty. Still, the unspectacular advertising of the 1930s left the company with just 18 percent of the blade market in 1938.

A $300 million ad campaign announced the arrival of Gillette's Mach 3 razor system in 1998.
Courtesy of The Gillette Company.

The Sports Connection

The company's most notable advertising successes came after Joseph P. Spang, Jr., took over as president in December 1938 and increased the advertising budget by 50 percent. Gillette advertising manager A. Craig Smith, although not a sports fan himself, saw immense marketing possibilities in sports promotions proposed by the Maxon agency. Gillette had solicited testimonials from baseball player Honus Wagner and manager John McGraw back in 1910, but the company then eschewed sports campaigns until 1935, when it sponsored the Baer-Braddock boxing match. The bout was a boring 15-round affair that caused Gillette temporarily to back away from using sports to reach male audiences. Four years later, however, Spang and Smith took another sports-related gamble, making Gillette the exclusive sponsor of the World Series over the Mutual Broadcasting System in 1939. Gillette committed more than $200,000 (20 percent of the annual advertising budget) for exclusive radio rights, radio time, and a "World Series Special" promotion during baseball's showcase series. The campaign proved remarkably successful; with renowned announcers Red Barber and Bob Elson hawking the blades, Gillette sold about 2.5 million World Series Specials, more than twice the projected amount. The World Series promotion proved so successful that Gillette spared little expense to remain the event's primary or sole sponsor from 1939 through 1963.

Under Smith's supervision Gillette also began pouring an increasing amount of money into other sports broadcasts, sponsoring several college football bowl games, the Kentucky Derby, and the professional football championships. Gillette furthered its involvement in sportscasting with the launch of the *Cavalcade of Sports* program in late 1941. (Its auspicious first broadcast was the epic Joe Louis–Billy Conn heavyweight fight.) For the next quarter-century, Gillette's sponsorship of most of the premier sporting events under the *Cavalcade* title rendered the blade maker's name synonymous with sports. Broadcast sports became such a productive marketing venue that by the mid-1950s, nearly 85 percent of the company's total annual advertising budget went to the *Cavalcade of Sports*. The Maxon agency handled the company's sports offensive.

Televised boxing also drew Gillette's advertising dollar; the company touted the benefits of its blades to boxing's male-dominated audience, starting with local New York City telecasts in 1944 and culminating in the famous *Friday Night Fights* on NBC through 1959 and on ABC from 1960 to 1963.

Despite these ventures into the promotion of other sports, baseball continued to serve as Gillette's primary promotional venue throughout the 1950s, especially after the company paid a then-staggering sum of $7.37 million for six years of exclusive radio and television rights to the All-Star Game and the World Series in December 1950. The company used the 1952 World Series as a platform for the revised "Look sharp, feel sharp, be sharp" campaign (originally trumpeted during the 1946 series broadcast) and the "How're ya fixed for blades" ads. The former campaign was characterized by the catchy "Look Sharp March," composed by Mahlon Merrick (who was otherwise known as the leader of the *Jack Benny Show* orchestra), while the latter took off with a memorable series of animated spots featuring Sharpie, the talking parrot, who in later broadcasts was superimposed over the action on the field in order to keep Gillette's presence visible as the sporting event unfolded.

Gillette broke racial barriers with some of its advertising in the 1950s, featuring black ballplayers such as Willie Mays in television commercials despite objections from southern broadcasters interested in maintaining segregation. The spots proved highly lucrative for the company, which controlled about 60 percent of the blade market by 1960.

Gillette's sports sponsorship has extended to events in other nations. The company is the longest continuous supporter of the World Cup, devoting millions of advertising dollars every four years since 1970 to soccer's signature event, with most of the money earmarked for campaigns in Europe and Latin America.

Postwar Years

Gillette began to diversify in the postwar era, tapping into the female market in 1948 by purchasing the Toni Company, a manufacturer of home permanent kits whose products did not have quite the same global appeal as Gillette's blades. Under Gillette's ownership, however, Toni sponsored the television hit *Arthur Godfrey and His Friends,* beginning in 1950, and became a sponsor of the Miss America Pageant in 1958.

Gillette's Super Blue Blade, the company's first new blade in nearly three decades, debuted in late 1959. It was designed to offset the inroads made by Schick and electric razor manufacturers into the shaving market and was promoted with quiet, unspectacular advertisements that stressed performance. The muted campaign marked a sharp turn away from the strongly masculine character of previous ads, setting the tone for a more low-key approach to advertising that would last for almost 30 years. The Super Blue Blade was not on the market for long, however; its brief life ended in 1963 when Gillette finally caught up to its competitors by becoming the last major razor company to produce stainless steel blades. The increasingly stale Gillette advertising of that era continued to be produced by Maxon, which followed "tried and true" approaches rather than innovative advertising during the 1963 World Series, the 25th, and (not coincidentally) last, year that Gillette served as the sole sponsor of the event.

The 1971 World Series served as a launching pad for the Trac II system, notable for the slogan hyping improved performance. "It's one blade better than whatever you're using now," claimed commercials during the $10 million advertising push overseen by Benton & Bowles. As Gillette capitalized on the popularity of disposable razors between the late 1970s and mid-1980s, however, its marketing paradigm shifted from emphasizing quality to stressing convenience, and the company's advertising budgets fell. Although Gillette's products set the industry standard for quality, research showed that older men purchased the blades because they had fond memories of the brand's 1950s ads and sports sponsorships, while younger men thought the brand name meaningless or associated it only with inexpensive plastic disposables.

A pioneer in the field of sporting event sponsorship, Gillette has sponsored every World Cup since 1970 and remains the event's longest continual supporter. *Courtesy of The Gillette Company.*

The Sensor and Mach III

With profits waning in the late 1980s, Gillette decided to revive its flagging sales by discontinuing ad support for disposable razors and returning to an emphasis on the "quality" shave afforded by a steel razor. Under the direction of Colman Mockler, the company chairman, and John Symons, president of Gillette's Blade and Razor Group division, the advertising budget for disposables such as Good News and Micro-Trac was slashed from $9.9 million in 1987 to zero in 1990. The Boston, Massachusetts, office of BBDO Worldwide created a campaign centered around the slogan, "The best a man can get," designed to reinforce the traditional image of Gillette as a brand bonding masculinity to high-quality products. Commercials positioned shaving as an emotional rite of passage and showed men as devoted family members as well as successful corporate leaders. "The best a man can get" was launched during the Super Bowl in January 1989, kicking off an $80 million international advertising campaign to support Atra and Contour Plus razors. The campaign used the same visual imagery (and, in broadcast media, the same music) in the 19 North American and European nations in which it ran, the slogan

translating easily into 14 languages. The slogan would remain in widespread use for at least a decade after its introduction.

In 1990 Gillette again initiated a major advertising campaign during the Super Bowl. Preceded since October 1989 by "teaser" ads promising that "Gillette is about to change the way men shave forever," the company unveiled the Sensor razor in a series of commercials that used the "best a man can get" slogan to pitch the Sensor's new type of blades. In support of the first synchronized worldwide product launch, nearly all of Gillette's $175 million multinational advertising budget was devoted to Sensor. The campaign, handled by BBDO, proved successful enough that Gillette had to pull some advertisements in April 1990 when demand exceeded supply, and the company shipped its billionth Sensor razor less than two years after the Super Bowl ads debuted.

With its corporate profile and market share growing, Gillette again pursued the women's shaving market, introducing the Sensor for Women product line in 1992. Supported by a $14 million advertising budget, the TV spots touting the redesigned razors aired during prime time rather than on daytime soap operas in the United States, and the previously impenetrable female market seemed suddenly receptive to Gillette shaving equipment. The product was also marketed internationally; Sensor for Women advertisements using the slogan "Finally, a razor worth holding on to" appeared throughout Europe. The advertisements were predicated on research that showed women viewed shaving as a chore whereas men viewed it as a skill, and the campaign sought to make women feel more enthusiastic about the activity.

Gillette's final major marketing development of the 1990s came in July 1998, when the company unveiled the Mach 3 razor system. The company backed this product, which took five years and $750 million to develop, with a $300 million promotional campaign. The only advertising budget in the 1990s to surpass the one for Mach 3 was Microsoft's $1 billion campaign for Windows 95 software. The campaign for the Mach 3 system stressed the aerodynamic design of the razor, using jet planes and sonic booms in conjunction with the familiar "The best a man can get" slogan to lure male shavers. The Mach 3 campaign, which helped the razor become the top seller in the market by a ten-to-one margin, won Gillette the Grand Edison New Product Marketer of the Year Award in 1998.

Gillette also devoted $40 million to its "Are you ready?" campaign in 1998, which positioned the company's products as a necessary part of a modern woman's physical and psychological beauty regimen. Seeking to extend the inroads made into the female market, the company spent $16 million in the United States to air commercials on such popular prime-time television programs as NBC's *Seinfeld* and Fox's *Party of Five*. The spots featured fashionable women answering "Yes I am" to the campaign's question. Print ads showed contemporary women preparing for the first day on the job or for a night on the town and asked them to consider the question, "But without soft, smooth legs, are you ready?"

Gillette remains the dominant manufacturer in the blade business, in part because it has successfully defined gender roles through its ads. The renewed emphasis on quality, historically central to its products' appeal, and the continuing strength of the "Best a man can get" slogan suggests that Gillette will continue to be an advertising and product innovator.

DOUG BATTEMA

Further Reading

Adams, Russell B., Jr., *King C. Gillette: The Man and His Wonderful Shaving Device,* Boston: Little Brown, 1978

Gagnon, Louise, "The Big One: Gillette Isn't about to Retire the Formula that Has Made its Cavalcade of Sports Such a Success for 27 Years," *Marketing Magazine* 102 (14 April 1997)

"Gillette: After the Diversification That Failed," *Business Week* (28 February 1977)

Grimm, Matthew, "Sports Marketing: Gillette Back Heavy in Sports," *Brandweek* 34 (15 March 1993)

"King Gillette, Who Built New Industry, Dies on West Coast," *Advertising Age* (16 July 1932)

Leonard, Albert S., "Gillette's Cavalcade of Sports Rode Early Boom in Broadcasting World Series, Boxing Classics," *Advertising Age* (22 October 1973)

"Management Brief: The Best a Plan Can Get," *Economist* (15 August 1992)

McKibben, Gordon, *Cutting Edge: Gillette's Journey to Global Leadership,* Boston: Harvard Business School Press, 1998

Smith, Richard Austin, "Gillette Looks Sharp Again," *Fortune* 45 (June 1952)

Symonds, William C., and Carol Matlack, "Gillette's Edge," *Business Week* (19 January 1998)

Taylor, Cathy, "With Sensor, Gillette Took Lead in 'Orchestration,'" *Adweek* (3 June 1991)

Weisz, Pam, "The Razor's Edge: Interview with Gillette's R. Rossi," *Brandweek* 36 (24 April 1995)

Global Advertising

At the dawn of the 21st century, two major trends were affecting consumers around the globe. The first was the extraordinary growth in the number of businesses operating on an international scale. Consumers around the world smoked Marlboro cigarettes, wrote with Bic pens, watched Sony television sets, wore Levi's jeans, and drove Volkswagen automobiles. The expansion of firms operating outside their domestic borders led to the rise of the second trend—the growth of international advertising. Increasingly U.S. agencies were looking abroad for clients. Overseas, agencies around the world were expanding rapidly, even taking control of some of the most prestigious U.S. shops. With expertise in advertising no longer a U.S. monopoly, the American advertising industry faced stiff competition from Tokyo, Japan; London, England; Paris, France; and even São Paulo, Brazil.

Growth of International Business

As far back as the late 1800s, a number of firms recognized the importance of global expansion, and by the early 1900s U.S. firms such as the Ford Motor Corporation, Singer, Gillette, National Cash Register, Otis, and Western Electric had commanding world market shares. The trend toward globalization slowed between 1920 and the late 1940s. These decades, marked by a world economic crisis and World War II, resulted in a period of strong nationalism. In the years after World War I, countries attempted to salvage and strengthen their own economies by imposing high tariffs and quotas to keep out foreign goods and protect domestic employment. Among the results of these policies was global depression. After World War II the number of U.S. firms operating internationally again began to grow significantly.

Several developments further spurred the growth of international business: the creation of the International Monetary Fund (IMF) and the General Agreement on Tariffs and Trade (GATT) at the close of World War II, along with the formation of the European Community (EC) in 1992 and the ratification of the North American Free Trade Agreement in 1993. As a consequence, according to a 2001 *Fortune* magazine survey, the top-500 multinational companies alone generated more than $14 billion in revenue in 2000. The United States led all countries with 185 companies on the list; Japan ranked second (104 companies), and Germany ranked third (34 companies).

Thousands of smaller U.S. firms also engage in international marketing. Indeed, the majority of U.S. exporters have fewer than 100 employees each. Corporations may look abroad for the same reasons they seek to expand their markets at home: where economies of scale are feasible, a large market is essential. However, if production capacity is not fully utilized in meeting the demands of one market, additional markets may be tapped. During seasonal fluctuations or economic downturns in one market, corporations may turn to new markets to absorb excessive output. Firms may also find that a product's life cycle can be extended if the product is introduced in different markets—products already considered obsolete by one group may be sold successfully to another. In addition, significant global changes have helped to fuel this phenomenal growth in international business. These changes include: saturated domestic markets, higher profit margins in foreign markets, increased foreign competition in domestic markets, trade deficits, and the emergence of new markets (such as the countries of the former Soviet Union).

In the last two decades of the 20th century alone, world trade expanded from $200 billion to well over $4 trillion. While the United States, once considered the hub of world trade, remains the major player, U.S. participation in world trade measured as a portion of world market share has declined drastically. Whereas in 1950 the United States accounted for nearly 25 percent of the world trade flow, its share at the end of the 20th century was less than 10 percent. These figures reflect the entrance of other trading partners into the picture rather than the decrease of U.S. exports during this period. In 1980, 23 U.S. companies made *Fortune*'s top 50, compared with only five Japanese firms. In 2000 only 16 American companies ranked among the top 50, while the number of Japanese companies had increased to 16. Competition for world markets comes not only from other industrialized countries but from newly industrialized countries as well. Three of the top 100 corporations on *Fortune*'s list are Chinese. A Venezuelan petroleum-refining firm, a South Korean electronics company, and a Mexican mining and crude oil company also ranked among the top 100.

Table 1. Top Global Ad Markets, 2000.

Rank	Country	Projected Advertising Spending (U.S. dollars, billions)
1	United States	$134.3
2	Japan	33.2
3	Germany	21.6
4	United Kingdom	15.8
5	France	11.1
6	Italy	8.3
7	Brazil	6.9
8	Spain	5.4
9	Canada	5.3

Source: Ad Age Global Web site <www.adageglobal.com/cgi-bin/pages.pl?link=425>

Growth in Advertising Worldwide

Patterns in the growth of international advertising have paralleled those of international business. At the end of World War II, the bulk of U.S. advertising activity was domestic, and 75 percent of recorded advertising expenditures worldwide were concentrated in the United States. Since then, the growth in global advertising spending has skyrocketed. In 1950 estimated ad spending totaled $7.4 billion worldwide—$5.7 billion in the United States alone. By the late 1990s it was estimated that more than $1.5 trillion was being spent annually to market goods and services.

The role of advertising varies significantly from country to country. Table 1 lists the top nine countries in terms of projected total ad spending for 2000. Countries ranked at the top of the list are primarily wealthy industrialized nations. For the most part, the developing countries in Asia, Africa, and the Middle East appear to be light advertisers. However, economic development is not the sole predictor of advertising expenditures. Some relatively rich countries—for example, Austria—are not even on this list, whereas Brazil is. This observation suggests that other variables, such as culture, must be considered in attempting to understand the role of advertising in a particular country. The figures in the table do not reflect the relative costs of media time/space in each of the countries. Media costs in many developing countries tend to be rather low, and this factor must be taken into consideration when making comparisons.

About two-thirds of all media dollars spent around the world are used to market consumer products and services. The remainder is spent by firms promoting their goods and services to other businesses (i.e., business-to-business advertising). In developing markets, the ratios deviate from this norm. Countries in the Middle East, for example, see nearly a 50/50 split between consumer and business-to-business marketing expenditures. The United States accounts for more than one-third of the world's media spending. But on a per capita basis, Japan spends more to advertise consumer goods and services. Table 2 lists per capita media spending for the top-ranking and bottom-ranking countries. Ad spending

Table 2. Media Spending Per Capita for Top-Ranking and Bottom-Ranking Countries.

Rank	Country	Per Capita Media Spending (U.S. dollars)
1	Japan	$2,137
2	United States	1,861
3	France	1,845
4	Germany	1,593
5	Netherlands	1,517
6	Denmark	1,504
7	Belgium	1,357
8	United Kingdom	1,286
9	Hong Kong	1,180
10	Australia	1,166
. . .		
126	Tanzania	4.10
127	Vietnam	2.92
128	Nigeria	2.77
129	China	2.62
130	Laos	0.41

Source: Cassino, Kip, "A World of Advertising," *American Demographics* (November 1997).

per person ranges from a low of less than $1 in Laos to more than $2,100 per person in Japan, the most intensely advertised-to population. Although these two countries are geographically close, they could hardly be more different economically. Note that at nearly $6, daily media spending directed at the average Japanese resident is 14 times greater than the amount aimed at the average Laotian in an entire year.

Total advertising spending among the top-50 global marketers decreased to $52 billion during 2000 (down from $59 billion in 1997). Anglo-Dutch consumer goods giant Unilever invested the most money in advertising outside the United States—nearly $3 billion (plus another $698 million within the United States)—according to an *Advertising Age* report that tracks ad spending in 56 countries and ranks advertisers by non-U.S. spending to reflect global trends. Procter & Gamble Company is ranked a close second with $2.6 billion, and Nestlé ranked third with its comparatively small budget of $1.5 billion.

Agency Trends

The first U.S. ad agency to establish itself overseas was the J. Walter Thompson Company (JWT), which opened an office in London in 1899 to meet the needs of its client General Motors. By the early 1920s, both J. Walter Thompson and McCann-Erickson had large global networks with offices in Europe, India, and Latin America. Overall, however, U.S. agency movement to international soil was rather slow prior to 1960 and nearly always led by client expansion. One prominent exception was Doyle Dane Bern-

bach, which opened an office in Frankfurt, Germany, in 1961 to serve a German client it had acquired—Volkswagen.

A study of 15 large U.S. multinational agencies conducted by Arnold Weinstein revealed that in the years between 1915 and 1959, these agencies had opened or acquired only 50 overseas branch offices. Yet in the subsequent 12-year period, 210 overseas branch offices were opened or acquired—a fourfold increase. When firms began to expand to foreign markets, their advertising agencies were faced with the following options: (1) allow a local agency abroad to handle the account, (2) allow a U.S. agency with an established international network to service their client, or (3) open or acquire an overseas branch. Initially, when multinational clients were the exception rather than the rule, the second alternative was the most common practice. However, allowing another agency to handle a client's international business became risky, often resulting in the loss of both the domestic and international account.

The 1960s were characterized by rampant expansion abroad by U.S. advertising agencies. Agencies began to see many advantages to joining their clients in foreign markets; they could service their domestic clients as well as compete for the foreign accounts of other U.S.-based multinational firms and for the accounts of local foreign firms. Thus, as domestic advertising volume began to taper off, foreign markets looked increasingly appealing. In addition, there was the attraction of potentially higher profits. Overseas, salaries of ad agencies employees in the 1960s were as much as 70 percent lower than in the United States, while average agency profits were often twice those in the United States. Setting up offices overseas had the additional benefit of freeing U.S. agencies from a total dependency on the performance of the U.S. economy as a whole. For example, during the 1970 recession, domestic advertising agency billings declined 1 percent, while the foreign billings of multinational agencies increased 13 percent.

In contrast to the 1960s, the 1970s were a period of consolidation and retrenchment for many U.S. ad agencies. While the combined annual billings of multinational agencies continued to increase, many smaller agencies with a limited presence overseas were forced to withdraw from foreign markets. Many realized that to compete successfully, they had to maintain offices in almost all of the important countries of Europe, Latin America, and the Far East—a commitment that only the largest agencies were prepared to make. In 1970 *Advertising Age* listed 58 agencies that had international billings; by 1977 that number had dropped to 36.

In the 1980s the profile of the industry changed substantially. On New York City's Madison Avenue, foreign accents were increasingly heard. London-based Saatchi & Saatchi purchased three U.S. agencies in 1986: Dancer, Fitzgerald, Sample ; Backer & Spielvogel, Inc.; and Ted Bates Worldwide, Inc. In 1989 the British WPP Group brought two of U.S. advertising's most glamorous names—J. Walter Thompson and the Ogilvy Group—into its family via hostile takeovers. French agencies, too, looked to the United States. In 1988 the Publicis Group formed the first big French-U.S. alliance with Foote, Cone & Belding Communica-

Table 3. Top Advertisers by Media Spending outside the United States, 2000.

Rank	Advertiser (Headquarters)	Media Spending (U.S. dollars, millions)		
		Outside U.S.A.	U.S.A.	Worldwide
1	Unilever (London/Rotterdam)	$2,967	$698	$3,664
2	Procter & Gamble (Cincinnati, Ohio)	2,610	1,542	4,152
3	Nestlé (Vevey, Switzerland)	1,560	327	1,886
4	Toyota Motor Corporation (Toyota City, Japan)	1,345	790	2,135
5	Volkswagen (Wolfsburg, Germany)	1,290	424	1,714
6	Coca-Cola Corporation (Atlanta, Georgia)	1,176	403	1,579
7	Ford Motor Company (Dearborn, Michigan)	1,127	1,196	2,323
8	General Motors Corporation (Detroit, Michigan)	1,028	2,951	3,979
9	PSA Peugeot Citroën (Paris)	1,004	0	1,004
10	Fiat (Turin, Italy)	988	2.0	990
11	Renault (Paris)	914	0	914
12	L'Oréal (Paris)	913	494	1,407
13	Kao Corp. (Tokyo)	715	42.1	757
14	McDonald's Corporation (Oak Brook, Illinois)	694	710	1,404
15	Mars, Inc. (McLean, Virginia)	692	288	980
16	Vodafone Group (Newbury, U.K.)	673	41.8	715
17	Nissan Motor Corporation (Tokyo)	665	619	1,284
18	Henkel (Düsseldorf, Germany)	654	8.4	663
19	Ferrero (Perugia, Italy)	633	34.5	667
20	Sony Corporation (Tokyo)	556	659	1,215
21	Phillip Morris Companies (New York City)	541	1,770	2,311
22	Danone Group (Levallois-Perret, France)	539	54.5	594
23	France Telecom (Paris)	527	1.5	528
24	DaimlerChrysler (Auburn Hills, Michigan/Stuttgart)	424	1,686	2,111
25	Telefonica (Madrid)	419	43.6	462

Source: Ad Age Global, vol. 2, no. 3 (November 2001).

tions of Chicago, Illinois, a relationship later dissolved. In 1989 Della Femina, McNamee WCRS, Inc., became a subsidiary of Eurocom, France's top agency; in 1990 Paris-based BDDP bought 40 percent of Wells, Rich, Green, Inc.; and in 1994, the Publicis Group acquired Bloom FCA, with offices in New York City and Dallas, Texas. Two Japanese agencies, Dentsu (Japan's largest) and Hakuhodo, also opened offices in the United States in the mid 1990s.

The United States has lost its long-unchallenged grip on advertising at home and abroad. European, Japanese, Australian, and Brazilian agencies have expanded or merged operations with agencies worldwide to meet the needs of their clients. Many of the largest multinational agencies have regrouped into multimillion- and multibillion-dollar multiservice transnational agencies that perform market research and other services along with creating advertising. To compete with these huge agencies, smaller shops have set up independent agency networks called "indies." These proliferated in the 1980s and particularly in the 1990s as marketers entered relatively new markets in Asia and the Pacific and in Eastern Europe.

Independent networks are typically sustained by participating agencies through initiation fees and annual dues. Dues are generally determined by the level of influence and activity at the secre-

tariats that govern most organizations. These central authorities may provide member agencies discounts on market research, media buying, and high-tech equipment and offer e-mail and Internet access. "Indies" generally represent themselves as alternatives to the multinationals, less burdened by bureaucracies than the larger agencies and more available to clients. In 2000, Worldwide Partners, based in Aurora, Colorado, was the largest independent network, with collective billings in excess of $4 billion from its 145 member agencies.

Each spring *Advertising Age* publishes a special report on the top 500 U.S. advertising agencies. The report lists top agency groups or holding companies, top agency brands, and top agencies by country. Data elements for each agency are worldwide, and U.S. gross income, volume, employees, and offices change from the previous year. Agency groups, the parent organizations (those that own more than 50 percent of their own operations), are ranked by equity gross income. Agencies are also listed by "brand," the individual core agencies that make up the groups. Agency gross income was propelled to $32.57 billion worldwide, up 12.4 percent on billings of $295.28 billion among U.S. agencies, according to the April 2001 report. The U.S. portion grew even faster, at $18.94 billion, giving U.S.-based agencies their second-best growth year of the past decade.

Table 4. Top Agency Organizations and Brands, 2000.

Rank	Company (Headquarters)	Worldwide Gross Income (U.S. dollars, millions)
1	WPP Group (London)	$7,971
2	Omnicom Group (New York City)	6,986.2
3	Interpublic Group of Companies (New York City)	6,595.9
4	Dentsu (Tokyo)	3,089
5	Havas Advertising (Levallois-Perret, France)	2,757.3
6	Publicis Group (Paris)	2,479.1
7	Bcom3 Group (Chicago)	2,215.9
8	Grey Global Group (New York City)	1,863.2
9	True North Communications (Chicago)	1,539.1
10	Cordiant Communications Group (London)	1,254.8

Source: Ad Age Global Web site <www.adageglobal.com/cgi-bin/pages.pl?link=466>

Advertising Age also ranks the top ten global agency organizations and the top ten global agency brands (see Table 4). For 2000, the WPP Group was ranked the top world ad organization, and Dentsu (with headquarters in Tokyo) was ranked the world's top agency brand.

BARBARA MUELLER

See also color plate in this volume

Further Reading

Cassino, Kip, "A World of Advertising," *American Demographics* 19, no. 11 (November 1997)
Endicott, R. Craig, "New Markets Nurture Indie Agencies," *Advertising Age* (15 May 1995)
Endicott, R. Craig, "Agency Report," *Advertising Age* (27 April 1998)
Kahn, Jeremy, "The Fortune Global 5 Hundred," *Fortune* 138, no. 3 (August 1998)
Mueller, Barbara, *International Advertising: Communicating across Cultures,* Belmont, California: Wadsworth, 1996
Rothenberg, Randall, "Brits Buying Up the Ad Business," *New York Times Magazine* (2 July 1989)
Weinstein, Arnold K., "The International Expansion of U.S. Multinational Advertising Agencies," *MSU Business Topics* 22, no. 3 (Summer 1974)

Goodby, Berlin & Silverstein

(Goodby, Silverstein & Partners)

Founded by Jeff Goodby, Andy Berlin, and Rich Silverstein, 1983; acquired by Omnicom Group, 1992; developed the "Got milk?" campaign for California Milk Processor Board, 1994; awarded $200 million Hewlett-Packard account, 1999; named "U.S. Agency of the Year" by *Advertising Age,* 1989 and 2000.

Major Clients

Anheuser-Busch Companies
California Milk Processor Board
E*Trade
Frito-Lay, Inc.
Hewlett-Packard Company
SBC/Pacific Bell
TiVo

In the 1960s San Francisco, California, was best known for its flower children and counterculture ethic of peace and love. It was not long, however, before the "city by the bay" also became known as a hot, innovative advertising-agency town where Foote, Cone & Belding crafted head-turning Levi's spots; Hal Riney launched his own, in-demand shop; and a group of young people from the creative side of advertising banded together to form Goodby, Berlin & Silverstein, later renamed Goodby, Silverstein & Partners.

Jeff Goodby cofounded the agency in 1983 with Ogilvy & Mather colleagues Rich Silverstein and Andy Berlin. A Rhode Island native, Goodby was a Harvard University graduate who had worked as a political reporter in Boston, Massachusetts, before migrating to San Francisco with his California-born wife. He was unable to find an opening for a reporter on any of the city's papers but won a job as a copywriter at the J. Walter Thompson Company, where he worked for four years on the Chevron and Teledyne accounts. He joined Ogilvy & Mather (O&M) in 1979, where he met art director Rich Silverstein. The pair won a number of advertising prizes, including the Advertising Research Foundation's David Ogilvy Award for their work for the Oakland A's baseball team.

Silverstein grew up in New York City and attended the Parsons School of Design in Manhattan. He began his career as a graphic designer in San Francisco and was an art director at *Rolling Stone* magazine. Then he began a series of one-year stints at San Francisco agencies, including Bozell & Jacobs; McCann-Erickson; Foote, Cone & Belding; and O&M.

Goodby, Silverstein, and Andy Berlin, another award-winning copywriter from O&M, forged their creative partnership when they collaborated on a freelance job for Amazin' Software. They suggested renaming the company Electronic Arts and created the burgeoning company's packaging, advertising, and posters in their spare time.

One day Berlin showed Goodby and Silverstein a computer spreadsheet that purported to show the financial viability of starting their own agency. The trio launched Goodby, Berlin & Silverstein in 1983 with a single client: Electronic Arts. Goodby later described the partnership as a "turbocharger that's made the most of our innate abilities." He added, "We dare each other to take risks and attempt outlandish things and then offer the moral support that makes it all seem reasonable."

After landing the Oakland Invaders United States Football League team—the football league failed, but the agency's spots scored big —other accounts quickly followed. "It's amazing how much of new business is dumb luck," Goodby has said. William Randolph Hearst III was in the audience when Goodby gave a speech about the ad effort for the Invaders, and the publisher decided to hire the new agency for the *San Francisco Examiner*'s advertising.

With billings of about $800 million, Goodby, Silverstein & Partners has captured numerous national and international awards for its advertising and netted multiple "agency of the year" honors, including *Advertising Age*'s "U.S. Agency of the Year" for 1989 and 2000. "Good advertising achieves whatever objectives are established at the outset," Goodby has said. "Some campaigns do this through sheer weight and repetition. Others do it by speaking to the consumer in an intelligent manner, as an equal, opting for the highest common denominator rather than the lowest. We prefer the latter approach. . . ."

The agency's big break came when it won the $10 million Royal Viking Cruise Line account, almost all of it print advertising. It won American Isuzu Motors and helped launch the automaker's sport-utility vehicles (SUVs). The agency also devised the signature "Sega!" scream for the electronic games developer of the same name.

In 1992 the Omnicom Group acquired Goodby, Berlin & Silverstein. Berlin left San Francisco to manage a turnaround team at Omnicom's DDB Needham New York City flagship office. Then, with John Wren (who became Omnicom chief executive officer in 1996), he helped launch Focus, an Omnicom integrated marketing company in Dallas, Texas. Berlin also started a specialized automotive agency, Berlin Wright Cameron, in New York. By 2001 Berlin was chairman–chief executive officer of New York City–based Berlin Cameron & Partners, a general-market agency he opened in November 1997 with Ewen Cameron.

In 1994 the renamed Goodby, Silverstein & Partners developed what would become one of the industry's most recognizable and successful campaigns. "Got milk?" (not to be confused with the "milk mustache" campaign for the National Fluid Milk Processor Promotion Board created by Bozell & Jacobs) was created originally for the California Milk Processor Board, which later took the droll spots national. Goodby penned the "understated punchline" and served as creative director on the campaign with Silverstein.

In late 1996 the agency leveraged Hewlett-Packard Company's (H-P) reputation for engineering excellence and humanized its technology company with its first TV spots for H-P's imaging division. Goodby directed the humorous commercials for color printers and copiers, with the theme "Built by engineers. Used by normal people." When H-P decided to streamline internally and create a single corporate-wide brand, it awarded the $200 million account to Goodby, Silverstein & Partners, which went on to launch the "Invent" campaign for H-P.

The agency took on the E*Trade account in early 1999 and by April debuted a $150 million campaign that was bold, fresh, and irreverent; it marked the start of a new era in financial services advertising, and the campaign went on to win a Clio award.

Goodby, Silverstein & Partners also tallied its share of losses. In January 1998 the agency lost the Porsche Cars North America, Inc., account, which it had won five years earlier. The agency had created award-winning campaigns for the luxury automaker's redesigned 1995 Porsche 911 and its new-in-1997 Porsche Boxter. In 2000 Goodby, Silverstein & Partners also ended its advertising relationship with Nike (which had moved some of its business to the agency in 1997) when Nike decided to consolidate all brand-level advertising in the United States with Wieden & Kennedy, Portland, Oregon, its primary agency for 16 years. Goodby, Silverstein & Partners had crafted the award-winning skateboarding campaign as its first Nike work as well as a highly popular campaign for the U.S. women's soccer team.

In 1999 the agency reported one-third of its billings in technology-related accounts, a 50 percent increase over the previous year. With H-P, E*Trade, the eBay on-line auction site, Sirius Satellite Radio, and others, Goodby, Silverstein & Partners remained strong in technology-related business. In July 2000 the agency launched a national campaign laced with plenty of humor to build brand awareness and educate consumers about TiVo's personal TV service.

According to Silverstein, the agency does not specifically target technology- or Internet-related accounts for new business. "We're interested in making products important brands whether they're on the Web or not," he has said. "They just have to be products we want to use."

Goodby has said that the way to craft a brand is to differentiate it from the herd and do something no one has done before. "It's about establishing a look and talking to people, treating people as if they have some intelligence and not relying on repetition and dumbness to get things across."

The agency's maverick, often humorous creative approach has been backed up by close client contact and intensive research that has yielded results for advertisers and long-lasting relationships for Goodby, Silverstein & Partners. "Advertising is art and commerce combined," Silverstein has said. "You have to sell the product."

CHRISTINE BUNISH

Further Reading
Farrell, Greg, "Wacky Investment Spots Win Lots of Hearts,"
    USA Today (10 October 1999)
"Good, Good, Goodby!" <www.clioawards.com/
    html.wsu.goodby.htm>

Mergenhagen, Paula, "How 'Got Milk?' Got Sales," *Marketing
    Tools* (September 1996)
Saba, Jennifer, "Advertising Agency of the Year 2000:
    Goodby, Silverstein & Partners," *Marketing Computers*
    (April 2000)

Good Housekeeping Seal

Since January 1910 the Good Housekeeping Seal has been a visible symbol of *Good Housekeeping* magazine's Consumers' Policy as well as a valuable and sought-after tool for marketers, which attach the seal to their products and advertising to bolster consumer confidence in their products and services. The seal is an extension of the long-standing "public policy" concept that has been a hallmark of the magazine since its inception in 1885. The magazine, published by Hearst Corporation, established the Good Housekeeping Institute as a product evaluation laboratory that considers marketers' applications to use the seal. The institute is located at the magazine's headquarters in New York City.

The goals of the Good Housekeeping Institute are to provide consumer education and product evaluation. The institute has individual departments that study engineering, chemistry, food, food appliances, nutrition, beauty products, home care products, and textiles. It reviews all advertisements submitted to the magazine, and only those that it finds acceptable are published in *Good Housekeeping*. Advertisers then become eligible to earn the Good Housekeeping Seal. Only products that have been accepted for advertising in the magazine, through a review by the institute, can use the Good Housekeeping Seal.

The magazine strives to maintain a high level of taste and exercises strict standards for reviewing advertising before it is accepted for publication. It has a long-standing policy that prohibits the acceptance of ads for tobacco and alcohol products, for example. Advertisers whose products are found acceptable may use the Good Housekeeping Seal in their advertisements, on packaging, and in other promotions at no additional fee. The magazine is unique in offering this kind of service, in essence functioning as a third-party clearinghouse to determine the effectiveness of products and services. In most issues, the magazine publishes a complete list of the marketers that have earned the seal since its inception as well as a list of the advertisers in that particular issue.

Good Housekeeping stands behind its recommendations, offering a limited warranty to buyers or recipients of products that have earned its seal. If any product bearing the seal proves defective within two years of purchase, *Good Housekeeping* will replace the product or refund a consumer's money. Each issue of the magazine contains instructions to readers that explain the procedures *Good Housekeeping* has in place to facilitate replacements or refunds.

In the September 1997 issue, *Good Housekeeping* celebrated its continuing tradition of standing behind products advertised in the magazine.
Good Housekeeping © 2001.

Many products and services, however, are explicitly excluded from this warranty, including insurance; housing of any kind; automotive and camping vehicles; public transportation; travel facilities; catalogs and merchandise portfolios; items featured in "Shopping by Mail," a section near the end of the magazine; premiums; schools, hotels, summer camps, and similar facilities; and prescription drugs and medical devices, as well as products and services in institutional advertisements. While the magazine has several international editions, in Great Britain, Latin America, the Philippines, and Russia, the guarantees for the most part are valid only within the United States—the main exception being for products bearing the Good Housekeeping Seal that are produced in the United States but sold overseas.

Over time, the seal's design has changed, although it always has remained an oval. One recent redesign, in 1997, rendered the seal in white and dark blue, with a red star and the word *Promises* also in red. In 1975 the wording within the seal was changed to comply with the new federal warranty law known as the Magnuson-Moss Warranty legislation. This statute required the modification of the terms of all warranties and guarantees extended by manufacturers and retailers to consumers. The current wording at the top of the seal reads, "Limited Warranty to Consumers."

The value of the seal to marketers was confirmed in 1990 by a national survey conducted by advertising agency Warwick, Baker & Fiore. The poll examined consumer attitudes concerning a number of often-used advertising slogans, including the phrase, "has the Good Housekeeping Seal of Approval." Warwick, Baker found that 42 percent of the American public perceived the presence of the phrase as "extremely important" in making a decision to buy a product, second only to "low cholesterol."

A 1996–97 study by the research firm Siegel & Gale found that awareness of the Good Housekeeping Seal among U.S. consumers was higher than that of any other consumer symbol, rating, or endorsement, including such ratings as the U.S. Department of Agriculture's "USDA Choice" shield or the American Dental Association's "ADA Accepted" emblem. During the 1980s and 1990s, the market research firm Roper Starch Worldwide conducted several studies that consistently showed the seal also had a positive effect on consumer purchasing decisions and product perceptions, further illustrating its role in attracting advertisers to *Good Housekeeping* as well as its value as a tool for marketers in general.

ELIZABETH GOLDSMITH

Further Reading

Good Housekeeping: The Way We Were! The Way We Are! New York: Good Housekeeping Institute, 1990

Mott, Frank Luther, *A History of American Magazines*, vol. 5, Cambridge, Massachusetts: Harvard University Press, 1968

Gossage, Howard Luck 1917–1969

U.S. Advertising Copywriter

Opinions vary widely concerning Howard Luck Gossage's place in the world of advertising. To some, the "Socrates of San Francisco" was a voice of reason, advertising's greatest defender. To others, he was an unconventional critic, continually railing against problems he perceived within the industry. David Ogilvy called him "the most articulate rebel in the advertising business."

Gossage was born in Chicago, Illinois, in 1917 and grew up in New York City; Denver, Colorado; New Orleans, Louisiana; and Kansas City, Missouri. After graduating from the University of Kansas, he went on to serve as a naval aviator in World War II. By the age of 30, Gossage had landed a job as promotion manager for radio station KLX in San Francisco, California. He later moved to CBS, where he worked for a few years until he began graduate work in sociology at the University of Paris, France, and University of Geneva, Switzerland, with his tuition paid for under the GI bill.

In 1954 he joined San Francisco ad agency Brisacher, Wheeler & Staff and, after being with the company for a year, was named a vice president. Gossage found his first commercial success there with his "Win Yourself a Kangaroo" campaign for the little-known Qantas Airlines, under the headline, "Be the first kid on your block to own a kangaroo!"

In 1957 Gossage and two partners, Stan Freberg and J. Joseph Weiner, formed Weiner & Gossage, setting up shop in the original San Francisco Firehouse No. 1. It was then that Gossage began to break advertising's rules of the day, creating a softer approach that proved effective. He also brought humor to his advertising, a fresh tack that contrasted with the serious ads being used at the time. His success showed that advertising could be restrained, informative, and entertaining, yet still meet its objectives.

Gossage's ads generally contained long copy and informal artwork. It was his belief that copy was vital. "Nobody reads advertising," he said. "People read what interests them, and sometimes it's an ad." He also frequently employed contests or reply coupons, believing that the job of an ad is to engage the consumer in a dialogue with the advertiser. In fact, the majority of his work was what later came to be known as direct response advertising. His ad coupons could be sent to advertisers, and sometimes they were designed to send to government agencies to urge policy changes.

Gossage's philosophy on advertising included the belief that advertising should involve the audience; audience members should receive some reward for their involvement with the message, whether it be in the form of entertainment, samples or brochures, or information. He also posited that it is better to plan properly for a single well-placed, well-written ad than to bombard the consumer with many frequent ads: "You do not have to bruise an elephant with 100 BB guns to kill him. One shot in the right place will do." Gossage also believed that an advertiser is more likely to succeed if it narrows its objectives to the ones best suited for the form of communication being used. He viewed advertising's greatest function as the establishment of identity for the client. After that was settled, all advertising campaigns, marketing, and client association flowed from this sense of corporate identity.

Gossage's important campaigns and clients included a 1969 effort for Heileman Brewing Company's Rainier beer that featured a 1,000-mile walk from San Francisco to the Seattle (Washington) World's Fair by a retired 79-year-old postman. This campaign introduced what was to become a nationwide fad, Beethoven and Bach Rainier sweatshirts. The shirts were initially sold as a gag with the claim, "It just seemed a brewer's idea of culture." Although the beer did not sell well, the shirts did, earning Gossage's agency and sweatshirt marketer Eagle Shirts significant profits.

The agency's 1967 Great International Paper Airplane Competition for *Scientific American* magazine drew entries from around the world. The campaign helped to establish the magazine as a viable place for air and travel advertising and sparked a book, *The Great International Paper Airplane Book,* sales of which continued into the 21st century. The Fina Oil and Chemical Company campaign featured an improvement on the compressed air offered at service stations throughout the nation; Fina's air contained a pink additive that supposedly made it better. Gossage's headline for Land Rover, "At 60 miles an hour, the loudest noise in this new Land Rover comes from the roar of the engine," drew praise from David Ogilvy, whose understated 1958 headline for Rolls-Royce ("At 60 miles an hour the loudest noise in this new Rolls-Royce comes from the electric clock") was the object of parody. Whiskey Distillers of Ireland and Paul Masson were also among Gossage's clients.

Despite the success of these efforts, a campaign for Anguilla Island perhaps best exemplifies the type of advertising Gossage espoused, because it led to the island's independence from Britain. He also did several environmental ads for the Sierra Club and was associated with the campaign that saved the Grand Canyon from being flooded, which ran with the headline, "Should we also flood the Sistine Chapel so that tourists can get nearer the ceiling?"

Gossage's unusual style led to commercial and financial success, which freed him to focus on the issues and causes that interested him. Gossage and G. Mason Feigen, a business associate, spent thousands of dollars promoting Marshall McLuhan, the University of Toronto professor who won acclaim for his discus-

Howard Luck Gossage (at work on the 1967 *Scientific American* paper airplane contest account).

sion of the mass media. Gossage believed in the power of advocacy advertising, feeling that advertising, in promoting goods for sale, was not being used properly; its proper place, in his estimation, was to provide information and education concerning specific issues. He was a critic of the consumer culture that had by then overtaken the United States and felt that advertising was in large part to blame for this state of affairs. He thought that the way the advertisers had taken over the media was comparable to hot dog vendors taking over a football field—no one could any longer watch the game.

Advertising was too valuable, Gossage believed, to be wasted on commercial products. Instead, it should be used to promote social causes. He believed that public-service campaigns would eventually become the primary function of ad agencies and that "an agency is in fact a medium and ought to regard itself so. Perhaps this is the answer to advertising's search for identity."

In addition to his unconventional yet successful work, Gossage was known for his articulate criticism of advertising's abuses, lack of restraint, and disrespect for audiences' sensitivities. He believed that there was simply too much advertising, causing diminished effectiveness as audiences grew inured to the ads.

Gossage was particularly outspoken against the commission system for ad agencies, which, he asserted, provided incentive for exploitation. He worked for fees and made arrangements with his clients so that he would be compensated proportionately for the growth of their businesses as a result of his advertising. This stance led him to establish Kickback Corporation in 1967 as "an out and out placement agency," which returned a substantial portion of its commissions to clients.

Outdoor advertising was another area of perceived abuse. Gossage did not oppose it on aesthetic grounds; instead, he wrote, "Outdoor advertising is peddling a commodity it does not own and without the owner's permission: your field of vision." Such a stance gained him the derision and animosity of many in the industry. He wrote in his defense, "I like outdoor advertising. I just think it has no right to be outdoors."

Gossage blamed advertisers for the demise of newspapers and other periodicals, saying that it was advertisers, not readers, who disliked the publications. He thought that an index should be developed that showed how much such publications were worth based on how much readers would pay not to be deprived of the next issue.

When he learned he had leukemia, Gossage took steps to ensure the continuation of his agency, which by then had become known as Freeman & Gossage. He and his partner, Robert B. Freeman, formed the Shade Tree Corporation as an umbrella agency for the various activities and causes of the agency. Jerry Mander, who had written much of the agency's copy in the time leading up to Gossage's death, was brought on board to take the reins of the business. The agency was renamed Freeman, Mander & Gossage, Inc., in November 1968. It closed in 1971.

Gossage died on 9 July 1969. He left behind an unusual legacy of thought and practice in advertising. He was posthumously inducted into the Copywriters Hall of Fame on 26 March 1970.

BARBARA KNOLL

Biography
Born 13 August 1917; opened his own agency, Weiner & Gossage, in San Francisco, California, 1957; agency became Freeman & Gossage, 1963; agency renamed Freeman, Mander & Gossage, November 1968; died on 9 July 1969; posthumously inducted into Copywriters Hall of Fame, 1970; agency folded, 1971.

Selected Publications
Is There Any Hope for Advertising? 1986
The Book of Gossage, edited by Jeff Goodby, Stan Freberg, and Jay Conrad, 1995

Further Reading
"Advertisers Are Killing or Altering Media, Heedless of Public: Gossage," *Advertising Age* (28 January 1969)
"Gossage Blasts Outdoor as 'Invasion of Privacy'; 'Not Even Ad Medium,'" *Advertising Age* (27 January 1960)
Ogilvy, David, *Ogilvy on Advertising,* London: Pan, and New York: Crown, 1983

Government Regulation

Even though the law has favored sellers over buyers for much of history, regulators and would-be regulators have never been far behind in their attempts to limit or outlaw advertising. Over time, a multiplicity of legal issues, distinctions, and regulations have evolved around advertising, including the development of a commercial speech doctrine, the concept of misrepresentation through false and misleading claims, and various consumer-protection laws. But all can be traced to a maxim of laissez-faire capitalism first articulated during the Middle Ages.

Caveat Emptor

The Latin phrase *caveat emptor* (let the buyer beware) made its first appearance as a legal principle in England in 1534 in an incident involving the sale of a horse. The phrase is believed to have been coined by the Romans, who offered no remedy to buyers of defective goods (but who, in any case, conducted such limited trade that legal protection was unnecessary). Only as trade grew and prospered during the Middle Ages did the need to regulate it—and related practices such as advertising—develop. Writing in the 13th century, the theologian St. Thomas Aquinas outlined rules that made sellers responsible for defects and put buyers on notice that they must admit if they received more than they had purchased. Aquinas did reflect one apparently traditional adage in his guidelines: that sellers need not reveal obvious defects. In a time of simple commodities, however, obvious meant obvious.

At the height of the Middle Ages, it was in the best interests of craft guilds and market towns to support consumers to ensure good future business relations. The monopoly status of the guilds allowed them to establish strict standards of workmanship and honesty in the goods and services they provided. Violators could be fined or thrown out of the trade. Although these organizations existed independently of government, they operated with local public approval. When necessary, traders used their own court system based upon principles that came to be called the Law Merchant, which advocated the rule of mutual trust. With such strict regulations for formal trade in place, the principle of caveat emptor probably developed outside of the law, involving fly-by-night traders and producers. Anxious to demonstrate their superiority to existing political institutions such as the churches and guilds and prevailing common laws and practices, Reformation-era monarchs such as Henry VIII of England frequently crafted new governmental regulations from whatever they pleased. Caveat emptor emerged in England probably more as a demonstration of Henry's authority and out of a need to encourage greater trade (and profit to him) than as a reflection of any broader legal or societal need.

The earliest reference in English to spoken statements about a business transaction appeared in the common law in 1367. However, in *Chandler v. Lopus,* an English case from 1603, the King's Bench made a pronouncement on caveat emptor that was cited repeatedly in years to come for no apparent logical reason. In its decision, the court distinguished between statements made and statements warranted during the course of a business transaction. The former were considered a normal part of business and were therefore not actionable even if they proved to be false. A buyer had cause for misrepresentation only when a seller warranted or promised a product or service he did not deliver or perform. In retrospect, *Chandler* was largely an accident of history, for there were many other, contrary rulings that judges could have used as precedent. However *Chandler* became the common law because courts wanted it to be, for political and personal reasons. Caveat emptor became commonplace in Great Britain and other parts of Europe in the 17th century as printed advertising became more widespread, and the principle served as an inspiration for English libertarian philosophers such as John Locke and Adam Smith.

Early Legal Precedents

An English jurist named Lord Holt attempted to reinterpret *Chandler* in a 1689 case, but his efforts only further muddied the issue of when an offhand claim represented a legal promise. Holt held in *Crosse v. Gardner* that a bare statement of ownership was a warranty of legal title. A century later, in an English case called

Pasley v. *Freeman,* another English judge cited *Crosse,* but only when the seller had intended the statement to be a warranty. The latter legal thought never appeared in the original *Crosse* decision. Nevertheless, *Pasley* emerged as a leading precedent in the law of misrepresentation.

The error was incorporated into the first American case involving advertising, *Seixas and Seixas v. Woods,* which was decided by the highest court of New York State in 1804. A claim about the species of wood in an advertisement for lumber was ruled to not amount to a warranty. Early in its history New York was the pacesetter for American jurisprudence, and a surprising number of its cases came to serve as precedents for other state courts in the 19th century. *Seixas* became common law in the country, and it was cited in the quintessential U.S. Supreme Court statement on caveat emptor, the 1871 *Barnard v. Kellogg,* which held that "no principle of the common law has been better established, or more often affirmed . . . [than] the maxim of caveat emptor." Interestingly, caveat emptor was allowed to exist only within the spheres of business and trade. A claim that interpersonal relations should be dictated by the same doctrine as expressed in *Barnard* was rejected by the Massachusetts high court in 1885.

The earliest grievance addressed by government regulation of advertising, misrepresentation, or the knowing false statement by either seller or buyer, dates to before *Chandler v. Lopus,* which held that open fraud had to be proved by a buyer. The 1663 English common law case *Ekins v. Tresham* found that there were certain facts in a transaction that sellers had to know, such as legal ownership, but subsequent courts were not moved to change the prevailing standard. In *Seixas and Seixas v. Woods,* the New York State high court held that the difficult open fraud standard "must be proved" in business transactions. This reasoning began to change in Great Britain in the 1801 *Haycroft v. Creasey* and was codified in the 1843 *Taylor v. Ashton,* which held that fraudulent behavior included making a claim insincerely, knowing that it was not true, or making it while knowing it to be false. At about this time British jurists also began distinguishing between fraudulent and negligent misrepresentation, the latter involving statements made by speakers who represented themselves as experts as opposed to a layperson without specific knowledge. In both kinds of misrepresentation, American courts largely observed English precedents, since Great Britain had more sophisticated business and advertising.

The introduction of "patent" medicines inspired the creation of the first U.S. law aimed at misrepresentation and led to the creation of the Federal Trade Commission (FTC). These products, named for the permission or patent granted by the king, first appeared in Great Britain in the 18th century and spread across the Atlantic Ocean over the next century. Although advertising for patent medicines remained localized up to the time of the Civil War, claims to cure heart attacks, venereal diseases, and even cancer were so outrageous that the American Medical Association was organized in 1848 in part to limit them. With the rise of N.W. Ayer and other early advertising agencies, patent medicines began to be advertised nationally and quickly became the mainstay of most agencies' profits. In 1890, 25 percent of all newspaper

SURGEON GENERAL'S WARNING: Smoking Causes Lung Cancer, Heart Disease, Emphysema, And May Complicate Pregnancy.

In the United States all cigarette advertising must include a warning from the Surgeon General about the health risks of tobacco use.

advertising in the typical Midwestern city of Middletown, Indiana, was for patent medicines, far more than any other type of product.

Their exaggerated claims and harmful ingredients—including such substances as petroleum distillates, heavy metals, and narcotics—scandalized publishers, but few felt they could afford to turn away patent medicine advertising dollars until the *Ladies' Home Journal* banned all such ads in 1892. The *Journal's* publisher, Edward W. Bok, launched a crusade against the industry in a series of muckraking articles that appeared between 1904 and 1906. Other periodicals and newspapers joined the battle, and Congress approved the Pure Food and Drug Act in 1906. The law did not ban patent medicines—that would not occur for another 32 years—but it did require their manufacturers to list the ingredients on each bottle and substantiate any claims their advertising made of curative power.

The Federal Trade Commission

The *Ladies' Home Journal* and its companion publication, the *Saturday Evening Post,* adopted a comprehensive advertising code in 1910 in an effort to weed out deceptive or fraudulent advertising. That code served as a prototype for a model statute advocated by the advertising trade publication *Printers' Ink* the following year. In turn, the *Printers' Ink* model was adopted by most American states, especially in its definitions of "untrue, deceptive, or misleading" advertising. The model statute also inspired Congress to pass the Federal Trade Commission Act in 1914. The original legislation empowered the FTC to regulate "unfair methods of competition in commerce." One of the nation's largest advertisers complained that such phrasing was ambiguous, but the 7th U.S. Court of Appeals ruled in the 1919 *Sears, Roebuck v. FTC* that Congress had made the agency's charge vague on purpose to leave judgments to its five commissioners. The U.S. Supreme Court overturned part of that interpretation in the 1920 case of *FTC v. Gratz,* but writing for the minority, Justice Louis Brandeis reiterated that Congress had intended such determinations to be the commission's right, and it was Brandeis's dictum that has prevailed.

During the hectic 1920s, the FTC struggled with its role as advertising regulator and did not hit its stride until *FTC v. Algoma.* In that 1934 case, the U.S. Supreme Court noted that advertisers were "not relieved by innocence of motive from a duty to conform." That was interpreted to mean that the FTC could not put advertisers out of business, as the original *Printers' Ink* statute had recommended, but it could stop misrepresentations in advertising simply if they appeared fraudulent or misleading. Intent did not matter. In the Wheeler-Lea Amendments of 1938, Congress strengthened the FTC's purview, giving the agency authority over "any false advertisement" for food, drugs, medical devices, or cosmetics. In *Moretrench v. FTC,* the 2nd U.S. Circuit Court ruled that the FTC's finding of unlawful misrepresentation in an ad was appropriate even though the statements apparently were made in good faith. That doctrine was reiterated in *DDD Corp. v. FTC* in 1942, in which the courts ruled that the use of the word "remedy" for a skin cream implied cure rather than relief.

Deceptive Advertising

The U.S. Supreme Court, which had upheld the FTC's creation in 1920, put its stamp of approval upon the agency's efforts against misleading advertisements again in the 1965 *FTC v. Colgate-Palmolive.* That case dealt with a television commercial for Rapid Shave, in which what purported to be a piece of "tough, dry sandpaper" was shaved by a razor. However, the commercial's creators used a piece of Plexiglas sprinkled with loose sand because real sandpaper looked smooth on grainy black and white television. "Apply . . . soak . . . and off in a stroke," intoned an announcer as the mock-up "sandpaper" came clean. Some viewers who tried unsuccessfully to repeat the experiment at home with real sandpaper complained to the FTC, and the agency responded by banning all mock-ups unless they were disclosed. In its decision, the Supreme Court claimed the Plexiglas demonstration was materially deceptive because it was used as "actual proof of an advertising claim." The court did allow mock-ups to be used if they were not employed falsely to prove a product claim, a distinction the public did not readily discern. When television personality Ed McMahon did a live commercial in 1966 for an ice cream topping that was poured onto vegetable spread made to look like ice cream (real ice cream melted too quickly under hot TV lights), *Tonight Show* host Johnny Carson complained, "There ought to be a certain amount of honesty." The FTC apparently came to agree. In 1973 it showed how far it would go in stopping what it considered misrepresentations when it made I.T.T. Continental Baking Company, the maker of Wonder Bread, stop advertising that it could help children grow "12 different ways," a claim the FTC said was true of all similar types of bread. In another case, ad agency Kastor, Hilton, Chesley, Clifford & Atherton argued in 1964 that it was not liable for placing ads it knew to be misleading for Regimen weight-loss pills because the agency did not create the ads. The agency changed its plea when state law specifically barred such a defense.

The FTC has a variety of legal tools to enforce its decisions. It publishes industry guides, which provide interpretations and general statements of policy. In any particular case it may issue an advisory opinion, which, if obeyed, protects an advertiser from being sued. If an advertiser fails to comply with the FTC's warnings, the agency can halt the ads through consent decrees, agreements in which a party voluntarily discontinues an objectionable advertising practice, or with a cease-and-desist order, which carries fines of up to $10,000 per day. If the public health is at risk, the FTC may issue an injunction. In cases involving cease-and-desist orders and injunctions, the FTC must identify a "specific and substantial" interest and follow a specific administrative procedure that gives the advertisers several opportunities to appeal. Trivial deceptions, which might be stopped by a consent decree, may not be serious enough for further agency action. More than 90 percent of FTC cases are resolved with consent decrees, and most cases originate with a citizen or competitor contacting the FTC in Washington, D.C., or at one of the several regional FTC bureaus.

Beyond halting deceptive ads, the FTC can also order alterations to ads, such as adding an affirmative disclosure (i.e., stating facts necessary to keep ads from being deceptive) or a corrective statement, to counteract a long-term, misleading advertising campaign. The Warner-Lambert Company, for example, was required to make statements in its advertising to correct a long-running campaign claiming that Listerine mouthwash could help prevent colds. The company was ordered in 1974 to include in its advertising the line that Listerine "will not help prevent colds or sore throats." Oddly, the ads had the unanticipated reverse effect of increasing mouthwash sales, as consumers strained to see or read the required correction notice.

A 1998 study of 66,000 U.S. advertisements found that ads in the period from 1971 to 1981—a time of strict FTC advertising regulation—contained fewer objective information claims than in the subsequent, less-stringent period from 1982 to 1992. The implication was that strict regulations reduced the amount of information contained in ads. At the same time, a 1994 study of six decades of advertising research revealed that 70 percent of American consumers continued to believe that advertising was often untruthful, that it sought to persuade people to buy things they did not want, and that it should be strictly regulated.

Unfair Practices

The FTC remained the model for the government regulation of advertising at the turn of the 21st century, working in tandem with other federal and state agencies. In addition to monitoring commerce for monopolistic and anticompetitive activities, it refined its purview to include a variety of unfair advertising activities. Unfairness in advertising is defined as any practice that "causes or is likely to cause substantial injury to consumers which is not reasonably avoidable by consumers themselves." A company is more likely to be unfair in the way it treats its customers than in its advertising, but certain acts involving health and safety will attract agency scrutiny. In one case, the FTC faulted a razor manufacturer for distributing free blade samples in newspapers, creating concern for small children. In 1994, the FTC closed a lengthy investigation into the unfairness of Joe Camel, a cartoon character used in advertising by the R.J. Reynolds Tobacco Company. A minority of commissioners charged that the ads inspired impressionable children and adolescents to smoke, a claim that could not be proven scientifically. The company eventually abandoned the ads as a result of a spate of litigation orchestrated by 40 states.

Deceptive advertising must possess a "tendency" or "capacity" to mislead a consumer or must be "likely" to mislead. Statements in question must be material to an advertisement and likely to affect a purchasing decision. Incidental deceptions are not a serious concern unless they contribute to an overall impression of falsity according to the FTC. Falsehoods are classified either as express (i.e., determined from the plain meaning of the words) or implied (i.e., a false meaning attributed to the words by the consumer even though the ad's claims are, on face, true).

The FTC recognizes more than a dozen varieties of implied falsehoods, including a reasonable basis implication, which requires advertisers to support substantive claims with scientific or other appropriate evidence; a demonstration implication, such as in the Rapid Shave case; and an omitted qualification implication, involving pertinent facts that are ignored. Significance implication (stating insignificant facts to create a false impression) can also be a form of implied deception, as are puffery implications (which go beyond product hyperbole to imply material assertions of superiority) and expertise and endorsement implications (such as when an expert endorser is really not an expert or when a celebrity falsely claims to use a product). Although advertisers no longer have to say that a celebrity is being paid for an endorsement, they must reveal if actors are being used to portray ordinary consumers, especially in infomercials, program-length television commercials.

As in other aspects of law, the deception must be apparent to a "reasonable" person. No reasonable person, for example, would believe that all of the passengers on an airplane would faint if one passenger took off his shoes, the premise of an ad for Dr. Scholl's foot deodorant. Some advertising is deceptive per se, so apparent that anyone can tell, but the FTC usually depends upon experts and public opinion research to gauge deceptiveness. Exceptions are made for children, the aged, the ill, and even otherwise healthy adults who might be especially vulnerable (e.g., obese

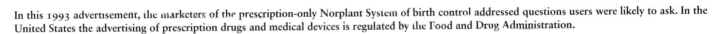

In this 1993 advertisement, the marketers of the prescription-only Norplant System of birth control addressed questions users were likely to ask. In the United States the advertising of prescription drugs and medical devices is regulated by the Food and Drug Administration.

individuals, who may be particularly susceptible to misleading weight-loss ads). Even though Congress banned tobacco advertising on television in 1971, tobacco companies have since agreed to stop placing advertising signs behind scoreboards and in other prominent locations at sporting events because children may be viewing a broadcast. The FTC halted the use of logos and signs for smokeless tobacco products at tractor and truck pulling events for the same reason. The FTC also took action against alcohol advertising directed toward children and teens.

Other Regulatory Agencies

In addition to the FTC, other federal and state agencies oversee certain types of advertising in the United States. The Securities and Exchange Commission regulates advertising of securities, including first-time stock offers. The Food and Drug Administration (FDA) regulates advertising for prescription drugs. Although the FTC is responsible for the advertising of over-the-counter drugs, cosmetics, and foodstuffs included in its 1906 enabling legislation, the FDA retains the jurisdiction over the labeling of these products. In the 1990s the FDA was moving toward regulation of

tobacco as a drug, an effort not entirely supported by the courts. In *Cipollone* v. *Liggett Group,* the Supreme Court ruled in 1992 that federal law did not bar smokers from suing cigarette companies for misleading advertising.

The Department of Housing and Urban Development monitors discriminatory practices in advertising related to the sale and rental of housing. The Civil Rights Act of 1964 forbids employment notices that appear to discriminate by race or sex and gives those harmed by such advertising the right to file civil suits seeking monetary damages. In *Metromedia* v. *City of San Diego* (1981), the U.S. Supreme Court held that some restrictions on outdoor advertising, such as contained in the Federal Highway and Highway Beautification Acts, are constitutional. Advertising involving alcoholic beverages has been the subject of extensive federal and state regulations, especially through the Bureau of Alcohol, Tobacco, and Firearms (BATF). For example, the BATF requires all alcoholic beverage advertising to contain certain kinds of information, including the company that produced the product, the nature of the beverage, and government warnings about the effects of consumption. In *Adolph Coors* v. *Bentsen,* the U.S. Supreme Court in 1995 invalidated restrictions on statements about the alcoholic content of malt beverage labels; those restrictions had been based on fears that such advertising would lead to a war over alcohol content claims among brewers. In 1994 a federal district court held in *Anheuser-Busch* v. *Baltimore* that the regulation of the outdoor advertising of alcoholic beverages was constitutional based on the assumption that there is a direct link between advertising and potential consumption by minors.

Federal laws govern the representation in advertising of a variety of objects and images—from U.S. currency to icons such as Smokey Bear and Woodsy Owl. State laws often deal with unfair competition, such as the "passing off" of one product as another through similarities in design or packaging. All but two U.S. states have regulations on the advertising of alcoholic beverages.

Regulation around the World

The regulation of unfair and deceptive advertising took on different guises around the globe at the turn of the 21st century. Canada's nongovernmental advertising watchdog, Advertising Standards Canada (ASC), was receiving more complaints involving taste and public decency than misleading claims. Meanwhile, Canada's Supreme Court overturned a ban on tobacco advertising in 1995. With the turnover of Hong Kong—and its free-market economy—to the People's Republic of China, the Chinese government struggled to regulate advertising in its burgeoning quasi-capitalistic economy. It prohibited tobacco advertising in both electronic and print media and required that all advertising be examined by "relevant authorities" prior to publication or broadcast. A commercial for instant noodles was banned because it showed an emperor enjoying the product. The regulators argued that the advertiser could not prove that the product was fit for an emperor because there were no more emperors. Other Asian countries struggled with a maze of government restrictions and unwritten laws, many involving tobacco and alcohol, in an effort to protect the region's diverse cultures and religions. In Australia and Japan regulatory laws were as complicated as those of the United States, while in Vietnam the strongly Western-influenced advertising industry was heavily regulated because consumers were deemed less sophisticated than in the United States.

The formation of the European Community (EC) led to efforts to coordinate and harmonize advertising regulations across the European continent and, indirectly, around the world. Many of the EC regulations were patterned after the U.S. Federal Trade Commission and the 1946 Lanham acts, which regulated trade and service marks. Nonetheless, local regulations persisted: Greece banned ads for toys, while Sweden prohibited all advertisement aimed at children, and Great Britain and Denmark limited who could sponsor sports broadcasts. France was notorious for a 1993 regulation called the Evin Law (*Loi Evin*). This statute, prompted by statistical evidence that tobacco and alcohol accounted for 20 percent of all deaths in France, restricted the advertising of wine, spirits, and tobacco. Such ads were outlawed in movie theaters, limited on radio and television, and restricted or banned on billboards and other outdoor venues. Also in 1993 France introduced the Sapin Law (*Loi Sapin*), which prohibited

the "undisclosed discounting" of ad space and airtime by advertising agencies unless they accounted for the true amount of the discount and the real value of the deal to clients. According to their critics, these laws resulted in a circulation decline among business publications and put undue constraints on the newspaper and periodical industries; they also spawned litigation from companies such as the U.S. brewer Anheuser-Busch.

Free Speech

Although misrepresentation has long been a concern of regulators, the protection of an advertiser's right of free speech is a much newer aspect in the law. Most experts assume that the authors of the U.S. Bill of Rights did not consider commercial speech, which includes advertising along with other forms of "lesser protected" speech, as being deserving of protection as individual political speech. The U.S. Supreme Court limited the First Amendment in 1833 when it held that the federal Bill of Rights did not apply to the states, a decision that was reversed in name if not in practice with the ratification of the 14th Amendment in 1868. But the Supreme Court did not make reference to commercial speech until 1939, decades after the introduction of mass media print and broadcast advertising, and it ruled three years later in *Valentine* v. *Chrestensen* that "purely commercial advertising" was not protected by the First Amendment. That remained the court's position until a case involving a state ban of a display advertisement for abortion services, *Bigelow* v. *Virginia,* which reached the court in 1975, two years after the individual privacy case *Roe* v. *Wade.* Virginia's ban on abortion advertising was a none-too-subtle attempt to limit a woman's constitutional right to seek an abortion and a repudiation of *Roe.* In *Bigelow,* the court ruled that the abortion ad went beyond a simple commercial transaction to offer "factual material of clear public interest." It stopped short of recognizing all commercial speech, but it did find that "advertising is not thereby stripped of all First Amendment protection."

The breakthrough in commercial speech protection occurred in the 1978 *First National Bank of Boston* v. *Bellotti.* The case involved paid political (rather than purely commercial) advertising by a for-profit corporation. In an effort to oppose a proposed graduated personal income tax, a Boston bank sought to purchase print and broadcast advertising opposing the tax. Massachusetts had a statute prohibiting banks and most other corporations from spending money to influence an election, and the state's attorney general threatened to prosecute the bank if the advertising appeared. The U.S. Supreme Court rejected arguments that allowing corporations to become involved in elections would overwhelm the free marketplace of ideas or drown out individual voices. Instead, the court argued that the statute "abridges expression that the First Amendment was meant to protect." After nearly 200 years, the original intent of the First Amendment by most accounts was reinterpreted.

The limits of commercial speech were defined in the 1980 *Central Hudson Gas & Electric Corporation* v. *Public Service Commission,* a case involving advertising to promote the use of

THE SOFT DRINK FOR DRY SKIN
Almay Deep Mist Moisture Treatments.
It's the pure thing—free of known irritants, of course.

Give dry skin what it really needs to feel refreshed and good—the purest *all-day moisturizing.* Unscented Deep Mist Moisture Cream and Deep Mist Moisture Lotion are specially formulated to care for your kind of skin—to fight dryness steadily, to keep skin feeling supple and smooth. Either way is the right way for you to start a makeup and keep it glowing all day long. Slipped on bare skin, only the results are visible. Deep Mist Moisture Cream: Reassuringly rich, yet beautifully light for daywear. Deep Mist Moisture Lotion: A delicate cloud of creamy liquid to give your skin the most softening, tender care. From the famous Almay Deep Mist day and night collection of cleansers, toners, night cream, eye cream, facial mask and body care. Almay—hypoallergenic, free of known cosmetic irritants. (If your skin's at all sensitive to the world, you wouldn't want to give it anything but the *pure* thing, would you?)

ALMAY
WORLD'S LEADING AUTHORITY IN HYPO-ALLERGENIC SKIN CARE.

INGREDIENT DISCLOSURE: The following ingredient disclosure is your proof of our purity. The products have been dermatologically tested, and are free of known irritants.
DEEP MIST MOISTURE CREAM: Water, mineral oil, propylene glycol, cetyl alcohol, stearyl alcohol, PEG-30 stearate, methyl paraben, propyl paraben, FD&C Red No. 2.

DEEP MIST MOISTURE LOTION: Water, mineral oil, sorbital, triethanolamine stearate, stearyl alcohol, magnesium aluminum silicate, methyl paraben, cellulose gum, propyl paraben, certified color.

At the bottom of this 1975 ad for Almay Deep Mist Moisture Treatments, the company listed the products' ingredients. This action demonstrated that the marketer was in compliance with government regulations that advertisements not mislead consumers.

electricity. In its decision, the court held that advertising promoting illegal products or activities was not protected nor was advertising that lied or was misleading. For government regulators, there must be a substantial reason for wanting to limit such speech, such as the public interest, and the regulations must advance that interest and go no further. Commercial speech remained different and had fewer protections than other forms of speech, but efforts by the New York State Public Commission to halt all methods of promoting electricity use by a utility were unconstitutional. The U.S. Supreme Court further refined its distinctions of commercial speech in *Posadas de Puerto Rico Associates* v. *Tourism Company of Puerto Rico* (1986), upholding a Puerto Rican law limiting the advertising of gambling. The court observed that the First Amendment did not prohibit a total ban of speech about a legal product or service that was not false, illegal, or deceptive, although lower courts subsequently demanded more proof than was given in *Posadas*. In *Cincinnati* v. *Discovery Network* (1992), the Supreme Court overturned a city ordinance banning advertising news racks on city streets. In *U.S.* v. *Edge Broadcasting* (1993), the Supreme Court upheld a federal regulation banning the broadcast of lottery ads in states that do not have a lottery. In all three cases, the court used and furthered the commercial speech standards established in the *Central Hudson* case. Legislative efforts by the federal and state governments to ban or limit the participation of corporations and labor unions in election campaigns set the stage for yet another showdown over how far government can regulate commercial speech at the turn of the 21st century. And a settlement between the tobacco companies of America and 40 states limited the types of advertising those companies could do.

Consumer Protection

Consumer protection is another, newer aspect of the government regulation of advertising. The consumer's perspective on caveat emptor was first articulated in the United States in the 1816 *Bradford* v. *Manly*. The high court of Massachusetts held that "a sale by sample is tantamount to an express warranty." The decision articulated a question overlooked in the 1603 English common law case of *Chandler* v. *Lopus*: Did consumers find it embarrassing to demand a warranty from sellers because it implied dishonesty in the transaction? In the *Bradford* decision, the court reasoned that most buyers would take a sample itself as an express warranty rather than risk jeopardizing an entire sale. The court also held that *Chandler* "would not now be received as law in England" or in the United States, an explicit rejection of the 1804 *Seixas and Seixas* v. *Woods*. New York State finally reversed *Seixas* in the 1872 *Hawkins* v. *Pemberton,* which ruled that a seller "is responsible for the language he uses, and cannot escape liability by claiming that he did not intend to convey the impression which his language was calculated to produce." *Hawkins* became the model for the drafting of the Sale of Goods Act in Great Britain in 1894 and the Uniform Sales Act and the Uniform Commercial Code in the United States in the 20th century, all designed to protect consumers' interests.

Upton Sinclair's 1906 novel *The Jungle* told a chilling tale of adulterated food sold to American consumers, but the original Federal Trade Commission Act of 1914 gave the agency authority over only unfair methods of competition and unfair or deceptive acts or practices affecting commerce. It was not until the Wheeler-Lee Amendments of 1938 that the FTC's scope was broadened to provide protection for consumers as well as competitors. The latter changes were spearheaded by Consumers Union, a politically liberal nonprofit organization established in 1936 to provide consumers with information and advice on goods, services, health, and personal finance.

Consumer awareness increased during the 1950s and 1960s, especially in the United States, as an outcome of the broadening role of women in society and commerce and the efforts of a new generation of crusaders, chief among them Ralph Nader. His career as an activist was launched with the publication in 1965 of *Unsafe at Any Speed,* a book that chronicled the safety hazards of the Chevrolet Corvair and provided the primary impetus for the National Traffic and Motor Vehicle Safety Act of 1966. Nader contributed to the enactment of the Wholesome Meat Act in 1967 and became involved in other consumer issues involving corporate ethics and human safety. During the 1970s inflation resulted in increased consumer awareness as the public became concerned about the cost and quality of goods and services.

To respond to changing consumer expectations, the FTC stepped up its regulatory efforts during the 1970s. At Nader's instigation, the agency ruled against I.T.T. Continental Baking Company in 1973 for visually implying that children who ate Wonder Bread grew more quickly than children who did not. It vigorously pursued other advertisers, Firestone, for example, which used white-jacked technicians in a TV tire commercial to create a false implication of scientific validity as well. Government-sponsored consumer advocates, either independent or operating within an existing state agency such as an attorney general's office, began advocating and litigating for consumer rights. Most consumer activism centered upon four concepts of the marketplace: ensuring products whose quality was consistent with their prices and claims; protecting against unsafe goods; providing truthful, adequate information about goods and services; and ensuring choice among a variety of products. New legislation required warranties to be written clearly and gave consumers "implied warranties"—unwritten guarantees that products were suited to the purposes for which they were sold. Standards authorities were created or strengthened to provide for pure, wholesome food and safety of products such as electrical goods and household items. New laws required that product labels list contents and provide the manufacturer's name and address. Other regulations required labels to show the nutritional content of foods and to display product freshness dates. Consumer activism was effective in the dismantling of telephone company and other monopolies, stemming the growth of the nuclear energy industry, and informing people of their legal rights in general.

Consumer groups proliferated around the world toward the end of the 20th century. In Great Britain, the Consumer Association tested goods, investigated services, and published the results.

In Australia, consumer affairs agencies operated in the states and territories. In most developing nations, however, consumer advocacy was either nonexistent or confined to urban areas.

In spite of the considerable effectiveness of consumer advocacy, the competition between advertisers and regulators is not likely to end soon. Transnational communication media such as the Internet, with its ability to advertise products globally, beyond the reaches of any single government regulator, will continue to test legal and ethical limits. Given technological advances and ongoing concerns about existing regulations, advertising scholar Ivan L. Preston has called for the reinvention of advertising regulation, based on what he calls a "reliance rule." Regulators should require advertisers to advocate that consumers make buying decisions on the basis of ad claims alone, without reliance on governmental or other external fact checkers. Such a practice, according to Preston, would reduce or eliminate much misleading, false, or confusing advertising. Regardless, as one advertising executive has said, "You can expect advertising to tell the truth and nothing but the truth, but you must not expect it to tell the whole truth." And as long as this philosophy prevails, government regulators of advertising will continue to be needed.

RICHARD JUNGER

Further Reading

Abernethy, Avery M., and George R. Franke, "FTC Regulatory Activity and the Information Content of Advertising," *Journal of Public Policy and Marketing* 17, no. 2 (Fall 1998)

Calfee, John E., *Fear of Persuasion: A New Perspective on Advertising and Regulation,* Washington, D.C.: American Enterprise Institute for Public Policy Research, 1997

Calfee, John E., and Debra Jones Ringold, "The 70% Majority: Enduring Consumer Beliefs about Advertising," *Journal of Public Policy and Marketing* 13, no. 2 (Fall 1994)

Gartner, Michael G., *Advertising and the First Amendment,* New York: Priority, 1989

Hovenkamp, Herbert, *Enterprise and American Law, 1836–1937,* Cambridge, Massachusetts: Harvard University Press, 1991

Mayer, Robert N., *The Consumer Movement: Guardians of the Marketplace,* Boston: Twayne, 1989

Mazis, Michael B., "Marketing and Public Policy: Prospects for the Future," *Journal of Public Policy and Marketing* 16, no. 4 (Spring 1997)

Middleton, Kent, Bill F. Chamberlin, *The Law of Public Communication,* White Plains, New York: Longman, 1988; 5th edition, by Middleton, Chamberlin, and Robert Trager, New York: Longman, 1999

Moore, Roy L., Ronald T. Farrar, and Erik Collins, *Advertising and Public Relations Law,* Mahwah, New Jersey: Erlbaum, 1998

Petty, Ross D., *The Impact of Advertising Law on Business and Public Policy,* Westport, Connecticut, and London: Quorum, 1992

Preston, Ivan L., *The Tangled Web They Weave: Truth, Falsity, and Advertisers,* Madison: University of Wisconsin Press, 1994

Grant Advertising, Inc.

Founded by Will C. Grant, 1935; purchased Abbott Kimball Company, 1958; purchased Chambers, Wiswell, Shattuck, Clifford & McMillan, 1960; acquired L.B. Singleton, 1963; announced public stock offering for international operations, 1964; acquired by Comcore Communications, 1972; sold to U.S. group led by J. Richard Harris, renamed Harris-Grant, 1974; ceased operation, 1975.

Major Clients
China Airlines
Chrysler Corporation
Dr Pepper Company
Ecko Products Company (Ecko S.A.)
General Foods Corporation
Mars, Inc.
Mobil Oil
Ryder System, Inc.
Wm. Wrigley Jr. Company

Founded in 1935 in Chicago, Illinois, by Will C. Grant, Grant Advertising, Inc., quickly grew into a worldwide network, opening its 25th overseas office, in Bangkok, Thailand, just 21 years later. To foster individual advertising philosophies for each country, corporate policy stated that no more than 25 percent of advertising handled by an overseas office could be from the United States or from other outside countries. By 1959 Grant had 42 offices worldwide, further expanding what it claimed in 1952 to be the largest network of wholly owned advertising-agency offices. In 1963 Grant established a foothold in Kenya, just before that East African country gained independence from Britain.

A fervent opponent of communism, Grant spoke frequently to industry trade groups about the value of advertising as a weapon, saying that exposure to American products would transform the lives of those living in developing nations and increase wealth. He was also convinced of the importance of radio and television to advertisers.

The agency got off to a fast start, signing the Mars, Inc., candy company as one of its first accounts. Within just a few years, it had added Old Dutch Cleanser, J.A. Folger & Company, Bendix Aviation Corporation, Florists' Telegraph Delivery Association, and American Chicle.

One of the agency's primary accounts throughout most of its existence was Chrysler Corporation; it supplied both domestic and foreign advertising for the automaker. Grant opened an office in Detroit, Michigan, in 1956 to handle Chrysler's Plymouth and Dodge brand advertising, creating a special group to handle the Plymouth-sponsored television programs the *Ray Anthony Show* and Lawrence Welk's *Top Tunes and New Talent.* In 1957 trucking and rental company Ryder System, Inc., of Miami, Florida, tapped Grant as its first advertising agency.

Grant acquired a portion of Chrysler Corporation's Canadian advertising from Ross Roy, Inc., in 1959 when the automaker decided to split its account along the lines of its marketing structure in that country. At the same time, Grant also acquired responsibility for all Chrysler Canada television advertising from the Leo Burnett Company and geared up Dodge's campaign to introduce its Dart line.

In 1960 Grant purchased Robinson, Fenwick & Haynes of Los Angeles, California, and Chambers, Wiswell, Shattuck, Clifford & McMillan, the third-largest agency in Boston, Massachusetts. By the end of the year, however, Grant and Robinson, Fenwick announced they were parting ways based on conflicts of interest among existing Grant accounts and those brought into the agency as part of the Robinson, Fenwick acquisition. For example, a conflict existed between Grant client Marquardt Aircraft Company and Robinson's Packard Bell Electronics Company. The Seventh Day Adventists, owners of Robinson client Loma Linda Food Company, also objected to Grant's winemaking clients: Almaden Vineyards, San Francisco, California, and Monarch Wine Company, New York City.

In 1961 the Dr Pepper Company expanded its U.S. advertising agreement with Grant to include responsibility for Canada, taking the account away from Kenyon & Eckhardt. The United States Time Corporation, however, moved its Canadian Timex brand advertising to Ronalds-Reynolds, costing the agency an estimated $250,000 in billings.

Grant jumped on the bandwagon of advertising agencies going public in 1964, announcing a public offering for its international operations, beginning with its South African subsidiary Grant Advertising Ltd., in Johannesburg. In papers filed with the U.S. Securities and Exchange Commission in 1964, Grant claimed $22.1 million in international billings. Gross billings, which totaled $37 million in 1966, had reached $49.8 million by 1969, of which $41.9 million was from non–U.S. operations, according to *Advertising Age.*

By 1971 Grant's international operations were in the red, posting roughly $1 million in losses. Worldwide operations had shrunk to 30 offices in 22 countries, including Chile and Pakistan. This decline occurred despite China Airlines' announcement that it was signing on with Grant, moving its $500,000 account from McCann-Erickson. A year later, Grant's independence came to an end. Batten Barton Durstine & Osborn subsidiary Comcore Communications of Toronto, Canada, purchased Grant, which had billed approximately $60 million in both its public and private units the previous year. Will Grant was relegated to the role of consultant, while Comcore President David Gillespie assumed the role of president for Grant's U.S. operations. Longtime Grant veteran Joe G. Wren continued in the role of president of Grant International, with Grant's son William R. Grant serving as the company's executive vice president.

Grant's domestic operation, which accounted for approximately $5 million in billings, was sold in 1974 to a group headed by J. Richard Harris, executive vice president of Comcore's U.S. operation, which had billings of $5 million–$6 million at the time of the sale. Two years later Harris-Grant, the parent of Grant Advertising, Inc., closed its doors after amassing $1 million in debt to 600 creditors when Cummins Engine Company of Columbus, Indiana, and the Curacao Government Tourist Bureau of New York City ceased advertising. Billings dropped to about $4 million, payments from clients were slow to come in, and projected billings increases failed to materialize. This forced the three remaining offices—in New York City, Chicago, and San Francisco—to close their doors after projections for 1975 "showed it was futile to continue," according to a letter to creditors. As for Grant International, the company once billed as the largest in the world was reported as insolvent in November 1974.

DEREK DATTNER AND AMY I.S. DATTNER

See also color plate in this volume

Further Reading

"Agency Stocks Perform Variously; Most Prices Rise," *Advertising Age* (26 August 1968)

"C'mon in—Overseas Is Fine, Grant Urges, Opening 25th Office Abroad," *Advertising Age* (16 January 1956)

"Grant Now Owned by Comcore," *Advertising Age* (17 April 1972)

"Grant Puts African Stock on Market, Hopes to Be All Public in 5 Years," *Advertising Age* (4 May 1964)

"Grant Sees Worldwide TV Audience of 2 Billion Viewers by 2000 A.D.," *Advertising Age* (24 October 1960)

"Harris-Grant Closes Doors; Cites Debt of $1,000,000," *Advertising Age* (6 January 1975)

"Robinson Agency Splits with Grant," *Advertising Age* (2 January 1961)

"You Ought to Know . . . Will C. Grant," *Advertising Age* (11 March 1946)

Grey Advertising Agency, Inc.

(Grey Advertising; Grey Worldwide)

Founded as Grey Advertising Agency, Inc., by Lawrence Valenstein, 1917; incorporated in New York in 1925 (changed its state of incorporation to Delaware in 1974); acquired Gross, Townsend, Frank, Hoffmen, Inc., health care agency, anchor of worldwide Grey Healthcare network, 1986; acquired interest in Font & Vaamonde Associates, Inc., 1987; purchased Regian & Wilson Advertising & Public Relations, largest full-service advertising and public relations agency in Fort Worth, Texas, 1998; acquired Innovative Customer Solutions LLC, Ohio-based advertising company, 1999; renamed Grey Worldwide when holding company Grey Global Group formed, 2000.

Major Clients

Block Drug Company, Inc.
Bridgestone/Firestone Tire Sales Company
Dannon
Hasbro
Panasonic (consumer and industrial products)
Procter & Gamble Company
SmithKline Beecham
3M Corporation
United States Department of Treasury

Since its inception in 1917, Grey Advertising, a multinational advertising agency, has been engaged in the planning, creation, supervision, and placement of advertising. Grey has 409 offices in 159 cities within the United States and in 90 countries and employs more than 10,000 people (10,086 in 1998) nationally and internationally. Some 50 percent of its total business is generated from the United States. The company has been publicly held since 1965, with approximately 50 percent of the stock employee-owned. It has offices in the Americas, Europe, the Middle East, Africa, and the Pacific Rim. In 1978 Grey's total billings were $607 million, with $433 million coming from the United States (or approximately 71 percent). In 1998 its billings had grown to $7.77 billion, with only $3.73 billion coming from the United States (or approximately 48 percent). In 1998 Grey ranked seventh among agencies worldwide in income. Within the United States, it was ranked number one in income. In 2000, in the first major restructuring in 30 years, Grey Advertising established a new holding company known as Grey Global Group, and the advertising arm was renamed Grey Worldwide. The latter had estimated billings of more than $8 billion from clients such as British American Tobacco, Mars, Oracle, Procter & Gamble, and SmithKline Beecham.

In the late 1990s Grey Advertising had the largest number of multinational accounts handled (91), followed in second place by McCann-Erickson with 60, and in third place by Doyle Dane Bernbach with 42. Some of its multinational clients included Oracle, P&G, 3M, Nokia, British Petroleum, Quaker Oats, and Microsoft. Grey had developed into a truly integrated marketing communications agency with numerous functional areas handled by the following Grey-owned groups: GCI/APCO (public relations and government relations), Grey Direct (direct marketing), Grey Interactive (interactive marketing), J. Brown/LMC Group (co-marketing and local marketing), Grey Healthcare Group (health care marketing), Great! Productions (corporate meetings and events), FOVA (Hispanic marketing), and Grey Design & Promotion (corporate identity, design, and promotions).

Beginnings and Growth

Grey Advertising was started in an art studio by 18-year-old Lawrence Valenstein, who borrowed $100 from his mother to start the agency. He conceived the name for the agency, Grey Art Studios, from the color of the walls of the first office. Originally, the agency specialized in direct mail. In 1921 Valenstein hired then 17-year-old Arthur Fatt, who later became an equal partner and chairman of the agency. Fatt was not interested in the limelight; he felt that all of the agency's attention should go to its clients or potential clients. Fatt believed in maintaining close relationships with clients so that he could learn to anticipate their wants and needs. He helped develop Grey's reputation as an agency that utilized a team approach to advertising. Grey was known for working very closely with its clients. Fatt also believed in studying client histories and product histories, thus giving agency personnel a better idea of why consumers purchase the clients' products and services. Although Fatt was known to encourage creativity and risk taking, he was also a firm believer in the value of research.

Grey moved into the ranks of top U.S. agencies in 1947 when its billings hit $10 million for the first time, having won the Gruen watch account. In a time when Madison Avenue was largely run by old-line WASP executives, Grey was widely perceived as a Jewish agency among the top American companies. In 1949 two Grey executives, William Bernbach and Ned Doyle, left the agency, taking with them the BVD account, to form a new agency that would also have a heavily Jewish reputation. Their agency, Doyle Dane Bernbach (DDB), recruited many of its early employees from Grey.

Grey landed the Block Drug account in 1955 and reached $30 million in billings. Block Drug became an international advertiser and proved to be one of the top accounts for Grey. In 1956 Fatt became president of the agency and Valenstein the chairman. In 1957 Grey created the "Leaving now for Trenton, Philadelphia and Cucamonga!" campaign for Greyhound Bus. The Greyhound tag line, "Go Greyhound and leave the driving to us," became one of the best-remembered slogans of the time. In the 1960s Grey produced the first global advertising campaign. The "Lilacs in the snow" (Revlon) campaign was shown in more than 20 countries.

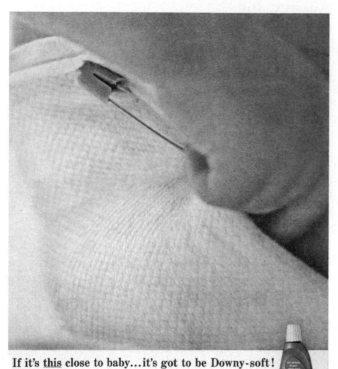

If it's this close to baby...it's got to be Downy-soft!

This diaper touches the most delicate skin in the world...baby's. That's why only a very special softness will do...the softness you'll get from Procter & Gamble's new Downy Fabric Softener. A little Downy in the final rinse makes baby's diapers, sleepers, undershirts, softer than you ever dreamed possible. Give all your family's wash deep Downy softness...the softness that satisfies even a baby's tender needs.

Grey Advertising launched the campaign to introduce Procter & Gamble's Downy Fabric Softener, which remained both a brand leader and a Grey client four decades later.
Courtesy of The Procter & Gamble Company.

Additional famous tag lines produced during this period included, "Ford has a better idea," "Choosy mothers choose Jif," and "For skin almost as soft as a baby's behind" (Mennen).

In 1961 Grey ranked 18th among U.S. agencies with $58.5 million in billings. That year it had a change in officers, with Herb Strauss becoming president and Fatt becoming chairman. This was the year that Grey helped with the introduction and launch of P&G's Downy Fabric Softener campaign. The following year, Grey opened an office in Los Angeles, California, creating the Grey Western Division. At about the same time, Grey acquired a London, England, agency, thus beginning its overseas expansion. In 1963 Grey-Daiko became the second U.S. agency to enter Japan. Grey Public Relations was also established in 1963. Grey's billings reached $100 million in 1964, and the company moved to its current location at 777 Third Avenue in New York City. In 1965 Grey Advertising decided to become a public company and began to have its stock traded on the Nasdaq exchange. Grey also began using psychographics in its advertising research on consumers in that year. (Psychographics is the analysis of consumer lifestyles.) In 1966 Grey broke into the top-ten ranks of U.S. agencies, and the next year Herb Strauss was named CEO and Ed Meyer, president. In 1969 Grey won the Post cereal account

(Kraft General Foods). The leadership changed again in 1970 when Ed Meyer was named CEO.

The 1970s were marked by the addition of several campaigns, including *Star Wars* toys from Kenner, aspirin and toothpaste from SmithKline, and Stove Top Stuffing from General Foods. During the 1980s Grey Direct and GCI Group were formed. In the early 1990s, Grey opened offices in Beijing and Guangzhou in China.

In 1991 Grey was awarded the Dannon Yogurt account. At that time the yogurt market was growing rapidly, and there was increased competitive activity within this market segment. In 1992 Grey utilized the "Dannon Consumer Awareness, Attitude and Usage Tracking Study" to create a research base for a strategic plan that would reestablish Dannon as the brand of choice in the yogurt market. By 1994 Grey's advertising had elevated yogurt into the mainstream of American food with the Dannon campaign. The ads highlighted numerous research findings (including the facts that consumers liked Dannon's product packaging and Dannon Yogurt's pure, natural ingredients). Based upon consumer perceptions, Dannon introduced several new products, including frozen yogurt, low-fat yogurt, and yogurt on a stick. The campaign stressed education and the introduction of new products and packaging, including a change from waxed cups to plastic cups, and tamper-proof covers were added. These changes prompted other yogurt companies to follow suit. "Taste why it's Dannon" was chosen as the campaign slogan. The campaign was an immediate success, and within a week of its launch, sales of the product increased significantly. The campaign was awarded the prestigious David Ogilvy Award by the Advertising Research Foundation. This award is presented to an agency that, in conjunction with its client, utilizes effective research in a campaign's development.

In 1994 Ed Meyer celebrated 25 years as Grey's chief executive officer, and its billings passed the $5 billion mark. In 1995, through its entertainment division, Grey introduced the Beatles to a new generation with its advertising for the *Beatles Anthology,* which aired on ABC.

In 1996 Grey was awarded the Los Angeles/Orange County (California) Mitsubishi Dealers Advertising Association account, estimated at $10 million. In 1997 Globalstar, a global satellite mobile-telephone system, gave its international advertising and public relations contracts to Grey Advertising. The campaign, launched in a variety of telecommunications publications, urged local service providers abroad to sign up for the service. In addition, the campaign encouraged regulators to allow Globalstar to offer its service in their countries. Additionally, in 1996 Grey took its media buying and planning worldwide with the launch of its MediaCom Worldwide unit. In 1997 Sprint Corporation employed Grey to handle its corporate brand-development strategy ($40 million). Grey had previously handled approximately $60 million of Sprint's advertising. Another major account acquired in 1997 was Reebok's media account, valued at $90 million.

In 1998 Grey became the agency for Dairy Queen. The agency developed a campaign that focused on the restaurant and its people rather than the products and was awarded the American Mar-

MENDOZA BEAVER

A Fur of Luxury ~with Economy

*H*AVE you ever desired a coat of Beaver—that deep, rich, luxurious fur—yet hesitated because of its cost? Then *Mendoza Beaver* will prove a dream come true—the answer to all your wishes.

Mendoza Beaver, the cleverest fashion discovery of the century, is made of only the finest New Zealand Coneys, dyed with the lustre, the silky softness, the deep brown color, the caressing beauty of natural Beaver—at a fraction of its cost.

Paris has designated Brown as the leading fur color for the coming season—and this decree is obeyed by *Mendoza Beaver*, the only Beaver-dyed fur guaranteed for color. Stunning fur coats and wraps of *Mendoza Beaver*—coats and suits of cloth and other furs trimmed with *Mendoza Beaver*—such modes are featured everywhere by stores noted for the undoubted quality and style authenticity of their offerings. Look for *Mendoza Beaver* in planning a Winter wardrobe that combines luxury with economy.

MENDOZA FUR DYEING WORKS, Inc.
722 East 133rd Street, New York City

The label above is your guide to garments of *Mendoza Beaver*—a symbol of beauty with economy.

The coupon will bring you a free copy of our new booklet on the advance mode in furs for 1926-1927.

> MENDOZA FUR DYEING WORKS, Inc.
> 722 East 133rd St., New York City
> Kindly send me a copy of 'The Advance Fur Mode *for* 1927'
> Name..
> Address...

COLOR GUARANTEED

Mendoza Fur Dyeing Works, Inc., was Grey Advertising's first national account, won in 1926.

---

keting Association's Gold Effie based on the sales increase realized from the Dairy Queen campaign. Also in 1998 Grey launched a $20 million TV and print campaign for Panasonic, which was one of the most aggressive worldwide efforts touting a company's digital offerings.

Legal Problems and Client Losses

That same year, however, Grey faced legal problems related to its advertising of "leasing" for Mitsubishi Motors of America, Inc. The Federal Trade Commission (FTC) charged the agency with misrepresentation, failure to disclose, and violation of the Consumer Leasing Act and the Truth in Lending Act. A settlement was reached in which Grey did not admit to violating any laws but was nonetheless required to adhere to certain FTC rules.

In 1998 Grey also lost several clients, including Barilla, Dannon, Kraft Foods, Lexmark International, and Mitsubishi. In addition, its stock value declined significantly. After these setbacks, Grey fought hard to prevent further client defections. In 1999 Hasbro, P&G, and Seagram gave Grey a combined $152 million in additional business.

At the close of the 20th century, some of the products promoted by Grey for P&G were Febreze and Pantene. Febreze's success was attributed to a two-year test-marketing program. Pantene's campaign focused on objects such as flowers and fruits to promote an association with a refreshing and healthy lifestyle. The campaign incorporated a diverse group of models that illustrated different hair types. Thomas Puckett, Grey's vice president and international creative director, summed up the theme of the campaign as "Love your hair, not someone else's."

Grey also won the $40 million print and broadcast advertising Glaxo Wellcome account in 1999 to promote a new migraine drug. Glaxo ranked third among drug makers in consumer advertising spending at $184 million.

Hasbro awarded Grey its creative and media-planning account for Micro Machines. Hasbro's Play-Doh and My First Game also went to Grey. Additionally, Grey gained in its "nontraditional" areas such as direct marketing, interactive advertising, and health care and within its public relations units. Grey's MediaCom unit (its media-buying unit) also made significant gains, generating more than $350 million in new business in 1999.

JAMES R. OGDEN

Further Reading

Kephart, P., "The Leader of the Pack," *American Demographics* (September 1995)

Lucas, S., "Grey to 'Reinvent' Itself," *Adweek* (8 February 1999)

Meyer, Edward H., "Arthur Fatt's Vision Helped Grey Prosper," *Advertising Age* (22 March 1999)

Smith, S.T., "Grey Lands $90 Million Reebok Media Account," *Boston Business Journal* 17, no. 10 (August 1997)

Strickland, Amanda, "Grey Wins Big Migraine Drug Account," *Triangle Business Journal* 15, no. 6 (15 October 1999)

Grocery and Supermarket

Until the onset of the Great Depression, the retail grocery business in the United States was essentially a storefront proposition. The stores, wedged in among other retail establishments along the main roads and neighborhood streets of cities and hamlets alike, were small, offered little or no off-street parking, and lacked any self-service component. The grocer, usually positioned behind a counter, took items off the shelves as requested by the customer. There were no wheeled shopping carts, no checkout counters, no magazine racks, no drug or household items department, and in many cases no meat—for that customers might have to visit the butcher down the block.

Although the mom-and-pop stores, as they were commonly known, dominated, grocery chains existed even in that bygone era. By far the largest was the Great Atlantic & Pacific Tea Company (A&P), which had been founded in 1859. During the pre-supermarket era, A&P had about 15,000 stores nationwide, almost all of them of the neighborhood variety.

Although the early supermarkets had little in common with today's giant outlets, they did, as William I. Walsh observed in *The Rise and Decline of the Great Atlantic & Pacific Tea Co.,* "introduce the concept of marketing the whole spectrum of food products, most on a self-service basis, under a single roof, at prices lower than any service store operator, including A&P, could match."

The first truly self-service grocery store, one of the Piggly Wiggly chain, opened in Memphis, Tennessee, in 1916; customers passed through turnstiles and were issued wooden baskets. (The wheeled grocery cart would not be introduced until 1937.) But like so many other American societal innovations, the supermarket first saw light in a major way in California. Those earliest West Coast stores, opened in the 1920s, were rudimentary by current standards, with little attention given to decor or display.

By the early 1930s, the big-store concept had moved east; in 1930 Michael Cullen, a former A&P employee, opened a supermarket in New York City's borough of Queens. Within a few years, he had a chain of King Kullen supermarkets in the borough, many of them in converted garages, factories, or warehouses. And just west of New York City in Elizabeth, New Jersey, another large supermarket, called Big Bear, opened in a former auto manufacturing plant. In their newspaper ads, both King Kullen and Big Bear stressed cost savings. An early King Kullen ad read, "Tell your friends and neighbors about this great price-wrecker. Tell 'em it's the lowest price grocery in all America. Tell 'em our prices are not for a day or a week, they are our regular everyday prices. Save 10% to 50%."

Rise of Supermarkets

By the late 1930s, the big grocery chains began responding to the challenge of these upstarts by developing their own supermarkets. After agonizing over entering the supermarket field, conservative A&P moved with uncharacteristic speed. The New York–based company started by opening 100 of the big stores in 1936. Two years later, A&P was operating more than 1,100 supermarkets and had closed many of its smaller stores. Other chains, including Kroger and National Tea, followed, although the growth of the supermarket concept was stifled by the onset of World War II and did not regain momentum again until after the war.

Grocery advertising in the pre-supermarket era was low profile and primarily confined to newspapers. Although A&P had been advertising in newspapers as early as the 1880s, it generally bought few ads, and those were invariably small fractions of a page. The larger food ads in the 1920s and 1930s—and even these were less than a full page—were bought by manufacturers, usually for a specific product, such as a brand of coffee, tea, canned fruit, or the like. In 1937, for example, General Foods spent $1.4 million for magazine ads and $2.9 million for radio advertising. By comparison, in the same year, A&P spent only $275,000, Kroger $235,000, and Safeway, a relatively new West Coast–based chain, $8,600—all on radio advertising. Through its agency Paris & Peart, Inc., A&P sponsored an early soap opera during 1932–33 and the singer Kate Smith in 1936–37, mainly to build awareness for its Ann Page and Jane Parker house brands. Kroger, through the Ralph Jones Agency, sponsored a syndicated serial, *Linda's First Love,* in the mid-1930s to cover its regional markets. Other radio efforts were sporadic.

After World War II, supermarket expansion picked up where it had left off. Over the next two decades, thousands of small independent grocers were driven out of business by the onslaught of the big stores, as the chains steadily increased their share of the market. In 1946 supermarkets accounted for only about 3 percent of the grocery stores in the United States, although their sales were 28 percent of the total volume. By the mid-1950s these big stores, now averaging about 18,000 square feet, still accounted for only about 5 percent of all outlets, but they accounted for almost half of the sales volume. The tremendous sales growth came at the expense of small stores, many of which closed during this period.

In 1962 the top ten food retailers by sales volume were A&P, Safeway, Kroger, National Tea, Acme, Winn-Dixie, Food Fair, First National, Grand Union, and Jewel Tea. These chains operated 12,445 supermarkets and had combined sales of $5.3 billion.

As the supermarket chains grew, so did their advertising and their influence. In the 1950s and 1960s, page ads from the marketers began appearing with increasing frequency in newspapers. Soon the larger metropolitan newspapers introduced a weekly food section, usually appearing on Thursday or Friday when most housewives shopped for the weekend; the food section featured recipes and other food-related stories and bulged with supermarket and other food advertising. For instance, on Friday, 22 February 1957, the *Chicago Tribune* premiered a "Weekly Illustrated Food Guide" and touted its arrival in a page 1 story. The 22-page premiere broadsheet section included a "Cook of

© 1930 P. W. A. C.

SHE PAYS $40 FOR HER HATS . . .

but she knows the price of oranges to a cent!

SHE can, and does, pay cheerfully for what she wants . . . but she doesn't want to pay more than she has to for *anything*.

What woman (and the larger her income grows, the truer this seems to be) really does?

That's why Piggly Wiggly attracts so many of her type. Women who pride themselves on their careful judgment . . . monied women who so often are among the thriftiest!

San Diego's Mission Hills . . . Mil-waukee's Whitefish Bay . . . each smart center the country over has its Piggly Wiggly stores, where the wealthy (and thrifty) women of that community shop daily.

They have found that at Piggly Wiggly they're sure of the finest foods at consistently low prices. Volume buying, volume selling, give Piggly Wiggly customers this advantage.

But low prices aren't the only reason Piggly Wiggly's 3200 pleasant stores are thronged daily. 2,500,000 women

prefer the Piggly Wiggly way of choosing for themselves—every day!

They like to compare prices on the big, swinging tags. They like to select the famous, packaged foods from neat shelves . . . the fresh, crisp produce from shining bins . . . unhurriedly, in-dependently. Shopping at Piggly Wiggly is smart . . . modern!

You, too, will enjoy this sensible vogue in marketing. Follow the trend of the times! Why not visit a Piggly Wiggly store in your neighborhood today.

P I G G L Y   •   W I G G L Y   •   S T O R E S

This 1930 Piggly Wiggly campaign emphasized the good value made possible by buying and selling in volume. The convenience—and modernity—of self-service was also a selling point.
Reprinted by permission, Piggly Wiggly Company.

the Week" feature, recipes, and a full week's menu for a family. Five supermarket chains took page ads, and other advertisers included Nabisco, Pillsbury, Gold Medal flour, Kaiser aluminum foil, Wonder Bread, Libby's baby food, Ken-L Ration, and a local liquor store chain.

Growing Competition

In the early postwar years, competition among the chains heated up. In the 1950s, as an incentive to attract more customers, most of the big food retailers introduced trading stamps, which could be redeemed for household items, furniture, sporting goods, and a wide variety of other products. The trading stamp frenzy reached its peak in 1960, when about 75 percent of all supermarkets issued them. But by the 1970s the fad had run its course, and the stores switched to promoting discount prices.

As popular as supermarkets had become with the U.S. public, they suffered a crisis of confidence in the 1960s as governmental and consumer groups assailed both the quality of supermarkets' food products and their high prices. A principal criticism of the foods themselves was the use of chemical additives, such as food colorings and flavor enhancers. Consumers also charged that the supermarket chains had increased their prices to cover the high costs of overhead, promotion techniques, and advertising.

Out of these dissatisfactions arose nonprofit food co-ops, which operated either as retail stores or as pre-order centers where members' orders were assembled and then delivered on a schedule. Membership was unrestricted, and each member had a vote in the co-op's policies. Co-ops, many of which were organized by community activists, shunned fancy trappings, preferring to display the food in a no-frills nonpromotional atmosphere. Although initially successful, co-ops eventually declined in number by the late 1970s for a variety of reasons—among them inadequate organizational structures, high turnover in membership, and a decline in governmental support of community organizations.

Though price competition had long been a major factor in grocery retailing, it reached a new level of intensity when many stores began offering unbranded generic goods among the most basic staple product categories such as salt, flour, sugar, soft drinks, cooking fats, soups, and paper products. Generics underpriced even house labels, though the quality levels were also well below those of national and house brands. Also, in the middle and late 1970s, as inflation in the United States soared and economic growth stagnated, no-frills grocery stores that reduced amenities to a minimum and required customers to bag their own purchases began to appear. They rarely promoted sale price items; their consistent promise was that prices were low at all times.

Bigger and Better

As economic conditions improved in the 1980s, generic and no-frills growth stalled at less than expected levels. Once again stores began to attract customers by building bigger and better stores and emphasizing quality. Kroger and its ad agency (since 1957) Campbell-Mithun, of Chicago, Illinois, believed that a store's meat department had a disproportionately large spillover impact on consumers' impressions of a store as a whole, so late in the decade the company put considerable money into building up the reputation of its meats. Even as this continued, it was still necessary for the store to protect its pricing front with its "cost cutter" scissors symbol. Kroger and many other chains tried to de-emphasize sales and loss-leaders to generate traffic and adopt the "everyday low price" theme of the no-frills stores. But their operating costs made it impossible for them to match no-frills price levels, and manufacturer discounts and co-op promotions ensured that special sale items would continue.

As the big chains came to increasingly dominate the grocery business, consolidation and change ensued. A&P steadily lost market share, yielding its number-one spot to Safeway in the early 1970s. Much of Safeway's strength was attributed to the California-based company's expansion in fast-growing western states, while A&P's greatest concentration was in the East, where population growth was minimal. Later Safeway was overtaken by Kroger with 13 marketing areas in the South and upper Midwest.

In an attempt to brake its slide, A&P and its agency, Gardner Advertising, New York City, in 1972 instituted the WEO ("Where Economy Originates") program, in which it converted stores overnight to discount operations. Within six months the company had converted an estimated 3,000 of its then 4,000-plus outlets to WEOs. Other marketers retaliated in various ways: Pathmark, which already discounted, took the then-radical step of keeping some of its stores open 24 hours; other chains extended their hours until midnight; and still others began to be open on Sundays, which previously had been unheard of in some areas of the country. In a business that traditionally operated on very low profit margins, usually 1 percent to 3 percent, this cutthroat competition threatened to slice those margins even thinner. The net result for A&P was that its WEO program, although initially successful in some markets, failed to stop the company's market erosion, which eventually relegated the once mighty chain to the second tier of grocery marketers.

As the grocery companies turned away from trading stamps, they increasingly embraced couponing. In 1976 advertisers distributed a record 45.8 billion cents-off coupons, more than 72 percent of them carried in newspapers, according to Nielsen Clearing House, a processor of redeemed coupons. The newspapers' share of the coupons distributed in 1976 included 9.5 percent in Sunday supplements and 7.2 percent in free-standing inserts (FSIs). Magazines' coupon share was 15.4 percent, with most of the balance in direct-mail and on-package coupons.

The trend toward couponing was reflected in newspapers and their food sections as they moved into the last decades of the 20th century. Although both chains and manufacturers still placed run-of-press (ROP) ads, they increasingly relied on FSIs to deliver both their advertising messages and their coupons. These inserts appeared both in the editions containing the food sections and on other days of the week, including Sundays. Similar ads were sent out in mass mailings. Many of the coupons in these FSIs and direct-mail pieces could be redeemed at a chain only when accompanied by that chain's preferred customer card.

The use of in-store coupons increased as well. In 1992 Norwalk, Connecticut-based ActMedia introduced its Instant Coupon Machine (ICM). The company claimed in its first year that ICMs were responsible for $55 million in sales. The company boasted redemption rates of about 17 percent, which it said was seven to nine times greater than the rate for FSIs. By 1999 ActMedia, part of News America Marketing (itself a unit of Rupert Murdoch's News Corporation), was operating its in-store coupon dispensers in 27,000 grocery stores. By the mid-1990s, couponing had also moved to the Internet, as a number of companies offered to deliver coupons directly to consumers' printers.

The merger-mania prevalent in almost all categories of business in the late 20th century penetrated the retail food world as well. By the 1980s Salt Lake City, Utah's American Stores had bought the Philadelphia, Pennsylvania-based Acme Stores, Chicago-based Jewel Companies, and California's Lucky Stores. And in 1999 the Albertson's chain of Boise, Idaho, acquired American Stores, giving the company 2,492 outlets in 37 states. Also in 1999 Safeway bought the Chicago-based chain of Dominick's Finer Food stores, the latest in a string of acquisitions that included the Randall's and Vons stores. And the Kroger Company of Cincinnati, Ohio, took over Dillon Companies in 1983 and Fred Meyer, Inc., in 1999.

Specialty Formats

As the grocery chains grew, so too did the sizes of their outlets. According to a 1995 report by the Food Institute, by the mid-1990s there were 14 distinct store formats in the food industry. Conventional supermarkets—those stores defined as carrying at least 9,000 items and usually having a service deli and a bakery—accounted for only 26 percent of the industry's total volume in 1994, compared with more than 50 percent in 1980.

Other major store formats as defined in the report included:

- convenience store—Small, higher-margin grocery store offering a limited selection of staple groceries, nonfoods, and other convenience items, including ready-to-heat and ready-to-eat foods as well as gasoline. Approximately two-thirds of traditional convenience stores sell gas. Petroleum-based convenience stores are primarily gas stations with a small convenience store component.
- superstore—A larger version of the traditional supermarket, with at least 30,000 square feet and 14,000 items.
- super warehouse store—A very large food and general merchandise store of at least 100,000 square feet. The food-to-general merchandise ratio is typically 60–40.
- wholesale club—A 90,000-square-foot-plus membership retail/wholesale hybrid with a varied selection and a limited variety of products presented warehouse-style. The grocery portion of the store—30 to 40 percent—consists of large sizes and bulk sales.
- mini-club—About half the size of the wholesale club, it carries about 60 percent as many items.
- supercenter—Food/drug combination store and mass merchandiser with an average size of 150,000 square feet with 40 percent of its space given over to grocery items.

It was through its supercenters—with a whopping 200,000 square feet of floor space—that Wal-Mart became the largest retailer in the United States selling groceries. According to the trade journal *Supermarket News,* as of 2000 Wal-Mart had 11.1 percent of U.S. grocery industry sales, or about $57.2 billion, at its 800-plus Wal-Mart Superstores. Groceries accounted for about 30 percent of total sales in these huge stores, or approximately $17.1 billion. Total supercenter sales (grocery and other merchandise) in turn represented about 30 percent of Wal-Mart corporate sales.

The rest of the top ten grocery operations in the *Supermarket News* rankings for 2000 (sales figures are estimates) were as follows: Kroger Company ($49.2 billion), Albertson's ($36.4 billion), Safeway ($33.2 billion), Ahold USA ($27.5 billion), Supervalu ($23.3 billion), Fleming ($14.7 billion), Publix Supermarkets ($14.0 billion), Winn-Dixie ($13.8 billion), and Loblaw Companies ($13.8 billion). A&P, which for much of the country's history had been its premier grocer, had by the end of the 20th century fallen to 12th in the rankings, with estimated sales of $10.6 billion, accounting for just 2 percent of U.S. grocery sales.

Among the developments of the late 20th century were on-line grocery services that enabled consumers to order food over the Internet for home delivery. Two companies, California based Webvan and Peapod, headquartered in a Chicago suburb, dominated the field in its infancy. But in July 2001 Webvan shut down, and several smaller competitors also went out of business or were absorbed by larger competitors.

These on-line services maintained large warehouses—some as big as 300,000 square feet—in several major markets. Using their own trucks or those of carriers such as United Parcel Service, they delivered groceries on order, and presumably on a well-defined schedule, to customers who placed their orders via the Internet. These businesses suffered because they lacked a substantial base of regular customers (i.e., those who placed orders at least weekly). By 2001 their volume had not yet become sufficient to offset the fixed cost of maintaining plant and equipment, and their futures remained problematical.

Food advertising at the beginning of the 21st century continued to be led by newspapers. In calendar year 2000, the media-by-media breakdown of the "food stores and supermarkets (chain)" ad category, as tabulated by Competitive Media Reporting, was as follows:

- newspapers (including national newspapers and Sunday magazines), $315.1 million (48.1 percent of the total of $655.4 million).

- television (including broadcast, spot, and syndicated TV and cable networks), $257.7 million (39.3 percent).
- radio, $63.9 million (9.8 percent)
- outdoor, $14.5 million (2.2 percent)
- magazines, $4.2 million (0.6 percent).

ROBERT GOLDSBOROUGH

See also color plate in this volume

Further Reading

Mayo, James M., *The American Grocery Store: The Business Evolution of an Architectural Space,* Westport, Connecticut: Greenwood Press, 1993

McAusland, Randolph, *Supermarkets: 50 Years of Progress: The History of a Remarkable American Institution,* Washington, D.C.: Food Marketing Institute, 1980

Seth, Andrew, and Geoffrey Randall, *The Grocers: The Rise and Rise of the Supermarket Chains,* London: Kogan Page, 1999

Walsh, William I., *The Rise and Decline of the Great Atlantic & Pacific Tea Company,* Secaucus, New Jersey: Stuart, 1986

H

Hair Care Products

The hair care market expanded significantly in the late 1940s and early 1950s with the introduction of the home permanent, which enabled women to perform for themselves a complicated—even risky—procedure previously available only at the beauty shop. By simplifying the process, the Toni Company, a unit of the Gillette Safety Razor Company, brought the permanent out of the salon and into the home. The initial print campaign from Foote, Cone & Belding (FCB) invited women to guess "which twin had the Toni" and which one had received a salon permanent.

Toni was so successful that by the end of the 1950s it had added Prom, Bobbi, Tonette, White Rain Shampoo, Tame Cream Rinse, and many other products to its line. The Procter & Gamble Company (P&G) introduced its Lilt Home Permanent about the same time, with advertising from the Biow Company, and later Party Curl (ads from Grey Advertising). Another leading brand name in the field was Richard Hudnut.

Toward the end of the decade and into the 1960s, the use of permanents began to decline as styles changed, and more natural-looking hair became the fashion. Hair sprays such as Spray Net and Suave began to grow in popularity, particularly with men, after Gillette began promoting "the dry look" as an alternative to the slicked-down appearance produced by traditional hair tonics. But these trends were largely a prologue to the force that truly drove the hair care market, beginning in the mid-1950s. The revolution began with a single phrase: "Does she or doesn't she?"

Does She . . . ?

Although Breck shampoo introduced its Breck Girl print campaign in the 1940s, hair care advertising really came to life when Clairol started promoting its hair-coloring product in 1956. Before that, American women had their tresses washed, styled, and colored at the corner beauty shop. Without the help of blow dryers and other styling aids not yet introduced, women relied on the experts. Even so, hair coloring was not popular. Rather, it was associated with a garish, vulgar kind of woman—that is, until FCB copywriter Shirley Polykoff wrote a simple ad for Miss Clairol Hair Color Bath that was taken directly from her own experience. The headline questioned, provocatively, "Does she . . . or doesn't she?" The

answer: "Only her hairdresser knows for sure." With the appearance of this ad, the market for hair coloring took off: 50 percent of American women started coloring their hair, and sales of hair coloring products jumped 413 percent in six years.

Advertising Age named the campaign number nine on its list of the top 100 advertising campaigns of the 20th century, rating the slogan itself among the century's top ten. Still, at the time it was developed, Clairol's print campaign was refused by some publishers, who cited as their reason a perceived double entendre in the headline. Subsequent research showed that women interpreted the slogan differently from men, with no sexual implications. At least women in the 1950s said they did not see any sexual reference in the text.

FCB and Polykoff followed that initial success in 1957 with a campaign that used the now famous slogan, "Is it true blondes have more fun?" Clairol's next hit came with Loving Care, a new hair color designed to cover gray hair. The tag line, "Makes your husband feel younger, too, just to look at you," suggested that it was all right for women to color their hair to please their partners—and also that men liked being associated with newly rejuvenated wives. This campaign coincided with a further jump in sales of hair coloring products. By the end of 2000, at-home hair coloring products constituted a $1.7 billion market.

Clairol had the U.S. business virtually to itself until 1970, when Paris, France-based L'Oréal ventured into the market. It launched L'Oréal Preference with the tag line, "Because I'm worth it," and the battle was joined. McCann-Erickson created the memorable Preference tag and ad campaign. L'Oréal has featured celebrities such as actresses Cybill Shepherd and Heather Locklear as spokeswomen; Clairol has countered with its own stable of stars, including Linda Evans, Julia Louis-Dreyfus, and Debra Messing.

The hair color market is dominated largely by product innovation. In 1996, to capture the market of women still afraid to color their own hair, Clairol introduced a water-based brand, Hydrience, via Wells Rich Greene BDDP, New York City. L'Oréal responded in 1998 with a color line called Feria, introduced by McCann-Erickson Worldwide; in early 1999, the company added four shades intended for men.

NOTE: *In the gardens of the Chateau de Lude in France. It was such scenes that the French chevaliers, the forefathers of the modern Creoles, left behind them to establish the colony of Nouvelle Orleans (New Orleans). The Creoles are of pure French and Spanish blood, and their wonderful hair is a mark of their descent as well as of the care given it. They have always retained the "secrets de toilette" as well as the charm bequeathed them by their aristocratic ancestors.*

For Beautiful Hair
Take the advice of highest medical authorities

THE Council of the American Medical Association has recognized Resorcinol Monoacetate for the treatment of dandruff (seborrhea) and baldness (alopecia)—the common foes of beautiful hair. Thus the most eminent authorities have prescribed the way to prevent the loss of the hair's life and luxuriance.

Resorcinol Monoacetate is an important ingredient of "La Creole" Hair Tonic. Abundant healthy hair is easily attained with this wonderful preparation.

Two or three times a week apply "La Creole" Hair Tonic to the scalp thoroughly. Massage with a rotary motion of the finger tips. Scalp circulation is then stimulated, the hair roots supplied with needed nourishment and dandruff quickly eliminated. You will quickly notice the new beauty of your hair.

Proper shampooing

Absolute cleanliness is essential for beautiful hair, healthy hair. If the pores and hair tubes are clogged with dirt and perspiration, a healthy condition is impossible. Regularly every ten days or two weeks shampoo the hair thoroughly with "La Creole" Liquid Shampoo.

This famous Shampoo is made from an exclusive Menthol formula of purest cocoanut and cochin oils. You will instantly notice the delightful, cooling effect from its use. The hair becomes soft and lustrous—dries quickly and the scalp and pores glow with clean health and vigor. Always apply "La Creole" Hair Tonic after shampooing. The tonic and the shampoo each aid the other.

"La Creole" Hair Dressing

is a treatment for the gradual restoration of the Natural Dark Color to hair that has grown gray, gray streaked or faded. Refinement approves its use.

If you cannot obtain these preparations at advertised prices, write us direct and we will see that you are supplied.

LA CREOLE LABORATORIES
Memphis, Tenn.

"La Creole"

"La Creole" Hair Dressing, $1.00

"La Creole" Hair Tonic, 75c   "La Creole" Liquid Shampoo, 50c

At Drug Stores and Department Stores

La Creole Laboratories, Memphis, Tenn.
Please send booklet, "La Creole—Hair Beautiful," teaching the hair dress becoming each individual.
Name...........................
Street..........................
City.................... State...........

Mademoiselle La Creole

A 1920 ad for La Creole hair care products invoked "medical authorities" as proof of its claims to make hair healthier and more luxuriant.

Men's haircoloring discovery!

Blends away gray in 5 minutes
...without changing your natural color

After years of testing, the world leader in men's haircoloring has perfected a unique product created especially for the needs of men. That's why it's called JUST FOR MEN.™

Here, at last, is a man's haircoloring that replaces gray faster and easier than was ever before possible. The results are so subtle, so natural, even men who hadn't thought of coloring their hair are changing their minds.

5-minute formula works faster

JUST FOR MEN is incredibly simple. Just apply it, and in 5 minutes, wash it out. That's right, in the time it takes to shave or shower—the gray is blended away. Just 5 minutes, not 40 like women's hair dyes.

And just one application is all you need—for up to six full weeks. With JUST FOR MEN, the color doesn't fade or wash out—shampoo after shampoo.

Hair regains its natural look

JUST FOR MEN works so subtly, it colors only the gray—without altering the rest of your hair's color. So gray is gone, blended away, and your natural-looking color is back.

Men all over the country are reporting their hair looks natural, healthier and even fuller—the way it used to be.

JUST FOR MEN is changing the way men think about coloring their gray hair. How about you?

JUST FOR MEN™
SHAMPOO-IN HAIRCOLOR

In the men's hair care section

Combe, Inc., was one of the first marketers to realize the potential in men's hair-coloring products. After its Grecian Formula line, it introduced Just For Men, featured in this 1988 advertisement.

Men came out of the hair-coloring closet in the mid-1980s. But Combe, Inc., of White Plains, New York, invented the men's hair color category in 1962 with its Grecian Formula. For a decade, Grecian Formula ads showed men how easily they could cover their gray hair. Combe did it all with a minuscule advertising budget and ads created in-house. In the 1990s Clairol also recognized the potential of the men's hair-color market and added Men's Choice to compete with Combe's Just for Men brand, which had been introduced in 1987 with in-house–developed advertising. Clairol added a second men's line, Natural Instincts for Men, in 1999. Though dwarfed by advertisers' spending on women's hair color, the men's portion of the business has continued to grow.

Shampoos

While modern hair care advertising got its start with hair coloring products, shampoos opened their own marketing wars in the 1970s. Marketers had a challenge: women at the time were abandoning many traditional personal grooming products in favor of more natural, botanical-based preparations. Once again, Clairol led the way in 1971 with a product that capitalized on a "natural" positioning, Clairol Herbal Essence Shampoo. Clairol turned to Young & Rubicam to create an animated image of an innocent blond sauntering through a fictional garden of earthly delights. She wore flowers in her hair and was featured in packaging on a clear bottle that showed the green color of the shampoo. The message was health, nature, and freshness— a change from the use of sex to sell shampoo.

The success of Herbal Essence opened the way to a succession of new products, such as Gee, Your Hair Smells Terrific; Body on Tap; Vibrancy; Ivory; and Faberge Organics. Faberge was known for a creative campaign by Nadler & Larimer, Inc. The TV commercial showed one woman telling another about Faberge. That friend told two friends, and she told two friends, and so on. The image on the screen broke into multiple faces to convey the point.

While Clairol was scoring points with hair care customers, Gillette Company was looking for a way to bring shoppers to its brand. Its solution was Silkience, and the campaign by the agency Advertising to Women showed that the shampoo could treat hair where it needed help the most. An electronic image was used to show different hair strands getting different "amounts" of cleaning.

Niche markets also emerged within hair care. P&G successfully created a market for dandruff-control shampoos with its Head & Shoulders line. Prior to the campaign by Tatham-Laird, Inc., dandruff had been a taboo subject. P&G also had a hit with Prell, which was touted for its rich formula, demonstrated by showing a pearl slowly sinking to the bottom of the Prell bottle. The agency was Benton and Bowles, Inc.

Specialty Labels

Designers also started making inroads into the hair care market in the early 1980s. Vidal Sassoon assured customers, "If you don't look good, we don't look good." Commercials featured Sassoon in his New York City salon promising that salon looks could be achieved at home. Other stylists, such as John Frieda, followed with their own brands. At first, Frieda did not have money to spend on advertising, so he made personal appearances at drugstores, generating sales by word of mouth. Eventually, he reached a larger audience, thanks to a $38,000 TV spot (created in-house under Frieda's supervision) that introduced women to his antifrizz hair serum. The spot helped turn Frizz-Ease into a $20 million brand. Another successful salon entrepreneur was Jherri Redding, who cofounded several successful brands such as Redken, Jherri Redding, and Nexxus. The brands were not widely advertised to consumers, relying instead on promotion through salons.

Helene Curtis, recognizing consumer demand for salon-quality products, ushered in a line called Salon Selectives that was marketed as a salon product available through mass merchandisers. The company pumped $14 million into advertising designed by J. Walter Thompson Company and $26 million into promotion to educate consumers about its positioning. Curtis also had a niche in the value segment of hair care with Suave, which it pitched as a "smart" buy.

Another marketing opportunity emerged in the form of hair care brands targeting African-American consumers. Companies marketing specialized items included Revlon, Johnson Products, and Soft Sheen. Little advertising supported these brands, but retailers began to create special departments within their stores to showcase the items.

Although most hair care advertising had been aimed at women—the primary purchasers—L'Oréal introduced a whimsical children's brand (L'Oréal Kids) in the early 1990s. Borrowing from its "I'm worth it" campaign, L'Oréal featured kids saying, "We're worth it, too," a tactic that spawned a flood of children's versions of shampoos.

Capturing Fickle Consumers

The massive amounts being spent on hair care advertising resulted in a huge but splintered market where even a 1 percent or 2 percent share of the market equated to millions of dollars. Shoppers became fickle, bouncing from one brand to another almost weekly. Along the way, marketers began to persuade women that they needed both shampoo and conditioner to achieve healthy locks. Revlon's Flex, handled by in-house Tarlow Advertising, was particularly adept at pitching the two-product punch. This trend continued until the late 1980s, when P&G took an existing brand, Pert, and conjured up Pert Plus to rival Flex. The advertising targeted harried consumers, who learned that they no longer needed to use both a shampoo and a conditioner—a single product could do both. Pert Plus enjoyed a two-year run of success until shoppers reverted to their former hair care regimens.

Although the return to multiproduct regimens helped build sales, the market for shampoos and conditioners was maturing and hit a sales plateau; there simply were not any more heads to wash. Salvation came from abroad when L'Oréal introduced Studio Mousse, a foamy hair-styling aid in a can. Working with McCann-Erickson, L'Oréal spent about $14 million to introduce American consumers to mousse in 1983. Other marketers followed, among them Alberto-Culver Company, Sassoon, and Revlon. Mousse sales quickly swelled from zero to more than $200 million in less than one year. Mousse and other styling products quickly became an important sub-sector of the hair care business.

In the slow-growing shampoo segment, however, Clairol's Herbal Essence sales declined, and the brand almost disappeared from retailers' shelves. Clairol decided to revive the brand in the 1980s. Sensing renewed consumer interest in natural and organic products, Clairol relaunched it as Herbal Essences. The advertisements, by Kaplan Thaler Group, a division of Bcom3, were known for the risqué tactic of playing off the similarity of the words *organic* and *orgasmic*. The tag line was, "A totally organic experience."

Clairol credited the campaign with making Herbal Essences one of the most successful relaunches ever. Clairol parent Bristol-Myers Company spent $30 million—via the Kaplan Thaler Group—on Herbal Essences shampoo in 1999, according to *Competitive Media Reporting*. The product line was extended into body washes, with plans for hair color as well. Clairol also spent $40 million to introduce Daily Defense shampoo and conditioner (also from Kaplan Thaler). Despite its success in hair care, Bristol-Myers decided to put Clairol on the market in 2000. P&G, looking to round out its beauty arsenal, snapped up Clairol in April 2001 for $4.9 billion.

Trying to counter Clairol's hold on the market, Unilever's Helene Curtis unit repositioned a languishing brand called Thermasilk in the late 1990s. An $82 million advertising blitz from the J. Walter Thompson Company helped convince women that blow-drying—which had been believed to damage hair—could actually help hair if used in tandem with Thermasilk shampoo.

P&G also reinvigorated its Pantene line in 1999. Traditionally, P&G's advertising from Grey Advertising had used the line's so-called pro-vitamins as a distinctive selling point. The fresh Grey campaign broke away from science to highlight imagery. The new creative effort featured fruits and flowers with a theme of "Love your hair."

FAYE BROOKMAN

See also Polykoff, Shirley; *and color plate in this volume*

Further Reading
Klepacki, Laura, "P&G is Here to Stay," *WWD Beauty Biz* (February 2002)

Polykoff, Shirley, *Does She . . . or Doesn't She? And How She Did It,* Garden City, New York: Doubleday, 1975

Hakuhodo, Inc.

Founded in Tokyo, Japan, by Hironao Seki as an advertising space broker for educational magazines, 1895; reorganized as joint-stock company, 1924; established a joint venture with McCann-Erickson, Inc., to create McCann-Erickson Hakuhodo Company, Tokyo, 1960; entered into an affiliation with SSC&B:Lintas Worldwide, 1982; opened an agency in The Netherlands with TBWA Group, 1992; sold stake in McCann-Erickson Hakuhodo to McCann, 1993; created G1 Worldwide with TBWA, 2000.

Major Clients
Amazon.com.
Hitachi
Nissan Motor Company
Sanyo Electric Company, Ltd.
Suzuki Motorcycles
Unilever

Hakuhodo was founded in 1895 by Hironao Seki as an advertising space broker specializing in placing advertising for companies in the publishing business, such as bookbinders and paper dealers. In 1910 the company, then known as Naigai Tsushinsha, began publishing the daily *Naigai Tsushin.*

In the late 1920s inexpensive books called *Yen Pon* (one-Yen books) became extremely popular with Japanese consumers. As the major advertiser for publishers in Japan, Hakuhodo benefited greatly from this vogue. The market for *Yen Pon* soon became saturated, however; book sales—and Hakuhodo's fortunes—declined.

It was not until 1947—when Japan was in the midst of a severe depression that followed World War II—that the agency added its first client outside the publishing business. A year later the company launched the marketing communications publication *Monthly Hakuhodo,* which was later renamed *Kohkoku* (and revived in 1978), and in 1950 the company name again changed, this time to Naigai Tsushinsha Hakuhodo, Inc. The following year it entered the radio advertising market, adding television advertising and sales promotion in 1953. One client in particular spurred its move into television: Sanyo Electric Company, Ltd., which wanted to use the medium to promote its television sets.

In the late 1950s the agency—which had changed its name to Hakuhodo, Inc., in 1955—adopted a more American-style advertising structure, setting up an account executive system and establishing a planning department that included planning, research, and creative functions, as well as a public relations division. With this transformation into a modern advertising agency, Hakuhodo grew rapidly, expanding over a five-year period from 209 employees to more than 1,000.

In 1960 the agency entered a partnership with McCann-Erickson, Inc., to create the McCann-Erickson Hakuhodo Company in Tokyo. In 1994 McCann bought out Hakuhodo's share of the agency, and it became McCann-Erickson Japan, one of the relatively few foreign-owned agencies in the country.

In 1972 the Seki family, which had continuously headed the agency since its founding, was forced out. With its business in internal turmoil, Hakuhodo went outside its ranks to hire Michitaka Kondo, the former commissioner of the Japanese National Tax Administration, as its new president and chief executive officer in 1975. The unprecedented move helped restore the agency's image, and business began to improve.

In 1978 *Advertising Age* ranked Hakuhodo as the tenth-largest ad agency in the world by gross income. The agency also was doing well creatively, winning a number of international awards, including a Grand Prix at the Cannes (France) International Advertising Festival in 1982.

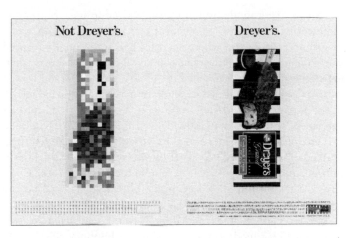

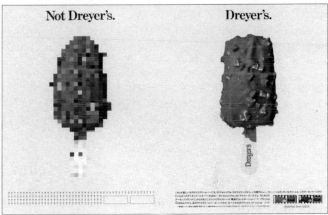

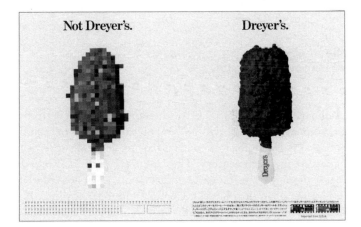

Hakuhodo received international recognition for its 1993 Dreyer's ice cream campaign.
Courtesy of Dreyer's Grand Ice Cream, Inc.

In 1981 the agency created the Hakuhodo Institute of Life and Living, Inc., an independent research organization, to gather data on the lifestyles of Japanese consumers, and in 1982 it entered into an agreement with SSC&B, Inc., to form Hakuhodo: Lintas, Tokyo. This move followed another foreign alliance, with South Korea's Cheil Communications in 1973, under the provisions of which Hakuhodo agreed to help train employees for the then-new Cheil; a joint agency, Hakuhodo Cheil, was established in Seoul.

In 1982 Hakuhodo announced it was adopting "Marketing Engineering Company" as its corporate philosophy. This was a new concept in Japan, where agencies had traditionally focused solely on advertising rather than on an all-encompassing marketing strategy. In 1991 it updated the philosophy to "Grand Design Partner," which established its reputation as a cutting-edge agency in the Japanese advertising market. In 1992 it entered into an agreement with TBWA Worldwide, setting up TBWA/Hakuhodo in The Netherlands. In 2000 the two agencies expanded their association to create G1 Worldwide, with offices in Japan, Europe, and North America, to handle the Nissan Motor Company's $1.1 billion global account; both had worked on the account in their respective regions of the globe.

In 2000 Hakuhodo expanded into several new media areas. It established Hakuhodo i-studio, an Internet boutique shop, and it entered a joint venture with Japan's third-ranking agency, Asatsu-DK, and mobile phone company KDDI to form A1 Adnet Corporation, an agency specializing in creating ads for Japan's Internet phone services and developing e-mail campaigns targeted at Internet phone users.

By 2000 Hakuhodo was the second-largest agency in Japan and the 11th-largest ad organization worldwide by income, according to *Advertising Age*. Its worldwide gross income was $1 billion in 2000, a 21.8 percent increase over the 1999 figure, and its billings were $7.6 billion. In 2000 the agency had 3,405 employees working in 15 offices in Japan and 42 offices in 16 other countries; its top foreign shops included Hakuhodo Cheil ($58.8 million in billings); Hakuhodo Deutschland, in Düsseldorf, Germany, ($39.8 million); HY Marketing, in Taipei, Taiwan ($34.8 million); Group Nexus/H, located in Kent, England ($20.3 million); and in China, Shanghai Hakuhodo Advertising ($19.2 million).

YUTAKA MIZUNO

Further Reading

<www.hakuhodo.co.jp/profile/e/history-fr.html>

Hallmark Cards, Inc.

Principal Agencies

Henri, Hurst & McDonald, Inc.
Foote, Cone & Belding
Young & Rubicam, Inc.
Ogilvy & Mather
Leo Burnett Company, Inc.

Hallmark Cards of Kansas City, Missouri, is the largest greeting card company in the world. "When you care enough to send the very best" is one of the most recognized and enduring advertising slogans of the 20th century. The *Hallmark Hall of Fame,* the longest-running dramatic series on television, is acknowledged as a major factor in that success. Company founder Joyce C. Hall played an important role in advertising and television history when he suggested the idea of a sponsored two-hour special television program that would air several times a year, rather than a weekly schedule of short programs.

Hall arrived in Kansas City at age 18, a traveling salesman for an illustrated postcard company with big plans for a mail-order postcard business. Taking a room at the local YMCA, he began his career with a couple of shoe boxes filled with illustrated postcards. But after a short time, Hall concluded that postcards could not clearly communicate people's feelings for one another, so he devised greeting cards to meet that need. One of his innovations was the introduction of envelopes for Valentines, which enabled the sender's message of affection to remain private. By 1915 Hall was in the business of manufacturing greeting cards. His brothers Rollie and William soon joined in the venture. When the business was incorporated as the Hall Brothers Company in 1923, the operation employed 120 workers in a new six-story facility.

Branding a Greeting Card

Ignoring advertising experts who told him consumers would not buy a greeting card for the brand name, J.C. Hall moved into national advertising with an ad in the *Ladies' Home Journal* prepared by Henri, Hurst & McDonald, Inc., in Chicago, Illinois. In 1936 Hall took his advertising to radio. Chicago "radio philosopher" Tony Wons would read poetry and bits of sentiment from Hallmark Cards and then, turning the card over, he would call listeners' attention to the company's trademark crown on the back. Greeting card dealers soon noticed customers doing the same in their stores: after reading the cards, they would look on the back for the Hallmark crown. The 13-week trial run of advertising on a small network of Illinois stations was just the first step. Soon afterward, Hall expanded the program to national coverage on the CBS radio network. The move into broadcasting would lead to television and national acclaim nearly 20 years later.

Before World War II, Hallmark was one of a half-dozen companies producing greeting cards. Hall's decision to advertise his product over the airwaves would change that significantly. In 1948 the *Hallmark Playhouse* was introduced, a 30-minute dramatic anthology on CBS hosted by best-selling British novelist James Hilton. In 1953 it became the *Hallmark Hall of Fame* and was hosted by the actor Lionel Barrymore, who presented stories

When you care enough to send the very best **Hallmark Cards**

This 1951 Hallmark ad included the marketer's long-running slogan, "When you care enough to send the very best."
Courtesy of the Hallmark Archives, Hallmark Cards, Inc.

of famous historical figures. The radio show would continue until 1955.

In 1944 Hall Brothers (the company would not adopt the "Hallmark Cards" corporate name until 1954) approached Foote, Cone & Belding (FCB) to handle the company's national advertising account. J.C. Hall emphasized the importance of excellence and high quality, visibly illustrated by the crown logo found on the backs of Hall Brothers cards. Thus when Hall Brothers Sales and Advertising Manager Ed Goodman suggested the slogan, "When you care enough to send the very best," it was favorably received. By late 1944, all Hallmark greeting card commercials on radio ended with those words. The original draft of the Hallmark slogan is proudly displayed on a three-by-five card in a glass case at the Hallmark Visitors' Center in Kansas City.

By 1951 Hallmark had enjoyed more than ten years of profit as a result of radio advertising and was amenable to the possibilities television presented. The greeting card company moved into television sponsorship with *Hallmark Presents Sarah Churchill.* Churchill (daughter of Hall's friend, the British Prime Minister Winston Churchill) hosted a series of 15-minute weekly interviews with notable people from stage, screen, and politics. A dedicated theater enthusiast, Hall followed the series in January 1952 with *Hall of Fame Theater,* 30-minute dramatizations of little-known events from the lives of famous people. The third program in the weekly series, "The Big Build-up," which aired 20 January 1952, starred an unknown actress named Grace Kelly. Soon the program's name was changed to *Hallmark Hall of Fame.*

The company received accolades from television critics for its cultural contributions and the quality of its advertising. The *Chicago Sun Times* praised Hallmark commercials: "There is a gentle artistry about these advertisements. They make an impression without intruding into the program." Consumers showed their appreciation, too. Research indicated that Hallmark cards were the choice of most greeting card buyers.

Substantive TV Programming

J.C. Hall continued to have direct input into Hallmark advertising, explaining, "I want the commercials to be as entertaining as the show. I'm opposed to the 'hard sell' because the people at home are our guests." With his focus on excellence, Hall continually sought substantive programming to sponsor. He had received enthusiastic acclaim in 1951 when the company had sponsored the first opera written for television, Gian Carlo Menotti's *Amahl and the Night Visitors,* on Christmas Eve. The program also made history two years later in a repeat telecast as the first sponsored program in color, broadcast only two days after the Federal Communications Commission had approved NBC's new color process.

Hall went on to sponsor *Hamlet* in April of 1953, the first Shakespearean drama to be presented on television. It was also the first TV special—that is, a two-hour entertainment program preempting regular fare and advertising in prime time. Sylvester "Pat" Weaver, president of NBC, recognized the potential of such programming when J.C. Hall requested it and today is known as the innovator who pioneered television specials.

Ever notice how you find this on the back of things that mean the world to you?

By 1996 the widely recognized Hallmark crown symbol was the only image needed in this advertisement, which appeared on the back of *National Geographic* magazine.
Courtesy of the Hallmark Archives, Hallmark Cards, Inc.

By 1954 Hallmark held a dominant position in the greeting card industry. "When you care enough . . ." was readily identifiable by shoppers. Hallmark cards could be found in large department stores throughout the country. In Kansas City, the company's $8 million headquarters was under construction.

Hall's insistence that the *Hallmark Hall of Fame* provide the best in entertainment resulted in outstanding scripts and distinguished actors being used in the series. After 1955 programs were broadcast as 90-minute specials up to six times per year. The series continued its tradition of innovation over the years as its producers experimented with new technology. In 1958 the recently introduced videotape format was used for *Kiss Me Kate.* The 1960 Hallmark presentation of *Macbeth,* filmed on location in Scotland, was the first made-for-television movie. The chroma key electronic process allowed angels to float dramatically in place in *The Littlest Angel* (1967). By the beginning of the 21st century, *Hallmark Hall of Fame* had become the longest-running dramatic series on television. It has also been the most honored, having been awarded 78 Emmys and 11 Peabodys, as well as the Golden Globe and Christopher awards. In 1961 J.C. Hall was the first sponsor to receive a special Emmy, which was presented with a paraphrasing of the familiar words: "Thank you, Mr. Hall, for caring enough to send the very best—in television." The dramatic series featured a wide variety of scripts including "Man and Superman," "A Doll's House," "Anastasia," and ten Shakespeare plays. Luminaries of the theater world were featured, including Alfred Lunt, Lynn Fontanne, Richard Burton, Julie Harris, Judith Anderson, and Orson Welles.

In the early days of television, agencies had a great deal of control over programs, from development to final production. Hall, however, maintained a significant presence in the *Hall of Fame* productions. FCB submitted 10 to 12 drama suggestions annually; Hall usually made the final choices. "We don't argue with him much anymore. He's been right too often," said FCB founder Fairfax Cone. Although Hallmark used both print and broadcast advertising, most of its advertising budget went to the broadcast side. In 1959 the advertising budget totaled about $3 million dollars; more than 70 percent of that amount went to television. By the end of the decade, FCB had written and produced more than 700 television commercials for Hallmark.

FCB: "Guardian of Quality"

FCB was Hallmark's lead advertising agency for 37 years. The agency maintained a production division dedicated entirely to Hallmark well into the 1970s. A writer once described the agency as Hallmark's "guardian of quality" because of the emphasis on entertaining yet tasteful soft-sell advertising. TV critics and viewers alike praised the quality of the commercials and their lack of intrusiveness.

Three FCB executives were credited with the high quality of workmanship of the *Hallmark Hall of Fame* and its commercials during the 1950s: Goodwin Alarik, account supervisor; John B. Rand, copy supervisor; and Homer Heck, vice president of television and radio. All commercials in early shows were produced live at the time of the broadcast. Two days before the air date, rehearsals began in New York City. Each spot ran only once between acts of the drama. A specific card or specialty item (party favor, gift wrap, ribbon) was featured during each commercial. Hallmark notified its dealers in advance as to which items were being promoted, thereby ensuring that all dealers had enough stock to meet the inevitable increase in demand after the *Hall of Fame* aired. By the mid-1960s commercials were being recorded on videotape and in color.

J.C. Hall played a much greater role in his company's advertising than most company presidents. Early on, Hall assured Duane Bogie, FCB's chief of productions, that the Hallmark account "will never be an easy one, but it will always be worthwhile." Throughout his advertising career Cone always took a personal interest in the account and in the production of *Hall of Fame*. He

conceded in the mid-1960s that the relationship had not always been an easy one: "We've had our ups and downs." In his autobiography Cone wrote with admiration for both Hall and *Hallmark Hall of Fame*, describing the program as "an exception to the common rules of television."

Hallmark's trademark slogan and soft-sell approach continued to be the backbone of its advertising through the 1960s, 1970s, and into the early 1980s (it was rated number one in credibility by an independent research firm). However, there were rumors that the company wanted to institute a somewhat more aggressive message, with a stronger product (as opposed to image) orientation.

Account in Play

In 1981 Hallmark invited four agencies to submit presentations for the $16 million account: FCB, Leo Burnett U.S.A., Ogilvy & Mather (O&M), and Young & Rubicam, Inc. (Y&R). Representatives from each agency traveled to Kansas City to present the two required campaigns. One was to include two finished and tested 30-second television spots; the second was to be presented in storyboard form. The agencies had to show how both campaigns could be used on a nonseasonal basis as well as for holidays. In addition, Hallmark requested a media plan and research design. Although insiders said the $100,000 Hallmark paid each agency came nowhere near the expense of producing the campaign, the prestige of the account was a major incentive.

At the end of the three-month competition, in February 1982, Y&R was declared the victor. A Hallmark executive said Y&R had "demonstrated to the complete satisfaction of Hallmark management that they could make our business grow." Very shortly after the announcement that Y&R had won the account, a new 30-second television commercial began running nationally. It was one of the spots Y&R had developed for its presentation, and this commercial continued the sentimental focus of Hallmark advertising. As a husband unhappily packed for an unexpected business trip, his wife slipped a Hallmark card into his suitcase. Unpacking in a distant city, he finds the card, and the discovery brings a smile to his face. The Y&R campaign was designed to encourage people to give cards any time, not just on holidays. The spot underscored a Hallmark spokesman's assertion that there would be no switch to hard-sell tactics, despite earlier industry rumors.

The relationship between Hallmark and Y&R was destined to be a short one, however. When the agency accepted the $20 million AT&T Communications long-distance telephone account, Y&R lost the Hallmark account, then billing at $40 million annually. Despite the fact that Hallmark provided a product and AT&T a service, the greeting card giant perceived a conflict of interest in the agency handling both accounts. In May 1984 a Hallmark representative said that both businesses promoted their enterprise as "the most effective way to share feelings and love with another person." With little ceremony the Hallmark account was shifted to O&M, one of the finalists from the competition held two years earlier.

But the relationship with O&M was not fated to be a long one, either. Hallmark put its account up for review in September

1988; five agencies, including O&M, made presentations. Hallmark chose the Leo Burnett Company, describing its award-winning work as "an excellent match with our strategy and style." The Hallmark/Leo Burnett association proved to be a successful one.

Burnett's Brand Building

In 1996 Hallmark increased its ad budget to $50 million and Burnett introduced a brand-building campaign to persuade shoppers to do what Hallmark refers to as "sneak a peek." Television commercials encouraged card shoppers to make sure they were buying one with the Hallmark brand name and logo on the back. A $10 million "brand insistence" print campaign focused on back-cover ads especially tailored for the specific publications in which they ran. The *National Geographic* ad read, "Ever notice how you find this on the back of things that mean the world to you?" Turning *Good Housekeeping* over to the back cover, readers saw, "When you find this on the back, you know you've got a seal of approval."

Hallmark commercials have consistently been named in the *Advertising Age* annual Best awards. Sentimentality tugs at the viewers' heartstrings in "Report Card" when a mother finds a thank-you card from the teacher in her son's book bag. The boy had stayed inside with an ailing friend who could not go out to play at recess. With "Dad's House," Burnett and Hallmark recognized societal shifts taking place in the 1990s. In this spot, a divorced mother buys a Christmas card for her son to take with him when he goes to stay at his father's house on Christmas Eve.

A Burnett/Hallmark commercial was also featured in Bernice Kanner's *The 100 Best TV Commercials . . . And Why They Worked* (1999). "Dance Card," which first ran in 1991, marking the 40th anniversary of the *Hall of Fame,* is one of the three most popular commercials in Hallmark's history. In this spot, four pre-teen boys having lunch in the school cafeteria discuss the most effective way to invite a girl to a school dance. When a female classmate interrupts their discussion to thank one boy for a Hallmark card and accept his invitation to the dance, the others reconsider their ideas. The reliable slogan, in use since the 1944,

underscores the brand image of quality and emotional connection: "Hallmark: When you care enough to send the very best."

J.C. Hall died at age 91 in 1982, but over the years Hallmark has remained a vibrant family business. Donald J. Hall followed his father as chairman and chief executive officer. In August 1999 Hallmark announced that it intended to triple its annual sales to $12 billion by 2010, a growth of ten percent per year. A company spokeswoman said the key to achieving the aggressive goal will be the founder's grandson, Don Hall, Jr., corporate vice president of strategy and development.

Hallmark cards are printed in 30 languages and distributed in more than 100 countries. The $3.5 billion corporation employs nearly 20,000 people, who own just over a third of the company through a profit-sharing and ownership plan. The Hallmark Entertainment division is the largest producer of family-oriented television films and miniseries in the world.

SANDRA L. ELLIS

Further Reading

Alter, Jennifer, "At Hallmark, 4 Agencies Present Their Very Best," *Advertising Age* (1 February 1982)

Alter, Jennifer, "Hallmark Selects Hot Y&R," *Advertising Age* (8 February 1982)

Alter, Stewart, "Conflict at Hallmark for Y&R," *Advertising Age* (10 May 1984)

Cone, Fairfax M., *With All Its Faults: A Candid Account of Forty Years in Advertising,* Boston: Little Brown, 1969

Hallmark Hall of Fame: A Tradition of Excellence, January 18/ April 18, 1985, New York: Museum of Broadcasting, 1984

Jervey, Gay, "Hallmark Keeps It Sweet," *Advertising Age* (8 March 1982)

Kanner, Bernice, *The 100 Best TV Commercials—and Why They Worked,* New York: Times Business, 1999

Kingman, Merle, "Hallmark Hall of Fame Starts 15th TV Year," *Advertising Age* (18 October 1965)

Kisseloff, Jeff, "A Half-Century of Quality, Paid for by Greeting Cards," *New York Times* (31 January 1999)

Mann, Jennifer, "Triple the Sales by 2010 Is Goal: Hallmark Reveals Aim, Not Tactics," *Kansas City Star* (18 August 1999)

Hal Riney & Partners, Inc. *See under* Riney

Hamlet Cigars

Principal Agency
Collett Dickenson Pearce

Hamlet cigars were created in 1964 by the long-established U.K. tobacco marketing company Gallaher. The origin of the company dates to 1857, when Thomas (Tom) Gallaher founded a one-man business in Londonderry, Northern Ireland, making and selling roll pipe tobaccos.

Gallaher, born in 1840, was one of nine children. His father was a prosperous farmer and corn mill owner. While working as apprentice to a tea merchant, Gallaher saw an opportunity in the tobacco leaf imported from the United States. With a demonstrable flare for marketing he displayed his tobacco products on a cart, which he paraded around the town.

A shrewd and hard-working businessman, Gallaher soon expanded into the growing city of Belfast. His business prospered and became a limited company in 1896 with a capital of £1 million, earning him the epithet "Tobacco King." In 1901 Gallaher rejected a bid from James Buchanan Duke, head of the American Tobacco Company, to buy his business. To resist Duke's advances, 13 other British tobacco companies merged to form the Imperial Tobacco Company.

For a year after Gallaher's death in 1927, the company was managed by his nephew, John Gallaher Michaels. It then passed into the hands of a company headed by London, England, financier Edward de Stein. In 1947, after a string of acquisitions, Gallaher purchased J.R. Freeman, manufacturer of small cigars. Gallaher's Freeman factory in Cardiff, South Wales, was still the largest single U.K. manufacturer of cigar products in 2001. Nearly half of all cigars smoked in the U.K. are made by Gallaher, and the company's Hamlet brand range accounts for more than four out of every ten cigars sold.

Hamlet owes its success to both innovation and advertising. Between the 1920s and the early 1960s two brands of cigars dominated the U.K. market. Both were short, dark, and strong. J.R. Freeman's Manikin, launched in 1917, was the best-seller, followed by Wills's Whiffs. In 1964 a new generation of cigar brands emerged, including Player's Doncella, Wills's Van Dyck, Churchman's Grandee, and J.R. Freeman's Hamlet.

Wanting a name that sounded quasi-European, Gallaher had toyed with the idea of calling the small cigar "Prince of Denmark," but decided that was too much of a mouthful. From there, though, it was a short step to "Hamlet." The cigar stood out from its competitors. It came in a light-colored hull and slide pack, while the others were in dark tins. It was longer, slimmer, and came wrapped in Connecticut shade-grown leaf, making it look and taste lighter than other cigars.

Early in 1961 Gallaher signed up a dynamic new London advertising agency, Collett Dickenson Pearce, which had opened its doors only the previous April. The agency immediately launched a major campaign for the little-known cigarette brand in a gold box—Benson & Hedges.

When faced with the new, distinctive cigar brand Hamlet, Collett embarked on what was then the unusual step of talking with consumers about why they smoked small cigars. This research showed that smokers felt a sense of inner relaxation and well-being. Cigars were seen as a small, affordable luxury that could punctuate their hectic lives. From this premise the proposition was developed that a Hamlet cigar brings "solace in the face of adversity."

Ian Warrener and Rob Curruthers made up Collett's creative team charged with the task of developing a strategy for the brand. Legend has it that they were waiting for a double-decker bus one evening in a howling gale. It was only when they ascended to the upper level of the vehicle that they were able to light up. Warrener inhaled deeply, leaned back, and said "Happiness is a cigarette on the top of a number 34 bus." Curruthers wrote it down, and the next day one of the most enduring theme lines in the history of British advertising was born: "Happiness is a cigar called Hamlet."

From the onset Hamlet ads introduced a new tone of voice. They were among the first to enjoy a joke with the audience. The ads shared the well-known and readily understood feeling that when the world seems to be against you, there may be little you can do about it. The best option, then, is to shrug off your cares and reach for a comforting cigar. The product did not claim to solve the problem but simply to make it easier to bear.

The advertising of many tobacco products at the time used idealized stereotypes, to which the target market—men in the 35-to-55 age group—could aspire. Hamlet took an opposing stance, showing a vulnerable main character in embarrassing or frustrating situations, finding refuge and relief in a quiet, restorative smoke. This became Britain's longest-running campaign, retaining its original strategy for more than 36 years.

Hamlet's debut TV commercial in black and white appeared in 1964. It showed a man with his leg in plaster, lying in a hospital bed, enjoying a cigar. This scenario developed into a three-stage story: problem, product, solution. The product enhanced the quality of life of the protagonist. This was exemplified by the "music teacher" commercial in 1966, in which a man tormented by his pupil's discordant piano playing finds solace in a Hamlet. The campaign was the first to use music as an integral element of the brand's personality. Hamlet became brand leader within eight years, toppling Manikin from the top slot in 1972, a position it has retained ever since.

Hamlet has run more than 100 TV commercials, approximately 50 print ads, and approximately 35 radio ads; Hamlet was the first advertiser on classical FM radio. Many of these ads have won awards. Perhaps the most memorable commercial—"Photobooth"—featured actor and comedian Gregor Fisher failing to have his photo taken. In 1995 a panel of international advertising journalists voted this "The best ad in the world. Ever."

Hamlet's advertising campaigns, including this TV spot from the early 1980s, have been among the most successful in British television history. *Courtesy of Gallaher, Ltd.*

Many Hamlet ads have covered topical events, such as the commercial that coincided with the launch of Channel 4 Television. The ad showed the station's logo coming together to form the number 5, instead of 4; the error was another of life's trials that a Hamlet cigar could help you cope with.

In the U.K. cigarettes and tobacco for hand rolling were banned from TV advertising in 1971, while ads for pipe tobacco and cigars (including Hamlet) were banned from TV in 1991. Anticipating that cinema tobacco advertising would be banned as of 9 December 1999, the agency made what was to be Hamlet's final cinema commercial. "Life" showed five scenarios based on the premise that everybody experiences "Hamlet moments." The agency hoped to perpetuate the memory of its ads by encouraging people to continue recognizing such moments in their own lives. In any event, tobacco advertising was granted a reprieve, and the total ban had not yet come into effect as of the end of 2001.

DAVE SAUNDERS

Further Reading

Salmon, John, and John Ritchie, *CDP: Inside Collett Dickenson Pearce*, London: Batsford, 2001

Saunders, Dave, *20th C Advertising*, London: Carlton Books, 1999

Hard-Sell/Soft-Sell Advertising

Among advertising professionals there has long persisted a debate over which advertising strategy is best, hard sell or soft sell. Indeed, advertising agencies have often been classified according to which of these two selling orientations underlies the firm's philosophy. The following passage from the "Tale of Two Salesmen" in the *Copywriter's Guide* (1959) highlights the differences between these two basic approaches to advertising.

Marmaduke Smith, a traveling salesman, spends a busy week in a small town. In his house-to-house selling, he concentrates his sales talk on the wonderful benefits the housewife will derive from using his products. This is the strategy of hard-sell advertising.

Now comes the second salesman. He likes the town and decides to settle down. So he sets about making friends first and sales afterward. He gives a picnic for the local Cub Scouts, takes part in varied civic activities, and shows the town he is a nice guy to have around. Then, when he offers his merchandise, he finds that people buy it with very little selling effort on his part because they like him and have confidence in him. This is the strategy of soft sell.

As the above anecdote suggests, hard-sell advertising uses a direct "reason why" approach that informs the headline, body copy, and visual components of the advertisement, all of which focus attention on how "you"—the consumer—can directly benefit from using the advertised product. The assumption about consumer decision-making underlying this approach is that such decisions are rational and reasoned. Soft-sell advertising, on the other hand, is more subtle and indirect—instead of emphasizing select rational benefits, such ads attempt to influence the consumer by evoking positive emotional responses that are then associated with the advertised product, brand, or company. Ad elements that are humorous or emit warmth and friendliness are used to elicit these emotional responses. The assumption about consumer decision-making underlying the soft-sell strategy is that such decisions are based on feelings.

The history of hard-sell advertising can be traced to the turn of the 20th century. In 1897 Charles Austin Bates described advertising as "salesmanship in print." However, Bates's notion did not gain much notice until 1904, when John E. Kennedy described advertising in similar terms to Albert Lasker in order to land a copywriting job at the Lord & Thomas advertising agency. Under

Kennedy's influence, Lord & Thomas pioneered the hard-sell strategy, an approach soon copied by numerous other firms.

Lord & Thomas was also to be responsible for the development of another style of advertising, which evolved from the hard-sell approach. Claude Hopkins, hired by Lasker as a copywriter, put his own stamp on the Kennedy style by creating brand images in advertisements. As Edward Applegate recounts in his book *Personalities and Products* (1998):

> Hopkins enjoyed visiting clients to see how products were manufactured. He visited Quaker Oats and observed how the company produced rice and wheat cereal, then he changed the name of one of the company's products from Wheat Berries to Puffed Wheat and employed the line "The cereal shot from guns."

Lord & Thomas had a major influence on the practice of advertising through the 1930s, when Lasker retired. In 1943 the agency became Foote, Cone & Belding (FCB), named for three executive vice presidents who purchased Lord & Thomas. FCB continued to have a significant influence, though not necessarily in the hard-sell tradition.

Another major innovator of the hard-sell method was Rosser Reeves, copy director and chief theoretician at the newly formed ad agency Ted Bates, Inc., in the 1940s. Reeves had a straightforward and direct style, best represented by his concept of the "unique selling proposition," or USP. Reeves insisted that every ad should offer a USP for the product being sold, and he taught that these propositions must be developed according to three distinct guidelines. First, the USP must involve a specific product benefit; second, the USP must be unique; and third, it must sell. Memorable USP's created by Reeves and the Ted Bates agency include: "M&M candies melt in your mouth, not in your hand," and "Colgate cleans your breath as it cleans your teeth." Once the USP was created, it could be repeated in advertising until it no longer worked to sell the product.

The Ted Bates agency was a major force in advertising throughout the mid-20th century, and Reeves in particular is remembered for his part in the history of political advertising. Although it does not resemble the ads used in campaigns today, Reeves's distinctly unflashy advertising for Dwight D. Eisenhower's 1952 presidential campaign was quite effective in its day. Typical of Reeves's hard-sell style, the campaign was called "Eisenhower Answers the Nation." The candidate was shown responding to questions asked on camera by typical voters. The questions dealt with such issues as inflation, high taxes, and foreign policy, and Eisenhower's answers were given in personal terms. In one commercial he noted that his wife had recently complained to him about high food prices.

In contrast to the styles of Kennedy, Hopkins, and Reeves was that of Theodore MacManus, whose agency MacManus, John & Adams had the Cadillac account. In 1914 MacManus wrote the classic model of the soft-sell or "impressionistic" ad. The headline was "The penalty of leadership," and beneath it was an eloquent and thoughtful essay on the burdens of being associated with

This 1903 house ad for the J. Walter Thompson Company—an example of hard-sell advertising—uses a direct, benefit-based appeal to market the agency's services.
Courtesy of J. Walter Thompson Company.

being the best in one's field. The copy never mentioned Cadillac; no illustration accompanied it. It ran in the *Saturday Evening Post* on 2 January 1915 and became one of the most influential single ads ever written. In subsequent surveys and polls of great advertising, it was frequently cited as the greatest advertisement ever written. Eighty-five years later *Advertising Age* ranked it 49th among the century's 100 best advertisements. In the 1920s and 1930s, Raymond Rubicam carried on the MacManus tradition in much of the work turned out by Young & Rubicam. In radio the agency became an early pioneer in integrating commercials into the flow of comedy and variety programs. Comedian Jack Benny's commercials for Jell-O, for example, often became part of the story line of his show.

The agency that best epitomized the soft-sell approach after World War II was Doyle Dane Bernbach (DDB). William Bernbach's approach emphasized creative execution, sometimes at the expense of content; Bernbach contended that a well-executed ad would stand apart from the clutter of other less distinctive ads. Entertainment and humor became trademarks of the Bernbach style. They were used both to gain the consumer's initial attention and to reward those who investigated the ads more fully.

Bernbach was responsible for a number of memorable ad campaigns. In 1962 DDB created the "We're number 2, we try harder" campaign for Avis rental cars. The agency also created for Volkswagen (VW) the memorable ad showing a picture of the original VW Beetle above the headline, "Lemon." When the VW ad debuted in 1960, the concept of humorously disparaging the advertised product was quite radical; the "Lemon" ad thus represented the birth of irony in modern advertising.

Whereas Reeves and Bernbach represent the hard-sell/soft-sell extremes, other agencies have blended the two approaches. David Ogilvy considered the content of the advertisement to be the most important element, stressing as his first commandment to copywriters that "what you say is more important than how you say it." His ads had a visual style that emphasized clarity of content, blending classic serif type fonts in capital and lowercase letters and using an editorial layout embracing illustrations that were already captioned. (Ogilvy's research revealed that more people read the caption under a picture than the body copy.) Ogilvy disapproved of printing headlines in all-capital letters because he thought they were too hard to read. The classic long-copy Ogilvy & Mather (O&M) ad is a model of easy readability, reflecting Ogilvy's conviction that content was vital. At the same time, Ogilvy believed in the importance of brand image, stating in his tenth commandment, "It is the total personality of the brand rather than any trivial product difference which decides its ultimate position in the market."

The Leo Burnett Company, in Chicago, Illinois, became known for creating dramatic ads that were both "warm" and "believable"—thus, Burnett created the "Jolly Green Giant," the "Marlboro Man," and other campaigns that developed a brand image through the use of drama (a soft-sell method), while at the same time providing information (a hard-sell approach).

Other agencies followed different paths. Young & Rubicam focused on product personality, often dramatically portraying the product as a hero. The J. Walter Thompson Company (JWT) stressed creativity in advertising execution. Saatchi & Saatchi developed a creative style similar to that of DDB, an agency that also influenced Lee Clow, creative director at Chiat/Day, who contended that advertising must create impact.

The debate rages on. In his 15 December 1997 *Advertising Age* column, Rance Crain observed that the ad community is still

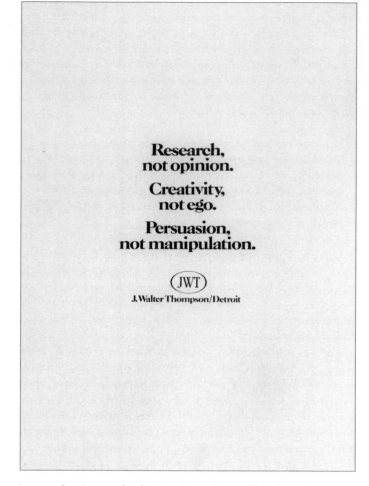

A 1973 advertisement for the Detroit, Michigan, office of J. Walter Thompson Company takes a soft-sell approach, emphasizing the abstract, intellectual qualities of its work.
Courtesy of J. Walter Thompson Company.

divided on which approach is the best, pointing out that some of the most memorable campaigns have been those that appeal to both "head and heart." Some of the classic ads that blend hard-sell and soft-sell methods include Ajax's White Knight, Nine Lives' Morris the Cat, and Clairol's "Does she or doesn't she?" campaigns.

Although individuals in the advertising industry may not want to admit to using both approaches, their agencies' philosophies suggest otherwise. The philosophy of JWT, for example (as described on the agency's Web site), emphasizes the importance of the brand, which "is represented as a set of convictions in the consumer's mind." To reinforce these convictions, a dialogue must be created between the advertiser and the consumer through the "big powerful idea," which can be either a "rational argument vividly displayed" (a hard sell) or an "emotional affinity vividly displayed" (a soft sell).

Burnett describes itself as a "brand-driven" agency. The firm's primary focus is the creation of a consistent brand image across all communication media used by an advertiser. According to its

Web site, Leo Burnett aims to produce advertising "so interrupting, so daring, so fresh, so engaging, so human, so believable and so well-focused as to themes and ideas that at one and the same time it would build a quality reputation for the long haul as it produced sales for the immediate present."

Ogilvy & Mather still adheres to David Ogilvy's philosophy of making "advertising that sells." This perspective is reflected in the agency's belief—similar to that of JWT and Leo Burnett—that advertising that builds brands is the most effective. Therefore, O&M works to enhance the relationship consumers have with a brand. BBDO also strives to reinforce the consumer-brand relationship. That agency states that advertising needs to provide a "positive experience" for its audience. According to BBDO, ads should also be likable and have substance. FCB echoes a similar philosophy: "Create ideas that sell today and build brand value over time."

Proponents of the two approaches continue to debate this issue. One particularly productive topic for discussion concerns the identification of those situations when one method or the other may be more effective. John Rossiter and Larry Percy, former ad agency executives, have attempted to provide direction for creative strategy by developing a two-stage planning model (known as the Rossiter-Percy Grid). Under this model, advertisers first focus on the communications objectives for their advertising (brand recognition or brand recall) and then they consider which strategies will be most persuasive given those objectives.

As the extensive discussion found in Rossiter and Percy's book *Advertising Communications and Promotion Management* explains, the grid analyzes the purchase motivations of consumers of particular types of products. Consumers purchase certain products, such as cleaning solutions, microwave ovens, and computer hardware, to solve problems (negative motivations). In these situations advertisements using informational creative tactics are often most effective. In other words, in this context the traditional "hard-sell" approach typically works best, although Rossiter and Percy suggest that ads may also succeed by combining emotional appeals with the benefit-claim approach.

Consumers purchase fashion items, accessories, perfumes, and other similar products to reward themselves (positive motivations). These products are considered transformational, since the use of the product is supposed to change the consumer for the better. In these instances the traditional soft-sell approach is recommended. Again, Rossiter and Percy provide alternatives for using a creative strategy based on either emotions or claims of benefit. Automobiles are often advertised through a two-tiered approach, in which the manufacturer builds an emotional relationship between the brand and the consumer while regional dealer associations compete on the more hard-sell basis of price.

The hard-sell/soft-sell debate remains a source of controversy among practitioners and academics. Because agencies typically combine elements of both approaches in contemporary campaigns, it seems likely that in the future parties in this debate will focus most closely on what degree of hard- or soft-sell is best.

HARLAN E. SPOTTS

Further Reading

Aaker, David A., and John G. Myers, *Advertising Management*, Englewood Cliffs, New Jersey: Prentice-Hall, 1975

Applegate, Edd, *Personalities and Products: A Historical Perspective on Advertising in America*, Westport, Connecticut: Greenwood Press, 1998

BBDO Web site, <www.bbdo.com/beliefs/body.html>

Crain, Rance, "Ad Industry Still Doesn't Know Which Half of Ad Budgets Wasted," *Advertising Age* (15 December 1997)

FCB Web site, <www.fcb.com>

French, Elbrun Rochford, *The Copywriter's Guide*, New York: Harper, 1959

J. Walter Thompson Web site, <www.jwt.com/jwt/philosophy/ttb/2.2.1.html>

Leo Burnett Web site, <www.leoburnett.com/content/beliefs/operating_philosophy.html>

Ogilvy, David, *Ogilvy on Advertising*, London: Pan, 1983; New York: Crown, 1983

Ogilvy and Mather Web site, <www.ogilvy.com/o mther/flash/o mather1 text.asp>

Rossiter, John R., and Larry Percy, *Advertising and Promotion Management*, New York: McGraw-Hill, 1987; 2nd edition, as *Advertising Communications and Promotions Management*, New York: McGraw-Hill, 1997

Harper, Marion 1916–1989

U.S. Advertising Executive

Marion Harper was the first advertising agency executive to create a huge international ad agency holding company that offered myriad marketing services and handled the accounts of competing clients. His activities during the 1950s and 1960s led to a burgeoning of mergers and acquisitions by other agencies during the 1970s, and his early experiments in providing multiple marketing services foreshadowed the integrated marketing communications agencies of the 1990s.

Harper was born in Oklahoma City, Oklahoma, in 1916. He attended Yale University, New Haven, Connecticut, graduating with honors in 1938. The following year Harper joined the McCann-Erickson agency in New York City and began a meteoric rise through the agency ranks. He began in the young men's training program, but he quickly impressed agency executives by devising a formula for predicting which types of creative executions would score best in Starch Readership Reports, surveys that measure the attention readers pay to print ads. The agency used his system to predict readership scores before the ads were published. Assigned to the research department, Harper became a potent member of the new-business team, and his extensive research on clients garnered many new accounts.

Harper was named research director and made a vice president in 1942 at the age of 26. Six years later he was named president of McCann-Erickson. By that time McCann-Erickson had a good reputation and international offices, but Harper felt the agency was lacking in creative talent. He reasoned that to attract bright creative people, he needed a larger business; for the business to grow, he needed good clients.

One obstacle to growth was the problem of competing accounts. In constructing a holding company he acted on the assumption that agencies in the company could handle competing accounts as long as competitors were not served by the same agency. To accomplish this separation of responsibility, each agency would have to maintain its own identity, and no agencies within the holding company could exchange information. Agencies would pay the holding company for legal, personnel, and other services. Harper first purchased the Marschalk & Pratt agency in 1954, and after success there, he acquired other agencies.

In addition to adding agencies, Harper expanded the business internationally, opening offices in approximately 16 countries. He also began establishing separate companies that specialized in different services, such as public relations, research, sales promotion, and market research. Each company was given a separate identity, which made paying extra for these services more palatable to clients.

Harper was able to attract many talented creative people. The advertising industry was skeptical, but Harper persevered, and the business grew. Within five years after he became president, McCann-Erickson's billings had doubled, reaching $100 million. Three years later, in 1956, billings again doubled. Harper's goal was to achieve billings of $1 billion.

During this time, McCann added some of its most important clients to its roster, including Bulova, Esso, Nestlé, and Westinghouse Electric. Harper shocked the industry when he resigned the Chrysler account, worth about $27 million in billings, in order to accept Buick, valued at $14 million. But the Buick account led to more business from parent company General Motors Corporation, including Chevrolet and GMC trucks, and eventually resulted in more than $100 million in billings. Harper won the Coca-Cola account by presenting a global strategy that turned Coca-Cola's business around. He was known for his exhaustive preparation before delivering a new business presentation to a client, and his methods proved successful in gaining many new accounts.

Marion Harper.
Photograph from the American Advertising Federation's 50th Anniversary Advertising Hall of Fame book.

In 1961 he placed all of the agencies under the Interpublic Group, the new conglomerate he had built. He continued to buy agencies, and the huge holding company grew at an accelerated pace. By 1966 Interpublic owned companies (agencies, research firms, etc.) in 100 cities in 48 countries and served 1,900 clients. The holding company's staff grew to 8,700 people, of whom 5,500 were outside the United States.

By 1967, however, the costs involved in acquiring agencies, hiring experienced people, and paying the high overhead required to run the conglomerate began to weaken Interpublic. Although its billings that year were $700 million, its losses were estimated to be $2 million to $3 million, and Harper ran into difficulty with several banks over loan agreements. When Interpublic was unable to satisfy the bankers through cost-cutting measures, they forced Harper's removal as chairman of the board in November 1967. He stayed with Interpublic for a few months but then resigned.

In his later years Harper indicated that he might have made a mistake in trying simultaneously to increase international business, acquire agencies, and expand marketing services. After his resignation from Interpublic, he engaged in several small ventures, then virtually disappeared for 12 years. He reappeared in Oklahoma City in 1979, when he talked informally with a reporter from *Advertising Age* about publishing a work on marketing and company organization. He was next heard from in 1982, in an interview published in Bart Cummings's *The Benevolent Dictators,* in which he spoke of his meteoric rise at McCann-Erickson and his reasons for building Interpublic. He died in 1989 at the age of 73.

CAROLYN STRINGER

Biography

Born in Oklahoma City, Oklahoma, 14 May 1916; graduated Yale University with honors, 1938; joined McCann-Erickson agency, 1939; became vice president and research director, 1942; named president, 1948; formed Interpublic Group of Companies and became its chairman and president, 1961; died in Oklahoma City at age 73 on 30 October 1989; named posthumously to Advertising Hall of Fame, 1998.

Further Reading

Cummings, Bart, *The Benevolent Dictators: Interviews with Advertising Greats,* Chicago: Crain, 1984

Daniels, Draper, *Giants, Pigmies, and Other Advertising People,* Chicago: Crain, 1974

Fox, Stephen, *The Mirror Makers: A History of American Advertising and Its Creators,* New York: Morrow, 1984

Johnston, Russ, *Marion Harper: An Unauthorized Biography,* Chicago: Crain, 1982

"What Makes Marion Harper Run?" *Newsweek* (30 March 1964)

C.F. Hathaway Shirt Company

Principal Agencies

Ogilvy & Mather
Eric Mower & Associates
TBWA Chiat/Day

Few companies have enjoyed a more successful long-term relationship with their advertising agencies than the C.F. Hathaway Company had with Ogilvy & Mather. In 1951 the "Man in the Hathaway Shirt" campaign, created by David Ogilvy, produced soaring sales for the company's unique three-hole button dress shirts and established the reputation of Ogilvy & Mather as a top creative shop. The campaign, which for the first four years ran exclusively in *The New Yorker* magazine, became the classic example of the power of a strong brand image.

The C.F. Hathaway Company of Waterville, Maine, established in 1837, pioneered the ready-to-wear shirt business in the United States. After operating for more than 100 years with no advertising, company management contacted David Ogilvy and asked him to handle the account. The ad budget was only $30,000, but the company promised Ogilvy that if he took the account, Hathaway would never fire him nor would it ever alter his copy. The agreement stood for more than 20 years, until well after Ogilvy left the agency.

For the original campaign, Ogilvy came up with the idea of using a distinguished-looking model with a patch over one eye to give the ad "story appeal," a provocative element in the creative concept that would build attention and memorability. In an interview with the American Association of Advertising Agencies, Ogilvy discussed the idea behind the creation of the eye-patch-wearing model who became known as the "Man in the Hathaway Shirt":

[Hathaway] came to us after not advertising for 106 years and they asked if we would take on the account. . . . Well, I had been reading a book titled *Attitude and Interest Factors in Advertising* by Harold Rudolph and in this book Rudolph said pictures had a certain story appeal and the more story appeal a photo had, the more people would look at your ad. So, I started writing down ideas about how to get story appeal and I wrote 18 and the man wearing the eye patch was the 18th. And that idea has lasted 19 years.

In 1983 the company left Ogilvy & Mather and moved to Eric Mower & Associates. No reason was given, but there was speculation that Hathaway was too small to remain with such a large agency. At that time, its advertising budget was approximately $1 million. During the association with Mower, the budget never topped $2 million.

Mower decided to keep the strong eye-patch brand image but bring new life to it by including real "Hathaway men." The list of models asked to don the eye patch during the seven years Mower had the account included media entrepreneur Ted Turner, former Texas governor and U.S. Treasury Secretary John Connally, *Megatrends* author John Naisbitt, and Marriott Corporation executive J.W. Marriott. Although the campaign was successful in maintaining the strong brand image developed by Ogilvy, Hathaway sales suffered as Americans began to dress more casually and the demand for dress shirts declined.

In 1988 Hathaway left Eric Mower & Associates for TBWA Chiat/Day. The reason given for the change was an inability to work well with a new management team. After a brief stay at TBWA, the account was moved in-house.

Until 1996 Hathaway was a Warnaco company offering dress and sports shirts and sportswear. In May 1996 Warnaco announced that the two plants producing Hathaway branded shirts would close. Only a six-month cooperative effort by workers, union officials, business, and government saved the plants. Eventually an investment group led by former Maine Governor John McKernan bought the Hathaway plant and label.

Hathaway's media budget for 1997 was $600,000. Ad dollars were primarily spent on newspaper, consumer magazine, and co-op advertising (local advertising whose cost is shared by the company and local retailers). That same year the company announced that it planned to revive what it called "one of the best icons of all time"—the man with the eye patch.

OLAN FARNALL

See also color plate in this volume

Further Reading

Ogilvy, David, *Ogilvy on Advertising*, New York: Crown, and London: Pan, 1983

Raphaelson, Joel, editor, *The Unpublished David Ogilvy*, New York: Crown, 1986

Havas Advertising

Havas Advertising, today a large agency holding company, traces its roots to 1835, when former shipping magnate Charles-Louis Havas created the world's first press agency, Agence Havas, and set out to become the principal supplier of foreign news to the burgeoning French media. At age 40, Havas had accumulated countless contacts and a command of several European languages during his years in the shipping trade, enabling him to obtain and translate foreign news unavailable to the leading French newspapers.

Havas was not only a competent press baron, he was also a shrewd businessman. His press agency traded its foreign dispatches to newspapers for advertising space that it later sold to shopkeepers and small businesses. The French writer Honoré de Balzac publicly criticized Havas's resulting monopoly on information and advertising as early as 1840, but his barbs drew little comment from newspaper owners, advertisers, and government officials, all of whom saw economic merit in the system. Historians now view Havas's business plan—which combined marketing advice, advertising materials, and media space—as a precursor to the integrated communications services offered today by the industry's leading groups, including Havas Advertising.

Havas's advertising activity blossomed in 1857, when Agence Havas, now run by second-generation scion Auguste Havas, joined forces with Charles Duveyrier, owner of the Sociéte Genérale des Annonces, France's principal advertising company. By the time Auguste Havas retired in 1879, the family operation had been transformed into a limited liability company with offices across the French provinces and foreign bureaus spanning Africa, Europe, and the Middle East.

Havas's activity was stoked in 1881 by a law that radically extended freedom of the press, creating new competition in the media business and fresh opportunities for raising advertising revenues. The company was split into two divisions, one for news coverage and another for advertising operations, and began working with an American advertising man, John F. Jones, whose Compagnie Genérale de Publicité brought new sales and communications methods to the French market. By the beginning of the 20th century Havas was producing and placing distinctive press-ready ads in newspapers and magazines for clients, including

Comio motorcycles, the Menier chocolate company, Pathé cinemas, and the Cosmydor line of soaps.

French executive Leon Renier, who had worked with many of these clients, took over the helm of Havas in 1916. Renier's tenure began slowly, as World War I stunted economic expansion worldwide, but Havas's advertising division experienced its own "golden age" from 1920 to 1939, operating as Havas Publicité.

The company won distribution rights to massive amounts of government advertising, which allowed for a rapid growth of private sector activities. Havas began offering clients brand counseling, consumer research, media planning, and ad creation. It ran ad sales networks for the print press, radio, and cinema, and operated an extensive stable of outdoor advertising infrastructure divisions.

Havas's campaigns from this period turned the antiflea powder Marie Rose into one of the country's leading brands. It hired crooner Charles Trenet to sing radio jingles that turned a brand of tea, Thé des Famille, into a national leader. Similarly, musician Ray Ventura led an orchestra at the Lustucru Théatre, which made the packaged foods company Lustucru a household name.

The 1920s were not without scandal, however. Havas came under attack for its near monopoly on providing the provincial press with financial and economic news, much of which was often little more than advertorials for its clients in the banking and investment sector. The group flexed its muscles in an advertising war against independent newspaper owner François Coty in 1928 after he refused to allow Havas to handle ad sales for his low-cost daily *L'Ami du Peuple* (Friend of the People). In a precedent-setting move, Havas retaliated by forcing its major newspaper clients to refuse advertising from any companies that circumvented Havas to advertise in *L'Ami du Peuple*. A series of French courts contested this practice as unfair, but none was able to force the newspapers to end the Havas-imposed ban.

The advent of World War II ended Havas's golden run. The Vichy government, coming to power in 1940, nationalized the news service, renaming it the French Information Office, and forced it to work under the orders of Germany's military occupation force. The office maintained a monopoly on government advertising, leading to resentment against Havas and charges of collaboration that lasted long after France was liberated in 1944.

France's first postwar government confirmed the Vichy government's nationalization. It turned Havas's former news service into Agence France Presse, an ongoing wire service, and moved many of its advertising assets into the newly created National Publicity Office. The office, based in Havas's headquarters, was granted wide-ranging powers over the advertising industry as well as a temporary monopoly on the distribution of government advertising.

It did not replace Havas, however, and the group gradually came out of hibernation during the late 1940s. By the early 1950s, under the leadership of Jacques Douce, recruited from Havas's provincial office in Grenoble, France, the agency was back on its feet. It once again assumed the principal role in distributing government advertising. It reclaimed its place as a leading provider of advertising and publicity services to the private sector. And it diversified into new activities, including directory services production, travel services, and media operations.

In 1958 the company's various advertising activities were grouped under a new state-owned company, Havas Conseil, which was completely separated from other businesses in 1968, when it reported $70 million in billings, or about 12 percent of all French advertising.

The 1970s marked a period of rapid growth and diversification for Havas Conseil. International division Univas, comprised of 21 Havas agencies in 13 countries, formed a nonfinancial partnership with S.H. Benson, of London, England, and Needham, Harper & Steers, Inc., of New York City, in 1971. The new joint venture created the world's 11th-largest agency network, with international billings topping $300 million, but never led to full integration of business activities.

In 1972 the government decided to restructure Havas, beginning with a partial privatization of Havas Conseil, France's largest agency, whose billings topped $100 million. In 1974 Havas management created the Eurocom holding company, which consolidated the group's various advertising companies into four principal divisions: Havas Conseil; Ecom, partnered with the Univas international agency network; Futurs; and the Belier Group.

Eurocom expanded internationally in 1976, when its Univas division bought a 50 percent stake in Boase Massimi Pollitt (BMP), of London, marking the first time a French agency had made such an important acquisition across the English Channel. Eurocom continued its expansion in 1978, picking up $70 million in billings with the acquisition of the U.S.-based agency Kelly, Nason, Inc., and winning its first business from a future anchor client, automaker Peugeot, for a series of campaigns for the 104 model.

Havas Conseil won the entire Peugeot automotive account in 1981, establishing itself as the carmaker's sole agency and laying a critical foundation for its future expansion. In 1982 Eurocom acquired a controlling stake in the packaging, retail, and restaurant holding company Goulet, of Paris, France, a controversial diversification strategy aimed at staking a presence in nonmedia areas linked to its main clients. Later that year, it acquired the Bazaine agency, securing its control over the top of the French advertising industry, and listed Eurocom SA on the Paris Bourse.

The death of Douce, at 57, president of Eurocom, Havas Conseil, and Univas and general manager of Agence Havas, sent ripples through the company's management structure. Shuffles at the top boded well for Alain de Pouzilhac, an up-and-coming 37-year-old packaged-goods specialist who was promoted to president of Eurocom's leading division, Havas Conseil. In 1984 de Pouzilhac showed the mettle that would eventually advance him to the position of chief executive officer of Havas Advertising by negotiating a new joint venture between Havas Conseil and Young & Rubicam's Marsteller, Inc., unit. The HCM network was born in January 1985, with billings topping $500 million and a blue-chip client roster led by Peugeot and Philips N.V. By year's end, it had added more than $140 million in new billings from clients such as Danone Group and the Jack-in-the-Box fast-food chain.

The HCM deal furthered the financial clout of Eurocom, by now a corporate holding company with 144 divisions, 6,000 employees, and billings topping $4 billion, spread across four advertising groups—HCM, Univas, Polaris, and Belier.

The year 1987 was marked by two events: the partial privatization of Eurocom's corporate parent, Havas, and a move toward internationalization across the advertising group. In May the Paris-based creative shop Alice joined the CDP international network, which had offices across Europe. In July the HCM joint venture with Y&R was extended to include a third party, the Japanese agency network Dentsu, and the newly formed entity was named HDM. In September, the Belier Group, already number one in the French market, allied itself with the U.K.-based WCRS Group, owned by Aegis, of London, creating an international agency network with a strong presence in both Europe and the United States. Finally, in December, Eurocom's Polaris division merged with Synergie, the French division of Bozell, Inc., to create a new French powerhouse linked to an international network with offices in more than 40 countries.

By the end of 1988, following the consolidation of prior acquisitions and the $90 million acquisition of top free-press publisher Comareg, Eurocom reported billings topping $5 billion, making it the world's number-six holding company. Billings hit $6.2 billion in 1989 after Eurocom increased its stake in WCRS from 20 percent to 60 percent, taking it to fifth place globally. De Pouzilhac, now president of Eurocom, rolled the WCRS holdings into a new network, EWDB: E for Eurocom, W for WCRS, D for Della Femina, McNamee WCRS, Inc., and B for the Ball Partnership, WCRS's Asia-Pacific unit. Eurocom also struck a deal with WCRS to buy a minority share in the Carat International media-buying unit, greatly expanding its presence in this sector.

Eurocom entered the 1990s with a new passion: restructuring. The company sold its packaging unit Techpack to Pechiney Group and began consolidating divisions. HDM, the three-way venture with Dentsu and Y&R, and recently created EWDB were both merged into a new holding company, Eurocom Advertising. But that entity would prove to be short-lived, giving way in October 1991 to Euro RSCG, formed from the surprising merger of Eurocom and French rival RSCG. The deal linked the unquestioned creativity of legendary French adman Jacques Séguéla and the business acumen of de Pouzilhac and his associates at Eurocom. It brought together more than $6 billion in billings and operations in 27 countries, to form the number-seven global agency. Its client list was a who's who of industry, including car brands Citroen and Peugeot, French carrier Air France, cosmetics leader L'Oréal, and various brands from food giants Nestlé and Danone.

Séguéla, a longtime critic of both the Havas media group and its Eurocom subsidiary, did a famous about-face on the day of the buyout, stating at a media conference that the deal marked "the happiest day of my life." In fact, Séguéla was probably happier to save his skin. Ill-timed network expansion and a global recession linked to the Gulf War had crushed ad sales in the 1990 to 1991 period, leading RSCG to rack up debts topping $150 million. The Eurocom buyout offered Séguéla and his colleagues the chance to cash in their investments and make a fresh start in key positions at Europe's largest network.

Not all of the group's clients supported the merger, however. Italian automaker Fiat withdrew its $70 million French account over concerns about the consolidation of the Peugeot and Citroen accounts under the same banner. Similarly, Euro RSCG was forced to resign an estimated $60 million in pan-European work with German packaged-goods marketer Henkel to appease rival packaged-goods giant Procter & Gamble Company.

While de Pouzilhac, Séguéla, and the rest of the upper management team at the various agencies dealt with the fallout from account losses, restructuring continued the following month. Euro RSCG merged the Belier agency and HDM into Eurocom France, making it Europe's largest agency with gross income of $250 million.

The 1992 to 1996 period marked the completion of the fusion between Eurocom, RSCG, and the remaining Havas agencies, as well as radical expansion of the Euro RSCG Worldwide network. The group struck a media-buying partnership with Young & Rubicam in 1994 and produced numerous award-winning advertisements, including a memorable television spot in which the blind singer Ray Charles drove a Peugeot 306 across Utah's Bonneville Salt Flats.

Euro RSCG was renamed Havas Advertising in 1996, taking into account the famed brand name of the company's largest shareholder, Havas, which held a 37 percent stake in what had become the fifth-largest global communications group. Euro RSCG Worldwide was retained as the name for a holding company unit of Havas that is comprised of its European Euro RSCG agencies as well as Messner Vetere Berger McNamee Schmetterer/ Euro RSCG in New York City and other shops.

Ever the strategist, de Pouzilhac, now president and managing director, divided Havas Advertising into four divisions:

- Euro RSCG, a global network with offices in 61 countries and a client roster that included Citroen, Danone, Kraft General Foods, L'Oréal, Nestlé, Peugeot, Philips, and Procter & Gamble.
- Campus, a European network with agencies in France, Germany, Italy, Spain, and the United Kingdom.
- Diversified Agencies, a group of 30 agencies across Europe specializing in the marketing services area.
- Mediapolis, the joint venture space-buying arm operated since 1994 with Y&R.

The French utilities and communications entity Compagnie General des Eaux—later renamed Vivendi Universal—acquired a majority stake in Havas, including the controlling stake in Havas Advertising, in 1997, and vowed to put the group at the center of an integrated communication and media division. Vivendi executives later decided that advertising was not a core business and gradually reduced their stake in Havas Advertising to less than 10 percent in 2000.

The new century brought another major development for the French group when Havas Advertising announced plans in February 2000 for a $2.1 billion all-share buyout of U.S.-based Snyder Communications, Bethesda, Maryland, parent of Arnold Communications. The transaction moved Havas to fourth place in the global rankings, creating an international holding company with 20,000 employees in 75 countries generating billings of nearly $20 billion and income topping $2 billion. The deal was completed with Havas Advertising listed on the U.S. NASDAQ exchange in September 2000.

Havas Advertising consolidated its media buying division in early 2001, announcing plans to pay a group of Spanish shareholders upward of $500 million in cash and stock for the remaining 55 percent stake in a joint venture created in 1999. The deal gave the Spanish shareholders control over 9.3 percent of Havas's share capital, but allowed the French giant to assume full control over a division that recorded billings of $8.45 billion and income topping $200 million from operations in more than 15 key advertising markets across Europe, Latin America, and the United States in 2000. Havas had worldwide gross income of $2.8 billion in 2000, up 7.8 percent from 1999, on billings of $26.3 billion.

In October 2001 Havas Advertising announced a wide-ranging restructuring program aimed at heading off revenue shortfalls linked to the economic downturn affecting the advertising industry. The restructuring focused primarily on the dismantling of the group's Diversified Agencies division, whose assets and operations were merged into Havas's three principal "brands": the Euro RSCG Worldwide and Arnold Worldwide Partners advertising networks and media specialist MPG. At the end of the year the company announced plans to officially drop the term *Advertising* from its corporate identity, reclaiming the Havas name under which the group was established in the 19th century.

LAWRENCE J. SPEER

Hearst, William Randolph 1863–1951

U.S. Publisher

William Randolph Hearst was America's first true media baron. At the height of his empire in the 1930s, he had built the country's first national newspaper chain and owned 25 daily newspapers, a handful of radio stations, and an impressive stable of magazines, many of which Hearst Corporation continued to publish into the next century. In fact, although the company in the early 21st century had far fewer newspapers than in Hearst's era, its overall holdings made it a vastly larger media player than during its founder's heyday.

Hearst was born into wealth in San Francisco, California. His father, George, was a gold- and copper-mining tycoon and a U.S. senator from California. The young Hearst attended Harvard University, but was expelled because of pranks. On returning home, he was given the San Francisco *Examiner* by his father. It became a financial success under the new editor's flamboyant leadership, and, in 1895 he bought the New York *Journal.* Thus began one of the great newspaper wars in U.S. history, as Hearst and his *Journal* battled Joseph Pulitzer and his New York paper, the *World,* for circulation, each trying to outdo the other with screaming headlines and sensationalized articles. The phrase "yellow journalism" grew out of this period, originating in the papers' dispute over the rights to the comic strip "The Yellow Kid," which appeared first in the *World* and then in the *Journal.*

Charges of journalistic sensationalism would dog Hearst for the rest of his long life—not without justification. His newspapers blatantly used the news columns to promote their chief's causes—including the United States's entry into the Spanish-American War. At its peak, the highly centralized Hearst chain had at least one daily paper in most of the largest U.S. cities. They looked alike and all carried the same editorials, often written by or at the behest of Hearst. He introduced bold headlines, halftone newsprint photos, and color comics, and he invested heavily in new technology and promotion. His worldwide publishing empire eventually included 32 major city papers; 13 magazines; King Features Syndicate; radio and TV stations; Metrotone News; and movie and book companies.

A larger-than-life figure, Hearst had political aspirations. Running as a Democrat, he was elected to the U.S. House of Representatives from New York in 1902 and unsuccessfully sought the party's nomination for president of the United States two years later. He also lost races for governor of New York and mayor of New York City.

An avaricious collector of objets d'art, Hearst built "castles" in which to house them, the grandest of which was at San Simeon on the California coast about 175 miles south of San Francisco. He lived there with his mistress, actress Marion Davies, and threw lavish parties attended by a who's who of the entertainment, business, and political worlds. The lavish house and grounds were later opened to the public as part of the California parks system.

In 1941 Orson Welles directed and starred in the movie *Citizen Kane,* a thinly veiled and somewhat fictionalized story of Hearst's life, including his fast-and-loose journalistic style and his 30-year relationship with Davies. The aging media tycoon reacted violently, using all his leverage to suppress the film. He was partially successful: some theater chains refused to screen *Citizen Kane,* and the Hearst papers refused to carry advertising for it. Nonetheless, it ultimately has been acknowledged as one of the greatest American films.

In his later years, Hearst adopted an archconservative stance, which was reflected in his newspapers' editorials—and often in their news columns as well. He became an outspoken foe of U.S. President Franklin D. Roosevelt's New Deal policies and an ardent anti-Communist. In the late 1930s and on into the 1940s, his publishing empire shrunk, and at one point he was near bankruptcy. Many of his newspapers were sold or shuttered, and his health steadily failed. He died in Beverly Hills, California, in 1951 at the age of 87, no longer the mighty press baron of earlier days.

William Randolph Hearst.
Courtesy of The Hearst Corporation.

In the decades since his death, Hearst Corporation has thrived, although newspapers have become relatively less important in the company's media mix. Of Hearst's remaining papers, only two are holdovers from the days of the founder. But in addition to such titles as *Cosmopolitan, Good Housekeeping, Harper's Bazaar,* and *Town & Country,* which were founded in Hearst's era, many magazines have been added to the Hearst stable since his death, among them *Esquire, Redbook,* and *Victoria.* The privately held Hearst Corporation ranked 15th among U.S. media companies in 1999, with net media revenue of $3.71 billion, according to *Advertising Age.* It ranked second in magazine revenue, seventh in newspaper revenue, and eighth in television revenue.

ROBERT GOLDSBOROUGH

Biography

Born in San Francisco, California, 29 April 1863; expelled from Harvard University, 1885; given the San Francisco *Examiner* by his father, George Hearst, 1887; bought the New York *Journal,* 1895; elected as a Democrat from New York state to the U.S. House of Representatives, 1902; unsuccessfully sought the Democratic nomination for U.S. president, 1904; ran unsuccessfully for governor of New York and mayor of New York City. Died in Beverly Hills, California, 14 April 1951.

Selected Publication

William Randolph Hearst, A Portrait in His Own Words, 1952 (edited by Edmond D. Coblentz)

Further Reading

Endicott, R. Craig, and John Fine, "100 Leading Media Companies," *Advertising Age* (21 August 2000)

Hearst, William Randolph Jr., with Jack Casserly, *The Hearsts: Father and Son,* Niwot, Colorado: Rinehart, 1991

Nasaw, David, *The Chief: The Life of William Randolph Hearst,* Boston: Houghton Mifflin, 2000

Presbrey, Frank, *The History and Development of Advertising,* Garden City, New York: Doubleday Doran, 1929; reprint, New York: Greenwood Press, 1968

Swanberg, W.A., *Citizen Hearst,* New York: Galahad Books, 1961

"We're Buying and Not Selling, Says Hearst Jr.," *Advertising Age* (24 March 1952)

Heineken

Principal Agencies

Kelly, Nason & Winston
MacManus, John & Adams
Fuller & Smith & Ross
Warwick Advertising, Inc.
Wells Rich Greene BDDP
Lowe & Partners/SMS

Heineken, a lager brewed in The Netherlands and brought to the United States by a Dutch immigrant after the repeal of Prohibition in 1933, has always been marketed as a premium beer for cultivated tastes. Until competition forced its hand, the company relied on the distinctive green bottle and the product within to speak for its brew. In December 1933 Leo van Munching, Sr., brought his family and 50 cases of Heineken with him to the United States, having talked the brewery into making him its sole distributor in the American market. The relationship lasted until late 1990.

Five years after the first imports of Heineken to the United States, the Heineken board decided to strongly support the market by sponsoring a Heineken pavilion at the World Expo in New York City in 1939. But the euphoria did not last; the Nazi invasion of Holland and Japan's entry into World War II curtailed exports. The Dutch government did not allow Heineken to restart its export business to the United States until 1946. Still, the war proved a fortuitous marketing opportunity because U.S. servicemen stationed in Europe acquired a taste for the sophisticated European lager and brought that thirst back home with them.

After the war van Munching hired the agency Hershon & Garfield and continued to play on the "foreign" cachet, primarily by not stooping to what he believed was commonplace advertising. Instead, in the 1960s he purchased quarter- and half-page ads in *The New Yorker* magazine, placed by MacManus, John & Adams. In the 1970s, however, the company's advertising began to change, under the leadership of Leo van Munching, Jr., who followed his father into the business and switched agencies, hiring Fuller & Smith & Ross, Inc. Color print ads were introduced to highlight the distinctive green bottle, and in the mid-1970s the first TV spots were aired.

Heineken's entry into television broke the mold of the traditional beer commercial. Previously, beer ads had featured back-slapping men sitting around in bars. Heineken's ads pictured only the bottle with the tag line, "America's No. 1-selling imported beer." The simple yet effective campaign, with subtle variations in wording and background settings, ran for 15 years, and by 1979

Heineken accounted for 41 percent of all import beer sales. It was always positioned as a high-class brew, so van Munching took care to preserve its niche. For instance, ads were never placed on television and radio programs or in publications with questionable plots or language.

When it came time to launch a light beer, the brewer dubbed it "Amstel Light," to separate it from its core product. In its brown bottle Amstel Light was positioned as a premium imported light beer and was targeted directly to women with the slogan, "95 calories never tasted so good."

Throughout the 1970s Heineken remained at the top of the still tiny import category, and the company saw little reason to tinker with the advertising. Import beers truly came into their own in the United States in the 1980s, as they were taken up by young urban professionals seeking a better life. Heineken frequently expanded its media budget to hang onto its crown. But it was not the only import yuppies were reaching for; increasingly, they ordered Corona Extra. By 1986 Corona, which appealed to a young audience seeking trendy new products, had surpassed Molson and Beck's to become the number-two import beer. Heineken realized that it needed a fresh approach to capture the younger end of the market while not alienating its longtime consumers.

In addition to Lintas's developing new approaches, van Munching, invited other agencies to bid for the company's business. The winner was Warwick Advertising, Inc., which positioned Heineken against faddish beers. For the first time, Heineken went directly after the competition with ads that all but spelled out what the fad beers were. The new tag line in 1988 became "When you're done kidding around, Heineken."

The 1990s brought a new team of competitors in the form of the microbreweries being spawned around the United States. Products such as Samuel Adams Boston Lager and Pete's Wicked Ale threatened Heineken's image with direct knocks at imports in advertising, marketing panache, and premium pricing.

Heineken's ad message remained the same in the early 1990s, despite a change in corporate control. Van Munching sold the rights to the brand in the United States back to Heineken, and Van Munching Company, Inc., became an operating company under the control of Heineken. The "When you're done kidding around" campaign of 1988 gave way to "Just being the best is enough" in 1991. But it was not enough. Sales continued to wilt, in part because of the effect of federal taxes. In 1997 Corona Extra dethroned Heineken as the top import.

The 1990s brought changes to Heineken's international marketing strategy as well. Since 1974, Heineken's slogan in the United Kingdom, created by Collett Dickenson Pearce, had been,

"Heineken refreshes the parts other beers cannot reach." The first TV commercials with this theme aired on British TV in 1986. One spot showed a gulp of Heineken restoring a piano tuner's bad hearing. In another, Humpty Dumpty's broken shell is fixed. The ads were well received and the tag line lasted 24 years, until 1998, when Lowe Lintas & Partners/SMS replaced it with a new tag, "How refreshing, how Heineken."

By the mid-1990s Heineken's U.S. marketing strategy was to focus on the now-filled-in red star on its bottle; the first new ads to come out of Wells Rich Greene BDDP, which won the business from Warwick after the ownership change, were simply a red star on a green background, similar in simplicity to the Nike "swoosh." A second phase of the 1996 print campaign, which used an indirect approach that eschewed mention of the brand name, added phrases such as, "How I wonder what you are?" A concurrent TV spot showed a red star being painted on a green wall, to the tune of the children's song "Twinkle, Twinkle Little Star." Again, there was no direct reference to the brand.

The indirect approach fizzled, however, and a few months later the pitch was altered again to feature "real-life" conversations among young adults but no talk of the product. "We needed to make ourselves hip and with it," Steve Davis, vice president of marketing for Heineken USA, told *Advertising Age*. That tactic, too, failed to resonate with consumers, and a year later, Heineken sought to position its brew as more of a mainstream product and not one reserved for special occasions.

Heineken's relationship with Wells Rich Greene ended in early 1998 after the agency's parent was sold to the Omnicom Group, a subsidiary of which handled the Anheuser-Busch Companies. Lowe & Partners/SMS won the estimated $40 million Heineken account and returned the focus to the product as a high-quality beverage suitable for everyday occasions.

MARY ELLEN PODMOLIK

See also color plate in this volume

Further Reading

Arndorfer, James B., "Imported Beers Find Edgy Ways to Tout Quality," *Advertising Age* (29 September 1997)
Arndorfer, James B., "Heineken Dims Red Star for Mainstream Appeal," *Advertising Age* (20 October 1997)
Kanner, Bernice, *The 100 Best TV Commercials and Why They Worked*, New York: Times Business, 1999
Van Munching, Philip, *Beer Blast: The Inside Story of the Brewing Industry's Bizarre Battles for Your Money*, New York: Times Business, 1997

H.J. Heinz Company

Principal Agencies
Maxon, Inc.
Doyle Dane Bernbach, Inc.
Ketchum, MacLeod & Grove, Inc.
Grey Advertising, Inc.
Leo Burnett Company

Iron, steel, and glass factories had already made Pittsburgh, Pennsylvania, a major industrial center when Henry John Heinz built a model factory complex along the Allegheny River that was to become a giant in the food-processing industry. Early on, Heinz also developed a reputation as an ad-savvy promotional wizard. "It's not so much what you say but how, when and where," he declared. One obituary would dub him "a genius in advertising."

Heinz was born in 1844 to German immigrants in western Pennsylvania and as a youngster sold produce from the family garden. He launched his business career when he saw an opportunity to earn extra money supplying "table delicacies." He dressed his mother's grated horseradish in a new way, bottled it, and peddled it door to door from a basket over his arm. As his business expanded, he used a barrow and then a horse and cart to sell the growing number of products from the Heinz family garden. Soon Heinz was selling to groceries.

First Factory

With a friend, L. Clarence Noble, Heinz established his first factory in Sharpsburg, Pennsylvania, in 1869; it was named Heinz and Noble, and it bottled horseradish in clear glass to demonstrate the product's purity. The company did well until a crop surplus in 1875 drove it to bankruptcy.

But Heinz was not about to give up. The following year he opened F&J Heinz, named for his cousin Frederick and brother John, to sell prepared foods, including his new tomato ketchup. In 1877 the company sold canned goods for the first time, and in 1880 it was the first to market sweet pickles. Heinz ordered the sides of his delivery wagons to be painted with pictures of the Heinz farms and products, especially pickles.

Heinz believed in letting the public help the H.J. Heinz Company, as it became known in 1888, advertise its products and promote its name. "We keep our shingle out and then let the public blow our horn and that counts," he wrote in July 1892. "But we must do something to make them do this." That year in New York City, Heinz contracted for "more advertising matter at one time to be used inside a year than ever before in my life: $10,000." It was spent on calendars, souvenir books, pickle cards and spoons, and small watch chain charms in the shape of a pickle.

Heinz and other U.S. food manufacturers showed their wares on the gallery floor of the Agricultural Building at the World Columbian Exposition in Chicago, Illinois, in 1893, but few fair-

goers were willing to climb the stairs after touring the main floor. So Heinz printed up a card promising the bearer a free souvenir at the Heinz exhibit on the gallery floor. Thousands of cards were handed out, and so many people flocked to receive their pickle charms that the supports of the gallery had to be strengthened to accommodate the crowds. The *Saturday Evening Post* called the pickle charm "one of the most famous giveaways in merchandising history." Heinz adapted the pickle charms into pins and continued to give them away, presenting them to those who toured his plant, another business first. Streetcars carried Heinz color cards with verses, and Heinz signs were posted along every U.S. mainline railroad.

In 1892 Heinz was riding in a New York City elevated train when he saw car cards for a shoe store offering 21 styles of shoes for sale. Although his company already boasted more than 60 products, the phrase "57 varieties" kept coming to his mind. Within a week the image of a pickle and the slogan "57 Varieties," which appeared inside the keystone symbol used by the state of Pennsylvania, were found in newspaper ads, on billboards, and "everywhere else I could find a place to stick it," Heinz wrote.

In 1898 Heinz leased, then purchased and remodeled a pier in Atlantic City, New Jersey. He had visited the resort almost 20 years earlier and estimated that by the end of the century, 20,000 people came daily to the shore town in season. Heinz Ocean Pier's glass-enclosed sun parlor offered free stationery, postcards, rest rooms, and Heinz product samples and pickle pins. Another pavilion with a 70-foot-high "57 Varieties" electric sign, featured an assembly hall and changing exhibits of art and curios collected by Heinz on his world travels. The pier remained open for 46 years until it was destroyed by a hurricane.

Working conditions at the Heinz factory in the late 1800s were far superior to those at other plants. A great believer in self-improvement, Heinz offered his employees opportunities to attend courses to further their education and gain new skills. He also had a world vision for his company. Heinz made its first sale abroad in 1886, and by 1900 Heinz salesmen had traveled to every inhabited continent, selling more than 200 Heinz products.

Always forward thinking, Heinz purchased an electric mercantile wagon in 1899, which he used as an advertising device while delivering donations to homes, churches, and other charities in Pittsburgh. The ad wagon drew crowds of the curious, and Heinz bought more electric wagons for Pittsburgh, Chicago, and New York City. Heinz was also among the first to advertise with electric outdoor signs. He designed a 40-foot-long pickle for a six-story electric sign promoting the 57 Varieties exhibited at Heinz's Atlantic City pier. The sign was located at the corner of New York's Fifth Avenue and 23rd Street, a site subsequently occupied by the Flatiron Building. Another electric sign at the same location later announced, "A Few of Heinz 57 Good Things for the Table."

A millionaire before the 19th century ended, Heinz was one of few in the food-processing business who endorsed government

The characteristic pickle and the number 57 were already an integral part of Heinz's advertising when this outdoor ad went up in Union Square, New York City, in 1893.

regulation of processed and preserved foods, which ultimately resulted in the Pure Food & Drug Act of 1906. Heinz died in 1919, leaving his son Howard to lead the company as president. The latter saved the company during the Great Depression by introducing baby food and ready-to-serve soup. He also increased promotions and cut costs but managed to do so without reducing wages. By 1937 business had doubled.

Association with Maxon

In 1934 Howard Heinz formed what was to be a 30-year relationship with Detroit, Michigan, agency Maxon, Inc. Heinz's Aristocrat Tomato man, a tomato-headed character clad in top hat and tails, was first used in mid-1930s print advertising to publicize Heinz tomato juice, the "aristocrat" of all tomato juices. Although he was originally designed to wear only formal attire, Mr. Aristocrat subsequently appeared in ads for ketchup, soup, and juice dressed as a farmer, Scotsman, and cowboy. After a brief sponsorship of the radio show *Joe Palooka* in 1932, Heinz made its first major venture into network radio in 1936 with the *Heinz*

Magazine of the Air. Maxon also put Heinz into *Information Please* on NBC from 1943 to 1945.

During World War II in 1941, Heinz U.K.'s Harlesden factory was bombed twice. Howard's son, Henry John "Jack" Heinz, took over the company as president-chief executive officer (CEO) and plunged the company into the war effort with such slogans as "Beans to bombers" and "Pickles to pursuit planes." After the war, Jack Heinz took the company public, expanded international operations, and embraced TV advertising. The company sponsored the aptly named prime-time dramatic series *Studio 57* from 1954 to 1955 on the DuMont TV Network, which went out of business in 1956. Heinz also sponsored the *Captain Gallant* show from 1955 to 1957 in syndication.

Heinz's advertising expenditures for 1954 were estimated at $6 million, with about $4 million in measured media. The company took advantage of serendipity by declaring 1957 the Year of Heinz. It ran spots on 86 major TV stations on New Year's Eve 1956 wishing viewers, "Our best to you in '57 from the 57 Varieties." It kept the "Our best to you in '57" slogan all year, coupling it with its "No other ketchup tastes like Heinz" print campaign. Heinz also issued a "Best of '57" record album for $1 and four soup labels, and promoted special offers in print and on radio and TV.

In the fall of 1958, Heinz moved heavily into daytime TV, cosponsoring four 15-minute contestant-based programs a week on NBC to expand its reach to homemakers. Pleased with the results, Heinz increased its sponsorship to eight shows a year later.

By 1960 Heinz's annual ad expenditures topped $11 million. Maxon launched the "Red Magic" ketchup campaign in 1960 and featured Mr. Aristocrat in Red Magic print ads for several years. In 1960 Heinz also began running print ads in farm publications to boost sales among rural families.

Heinz's agricultural specialists, working with universities, the United States Department of Agriculture, and government research stations, provided growers with new and improved strains of tomatoes and other plants. Its tomato tonnage per acre had increased 45 percent over five years and pickle productivity was up 64 percent per acre.

Moving to Other Agencies

Heinz ended its long relationship with Maxon in April 1964, moving its ketchup, chili sauce, and soup business to Doyle Dane Bernbach (DDB), New York City; pickles, relishes, and baby food to Grey Advertising, New York City; and beans, sauces, vinegars, and other products to Ketchum, MacLeod & Grove, Pittsburgh and New York City. In 1965 the first non-Heinz family CEO was named. R. Burt Gookin, a 20-year company veteran, had restructured the company and led two domestic acquisitions: StarKist in 1963 and Ore-Ida in 1965. Heinz invested an estimated $21 million in advertising in 1968. The company celebrated its centenary in 1969. Its Heinz 57 logo was dropped in favor of stylized text reading "Heinz" on a bright red background; the marketer retained Heinz 57 primarily as a product trademark and promotional device.

A probe initiated by Heinz led to a Federal Trade Commission (FTC) attack on the Campbell Soup Company's advertising in 1969. The complaint charged that Campbell and its agency, Batten Barton Durstine & Osborn, put clear glass marbles into bowls of Campbell's soup used in TV spots to misrepresent the amount of solid ingredients in a typical serving. Although the FTC did not order corrective ads from Campbell's, it held that such ads could be required in future deceptive advertising cases.

In October 1970 Heinz moved its baby food and pickles accounts from Grey Advertising to DDB and Ketchum. At about that time Heinz Great American Soups made headlines with a TV spot from Ketchum that was said to cost the then-large amount of $154,000 to produce. Stan Freberg directed the musical extravaganza, which starred dancer Ann Miller, was choreographed by Hermes Pan, and featured Freberg's satiric song, "Let's Face the Chicken Gumbo and Dance."

Sales at Heinz topped $1 billion for the first time in the company's history in 1971. The company's Heinz USA unit assigned its ketchup account to Leo Burnett USA of Chicago in 1974. Bur-

nett had created the Charlie the Tuna character (a low-class fish who had delusions of being good enough for StarKist) in 1961, prior to the brand's purchase by Heinz, and continued working on it under Heinz ownership. Another StarKist product was 9-Lives cat food, for which Burnett created another of its most famous characters, Morris "the finicky cat," in 1969. Heinz spent $36 million in domestic advertising in 1974, according to *Advertising Age*, $20.5 million of it in measured media.

Ketchup Campaigns

Ketchup sales had been stagnant for several years, and Heinz had a 37 percent market share when DDB created what would be its swan song effort for Heinz, "Heinz is what ketchup tastes like." But Burnett decided to focus on the product's thickness and slow speed out of the bottle. It created an extremely popular campaign featuring the Carly Simon song "Anticipation," which it licensed for $50,000. Consumers responded to the campaign, which ran through 1979, and market share grew to 40 percent in the campaign's first two years.

Heinz was engaged in a new battle with the Campbell Soup Company in 1976, with Heinz charging it was victimized by Campbell's allegedly deceptive advertising and predatory pricing practices in the canned soup market. Heinz filed antitrust charges against Campbell and asked $105 million in damages. The case was settled soon after.

TV spots from 1980 to 1983 featured strainer and plate tests, as Leo Burnett turned to competitive demonstrations to link Heinz ketchup's thickness with quality and taste. Market share grew to 46 percent during this period.

In 1983 Heinz introduced new packaging for its ketchup: the plastic squeeze bottle. The following year, the marketer broke a new Burnett campaign, titled "Thick, Rich One"; by year's end, Heinz had increased its share of the ketchup market to almost 50 percent. Heinz would increase that to 55 percent in 1986 and 56 percent in 1987. Heinz invested $340 million in domestic advertising in 1988, according to *Advertising Age*, $150 million of that in measured media. Its media spending for ketchup grew to $17.3 million, a 50 percent increase largely attributed to promotion of its revamped 64-ounce Ketchup Lover's plastic bottle.

Burnett's ketchup campaign themed "The best things in life never change" kicked off the 1990s. But Burnett resigned the Heinz USA account in 1994 owing to ad budget cuts. William R. Johnson became president-CEO of Heinz in 1998, and by October Heinz had returned to Burnett, selecting the agency to handle global advertising and brand positioning for Heinz ketchup and other condiments and sauces.

Burnett's next work for Heinz USA was the "Ketchup With Attitude" campaign targeting teens by focusing on fun attributes of the product. In October 2000 Heinz introduced green ketchup, the hottest product in the company's history. Heinz met its full-year sales goal for the new product in just 90 days, and green ketchup quickly acquired a 6 percent market share. Burnett's ad campaign for green ketchup began in January 2001 with two TV spots for children.

At the same time, the company's North American operation launched a multimedia advertising and promotion campaign building on the successful introduction of the first ketchup product made especially for kids, Heinz EZ Squirt, which also debuted in 2000. Heinz partnered with TV's Kids' WB! network to develop an on-line art sweepstakes and premiered spots featuring kids using the container's special squirt-top feature in creative ways.

Early in 2001, owing to popular demand, a promotion from Burnett brought Heinz ketchup's wisecracking "talking label" bottles back to supermarket shelves after a one-year hiatus. The paper labels sported humorous commentary, such as "Sunscreen for french fries."

A far cry from Henry John Heinz's original 57 varieties, by the end of the 20th century H.J. Heinz Company was marketing more than 5,700 varieties and tallied sales of more than $9 billion. Its 50 companies were operating in 200 countries. Nearly half of the company's sales were coming from non-U.S. operations and nearly 70 percent of sales from non-Heinz branded products. Among the company's brands were StarKist, Ore-Ida, 9-Lives, Weight Watchers, The Budget Gourmet, Skippy, Kibbles 'n Bits, and Pounce.

CHRISTINE BUNISH

Further Reading

Alberts, Robert C., *The Good Provider: H.J. Heinz and His 57 Varieties,* Boston: Houghton Mifflin, 1973; London: Barker, 1974

Edwards, Larry, "Book Tells How Heinz Picked 57," *Advertising Age* (3 December 1973)

"FTC Data Reveal Heinz As One That Blew Whistle on Campbell's Marbles," *Advertising Age* (6 December 1976)

Heinz <www.heinz.com>

Henderson Advertising, Inc.

Founded by James Henderson in Greenville, South Carolina, 1946.

Major Clients
Michelin
Procter & Gamble Company
SouthTrust (banks)
Texize Chemicals, Inc. (later DowBrands, Inc.)

Henderson Advertising, Inc., was created in 1946 by James Henderson with a $500 loan from his wife after Curt Freiburger, who had given Henderson his first agency job two years earlier, refused to give him an ownership interest in what was then the largest advertising agency in Denver, Colorado. Henderson moved back to his boyhood roots in Greenville, South Carolina, and built an agency that in 1979 would become the first outside the advertising capitals of New York City and Chicago, Illinois, to win *Advertising Age*'s prestigious Agency of the Year award. Henderson Advertising, which became known as "Madison Ave., South Carolina," built its business on Texize (later to become DowBrands) cleaning brands and its reputation for employing brand-building strategies with personalities for national advertisers.

Henderson was a disgruntled engineering student at Clemson University who enjoyed working as advertising manager for the college newspaper and producing his own radio show for the campus station. After receiving career counseling that suggested he try sales, Henderson landed a job with General Foods, advanced to district manager, relocated to Denver, and met Freiburger, who gave him his first advertising job. Having failed to get an ownership interest in Freiburger's firm, Henderson returned to Greenville to open his own agency. However, he soon realized a limitation of the Blue Ridge Mountain area: although there were many industries in the area, none was headquartered nearby, and so he had no access to the advertising decision makers to whom he needed to sell his agency's services.

Henderson began by servicing small retail accounts in the area, but he remained committed to landing consumer goods accounts. One day he got a call from Texize Chemicals, Inc. The company made an industrial cleaner for area textile mills, and it wanted to market the product for consumer use. Henderson did not own an automobile, so he took a train that delivered him to Texize at 5:30 A.M., hours before anyone arrived at the office. He kept his transportation mode a secret until the day a Texize executive called to say Henderson was needed immediately. Henderson admitted that he could not arrive until the next morning's train, so the executive came to pick up Henderson and offer him the cleaner account. The Texize cleaner soon became the well-known brand Janitor-in-a-Drum. In 1960 the agency's billings were estimated at $6 million; by 1965 they had increased to $7.3 million.

From that humble beginning, Henderson Advertising grew steadily, always remaining rooted in a core set of principles. The agency refused to accept cigarette accounts, and it focused on training and promoting from within. Henderson built a $3 million state-of-the-art building with solar heating designed with the idea of enhancing creativity among employees. By 1972 the agency ranked 77th and billed $18.6 million.

In the midst of this important growth phase, Henderson trusted his employees enough to take a leave from the agency to become assistant postmaster general in the administration of President Richard M. Nixon. He was instrumental in convincing the U.S. government to print stamps with pictures taken by astronauts on the Moon. More than 140 million of the stamps were sold, many of which were saved by consumers as souvenirs and never used for postage. Henderson was a man of many interests, but his most passionate interest was to prove that regardless of location, a person could establish a good advertising agency.

Growth throughout the 1970s, 1980s, and the early 1990s led to the opening and closing of offices in Atlanta, Georgia (twice); Charlotte, North Carolina; New Orleans, Louisiana; and Chicago, Illinois. The company had increased its billings to $54 million by the time it was named *Advertising Age*'s "Agency of the Year" in 1979. In 1986 Henderson sold his interest in the agency to eight executives within the firm; billings stood at nearly $80 million.

The next few years were marked by leadership turmoil, as several of the executives departed and outsiders were hired. As the mid-1990s approached, Henderson Advertising fell victim to several peculiarities of the advertising business. Clients' shifting from agency to agency and consolidation of advertising for all brands of a company with a single agency left Henderson on the short end of many such decisions. In 1995 Dow Brands consolidated its work for Fantastik, Glass Plus, and Spray 'N Wash, longtime Henderson accounts, with a single agency worldwide: Saatchi & Saatchi. This was followed in 1995 by the loss of the $6 million Quincy Steakhouse account, leaving Henderson without two of its largest clients. Henderson died that year at the age of 74.

But Henderson Advertising not only survived, it expanded its client roster and brought in high-powered executives. In 1999 the agency had 62 employees at its single Greenville location and handled about $57 million in billings annually.

James Henderson had widespread influence not only on his agency but also on American advertising. "Jim had incredible vision and would not accept mediocrity in any form," Ralph Callahan, president and chief executive officer at Henderson, told *Adweek* after Henderson's death. "He established the credibility of Southeast advertising agencies as competitive to any in the nation." In 1984 Henderson was featured as one of the leading figures in advertising in the book *The Benevolent Dictators* by Bart Cummings.

JAMES V. POKRYWCZYNSKI

See also color plate in this volume

Further Reading

Cummings, Bart, *The Benevolent Dictators: Interviews with Advertising Greats*, Chicago: Crain, 1984
Millman, Nancy, "Henderson Advertising Named Agency of the Year," *Advertising Age* (19 March 1980)

Hershey Foods Corporation

Principal Agencies
Ogilvy & Mather, Inc. (later Ogilvy & Mather Worldwide)
Doyle Dane Bernbach, Inc. (later DDB Worldwide)

The Hershey Foods Corporation produces some of the top-selling candy brands in the United States, including the Hershey's milk chocolate bar, Reese's Peanut Butter Cups, and Hershey's Kisses. The company has used acquisitions as a principal method of diversification and increasing market share. Until 1999, when the company sold its pasta unit, Hershey's food division accounted for 27 percent of the U.S. pasta market.

In the United States, Hershey and its principal competitor, Mars, Inc., continually engage in marketing duels that rival the "cola wars" between Coca-Cola and Pepsi. Closely guarding their production methods, the two candy companies rarely allow access to outsiders. A publicly traded company, Hershey rarely discloses more information about its operation than is required by law; rival Mars, a privately held company, reveals even less. The competition between the chocolate leaders may be less publicized than the one between Coke and Pepsi, but it is no less intense.

Milton S. Hershey started the Hershey Chocolate Company in 1894 as a subsidiary of his Lancaster Caramel Company in Lancaster, Pennsylvania. He sold his company in 1900 but kept his chocolate subsidiary and manufacturing equipment, moving them to a rural area outside his hometown, Derry Church, Pennsylvania. While struggling to create a reliable, consistent recipe for milk chocolate, Hershey began construction of a manufacturing plant, which was completed in 1905 and opened as the Hershey Chocolate Company. Adjoining his operation, he also planned and built a town, which would become Hershey, Pennsylvania, with modern housing, stores, schools, and a park for his workers. With its ability to mass-produce milk chocolate, the company introduced the U.S. public to affordable milk chocolate in the form of the five-cent Hershey's bar. In 1907 the company began selling Hershey's Kisses, bite-size pieces of milk chocolate hand-wrapped in foil.

1907

1990

A kiss is still a kiss.

——— HERSHEY'S KISSES ® ———

This 1990 ad shows Hershey's Chocolate Kiss, a product that has remained unchanged for nearly a century.
Advertisement reproduced with permission of Hershey Foods Corporation.

Milton Hershey's main interest was in product development—he had little use for financial statistics—and he considered advertising to be immaterial if the quality of the product were high. The founder's philosophy about advertising became entrenched within the company and continued well after his death in 1945. Hershey was the only Fortune 500 company that did not have a marketing department by the mid-1960s, and the company did not fully advertise its products until 1970, when it hired New York City agency Ogilvy & Mather. Critics of Hershey maintain that its resistance to advertising contributed to its slight international presence. "Hershey's cautious ways have cost it huge opportunities," declared one analyst in *Forbes* magazine in 1992. "At the end of World War II Hershey had as much international brand recognition as did Coca-Cola." Other critics, however, say the company's lack of international distribution has more to do with the taste of its chocolate, which many Europeans find unappealing.

Hershey's conservative marketing practices can be explained in part by the fact that its primary stockholder is the Milton Hershey School through the Hershey Trust Company. The school, founded in 1909 by Milton Hershey, cares for and educates orphans and disadvantaged children through their high school graduation; in 1918, three years after his wife's death, Hershey signed over all his shares in Hershey Chocolate Company to the school to ensure its continuation. It controls 31.4 percent of the corporation's common stock and 76 percent of its voting shares. Lee Smith of Ogilvy told the *Wall Street Journal* in 1970 that the agency always had to prove to Hershey "that advertising is really paying off. After all, every dollar they spend with us means one dollar less for the orphans."

Hershey was facing several challenges when it hired Ogilvy. The company had been forced to discontinue its five-cent Hershey's bar in 1969 owing to rising costs, but the decision had proved to be unpopular with consumers. Additionally, Hershey had problems with product distribution. Nationwide surveys showed that 30 percent of the company's products were out of stock at grocery stores and other sales venues in 1967.

The initial campaign by Ogilvy hinged on consumers' nostalgic sentiments about the Hershey's bar. The campaign's slogan, "The great American chocolate bar," reflected the consistency symbolized by the bar's familiar silver-and-brown wrapper. The campaign for Reese's, which Hershey had acquired in 1963 for $23.5 million, was also successful. It featured comical collisions between peanut butter eaters and chocolate eaters, who accused each other: "You got peanut butter in my chocolate . . . You got chocolate in my peanut butter!"

Hershey's sojourn into advertising was brief, as the company decided to pull the otherwise successful campaigns only two years after they began. It cited President Richard M. Nixon's introduction of wage and price controls and the escalation of sugar and cocoa prices as reasons for its decision. However, the company returned to advertising by the late 1970s, adding Doyle Dane Bernbach, Inc. (DDB), to its agency roster in 1978.

Given the company's generally conservative marketing history, it is somewhat surprising that Hershey participated in a major marketing coup that pioneered the appearance of brand-name products in feature-length films: the placement of Reese's Pieces candy in Steven Spielberg's movie *E.T. the Extra-Terrestrial.* Spielberg's script had originally called for M&M's to be used to lure the film's alien from the woods, but Mars refused to participate. Universal Studios then turned to Hershey, which had recently launched Reeses Pieces, a coated peanut butter candy that was languishing in sales. Jack Dowd, head of market research at Hershey, agreed to sponsor the movie with $1 million worth of promotions; in turn, Hershey was granted the right to use the E.T. character in ads for its product extension. The practice of advertisers paying studios to display brand-name products is ubiquitous today; in 1982, however, the product tie-in appeared to many to be a risky venture. The naysayers were proved wrong. The product placement was a wild success for Hershey; the film broke box office records, and sales of the candy tripled within two weeks of the film's release. It is still the company's most successful marketing campaign, and one of the most successful in advertising history.

In the 1980s and 1990s Hershey's developed into a company committed to mass marketing. In 1988 Hershey acquired Peter Paul/Cadbury, the U.S. subsidiary of Cadbury Schweppes PLC, for $300 million. The deal brought to Hershey several established candy brands, including Peter Paul Mounds, Almond Joy, and York Peppermint Patty, and the merger allowed Hershey to take back the lead in market share, with 37 percent, over Mars's 33 percent. Under the leadership of chief executive Richard Zimmerman, Hershey also focused on product extensions, including the successful Hershey's Kisses with Almonds (1990) and the white chocolate/milk chocolate kisses called Hugs (1993), which

became a $100 million brand by 1995. Adding to its U.S. brands, Hershey acquired several international candy manufacturers during the 1990s, including chocolate makers in Germany, Norway, Italy, and The Netherlands. In another major acquisition, Hershey in 1996 bought Leaf North America's confectionary operations, including Good & Plenty, Heath, Jolly Rancher, Milk Duds, PayDay, and Whoppers.

By 1999 Hershey Food Corporation was the 74th largest advertiser in the United States, according to *Advertising Age,* spending $395.5 million. Its brands were divided between two agencies, DDB, which handled Heath, Kit Kat, Mr. Goodbar, PayDay, Reese's Pieces, Twizzlers, York Peppermint Patties, and other products, and Ogilvy, which oversaw Almond Joy, Hershey's Kisses, Hershey's Hugs, Hershey's milk chocolate bar, Reese's Peanut Butter Cups, Jolly Rancher, and Mounds, among others.

DARYL UMBERGER

Further Reading
Brenner, Joël Glenn, *The Emperors of Chocolate: Inside the Secret World of Hershey and Mars,* New York: Random House, 1999
Kleinfield, N.R., "Hershey's Bites Off New Markets," *New York Times* (22 July 1984)
Koselka, Rita, "Candy Wars," *Forbes* (17 August 1992)
McMahon, James D., Jr., *Built on Chocolate: The Story of the Hershey Chocolate Company,* Santa Monica, California: General, 1998
Morris, Jack H., "Hershey's Troubles," *Wall Street Journal* (18 February 1970)

Hertz Corporation

Principal Agencies
Campbell-Ewald
Norman, Craig & Kummel, Inc.
Carl Ally, Inc.
Ted Bates & Company, Inc.
Scali, McCabe, Sloves, Inc.
Wells, Rich, Greene, Inc.
Moss/Dragoti

The world's leading vehicle-rental company, the Hertz Corporation, pioneered its field. The company's recognition of the value of advertising—from the first day of its founding—has helped Hertz maintain its first-place position in its industry for more than 80 years.

In 1918, at the age of 22, Walter L. Jacobs borrowed $2,500 and opened "Rent-a-Ford" in Chicago, Illinois, with a dozen

Model Ts. It was the first company of its kind in the country. For his first year in business, Jacobs budgeted approximately $1,000 for advertising, which he spent on classified ads in telephone books, one-column ads in the *Chicago Tribune,* direct mail, and outdoor posters.

Within five years Jacobs's business was generating annual revenues of approximately $1 million. His target market consisted almost entirely of men who did not own cars and who lived in the towns where they rented cars for pleasure travel.

Jacobs maintained the same ad schedule until 1923, when he sold his car-rental operation to John Hertz, president of the Yellow Cab and Yellow Truck and Coach Manufacturing Company. Hertz gave the rental company his name and its now-familiar hallmark yellow color. Jacobs continued as the company's president and chief operating officer. Hertz wanted to expand the company and in 1925 sought the advice of advertising strategist Albert D. Lasker, chairman of Lord & Thomas, who suggested running an ad spread in the *Saturday Evening Post* to enlist licensees. Hertz's "Wanted: Men of Character" ad received an enormous response and enabled him to establish a national car-rental system practically overnight. A few more *Saturday Evening Post* ads followed in 1926, propounding the idea that it was cheaper to rent than to own a car.

The General Motors Corporation (GM) acquired Hertz's Driv-Ur-Self System when it bought Yellow Truck from John Hertz in 1926. That year Jacobs and Hertz introduced a rail-drive program targeting railway passengers. Another innovation was the National Credential card—forerunner of another product, the Hertz International AUTO-matic Charge Card, a credit card for Hertz customers.

When GM dealers protested the acquisition of a car-rental company—fearing competition for access to vehicles—GM in 1929 sold the division to a group made up of 35 members of its management team; however, in 1932, as the division continued to lose money, GM repurchased it. About that time GM named Campbell-Ewald (C-E) as the rental division's advertising agency.

The Airline Link

Hertz was quick to see a potentially profitable link between flying and driving, opening the first airport car rental location at Chicago's Midway Airport in 1932 and launching the industry's first fly-drive program. It entered the Canadian market in 1938.

During World War II, with gas, tires, and cars being either scarce or rationed, the car-rental business suffered. By the end of the war in 1945, Hertz owned 600 cars and 4,000 trucks, all in poor mechanical shape. Nonetheless, because of the shortage of vehicles immediately after the war, people lined up to rent them. Hertz began the process of replacing its aging fleet and, since there was such a demand for its old vehicles, it began to sell them to the public, creating a new source of revenue.

The rental company ran scattered local ad drives until 1947, when Hertz executives convinced GM the time was right for national advertising. With a budget of approximately $250,000, and still with C-E, Hertz began its first national ad effort, which was almost entirely a print campaign. Its initial national ad depicted an angled sign over a map of North America. "This is the sign of America's only coast to coast and Canadian driv-ur-self system," it proclaimed. Hertz showed steady growth from 1947 to 1953, with gross revenue rising from $17.2 million to $56.9 million over that period. Part of that growth was due to the opening, in 1950, of the company's first European location in France.

Although fly-drive travel was a Hertz innovation from the early 1930s, the concept came into its own in the postwar period. Competitor Avis Airlines Rent-a-Car Company was launched in 1946 and began setting up airport rental locations around the country, becoming the nation's second-largest rental car company in 1953. That year, Hertz countered its competitor's airport strategy, running co-op print ads featuring Hertz and American Airlines, TWA, and Braniff International Airways. Approximately 60 percent of Hertz's nonresident car-rental business, which comprised more than half of all Hertz business, came from fly-drive travel.

Sale to Omnibus

In 1953 the Hertz properties were purchased from GM by the Omnibus Corporation, which divested itself of its bus interest to focus exclusively on car and truck rental and leasing. In 1954 Omnibus renamed itself the Hertz Corporation and listed itself on the New York Stock Exchange. Jacobs became Hertz's first president and served in that post until his retirement in 1960.

Hertz's national ad budget rose from $1 million in 1953 to $1.3 million in 1955. Joseph Stedem, Hertz's executive vice president in charge of advertising at the time, said that national magazines were the only medium that satisfied the majority of licensees, many of whom were in small towns where radio and TV did not reach potential customers.

Starting in 1954 Hertz's national ad fund was bolstered by funds from the Ford Motor Company, which paid an undisclosed amount in return for Ford cars and trucks being featured exclusively in Hertz ads. By 1956 Hertz had a three-tiered ad schedule. Major national magazines targeted the general public; specialty publications reached teachers who traveled extensively during school breaks; and travel and transportation journals, including official airline and railway guides, targeted the travel industry.

From 1947 to 1955 Hertz ads had been largely educational. The company explained the advantages of car rental to the general public, often using testimonials. It sold teachers on the benefits of group rental and promoted its rail-drive and fly-drive packages to travel agents. But in 1956, at the urging of C-E, Hertz decided to switch tactics. The company adopted a more hard-sell approach with the tag line, "More people by far . . . use Hertz rent a car." Avis and another rival, National Car Rental, had adopted hard-sell approaches the previous year.

In 1958 Hertz built large electric signs in four cities, its first use of such an ad medium. That year, for the first time, its ad campaign put the spotlight on celebrity spokesmen such as adventurer and author Lowell Thomas. Walter Cronkite, prior to achieving fame on television, reported *Hertz Business and World News* on the CBS Radio Network 13 times a week. TV buys included *The Jackie Gleason Show* and Jack Paar's late-night program.

In July 1959 Norman, Craig & Kummel, Inc. (NC&K), of New York City, won the Hertz account, succeeding longtime agency C-E. Hertz budgeted a record $5 million for advertising for the year. Its new agency planned a 52-week spot TV blitz in 11 key U.S. markets supplemented by other media.

In 1961 NC&K unveiled a TV campaign later ranked 65th by *Advertising Age* among its top 100 ad campaigns of the 20th century. Using what were then state-of-the-art visual effects, the spots showed a "flying man" gliding through the air and into a moving, open convertible. The attention-getting commercial had an equally catchy jingle composed by Broadway's Richard Adler, best known for the musicals *Pajama Game* and *Damn Yankees*. Across America, TV audiences and radio listeners sang along: "By the hour, by the day / By the week, or any way / Just let Hertz put you in / The driver's seat — today." In 1962 Hertz distributed 50,000 free copies of sheet music for the 36-bar jingle. That summer the company ran a $500,000 print and network

This 1962 execution of Hertz's most famous campaign shows how the car rental company helped put different types of people "in the driver's seat."
© 2001 Hertz System, Inc. Hertz is a registered mark and trademark of Hertz System, Inc.

TV variation of its popular campaign. It showed a family in a convertible with the message, "Instant vacation: just add Hertz and steer."

International Growth

Hertz continued the overseas expansion it had begun in France in 1950, launching operations in South America in 1961, the Caribbean in 1965, and the U.S.S.R. in 1969. At the same time, things were getting interesting on the domestic ad front. In 1963 Doyle Dane Bernbach (DDB) created the "We try harder" campaign for

number-two Avis. It was later reinforced by Avis's "We're No. 2" message.

In March 1964 NC&K created a newspaper ad based on what the agency termed "The Fable of the Tiger & the Cat." The cat, presumably Avis, has visions of growing into a tiger, presumably Hertz. Although the cat grows bigger over a year's time, the tiger grows even more. The moral of the tale was "to tell the difference between a tiger and a cat, take a look at the kitty"—meaning Hertz's and Avis's respective revenues for 1963.

Hertz made fun of the media battle with Avis in a 1967 ad showing Avis and Hertz clerks side by side. The headline read,

"Aha! You were expecting another get tough with Avis ad." The copy promised, "All future advertising will be devoted solely to acquainting you with how reliable, resourceful, helpful, and pleasant we are."

In 1967 Hertz was acquired by the RCA Corporation but continued to operate as an independent unit. In August of that year, Hertz ran a print and TV campaign promising frazzled travelers that they would find more than a set of car keys at the Hertz counter.

The following year Hertz split its account into two, awarding its domestic advertising to Carl Ally, Inc., while NC&K retained the overseas business. Ally created a campaign that responded to Avis's "We try harder" claim with ads in New York City newspapers and the *Wall Street Journal*. The ad depicted a man's hand with index finger upraised and the headline, "For years Avis has been telling you Hertz is No. 1. Now we're going to tell you why."

In 1974 Hertz and Avis took aim at each other in the business car-rental segment. Ted Bates & Company, which had taken over the Hertz account from Carl Ally in 1973, aimed to increase confidence among business travelers with the theme, "Your Hertz car. One less thing to worry about." Avis struck back at Hertz's number-one positioning, claiming that while Hertz may be number one in size, Avis was number one in service.

Bates signed Buffalo Bills running back O.J. Simpson as Hertz's spokesman in 1975. The campaign that ensued—showing Simpson dashing through airport terminals and hurdling suitcases—touted Hertz as "the superstar in rent-a-car." The ads received high marks for increasing consumer awareness, aiding recall, and positioning Hertz as the "best" car-rental company. Avis responded with a commercial showing an ordinary customer sprinting through an airport terminal, then being assured by an Avis employee that it was OK to walk to the Avis counter. Meanwhile, Simpson went on to do car and truck rental spots for Hertz, and in 1977 his role expanded to include car leasing and other corporate advertising.

In 1979 Hertz moved its domestic account to Scali, McCabe, Sloves, Inc. (SMS). During this period Hertz further expanded overseas, opening operations in Asia in 1978 and in Australia in 1980.

In 1984 SMS produced a TV spot that alluded to the Miller Brewing Company's popular "Tastes great/less filling" (for Miller Lite) with a "More reliable/less money" campaign for Hertz. The TV spot paired Simpson with golf legend Arnold Palmer. Football greats Dick Butkus and Bubba Smith, in roles similar to those they had played in the Miller Lite spots, joined Simpson and Palmer to deliver the punch line. Simpson went on to appear with Palmer in additional spots promoting Hertz service.

Short-lived Merger

Hertz was acquired by UAL, Inc., United Airlines' parent company, in 1985. Both companies gained opportunities for joint land-air promotions. Hertz founder Walter Jacobs died in 1985 at the age of 88. Hertz continued to expand its service, introducing computerized driving directions in 1984 and Instant Return Service in 1987. In January 1986 Scali launched a campaign themed, "There's a big difference between Hertz and the competition. And it's not the price," which put the accent on service. The agency developed the tag line, "Hertz: You don't just rent a car, you rent a company."

Hertz's stint under the UAL banner proved short-lived. On 30 December 1987 Hertz was sold to Park Ridge Corporation, a company formed by Ford and Hertz management for the purpose of purchasing Hertz. In fall 1987 SMS featured actor E.G. Marshall, star of the 1960s TV series *The Defenders*, in a courtroom spot touting Hertz's superior liability protection program. In 1988 Volvo North America Corporation joined Ford and Hertz management as an investor in Park Ridge.

Early that year SMS added actress Jamie Lee Curtis to Hertz's roster of celebrity endorsers to reach a growing number of women renters; over the previous decade, women customers had increased to as much as 25 percent of the overall market. Hertz launched #1 Club Gold, its premier, expedited rental service, in 1989.

In September 1989 the $25 million Hertz domestic account moved to Wells, Rich, Greene (WRG). When WRG became part of the BDDP Group, the account moved to Moss/Dragoti Advertising, a boutique shop created from within WRG. Moss/Dragoti launched "America's Wheels" in May 1990, a warmer and more personal campaign than previous advertising. The campaign was targeted to the leisure market and ran about three years on TV, radio, and in print.

In 1993 the Park Ridge Corporation merged with the Hertz Corporation. To celebrate Hertz's 75th anniversary that year, Moss/Dragoti created special ads with the theme, "Hertz. . . . The people's choice." One ad showed a picture of a Ford Model T alongside a 1993 Ford Thunderbird available at Hertz. The caption read: "It's not the first time we're offering you a great deal on a T."

In 1994 Ford purchased the outstanding shares of Hertz, and the rental company became a subsidiary of the automaker. At about that time, Moss/Dragoti developed another new campaign, "Exactly," which portrayed the car-rental battles as Hertz versus everybody else and targeted both business and leisure travelers. At the turn of the new century, Hertz was still running the campaign.

Hertz reported its seventh consecutive year of record net income in 2000. In January 2001, Ford announced a proposal to acquire any shares of Hertz stock it did not already own. (In 1997 the automaker had sold 20 percent of the car rental unit, and it was this stake it proposed to recover.) At the beginning of 2001, Hertz was represented in more than 140 countries and operated a fleet of 525,000 vehicles from approximately 6,500 locations.

CHRISTINE BUNISH

See also color plate in this volume

Further Reading
Curme, Emmett, "Ads Built Hertz Car, Truck Rental Business to $89,100,000 Operation," *Advertising Age* (23 April 1956)
Haugh, Louis J., "Hertz, Avis Set New Drives in Battle for Business User," *Advertising Age* (12 August 1974)
Hertz History <www.hertz.com/company/hist.html>

HHCL and Partners

(Howell Henry Chaldecott Lury)

Founded in London, England, as Howell Henry Chaldecott Lury, 1987; revamped focus to become a total marketing communications shop, 1994; became the first U.K. advertising agency to register for an Internet domain name and set up a Web site, 1994; purchased by Chime Communications, PLC, 1997.

Major Clients
Automobile Association (U.K.)
British Airways
Britvic Soft Drinks
Egg (on-line banking)
Fifa (Federation Internationale de Football Association)
Go (airlines)
Guinness Ireland
Mars, Inc.
Molson Brewery (Canada)
Texaco
Unilever

Howell Henry Chaldecott Lury (HHCL) was founded on 1 October 1987 by Rupert Howell, formerly of Young & Rubicam; Steven Henry, group director at agency WCRS; Axel Chaldecott, group director at WCRS; Adam Lury, from Boase, Massimi, Pollitt; and Robin Price, of the London, England-based video production company Frontline Video Limited. Early clients included *Marie Claire* magazine and the Danish bacon marketer Danepak.

Two years later, the company's work for Maxell Tapes, using Desmond Decker's song "Israelites," was recognized worldwide when HHCL was named "Agency of the Year" by the U.K's *Campaign* magazine. By 1990 the agency had also launched the First Direct "no-counter banking" concept for Midland Bank, utilizing telephone and Internet banking, and relaunched Fuji Film in the United Kingdom. The agency's early success was attributed to its department-free, collaborative organizational style. The agency became known for using a multisolution approach to creating campaigns and for its "tissue meetings," where a range of campaign and branding approaches are discussed.

The drink brand Tango, part of Britvic Soft Drinks, became a client in 1990. The agency developed a youthful approach for the brand's ads that continued to draw attention into the 21st century. The initial TV commercials featured a nearly naked, rotund man running up and slapping or kissing a man drinking Tango. The video was shot in slow motion and accompanied by a sports-style narration. It proved to be a significant campaign, helping establish HHCL in the British advertising hierarchy; it also raised the hackles of educators and doctors concerned about children repeating the ad's cheek-slapping action.

HHCL drew criticism—and a ban by the Independent Television Commission, Britain's television regulation agency—in 2000 for its spot for Britvic's Tango megaphone, a Tango-branded megaphone that customers could purchase for $4.48. About 60,000 of the megaphones were sold, spurring concerns among the medical community and others about the potential for hearing loss from "megaphoning."

The work for Tango helped the agency win the Automobile Association (AA) account in 1992. The U.K. motoring organization's emergency repair service message was in need of repair itself, and the agency proposed a potentially radical approach: position the company as the United Kingdom's "fourth emergency service" after the police, fire, and ambulance services. The campaign had an impact; AA membership in the United Kingdom grew from 7.5 million in 1992 to more than 10 million in 2001.

Another victory in 1992 came from across the Atlantic when the agency won the review for the U.K. launch of Molson Ex (Export) beer from the Canadian brewer Molson. In 2000 HHCL again provided a television-focused ad campaign for Molson Ex in its home market.

In 1994 the agency closed its doors to outside new business, accepting new assignments only from its existing clients. The move signaled a major change in the agency's focus. It streamlined its name to HHCL and Partners in October 1994. Chris Satterthwaite, former chief executive of IMP, Ltd., a leading sales promotion and direct marketing agency in Britain, and nine other executives were recruited to provide direct-marketing capabilities, and the agency broadened its corporate focus to total marketing communications solutions. To coincide with the name change, HHCL published a book, *Marketing at the Point of Change*, outlining the agency's agenda for advertising and marketing. That year the agency also became the first ad agency in the United Kingdom to register an Internet domain name and launch a Web site. In 2000 it increased its on-line presence by launching howellhenryland, an Internet/intranet/extranet-in-one (www.hhcl.com).

In 1995 *The Independent on Sunday* included the agency on its list of the "Top 100 fastest growing independent companies in the U.K.," and by the next year it had made it into the top 50. The drink brand Martini joined the client list and by the end of the year had began to run HHCL's "Beautiful People" campaign. Subsequent campaigns followed for new Martini-linked brands, including Metz, V2, and Citro. The agency relaunch paid dividends in 1995 when HHCL and Partners was selected for a second time as *Campaign* magazine's "Agency of the Year."

In 1997 HHCL and Partners was purchased by marketing services group Chime Communications PLC—in which the WPP Group held a minority share—and brought into a corporate portfolio of widely known media-related holdings, including public relations specialist companies Bell Pottinger and Good Relations. This move gave HHCL access to the international resources of WPP.

A year later the agency celebrated a major coup when it captured the $15 million account for British independent television network ITV. The campaign was largely focused around individual shows, including the long-running soap opera *Coronation Street* and the talent competition *Popstars*. In the latter, a guerrilla marketing campaign revolved around the tag line, "Nigel, pick me," a play on the talent-spotting abilities of Nigel Lythgoe, a TV executive-turned-presenter and impresario who chose a few lucky individuals from thousands of entrants in a televised competition to create a new pop band called Hearsay.

In 1998 the company launched the Go airline brand and the Egg banking brand. In the case of Go, HHCL and Partners provided brand-consultancy and business-plan support for what was (until it was spun off) British Airways' new low-cost domestic airline unit. Working with design consultancy Wolff Olins, the agency developed the Go logo and brand identity, and the airline grew from 2 to 13 aircraft.

The agency's work for Egg, an on-line banking company, involved a fully integrated brand launch that included Teletext and Internet services alongside a general media effort. The campaign resulted in 100,000 phone calls and almost 1 million hits on the Egg Web site. The agency also created advertising for the Egg credit card.

Another client, Bestfoods U.K. Ltd., saw its Pot Noodle snack brand repositioned as a youth snack with the "Spanking Gorgeous" campaign that broke in 1997. Pot Noodle became U.K. teenagers' second-favorite hot-food snack after McDonald's, and the brand was estimated to be worth more than $150 million in 2001.

In 1999 HHCL signed ten new clients, including Amazon.co.uk, Guinness Draught in a Bottle, and British Airways London Eye. Rupert Howell, joint chief executive of the Chime Group and chairman of HHCL, became the youngest-ever president of the Institute of Practitioners in Advertising. Billings for the year ended in September 1999 were up 85 percent from fiscal year 1998 to $270 million.

In January 2000 *Campaign* magazine named HHCL "Agency of the Decade." The Internet company 365 Corporation signed HHCL as its inaugural agency of record. Following a multiagency pitch, computer mail-order retailer Time Computers awarded its $45 million account to HHCL; however, since then the retailer has run only seasonal sales campaigns.

Other HHCL projects included a multimillion-dollar 2001 campaign for The Studio, a film channel being launched by the cable television company NTL and U.S.-based Universal Studios, and a campaign to promote Internet search engine Yahoo! HHCL also created "The Yummies" cartoon characters as part of the delivery for the $4.5 million Ambrosia account, which it

An audacious commercial for the drink brand Tango helped establish HHCL's reputation in the British ad industry.

won from Delaney Lund Knox Warren & Partners. Other new clients included AITC investment trusts; *Industry Standard Europe;* Mars, Inc. (Topic chocolate); British retailer Littlewoods; U.K. refrigerated foods company St Ivel; and Securicor e-solutions.

Founding partner Adam Lury retired in 1998. As the agency entered the 21st century, it continued to evolve, adding an impressive line-up of creative directors and channel strategists to its staff. In 2001 HHCL launched a new creative business consultancy division, Heresy.

The agency continued to pride itself on delivering the goods under budget, claiming that its 30-second commercial costs were under the industry average of $225,000. It also claimed to have surprised more than one client with refunds of as much as $15,000 based on estimated outset budgets. HHCL and Partners had a staff of 225 and reported billings of $300 million at the beginning of 2001.

SEAN KELLY

Further Reading

Goffee, Robert, and Gareth Jones, *The Character of a Corporation: How Your Company's Culture Can Make or Break Your Business,* New York: HarperBusiness, and London: HarperCollinsBusiness, 1998

HHCL and Partners <www.ehhcl.net/~moo/hhland/html/hhcl.html>

Reynolds, Bob, *The 100 Best Companies to Work for in the UK,* London: Fontana Press, and Collins, 1989

Hill and Knowlton, Inc.

Originated in Cleveland, Ohio, when Don Knowlton became a partner in John Hill's publicity firm, 1933; Hill and Knowlton, Inc., established in New York City, 1947; acquired by JWT Group, 1980; acquired by WPP Group in takeover of JWT, 1987.

Major Clients
American Iron and Steel Institute
Citizens for a Free Kuwait
Standard Oil Company
Tobacco Industry Research Committee

John Wiley Hill, the man who would found what would become one of the world's biggest public-relations firms, was born outside Shelbyville, Indiana, on 26 November 1890. In 1911 he entered Indiana University, where he studied English and journalism but did not graduate. After leaving school, Hill worked for a number of years as a journalist.

Hill's first venture into public relations was in 1920, when he created a newsletter for Union Trust Company, Cleveland, Ohio. The experience he garnered and the contacts he established while in the service of Union Trust and in a concomitant position—financial editor of the *Daily Metal Trade*—facilitated the opening of what was called a "corporate publicity office" in April 1927. Union Trust became the new firm's first account, and its president, John Sherwin, Sr., was instrumental in facilitating Hill's entry into the world of steel when he secured for Hill his second account, Otis Steel. The Otis account led to other steel accounts, including United Alloy Steel and Republic Steel. The steel industry would figure prominently in the history of Hill and Knowlton (H&K).

When Hill and Don Knowlton became partners in 1933, the United States was in the throes of the Great Depression, a disaster that actually proved salubrious for the firm. The causes of the Depression were not well understood at the time, but many Americans believed that the nation's business leaders were to blame. An image problem of such magnitude could only benefit a fledgling firm such as H&K. In fact, the partnership with Knowlton, the advertising and publicity director at Union Trust, was established after that financial institution had collapsed.

H&K's most important account in the early days of the firm was the American Iron and Steel Institute (AISI). The steel industry had long been opposed to unionism, but the advent of the New Deal, with its pro-labor stance, encouraged the labor movement to attempt unionization of the industry. H&K prepared full-page advocacy ads for AISI that ran in 382 newspapers. The advertisements asserted that outside agitators had pressured steel mill employees into becoming union members and that workers hired under closed-shop conditions were actually being forced to pay for their jobs. In response to an AISI request, H&K established a branch office in New York City.

A New Agency

In 1947 Hill, having relinquished 95 percent of the ownership of the Cleveland agency (Hill and Knowlton of Cleveland) to Knowlton, founded a separate firm in New York City—Hill and Knowlton, Inc. The new agency had a number of characteristics that distinguished it from many of its competitors. It projected a staid image, participated in the policymaking of its clients, and engaged in client selectivity. The firm refused, for example, to accept religious or political accounts. There was also an anti-Communist tinge to much of the agency's output during the postwar period.

H&K became embroiled in the dispute over butter versus margarine during the late 1940s when it accepted as clients the American Butter Institute, the National Creameries Association, and the National Cooperative Milk Producers Federation. Although early margarines had a somewhat off-putting taste, by the late 1940s the product had acquired a much better flavor and a more favorable image, the result of improvements made before and during World War II. At issue during the dispute was the repeal of an onerous tax and color restrictions designed to impede the sale of yellow margarine. There was significant support for the repeal among journalists and ordinary citizens, which was not surprising considering the fact that consumers were forced to add yellow food coloring to the product and then mix, mold, and refrigerate it before use. Taking into account the formidable opposition to its clients' interests, as well as the success of pro-margarine legislation in the U.S. House of Representatives, H&K urged the dairy groups to change tack, suggesting that they accept the repeal of the tax but continue to insist on the color ban. Justification for the latter would focus on the potential for fraud if the proscription were lifted—specifically, the possibility that retailers would sell colored margarine to customers who requested and were being charged for butter, a practice known as "butterlegging." The color issue failed, however, as supporters of margarine were quick to note that yellow coloring was also added to butter. A pro-margarine bill was passed by the U.S. Senate in January 1950 and signed by President Harry S Truman in March.

The Steel Strike

The steel strike of 1952 pitted H&K, working on behalf of the large steel companies, against the government and labor. At the heart of the crisis was labor's demand for a wage increase and benefits that would establish parity with what was being offered other union members, such as coal miners. The big steel companies asserted that they could raise wages only by raising prices. Because the Korean War was in progress, government stabilization agencies had to authorize all wage and price policies, and so a direct settlement was not possible. The government came down on the side of labor when the Office of Price Stabilization determined that the companies could offer a wage hike without increasing prices. On 20 March 1952 the Wage Stabilization

Board released its recommendations, which labor accepted and the steel companies rejected. Labor agreed to resume negotiations, the companies balked, and President Truman ordered the seizure of the mills, which were operated on behalf of the government until the order was overturned by the U.S. Supreme Court. The steelworkers walked out, bringing about a 54-day strike, but an agreement was finally reached on 26 July 1952. The real struggle during the crisis was not so much between big steel and labor as it was between the steel companies and government, with the former resenting the latter's role in setting prices and for its perceived collusion with labor.

The approach H&K employed before President Truman ordered the mills seized differed from the one used subsequent to the seizure. On 4 April 1952, H&K released a statement on behalf of the steel companies that attributed the problem to the demands of avaricious workers, already among the country's highest-paid industrial laborers. If their demands were realized, the statement claimed, it would have a negative impact on the nation as well as the industry. Any increase in wages would result in price increases, with the potential of launching the nation into an inflationary spiral. Not surprisingly, H&K put forth different arguments after the seizure. The dominant issue then became the administration's involvement and the constitutionality of the president's action, with frequent allusions made to the specters of socialism and totalitarianism. This approach helped to deflect attention from what was perhaps the real impediment to a resolution of the crisis: the industry's price demands.

During the 1950s tobacco fell from grace. A growing body of research suggested that tobacco was the culprit behind a number of illnesses, ranging from lung cancer to heart disease. In 1953, when cigarette sales started to decline, manufacturers became alarmed and engaged the services of H&K. With the support of nearly all of the major manufacturers, H&K embarked on a public relations campaign that saw the establishment of the Tobacco Industry Research Committee (TIRC), a technically independent agency but one that worked for the interests of the manufacturers. The approach taken in support of tobacco focused upon alleged scientific disagreement with respect to the dangers of smoking. H&K developed a number of arguments based on the idea that the final conclusions about the hazards of smoking were not yet available. Scientists were forced to defend their methodologies and their results, and the motives of some antismoking doctors, who were portrayed as being either puritanical fanatics or publicity seekers, were impugned. In addition, the TIRC's putative large allocations for research were publicized (in reality, these were small compared with profits and allocations for PR and advertising). In 1969, after well over a decade and a half of work on behalf of tobacco, H&K severed its relations with the industry.

After having established a network of affiliated firms outside the United States, H&K established international headquarters in Paris, France, in December 1954. The agency initially had little international business, but the situation changed when it landed the account for the World's Fair to be held in Brussels, Belgium, in 1958. The fair was a great success, and although clients did not rush to H&K in its wake, the firm's international business eventu-

John Hill.
State Historical Society of Wisconsin.

ally increased to such an extent that by 1960 its network encompassed 30 countries. H&K then moved its international headquarters to Geneva, Switzerland, severed the agreements with its European affiliates, and opened its own offices. The headquarters of Hill and Knowlton International, N.V., were later moved to London, England.

Hill relinquished his post as president to Bert Goss in 1955, but he remained involved with the firm, serving as an active chairman. Goss was succeeded by Dick Darrow, who died before Hill himself died in 1977. Loet Velmans became president in 1976, and with Velmans's retirement the agency began to change.

Branching Out

By 1990 H&K was the largest public-relations firm in the world. Its new chief executive officer, Robert Dilenschneider, had launched a program of acquisitions that involved the purchase of lobbying firms and ten other public-relations agencies, including Carl Byoir and Associates. In 1990 H&K merged with the lobbying firm of Wexler Reynolds. Under Dilenschneider's stewardship, Hill's selective approach to the acquisition of clients was abandoned in favor of working for virtually anyone in need of representation. The agency took on accounts that Hill likely would have turned down. Dilenschneider abrogated Hill's proscription against the representation of religious and political groups and took on such controversial accounts as the Baha'is, the Church of Scientology, the Bishops Pro-Life Committee of the United States Catholic Conference, the evangelist Larry Jones, and a number of political clients, including Citizens for a Free Kuwait (CFK).

Records of the U.S. Department of Justice indicated that the Kuwaiti government had contributed $11.8 million to CFK's budget, whereas 78 people residing in the United States and Canada had contributed about $18,000. H&K's efforts on behalf of CFK included producing news releases, monitoring the media, organizing Kuwait Information Day on college campuses, and preparing exhibits for the United Nations Security Council, to name only a few. After the Persian Gulf War, H&K was accused of having culled and coached Kuwaiti refugees so that those with the most riveting stories and those with stories most in harmony with the H&K agenda received exposure. The case of Nayirah, a Kuwaiti teenager, was especially noteworthy. In her testimony before the U.S. Congress she claimed to have seen Iraqi soldiers rip premature babies from their incubators. The *New York Times,* in a story that appeared a year after the war, revealed that Nayirah was, in fact, the daughter of Kuwait's ambassador to the United States, Sheik Saud Nasir al-Sabah. Further aspersions were cast on the so-called incubator atrocity when a reporter for ABC News, John Martin, interviewed employees of the hospital in which the incident had allegedly taken place. Those interviewed said that no

such incident had occurred. H&K's activities with respect to the CFK account were addressed at length in John R. MacArthur's book *Second Front.*

Dilenshneider left H&K in September 1991. With his departure the firm made an attempt to return to its roots. Client choice was once again given prominence, and an effort was launched to rehabilitate the agency's image. H&K also increased its efforts in Asia, especially China.

WILLIAM F. O'CONNOR

Further Reading

Aspley, John Cameron, and L.F. Van Houten, editors, *The Dartnell Public Relations Handbook,* Chicago: Dartnell, 1956; 4th edition, as *Dartnell's Public Relations Handbook,* edited by Robert L. Dilenschneider, Chicago: Dartnell, 1996

Dilenschneider, Robert L., *Power and Influence: Mastering the Art of Persuasion,* New York: Prentice Hall, 1990; London: Business Books, 1991

Hill, John W., *Corporate Public Relations: Arm of Modern Management,* New York: Harper, 1958

MacArthur, John R., *Second Front: Censorship and Propaganda in the Gulf War,* New York: Hill and Wang, 1992

Miller, Karen S., *The Voice of Business: Hill and Knowlton and Postwar Public Relations,* Chapel Hill: University of North Carolina Press, 1999

Hill, Holliday, Connors, Cosmopulos, Inc.

Founded in Boston, Massachusetts, 1968; acquired Wang account, 1977, and grew rapidly in early years of the computer revolution; bought by Interpublic Group of Companies, 1998.

Major Clients

Gillette Company (White Rain, Dry Idea)
John Hancock Companies
Hyatt Hotel Corporation
Nissan Motor Corporation (Infiniti)
Pitney Bowes Corporation
Sony Corporation
Wang Laboratories

Hill, Holliday, Connors, Cosmopulos, Inc. (HHCC), was founded in August 1968, in offices at 143 Newbury Street, Boston, Massachusetts. The biggest agency in Boston at that time was Batten Barton Durstine & Osborn (BBDO), and it was there that the partners of HHCC found each other. Senior partner Stevros Cosmopulos was a dedicated art group head who often started his

day at 4 A.M. George Jackson (Jay) Hill III was a BBDO copy chief who came from a long line of Boston natives.

Both men felt the much-discussed "creative revolution" of the 1960s was either finished or unable to find its way to Boston. They believed advertising was becoming a commodity and wanted to reverse that trend. Their first plan was to buy an agency. They considered purchasing a small shop in the theater district that billed around $1 million on 150 different accounts, but they then decided that starting from scratch would be easier. Together, Cosmopulos and Hill would serve as HHCC's first creative department.

Alan Holliday had been an account executive at BBDO before becoming a partner in the new agency. At HHCC he found himself taking on everything the other partners were not doing, and he later admitted that he had been "clueless" about many of his new responsibilities. After only eight months, he became the first of the original partners to leave. He later attended Harvard Divinity School and joined the faculty of Boston University.

The junior member of the founding group was John Michael Connors, who idolized William Bernbach and Young & Rubicam chief executive officer Ed Ney and was the group's most fearless salesman. Cosmopulos worked out every permutation of the four partners' names to create a title for the agency. The final name-order was a matter of sound, not seniority: Hill, Holliday, Connors, Cosmopulos seemed to have an optimistic rhythm to it. Even as the partners later departed, their names would remain on the masthead.

Each of the founders contributed $1,500 to the venture, but a month's rent for the tiny attic offices cost that much. They needed another $10,000, minimum, to start the agency. Connors cashed in on old college connections, calling on a banker who was a fellow alumnus of Boston College, and arranged the necessary loan.

HHCC started with billings of less than $250,000, but it soon managed to build up to around $1 million by working with various local businesses. The agency's breakthrough account came in July 1969 when the state of Maine's Department of Economic Development picked HHCC over a dozen New York City and New England agencies to handle the department's advertising.

Maine gave the agency a total of $250,000, but only $150,000 of that fee was allocated for tourism advertising, a sum decidedly smaller than the client's expectations. An older and wiser agency might have made quick work of the job, with an efficient, if routine, effort. But neither age nor wisdom had yet come to HHCC, which devised a witty campaign of small black-and-white ads exploiting the state's postal abbreviation, "Me.": "Come up and see Me. Sometime"; "Lover come back to Me."; and "Come to Me. My melancholy baby."

A steady influx of commissions from small regional businesses over the next few years fueled the agency's slow but steady growth. The Howdy Beef Burger chain, a subsidiary of Dunkin' Donuts, added $200,000 to the agency's coffers in the fall of 1970. Howdy later went out of business, but HHCC's relationship with Dunkin' Donuts continued. Other high-profile work included the 1972 reelection campaign of Boston Mayor Kevin White, who was a close friend of Connors. Later, when the agency worked with the *Boston Globe*, HHCC was obliged to stop creating all political advertising.

The agency ended 1972 with billings around $6.5 million. Just as Maine tourism had turned HHCC into something of a "boutique," another account—Wang Laboratories—would soon push it to the next level and turn it into a powerful regional agency.

A person could not live in Boston for long in the 1970s without sensing the excitement building in the high-technology industries. Wang Laboratories, in Lowell, Massachusetts, was emerging as a leader in the field. Its founder, An Wang, had left China in 1945 to study physics at Harvard, where he invented the magnetic pulse memory core, a standard element in early large computer systems. In 1951 he left Harvard to form Wang Laboratories. In the mid-1960s, Wang, which was well known for its desk calculators, began moving into the computer industry.

HHCC had developed a budding reputation as a specialist in electronics advertising when, in the spring of 1977, Connors received a call from the secretary of John Cunningham, Wang's marketing chief. She said that Cunningham had been impressed with a speech that Connors had given at Boston College and

would like him to pitch the account. In fact, Connors had never spoken at the college, but he did not tell the secretary that she had the wrong man. Instead, he made an appointment, at which he convinced Cunningham to listen to his ideas.

At that meeting, Connors pointed out that Wang had been in business for 25 years, yet only 4 percent of all U.S. managers were aware of the brand name. Connors then promised that if Wang gave HHCC $500,000 for six weeks of network TV ads, the agency would raise the awareness statistic to 20 percent. Wang accepted HHCC's offer. The commercial, which debuted just before the Super Bowl in 1978, was an adaptation of the story of David and Goliath. Within six months, national awareness of Wang stood at 80 percent. The company found itself with instant credibility, and the agency had a grateful client, whose spending at HHCC would rise to $45 million by 1982.

In 1978 HHCC lost Cosmopulos, the second of its original partners. Cosmopulos did not share Connors's appetite for expansion. Early in the year he resigned his position as chairman and co-creative director, although he functioned as a consultant until October, when he moved to Arnold & Company, another Boston agency.

HHCC grew, almost exclusively on the strength of Wang's growth, during the 1980s. By the end of 1980, total billings for the agency had tripled in three years, to about $45 million, and the agency had small service offices in New York City and London, England, and plans for branches in Frankfurt, Germany; Sydney, Australia; and Singapore. In July 1982 HHCC opened in Paris, France. At that time, there was also talk of offices in Los Angeles, California; Chicago, Illinois; and Atlanta, Georgia—all to serve Wang. These offices never materialized, however.

In January 1981 the agency moved into Boston's Hancock Tower after winning the John Hancock account. HHCC leased the entire 39th floor, even though it did not initially need that much space. In March 1982 billings were at $60 million, and Connors was predicting billings of $250 million in 1990. By 1998 the agency was billing nearly $700 million, and it occupied five floors of office space, some of which was used by HHCC's research department, which had been launched in July 1982 when Jack Sansolo was hired away from a New York firm to provide long-range market planning. The agency's expansion in the 1980s and 1990s was partially due to the demands created by Wang's growth; Connor was also motivated by his race with his arch rival, Humphrey Browning MacDougall (HBM), to be Boston's top agency.

HHCC stumbled as it tried to expand beyond its Boston base. In 1981 the agency formed HHCC International (HHCCI), with headquarters in London, to build its billings from companies marketing outside of the United States, which stood at around $13 million by 1983. HHCCI, like its parent agency, was overwhelmingly dependent on billings from Wang, which in 1982 accounted for 90 percent of HHCCI's overseas volume and 50 percent of HHCC's domestic billings. This fact left the agency not only dangerously vulnerable to the fortunes of Wang but also reinforced HHCC's reputation as a "tech shop," despite its work for Gillette, Hancock, and others.

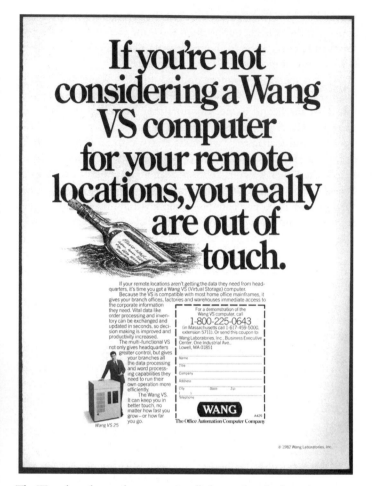

The Wang brand name became nationally known largely through
advertising such as this 1982 print ad created by the Boston,
Massachusetts, shop Hill, Holliday, Connors, Cosmopulos, Inc.
Courtesy of GetronicsWang Co. LLC.

"Coordinated decentralization" became both a strategy and a
slogan for the agency, which sought to create a flexible and balanced relationship between its Boston and European operations
that would assist in HHCC's drive for new clients. Unfortunately,
Wang's momentum sagged badly in the mid-1980s before HHCCI
could secure a solid international presence. Cunningham, who
had become president of Wang in 1983, resigned in 1985, along
with other senior executives, and Wang losses grew to $70 million
in 1987 and $90 million the next year.

Wang's collapse left HHCCI stranded. The Sydney office
closed after three years. In an effort to build its London base,
HHCCI bought Aspect in 1985 (becoming Aspect Hill Holiday in
London) and another U.K. shop in 1986; in September of that
year the agency won Reebok International. However, the biggest
part of the Reebok account went to Ogilvy & Mather a few
months later. That loss triggered an exodus of both staff and clients from the London agency, amid complaints that the Boston
office was too controlling.

Unwilling to surrender London, Connors hired an experienced
London-based executive, Jennifer Laing, from Saatchi & Saatchi
in September 1987 to rescue the operation. Laing used her contacts and knowledge of advertising in England to great benefit,
and after a year she and Max Henry, the creative director, became
partners, and the agency was renamed Laing Henry Hill Holliday.
A few years later Laing and Henry went independent.

Efforts on the part of Boston to build a viable New York office
proved almost as rocky as the London experience. The first serious effort came in May 1984 when Malcolm MacDougall—formerly a partner at rival HBM and, before that, boss to Hill and
Cosmopulos at BBDO—was hired to lead the New York office,
which was then languishing at billings of around $5 million. Over
the next four years the New York billings climbed to more than
$60 million, although much of the business (Hyatt, Royal Crown,
Pitney Bowes) was still shared with Boston. MacDougall left
HHCC in September 1987 and was succeeded the following
August by J. Walter Thompson veteran Wally O'Brien.

Billings from the New York office shrank to $30 million with
the loss of Revlon and Royal Crown in 1989, and O'Brien quit in
November, leaving the office, which had gone through four chiefs
in five years, without a president. Despite these troubles, Connors, who had spent years shuttling between New York and Boston, insisted that his commitment to a large agency was as strong
as ever.

HHCC bought Reichfeld-Altschiller from Omnicom in 1995.
Hill, Holliday/Altschiller could not secure more than one-tenth of
1 percent of the New York market, but Connors seemed satisfied
with this performance. Even as it pursued glory on the global
stage, HHCC creative fires were blazing in Boston. As Wang
began to weaken, the agency gathered creative momentum on
other accounts and attracted clients willing to sponsor ads that
were showcases for creative brilliance. Along with veteran creative directors Jay Hill and Dick Pantano, writer Bill Heater and
art director Don Easdon played major roles in the agency's growing creative profile.

When the editors of *Advertising Age* named HHCC Agency of
the Year in April 1986, John Hancock Financial Services was its
largest client and sponsor of one of the most remarkable campaigns of the decade, which was created by Heater and Easdon:
"Real life, real answers." (Heater, at director Joe Pytka's suggestion, actually appeared in one of the commercials, playing a new
father reflecting on his expansive plans for his new daughter.)
Later in 1986, Jay Hill and Pytka collected the Grand Prix at the
Cannes International Advertising Festival for their work for Hancock. Their victory was somewhat controversial: although the
judges had unanimously picked the campaign, others considered
it sentimental.

In April 1988 the agency, now highly regarded for its creativity, was among three finalists vying for the launch of General
Motors' new Saturn, the most anticipated new car since the Mustang. HHCC lost the bid for the Saturn account, but its efforts
were greatly noticed by other advertisers. In July HHCC won the
$60 million Nissan Infiniti account. A year later, the first nine
commercials for the luxury car aired, and not a single spot
showed the vehicle. Instead, viewers (who were presumably
young, rich, and spiritual) were invited to contemplate water,

geese, trees, wind, and lightning. The result was one of the most controversial ad campaigns of the decade, and it drove the curious into Nissan showrooms by the thousands. "We never showed the car until the third or fourth round of commercials," Pantano, creative director on the account, told *Advertising Age* in 1998. He continued:

> Actually it came out of the whole Japanese feel of the product. The door handles were ovals. The crust was like baked enamel. It was a funny looking car, with no grille. It was a very Japanese kind of product, and it called for a very oblique advertising. They loved it when we presented it. We went with two campaigns, the other a more traditional campaign which had everything from soup to nuts in it. But we went with the first one.

After the success of the initial Infiniti campaign, agency executives at the Los Angeles office struggled to create another winner but to no avail. In November 1992, just days after the agency had resigned its Hyatt business, Connors was summoned to a meeting, where, without warning, Nissan told him that the agency had lost the $75 million Infiniti account. "Efficiency" was the excuse of record, but Connors later admitted that the creative work had not met Nissan's expectations. The loss of the Infiniti account cost Connors nearly a third of his company. The Los Angeles office shut down, and not even the subsequent return of Reebok and Lotus to HHCC eased the agency's immediate troubles.

Anticipating his own retirement, Connors took steps to transform what was essentially a family business into an institution. In September 1996 senior managers became equity partners in the company's future growth, and the agency began looking for additional partners. This was not the first time that HHCC had considered such partnerships. Connors had first met with the Interpublic Group of Companies in 1980, when Interpublic offered him and his remaining original partner, Hill, $6 million for an agency grossing $7.2 million on billings of $46 million.

Connors and Hill declined that offer but kept in touch with Interpublic. Connors also met with Carl Ally, whose Ally & Gargano Agency (A&G) had gone public only to see its stock fall to $6 per share. The proposed partnership would have joined HHCC's business skills to A&G's creative reputation, while taking HHCC public in the process, but A&G's board vetoed the idea.

Finally, in the spring of 1998 three propitious events occurred: a bull market on Wall Street, the enactment of new capital gains legislation in the U.S. tax code, and a remarkable rise in billings that brought HHCC billings to $600 million, making it among the largest and strongest U.S. agencies still in private hands. After approaches from Publicis S.A. and Havas, Connors decided to accept the offer of Interpublic. The acquisition was announced in February 1998 for an undisclosed amount. At the time of the takeover, Connors told *Advertising Age* that in an era of expanding media alternatives, he wanted to see HHCC evolve into a "communications consultancy." At the time, he said, 50 percent of the agency's volume was in traditional advertising and 50 percent in other media.

JOHN MCDONOUGH

Further Reading

Alter, Stewart, "HHCC Agency of the Year," *Advertising Age* (28 April 1986)

Arnold, Peter, "A Tale of Two Not-So-Giant Shops," *Advertising Age* (1 May 1982)

Garfield, Bob, "Ad Review: Infiniti Ads Touch Inner Chord by Taking No-Car Philosophy," *Advertising Age* (26 August 1989)

Horton, Cleveland, and Gary Levin, "Hill Holliday Wins Big," *Advertising Age* (4 July 1988)

McDonough, John, "Hill Holliday at 30," *Advertising Age Special Section* (14 December 1998)

Oliver, Brian, "Aiming for the Best of Two Worlds," *Advertising Age Focus* (January/February 1984)

History: Pre–19th Century

The history of advertising as it is thought of today begins in the 19th century with the convergence of mass production, new forms of print technology, and the advent of the advertising agent. These developments laid the foundations for marketing on a national and eventually global scale. "Modern" advertising encompasses any form of paid, nonpersonal communication that has a clearly identified sponsor. Yet if advertising is loosely defined as any human communication that is intended to persuade or influence buyers in their purchase decisions, the practice can be traced to ancient times.

The Ancient Marketplace

For thousands of years tradespeople made use of trademarks, posters, pictorial signs, and hawkers. Farmers branded cattle to mark ownership, while craftsmen imprinted trademarks on goods to identify the maker or the article's origin, thus assuring the quality of goods. In Babylon, barkers enticed buyers with descriptions of wines, spices, rugs, and other wares from newly arrived ships. In Egypt, citizens posted announcements on papyrus in temples, offering rewards for runaway slaves, bond servants, and later for lost articles. Like shopkeepers of later periods, early Egyptian, Greek, and Roman merchants hung carved signs and painted storefronts, using symbols and pictures instead of words, so that even illiterate passersby could identify the nature of the business. And in the volcanically preserved city of Pompeii in Italy, ancient wall writing, some of it advertising, painted in black and red is still legible today. Some notices were political in nature whereas others advertised sales, theatrical performances, sports exhibitions, and taverns.

In China, commercial advertising dates back some 3,000 years to the Western Zhou Dynasty, when trade fairs began to appear. Displays of wares and street hawking were the major forms of advertising. Moreover, the Chinese introduced paper around 105 BC and several centuries later introduced printing, using blocks to make an imprint on the page. Although contacts between the West and the Far East were sporadic, these inventions would lay the foundation for the development of mass communications. With the fall of the Roman Empire in the fourth century AD, many early advertising practices ceased in the Western world for nearly 1,000 years.

The Medieval Period

During the Middle Ages, urban commerce, markets, and handicrafts dwindled in Western Europe; increasingly, the population was decentralized into small villages. Piracy on the seas hampered maritime trade, and the Saracens blocked Europe's exchange with the East. With the decline in literacy, the painted wall announcements disappeared and street-sign advertising ebbed. Few beyond the clergy could read, since to know how to read and write was considered an unmanly accomplishment, even for noblemen. Only the town criers pursued their practice, initially restricted to official uses in Europe.

As law and order returned in the 13th century, trade and commerce began to stir again. Cities were revived, craft guilds formed, and a middle class, consisting of craftspeople, merchants, and other professionals, emerged. The rise of this new class contributed to the decline of the feudal aristocracy's domination. Trade with the East resumed, and ships now traveled to distant ports and returned with exotic items. With this commerce, entrepreneurship developed.

Merchants paid town criers to advertise their goods and hung signboards to identify their businesses. In medieval England, customers could locate the shoemaker by his boot-shaped sign, the baker by a sign in the form of a sheaf of wheat, or the barber by his red-and-white striped pole. Advertisers also used hand-lettered flyers and posters to attract attention.

It was this enlightened climate that embraced the revolutionary idea of printing. During the Sung Dynasty (960–1279), the Chinese improved printing technology with the refinement of two features: blocks for printing whole pages and moveable type cast in metal. Chinese book-making and government-issued printed paper currency can be traced to the tenth century. Popular advertising media included high-flying banners, lanterns, pictures, wooden signboards, decorated structures, and printed wrappers for products. Printed advertisements also came into existence.

Although Europeans were slow to adopt the concept of printing and initially confined their efforts to religious subjects and playing cards, three developments gave printers the impetus to further develop the printing process and speed book production. First, the demand for books and other forms of communications grew as literacy spread. In the 13th century, Europeans also began to produce their own paper, which was considerably cheaper than parchment material or papyrus. Finally, the Chinese refinement of wood-block printing and movable type provided the technology. The first use of movable type was in 1041, when the Chinese shaped it from clay. In 1403 the Koreans cast metal type from porcelain forms and printed with it. Forty years later the West improved upon the concept.

The Printed Word, 1450–1600

The most important development in the history of advertising was the introduction of the printing press around the mid-1440s. In Germany, Johannes Gutenberg perfected a system of movable type that could be used again and again to produce books and other printed matter. The first book issued by Gutenberg, the Bible, set a high standard. Within 50 years, presses were in operation all around Europe, replacing slow hand-replication.

Before the invention of the printing press, only a few monks and scholars could read and write, and news traveled by word of mouth. Printing provided a way to record information so that people no longer had to rely on their memories. Many more people learned to read and write, and ideas spread quickly. Also, the new technology enabled the development of the first forms of advertising—printed handbills, posters, trade cards, and the first mass medium, newspapers.

In the late 15th century, posted advertisements appeared in England where crowds gathered. The ad was called a *siqui* (from the Latin for "If anybody . . .") because the notice usually started with the Latin phrase, "If anybody knows" or "If anybody desires." Initially, hand-lettered announcements, and later printed notices, appeared on church doors or inside cathedrals. In 1477 William Caxton, a London, England, printer, posted the first printed advertisement in English, a three-by-five-inch handbill announcing his prayer book for sale. The church used printed material to spread its liturgy, raise contributions, and recruit clergymen. Tradespeople handed illustrated shop bills out over the counter or door-to-door to prospective customers. And producers of medicinal remedies began to attach posterlike labels to their bottles, a forerunner of modern packaging. Other printed communication appeared in the form of official announcements, programs, menus, and guides to exhibitions, museums, churches, towns, and hotels.

The first newspapers appeared during the 16th century. Professional writers penned hand-written manuscripts, or "newsletters," for sale to nobles or others requiring the latest news. These letters eventually appeared sporadically in mass-produced printed

> ## If it plese ony man spirituel or temporel to bye ony pyes of two and thre comemoracios of salisburi vse enpryntid after the forme of this preset lettre whiche ben wel and truly correct, late hym come to westmonester in to the almonesrye at the reed pale and he shal haue them good chepe ∴
>
> ### Supplico stet cedula

William Caxton's announcement of the publication of a prayer book in 1477 is believed to be the first printed English advertisement. Roughly translated into contemporary English, the text reads: If it please any man spiritual or temporal to buy any pieces of two and three commemorations of Salisbury use imprinted after the form of this present letter which is well and truly correct, let him come to Westminster into the almonesrye at the reed pale and he shall have them for a good price. Please do not remove this notice.

form. News periodicals printed on a regular basis later took the form of a pocket-size publication, called a "newsbook."

In 1625 the first newspaper advertisement in English— promoting a book—appeared on the back page of a newsbook. In subsequent editions, advertisements appeared either on the last page or sandwiched in among the news. To bring the reader's attention to these notices, newsbook publishers headed them with the word "advertisement," which was derived from the Middle English word *advertisen,* meaning to notify. By mid-century, newsbooks carried advertisements not only of newly published books but of patent medicines, professional services, and seekers after lost horses.

Single sheets later replaced the book form, and by the early 17th century "newspapers" appeared in many major European cities. In Italy, the publications became known as *gazettas* from an old Venetian word for a coin (the price of the pamphlet), hence the origin of the modern word *gazette.*

In the 17th century the art of advertising also developed in the form of illustrated shop bills distributed by tradesmen, called trade cards or tradesmen cards. These announcements ranged in size from 1.75-by-2.75 inches to 10-by-16 inches and were handed out over the counter or door-to-door to prospective customers. The heading of the trade card often bore an engraving of the picture sign hanging outside the shop. Over time, the cards developed from a formal announcement of the nature of the business to persuasive advertisements, listing and illustrating the wares offered.

England, 1600–1800

The first modern media to carry advertisements were British-run newspapers. In England, the *London Gazette,* the first officially recognized newspaper, initially refused advertising, stating the paid notices of books, medicine, and other such items were not the business of a paper of intelligence. The publication eventually carried text-only advertisements similar to today's want ads, but they appeared on a separate sheet.

Although the founders and theoreticians of early modern advertising were mainly American and British, the inventor of the advertising agency in a primitive form was a Frenchman, Théophraste Renaudot. In 1630 the promoter of the *Gazette de France,* the ancestor of the modern French newspaper, opened an office in Paris where advertisements could be posted for three sous each. In London, Henry Walker set up business in 1659. Like modern agencies, these offices accepted advertising. Unlike agencies today, they did not place copy in external media, but in one medium, their own, and charged buyers and sellers a fee to use it. They offered no other services. Not for some time were other agency services offered.

Others, like one-time apothecary and general dealer John Houghton, also saw a greater future for advertising. In 1692 he launched a publication, *A Collection for Improvement of Husbandry and Trade,* primarily for advertisements. At first he merely listed products and prices and offered to tell callers where they could be obtained. After experimenting with blind ads, Houghton

Public Notice is hereby given,

THAT a GENERAL INOCULATION is permitted to take place within this city, to commence on the *twenty-fifth instant*, and to continue until the twentieth day of February next-----and that all persons disposed to avail themselves of this license, are hereby permitted, during that period, to have any person or persons inoculated within this city; and that all those who may be aiding or abetting the continuance of the aforesaid disorder by inoculation, after the period aforesaid, may depend on being prosecuted agreeable to law.

It is therefore desired that the several persons within this city, whose situation in life prevent their applying to the faculty for aid, that they are requested to give a statement of their situation, and a list of the number of persons of their respective families, that they may wish to have inoculated; as the several gentlemen of the faculty have humanely offered their service and attendance to such as they may be requested to extend it to.

And for the better information of the Citizens requiring the assistance of the magistrates and of the faculty, application is to be made as follows:

All persons from Gillie's Creek to the street leading to the Church, are to apply to Mr. M'Roberts; from thence to the Courthouse, to Mr. Scherer; from thence to the cross-street by Mr. Hyland's Tavern, to Mr. Lambert; from thence to Shockœ-creek, to Mr. Mitchell; and from Didier Collins' to the brick house of Mr. Davis, opposite to Mr. Boyce's and down to the bounds of the city, to Mr. Lyne; and from Mr. Kibble's to Mr. Harris's brick house, and back to the north-west bounds of the city, to Mr. Greenhow; and from A. Dunscomb's house up to Mr. Cock's, and to the north-west bounds of the city, to said Dunscomb; and from Doctor M'Clurg's to aforesaid Cock's, and down towards the river to the bounds of the city, are to apply to Mr. Barrett; and that the said applications be made on or before the 25th instant.

JOHN BARRETT, Mayor.—DAVID LAMBERT, Recorder.
ALEX'R. M'ROBERT, AND'W. DUNSCOMB, JOHN GREENHOW, } Aldermen.
JOHN LYNE, SAMUEL SCHERER, ROBERT MITCHELL, }

RICHMOND, Jan. 21, 1794.

A 1794 public notice from Richmond, Virginia, advertised inoculations against smallpox.
Courtesy of the Rare Book, Manuscript, and Special Collections Library, Duke University.

began to give the names and addresses of those who could supply lumber, lodgings, brimstone, wigs, servants, a wet nurse, or a suitable school for children. He also employed such attention-getting graphic devices as the two-line bold initial letters, all-capital first words, the pointing finger, and italics, as well as the long dash and triple asterisk to mark a paragraph.

During the early 18th century, however, the British government curbed the press by imposing a stamp duty and an advertisement tax. As English publishers faced increasing costs and government taxation, many ceased publication, while others flourished with the support of advertising revenues. The *London Country Gentleman's Courant* was the first paper to establish a "line rate" instead of a flat rate for an advertisement, which seldom departed from a length of eight or ten lines. Next, the literary periodical the *Tatler* (1709–11) introduced the "frequency rate," a reduced charge for an ad that ran a certain number of times within a given period, an advantage for regular advertisers. In 1710 Joseph Addison, after appearance of the *Tatler,* agreed to write an advertiser's copy on the condition that he be given exclusive rights to do so and that he place all the advertising he wrote in one medium. The net effect was an increase in both the size and frequency of advertisements.

For a century, advertisements were directed to a limited market, mainly the frequenters of coffeehouses where the newspapers were read. There was little or no advertising of household goods. Instead, notices offered the wealthy coffee, tea, books, wines, wigs, cosmetics, and medicines; notified them of plays and concerts; offered lottery tickets; or sold servants and slaves. About the state of advertising, Samuel Johnson wrote in the *Idler* in 1759: "Promise, large promise is the soul of an Advertisement." The learned doctor also noted, "The trade of advertising is so near to perfection that it is not so easy to propose any improvement."

The New World, 1600–1800

It could be argued that America began with efforts by English entrepreneurs to attract settlers to the newly discovered land, one of the first sustained advertising campaigns in the modern world. Throughout the 17th and 18th centuries enterprising promoters printed a variety of books, brochures, and posters to promote America to their countrymen. English entrepreneurs lured settlers with promises of the good life: gold and silver, fountains of youth, abundant fish and game, and productive land. Reports of earlier explorers also led them to expect a Garden of Eden—an idyllic place where food could be effortlessly plucked from the land; clothes and shelter were hardly needed; docile native people would perform laborious tasks; and the word of Christianity could be spread.

Once in the New World, men and women made the first colonies viable, organized local governments, and adapted their Old World ways to their new home. European colonists brought the idea of advertising with them to America, but the concept was slow to take hold. Colonists simply had little need, and virtually no media, to advertise their goods for sale over a wide area. They also found printing equipment and supplies to be scarce and expensive. The English government licensed printing presses and restricted what the colonists could print in order to suppress any criticism of the government. Without newspapers, news spread primarily through gossip or by the town criers. All printed matter came from Europe, and few people could read. Despite these limitations, the first printing press in America arrived in the Massachusetts Bay colony (Harvard University) in 1639. The sponsors planned to turn out mainly Puritan theology and some classical writings.

In 1704 *Boston News-Letter,* the first regularly printed newspaper in America, carried advertisements. But it would be Benjamin Franklin who would capitalize on advertising as John Houghton did. In 1728 he founded the *Pennsylvania Gazette.* Its lucid style of writing, appealing typography, and pictorial details made a good-looking sheet, and circulation quickly increased. The large readership attracted more advertising than any other colonial newspaper, including a new class of advertisers, particularly in the retail field. Franklin printed ads on the front page, a marked contrast to other publishers, who started notices from the last column of the back page and moved forward. The paid announcements later appeared next to news matter on every page. Franklin's *General Magazine and Historical Chronicle,* appearing 16 February 1741, was the first to be conceived in the colonies, but Andrew Bradford issued his *American Magazine* three days earlier. Although both periodicals were short-lived, the first magazine advertisement appeared in the May 1741 issue of Franklin's publications. But magazines did not succeed as vehicles for advertising for another century.

Well before 1800, most American newspapers were not only supported by advertising, they were primarily vehicles for the dissemination of advertising. The front and back pages of almost all of the four-page Boston, Massachusetts, New York City, and Philadelphia, Pennsylvania, newspapers were generally solid advertising, often with two or three columns of additional advertisements on page three.

The majority of advertising centered on real estate, runaway apprentices and slaves, and transportation; lost articles, books, and merchants' lists of goods accounted for the rest. These notices were simple announcements that posed two basic questions—where and when. (Has anyone got any flour? Will there be a stagecoach to Savannah? When is the ship arriving with the cargo of farm tools?)

Notices of slaves for sale constituted a good percentage of these advertisements. Posters, flyers, and newspaper ads advertised slaves available for purchase in the same way a merchant sold goods—as an inanimate article. Slavery formed the foundation of Southern society, which plantation owners argued might collapse if they paid fair wages to the enslaved workers. Yet slavery would not have been such an effective institution without advertising.

Advertising human merchandise involved a number of innovative techniques. Promoters described newly arrived cargoes of "prime, healthy Negroes" with eye-catching graphics, illustrations, "product" liability disclaimers, and descriptive copy. Traders often used branding irons to mark slaves' bodies. Advertisements offered "a lusty negro man-slave," "a likely young Negro wench," and a "good House-Negro who can do all manner of house work, and can knit and spin." For runaways, the ads generally emphasized any noticeable characteristics that could identify the slaves, the kind of work they performed, and other features of their lifestyle. The detailed descriptions increased the chances of capturing the runaway.

By 1765 an estimated 2 million people lived in the colonies. The literate part of this audience noticed almost anything in print, since cheap reading matter was still a rarity. A mere 25 publishers printed approximately 15,000 four-page weekly newspapers that had an even greater secondhand circulation. Colonists commonly read newspapers aloud in group gatherings or at coffeehouses. People gave primary attention to local news and to advertising rather than foreign events, because these matters affected their daily lives. They read and reread announcements about the arrivals of new shipments of tools, food, or drink.

The demand for news about the American Revolution enlarged newspaper circulation, and subsequently the chronic paper shortage became even more acute. At the time, paper consisted of 100 percent rag. Yet the shortage of rags for paper making made this type of paper scarce. People frugally used the same fabric over and over, since the home production of cotton and linen involved laborious spinning and weaving. They used remnants to patch old clothing, fashion quilts, and braid rugs, but even then it took years for the rags to deteriorate to the point where people sold them by the pound to printers. Despite editorial pleas for people to save their rags to make newsprint, the paper shortage often limited many major city newspapers to a mere 300 to 400 copies per day. Others were forced to suspend publishing.

To solve the chronic paper shortage problem, publishers crammed more type into less space and restricted advertising for the next 70 years. Seven or eight columns crowded a page, where before there had been three to five. Publishers also dropped rules between columns and shrank type size from the standard 12-point down to an almost illegible six-point in both news and advertisements. White space all but disappeared, and advertisements were limited to abbreviated announcements of product lists with an occasional exception, such as a thumbnail-size cut of a ship or stagecoach in transportation announcements.

Many advertisers responded by moving their creative announcements to posters called "broadsides," handbills, and trade cards. The broadsides typically were twice the size of a newspaper page, providing plenty of space to make the message interesting. Similar to magazines today, broadsides announced the arrival of new merchandise and listed what merchants had for sale. Broadsides also proved a popular news medium. Publishers printed their message on single sheets and hired runners to distribute them throughout the city. Selling for a penny, the notice might contain official declarations, political propaganda, dying confessions of convicted criminals, or even poetic verses.

By the end of the 18th century, advertising was thoroughly established in both Great Britain and the United States, and the newspaper, then the only general means of public communications, had established itself as an advertising medium. What magazines there were carried no advertising, or little of any account, and would not for another half century. It took an industrial revolution and the development of national advertising media to make this expansion possible and economically necessary.

Until this time, businesses had little need to create new demand or to advertise to attract customers, and most people had little money to spend. People made a living from their farms, growing and making nearly everything they needed. Because employers often provided room and board in exchange for labor, with perhaps a very small amount of money thrown in, most workers earned little cash. Small family operations produced items in modest amounts and found buyers in the village marketplace. Nearly anything they could make could be sold—wagons, shoes, flour, houses. The problem was rarely to find a market for the goods, which were very much in demand. The problem was finding someone with money to pay for them. When this condition changed, advertising, as it is known today, began in earnest.

JULIANN SIVULKA

Further Reading

Goodrum, Charles, and Helen Dalrymple, *Advertising in America: The First 200 Years,* New York: Abrams, 1990

Meggs, Philip B., *A History of Graphic Design,* New York: Van Nostrand Reinhold, and London: Lane, 1983; 3rd edition, New York: Wiley, 1998

Presbrey, Frank, *The History and Development of Advertising,* Garden City, New York: Doubleday, 1929; reprint, New York: Greenwood Press, 1968

Sivulka, Juliann, *Soap, Sex, and Cigarettes: A Cultural History of American Advertising,* Belmont, California: Wadsworth, 1998

Turner, Ernest Sackville, *The Shocking History of Advertising,* London: Joseph, 1952; New York: Dutton, 1953; revised edition, London: Penguin, 1965

Wood, James Playsted, *The Story of Advertising,* New York: Ronald, 1958

History: 19th Century

The Industrial Revolution, which began in England in the mid–18th century and reached North America in the early 19th century, affected both businesses and households. Manufacturers were able to produce a stream of low-cost, uniform-quality goods, and for the first time it cost people less to buy a product than to make it themselves, thus fueling customer demand. On both sides of the Atlantic, advertising played an ever-larger role in the economy, helping to both stimulate demand and create a new medium of information.

England, 1800–1880

At the start of the 19th century, heavy taxation continued to restrict the British press. Government advertising, another important source of revenue, was withheld from those papers that dared to criticize the way the country's affairs were conducted. Although the Industrial Revolution was well under way and illiteracy was receding, there were fewer papers in the 1840s than there had been a hundred years earlier, even though the advertisement tax had been lowered in 1833.

The nature of advertising was changing, however. Instead of pandering to the rich, manufacturers of hair-dressing products, tooth powder, and various household goods were beginning to woo a nascent mass market. Warren's Shoe Blacking is often cited as having marketed the first nationally advertised household article, launching the campaign on a virtual sea of poetry. One of its much-admired ads pictured a cat spitting at its reflection in a highly polished Hessian boot. Advertising also made Rowland's

Macassar Oil popular, starting around 1793. Within 20 years the product was widely known. Several of London's earliest advertising agencies date to the early years of the 19th century, including John Haddon & Company (1814); G. Street & Company (1830); C. Mitchell & Company (1837), publisher of the first newspaper directory in 1845; and Mather & Crowther, Ltd. (1850), precursor to Ogilvy & Mather.

Yet many ambitious merchants were far from convinced that the press was the best advertising medium. There were hundreds of thousands who did not read newspapers. To reach this audience, merchants enlisted bill-posters, who pasted their announcements on walls everywhere. Bills were not subject to the advertisement tax. In the 1830s and 1840s just about every vacant wall in London was pasted over with clamorous announcements. In response, the Metropolitan Police Act of 1839 made it an offense to post bills without the property owner's consent, but the law proved difficult to enforce. Another form of outdoor advertising was the "sandwich man." Advertisers sent men out in droves, wearing placards back and front. Other resourceful contractors put placard-carrying men on horseback. Advertising banners streamed from hand-carried poles, advertising boats appeared on the Thames during regattas, and ad messages even began to appear on umbrellas.

The increasing trend toward "puffery" aroused much disdain. No one can read the advertisements of this period without marveling at the overblown writing style. Decayed teeth were filled with "mineral marmoratum," hair cream was an "aromatic regenerator," and hair dye was "an atrapialatory." In the 1840s poetic advertisements became an English craze. Another advertising fashion was that of capturing readers' attention by printing an arresting phrase in bold type. For example, one shirtmaker ran the line: "A Beautiful Young Girl Strangled," followed in small type by a phrase such as "by a cry of admiration when she saw our new blouses." Numerous items were advertised as being used in Queen Victoria's household—often, no doubt, without authority. Help-wanted and jobs-wanted notices began to appear along with offers of employment and railway advertisements, providing a new source of revenue for the popular newspapers.

Most advertising followed a standard pattern, but there were curious announcements for patent medicines. Of the leading pill-makers, James Morrison was among the most provocative. The self-styled "Hygiest" created the "Universal Pill," which one need swallow only once and all would be well. Another prolific British medicine man was "Professor" Thomas Hollaway, who popularized his pills and ointments through paid announcements. In 1842, four years after starting his business, he was spending £5,000 a year on advertising; by the 1870s he spent £40,000 to £50,000 a year, taking a similar sum in profit.

The Industrial Revolution brought bigger and faster steam-powered presses, lithography, new methods of paper-making, and color-reproduction techniques that made volume printing cost-effective by mid-century. At the same time, the costs of running a newspaper were growing owing to the news services and features the public had grown to expect. Yet many editors were still reluctant to admit that advertising provided a vital source of revenue.

By common consent, the newspapers banned advertisements that used large type or illustrations and extended over several columns. The editorial argument was that display advertising was unfair to the daily small-space advertisers.

The typical newspaper ad looked much the way present-day want ads or legal announcements do, with little white space and few illustrations separating the ads from editorial text. Creative advertisers maneuvered around the stringent restrictions, filling advertising columns with endless repetitions of a firm's name or a phrase for as many as 1,000 lines. Others discovered the trick of building up large capital letters by grouping together single letters in appropriate type to form novel images. This so-called iteration advertising eventually led to the breakdown of the every-ad-the-same-size rule.

In 1861 the last remaining duty on newspapers was lifted in England. Still, all but a few manufacturers had yet to be convinced that advertising was necessary. The traditional way to do business was to surround oneself with a circle of loyal customers and to cultivate personal relationships with them; superior goods and word of mouth would do the rest. If wider markets were needed, manufacturers would send respectable traveling peddlers out on the road and pay them commissions. The last thing they would consider was inserting paragraphs in newspapers or posting bills in the company of dubious claims. Generally, advertising was still held in widespread contempt.

Yet what if an honest manufacturer planned to market a complex machine such as a sewing machine or a mechanical piano? With hundreds of processes involved in making these things, the selling price would be prohibitively high if only a few consumers bought them. A manufacturer who invented a new processed food faced a similar problem. How could the maker offset the cost of the plant and machinery without the certainty of buyers? Who would buy a product they never heard of? Distasteful though the idea might be, advertising seemed to be the only way of ensuring a market. But since advertising was still held in widespread contempt, manufacturers did little more than state the firm's name and product, using the technique of proclaiming rather than persuading.

Hence, unsubtle and repetitive phrases typified ads in the latter part of the century. Reminder phrases—"Pears' Soap," "Mellin's Food," and "Hot Bovril"—were regarded as complete and sufficient advertisements. But the population was growing quickly, and the ambitious middle class demanded the outward trappings of prosperity and progress. For the most part, however, this class still lived within its income. Although the idea of installment buying had been introduced, it was not until the 20th century that the system took hold.

America, 1800–1880

At the start of the 19th century in America, most advertising was by local merchants selling to their own communities. As the communities grew larger and got richer, general stores sprang up, and the demand for goods increased. However, self-service supermarkets with attractive, packaged merchandise on easy-to-reach

ILLEGAL ADVERTISEMENTS.

WHEREAS a number of Adventurers in the character of Dealers in Wood, Cattle, Barley, Spirits, and other produce of the country, as well as Emigrant crimps; cause various Meetings, and calls for Meetings to be proclaimed, and fixed on the Church doors of the Lovat Estate, in the Shires of Inverness and Ross, without the sanction of an Heritor of the Parish countenancing the same.—The Clergy, their Kirk-officers, Ground-officers and Constables, are hereby enjoined not to permit under any pretext whatever, any Advertisement to be called at, or affixed to the Kirk-doors as said is, unless the same be sanctioned by a written authority of an Heritor within the Parish where the Proclamation is made, who can answer for the character and conduct of the Person meaning to Advertise.

Beaufort, 1st Feb. 1803.

(Young and Imray, Printers, Inverness.)

An 1803 public notice bans the unauthorized posting of advertisements on church doors in Beaufort, Inverness, Scotland.
Courtesy of the Rare Book, Manuscript, and Special Collections Library, Duke University.

shelves had yet to be invented. Instead, the shopkeeper portioned out bulk food from open containers and sold by weight—one cereal was as good as the next. Products were sold as commodities, not brands. With the invention of the refrigerator a long way off, perishable products lasted only a few days. In the cities, people depended on noisy, smelly, crowded—and sometimes filthy—city markets. Urban groceries lacked marked prices, so shoppers had no way of knowing what a given item cost from one week to the next.

The country's burgeoning population, booming economy, and western expansion created a demand for news about business, travel, entertainment, and the availability of goods and services. This led many newspapers to consider advertisements as a vital source of revenue—some even included the term *advertiser* in their name. Unlike the British publications restricted by taxation, the American newspapers in the 19th century expanded rapidly. The price of a newspaper was only three cents, less than one-fourth of a British issue.

As in England, the typical U.S. newspaper ad looked much the same as present-day classified ads. In 1846 publisher James Gordon Bennet with his huge *New York Herald* banned all display advertising, stating it was unfair to the daily small-space advertisers. He also insisted the ad copy could run no longer than two weeks to keep the announcements fresh. Other American papers soon followed this practice. By 1850 illustrations had almost disappeared from penny papers, though the six-cent papers occasionally used thumbnail-size engravings. To overcome this limitation, advertisers built up big letters from scores of smaller ones and repeated copy blocks to look different from adjacent ads. To meet the two-week copy rule, they created several variations. From this came familiar ad slogans such as "Use Sapolio" (a popular soap) and "Eat H-O" (a brand of farina) later seen across the country.

But it was showman P.T. Barnum who popularized a number of advertising and publicity methods on both sides of the Atlantic. In 1841 he acquired the American Museum in New York City and ran nonstop entertainment featuring ventriloquists, albinos, dwarfs, and a wide variety of other curiosities. Barnum is remembered not for his newspaper advertising, but for the effort he put into rousing posters, handbills, flags, banners, and bands.

Following Barnum's example, exaggeration became the rule in advertising, and customers learned by experience to discount everything they read. Promoters posted notices at taverns and other common places. Handbills and broadsides advertised theaters, museums, patent medicines, clothing stores, and auctions. Advertisers painted notices on walls and on the sides of barns. Sandwich men became a common sight. Horse-drawn wagons bearing advertisements paraded along downtown streets, and announcements later appeared on rail cars.

Advertising as a "profession" did not exist until the mid–19th century. There were no copywriters, art directors, account executives, or marketing professionals. As long as advertising was aimed only at local readers, advertisers had little need for outside assistance and dealt directly with newspapers.

As transportation improved, manufacturers distributed their goods over wider areas and thus required sales promotions that reached beyond their own region. Advertisers often found that the placing of printed announcements involved a myriad of details and time-consuming tasks. These included identifying effective newspapers, negotiating rates, directing the printer, confirming the insertion, and sending in payment. To take care of these chores, newspapers began paying agents to sell space to advertisers, thereby starting an entirely new business: the advertising agency.

The earliest known advertising agent in the United States was Volney B. Palmer, who set up shop in Philadelphia, Pennsylvania, in the early 1840s. Palmer called himself an "agent for country newspapers." He worked for the newspapers he represented and also acted as an agent for the advertisers. When he persuaded a firm to buy space in a paper, he passed along the copy he received, and the newspapers paid him part of the revenue (usually 25 percent). Following in Palmer's footsteps, a number of agents operated as authorized representatives for the newspapers. Among these advertising agents, John L. Hooper did things a little differently, buying large orders of space at a substantial discount. He then divided the space into smaller units and resold them at a higher price—yet considerably lower than what advertisers could obtain elsewhere. The idea caught on quickly, and by the beginning of the Civil War, there were about 30 such agencies, with more than half of them in New York City.

By 1850 the economy of the United States was booming. A network of waterways, roads, and railroads opened new markets and dramatically reduced transportation costs. The railroads themselves became a big business, hauling lumber, coal, and farm goods to the growing markets. Innovations such as the steel plow and the horse-drawn reaper greatly increased food production. On both sides of the Atlantic, more and more goods from previously limited local markets were sold in both Europe and the United States. Prime examples of these products were Samuel Colt's handgun and Elias Howe's sewing machine. Other manufacturers bottled, canned, and packaged not only new foods but familiar ones. Gail Borden and Henri Nestlé succeeded in condensing milk. Baker and Fry branded cocoa. Liebigh Extract of Meat Company supplied extract of beef, while Philip Armour and Gustavus Swift developed meat by-products.

The U.S. Civil War (1861–65) advanced the advertising profession and dramatically changed manufacturing, giving rise to a consumer economy. Wartime shortages and the demand for war news spurred innovations in publishing, including new methods of reproducing illustrations, improved printing techniques, and advances in paper-making technology.

The Civil War created a whole new generation of customers who had never before bought ready-made food or clothing from a store. Previously, food and dry goods had been shipped, stored, and sold in bulk. With the onset of war, the need to feed thousands of soldiers in sometimes remote locales led to innovations in packaging and food preservation. Although canning had been available in the early 19th century, consumer use of canned goods lagged until a generation of soldiers became accustomed to eating canned vegetables, fruits, and condensed milk. The invention of the can opener removed another troublesome obstacle to the widespread use of processed foods. And the need for thousands of soldiers' uniforms, underwear, and shoes brought the sewing machine into wider use, and ready-made clothing evolved into a big business.

Before the Civil War American families living on farms formed a tightly knit economic unit. The women performed such important functions as preserving foods, spinning, sewing, making clothes, and processing ashes into soap. The men worked in the fields, managed the family's money, and made most of the purchases. And the children pitched in wherever they were needed—in the fields, the barnyards, and the home.

With the men gone to war, it was women who shopped in the stores and purchased goods from peddlers. Having less time for household tasks, women bought clothing, canned goods, bakery items, and soap—items they would previously have made themselves. Thus, women assumed the task of choosing what and how much to buy.

After the war this purchasing trend continued as many people left the farm to work in urban factories. As a result, they came to rely less on their own production and bought more affordable mass-produced goods. They simply could not match the variety, attractiveness, and particularly the prices of the articles produced by U.S. manufacturers—from food and drink to clothing and furniture. As manufacturers mass-produced foodstuffs, urban food retailing became specialized. In large cities, a customer might have to shop as many as half a dozen specialty stores to obtain basic

Lieutenant (later Admiral) Robert Peary testified to the reliability of the Kodak camera in this 1893 print ad.
Courtesy of Eastman Kodak Company.

foods: produce, dairy products, meat, baked goods, tea, coffee, liquor, and candy. The shopper typically found goods sequestered behind a counter; a salesclerk searched the shelves or portioned out goods from open containers.

A new breed of merchandisers brought the European idea of large retail shops—or "department stores"—to America. A.T. Stewart and R.H. Macy in New York City, John Wanamaker in Philadelphia, and Marshall Field in Chicago, Illinois, set up department stores and competed by offering customers elegant surroundings, broad selection, and prompt and courteous service. Previously, the finer stores had kept their goods out of sight, bringing them out only for the most serious customer. In the new showrooms, any shopper could examine the merchandise, ask questions, and compare prices. To facilitate sales, the age-old practice of negotiation eventually gave way to a system of fixed prices. And shopping became grander as block-size establishments gave way to enclosed, multitiered arcades with space for shops, restaurants, and doctors' and lawyers' offices.

By the late 1860s publishers recognized that retailers and other advertisers were willing to spend a lot of money to attract attention and began to give them greater freedom. As department stores increased in size and sales, their store announcements expanded down the column, spanned adjoining columns, and eventually filled the whole page. Sewing machines and typewriters, the most heavily advertised machines of the time, were the first products pictured in large newspaper ads. Yet no one in business really seemed to have any idea of which papers existed, where and how they published, and to what size audience.

Although George P. Rowell published the *American Newspaper Directory* after the Civil War, providing agencies and advertisers with the first sound basis for estimating a fair value of media space, these details were not fully sorted out until 1914, when the Audit Bureau of Circulations was formed. Another who contributed to the honesty of advertising was Francis W. Ayer, who started his Philadelphia agency, N.W. Ayer & Son in 1869. (In deference to his father, he named the agency for him, Nathan Wheeler Ayer.) Although Ayer adopted Rowell's basic approach, he added another strong selling point to his practice—the open contract. Other agents had kept advertising rates strictly confidential so that the customer never knew the net publication prices. Ayer, however, fixed his commission at 15 percent, giving the advertiser the benefit of all discounts and the agent's shrewd bargaining. Typically, though, advertising agents struggled to get by in a dubious profession.

New Role for Advertising, 1880–1900

By the 1880s a number of firms realized unprecedented economies of scale, expanded their distribution, and reached for coast-to-coast markets. Dramatic changes accompanied the enormous economic growth. For example, coal took the place of wood as the major source of energy. Mechanized reapers, sewing machines, and other innovations in machinery led to new production processes. Factories increased in size, and raw materials flowed through them at a faster rate and lower cost than ever before. Inventions such as the electric lightbulb, telephone, motorized streetcar, phonograph, and motion picture appeared. Direct and mail-order selling flourished with the development of the national railroad system and the introduction in 1896 of rural free mail delivery. Getting goods to out-of-the-way places was no longer a problem.

But continued economic progress depended on the addition of new customers. To gain those customers, manufacturers had to persuade formerly self-sustaining households to purchase soap, bread, clothing, and other necessities instead of making their own, as well as to convince the prospects to select their branded product over another. Businesses began to recognize that advertising could do more than reduce production costs by increasing sales. It could also create desires—desires that could fuel a consumer economy. People bought articles they did not know they wanted until advertising told them why they could not live without it. The success of patent medicines and the great expansion of mail-order houses such as Montgomery Ward & Company and Sears, Roebuck & Company demonstrated the possibilities for sales on a national scale.

Moreover, advertising emerged as only one aspect of a national marketing effort. Early mass-marketing firms also developed national organizations of managers, distributors, salesmen, and buyers. Firms also set up extensive marketing organizations and established ties among managers, jobbers, and retailers. This enormous market power forced many retailers to distribute their products without any price breaks, often creating a monopoly and limiting competition.

Meanwhile, advertising played a major role in two different aspects of the post–Civil War consumer's life. First, national advertising of mass-produced, brand-name packaged goods emerged as one of the most significant developments of the era. When the Industrial Revolution began in England in the mid–18th century and reached North America in the early 19th century, both businesses and households felt the effect. Mechanization enabled manufacturers to produce goods in multiples rather than one at a time. Advertising provided manufacturers with a way to stimulate demand for their output. It also made specific products so appealing that customers would accept no substitutes, and in turn, they urged stores to stock these products regardless of the price set by the manufacturer. Advertising thus permitted higher profits, not just more sales.

Before the 1880s the names of most manufacturers and marketers had been virtually unknown to the people who bought their products. Tobacco was tobacco, flour was flour until companies found a way to promote their names to customers. Patent medicine manufacturers, in particular, pioneered new techniques for advertising brand-name goods, providing marketers with an advertising vehicle in the form of labels, wrappers, and boxes. They also established the foundation for today's multimillion-dollar health products industry with their promotion of over-the-counter medicines and mail-order remedies.

The early patent medicine peddlers had perfected one of the oldest selling styles, the "hard sell." To make sure buyers selected the right bottle from the shelf in a store, the medicine makers experimented with elaborate and distinctive labels, often featuring an easily remembered name. Thus Radway's Ready Relief, Kickapoo Indian Sagwa, and dozens of others vied for attention. The hard sell also included the claim of being the best, the greatest, or the most wonderful product in the world, along with phrases such as "send no money," "money-back guarantee," and other attention grabbers. Lydia Pinkham's Vegetable Compound, a mixture of roots and alcohol for "female complaints," became one of American advertising's most widely publicized early success stories. Although Pinkham died in 1883, her famous face continued to appear in newspapers and magazines, on billboards, and in streetcar ads.

Tobacco companies also advanced the use of appealing proprietary names, commercial symbols, and packaging. Manufacturers packed bales of tobacco under named labels and began to literally "brand" their products with hot irons that burned the maker's name into wooden packages—hence, "brand names" such as Black's Twist and Smith's Plug and Brown. This was hardly a new idea. Since antiquity people had imprinted symbols on livestock, barrels, boxes, and tools to mark ownership. Still other manufacturers burned Xs on barrels of whiskey and sugar to aid clerks who could not read. By the 1860s the makers of tobacco products began to package their goods for sale directly to the consumers. Creative names acquainted consumers with a product's special qualities—Cherry Ripe promised a rich, aromatic tobacco, while Bull Durham meant a stronger smoke. Like the patent medicine bottlers, they also experimented with picture labels and decorations to make the packages attractive.

From 1860 to 1920, factory-produced merchandise in packages largely replaced locally produced goods sold in bulk. At first most people considered packaged goods a luxury suitable only for gifts or as a personal indulgence. Decorative bottles suggested the allure of Pears' toiletries. Printed labels on pottery jars enhanced the appeal of Keiller's Dundee marmalade. Individually foil-wrapped candies created an elite image for British Cadbury chocolates.

In the move to standardized packaging, the next significant innovation in distribution and marketing was the folding box. In 1879 the cereal industry mechanized the printing, folding, and filling processes. Quaker Oats oatmeal, which still appears on the standard breakfast menu, became a prime example of how marketers could turn relatively generic bulk goods into far more popular and identifiable products. A manufacturer put a commodity in a small box, injected "personality," added information to increase its usefulness, and turned the goods into something both desirable and extremely profitable. The success of selling packaged goods also depended on advertising a "name." Yet it was something more than a name—it was the established identification of a "brand name." This identity differentiated the product from others of the same category and enabled buyers to appraise its value before buying.

Thus early marketers packaged cereals, soaps, flour, cigarettes and matches, and canned vegetables, fruits, milk, and soup. Then they put their name on the package and began to develop a loyal following: Campbell soup, Procter & Gamble soap, Pillsbury flour, Heinz condiments, Borden dairy products, Coca-Cola soft drinks, Levi Strauss jeans, Hires root beer, National Biscuit Company (later Nabisco) cookies and crackers, and Hills Brothers coffee, to name a few. As the use of brand names and commercial marks spread, so did the practice of imitation, but the protection provided by the new trademark laws encouraged companies to rely more heavily on well-advertised commercial symbols.

In the new era of packaged goods, advertising no longer focused on a blaring hard sell to provide product information, because people were already familiar with most of these commodities. Instead, the emphasis shifted to a "soft-sell," feel-good style that focused on establishing the brand name and the reputability of the manufacturer with favorable and memorable associations. People came to rely on these brand names for assurance that the products they bought came from a reliable source.

Still another role of advertising was the introduction of new products. National advertising of cameras and bicycles demonstrated that people would buy something they did not even know they wanted until advertising pictured the product and sang its praises. Moreover, they would do so even if the cost of the item exceeded their standard of living. During this period, the phonograph, telephone, bicycle, and electric lightbulb appeared. Eastman's Kodak camera appeared in 1888, and Daimler and Benz started producing automobiles in 1885. In almost every case, manufacturers spent a great deal on advertising to stimulate enough demand to justify the mass production needed to make a profit. The advertisement had to explain the benefits of owning the product, and advertisers became skilled at justifying how it was going to make the reader's life brighter, easier, and more fun. Products old and new jammed the marketplace, and advertisers sought new ways to reach potential consumers. The emergence of magazines reflected this effort.

The Communications Revolution

The Industrial Revolution brought technological advances that created the greatest changes in communications since the introduction of the printing press. The invention of photography in 1839 and the ability to print detailed illustrations gave advertisers a new way of showcasing their products. Illustrations remained the basis of most print advertising until the 1950s. Railways, postal routes, telegraph, typewriters, and telephones speeded communication. Meanwhile, society was becoming more educated, urbanized, industrialized, and faster-paced. The combination of rising literacy and falling printing costs expanded the reading audience. This literate audience, concentrated in cities and larger towns, became the target of what is now known as the mass media—newspapers, magazines, books, and advertising. The age of mass communications had arrived.

Unlike newspapers, magazines made most of their money from subscriptions. Recognizing that their subscribers—who were refined or aspired to be so—regarded most product advertising as dubious, magazine publishers were slow to accept paid notices. Thus most magazines carried little if any advertising until the 1870s, at which time publishers began to accept ads but only in a separate section at the back of the issue.

In 1872 Aaron Montgomery Ward, a traveling salesman, produced the first mail-order catalog and devised the first mass-produced color pictures in a printed publication. Ward's catalog techniques of color reproduction were later adopted by magazine publishers.

It was Boston, Massachusetts, advertising solicitor Cyrus H.K. Curtis who truly established the magazine as a high-grade advertising vehicle, first with the *Ladies' Home Journal* in 1883 and then the revamped *Saturday Evening Post* in 1897. Like Curtis, New York advertising agent J. Walter Thompson also transformed previously staid magazines into eye-catching publications that were underwritten by advertising and reached millions of homes. Whatever their content, these magazines had one thing in common: they depended on a new class of subscribers—middle-class readers eager to buy consumer goods advertised in an appropriate fashion. These new magazines created new opportunities for national advertisers as well as new demands on agencies. Art, copy, and layout had to be carefully considered to reflect the broader marketing strategy of product image, pricing, and distribution.

With the development of color lithography in the 1880s, Europe had taken the lead in the production of artistic posters and advertisements. The poster as an advertising form was used widely in Italy, France, and Germany before it found its way to England. Art Nouveau–style posters coming out of Paris and London fascinated the art world. The work of poster artists such as Jules Cheret, Henri de Toulouse-Lautrec, and Alphonse Mucha sold everything from cough drops to world's fairs. These artists functioned as both designers and illustrators, producing magazine covers, literary posters, and better advertisements.

But it was a long time before British painters of repute would allow their works to appear on billboards. In 1887 Sir William Ingram bought a painting by Sir John Millais and resold it to Thomas Barrat's firm of Pears' Soap for 2,000 guineas. Although Millais did not paint the picture for Pears', the color reproduction shows a little boy blowing bubbles of Pears' Soap. Soon works by other British artists, including Dudley Hardy, Aubrey Beardsley, and the Beggerstaff brothers (James Pryde and William Nicholson), came to be seen on billboards. Some of the best posters in America during this period were produced in the Beggerstaff style by Edgar Penfield. Beardsley's designs were also widely imitated.

By the 1880s ambitious pictorial advertisements began to appear in British illustrated magazines. Ad makers reproduced original paintings, wash drawings, and sketches as full-page advertisements to give the product the right image. Among the early American artists to be taken up by advertisers, Frederick Remington painted Western scenes for Smith & Wesson guns and Jesse Wilcox Smith created illustrations for Ivory Soap and Kodak. Under the influence of the new printing methods, trademarks evolved from simple marks into complex pictorial symbols. One of the earliest came from Walter Baker & Company, which identified its cocoa and chocolate with a demure waitress bearing a tray of hot chocolate. The Quaker Oats trademark Quaker gentleman appeared on a cereal package as did the Cream of Wheat chef, while the Michelin Man represented tires, and Aunt Jemima became synonymous with pancakes.

Ad copy had its own unique pattern of development. Until the advent of John E. Powers, advertising typically appeared either as blaring overstatements or numbing lists of merchandise. Powers, a U.S. copywriter, suggested that sincerity, a commonplace approach, and skillful support for claims would convince the customer to buy the product. In this period, slogan-making developed into a specialty to encapsulate a key theme or idea, such as National Biscuit Company's "Do Uneeda Biscuit?" and Procter & Gamble's Ivory Soap's "99 and 44/100% pure" and "It floats," among others. Also at this time, ad makers revived the jingle. For nearly a century, advertising rhymes had appeared in England with great success. The jingle had the virtue of being easily remembered. For example, a series of lighthearted streetcar ads made Sapolio Soap synonymous with cleanliness, praising the qualities of Sapolio in verse:

This is the butcher of Spotless Town,
His tools are bright as his renown.
To leave them stained were indiscreet,

For folks would then abstain from meat.
And so he brightens his trade you know
By polishing with Sapolio.

The ads introduced new characters—the doctor, the mayor, and so on, eventually 12 in all—as the series about Spotless Town, a quaint cobble-stoned Dutch village, grew.

Emergence of the Agency

By 1900 the agencies began to expand with the rise of national advertisers and the advent of new media to meet the demands of businesses. Agencies grew beyond their initial role as sellers of newspaper space. They began to offer multiple services to advertisers—writing the ads, seeing that they were placed in the best possible location, and trying to get the best possible price for the space. Agencies also learned how to create advertising campaigns, plan marketing strategies, and prepare ads. Some agents formed their own bill-posting companies, which erected their own boards and leased space. Others organized streetcar and magazine advertising, selling on a national basis.

These efforts solved many of the problems that entrepreneurs faced when they set out to advertise beyond their immediate community. At the same time, they also led to the creation of national and eventually global advertising organizations. New York, America's leading city in domestic and foreign trade, emerged as the nation's center of advertising as major agencies opened up shops: N.W. Ayer & Son (1869); the J. Walter Thompson Company (1878); Lord & Thomas (later Foote, Cone & Belding; 1873); and George Batten Company (later Batten Barton Durstine & Osborn; 1891).

The largest of the modern British agencies, T.B. Browne Ltd., set up shop in 1876 and soon bought space for Pears' Soap and other international advertisers. Other large agencies in London included S.H. Benson, Ltd. (1893), C. Verson & Sons, Ltd. (1894), Paul E. Derrick Advertising Agency (1894), and Erwood's Ltd. (1895).

Advertising and Imperialism

By 1900 Britain, the United States, and Japan to a large extent controlled the economies of the developing nations. From the onset, the burgeoning advertising industry was American and British dominated. Because the developing areas were largely colonial possessions, the major advertisers as well as the most prominent advertising companies operating in the region were those of its colonial masters. As a result, the colonial mentality—a preference for things foreign, particularly American or British—became prevalent.

The history of advertising in Asia and Africa is almost as old as the history of modern print media in the countries. During the colonial period, Britain had gained footholds in South Africa, Australia, Hong Kong, India, and Malaysia. British-made goods were sold in the colonial markets by British trading companies. As a result, most of the commercial advertisers in these colonies were initially British businesses, and foreign advertising networks formed part of a global strategy. The French, Germans, and Dutch were also active colonial empire builders.

Advertising in Britain's colonies was British in character, modified to accommodate the needs and resources of the local people. For example, the notion of modern advertising using mass media was entirely foreign to the Chinese until the British introduced the practice. The practice was first popularized by foreign tobacco and petroleum companies in the middle of the 19th century. In the 1840s Britain had won Hong Kong Island from China and declared it a free port, using it for the sole purpose of trade.

In the second half of the 19th century, the colonization by Britain had a strong influence on advertising in both China and Hong Kong. More than 300 foreign-run newspapers and magazines were circulated in China, with most published in Shanghai, the commercial center of the country. These publications, many of which were in Chinese, became the major mass media for advertising in the country. Westerners introduced modern advertising media practices and skills, which closely resembled painting and fine arts. Companies hired artists who practiced the traditional style of painting. Calendars, matchbox covers, newspapers, magazines, and painted signs and posters reflected the adaptation of traditional Chinese painting to product promotion.

The earliest advertising in Malaysia and Singapore primarily took the form of newspaper advertisements featuring imported products and shipping information from Britain to colonies in Southeast Asia, while other notices included hotels and medicinal products. Early advertising also included posters, handbills, and sandwich boards.

Almost 200 years of British rule had a lasting influence on advertising in Indian society. The first newspaper in India was published in 1780, and the paper did carry a few advertisements in its first issue. Other newspapers published during the same decade also carried advertisements. Most of the commercial advertisers in India were British business houses. Advertising agencies did not exist in India at this time.

By the turn of the century, American advertising networks also began to aggressively expand into other countries. The J. Walter Thompson Company (JWT) became the first multinational agency when it set up shop in London in 1899. The objective of this first sales bureau was to urge European businessmen to sell in America and advertise their products there. JWT had already published (1888) the first bilingual (French-English) annual to initiate Europeans into the workings of the U.S. market and its press. It was also at this time that a Latin American department was set up. But it would not be until the 1920s that JWT would sign its first campaign in England for the account of an American client.

Around the turn of the century, America also established a presence in the Philippines, where there was already evidence of early forms of advertising. During the Spanish period, whatever advertisements there were in newsletters, journals, and magazines were wholly business announcements. Publications were generally short-lived and quite specialized. However, some forms of outdoor advertising were evident, such as posters put up in cockfighting rings and in plays. The first transit advertising also appeared in the form of horse-drawn carriages on which barkers called public attention to their announcements with a drum.

In Canada advertising generally developed about 20 years later than similar beginnings in the United States. In 1881 the owners of the *Daily Mail* newspaper, published in Toronto, set up an advertising agency, and three years later they placed James T. Wetherald in charge. Wetherald was possibly the first Canadian newspaper representative sent to another city to look after its advertising business, but there were few national advertising accounts then, and two years later Wetherald joined the Pettingill agency in Boston. From 1880 to 1900, the advertising business grew slowly; accounts were small and so were the advertisements, as they followed the English models.

Although America and Britain had the most impact on advertising, the practice of advertising as a modern industry in Japan also dates back to the establishment and popularization of mass media. In 1867 the first newspaper advertisement placed by a Japanese company appeared in a Japanese language newspaper, and the publications soon began to increase their circulation as well as advertising revenue. In 1873 the first Japanese advertising agency is said to have been founded, although advertising was just a sideline for this firm, whose main businesses were news wire service, shipping, and insurance. In the 1880s and 1890s the first truly professional advertising agencies were founded, including Kohodo, Kokoku-sha, Man-nen-sha, and Hakuhodo. In the 1890s the first weekly magazines started. The primary advertisers were cosmetics, pharmaceuticals, and publications. The skills of advertising expression were gradually refined through these publications.

JULIANN SIVULKA

See also color plate in this volume

Further Reading

Fox, Stephen, *The Mirror Makers: A History of American Advertising and Its Creators*, New York: Morrow, 1984

French, George, *20th-Century Advertising*, New York: Van Nostrand, 1926

Frith, Katherine Toland, *Advertising in Asia: Communication, Culture, and Consumption*, Ames: Iowa State University Press, 1996

Goodrum, Charles, and Helen Dalrymple, *Advertising in America: The First 200 Years*, New York: Abrams, 1990

Lears, T.J. Jackson, *Fables of Abundance: A Cultural History of Advertising in America*, New York: Basic Books, 1994

Pope, Daniel, *The Making of Modern Advertising*, New York: Basic Books, 1983

Presbrey, Frank, *The History and Development of Advertising*, Garden City, New York: Doubleday, 1929; reprint, New York: Greenwood Press, 1968

Schudson, Michael, *Advertising, the Uneasy Persuasion: Its Dubious Impact on American Society*, New York: Basic Books, 1984; London: Routledge, 1993

Sivulka, Juliann, *Soap, Sex, and Cigarettes: A Cultural History of American Advertising*, Belmont, California: Wadsworth, 1998

Strasser, Susan, *Satisfaction Guaranteed: The Making of the American Mass Market*, New York: Pantheon, 1989

Tedlow, Richard, *New and Improved: The Story of Mass Marketing in America*, New York: Basic Books, 1990

Turner, Ernest Sackville, *The Shocking History of Advertising*, London: Joseph, 1952; New York: Dutton, 1953; revised edition, London: Penguin, 1965

Wood, James Playsted, *The Story of Advertising*, New York: Ronald, 1958

History: 1900–1920

By the turn of the 20th century, the United States had taken the lead from Great Britain in the field of advertising. Ad makers expanded on what the British had taught them and introduced new ideas. In a reversal of tradition, the European advertising industry now eagerly looked to the United States for the latest trends in advertising, marketing, and research.

Order, efficiency, and scientific principles became the key words of progressive America in the early 1900s. Public education brought literacy to native-born Americans and a rising tide of immigrants. Cities became cleaner and healthier. Electricity illuminated homes and streets and powered streetcars and appliances, while gasoline engines powered automobiles, trucks, and buses. Developments in steel making and architecture made skyscrapers possible. Science and technology produced such wonders as elevators, escalators, telephones, gasoline engines, rayon fabric, and plastics. Advertising, too, responded to these influences, using science to form the basis for advertising campaigns.

The United States emerged as the world's leading industrial power, and during subsequent decades economic output continued to increase. Manufacturers produced an increasing variety of products, the means to distribute them coast to coast, and ways to deliver their advertising messages through newspapers, magazines, and direct mail. The great monopoly trusts built in the late 19th century were substantially broken up by government action. Their competing spin-offs then grew into multimillion-dollar ventures. Advertising expenditures skyrocketed from thousands of dollars a year to millions, and as a consequence, advertising agencies, assuming full responsibility for campaigns, evolved into their present form. Advertising became a social and economic fixture in the world, despite its lingering dubious reputation.

Emergence of the Consumer Economy

The signs of a consumer economy continued to appear everywhere as a growing number of Americans enjoyed increasing wealth. Americans now spent hundreds of millions of dollars annually for wrapped soaps, packaged cereals, canned vegetables, bakery-baked bread, and ready-made clothes. Urban department stores, mail-order companies, and chain stores brought new places to shop, while new products were routinely introduced with a flurry of advertising.

U.S. industry responded by expanding the production of new consumer goods—everything from food and drink to home furnishings and automobiles. A flood of immigrants provided both a source of labor and a new class of consumer. Innovative packaging techniques and the development of chain stores helped keep consumer goods moving.

The American business scene changed dramatically at the turn of the century as big business became bigger. From 1898 to 1902, a wave of mergers consolidated 2,653 independent firms into 269 companies with $6.3 billion of capital. These large-scale corporations, called "trusts," controlled such basic industries as railroads, coal, iron, copper, oil, steel, sugar, and tobacco. These firms quickly recognized that if they were to make the huge capital investments necessary to control production under a central management and bring together the large labor forces required to operate the factories, demand could not be left to chance. The economic health of the trusts and the need for social stability required that demand be controlled and expanded with the same care given to the building of production capacity. Thus, marketing and advertising joined production and distribution as the third great institution of the U.S. industrial establishment. Although these newly consolidated companies had relatively few brands, they wielded great blocks of capital and dominated large shares of the markets in which they operated. Here advertising also played an important role in maintaining market power. Advertising benefited consumers too, informing them of new products and establishing brand distinctions.

Advertising helped manufacturers move from selling fairly small quantities in limited markets at high prices to selling mass-produced goods at convenient locations and affordable prices. Scouring pads, toothpaste, and denim jeans, for example, found national markets. Packaging and promotion of soaps, crackers, and flour turned these essentially undifferentiated commodities into desirable products. Other manufacturers shifted their selling pitches, matching their advertising to the uses to which consumers had put their products. Coca-Cola's soft drink started as a medicinal tonic. A Methodist congregation created Welch's grape juice as a substitute for wine, and W.K. Kellogg originally created food products for patients with digestive problems.

Advertisements did more than inform the customer; they relentlessly tried to persuade Americans to buy particular brands and above all to accept no substitutes. The annual volume of advertising surged nearly sixfold in the 20-year period following 1900, from $540 million to just less than $3 billion. As big business got bigger, industrial growth reached new heights. Fundamental to this economic boom were electricity and the abundant supply of immigrant labor, both cheap. Advances in production coincided with the country's explosive growth from 31 million people in 1860 to 105 million in 1920.

In this era of economic prosperity, incomes steadily increased, and many had money left over after they paid for necessities. This increased purchasing ability created a demand for more consumer goods: ready-to-eat breakfast cereals, lightbulbs, vacuums, irons, toasters, washing machines. Other products, such as player pianos, phonographs, and board games, appeared entirely for consumers' enjoyment, while the automobile changed the way millions spent their leisure time.

Henry Ford brought the automobile within reach of millions of Americans and, as road travel increased, the billboard industry developed as a means of addressing the newly mobile public. In 1900, the first standardized structure for displaying posters was developed. Before this, outdoor advertising had been limited to the placing of messages on buildings, fences, and other existing structures. After 1900 standardized billboards could be erected anywhere. By 1915, roadsides had become important advertising venues for companies such as U.S. Rubber, Firestone Tire and Rubber Co., and Goodyear. Other billboards went up for Ford Motor Company, Carnation, and Coca-Cola, to name a few.

Retail Revolution

Yet perhaps more than anything else, marketing and packaging stimulated the consumer economy and created a revolution in retailing. The soaring number of retail stores and mail-order catalogs took advantage of innovations in packaging. Improved transportation and distribution systems allowed canners and bakers to ship their goods beyond their established markets. Inevitably, the need for other forms of packaging appeared. Some bakers packaged crackers in tins and in printed cardboard cartons. Later, wax-sealed cartons preserved the freshness of such foods as breakfast cereal, grains, biscuits, cookies, and snack food. Other innovative packaging included wood containers, sealed glass jars and bottles, cans, tins, and metal tubes. Colorful descriptive labels on packages further assisted shoppers, transforming generic products into unique ones. Packages also allowed cost comparison as more stores affixed prices to the merchandise.

In the cities, shoppers flocked to department stores, which provided luxury, comfort, and convenience as well as strong point-of-purchase selling incentives. Sales floors displayed the latest fashions in dresses, kitchenware, home furnishings, and other amenities. At the same time, giant mail-order firms offered to fulfill rural Americans' every need, from patent medicines to the latest gadgets for home or work; even livestock could be ordered by mail.

The next step in mass retailing was the chain store. Previously, the typical shopkeeper had handled everything from purchasing and selling to display and advertising. Then general merchandis-

ers and food retailers began to bring the same economies of scale that had been applied to manufacturing to selling. A centrally managed operation placed large orders at low prices, established low profit margins, and made money through volume sales. Consumers benefited, with a wider selection at affordable prices. Great Atlantic and Pacific Tea Company (A&P), Woolworth's Five and Dime Stores, and J.C. Penney Company profitably expanded to hundreds of outlets, called chain stores.

As the consumer society emerged, women became the nation's primary purchasers of consumer goods. Although advertisers accepted that women made 85 percent of consumer purchases, no one could cite a source for that number. Yet, men created most of the ads and images were intended to influence women to purchase a variety of products. As the industry gained prestige, men came to dominate the field. Women in advertising worked on products for the women's market (food, soap, fashions, and cosmetics). Men moved through training programs, working through all the departments to find the right job. Women, who did not have the right to vote until 1920, started lower, as secretaries or researchers, trying to get noticed as copywriters.

Despite this climate, a few women rose to prominence. On the agency side, Helen Lansdowne Resor had a brilliant career as a copywriter and creative supervisor at the J. Walter Thompson Company (JWT). Helen Rosen Woodward, one of the first prominent female account executives, worked for the Presbrey and Gardner agencies before becoming an author. Later, the manpower shortage during World War I and the postwar economic boom would reopen opportunities for women in advertising

Growing Sophistication

By the turn of the century, successful marketers recognized the importance of well-coordinated promotional planning that pushed the sale of particular brands and continually introduced new ones. Thus manufacturers routinely introduced new brand-name products with a wave of advertising. Advertisers gradually began to turn entirely to advertising agencies. With full responsibility for campaigns, the agencies evolved from space agents (who brokered the purchase of advertising space for marketers) into their present form in the first decade of the century. Advertisements now were but one component of planned campaigns that had to be integrated into appropriate marketing strategies.

Skilled copywriting, layout, and illustration became important in achieving continuity and strengthening selling appeals. In agencies' early years, agency principals wrote the copy. For important accounts, some employed prominent freelance copywriters who also assisted with trademarks, slogans, and other program needs. Although agencies began to hire full-time established writers to pen advertising copy, "art managers" typically sent an advertisement in its rough layout form to the printer. This changed, however, when designers and artists joined the staff and asserted that the "look" of an ad was just as important as the words.

The role of the account executive expanded from one of bringing in new business to one of serving as a liaison between the client and the creative staff, while media buyers continued to see

along with the catchy slogan: "Lest you forget, we say it yet, Uneeda Biscuit." In 1899 Ayer launched the first multimillion-dollar advertising campaign in the United States.

Using Uneeda as an example, the N.K. Fairbank Company of Chicago, Illinois, made the Gold Dust twins symbols of one of the most heavily advertised products after the turn of the century—Gold Dust washing powder. Other familiar personalities became the trademarks of the products they advertised and as famous as national heroes: Sir Thomas Lipton, the Dutch Cleanser house-keeper, Aunt Jemima, the Campbell's Kids, the Morton Salt girl, Buster Brown, Planter's Mr. Peanut, and Cracker Jack's Sailor Jack, to name a few. Animals also became famous symbols: Camel cigarettes' Joe Camel and the RCA dog, Nipper.

Printing innovations also encouraged creativity. The reproduction of gradations of light and dark tones and multiple-plate color printing allowed printed pictures to look like opulent oil paintings, instead of hand-sketched black-and-white line drawings. When four-color front and back covers and one- and two-color interior ads became standard by 1900, magazines exploded with color. The look of the ad became a key responsibility of the advertising agencies.

Earnest Elmo Calkins, of the New York City-based agency Calkins & Holden (C&H), elevated the art of the advertisement, emphasizing the ad itself instead of the media selection or the size of the advertiser's budget. If an ad had the "look," it would stop a reader from turning the page of the magazine or newspaper. This look built an image for the product and integrated branding, advertising, and other promotions. To execute his visions, Calkins hired artists such as Joseph Leyendecker, known for his *Saturday Evening Post* covers, who painted the Arrow Collar Man for Arrow Shirts. Other successful C&H soft-sell campaigns were developed for Force cereal, Pierce-Arrow cars, and the Lack-awana Railroad. Calkins's richly illustrated ads were soon imitated, as other agencies hired gallery artists to create memorable illustrations. Maxfield Parrish's meticulous painting style appeared in stunning ads for Fisk Tire and Community Plate Silver. The illustrator N.C. Wyeth filled ads for Cream of Wheat with cowboys and gold miners. Norman Rockwell painted realistic figures with a humorous touch for everything from Heinz Baked Beans to Grape Nuts.

While humor, jingles, and trade characters kept the names of products in the public's mind, they did not always sell them. For a familiar product, such as Sapolio soap, the devices effectively reminded the customer of an already well-established brand. People may have found the characters and verses for a new product entertaining, but more often they failed to discover the benefits of using the product and why the product was better than rival brands. As a result, many ad makers shifted from soft-sell styles to hard-sell copy approaches that offered specific reasons to purchase.

Dueling Theories

A successful ad works because it creates a connection between the product being advertised and some need or desire that the audience feels. These links, called *appeals,* fall into two categories.

This 1920 photo of New York City's Times Square shows both the density of advertising and the range of advertising media, from trade bills to lighted signs and neon graphics.

that the ads were placed in the best possible location and shopped around for the best possible deals from newspapers or other ad media. Market research, however, proved slower in getting started than skilled copywriting, layout, and account management.

Uneeda Biscuit set the standard for a well-coordinated advertising plan that introduced a new product. The newly formed National Biscuit Company's (later called Nabisco) first move was to create a brand-name cracker and to sell it in a package that preserved its freshness. Previously, grocers had sold biscuits from open barrels, making no claims about their crispness or cleanliness. National Biscuit settled on a light, flaky soda cracker in a distinctive octagonal shape. To preserve the crackers' crispness, they packaged them in airtight, waxed-paper-lined packages. For the name, the N. W. Ayer & Son agency in Philadelphia, Pennsylvania, suggested "Uneeda" (pronounced "You-need-a"). Ayer also created the Uneeda trade character, a boy in a rain slicker,

Logical (or rational) appeals present selling pitches based on performance features or a product's ability to solve a problem. Emotional appeals try to sell a product based on the satisfaction that comes from purchasing the product. An extremely strong appeal tells the reader: "This is *the* product that will meet my needs or fulfill my desires."

Although fundamental today, these ideas seemed revolutionary in 1905, especially the idea that the skillful use of emotional appeals could move products faster than logical appeals. Nevertheless, the emotional approach did not just suddenly appear. In the early 1900s pioneering admakers first introduced the idea of the sales argument, called "reason-why copy," as opposed to brand identification. The new approach shifted the selling pitch to sales arguments designed to overcome any resistance. This hard sell was in sharp contrast to simple brand identification, which merely kept the advertiser's name before the people.

Reason-why practitioners such as John E. Kennedy, Claude Hopkins, Albert Lasker, and Helen Lansdowne Resor established the copywriter as crucial to the operation of the American advertising agency. Kennedy, hired as Lord & Thomas's chief copywriter for the Chicago office in 1904, treated advertising as business news to be told in a detailed, straightforward style. "Advertising is salesmanship in print," Kennedy explained. Instead of soft-sell pictures and general claims, advertising should state in print what the salesman would say in person to a customer. That is, it should offer a sensible argument with specific reasons why the product was worth buying. Kennedy's copy style owed a debt to hard-selling patent medicine arguments—testimonials, samples, coupons, money-back guarantees, specific claims, and other attention-getting devices. Kennedy taught Lord & Thomas account executive Lasker, who passed the reason-why gospel along to his apprentice copywriters.

At Lord & Thomas, Hopkins emerged as one of the most influential copywriters in advertising, developing the preemptive claim technique that established a product's uniqueness. His classic strategy theorized that an ad should be built around a single selling point. He then gave readers scores of reasons why they should buy the product. He theorized that if one took a product feature or quality that might be common to the industry and made the claim first, one owned it. Typically his ads included free or inexpensive samples, premiums, coupons, hard-selling arguments, and functional illustrations with informative captions. This technique worked for Schlitz beer, Pepsodent toothpaste, Van Camp's pork and beans, and Sunkist, the brand of the California Fruit Growers Exchange. In 1911 JWT copywriter Helen Lansdowne (who later married then-JWT-President Stanley Resor) added the essential emotional appeal to the sales argument with her celebrated ad for Woodbury's Facial Soap. The ad featured a painting of an attractive couple locked in an embrace; a provocative headline invited the audience to read further: "A skin you love to touch." The ad copy featured a skin-care regimen and closed with an offer for a week's supply of soap and a reproduction of the art from the advertisement. The landmark ad talked about the benefits of using the product, suggesting softness, sex appeal, and even romance. Lansdowne understood women's motivation for buying—whether

soap or shortening—and presented provocative arguments about self-improvement and aspiring to the habits of the wealthy.

The next new strategy represented a subtler approach than Hopkins and Resor's reason-why, claim-and-coupon styles. With this soft-sell style, the pitch revolved around conveying the impression of integrity, quality, and prestige as it showcased the products in a unique selling environment. The intent was to differentiate these products from those associated with hard-selling arguments. The theories of psychoanalysts Sigmund Freud and Carl Jung and the influential book *The Psychology of Advertising* (1908) by Walter Dill Scott further justified this psychology of suggestion to make an impression. Instead of scientifically describing the item, as was the practice in reason-why copy, Scott urged ad makers to focus on the pleasure it would provide the purchaser.

The eloquent "Penalty of Leadership" essay for Cadillac, which positioned the marque as the standard for American luxury cars, established copywriter Theodore MacManus as the leader in the atmospheric soft-sell school. The ad copy opened with this memorable line, "In every field of human endeavor, he that is first must perpetually live in the white light of publicity." Many consider this image ad for Cadillac one of the all-time great advertisements. (It ranked 49th in *Advertising Age*'s top 100 ads of the century.) Astonishingly, the ad, which had no illustration—and no mention of automobiles—ran only once, in the *Saturday Evening Post* of 2 January 1915. Another atmospheric copywriter of the time, Raymond Rubicam, used suggestive sales pitches along with lavish art and layouts to make a favorable impression. Notable campaigns from Rubicam included work for Steinway, E.R. Squibb, Rolls-Royce, and the International Correspondence School.

The two schools of advertising theory, reason-why and atmospheric, coexisted for some time. The effectiveness of the style depended on the product. The Hopkins reason-why style worked best for small, inexpensive, frequently purchased items—such as cigarettes, toothpaste, and soap—that could be offered as samples and easily sent through the mail. The MacManus soft-sell style, however, built prestige for large, expensive items—automobiles, pianos—bought infrequently and seldom on impulse.

Agencies multiplied in size, number, and services offered as the volume of advertising increased. New agencies began to offer the same services available today—planning, research, ad creation, and implementation of advertising campaigns. In particular, ad preparation, education in advertising practice, and market research marked key steps in the industry's development.

Beginning around 1900 correspondence schools began to offer courses in advertising technique, an indication of advertising's increased legitimization in the business world. A decade later, institutions of higher learning, including Harvard University, New York University, Boston University, Northwestern University, and the University of Missouri, began to take advertising seriously enough to be studied as essential to business success.

The concept of marketing research, however, was slower to be developed. Who is the buying public? What are its tastes and desires? Which ads pull the best? To understand their audience, some ad makers went into the field to sell products, observed them in use, or interviewed housewives to acquire a feel for consumer tastes and retail problems—research efforts that were primitive by today's standards.

A JWT study, combined with Curtis Publishing Company's own findings, provided a factual base on which future marketing researchers would build. In 1912 JWT commissioned a study entitled "Population and Its Distribution," which listed virtually every store by category and by state. The agency continued to update the research and began to track the growth of wholesale and retail stores in large cities.

Mail-order response testing emerged as the major form of research, providing a rough idea of advertising preferences. For example, coded advertisements ran with coupons, which readers could cut out and return for information, product samples, booklets, or premiums. In test cities, identical ads appeared in different magazines and the results were compared. "Split runs" compared different versions of an ad in partial pressruns of the same issue of a magazine. From these new studies, agencies identified the best medium or media for the advertising of a given product. In addition, researchers sent crude surveys, such as questionnaires, to employees' friends, women in the agency's own office, or to the "typical" consumer (the ad executive's wife). Independent research firms also emerged, and departments began to form within agencies to obtain detailed data to assist advertising planning.

Agencies were no longer primarily space-brokers. The quality of the ads they prepared became one of the greatest methods of attracting clients. Agencies used portfolios of their advertisements to make a favorable impression on prospective clients.

Professional organizations, notably the Association of National Advertisers (established in 1910) and the American Association of Advertising Agencies (1917), brought together advertisers, agents, publishers, and others associated with advertising. Their efforts established standards for codes and ethics and simplified the mechanics of advertising. Another organization, the Audit Bureau of Circulations, formed in 1914, verified which papers existed, how frequently they published, how much they charged readers to receive the publication, and how large their audiences were. Participating publishers also agreed to establish uniform page and column sizes for newspapers and magazines.

Regulation of Advertising

On both sides of the Atlantic, the advertising of cure-alls and health devices underwent scrutiny in this period. The reform began when the *Ladies' Home Journal* refused to print medical advertising in 1892; other magazines soon followed. A decade later, the *Journal* shocked the public when it printed chemical analyses of medicines showing that they contained such addictive substances as cocaine and morphine. Other leading magazines and major newspapers joined the campaign.

In the United States, the resulting consumer movement led to government regulation and industry efforts at self-regulation. One outcome was the passing of the Meat Inspection Act and the 1906 Federal Food and Drugs Act, as well as laws requiring lists of ingredients on food containers, medicine bottles, and pill boxes.

Also, the activities of long-time promoters of worthless stock certificates, deceptive retail announcements, and other advertising inaccuracies led to the truth in advertising movement and the formation of the National Better Business Bureau.

The situation was different in Great Britain, where the government derived appreciable revenue from the trade in dubious medicinal products in the form of a stamp duty. To some consumers, the government stamp on a bottle appeared to be an indication of integrity. Some manufacturers even claimed that the stamp was a guarantee of excellence. As long as the law stood, however, British manufacturers could say what they liked in their advertisements, providing that they avoided gross impropriety.

The entry of the United States into World War I in 1917 provided a boost for advertising. Many manufacturers converted their production from consumer goods to war materials, and others felt constrained from promoting nonessential consumer products during this time of crisis. Yet the shortages fueled an increase in the "institutional" advertising that kept company names and trademarks in the public eye. Eloquent essays sang the praises of firms' commitment to noble ideals, explained how their products assisted in winning the war, and appealed to the public to buy war bonds. The government created national advertising programs to gain public support for the war effort. The newly created Federal Committee of Public Information helped shape public opinion, developed wartime patriotism, and told the public what they could do to help win the war. Within the committee, artist Charles Dana Gibson formed a "Division of Pictorial Publicity" that contracted with professional designers and leading illustrators to contribute their artwork to the war effort. Printers donated their services as well. After the war, the tradition of making free space available for public causes continued.

Advertising in Great Britain

As literacy spread and new media outlets opened, the modern advertising agency in Great Britain developed along the same lines as in the United States. Several of London's large agencies date to this period, including Dorland Advertising, Ltd. (1906), Pools Advertising Service and Charles F. Higman, Ltd. (1908), and W. S. Crawford, Ltd. (1914). London-based agencies including T.B. Browne operated internationally, with offices in colonial and U.S. centers.

From the 1890s onward, U.S. competition forced many British manufacturers to expand their advertising budgets. U.S. cocoa, cereals, and cigarettes were finding their way onto British store shelves. Energetic Germans were also selling their wares abroad.

During the first decade of the 1900s, the cry of "Wake up, England!" echoed, referring to the "take it or leave it" way in which British goods were offered. The call was first articulated in 1901 in a speech by the Prince of Wales (later George V) remarking on increasing foreign competition in Great Britain's colonial trade. Thus British advertisers were put on notice that to maintain their position of preeminence, they would have to be more solicitous toward consumers. The speech came at a time when British tobacco marketers were battling foreign rivals at home. The

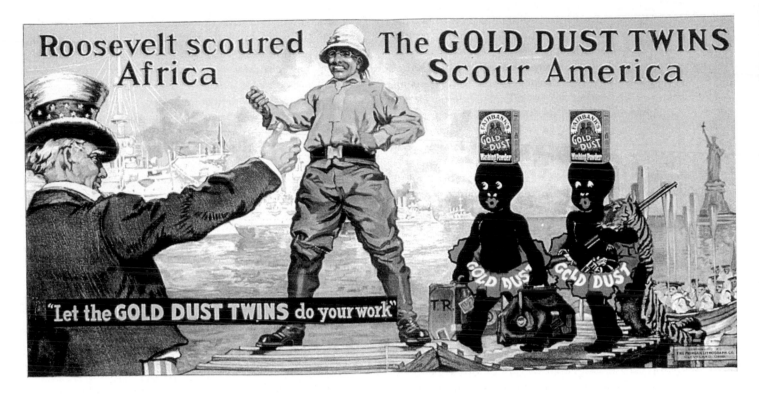

In what was perhaps the most widely noted and remembered billboard of its day, the "Gold Dust Twins" are pictured amid a collection of American patriotic symbols.

American Tobacco Company, for example, ran half-page newspaper ads with large pictures. Such competition stimulated British tobacco companies to run their own advertisements and issue trade cards. Little or no attempt was made to tell people why they should smoke, however, or what benefits they might expect to derive from so doing. Like the cocoa producers, the tobacco companies contented themselves with stressing the purity of their products. The immediate result of this advertising was that both the U.S. and British tobacco industries prospered.

Other countries also launched well-planned advertising campaigns in Great Britain. The Greeks sold surplus currants, while Brazil sold its overproduction of coffee. How could Great Britain counterattack? Only by better-planned advertising campaigns overseas, pointed out leading agents, using their specialized knowledge of foreign markets, tastes, and techniques. British advertisers, however, faced resistance from consumers in Great Britain who preferred many imported products to domestic ones. They also faced the problem of a market with lower purchasing power than that of the United States.

Advertising in Great Britain had not yet become as unified and regulated as it was in the United States. Although there was talk of ethical issues in advertising, no code of ethics could be set up without cooperation among advertisers, which were, for the most part, individualists. Nevertheless, the Advertisers' Protection Society (later the Incorporated Society of British Advertisers) was formed in 1900, although the media and agencies did not readily

form associations to work together in the development of advertising as a business.

Moreover, Great Britain had not yet generally adapted to the idea of research as the basis for an advertising campaign. By trial and error, agents could discover that ads in certain publications brought better results than ads in others, but many publications concealed both circulation figures and net sales, data that were needed to conduct more accurate tests. What might be called basic tenets of American advertising—such as the need for a fundamental merchandising idea and sound, scientific market research—took hold slowly within Great Britain.

The practice of advertising was not without its detractors. Socialists continued to be critical of the new extravagances of advertising. For the Marxist, the advertiser was just another servant of capitalism, whose role was to persuade the public to misspend money on nonessentials instead of goods and services produced by common agreement for the common good; they argued that the advertiser should serve, not rape, the community. In 1914 the English Socialist theorist Sidney Webb elaborated on the Socialist attitude to advertising in an introduction he wrote for G.W. Goodall's *Advertising: A Study of a Modern Business Power*. In short, Webb wrote, the purpose of advertising should be to influence consumers as to how to spend their income for the general good of the community. Over the next four years, there were enormous developments in advertising, but they were very different from those envisioned by Webb.

On the surface, it appears that Great Britain was far behind the United States in every phase of advertising development. Yet it is not a question of whether British advertising was as efficient as American advertising, since there were other differences in social and economic conditions. One major obstacle to advertising response was the lower level of income in England. In the United States, a working woman thought she needed two or three dresses a year, while her counterpart in England would be content with one. The average English woman did not have the same freedom to spend her husband's earnings, so she was a shrewd buyer, difficult to influence. The lower level of class-consciousness and greater social mobility in the United States gave American women social aspirations that their European counterparts did not possess. Thus, among the English working class, advertisers did not have such a highly receptive audience.

During World War I, however, advertising matured in Great Britain as it had in the United States. It fell to the government to recruit men for the armed forces, encourage women to volunteer on the domestic front, sell war bonds, and promote conservation of war materials. The publicity campaigns emerged as outright appeals to the emotions—pride, shame, fear, vengeance—which drastically departed from traditional low-key British ad appeals. One famous recruiting campaign featured children asking, "Daddy, what did YOU do in the Great War?" In another women were asked whether their husband or son had "to hang his head" because they had prevented him from going off to fight. At the same time, advertisements by commercial firms sought to give their products a patriotic glow, a tactic practiced earlier during the war in South Africa. By the end of World War I, advertising had proved a force for selling ideas as well as soap.

Advertising and Imperialism

During the first two decades of the 20th century, the pioneering phase of international advertising networks continued, with the United States and Great Britain as both the leading players and the foremost imperialists, spreading the notion of a consumer economy to other cultures. Although the volume of advertising exported from the United States and Great Britain continued to increase, in other countries advertising did not increase in proportion to the growth in industry.

After World War I, Canada sought to exert its independence from Britain, as foreign capital flowed in, especially from the United States, which displaced Great Britain as the chief investor in Canadian business. As general trade and manufacturing expanded, so did advertising. In contrast, Germany had not yet recovered from the war, and advertising was greatly reduced. In Central European countries, advertising was not considered an essential business-building method, as it was in Great Britain and the United States. Here, advertising was handled by large agencies that had control of publications, such as Rudolph Mosse, Agence Havas, and Société Européenne. Among the Scandinavian countries, Sweden expressed an interest in American-style advertising, notably from prominent publisher Louis F. Henius.

U.S. companies sought to capture foreign markets for their products and technologies by increasing their outlays in advertising. As a result of their willingness to penetrate regional markets in Europe and Asia, new media outlets opened to transnational as well as domestic advertisers.

In the Philippines, U.S. rule began around the turn of the century and was especially conducive to the development of Filipino advertising. During the last decade of the 1800s and the first of the 1900s, newspapers catered to various audiences, such as the Spanish-speaking elite and middle class, U.S. servicemen, bureaucrats, and businessmen. These publications carried advertisements, many of which were rather simple boxed announcements in a format similar to present-day classified advertisements (for example, names, addresses, and hours of operation of professionals such as doctors and dentists and goods for sale in department stores). By the 1920s, Filipino ads began to include pictures and illustrations.

Great Britain continued to dominate advertising in its dominions. In Australia, New Zealand, and South Africa, the chief advertising interests were the exporters from Great Britain and the United States. In India, local advertising agencies emerged in the early part of the 20th century, The first recognized advertising agency in India was B. Dataram and Company, founded in 1905. The Ind-Advertising Agency was established in Bombay in 1907, followed by the Calcutta Advertising Agency in 1909.

In other British colonies, however, local agencies did not set up shop until the 1920s. By World War I, British Malaya had become the world's largest producer of tin and rubber, while Singapore emerged as a major trade center. The earliest evidence of advertising agents and agencies seeking clients in Singapore dates to 1919, when a Mr. J.R. Flynn advertised his services and Mr. Siow Choon Leng offered his expertise to merchants. Under British rule, Hong Kong's position as a trade center declined relative to Shanghai's during the first half of the 1900s, and local agencies did not begin to operate until the late 1920s.

Unlike the concerted efforts of U.S. agencies to expand internationally, Dentsu Advertising of Japan, established in 1901, operated exclusively in Asia, functioning as both an advertising firm and a news service agency. Advertising in Korea can be traced to the early 1900s, during which time the country was dominated by Japan. However, only a few Japanese agencies operated in Korea during its occupation.

JULIANN SIVULKA

See also color plate in this volume

Further Reading

Fox, Stephen, *The Mirror Makers: A History of American Advertising and Its Creators,* New York: Morrow, 1984

French, George, *20th Century Advertising,* New York: Van Nostrand, 1926

Frith, Katherine Toland, *Advertising in Asia: Communication, Culture, and Consumption,* Ames: Iowa State University Press, 1996

Goodrum, Charles, and Helen Dalrymple, *Advertising in America: The First 200 Years,* New York: Abrams, 1990

Lears, T.J. Jackson, *Fables of Abundance: A Cultural History of Advertising in America*, New York: Basic Books, 1994

Pope, Daniel, *The Making of Modern Advertising*, New York: Basic Books, 1983

Presbrey, Frank, *The History and Development of Advertising*, Garden City, New York: Doubleday, 1929; reprint, New York: Greenwood Press, 1968

Schudson, Michael, *Advertising, the Uneasy Persuasion: Its Dubious Impact on American Society*, New York: Basic Books, 1984; London: Routledge, 1993

Sivulka, Juliann, *Soap, Sex, and Cigarettes: A Cultural History of American Advertising*, Belmont, California: Wadsworth, 1998

Strasser, Susan, *Satisfaction Guaranteed: The Making of the American Mass Market*, New York: Pantheon, 1989

Tedlow, Richard, *New and Improved: The Story of Mass Marketing in America*, New York: Basic Books, 1990

Turner, Ernest Sackville, *The Shocking History of Advertising!* London: Joseph, 1952; New York: Dutton, 1953; revised edition, London: Penguin, 1965

Wood, James Playsted, *The Story of Advertising*, New York: Ronald, 1958

History: 1920s

Since 1919, the circumstances of American life have been transformed.
—Frederick Lewis Allen in *Only Yesterday* (1964)

Americans of the 1920s were ready for a change from rationing and war preparedness and "doing without." A new enthusiasm infused daily life. World War I was over. An economic depression in 1921 was brief and soon forgotten. The economy was healthy, and factory jobs multiplied. The mass production methods that had supplied the war effort could now be applied to the manufacture of toasters, teapots, and Model Ts. The consumer economy, which had begun around the turn of the century, was flourishing. A mass market was in the making.

By 1925 nearly 40 percent of the workforce earned $2,000 or more a year, and the six-day workweek was reduced to five. People had free time and could take vacations. There was money to spend, and advertisements, appearing in newspapers and magazines, described what to buy, why, and where.

Probably the best example of the rise of popular media during the 1920s is *Time* magazine. In 1923 Henry Robinson Luce, then 25, and a former Yale University classmate, Briton Hadden, founded *Time*, the first weekly news magazine in the United States. Luce and Hadden were the first publishers after World War I to break away from past models of general interest magazines and offer something radically new—news and information. The name for the publication (which nearly was called *Facts*) came from the emphasis on short (under 400 words) stories that would amass facts on subjects of general interest and would be departmentalized for easy reference, in categories such as sports, business, and national affairs. Brevity was key to the format, separating the publication from other weeklies. *Time* was also distinctive in its focus on news rather than commentary.

The Rise of Radio

Among the many important innovations of the time (automobiles, retail chains, credit), the most crucial was radio. Its development as a medium of entertainment also radically changed the world of advertising. Prior to the 1920s, advertisements for consumer goods had been limited to print media—newspapers, magazines, and billboards. The information and entertainment presented on the radio was considered "pure," and many contended that commercials would defile the medium.

A debate of enormous and far-reaching importance dominated the 1920s: who would pay for radio? The answers would help make the decade one of the most crucial in advertising history because they laid the foundations for broadcasting in the United States and Europe.

The technology of voice broadcasting had been developed more than 25 years earlier. It was during the 1920s, however, that radio became the mass communication technology it is today, growing out of a combination of institutional and technological innovations and individual ideas.

Radio developed in many of the industrialized countries during the 1920s when technological developments, stimulated by World War I, made possible the broadcasting of sound. Although The Netherlands claims the first radio broadcasts in 1919, information was already being transmitted via radio in England, Germany, and France. It was in the United States, however, that commercial radio broadcasting found its foothold as a form of entertainment. Historian Susan Douglas suggests four factors that helped shape the development of radio during this time: (1) economic depression, (2) the role of corporations, (3) urbanization and electrification, and (4) recognition of production, consumption, and distribution.

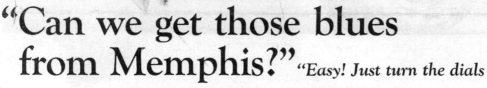

"Can we get those blues from Memphis?" *"Easy! Just turn the dials*

to 64, Mary, and we'll have 'em right away."

You never imagined that radio *could be* so sure—so simple to use. Just think! Once you've tuned in a station with WorkRite Super Neutrodyne Receivers, you can turn to it instantly, at any time, simply by referring to your "log."

Select what you want to hear from the daily programs—and know in advance that WorkRite will get it for you—clear as a bell, with no loss of quality, richness or brilliance, and free from distracting howls or whistles.

WorkRite brings in distant stations—not just once in awhile—but regularly and distinctly on the loud speaker. Under favorable conditions, it will bring in broadcasting from across the continent.

Amazing Selectivity

There's another great WorkRite advantage that you'll appreciate. It's this. No matter how powerful your local stations may be, you can easily tune them out and bring in other stations using practically the same wave length.

The first time you operate one of these beautiful, companionable sets, you'll think it's almost magical. But, there's really no secret to WorkRite's remarkable range

and selectivity. They are due largely to two things: First—WorkRite's ingenious Super Neutrodyne "hook-up." Second—the way WorkRite is built—the fine materials that go into every set—the intimate, careful attention given to every detail of manufacture.

Already Tremendously Successful

WorkRite has already won a host of enthusiastic friends. Dealers in many cities find themselves pressed to meet the demand for WorkRite. So, if the store you visit is unable to demonstrate WorkRite for you, write us and we will send you the name of a store that can. Or, if you want to know more about WorkRite sets before you see them, mail coupon below and we'll send a beautiful illustrated rotogravure folder giving full information on all WorkRite models.

By all means, know what WorkRite will do. It would mean so much to you and your family—a new delight, a fresh treat, every day.

THE WORKRITE MANUFACTURING COMPANY
1812 EAST 30TH STREET   CLEVELAND, OHIO
Branches: Chicago, 536 Lake Shore Drive; Los Angeles, 239 South Los Angeles Street

DEALERS—If you don't know about WorkRite Super Neutrodyne Receivers, by all means write us immediately for full particulars.

WORKRITE AIR MASTER
Like all WorkRite models, this is a 5 tube set, encased in genuine brown mahogany cabinet with graceful sloping panel. Almost identical with WorkRite Radio King, shown in main illustration, except the latter has a loud speaker built into cabinet behind a handsome grille. Both furnished with plug and special cable carrying all battery wires.
Price, Air Master, without accessories, $160
Price, Radio King, without accessories, $220

WORKRITE ARISTOCRAT
In this beautiful mahogany console, the loud speaker with special horn and reproducing unit is placed on one side and compartment for A and B batteries on other side. All connections made inside with cable and plug. Front drops, forming arm-rest for tuning or writing. Drawer beneath drop is provided for log sheets, etc. A set unsurpassed in any respect.
Price, Aristocrat, without accessories, $350

Send Coupon for FREE Rotogravure Booklet

The WorkRite Manufacturing Co.
1812 East 30th Street   Cleveland, Ohio

Please send me FREE a copy of the Rotogravure booklet which describes WorkRite.

Name...............................
Address...........................
City.................... State........

WORKRITE
SUPER NEUTRODYNE RADIO SETS

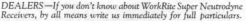

In the 1920s listening to the radio became a social activity, as depicted in this ad for WorkRite radio sets.

The United States had also just recovered from 25 years of wild economic fluctuations, economic depressions, an unusual amount of concentration of corporate wealth, political turmoil, and labor unrest. Conflicts between immigrants, nativists (those opposed to immigration), workers, managers, the wealthy, and the poor led many to believe that capitalism had led to a loss of control over the economy and traditions. Radio entered this arena at a time when a handful of major corporations were becoming increasingly powerful and consolidation of ownership was once again on the rise at the end of the Progressive Era.

At the same time, the technology that had supported mass production of defense-related products was now turning out consumer goods. This required a new way of thinking on the part of consumers. People needed to be convinced to buy their bread, rather than make it themselves. With corporate interests expanding westward, the system of distribution improved. Media of the day carried advertisements for products and services that had previously been available only in the cities and only to the wealthy. Advertising agencies that had operated primarily as intermediaries and couriers now rose to the challenge of positioning the consumption of goods as "the American way." Radio developed at the same time. Manufacturers were looking for new ways to reach customers. Broadcasters knew little about audience makeup or listening habits. As a result most programming reflected the broadcasters' tastes. Station coverage was deduced from postmarks on listener comment cards. This information became valuable once advertising became the medium's main support.

David Sarnoff, founder of the Radio Corporation of America (RCA), is generally credited with taking radio from the margins into the mainstream of American life. A former wireless operator, Sarnoff recognized that radio's financial potential depended on its being thought of as a household appliance. In the early 1920s radio listeners were regarded as hobbyists—a subculture of men and boys who found amusement and relaxation tinkering with crystal sets—and listening was considered simply a pastime. Mail-order businesses thrived as enthusiasts sent away for headphones, tubes, and other tools for radio building. It was a time when "an army of tinkerers retired to cellars, attics or barns" (as descibed by Douglas in her book *Inventing American Broadcasting, 1899–1922*) to construct crystal sets that, during the evening, could bring in Philadelphia, Pennsylvania, or New York City. An advertisement of the day announced, "Radio is no longer an experiment!"

True to his mission of making home radio an economic success, Sarnoff oversaw the introduction of the "Radiola" by American Marconi (later RCA) in 1922. The radio sold for $75—a hefty sum in those days—but a price within reach of America's burgeoning middle class. The rate of adoption of this innovation was impressive. First year sales alone were $11 million, and by 1925 they totaled more than $60 million—"home entertainment" would never be the same.

Resistance to Radio

Despite widespread interest, many people considered radio to be, at the least, in poor taste and a waste of resources. To them, radio was the technological manifestation of society's ills, a symbol of modernity and creeping consumerism and a threat to traditional family values. A 1922 article in the advertising trade journal *Printers' Ink* warned that "the family circle is not a public place and advertising has no business intruding there unless it is invited." Radio was viewed as a particularly intrusive nuisance by the newspaper industry. Newspaper owners felt that the medium infringed on the formerly undisputed role of newspapers as the purveyor of daily information and entertainment in the home. A quote from *Printers' Ink* illustrates this point:

> The radio is imperative. It is immediate. To utilize it, to enjoy it, all else must be dropped and all attention concentrated on the instrument. It offers no permanent record. It has not the flexibility to handle the most important and most vitally interesting type of news—the totally unexpected.

Historian Roland Marchand has pointed out that advertising agencies quickly responded to this concern by suggesting that "radio could never become anything but a good will supplement to print advertising." This, however, did not prove to be the case.

Funding Models

Little thought was given in the early 1920s to the financing of radio stations. Early stations such as KDKA in Pittsburgh, Pennsylvania, were not expensive to run. Frank Conrad, chief engineer at Westinghouse Electric and Manufacturing, began his radio career by sending signals from his garage. From his makeshift station (8XK, later KDKA), Conrad sent music from borrowed phonograph records. Conrad's popular musical broadcasts caught on and listeners began asking for a wider variety of entertainment and for longer broadcasts. The days of spinning a few borrowed phonograph records, reading headlines from the local newspaper, or featuring a friend's wife at the piano were short-lived. Professional talent was in demand, and that required money. By 1925 funding reached the crisis stage.

Sarnoff, committed to having a radio in every home, explored a range of funding proposals—among them philanthropy, listener support, a common fund, dedication of a percentage of radio sales to support stations, and government funding. Station owners also explored several European models. These included a mix of private and government ownership (France), private ownership (Canada), a limited advertising model (Germany), or a government-supported model (Great Britain). In the United States, radio at first was the "voice" of various businesses and commercial institutions. The Chicago Federation of Labor established WCFL. The *Chicago Tribune* had WGN (for "world's greatest newspaper"). Department stores, churches, and governments saw radio as a way of putting themselves before the public as "public service."

None of these models seemed adequate or appropriate. If there was private or government ownership, then owners feared their rights to free speech would be at risk. Private ownership could mean a private agenda, and limited advertising meant limited profits. The U.S. government was also squeamish about the "slippery slope" of radio regulation. Advertising appealed to proponents of the free enterprise system of capitalism, yet the notion of direct advertising was troubling. Overall, the consensus was that radio should be privately owned and that advertising should be kept out—at all costs.

Resistance to Radio Advertising

The financial survival strategy that did win out was direct advertising—that is, the purchase of time from a station for the presentation of commercial messages. Concerns about an advertising-supported model were shared not only by the general public but also by the newspaper industry, where advertising was considered to be a threat to pure information, a frivolity, and in opposition to the "public service" model of radio. Even more important, it was radio advertising's threat to newspaper's advertising base that was at the heart of the debate.

John O'Donnell, editor of the *Oil City* (Pennsylvania) *Derrick,* declared that he was far more concerned about radio's possible invasion of news than its invasion of advertising. "With a few exceptions," he said, "radio advertising is a very doubtful quantity. But it is an easy thing to sell. It has the charm of novelty. It caters enormously to vanity. Yet its very attractiveness is fatal to advertising."

There was so much concern over radio advertising that a bill was about to be introduced in the U.S. Congress designed to abolish all radio advertising. Before this could happen, however, an alternative came forth from a most unlikely source—the telephone company.

Advertising Enters the Mainstream

The American Telephone and Telegraph Company (AT&T), established its anchor station, WEAF, in New York City, as a "toll station" in 1922. The thinking behind this plan was that people who had something to broadcast would pay to do so, a model based on how telephone time was paid for.

AT&T treated its investment in radio as a public service effort. At first WEAF management stated that it would provide no material of its own but soon realized few were likely to step forward to pay a toll to broadcast on the radio. For the first six months in fact, no one stepped forward. Those willing to pay trickled in eventually, and the first "commercial" (named from AT&T accounting practices) aired on WEAF between 5:00 and 5:30 P.M. on 24 August 1922. It was for the Queensboro Corporation, which paid $50 for a ten-minute message promoting the sale of apartments in Queens, New York. The announcement was repeated four times, and an additional half-hour of evening programming was purchased. Several apartments were sold as a result. Direct advertising was pronounced a success.

One month later, two more companies broadcast messages—Tidewater Oil and the American Express Company. In less than a year, WEAF had 25 advertisers including the R.H. Macy Department Store, Greeting Card Association, American Hard Rubber Company, Bedford YMCA, National Surety Company, and Metropolitan Insurance Company. The announcements were not sales pitches per se, but they were not public service broadcasts either. For example, *The Story of the Christmas Card,* which aired on WEAF on 21 December 1922, was presented by the Greeting Card Association. The same year *The Story of the Haynes, America's First Car* was presented by the Haynes Automobile Company.

Station managers, politicians, and other public officials were concerned that advertising on the radio would compromise the dignity of the medium. In fact, the pressure brought by potential advertisers—and the financial pressures ad revenues relieved—led to advertising's becoming the primary source of financial support for radio with the proviso that the advertiser provide the program content in which to place its ad message.

Acceptance and Growth

Once criticized as a divisive tool that would debase other media and destroy the family, radio was positioned as a "civilizing force" by bringing classical music and famous orchestras into otherwise mundane lives. Proponents of radio claimed that it had the potential to elevate the popular taste. The most obvious example of this view can be found in advertisements for radio receivers. The ads showed elegant homes and tastefully decorated rooms where couples in eveningwear listened to the classics. If radio was such a dignified purveyor of the finer things in life, certainly the association of a corporate name with radio would be good business. Given the "public service" view of radio, this association could build good will among the listening public and earn eternal gratitude from listeners.

Prior to the mid-1920s advertising agencies had largely ignored radio advertising. Station brokers sold the limited amount of time available. RCA eventually dismissed its policies against commercial programming. In 1926 RCA, which already owned WJZ in New York City, bought WEAF from AT&T and formed the National Broadcasting System (NBC). In November of that year NBC launched two separate broadcasting networks, the Red and the Blue. It was at this time that its advertising rate cards were created. Ad executive Frank Arnold was hired by NBC to sell radio time to the remaining skeptics. Promoting radio as having "voice appeal," as opposed to the eye appeal of print, Arnold positioned the medium as a fourth component of advertising (after newspapers, outdoor signs, and magazines). The Columbia Broadcasting Company—CBS—was started in 1927 and was acquired in 1928 by William Paley.

What truly spurred on the commercialization of radio was competitiveness. WEAF was committed to beating rival station WJZ in talent and programming. Part of its strategy included moving to fancy new offices and buying fancy new equipment—all at fancy new prices. To support all this fanciness, WEAF created a sales staff to promote radio to potential advertisers. Just

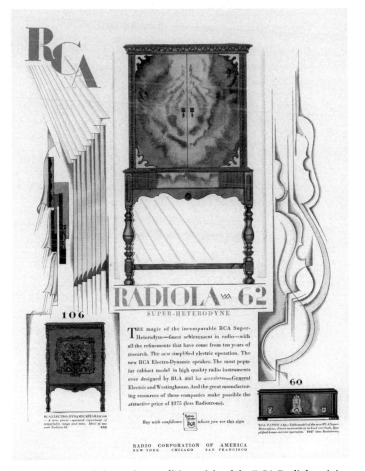

This 1928 print ad shows three stylish models of the RCA Radiola, a joint design project of RCA, General Electric, and Westinghouse.

Creative Challenges

The new medium of radio presented advertising agencies with creative challenges. The purely aural nature of radio brought a new emphasis to words. Agencies experimented with sounds, music, voices, and sound effects—anything to grab a listener's attention.

Initially radio ads were merely segments of airtime filled with promotional messages. Some agencies experimented with creating programs devoted entirely to a product. The Gillette Company hosted a talk show on fashions in beards. However, by 1927 only 20 percent of radio programs had sponsors. As advertisers began supporting radio, programming picked up, too. Vaudeville acts, musical variety shows, song-and-dance teams, and comedy acts were brought to the listener by sponsors such as Ever Ready Batteries (*The Ever Ready Battery Hour*) and A&P grocery stores (*The A&P Gypsies*).

By 1928 radio had become an advertising-supported medium, and advertising agencies became involved with the development of programs that fit the needs and interests of their clients. Even ad agencies that had resisted radio in the beginning became involved. According to radio pioneer Carroll Carroll, "You can't imagine with what crushing surprise radio made its guerrilla attack on advertising agencies. It caught few ready for it but all prepared to fake it."

Despite resistance by many advertising agencies, two are considered the leaders in early radio advertising: Lord & Thomas (L&T) and the J. Walter Thompson Company (JWT). It was L&T, for example, that produced the *Lucky Strike Show,* which evolved into *Your Hit Parade* by 1935 and Pepsodent's *Amos 'n' Andy.*

Program Sponsorships

World War I may have just ended at the outset of the 1920s, but the "tobacco wars" were just starting. From 1917 until the end of World War II, three major tobacco brands battled it out—Camel, Lucky Strike, and Chesterfield. The American Tobacco Company (ATC) wanted to win this war and hired Albert J. Lasker, of L&T, to help. Lasker's so-called reason-why copy (he insisted that the headline was 90 percent of the ad) focused on a key slogan or phrase heard repeatedly. On the newly created Lucky Strike radio shows, listeners heard slogans ("Reach for a Lucky instead of a Sweet," "So Round, So Firm, So Fully Packed, So Free and Easy on the Draw") repeated after every song. ATC spent a fortune on Lucky Strike and eventually won the tobacco wars. This spending also helped move L&T into the ranks of the major advertising agencies in 1929 by contributing 25 percent of the agency's $40 million in billings.

The other ad agency associated with early radio advertising was JWT, which launched several musical variety hits such as *The Fleishmann Yeast Hour with Rudy Vallee* and in the 1930s *The Chase & Sanborn Hour* and *The Kraft Music Hall.* Despite early resistance from its chief executive officer, Stanley Resor, JWT became known as one of the earliest and most important supporters of radio.

when things were looking up, and about the time the sales staff at WEAF was beginning to bring in advertisers, *Printers' Ink* ran an editorial titled "Radio, an Objectionable Advertising Medium." The trend toward sponsored programs was characterized as "full of insidious dangers." The editorial went on to declare that mixing advertising with programming was objectionable if radio was supposed to be "pure" and in the public interest: "We are opposed to advertising for the same reason we are opposed to skywriting. People should not be forced to read advertising unless they are so inclined."

The power of a single announcer to reach thousands of people was very attractive to product manufacturers and, therefore, to their advertising agencies. By the end of 1921 approximately 1 out of every 500 U.S. households had a radio receiver. A half-million were sold during a six-month period in 1922. By 1926 the ownership ratio was 1 out of 6 households. The novelty of radio was wearing off, and people began turning the dial for content. Radio came to resemble the telephone less and an entertainment medium more. *Printers' Ink* exclaimed, "Who would have dreamed that the radio phone would today be the subject of such widespread advertising! The merchandising attention being given to this new means of communication is perfectly astonishing."

Other agencies eventually jumped in and overtook L&T and JWT with radio success stories. Young & Rubicam (Y&R), founded in 1923, offered its *Radio Household Institute* (sponsored by Borden and General Foods products) as a morning program featuring recipes and homemaking tips. Agency founder Raymond Rubicam, however, was never impressed by radio, even though it would bring in one-third of Y&R's billings by the late 1930s. Instead of dealing with the new medium, he turned all radio activities over to Chester LaRoche, who eventually became president of the agency. The other major agency to rise in the 1920s was Batten Barton Durstine & Osborne (BBDO), which attracted such corporate clients as General Electric, General Motors, and Lever Brothers.

The 1920s saw the creation of the sponsored program and marks the point where advertising took control of programming by way of sole sponsorships. There are remnants of sole sponsorships in the 21st century's media world (the *Hallmark Hall of Fame* TV specials), but in the 1920s the sponsor's name was the program's name. Radio advertising in the 1920s set the stage for what many consider to be radio's Golden Age—the 1930s—typified by that ever-popular program, the soap opera.

DEBRA MERSKIN

See also Radio; Sarnoff, David

Further Reading

Barnouw, Erik, *A Tower in Babel: A History of Broadcasting in the United States, to 1933,* New York: Oxford University Press, 1966

Douglas, Susan, *Inventing American Broadcasting, 1899–1922,* Baltimore, Maryland: Johns Hopkins University Press, 1987

Maltin, Leonard, *The Great American Broadcast: A Celebration of Radio's Golden Age,* New York: Dutton, 1997

Marchand, Roland, *Advertising the American Dream: Making Way for Modernity, 1920–1940,* Berkeley: University of California Press, 1985

Sterling, Christopher, and John M. Kittross, *Stay Tuned: A Concise History of American Broadcasting,* Belmont, California: Wadsworth, 1978

History: 1930s

If the major story of the 1920s in U.S. advertising was the decision that radio should be a commercially supported enterprise rather than a publicly funded one, then the key theme of the 1930s was the growth of network radio as a national advertising medium. In 1927, the first full year of U.S. radio network operation, the revenues of NBC (the only network at the time—CBS was not established until 1928) were $3.8 million. The combined income of NBC and CBS the following year was $10.2 million, and by 1929 it had grown to $18.7 million. Whereas revenues in many other industries declined after 1930, increases continued in radio. By 1934, total network gross, excluding the new Mutual Broadcasting System, had climbed to $42.6 million. By 1939 network volume had risen to approximately $80 million, counting only those advertisers spending more than $100,000 and exclusive of non-network local radio ad volume.

What was true for radio, however, was not necessarily true for the rest of the advertising business. According to ad historian Stephen Fox in his book *The Mirror Makers,* total ad volume in all media declined from a high of $3.4 billion in 1929 to $2.3 billion in 1931—and then to only $1.3 billion in 1933.

Radio's Rising Tide

In contrast to the overall decline of the ad business in the 1930s, the rise of radio is one of the remarkable advertising stories of the Great Depression. But then radio was free, could speak to the whole nation at once, and came into the home or car at the flick of a wrist. It also had one other advantage that traditional print lacked—it transcended the limitations of illiteracy. On the rising tide of radio there arose advertising agencies, many of which were formed to respond to the reality of broadcasting, often on the basis of a single major account. Among the agencies founded in this decade that established a strong radio presence for their clients were McCann-Erickson, handling Nabisco, and opened in 1930; William Esty and Company (Camel), founded 1932; Campbell-Mithun (General Mills), established in 1933; D.P. Brother (Oldsmobile), founded 1934; and the Leo Burnett Company (Minnesota Canning) and Kudner Advertising (General Motors), founded in 1935.

At first, established agencies took the lead in the new medium: Lord & Thomas for Pepsodent and Frigidaire; the J. Walter Thompson Company (JWT) for Chase & Sandborn; Batten Barton Durstine & Osborn (BBDO) for Wrigley; Young & Rubicam (Y&R) for General Foods; and Ruthrauff & Ryan for Lever Brothers. The most successful agencies became to radio what the major Hollywood studios were to motion pictures—a primary production source of U.S. popular culture and entertainment. In 1935 a young radio director named Sylvester ("Pat") Weaver came to New York City from California eager to work in network radio. In his 1994 memoir, *The Best Seat in the House,* he recalled going to CBS to look for a job in programming and was astonished to find that CBS lacked a programming department and that radio was run by the ad agencies, not by the networks. Weaver soon found his way to Y&R, where he began a career that would

Gang Busters, sponsored by Palmolive shave cream, was a popular radio show in the 1930s.
Courtesy of Colgate-Palmolive Company.

one day take him to the presidency of NBC. Because radio had developed in the United States as an advertiser-supported medium, it fell to the ad agencies to create the programming that would showcase its clients' products. Y&R supervised the casting, writing, and production of the Fred Allen and Jack Benny programs for Sal Hepatica and Jell-O, respectively. JWT did the same for Standard Brands and Fleischmann's Yeast, bringing Edgar Bergen and Rudy Vallee to the air. BBDO controlled all aspects of the *DuPont Cavalcade of America*. Benton and Bowles produced *Gang Busters* and *Hilltop House* for Colgate. William Esty brought Benny Goodman to radio for Camel Cigarettes. Lord & Thomas produced *Your Hit Parade* for Lucky Strike Cigarettes and later introduced Bob Hope to the air for Pepsodent. Blackett-Sample-Hummert became the largest radio buyer and producer of all, creating a procession of daytime serial dramas, or "soap operas," for American Home Products, General Mills, and Kolynos Toothpaste. Because advertisers owned the programs they sponsored, their agencies could build long-term associations between performers and brands. For 15 years Needham, Louis & Brorby made the homespun character Fibber McGee synonymous with Johnson's Wax.

Advertising and the Economy

For many advertisers, however, national radio lay beyond both their budgets and their marketing requirements. Hence a parallel broadcast system of regional networks and local stations in major markets arose to perform functions similar to what regional magazines and local newspapers had been doing for decades. They served local advertisers, as well as national advertisers targeting specific markets, through "spot" buys (i.e., the purchase of radio time on a station-by-station basis). All this was played out against the background of fundamental economic reform during the Great Depression, which brought an increased role for govern-

ment in the private sector, including its power to act on behalf of the consumer and compel compliance with basic standards of truth in advertising.

In 1930 advertisers in the advanced Western economies and particularly in the United States were in the final stages of a shift in fundamental purpose. The ability to manufacture goods on a large scale had been essentially accomplished through the development of the production line and the use of cheap, unskilled labor. It was a historic step that for the first time in history had brought the supply of most goods into line with demand and, in some cases, pushed it beyond natural demand levels. This created a new phenomenon—overproduction—which could cause sudden price drops. In the early years of the Great Depression, government policy was heavily committed to maintaining price levels in the face of a shrinking supply of money. This initially caused manufacturers to turn their attention more than ever to the uses of distribution and demand stimulation through advertising. What was bad for many businesses was seen at the time to be good for the advertising business, especially with the packaged goods mergers that a short time earlier created Colgate-Palmolive-Peet, Standard Brands, and General Foods, together with their large pools of advertising dollars. As shrinking markets slowed the rate of production, however, advertising began to contract as well.

The advertising business had other problems unrelated to the economic crisis. It somewhat meekly entered the decade after many years of being considered a marginal, even disreputable, element in the marketing scheme. It therefore tended to be a highly conservative industry in the way it regarded itself. As an industry, advertising still labored under a public reputation formed during earlier ethical lapses in the era of patent medicines. It was a problem that major older agencies such as BBDO and Calkins & Holden took great pains to counteract through declarations of principles, self regulatory agreements, and other attempts at institutionalizing responsible behavior. Others in the business regarded such self-imposed restraints as a major interference with the power of advertising to sell. This was all a lively topic of debate within the industry at the time. Major advertisers began moving into radio in the early 1930s with great caution. The tone of early messages for products such as Woodbury Soap and Chevrolet was delivered with a sense of well-mannered propriety. Most advertisers seemed acutely aware that they were selling to people in the privacy of their homes and must behave accordingly; however, not all advertisers did. In the debate over good taste in advertising, Lucky Strike cigarettes and its agency, Lord & Thomas, became symbolic of everything that was rude and intrusive about advertising. Its campaigns, created under the supervision of American Tobacco Company Chairman George Washington Hill, were aggressive and endlessly repetitive. Yet many admitted that such advertising had the quality of what *Fortune* magazine called in March 1930 "force."

The State of Print

At the start of the decade, print advertising was still the major form of communication. U.S. ad volume in newspapers and magazines stood at about $1 billion in 1929; more than three-quarters of this sum was still being spent in newspapers. Network radio represented less than 3 percent of the total. The two main trade publications in the field of advertising were *Printers' Ink* and *Advertising & Selling,* though neither covered day-to-day news of the industry in any depth, preferring instead profile and issue articles. *Advertising Age,* which would soon become the industry's key trade publication, was launched in Chicago, Illinois, by G.D. Crain, Jr., on 11 January 1930, to fill this news gap. Its primary focus was advertisers and media companies, and it covered those well. While agency account shifts were tracked, the details of agency business, finance, and billings received less intense coverage. This was because the role of even the largest agencies, all still privately held at the time, was treated with discretion, if not outright secrecy. Most agencies preferred to keep a low profile in deference to the clients they publicized, notwithstanding agency heads, such as Maurice Needham, who spoke out early in favor of open disclosure by agencies. A month after *Advertising Age* was founded, Time, Inc., launched another influential business publication, *Fortune,* targeted to top management. Many of the major U.S. ad agencies advertised their own services regularly in the magazine.

As most of Europe and the United States settled into the worst of the Great Depression in 1932, there was enormous pressure on newspapers and magazines to cut their rates, resulting in rate wars and widespread distrust of circulation claims by advertisers. Lord & Thomas made it a matter of policy that any invoice received from a publication must come with a statement of circulation for the previous 30-day period. The commission system, which was beginning to take root, became a subject of great controversy as advertisers pressured their agencies as well as the media for rebates and deep discounts. Many had no choice; if they did not cut their rates, a competitor would. Agency pioneer Earnest Elmo Calkins regarded the commission system as being in such a shambles that he suggested a sliding fee scale of agency payment. Meanwhile, former JWT executive James Webb Young took an academic post at the University of Chicago and thoroughly studied the commission issue. In 1933 he issued a report, "Advertising Agency Compensation in Relation to the Total Costs of Advertising," supporting the existing 15 percent commission. The National Recovery Administration seemed to support the system as a means of stabilizing prices. Agencies and media companies applauded it; advertisers, however, turned to their own study by A.E. Haase, a former director of the Association of National Advertisers. The Haase report, issued in November 1934, made the case for a negotiable fee system; agencies feared this would set off a bitter price war within the industry. The same report, however, conceded some advantages to the status quo. As the debate continued, the 15 percent commission system continued to take root, and more advertisers decided to accommodate it. Ultimately, it survived.

New Horizons: Sports and Politics

With national radio at their disposal, advertisers began to more seriously look at sports events as commercial vehicles. In 1934

Ford sponsored the World Series, and Chevrolet bought a series of college games. The following year the Brown & Williamson Tobacco Company sponsored the first Kentucky Derby with pioneer sportscaster Graham MacNamee. Although parts of the 1936 Olympics from Berlin, Germany, were carried as "special events" broadcasts, they were not sponsored. Nevertheless, a pattern was set in the mid-1930s for the sports-advertising partnership that would come to dominate sports broadcasting in the television era. No company made a more complete commitment to sports than Gillette, whose agency, Maxon, Inc., made a major investment in the 1939 World Series, a move that would prove so successful for the marketer that it would soon become the largest sports advertiser in broadcasting.

Outdoor advertising continued to be an inexpensive and efficient way to reach local consumers on a highly specific geographic basis. In 1928 Henry Ewald, president of Campbell-Ewald in Detroit, Michigan, an agency that had been a major force in billboard advertising, founded the National Outdoor Advertising Bureau, which he would chair until after World War II. It was appropriate perhaps that his agency would unintentionally play a key role in the creation of one of the most famous and iconic photographic images of the Great Depression—if not the 20th century. In 1936 Campbell-Ewald won the account of the National Association of Manufacturers (NAM), a trade group intent on promoting the values of capitalism in the face of what its members viewed as "New Deal socialism." In January 1937 the agency unveiled an outdoor campaign of 24-sheet posters with one simple tag line: "There's no way like the American way." The first in the series carried the headline, "World's highest standard of living," an idea embodied in a huge illustration of an ideal American family of four out for a bucolic Sunday drive.

In the spring of that year, Louisville, Kentucky, was hit with massive floods. One of the billboards happened to be posted on a street where homeless flood victims had gathered to receive emergency provisions. As a long bread line of impoverished, mostly black, flood victims gathered waiting for food relief, the NAM billboard, with its vision of prosperity and contentment, loomed above. The disparity was a devastating irony that *Life* photographer Margaret Bourke-White quickly recognized and photographed. The photo became one of the defining symbols of the social and political polarities of the 1930s.

Politics and advertising were first connected during the 1936 U.S. presidential campaign when NBC and CBS each made a decision to sell airtime to the political candidates. Hill Blackett of Blackett-Sample-Hummert directed the radio effort for the Republican Party, creating transcribed dramatizations of such issues as the national debt and high taxes for the working class. Although NBC and CBS declined to run the programs because of a policy requiring that everything fed by the network must be live, Blackett placed them on local stations—not bound by such restrictions—around the country. The live policy created a dilemma at CBS when Blackett bought program time on election eve for a "debate" between the influential Republican Senator Arthur Vanderberg and President Franklin D. Roosevelt, the Democratic incumbent (who was running against Republican

CHICAGO
PUBLISHED WEEKLY AT 537 S. DEARBORN ST. HAR. 7504

Advertising Age

THE NATIONAL NEWSPAPER OF ADVERTISING

NEW YORK
GRAYBAR BUILDING, 420 LEXINGTON AVE. LEX. 1572

Vol. 1, No. 1 — CHICAGO, JANUARY 11, 1930 — Three Cents a Copy $1 a Year

Rough Proofs

The publisher who tried to popularize a bridge magazine went into bankruptcy. Evidently he failed to make his contract.

• • •

"Telephone growth is essential to the new American civilization of better opportunity for the average man."

Certainly; doesn't the new Declaration of Independence guarantee the inalienable rights of life, liberty and the pursuit of wrong telephone numbers?

• • •

The New Yorker says that mornings are a burden to humanity and should be abolished. The chap who wrote that had probably just finished reading the bright and cheery alarm-clock advertisements which tell how to roll out smilingly at 6 a. m.

• • •

"On tender hot tea biscuit learn the delicate new-churned goodness of Brookfield creamery butter."—Swift & Co.

In fact, if the biscuit is tender to the point of being sentimental, you might even add a bit of honey.

• • •

"Buick," we are assured, "pursues a constant program of service education, including field service clinics for its representatives."

Such a clinic might well present a major operation on an automobile engine, with the anesthetic applied to the owner.

• • •

The Towle Silversmiths offer a suggestion to "the friends of brides." The best suggestion is that they remain discreetly in the background.

• • •

"They haven't the grasses, the herbs, the water that Switzerland has," so of course they can't make Swiss cheese anywhere else. And besides, where else could they produce holes like those that are made in Switzerland?

• • •

Speaking of cheese, the makers of Roquefort are advertising that it is made of sheep's milk. But what I would like to know is how they separate the Roquefort sheep from the goats.

• • •

"Rubinstein himself would have placed your child before a Steinway."

But not even Rubinstein himself would have guaranteed that the results would be worth the effort.

• • •

"Remember," says the Fruit Dispatch Company significantly, "you can always buy bananas."

Thus putting the official seal of denial on the faint echo of that once famous canard, "Yes, we have no bananas."

• • •

"Subtle individuality—this is the gift of Tangee to every woman, blonde, brunette or titian."

Did you ever hear of a subtle redhead?

• • •

The new Ruxton announces that included in its line is a saloon for five passengers. The details are not given, but of course a brass rail and a sawdust box are among the appointments.

• • •

Printer's Ink recently reported that a new publication was being started "at" Chicago. It's permissible to say "at" Horse Cave, Ky., or "at" Kennebunkport, Me., but in referring to New York and Chicago, *P. I.*, let's say "in."

COPY CUB.

EDWARD W. BOK, HARVARD AWARD FOUNDER, DEAD

Famous Editor Victim of Heart Attack in Florida

(By wire to Advertising Age)

Philadelphia, Jan. 10.—The death of Edward W. Bok, former editor of the *Ladies' Home Journal* and for thirty years the right-hand man of Cyrus H. K. Curtis in the publication of that magazine, at Lake Wales, Fla., yesterday brought to a close one of the most romantic and spectacular careers America has seen.

Mr. Bok, famous as the founder of the Harvard Advertising Awards, and as a philanthropist in many fields, died four days after reaching his winter home, the end coming as the result of a heart attack. His home was at Merion, a Philadelphia suburb.

He was sixty-six years old, having been born in Holland, October 9, 1863. He is survived by his widow, who was Mary Louise Curtis, daughter of the publisher, and two sons, Curtis and Cary. The funeral was held at Lake Wales this afternoon, and burial was in crypt in the Singing Tower, a remarkable bird sanctuary containing a carillon of sixty-one bells, which he erected at his winter home shortly after his retirement in 1919.

Mr. Bok came to America with his parents in 1870. His first employment was as an office boy for the Western Union. At 19 he was editor of the *Brooklyn Magazine*. He had an experience with newspaper syndicate work, featuring as one of his writers Ella Wheeler Wilcox and at twenty-one joined the publishing house of Charles Scribner's Sons. There he had many intimate contacts with famous authors. He was later advertising manager of *Scribner's Magazine* and some of the other Scribner periodicals.

Editor at Twenty-six

In 1889 he became editor of the *Ladies' Home Journal*, when he was only twenty-six years old. He held the post for thirty years, and under his aggressive and at times inspired editorial direction the magazine became one of the great publishing properties of the country. He retired in 1919 in order to devote himself to community work and civic activities of all kinds.

In "The Americanization of Edward Bok," which Mr. Bok wrote in 1921, he told the story of his life, using the third person, and described vividly his career on the *Ladies' Home Journal*. In addition to getting the work of many of the famous authors of the day, as well as such important personages as Theodore Roosevelt, Mr. Bok was responsible for the cleaning up of patent-medicine advertising, undertaking a campaign against untruthful advertising of spurious medicines which lasted for two years.

"The magazine attacked the evil from every angle," Mr. Bok said in his autobiography. "It aroused the public by showing the actual contents of some of their pet medicines. The editor got the Women's Christian Temperance Union into action against the periodicals for publish-

(Continued on page 11.)

Federal Expert Tells Food Advertisers to Get Housewife's View

New York, Jan. 10—Dr. Louise Stanley, chief of the bureau of home economics of the Department of Agriculture, gave food advertisers a lot of good advice at a luncheon at the Union League Club attended by food manufacturers, advertising agency men and others. She told them to quit emphasizing "vitamines" so much, to get the housewife's point of view in the matter of

Dr. Louise Stanley

recipes, packages, etc., and above all not to standardize their products to the point where flavor is eliminated—a mistake she attributed to the bread bakers.

The luncheon, which was under the auspices of *The New Era in Food Distribution*, Chicago, was presided over by F. M. Feiker, chairman of the advisory committee for the census of distribution and managing director of the Associated Business Papers, Inc. The other principal speaker was O. H. Cheney, vice-president of the American Exchange Irving Trust Company, New York, who commented amusingly on the jealousies of the various trade groups in the food field, and suggested that they get together on the basis of efficiency in food distribution.

"Food does not lend itself to high-pressure salesmanship," said Dr. Stanley, in the first of her salty comments on modern food merchandising. "We have had doughnut weeks and other kinds of weeks, but it must be remembered that the total amount of food to be eaten cannot be increased. The capacity of the stomach is limited.

"One means of selling food which has been most overdone is the exploitation of nutrition values by unscrupulous advertisers. There is a growing prejudice among consumers against excessive advertising of nutrition values, because there has been so much misrepresentation. The public has been particularly gullible along this line. Your product is not eaten alone. You should fit it in with the picture of other foods.

"Many of you have not taken advantage of your opportunities in putting your foods forward in their best light. Some of you might increase the value of your foods by saving portions now being discarded. The protective portion, particularly the germs of cereals, could be saved and used in various forms to safeguard diets. Natural syrups and sugars have certain constituents which we do not find in the purified form, yet the house-wife finds it difficult to buy brown sugar, and the natural syrups are becoming more difficult to obtain.

Palatability Big Urge

"Habit, palatability, economy and convenience are the four factors which most influence food choice by the consumer. Habit is largely racial or family preference. Over-

(Continued on Page 11)

Why We Are Here

Advertising Age, The National Newspaper of Advertising, has been developed to meet a definite need.

Presenting the news of advertising—a business of widespread interests and ramifications, involving expenditures of two billion dollars a year—has never been the primary, exclusive function of any advertising publication.

That is the task to which Advertising Age will devote itself. Each week in these columns will be found the record of events in the world of advertising: the news of advertisers, of agencies, of publications and other mediums, and the news of general developments which affect marketing and hence advertising.

With an organization which has had fourteen years of successful publishing experience, with a staff familiar with the activities and personnel of the advertising and publishing fields, with a group of news-gatherers covering not only the chief centers of advertising, but the whole country, Advertising Age, The National Newspaper of Advertising, is ready to function.

We hope to merit the appreciation and good-will of our readers and advertisers.

FIVE-DAY WEEK WON BY PRINTERS AND ENGRAVERS

Production Gets Larger Share of Advertising Dollar

Printing, photo-engraving, and other processes necessary in the production of advertising, will take a larger bite out of the advertising appropriation in 1930. The five-day week, the goal of union printers throughout the country, has been agreed on in Chicago. While Chicago journeymen were actually getting what they wanted, effective at a later date, progress toward this end was made in other parts of the United States.

The Chicago agreement, just sealed by employers and employes, provides the following salient changes:

For union job compositors, an immediate wage increase of $3 for day workers, making the scale $57 per week; an increase of $2 for night shift, making the scale $60.

Introduction of the forty-hour work week for day workers, for three months (June, July and August) of 1931 and corresponding months of 1932, with the forty-hour week in full operation after April 1, 1933.

Linotype and monotype operators to receive $1.40 in excess of scales in effect for hand compositors.

Increase Passed On

It is estimated that this contract means the payment of an additional $3,000,000 by employing commercial printers to 4,000 job compositors during the five years the contract covers. The employers are passing the increase on to the buyer.

This agreement, effective Jan. 1, was concluded in November, 1929, and many advertisers, seeing the handwriting on the wall, renewed 1930 contracts with employing printers as early as possible. A number of large advertisers and agencies were able to protect themselves in this way on 1930 requirements. While those who did not get in under the wire may scan the horizon for less expensive printing, the full results of the increase, it is believed, will not be manifest for another year.

One specific result, however, is indicated by the new estimating schedule adopted by Chicago trade compositors. Hand composition, formerly priced at $4, has been increased to $4.20; linotype time work has been increased from $5 to $5.40; monotype time work, from $6.50 to $7, and Ludlow work, from $5 to $5.40.

More Pay in New York

Substantial increases in pay have been secured by union printers of New York. The 44-hour week has not been altered, but changes in the wage scale are indicated by the following figures applying to a single type of workers—pressmen.

One-cylinder (over 68 inches), old scale, $56; new scale, $58. This scale is in effect to Jan. 1, 1931, when a $1 increase goes into force for each classification. Another $1 increase becomes effective Jan. 1, 1932.

Conditions existing in the printing trade are paralleled in the photo-engraving industry. Louis Flader, commissioner of the American Photo-Engravers Association, Chicago, recently summarized developments as follows:

"Agreements for introduction of the five-day, forty-hour week have been made, with slight variations, in

Advertising Age, which became the premier trade publication for the U.S. advertising industry, made its debut with this 11 January 1930 edition.
Reprinted with permission from the 11 January 1930 issue of Advertising Age. *Copyright, Crain Communications, Inc., 1930.*

Alfred M. Landon). In fact, Vanderberg would be debating recorded excerpts of Roosevelt's speeches. CBS cut off the program after several minutes on the grounds that it violated the network's ban on recordings, though the network had earlier approved the idea as "public service exception." Blackett accused CBS of suppressing the Republican Party's right to free speech. After the election, a Senate committee investigated the 1936 campaign at all levels—local, state and federal—and estimated that the total amount spent was about $50 million. Of this sum, money spent on the presidential contest came to $5.6 million for the Democratic Party and $8.8 million for the Republican Party. The report called it the most expensive presidential race in history, and it noted with a sense of warning that the largest single political contribution of the campaign came from one individual, Lammot du Pont, who gave $183,500 to the Republicans. Thus, the outlines of a soon-to-be-familiar pattern began to emerge in the 1930s, although at that time the vast majority of the money spent by both parties was on travel and staff expenses, not advertising.

Application of Scientific Testing

In a decade in which science began to reveal itself in the trend toward streamlining, the rise of commercial aviation and other advances in transportation, and the creation of a national radio system, advertising sought to make itself more scientific as well. Improved sampling and analysis models began to refine the basic techniques of mass market research, and agencies worked with the radio networks to develop more reliable methods of audience measurement, or "ratings." One particularly controversial technique received a great deal of attention in 1938, when the consulting firm Townsend & Townsend introduced a 27-point system for evaluating advertising copy. For most agencies and advertisers, an advertisement's copy was judged through trial and error. Direct mail specialists, who asked for the sale directly and provided a means of purchase, had a reality check in understanding the link between specific copy and selling power. For other media advertisers, however, the variables were too vast to systematize.

The Townsend system insisted on a "fixed relationship between the sales results produced by an advertisement and the number of 27 basic selling elements contained in that advertisement and the sequence in which the elements are used." In short, it offered advertisers scientific certainty in place of the agency guesswork. In 1938 the Townsends began the evolution of copy testing as a motivational subspecialty within advertising research. For $50,000 in the first year and 1 percent of the advertising budget for the next four years, their firm would unlock the motivation selling codes of an advertiser's ad copy. They marketed their services directly to advertisers, in many cases interposing themselves between agency and client. When Quaker Oats insisted that all of the ad copy written at Lord & Thomas be evaluated against the 27 points, agency President Albert Lasker, who in 1904 had been profoundly influenced by John E. Kennedy's reason-why theories

of copy effectiveness, refused to put his experience and expertise up against a "scientific" system. When he resigned the Quaker business, he dealt a blow to the Townsends but not to advertiser curiosity about the motivational factors of copy.

Toward the end of the decade, a revitalized consumer movement began to be felt in Washington, D.C., as a kind of rearguard action in a decade of vast progressive reform. Legislation was passed governing aspects of the manufacture and marketing of cosmetics. In 1939 the Federal Trade Commission (FTC) lodged a complaint against *Good Housekeeping* magazine's "seal of approval," but the most far-reaching legislation of the decade was the Robinson-Patman Act of 1936, which was a response to the growth of chain stores and mass nationwide distributors and the power they had over small independent businesses. Discriminatory pricing by large companies was the main target of the act. The Wheeler-Lee Amendment of 1938, however, broadened the power of the FTC to move in many directions where advertising promoted and furthered unfair trade practices. For the first time ad agencies became parties to consent decrees. Another controversy later in the decade occurred when Roy Durstine, president of BBDO, recommended that testimonial advertising be banned by law. His suggestion was ignored, however, and he left BBDO in 1939 to form his own agency.

In April 1939 President Roosevelt opened the New York World's Fair before an RCA television camera. Television was further along in England at the time, where the government-owned BBC was unconcerned with the economies of sponsorships and ad revenues. In the United States, agency leaders were doing little else but debating the possible impact of the new broadcasting technology. Another new technology that came out of the 1930s was frequency modulation, or FM, radio, invented in 1935 by Edwin Armstrong, who had been commissioned by NBC Chairman David Sarnoff to build a radio that was free of static. But both these technologies were largely undeveloped as the 1930s ended.

Among the early ad pioneers who died during the decade were: Lord & Thomas founder Daniel Lord, Lennen & Mitchell founder J.T.H. Mitchell, and John T. Dorrance of Campbell Soup (1930); copywriter Claude Hopkins, Procter & Gamble founder James Gamble, chewing gum magnate William Wrigley, and Kodak Chairman George Eastman (1932); publisher Cyrus Curtis and inventor Thomas Edison (1933); radio pioneer Don Lee and publicist Ivy Lee (1934); agency pioneer Frank Presbrey, McCann-Erickson founder A.W. Erickson, and ad pioneer Charles Austin Bates (1936); washing machine pioneer Frederick Maytag (1937); tire baron and sponsor of the *Voice of Firestone* Harvey S. Firestone (1938); and in 1940, agency pioneer Theodore MacManus, agency chief J. Stirling Getchell, R.C. Desirens (who created the B&O Railroad's "Chessie" the cat), and Leon Douglass, the RCA Victor founder who made the dog Nipper and "His master's voice" a legendary trademark.

JOHN MCDONOUGH

History: 1940s

During the decade of the 1940s, advertising in the United States faced two remarkable challenges. First, in an era of full employment and relatively broad-based prosperity, when consumers had huge amounts of discretionary income and were eager to spend it, acute wartime shortages largely deprived the economy of goods to advertise and sell. This forced marketers to use advertising to maintain brand awareness and market share even though production capacity could not satisfy existing, let alone fresh, demand. During World War II, advertising became a way for marketers to fortify their future postwar positions for the tidal wave of pent-up demand likely to come with peace. And second, although the decade ended with network radio still the dominant broadcast medium, no one doubted that television, introduced with great fanfare in the late 1930s and then shelved for the duration of the war, would soon be the medium into which all major advertisers would be moving. Late in 1946, the RCA Victor division of Radio Corporation of America became the first manufacturer after the war to market and advertise television sets, launching the effort in six U.S. markets.

Just as the major radio networks continued to shape early television, the major ad agencies that had come of age with network broadcasting continued to dominate the advertising field (see Table 1). Several of these agencies (or their successors) remained among the top ten shops for the duration of the decade. They had helped shape radio, and they now had the resources to do the same in television.

Total advertising billings among the top agencies in 1943 (those billing $10 million or more) was $450 million, according to *Advertising Age* estimates at the time. In 1944, the year *Advertising Age* began tracking the relative size of all U.S. shops on an annual basis, there were 22 agencies billing $10 million or more, with combined billings of $515 million. The J. Walter Thompson Company (JWT) was the number one agency that year, with $72 million in billings. By 1950 the list of major agencies had more than doubled, to 47, and their combined billings totaled approximately $1.34 billion. JWT remained number one, with billings of $130 million. In 1944 *Advertising Age* also charted 29 "midsize" agencies (those billing $5 million to $10 million), for additional billings of about $200 million. In 1950 this second tier of agencies added an additional $260 million. By 1950 nearly all the shops among the top 20 had been equally prominent a decade before. Only two new agency names appeared on the list in 1950: Ted Bates & Company, founded in 1940, and the Leo Burnett Company, founded in 1935. Postwar agencies that would make their mark in the 1950s and beyond were still far down on the list as the 1940s ended: Doyle Dane Bernbach; Hewett, Ogilvy, Benson & Mather; and Tatham-Laird.

Legal Ramifications of Advertising

The war triggered a huge expansion of government bureaus and administrative power, some of which affected advertising. Short-ages and rationing deprived magazine publishers of quality paper, forcing major magazines such as *Life* and *Time* to go to press on stock barely better than newsprint. Although war news flowed in a generally open manner within agreed-upon bounds of censorship, the government presumed in at least one case to take unjustified liberties with constitutional press freedoms. On 30 December 1943, the U.S. postmaster general denied *Esquire* magazine a second-class mailing permit, alleging that the publication featured indecent pictures of partially naked "Petty girls" drawn by artist George Petty —in addition to literary works by America's finest writers and journalists. The denial was challenged in a court battle that finally went to the U.S. Supreme Court; the court's decision in 1946 vindicated *Esquire*. The publisher of *Esquire*, as well as other publishers and interested unions, used advertising to help make their case and create a favorable public atmosphere for the *Esquire* cause.

Another legal case, this one carried over from 1939, would have a far-reaching effect in stabilizing the reliability of circulation data on which ad rates were calculated. Tower Magazines, which published a group of magazines distributed by the F.W. Woolworth retail chain, had submitted false circulation figures to the Audit Bureau of Circulations (ABC). When the fraud was uncovered, the publisher, Catherine McNelis, and other Tower officers were indicted and, after a lengthy trial, convicted. But almost as much damage was done to the ABC, whose certification of circulation had been regarded as incorruptibly accurate. The ABC, which was not indicted, had failed to audit Tower and instead accepted a letter, supposedly from Woolworth, containing circulation data. The incident spurred reforms at the ABC that ultimately strengthened its credibility.

Other legal skirmishes that marked the decade included a 1941 investigation led by James Fly, chairman of the U.S. Federal Communications Commission (FCC), into the monopoly status of newspapers and radio stations in the same market. Some ad industry associations regarded the move as a first government step in the ultimate abolition of advertising. The industry responded with moves to preempt government action.

Radio

The 1940s began with the introduction of Swan Soap from Lever Brothers, Nescafé from Nestlé, and the Audimeter from A.C. Nielsen Company (which would take the device national in 1945). W.H. Weintraub opened the agency that would become Norman, Craig & Kummel in 1955. And the H.W. Kastor & Sons agency launched radio's first big-money quiz show, *Pot o' Gold,* for Tums, a product of the Lewis Howe Company. The program quickly provoked movie theater owners to complain to the Justice Department. They argued that the program's offer of $1,000, a considerable sum in 1940, to anyone who was home to answer a random phone call from the show was keeping people out of movie houses every Tuesday. The Justice Department declined to

Table 1.   **Top Ten Network Radio Advertisers of the 1940s.**

Rank	Marketer	Agency/Agencies
1	Procter & Gamble Company	Compton; Blackett-Sample-Hummert; H.W. Kastor; Pedlar & Ryan
2	General Foods	Young & Rubicam; Benton & Bowles
3	Lever Brothers	J. Walter Thompson Company; Ruthrauff & Ryan
4	Sterling Drug, Inc.	Blackett-Sample-Hummert; Thompson-Koch
5	Standard Brands	J. Walter Thompson Company
6	Colgate-Palmolive-Peet	Benton & Bowles
7	Campbell Soup Company	F. Wallis Armstrong; Ruthrauff & Ryan;
8	American Home Products	John F. Murray Advertising Agency
9	American Tobacco Company	Lord & Thomas; N.W. Ayer
10	General Mills	Blackett-Sample-Hummert; Knox Reeves

act, but United Artists and part-time producer James Roosevelt decided to fight fire with fire by documenting the national phenomenon in a Frank Capra–style movie comedy called *Pot o' Gold*, starring James Stewart and Paulette Goddard, who were not on the radio program, and bandleader Horace Heidt, who was.

Other forces were at work that would fundamentally change radio. In 1935, at the invitation of NBC Chairman David Sarnoff, Henry Armstrong had invented a static-free radio broadcast system called frequency modulation, or FM. It sounded so brilliantly lifelike that the FCC considered it as the basis for the sound component of the coming U.S. system of television. The FCC also allocated a band segment for FM radio to begin experimental broadcasts. FM radios began to be manufactured in limited quantities, and by 1940 and 1941 in something closer to mass production. License applications boomed as well, spurring the need for greater bandwidth. So the FCC reviewed the space it had allocated to experimental television, which covered 18 channels in the 30- to 300-megacycle range, and decided to detach channel 1 and assign its 42- to 50-megacycle space to FM radio. Commercial operation was authorized in May 1940, and shortly thereafter FM officially became part of the U.S. television specifications. But Sarnoff, an early proponent of FM who quickly became an enemy, recognized the threat it posed to the AM (amplitude modulation) network structure over which he presided.

For Sarnoff and much of the radio establishment, the war could not have come at a better time. FM was shelved, manufacturing stopped, and station activity was curtailed. General Electric Company continued to be a vigorous proponent, placing ads for its FM radios in *Life* and *Look* magazines. "Only FM brings you these artists in glorious natural color," said one 1944 *Life* ad by

Batten Barton Durstine & Osborn (BBDO), though with the caveat that "all G.E. radio equipment now goes to the armed forces. But after Victory [it] will be an even finer instrument than it is now." By the end of 1941, 46 FM stations were operating in the United States and more than 500,000 receivers were in use, none of which were made by RCA. But much politicking went on behind the scenes as the AM industry sought to influence future government policy. By 1945 a quite different FCC looked once more at FM and decided for various technical reasons to move it up the spectrum to just above television channel 6. The effect was to make every FM radio in the country obsolete and kill off what little audience FM had. The AM network system, through which advertisers could easily reach the entire country from coast to coast, would remain dominant, and the challenge of FM would be postponed for nearly 20 years. By the mid- and late 1940s the entertainment programming heard and seen by all Americans was effectively in the hands of three networks and a handful of powerful ad agencies, with television still only a minor factor. Never again would so much advertising and communication power be concentrated in network radio.

The power of the U.S. radio industry was so concentrated that it drew the attention of the Justice Department and the FCC, which had been probing the network chain broadcasting situation since 1938. In 1941 NBC was held by the FCC to be a monopoly and told it could no longer own two networks. Since 1926 the NBC Red network had been fed by RCA's New York City flagship station WEAF; NBC Blue was fed by WJZ, New York City. Both were owned by NBC and its parent, RCA. The Red network was the more prestigious chain; the Blue had more of a small-town image. NBC decided to set up the Blue network as a separate company, then sell it. In October 1943 Edward J. Noble, who had built Life Saver Corporation, bought the Blue network for $8 million and formed a new network that soon was renamed the American Broadcasting Company, or ABC.

World War II

When the United States entered the war in December 1941, the impact on advertisers was immediate. Rubber and fuel became subject to strict ration allocations. Automobile production ceased as factories converted to military production. The 1942 model year would be the last the country would see until 1946. Ad agencies faced the problem of what to advertise when there was nothing to sell and soon decided the best thing to sell was the promise of tomorrow while protecting the power of their clients' brands today. Ads emphasized two constant themes: what the advertiser was doing to help the war effort now, and how today's sacrifices would pay off in a dazzling array of new products consumers would enjoy after the war. "You can look forward to the day when you can home launder shirts," said a Westinghouse ad in 1944. "[It's] worth waiting and saving for." Patriotic copy boasted of the pride manufacturers felt in taking on vital military jobs. "Fire power is our business," General Motors proclaimed in an Oldsmobile ad. "Buick powers the liberator," said another, adding, "As of September 1, 1944, Buick has built more than

Like many wartime ads, this 1944 A.B. Dick Company advertisement kept the brand in the public eye while supporting the war effort.
The A. B. Dick Company.

55,000 Pratt & Whitney aircraft engines." Even musical instrument manufacturers converted to military production, and fan magazines such as *Down Beat* were full of ads explaining how a trumpet factory was now turning out valves for B-17G fuel systems. Hundreds of ads piggybacked a reminder to buy war bonds, and New York City daily papers had a "victory rate" discount of 24 percent for war advertising.

But there was more at work behind this trend than patriotism. A serious threat to advertising was taxation. Many advertisers selling principally to the government used advertising as a public relations tool. When Senator Harry Truman of Missouri investigated the whole range of defense spending, he questioned why the cost of advertising and the attendant commissions to agencies were being deducted from corporate income tax returns as "necessary business expenses" when the government was the only buyer of the product being advertised. Much of the money going into ads and radio production, the government argued, would otherwise go to the war effort through a wartime excess profits tax aimed at potential profiteers. The effect of the deductions was a government subsidy of advertising. When the Internal Revenue Service (IRS) announced in October 1942 that it would carefully examine advertising deductions, agencies, advertisers, publishers, and broadcasters rushed to Washington, D.C., to lobby against such scrutiny.

The government soon learned that the issue was not so simple. The war effort itself, it became clear, required advertising if war bonds were to be sold, rubber and scrap drives were to be effective, rationing was to be accepted, and a whole range of civilian controls and policies were to be effectively publicized. Rather than make advertisers adversaries of the IRS, it seemed wiser to make them partners in these and other priority communication efforts. Using radio stars and advertisers to help broadcast government information was a trend that was already under way before the Japanese attack on Pearl Harbor. In the fall of 1941 the Association of National Advertisers and the American Association of Advertising Agencies met and laid the basis of what was to become the Advertising Council, which became the industry's chief public relations instrument. Early the next year, the War Advertising Council (WAC) was formed to provide government liaison and leadership in helping advertisers promote the war effort. The WAC became the facilitator of government-advertiser cooperation, which soon became standard operating practice. Elmer Davis left his post as chief news analyst at CBS News to head the Office of War Information (OWI), which set priorities and worked closely with radio writers and performers as well as ad agencies to present information.

Shortly after the IRS announcement in the fall of 1942, Washington relented on the tax question and told the industry that "reasonable" ad costs would continue to be deductible. The move proved a huge windfall to radio, which did not have to wrestle with the paper allocations that forced newspapers and magazines to cut back on ad space. Radio not only had time for more ads, it could work government messages into comedy and drama content. The war made radio the most powerful communications medium in the United States. After the war, the OWI was dissolved and the WAC continued as the Advertising Council, setting its own priorities in choosing worthy causes and creating public service messages.

In 1942 the *New York Times* launched its *Sunday Magazine,* which became a much sought-after medium for fashion marketers. Three years later in Chicago, Illinois, Johnson Publishing began publishing *Ebony,* a *Life*-like photojournalism magazine aimed at a national Negro market. Soft goods, such as clothing and shoes, and packaged goods, such as cigarettes, canned foods, toilet articles, and soaps, continued to be advertised and sold, although to save on material, "Victory suits," as they were called, had no lapels.

News became more important than ever on radio, and network representatives were constantly meeting with agency executives to reach increasingly formal understandings governing preemptions and reimbursements when war news required the cancellation of scheduled sponsored programs. Agencies were as sensitive to these matters as anyone, perhaps more so. They established policies to immediately withdraw all commercial announcements when breaking war news made product promotion inappropriate. The Domestic Radio Bureau of the War Department's OWI prepared an inventory of patriotic messages that advertisers were free to use in an emergency. On D day, 6 June 1944, virtually all network advertisers ceased selling. No detail was too small to overlook. H.W. Kastor & Sons, which produced the show *Abie's Irish Rose* for Procter & Gamble (P&G), ordered that the burst of laughter that normally opened the program be eliminated in the event the show were to air on invasion day. BBDO had a standing order to 91 stations to cancel all spots for Wildroot hair tonic as of H-hour on D-day (the day and hour on which the invasion was to be launched).

Agency Developments

The agency landscape was changing in significant ways in the 1940s. Duane Jones left the Maxon agency in 1942 to start the Duane Jones Company. And at the end of the year Albert Lasker, who had built Lord & Thomas into one of the country's most powerful agencies, suddenly resigned, retired the agency name (which he owned) and turned the company over to the heads of its three principal offices—Emerson Foote (New York City), Fairfax Cone (Chicago), and Don Belding (Los Angeles, California), who reopened it after the New Year's break as Foote, Cone & Belding (FCB). The agency, which would create Smokey the Bear for the Advertising Council, continued to hold its major clients, which included Pepsodent and Lucky Strike. The agency made history in 1948 when it voluntarily resigned the $12 million American Tobacco Company business over marketing differences. It was the largest account any agency had ever chosen to walk away from at that time, and FCB was much admired for its courage. The same year FCB was born, Hill Blackett left Blackett-Sample-Hummert, which continued as Dancer, Fitzgerald, Sample and established Hill Blackett, Inc. C.J. LaRoche departed Young & Rubicam (Y&R) and later formed C.J. LaRoche & Company (which became McCaffrey & McCall in 1972). Four senior officers at Pedlar & Ryan departed in 1944 to form Doherty, Clifford & Shenfield, taking the Bristol-Myers account with them. (The company would later merge with Needham, Louis & Brorby to form Needham, Harper & Steers in 1964.) In 1946 a similar defection from Ruthrauff & Ryan produced one of the hottest post-war agencies, Sullivan, Stauffer, Colwell & Bayles (SSC&B), which rose to the rank of a major agency within two years on the strength of the Lever Brothers' Lifebuoy brand and American Tobacco's Pall Mall cigarettes. (In November 1979 SSC&B was acquired by the Interpublic Group.) And in 1948 McCann-Erickson named Marion Harper as president, although it would be more than a decade before he would change the structure of the industry by inventing Interpublic and the multi-agency model of the holding company.

After the war, advertisers worried about a depression that never came. In 1948 total national advertising volume was estimated by *Advertising Age* at $1.224 billion. What did come was a major spurt of inflation as the Office of Price Administration was killed off, wartime price controls were lifted, and prices rose to catch up with the money supply. New products came fast. P&G launched Prell, a shampoo in a tube, via Benton & Bowles. In 1947 the Toni home permanent (which was acquired by Gillette in 1948) became the wonder of the postwar world, as the ad budget given to FCB shot from $5,000 to $6 million almost overnight ("Which twin has the Toni?"). P&G came out with its Lilt permanent, but Toni had defined the category. Other new wonder brands and categories to emerge after the war were Gold Seal Glass Wax, Dial soap, synthetic detergents, antihistamines for relief from colds, the long-playing record, and the stick-on bra, which became such a sensation after it was advertised in *Life* magazine that the manufacturer was overwhelmed with demand and sold out to Textron.

Television

But the greatest postwar wonder of all, both to advertisers and consumers, was television. For much of the decade there was little to talk about but its "promise." During the war much of the promise was based on the optimistic notion that it would have the opportunity to start completely fresh, that it could be free of radio's problems and shortcomings, whatever they might be. Among those who were less than eager to see the arrival of television were some in the radio business, most in the movie industry, and newspaper and magazine publishers, who had special reason to fear the volume of ad revenues TV might drain away from their media.

In any case, the promise was slow in materializing, as it had been for years. In the late 1920s, television was predicted within five years. In 1939 it seemed to be looming just over the horizon. Depression and war intervened, however, and in the end television was better for the wait. In 1929 a rough television picture could be mechanically scanned on a 60-line grid offering minimal detail. By 1936 electronic scanning boosted the level to 343 lines. Finally the standard of 525 lines synchronized at 30 frames per second was set in 1941 by the National Television Standards Committee,

The Public Is Demanding FM
...And Zenith Has The Answer

$59.95
And Up!

It will shortly be very difficult to sell any radio (except in the lower price brackets or portables) which does not incorporate FM. Zenith has long recognized the universal appeal of this new kind of static-free, true fidelity broadcasting as developed by Major Edwin H. Armstrong. To meet it, Zenith engineers have perfected two-band Armstrong FM in table model sets designed to appeal to the mass, volume market, as well as in the finest console combinations . . . all with Zenith's patented built-in light-line antenna. That is why Zenith is recognized by broadcasters, dealers and the public as the outstanding manufacturer of FM receivers.

ONLY ZENITH HAS THIS!

★ Genuine Armstrong FM On Both Tuning Bands
★ Super 6-Purpose Tube
★ Built-in FM Antenna, Even for Table Models
★ Big, Easy-Tuning Dial
★ Permeability Tuning
★ Compact Chassis
★ Built-in Wavemagnet
★ Sensitive, Selective Circuit

Zenith Is Building A Mass FM Audience:

70.10% of all the FM equipped table model sets produced during the period from January 14, 1946 to January 4, 1947 were Zeniths. These latest available figures (February 5, 1947) are from Haskins & Sells, the official reporting agency of the Radio Manufacturers Association.

ZENITH RADIO CORPORATION   CHICAGO 39, ILLINOIS

In this 1947 ad, Zenith's answer to the demand for more programming was a radio that included the higher-megacycle FM band opened by the Federal Communications Commission in 1945.
Zenith Electronics Corporation.

a technical panel of the FCC whose initials, NTSC, continue to reference the American television system. Also by 1941, the basic patents had been joined in a patchwork of licenses and agreements, and AT&T was tackling the problem of coast-to-coast broadcasting with plans for a national coaxial cable hookup of landlines.

Just before the war, a TV set could be bought for somewhere between $150 and $400. RCA, which had invested $10 million in television by then and was eager to see some prompt payoff, made its first attempt to launch the new medium in March 1940. It opened a full-scale ad campaign, cut the price of receivers to the bone, and appeared to suggest that a full-scale TV schedule was already on the air, which it was not. The campaign, which was confined to the New York area, was indeed premature. Technical standards were still in flux, and other makers, such as the Philco Corporation and DuMont Laboratories, feared that RCA was trying to preemptively force its system on everybody else by gaining marketplace equity. By the time the United States entered the war, there were eight commercial stations on the air broadcasting to about 10,000 sets, mostly in New York City. By the end of the war, however, they would all be obsolete.

A great debate surrounded the future of television in 1944 and 1945. One camp (RCA, DuMont, and Philco) wanted a system set in the very high frequency range (VHF) of 30 to 300 megacycles, where proven technology and most of RCA's accrued investment could get TV off to a fast postwar start. The other camp (CBS, Zenith) favored a system in the less-crowded ultrahigh frequency (UHF) of 500 to 1,000 megacycles, where TV would have space to grow even though it would take several years longer to set up. Caught between the pressures of speed versus space, the FCC in May 1945 kept television in the VHF range but broke the original continuous 18-channel allocation of 1940 into two smaller band segments totaling 12 channels, with 2 to 6 in one slot and 7 to 13 in the other. In between lay FM radio and government space. The FCC, taking advantage of the higher frequency opportunities opened up by the war, also gave television broad space in the UHF range. This was experimental, however, and few receivers would be equipped to tune in UHF channels until the mid-1960s. These frequency allocation decisions were the most critical factors in shaping the next 50 years of commercial television in the United States. Their effect was to create an artificial scarcity of spectrum space that in turn concentrated great economic power in the hands of VHF broadcasters and particularly RCA.

BBDO had put three of it clients into television as an experiment as early as 1943. Executives at Lennen & Mitchell and the talent agency William Morris were advising advertisers to get into TV early in order to stake out a "time franchise" (broadcast time period) that would be theirs when the medium took off. As the audience grew in 1946 and 1947, advertisers moved toward TV in earnest. Maxon, Inc., put Gillette on NBC in *The Gillette Cavalcade of Sports*, and JWT produced the *Kraft Television Theater*, a live drama anthology that became a standard format for many advertisers over the next decade. In 1948 the new medium had its first three runaway hits capable of generating large-scale set purchases: *Arthur Godfrey's Talent Scouts*, produced by Y&R for Lipton tea; *Toast of the Town* with Ed Sullivan, produced by Kenyon & Eckhardt for Ford Motor Company's Lincoln-Mercury division; and the biggest hit, *The Texaco Star Theater* with Milton Berle, produced by the Kudner Agency for Texaco. All were migrants from radio (*Talent Scouts* was actually simulcast), and all were run with heavy ad agency involvement, indicating that TV was not starting "fresh," as some had hoped, but was becoming an extension of the radio business model. The one element of that model that worried broadcasters most was the dominant role of ad agencies in programming, production, and scheduling. Agency television directors routinely supervised the networks' technical and crew people during rehearsals and telecasts. In 1949 five of the top ten shows on television were in-house productions of Y&R.

One reason for this was that broadcasters and advertisers knew, though they were not necessarily admitting it publicly, that network radio was doomed and that television was their only hope of survival. Yet, no real network TV system was up and running through 1948, denying a national platform to major advertisers. That alone granted a stay on the demise of radio's supremacy. Live TV programs could only be seen along the upper East Coast as coaxial cable construction was rushing toward Cleveland, Ohio; Chicago; St. Louis, Missouri; and points west. "Never before . . . have so many men lost so much money so fast," wrote *Fortune* magazine, "and so willingly." The costs of constructing a basic TV station ran close to $500,000, a far greater investment than that required for radio in the same market. And ad revenues remained sparse. In 1948 WPIX, an independent New York City TV station, was peddling commercial time to local department stores for $250 a commercial. To recoup as much revenue as possible, stations were breaking with the radio tradition of single program sponsorship and offering segments of a show to noncompeting advertisers. "Participating sponsorship," as it was called, soon became a new trend in TV time sales, in some cases bringing in advertisers that had never used radio. In April 1948 there were 301 advertisers on all TV stations. A year later there were 1,350, and NBC said that 30 percent were coming into broadcasting for the first time. Then the flood began. In 1950 *Variety* magazine called the exodus of major advertisers out of radio and into television "the greatest exhibition of mass hysteria" in show business history.

Television Traffic Jam

The rush to get into television, however, created a traffic jam in the narrow 12-channel corridor of space allocated for the burgeoning industry. In September 1948 the FCC clamped a freeze on further expansion. Stations already running (37 outlets in 21 cities) or licensed (another 71) could continue. But no new licenses would be granted until various technical issues were worked out. The freeze came at a time when television coverage was still spotty and unbalanced. New York had six stations and Chicago had four, while a major market such as Denver, Colorado, had none. Expected to last only six months, the freeze dragged on for nearly four years, keeping 14 states and their cities blacked out while at the same time permitting stations already on the air to solidify network, advertiser, and market relationships totally protected from new competition. During that time, receiver penetration nationwide soared from 0.5 percent of the population to more than one-third by the end of 1952. Clearly, the freeze also further entrenched the VHF system. By the end of the freeze in April 1952, the entire U.S. television system consisted of only 108 stations and a huge pent-up urge to catch up. The lifting of the freeze would trigger the great television boom of the 1950s.

Quiz programs came back into fashion on radio in the late 1940s with *Stop the Music* from Old Gold and *Take It or Leave It* from Eversharp, which put the phrase "the 64-dollar question" into the national idiom. Lennen & Mitchell and the Biow Company were the respective agencies. Taking a cue from radio, advertisers returned to the contest as a promotional vehicle. Borden drew almost 1 million entries in 1948 when it asked for suggestions on naming the calf of its much-beloved icon, Elsie. (Beauregard was the winning name.) And that same year, the Pepsi-Cola Company offered $203,725 in prizes in a contest that so confused the public that the company switched agencies from Newell Emmett to Biow.

By the end of the decade, advertising was developing enough of a sense of its own that the Advertising Federation of America and the New York Ad Club created the Advertising Hall of Fame. Among the ten first inductees in 1949: retail pioneer John Wanamaker, *Printers' Ink* Editor John Irving Romer, and legendary copywriter Theodore MacManus. The decade included many smaller milestones as well: vitamins and vitamin content became a strong selling point early in the decade, as Standard Brands launched Stamms and Lever Brothers came out with Vimms. For the first ten months of 1941, the American Society of Composers, Authors and Publishers (ASCAP) refused to license its music catalog, which included virtually every popular song written for theater, movies, or tin pan alley since 1914, to the radio networks. It was a move that triggered the formation of an alternative licensing organization by the networks, Broadcast Music Inc. (BMI). Newsman Elmer Davis left CBS to head the Office of War Information (OWI), and CBS's WJSV in Washington, D.C., became WTOP. The networks canceled vast amounts of commercial programming and advertising to accommodate breaking news of the invasion of Europe in June 1944, a practice that would be repeated as the war came to an end in 1945. In Chicago in 1947, Marshall Field bought the *Chicago Times* and merged it with his own *Sun* to form the *Sun-Times*.

Throughout the decade, advertising continued to see the first generation of its great pioneers pass from the scene. MacManus, who came out of retirement briefly in 1940, died that same year. So did Walter Chrysler, founder of the Chrysler Corporation; O.B. Winters, noted copywriter at Erwin Wasey & Company; agency founder J. Stirling Getchell; R.C. Desirens, creator of the Chesapeake & Ohio Railway's mascot "Chessie," the cartoon kitten that became a symbol of the company's freight service; and Leon Douglass, who put Nipper the dog into Victor Talking Machine advertising.

Others who died during the decade included: Ruthrauff & Ryan founder Wilber Ruthrauff and H.J. Heinz Company executive Howard Heinz (1941); Kenyon & Eckhardt founder Henry Eckhardt, publishers Moses Annenberg and Condé Nast, mail order pioneer E.T. Gundlach (1942); agency founder Arthur Kudner, BBDO Chairman William Johns (1944); *New York Daily News* Publisher Joseph Medill Paterson and American Tobacco Company boss George Washington Hill (1946); General Motors founder William C. Durant and type designer Frederic Goudy (1947); McGraw-Hill founder James H. McGraw and Burridge Butler, owner of the *Prairie Farmer* and Chicago's WLS radio (1948); and Buchanan & Company founder Thomas Buchanan, Lever Brothers chief Viscount Leverhulme, Kenyon & Eckhardt founder Otis A. Kenyon, and F. Wallis Armstrong, who hired Raymond Rubicam in 1919 and whose agency later became the Ward Wheelock Company (1949).

JOHN MCDONOUGH

See also color plate in this volume

Further Reading

Barnouw, Erik, *A History of Broadcasting in the United States*, 3 vols., New York: Oxford University Press, 1966–70; see especially vol. 2, *The Golden Web, 1933–1953*

Boddy, William, *Fifties Television: The Industry and Its Critics*, Urbana: University of Illinois Press, 1990

Fox, Stephen R., *The Mirror Makers: A History of American Advertising and Its Creators*, New York: Morrow, 1984

MacDonald, J. Fred, *One Nation under Television*, New York: Pantheon Books, 1990; updated and enlarged edition, Chicago: Nelson Hall, 1994

"The Promise of Television," *Fortune* (August 1943)

"Television: The Next Great Development," *Life Magazine* (4 September 1944)

"The Television Freeze," *Fortune* (November 1949)

"TV: The Money Rolls Out," *Fortune* (May 1949)

History: 1950s

Tempered by the Great Depression and a world war, Americans greeted the relative peace and prosperity of the 1950s with an unbridled passion to consume. A new medium, television, promoted lifestyles and needs, and the economic shift from wartime manufacturing to consumer manufacturing increased employee salaries and disposable income. Globally, nations hardest hit by the war's devastation were rebuilt through the Marshall Plan and other outside funding. Advertising in these countries not only sold products but also shaped culture and national identity.

In the United States far-reaching advertising trends first became established in the cultural and economic environment of the 1950s. Traditional media such as radio, newspapers, and magazines remained vital conduits for advertising during the early years of the decade, but television quickly replaced radio and magazines as the cornerstone in many advertisers' national media plans. Throughout the decade, advertising expenditures increased to unprecedented numbers. The J. Walter Thompson Company saw its billings increase from $78 million in 1945 to $172 million in 1955 and $250 million by 1960. Overall, the decade saw gross annual advertising industry expenditures quadruple, going from $1.3 billion in 1950 to $6 billion in 1960.

Advertising and consumerism in the 1950s can be divided into two distinct periods. The first period, lasting approximately until 1953, was a time of "catching up." Products such as clothing, refrigerators, automobiles, and appliances—unavailable or in short supply during the war—were again plentiful. Pent-up demand for consumer products fueled a steady growth in manufacturing.

Conversely, the middle to end of the decade was, for consumers, a period of acute "consumption anxiety." Marketers analyzed variations in the economic landscape and continued to offer "new and improved" products to maintain high consumer demand. This focused selling technique used newly popular methods such as motivational research, demographic targeting, and generational marketing.

The postwar years saw a huge increase in population. From 1945 to 1964 a global "baby boom" occurred. Reunited families made up for lost time, and the birthrate—which had fallen in the mid-1930s—soared by 25 percent following the end of the war and remained elevated throughout the decade.

The baby boom's significance became evident in new housing starts. During the economic depression of the 1930s, new-home construction virtually ceased. Homes built in the suburbs during this period were primarily for the wealthy. Average Americans lived either in urban apartments near their employment and near convenient transportation, or shared housing with parents or in-laws.

As family size grew, so did the need for affordable housing. Contractor William Levitt took his inspiration from automobile manufacturer Henry Ford and built inexpensive, attractive single-family houses for ordinary citizens. It was Levitt and his New York community, Levittown, that made the American dream possible for people who had never thought of themselves as middle class before, according to David Halberstam, author of *The Fifties*.

Catering to Suburbanites

Levitt, a shrewd businessman, enticed returning veterans to buy his homes with little or no money down. As incentives, he included a television set and a washing machine with every home purchase. Ads, such as the following from the *New York Times*, promoted the new houses:

> This is Levittown! All yours for $58. You're a lucky fellow, Mr. Veteran. Uncle Sam and the world's largest builder have made it possible for you to live in a charming house in a delightful community without having to pay for them with your eye teeth . . . .

By the mid-1950s Levitt-style subdivisions were being built nationwide and represented 75 percent of new housing starts. Critics denounced these subdivisions as symbols of conformity and materialism. Yet, the shift from urban to suburban living had

begun. Suburbs grew by 46 percent. By the close of the decade, one-third of the population lived in suburban areas surrounding metropolitan centers.

Suburbanites realized the need for appliances and other necessities to fill their homes, and marketers rushed to introduce a vast array of products while manufacturers churned out new appliances, automobiles, and consumer electronics. Many advertised products promoted labor-saving automation for increased productivity and leisure time. Heating and cooling products, kitchen and laundry appliances, furniture and decorating accessories, and frozen and prepared foods all promoted time-saving benefits.

Typifying this trend was a 1950 Hotpoint ad headline that pleaded, "Please . . . let your wife come into the living room!" As her husband and children watch television, the wife struggles in the kitchen over a stack of dirty dishes. The ad claims that by taking advantage of Hotpoint's new automatic dishwasher the wife gains an extra hour a day—seven hours a week. The accompanying copy reads:

> Don't let dirty dishes make your wife a kitchen exile! She loses the most precious hours of her life shut off from pleasures of the family circle by the never-ending chore of old-fashioned dishwashing! It's easy to banish the dishpan drudgery and let her join the family fun—the modern, work-saving, Hotpoint automatic way!

Capitalism claimed the technical innovations of wartime and transformed them into labor-saving convenience products. The aerosol spray can was a by-product of the war's South Pacific "bug bomb." Adding a spray top transformed the "bug bomb" into a dispenser for everything from processed cheese, whipped cream, shaving cream, hairspray, and deodorant to furniture polish. Nylon, initially developed for parachutes, replaced expensive silk in stockings. Plastics and Styrofoam found new applications in everything from furniture to insulation.

Advertising reflected a conscious return to traditional family values. In a single generation, lingering memories of Depression and war were replaced by positive futuristic portrayals of the idealized modern family—mother, father, son, and daughter enjoying the comforts of their new home, the convenience of their automobile, and the added leisure time together. Children became targeted consumers for the first time as advertising tapped their newfound affluence. Phonographs, records, radios, magazines, clothing, and soft drinks, among other products, found a receptive teen audience.

Advertising reflected society's upward mobility and prosperity, its technological superiority in products and manufacturers, and its renewed optimism of a rebounding from war. Expanded highways and expressways connected suburbs to downtown workplaces. As automobile ownership became commonplace, suburban workers could conveniently commute to their jobs, and housewives could enjoy shopping centers and supermarkets located in the new communities.

The necessity of becoming a two-car family was heavily promoted throughout the 1950s—a decade that began with a mere

In the 1950s ads from American automakers reflected the rise of the two-car family and the growing importance of the automobile in family life. *Courtesy of Ford Motor Company.*

59 percent of American families owning a car. A 1950 Ford advertisement, for example, touted the convenience of owning two cars and the added economy of owning a Ford. Its headline read, "Now thousands own two fine cars!" Within a few years, nearly every family owned at least one car while many owned several.

By the mid-1950s, automobiles surpassed packaged goods and cigarettes as the most heavily advertised products. In *The Mirror Makers,* historian Stephen Fox cites Chevrolet (at $30.4 million) and Ford (at $25 million) as having the largest individual advertising budgets in 1956. Other automobile manufacturers—Buick, Dodge, Plymouth, Mercury, Chrysler, Pontiac, and Oldsmobile—followed. Only stalwart advertiser Coca-Cola Company broke through the mix of Detroit, Michigan-based standouts.

Car owners of the mid-1950s began to see their vehicles as extensions of themselves. As chairman of General Motors Corporation (GM), Alfred P. Sloan had implemented the strategy of planned obsolescence, stressing marketing segmentation among GM products. As early as the 1920s, Sloan dreamed of annual model changes to hasten consumers' desire to purchase new and more expensive cars. Under the leadership of GM chief designer Harley Earl, Sloan's planned obsolescence strategy was rediscovered and became the "dynamic obsolescence" of the 1950s. Earl's ever-changing designs pushed consumers to replace their cars yearly—not for lack of performance, but for lack of style. It was Earl who gave Cadillac and other 1950s GM cars their distinctive tail fins. Automobile design and advertising reflected the nation's infatuation with new technology, jet planes, and the atomic age. Soon other manufacturers introduced cars with large panoramic windshields, shiny chrome trim, and menacing "gun turrets" on the hood.

Consumers rejected excessive style changes, however. The Ford Edsel, introduced in September 1957 and named after Henry Ford's son, remains one of the automobile industry's most infamous marketing failures. Even with a $30 million consumer advertising campaign, Edsel's unique styling and push-button performance failed to connect with consumers. Fairfax Cone, of Foote, Cone & Belding, said, "The trouble with Edsel was almost everything." Trade publications promptly reported Edsel's demise and speculated that consumers had tired of artificial design obsolescence and instead sought tangible product improvements.

TV's Coming of Age

Perhaps the most important factor influencing advertising in the 1950s was the growth of television and its maturation into a viable ad medium. Advancements in television technology, suspended during the war, quickly regained momentum at war's end. By 1951 regular live network service reached the West Coast via microwave transmitters, establishing coast-to-coast national coverage. As with radio, early television programming was advertiser sponsored and dominated. Advertising agencies produced TV shows, with networks providing little more than facilities, airtime, and occasional guidance. Sponsors benefited from dictating the environment and how and when their messages were inserted. Programming typically promoted the name of the sponsor and not

the star: *Hallmark Hall of Fame, Texaco Star Theater, Colgate Comedy Hour, Goodyear TV Playhouse,* and *Kraft Television Theater.*

Large U.S. agencies such as the J. Walter Thompson Company, Young & Rubicam, Inc., Batten Barton Durstine & Osborn (BBDO), and McCann-Erickson benefited by handling major packaged and durable goods advertisers such as Procter & Gamble, Bristol-Meyers, Westinghouse Electric, and Colgate-Palmolive. As the advertisers' business grew, so did their agencies' potential for growth. In 1949 Ben Duffy of BBDO spent 80 percent of his media time on television and only 20 percent on radio. By 1950 the BBDO television department had grown from 12 employees to 150, and the agency was billing $4 million in the new medium.

Likewise, Madison Avenue continued to profit from spiraling TV spending. In 1949 the advertising industry's television spending was $12.3 million. Within two years it had grown to $128 million. By 1954 television had become the leading medium for advertising. It was, as author Martin Mayer described it, a world "in which everyone watched one of three networks and [an advertiser] could reach 60 percent of the country with a budget that was affordable." Meanwhile, network radio suffered losses as major stars and their audiences moved to television. Although network radio lost national prominence, individual stations remained outlets for local advertising and niche marketing throughout the decade.

While television was busy siphoning media dollars away from radio, newspapers and magazines were profiting by selling a new product category—television sets. New sets cost between $200 for small models and $2,500 for large consoles. Purchasing a television set was a major family event as well as a significant status symbol. By 1957 Americans owned 37 million television sets, and 450 TV stations were in operation. By 1960 television had approached 90 percent household penetration.

Advertisements featuring television reflected family togetherness and new technologies. Unlike radio, television demanded complete attention by the viewer. Families gathered to watch television, and products such as Swanson TV dinners were introduced to keep them in front of the set at mealtime.

Since videotaped programming was not widely available until after 1956, most early broadcasts and advertisements were performed live or on film. Spokespeople became readily identified with the product as product demonstrations gained significance in this visual medium. Betty Furness, a B-movie actress of the 1930s, became spokeswoman for Westinghouse appliances in 1949 on *Studio One.* For 11 years her popularity soared, as did the popularity of Westinghouse refrigerators, stoves, and other household appliances. Furness understood the new medium from her days as an actress. Most television spokespeople came directly from radio, and their presentations were often stiff and boring. Furness's film training helped her memorize lines and deliver them in a comfortable, believable manner. As a bright, confident, modern housewife, she epitomized the American dream. In the process, as the presenter of the all-American kitchen, she became one of television advertising's first celebrities.

Demonstrations also helped differentiate similar packaged goods. Notable televised product demonstrations included Band-Aid brand's "Super-Stick" bandages clinging to an egg in boiling water, Remington shaver's peach test in which a razor was used to shave peach fuzz, and the series of shock tests inflicted on Timex watches.

Other memorable television commercials include the stop-motion antics of Speedy Alka-Seltzer; Old Gold's dancing cigarette boxes; Dinah Shore's singing "See the USA in Your Chevrolet"; newsman John Cameron Swayze's matter-of-fact delivery of "It takes a licking and keeps on ticking" for Timex; and animated depictions of the Ajax Pixies, Tony the Tiger, Hamm's beer bear, and beer mavens Bert and Harry Piel.

Picked as one of the best advertisements of the decade by *Advertising Age*, Anacin pain reliever showed how beneficial and intrusive television advertising could be. Through slogans, demonstrations, mnemonics, and repetition, Anacin positioned itself as the "tension headache" remedy by repeating the phrase "Fast, fast, fast relief" and diagramming an imaginary headache with lightning bolts and hammers. The ad's tactic of repetition, created by agency Ted Bates & Company, drew harsh criticism, yet it increased Anacin's sales and stature. Motivated by Anacin's success, similar hard-hitting and repetitive ads followed.

The system of advertiser control over program content and scheduling that evolved in the heyday of radio was not a practice the networks were eager to see continue in television. As the stakes mounted and the competition between the networks intensified, broadcasters felt that they needed the authority to remove weak programs and strategically schedule strong ones to maintain viewer numbers during the valuable evening hours.

William Boddy, whose book *Fifties Television: The Industry and Its Critics* (1990) offers the most complete description of the advertiser-network struggle, cites this example of a growing network aggressiveness. *The Voice of Firestone* came to television from radio in 1949 at a time when networks still permitted advertisers to select and hold a time period of their choice as long as they were willing to pay for it. Under this practice, called sponsor time franchise, Firestone had held onto the same Monday night time-period (8:30 to 9:00 P.M.) for season after season. But the stodgy classical music format created a huge drop in NBC's ratings in the middle of its Monday prime-time schedule. Executives pleaded with the sponsor and its longtime agency, Sweeney & James Company, to yield the position, but it refused. Finally, in 1954 NBC took the then-unprecedented action of removing the show. Despite anger and threats of lawsuits, NBC effectively ended the time franchise.

The president of NBC at that time was Sylvester L. ("Pat") Weaver. He had seen the problem of advertiser control from all sides—agency, marketer, and network. Weaver started at Young & Rubicam in 1935, then moved to the American Tobacco Company, and finally went to NBC. Like many television executives, he believed that networks, not advertisers and agencies, should control programming. To this end Weaver decided that NBC not only should produce an inventory of shows but also should sell them to a variety of "participating" sponsors rather than a single

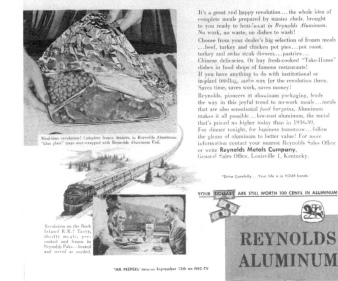

This 1953 print ad shows Reynolds Aluminum products at the forefront of the 1950s culinary revolution: time-saving "heat-'n-eat" meals made possible by aluminum containers and wraps.
Courtesy of Reynolds Consumer Products.

advertiser. This was the real strategy that lay behind such NBC programs of the 1950s as *Today, The Tonight Show, Your Show of Shows*, and *The Comedy Hour*. By selling one-minute commercial windows in network-produced programs, instead of 30- or 60-minute time blocks in which advertisers could dictate content, Weaver hoped to draw creative authority to the network as well as expand the access of smaller advertisers to network television. He was not always successful; Colgate ended up taking over *The Comedy Hour* and turning it into *The Colgate Comedy Hour*.

But the networks had an ally in economics. As the 1950s progressed, production costs rose dramatically to the point where many advertisers began to feel the strain. Increasingly programs that had started the decade with a single sponsor retreated to "alternate sponsorships" in which one advertiser would have the program one week, and another the alternate week. By 1957 Lucky Strike and Richard Hudnut shared *The Hit Parade*, and Stopette deodorant and Remington Rand alternated on *What's My Line*. Ad agencies remained an important part of the process, however. An agency might produce a program and offer it to two different clients on an alternate basis or it might switch sponsors.

The Kudner Agency produced *The Texaco Star Theater* with Milton Berle for its client, Texaco, for example, but when Texaco decided to withdraw in 1953, Kudner sold the program to another of its clients, General Motors, and it became *The Buick-Berle Show.*

Control over content finally shifted from advertiser to network in the wake of the quiz show scandal of the late 1950s. Long a staple on radio and television, quiz shows were among the most popular programs. Revlon sponsored *The $64,000 Question* and controlled program content so tightly that corporate heads chose the game's winners and losers. Revelations about a similar game show, *Twenty-One,* shocked the nation when it was reported that contestant Charles Van Doren had been given the answers to the questions in advance. Congressional hearings ensued, and the networks established control over the content of their broadcasts by 1959.

Advertising Age columnist Bob Garfield said of the change from program sponsorship to the modern U.S. system of TV advertising, "Whatever else can be debated about the legacy of 50 years of TV advertising, this is undeniable: it underwrote the revolution."

Selling of the Presidency

Further revolutionizing the medium of television was the 1952 presidential campaign between Republican Dwight D. Eisenhower and Democrat Adlai E. Stevenson. Rosser Reeves of Ted Bates & Company, creator of the Anacin campaign, developed the strategy for Eisenhower's TV ads. A firm believer in the television spot, Reeves is remembered for hard-hitting, straight to the point, repetitive television advertising, and for his promotion of the "unique selling proposition," or USP, to break through the ad clutter in the mass media.

He positioned Eisenhower as "The man from Abilene" and a "Man of peace." Through a series of brief television spots entitled "Eisenhower Answers America," Reeves prerecorded Eisenhower as if he were speaking directly to the American people. Reeves then intercepted a tour bus at Radio City Music Hall in New York City and filmed average Americans asking the candidate questions such as, "Mr. Eisenhower, are we going to have to fight another war?" Careful editing showed the citizen's questions matched with Eisenhower's prerecorded answers. Eisenhower was reluctant to participate, but acquiesced to Reeves's persuasive arguments. At the close of filming, Eisenhower was said to have remarked, "To think that an old soldier should come to this."

Eisenhower won the election, but critics charged that Reeves had denigrated the office of presidency by selling it like toothpaste. Stevenson voiced his concern over merchandising the presidency and refused to recognize the medium. Stevenson's objections were too late as television and politics now formed an inextricable union.

Era of the Hidden Persuader

Mid-century advertising was a fertile ground for critics. As the Cold War raged, critics claimed that new mind-control methods were used to manipulate unsuspecting consumers. Motivational research (MR) tapped into hidden desires and influenced consumers to purchase goods through their need for security, sex, social acceptance, style, luxury, and success. The leading proponent of motivational research was consultant Ernest Dichter. Dichter and his associates claimed to use psychological tools to analyze consumer buying habits and attitudes toward products, brands, packages, colors, and other motivations. Dichter proposed that one of the main dichotomies advertisers should resolve was what he called "the conflict between pleasure and guilt" among adults more affluent than their Depression-era parents.

Many ad agencies formed MR departments, and new brand personalities were born. The Marlboro man, Maidenform woman, and Hathaway man brought parity products (those with no easily discernible differences from others in the same category) to life and offered such attachments as emotional security, reassurance, creativity, and power. Vance Packard introduced MR to a Cold War–weary public in his best-selling book, *The Hidden Persuaders.* Revealing little about advertising technique, its ostensible subject, the book instead fueled Americans' fear of manipulation and mind control and became one of the most widely read exposés on advertising since the 1930s.

Though the 1950s seemed to be a serene decade of family values, suburban expansion, and increased prosperity, it also laid the groundwork for the turbulent decade to follow. While highways and supermarkets were expanding, so too were the communications needs and challenges of a new generation. For this expansion, historians claim that advertising served as handmaiden, cheerleader, and publicist. Critics claim that 1950s advertisements were not only bland and unimaginative but also reflected the conformity of the decade. Soon the compulsively obedient "organization man" of William Whyte's 1956 study by the same name would give way to the "creative revolutionary" of the 1960s.

KEN OHLEMEYER, JR.

Further Reading

Boddy, William, *Fifties Television: The Industry and Its Critics,* Urbana: University of Illinois Press, 1990

Cone, Fairfax M., *With All Its Faults: A Candid Account of Forty Years in Advertising,* Boston: Little Brown, 1969

"50 Years of TV Advertising," *Advertising Age* 66 (Spring 1995) (special issue on 50th anniversary of television advertising)

Fox, Stephen, *The Mirror Makers: A History of American Advertising and Its Creators,* New York: Morrow, 1984

Frank, Thomas, *The Conquest of Cool: Business Culture, Counterculture, and the Rise of Hip Consumerism,* Chicago: University of Chicago Press, 1997

Halberstam, David, *The Fifties,* New York: Villard, 1993

Jamieson, Kathleen Hall, *Packaging the Presidency: A History and Criticism of Presidential Campaign Advertising,* New York: Oxford University Press, 1984; 3rd edition, 1996

Matthei, Hany, "Inventing the Commercial," *American Heritage* 48, no. 3 (1997)

Mayer, Martin, *Madison Avenue, U.S.A.*, New York: Harper, and London: Bodley Head, 1958

Packard, Vance, *The Hidden Persuaders*, New York: McKay, and London: Longmans, 1957; revised edition, New York: Pocket, 1980; London: Penguin, 1981

Reeves, Rosser, *Reality in Advertising*, New York: Bates, 1960

Sivulka, Juliann, *Soap, Sex, and Cigarettes: A Cultural History of American Advertising*, Belmont, California: Wadsworth, 1998

Wood, James Playsted, *The Story of Advertising*, New York: Ronald, 1958

History: 1960s

The 1960s were advertising's "coming of age," when the industry reached its full potential as a communications tool. It mastered the language of television, appropriated the medium of photography, and produced work of unprecedented creativity. Influenced by the cultural and social changes of the decade, advertising reflected a trend toward innovation, sophistication, and a growing youth culture. In the United States the postwar abundance of the 1950s continued into the early 1960s, providing a profusion of mass-produced goods to eager consumers who enjoyed more leisure time and greater disposable income than any previous generation.

Advertising provided the information and incentive to keep consumption at an all-time high, but it was perhaps best known during this decade for its "creative revolution"—in which traditional styles and formats were discarded in favor of the "new advertising" characterized as irreverent, humorous, self-deprecating, ironic, and resonant. Advertising was also beset during the decade by criticism and regulatory concerns as consumer advocates sought new rights and protections for buyers.

Political and Social Upheaval

The 1960s in America were a time of enormous social and political change. Long hair became a symbol of revolution, hard hats an icon of reaction. The war in Vietnam was played out alongside prosperity at home, while freedom for white Americans existed alongside segregation for blacks. The contrasts conveyed disparate messages about the United States, which many young people interpreted as hypocrisy. Old attitudes toward war, race, gender, age, tradition, and authority were challenged. Idealistic young people protested against the materialism, consumerism, capitalism, and conformism of their parents' generation. This counterculture movement found expression in, among other places, the art schools of London, England; the music of the Beatles; and the images of the so-called pop artists.

The anti-establishment mood grew to be a sort of *cause célèbre* as rebellion spread across college campuses and became fashionable with the middle class. A revolution of tastes, technology, production, art, fashion, and music invigorated a new youth-oriented culture rebelling against the ways of its elders. The postwar baby boom generation came of age in the 1960s, with almost 50 percent of the U.S. population being under the age of 25 by the middle of the decade. A youthful sense of freedom and irreverence and a drive to break down old barriers was felt globally as young people around the world took to the streets to protest against authority of all kinds.

In this context of change and upheaval, advertising faced a number of challenges. Probably more than at any time in its history, advertising was subject to unprecedented criticism, not necessarily because of its practices but because the climate of upheaval and the challenge to the establishment brought advertising practices under closer scrutiny than ever before. The consumer movement gained force in the 1960s, fueled in part by a number of social critiques of advertising ethics. Advertising was castigated for its tendency to promote materialism and for exaggerated and often deceitful practices such as presenting doctors (played by actors) who made claims about the healthful aspects of cigarettes. Portrayed as "waste makers" and "subliminal charlatans" by their critics, advertisers were threatened with increased government regulation and, in some countries, taxation. Advertising entered the decade at the low end of public opinion polls and was perceived as "untrustworthy" by the antimaterialistic and skeptical youth culture.

One of advertising's major challenge during the decade was to improve its image. It needed not only to appease and disarm its critics, but also to capture the lucrative new youth market. With innovative campaigns such as Pepsi Cola's "Think Young" and "Pepsi Generation" from Batten Barton Durstine & Osborn (BBDO), advertisers made an effort to tone down their claims and establish a relationship with their audiences. Whereas it had previously treated the counterculture as deviant, undesirable, and marginalized, advertising now embraced it and attempted to connect with the youth market as well as with consumers fascinated with the counterculture phenomenon. No brand made this connection better than Coca-Cola, which embraced peace and love at the end of the decade in a commercial featuring a multiethnic chorus of young people singing "I'd Like to Teach the World to Sing" (from ad agency McCann-Erickson).

The "Creative Revolution"

Relying less on research than in previous decades, advertising turned to its creative instinct. Eschewing portrayals of elitism,

The tenor of the times is apparent in this 1968 poster protesting the military draft.
National Museum of American History, Smithsonian Institution.

materialism, authoritarianism, reverence for institutions, and other traditional beliefs previously heralded in ads, advertising attempted to win over consumers with humor, candor, and, above all, irony (which had the additional benefit of seeming very hip to those who "got it")—strategies decidedly more in line with the mood of the 1960s. Reflecting the culture's rejection of the "old ways," advertising made history during its own "creative revolution" by adopting popular 1960s icons to adorn its advertisements, along with clever headlines and visuals. Campbell's soup became "M'm, m'm, groovy!" and pop art found a place in advertising messages—and vice versa—as Andy Warhol brought commercial images to fine art with his Brillo pads and Campbell soup cans. The melding of art and commerce became legendary during the decade. The "new advertising" took its cue from the visual medium of television and the popular posters of the day, which featured large visuals and minimal copy for a dazzling, dramatic effect. Relying more on photography than illustration, print ads took on a realistic look, and television commercials gained sophistication as new editing techniques were mastered.

Advertising was gaining momentum, and the media praised the industry's creativity and humor. The 1960s are remembered for a number of these critically acclaimed campaigns. The trend-setting U.S. agency Doyle Dane Bernbach created perhaps one of the most famous campaigns in advertising history. Volkswagen hired the agency to promote its tiny Beetle in the United States at a time when Americans were mesmerized by large, tail-finned, super-powered automobiles. The Volkswagen could not hope to compete with these sleek vehicles, so DDB decided to capitalize on the car's "liabilities" and advertise it with honesty. DDB's headlines—"Lemon," "Ugly," and "Think small"—broke a time-honored "rule" in advertising by employing negativity to address a product's features. In the case of Volkswagen, that meant no frills, no glamour, no model changes, and very little horsepower. The effort's candor, in addition to its simplicity, humor, and a minimalist approach, made it one of the most popular campaigns during the decade. In 1999 *Advertising Age* named it the number one campaign of the 20th century.

Similarly, Wells, Rich, Greene's "The Disadvantages" campaign for Benson & Hedges 100s focused on a product gimmick—an extra-long cigarette. Rather than emphasizing the extra puffs a smoker got, the campaign humorously showed the number of ways a long cigarette could get in the way. The campaign ran successfully throughout the 1960s.

Other notable campaigns during the decade were characterized by catchy slogans, such as Avis's "We try harder," Esso's "Put a tiger in your tank," Foster Grant's "Who's that behind those Foster Grants?" Alka Seltzer's "I can't believe I ate the whole thing," Blackglama furs' "What becomes a legend most," and Wisk detergent's "Ring around the collar." Others were characterized by their impact, such as the 1964 "Daisy" TV spot for the Lyndon Johnson for President campaign, which showed a girl counting daisy petals while a voice-over intoned a countdown leading to the detonation of a nuclear bomb—the likely outcome, it was implied, if Senator Barry Goldwater were elected president.

Some campaigns became memorable for characters such as the Maytag repairman, the Pillsbury Doughboy, Ronald McDonald, and Charlie the Tuna. Others, such as a series of Canada Dry ads, were noteworthy for their visuals. Using effective layering of art, copy, and photography, these attention-getting ads also used clever headlines and confessional strategies. Presenting the drink as less than perfect, Canada Dry headlines read "Sure we could make it cheaper," or "We always said that nothing could compare with an ice-cold bottle of Canada Dry. We were wrong." The copy offered further explanation—and the sales pitch—while the ads appealed to consumers' sense of humor, candor, and irony.

The decade was also marked by its advertising greats, some with long histories in the industry. Preaching both the hard- and the soft-sell approach, David Ogilvy had done his defining work in the 1950s. But Ogilvy became the most famous man in advertising in October 1963 with the publication of his memoir *Confessions of an Advertising Man*, which sold a million copies and was translated into 14 languages. Ogilvy & Mather used the hugely influential book as the basis for a series of house ads that were quickly tacked onto many agency office walls. The book was

A concert promotion poster by artist Victor Moscoso typifies the revolution in art and graphic design set off by the counterculture of the 1960s.
© 1967 Neon Rose. Designer, Victor Moscoso.

also iconoclastic in that it spared neither Ogilvy nor his trade. Ogilvy's emphasis on ethics loosely associated him with others exposing questionable practices—environmentalist Rachel Carson, consumer advocate Ralph Nader, and muckraker Jessica Mitford, all of whom had successful books on the market. Ogilvy had said he regarded much of advertising as just plain stupid, an attitude that, coming from an insider, consumers found refreshing.

The Leo Burnett Company was another hot agency that made history during the 1960s with a number of innovative campaigns. Perhaps its most notable achievement was for Marlboro cigarettes. Although the western theme and the Marlboro cowboy had been launched in 1955, they reached a critical mass in the 1960s, and composer Elmer Bernstein's score for the movie *The Magnificent Seven* (1960) remained its theme music in countries where cigarette advertising was still permitted on radio and television.

Some believe the decade's most influential single figure was William Bernbach (named *Advertising Age*'s "Advertising Person of the Century" in 1999). Bernbach spoke to a new generation of consumers with a number of memorable campaigns during the 1960s, including Avis, Volkswagen, and Ohrbachs. He restructured Doyle Dane Bernbach around a partnership between copywriters and art directors, and the agency's revolutionary creative work challenged advertising rules while at the same time making industry history.

Another advertising superstar of the decade was Mary Wells Lawrence, who opened her agency Wells, Rich, Greene, Inc., in 1966 and quickly became one of the most influential women in advertising history. In 1969 she became the industry's highest-paid executive. Her Alka-Seltzer campaign, "No Matter What Shape Your Stomach's In," caught the public's eye with its humor, human-interest approach, and innovative style. Her sitcom-style Benson & Hedges commercials increased sales from 1.6 billion units in 1966 to 14.4 billion in 1970, and she brought Braniff International out of obscurity with clever and humorous spots themed "The end of the plain plane."

Other Changes

The decade saw the final deterioration of the agency–television network relationship, in which the advertiser had complete control over the programming environment for its ad messages and the network provided the airtime and physical facilities—a system that had supported network broadcasting since 1926. Nevertheless, throughout the 1950s, powerful advertisers and agencies resisted network efforts to take control of programming. By the 1960s, however, the costs of programming were becoming so great that few advertisers could shoulder such a burden alone. Shared sponsorships and alternate sponsorships became more common. By the end of the decade, participating sponsorship, in which national advertisers bought commercial slots from an inventory of network-supplied programming, was the norm.

The quiz show scandal of 1959, which centered on advertisers' efforts to rig the outcomes of big-money quiz programs, not only undermined the prestige and moral position of advertisers, it also brought the federal government into the picture. The networks exploited the weakness of the old advertiser-dominated system and argued that they, not advertisers, would be the most responsible custodians of the public interest. A few agencies remained active in program production. Procter & Gamble continued to hold on to several daytime soap operas and also financed the pilot of the successful *Dick Van Dyke Show* through Benton & Bowles and sponsored the show's first season on TV. For the most part, however, during the 1960s control of programming and scheduling shifted from the agencies to the networks.

While magazines lost advertising revenue to television, newspapers, relying less on national advertising, remained the dominant medium for most local advertisers, and the potentially large audiences for programs of recorded music continued to draw advertisers to radio. The oversize mass-audience magazines were the hardest hit by competition from television. The *Saturday Evening Post* ceased publication in 1969. (*Collier's* had published its final issue in 1956, and *Look* and *Life*, once the most widely read magazines, would succumb to the power of television in 1971 and 1972, respectively.) While advertisers generally withdrew from magazines with broad readership, they did use special interest publications to reach more narrowly defined audiences. Among the specialized magazines that emerged in the 1960s were regional and city magazines such as *New York, Texas Monthly,* and *Washingtonian*.

Changes in the manufacturing and distribution of mass-produced products also had an effect on advertising's task in the 1960s. Small independent retail stores were giving way to larger operations such as supermarkets, discount stores, and other self-service outlets, requiring a different type of promotion. The trend toward prepackaged products and self-service put the onus on advertising to promote specific brands and highlight their distinguishing features. Giving products a personality or "image" was rewarding if the image caught on, and many did. Avis became the underdog, Volkswagen the minimalist, and Esso the "tiger in your tank." The economies of scale in manufacturing and retailing meant an era of mergers and expansion, and the decade saw increasing numbers of companies, many of them U.S.-based, becoming international in scope. The decade saw the growth of franchises and retail chains and, of course, concentration of ownership. By 1963, for example, regional chains such as A&P and Safeway controlled nearly half of all retail food sales.

Advertising agencies expanded operations as well, dealing with different types of clients and facing new marketing challenges. Mergers and acquisitions transformed agency identities, and a number of agencies went public. The first Madison Avenue agency to do so was Papert, Koenig, Lois, Inc. (PKL), in 1962, but not without industry criticism. At the time PKL was accused of compromising the concept of agency independence and integrity. But other agencies soon followed, and the initial public offering, or IPO, became an industry trend. Although not known at the time, this financial arrangement would later make some of the top agencies vulnerable to hostile takeovers at the height of their success. In fact, much of the growth in the advertising industry was driven by acquisitions. Marion Harper masterminded the financial growth of McCann-Erickson during the decade partly through the acquisition of other agencies. His parent company, Interpublic, held a number of agencies functioning independently, thereby eliminating any problems with client conflict of interest.

Toward the end of the decade, with an economic recession looming, clients were demanding that advertising justify its costs. In the agencies, accountants and business administrators were finding their way into positions once held by those from the creative side of the business. Market research again assumed a priority, edging out creativity as the hoped-for solution to the economic slowdown. Some clients canceled advertising, while others met their promotional needs in-house. The recession and a trend toward conservatism marked the end of a decade noted for its unprecedented creative surges in both advertising and culture as a whole.

While the major established agencies of the decade prospered, new agencies were founded and new reputations made. Jack Tinker, Mary Wells, Jerry Della Femina, Jay Chiat, Julian Koenig, Eugene Case, Helmut Krone, and Carl Ally were among the individuals advertising people would be talking about for years to come. Wells, Rich, Greene gained fame for its award-winning Benson & Hedges campaign; Jack Tinker & Partners added its creative genius to the Alka-Seltzer ads; PKL set a creative precedent with the Wolfschmidt Vodka campaign; Carl Ally put Hertz and Volvo in the limelight; and Chiat/Day, established in California in 1968, would become one of the most successful agencies of the 20th century.

Among the prominent advertising-related figures whose obituaries appeared during the 1960s were Vincent Riggio, former American Tobacco president, whose differences with Foote, Cone & Belding (FCB) in 1948 had precipitated the largest account resignation in history to date by an agency, and Walter Dorwin Teague, pioneer industrial designer, both in 1960. Arthur Pinkham, grandson of Lydia Pinkham and president of the company she founded; Masius & Fergusson founder Leonard M. Masius (later of D'Arcy-MacManus & Masius); and agency founder Duane Jones, all died in 1961. BBDO founder Roy Durstine and former J. Walter Thompson CEO Stanley Resor died in 1962. Others who died during the decade included pioneering copywriter Helen Lansdowne Resor; Cunningham & Walsh founder Frederick H. Walsh; Mather & Crowther, Ltd., President Francis F. Ogilvy (brother of David Ogilvy); Austin Croom-Johnson, author of the "Pepsi Cola Hits the Spot" jingle; pioneer copywriter Earnest Elmo Calkins; MacManus, John & Adams founder W.A.P. John; Alex Osborn and Bruce Barton, the surviving founders of BBDO; and Kenyon & Eckhardt Chairman Thomas Brophy.

HAZEL G. WARLAUMONT

See also color plate in this volume

Further Reading

Dobrow, Larry, *When Advertising Tried Harder: The Sixties, the Golden Age of American Advertising*, New York: Friendly Press, 1984

Glatzer, Robert, *The New Advertising: The Great Campaigns from Avis to Volkswagen*, New York: Citadel, 1970

Iams, Jack, "Advertising's Creative Revolution," *Newsweek* (18 August 1969)

Nevett, T.R., *Advertising in Britain*, London: Heinemann, 1982

Rutherford, Paul, *The New Icons? The Art of Television Advertising*, Toronto and Buffalo, New York: University of Toronto Press, 1994

History: 1970s

Total U.S. advertising agency billings increased substantially in the 1970s but not by record multiples. The advent of television, for example, had carried total U.S. billings from $1.3 billion in 1950 to $6 billion in 1960, an increase of nearly 500 percent. Between 1960 and 1970, however, only about $4.5 billion was added to that total, for a growth rate well under 100 percent for the decade.

The 1970s began on an even less promising note. In the midst of a minor recession, ad billings were flat in the first year of the decade, then took off slowly, growing in progressively larger increments after 1976, the year the J. Walter Thompson Company (JWT) became the first agency in history to break the billion-dollar mark in worldwide volume. By 1979 total U.S. industry billings had nearly tripled for the decade. (See Table 1.)

The 1970s presented U.S. manufacturers with some real challenges. In electronics—especially in television and radio sets and video cassettes—the Japanese practically swept U.S. manufacturers from the marketplace. The gasoline shortages that surfaced starting in the fall of 1973 had an enormous impact on all segments of the economy, especially the automobile industry. Americans paid more for necessary items such as gasoline, and foreign automobile manufacturers pressured U.S. carmakers to rethink their products.

Political events of the 1970s also contributed to the unrest of the decade. The Watergate scandal and subsequent resignation of President Richard M. Nixon, as well as the divisiveness caused by the war in Vietnam, resulted in a growing lack of support for and suspicion of the government. Inflation, the apparent influence of

Table 1.   U.S. Ad Billings in the 1970s.

Year	Total Billings (billions)
1970	$10.58
1971	$10.5
1972	$11.3
1973	$12.9
1974	$13.6
1975	$14.6
1976	$17.2
1977	$19.4
1978	$23.3
1979	$27.9

Source: Advertising Age.

foreign business, and the visible success of foreign manufacturers in winning large portions of the American market further eroded faith in both government and business. Moreover, a perceived U.S. vulnerability to foreign oil imports also caused concern.

In spite of an economy slowed by economic pressures and political unrest, by the middle of the decade billings at the top agencies and total advertising expenditures increased faster than the gross national product (GNP), inflation, or any other economic indicators. (See Table 2.)

It was reported by the American Association of Advertising Agencies (AAAA) that during the 1970s an average American consumer was exposed to 1,600 ads per day, although it was acknowledged that fewer than 80 ads were consciously noticed, and only 12 provoked some type of reaction. Advertising was an integral part of American culture. As historian Daniel J. Boorstin wrote in 1974, "While advertising was not, of course, a modern invention, the American elaboration and diffusion of advertising, and its central place in the consciousness of the community, were new. The proportion of the national ingenuity, energy, and resources that went into advertising was unprecedented." Boorstin called advertising the most characteristic form of American literature.

By the beginning of the 1970s, television viewing had emerged as a core experience of American culture. The growing trend toward the use of television as a preferred ad medium continued throughout the decade. In 1976, with more than 69 million U.S.

Table 2.   Leading U.S. Agencies of the 1970s.

Agency	Total Billings (millions)		
	1970	1975	1977
J. Walter Thompson Company	$438.0	$432.8	$619.5
Young & Rubicam, Inc.	$366.4	$476.6	$619.0
Batten Barton Durstine & Osborn	$324.4	$369.9	$456.5
Leo Burnett Company, Inc.	$283.6	$400.0	$575.0
Ted Bates & Company	$254.0	$280.2	$373.3

homes containing at least one TV set and viewing-per-home topping six hours per day, advertiser investment reached nearly $5.9 billion.

Clients of the 1970s looked for accountability and efficiency in their advertising agencies, and campaigns used "positioning" as a more scientific technique for placing ads in the minds of consumers. And throughout the advertising industry the use of computer technology grew, reflecting a rediscovery of and growing emphasis on "empirical advertising"—research and fact-based marketing—during the decade. This practice was a reaction to the "creative revolution" of the 1960s and indicated a marked shift to a preference for discipline and accountability.

At least three intense pressures challenged the advertising business during the 1970s. First, the business was experiencing a threat from growing government regulation early in the decade. Second, the public was increasingly suspicious of and disenchanted with advertising practices. And third, advertising agencies were making increased efforts to increase diversity within their own professional ranks and among the population portrayed in the advertisements themselves.

In addition to the expanded use of television as an advertising medium, a second practice distinguished the advertising business in the 1970s. In contrast to the "product era" of the 1950s and the "image/impression era" of the 1960s, "positioning" emerged as a primary advertising strategy of the 1970s. In a media-oriented culture, manufacturers found it important to "position" a product in the public's mind, both within the context of its own merits and strengths and in relation to its competitors. Therefore, the practice of comparative advertising flourished. Seven-Up's "Un-Cola" campaign took aim at Coca-Cola and doubled Seven-Up's sales, for example. And the cola manufacturers—Pepsi and Coca-Cola—went head-on with Coke's "It's the real thing" campaign, and later with Pepsi's hidden cameras that recorded blind taste tests against Coke, increasing Pepsi's market share in a year. The subsequent cola price war resulted in the temporary reformulation of Coke. Tylenol's "for the millions who should not take aspirin" campaign positioned the product among its competitors and helped it to become the best-selling nonaspirin pain reliever on the market. Both advertisers and the public seemed to respond to comparative advertising. Some campaigns directly named competitors, while others merely alluded to them. For example, a campaign for Scotti Automobile Mufflers explicitly scoffed at "the Midas touch," pointing out that Midas's famous lifetime replacement muffler guarantee did not include other parts of the exhaust system installed by the company, whereas Scotti promised that guaranteed customers could get off "Scott free." In a similar fashion, a Dictaphone commercial proclaimed, "Bad news for IBM."

Industry code review boards and federal government officials monitored this practice carefully, often banning unclear, exaggerated, and untrue claims. Moreover, the "watchdogs" often discouraged disparaging comments about competitors. An advertiser could claim that "our product is better than their product" but not that "their product is worse than our product." Nonetheless, the practice of positioning expanded in use. Even the tenacious regulator of advertising, the Federal Trade Commission (FTC), allowed light-beer manufacturers to compare the calorie counts of products. "Light" had become the magic word in beer, and "diet" the secret of soft drink sales during the decade, according to *Advertising Age*.

These strategic approaches and the trends toward increased television advertising, positioning, and comparative advertising were accompanied by four distinctive management practices during the decade. First, many large agencies "went public"—that is, they converted their proprietorship into shares that were traded on the stock market. Some agencies even diversified into auxiliary businesses to generate increased profits for principals and stockholders. Doyle Dane Bernbach, for example, went into the sailboat business.

Second, in addition to innovative efforts to raise money, the understanding of and use of computers increased, revolutionizing many facets of the advertising industry's day-to-day operations. Empirical methods for accounting, billing, and reporting became regular tools of the business and provided ad executives with detailed data and analyses necessary for making sound decisions. In addition to these "clerical" functions, the new technology provided advertisers with information about market segmentation, product proliferation, automated distribution, demographics, and profits. The computer was used to analyze consumers, to calculate cost efficiencies in relation to client objectives, and to make projections.

Third, advertising management was plagued by the fluidity of client relationships. For a variety of economic reasons—including the Vietnam War and volatile oil prices—the U.S. economy was in recession at the beginning of the decade, and most large advertising agencies suffered losses in total domestic billings (a loss of $15 million in U.S. billings in 1971 alone, for example). For many firms the financial loss was aggravated by a loss of clients to other firms. Observing their declining profit margins, many clients broke long-standing relationships with ad agencies. American Motors abandoned Wells, Rich, Greene in 1972 after becoming concerned about declining sales, taking its $22 million worth of business to Cunningham & Walsh. Lever Brothers, Whirlpool, Sara Lee, Quaker Oats, and others left often long-standing relationships, resulting in a total account loss of about $33 million in 1972 to various agencies. And in 1973, a decline in U.S. billings of nearly $11 million continued the trend, although not as precipitously. By various accounts, 20 percent to 25 percent of all advertising accounts in the nation moved from one agency to another during the decade.

Fourth, a number of mergers occurred. Large advertising agencies merged with smaller agencies in order to keep their business volume high. As a representative of one agency said, "In our business perception is everything; and we don't need to be perceived as losing, as failing." One of the decade's largest domestic mergers brought together MacManus, John & Adams and D'Arcy Advertising. A second merger, finalized in 1976, created D'Arcy-McManus & Masius, Inc. Other agencies accelerated the merger trend. Interpublic bought Campbell-Ewald (1972); Ogilvy & Mather purchased Scali, McCabe, Sloves (1976), one of the hottest new agencies in the 1970s. Ted Bates & Company bought out

The 1970s saw a revival of fact-based comparative advertising techniques, as exemplified by this 1972 ad for the Dictaphone Thought Tank dictating machine.

Campbell-Mithun (1979), and the three largest public relations firms were absorbed by JWT, Young & Rubicam, and Foote, Cone & Belding. By the end of the 1970s no major independent U.S. agencies remained on the West Coast.

American ad agencies also looked overseas for new markets and growth. Needham, Harper & Steers became the North American component in the Benson, Needham, Univas firm, along with S.H. Benson of London and Univas/Havas Conseil of Paris. SSC&B acquired 49 percent interest in Lintas, Europe's largest agency. Other agencies strengthening their global position included the Leo Burnett Company; Ketchum, MacLeod & Grove; and Batten Barton Durstine & Osborn.

Several social issues plagued the advertising business and threatened to weaken it. The early years of the decade brought an increased threat of government regulation, triggered largely by concerns from many quarters—parents, legislators, consumer groups—that advertising was capitalizing on the inability of children to distinguish between commercials and programs. TV advertisers were spending millions of dollars annually pitching

For your child! The most marvelous, expensive, crazy (like a fox) Christmas gift of all time. A <u>personal</u> computer.

Not just any computer. The Radio Shack TRS-80 system that teaches, remembers, plays, displays, and makes it possible for kids to understand the problems and delights of today's electronic world.

An educator thanks us "for making possible the tapping of human innovation and creativity on an unprecedented scale."

A father writes to tell us his investment in a TRS-80 is "one of the most significant in value to our family and to the future education of our child that we have ever seen."

Before this year our "tomorrow machine" would not have been available at an affordable price or in a convenient size. Now it is, thanks to Radio Shack's famous breakthrough design. For the price of a good camera you get it all — computer with typewriter keyboard, 12" video screen, cassette recorder, 232-page beginner's manual.

For the parent who cares enough to invest $599 in a child's tomorrow, Radio Shack and its participating dealers have a Christmas gift of meaningful and lasting significance. And your family will benefit beyond your fondest dreams. And that's a promise!

232-page manual makes it easy to start with no computer experience

Radio Shack®
The biggest name in little computers™

A Division of Tandy Corporation   Fort Worth, Texas 76102

Radio Shack was one of the first marketers to realize the potential of the "personal" computer, as seen in this 1978 ad.
Radio Shack Corporation.

products to children. Empirical research suggested that children under the age of eight generally could not distinguish between a product commercial and the main program fare. The data suggested this remained true until about the sixth grade. Public con-

cern led a group of women in Boston, Massachusetts, to form Action for Children's Television (ACT). The group won some important skirmishes by forcing the withdrawal of vitamin ads appealing to children, reducing commercials during weekend children's programs, and garnering support to ban stars from making pitches to children. ACT won other battles as well, including the provision for public service spots about good nutrition habits and the requirement that advertisers portray the size and speed of toys accurately and in some "meaningful and understandable" manner for children.

No discussion of the 1970s would be complete without noting another criticism of the advertising business that caught the attention and interest of a great many people—in the charge by journalism professor Wilson Bryan Key that Madison Avenue was engaging in subliminal sexual manipulation of the buying public. Specifically, Key charged that "sexual embedding"—placing the word "sex" somewhere in an ad—was practiced in political campaigns, on magazine covers, and even in the promotion of Ritz crackers.

Such concerns as those expressed by ACT and Key resonated with a public growing increasingly suspicious and skeptical of advertising. A 1976 Gallup Poll asked Americans to rate the honesty and ethical standards of those engaged in 11 fields of work. The professional at the bottom of the list—dead last—was the advertising executive. It is not surprising that new and intense regulation ensued through the FTC and the industry's own National Advertising Review Board (NARB), holding the advertising business to unprecedented standards of accuracy, honesty, and disclosure. This led to another distinctive quality of the business during this decade, the practice of "corrective advertising." The FTC, for example, ordered the manufacturer of Listerine to spend $10 million to correct its claim that Listerine prevented colds or sore throats and required the makers of Anacin to spend $24 million on ads explaining that the product did not relieve tension, as previously claimed. The use of corrective advertising had waned by the late 1970s, however, within the general context of deregulation.

The move to deregulate was given landmark expression in 1976 when the U.S. Supreme Court extended First Amendment protection to commercial speech. Whereas the amendment had long been applied to matters of defamation, privacy, and prior restraint, the Supreme Court gave advertising legal standing and protection.

And finally, reflecting a trend that grew out of the 1960s in American culture to demonstrate greater sensitivity to gender differences and ethnic minorities, the advertising business in the 1970s worked to improve diversity in its advertisements and within its own ranks. Some progress was made with ad content. Whereas blacks appeared in only 5 percent of all TV ads in 1967, for example, this number grew to 13 percent in 1976, reflecting a concerted and publicly discussed effort to have advertising more accurately reflect the diversity within American culture. Progress was also made in the employment arena. Between 1970 and 1975 minority employment at the two dozen largest agencies rose from 8.9 percent to about 10 percent overall. It was noted, however, that at mid- and top-management levels, the percentage was lower and actually decreasing. A number of individuals pursued employment discrimination suits against agencies during the 1970s, making it a most litigious period for the industry. Members of minorities also launched a number of agencies during the decade, but for a variety of reasons, these firms were generally short-lived. Women seemed to be more successful than ethnic minorities at improving their lot within the industry, some even reaching the upper ranks.

Thus, the 1970s can be characterized as a decade of change for American culture generally and for the advertising business in particular. During this decade of political and economic uncertainty, the ad industry experienced shifts socially—with changes in infrastructure created by mergers and acquisitions and with expanded international activities and markets. The industry also experienced changes technologically with enhanced computer applications for clerical as well as market diagnostic tasks and with the growing use of television as a preferred advertising medium. Cultural changes were also evident. The profession was subject to growing criticism of its motives and practices. It was pressured to more accurately reflect the multicultural nature of American society and to assume a responsible role in that society.

J. DOUGLAS TARPLEY

See also Children: Targets of Advertising; Comparative Advertising; Corrective Advertising; Minorities: Employment in the Advertising Industry; Minorities: Representations in Advertising; Subliminal Advertising; *and color plate in this volume*

Further Reading

Boorstin, Daniel G., "Advertising and American Civilization," in *Advertising and Society*, edited by Yale Brozen, New York: New York University Press, 1974

Buxton, Edward, *Promise Them Anything: The Inside Story of the Madison Avenue Power Struggle*, New York: Stein and Day, 1972

Dyer, Gillian, *Advertising as Communication*, London and New York: Methuen, 1982

Price, Jonathan, *The Best Thing on TV: Commercials*, New York: Viking, 1978

Ries, Al, and Jack Trout, *Positioning: The Battle for Your Mind*, New York: McGraw-Hill, 1981

History: 1980s

In the 1980s, as manufacturers produced goods and services for an affluent, growing American population, advertising expanded. Under the administration of President Ronald Reagan, a decade of deregulation, spending, and affluence was launched, and advertising continued to be a prominent source of support for industry and the mass media.

Approximately $130 billion was being spent annually on advertising by the end of the decade. Newspapers accounted for the biggest share of advertising revenue with 25 percent, followed by television with 22 percent, direct mail with 18 percent, radio with 7 percent, magazines with 8 percent, and outdoor advertising, 1 percent. Miscellaneous venues constituted the balance. At the end of the 1980s, approximately $32 billion was spent annually on newspaper ads, $28 billion on television ads, and about $23 billion on direct advertising.

A significant change occurred in the advertising industry during the decade: newspaper advertising expenditures dropped nearly 4 percent, magazine ad spending dropped a little over 3 percent, and radio spending only very slightly. Television, however, increased nearly 5 percent and direct mail just over 3 percent. According to *Advertising Age,* there was a total work force of approximately 125,000 advertising professionals in the early 1980s.

Advertising of the 1980s was marked by several distinguishing qualities and trends. The most noteworthy were the result of technological innovations. Specifically, cable television permanently changed Americans' television viewing habits. Further, TV viewers became enamored of two other items of new technology—the videotape recorder and the remote control, both of which created enormous new challenges for the advertising business. As television viewing shifted to include independent and cable fare, advertising revenue derived from TV continued to grow at the expense of other media.

Cultural and social factors linked with these technological advances posed several additional challenges to the advertising industry. Ad agencies shifted away from formulaic approaches, placing a renewed emphasis on creativity, much like that in the "creative revolution" of the 1960s. This revival was a backlash against the factual and more rigid style of advertising of the 1970s and surfaced slowly in the mid-1980s.

The infrastructure of the advertising industry also changed, as ad agencies, flush with funds, surveyed the horizon for merger or acquisition candidates. Driven by a desire to increase profitability and fueled by their own profits, several major advertising agencies evolved into a few international mega-agencies. This development, in turn, had the curious effect of spawning numerous smaller agencies around the country, and these gave consumers some of the most memorable commercials of the decade. With a growing international focus, the advertising agencies ushered in another unique quality of the decade. Whereas advertising theory and practices had been essentially a U.S. phenomenon, innovations now flowed into America from foreign shores.

Economic factors, too, shaped the business. The growing international competition for U.S. dollars pressured domestic manufacturers and influenced advertising strategies, themes, and messages. The stock market crash of 1987 had an influence on the industry as well. And because all media and media-support agencies of advertising and public relations exist as part of a social system, they influence and, in turn, are influenced by society, culture, and technology. The decade of the 1980s was no exception in this respect.

"Decade of the Deal"

Affluence, improved transportation, and changes in mass communication during the 1980s inspired the development of extremely large advertising agencies with branches throughout the world. In 1982 and 1983, for example, eight sizable agencies were bought by larger ones, with one Los Angeles, California, agency selling for $22 million and another for $57 million. Saatchi & Saatchi bought McCaffrey & McCall for $15 million, and the Interpublic Group of Companies bought Dailey & Associates for $22 million.

By the end of the decade agencies once considered secure were also changing hands. In 1987 Martin Sorrell's WPP Group acquired the J. Walter Thompson Company (JWT) for $566 million. Although it was not a hostile takeover, the partners of Lord, Geller, Federico, Einstein, Inc., itself a JWT acquisition, quit in protest, resulting in a court battle that cost them $7 million. Two years later the Ogilvy Group—which included Ogilvy & Mather—followed JWT and was acquired by WPP in a very bitter hostile takeover (the first in advertising history), in which David Ogilvy publicly characterized Sorrell as "an odious little shit." Saatchi went on to absorb Dancer, Fitzgerald, Sample and Backer & Spielvogel, Inc., and finally Ted Bates & Company in a deal that also included Bates subsidiaries Campbell-Mithun and William Esty. The Bates acquisition in 1986 was followed one week later by the creation of Omnicom, a triad that merged Needham, Harper & Steers Advertising and Doyle Dane Bernbach into DDB Needham and maintained Batten Barton Durstine & Osborn (BBDO), the third agency in the deal, under its own name. Of the top 15 U.S. agencies at the start of the decade, only four survived the 1980s with their ownership intact: the Leo Burnett Company, Young & Rubicam (Y&R), McCann-Erickson, and Grey Advertising Agency.

The "decade of the deal," as *Advertising Age* called it, affected advertisers as much as agencies. Financiers Kohlberg Kravis Roberts & Company scored the greatest leveraged buyout of the decade with its purchase of Nabisco for $25 billion, a deal that also included Standard Brands, which Nabisco had already absorbed. Philip Morris bought Kraft, Kodak bought Sterling Drug, and Grand Metropolitan of England bought Pillsbury. Companies such as the grocery retailer Kroger Foods fought the takeovers but found them expensive, and much of the cost was reflected in diminished ad spending. Of the 100 largest advertisers in 1980, only a third were still independent by 1990.

Agency consolidations were driven mostly by three factors. First, agencies that were bringing in huge profits had money to spend on acquisitions and looked for other profitable operations. Second, banks and other lending institutions were willing to finance highly leveraged acquisitions. Third, agencies were looking for ways to increase profitability. It is important to note that this buying "binge" came to a halt with the recession that developed late in the decade.

The mega-agencies expanded their international billing during the decade. The top ten agencies alone, for example, placed more than $3.3 billion annually in international advertising. The top ten U.S. advertising agencies collected nearly half of the world's advertising revenue. Several companies long a part of the international field—such as Coca-Cola, IBM, General Motors, Monsanto, and McDonald's—were joined by countless others seeking their share of the world market as they made international advertising part of their general advertising strategy. Cable television contributed to the internationalization of advertising. CNN sold advertising worldwide, offering companies the ability to advertise their products to a worldwide audience. Overall, during the decade, billings outside the United States commanded an increasing share of the U.S. agencies' business.

Effects of Technology

In addition to the social changes in advertising, the industry experienced a dramatic metamorphosis as a result of the innovations in mass media technology. Television, which had grown in importance to advertising since the 1950s, changed dramatically during the decade of the 1980s, when a combination of technological advances resulted in a decline in the influence of the traditional television networks. Specifically, the introduction and explosive growth of cable television and the widespread use of the home videocassette recorder (VCR) and remote control devices revolutionized TV viewing and advertising.

Cable television had a profound impact in reshaping the television industry during the decade. Just ten years earlier, a station broadcasting news throughout the day would have been unthinkable, as would one airing music videos. The public was at first indifferent to, then curious about, new modes of communication for information and entertainment. Finally, these new media became indispensable. Moreover, as cable channels prospered—to the surprise of many people—they undermined the influence of traditional broadcast networks. By the early 1990s the once-dominant major broadcast networks had seen their portion of the evening TV audience slip to less than 60 percent. *Advertising Age* reported that whereas ABC, NBC, and CBS each claimed about 19 percent of the television audience, "independent" television and cable television captured more than 40 percent. The balance of power shifted away from the networks; the television viewing habits of Americans changed, and so did advertising.

The shift to cable TV also created an expectation by viewers that they could watch whatever they wanted. This concept was furthered by another piece of technology that transformed the television viewing experience: the VCR. It allowed viewers to

The deadpan "Cheer man" and his silent demonstrations of the cleaning power of Cheer detergent were the centerpiece of a memorable ad campaign of the 1980s.
Courtesy of The Procter & Gamble Company.

manage, organize, and control the programs available to them on the myriad of channels. They could videotape and view whenever they preferred any number of programs—sports, children's shows, religious fare, news, cartoons.

Not only did VCRs and the increased number of channels available through cable television affect the television medium in the 1980s, but remote control allowed television viewers to "zip" and "zap" their way through television commercials. The term *zipping* was coined to describe the practice of using the remote control to change channels during commercials. Viewers could also "zap" commercials out of recorded programs by fast-forwarding through them, thus ignoring advertising messages created with the hope of reaching potential consumers. Eventually, certain VCRs were marketed that could be programmed to automatically skip commercials, compounding the problem for advertisers.

Technology also provided benefits to the ad industry. Continuing a trend begun before the 1980s, computer technology helped the business side of ad agency operations, improving accounting and enhancing research efforts. Expanding applications of computer technology and computerized data services opened new avenues for advertising, which grew through the 1990s with use of the World Wide Web.

A new form of electronic advertising was developed in the 1980s: direct-response home shopping services. Cable networks—such as the Home Shopping Network and QVC—sold discounted goods directly to viewer-consumers, who called in orders to telephone operators. Instead of purchasing airtime for advertising from cable operators, home-shopping networks paid cable operators a percentage of the profits from sales generated in their viewing area. This form of direct selling was poised to take on new dimensions as interactive TV and virtual-reality technologies found their niche in the marketplace.

Another new advertising vehicle was developed—the infomercial—which became one of the fastest growth areas of television advertising. These 30-minute commercials often featured celebrities and appeared to be news or information programs, when in reality they were promotional pitches for all types of products, from kitchen gadgets and exercise machines to money-making and investment programs. In 1988 the infomercial industry was a $350 million business, expanding to more than $4.5 billion over the next ten years.

In an effort to maximize profits and enhance ad effectiveness, agencies made a shift in the mid-1980s to 15-second TV spots, moving away from the earlier 30-second standard established in the 1970s. The new "15s" theoretically allowed advertisers to double the number of ads run and reduce the cost per ad, maintaining and often increasing revenue levels. These shorter spots posed a new creative challenge to the industry, which had to pack incentive to purchase and product information into a shorter message.

"Neotraditional" advertising also took root in the 1980s. Psychographic research, a growing practice for advertisers during the decade, focused specifically on values and lifestyles. While such research existed prior to the 1980s, studies conducted during this decade revealed that viewer-consumers were blending the "liberal" values of the 1960s with more traditional values, a trend labeled "neotraditionalism." For example, research showed that consumers in 1985 were buying sport-utility vehicles (SUVs) such as the Jeep Cherokee and using them in much the same way as their parents had bought and used station wagons.

Advertisers also began to explore "alternative" environments such as movie theaters. Although long-established in Europe, the practice did not go over well with U.S. audiences. For example, the traditionally untapped audience of moviegoers was targeted in the 1980s by such advertisers as Coca-Cola, which began to run advertisements before the previews preceding the feature film. A 1988 survey concluded that one-third of the audiences were opposed to the advertising, one-third in favor of it, and one-third neutral. Within ten years, however, it was reported that two-thirds to three-quarters of moviegoers liked the commercials. Advertisers experimented with the length of these ads, too, borrowing from their European counterparts to increase the advertising time.

Innovations

One kind of advertisement that took a twist in the 1980s was the traditional "slice-of-life" ad. Advertisers had used this technique for television for years, creating brief stories in which a product appeared as an element in the plot line. For example, a young boy moved to a new area and was surrounded by new faces but quickly found that they all shared a universal experience: McDonald's fast-food. Although fear had always been used as an emotional appeal in advertising, advertisements in the 1980s embraced it directly and blatantly. Consumers saw men afraid they would lose their jobs because they had purchased the "wrong" computer hardware or software for the work environment. Telecommunications companies used similar tactics, with ads featuring business owners who were losing customers and business because of ineffective telephone systems.

The threats posed by "zipping" and "zapping" were credited with gradual and continual improvements in the quality of TV commercials during the decade. At the very least, they became more interesting and entertaining for the audience. If the ads were to be effective, it was argued, they had to be compelling. Some experts have noted, however, that this increased attention to creativity and entertainment fueled the trend toward a decline in the amount and nature of product information in television commercials.

Noteworthy Advertisements

Several specific advertisements of the decade are noteworthy. Coca-Cola introduced its Polar Bears, using computer-animated imagery not seen before in TV commercials. The Coca-Cola Polar Bears became part of the company's "Always" campaign, which also introduced a notable jingle. Not to be outdone, Pepsi-Cola changed its slogan in the 1980s from "Pepsi generation" to "Choice of a new generation" with the help of BBDO and contracted with music icon Michael Jackson in one of the largest celebrity endorsement agreements in the history of American advertising.

Other popular and memorable commercials from the decade include "Lunch Box," for the California Raisin Advisory Board, in which hip clay animation raisins wearing sunglasses shuffled to the 1960s hit tune "I Heard It Through the Grapevine." Foote, Cone & Belding was the ad agency. Memorable as well was the

It sounds like it weighs a ton.

**The Sony Walkman.
Our smallest stereo cassette player.**

Sony has long been famous for reducing size and increasing performance. This time we have outdone ourselves. The Walkman produces such a big, rich sound it can only be compared to a very elaborate and expensive component stereo system. Yet, it's so small you can take it anywhere you go.

There is really no way to convey the remarkable sound quality of this little machine. You've got to hear it.

If you are like most people, when you put on the incredibly efficient headphones, you will shake your head in amazement and then ask, "How can I get one?"

And there has never been a better way to make bike riding, roller-skating, skiing, or just taking a walk more fun. Because there's no easier way to take your music along for the ride.

The Walkman comes with featherweight (1.4 oz.) stereo headphones, carrying case, and an extra jack for a second set of headphones. And an exclusive Hot-Line button that lets you carry on a conversation or sing along over the music.

Stop by a Sony dealer and hear one for yourself. Your eyes won't believe your ears. Because nothing this small ever sounded this big.

SONY
THE ONE AND ONLY

Introduced nationally in the United States in 1980, the Sony Walkman personal stereo went on to become one of the most successful products of the decade.
Courtesy of Sony Electronics, Inc.

Cheer commercial in which the silent deadpan presenter smudged a handkerchief and put it in a cocktail shaker with water, ice, and a dash of the detergent. With an opera aria as background music, viewers saw that the hankie, of course, was spotless when pulled from the shaker. The Energizer Bunny, ranked among the top icons in advertising history by *Advertising Age,* was also introduced in the 1980s. The commercials (from Chiat/Day) were called the "ultimate product demo" because they showed the product's unique selling proposition—long-lived batteries—in an inventive, fresh way. The Bunny appeared in more than 125 spots in English and Spanish, with new commercials debuting annually.

Perhaps one of the best commercials—and marketing strategies—of all time was the Orwellian Apple Computer advertisement entitled "1984," which launched the Macintosh revolution. The commercial broadly suggested that Big Brother and IBM were one and the same. The one-time showing of the commercial during the 1984 Super Bowl became a watershed of American advertising. That same year, a senior citizen named Clara Peller became a star after she appeared in a now-classic Wendy' s commercial ("Where's the beef?"), produced by Dancer, Fitzgerald, Sample and directed by Joe Sedelmaier. Also that year, JWT introduced "Herb," a man who had never tried a Whopper, for Burger King. Viewers were urged to be on the lookout for Herb in Burger King outlets, but the campaign was less than successful and was dropped four months later. In reaction to the inroads that foreign automakers were making on the U.S. market during the decade owing to the perception that foreign cars were of better quality than their American counterparts, U.S. advertisers responded with increasing defensiveness. Ads told the American people, "At Ford quality is job one" and "GM puts quality on the road."

Politics, Critics, Milestones

Among the most effective ads of the decade were some for political candidates. No discussion of advertising in the 1980s would be complete without noting the high priority placed on television advertising by the reelection campaign of President Ronald Reagan. The Reagan "feel good" spot for the 1984 campaign included a number of patriotic vignettes on the theme "It's morning again in America" and marked an imaginative use of political advertising. But the use of "political advertising" went beyond the direct advertisement. In 1984, as historians have noted, Reagan took full advantage of the media in order to project his "presidential image." He was often called a master communicator who understood the power of the media to inform and persuade. In a successful effort to influence—some critics say to control—the media, Reagan dramatically altered the traditional relationship of the press and politics. He and his aides staged news events for maximum press coverage, timed announcements to be seen by large television audiences, and demonstrated an understanding of the power of visual media at a time when television was the dominant means by which the U.S. public received information.

The 1980s were marked by some serious criticism and challenges for the advertising industry. For example, long-held assumptions about advertising's effectiveness were challenged by

Gerald Tellis, who put together a sophisticated statistical model and concluded that people are relatively unmoved by television advertisements in making brand choices, especially with regard to everyday products. His 1983–84 examination of consumer purchasing patterns generated discussion and concern. The research continued into the 1990s.

During the 1980s advertisers became increasingly concerned about the loss of control over media and audiences. They were concerned with the "empowerment" extended to audiences, resulting from such "anti-advertising devices" as the remote control. They also grew concerned about "ad clutter," which developed when media outlets were permitted to carry more advertising per half-hour unit.

Although advertisers' strategies and techniques reflected their perceived loss of traditional audience and media control, they enjoyed a newfound freedom in at least one other significant area—government control. Government deregulation under President Reagan ushered in a philosophy of "less government" and more free marketplace decision-making and autonomy. During Reagan's presidency a political and economic environment was created that allowed for mergers and acquisitions and also tolerated tremendous media corporate growth in the decade. General Electric was allowed to purchase RCA, which owned NBC, in 1986. In 1989 Time bought Warner Communications, Inc., and formed Time-Warner, Inc., bringing under a single corporate umbrella an empire consisting of magazines, motion picture and television production companies, cable TV networks, book publishers, record companies, and a major comic book company.

Other significant milestones of the 1980s include the introduction of Rely tampons by the Procter & Gamble Company in May 1980 and the withdrawal of the product four months later when the U.S. Centers for Disease Control linked it to toxic shock syndrome. Two years later Tylenol capsules were pulled from shelves after an incidence of product tampering that resulted in seven deaths. The decade saw the sudden rise of blue jeans into the realm of high fashion with such brands as Sergio Valente, Bon Jour, Calvin Klein, Gloria Vanderbilt, and Jordache. Hershey's Reese's Pieces saw sales leap 70 percent in 1982 after its exposure in the movie *E.T. The Extra-Terrestrial.* Caffeine-free soft drinks were introduced in 1983, and AT&T divested itself of its local phone companies, which became a series of seven independent regional companies. ACNeilsen Corporation was sold to Dun & Bradstreet Corporation in 1984, and Nike signed Chicago Bulls rookie Michael Jordan in a deal said to cover five years at $2.5 million. In response to the AIDS epidemic, magazines such as *Bride's, Family Circle, Parents,* and *Vogue* began accepting ads for condoms in 1986.

The Cosby Show commanded a record $400,000 for a 30-second advertising spot in 1986. Oat bran became a sensation in 1989 when research suggested it might help reduce cholesterol. Kellogg, General Mills, Quaker, Nabisco, Post, and even Mrs. Field's competed for their share of the oat bran market. Several people who had made an impact on advertising died in the 1980s: Colonel Harland Sanders, founder of Kentucky Fried Chicken (1980); DeWitt Wallace, founder of *Reader's Digest* (1981); William Bernbach, founder of Doyle Dane Bernbach (1982); Rosser Reeves, former chairman of Ted Bates (1984); and Jack Tinker, the creative innovator at McCann Erickson (1985).

J. Douglas Tarpley

See also color plate in this volume

Further Reading

Applegate, Edd, *Personalities and Products: A Historical Perspective on Advertising in America,* Westport, Connecticut: Greenwood, 1998

Fallon, Ivan, *The Brothers: The Rise and Rise of Saatchi & Saatchi,* London: Hutchinson, 1988; as *The Brothers: The Saatchi & Saatchi Story,* Chicago: Contemporary Books, 1989

Gartner, Michael, *Advertising and the First Amendment,* New York: Priority, 1989

Norris, Vincent P., "Advertising History—According to the Textbooks," *Journal of Advertising* 9 (1980)

Schudson, Michael, *Advertising, the Uneasy Persuasion: Its Dubious Impact on American Society,* New York: Basic Books, 1984; London: Routledge, 1993

History: 1990s

Advertising confronted many social and economic changes in the 1990s and adapted to both accommodate and reflect those changes. In the United States, as the baby boomers aged, the birth rate declined, and family units became smaller. At the same time, immigrant and minority populations grew, the population shifted toward the Sunbelt states, new consumers entered the economy, and new market segments emerged. The decade also witnessed technological breakthroughs that stimulated rapid change in the economy, forced changes in business operations, and gave rise to new enterprises and forms of commerce and trade. While advances in technology expanded the mass media audience, new technologies such as the Internet fragmented that audience. The mass media environment grew increasingly sophisticated, complex, and expensive as consumers were provided with more choices, more control, and a greater capacity for interacting with the sources of information.

Agencies: New Challenges

Advertisers faced increased choices too, as consultants began to insert themselves into the traditional agency-client relationship. These consultants included specialists in database marketing, interactive media, and all manner of market segments defined by race, ethnicity, values, and other factors. As agencies awoke to this challenge, many moved to expand their capabilities so as not to see valued clients torn by divided loyalties that might undermine agency relationships. Advertising entered a period of transition: the size, structure, and functions of agencies changed, along with the nature of advertiser-agency relationships. Beginning in the mid-1980s and continuing through the early 1990s, some advertisers moved to consolidate accounts at fewer agencies, while others sought the services of several agencies. The move by advertisers to consolidate or change agencies resulted from increased global competition and business mergers and acquisi-

tions. With the growing need to reach a global audience in an expensive mass media environment, advertisers began to cut back on spending. These cutbacks put pressure on the structure and size of agencies and altered their functions and relationships with advertisers. Given increasingly fragmented audiences, advertisers and agencies were under pressure to find the most distinct and effective media outlets in which to place their advertisements to reach the largest audience at the lowest possible cost. To deal with these challenges, some advertisers (e.g., Nestlé and McDonald's) maintained the traditional centralized structure, wherein the advertising agency works with the corporate staff to make decisions on promotions, while others (e.g., General Motors, Ameritech Corporation, and General Mills) operated on a more decentralized basis, allowing brand, category, and regional managers to work with their agencies to make decisions on advertising and promotional activities. Decentralization allowed managers to make decisions fast, as market forces dictated. It was a trend that swept through top management in all business categories with the publication of a best-selling book, *In Search of Excellence,* by management guru Tom Peters.

As advertisers reinvented their structures and operations, so did agencies. In the late 1980s, some agencies had reacted by consolidating or merging with other agencies to form "mega-agencies" or holding companies of agency networks. For example, one of the world's largest agencies, Cordiant, was created by merging smaller and unknown shops with well-established agencies such as Saatchi & Saatchi, Compton Worldwide, Dancer Fitzgerald Sample, Backer Spielvogel Bates, and several other smaller agencies into one corporate structure. Mega-agencies all over the globe purchased smaller agencies, wholly or in part, as the smaller agencies landed the accounts of some *Fortune* 500 companies. The larger agencies assumed that acquiring or cooperating with smaller agencies would enable them to offer clients a greater reservoir of talent and the ability to shift their business

Mountain Dew's "Do the Dew" campaign featuring the "Dew Dudes" captured the bravado of the 1990s youth culture. *Pepsi-Cola Company.*

from one agency to another. There were disadvantages, however; many advertiser-agency relationships became strained and produced conflicts between the agencies for competing accounts.

Advertisers demanded less and less in the way of traditional agency services as they began to divide their accounts among different agencies and began moving their spending from advertising to promotion. In 1994, when Anderson and Lembke landed the coveted Microsoft Corporation account, it marked a distinct shift in advertiser-agency relationships. Advertisers were relying less on traditional agency review procedures, courting agencies that would produce results. In the 1990s Coca-Cola moved its accounts among 26 agencies, though without cutting its long-time ties to McCann-Erickson. Many corporations changed agencies frequently, dissolving long-term relationships. Methods of compensation changed as they become linked to the profitability of clients. Several factors contributed to these changes: the growth of client marketing departments, the rise of consult-

ant specialists, the process of agency acquisition and merger, and the impersonal nature of the mega-agencies. The emergence of interactive media, the burgeoning of electronic commerce, and the explosion of new firms also contributed to the change in advertiser-agency relationships.

As advertisers became more demanding and their needs more varied and complex, both advertisers and agencies realized that success did not necessarily depend on agency size, structure, or location. Small regional shops sprang up in cities such as Minneapolis, Minnesota; Portland, Oregon; Richmond, Virginia; and Peoria, Illinois. Technological innovations made the physical location of an agency less important as advertisers and agencies relied on new forms of communication to receive and provide services from various regions. Some small creative boutiques developed during the decade, and older agencies began losing creative talent as their most productive personnel left to start their own new ventures. The established agencies reacted by creating niche units to

The rigors of pizza delivery boot camp were the premise of this 1995 commercial for Little Caesar's.
"Training Camp" used with permission of Little Caesar Enterprises, Inc. © 1995, Little Caesar Enterprises, Inc. All rights reserved.

serve particular clients. Specialized ethnic agencies focused on particular population groups. Small creative shops concentrated on developing ideas, while others concentrated on execution. As the array of media grew in complexity, big agencies separated, or "unbundled," their media departments to provide full media services and permit them to seek clients outside the parent agencies. The spin-offs arose as advertisers demanded the most effective media outlets at the lowest rates.

Among the leading independent media companies to be spun off from traditional agencies in the 1990s were: MindShare (WPP), OMD Worldwide and PhD (Omnicom), Zenith Media (Saatchi & Saatchi and Cordiant), Initiative Media Worldwide and Universal McCann (Interpublic), Media Edge (Young & Rubicam), MediaCom (Grey), TN Media (True North), and Starcom and MediaVest (Bcom3). The mega-agencies created independent agencies or units to perform particular functions. To meet the demands of a major client, DDB Needham formed Team

Frito Lay, based near the Plano, Texas, headquarters of the Frito-Lay Company. As technology became an increasingly important tool in advertising, many agencies added separate technology departments. The 1990s also reinforced the growth of specialized agencies such as farm market specialist Gilmore Communications, in Kalamazoo, Michigan, and Lecazon Associates, Miami, Florida, a specialist in the ethnic market. Others focused on the high-tech or business-to-business markets. About a decade after its founding, Cordiant split into two independent agencies, the Saatchi & Saatchi and Bates networks, to deal more efficiently with client needs.

In another major trend of the 1990s, advertising agencies began to provide integrated marketing activities ranging from sales promotion, direct response, and public relations to high-tech alternatives such as on-line services and Internet pages and advertising. The process, known as integrated marketing communication, became a popular service agencies offered their clients.

In order to keep pace with the changing times, full-service agencies were compelled to keep reinventing themselves. Reengineering enabled agencies to devote more time (about 60 percent) to dealing with their clients' ancillary needs across the entire spectrum of nonmedia marketing activities, including public relations, promotion, direct marketing, package design, and media placement. For example, McCann-Erickson bundled its services to put its menu of tools at the disposal of a worldwide client, Selvage and Lee, while Leo Burnett unbundled its services to focus on creativity.

The Internet: New Frontier

As the 1990s progressed, electronic commerce grew and Internet advertising came into vogue. The technology that made electronic business and Internet advertising possible originated some 30 years ago at the height of the Cold War. Invented by the U.S. Department of Defense, it was a military technology developed to enhance communication among research facilities. The new technologies included the so-called information superhighway (using computers, television, and other electronic means to send large quantities of information to large groups); the Internet (connecting computer networks, each containing varying forms of information); the World Wide Web (developing a place on the Internet where corporations can place information about themselves and their products and services for consumers to access); and interactive media (two-way communication over a computer network).

As a selling environment, the Web provided businesses with the opportunity to connect easily with consumers individually and globally. The promise of being able to reach millions of consumers instantaneously in an interconnected world contributed to the growth of electronic commerce. The vision of commerce promised by the Internet fueled the launching of many "dot-com" companies such as ebay.com and Amazon.com. The system provided consumers with the ability to purchase the precise goods and services they needed, quickly and at competitive prices, while shopping from the comfort of their homes. Many Internet companies initially offered only a single product or service, but as electronic commerce grew and bricks-and-mortar companies entered the fray, competition grew. Internet companies began offering consumers a variety of goods and services. On-line auctioning opened the door for sellers to get the highest possible prices from the broadest possible group of bidders. From the mid- to the late 1990s, Internet commerce reached $8 billion and was expected to grow to $3 trillion by the end of the first decade of the 21st century, although its failure to show profits and its consequent decline in the latter half of 2000 put such predictions at grave risk.

Internet advertising arrived about a decade after commercial on-line services began, in 1994, with the launch of Hotwired. Hotwired charged sponsors a fee of about $30,000 to place advertisements on its Web site for 12 weeks. The initial sponsors included AT&T, MCI, Club Med, Coors's Zima brand, IBM, Harman International Industries' JBL speakers, and Volvo Cars of North America. To access these advertisements, agencies had to create sites and "micro-sites" to link to a sponsor's ad on its own Web site. Modem Media tracked an average 40 percent "click-through" rate for its clients, which included AT&T and Zima. Click-through occurs when a computer user places the cursor on a Web link and clicks to go to another page. Also known as click rate, it is determined by the number of clicks on an advertisement divided by the number of ad requests. It is one of three measurements used to track Internet audiences. The second parameter, "ad request," occurs when a user loads a Web site with advertisements on it and the browser pulls an ad from the host server. The third gauge is cost per lead acquisition. Although both ad request and click rate can be translated into cost per thousand, or CPM, they have a major limitation—they can reach individuals only, not a mass audience.

Based on the success of Hotwired, established on-line services that already had large clienteles started attracting advertisers to their sites. When Hotwired offered the first full-fledged Internet advertising in 1994, it had 25,000 names on its e-mail list and a sizable number of users who visited the America Online (AOL) Wired site. These names and users became the main audience for advertisers. By 1997–98, the Internet audience was estimated to be more than 60 million in the United States and hundreds of million around the world.

Internet advertising can take several forms: Web sites, banners, buttons, sponsorships, and interstitial and classified advertisements. A Web site provides information on a company and its mission and promotes its products and services. Banners display billboards that spread across the top or bottom of a Web page. Buttons link a computer user to a page with more information about the advertiser. Sponsorships enable organizations to sponsor entire sections of a publisher's Web page. Interstitial animated advertisements pop up on the screen while a computer is downloading a Web page. Classified ad Web sites, often used by local advertisers, are primarily supported by ad banners of other advertisers. Search engines and local newspapers also sponsor classified ad Web sites. The cost of Internet advertising ranged from zero for the free classified advertisements to more than $15,000 per banner or $1 million per Web page per sponsorship. Total Web ad spending reached $300 million in the mid-1990s and more than triple that amount by 2000, according to Jupiter Research.

Internet technology can help companies compile data on consumers and target advertising to reach particular consumers. The promise of reaching targeted consumers, it is believed, will enable advertisers to better utilize their advertising dollars. The ability of consumers to be actively involved has compelled advertisers to production of informative, interactive advertisements, but the growing complexity and vastness of traditional mass media such as radio and TV have made it more difficult to assess the success of highly targeted Internet advertising. This very difficulty in determining the effectiveness of Web advertising represents a major failure of the Internet as a forum for advertising, promoting, and marketing goods and services. The medium is hampered by a lack of knowledge of advertising effectiveness, market research, and standardized measurement for ad exposure and pricing. Other problems related to Internet advertising include

first set of clubs: $175

first pair of golf shoes: $25

first 18 holes: $33

first love:

priceless

Justin Leonard, Age 8

there are some things money can't buy

for everything else there's MasterCard.

PINEHURST
1895

Preferred Card of Pinehurst, site of the 1999 US Open.

MasterCard

The late 1990s "Priceless" campaign—which focused on the intangible benefits of MasterCard purchases—was one of the most well received and frequently copied ad campaigns of the decade.
MasterCard International.

fears of loss of security and privacy, inappropriate placements, and slow downloads

The number of Web sites in existence grew exponentially in the late 1990s. By the year 2000 various estimates put the number in the hundreds of millions. Less than a year later, however, hundreds of those e-commerce and media sites were shuttered, victims of a downturn in dot-com values on Wall Street that dried up venture capital. More than ever, expectations that the Internet would lead to the demise of traditional mass media such as television, radio, and newspapers appeared unfounded, as Internet companies continued to rely on these traditional media to promote their brands, products, and services.

Advertising's "New Look"

The development of new technologies and software in the 1990s altered the way advertising was created and produced. Art directors and graphic designers were compelled to complement their brushes and paints with computer animation, as computers became integral to the creative and production processes. The use of computers to create and alter images meant that ads could be made quite simple or extremely complex, but it led to an emphasis on nature and outdoor imagery (which could now be produced without costly trips to picturesque locations) as seen in ads where polar bears drink Coke or Jeeps cruise through snowdrifts.

New technologies enabled designers to turn type into images and images into type, greatly expanding design possibilities. The application of new technologies to the creation of advertising messages also revolutionized the way consumers see words and pictures, the way they read and speak. Other changes were apparent in ads of the 1990s: overblown language was largely abandoned, stereotyped characters were exchanged for multicultural images, and predictable headlines and tag lines gave way to language that surprised—and sometimes shocked—consumers.

EMMANUEL C. ALOZIE

See also E-Commerce; Internet/World Wide Web

Further Reading

Bovée, Courtland L., and William F. Arens, *Contemporary Advertising*, Homewood, Illinois: Irwin, 1982; 7th edition, by Arens, Boston: Irwin/McGraw-Hill, 1999

Hicks, J., "The Demise of Traditional Agencies," *Advertising Age* (6 October 1997)

"The Interactive Future," *Advertising Age* (March–April and Special Issue, 2000)

Morrison, D., and P. Patricia, "Bye to the Creators, Hi to the Inventors" *Marketing News* 30, no. 7 (1996)

"The Next Century," *Advertising Age* (September–October and Special Issue, 1999)

Sissors, Jack Zanville, and E. Reynold Petray, *Advertising Media Planning*, Chicago: Crain Books, 1976; 5th edition, by Sissors and Lincoln Bumba, Lincolnwood, Illinois: NTC Business Books, 1996

Steinberg, H., "The Future of the Agency Business: Integrated Business," *Advertising Age* (6 October 1997)

Vanden Bergh, Bruce G., and Helen Katz, *Advertising Principles: Choice, Challenge, Change*, Lincolnwood, Illinois: NTC Business Books, 1999

H.J. Heinz Company. *See under* Heinz

Holding Company

The advertising holding company developed out of the need for agencies to service large clients. Under a central management, the holding company could gather independent, competitive service companies that could represent competing marketers, something that a single, independent agency could not do. The concept evolved in the mid-1950s out of advertising agency McCann-Erickson and the fertile mind of its president, Marion Harper, Jr., and materialized first as Interpublic, Inc., in 1960 and then as the Interpublic Group of Companies in 1964.

Forty years later few agencies of any size remained outside the world's top ten ad organizations—industry nomenclature for holding companies. These ten amassed worldwide gross income of $30.3 billion on billings of $245.9 billion in 1999, or about 80 percent of the world's total advertising handled by agencies, according to *Advertising Age*. The Interpublic Group, top-ranked agency holding company in early 2001 with $6.73 billion in gross income on billings of $62.5 billion, was light years from the $55.6 million gross income on billings of $371 million that Interpublic, Inc., registered at its founding in 1960.

By 2001 Interpublic, the WPP Group, and the Omnicom Group were the dominant power brokers among the agency holding companies. WPP was only slightly behind Interpublic, with $6.69 billion in gross income on billings of $53.83 billion; and Omnicom had $5.74 billion on billings of $45.55 billion. That ranking included WPP's buyout of Young & Rubicam in the fall of 2000 and Interpublic's acquisition of agency holding company True North Communications in mid-March 2001.

Holding Companies and Consumer Growth

The idea of the agency holding company began at McCann-Erickson at a time when marketers were expanding product lines and increasing production to meet the needs of a growing postwar consumer market both in the United States and abroad. "To attract good people, we had to have a larger business; the very best clients made the best agencies," Marion Harper told interviewer Bart Cummings in *Advertising's Benevolent Dictators*. Harper added, "These clients would have new products and concepts, and those new products should not routinely be given to some other agency because of some idiosyncrasies of management or possible product conflict."

In 1954 McCann-Erickson purchased Cleveland, Ohio, agency Marschalk & Pratt. Rather than merging it into McCann, Harper decided to keep Marschalk, which had a largely industrial client list, as a separate agency. A year after the Marschalk purchase McCann won Coca-Cola's Coke business. McCann saw potential profit in representing other Coca-Cola products and local and regional bottlers, though in the case of the latter, their high degree of independence would preclude any national agency from gaining their business. Marschalk was called upon to pitch the local New York City bottler; in 1960 Coca-Cola expanded its brands and made Marschalk a roster shop. By then, Marschalk had transformed itself into a consumer agency.

"It became clear that supervising all the aspects of the Coca-Cola account out of McCann-Erickson at the same time we were trying to foster the independence and competitiveness of Marschalk wasn't going to work," Neal Gilliatt, longtime McCann executive, told Cummings. The answer to this supervisory need and the advent of Interpublic, Inc., emerged virtually simultaneously. In Interpublic, the McCann hierarchy was basically collapsed, with the traditional McCann agency and Marschalk as separate units on one side of the family tree, and former McCann units like the Marplan research function (later, Allied Communications) among the nonadvertising services on the other side.

This model for corporate structure swept the agency community, and the ad industry rapidly consolidated into large holdings. The autonomous nature of the agency networks created in these holding companies eased most client concerns regarding the proprietary nature of their agency relationship. Clients did not invest such trust overnight, though. Today most of the large ad organizations have multiple food, airline, and car accounts, for example, within different operating units, though it is unlikely that Interpublic, with its huge General Motors Corporation (GM) billings, would risk seeking Ford or Chrysler business.

Multinationals

By the turn of the 21st century a new trend had developed. Multinationals were consolidating creative staff for their accounts drawn from many agencies—independents to operating units of holding companies—into these big holdings. The reasons for this change were varied; a significant factor was aggressive pitching at the holding-company level rather than the normal pattern of leaving pitching to agencies. Behind this trend was money. Both Omnicom and its DDB Worldwide network simultaneously sought the Chrysler Group account of DaimlerChrysler, winning it from FCB Worldwide, whose executives were joined in the pitch by those from their parent, True North. Little wonder True North's top executives entered the fray. The Chrysler Group account was valued at about $2 billion in billings, a tally equivalent to 9 percent of True North's revenue and 25 percent of net income. Following the loss of Chrysler, True North became more attractive as an acquisition target. Interpublic did not have to worry that its client, GM, would balk at its acquisition of an agency enriched by billings from an auto competitor.

In 2000 the WPP Group created a worldwide coordinator for the Ford account, possibly to keep Ford happy as well as to unify marketing efforts. As of March 2001 Ford's two major agencies worldwide were WPP's J. Walter Thompson Company and Ogilvy & Mather Worldwide, although through acquisition Ford had added other agencies, including Messner Vetere Berger McNamee Schmetterer, which served its newly acquired Volvo subsidiary. Interpublic deepened its relationship with Coca-Cola (McCann is Coke's lead agency) at the end of 2000 by agreeing to coordinate communications for Coca-Cola's flagship soft-drink brand. Coke has worked with a host of agencies to get the widest range of ideas in the past, but its brand has struggled to maintain a consistent marketing message. The new arrangement no doubt enhances Interpublic's chances of landing additional Coke business.

One-Stop Shopping

Since 2000 other advertisers have joined the Chrysler Group in consolidating their business at one or two agency networks, including United Airlines, the Guinness division of Diageo, Exxon Mobil, Hasbro, Ford Motor Company, Kellogg Company, the Philip Morris Companies, Unilever, Volvo, and Compaq Computer Corporation.

Clients see several benefits in doing business with holding companies, including multinational coverage, economies of scale, and one-stop shopping. Of the top ten holding companies in 1999, the billings split was 44 percent United States and 56 percent non-United States, a geographic distribution nearing the 50/50 split most global ad organizations were seeking. The consolidation of the media functions of multiple networks into a single operating unit under a holding company is a prime example of economies of scale. Independent media units of the top ten ad organizations in 1999 accounted for $49 billion in U.S. media placements. By handling huge media purchases, these media specialist companies save costs. Their commissions of 2 percent–4 percent for TV purchases and 5 percent–8 percent for print are far below the increasingly obsolete 15 percent commission that agencies once pocketed when their livelihood depended on media billings. Fees have become the currency of agency payment.

As a "supermarket" of services beneath a single roof, the holding company not only accommodates an advertiser's multiple marketing needs but shores up its own bottom line. Specialty services, the so-called below-the-line components of advertising and marketing, typically carry higher margins than traditional advertising. Most holding companies are seeking to derive at least 50 percent of their revenues from marketing services. Cordiant Communications Group is aiming at 60 percent by 2003.

Agencies have benefited from the holding company structure because it gives them a means to "finance" the billings outlays of large advertisers. Holding companies have cushioned the impact of account losses and enhanced management succession plans among subsidiary agencies by broadening the ownership base with stock and other financial incentives. Expansion needs have encouraged holding companies to become public, thereby further opening the door to capital markets. Their stock has become their chief means of making acquisitions. Just after Interpublic went public in 1971 it used stock to purchase Campbell-Ewald in 1972 and, in 1979, to acquire Sullivan, Stauffer, Colwell & Bayles and its 49 percent ownership in Lintas (it later bought all of Lintas from owner Unilever).

Interpublic stock gave agencies value, making them attractive even to nonadvertising/communications companies such as meatpacker Mickelberry Corporation, which became a holding company for ad agencies in 1982 when it bought agencies Laurence, Charles & Free, Nadler & Larimer, and Cunningham & Walsh (C&W) that year under a holding company structure.

C&W had been coveted as a building block for expansion into the United States by British agency Saatchi & Saatchi. Saatchi instead bought Compton Advertising and its string of subsidiaries in 1982. Saatchi soon took the holding company idea to a new level. It announced it would become the world's largest holding company, a boast that raised hackles on Madison Avenue. But it followed through on its claim. In 1986 Saatchi literally bought that title by purchasing Dancer Fitzgerald Sample, Backer & Spielvogel, and Ted Bates Worldwide (which included the William Esty Company, Campbell-Mithun, and AC&R Advertising, among others). Owing to account conflicts, Saatchi lost $70 million in Procter & Gamble Company business with the deal.

Partly to counter Saatchi's move, Omnicom was formed in 1986 as a holding company for three agencies: BBDO Worldwide, Doyle Dane Bernbach; and Needham, Harper & Steers. Clients, citing conflicts, peeled away $117 million in billings from Omnicom. Under the Omnicom mantle, agency networks were formed out of BBDO and the merger of DDB and Needham, Harper & Steers. Omnicom's TBWA Worldwide network later emerged in two phases, through the 1992 acquisition of TBWA Worldwide and the 1994 acquisition of Chiat/Day. Agency specialties from these various units were moved laterally into the Diversified Agency Services unit in the same way that Interpublic isolated specialties in its Allied Communications operation.

Martin Sorrell, Saatchi's finance director during its early growth period, left to form the WPP Group in 1985. After a series of small acquisitions he acquired the JWT Group in a hostile takeover in 1987. Two years later he added the Ogilvy Group. Both JWT and Ogilvy were already holding companies. WPP was deep in debt when the world economy went into recession at the end of the 1980s, forcing it to restructure to avoid receivership. Interpublic had survived a similar economic turndown in the late 1960s. Overextended from debts incurred from heavy acquisitions and free spending by Marion Harper (Interpublic made nearly 50 acquisitions from 1959 to 1967), the agency discharged Harper. Newly named Chief Executive Officer Robert Healy restructured the company by merging units, cutting staff, and obtaining credit agreements with banks.

The French attempted to add mathematical certitude to the holding company equation in 1988, when Paris-based Publicis and Foote, Cone & Belding, a public agency since 1963, bought minority positions in each other and then linked their European operations outside of France into a single network. This arrangement worked so well for Publicis that when the two split up in 1997, FCB was left without its European agency network, which had been substantial before the alliance. Just as McCann had earlier evolved into Interpublic, FCB evolved into holding company True North Communications by the end of 1994. True North used stock to buy traditional and specialist agencies, culminating in its 1997 acquisition of Bozell, Jacobs, Kenyon & Eckhardt, the parent of Bozell Worldwide and other shops. Following its breakup with True North in 1997, Publicis went on a buying binge, picking up Hal Riney & Partners, Fallon-McElligott, and Burrell Communications, and in 2000, Saatchi & Saatchi. Saatchi, the holding company, had split its properties in half in 1995, the agency network of the same name remaining at Saatchi while the other Saatchi network, Bates Worldwide, moved to newly created Cordiant.

The other big French agency holding company, Havas Advertising, got its start in 1958 when the French government-created Agence Havas to take care of state-controlled businesses. The government sold 55 percent of Havas to private investors in the early 1970s. Havas changed its name to Eurocom and in 1975 exchanged minority shares with Needham, Harper & Steers to establish the International Needham Univas network. Eurocom (Havas) expanded rapidly in the 1980s and made its first strike with a 51 percent stake in Young & Rubicam agency Marsteller, Inc.

Eurocom then merged with WCRS in 1989, taking a 60 percent position in the merged network called EWDB Worldwide. Eurocom bought Paris-based pan-Europe agency Roux Seguela Cayzac & Goudard (RSCG) in 1991 forming Euro RSCG and, in

1992, created Messner Vetere Berger McNamee Schmetterer out of the former Della Femina, McNamee shop that had been part of WCRS since 1986. It reestablished the Havas name as its holding company in 1995 and soon afterward moved Euro RSCG headquarters operations to New York City, home of its lead agency, Messner. Havas's biggest acquisition came in 2000 with the $2.1 billion buyout of Snyder Communications, a marketing services company with a sizable advertising component, Arnold Communications.

The "Whole-Egg" Approach

Young & Rubicam offered another twist to the holding company concept with its so-called "whole-egg" approach to treating the multiple marketing needs of clients. It did this by assembling agency specialties—healthcare, Latino, direct marketing, sales promotion, design, interactive—as satellites to work with lead agency Y&R Advertising on all aspects of a client's advertising and marketing needs. These multidisciplinary shops also maintained their own clients. Young & Rubicam went public in 1999. It was bought out by WPP in 2000, but not until Y&R's negotiations with white knight Publicis had fallen through. WPP paid $4.7 billion in stock for Young & Rubicam, the biggest takeover in agency history, and made it WPP's third-largest agency network, joining Ogilvy & Mather Worldwide and the J. Walter Thompson Company. A fourth WPP network for smaller clients, Red Cell, was formed in 2001 out of various independent units within WPP—Conquest Europe, a small network of shops developed in the early 1990s to handle the Alfa Romeo account; Cole & Weber, of Seattle, Washington; and Batey Group, a Singapore-based agency network that had been 30 percent owned by WPP. WPP increased that ownership to just over 50 percent at the creation of Red Cell.

Bcom3, a renaming of BDM, emerged in 2000 as a privately held holding company formed by the Leo Group (the Leo Burnett Company) and the MacManus Group (D'Arcy Masius Benton & Bowles), with Dentsu, Inc., of Japan owning 20 percent equity. Burnett and D'Arcy Masius Benton & Bowles represent its two big agency networks. An initial public offering had been planned for Bcom3 in 2001, but the market downturn delayed the action. The publicly held holding company Grey Global Group is closely owned (75 percent) by its chairman, Ed Meyer. Grey reconfigured itself into a holding company in 2000 largely to bring in new management at the operating level (the old guard moved to the holding company). Grey also sought to establish a more even-handed approach to managing subsidiaries than prevailed in the days when decisions came from Grey Advertising, an agency higher in the hierarchy than its siblings.

Concentration of Wealth

Other holding companies emerged in the late 1990s, largely as a means of concentrating the wealth of specialized marketing services under a single umbrella. They included:

- Envoy Communications Group, Toronto, Canada, a publicly traded holding company specializing in design, marketing, and technology. Its traditional agency component was Hampel/Stefanides, New York City. Envoy sought to acquire the traditional British agency Leagas Delaney, based in London, England, through a stock deal, but the deal fell through in July 2001 when the two parties were unable to agree on a valuation for Leagas Delaney. Envoy also owned Devlin Applied Design, specializing in Web site design, and Sage Information Consultants, providing back-end electronic-business solutions.

- Incepta Group, a publicly held London-based advertising/communications company largely shaped by two units, Citigate Albert Frank, a financial advertising company, and Dewe Rogerson Incepta, a public relations firm. As of 2001 Incepta's primary operations were in the United States and the United Kingdom. In July 2000 the company bought Cunningham Communications (renamed Citigate Cunningham), a sizable Palo Alto, California, public relations and marketing agency with fee income of more than $24 million.

- Maxxcom, a unit of MDC Communications, with agencies in the United States and Canada. As of 2001 these included Colle & McVoy (Minneapolis, Minnesota); Margeotes/Fertitta & Partners (New York City); Fletcher Martin Associates (Atlanta, Georgia); 49 percent ownership of Crispin Porter & Bogusky (Miami, Florida); CyberSight (Portland, Oregon); Source Marketing (Westport, Connecticut); and Accent Marketing Services (Louisville, Kentucky). In July 2000 Maxxcom bought TargetCom, a Chicago, Illinois–based direct/relationship marketing agency that owned Bang!zoom, a San Francisco and London-based technology and dot-com company, and Etelligence, an Internet-specific relationship marketing unit with offices in Chicago and St. Louis, Missouri. Maxxcom bought Mackenzie Marketing, Minneapolis, Minnesota, in August 2000. Maxxcom also owned ad agencies Ambrose Carr Linton Carroll, Toronto; Cormark Communications, London, Ontario; and Allard Johnson, Toronto and Montreal; sales promotion shop Accumark Promotions Group, Toronto; four Toronto public relations firms—Bryan Mills & Associates, McManus Elliott Communications, News Canada, and Veritas Communications; consulting company Integrated Health Care, Toronto; corporate identity/branding company Strategies International, Toronto; and research/consulting business, Northstar Research Partners, Toronto.

- SPAR Group, Tarrytown, New York, which had grown through acquisitions in the late 1990s. These included PIA Merchandising Services, of Irvine, California, a supplier of in-store merchandising, which accounted for nearly 50 percent of SPAR's billings in 2000. The company's goal was to create one of the nation's largest providers of retail merchandising and other marketing services using SPAR's Internet reporting and control services, which allow clients real-time access to their accounts and on-demand marketing services. Aside from in-store merchandising SPAR offered incentive marketing, teleservices, database marketing, and marketing research services.

- Panoramic Communications, New York City, a marketing communications holding company encompassing the 16 independent operating companies of Epb.communications. Along with lead agency Earle Palmer Brown, of Bethesda, Maryland, other companies included R.J. Palmer, a media specialist company; three Web site design companies; two design operations; and a consulting firm. The holding company was a 50/50 partner of Epb.communications and the Destination Group, a private equity firm in Los Angeles, California. The Destination Group also provided capital, management, and services such as recruiting and retaining talent.
- Aspen Marketing, Los Angeles, an integrated marketing services company that grew out of the company of the same name and from acquisitions of marketing services companies such as Hanig & Company, MAP Promotions & Incentives, and Schmidt-Cannon International. The company grew during the 1990s through a flurry of acquisitions: Creative Marketing International (West Chicago, Illinois); PhoneWorks (St. Petersburg, Florida); Corporate Trademarks (Alpharetta, Georgia); and Premium Source Merchandising (Los Angeles). The company had four divisions: Aspen Direct, Aspen Promotion, Aspen Identity (corporate logos, programs, and merchandising), and Aspen Interactive, which included interactive agency B-12, New York City.
- Lighthouse Global Network, Chicago, a marketing services holding company purchased in 2000 by Cordiant Communications Group, London. Cordiant, which dropped the Lighthouse name at the merger, gained agencies covering a broad spectrum of marketing disciplines in the deal. The network was divided into three divisions: a marketing services division called Communicator Group, LGN Design & Development (product development and brand consulting), and LGN Business Communications (investor, financial, and crisis communications at the corporate level). Communicator

Group was created by the merger of six marketing services agencies dealing with sales promotion, new media, sports marketing, event management, and direct marketing.

- Hawkeye Communications, New York, a business communications holding company formed in 1999. Through extensive acquisitions, it gained specialized capabilities—market research, corporate identification programs, media analysis, sales literature, Web site design and support, direct marketing, public relations, trade show programs, and video and film production.

CRAIG ENDICOTT

See also Bcom3 Group; Cordiant Communications Group; Havas Advertising; Interpublic Group of Companies; Omnicom Group; Publicis Group; WPP Group

Further Reading

"An Awesome Feat," *Advertising Age* (12 June 1972)

Brown, Stanley H., "Under Marion Harper's Big Tent," *Fortune* 69 (May 1964)

Cummings, Bart, *The Benevolent Dictators: Interviews with Advertising Greats,* Chicago: Crain Books, 1984

Endicott, R. Craig, "Top 100 in 45th Agency Report," *Advertising Age* (29 March 1989)

Endicott, R. Craig, "56th Annual Agency Report: At Agencies, a Growth Year for the Ages," *Advertising Age* (24 April 2000)

Endicott, R. Craig, "57th Annual Report: Agency Report: U.S. Shop Billings Top $259 Billion," *Advertising Age* (23 April 2001)

"Harper Era Is Seen Ending at Interpublic," *Advertising Age* (20 November 1967)

"Marion Harper Makes It," *Advertising Age* (21 October 1963)

O'Gara, James V., "Profiles of 514 Agencies: Here Are the Details in Billings, New Accounts, Media, Employees, Mergers," *Advertising Age* (26 February 1962)

Quinn, Hugh, "Stockholders Clear Big C-E, Interpublic Union," *Advertising Age* (20 November 1972)

Honda Motor Company

Principal Agencies
Gumpertz, Bentley & Dolan
Grey Advertising Agency, Inc.
Needham, Harper & Steers, Inc.
Rubin Postaer & Associates
Dailey & Associates
Suissa Miller
Dentsu
Hakuhodo

Although the Honda Motor Company did not begin exporting automobiles to the United States from Japan until the 1970 model year, by the end of the decade it was already becoming a significant player in the U.S. auto market. In ads for Honda's 1978 models, Needham, Harper & Steers, then the agency for the auto division of American Honda Motor Company, devised a campaign that drew on Honda's quickly developing reputation as a marketer of dependable, efficient small cars. The ads had a clean look, showing cars on plain backgrounds, often with no models or distractions other than clear, legible copy. The famous tag line, used for six years, was, "Honda, we make it simple." The theme crystallized what Honda meant to its U.S. customers at the time—sensible, reliable cars that were an economical alternative to the big, gas-guzzling Detroit models of the era.

Honda Motor Company had its origins in the postwar Japan of 1946, when Soichiro Honda, a mechanic, founded the Honda Technical Research Institute in Hamamatsu. The company initially produced auxiliary engines that could be fitted to bicycles. In 1948 it was renamed Honda Motor Company, and by 1949 motorcycle production was under way with a model called the Dream. Honda moved its headquarters to Tokyo in 1952 and began its first exports of the famous Cub motorcycle to Taiwan and the Philippines. By the mid-1950s Honda was building its reputation by participating in motorcycle racing around the world and also had begun producing small engines for agricultural use. Honda's Power Equipment division continues to market lawnmowers, generators, and other small engine powered machines worldwide.

First U.S. Foray

When it established the American Honda Motor Company in a Los Angeles, California, storefront in 1959, Honda was not yet an automaker. Motorcycles were still its primary line of business. In 1961, Honda's first year of sustained U.S. advertising, its ad budget was $240,000. In that conservative era, motorcycles had what many regarded as an undesirable "bad-boy" reputation. Honda sought to combat this image and appeal to a broader market. The company's first U.S. advertising agency, Gumpertz, Bentley & Dolan, of Los Angeles, produced ads showing well-dressed people riding the small motorbikes. In 1963 Honda appointed a new U.S. agency, Grey Advertising, Beverly Hills, California, which took Honda's message a step further with the tag line, "You meet the nicest people on a Honda." The successful campaign, which eventually ran on network TV, radio, and in magazines, continued to feature the images of clean cut people riding Hondas in everyday situations.

Honda quickly built itself into the leading motorcycle brand in the United States, claiming as much as 70 percent of the rapidly expanding market in the early 1960s. Furthering its international expansion, Honda established its first European arm in Hamburg, Germany, in 1961. When the U.S. account was switched to Grey in 1963, Honda's U.S. ad budget was increased to $2.18 million. The "nicest people" campaign was eventually used in other select international markets. Despite the arrival of other Japanese-made motorcycles in the United States in the 1960s, Honda continued to lead the pack.

In 1967, with the demand from first-time buyers exhausted, the bottom dropped out of the U.S. motorcycle market, but Honda continued to hold the top spot. By 1972 Honda motorcycles were receiving $3.5 million in advertising support in a full range of U.S. media. The latest tag line from Grey was, "From mighty to mini, Honda has it all." Honda's early U.S. strategy

This 1963 ad featured the memorable slogan that helped make Honda the most popular motorcycle in the United States for nearly 40 years.

was by now obsolete, as U.S. motorcycle buyers began to be attracted to the leather-clad biker mystique defined by the 1969 movie *Easy Rider*. Honda started marketing road bikes and cruisers to address new market segments. With the motorcycle heyday of the early and mid-1960s over, and with increased competition from other Japanese brands, Honda's dominance of the fluctuating U.S. motorcycle market remained at an impressive 40 percent in 1973.

In 1979 Honda of America Manufacturing was set up to begin building motorcycles in a new facility in Marysville, Ohio. The same year Honda switched its motorcycle and power products accounts to Dailey & Associates, Los Angeles. The new slogan for the 1979 motorcycles ("Honda, follow the leader") capitalized on Honda's market position. Complementing the motorcycles was a lineup of scooters and all-terrain vehicles, or ATVs, which were becoming popular in the United States. Through the 1980s Honda introduced a spate of new cycles, and 1988 saw a huge $75 million ad push with the tag line, "Come ride with us." Honda's share of a shrinking U.S. motorcycle market had declined, but by 1991 its 28.7 percent share was still enough to hold on to the number-one position. Honda maintained leadership of the U.S. market until 1999, when a resurgent Harley-Davidson, Inc., claimed the sales leader title.

Why some garages are happier than others.

Have you ever noticed how some garages have all the luck? Imagine being home to not just one Honda product, but many.

Sure, we're best known for our automobiles. But we are, first and foremost, an engineering company. And, along with our world-renowned cars, we manufacture some of the world's most reliable motorcycles, marine engines, generators, snowblowers, lawnmowers, all-terrain vehicles and tillers. Products designed to balance your desires for fun and performance with society's needs for better fuel efficiency and cleaner air. And, all powered by Honda.

From our low-emission automobiles to our tremendously clean and quiet marine engines, Honda thinking has led to many breakthrough innovations in virtually every product we make. Which, ultimately, helps improve the quality of your life. Not to mention your garage.

HONDA

From the top left by row: XR400R, Accord EX V-6 Sedan, Honda 4-Stroke Trimmer, Honda Harmony™ lawnmower, Honda BF130 outboard motor, Honda Super Quiet Generator, Honda Harmony™ Mini Tiller, Acura MDX with Touring Package, Honda Track-Drive Snowblower, Gold Wing® SE, FourTrax® Foreman. ©2000 American Honda Motor Co., Inc. honda.com

A 2000 corporate ad for the Honda Motor Company emphasized the company's versatility and high standards.

Entering the Car Market

In the early 1960s the worldwide popularity of Honda motorcycles was indisputable, but Soichiro Honda had a vision of his company as an automobile manufacturer as well. Honda first introduced its T360 light truck and S360 sports car in Japan in 1962. By 1968 Honda was preparing to enter the U.S. auto market, and Grey Advertising, Honda's U.S. agency, was ready to take on the assignment. There was a problem, however—Grey had won Ford Motor Company's corporate account in 1966. Grey initially contended that having both accounts posed no conflict as the two companies targeted different segments of the auto market, but once Ford began to grumble, Grey conceded, and the Honda car account went to Chiat/Day, Los Angeles, California. Grey retained the motorcycle business.

The first Chiat/Day ads for Honda cars, for the 1970 model year, touted the tiny 600 as the "New little car in town," and later ads introduced it simply as "The Honda car." Magazines were the main venue, though there was some spot TV and radio support. Annual spending on the car account was $2 million by 1972; 12,000 vehicles were sold. That year, using network TV for the first time for its auto campaign, Honda introduced the Coupe, a car even more diminutive than the 600. The campaign

targeted the 18-to-24-year-old age group with a tag line ("It makes a lot of sense") that poked fun at the idea of keeping up with the Joneses.

The Honda Civic, first introduced in Japan in 1972, was brought to the United States in 1973, the same year that Soichiro Honda retired and became "Supreme Adviser" to the company. Although still small, the Civic was a larger, more refined car than the 600 or Coupe. Advertising for the Civic began in March 1974 and touted the fact that the car had ranked highest in the U.S. Environmental Protection Agency's mileage rankings. The tag line, "More miles per gallon than anybody," hit home during the energy crisis—a time when most American cars had abysmal gas mileage. Ads ran on network TV, radio, and in print. The year was one of decline for the U.S. auto market, but Honda managed to increase its sales to 41,638 units and more than doubled its auto ad spending to $6 million. In a memorable 1974 campaign, Chiat/Day developed ads aimed at marketing Honda cars to women. Print ads ran in women's magazines, emphasizing that women valued the same things as men when buying a car. The campaign avoided the condescending tone of many other efforts aimed at women. One popular TV spot showed a young woman picking up a date in her Honda Civic and presenting him with flowers.

Those ads were among the last Chiat/Day would do for Honda. In late 1974 the company moved its auto account to Needham, Harper & Steers, Los Angeles. The next year was a huge one for Honda autos in the United States, despite—or more accurately, because of—the energy crisis and recession. The company introduced its high-tech, clean-burning CVCC engine in the 1975 Civic, at the same time as it curtailed production of the older mini cars. Honda put its ad efforts behind the Civic, initially forecasting a 20 percent increase in sales. The first major creative effort from Needham, Harper & Steers, under account supervisor Gerry Rubin, focused on the CVCC engine technology and touted the Honda Civic as "What the world is coming to." Sales jumped dramatically, and by the end of the year Honda was offering a version of the Civic that was the lowest-priced car on the U.S. market, wresting that title from rivals Toyota and Datsun. The Civic turned out to be a car well-suited to the times—economical, fuel-efficient, environmentally responsible. Honda's 1975 U.S. sales were up more than 145 percent over the prior year, to 102,383 units.

The success of the Civic was quickly followed by the introduction of the larger Accord in 1976, a year that saw Honda's worldwide revenue increase 32 percent and worldwide sales of Honda autos exceed 500,000 for the first time. The introductory U.S. campaign for the Accord, exclusively in print, proclaimed, "A little bigger car from Honda." The ad occupied four consecutive color pages. The first spread featured the Civic, and the second the new Accord. The cars were shown large, on plain backgrounds, a graphic technique that would later be used in the "We make it simple" campaign and other Honda ads for years to come. The Accord was another immediate hit with the public. As Honda's U.S. auto sales increased another 47 percent, filling demand became an issue, and the company began considering the possibility of building cars in the United States.

First U.S. Auto Plant

In 1981 Honda announced plans to establish U.S. auto production, becoming the first Japanese company to do so. The first car produced at the company's Ohio plant was the Accord, starting in late 1982. The decision to build plants in the United States was well timed, as Honda's U.S. car sales had declined slightly for two consecutive years owing to import restrictions imposed in 1980 on Japanese auto manufacturers. The Ohio-built Accords allowed Honda to increase U.S. sales in 1983 despite those restrictions. In another push for overseas expansion, Honda Motor Company signed an agreement with British Leyland (later Rover Group) in 1979 to jointly design and produce cars in the United Kingdom. Honda eventually took a 20 percent equity stake in Rover, which it relinquished in 1994 when BMW acquired the other 80 percent.

In 1984 Honda became the first Japanese automaker to announce the creation of a luxury division in the United States. Japanese cars had always been economy cars, though the Japanese reputation for quality was by now well established and the Accord had gone a long way toward moving the Honda image upscale. The Acura division was launched in 1986 with two mod-

els, the Legend and the Integra. Honda awarded the U.S. account to Ketchum Advertising, San Francisco, California, and put $24.5 million behind the introductory campaign, which used the tag line, "Precision crafted automobiles—from a new division of American Honda." First year Acura sales were 52,869 units; the number more than doubled in 1987, as did the division's ad budget. In 1989 Acura was challenged by upscale divisions of both Toyota (Lexus) and Nissan (Infiniti). For 1990, Acura ad spending was $100 million, but the division's sales peaked in 1991 at 143,708 units. In 1996 the account was moved to Suissa Miller, Santa Monica, California.

By 1986 nearly 70 percent of worldwide Honda revenue was from its overseas markets, and approximately 50 percent of that came from North America alone. In the spring of that year, however, an event occurred that had a direct impact on Honda—the giant ad agency merger of Batten Barton Durstine & Osborn (BBDO), Doyle Dane Bernbach (DDB), and Needham Harper Worldwide. DDB was Volkswagen of America's longtime agency, and under the new agency organization, soon to be called Omnicom, DDB and Needham Harper were to be merged, creating an account conflict between Honda and Volkswagen. Gerry Rubin and Larry Postaer of Needham agreed to buy the agency's Los Angeles office and set up shop as Rubin Postaer & Associates to handle the Honda account. American Honda was happy with this arrangement, and much later, in 1999, consolidated its entire auto account with Rubin Postaer, awarding it the Acura division business as well.

The 1980s turned out to be another decade of huge growth for Honda. By the end of 1989, U.S. auto sales for both divisions had reached 783,102 units, and the Honda Accord had become the best-selling car in the country—the first foreign-branded model to do so. The Accord theme for 1989 was "You have to drive it to believe it." The Accord maintained its best-seller status for three years. By 1990 Honda was selling more than two cars in North America for every one sold in Japan, underscoring the importance of the North American market to the company.

Soichiro Honda died in 1991, at age 84. Two years later, in 1993, Honda made its first tentative steps into the growing U.S. light truck market with an agreement to sell rebadged American Isuzu Motors sport-utility vehicles (SUVs). Honda increased its total U.S. ad spending by a huge 39.5 percent in 1994, to nearly half a billion dollars. In 1997 Honda launched its own small SUV, the CR-V, in the United States. By 1998, Honda's total U.S. auto sales for both divisions topped 1 million units for the first time. Honda's U.S. spending was $749.5 million in 1999, the year that it lost its longtime dominance of the U.S. motorcycle market. In its home market, where both Hakuhodo and Dentsu are Honda agencies, Honda achieved the status of Japan's second-largest automaker in 2000, displacing Nissan Motor Company for the first time.

SCOTT MACDONALD

Further Reading
Mair, Andrew, *Honda's Global Local Corporation*, London: Macmillan, and New York: St. Martin's Press, 1993

Sakiya, Tetsuo, *Honda chohasso keiei: Honda Soichiro to Fujisawa Takeo no sekai*, Tokyo: Daiyamondosha, 1979; as *Honda Motor: The Men, the Management, the Machines*, translated by Kiyoshi Ikemi, edited by Timothy Porter, Tokyo: Kodansha International, and New York: Kodansha International USA, 1982

"The Sales Statistics in *The-100 Year Almanac and 1996 Market Data Book*," *Automotive News* (24 April 1996)

HongkongBank

(HSBC)

Principal Agency
Bates Hong Kong Advertising

In 1998 HongkongBank was renamed HSBC (Hongkong and Shanghai Banking Corporation). The corporation included other banks such as Midland Bank, Marine Midland Bank, and the British Bank of the Middle East, all of which had been held by the Hongkong and Shanghai Banking Corporation Group. The HSBC Group was named after its founding member, the Hongkong and Shanghai Banking Corporation Limited.

The bank, founded by a group of British and other foreign businessmen, opened at 1 Queen's Road in Hong Kong in March 1865, and the first branch office opened in Shanghai shortly afterward. The name in Chinese (*Wayfoong*) means "a focus on wealth." By the late 1990s the HSBC Group had operations in 19 countries in Asia and the Pacific region, the Americas, Africa, Europe, and the Middle East, and more than 5,000 offices worldwide.

Initially the bank worked locally in Hong Kong and within Asia, but it quickly set up offices in London and India. It was the sole British overseas bank with its headquarters in Hong Kong. As well as being the dominant local bank, it became powerful in China by 1900. It played a leading role in helping to finance the post–World War II recovery and in developing Hong Kong's industrial economy. The name HongkongBank and its hexagon logo were adopted in the 1980s. Into the early 21st century, HSBC served as a central bank for Hong Kong that produced most of the local currency. The local advertising promotion of Hongkong-Bank/HSBC Group around the retail banking services from the 1970s to the 1990s best represented the development and expansion of the HSBC Group into new international markets, new acquisitions, and new products and services.

The bank's earliest television campaign, launched in 1972 by Bates Hong Kong Advertising, featured a cartoon lion and focused on the bank's facilities and services. The lion image was already a well-known symbol of the corporation: two bronze lions have stood outside its headquarters since the bank's establishment. Subsequent TV commercials emphasized new services provided by advances in technology and ease of use and convenience. For example, in the first ad for the direct debit service Autopay, "Jumping Man," which was produced in 1976, Autopay was described as a convenience that made everyday life easier.

The Electronic Teller Counter, which allowed customers to withdraw cash at any time through an automatic teller machine, was introduced in 1980. The initial campaign included three ads, "Sword Man," "Lydia Shum," and "Amah," all with the slogan, "Just like money in your pocket." The ads explained the service, how to apply for it, and the convenience it could provide to the individual user. A catchy line in the "Sword Man" spot—"So easy you can do it with one hand"—made the commercial a classic of Hong Kong advertising.

Advertising campaigns in the 1980s focused on various financial services and products as they were introduced. The first HongkongBank Visa campaign, "Colour TV," which was launched in 1980, claimed that the card was "the world's biggest card, from Hong Kong's biggest bank." A follow-up ad, "Suit," which was aired later in the year, included more purchasing scenarios. The same series of ads included "Extended," "Airline," and "Visa-bility," which were launched between 1980 and 1982. Another service provided by HongkongBank was the Personal Installment Loan. The service was launched in 1983 with an ad called "Thank You HongkongBank," which positioned the bank as a friend that helped customers solve their financial problems.

With the signing in December 1984 of the Sino-British Joint Declaration, providing for the return of Hong Kong to Chinese sovereignty in 1997, colonial control began to diminish. As the transition drew near, many people found it difficult to identify either with the British colonial government or with the typical image of China as backward, poor, and unsophisticated. It was under these circumstances that, from April 1993 to July 1995, HongkongBank ran a local corporate image campaign under the theme "Partnership." The campaign was successful in establishing and reinforcing the bank's connection to the local community and its commitment to the territory. From this point on the bank developed its corporate advertising strategy against the background of the political and cultural changes taking place in Hong Kong.

In September 1995 the "Hongkongers" corporate image campaign was launched. It included the ads "Fisherman," "Grand-

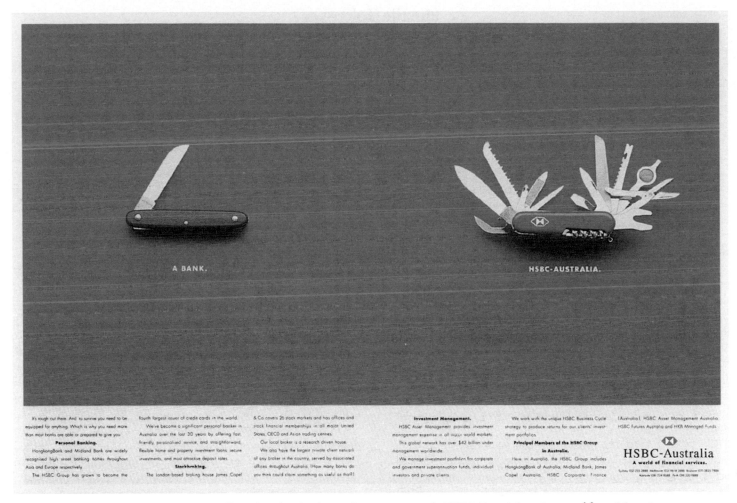

This award-winning 1995 Australian ad used a visual metaphor to represent the HSBC Group's broad range of financial services.
Courtesy of HSBC Bank Australia Ltd.

son," and "Daughter," all using the slogan "Your future is our future." The strategy evolved from the previous "Partnership" campaign. The "Hongkongers" campaign not only won numerous international advertising awards, including finalist in the corporate image category at the 1996 Cannes (France) International Advertising Festival, but also was popular with the people of Hong Kong. The campaign became a topic of conversation in Hong Kong soon after it was launched, and the creativity of its epic storytelling approach was quickly imitated by other advertisers. The campaign recalled people's memories of both the good and bad times Hong Kong had experienced, including its remarkable rags-to-riches development in the 1990s, and it called on people to have the confidence to work together for the best in the future.

Bolstered by the success of its corporate image campaign, HongkongBank continued to position itself within the political and cultural changes taking place. The "Life-Stage" campaign, which included the ads "Gold Fish" and "Clock" and which also used the tag line, "Your future is our future," was launched in April 1997. The campaign responded to the approaching change

in July by emphasizing the commitment of the bank to Hong Kong. It pledged the cooperation of the bank with the ambitious and hardworking people living in the newly formed Hong Kong Special Administrative Region of the People's Republic of China. Such corporate ads, using forward-looking and lighthearted approaches, remained the basic direction of the bank's image advertising in the years immediately after the changeover.

WENDY SIUYI WONG

Further Reading

HSBC Holdings <www.hsbc.com>

Jao, Yü Ching, *Hong Kong's Banking System in Transition: Problems, Prospects, and Policies*, Hong Kong: Chinese Banks' Association, 1988

King, Frank H.H., *The History of Hongkong and Shanghai Banking Corporation*, 4 vols., Cambridge and New York: Cambridge University Press, 1987–91; see especially vol. 4, *The Hongkong Bank in the Period of Development and Nationalism, 1941–1984: From Regional Bank to Multinational Group*, 1991

Hostile Takeover

In a hostile takeover, a company or an individual seeks to gain control of another company by increasing its stock ownership against the wishes of the management or board of directors of the target company. Once it owns a majority of shares, the acquiring company may place its own managers in control of the target's daily operations. Until the late 1980s, no advertising agency had ever attempted or been subjected to a hostile takeover.

During the "creative revolution" of the 1960s, the advertising industry experienced an entrepreneurial explosion as art directors and creative teams deserted large advertising agencies to form their own shops. The enthusiasm for advertising agencies carried over onto Wall Street. Between 1962 and 1973, 24 ad agencies went public, selling their private stock to outside investors through initial public offerings (IPOs). For these companies, the primary goal of the stock sale was to raise money to re-invest in the business or to permit the founders and senior executives to sell their interest in the company. Among the agencies that went public during this period were Foote, Cone & Belding, Ogilvy & Mather (O&M), the Interpublic Group of Companies, the J. Walter Thompson Company (JWT), Doyle Dane Bernbach (DDB), Batten Barton Durstine & Osborn (BBDO), and Grey Advertising. Each entered the IPO arena so that it could acquire capital to use in expansion, acquisitions, and employee stock-option programs.

By the late 1970s the investor enthusiasm that had accompanied the early IPOs had given way to tighter ad budgets and lack-luster profits. Several agencies went out of business, some reverted to private status, and others were acquired by or merged into other companies. The market for IPOs remained cool well into the late 1990s.

However, other trends emerged in the advertising industry. The U.S. economy's robust growth in the 1980s fueled activity in mergers and acquisitions, and the advertising industry was no exception. U.S. ad agencies grew by acquiring agencies and complementary businesses (such as public relations and marketing research) both at home and overseas to accommodate global clients in need of a full range of services. These transactions were primarily friendly business deals. Buyers and sellers came together seeking mutually agreeable combinations.

Historic Move

In June 1987 the WPP Group, originally a small maker of wire shopping carts, shocked the advertising world. Led by its Chief Executive Martin Sorrell, the British company launched the first hostile takeover of an advertising agency, JWT. Just one year earlier Sorrell had been the chief financial officer of the British agency Saatchi & Saatchi. There he had been instrumental in building the company into the world's largest advertising agency through a series of consensual acquisitions. With the purchase of JWT, he now sought to turn WPP into a marketing conglomerate. Within two weeks after the initial tender offer, JWT gave in to WPP for $566 million.

JWT was an attractive target for acquisition. Poor earnings and a highly publicized management upheaval earlier in the year had kept its stock price low. The 123-year-old agency also had a premier client roster that included Eastman Kodak Company, Ford Motor Company, Goodyear Tire & Rubber Company, IBM Corporation, and Sears, Roebuck & Company. It owned the world's largest public relations agency, Hill & Knowlton, and other advertising and marketing research companies. But JWT clients did not sit quietly observing the action. Goodyear, itself a target of a failed takeover attempt, announced its objection to the sale as did Ford. Immediately after the sale, Goodyear put its account in review. Ford moved its international accounts to other agencies but retained JWT for its U.S. advertising.

Almost two years after acquiring JWT, WPP struck again. This time the target was the Ogilvy Group. Founded by David Ogilvy in 1948, the Ogilvy Group was noted for producing memorable advertising campaigns for its clients, including the "Man in the Hathaway shirt" and, for American Express Company, "Do you know me?" The agency also produced ads for other popular brands, such as AT&T, Polaroid, Merrill Lynch & Company, and Maxwell House.

In May 1989 the Ogilvy Group disclosed that it had received a letter from WPP offering to buy the company. The agency spurned WPP's offer, saying it was unsolicited and unwelcome. Ogilvy had been prepared for such an action, having adopted a "poison pill" financial strategy designed to protect against advances from unwanted suitors. The New York state legislature even intervened to protect the agency by renewing the state law that permitted the agency's anti-takeover strategy.

In the end, however, WPP's offer was too tempting to reject. Rather than undergo a demoralizing takeover process, Ogilvy agreed to be purchased for $864 million, the highest price ever paid for an advertising agency up to that time, and at least some satisfaction for Ogilvy himself, who fought the takeover to the end.

The acquisition of Ogilvy along with JWT Group put two of the most reputable advertising agencies under one parent company. WPP had become the world's largest advertising and communications company. More than half of its clients were among the Fortune 500. After WPP's takeover of JWT Group and Ogilvy, such hostile financial maneuvers would not be employed by an agency again for eight years.

Thwarted Attempt

In December 1997 the French ad giant Publicis S.A. announced a $268 million hostile bid for True North Communications, a Chicago, Illinois-based company that owned FCB. The client roster of FCB included AT&T, S.C. Johnson & Son, and Levi Strauss &

Company. Nestlé and L'Oreal were among key clients of Publicis. No strangers to each other, the two companies had entered into a joint venture agreement in 1989. The relationship soured, however, and ended in 1997, leaving the companies as bitter rivals. Despite the separation, Publicis retained its 18.5 percent ownership stake in True North. It continued to explore other ways to bring the two companies together before proposing a merger in December 1997.

True North executives rejected the merger proposal and instead authorized the acquisition of privately owned Bozell, Jacobs, Kenyon & Eckhardt. Publicis opposed the acquisition, claiming that the deal was too expensive and would not help True North expand internationally. One FCB client, S.C. Johnson, said it would leave the agency if the takeover attempt by Publicis were successful. After a series of legal and financial maneuvers by both companies, the courts restricted Publicis from interfering with the acquisition and from pursuing its offer, ending its takeover effort.

True North's shareholders voted to acquire Bozell several days later.

PATRICK O'NEIL

Further Reading

Enrico, Dottie, "True North Fights Bitter Takeover Bid by Ad Giant Publicis," *USA Today* (8 December 1997)
Horovitz, Bruce, "Ogilvy Group Agrees to Deal with WPP for $864 Million," *Los Angeles Times* (18 May 1989)
Lipman, Joanne, "JWT Illustrates Danger of Neglecting Takeover Threat—Dismissal of WPP's Overtures Was Based on Belief of Invulnerability," *Wall Street Journal* (2 July 1987)
McEwan, Fiona, "Marketing and Advertising: Megalomania or a Real Service for International Advertisers?" *Financial Times* (6 August 1987)
Rothenberg, Randall, "WPP's Bid Is Accepted by Ogilvy," *The New York Times* (16 May 1989)

House Agency

A house, or in-house, advertising agency is an agency owned and operated by an advertiser as a company department or subsidiary. It may fulfill some, most, or all of the functions of a traditional ad agency. A house agency may mirror the structure of a full-service agency with a host of regularly staffed positions; it may perform key tasks such as media buying or creative development and outsource other work; or it may operate as an administrative hub, coordinating advertising campaigns and contracting with outside specialists on an as-needed basis.

Companies choose to keep their advertising in-house for a variety of reasons. Relatively small retail businesses often opt to organize advertising in-house because they consult with local media representatives to develop ideas; because their advertising budgets are too limited to attract agencies; or because their advertising schedules stress tight turnaround times, making it cumbersome to deal with an intermediary. Although many house agencies are small shops that service a local or regional business, a fair number of large companies also choose the house agency approach. Reasons for choosing a house advertising agency instead of an external agency differ, but six general advantages are apparent: lower cost; intimate knowledge of the product or service; continuity; confidentiality; flexibility; and speed.

Saving money has long been credited as a key reason for either keeping or moving ad agency functions in-house. Businesses anticipate that a house agency will reduce overhead, eliminate redundant personnel, avoid markups, and—perhaps most important—internalize media-buying functions, thereby saving the media commission fees customarily paid to external ad agencies.

A company's need for an agency with specialized insight into products or services may also motivate it to create a house agency. Creating ads for certain types of goods and services can require a high level of technical expertise, as well as knowledge of a specialized vocabulary. Technology, scientific, medical, and industrial firms can find it especially difficult to train new account executives or copywriters, particularly because agency teams are often transient. Continuity of personnel (as well as a consistency of vision and a broad perspective of a company's marketing aims) may be easier to maintain in internal agencies.

A company's desire to maintain confidentiality may also factor into the decision to choose an in-house approach. Keeping facts about sensitive projects, such as the introduction of new products, within the confines of the company reduces the likelihood of information leaks and eliminates the potential conflicts of interest that may arise when an outside agency also has contact with a company's competitors.

Finally, an in-house agency offers increased flexibility and the related benefit of priority handling for specific projects. A traditional agency typically works for many clients, and although an agency strives to be responsive to the special needs of each of its client companies, it is unrealistic for any client to assume that its work will receive the agency's undivided attention. In contrast, a house agency has the freedom to evaluate and rearrange work assignments on a regular basis, and it can concentrate resources on a particular program or plan.

Throughout the 20th century many notable corporations used house agencies to design and implement advertising campaigns.

For example, Bristol-Myers, Nabisco, General Electric, American Home Products, Quaker Oats, Macy's, Revlon, Ralston Purina, Sony, Lever Brothers, and Gillette have all launched campaigns created by house agencies. In the late 1990s companies with either full-service or substantially staffed house agencies included Avon, The Gap, Benetton, Best Buy, NBC, Prudential Insurance Company of America, Fidelity Investments, MasterCard International, and the National Football League.

House agencies do have drawbacks. An agency so closely linked to the advertised service or product may lack objectivity and creative independence. House agency personnel are also less likely to have the versatility or the range of creative experience found in an external agency. Some house agencies address these issues by bringing in specialists to work on some or all aspects of a campaign.

Despite the potential shortcomings of operating a house advertising agency, memorable in-house campaigns have left a mark on advertising history. In the late 19th and early 20th centuries, three of the largest and most influential U.S. advertisers used in-house operations: Royal Baking Powder, Ivory Soap, and Sapolio Soap. Another soap company, A&F Pears of England, created its campaigns in-house and was a pioneer in international advertising. Under the leadership of Managing Director Thomas A. Barratt, Pears' Soap ads were acclaimed for their use of fine art and illustrations. Celebrated campaigns developed by house agencies include: Proctor & Gamble's Ivory Soap's "99 and 44/100% pure"; Calvin Klein's "Know what comes between me and my Calvins? Nothing!"; and Springmaid linens' "A buck well spent."

In-house agencies have nurtured many honored advertising personalities and have also been the starting points for some notable, now independent, agencies. Procter & Gamble's agency, Procter & Collier, in Cincinnati, Ohio, launched the careers of Stanley Resor and Helen Lansdowne Resor of J. Walter Thompson. McCann-Erickson founder Harrison King McCann worked as ad manager at Standard Oil until the U.S. Supreme Court dissolved the company. McCann created his eponymous agency in 1912, with the re-formed Standard Oil as his primary client. In 1928 Unilever formed Lintas (Lever International Advertising Services) to serve its interests in England, The Netherlands, and Germany. Lintas Worldwide eventually dissolved its formal ties to Unilever and ultimately became Ammirati Puris Lintas and Lowe & Partners. Similarly, the AdCom advertising agency opened in 1969 as an in-house shop for Quaker Oats, only to split off in 1985, becoming Bayer Bess Vanderwarker (which was absorbed by Foote, Cone & Belding in 1996).

On the other hand, external agencies have sometimes been transformed into house agencies. In 1989 Revlon bought the independent Tarlow Advertising agency to function as the Revlon in-house organization. Coca-Cola made a similar move in 1995, when it hired three creative consultants from Creative Artists Agency to head a new in-house agency called Edge Creative.

It can sometimes be difficult for historians to identify clearly whether external or house agencies deserve the greater credit for successful campaigns. For example, in the late 1890s Prudential Insurance sought outside help with its company image; the celebrated freelance writer and early advertising educator Nathaniel C. Fowler, along with Mortimer Remington, who worked for J. Walter Thompson, came up with the idea of using the Rock of Gibraltar to symbolize the strength and stability of Prudential. However, subsequent advertising building on that image through the 1920s was created in-house.

Similarly, Procter & Gamble went outside its house agency for the first time in 20 years when it enlisted Helen Lansdowne Resor to oversee the introduction of Crisco in 1911, but Procter & Gamble advertising from that era is generally credited to the company's successful house advertising agency.

The Gap offers a contemporary example of agency cross-pollination. Throughout the 1980s The Gap created all ads in-house, but in 1993 the clothing retailer brought in Wieden & Kennedy to inject new ideas into its campaigns. After vetoing Wieden & Kennedy's suggestions, the company returned to its all-house strategy in 1994, only to assign advertising for its Banana Republic store chain to the Arnell Group later that year.

CLAUDIA CLARK

Further Reading

Fox, Stephen, *The Mirror Makers: A History of American Advertising and Its Creators*, New York: Morrow, 1984

Laird, Pamela Walker, *Advertising Progress: American Business and the Rise of Consumer Marketing*, Baltimore, Maryland: Johns Hopkins University Press, 1998

Mayer, Martin, *Whatever Happened to Madison Avenue: Advertising in the '90s*, Boston: Little Brown, 1991

Pope, Daniel, *The Making of Modern Advertising*, New York: Basic Books, 1983

Presbrey, Frank, *The History and Development of Advertising*, Garden City, New York: Doubleday, Doran, 1929

Household Cleansers

For a seemingly mundane category of products, household cleansers have produced a rich heritage of advertising. Among the earliest ad campaigns in history, and one of the first to make use of the advertising jingle, was one for Sapolio, a scouring soap. The category also spawned a memorable collection of ad icons during a post-World War II explosion of branding efforts, ranging from Mr. Clean to the Dow Bathroom Cleaner "scrubbing bubbles." Some of the advertising industry's greatest talents have lent their genius to cleanser advertising: the novelist Bret Harte wrote the first Sapolio jingles; advertising legend Jerry Della Femina created the scrubbing bubbles.

Household cleanser advertising also has been something of a chronicle of women's progress in society—or lack thereof. Magazine advertising for Lehn & Fink's Lysol disinfectant brand from 1928 to 1948 actually made the medically questionable suggestion that women use Lysol as a douche during menstruation. While most ads showed women as housewives, in the 1960s Comet cleanser, from the Procter & Gamble Company (P&G), ran ads that featured a female plumber. And in the 1990s Dow-Brands took the working woman approach one step further, showing real Dow Chemical Company scientists in their roles as product developers and mothers, developing products to make household cleaning easier.

Odes to Soap

Most household cleanser advertising, however, left no question as to whose job it was to clean up. When men did appear in the ads, they were portrayed as all-knowing purveyors of cleaning wisdom or as fantasy helpers, in the form of the Ajax knight in shining armor or Mr. Clean.

Cleanser advertising got off to a poetic start in the mid-1870s, when Enoch Morgan's Sons, a New York City soap maker, began branding a small gray cake of scouring soap "Sapolio." The Morgan family sought medical advice in developing the brand name, asking their family physician for help with a Latin-sounding name. Early advertising came in the form of pamphlets supplied to retailers. One was written by Bret Harte, whose best days were behind him, as he eked out a living in New York City writing verse such as this:

The shades of night were falling fast
As through an Eastern village passed
A youth who bore, through dust and heat,
A stencil-plate, that read complete
"Sapolio."
On household fences, gleaming bright,
Shone "Gargling Oil" in black and white;
Where "Bixby's Blacking" stood alone,
He straight beside it clapped his own—
"Sapolio."

Harte moved to Europe and ended his advertising career, and in 1884 the Morgans hired advertising manager Artemus Ward, who over the following two decades made Sapolio the best known brand name of its era. At the time Sapolio was sold seasonally for spring and fall cleanings. Ward's job was to make it a year-round product.

He directed his initial ad budget of $30,000 toward brief slogans such as, "Be clean! Sapolio scours the world," which appeared in rural weeklies and on the sides of city streetcars. He promulgated the spurious legend that the words "Oilopas esu" had been found in an Egyptian tomb; the "mysterious" phrase could be solved by reading it backward. In an early stab at global branding Ward hired a sailor to take a 14-foot sloop from Atlantic City, New Jersey, to Spain, with the Sapolio brand displayed prominently on the sail. Ward also greeted travelers arriving in New York City harbor with a 1,000-foot sign advertising Sapolio.

Spending then unheard-of thousands of dollars daily, Ward made Sapolio virtually ubiquitous. It joined P&G's Ivory soap (positioned primarily as a toilet soap for personal cleansing), Royal Baking Powder, and the Douglas Shoe as the best known brands of the day.

In 1900 Sapolio again turned to verse, when Ward hired recent Cornell University graduate James K. Fraser to develop a new campaign for what was already a household name. One night, after a dinner of Welsh rarebit, Fraser dreamed of a town where all the inhabitants testified to Sapolio's superiority. The next day he started drawing pictures and writing jingles for streetcar ads:

This is the maid of fair renown
Who scrubs the floors of Spotless Town.
To find a speck when she is through
Would take a pair of specs or two,
And her employ isn't slow,
For she employs Sapolio.

Soon the public was anticipating Sapolio ads with the same eagerness that it awaited installments of serial novels. The campaign ran for six years, ultimately inspiring real towns to pass resolutions to become as spotless as Spotless Town. Spotless Town found its way into political cartoons, books, plays—even children's toys.

As the 20th century moved onward Sapolio gave way to more versatile products such as Lysol, ammonia, and soap flakes. Advertising for these products tended toward the mundane and focused on the benefits to be gained by their use. The economic privations of the Great Depression and shortages of animal fat for production of household detergents during World War II crimped cleanser advertising.

Betty Boop Meets Mr. Clean

What could be called the golden age of cleanser commercials dawned after World War II as such companies as P&G and the

A 1928 ad for Sapolio, the ubiquitous household cleanser of the late 19th and early 20th centuries, featured the tidy residents of the mythical Spotless Town.

Colgate-Palmolive-Peet Company returned to full peacetime production and more imaginative ways of marketing their products. When P&G's Mr. Clean emerged from magazine ads to television in 1959, he ushered in a resurgence of cleanser advertising icons that lasted into the mid-1970s, spawning the hip, well-ahead-of-his-time Mr. Clean (from Tatham-Laird); Josephine the Plumber spreading the Comet cleanser gospel even as she unplugged drains (from Compton Advertising); the Ajax White Knight and "White Tornado" campaigns (from McCann-Erickson) with their impossible-to-forget "Stronger than dirt" reprise; and Dow Bathroom Cleaner's scrubbing bubbles.

Even cartoon legend Betty Boop made a cameo appearance singing the praises of Formula 409 in the early 1960s, as Spinney Manufacturing Company, a small West Springfield, Massachusetts, company, used saturation advertising from Wesley Associates, New York City, in spot markets to force distribution of the new product in stores.

Brand proliferation was the order of the day as P&G and Lever Brothers competed against a host of smaller manufacturers trying to elbow their way to dominance in the postwar household cleaning business. Once regionally important but now long forgotten brands such as Old Dutch, Kitchen Klenzer, Vano, Nylofoam, Liqua-Zone, Tish, Scoop, and Zeen came and went. The postwar cleanser business approximated something similar to a gold rush mentality. In 1946 *Advertising Age* estimated that more than 200 companies were competing in the cleanser business, of which 125 advertised, 85 using national magazines and 14 using network radio. The number of competitors had doubled between 1940 and 1946.

P&G ultimately carried the day using multiple brands with multiple positions, including Mr. Clean, Top Job, Spic and Span, and Lestoil. The technology behind its Tide synthetic heavy-duty laundry detergent began finding its way into household cleansers, helping give P&G an edge that knocked many regional competitors, along with Unilever, out of the U.S. household cleanser business.

Of all the cleaning aisle's advertising icons, P&G's Mr. Clean still towers above the rest, both literally and figuratively. The bald, muscle-bound, earring-wearing, eyebrow-raising creation of Tatham-Laird, Chicago, Illinois, premiered in magazine ads in 1958 and TV in 1959. In *Advertising Age* in 1959, ad reviewer Andy Armstrong wrote that Mr. Clean fulfilled the dual roles needed to appeal to housewives of the time in that he was both sexy and helpful around the house. "Never until now in one male torso has so much sex appeal joined so much backstairs efficiency," Armstrong wrote. He was, however, much more impressed with the print than the TV execution of Mr. Clean where, Armstrong said, he "capers jerkily and makes silly faces." He wrote: "In television, this is no doubt compulsory. Costing all that money, characters should do something. But when Mr. Clean does something, he ceases to be great and begins to look foolish. . . . Mr. Clean is a fine fellow, an inspired concept—in print. But he is lousy on TV. Maybe his uncles will take him off before he defeats his illusion and the product's, too."

Mr. Clean captured leadership of the household cleanser aisle in the 1960s. In a 1985 survey Mr. Clean had name recognition among 93 percent of Americans, according to a survey commissioned by P&G, almost twice the name recognition of then-U.S. Vice President George Bush.

Mr. Clean's undisputed pre-eminence came under challenge, however, from the Clorox Company, which acquired Formula 409 and Pine Sol in the 1990s to dominate the category. Mr. Clean really stuck his foot in the bucket in 1994, when P&G made the strategic misstep of concentrating the product so that it would take less shelf space, a step intended to please retailers. Clorox did not follow suit with its products, which appeared bigger and better priced on store shelves, accelerating their market share gains over Mr. Clean. As P&G celebrated Mr. Clean's 40th birthday in 1998, the company reverted to the original nonconcentrated formula but without doing much to regain market share. When P&G extended Mr. Clean to antibacterial cleaning wipes in 2000, he was beaten two-to-one by Clorox Disinfecting Wipes, which rolled out simultaneously. Production and supply glitches that kept P&G from stocking some stores with the wipes contributed to Mr. Clean's woes. But even if Mr. Clean was being pushed around like a 98-pound weakling by Clorox, the strength of the icon endured. Both the Honda automobile and EconoLodge motel chain borrowed him for ad campaigns of their own in the late 1990s.

Josephine the Plumber

As was the case with Mr. Clean, Josephine the Plumber's impact spread beyond her category. Launched in 1963 in a campaign by Compton Advertising, Josephine, played by actress Jane Withers, spent 11 years praising Comet and proving its effectiveness against "another" leading brand in side-by-side comparisons removing stains from sinks, bathtubs, and kitchen countertops. Josephine was retired in 1974, but she served as a role model for another P&G working-class heroine, Rosie the Waitress, played by actress Nancy Walker, who likewise made use of side-by-side demos to prove that Bounty paper towels were the "Quicker picker upper." Former P&G chief executive officers Edwin L. Artzt and Durk Jager list Bounty's Rosie ads, from Jordan McGrath Case & Taylor, New York City, as among P&G's five best of the 20th century because they turned the side-by-side demo into something of an art form.

Josephine's archrival in the powder cleanser business was Colgate's Ajax, introduced in the 1940s, via ad agency Sherman & Marquette, Inc., with the long-running jingle:

Ajax, the foaming cleanser,
Floats the dirt right down the drain.
Ba ba ba boom . . .

Increased competition in the category, however, forced Colgate to become more aggressive in its advertising. In 1963 a new campaign by Norman, Craig & Kummel depicted Ajax as having the cleaning power of a "white tornado." The campaign ran through the early 1970s. Buttressing those efforts were ads for Ajax laundry detergent featuring a knight in shining armor galloping on horseback. The memorable musical tag line, "Stronger than dirt," linked both campaigns.

Another working-class heroine, Madge, appeared on behalf of Colgate's Palmolive dish soap via Young & Rubicam, Inc., doing a decade's worth of Palmolive manicures to demonstrate the light-duty liquid's gentleness on hands.

From Drudgery to Dream

Though cleansing benefits, ease of use, and gentleness have been staples of cleanser advertising over the years, some have recognized the simple drudgery involved in the products' use and concentrated instead on the idea of taking consumers away from it all.

Though P&G's Spic and Span, acquired from Spic, Inc., in 1945 (and sold in 2001 to Shansby Group, San Francisco, California), made plenty of superior cleaning claims over the years, contests were a staple of the brand's appeal, too. In its first post-World War II contest, P&G offered a chance to win a new HomeOla prefabricated home plus $4,000 for a lot and landscaping to boost Spic and Span, plus a second prize of a 1947 Chevrolet Fleetmaster sedan, and additional prizes of 10 Eureka home cleaning systems and 100 Eureka cordless irons. In a 1986 promotion P&G went one better by packing diamonds, sapphires, emeralds, and garnets into Spic and Span floor cleanser, as well as into packages of Safeguard and Camay soaps and Bounce fabric softener. Every package had at least a garnet, with one in 10,000 containing a diamond.

Adopting a different approach, some marketers depicted women not as eagerly receiving cleansing technology from men but as developing the technology. The Dow cleansing brands, including Dow Bathroom Cleaner and Fantastik household cleaning spray, had received little ad support for nearly a decade when the Dow Chemical Company in 1996 launched a campaign from Campbell Mithun Esty, of Minneapolis, Minnesota, portraying Dow research scientists in their dual roles as developers and users of cleansing products. The ads, which supported a move to develop a common identity for Dow brands products by adding the Dow diamond to all packages, ultimately helped Dow in its quest to shed its consumer products business, which was sold to S.C. Johnson & Son a year later.

S.C. Johnson had developed its own Johnson Wax and Pledge furniture polish brands in the 1930s and built its reputation through sponsorship of radio's *Fibber McGee and Molly* via Needham, Louis & Brorby. Johnson became an even bigger force in the cleanser business with its 1992 purchase of Bristol-Myers Squibb's former Drackett household products business, including Windex window cleaner. Within five years S.C. Johnson had doubled the business of the former Drackett brands to more than $1 billion through a combination of new product support and increased advertising by FCB Worldwide, Chicago, Illinois. Windex was supported with sponsorship of basketball games on ESPN, where announcer Dick Vitale referred to rebounds as "cleaning the glass." New products included a "no drip" version and Windex Outdoor, a product that attached to garden hoses for

Procter & Gamble first brought its Tide "washday miracle" to U.S. homes in 1947; the product eventually became the most recognized laundry detergent in the world.
Courtesy of The Procter & Gamble Company.

"touchless" outside window cleaning and that was launched in 1997 with a newspaper campaign timed to run on Fridays only in cities where the weather forecast called for sunny weekend weather.

Renewed Efforts

By the end of the 1990s, cleansing power was no longer the drawing card it once was, as house cleaning took second priority to work and leisure activities. Household products makers turned renewed attention to the category with new brands and benefits.

In an effort to bring its dominant position in Mexico with it to the United States, Colgate introduced its Fabuloso cleaner brand north of the border in 1996. Despite minimal advertising, Fabuloso did well in U.S. Latino markets, helped by its floral scent. Colgate applied the idea of adding fragrance to dishwashing liquid, launching Palmolive Spring Sensations with "aromatherapy" scents, carrying such names as Ocean Breeze and Spring Blossom. Backed by ads from Young & Rubicam featuring homemakers talking only about scent, not cleansing power, Spring Sensations helped Palmolive close the gap with P&G's Dawn dishwashing liquid.

While fragrance was a selling point for some, eliminating odors was the idea behind P&G's Febreze brand, launched in 1998 with ads from Grey Advertising, New York City. Febreze transferred a benefit from the air freshener category into household cleaning, promising a spray that "permanently cleans away" odors with molecules that chemically bind odor particles. Febreze had sales of more than $250 million in the United States its first year, making it second only to Nabisco Foods's SnackWells fat-free cookie and cracker line among new packaged-goods brands in the 1990s.

Convenience also became a chief selling point. In 1994 the Kao Corporation in Japan launched the Quickle Wiper, a swivel-head mop with an electrostatic dust cloth attached that could be used for mopping floors or dusting other surfaces, with the benefits of holding onto dirt and eliminating the need for dustpans or bending over to use them. Noting the success, P&G launched its Swiffer brand into test market in 1998 and global distribution a year later, with ads from D'Arcy Masius Benton & Bowles, New York City, featuring a tag line suggested by Barefoot Advertising, of Cincinnati, Ohio: "When Swiffer's the one, consider it done." S.C. Johnson licensed Kao's Quickle product and rolled it out in the United States and Europe under the Pledge Grab-It brand, placing second in the United States and vying for leadership globally.

Only a year later P&G had two Swiffer line extensions—Swiffer Max, a larger, better-performing version, and Swiffer Wet, a wet cloth for bucketless floor cleaning. Waiting in the wings was Swiffer Wet Jet, a battery-powered product with replaceable cleaning solution, which P&G introduced in Canada and Belgium. P&G rolled out Swiffer WetJet in the United States in August 2001 at the heretofore unheard-of price of nearly $50, after successful runs in Belgium and Canada. Clorox was poised to counter with its own pump-operated Clorox Ready Mop, another bucketless floor cleaning system operated by pump rather than motor.

Swiffer ads took a step few cleaning brands had before by showing men cleaning. One execution for the original Swiffer featured an all-male song-and-dance routine singing the praises and showing the ease of using Swiffer. In another reversal of traditional roles, an ad had a fictional female researcher introduce Swiffer Wet by leaving a mess on a diner floor and a Swiffer Wet mop next to a male diner. The ad shows him break into an uncontrolled cleaning frenzy when presented with the ease of using Swiffer Wet.

After 130 years in business, some things have changed in the cleanser industry and its advertising—and some have not. Housecleaning has again become a priority for household products companies, but men are actually seen doing some of the work.

JACK NEFF

See also Procter & Gamble Company; *and color plate in this volume*

Further Reading

Armstrong, Andy, "The Screen and Mr. Clean," *Advertising Age* (24 August 1959)

Beatty, Sally Goll, "Honda to Use Mr. Clean to Add Muscle to Environmental Claims," *Wall Street Journal* (26 September 1997)

Fox, Stephen R., *The Mirror Makers: A History of Advertising and Its Creators*, New York: Morrow, 1984

Murray, Robert W., Jr., "Hordes of Newcomers Battle for Cleaner Sales: Competitors Have Doubled since '40; Data Is Scrambled," *Advertising Age* (29 April 1946)

Neff, Jack, "Brand in Trouble: P&G's Mr. Clean Gets Friendlier in Bid for a Rebound," *Advertising Age* (1 December 1997)

Neff, Jack, "Struggling Mr. Clean Axes 'Ultra'; Readies New Scent: P&G Household Cleaner Prepares $10 Million in Ads As Brand Marks 40th Birthday," *Advertising Age* (3 August 1998)

Presbrey, Frank, *The History and Development of Advertising*, Garden City, New York: Doubleday, 1929; reprint, New York: Greenwood Press, 1968

Solomon, Jolie, "Procter & Gamble Plans a Real Jewel of a Promotion—Firm to Pack Some Products with Emeralds, Garnets, Diamonds, and Sapphires," *Wall Street Journal* (27 January 1986)

Weisz, Pam, "Ultra-Clean: Retail Cheers Still More P&G Concentrates: Procter & Gamble Introduces Superconcentrated Versions of 'Ultra' Liquid Cleaners," *Brandweek* (22 August 1994)

Howell Henry Chaldecott Lury. *See* HHCL and Partners

Humor

Most of the influential pioneers of advertising took a serious approach to their craft. Still, a few of the more daring copywriters gambled on the chance that humor could be used to sell. These risk takers were right—sometimes. Humor is a viable strategy, but it is by no means a sure bet. Traditional hard-sell pioneers such as Claude Hopkins of Lord & Thomas deplored the use of humor in advertising, saying in 1923, "People do not buy from clowns." Yet the fact that Hopkins found it necessary to condemn humor is evidence of its use in that comparatively early period in the development of the U.S. advertising industry.

Humorous print advertising in the United States dates back to the 1880s or possibly earlier. Even the venerable Ivory Soap, manufactured by historically conservative Procter & Gamble Company, employed humor in its advertising as early as the 1920s. An Ivory ad in the *Saturday Evening Post* in 1924 featured the headline "Soap Fisherman" over an illustration of a man in a tub feeling under the water for a lost bar of soap. Despite increasing use of humor in the decades that followed, there was strong conventional wisdom on the part of many in advertising, including the influential ad executive David Ogilvy, that good copywriters should resist the temptation to entertain. It was not until 1982 that Ogilvy altered his view, writing, "I have reason to believe that . . . humor can now sell."

In fact, through much of the 20th century humor in advertising was regarded with suspicion, and this view only began to change in the early 1980s—and then only gradually. It was with the advent of broadcasting that humor became a major executional tactic. In a 1995 survey of U.S. media, only 9.9 percent of consumer magazine ads had a humorous intent; in TV the percentage was 24.4, and in radio 30.6. Clearly, broadcasting is seen as the medium where humor has its best chance of success.

Radio

In its earliest form, radio advertising was comprised of formal sponsorships—for example, the *Lucky Strike Radio Show* and the *Maxwell House Showboat*—rather than actual sales messages. Even as advertising shifted from the subtle tactic of sponsorships to the use of distinct "plugs," the association between program content and advertising remained strong because the programs were owned by the advertisers rather than the networks. Consequently, radio talent was employed directly by advertisers, and commercial spots were performed live within the program, often by the stars of the programs themselves. Humor was an important part of programming during the glory days of radio.

The first program to integrate a humorous commercial into the fabric of the show was the *Fibber McGee and Molly Show*, packaged for Johnson Wax by the Chicago, Illinois, agency Needham, Louis & Brorby (predecessor to Needham, Harper & Steers). The announcer, Harlow Wilcox, became a regular member of the cast, who would drop by the McGee home in the middle of the program. The premise was always that McGee knew a commercial was coming, but that he did not know how Wilcox would work it

in. Bob Hope kidded his radio sponsor Pepsodent to the point where he would drop references to his sponsor into his motion pictures. Among the best integrated commercials were those done by Jack Benny, first for Jell-O (Young & Rubicam) and after 1944 for Lucky Strike (Ruthrauff & Ryan and Batten Barton Durstine & Osborn [BBDO]). In the late 1940s the musical act on the show, the Sportsmen Quartet, would perform one chorus of a popular song, then turn it into the singing commercial for Lucky Strike in the second chorus.

As network radio declined in the 1950s a new kind of approach to radio humor emerged whereby advertisers could no longer produce and control the program environments that had traditionally drawn audiences for their selling messages. The new radio humor was such that the commercial itself now had to be appealing enough to draw an audience. Its practitioners, in effect, created free-standing 60-second programs.

No one pioneered this technique more skillfully than Bob Elliott and Ray Goulding, whose work took humorous advertising to a new level and paved the way for other comics. They not only performed low-key, funny commercials on their own shows, but they also were available for hire to other advertisers for the purpose of creating and performing ad campaigns to run on a spot basis. Starting in the early 1950s with Piel's Beer, when the two portrayed the characters Bert and Harry Piel, they formed Goulding-Elliott-Greybar Production as a kind of creative boutique. The D.P. Brother Agency in Detroit, Michigan, retained Elliott and Goulding on behalf of General Motors's Guardian Maintenance Service for a campaign that continued for nearly a decade. Other clients included General Electric lamps (via BBDO), Nationwide Insurance (Ogilvy & Mather), and the Radio Advertising Bureau.

The second major innovator in radio advertising humor was Stan Freberg, who came to prominence in 1951 when his recorded parody of a fictional radio soap opera, *John and Marsha*, became a hit for Capitol Records. He formed Freberg, Ltd., in the late 1950s to market his talents as a satirist to advertisers. Its motto was *Ars Gratia Pecuniae* (Art for money's sake). A typical Freberg commercial took a familiar premise and played it as a joke, working in selling points almost as an afterthought. For Kenyon & Eckhardt, Freberg sold Prince spaghetti by creating a parody of the James Bond film *Goldfinger*. Since 1956 he has turned out hundreds of commercials for such brands as Contadina tomato paste, Chun King chow mein, Meadowgold Dairies, Sunsweet prunes, and the United Presbyterian Church.

In the 1970s and 1980s the most in-demand radio humorists in U.S. advertising were Dick Orkin and Bert Berdis, whose Radio Ranch Productions was based in Chicago. Orkin and Berdis created and performed their own commercials in an easygoing, naturalistic manner. Unlike Freberg, they avoided satire and premised their commercials on small situations that emphasized recognizable human foibles. Their series for *Time* magazine in the 1970s ran for several years and received countless awards. Orkin and Berdis split up as a team in the early 1980s, but Orkin continued

The Richards Group created this tongue-in-cheek bovine public-service ad for a campaign for the Chick-fil-A restaurant chain. The billboard was a finalist for an Obie Award in 1999.

on his own through the 1990s and beyond. Other boutiques specializing in radio humor include the Chuck Blore Company, Joy Radio, and Radio Radio!

Television

When World War II ended, television expanded rapidly. By 1948 *Howdy Doody*, *Toast of the Town* (later called the *Ed Sullivan Show*), and the *Texaco Star Theater* (with Milton Berle) had all debuted. Freberg, again, was one of the pioneers in exploring the creative potential of television advertising. By the early 1960s Freberg, Ltd., was producing highly regarded humorous television spots, such as its much-publicized minimusical for H.J. Heinz Company, which starred dancer Ann Miller and cost an extravagant (for 1970) $50,000 to produce. Freberg's work garnered numerous creative awards and established humor as a viable television strategy.

Humor's role in television advertising has continued to grow. Alka-Seltzer's spots from the 1960s and 1970s ("Atsa some spicy meatball" and "I can't believe I ate the whole thing"), the work of Joe Sedelmaier for Federal Express and Wendy's ("Where's the beef?"), Budweiser's frog-hating lizards, and other humorous television ads have become part of American popular culture. Indeed, for Super Bowl commercials, typically the highest-priced broadcast time, humor has become the dominant strategy.

Important Variables

Humor is a universal human phenomenon, yet it is an elusive concept that has defied a precise definition. People have an implicit sense of what is humorous, just as they have an implicit understanding of sadness. And yet, of course, not everyone finds the same things funny.

In the advertising literature, Paul Speck suggested in a 1991 study three basic humor processes: arousal-safety, incongruity resolution, and humorous disparagement. Most advertising uses incongruity; disparagement is used infrequently. The three processes further combine to create five humor types: comic wit, sentimental humor, satire, sentimental comedy, and full comedy. Studies show that different kinds of humor work better in some media than in others. Moreover, different products benefit from different approaches. In magazine ads, for example, research indicates that incongruity works especially well for so-called low-risk products (i.e., those with low financial, performance, and social risk) such as snack foods and beer. For these products, magazine ads that use humor in a dominant role or in messages that are focused on image (rather than on information) score well. Humor-dominant ads do not work well in magazine advertising for any other product categories.

A survey of executives at the largest ad agencies in the United States and Britain revealed that both groups generally favor the use of humor in advertising; the British executives, in particular, were proponents of humor. Compared to the Americans, they were significantly more positive about the value of humor in achieving seven key communication objectives (attention, comprehension, recall, communication of complex information, persuasion, intention, and action). Moreover, the potential harmful effects of humor on recall and comprehension were of comparatively less concern to the British group. Whereas the U.S. executives saw humor as best suited to messages for younger, better-educated, male, upscale, and professional audiences, the British group was generally less biased toward humor aimed at these subgroups and more positive toward the use of humor in communicating with a broad array of audiences. The two groups of executives agreed that the best use of humor was in ads targeting younger adults, while the least appropriate use was in ads aimed at older audiences. The British bias in favor of humor is evident in the fact that 35.5 percent of U.K. television ads are intended to be humorous, compared to only 24.4 percent in the United States. Both groups of executives agreed that TV and radio are the advertising media best suited to the use of humor. In advertising for

Fortunately, every day comes with an evening.

This early 1990s ad for Windsor Canadian whiskey was part of an award-winning series that highlighted some of the frustrations encountered in a typical workday.
Courtesy of Jim Beam Brands Co.

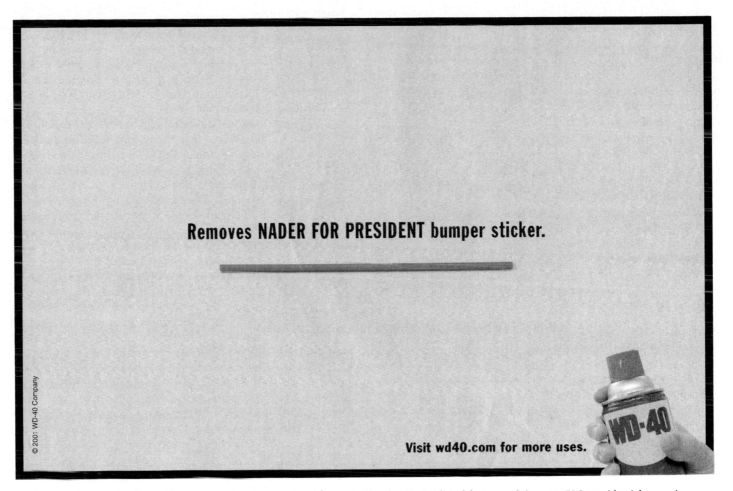

Removes **NADER FOR PRESIDENT** bumper sticker.

Visit wd40.com for more uses.

© 2001 WD-40 Company

An advertisement for the multipurpose product WD-40 found humor in the changing political fortunes of the 2000 U.S. presidential campaign. *Courtesy WD-40 Company.*

low-risk product categories, the British use humor in more than 50 percent of their TV ads.

Humor is not appropriate for every product or advertising goal. But in a review of the literature, Marc Weinberger and Charles Gulas concluded in 1992 that, not surprisingly, people like humor. While this finding may seem obvious, it should not be overlooked. The link between humor and liking is very strong, and liking is positively correlated with measures of advertising success.

Humor also draws attention, an important function in an increasingly cluttered advertising landscape, but it apparently does so without interfering with comprehension. Although there are some examples of increased persuasion linked to humor, it appears that a humorous approach does not offer significant advantages over a more serious one when persuasion is the goal. Nor does humor enhance source credibility—quite the opposite in some circumstances.

Comparative studies have shown that humor related to the product or to the message is superior to humor that is unrelated. Audience factors also affect response. What is funny to people in a certain gender, ethnic, or age group must be assessed in relation to the group's perspective. Another important consideration: who is the object of the humor? Research from the 1990s indicated that if an ad intended as humorous is not perceived as humorous, the ad's effectiveness can be compromised.

The nature of the product also affects the appropriateness of a humorous treatment. Humor appears to be more successful in ads for existing rather than new products. It is used much more often and appears to be most effective for so-called low-involvement products (e.g., household cleansers, soft drinks, light bulbs) in general and, in particular, for inexpensive treats such as snack foods, candy, and beer.

Risky Business

The use of humor as an advertising strategy and tactic has grown over the years. Perhaps more than any other form of commercial speech, the humorous broadcast commercial has become a part of American popular culture. Television broadcasters have aired humorous ads as program content, and humorous ads such as Wendy's "Where's the beef?" and the "Energizer Bunny" have become fodder for stand-up comedians and politicians alike.

Widespread use notwithstanding, humor has inherent risks. As noted above, it is more appropriate for certain product categories than others. Also, it is more likely to gain attention and be liked than to create credibility or be persuasive. More important, humor has the potential to cause negative effects. It can be offensive—indeed, most humor walks a fine line between funny and offensive. While this is not a serious problem for a comedian, an offensive ad could have dire consequences for an advertiser. In 1999 Just For Feet ran an ad in the Super Bowl that was intended to be humorous. However, many considered the ad racially insensitive and offensive. Just For Feet sued Saatchi & Saatchi, the agency that created the ad, for malpractice. Just For Feet claimed that the ad had caused its business to suffer and "created the unfounded and unintended public perception that it is a racist or racially insensitive company." In January 2000 Just For Feet filed for bankruptcy. Another risk run by advertisers that opt for humor is that the audience will not understand the joke. Intended humor is not synonymous with successful humor, and research has shown that a failed attempt at humor is less effective than a more serious approach. All of these considerations suggest that, perhaps more than in other forms of advertising, humor needs to be tested on the audiences that it is intended to influence.

When print advertising was in its infancy, humor played a peripheral role in advertising strategy. This was also the case with radio and TV advertising. As each of these media matured, however, the role of humor became more firmly defined. It remains to be seen if humor will also become a common strategy in Internet advertising and other forms of emerging media.

CHARLES S. GULAS AND MARC G. WEINBERGER

Further Reading

Advertising Age 66 (Spring 1995) (special issue entitled "50 Years of TV Advertising")

Herold, Don, *Humor in Advertising, and How to Make It Pay,* New York: McGraw-Hill, 1963

Ogilvy, David, *Confessions of an Advertising Man,* New York: Atheneum, 1963; London: Longmans, 1964

Ogilvy, David, and Joel Raphaelson, "Research on Advertising Techniques That Work—and That Don't," *Harvard Business Review* 60, no. 4 (July/August 1982)

Speck, Paul Surgi, "The Humorous Message Taxonomy: A Framework for the Study of Humorous Ads," in *Current Issues and Research in Advertising,* edited by James H. Leigh and Claude R. Martin, Jr., Ann Arbor: Division of Research, Graduate School of Business Administration, University of Michigan, 1991

Spotts, Harlan, Marc G. Weinberger, and Amy L. Parsons, "Assessing the Use and Impact of Humor on Advertising Effectiveness: A Contingency Approach," *Journal of Advertising* 26, no. 3 (Fall 1997)

Weinberger, Marc G., Leland Campbell, and Beth Brody, *Effective Radio Advertising,* New York: Lexington, 1994

Weinberger, Marc G., and Charles S. Gulas, "The Impact of Humor in Advertising: A Review," *Journal of Advertising* 21, no. 4 (December 1992)

Weinberger, Marc G., and Harlan Spotts, "Humor in U.S. versus U.K. TV Commercials: A Comparison," *Journal of Advertising* 18, no. 2 (1989)

Weinberger, Marc G., et al., "The Use and Effect of Humor in Different Advertising Media," *Journal of Advertising Research* 35, no. 3 (May/June 1995)

Hunt Lascaris

(TBWA Hunt Lascaris)

Founded in 1983 by Reg Lascaris, John Hunt, Graham Medcalf, and Jenny Groenewald in Johannesburg, South Africa, as Hunt Lascaris & Medcalf; sold 10 percent stake (later increased to majority holding) to TBWA, Paris, France, 1984; awarded the BMW account, 1988; reorganized, 1999; sold 25 percent stake to a black-owned investment group, Millennium Consolidated Investments, June 2001, leaving TBWA with 53 percent and management with 22 percent.

Major Clients
BMW
Kelly Girl
Nashua (photocopiers)

Sara Lee Corporation (Wonderbra)
Seychelles tourism
Shangrila Hotels (Hong Kong)
Standard Bank
TAG Heuer

From the start, the founders of TBWA Hunt Lascaris sought to build the first world-class ad agency to come out of Africa. Less than two decades after Reg Lascaris and John Hunt hung out their shingle in 1983, that far-fetched goal had been achieved. The agency was named by *Advertising Age International* as "International Agency of the Year" in 1994. *Campaign* magazine, the Brit-

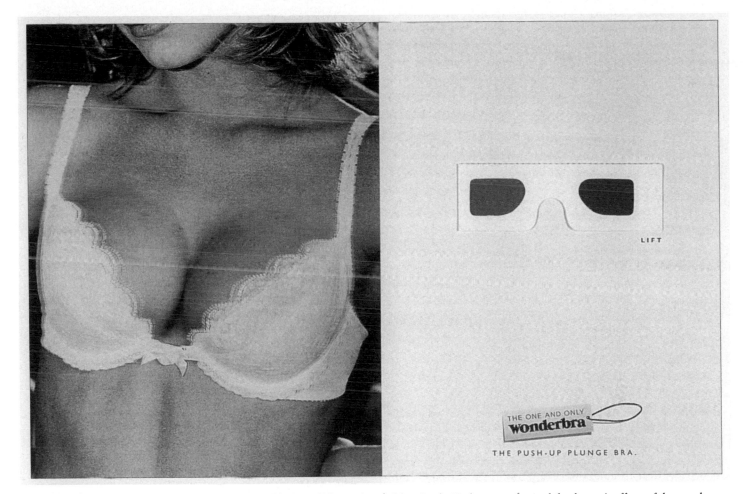

In Hunt Lascaris's award winning 1996 magazine ad for Wonderbra, a detachable pair of 3-D glasses emphasized the dramatic effects of the popular push-up bra.

ish advertising trade publication, included Hunt Lascaris in its list of the ten best agencies around the world in 2000, and that same year the *Financial Mail*, South Africa's leading weekly business magazine, named it the country's "Ad Agency of the Century."

The agency built itself on creativity. "Everything we do has to be with a creative twist," Lascaris has said. "Even the tea lady is expected to be creative." For example, the agency created an award-winning magazine advertisement with a three-dimensional photograph of a well-endowed model wearing a Wonderbra, with 3-D viewing spectacles pasted to the page.

Lascaris and Hunt met in 1975 when they were working for a small South African agency called Hands. They talked about starting their own agency, and by 1981 Lascaris was ready to propose a start-up. But Hunt had already decided to take a year's sabbatical to write a novel, and the launch was postponed until 1983. Meanwhile, Lascaris prepared a business plan and raised financing.

The agency was launched in 1983 as Hunt Lascaris & Medcalf, with a third partner, Graham Medcalf. The partners did not draw a salary for their first eight months, and Medcalf pulled out of the venture before the agency became viable. A fourth founding partner, whose name was not on the shingle, was Jenny Groe-

newald, an art director, who stayed with the agency until her retirement several years later.

The shop's first clients were Nashua, a photocopier company that was still with the agency in 2000, and Kelly Girl, a secretarial recruitment business. Within its first year the agency won a third client, Big Jack pies. But the agency's breakthrough came when it was awarded the BMW account five years later, a win that gave it credibility.

In the meantime, the agency affiliated with TBWA, then a relatively unknown Paris, France-based agency, in 1984, when South Africa was becoming an international pariah because of the government's policy of apartheid. TBWA initially took a 10 percent stake and increased it to 20 percent at a time when South Africa was suffering a wave of disinvestment. TBWA later gained equity control, but in 2001 it sold 25 percent of the equity to Millennium Consolidated Investments, a black-owned investment group, in response to pressure from the government on all ad agencies. Only by signing this deal was the agency able to qualify for the (government-owned) SA Tourism account. The head of Millennium is Cyril Ramaphosa, a prominent businessman who was once an unsuccessful candidate for leadership of the ruling African National Congress. Increasingly, governmental and quasi-governmental bodies are insisting on a 26 percent level of black ownership before considering an agency. TBWA Hunt Lascaris exceeds this threshold by virtue of Millennium's 25 percent and another 2 percent held by black executives of the agency.

While the agency's creative ethos may have been the driving force behind its climb to become one of the top agencies in South Africa, it was supported by an equal talent for self-promotion, usually by provoking outrage. Early on, Hunt Lascaris built a reputation for flouting convention—and often for breaking the rules, too. This helped it build unparalleled public awareness but earned some criticism from competitors for undermining the ad industry's standing with a government many feared could easily be tempted to impose regulatory controls on advertising.

For example, comparative advertising, in which rival products are named, was banned under the Advertising Standards Authority code of practice, but Hunt Lascaris repeatedly was sanctioned by the authority (while gaining approval from an iconoclastic public) for making comparisons in subtle ways that tested the limits of public and regulatory acceptance.

A marketing war between Hunt Lascaris client BMW and Mercedes-Benz for domination of the luxury car category in South Africa produced many blows and counter-blows but resulted in BMW gaining a share of the market unequaled anywhere else in the world. In one early battle, a Mercedes commercial reenacted the true story of how a driver had survived a 100-foot plunge in his vehicle off a mountainous coastal road. Hunt Lascaris responded with a commercial showing that BMW had the ability to negotiate the bends without accident. The voice-over was provocatively ambiguous: did it say "beat the bends" or "beat the Benz"?

BMW, an important client for the agency, was willing to play along with this strategy because it positioned the brand as an irreverent alternative to the safe, staid Mercedes. And it was a sufficiently respectable brand name to open the doors of other big clients to the growing, young agency. Hunt Lascaris became a lead agency for BMW on a global scale, and other clients soon followed. The agency aimed to get 5 percent of its creative work from beyond South Africa's borders in 2001 and to raise that to 10 percent by 2002. This would leverage the weak South African currency into a financially winning position for the agency, Hunt said. International clients included Seychelles tourism, watchmaker Tag Heuer, and Hong Kong's Shangrila Hotels.

As it entered the 21st century, however, the agency began responding to client demands by adopting a more strategic approach, positioning itself as a seamless all-around marketing resource. In an attempt to find new growth areas in a small marketplace, it began to diversify into specialized units, including direct response, retail advertising, promotions, and sponsorships. In 1999 it reorganized to move these nontraditional advertising activities out of the agency and into the local unit of TBWA's nontraditional marketing arm, Tequila, leaving Hunt Lascaris to focus on creative work. At the same time, Lascaris was appointed TBWA regional director for Africa, the Middle East, and Eastern Europe, and he became the agency's co-chairman with Hunt. Richard Reast was brought in from TBWA in London, England, to take on the managing director role of the flagship agency. In 2000 the agency had gross income of $26.4 million, a 12.3 percent increase over 1999 on billings of $228.6 million, and a staff of 544.

TONY KOENDERMAN

I

IBM Corporation

Principal Agencies
Cecil & Presbrey
Benton and Bowles, Inc.
Marsteller, Rickard, Gebhardt & Reed, Inc.
Ogilvy, Benson & Mather (later Ogilvy & Mather)
Lord, Geller, Federico, Einstein, Inc.
Wells, Rich, Greene, Inc.
Lintas:Worldwide
GGK (Paris)

Since its beginnings as a manufacturer of punch cards and meat slicers, IBM Corporation has continuously redefined itself in an effort to establish and maintain its leadership in an industry undergoing vast technological changes. At the beginning of the 21st century, the company, with revenue of $88.4 billion, was considered the blue-chip leader in the Internet and electronic-services industry.

IBM was incorporated in 1911 as the Computing-Tabulating-Recording (C-T-R) Company. It was created by the merger of the Tabulating Machine Company, Computing Scale Company of America, and International Time Recording Company. The new entity, C-T-R, with 1,300 employees, made and sold a wide range of machinery, including commercial scales, industrial time recorders, tabulators, and punch cards.

The First Mr. Watson

In 1914 Thomas J. Watson, a tenacious salesman from the National Cash Register Company of New York City, joined the company as general manager and was promoted to president within 11 months. In his first ten years of management of C-T-R, Watson recognized the increasing opportunities in global markets and the power of the company's tabulating machine to revolutionize business operations. Watson expanded the company globally and divested all nontabulating business. In February 1924 the company's name was changed to International Business Machines Corporation (IBM) to reflect its growth.

IBM's first sales messages and overall philosophy were deeply impressed on its salesmen, who were the first to sport the white-collared, blue-suited professional image that would be associated with the company until the early 1990s. Watson made sure that the sales staff was well versed in a strict code of conduct; a priority was assuring customers that their concerns were of primary importance to the company. In fact, the first slogans and jingles for the growing company were created in-house to foster a strong company image among its employees. Watson's motto, "Think," became a symbol of IBM and its innovations, with framed placards of the word posted throughout all company offices. Employees even sang catchy songs praising the company and Watson himself: "With Mr. Watson leading / to greater heights we'll rise / and keep our IBM / respected in all eyes."

Although Watson believed that investing in his sales force was far more important than traditional advertising spending, the company did retain an agency, Frank Presbrey Advertising, New York City, in 1924. Watson wanted to promote a strong national image of IBM performing its industrial duty to the United States and the world. He adopted an ambitious and internationally known slogan for the company, "World peace through world trade." During World War II, he joined other U.S. industrial leaders to promote the sale of war bonds in several print advertising campaigns. As part of this wartime effort, Watson turned over all IBM facilities to the U.S. government, which used them for military manufacturing.

Changing Direction

By 1950 IBM was again marketing typewriters, which it had introduced in 1933, and its massive punch card machines—such as the Mark I and the IBM 701—which were primarily sold to government and research projects. But a new development was about to change the company's direction. In the 1940s, the first computer, ENIAC (Electronic Numeral Integrator and Computer), was created for the U.S. military and soon was put into development in the private sector; in 1951 Remington Rand delivered the first Univac computer to the U.S. Census Bureau and

A 1929 ad showed the broad range of business equipment offered by IBM.

IBM 7070

SEPT. 2, 1958...MILESTONE IN COMPUTER HISTORY

A few months ago, the first in a line of fully transistorized IBM data processing systems was introduced. Orders from outstanding leaders in manufacturing, banking, utilities, and transportation signal enthusiastic recognition of the special abilities of the IBM 7070 to handle medium volume data processing problems. The big reason: IBM 7070 offers more performance per dollar than any other system in its class. How? Through unique efficiency and economy engineered into the IBM 7070 with advanced features like these:

Transistor Design . . . simplifies installation, cuts installation costs, saves space, minimizes cooling power and maintenance.   **"Building Block" Units** . . . modular concept means that IBM 7070 can grow as you grow.   **Maximum Processing Economy** . . . IBM 7070 "reads," "writes," computer simultaneously, provides "automatic priority processing," furnishes immediate access to data.   **Pretested Programming** . . . a library of advanced programs at no extra cost.   **Exclusive Operating Features** . . . for the first time in a solid-state system, the IBM 7070 combines higher storage capacity and faster computing speed with high-speed input output.   **Unrivaled Service** . . . from education of your personnel to top-notch service engineering, from program planning to testing—IBM men and methods help put modern data processing to work for you sooner.

For further details on the new IBM 7070 . . . call your local IBM representative or write to: International Business Machines Corporation, 590 Madison Avenue, New York 22, N. Y.

A logic component in a standard modular system of the IBM 7070. Each transistor panel is the functional equivalent of several conventional vacuum tubes.

LEADERSHIP IN DATA PROCESSING

Celebrating a "Milestone in Computer History," IBM introduced the IBM 7070, the first fully transistorized data processing system, in 1958.

eventually sold 46 Univacs at a cost of $1 million each. Seeing this as a threat to its own business, IBM began work in this new area, developing advanced calculating machines, taking advantage of newly downsized transistor tubes to create equipment that was increasingly affordable for business as well as the government.

In 1950 Watson, 76 years old but still in power at IBM, greeted the new decade with an ambitious print campaign that sought to sell America on the benefits of capitalism, which was treating his own company so well. Designed by Cecil & Presbrey, the successor agency to Frank Presbrey Advertising, "Capitalism: Nothing is superior except by comparison," included an essay by Watson exalting the dollar benefits of capitalism in the United States and seeking to erase the fears of the Great Depression of the 1930s and uncertainty in the age of World War II. The ad was a forerunner of IBM dominance of the next decades in many product categories.

In December 1954, after a final campaign—for the new 705 electronic data processing machine—and following the death of James M. Cecil, Cecil & Presbrey closed its doors. Forced to consider a new agency and strategy for the first time in 30 years, IBM decided to give its advertising budget of more than $1 million to

Benton and Bowles, New York City. The money was spent primarily for IBM's new electric typewriters in consumer, business, and women's publications. IBM had not yet entered TV or radio broadcast advertising (despite Remington Rand's heavy television schedule), but the well-executed artistry of various Benton and Bowles print campaigns of the late 1950s and 1960s was proof that print advertisements still worked well in the new broadcast age, helping IBM eventually become the global leader in typewriter sales.

Although secretaries of the day were not actually purchasing the product, Benton and Bowles was careful to target many of the new ads directly at them as a way of influencing their bosses, promising that the electric typewriter would drastically improve their efficiency and overall job. Later tag lines accompanying color pictures of a new IBM typewriter model underlined its beauty of design: "The IBM Electric: Its beauty is just a bonus." Some trade journalists criticized the ads for their lack of substantial product information that could justify the IBM product's incredible cost compared with the price of a manual typewriter. Although it was the most visible product to consumers and drew the bulk of IBM's ad spending, the electric typewriter did not represent the future for IBM. Nonetheless, the IBM Selectric, a typewriter with error-erasing capabilities, introduced in 1961, would be popular for decades.

Tom Watson, Sr., died in 1956, just six weeks after relinquishing the position of chief executive officer (CEO) to his son, Tom Watson, Jr. It would be the younger Watson who would lead IBM to its ultimate place as the overwhelming market share leader in the growing computer industry. Through the years, IBM was careful to establish an ongoing message to consumers that any advancement in IBM's computer technology was an advancement for America. After IBM computers were used to tally the 1960 election, a print campaign spread in major U.S. daily newspapers began, "Who won the computer battle last night? You did," and went on to explain the exciting changes that awaited Americans in a computer-driven world.

By 1960 Benton and Bowles had become IBM's agency of record for office products; World Trade Corporation, IBM's subsidiary responsible for business operations outside the United States; Service Bureau Corporation, IBM's computer subsidiary; and IBM's recruitment advertising. But IBM was also expanding its advertising efforts, hiring Marsteller, Rickard, Gebhardt & Reed, Inc., New York City, in 1960 as the new agency for its data processing division as well as some corporate work; in March 1963 it named Ogilvy, Benson & Mather, New York City, to handle $600,000 in corporate billings that had been at Benton and Bowles, which remained a principal IBM agency in both the United States and England. Ogilvy was responsible for introducing IBM to network television in 1965, boosting its corporate image as well as its media expenditures.

By the late 1960s IBM had also created a strong identity for itself internationally. While the company made sure its advertising carried a unified look worldwide, IBM hired agencies in each of its foreign markets to tailor its advertising efforts for the local audience. Marsteller, Inc., would help create and place international corporate campaigns, working with a family of smaller international agencies to ensure that all advertising was suitable to each local culture and not merely a translation of the English version.

In 1971 Tom Watson, Jr., stepped down as CEO, handing over the post to Vincent Learson, an IBM employee of 38 years. Learson retired in 1973 and was succeeded by Frank Cary, a 25-year veteran of IBM who would lead the company into the personal-computer age.

Market Dominance

By this time IBM had captured almost 70 percent of the computer market. The company was so dominant that it had earned the nickname "Snow White," the seven dwarfs being its competitors; its closest rival, Honeywell, Inc., had a 9 percent market share. As the industry leader, IBM was considered the prime target of competitors' advertising efforts that attempted to match IBM ad dollar for ad dollar and encroach on its market share by claiming their products were superior to IBM's. Their struggles against the IBM powerhouse drew the attention of the U.S. Justice Depart-

ment, which filed an antitrust lawsuit against the company in 1969; the suit against IBM and its "monopolistic practices" stood for 13 years until it was finally found to be "without merit." IBM, which had been embroiled in other such actions throughout its history, countered the 1969 suit with a public relations campaign from newly renamed Ogilvy & Mather, proclaiming in a print campaign that the company was "a tough competitor but a fair one."

IBM had achieved dominance largely through its massive worldwide sales force and its competitive pricing. But by the late 1970s, the Justice Department's anticipated ruling in the still-pending trial began to take its toll, as a wary IBM proceeded cautiously in new markets. By the decade's end, IBM saw its market share slipping toward 40 percent.

At the same time, other companies were working to develop minicomputers that would soon make IBM's massive machines and market dominance almost obsolete. In April 1977 the one-year-old Apple Computer, Inc., introduced its Apple II at a West Coast computer fair. The small but complete computing unit was a hit at the show, and Apple began an all-out industry sprint to produce and advertise its most powerful and marketable minicomputer.

It was clear that the minicomputer was creating new markets that IBM had to enter quickly or be left behind. In response, IBM mobilized a secret task force, code named "Project Chess," to create a minicomputer, pushed in part by IBM president John Opel, a member of IBM's Corporate Management Committee; he would later serve as CEO from January 1981 through 1984. The group emerged with the IBM Personal Computer (PC), which was ready for shipping in August 1981. It was based on a single operating standard that was compatible with other brands—a stroke of genius some said, although this very compatibility would later plague the company as IBM-compatible "clones" flooded the market in the late 1980s.

PC Wars

Apple Computer welcomed IBM to the market in an ad that ran in major U.S. daily newspapers the day after the "PC's" unveiling. "Welcome, IBM. Seriously," the ad read. "Welcome to the most exciting and important marketplace since the computer revolution began 35 years ago." Although some IBM loyalists may have seen the ad as a dig at the company's lateness to market, Apple was serious; the company did welcome IBM to the market because IBM's solid image gave the so-called PC revolution the legitimacy it needed. The slap in the face would come a few years later in another ad introducing Apple's new Macintosh: the "1984" spot that ran during the January 1984 Super Bowl. The commercial, a play on George Orwell's novel of totalitarian repression, 1984, showed a technology-crazed tyrant enslaving the masses, implying that IBM was the equivalent of the despotic Big Brother.

The image of a drab monolithic giant is precisely the image IBM sought to counter in advertising for its new personal computer in 1981. For the first time, the company had to rely completely on a national media campaign to sell the product rather

SIX ANCIENT MACHINES. AND ONE NEW ONE.

The first six are the basic machines. The seventh is a silicon chip.

Basic machines provide a mechanical advantage.

Silicon chips are different. They provide a *mental* advantage. Etched with microscopic circuits, they're the heart of the modern computer.

We make the comparison because, today, mechanical advantage isn't enough. America's waning productivity won't be improved just by working harder.

We have to work smarter, and silicon chips will help.

Armed with computers, old factories can behave like younger ones. With better use of information, assembly lines can be made to work with the assemblers instead of against them.

Heavy industry, technology firms, service companies must all become more productive, a challenge that demands ideas.

And just as levers alone don't move rocks, computers don't have ideas. But they give us an advantage.

They help us find solutions in time to solve the problems. You can't get more basic than that. **IBM®**

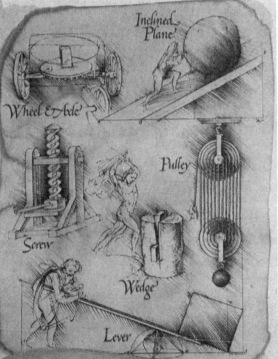

This 1980 corporate ad for IBM portrayed the silicon chip as the newest problem-solving machine and the key to increased productivity.

than using its vast army of salesmen. IBM enlisted one of its roster agencies, Lord, Geller, Federico, Einstein, New York City, to design a campaign for the new desktop machine that would dispel new users' fear of computers, which IBM's research had suggested would be the biggest hurdle to overcome. IBM also wanted the campaign to change the perception that the company was as heartless as the technology it sold.

IBM's new spokesman emerged in August 1981 as the Charlie Chaplin "tramp" character (played by actor Billy Scudder) in an effort to personify the qualities of a new computer that was uncomplicated and fun. "A tool for modern times"—alluding to Chaplin's 1936 film *Modern Times*—was the tag line. The campaign was such a success that IBM PCs practically flew out of dealer stores. In the first year of the IBM PC, sales went from a zero market share to a 28 percent share and grew from there.

IBM followed the success of its PC with a flop, the IBM PCjr—an attempt to directly tap the home computer market with a cute, less expensive model—launched in February 1984. Seeking to maintain the enthusiasm roused by the initial PC, IBM used an aggressive direct-mail campaign offering PCjr and software incentives to households with college-bound children. However, no amount of advertising support made up for the product, which critics said was poor in design and had a toylike keyboard and weak capabilities.

One failure, although humiliating, did not change the fact that IBM was among the most profitable companies in the world in 1985 when a new CEO, John Akers, took over from Opel. IBM's entry into the home computer market had increased its advertising expenditures, which it sustained throughout the decade, but critics saw IBM's efforts of the mid- to late 1980s as generally ineffective. The company unleashed aggressive advertising to market its new business of computer printers and to battle PC-clones that were taking over the market with claims that the products were equal to IBM's.

In January 1988 Lord, Geller created a campaign themed "The bigger picture," emphasizing the advantage of the long-term partnership between IBM and its customers without focusing on specific products. Later that year, the agency launched IBM's "Thanks a million" campaign, thanking customers for buying 1 million of its new model PS/2s. But while IBM was growing, the PC compatible market was growing twice as fast.

In June of that year executives from Lord, Geller left the agency to form their own shop—Lord, Einstein, O'Neill and Partners—and attempted to take IBM with them. A lawsuit ensued, and IBM began searching elsewhere to place its $135 million corporate account. By September 1988 IBM had settled on two new agencies, Lintas, New York City, to handle the PS/2 personal computer line domestically and assist overseas, and Wells, Rich, Greene, New York City, to oversee global corporate brand strategy. Research showed that many businesspeople who would consider IBM for their companies still viewed the company as unapproachable; at the same time, IBM's rivals were effectively reaching corporate America. A 1989 effort by Lintas for IBM's PS/2 to make IBM a "hip" competitor by using rap music was criticized for severely underestimating the intelligence of potential buyers.

In 1990 IBM sold off its typewriter, keyboard, and printer business to focus on a computer industry that looked nothing like it had only a decade before. Dual revolutions, one in desktop computers and their operating systems and a second in finding a way to link multiple desktop computers to new powerful "servers," rocked IBM's business model. In late 1992, Lintas launched another extensive print campaign with hundreds of sales promotion events to push IBM's new OS/2 operating system, which worked with Microsoft Corporation's Windows 3.1 platform.

Despite aggressive advertising, IBM ended 1992 with 40,000 fewer employees and plans to lay off another 25,000. The cuts were blamed on the then-current recession and the declining market for mainframe computers. IBM was losing the battle of creating an image for itself as a technology leader to more narrowly focused competitors. With IBM facing a loss in profits of $16 billion over three years, Akers resigned in February 1993.

Salvaging the Brand

IBM's new CEO, Louis Gerstner, an outsider, had been CEO at RJR Nabisco, Inc., for four years and, before that, chairman-CEO of American Express Travel Related Services Company; during his tenure at American Express, he had launched the company's well-known "Do you know me?" advertising campaign (done by Ogilvy & Mather). Gerstner did not know as much about computers as he did about branding, but his management style and trust in advertising would go far to salvage IBM's brand and the company.

In 1993 Gerstner recruited a veteran American Express marketing executive, Abby Kohnstamm, to head IBM corporate advertising and help plan a new marketing strategy. During this period, IBM's advertising remained much the same, with aggressive, expensive product campaigns and a growing agency roster. Lintas was handling IBM PS/2 PC campaigns, including an April 1993 print campaign in partnership with IBM's European lead agency, GGK of Paris, that touted IBM's service capabilities using the image of the Pink Panther. Other IBM agencies included Merkley Newman Harty, DDB Needham, D'Arcy Masius Benton and Bowles, and the J. Walter Thompson Company. Overall, IBM had built a roster of more than 40 domestic and international advertising agencies.

On 25 May 1994, IBM unexpectedly moved its entire $500 million advertising account to Ogilvy & Mather. The agency's North American division head, Shelley Lazarus, had worked on Gerstner's American Express brand years before as an Ogilvy account executive. Lazarus knew that Gerstner believed in the importance of branding, and her pitch to the IBM executives was based on the notion that years of disjointed advertising by multiple agencies had crippled the impact of the IBM brand. Gerstner, Lazarus, and Kohnstamm agreed that to counter this trend, IBM needed a unified, global, well-funded corporate branding strategy. The move was the largest account switch in advertising history at that point, and the largest global advertising strategy ever taken on by a single agency.

Presenting the IBM PC Server 320 Internet Series Solution.
It doesn't get much easier than this.

Call 1 800 426-7255, ext. 4116.* Or visit us at www.pc.ibm.com/servers/.

Solutions for a small planet™

IBM's "Solutions for a Small Planet" campaign of the late 1990s marked the company's commitment to networking, Internet, and e-business services.

A New Face

As Lazarus and Ogilvy struggled to devise a new strategy, early research using focus groups composed of corporate leaders revealed strong, bitter feelings toward the IBM brand name; customers felt let down by the industry leader and believed that the company did not care about them.

Early efforts from Ogilvy attempted to put a new face on IBM's products. Particularly successful was a huge U.S. and international print and television campaign for IBM's new OS/2 Warp software, launched in October 1994. The ads featured real users being "warped" after realizing the power of their new PCs. Particularly notable was a commercial that showed Czechoslovakian nuns in traditional habits discussing, in translated subtitles, the advantages of IBM's new operating system. The idea that the computer revolution could reach such an obscure corner of the Earth got audiences' attention, but in 1996, after some repositioning, IBM surrendered the consumer market to Microsoft Corporation's Windows.

In 1996, after the company had begun receiving accolades for successful product launches such as its ThinkPad notebook computer, its strategy took a new turn. IBM focused its advertising solely on what it termed "e-business," at a time when e-commerce—selling products and services on the Internet—was all the rage. IBM's new "e-business" logo made a play at the ever present "@" in e-mail addresses, designing the "e" the same way. Over the next two years, IBM continued its "e-business" focus, profiling actual IBM employees in edgy, ethnically diverse commercials with the tag line, "Are you ready for e-business?" These were not the blue-suited IBM employees of yesteryear.

In April 1998, Ogilvy began tying IBM products, or "e-business tools," into the corporate brand campaign. It also launched a testimonial kind of campaign to further persuade consumers of IBM's dominance in an Internet-driven world. This included marketing hundreds of IBM client Web sites with the company's well-known "circle-e" e-business logo.

Ogilvy's massive campaign sought to define IBM as a solutions and services provider, offering products with the power to make business-related lives easier, much in the way IBM's advertising had gone in the 1960s. Ogilvy used a variety of media to reach both Internet-reluctant corporate heads and the 25-to-35-year-old industry movers and young executives on the Web. The results: "e-business" became a part of the business lexicon, and the IBM brand name helped legitimize the Internet as a tool to enhance business.

As it entered the 21st century, the world's leading computer company had redefined itself as a major force in the Internet and computer services industry, thanks in large part to its radical change in advertising strategy. In 2001 about 40 percent of company revenue still stemmed from IBM's hardware, according to the company, but IBM had become a $32.2 billion information technologies services company.

MEGAN CASSADA

Further Reading

Chposky, James, and Ted Leonsis, *Blue Magic,* New York: Facts on File, 1988; London: Grafton, 1989

Delamarter, Richard Thomas, *Big Blue,* New York: Dodd Mead, and London: Macmillan, 1986

Garr, Doug, *IBM Redux: Lou Gerstner and the Business Turnaround of the Decade,* New York: HarperBusiness, 1999; Chichester, West Sussex: Wiley, 2000

IBM <www.ibm.com>

McKenna, Regis, *Who's Afraid of Big Blue?* Reading, Massachusetts: Addison Wesley, 1989

Rodgers, F.G. "Buck," and Robert L. Shook, *The IBM Way,* New York and London: Harper and Row, 1986

Illustration

The beginnings of both commercial illustration and modern art, closely intertwined as they are, can be found in the late 1880s in Paris, France. Advertising art owes its existence to a felicitous combination of technological advancements, innovative artists, and political change. In 1881 a new law in Paris gave greater leeway to those wishing to paste advertisements around the city, both by prohibiting the defacement of posters and by giving building owners more rights in the licensing of their walls for commercial purposes. This legislation, along with the improvement of lithographic processes, paved the way for the creation and proliferation of posters.

First and foremost among the poster pioneers was Jules Chéret, who began producing color lithographic posters in 1866 after a seven-year apprenticeship with a printer in England. In his shop in Paris, Chéret used lithography, which until then had mainly been used in reproduction, to make his own original designs. These were expressive images of a fancifully conceived Parisian nightlife, awash with delicate veils of color, and composed with an eye to the works of Watteau, Tiepolo, and Fragonard. Chéret's work had a significant impact on the art world of the time, most notably on the burgeoning Art Nouveau movement, which evolved from the nostalgic esthetics of the Pre-

ILLUSTRATION   839

Raphaelites, and on the artist Henri de Toulouse-Lautrec, who adapted Chéret's fluid lines and bold, flat silhouettes in his own, more experimental theater posters. Toulouse-Lautrec, Pierre Bonnard, the Swiss poster artist Théophile Alexandre Steinlen, and the Czech artist Alphonse Mucha all contributed to a movement in poster art away from realism and toward a graphic interpretation of form.

This movement was mirrored in Germany in the illustrations of Thomas Theodor Heine; in Vienna in Gustav Klimt's paintings; and in England in the Arts and Crafts movement and the work of the artist William Morris, illustrator Aubrey Beardsley, and the poster artist duo known as the Beggarstaff brothers (James Pryde and William Nicholson), who created their simplified compositions by combining and gluing paper cutouts on board. Beardsley, who began selling his highly stylized black-and-white illustrations at the age of 20, had an enormous influence on U.S. poster artists, most notably Will Bradley and Edward Penfield, who absorbed the Art Nouveau style as they saw it in Aubrey's work, and in Mucha's ads for actress Sarah Bernhardt's appearance in New York City.

Most noteworthy among U.S. illustrators of the time who owed a debt to the new traditions of Art Nouveau, the Arts and Crafts movement, and the Pre-Raphaelites, were Howard Pyle, Maxfield Parrish, and N.C. Wyeth. Pyle, best known for his theatrically composed children's book illustrations, educated legions of reputable illustrators (among them the magazine illustrator Jessie Wilcox Smith) while teaching at the Art Students League in New York City, at the Drexel Institute in Philadelphia, Pennsylvania, and at his own summer school in Chadds Ford, Pennsylvania. Parrish went on to become one of the best-loved commercial artists of the century, and images from his calendars and ads decorated the walls of homes across the United States. His paintings, somewhat more realistic in style than those of Beardsley or Toulouse-Lautrec, but still retaining their use of dark outline and bold contrast, often used the medieval, romantic themes favored by the Pre-Raphaelites. For example, an ad he produced in 1918 for the Fisk Rubber Company featured a pair of tunic-wearing pages presenting a tire to a king on his throne.

N.C. Wyeth, another of Pyle's well-known pupils (and father of painter Andrew Wyeth), also retained the high-contrast, imaginative approach of fin de siècle Europe, but like Pyle, his subject matter was usually rooted in a world of adventure, often American in flavor. Besides providing dazzling illustrations for the books *Treasure Island* and *Tom Sawyer*, he also created many advertisements throughout his career, including ads in 1907 for Cream of Wheat cereal set in the Wild West.

The artist whose illustrations best defined the western United States in the 1880s was Frederic Remington. Remington, who began publishing his paintings in *Harper's* magazine in the early 1880s, captured the western scenery and way of life as he experienced it himself as a rancher, military scout, and reporter.

Among the other illustrators who helped define the image the United States had of itself both before and during World War I were Charles Dana Gibson, Joseph Christian (J.C.) Leyendecker, and James Montgomery Flagg. Each was known for the charac-

The American illustrator Charles Dana Gibson was one of many artists who created posters supporting the U.S. war effort during World War I.

ters he invented for his ads: Gibson for his small-waisted, long-skirted "Gibson Girls," role models for young women of the time, and Leyendecker (later, in the 1920s) for his Arrow Collar Man, who served the same function for young men. Flagg, though he also defined fashion with his ads for clothing, is still best known as the creator (and model) for Uncle Sam in his 1917 "I Want You" armed forces recruitment poster, which debuted in World War I and was also used during World War II.

Flagg, along with Gibson, Leyendecker, and other leading illustrators of the day such as Howard Chandler Christy, were recruited as propagandists during World War I. Gibson headed the Division of Pictorial Publicity under the federal Committee on Public Information. In Europe, while some illustrators such as the English poster artist Alfred Leete (whose 1914 poster featuring a pointing British officer prefigured Flagg's design), were turning their talents to the war, practitioners of the fine arts were developing the tenets of cubism, de Stijl, and constructivism. All these movements left a great and lasting impression on commercial

Long on leg room –

GO PULLMAN
comfortable, convenient and safe!

William Steig, a cartoonist whose work often appeared in *The New Yorker,* also created illustrations for advertisements, as seen in this 1953 Pullman Company ad.
Illustration © William Steig.

design and art, and furthered the reinterpretation of form in abstract terms. Cubism did so by portraying objects from different perspectives and in terms of basic, geometric shapes; de Stijl by introducing the exclusive use of primary colors and the juxtaposition of different kinds and sizes of type; and constructivism by its ingenious use of photo-montage, type, and collage. (Some of the best examples of constructivism can be found in the work

of the Russian artist El Lissitzky). The aggregate of these various movements found its expression in the 1920s at the Bauhaus school in Germany, where artists such as László Moholy-Nagy synthesized modernist ideas into a conception of graphic design that took into account the importance of all visual elements.

It was the poster artist A.M. Cassandre, however, who helped translate the new ideas into advertising and best understood the future role of commercial art. "Painting is an end in itself," he wrote in 1933. "The poster is only a means to an end, a means of communication. . . ." The Ukraine-born artist, who worked in Paris in the late 1920s and early 1930s, produced ads for the French railway and for Dubonnet, among others, that gave modernism a more accessible twist. This style, somewhat analogous with Art Deco, contained imagery consisting of clean, much-simplified shapes in a limited range of colors, often based on the forms found in machinery. The U.S. artist McKnight Kauffer, who worked in England in the 1920s creating posters for the London Underground, shared this sensibility, which continued to shape his work throughout the following two decades.

Variations on the Art Deco style appeared in the 1920s in the United States in the work of Rockwell Kent, whose engravings and lithographs decorated ads for Rolls-Royce and Steinway & Sons. Coles Phillips's "Fadeaway Girl"—an image he created by using the overall color of the background to form part of the foreground figure—shows some of the influences of modernism. But it was John Held, Jr., who most effectively defined the era with his cartoonish, colorful flappers and college boys, often featured in *The New Yorker* magazine. Held also worked on a campaign for Lorillard Tobacco Company's Old Gold cigarettes (from ad agency Lennen & Mitchell) themed "Not a cough in a carload."

As the 1930s approached, photography began to gain ground as a means to illustrate advertising. Legendary photographers such as Edward Steichen and Ansel Adams got their start in advertising in this period, though illustrators continued to making a name for themselves in the field. In fact, perhaps the most popular commercial artist ever to work in the United States had become, by the 1930s, a household name. Norman Rockwell began enhancing ads with his paintings in 1914, and by the 1920s he was creating full-color ads for the likes of Grape Nuts cereal and the Fisk Tire Company. He went on to produce more than 300 covers for the *Saturday Evening Post,* most featuring his wholesome paintings of an idealized small-town America. In the early 1940s, as the United States entered World War II, Rockwell contributed his talents to (slightly grimmer) posters for the war effort. It is worth noting that Rockwell's realistic illustrations, which continued to be extremely successful even in the photography-laden 1960s, were themselves modeled on photographs: Rockwell generally based his paintings on carefully-posed photographic studies.

Rockwell's illustrations weren't the only ones in the 1940s to feature dramatic realism. McClelland Barclay, who was killed during the war when his ship was torpedoed, made illustrations for Texaco and General Motors Corporation in a painterly style, peopled with the well-heeled, sporty, and young. George Petty

ILLUSTRATION   841

used an airbrush to create his trademark pin-up girl, who debuted in *Esquire* magazine and figured in ads for Jantzen swimsuits. Opposite this realistic trend was the work of the cartoonists. James Thurber and William Steig, both regulars in *The New Yorker*, also illustrated ads ("So long, Junior. I warned you if you didn't use Lifebuoy, I'd drop you from the act," says a stern trapeze artist in Steig's 1944 soap ad, as he lets his less-than-fresh-smelling partner fall free).

Behind the front lines of prominent artists in advertising, however, there labored a small army of highly specialized illustrators who produced the majority of print artwork. In the automobile field, for example, a whole network of art studios, suppliers, and illustrators became a Detroit mini-industry, proliferating into astonishing auto sub-specialties. "We would work from photos or tight renderings from the agency," according to Ferd Prucher, whose Prucher Studios was a major artwork supplier to the Campbell-Ewald Company and D.P. Brother from the 1930s through the 1950s. He described the process to *Advertising Age* in 2000. "We would assign one artist to illustrate the basic car body. Then it would go to another artist who specialized in drawing nothing but wheels or interiors. Someone else would then come in whose specialty might be landscapes, trees, houses, or people. One artist might do just women, another men. Typically, no illustration was the work of just one artist. Every element of a picture came to have its own group of specialists because every product representation had to be not just perfect but idyllic."

A light stylistic touch predominated in the United States at the war's end, though often that touch was provided by European artists. In 1951 French painter Raoul Dufy enhanced ads for DeBeers Consolidated Mines with a continental seaside scene; Austrian-born Ludwig Bemelmans, while creating the *Madeline* series of books for children, made whimsical ads for Walker's Deluxe Bourbon around the same time; and even Salvador Dali, in the late 1940s, lent a surrealistic yet decorative flavor to ads for Bryan nylons. Less sophisticated but still playful were American Peter Hawley's ads for Jantzen and Bell Telephone, and the cartoon-style drawings of Whitney Darrow, Jr., for Post Toasties cereal and Simoniz floor wax.

In the 1950s and early 1960s photography became advertising's preferred form of imagery. The period also saw revolutions in art and style that were expressed in the work of the visually savvy and successful illustrators/designers Milton Glaser and Seymour Chwast, cofounders in 1954 of Push Pin Studios (Glaser's silhouetted poster-insert for Bob Dylan has become an icon); in the posters of Jaqui Morgan; and in the early advertising work of Andy Warhol, who began his career drawing shoes for I. Miller & Sons in the early 1950s. Warhol well understood the dynamic and convoluted relationship between art and advertising. His Campbell's Soup can series turned the idea of art for product promotion on its head. In his work product, ad, and art became indistinguishable from each other.

Poster art saw something of a revival in the late 1960s and early 1970s, with the concert and theater posters of artists such as David Edward Byrd and Bob Massé. Interestingly their work, along with that of Peter Max, harked back to the Art Nouveau posters of the 1890s. Byrd's 1970 poster for the Broadway musical *Follies* is a case in point, combining the curling lines and dark outlines of Mucha's work with the brighter colors and surreal imagery of the psychedelic movement.

Other standout illustrators of the 1970s, many of whom continue to work prolifically, had more divergent styles. Already a celebrated illustrator and artist by the early 1970s, Bernard Fuchs is known for his accomplished figural paintings for magazines, including *McCall's, Sports Illustrated,* and *Cosmopolitan.* David Levine has created caricatures for the pages of the *New York Review of Books* since the early 1960s, and his work has adorned the covers of *Time* and *Newsweek.* Brad Holland has contributed his edgy illustrations to *Playboy* magazine and to the opinion/editorial section of the *New York Times.* And Paul Davis, who first published in *Esquire* magazine in 1959, has since illustrated for many other publications, including *Harper's* and *Time,* and has also worked on advertisements for Mobil Oil (for its *Masterpiece Theatre* television program).

All these illustrators worked largely in an editorial context, which is still the arena in which many illustrators find the majority of their assignments. The art of the best illustrators working at the beginning of the 21st century—among them John Collier, Mirko Ilic, Marshall Arisman, Mark Summers, Steve Brodner, Gary Kelley, Brian Cronin, Maira Kalman, Henrik Drescher, Chris Ware, Christoph Niemann, Gary Baseman, Gary Panter, James McMullan, and Philip Burke—can be found in many major publications, from the *New York Times Book Review* to *Entertainment Weekly,* as well as in ads and promotional material for clients from Barnes & Noble to McDonald's Corporation. Though the era when illustration ruled advertising is past, commercial art continues to thrive. With the Internet offering new venues for visual art, it seems that illustration's variety of applications will continue to expand.

CAITLIN DOVER

Further Reading

Artcyclopedia <www.artcyclopedia.com>

Barnicoat, John, *A Concise History of Posters: 1870–1970,* New York: Abrams, and London: Thames and Hudson, 1972

Goodrum, Charles, and Helen Dalrymple, *Advertising in America: The First 200 Years,* New York: Abrams, 1990

Holme, Bryan, *Advertising: Reflections of a Century,* New York: Viking Press, and London: Heinemann, 1982

Illustration House <www.illustration-house.com>

Reed, Walt, *The Illustrator in America, 1900–1960s,* New York: Reinhold, 1966; revised edition, as *The Illustrator in America, 1880–1980: A Century of Illustration,* by Reed and Roger Reed, New York: Madison Square Press, 1984

Traditional Fine Arts Online <www.tfaoi.com>

Varnedoe, Kirk, and Adam Gopnik, editors, *High and Low: Modern Art, Popular Culture,* New York: The Museum of Modern Art, 1990

Watson, Bruce, "Beyond the Blue: The Art of Maxfield Parrish," *Smithsonian Magazine Online* (July, 1999) <www.smithsonianmag.com>

India

India is the world's second most populous nation, inhabited by more than 1 billion people. Successive invasions by intruders from a variety of cultures and later colonization by the British (who ruled the country from 1757 to 1947) had a strong influence on Indian culture and the country's sociopolitical institutions. After attaining independence from the British, India formally adopted a constitution in 1950, proclaiming itself to be a sovereign democratic republic. The country has a parliamentary form of government, with the president as the ceremonial head of state and the prime minister as the head of the government. With a federal structure consisting of 29 states and six centrally administered Union Territories, India is a multicultural and multilingual country. There are more than 15 official languages, along with hundreds of dialects. The official national language is Hindi, but most business in the corporate sector is conducted in English, and many Indians consider familiarity with English to be a prerequisite for a successful career. Many Indian advertising campaigns are first created in English and then translated into other languages.

In order to understand the development of advertising in India, it is important to view it in the larger context of the country's economic policy. Inspired by socialist ideals, India adopted a mixed economy model in the 1950s under the guidance of its first prime minister, Jawaharlal Nehru. Within the overall framework of a free market, the government retained control over certain core sectors, including air and rail transportation, telecommunications, and steel production. The policy had strong overtones of protectionism, and virtually no imports of consumer products (including automobiles) were permitted from the 1950s through the early 1990s. Major reforms in economic policy were instituted in the mid-1980s, paving the way for a substantially more liberal policy in the 1990s.

Rise of Advertising Agencies

The history of advertising in India is almost as old as the history of modern print media in the country. The first newspaper in India, the *Bengal Gazette or Calcutta General Advertiser,* was originally published by a Briton, James Augustus Hickey, on 29 January 1780. The newspaper carried a few advertisements in its inaugural issue, as did other newspapers published later in that decade. During the 19th century most of the commercial advertisers in India were British business houses. The industrial revolution in Great Britain had resulted in the creation of mass-produced goods, many of which were imported by these trading companies for the Indian market. However, advertising agencies did not exist in India at that time.

Advertising agencies began emerging in India in the early part of the 20th century. The first recognized agency in the country was B. Dattaram Company, which was founded in 1905. Other early ad agencies were the Ind-Advertising Agency, which was established in Bombay during that same period, and the Calcutta Advertising Agency, founded in 1909. Some leading newspapers also set up studios to provide assistance to advertisers in copywriting and illustration.

Within the next two decades, a few multinational agencies began to establish a presence on the Indian advertising scene. A British agency, S.H. Benson, commenced operations in India in 1928. This agency eventually became part of Ogilvy & Mather (O&M). Other multinational agency networks began operations in India in the next three decades. The J. Walter Thompson Company (JWT) began operations in 1929. JWT's Indian affiliate, known as Hindustan Thompson Associates (HTA), is now one of the largest agencies in the country. Lintas India Limited was founded in 1939. McCann-Erickson formed an alliance with Calcutta-based Clarion Advertising in 1956. A few smaller multinational agencies also began operations in India, such as the now-defunct Grant, Kenyon and Eckhardt (India) Private Limited.

In the late 1960s and early 1970s, the fortunes of multinational enterprises in various sectors were adversely affected by the political climate of the country. With the objective of promoting domestic business enterprises, the government of India began to impose restrictions on foreign ownership of equity in companies that were not involved in "core sector" activities. Several multinational corporations, most notably the Coca-Cola Company and the IBM Corporation, closed their doors after refusing to dilute their shareholding.

The protectionist economic policies of successive governments in the 1960s and 1970s had a dampening effect on multinational advertising agencies operating in the country. In the 1960s, JWT divested its equity stake in HTA, which became a wholly employee-owned company. Lintas India Limited was also "Indianized" in 1969. Despite these setbacks for multinational Western agency networks, the advertising industry experienced record growth during this decade. The number of advertising agencies registered with the Indian Newspaper Society during this period grew by 58.5 percent, from 106 agencies in 1969 to 168 agencies in 1979.

While multinational agencies cut back their presence in the 1960s and 1970s, a number of indigenous agencies were founded during this period. Several of these became major players in the industry, such Chaitra, daCunha, Enterprise, Everest, Frank Simoes Advertising, Mudra, RK Swamy, Rediffusion, Sista's, Trikaya, and Ulka. In subsequent decades, many of these agencies entered into joint ventures with multinational agency networks that were eager to establish (or in some cases reestablish) a presence in India.

While many of these ad agency joint ventures were loose affiliations without any financial commitment by either party, this trend changed in the 1990s. Despite the fact that most Indian agencies were privately held (and therefore less susceptible to hostile takeovers), many agreed to allow their multinational partners to increase their shareholding in return for the infusion of fresh capital. Consequently, multinational agency networks steadily increased their financial stake in their Indian joint ventures. JWT repurchased a controlling interest in its Indian affiliate, HTA, and acquired HTA subsidiary Contract Advertising. In addition to JWT, Lintas, and O&M, which had enjoyed long-term presences in India, several other multinational agency networks established (or in some cases, reestablished) a presence in the late 1980s and throughout the 1990s, primarily through joint ventures with indigenous agencies. Some of the more prominent multinationals involved in joint ventures were Leo Burnett (Chaitra Leo Burnett Private), BBDO Worldwide (RK Swamy BBDO Advertising), Bozell (MAA Bozell, now MAA Group), Dentsu Young & Rubicam (Rediffusion/DY&R), DDB Worldwide (Mudra Communications), FCB (FCB Ulka), Grey (Trikaya Grey), and Saatchi & Saatchi (Sista's Saatchi & Saatchi). McCann-Erickson, which had previously had a partnership with Calcutta-based Clarion Advertising, also reentered the Indian market in the 1990s as McCann-Erickson India. The search for a joint venture partner was not always smooth sailing, and there were occasional divorces between shops. Bozell, a U.S.-based multinational, initially had a joint venture with ARMS advertising before aligning itself with MAA. Likewise, the Indian agency Rediffusion initially aligned itself with the U.S. agency Ted Bates Advertising in the mid-1980s, but the partnership was quickly dissolved after Bates was taken over by U.K.-based Saatchi & Saatchi. Rediffusion then aligned itself with Dentsu Young & Rubicam (DY&R) and is now known as Rediffusion/DY&R.

An analysis of the data from the annual agency reports published by *Advertising & Marketing* magazine (India's leading trade journal in the advertising field) shows that the 20 largest agencies in India account for almost three-quarters of the total billings (among more than 100 agencies participating in the survey). In the near future, too, one can expect the larger agencies to reap the greatest benefits from the entry of an increasing number of multinational brands into the Indian market. Multinational advertisers are likely to prefer agencies with transnational alliances, or at least those with a national presence, a condition that will exclude many smaller agencies from the race.

An exception to this trend may be financial advertising agencies, many of which became prominent in the 1970s. These agencies have little involvement in corporate or brand advertising for their clients, but they derive a major proportion of their business from publicizing stock and bond issues. Financial agencies differentiated themselves from the competition by undertaking nonadvertising activities that traditional agencies were initially reluctant to handle, such as arranging stockbroker conferences and handling media relations. In the process, such firms have created an attractive niche market for themselves.

Leading Advertisers

The products that account for the largest advertising expenditures in India are bath soaps, laundry detergents, soft drinks, toothpaste, textiles, tires, confectionery, cigarettes, and tea. Not surprisingly, the majority of these are consumer nondurables that demand high-frequency advertising. Consumer durables (such as TVs and VCRs) and appliances (such as refrigerators and washing machines) are also heavily advertised.

"The first full fledged Indian Advertising Agency is the National Advertising Service launched in 1931"

Advertisers' Vade-mecum 1959.

A house ad for India's oldest indigenous ad agency, the National Advertising Service, founded in 1931, listed all of the agency's clients. *Courtesy of National Advertising Service Private Ltd., in its 70th year.*

According to *Advertising & Marketing* magazine, in 2000 the top eight corporate advertisers in India were (in descending order) Hindustan Lever (the Indian arm of Unilever), Colgate-Palmolive, ITC (a tobacco, hotels, and food products conglomerate), Dabur, Nestlé India, Britannia Industries, Bajaj Auto, and Tata Chemicals. While most of these large advertisers are packaged-goods marketers, the presence of durable-goods marketer Bajaj Auto (which makes scooters and motorcycles) is noteworthy. It is also noteworthy that indigenous companies such as Bajaj Auto, Tata Chemicals, and Dabur are in the list of leading national advertisers alongside such multinational corporations as Unilever, Colgate-Palmolive, and Nestlé. In addition to corporations, the government (both central and state) accounts for a large share of total newspaper advertising, mostly in the form of contract notices and recruitment advertising.

Media Picture

Print media in India have a long history dating back to the late 18th century. The ownership of print media has mostly been in private hands, and the press in India has operated without any fear of censorship. According to some estimates, more than 32,000 newspapers and magazines are published in India. Only 715 of these are members of the Indian Newspaper Society (INS), the leading trade association in the field, and 345 are members of the Audit Bureau of Circulations. Print media still have the largest share of advertising expenditures in India, although they have been steadily losing ground to television since the mid-1980s. According to estimates provided by Rediffusion DY&R, newspapers and magazines together accounted for 48 percent of advertising expenditures in 1997–98, down from 57 percent in 1996–97 and 65 percent in 1995–96.

Newspapers and magazines are published in all of India's official languages, and some are published in dialects as well. There are distinct regional variations in circulation levels, reflecting differences in literacy levels across states. Some of the newspapers and magazines with the highest circulations are published in Malayalam (the regional language of the state of Kerala) and Bengali (the regional language of the state of West Bengal), as these states have higher literacy rates than others. English-language newspapers and magazines do not have the largest circulation in any single region, but they are extremely influential in terms of opinion leadership and agenda setting, and they are therefore considered important, especially for national advertising campaigns. Foreign magazine titles were largely unknown until the 1990s (with the exception of *Reader's Digest,* which has had a presence in India for many decades), but magazines such as *Cosmopolitan* and *Elle* now publish Indian editions.

While the first TV station in India started broadcasting as early as 1959, it was not until 1984 that a nationwide television network was established. Broadcast television is a monopoly in India, controlled by Doordarshan, a government-run network. Doordarshan has been supported by advertising ever since the introduction of its national network. Until the late 1980s, most parts of the country had access to only a single television channel that broadcast for a limited number of hours daily. This scenario has since changed substantially, due in large part to the entry of satellite transmission of television signals by Star-TV, a Hong Kong–based satellite broadcaster. The advertising agency Rediffusion DY&R estimates that around 8 million urban households (30 percent) and 13 million total households had cable connections in 1998. Households with cable connections in some cities have access to as many as 65 channels of programming originating both in India and abroad. Although cable television (satellite television) is growing in popularity, its audience is still quite small compared to the 250 million viewers reached by Doordarshan. In response to the competition from cable programming, Doordarshan has diversified its offerings and now has multiple channels in many markets, offering more than 1,000 hours of programming per week. Along with the number of channels, television's share of total advertising expenditures has also grown, from 25 percent in 1995–96 to 35 percent in 1996–97 to 44 percent in 1997–98. Much of this growth has come at the expense of print media.

Like broadcast television, radio is a government monopoly in India. The sole broadcaster is All India Radio, which operates a nationwide network of stations, primarily in the AM band. Advertising is accepted on a limited basis. A small number of FM stations in the largest urban markets carry a limited number of privately produced programs. Radio accounts for about 2 percent of total advertising expenditures, a figure that remained constant throughout the 1990s.

Outdoor media (primarily billboards) account for the third-largest share (3 percent to 5 percent in the 1990s) of advertising expenditures after print media and television. Advertising in movie theaters was the sole audiovisual medium before the advent of network television in 1984, but it accounted for only about 2 percent of total ad expenditures in the 1990s. The Internet, especially the World Wide Web, is likely to emerge as an important medium in the years to come, especially among urban youth. In 1997 there were estimated to be fewer than 80,000 Internet connections nationwide, but the government's ambitious telecommunication policy proposes to increase that number to more than 1 million by 2005. Many of India's English-language dailies (and a few regional-language papers as well) already publish on-line editions, most of which carry advertising.

Industry Groups

The top trade organizations representing various aspects of the advertising industry include the Indian Society of Advertisers, the Advertising Agencies Association of India, and the Indian Newspaper Society. The Advertising Standards Council of India is a self-regulatory body formed by a coalition of advertising agencies, advertisers, and media companies.

There is also a small but growing consumer movement. Advertising regulation is supervised by the Monopolies and Restrictive Trade Practices Commission (a body similar to the Federal Trade Commission in the United States). The Securities and Exchange Board of India also has regulatory authority with respect to the content of financial advertising. Total gross income in India from advertising in 2000 was $256.2 million, up 21 percent from the year earlier, on total billings of $1.7 billion.

KARTIK PASHUPATI

See also color plate in this volume

Further Reading

Banerjee, Subrata, "Advertising in India: Evolution and Technique," in *Mass Media in India,* New Delhi: Ministry of Information and Broadcasting, Government of India, 1981

Pashupati, Kartik, and Pushkala Raman, "Web Banner Ads on India's Online Newspapers: Who's Talking and to Whom?" *Proceedings of the 1999 Annual Conference of the American Academy of Advertising,* edited by Marilyn S. Roberts, Gainesville, Florida: University of Florida, 1999

Sengupta, Subir, and Kartik Pashupati, "Advertising in India: The Winds of Change," in *Advertising in Asia: Communication, Culture, and Consumption,* edited by Katherine Toland Frith, Ames: Iowa State University Press, 1996

Sethi, Mohini, and Premavathy Seetharaman, *Consumerism: A Growing Concept*, New Delhi: Phoenix Publishing House, 1994

Shiva Ramu, S., *Advertising Agencies: Global and Indian Perspectives*, Jaipur, India: Printwell, 1991

Venkateswaran, K.S., *Mass Media Laws and Regulations in India*, Singapore: Asian Mass Communication Research and Information Centre (AMIC), 1993

Vilanilam, John, "Television Advertising and the Indian Poor," *Media, Culture, and Society* 11 (1989)

Infomercial

The term *infomercial* was originally coined as a pejorative label for television commercials designed in length and format to resemble news programs or talk shows. Though the term gained early usage among academics and those who produced the program-length commercials, it was only in the 1990s that it was uniformly adopted by broadcast managers. Earlier, each broadcast or cable company had devised its own term, such as "program buy," "program-length commercial," "DR" (for direct-response program"), or "sales program," in addition to "infomercial."

Advertising practitioners distinguish between advertising and publicity on the basis of the advertiser's payment for the time or space that carries the message. If the medium controls the time or space, the content is classified as "editorial" (in print) or "news and entertainment" (in broadcast and cable), and any mention of the advertiser or its products in this context is considered publicity. If an advertiser pays the publisher or station for printing or telecasting a message, the content of the message is deemed to be advertising. At today's broadcast and cable operations, those in charge of entertainment content clear the available time for infomercials. However, the operation's advertising managers sell the time periods, screen infomercial content for acceptability, and otherwise control the infomercial process. As one broadcast standards-and-practices officer said, "An ad is an ad is an ad. Thirty seconds or 30 minutes—these are all advertising."

For many in the advertising profession, however, the distinction between advertising and publicity is an important one. It is well established that consumers' responses to and acceptance of a message are affected by their perceptions of the message itself; they regard paid advertising with considerably more skepticism than they do unpaid publicity. Newspapers tend to have internal rules requiring that all advertising be easily distinguishable from editorial content or that it carry a label clearly identifying it as advertising. Many magazines have similar rules. In broadcasting, consumers often have presumed that commercials are restricted to the breaks during and between programs and that anything longer was, in itself, a program.

Blurred Boundaries

The neologism *infomercial* acknowledges that such programs are not always clearly presented to or recognized by viewers as advertising. The boundaries between commercial and noncommercial messages are blurred; the infomercial incorporates elements of newsmagazines and talk shows associated with informational programming, though it is produced and programmed as a commercial sales message. Moreover, since television newsmagazines and talk shows have become the primary vehicles through which issues are presented and analyzed in our society, these formats were seen to lend infomercials a kind of credibility that goes to the heart of many audience comprehension, miscomprehension, and deception issues.

Infomercials initially were criticized by both independent and governmental observers who said their programming formats distracted viewers from the fact that the information was a sales message. They were also considered questionable because of the claims they made for products. Several early infomercials prompted legal action by the Federal Trade Commission (FTC). The FTC acted against a sales program for sunglasses, for example, that presented itself as an independent, investigative consumer program; the agency also acted against a major distributor of several infomercials.

Infomercial producers have used a variety of program formats—including talk-show, newsmagazine, documentary, and even faux investigative consumer report—to sell their products. In some cases, they have even inserted "commercial breaks" within the programs to enhance the illusion that the ad is a regularly scheduled program. Some insidious examples have employed the conventional trappings of newscasts to make viewers think they are watching bona fide news. These frequently involved questionable products and pitches, alleging support from tests, reports, or surveys, demonstrations and mock-ups of product usage, and celebrity and consumer endorsements. Often the goods and services advertised in these infomercials had the potential for consumer abuse, among them ads for psychic services and hot lines, personal wealth and financial investment plans, weight-loss plans, hair-loss remedies, anti-aging products, and schemes for avoiding the payment of taxes.

The half-hour infomercial *Consumer Challenge*, for example, produced by the seller of MDR fitness tablets, which also bought the time in which to run the show, began with an announcer proclaiming that the show's two "investigative reporters" would determine for "you, the consumer" whether this product was genuine or a "consumer rip-off."

Another infomercial for a hair-loss program was presented as a live, investigative program hosted by a major television star. He presented questions to and appeared to interact with the advertiser's paid experts, whose side of the conversation had actually been taped in advance.

The Advertising-Media Relationship

Although the exact nature of the relationship between the program producers and the television vehicles is new, the idea of lengthy programs aimed at selling is not. Advertising has been an integral part of the electronic media from the earliest days of radio. The first paid commercial broadcast was made on radio station WEAF in New York City on 22 August 1922. It was a 30-minute sales presentation by the Queensboro Corporation promoting an apartment development in Jackson Heights, New York—in effect an infomercial. And as late as the 1950s and 1960s *The Kiplinger Newsletter* sold subscriptions through regular 15-minute radio programs purveying the kind of financial management tips offered in the newsletter.

In the 1930s and 1940s all sponsored radio programs were produced by the advertiser's agency or a producer hired by the agency, which in either case was the final authority on content. It prepared the commercials and often interpolated sales plugs into the program content. The salutation, "Jell-O again, this is Jack Benny," began every broadcast of *The Jack Benny Show* during the years Jell-O sponsored the program (1934–42). Brand names were often part of a show's title, and characters from the program would sell the products. Sometimes mention of the product was worked into the show's script. At the extreme, some programs, especially the early quiz shows, were created by advertising agencies and sold to their clients as advertising vehicles and also to stations or networks as programs. Sometimes scriptwriters also wrote ad copy, or agency personnel screened the scripts of sponsored program for acceptability.

This practice carried over into the early days of television, with advertisers controlling the content of daytime programs, in particular the "soap operas." Though the advertisers and agencies might have had less direct interest in origination or production of prime-time programs, the programs themselves still carried the sponsor's names in the title, such as *Texaco Star Theater* with Milton Berle and *Camel News Caravan*. Ad agencies exerted strict control over the content of those programs. The relationship of the Kudner Agency to the Milton Berle program is a case in point. When Texaco had Kudner shift its sponsorship from Berle to Jimmy Durante in 1953, the agency simply sold the Berle program to another of its longtime clients, the General Motors Corporation; the *Texaco Star Theater* became the *Buick Berle Show*, with Kudner continuing to oversee it. Though the content of these and other programs was routinely peppered with humorous references to their sponsors, they were not considered infomercials.

For a variety of reasons sole sponsorship died as the predominant form of program support by the early 1960s. Advertisers shifted to the practice of participating in sponsorships with other advertisers within programs that were purchased by the stations or networks. The result was the erection of a kind of firewall between advertiser and program content. And in keeping with this development, in the 1960s the Federal Communications Commission (FCC) and the National Association of Broadcasters (NAB) set limits on the number of commercial minutes allowed per hour of programming, requiring that all commercials be clearly identified. These restrictions barred anything akin to the infomercials of today. Such programs as *Great Moments in Music* and *100 Paintings,* essentially 15-minute commercials in the guise of cultural programs, were forced off the air in 1973 following action by the FCC.

These restrictions did not affect cable television systems, which provided an outlet for program-length commercials through the 1970s and 1980s. As cable television grew, so too did the number of outlets for these programs, and cable networks were not required to label such programs as advertising.

In 1979 the Justice Department sued the NAB on antitrust grounds, asserting that limits on the number of commercial minutes per hour artificially restricted the availability of airtime and inflated prices. Following some adverse preliminary rulings, the NAB dropped its code in 1982. Infomercials returned to broadcast television in 1984 after the FCC, following a philosophy of deregulation that characterized the administration of U.S. President Ronald Reagan, lifted its restrictions on the amount of commercial time permitted during the broadcast day.

Sponsor Is the Program

Infomercials, however, are more than simple program sponsorships. While sponsored programs are seen as a concern for programmers, they are not a problem for advertising salespeople. With an infomercial, the sponsor no longer simply buys and supplies the program; instead, the sponsor is the program. In fact, the sponsor is often the guest expert interviewed by the program's host.

At the end of the 20th century, the only remaining FCC controls on infomercials required TV stations to clearly identify them as advertisements. Such identification is not always built into the programs, however, and the FCC has cited some stations for failure to properly identify such programming. The reporting of violations is largely up to the viewing public, as the agency lacks sufficient resources to monitor such practices. Nonetheless, the FCC has stated that "existing statutory requirement(s) for identification of sponsored material, along with other requirements of law pertaining to false, deceptive, or misleading advertising should, in our view, be sufficient to assure that the public is informed when it is viewing paid-for broadcast matter."

There is a significant economic incentive to create infomercials: they are inexpensive to produce and returns can be quite high for various direct-mail efforts. Response rates run about 5 per 1,000 viewers, or up to 20 per 1,000 viewers if a bonus is offered, and revenue can run to three times the media cost.

There is also considerable incentive for various broadcast stations and cable networks to run infomercials. Since station operators do not pay for the program material, infomercials can generate up to 400 percent more revenue than buying and airing syndicated reruns that carry traditional, 30-second commercial spots. Local affiliate and independent broadcast stations consider this an economic benefit. In addition, infomercials are time-fillers; they provide programming to fill scheduling gaps or allow new cable networks to round out a 24-hour schedule without incurring their own programming costs. As one television station manager stated, "They come to me with money and all it costs me is electricity to stay on an extra hour plus paying someone to supervise the transmitter."

On the other hand, infomercials have been viewed as audience killers, providing an undesirable downturn in ratings and reducing the lead-in audience for programs that follow the infomercial. In the early days of the Turner Broadcasting System's WTBS, the "superstation" carried a large number of infomercials and was denigrated by some as the "Infomercial Network." The company's decision to forgo its dependence on infomercials resulted in a major drop in the station's short-term profits, but the action allowed the station to build a stable of regular programs and attract more "reputable" advertisers.

Infomercials first appeared during low-cost, readily available time periods—late at night and during weekends on cable television networks and independent TV stations. But as their numbers grew, infomercials began to occupy other time slots; they now appear at all times of day, on all types of cable networks or broadcast stations, including those owned and operated by the major networks; the only determinate is whether the station has time available and needs an inexpensive means for filling that time.

Gaining Acceptance

Despite lingering concerns, by the turn of the 21st century infomercials were increasingly gaining acceptance. Some, it could be argued, provide extensive, beneficial consumer information that could aid consumers in making purchase decisions. Many advertisers are turning to the infomercial format when long explanations are needed to communicate basic sales points or product benefits. For example, local real estate companies produce video tours of properties that are for sale. Sellers of exercise equipment take advantage of lengthy commercials to provide detailed demonstration of their products. An Apple Computer infomercial showed audiences "meeting" a family to see how simple it is to install a home computer and how quickly ordinary people can learn to use it. A Magnavox infomercial presented the many technological innovations in a newly introduced television set, also using segments of the sales program in many traditional 30-second spots. Some infomercials are also distributed as videotape "brochures."

TV Guide and other, local TV publications have become better at identifying commercial programs in schedules of telecasts, as have television stations and networks. Although some advertisers place their logo or commercial identification in a corner of the screen during an airing, some on-air identifications, as in the early days of these programs, appear only at the start of the programs. Viewers who tune in after the first couple of minutes may not see such notices. Yet the viewing public has become accustomed to these programs and recognizes them as sales efforts, so attempts to make them resemble a regular news or entertainment program could backfire on a sponsor. Some observers hold that the infomercial's special ability to deceive consumers has been declining—may, in fact, already be lost—as the format itself has become more readily recognized.

Some "mainstream" advertisers, such as Apple Computer and Magnavox, have made use of infomercial programs for introductions of new products or innovations. The most common users of infomercials, however, are mail-order sales companies with new products to demonstrate or investment plans to explain; psychics and sellers of exercise machines or programs also remain among the most prominent users of the infomercial format.

HERBERT JACK ROTFELD

Further Reading

Chester, Jeffrey, and Kathryn Montgomery, "TV's Hidden Money Games: Counterfeiting the News," *Columbia Journalism Review* 27 (May/June 1988)

Ferrall, Victor E., Jr., "The Impact of Television Deregulation on Public and Private Interests," *Journal of Communications* 39 (Winter 1989)

Hayes, Rader, and Herbert J. Rotfeld, "Infomercials: The Shame of Cable Network Programming," *Advancing the Consumer Interest* 1, no. 2 (1989)

Maddox, Lynda M., and Eric J. Zanot, "Suspension of the NAB Code and Its Effect on Regulation of Advertising," *Journalism Quarterly* 61 (Spring 1984)

Parsons, Patrick, John Finnegan, Jr., and William Benham, "Editors and Their Roles," in *Press Concentration and Monopoly: New Perspectives on Newspaper Ownership and Operation,* edited by Robert Picard et al., Norwood, New Jersey: Ablex, 1988

Parsons, Patrick, and Herbert J. Rotfeld, "Infomercials and Television Station Clearance Practices," *Journal of Public Policy and Marketing* 9 (1990)

Rotfeld, Herbert, et al., "Television Station Standards for Acceptable Advertising," *Journal of Consumer Affairs* 24, no. 2 (Winter 1990)

Wicks, Jan LeBlanc, "Varying Commercialization and Clutter Levels to Enhance Airtime Attractiveness in Early Fringe: How TV Sales Managers May Be Responding to Deregulatory Freedoms," *Journal of Media Economics* 4 (Summer 1991)

Insurance

The history of insurance advertising is filled with some of the advertising industry's most enduring efforts. Slogans such as Allstate Corporation's "You're in good hands," advertising sponsorships such as *Mutual of Omaha's Wild Kingdom,* and integrated campaigns such as Metropolitan Life Insurance Company's "Peanuts" campaign are among the most memorable. Indeed, a look at the history of insurance advertising reveals that notable campaigns are abundant, as are consistent themes and trademark icons. Among the most common themes are the recurring ideas of reliability, fear of death and disaster, and humility. The insurance industry has also, curiously, been quick to incorporate the use of animals in logos and in advertising to convey widely different messages.

As soon as a group of Connecticut businessmen formed the Hartford Fire Insurance Company in 1810, it was clear that advertising was a top priority. The fledgling insurer immediately began to place earnest, text-heavy ads in both local and regional newspapers that declared its charter, purpose, and trustworthiness. This straightforward approach would continue for the next several decades.

One such Hartford Fire ad, which ran in 1837, emphasized the company's age and financial soundness. "This institution is the oldest of the kind in the state," ran the ad. "It is incorporated with a capital of 150,000 dollars, which is invested and secured in the best possible manner." Hartford Fire sought to convey the message that it was a legitimate company, one that would pay a claim should disaster strike. In an age when both disreputable enterprises and city fires were commonplace, the approach sought to separate Hartford from its rivals.

By the 1920s Hartford Fire had forsaken its no-nonsense ads for a more emotionally charged approach. The company capitalized on the twin themes of fire and fear when in 1925 it launched its "Grim Reaper" campaign. Created in-house and run in magazines such as the *Saturday Evening Post,* it featured a cloaked Grim Reaper who warned of the damage fire could cause. "An unhappy New Year to you!" read one ad, "That's fire's New Year message to property owners." Beneath it is the smirking reaper, skeletal fingers intertwined and leaning forward on a counter, as though confiding in the reader. Above him is a quote: "I am Fire. I am Destruction. I am Loss." Beneath him is Hartford Fire's moniker.

Hartford Fire's dour tack, with ads created by N.W. Ayer & Son in the 1930s and 1940s, helped it grow from a regional business into one of the first nationally recognized insurance companies. Its timing reflected national events. Rampant fires were the most common and destructive calamities early in the century, as the United States was being transformed from a rural nation to an urban one. Hartford Fire's business grew markedly, particularly in larger cities such as Chicago, Illinois, and New York City.

Hartford Fire continued to use fear-mongering as a primary advertising method through the 1950s (when it switched agencies, hiring Marchalk & Pratt, Inc.), but it added additional appeals.

From its inception, the company had depicted a stag on its logo, a design element still in use in the 21st century. The image of the stag has been reproduced in every medium from magazine ads to the company's stationery. It appeared, for example, on the insurance policy that was written for the Springfield, Illinois, home of Abraham Lincoln.

It would be decades, however, before it occurred to the company to use a live deer in television commercials. In a 1980 TV ad campaign developed by Marchalk's successor, McCann-Erickson Worldwide, "Vladamir," an impressively antlered stag, appeared on the front walk of a suburban home and behind the locked gate of a business. The message was that the company, by then rechristened "The Hartford," would protect what it insured. The stag is still included in nearly all of the advertising and branding efforts of what is known as the Hartford Financial Services Group, Inc. One example is the company's "Bring it on" TV ad campaign (1997–98) from Arnold Communications. It promoted not only insurance policies but also mutual funds and estate-planning services.

The Hartford's use of the stag echoes the widespread use of animals, both real-life and in cartoon form, as among the most common of recurring icons in insurance advertising. Among the most noted animal-centric branding efforts and ad campaigns are those that have been run by the Mutual of Omaha Companies, Metropolitan Life Insurance Company, and American Family Life Assurance Company, Inc. (AFLAC). The use of animals, which came to the fore in the mid-1950s, underscored a major change in insurance advertising, as positive associations began to replace negative ones. While fear is still a common advertising theme, it is rarely given a heavy-handed treatment and is usually seen only as a minor aspect of a broader, more positive approach to selling insurance.

The animals in advertising trend began in earnest with the 1950 launch of Mutual of Omaha's *Zoo Parade with Marlin Perkins,* a TV program handled by ad agency Bozell & Jacobs. The brainchild of naturalist Marlin Perkins, who acted as host of the show, and Mutual of Omaha Chairman-Chief Executive Officer V.J. Skutt, the program ran through 1957. As its name suggested, *Zoo Parade* featured zoo animals. By the late 1950s, when many urban TV viewers could easily take a subway to their local zoo to see a live polar bear or boa constrictor, watching one on TV was of little interest, and the show was dropped.

No TV show, however, had yet depicted animals in their natural environments, a fact that had not escaped Perkins and Skutt. The two soon collaborated on *Mutual of Omaha's Wild Kingdom.* The show premiered 6 January 1963 and won many awards (including four Emmys) while greatly enhancing the insurer's image with consumers. *Wild Kingdom,* which regularly depicted Mutual of Omaha's "chief in headdress" corporate symbol, was on prime-time network television until 1971, when it went into syndication. *Wild Kingdom* remains a valuable marketing franchise for Mutual of Omaha, which maintains Web sites dedicated to the program and its late host.

WHILE FIRE LOOKS ON AND SMILES

MEN who smoke, or carry lighted cigars, cigarettes, pipes or matches while handling gasoline are inviting Fire, and thousands of blackened ruins bear testimony to their unpardonable carelessness.

Fire is a public enemy against which we are fighting a defensive battle. We *must* be more careful. We must do everything in our power to protect our homes, schools, public buildings and places of business, and to safeguard the investment that they represent. The Hartford Fire Insurance Company will help you in your efforts to prevent fire and will make good your loss if fire does come.

There is a local agent of the Hartford near you. He will see to it that you are protected by the service and policies of a Company that has been serving property owners faithfully for 114 years.

HARTFORD FIRE INSURANCE COMPANY, Hartford, Conn.

The Hartford Fire Insurance Company and the Hartford Accident and Indemnity Company write practically every form of insurance except life

A 1920s ad for the Hartford Fire Insurance Company personified fire as a malevolent black-robed figure.
Courtesy of Hartford Financial Service Group, Inc., with cooperation from Arnold Communications.

While Mutual of Omaha's advertising is associated more than any other insurer's with live animals, the Metropolitan Life Insurance Company's ads have been inextricably linked to cartoon animals—specifically, Snoopy and Woodstock of "Peanuts" fame. In 1985, with the help of its longtime ad agency Young & Rubicam, Inc., Metropolitan Life launched its first "Peanuts" campaign, which appeared on TV and in print. Critics within the insurance industry bemoaned the decision to link the stolid insurer with whimsical cartoon characters.

Criticism notwithstanding, the "Peanuts" campaign has been one of the industry's best remembered. It has also been one of the longer-running campaigns, continuing into the 21st century. Although the ads resonate in particular with the baby boomers who grew up reading the late Charles Schulz's daily comic strip, they have also gained widespread recognition among a younger age group. This nearly universal appeal comes from the fact that Metropolitan Life, more than many other insurers, integrated the themes from its TV advertising into nearly all its external communications. For example, its ubiquitous *Life Advice* pamphlets, which give advice on everything from becoming a grandparent to getting divorced to enjoying retirement, are replete with "Peanuts" characters such as Snoopy, Peppermint Patty, and Marcy. Metropolitan Life has also built much of its Internet advertising and branding strategy around "Peanuts," using Snoopy throughout the company's Web site.

Snoopy's ongoing presence is a reminder that, while insurance companies allow their ad campaigns to evolve and change, they understand that longstanding brand associations are worth cultivating. In part that is because consumers buy their products—term- and whole-life policies, for example—with the intention of keeping them for decades.

In more recent years, Metropolitan Life, like other insurers, has broadened its product line to include several types of investment products. Metropolitan Life's circa-2001 advertising reflected this shift. Its TV ads featured company agents working their sales territories, from a farming hamlet to an urban Chinatown. The message: Metropolitan's agents are part of their communities and develop financial plans that fit each customer's distinct needs. The Chinatown commercial in particular was a nod to Metropolitan Life's new client base, about 30 percent of whom were immigrants.

Another popular animal-centric ad campaign has been that launched in 2000 for AFLAC. The $40 million "talking duck" campaign, created by Kaplan Thaler Group, New York City, is among the most aggressive by a supplemental insurance company. Supplemental insurance is targeted at businesses, to be included as a payroll option. Typically only salesmen market such products. AFLAC's campaign was indicative of a changing business-to-business insurance marketplace, one in which competition had become sharp, and image and brand were becoming more important than standing relationships.

AFLAC's campaign broke at an auspicious time on a much-watched venue: CNN's celebration of the new millennium. It set an aggressive tone for the campaign's media placement. The insurer's spots were assertively positioned, often on popular

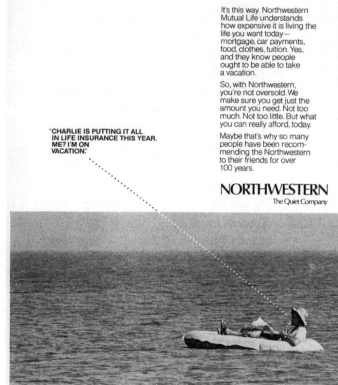

"CHARLIE IS PUTTING IT ALL IN LIFE INSURANCE THIS YEAR. ME? I'M ON VACATION."

It's this way. Northwestern Mutual Life understands how expensive it is living the life you want today—mortgage, car payments, food, clothes, tuition. Yes, and they know people ought to be able to take a vacation.

So, with Northwestern, you're not oversold. We make sure you get just the amount you need. Not too much. Not too little. But what you can really afford, today.

Maybe that's why so many people have been recommending the Northwestern to their friends for over 100 years.

NORTHWESTERN
The Quiet Company

NML THE NORTHWESTERN MUTUAL LIFE INSURANCE COMPANY-MILWAUKEE

In 1972 the Northwestern Mutual Life Insurance Company introduced its long-running slogan, "The quiet company," underscoring the company's low-key approach to selling insurance.
Courtesy of Northwestern Mutual Life Insurance Company.

prime-time TV programs such as *The West Wing* and during highly visible sporting events such as Major League Baseball games. AFLAC's prime-time approach has been consistent with its goal of reaching the 35- to 54-year-old age group, which is largely responsible for selecting supplemental insurance policies on behalf of their employers.

AFLAC's TV commercials have been noted for their creativity and humor, attributes that had been practically nonexistent in supplemental insurance advertising. The commercials' consistent star is a white duck that waddles through scenes of daily life, unnoticed by all, raucously quacking "AFLAC." The comedian Gilbert Gottfried does the duck's voice-over. In one commercial, a young couple lies in bed discussing whether or not to start a family. Pondering the financial implications of children, they wonder aloud where to go for answers. The frustrated duck quacks "AFLAC!" throughout, to no avail.

Some in the industry considered AFLAC's humorous approach ill-suited to the marketing of a product as serious as supplemental insurance. However, the campaign's results proved such critics wrong. AFLAC's name recognition jumped to 71 percent in 2000 (from only 2 percent in 1990), while the campaign itself was voted one of the best-liked advertising campaigns of 2000 by a *USA Today*/Harris poll. It was also cited as one of the top-ten ad campaigns of 2000 by the *Wall Street Journal*.

Pacific Mutual Life Insurance Company, based in Newport Beach, California, amassed its influence and grew in size without doing any advertising from its founding in 1858 until near the end of the 20th century. Its business was built through the efforts of its agent sales force, which is regarded as one of the industry's best. But Pacific Mutual's nonadvertising approach ended in 1997, when it launched its first TV campaign. Developed by Goddard Claussen Porter Novelli, it featured stock footage of a humpback whale and its calf swimming gracefully. A voice-over likened Pacific Mutual's strength to that of the humpbacks. The campaign not only markedly boosted the company's brand recognition, it also led to the company's choosing an image of a humpback as its new corporate logo, replacing an infinity symbol.

Northwestern Mutual started its advertising in earnest in 1948, but only began to see real results for its efforts some 28 years later. In the years following World War II, the Milwaukee, Wisconsin-based insurance company began to run print ads in national magazines. These ads consisted of straightforward testimonials from policyholders. While popular with the insurer's sales agents, the testimonial ads were far less well received by consumers. A 1970 Gallup poll revealed that only 10 percent of the nation's men had ever heard of Northwestern Mutual. This was crushing news, since at the time men bought nearly all insurance policies.

Northwestern Mutual and its agency, the J. Walter Thompson Company (JWT), set out to boost the company's image in 1972 through a national TV advertising campaign, themed "The quiet company." It was a new tack for Northwestern Mutual; it was also an unusual move for an insurer strongly associated with a region, as Northwestern Mutual was with the Midwest.

The company made its first major TV media buy as a corporate sponsor of the 1972 Olympic Games in Munich, which took a tragic turn when terrorists attacked the Israeli team. Some 90 percent of homes with TV sets across the United States tuned in to ABC's coverage of the attack and saw "The quiet company" campaign. Northwestern Mutual's $1.4 million media buy ended up gaining the company recognition worth many times that figure.

Surveys following the Olympics revealed a stunning turnaround in Northwestern Mutual's brand recognition. The company was now the third-most-recognized U.S. insurer. The campaign was wildly popular with agents as well as consumers: some began writing checks for policies from "The quiet company."

Bolstered by its success, Northwestern Mutual increased its U.S. ad presence with JWT buying time on programs such as *60 Minutes* as well as during Major League Baseball telecasts. In 1976 it spent $2.5 million in advertising, a good deal of which went toward yet another Olympic sponsorship, this time at the Montreal Games. Over the next 25 years, while Northwestern Mutual's advertising budget continued to increase, its slogan remained unchanged.

Allstate Corporation, State Farm Insurance Companies, and Nationwide Financial Services, Inc., have departed from North-

HELP IN A HURRY

You can count on it with Allstate auto insurance

Wherever you drive, in the U.S. or Canada, help is always as near as the nearest phone

When you have an accident, and somebody's hurt, you want help—that's what insurance is for. And whether it's night or day you want help fast—that's what Allstate Insurance is for.

As an insurance company, we expect to help out, we expect even careful drivers to need us—that's why more than 4,000 Allstate claims people stand ready to help our policyholders in a hurry.

So if you have an accident even in the middle of the night and somebody is injured—help is as near as the nearest phone. The first words you'll hear are: "May we help you?" This is more than just a polite greeting; we really want to know how we can help, and we're prepared to do something about it fast. Allstate claims people have the authority to do something about your problem right "on-the-spot." There's no long-distance red tape to slow you down.

Low rates, too. Fast, fair claims settlement is one good reason Allstate's rates are so low. By eliminating home-office red tape, Allstate cuts down on costly paper work and long-distance phone calls. Savings are reflected in Allstate's low rates. Allstate keeps selling costs low, too—and passes savings on to policyholders.

You may save $10...$20...$30 or more! As you'd expect, savings depend on where you live and how your car is used. It is not uncommon for Allstate policyholders to save $10...$20...$30 compared with rates of most other companies for similar coverage. Some folks save even more. (Standard rates in Texas where eligible policyholders have always saved through dividends.)

With insurance rates generally at an all-time high, wouldn't you be wise to compare values and join the more than 5 million policyholders now insured with us? Stop at the Allstate Booth in Sears, the Allstate Insurance Center in your neighborhood, or phone for an Agent to visit your home. Allstate Insurance Companies. Home Offices, Skokie, Ill. *May we help you?*

You're in good hands with ALLSTATE INSURANCE COMPANIES

AUTO · PROPERTY · ACCIDENT and SICKNESS · LIFE

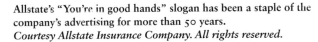

PAUL SCHMIT, Mayor of Port Washington, Wisconsin. Mr. Schmit, blinded by headlights of an on-coming car, ran his brand-new Chrysler into a tree. Time: about 3 A.M. Mr. Schmit was insured. One phone call to Allstate, and he got help in a hurry. The same morning, his car was in a garage with...

Allstate's "You're in good hands" slogan has been a staple of the company's advertising for more than 50 years.
Courtesy Allstate Insurance Company. All rights reserved.

western Mutual's message of humility, instead using individual approaches that appeal to trust. While all three have run advertising campaigns with real staying power, none resonates better than Allstate's. Its best-known campaign is centered on the idea of misfortune, which, for better or worse, is inseparable from insurance.

Allstate's slogan had its origins in 1950, when an Allstate sales manager's daughter was stricken by hepatitis and hospitalized. Upon returning home from work several days into her illness, the manager, Davis Ellis, was told by his wife that the hospital personnel had said that the parents need not worry: the staff had told her, "We're in good hands with the doctor."

Soon afterward, Ellis brought up the phrase during an Allstate meeting, where it was adopted as the company's slogan. The marketing team, with help from Leo Burnett Company, Chicago, shortened the core slogan to "You're in good hands." A sketch of outstretched cupped hands was positioned above the words. Between the hands and the slogan was the company's name. Allstate ran its first ad with the phrase in late 1950, in the *Saturday Evening Post* and *Colliers*.

Soon thereafter, Allstate launched its first TV ads, with actor Ed Reimers as spokesman. In the spots, Reimers's pitches for Allstate were aimed at young men with new families. And while the "You're in good hands" slogan was mentioned, it was not the centerpiece. Instead, the commercials focused on Reimers, who emphasized the affordability of Allstate's policies. Different commercials focused on various products: family insurance, endowment policies, convertible term, and mortgage protection. The approach emphasized Allstate as one of the first full-service insurers in the United States.

Although the sketch of the sheltering hands has been updated many times over the years, it had changed little as of the outset of the 21st century. Allstate's "You're in good hands" slogan has endured, as has the insurer's relationship with Burnett, which continued to handle Allstate's advertising in 2001.

Allstate's ads continued to evolve to fit both the times and its expanding product line. A 1987 print ad, which ran in major newspapers and magazines, began with copy that proclaimed, "Now you can get customized protection for all of these." Beneath were sketches of a home, a satellite dish, a tool shed, a lawnmower, a horse, and a barn accompanied by the line, "With just one of these." The ad was well timed and targeted an affluent group that was becoming a favored audience for insurance ads.

A 1999 Allstate TV, print, and radio advertising campaign, titled "Mine," featured Allstate agents doing good works in their local communities. One showed an employee who had handed out some 25,000 anti–drunk-driving brochures. The concept reflected the era, a time when insurance companies were increasingly taken to task for their purported lack of ethics.

The State Farm Insurance Companies also retained the same theme, with variations, for decades—"Like a good neighbor, State Farm is there"—as well as a single ad agency, Doyle Dane Bernbach (later DDB Worldwide). As with Allstate's, State Farm's slogan was intended to inspire trust. Moreover, it was intended to make State Farm resonate in the mind of the consumer as a local agency. This proved to be valuable at a time when many other insurance companies were forgoing regional strategies in order to focus on national and global ones. The slogan, written by singer Barry Manilow, was first used in 1971. It was adapted to television and radio spots, as well as print ads. Its use continued into the 21st century.

Yet another stolid midwestern insurer, Nationwide Financial Services, Inc., also relied upon the same theme over the decades. The "Nationwide is on your side" tag line underwent various incarnations under different ad agencies—from Ogilvy & Mather in the 1960s to Ketchum Advertising to Temerlin McClain in the 1990s.

New York Life's "Cityscapes" campaign, created by Berlin, Cameron & Partners, consisted of TV spots and print ads. One commercial depicts historical events unfolding with New York Life's own history set against them. For instance, a group of 1960s-era executives gather around a TV set in an office in New York Life's Park Avenue tower to watch the astronauts land on the moon.

Another top New York–based insurer, American International Group, Inc., also launched a historical theme-based campaign at about the same time as New York Life. Where New York Life's campaign culminated in the future, however, American International's is a celebration of the past.

Ogilvy & Mather Worldwide developed the campaign titled "The greatest risk is not taking one," which consisted of four commercials that depict famous Americans who took great risks and achieved great things. One spot features clips of baseball great Jackie Robinson. His wife provides voice-over in the form of an excerpt from Theodore Roosevelt's heralded "The Man in the Arena" speech.

PHILIP B. CLARK

See also Prudential Insurance Company

Further Reading

Gurda, John, *The Quiet Company: A Modern History of Northwestern Mutual Life,* Milwaukee, Wisconsin: Northwestern Mutual Life Insurance, 1983
The Hartford <www.thehartford.com>
Northwestern Mutual Life Insurance Company <www.northwesternmutual.com>

Integrated Marketing

The concept of integrated marketing emerged in the 1990s as a new discipline within the advertising industry, quickly becoming an essential element of most brand management operations. A pure integrated marketing strategy does not assume any particular solution or tactic but instead begins by considering the brand's marketing objectives along with the mind-set, lifestyle, and habits of the target audience. Only then is a communications solution, such as a TV campaign, a print ad, or a promotion, developed.

The integrated marketing model's most important legacy has been putting advertising and marketing messages into appropriate context and unifying those messages in a clear and consistent communications strategy. Another legacy of the rise of integrated marketing is the emergence in the 1990s of the position of chief marketing officer, an executive at a corporation or organization charged with orchestrating a coherent marketing program through diverse channels. "When the concept of integrated marketing took hold, it helped elevate the role of marketing right up the corporate ranks so it became part of the chief executive officer's agenda," according to Randall Rothenberg, author of *Where the Suckers Moon*, a book that traces the roots and dynamics of consumer perceptions of advertising.

Also referred to as integrated marketing communications, the discipline was originally defined as the process of unifying the themes of a brand marketing program so that advertising, sales promotion, direct response, direct and database marketing, and public relations had a consistent look and feel. The goal of basic integrated marketing was to leverage an organization's investment in a brand campaign across all communications channels to increase impact, while improving efficiency and effectiveness. Through such synergy, organizations hoped to bring diverse communications resources together, including coordinating the efforts of the advertising agency with an unrelated direct marketing agency, to achieve a seamless campaign sharing the same imagery and attitude.

The forces driving the creation of integrated marketing were diverse. As far back as the 1970s, major agencies began developing or acquiring related services such as public relations and sales promotion. Young & Rubicam, Inc., tried to put various diverse disciplines together under one roof and called it the "whole egg." But the concept was more a one stop service source than a systematized discipline. Another factor was the recognition in the late 1980s of a shift in the balance of spending on brands. Spending was moving away from traditional print and TV advertising in favor of promotion, point-of-sale efforts, couponing, direct marketing, sponsorships, and local, grassroots events, to the consternation of many advertising agencies whose main operations were creating TV and print ads.

By 1990 major advertisers, including the Procter & Gamble Company, had acknowledged that traditional budget allocations had been reversed; instead of 60 percent for advertising and 40 percent for promotion, 60 percent was now being spent on overall promotion practices, and 40 percent was going toward print and TV advertising. Advertisers and retailers were unhappy about spreading so much money into disparate channels where its effect was muted. But the competitive demand for in-store promotions, contests, sweepstakes, and coupons was too fierce to ignore.

At the same time, academics began to point out the benefits of coordinating all marketing and advertising messages under a unifying theme to achieve greater impact. Such practices would improve efficiency and effectiveness and make better use of corporations' investments in brand images. Universities with advertising departments, including Northwestern University in Evanston, Illinois, began offering graduate degrees in integrated marketing communications in the mid-1990s; awards programs were developed to recognize leaders in the field; and advertisers began to embrace the concept. Another major force behind the integrated marketing movement was the growing restlessness of agencies involved in creating materials traditionally considered below-the-line marketing, such as promotions, direct mail, and public relations. As consumers' lifestyles and leisure habits began to change in the 1980s and network TV ratings began to fall, media channels splintered. Nonadvertising communications began to play a bigger role, as public relations campaigns were used to introduce products and event marketing became a key strategy for companies to develop brand identities at the grassroots level.

By 1990 it had become apparent that nonadvertising programs were generally far less expensive than network TV commercials to produce and support, and in many cases they were extremely effective. The agencies creating these nonadvertising campaigns began to promote the results of lower-cost efforts, getting the attention of advertisers. For the first time, promotion agencies were being invited into corporate boardrooms alongside advertising agencies to pitch ideas for introducing new products and marketing campaigns. Many corporations assigned executives to manage the integrated marketing aspects of brands, to make sure the work of various agencies on advertising and promotion efforts was synchronized.

Soon, agencies that had been limited to handling only "below the line" marketing duties such as promotions seized the opportunity to pitch themselves to clients as full-service providers of integrated marketing and advertising solutions. Frankel & Company, a longtime Chicago, Illinois-based promotions agency, used integrated marketing to catapult itself out of the below-the-line category for clients such as McDonald's Corporation and Visa U.S.A., for the first time creating TV advertising in addition to its usual sweepstakes and in-store promotions.

At the same time, big agencies saw the arrival of integrated marketing as a wake-up call to reorganize. Many agencies had acquired subsidiaries during the 1980s and early 1990s; consequently, they had several divisions that handled direct marketing and promotion, but these were in different locations and under different management.

A number of agencies chose to reorganize their operations under a single umbrella. Others established integrated marketing specialties within the traditional agency structure. DDB Chicago harnessed the concept of integrated marketing to capture a greater share of overall advertising and marketing expenditures from clients by developing its own integrated marketing department, dubbed Beyond DDB. During the mid-1990s, DDB Chicago used this new integrated department to pitch clients its "whole egg" marketing services concept. For example, it synchronized Discover credit card's sweepstakes and point-of-sale efforts, as well as its event marketing, with the general advertising campaign's theme and imagery, which was also handled by DDB Chicago.

In the late 1990s integrated marketing underwent another evolution, as the principles of customer relationship management (CRM) seeped into the industry. The CRM revolution underscored the need to create relationships with customers through one-to-one marketing, recognizing the uniqueness of individuals. By the close of the century, integrated marketing had come to recognize diverse communication channels; it took the context of those communications into account, and it sought opportunities to establish ongoing dialogues or relationships with consumers.

KATE FITZGERALD

Further Reading

Grönstedt, Anders, *The Customer Century: Lessons from World Class Companies in Integrated Communications*, New York: Routledge, 2000

Rothenberg, Randall, *Where the Suckers Moon: An Advertising Story*, New York: Knopf, 1994

Schultz, Don E., Stanley I. Tannenbaum, and Robert F. Lauterborn, *Integrated Marketing Communications*, Lincolnwood, Illinois: NTC Business Books, 1993; as *The New Marketing Paradigm*, Lincolnwood, Illinois: NTC Business Books, 1994

Intel Corporation

Principal Agencies
Chiat/Day, Inc.
Dahlin Smith White (later Euro RSCG/Dahlin Smith White)
Messner Vetere Berger McNamee Schmetterer/Euro RSCG

Intel Corporation was founded in Mountain View, California (it later relocated to Santa Clara, California), in 1968 by Robert Noyce, Gordon Moore, and Andrew Grove, all former engineers from Fairchild Semiconductor, to advance large-scale integration technology for silicon-based chips. Intel pioneered an innovative advertising strategy focused on branding its components. The concept, perhaps the greatest technology campaign of all time, helped Intel become a global brand and the world's largest supplier of semiconductors.

In 1971 Intel invented the microprocessor, a computer on a fingertip-sized chip. For more than a decade Intel's marketing was essentially business to business, targeting design engineers at original equipment manufacturers (OEMs). Although these efforts were primarily sales-force driven, Regis McKenna, a Silicon Valley public relations expert, handled public relations and advertising.

Chiat/Day, Inc., acquired the Intel account in 1980 after buying McKenna's advertising business. Chiat/Day's advertising for Intel was highly respected for its simple design and nontechnical copy. However, an emerging computer industry trend would take Intel in new directions and revolutionize microprocessor and personal computer (PC) advertising.

PCs flooded the market in the 1980s, leading users to seek a point of differentiation among machines. Everyone, from industry insiders to business and consumer end users, began referring to computers by configuration, and Intel's "286" and "386" chips became that reference point. Intel seized this "configuration branding" opportunity. Worried that "386" and future microprocessor names would eventually become generic nouns, such as Band-Aid or Xerox, Intel launched a trademark effort mandating that its name appear in all ads that mentioned its microprocessors. Moreover, Intel recognized that end users were key targets for these messages.

Despite Chiat/Day's "gold standard" reputation for computer advertising, in May 1989 Intel placed its account into review.

Meanwhile, as a result of slack consumer demand, OEMs were not embracing Intel's 386 chip. Shafer & Shafer of Irvine, California, a little-known agency, was tapped to create Intel's first ad campaign that promoted microprocessors to end users. The $20 million print and outdoor effort encouraged 286 users to upgrade to 386 machines. The ads showed a red "X" painted over the number 286 followed by a 386.

Intel appointed Dahlin Smith White, Inc. (DSW), of Salt Lake City, Utah, as its agency in January 1990. Their collaboration led to an ongoing, multifaceted brand-building effort featuring the "Intel inside" theme and logo. Intel launched a multimillion-dollar campaign in April 1991 for its new 486 chip. Print and—for the first time—television ads drove consumers to demand 486 machines. With little choice but to use the chip, over a period of days computer makers announced new 486-based PCs.

The "Intel inside" slogan debuted in July 1991 in a global corporate print, television, and outdoor campaign. The first TV ad took viewers on a virtual trip inside a PC, entering through the disk drive, winding past the hard drive, and coming to rest on the central processing unit stamped with the Intel logo.

By fall 1991 the "Intel inside" cooperative advertising program, the world's largest co-op effort, was under way. Intel allocated funds for participating hardware manufacturers to use in advertising that incorporated the "Intel inside" theme or logo. Within a few months more than 300 OEMs in the computer industry were participating. By mid-1997, 1,500 manufacturers were participating, and Intel extended the program to Internet advertising.

Despite great initial success with configuration branding, as Intel had feared, a U.S. federal court ruled in 1991 that terms such as "386" were generic and not protected. Intel responded with the "Pentium," a new global brand of chip trademarked in all Intel's markets. In February 1994 DSW and Intel launched a consumer and business television and print campaign, spending more than $150 million to communicate that Pentium processors provide "instant access" to software. Driven by ongoing "Intel inside" advertising, 1994 revenue for Intel reached $8.8 billion, up more than 50 percent since 1992.

March 1996 saw Intel consolidate its $100 million account (previously divided between Dahlin Smith White in the United

States and some overseas markets, Publicis in Europe, and DPTO Propaganda and Marketing and Adler Publicidad de Occidente, S.A, de CV, in Latin America) at Euro RSCG, Paris, after Euro RSCG acquired a majority interest in Dahlin Smith White. The new team introduced multiple campaigns in 1996 to build the Pentium brand and extend into interactive media. A worldwide consumer effort, "Pentium Processor: On the 'Net/Off the 'Net," broke in March and demonstrated in television and print the Pentium's ability to access multimedia-rich Internet or desktop applications. New on-line banner ads also pointed end users to a redesigned Intel Web site. Young adults were targeted in October with the "Connected PC" theme in television, print, and Web sponsorships. Intel placed its first interactive ad on a connected CD-ROM called *LAUNCH,* and Web sponsorships surfaced in storylines, product placements, and full-screen animated ads. Dominating the microprocessor market with an 80 percent share, Intel's 1996 sales reached $20.8 billion.

Intel and Euro RSCG/Dahlin Smith White's advertising efforts continued in 1997 with a January campaign showcasing the MMX Pentium processor in two series of commercials. In one, *Seinfeld* television star Jason Alexander tried to impress potential dates while using Intel's videoconferencing technology. The other campaign, "Bunny people," debuted during the Super Bowl and showed technicians in "Bunny suits," the garments worn in sterile chip-manufacturing environments, dancing to hit music as they "put fun" into MMX Pentium processors.

In May Intel launched the Pentium II with an estimated $20 million global print and World Wide Web business campaign. Media used included newspapers, business and computer publications, and the Internet; the ads directed corporate buyers to a new section of Intel's Web site.

Intel's largest on-line advertising effort to date broke in September as part of the Pentium II consumer campaign. Sponsorships ran on Web sites such as MTV On-line, InterZine, and Mplayer and featured the "Bunny people" in ads designed to demonstrate Pentium II multimedia capabilities. Intel's 1997 ad budget reached $900 million—$150 million for its own ads and $750 million in co-op placements—making it the world's leading tech advertiser and one of the largest consumer advertisers.

Early in 1998, Messner Vetere Berger McNamee Schmetterer/Euro RSCG, New York City, joined Intel's roster of agencies to handle consumer advertising, while Euro RSCG/Dahlin Smith White retained business-to-business and interactive duties. Messner Vetere's first ad launched in September with television spots showing that, in a world short on processing power, a parachute does not open on time and a baseball does not reach home plate. The ads close with the question, "Time for a Pentium II processor?"

In November the animated television character Homer Simpson of *The Simpsons* was tapped for new Pentium ads created by Euro RSCG/DSW. "Homer's smarter brain" shows Simpson's inferior brain being fitted with a Pentium chip, turning him into a college professor.

With competition intensifying and its market share eroding to less than 80 percent, Intel supported the February 1999 introduc-

tion of Pentium III chips with $300 million in billboard, newspaper, television, and radio advertising. The ads replaced the Pentium II "Bunny people" with a blue door to represent the chip and a new tagline, "This way in," to link the chip with Internet usage. In the meantime, faced with the daunting challenge of competing with Intel, lesser-known chip manufacturers began advertising to consumers, with number-two chip maker Advanced Micro Devices (AMD) becoming Intel's chief rival.

Intel further adjusted its agency roster in April 1999 by awarding Messner Vetere Berger McNamee Schmetterer/Euro RSCG its business-to-business advertising responsibilities, taking the assignment from nine-year incumbent and sister agency Euro RSCG/Dahlin Smith White. By September, amid the 1999 dot-com frenzy, Messner Vetere Berger McNamee Schmetterer/Euro RSCG had its chance to craft both business-to-business and consumer sides of a new, $150 million global Internet technology campaign for Intel. Print and on-line media were used to promote Intel's e-commerce prowess to businesses while consumer-targeting television commercials tagged, "Don't just get onto the Internet, get into it," showed Pentium III processors enabling people to experience fantasies on the Internet. One month later, AMD took its challenge to a new level by launching its Athlon chip as the world's fastest computer processor. The October 1999 $15 million to $18 million multimedia campaign by agency Hill, Holliday, Connors, Cosmopulos, Boston, helped raise AMD's presence among consumers and corporate buyers, but the Intel marketing juggernaut rolled on.

The fall of 2000 saw the Pentium III campaign freshened by avant-garde performers the Blue Man Group pitching the processor with dramatic television spots that incorporated the group's trademark music and green paint to spell out the Roman numeral III. The year ended with Intel's market share holding at about 78 percent and AMD a very distant second with approximately 17 percent of market. Intel's advertising budget had reached approximately $800 million, and spending on the decade-old Intel Inside co-op program was approaching $1.5 billion globally. For the $300 million February 2001 launch of the Pentium 4, Intel executed a worldwide, multimedia effort featuring the Blue Man Group building the number "4" with white tubes and the tagline, "The Pentium 4 processor. The center of your digital world." By May 2001 AMD once again took the advertising stage to further penetrate the corporate chip market with a $25 million global print campaign featuring testimonials of success stories from firms that use AMD chips. As 2001 neared an end, Intel revised its Pentium 4 campaign. Under the existing tag the campaign, named Technology Quest, showed aliens searching for advanced technology on Earth. After locating a Pentium 4–powered personal computer, the aliens experiment with digital media. As the year drew to a close an industry debate over market share estimates ensued, with Intel responding to reports of AMD capturing a 21 percent share by challenging their accuracy and claiming that Intel's share figure "begins with an eight."

RANDY JACOBS

See also color plate in this volume

Further Reading

Brandt, Richard, "Intel: Way out in Front, but the Footsteps Are Getting Louder," *Business Week* (29 April 1991)

Glitman, Russell, "Valley Ad Agencies Seek New Ways to Sell Intel," *PC Week* (1 October 1990)

Johnson, Bradley, "Intel's Pentium II Gets $20 Mil Intro," *Advertising Age* (5 May 1997)

Johnson, Bradley, "Challenge for Intel: Boosting Tech Market," *Advertising Age* (15 September 1997)

Tapellini, Donna, "Intel's Amazing Flexibility Keeps It on Top," *Marketing Computers* 9 (November 1989)

International Advertising Association
(IAA)

The International Advertising Association (IAA)—the only global partnership of advertisers, agencies, media, and marketing communications professionals—was founded in 1938 as the Export Advertising Association. The group took its present name in 1953. The association's World Secretariat is located in New York City.

The IAA has more than 4,500 individual and associate members worldwide, 90 percent of whom reside outside of the United States. The organization also has 80 corporate members and more than 60 organizational members—among them the American Advertising Federation, American Association of Advertising Agencies, Ad Council, and American Academy of Advertising—along with scores of professional associations in international markets, 61 chapters in 59 countries, 21 associate chapters, and 47 accredited institutes (universities, colleges, and professional schools). Its elected world president in 2001 was David Hanger (publisher of *The Economist*). Wally O'Brien (director general) and Richard Corner (executive director) headed the professional staff at the IAA's World Secretariat.

The association was founded by Henry Ashwell, publisher of *Export Trade and Shipper Magazine,* and 12 others involved in export advertising. The original purpose was for the members to exchange ideas about and experiences in their profession of overseas advertising. Ashwell was elected honorary president, and Shirley Woodell, advertising manager of Packard Motors Export Corporation, became the group's first president. By year's end, membership had grown to 67. World War II slowed the organization's growth, but by 1949 membership had reached 300, and that same year the association held its first World Congress in New York City.

Overseas membership rapidly expanded. The 1955 IAA World Congress in Zurich, Switzerland, was the first held outside the United States. In 1956, as a means of promoting self-regulation in the industry, the IAA published *The International Advertising Code of Ethics and Standards of Practice.* World congresses were held in The Hague, The Netherlands, in 1957, and in Vienna, Austria, in 1959, and by the close of the decade, the IAA's constitution and bylaws provided for the establishment of local chapters and global board representation.

An associates group for young professionals was organized in 1964, and other associates groups soon followed. By 1969 membership totaled 2,100—the majority residing outside the United States—in 15 chapters. During the 1960s the bylaws were broadened to permit a greater role in promoting the benefits of advertising. Association growth slowed during the 1970s. Nevertheless, a report entitled "The Global Challenge of Advertising," presented at the 1973 Dublin, Ireland, World Congress, further expanded the association's leadership role to include professional development and advocacy. In 1974 the organization initiated corporate memberships as a means of broadening its base and attracting needed financial support.

Throughout the 1980s IAA membership continued to expand worldwide. As trade barriers were reduced, however, and new technologies facilitated commerce across national boundaries, the profession underwent profound changes, producing both opportunities and problems. In response to these changing conditions, the IAA established its Accredited Institute Program to prepare young people for careers in advertising and subsequently started an international internship program and expanded its advocacy programs to address what it considered unwarranted legislation and restraints.

INTERNATIONAL
ADVERTISING
ASSOCIATION

Courtesy of the International Advertising Association (IAA).

Prompted by the economic transformations occurring with the collapse of the Soviet Union, the IAA's European growth accelerated dramatically in the early 1990s. Chapters were formed in Poland, the Czech Republic, Hungary, Bulgaria, Romania, and the newly independent countries of the former Yugoslavia, as well as in several former Soviet republics. Membership continued to grow in Latin America and in the rapidly developing Asian markets until 1997, when the latter region was beset by an economic downturn. IAA world congresses have convened in countries from Mexico (1994) to South Korea (1996) to Egypt (1998) to London (2000). The event in 2002 will be staged in Lebanon, and in 2004 it will take place in China.

The 1990s' Campaign for Advertising was aired in more than 220 countries and territories; its theme, "Your right to choose," emphasized the importance of consumers' rights to free choice and demonstrated how advertising works. The campaign received more than $750 million in donated media time, with an additional $8 million contributed (by companies such as Procter & Gamble) for production.

The association continuously works in area markets to enhance the role of advertising and demonstrate its value. The IAA has conducted economic impact studies—in, among other countries, Estonia, Mexico, and Poland—aimed at quantifying advertising's economic contributions and documenting its role in generating economic growth. The organization also undertook consumer attitude studies in central and eastern Europe.

The current professional development goal of the IAA is to integrate all programs and activities to encourage lifelong relationships between talented individuals, the marketing communications profession, and the IAA. Efforts to strengthen the performance of the advertising industry within international markets are an integral part of the organization's professional development programs and initiatives. The IAA's accredited institutes have conferred the IAA diploma in marketing communications on more than 14,000 graduates. Its global internship program, launched in 1995, enables qualified students from its accredited institutes and other schools where advertising is taught to obtain hands-on professional experience. The program is being extended to marketing communications faculty for the purpose of fostering mutually advantageous relationships between employers and faculty participants.

In 1996 the IAA introduced the InterAd international student advertising competition. Each year a comprehensive case project is prepared by a global marketer. Students from all over the world are then invited to form agency teams to address an actual marketing communications problem. Student teams' recommendations are judged regionally by industry professionals, and the InterAd World Champion is selected by an international panel composed of the client's marketing executives, agency principals, and IAA directors. Clients have included the Jeep division of Chrysler, Merrill Lynch, MilkPEP (an association of independent dairies), and Compaq.

The IAA's biennial world congresses provide a global forum for the presentation and discussion of issues important to the profession. The association also works with its chapters to sponsor

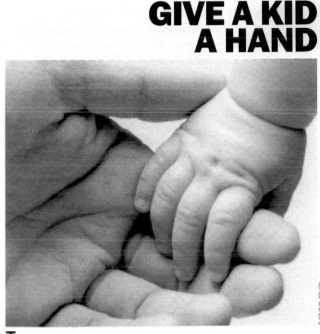

GIVE A KID A HAND

The first five years of a child's life are critical, the experts tell us. That's when their characters are formed. That's when caring counts. Someone to show them how to do things. Someone just to hold them. Unfortunately, for many of the world's children, that's just what they don't get. And society suffers as a result—because a deprived child has a lot less chance of growing up an adjusted adult. Some of us believe we can change things—or at least try. And we need your help. No, don't reach for your pocket. It's not your money — it's you we want. In your community there are dozens of ways you can make personal contact with kids and make a difference to their lives. Maybe you'll help one to read, to play a game, to learn to laugh. Maybe you'll just be the hand that holds out a little hope...

COME ON – HELP US GIVE A KID A HAND

Through its "Give a Kid a Hand" campaign, the International Advertising Association encouraged people around the world to participate in the many community organizations dedicated to helping children. *The International Advertising Association (IAA).*

local and regional conferences and events addressing its mission-related issues in contemporary marketing communication. In addition it sponsors education conferences designed to elevate the level of marketing communications education within international markets.

In recent years the IAA has refined its mission; it is now a global and grassroots partnership among successful brand builders, working to champion the cause of brand building. Because the elements that create a brand's reputation require the freedom to flourish without restriction, the IAA works to fight unwarranted regulation on behalf of responsible commercial communications. The association is an advocate for freedom of choice across all consumer and business markets.

JOHN H. HOLMES

Further Reading

Advertising and the Media in an Open Society: An International Symposium, New York: International Advertising Association, 1991

Boddewyn, Jean J., *The Case for Advertising Self-Regulation: An Essay*, New York: International Advertising Association, 1991

Calfee, John E., *Fear of Persuasion: A New Perspective on Advertising and Regulation*, Washington, D.C.: American Enterprise Institute for Public Policy Research, 1997

Day, Barry, *The Case for Advertising*, New York: International Advertising Association, 1998

Giges, Nancy S., editor, *Open Communications in the 21st Century*, London: Atalink, 1998

Giges, Nancy S., editor, *Technology and the World of International Marketing Communications*, London: Atalink, 1999

Giges, Nancy S., editor, *A New Connectivity: How Technology is Changing the Marketing World*, London: Atalink, 2000

International Business Machines Corporation. *See* IBM Corporation

Internet/World Wide Web

The Internet was originally created as a computer network for the sharing of information among universities; the network, set up in 1969, was called the Arpanet and linked four California universities at 50 Kbps (kilobits per second, a measure of modem speed). Twenty years later, in 1989, Tim Berners-Lee developed the World Wide Web at CERN, the European Particle Physics Laboratory, and the following year he introduced the first Web client and server. In 1991 the ban on business use of the Internet was lifted. And in 1994 the Internet's first banner advertisement—an AT&T Corporation ad from Modem Media—appeared on HotWired, the online version of *Wired* magazine. Proprietary services such as America Online (AOL) and Prodigy were already running banner ads, but this was the first banner on the Web. HotWired was designed to be a professionally published site with original content and advertising; as such, the startup service sold 12 companies a 12-week sponsorship; the cost per advertiser was $30,000. In addition to AT&T, sponsors included MCI Corporation, Sprint Corporation, Club Med, Coors Brewing Company's Zima brand drink, and IBM Corporation. In the late 1990s, fueling—and in turn being fueled by—the economic boom, the Internet underwent explosive growth.

The explosion was short-lived, however. By mid-2000, the dot-com gold rush was in decline. Even as consumers continued to flock to the Internet at the end of 2001, many marketers remained on the sidelines following a disastrous period for most Internet-focused companies, which found themselves uncertain as to whether the medium would become a viable place to spend advertising dollars. Steady growth in consumer penetration was not enough to convince advertisers. After the crash of the Nasdaq stock index in April 2000, industry bellwethers such as AOL and Yahoo! continued to increase their audiences despite faltering stock prices. In March 2000, Yahoo! had a total audience of 145 million unique users who saw an average 625 million pages on the service daily. By June 2001 those numbers had increased to 200 million unique users and a 100 percent increase in daily page views to 1.2 billion. In the same period, AOL's subscriber base grew from 22.2 million members to 30.1 million.

But marketers remained largely indifferent to the medium, blaming the ubiquitous banner, the same advertising format widely credited for the Internet advertising industry's early growth. In fact, the banner was by this time being identified as a significant contributor to the Internet's downfall. Companies—many of them dot-coms flush with venture capital money—invested heavily in the format during the boom, despite evidence that consumers were tiring of banner advertisers' often hard-sell come-ons. When the flow of investor capital dried up, people began to listen to naysayers; the result was a slowdown both in on-line advertising overall and a decline in the use of banner ads in particular.

Evidence of disenchantment with the banner had been apparent for some time. Data from a July 2000 Nielsen/NetRatings study showed that the average on-line user at the time was exposed to more than 400 banner ads each month but clicked on (i.e., requested further information) only 0.5 percent of them. During the dot-com boom, such low rates of follow-through hardly seemed to matter. From January to June 2000, Internet advertising increased 54 percent, from $818 million to $1.3 billion, according to AdZone Interactive. But the Interactive Advertising Bureau (IAB), an industry trade group, found in a September 2001 study that ad spending for the first six months of the year declined by 7.8 percent compared with the same period during 2000. While that decline was only in the middle range among all media in an advertising industry hit by an overall recession, the data showed a shift in on-line ad formats away from models such as banners. The percentage of advertising banners on the Web declined dramatically, from 51 percent of the overall on-

A 1998 print ad for SportsLine.com sought to persuade advertisers that ads on the Web site would reach a large audience.
SportsLine.com, Inc.

line ad market in 2000 to only 36 percent for the first six months of 2001. Further, classified advertising increased to 15 percent of total Internet spending, from 5 percent in the year earlier, while other formats—such as sponsorships; interstitials (full-screen ads that play between pages); and rich media (enhanced ads)—remained stable.

Early in 2001 the IAB came out in support of a variety of new ad formats designed to bring greater effectiveness to on-line advertising. The most popular of these, the so-called skyscraper, appears on the computer screen as a long, vertical box. By April, the IAB was reporting that sites ranging from Microsoft Corporation's MSN and Slate to Yahoo! and New York Times Digital's nytimes.com were accepting the "skyscraper" format. Studies released later in the year demonstrated that some of these new formats achieved a greater level of effectiveness than more established forms of Internet advertising.

Effectiveness itself remained an issue, however, and the absence of a system for measuring it served to restrict spending. The on-line ad industry had not yet devised universally agreed-upon definitions for such standards measures as hits and page views.

The outlook for the industry was not entirely bleak. The inexpensiveness of on-line advertising led some major brands to go on-line, especially those whose teen or young adult audiences are fluent in the medium. Anheuser-Busch Company's Budweiser found a way during 2000 to translate its popular " Whassup?" campaign to the Web, which included a site from which consumers could download the campaign catchphrase in 36 languages. The brand also experimented with on-line "daypart buys," a rela-tively new concept, placing ads for Bud on the home page of the CBS MarketWatch site on Friday afternoons. The American Honda Motor Company spent less than $1 million on-line to promote its revamped Civic Si model in an on-/offline sponsorship that linked the brand with the bands Everclear and blink-182.

An October 2001 survey by the Association of National Advertisers showed that 79 percent of respondents had advertised on-line in 2000, an increase of nearly two-thirds compared with the previous year, and that they spent on average $2.4 million each, up 24 percent. A total of 92 percent used banners. However, only 42 percent said that they planned to increase Internet ad spending in 2001.

Such numbers would seem to indicate that advertisers are willing to experiment with the Web but that adoption of the medium is slower than had been anticipated. Still, the data are irrefutable that not only greater numbers but a broader cross-section of the population is continuing to flock on-line. The data paint a portrait of an on-line audience that has changed radically from the days when the Internet was considered the province of college-educated males. By 2002 the question was not whether, but when, the on-line advertising industry will match the growth of its audience.

CATHARINE TAYLOR

See also E-Commerce; History: 1990s

Further Reading
Riedman, Patricia, "In the beginning," *Advertising Age* Special Issue (Volume 71, Number 16), 2000

InterOne Marketing Group. *See* Ross Roy, Inc.

Interpublic Group of Companies

The beginnings of the Interpublic Group of Companies date to the early 20th century, with the founding of two separate advertising agencies: the Alfred W. Erickson agency in 1902 and the H.K. McCann Company in 1911. In 1930 those two agencies merged to form McCann-Erickson Advertising, an ad giant that grew to encompass a number of agencies and marketing communications companies.

Pioneering ad executive Marion Harper, at 32 the youngest person ever named agency president at McCann, helped mold the fledgling shop into the modern agency it was at the beginning of the 21st century. It was Harper who advanced the idea that multi-ple agencies could thrive as separate entities under one corporate parent. The Interpublic Group of Companies (Interpublic) "is an outgrowth of Harper's idea of competing parallel agencies," according to company documents.

Harper first mentioned his competing agencies vision in 1951 under the broad heading of "agency of the future." He believed that there were significant benefits and advantages to keeping an acquired agency as a separate division, one with its own name and clients. His first chance to implement that vision came in December 1954 when McCann-Erickson purchased Marschalk & Pratt Company; instead of simply absorbing that agency, the Marschalk &

Fallon Worldwide.
Fallon McElligott created this award-winning advertisement for the Episcopal Church.
Courtesy of the Domestic and Foreign Ministry Society.

Feminism, Impact of.
The goal of a number of women by the early 1980s was to have a career without sacrificing family life or femininity. In this ad for Revlon's Enjoli fragrance, "having it all" was summed up in the jingle boasting of the liberated woman's ability to "bring home the bacon. Fry it up in a pan. And never let him forget he's a man!"
Courtesy of Revlon Consumer Products Corporation.

Firestone Tire & Rubber Company.
The influence of the Art Deco movement is evident in the striking graphics and sophisticated color scheme of this 1929
Firestone tire ad.
Courtesy of Bridgestone/Firestone, Inc.

Ford Mustang Hardtop

New Ford Mustang

$2368*f.o.b. Detroit

This is the car you never expected from Detroit. Mustang is so distinctively beautiful it has received the Tiffany Award for Excellence in American Design ... the first time an automobile has been honored with the Tiffany Gold Medal.

You can own the Mustang hardtop for a suggested retail price of just $2,368—f.o.b. Detroit. *This does not include destination charges from Detroit, options, state and local taxes and fees, if any. Whitewall tires are $33.90 extra.

Every Mustang includes these luxury features unavailable—or available only at extra cost—in most other cars: bucket seats; wall-to-wall carpeting; all-vinyl upholstery; padded instrument panel; and full wheel covers. Also standard: floor-shift; courtesy lights; sports steering wheel; front arm rests; a 170 cu. in. Six, and much more.

That's the Mustang hardtop. With its four-passenger roominess and surprisingly spacious trunk, it will be an ideal car for many families. Yet Mustang is designed to be designed by you. For instance, the trip to the supermarket can be a lot more fun when you add convenience options like power brakes or steering, Cruise-O-Matic transmission, push-button radio, 260 cu. in. V-8.

Or, you can design Mustang to suit your special taste for elegance with such luxury refinements as: air conditioning; vinyl-covered roof; full-length console; accent paint-stripe, and convertible with power top.

If you're looking for action, Mustang's the place to find it, with a 289 cu. in. V-8; 4-speed fully synchronized transmission; Rally-Pac (tachometer and clock) and other exciting options.

For an authentic scale model of the new Ford Mustang, send $1.00 to Mustang Offer, Department LH-1, P.O. Box 35, Troy, Michigan. (Offer ends July 31, 1964)

TRY <u>TOTAL</u> PERFORMANCE
FOR A CHANGE!

FORD

Mustang · Falcon · Fairlane · Ford · Thunderbird

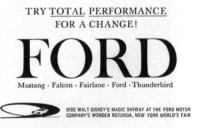

RIDE WALT DISNEY'S MAGIC SKYWAY AT THE FORD MOTOR COMPANY'S WONDER ROTUNDA, NEW YORK WORLD'S FAIR

Ford Motor Company.
The distinctive styling of the Ford Motor Company's Mustang was featured in this print ad from 1964, the year the automaker introduced the sports car.
Courtesy of Ford Motor Company.

General Mills.
Among General Mills' cast of cereal spokes-characters are
Lucky the Leprechaun (Lucky Charms), Count Chocula, the
Trix rabbit, and Sonny the Cuckoo Bird (Cocoa Puffs), all
pictured on packaging in this 1988 coupon supplement.
Courtesy of the General Mills Archives.

General Motors Corporation.
This 1927 ad for Frigidaire refrigerators, marketed by a
division of General Motors Corporation, stressed the economy
of electric refrigeration and helped transform a luxury item
into a common household appliance.
Courtesy of Frigidaire.

Global Advertising.
This print ad from the late 1990s highlighted the global
reach of the Visa card.

Grant Advertising, Inc.
Grant Advertising created this colorful ad for Old Dutch
Cleanser in 1943.
Courtesy of The Dial Corporation and Fitzpatrick Bros., Inc.

In cold ALASKAN WATERS
where the silvery SALMON run

The Petrel, flag-ship of A&P's Alaskan salmon fishing fleet.

A&P nets and packs for you
these beauties of the deep

RIGHT NOW the silvery salmon are running. Great schools of them rushing through Alaska's icy waters, bound for the raging rivers swollen by melting snows. Off shore, lying in wait for them is A&P's trim fleet of vessels, manned by hardy fishermen of that north country. On shore are A&P's six great salmon canneries waiting to receive the fleet's prize catches of the deep . . . shimmering, silvery salmon.

Direct from the boats, these salmon are expertly packed for shipment to the A&P Food Stores in your neighborhood. Their delicate flavor . . . their fine, firm freshness never fails to delight, however you choose to serve them.

Going to the icy waters of Alaska for salmon is typical of the great lengths to which A&P goes to provide its customers with better foods.

5,000,000 women throughout the United States and Canada shop daily at the A&P Food Stores because experience has convinced them that rarely, if ever, are A&P's fine quality and low prices equalled elsewhere. Why not cut your food bills? Shopping at the A&P Food Stores will do it.

THE GREAT ATLANTIC & PACIFIC TEA CO.

A&P
ESTABLISHED
1859
"WHERE ECONOMY RULES"

PINK SALMON

Grocery and Supermarket.
As seen in this 1930 print ad, A&P responded to upstart supermarket rivals with advertisements that emphasized the high quality of its products.
The Great Atlantic & Pacific Tea Company, Inc.

Hair Care Products.
Since 1936 the Breck Girl has been among the best-known icons in hair-care advertising. Cybill Shepherd, seen in a 1969 advertisement, was one of several former Breck Girls who went on to achieve celebrity.
Courtesy of The Dial Corporation and Cybill Shepherd.

C.F. Hathaway Shirt Company.
In the 1950s ad executive David Ogilvy introduced the "Man in the Hathaway Shirt" campaign, which created a strong brand identity for the C.F. Hathaway Shirt Company. Hathaway, Waterville, Maine.

Heineken.
Playing on the brand recognition of Heineken, at the time the top-selling imported beer in the United States, this 1991 print ad for Buckler nonalcoholic brew showed the Heineken bottle standing behind the new introduction from its parent company.

Henderson Advertising, Inc.
In the 1960s campaigns from Henderson Advertising, Inc., depicted women in roles other than those of housewife and mother.
Fantastik® advertisement courtesy of SC Johnson.

Hertz Corporation.
A 2001 print ad for Hertz Corporation's special programs for small business targeted readers of business magazines.
© 2001 Hertz System, Inc. Hertz is a registered mark and trademark of Hertz System, Inc.

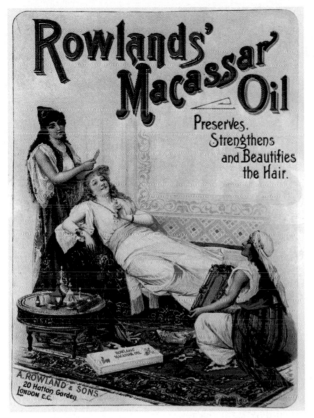

History: 19th Century.
The harem scene in this advertisement for Rowlands' Macassar Oil, a hair-care product sold in the 19th century, typified the era's fascination with the exotic.

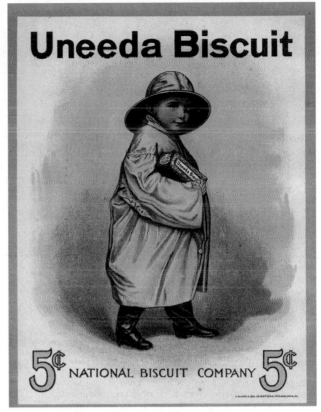

History: 1900–1920.
N.W. Ayer & Son, a New York City ad agency, created the Uneeda name and the "Slicker Boy" character, shown here in a 1919 ad, for the National Biscuit Company.
Courtesy of Kraft Foods Holdings, Inc.

History: 19th Century.
The U.S. showman P.T. Barnum was one of the first to recognize the persuasive power of advertising, as evidenced in this poster from 1870.
Image courtesy of Ringling Bros. And Barnum & Bailey® The Greatest Show On Earth®.

We just canned our top salesman.

We had to—our customers demanded it. You see, folks have been enjoying Canada Dry Ginger Ale in bottles since 1906. But when they wanted our Ginger Ale in cans, well, they just had to settle for a substitute. And let's face it: there just isn't any substitute for Canada Dry quality.

We use better ingredients and pinpoint carbonation to create

Special Sparkle. And it goes into every can we fill. That includes the original Pale Dry Ginger Ale, a tingling Grapefruit, refreshing Cola, lip-smacking Orange, old-fashioned Root Beer, and even five full-flavored, low-calorie beverages.

Canada Dry beverages always were unbeatable. Now they're unbreakable, too.

History: 1940s.
Rosie the Riveter, the symbol of millions of American women who joined the industrial workforce during World War II, was created by artist J. Howard Miller for the War Production Coordinating Committee.

History: 1960s.
The "confessional" headline in this Canada Dry ad from the 1960s was a hallmark of the new style of advertising that emerged during the decade.
CANADA DRY and the Shield are registered trademarks of Dr Pepper/Seven Up, Inc. ©2001.

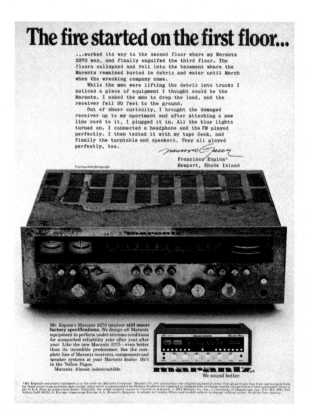

History: 1970s.
A testimonial-style print ad from the 1970s told the story of a Marantz 2270 stereo receiver that survived a house fire as well as a fall from a second-story window and still worked.

History: 1980s.
Launched in 1981, this campaign for Grey Poupon Dijon mustard continued to run for almost two decades. The tag line "Pardon me, would you have any Grey Poupon?" became a part of American pop culture.
Courtesy of Kraft Foods Holdings, Inc., with cooperation from Rolls-Royce & Bentley Motor Cars, Ltd.

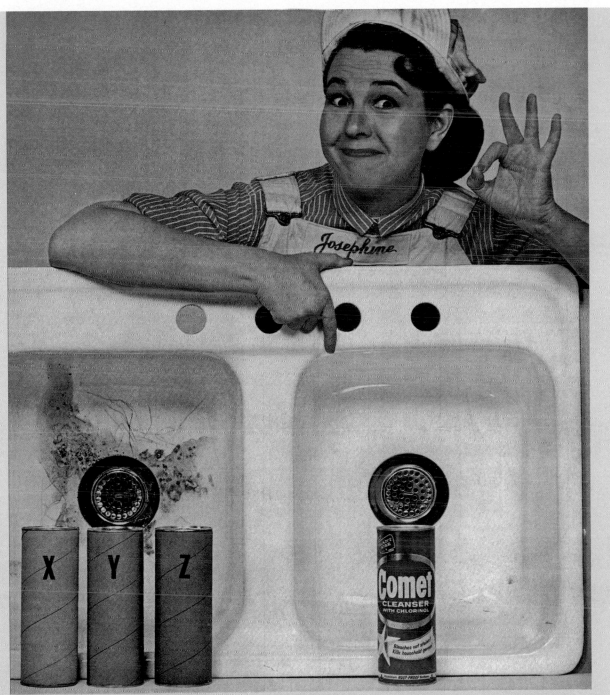

JOSEPHINE, TV'S LADY PLUMBER, SAYS:

"Compare cleansers. Comet removes both food stains and potmarks better than any other leading cleanser"

"What a difference! Other cleansers have problems with both food stains and potmarks. But not Comet. It gets out both kinds of stains best. Know why that is? Because only Comet has Chlorinol, the best cleaning, bleaching and disinfecting stuff in any cleanser. Even if you think you've got the world's worst stains, don't give up the sink! Get Comet and make it white as china. Comet cleans deep —bleaches right through old dried food stains, makes pesky, scratchy potmarks disappear. Comet removes those stains best—and you can't be any better than that!"

Household Cleansers.
Introduced in 1963 Comet's Josephine the Plumber quickly became a blue-collar heroine and an enduring advertising icon.
Courtesy of The Procter & Gamble Company.

India.
The year 1997 marked the 50th anniversary of Indian independence, as well as Cadbury's 50th year in business in India. This ad from "The Real Taste of Life" campaign celebrated both milestones.
Reprinted with permission of Cadbury Schweppes plc.

Intel Corporation.
The dancing technicians in shiny "Bunny Suits" first appeared in Intel ads in 1997. In this print ad focusing on Intel's media enhancement technology—"the technical term for fun," according to the copy—the technician was shown dancing to the strains of a mariachi band.
Intel Corporation.

Intimate Apparel.
Maidenform produced hundreds of advertisements during its
long-running "I Dreamed . . . ." campaign, including this
light-hearted execution from 1967.
Maidenform, Inc. All rights reserved.

Johnson & Johnson.
Following a highly publicized product-tampering incident in
1982, Johnson & Johnson embarked on a marketing and
public relations campaign that became a textbook example
of how to recover from disaster.
Courtesy of Johnson & Johnson.

S.C. Johnson & Son, Inc.
S.C. Johnson had been a national advertiser for almost four
decades when this ad for Johnson's Liquid Wax appeared in
the *Ladies' Home Journal* in 1925.
Courtesy of SC Johnson - a family company for over a century.

Kowloon-Canton Railway Corporation.
After Hong Kong reverted to Chinese rule in July 1997, the
Kowloon-Canton Railway began to target business travelers
with the "Peace of Mind" campaign, which emphasized the ease
of crossing the border with China via the company's coaches.
Courtesy of Kowloon-Canton Railway Corporation.

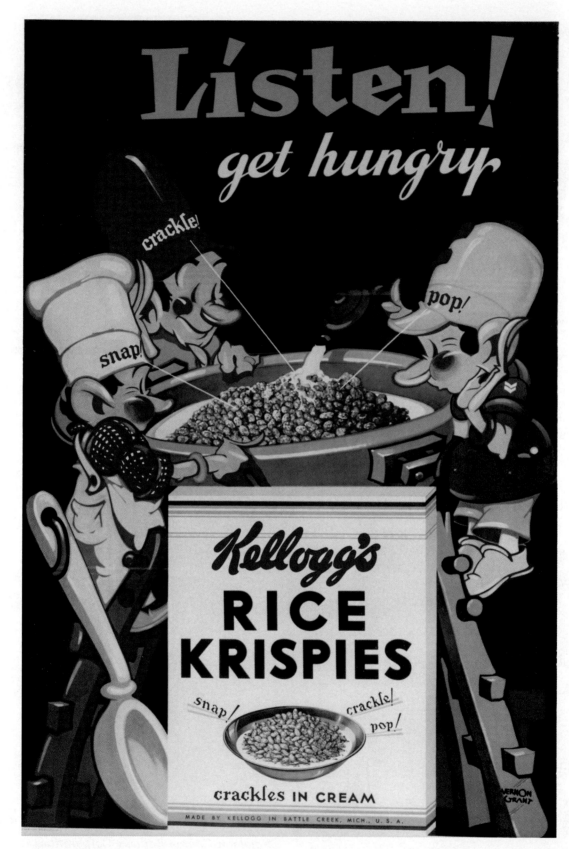

Kellogg Company.
This 1934 ad for Rice Krispies cereal was one of the first to feature all three of Kellogg's earliest spokes-characters: Snap, Crackle, and Pop.
Kellogg's® logo, Snap®, Crackle®, Pop®, and Rice Krispies® are registered trademarks of Kellogg Company. All rights reserved. Used with permission.

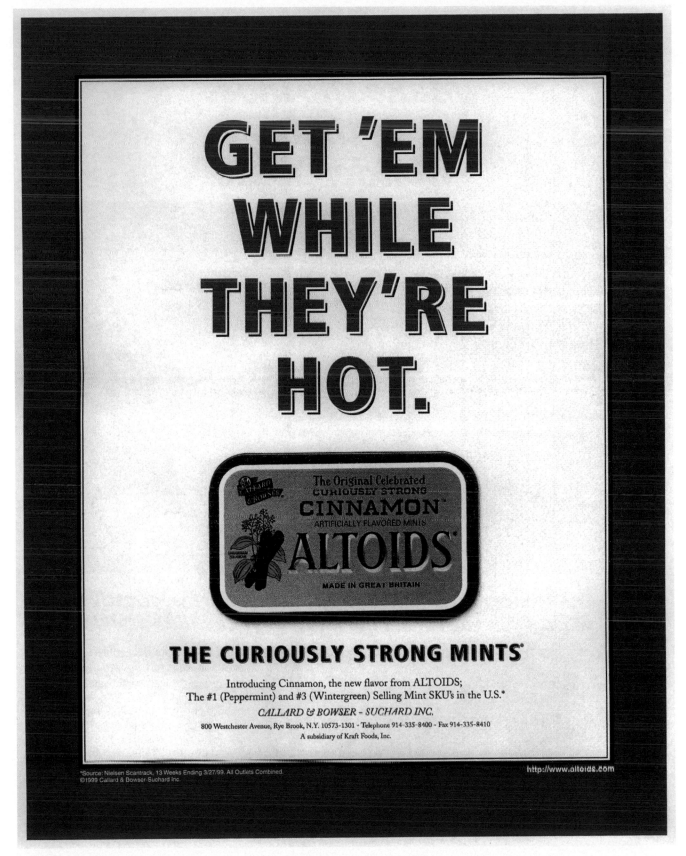

Kraft Foods, Inc.

In the 1990s Altoids became the best-selling candy mint in the United States. The product's strong brand identity was established through a combination of retro-style packaging and a highly visible ad campaign.

ALTOIDS is a registered trademark of Kraft Jacobs Suchard Limited and Kraft Foods Holdings, Inc.

Make the most of their "Wonder Years"

The "Wonder Years"—one through twelve—are the formative years when you can do the most for your child's growth

WONDER.

ENRICHED BREAD

helps build strong bodies 12 ways.

During these years your children develop in many ways — actually grow to 90% of their adult height. Every delicious slice of Wonder Bread is carefully enriched with foods for growing bodies and minds. The "Wonder Years" come only once. Make the most of them. Serve your children nutritious Wonder Bread.

Wonder Bread helps build strong bodies 12 ways! ®

Legal Issues.
The advertising slogans and claims of many products—Wonder Bread among them—drew increased scrutiny and legal challenges in the 1970s.
Interstate Brands Companies, subsidiaries of Interstate Bakeries Corporation.

Presenting Some Of The 2000 Body Parts You Can Clean With New Lever 2000.®

The Deodorant Soap That's Better For Your Skin.

- Lever 2000 has special skin-care ingredients.
- It won't dry your skin like other deodorant soaps can.
- It's been clinically proven better for your skin than any soap—not just any deodorant soap.

- You can use Lever 2000 everywhere. On hard parts. Soft parts. Tough parts. And pretty parts. All your 2000 parts.

© 1990 Lever Brothers Company

Lever Brothers Company/Unilever.
The 1990 campaign introducing Lever 2000 deodorant soap was the Lever Brothers Company's most successful ad campaign of the decade.
Courtesy of Unilever HPC.

The Safe Solution of Women's Greatest Hygienic Problem

Which 8 in 10 Better-Class Women Have Adopted

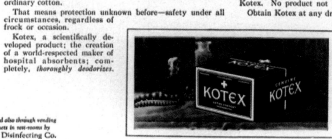

Easy
Disposal

and 2 other
important factors

① Disposed of as easily as tissue. No laundry.

② True protection—5 times as absorbent as cotton.

③ Obtain without embarrassment, at any drug or dry goods store,* simply by saying "Kotex."

Positive Protection Under ALL Conditions and An End Forever to the Embarrassing Difficulty of Disposal, This NEW Way

By ELLEN J. BUCKLAND, *Registered Nurse*

WITH this new way the hazards and uncertainties of the old-time methods are ended.

You wear sheerest frocks and gayest gowns without a moment's fear or doubt. You go about for hours; motor, dance, walk; meet all situations without a second thought.

The name is Kotex. Doctors urge it. Nurses employ it. Women find in it the scientific solution of their greatest hygienic problem. Its use will make a great difference in your life.

The difference between Kotex and ordinary pads

Kotex is the *only* sanitary pad filled with *Cellucotton* wadding, the extraordinary hospital absorbent recently discovered.

Thus Kotex provides the amazing absorbency of 16 times its own weight in moisture! It is 5 times as absorbent as ordinary cotton.

That means protection unknown before—safety under all circumstances, regardless of frock or occasion.

Kotex, a scientifically developed product; the creation of a world-respected maker of hospital absorbents; completely, *thoroughly deodorizes*.

A process applied under a secret and exclusive method, which ends an annoying problem.

Kotex eliminates utterly the problem of disposal—one discards Kotex almost as easily as tissue. No laundry.

* * *

Kotex is scientifically designed for safety in wear. That means a special quality gauze. It means ample gauze covering and strong gauze attachment ends, to eliminate absolutely all chance—all hazard.

Thus, from personal experience and from what other women told them, *80% or more better-class* women have discarded ordinary ways for Kotex. Once a woman tries Kotex, she rarely again invites the hazards of less scientific ways.

Only Kotex is "like" Kotex

Look for the name "Kotex" on the box of any sanitary pad you are asked to buy. If that name isn't there, you are not being given genuine Kotex. No other product is "like" Kotex. No product not plainly marked "Kotex" is Kotex.

Obtain Kotex at any drug, dry goods, or department store. 12 pads to the box. Two sizes of pads: Kotex Regular and Kotex-Super.

Kotex Company, 180 North Michigan Ave., Chicago, Ill.

Supplied also through vending cabinets in rest-rooms by West Disinfecting Co.

"Ask for them by name"

KOTEX
PROTECTS — DEODORIZES

No laundry—discards as easily as a piece of tissue

Lord & Thomas.
In the 1920s Lord & Thomas's advertisements for Kotex sanitary pads broke the taboo on talking about feminine hygiene in print. Copyright Kimberly-Clark Corporation. Used with permission.

Lorillard Tobacco Company.
This ad, part of Lorillard's "Tobacco Is Whacko" campaign to discourage smoking by young people, appeared in a 2000 issue of *Teen People.*
Courtesy of Lorillard Tobacco Company's Youth Smoking Prevention Program.

U.S.D.A. Inspected 100% Beef.

Twoallbeefpattiesspecialsaucelettuce-
cheesepicklesonionsonasesameseedbun™

You just read the recipe for McDonald's® Big Mac™ sandwich.

It starts with beef, of course.

Two lean 100% pure domestic beef patties, including chuck, round and sirloin.

Then there's McDonald's special sauce, the unique blend of mayonnaise, herbs, spices and sweet pickle relish. Next come the fresh lettuce, golden cheese, dill pickles and chopped onion.

And last, but far from least, a freshly toasted, sesame seed bun.

All these good things add up to the one and only taste of a great Big Mac.

Nobody can do it like McDonald's can™ **McDonald's®**

© 1979 McDonald's Corporation

McDonald's Corporation.
The headline of this print ad from the 1978 "Nobody Can Do It Like McDonald's Can" campaign doubled as a jingle in the TV commercials.
Courtesy of McDonald's Corporation.

Kids just eat him up.

© 1969 Hanna-Barbera Productions, Inc.

Fred, Barney, Pebbles, Bamm-Bamm, Dino, the Flintmobile—what a great way to get your kids to take their vitamins! In six fun shapes and bright lively colors, Flintstones© really are good to chew. And just one each day has all the vitamins kids normally need to take—if they don't eat right. Get the Flintstones, Regular or Plus Iron. They're all for the best.

FROM THE MAKERS OF

ONE A DAY®

©1969 Miles Laboratories, Inc.

GUARANTEED
PARENTS'
MAGAZINE

Miles Laboratories, Inc.
The J. Walter Thompson Company created this ad in 1969, a year after the agency introduced Flintstones vitamins for Miles Laboratories.
© Miles Laboratories and used with permission of Bayer Corporation. All rights reserved. Permission is also granted by Warner Bros. Consumer Products.

Military Advertising.
U.S. artist Howard Chandler Christy created the flirtatious Christy Girl for the Navy Publicity Bureau, which was seeking to attract recruits during World War I.

If you've got the time,
we've got the beer.

© 1972 The Miller Brewing Co., Milwaukee, Wis.

Miller Brewing Company.
During the 1970s Miller became the number-two U.S. brewer. A slogan introduced in 1971, "If you've got the time, we've got the beer," was credited with helping to boost Miller's sales.
Courtesy of Miller Brewing Company.

Nokia Corporation.
By incorporating a Nokia phone into a well-known British landmark, this 2000 ad suggested Nokia's standing as a global brand.

Pratt organization remained intact with its own staff and clients. According to the book *Truth Well Told: McCann-Erickson and the Pioneering of Global Advertising*, Harper quoted H.K. McCann as saying that he did not see why various forms of corporate organization were not as readily applicable to the advertising agency business as they had been to other businesses.

Harper's rationale for the new business strategy: Marschalk & Pratt could take on smaller clients more easily than the larger parent company could, and the agency could service those clients in a more profitable manner. More controversially, Harper believed that McCann-Erickson and Marschalk & Pratt could even handle some competitive accounts, since they operated under different names. Of Harper's new "agency within an agency model," *Advertising Age* wrote in December 1954 that it "may be a wholly new tactic for the agency business. It is probably the first time that any agency has undertaken to run a specialized advertising agency as a division, and the first time a division has been set up in the same city."

Harper's initial idea for this kind of agency structure was met with skepticism. The advertising industry—both agencies and advertisers—was not yet willing to accept the idea that two ad agencies owned in common could operate independently while preserving the confidentiality of conflicting accounts and competing for the best media opportunities on behalf of their clients. Indeed, company records show that McCann-Erickson initially lost two clients, American Mutual Life and Fuller paints, and Marschalk lost Tile-Tex, because of McCann's new philosophy.

At the time of the Marschalk merger, McCann operated 33 offices, 11 in the United States, and employed 2,300 people. Since 1945, McCann had opened 3 of those offices in the United States and 11 overseas. In 1945 billings were reported as $40 million; in 1953 *Advertising Age* reported billings of $106 million.

The idea of an agency holding company took root with Marschalk and continued to grow under Harper's supervision. Interpublic, Inc., was officially created in 1960, becoming the holding company for two wholly owned subsidiaries, McCann-Erickson, the larger of the two agencies, and Marschalk & Pratt. In 1964 the corporation was formally renamed the Interpublic Group of Companies, Inc.

During the early 1960s Interpublic rapidly added to its family of agencies, purchasing existing agencies in the United States and abroad, as well as opening new offices around the world. By January 1964 it listed 19 advertising and marketing companies as its components; expansion included international holdings, such as new operations throughout Central America. Among other moves, Interpublic brought Pritchard Wood, the London, England-based agency it acquired in 1961, to Mexico City, Mexico, merging it with Publicidad Stanton, and opened a Mexico City office for Marplan, which was the name for McCann's specialized marketing research service. As the agency continued its acquisitions-and-expansion strategy, the company presented its philosophy to clients as "a group of independent, competitive service companies, under a central business management."

Harper oversaw 38 acquisitions between mid-1959 and 1965 and supervised the opening of new offices in Africa, Australia,

and the Far East. In 1963 Interpublic signed a then-historic collaborative arrangement with the China Commercial Agency. The new Ling-McCann-Erickson agency operated out of an office in Hong Kong.

But the business environment in general began weakening, and Interpublic was stuck with debt from Harper's acquisition binge. In filings with the Securities and Exchange Commission, the company reported that "rapid expansion undertaken by Interpublic for several years prior to 1968 culminated in losses of about $250,000 in 1966 and about $3.9 million in 1967." Interpublic's bank debt, which the agency reported was only $1 million in 1962, had jumped to $9 million by 1967. "Cash requirements for acquisitions and to finance loss operations necessitated substantial bank borrowings," the company reported. Bank agreements, however, required Interpublic to maintain working capital of more than $10 million. By May 1967 the company was forced to inform its creditors, including Chase Manhattan Bank, that it could not meet those terms. These events culminated in the ouster of Harper on 9 November 1967. A dramatic Interpublic board meeting was covered widely by media organizations, including a story headlined "The Coup D'Etat at Interpublic," which ran in *Fortune* magazine several months after the event.

The board of directors named Robert Healy chief executive officer (CEO); he was given the title of chairman in February 1968, after Harper left the company. Healy immediately began a plan to reduce costs and restructure operations. He arranged for $10.2 million in revolving credit to restore the company's cash flow, "helped by the willingness of three major clients, Coca-Cola, Heublein and Carnation, to advance media commissions," according to company documents. The company announced that it returned to profitability in 1968 with profits of $3.7 million. It was a turnaround that *Advertising Age* described as "miraculous."

Interpublic went public in March 1971 at $17.50 per share and joined the New York Stock Exchange (ticker symbol: IPG) that August. Paul Foley, who had headed McCann-Erickson since 1968, succeeded Healy as CEO of Interpublic in 1971 and then assumed the title of chairman in 1973.

In 1972 Interpublic acquired the Campbell-Ewald Company, at the time a $123 million agency with 11 U.S. offices. This was Interpublic's largest purchase to date, a record that stood until 1979, when it acquired Sullivan, Stauffer, Colwell & Bayles (SSC&B) and its ownership position in the Lintas network.

Philip H. Geier, Jr., was named Interpublic's chairman-CEO on 1 January 1980. Except for one year at another agency, Geier served in various positions at McCann-Erickson and Interpublic his entire advertising career until his retirement in December 2000. Geier continued to be involved with Interpublic as chairman emeritus and as an adviser to the Interpublic board.

Geier oversaw the addition to the Interpublic network of Ammirati Puris Lintas (New York City) in 1994; DraftDirect Worldwide (Chicago, Illinois; formerly Kobbs & Brady and then Draft Worldwide) in 1996; and Hill, Holliday, Connors, Cosmopulos (Boston, Massachusetts) in 1998. He was endlessly mixing and matching his assets in various combinations. Campbell-Ewald merged with Marschalk in 1980, then parted ways in 1985. In

1987 Geier joined Campbell-Ewald to Lintas, then dissolved it ten years later. In 1999 Ammirati Puris Lintas was merged into the operations of another Interpublic acquisition, Lowe & Partners Worldwide, itself the main advertising unit of the Lowe Group. The merger created a global group with billings of more than $11 billion, putting it among the world's top five agency groups. By 2001 the new agency network had offices in 80 countries and operated as Lowe Lintas & Partners Worldwide (later Lowe & Partners). The Lowe Group management team was led by Frank Lowe as chairman and CEO; deputy chairman was Michael Sennott, who had been vice chairman of McCann-Erickson World-Group.

In November 2000 Interpublic announced the acquisition of Deutsch, Inc., a U.S. advertising and marketing communications agency regarded in the advertising industry as an innovative and creative company. Terms of the acquisition were not disclosed. Deutsch, with 1999 reported billings of $1.2 billion, at the time was ranked by *Advertising Age* as the largest independent agency in the United States. Deutsch operated as an autonomous Interpublic unit, headed by CEO Donny Deutsch.

In March 2001 Interpublic acquired True North Communications, the parent company of FCB Worldwide, Bozell Group, and other agencies. In addition to True North, Interpublic's primary holdings in 2001 included two other wholly owned global advertising agency networks, McCann-Erickson Worldwide and the Lowe Group, as well as five global specialized-services networks: Initiative Media Worldwide, Draft Worldwide, NFO Worldwide, Octagon, and Zentropy Partners, Interpublic's Internet-services company. Its eighth primary unit was the Allied Communications Group, managing Interpublic's holdings in a variety of specialized communications enterprises.

In 2000 Interpublic had realigned its public relations operations into two worldwide brands. The technology practice of Weber Public Relations Worldwide was combined with Shandwick International into Weber Shandwick Worldwide, an agency specializing in technology, public affairs, and lifestyle/entertain-ment. Golin/Harris International added 14 Weber offices in the United States, Europe, and Asia to its network. The public relations companies remain part of the Allied Communications Group of marketing services companies headed by Larry Weber, chairman and CEO of Allied.

Interpublic reported worldwide gross income of $6.6 billion in 2000, up 16.9 percent from the prior year. Domestic gross income in 2000 jumped 20.6 percent to $3.9 billion. For the first nine months of 2000, net new business jumped 40 percent to $2.1 billion, compared to $1.5 billion in 1999.

In March 2000 John J. Dooner, Jr., was named president-chief operating officer of Interpublic and, effective 1 January 2001, succeeded Philip H. Geier, Jr., as the holding company's CEO. With its acquisition of Chicago-based True North Communications, Interpublic surpassed the U.K.'s WPP Group as the world's largest advertising holding company.

LAURIE FREEMAN

Further Reading

Alter, Stewart, *Truth Well Told: McCann-Erickson and the Pioneering of Global Advertising,* New York: McCann-Erickson Worldwide, 1994

Bernstein, Henry, "Interpublic Prospectus Is Stormy Chronicle," *Advertising Age* (18 May 1970)

Budd, James H., "Interpublic Expands in Central America," *Advertising Age* (26 August 1963)

Heady, Robert, "Interpublic's SCI Unit Enters New Area—Ads," *Advertising Age* (15 April 1963)

"Interpublic Buy Presages Second Worldwide Shop to Vie with McCann," *Advertising Age* (13 February 1961)

The Interpublic Group of Companies <www.interpublic.com>

"Marschalk Agency Is a Division of McCann," *Advertising Age* (13 December 1954)

Mayer, Martin, *Madison Avenue, USA,* New York: Harper, and London: Bodley Head, 1958

Intimacy Products. *See* Feminine Hygiene and Intimacy Products

---

Intimate Apparel

Intimate apparel is one of the rare areas of advertising in which marketers have had to battle to show their products—or at least to show them on live models. Many of the companies whose brands are popular today trace their origins to the end of the 19th century and have seen every imaginable social change reflected in both their products and their advertising.

In the Victorian era, corsets for women were promoted via trade cards that, like the contemporary Victoria's Secret catalog, were designed to sell the product to women but were also enjoyed by men. Warnaco began in 1874 as the Warner Brothers Company (not related to the movie studio) with a "sanitary corset," developed by two physicians, Lucien and I. DeVer Warner; the garment was designed to produce appealing curves in a woman's body with less pressure than its stiff, confining predecessors.

Who Says It Has to Be White?

Jockey International, Inc., founded in 1876 as Cooper's, Inc., began advertising its men's underwear in magazines such as the *Ladies' Home Journal* and the *Saturday Evening Post* as early as the 1890s. Over the years, it used print ads with illustrations to introduce such innovations as the Kenosha Klosed Krotch (named for the site of the company's Wisconsin headquarters), a 1910 design that allowed a man to open a back flap with a single rubber button instead of a row of fasteners. The company also used print ads when it introduced the Jockey brief in 1935. That launch was so successful that when the briefs first went on sale at Marshall Field & Company in Chicago, Illinois, the store sold 50 dozen pairs before noon—in the middle of a blizzard.

In the 1960s Jockey capitalized on the revolutionary spirit of the times to sell "fashion colors" to men who had previously worn only traditional white underwear. One TV spot, from ad agency Henri, Hurst & McDonald, Inc., featured baseball player Yogi Berra in plain white shorts surrounded by his sons, wearing colorful Jockeys and urging their father to update his image. In another, the black comedian Godfrey Cambridge appeared in a close-up, asking, "Whoever said underwear had to be white, anyway?" In the 1970s Jockey worked with Campbell-Mithun, of Minneapolis, Minnesota, to balance the advertising for its men's line with that for its women's products. The campaign, "Jockey for her," proved successful and enduring.

Maidenform combined innovation with widespread marketing, including the first TV ads for brassieres. The "I dreamed . . ." campaign ran for 20 years starting in 1949. The original Maidenform ads were created by Norman, Craig & Kummel, Inc., and showed women acting out their fantasies. In one, a woman lawyer confides, "I dreamed I swayed the jury in my Maidenform bra." The campaign eventually collided with the social changes of the 1960s and 1970s, most notably the rise of feminism and the women's movement's disdain for what it saw as traditional images of women. When young women started burning their bras in the 1970s, Maidenform shelved the "I dreamed . . ." campaign for 11 years.

Playtex Apparel, one of Maidenform's chief competitors in department stores, also went into television early, starting in 1955 with ads on daytime shows for its bras and girdles. In 1971 it introduced what became a famous campaign from the Grey Advertising Agency, featuring the well-endowed 1950s film star Jane Russell selling its 18-Hour bra. Russell remained the primary spokeswoman for the brand until 1986. She demonstrated the bras in every possible way—slung over her forearm like a basket, worn over a tight turtleneck sweater, and on a mannequin—except worn on a real, live woman.

It was not until 1987 that Playtex became the first to show its bras on models in broadcast TV commercials, from Grey Advertising. The spots showed women walking by and then, for a few seconds, the same shot of the model wearing only her Cross Your Heart bra. Flexnit's Ce Soir was the first to advertise on cable TV, in early 1982, with a spot from Hicks & Griest tagged, "So sensuous, we can't show it on television."

Ads for men's underwear had more leeway to show the product, but the category was not without controversy. In 1986, when Grey created a spot for Fruit of the Loom men's underwear, it had to show a female model holding a pair of briefs across a man's midriff while he wore pajama bottoms. In a debate over another Fruit of the Loom spot, Grey's lawyers had to argue with network censors who objected to the male models' extremely hairy legs.

Celebrities and Real Folks

In 1975 Jockey broke ground with a print campaign from Bozell & Jacobs (now Bozell Worldwide) featuring star athletes modeling underwear. The models included Major League Baseball players Jim Palmer, Steve Garvey, and Pete Rose. Palmer emerged as the favorite pinup of women, who make the majority of underwear purchases, and his ads became popular posters. In 1980 Palmer was chosen as the sole spokesperson for Jockey and helped make Jockey sports underwear the number-one brand in the marketplace. He continued as Jockey's spokesperson until 1995.

Fruit of the Loom also tried celebrity endorsements, with a 1990 TV campaign from Grey. Spots featured a jingle ("Whose underwear is under there?") over shots of popular TV stars of the era wearing only their Fruit of the Loom briefs. Fruit of the Loom created its famous logo in 1875, but it was not until 100 years later that it used it in advertising. "The Fruit of the Loom Guys"—a trio of pitchmen dressed as pieces of fruit—first appeared in an ad campaign from Grey in 1975. The "Guys" became such popular icons that Fruit of the Loom has twice revived them, most recently in 2001 while in the middle of bankruptcy proceedings.

Although Grey eventually lost the Fruit of the Loom account in 1992, the agency went on to create a memorable campaign for Jockey that used real-life people as models. Print ads and billboards proclaimed, "Let them know you're Jockey," over pictures of such professionals as doctors, firefighters, and—in one controversial ad—women stockbrokers modeling hosiery. The campaign ran from 1996 until 2001, when Jockey once again decided to change direction and moved its account to a new shop, the Octopus Agency. Maidenform also revived a successful campaign from the past in 1980, when it launched an effort similar to its "I dreamed . . . " campaign. Ads from agency Daniel & Charles, with the tag line "The Maidenform Woman. You never know where she'll turn up," showed the Maidenform Woman in scenes such as commuting to work, reading the *Wall Street Journal,* and going to the theater—dressed in a matching bra and panties. Men in the scenes seemed oblivious to her state of undress. But times had changed, and the campaign received a less-than-enthusiastic

© 1996 SARA LEE INTIMATES. WONDERBRA IS A REGISTERED TRADEMARK OF CANADELLE, INC.

GRAVITY SCHMAVITY.

THE ONE AND ONLY
Wonderbra

THE LIFT BRA

AN EVERY DAY WONDERBRA DESIGNED TO PUT MOTHER NATURE BACK IN HER PLACE.

GAYFERS, MAISON BLANCHE, J. B. WHITE, THE JONES STORE CO., JOSLINS, BACONS, McALPINS, CASTNER KNOTTS, LION, HENNESSYS

The Wonderbra, introduced in 1994, revolutionized the lingerie industry and quickly became a household name. In this 1996 ad, support was sold with humor.

reception from the women's movement. It was finally abandoned in 1984 after health professionals complained about an ad in which the Maidenform Woman turned up as a doctor wearing a white lab coat.

Maidenform tried other approaches, and in 1988, Levine, Huntley, Schmidt & Beaver created a radical departure in lingerie ads. The TV spots featured neither women nor product, just male celebrities such as actors Omar Sharif and Corbin Bernsen, breathlessly expounding on women's lingerie and their personal experiences with it. The spots briefly revived Maidenform, but the company was suffering from other business woes that eventually prompted it to file for Chapter 11 bankruptcy protection in 1997. By then, Maidenform had switched agencies several times—first when Levine Huntley closed in 1991—always trying to establish a brand identity that fit the times. One spot from Ogilvy & Mather even took a stab at socially relevant advertising with chest shots of different women wearing political buttons and ending with a message encouraging women to vote in the 1992 election.

Maidenform eventually finished its reorganization and emerged from Chapter 11 in June 1999 with a new campaign and a redesigned identity from Frierson, Mee & Kraft (later Frierson, Mee & Partners). The campaign was built largely around in-store displays and outdoor boards near major retailers, in an effort to rebuild relationships with the company's most important vendors.

Catalog and Internet Marketing

The traditional underwear manufacturers were fighting a battle on many fronts in the 1990s. While the influence of department stores in fashion was declining, consumers were increasingly switching to discount retailers and specialty stores. One specialty store in particular reshaped the intimate apparel marketing in the 1980s and 1990s: Victoria's Secret. The company started in 1977 in San Francisco, California, as a chain of low-brow lingerie stores and a mail-order catalog better known for steamy photographs than for its merchandise. In 1982, retailer The Limited bought the business for $1 million and set out to rebrand Victoria's Secret in a manner acceptable to Middle America. Leslie Wexner, head of The Limited, overhauled the catalog, gave the stores an upscale image, and in the process changed how lingerie was marketed. Victoria's Secret legitimized the marketing of underwear to housewives and career women as an indulgence rather than as practical "foundation garments" or tasteless Frederick's of Hollywood seduction wear. Victoria's Secret managed to translate its nice-but-sexy attitude to television with spots by Tarlow Advertising in 1996. The ads were considered so racy that the major TV networks insisted on cuts before airing them.

Sex appeal is, nonetheless, the mainstay of the company's marketing appeal. Although the catalog remains its most successful marketing tool, Victoria's Secret also took steps into the Internet, starting with a Web broadcast of its popular Valentine's Day fashion show in 1999. The Webcast was promoted with a single TV spot during the broadcast of Super Bowl XXXIII, created by Resource Marketing, a local ad agency at The Limited's headquarters in Columbus, Ohio. While critics condemned the TV commercial, response to the ad was so enormous that the fashion show Web site overloaded and crashed; even before the fashion show, the Web site recorded 1 million hits in the half-hour after the spot aired.

In the mid- to late-1990s push-ups and padding revived intimate apparel sales in department stores and created a new marketing battleground for companies. The Sara Lee Corporation kicked off the battle with the launch of its Wonderbra in 1994. The padded push-up bra was first launched in the United Kingdom with an outdoor and print campaign from TBWA/Simons Palmer, in which model Eva Herzigova greeted passersby with a broad stretch of cleavage and "Hello, boys!" In spite of protests from feminists, the Wonderbra was an instant hit, and rivals quickly launched similar models with advertising just as racy. VF Corporation's Lily of France unit rolled out its X-Bra, a padded bra that allowed women to adjust their cleavage, with ads from D'Arcy Masius Benton & Bowles that showed an aggressive-looking woman under headlines such as "Adjust to Stun."

As the 20th century came to a close, intimate apparel marketing was both revived and more heavily contested. Apparel conglomerates such as Sara Lee and Warnaco joined in licensing agreements with upscale designers such as Ralph Lauren and Calvin Klein, respectively. The underwear business had become so profitable that it even generated legal actions. Calvin Klein ultimately sued Warnaco, claiming that the conglomerate had cheapened the designer's brand by selling it at discount stores. Warnaco countersued, saying Klein's provocative and controversial ads, created by its in-house agency, CRK Advertising, had hurt the brand's image.

MERCEDES M. CARDONA

See also color plate in this volume

Further Reading

Finnegan, Margaret Mary, *Selling Suffrage: Consumer Culture and Votes for Women*, New York: Columbia University Press, 1999

Leach, William, *Land of Desire: Merchants, Power, and the Rise of a New American Culture*, New York: Pantheon Books, 1993

Levine, Joshua, "Fantasy, Not Flesh," *Forbes* 145, no. 2 (January 1990)

Monget, Karyn, "From Corsets to Consciousness," *Women's Wear Daily* (28 September 1998)

Monget, Karyn, "Sex and Money Fuel Megabrands," *Women's Wear Daily* (24 January 2000)

Morse, Libby, "Briefly Speaking: Men's Underwear Exhibit Revealing," *Chicago Tribune* (1 October 1993)

Steele, Valerie, *Fashion and Eroticism: Ideals of Feminine Beauty from the Victorian Era to the Jazz Age*, Oxford and New York: Oxford University Press, 1985

Ipana Toothpaste/Sal Hepatica

Principal Agencies

Benton and Bowles, Inc.
Pedlar & Ryan, Inc.
Doherty, Cobb & Shenfield, Inc.
Young & Rubicam, Inc.

In 1915 Henry Bristol, the eldest son of William Bristol, became general manager of Bristol-Myers. William Bristol, Jr., handled manufacturing, while a vice president oversaw advertising. After a post–World War I recession forced the company to discontinue its line of ethical, or prescription, drugs, Bristol-Myers moved to Manhattan and focused production on its two best-selling specialty products, Ipana Toothpaste and Sal Hepatica (a mineral salt laxative), along with other toiletries, antiseptics, and cough syrups. These changes were accompanied by a new emphasis on advertising to consumers rather than the traditional audience of doctors and dentists.

In contrast to many ads of the period, which used copy only or employed artwork in a limited manner as background to the copy, Ipana ads were visually alluring, making use of artistic renderings of café and restaurant scenes and depicting elegantly dressed people. A favorite artist was Henry Raleigh, a chronicler of sophisticated, high-society fashion who also illustrated the stories of F. Scott Fitzgerald, William Faulkner, and other great writers of the era. In the advertisements he rendered for Ipana, his ink sketches were overlaid with colored washes. Raleigh carried with him the patina of Manhattan and Hollywood, and his artwork gave the ads a sense of glamour.

The message of these ads, launched in 1934, was that soft foods deprive the gums of stimulation, thereby encouraging bleeding. A sample headline reads, "How Ipana and massage defeat 'pink toothbrush.'" The ad copy encouraged the massaging of the gums twice daily: "Clean your teeth, massage your gums with Ipana twice a day for one full month, and learn the double joy of sparkling teeth and firm healthy gums." The ads included a coupon for a ten-day trial of Ipana: "Ten days will amply demonstrate Ipana's superb cleaning power, its delicious taste." The ad warned, however, that the sample could only begin the work of restoring gums to health and exhorted the reader to get a full-size tube, enough for a hundred brushings.

In the 1920s, the fledgling age of commercial radio in the United States, Ipana was one of the first brands to sponsor a song-and-patter program, a genre introduced by the Happiness Boys (a musical-comical act featuring Billy James and Ernest Hare). Ipana's radio show starred the Ipana Troubadours (who recorded a few songs, including "Prisoner's Song" and "After the Ball") and promoted the slogan "Ipana for the smile of beauty," which was repeated frequently in hopes of embedding the brand name in the nation's consciousness.

Ipana print ads of the same decade exemplified a trend seen in many advertisements of that era, which associated modern civilization with images of sloth, luxury, or decadence. In one ad, Ipana juxtaposed the warning "Eating today is a lazy pleasure" with an illustration showing a prosperous-looking couple dining in a restaurant. Other Ipana print ads explicitly described the sufferings of rich men, yacht-owning millionaires who were burdened with the affliction of "pink toothbrush."

In the 1930s Ipana and other advertisers faced the challenge of attracting the thousands of newly arrived immigrants and others who could not read English (at that time only 1 adult in 20 in the United States was literate) to their products. Ipana responded to this difficulty by referring to itself as "the one in the red and yellow tube" on its radio commercials, hoping that this identification would enable every listener to find Ipana on store shelves.

In the early 1930s Bristol-Myers's principal ad agency, Benton and Bowles (B&B), was handling the campaigns for Ipana and Sal Hepatica. In January 1934 the agency decided to sponsor a pair of back-to-back programs on NBC. Ipana led off with the *Ipana Troubadours,* and Sal Hepatica followed with comedian Fred Allen in *The Sal Hepatica Revue.* It was soon clear that Allen was drawing far more listeners than the Troubadours, so B&B convinced Bristol-Myers that the two brands should jointly sponsor a single one-hour program to be created around Allen. This move was virtually unprecedented, defying conventional wisdom, which dictated that advertising was most effective when it was associated with a single personality or program. In March 1934 Allen became star of *The Hour of Smiles* (renamed *Town Hall Tonight* in July), and the two sponsor slogans were joined: "Ipana for the smile of beauty and Sal Hepatica for the smile of health."

In 1935 Bristol-Myers replaced B&B and divided its business between two agencies. Pedlar & Ryan represented Ipana, and Young & Rubicam, Inc. (Y&R), got Sal Hepatica. Y&R produced the Fred Allen series until Bristol-Myers ended its sponsorship in 1940.

The Copeland Act (1934) extended to the U.S. federal government new power over the sale of drugs. The Wheeler-Lea Amendment to the Federal Trade Commission (FTC) Act (1938) also strengthened state regulation of the sale and advertising of drugs, declaring deceptive acts of advertising "unlawful" and thereby adding power to the FTC's cease-and-desist orders. Over the next several years, the FTC handed down several injunctions against advertisers and in 1942 filed a complaint against Ipana. The issue was the brand's successful "pink toothbrush" campaign. Litigation went on for three years before the FTC finally rejected the claim in 1949. The ad agencies involved were cleared of any responsibility and deemed to have acted under the direction of the advertiser. The FTC also objected to the slogan "Ipana for the smile of beauty," on the grounds that a smile "does not necessarily involve a display of teeth or gums"; "Beautiful teeth will not insure a beautiful smile or social popularity"; and teeth that are not naturally attractive "will not be rendered beautiful by the use of Ipana toothpaste." But in the

"What?...You haven't tasted NEW IPANA?"

Ipana-a-a-ah!

Tune in Garry on CBS Television Network, Mon. through Fri. See local paper for time and channel.

"Your teeth never had it so good", says Garry Moore.
"It's the BEST-TASTING way to FIGHT DECAY"

"Cavities are no fun," says fun-loving Garry, "so we Moores use the paste with the taste that makes it fun to fight decay. I mean new Ipana."

And most people are just as enthusiastic as Garry about Ipana's new flavor. It beat every other leading tooth paste hands down—after nationwide "hidden-name" home taste tests.

Destroys decay and bad-breath bacteria with WD-9

More good news is the way wonder-ingredient WD-9 in new-formula Ipana fights tooth decay and stops bad breath all day. It destroys most mouth bacteria with every single brushing.

"The only thing about Ipana they haven't improved is the stripes on the carton," Garry adds. So try new Ipana yourself . . . enjoy it . . . and trust your family's precious teeth to it.

New-Formula IPANA®
WITH BACTERIA-DESTROYER WD-9

CLIP THIS—AND JOIN ME IN A TASTE TEST

Let me send you a generous trial tube—mail coupon today.

GARRY MOORE, BRISTOL-MYERS CO., DEPT. H-35, HILLSIDE, N.J.

Please send me a trial tube of new-formula Ipana. Enclosed is 3¢ stamp to cover part cost of handling.

Name_____

Street_____

City_____ Zone____ State_____

(Offer good only in continental U.S.A. Expires June 1, 1955.)

Ipana A/C Tooth Paste (Ammoniated Chlorophyll) also contains bacteria-destroyer WD-9 (Sodium Lauryl Sulfate)

BETTER HOMES & GARDENS, MARCH, 1955

3

A 1955 print ad for Ipana toothpaste featured an endorsement by television personality Garry Moore.

"FROM SUN-UP...

TO SUN-DOWN...

I'M DOING CHORE...

AFTER CHORE, AFTER CHORE."

If your day makes you hurry, Sal Hepatica solves a worry!

If you're as busy all day long as Mrs. Veronica Svetlat of Farmingdale, New Jersey, you know what can happen.

Some days you're so pressed for time . . . your regularity is upset . . . and you get that headachy, logy feeling of constipation.

But if you can't afford to let constipation interfere with your chores any more than Mrs. Svetlat can, do what she does. Take speedy Sal Hepatica . . . and feel good again.

Taken before breakfast, Sal Hepatica brings relief usually within an hour. Taken ½ hour before supper, it brings relief by bedtime. Also sweetens a sour stomach. So keep Sal Hepatica handy on the farm.

SAL HEPATICA®

Gentle, speedy—Antacid laxative

A PRODUCT OF BRISTOL-MYERS

Ads for Sal Hepatica, a laxative mineral salt that was heavily marketed to rural and working-class consumers, frequently showed ordinary people going about their daily chores, as in this piece from 1955.

same 1949 judgment, the FTC permitted it on the basis that it was harmless "puffery."

In 1944 Francis Doherty, account manager for the Bristol-Myers Ipana business, left Pedlar & Ryan to form Doherty, Cobb & Shenfield. The Ipana account followed and remained with the agency with other Bristol-Myers brands until the agency merged with Needham, Louis & Brorby in 1964 to form Needham, Harper & Steers. Young & Rubicam continued as a Bristol-Myers agency through the 1970s.

In the 1950s Doherty, Cobb & Shenfield created a series of TV commercials aimed at encouraging children to brush their teeth. The ads featured the cartoon character Bucky Beaver in scenarios such as the "space man" and "one-man army," spots in which the mascot fought off evil "decay monsters" from space. The campaign was quite popular and had a lasting impact on American culture. Bucky Beaver had a fan club and was featured in a series of trading cards by Tick Tock Toys along with Bazooka Joe, Bosco, and Captain Go Go. The memorable Bucky Beaver song, beginning with the lines "Brusha, brusha, brusha, here's new Ipana toothpaste/Brusha, brusha, brusha, it's dandy for your teee-eeth," was featured in the movie *Grease,* and in the 1990s a Bucky Beaver Beanie Baby stuffed animal attracted many toy collectors before it was "retired" in 1998.

Despite the appeal of Bucky, the Ipana brand was discontinued in 1968 as a result of declining demand. Sal Hepatica also ceased production in the 1960s for the same reason.

SHARON KISSANE

Further Reading

Eastman, Susan Tyler, Sydney W. Head, and Lewis Klein, *Broadcast Programming: Strategies for Winning Television and Radio Audiences,* Belmont, California: Wadsworth, 1981

Goodrum, Charles, and Helen Dalrymple, *Advertising in America: The First 200 Years,* New York: Abrams, 1990

Maltin, Leonard, *The Great American Broadcast: A Celebration of Radio's Golden Age,* New York: Dutton Books, 1997

Marchand, Roland, *Advertising the American Dream: Making Way for Modernity, 1920–1940,* Berkeley: University of California Press, 1985

"Pink Toothbrush Theme of Ipana Finally Banned," *Advertising Age* (5 December 1949)

Preston, Ivan L., *The Great American Blow-Up: Puffery in Advertising and Selling,* Madison: University of Wisconsin Press, 1975; revised edition, 1996

Israel

Advertising is a thriving business in Israel. By 2001 there were nearly 100 agencies, many of them affiliated with large multinational advertising companies such as BBDO Worldwide, McCann-Erickson Worldwide, and Young & Rubicam. But the industry, which serves a market of seven million people in a full range of media, from newspapers and magazines to radio, TV, and the Internet, has come a long way since the 1930s and 1940s, when the Jewish population in what was to become the state of Israel amounted to only a few hundred thousand.

In the early 1940s only about ten agencies were doing business in Israel. Two of these, both owned by German Jews who had fled the Nazis, were in Haifa. The approach of ad agencies then was stiff and conservative; institutional style ads full of references to the Bible were the norm.

Most of the ads at this time appeared in two of the daily newspapers, the Hebrew *Ha'aretz* and the *Palestine Post*, as the *Jerusalem Post* was known before Israeli independence in 1948. The other papers of the day—*Hamashkif* of the revisionist Zionist political movement, *Davar* of the Histadrut trade union federation, and *Yediot Aharonot*, which eventually became a mass-circulation daily with dozens of pages of advertising—carried virtually no ads.

The only other effective ad medium through the 1950s were the so-called trailers shown at movie theaters. Israel had no TV station of any kind until 1969, and the state-run radio monopoly began accepting commercials only in the 1960s. Films, which could be subtitled in a variety of languages, were the major form of entertainment for the immigrants from Middle Eastern countries and displaced persons from Eastern Europe, who flowed into the country after its independence and did not yet understand Hebrew—the national language. (To this day, Israel Radio has special programs in a variety of tongues, from Amharic for Ethiopian immigrants to Russian and Romanian.) Eliyahu Tal, who during the 1960s and 1970s headed Tal Arieli, then the country's largest ad agency, has observed that some of this early cinema advertising, produced on extremely low budgets, was surprisingly good, winning gold medals at the New York Festival. Tal, who also served as the Israeli correspondent for *Advertising Age,* recalls a visit in the 1950s from that paper's long-time editor, Sid Bernstein. "He came to my agency in Tel Aviv, and saw a poster with a figure called Mr. Clean. Procter & Gamble Company had just started using the figure for its detergent ads, but we had hit on the idea a year before."

Those years also posed a special challenge for advertising professionals. Some immigrants from less developed nations knew nothing about modern appliances; others, from countries such as the Soviet Union, which lacked a modern economy, had to be taught about bank accounts and insurance policies.

As in Europe at the time, radio stations in Israel were controlled by the central authorities and carried no advertising; daily newspapers were the main advertising medium during the first years after statehood in 1948, as they had been under the British mandate, carrying about 60 percent of all advertising. The main papers founded after statehood—*Ha'aretz*, the *Post*, *Yediot Aharonot*, and *Ma'ariv*—were joined by a host of smaller publications written in the languages of the new immigrants, including Arabic, Polish, Russian, German, Romanian, and, of course, Yiddish, the vernacular of Eastern European Jews.

Broadcast advertising began in the 1960s when the Israel Broadcasting Authority opened Reshet Bet (B Network), a popular news and music radio station, to operate alongside the official state station, Kol Yisrael. The country's newspapers initially opposed allowing advertising on radio, arguing that the limited advertising budgets in Israel at the time would not be able to support the new medium. But instead of hurting the papers, radio stimulated a major increase in advertising budgets.

Even then, according to Tal, the culture of Israel had not really adapted to modern advertising practices. Advertisers wanted immediate results and did not understand the slow process of image building and the value of repetition. After using a particular slogan or image for a time, advertisers worried that it was becoming boring or stale and would seek something new.

Another part of the process of modernization was the founding of the Israeli Advertisers Association in 1961. As its first director, Bronislaw Tau helped the new professional organization shape the industry along Western lines, bringing in expert consultants and teachers from England, Germany, and the United States. In addition, Tau was instrumental in setting up programs in advertising and communications at Tel Aviv University and the Hebrew University of Jerusalem.

But while some foreigners came as consultants, the big international agencies shied away from actually doing business with Israel. Tal once offered legendary advertising executive David Ogilvy an affiliation with his agency, or even with one of his Israeli competitors. "Ogilvy said he could not because it would endanger his relations with his clients and some of their Arab customers," Tal recalled.

Although the Americans and British were not establishing affiliations, their way of doing things slowly began to penetrate the Israeli ad industry. Moshe Theumim, a co-founder and chairman of Gitam/BBDO, recalled that when he entered the business in 1973, the Dahaf agency, headed by Eliezer Zorabin, was the largest agency and handled most of the political accounts because of Zorabin's involvement with the political establishment.

Arieli, on the other hand, was the first modern agency, with a Western-style division of labor between account executives and creative people. The son of the owner came back from studying abroad and established separate departments. "Before that," Theumim recalled, "the account executive in Israel was a jack of all trades who did everything." The Arieli model was followed by a growing number of agencies in the 1980s. The metamorphosis took a decade to complete, and Israel was ready for the events that would make it part of the globalized world market.

the United States. While multichannel cable TV has served Israel for a decade, no local commercials are permitted. Some local advertisers get around the ban on local ads by advertising on the European MTV station, which is seen in Israel.

The advent of commercial TV changed the focus of Israeli advertising and, said Gitam/BBDO's Theumim, accentuated the division between the top agencies and all the rest. By the turn of the century, he said, there had emerged a "top five" in the Israeli ad world, each linked to a major world player: Kesher Barel McCann-Erickson; Bauman-Ber-Rivnay, formerly associated with Saatchi & Saatchi; Tamir-Cohen, linked to the J. Walter Thompson Company; Shalmor-Avnon-Amichay Young & Rubicam; and Gitam/BBDO. Together these five account for 30 percent–40 percent of the total ad billings in Israel and most of the major national and international accounts.

But the major ad agencies were not the only ones coming to Israel in the 1990s. Dozens of international chains, from Pizza

The cover of a 1968 Passover Haggadah from Carmel Wineries marketed the vintner's product as an important feature of a gracious holiday meal.

Since the early 1990s all of the major multinational agencies have set up operations in Israel, many with equity positions in local agencies. They began coming for three reasons: The lifting of the Arab boycott in the 1990s; rapid economic growth of more than 5 percent per annum in the first half of the 1990s, due to the boom in high-tech industries and the arrival of approximately 800,000 immigrants from the former Soviet Union; and the arrival, finally, of commercial TV.

Israel got its first TV station in 1969, but the government station was built on the model of the early British Broadcasting Corporation in the United Kingdom and did not carry commercial advertising. TV advertising only came to the country in 1994, with the introduction of Channel 2, Israel's first commercial station—and its only one in the early 21st century. There were, however, several anomalies to the setup: Channel 2's broadcasting week is divided among three franchise holders that run separate "stations"; there is, however, a common news department. Each franchisee gets two broadcasting days each week, and the seventh day, Saturday, rotates among the "stations" each year. Meanwhile, Israel TV, the non-commercial station, can raise revenue with public service spots or institutional sponsorships of programs, much along the lines of the Public Broadcasting Service in

The daily *Ha'aretz* was an early champion of advertising in Israel. This business-to-business ad—dating from before Israeli statehood—promoted the newspaper as a venue for publicity.
Published by Ha'aretz, *1936.* © *Ha'aretz Publishing House.*

Hut and McDonald's Corporation to Zara and Tower Records, suddenly found economic promise in the Promised Land. These chains and global franchise operations brought with them marketing demands of their own.

Still, Theumim said, Israeli advertising developed its own special flavor. Around the turn of the 21st century, campaigns from his agency featured Mediterranean music (for a dairy product) and full-figured women (for a line of prepared chicken parts) rather than the usual fashionably thin models. Theumim regarded such ads as the wave of the future for Israeli advertising, reflecting the continuing impact of U.S. television and marked by an increasing use of laid-back humor that appeals to Israel's growing Yuppie class. References from the Bible are quickly becoming a thing of the past. "The society," Theumim said, "simply isn't as biblically literate as it once was."

In 1999, the last year that official figures were available, Israeli ad spending topped the $1 billion mark for the first time, an increase of 10.2 percent over 1998. Part of the increase, though, was due to the country's high economic growth rate in 1999, as Israel emerged from a three year recession. Daily newspapers remained the dominant medium, with 48.3 percent of all ad expenditures. Print media, including the daily press, accounted for 61 percent of ad expenditures, followed by TV ($256 million, 24.7 percent), radio ($77 million, 7.4 percent), outdoor advertising ($70 million, 6.7 percent), and advertising in cinemas ($3 million, less than 1 percent). Over a five-year period these figures have remained relatively stable, with print media continuing to command upward of 60 percent, TV in the 22 percent–25 percent range, and radio rising slightly, from 5.6 percent in 1995 to 7.4 percent in 1999, while a corresponding decrease was felt in outdoor ads.

HANAN SHER

Italy

The history of advertising in Italy can be divided into three periods. The first began in 1861, the date of the founding of the Kingdom of Italy, and ran until 1918, the end of World War I. The second was the period from the end of World War I to 1968, when the modern Italian advertising industry came into being. The third period began in 1968 with the rise of social responsibility in advertising and has continued into the present.

Two of the first practioners of advertising in Italy were the chemist Attilio Manzoni, who founded not only a pharmaceutical industry but also a business that acted as an agent for the press, and Giulio Ricordi, head of the world-famous musical company. Much of the early advertising was created by artists, including many who worked for publishers and graphic firms, in collaboration with businesses. Early advertising was the subject of two shows at the end of the 19th century, an international exhibition in Milan in 1894 and a national exhibition in Genoa in 1899.

Changes began to take place in the Italian economy in the late 1890s. During the next 20 years Italy became an industrial nation, a development that was accompanied by changes in people's ways of living, including the growing use of consumer goods. The number of businesses—particularly industrial concerns—increased, and in order to compete, businesses made more and more use of advertising. In turn, advertising itself became more specialized, with experts acting as consultants to those who actually created the ads.

In spite of disparities in development among regions and sectors of the economy, in the half century after World War I, Italy consolidated its position as an industrial nation. The country's industrial policy of the late 1920s and early 1930s and the economic boom of the late 1950s and early 1960s were particularly important in this regard. Nonetheless, the interruption caused by World War II had a devastating effect on the economy and consequently on advertising. In particular, in the second half of the 1930s and the first half of the 1940s, advertising expenditure decreased and propaganda expenditure (economic, political, and social) rose. International advertising agencies such as Erwin, Wasey & Company (EW), a branch of which was established in Italy in 1925, disappeared, and Italian agencies such as Enneci (derived from EW and managed by Nino Caimi) and I.M.A. (managed by Anton Gino Domeneghini) were involved in state propaganda campaigns, beginning with economic campaigns on behalf of wheat, milk, fish, rayon, aluminium, and other commodities. Previously EW had worked for leading advertisers such as Ford, Palmolive and Mobil Oil, while I.M.A. dealt with Liebig, Philips, Singer, and others.

Although monopolies dominated the Italian economy during the period between the two world wars, advertising became more sophisticated and widespread. Italian entrepreneurs, particularly the owners of industrial concerns, wanted to use the new media—especially radio, which was introduced as an advertising medium in 1926—in addition to traditional press and outdoor advertising. With an increased demand for advertising, agencies and studios developed, as did advertising departments within businesses themselves. With the development of the profession, research studies proliferated, and new advertising associations—among them, the National Advertising Federation—were established. In 1933 the International Advertising Congress held its

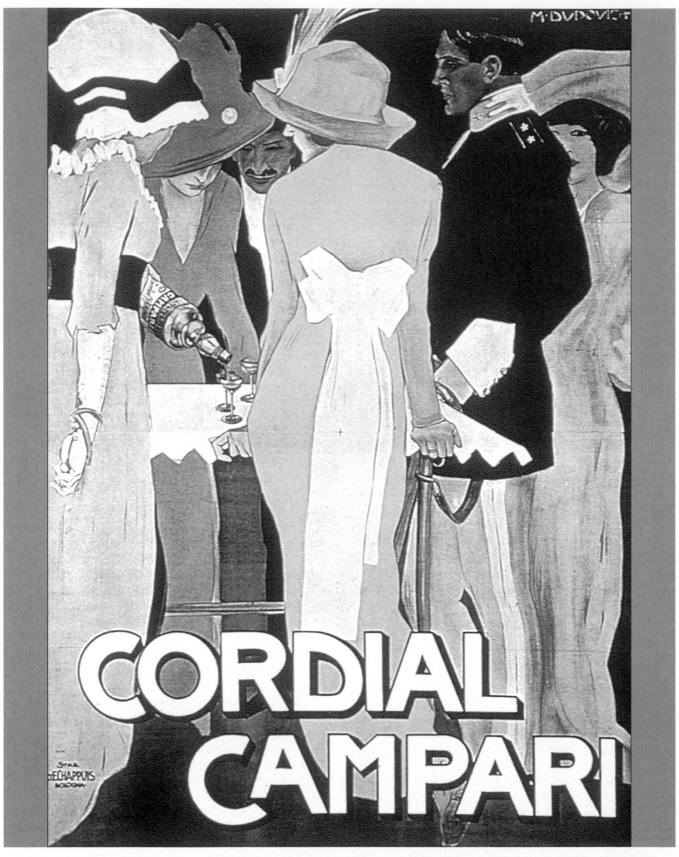

During the early years of the 20th century, traditional Italian products such as Campari aperitif significantly increased their advertising.

XXXIV. G. De Chirico, Fiat, 1950, manifesto.

In this 1950 advertising poster for Fiat, one of Italy's oldest advertisers, artist Giorgio de Chirico juxtaposed the images of the mythical winged horse Pegasus and the Fiat 1400.
Courtesy of Fiat.

centages in areas such as clothing, household goods, and certain services were still unbranded.

Another development in the Italian economy that affected advertising was a change in the methods of retailing. Beginning in the 1980s supermarkets and other large retail stores began to appear in greater numbers, and by the 1990s it was estimated that perhaps 60 percent of fast-moving consumer goods were sold in such establishments. Along with these changes in the retail sector came the introduction of private-label brands, a new type of product in Italy that became the object of new ad campaigns. Nonetheless, at the end of the 1970s the Italian advertising market was still comparatively small, with less than 1 trillion liras (approximately $1.2 million U.S.) in expenditures.

The Sixty-Eight Movement, the student activist movement of 1968, focused on the social responsibilities of business, a development that had an effect on Italian firms and Italian advertising and continues to influence both in a significant way. From the late 1970s to the early 1990s there was a period of especially rapid economic growth. This was followed by a short retrenchment, but growth resumed again beginning in 1996–97. Advertising was, of course, affected by this growth, as it was by the development of commercial television, introduced in Italy in 1976 following a struggle against the state monopoly on television broadcasting. Commercial broadcasts boomed in the 1980s. The time devoted to commercial spots grew rapidly, from 2,100 hours in 1980 to 4,738 hours in 1992, with the number of advertisers increasing from 500 to 1,500. Private consumption during this period increased an average of 2.8 percent a year, with branded products taking an ever larger share of the market. All of these factors produced additional work for advertising agencies as well as for audiovisual production houses and related businesses.

The Italian economy went into a slump in the early 1990s. Consumption fell, and intense price competition led to the use of discount outlets as a marketing tool. As an indication of the severity of the country's problems, the lira was devalued, and Italy withdrew from the European Monetary System (which it had joined in 1979). But as the economy began to rebound in 1996, advertising benefited once again from the increase in the sales of consumer goods, particularly of branded products, and in the trend toward the advertising of services. Italy joined other developed European countries in the growth of telecommunications and the so-called information economy. Banking, health services, education, entertainment, and tourism were among the industries beginning to avail themselves of the benefits of advertising.

According to *Advertising Age*, total gross advertising income for 2000 in Italy was $612 million on billings of $6.45 billion, a 6.8 percent increase over the previous year's total. The top five agencies in Italy (in terms of gross income) were Armando Testa Group, McCann-Erickson Italiana, Young & Rubicam Italia, J. Walter Thompson Company, and D'Arcy. The top five advertisers in 2000 were Telecom, Fiat, Vodafone, Unilever, and L'Oréal.

meeting in Milan (capital of the Italian ad industry) and Rome (political capital of the country).

The years after World War II were ones of reconstruction, much of it undertaken with the financial and technical help of the Marshall Plan and other Western aid. In the early 1950s Italy entered into an economic boom that lasted for a decade, and during this time it joined the European Economic Community. As the economy grew, branded products increased their presence in the market, something that had a major impact on advertising. The introduction of the Mulino Bianco (White Mill) line of oven products (biscuits, pastry), made by Barilla, at the beginning of the 1980s might be taken as a particularly instructive example. The new line was marketed with a campaign that evoked nostalgia for an older, rural Italy. Nonetheless, the majority of Italian consumer goods continued to be unbranded until the 1990s, when it was estimated that 11 percent of food products and even larger per-

EDOARDO T. BRIOSCHI

Further Reading

Brioschi, E.T., *Elementi di economia e tecnica della pubblicità,*
Vol. 1, *Dai primordi alla pubblicità moderna,* 2nd edition,
Milan: Vita e Pensiero, 1995

Ceserani, G.P., *Storia della pubblicità in Italia,* Bari: Laterza,
1988

Falabrino, G.L., *Effimera & bella. Storia della pubblicità italiana,*
2nd edition, Cinisello Balsamo: Silvana Editoriale, 2001

Ioppolo, D., *Nascita e sviluppo del mercato pubblicitario in Italia,*
Milan: Pro-manuscripto, 1999

Villani, D., et al, *Cent'anni di pubblicità nello sviluppo economico
e nel costume italiano,* 2 vols., Torino: Sipra, 1975

Ivory Soap

Principal Agencies

Procter & Collier Company

Blackman Company (later Compton Advertising, Inc.)

Grey Advertising Agency, Inc. (later Grey Global Group)

The story of advertising at the company that became the world's biggest advertiser begins squarely with one product: a small, air-puffed cake of soap with the brand name Ivory. Ivory's inauspicious beginning dates to 1878, when James Norris Gamble, son of a cofounder of Procter & Gamble Company (P&G), purchased a white soap formula from a rival manufacturer. His goal was to develop a product to compete with high-quality imported castile soaps becoming popular in the United States at the time. The product was first called simply White Soap.

Early in 1879, a workman accidentally left his soap-mixing machine running during lunch hour, causing more air to be mixed into a batch of the soap. A supervisor decided no harm was done, and the soap was shipped. Weeks later, P&G began getting orders for more of the "floating soap."

It would take the input of another founder's son, Harley T. Procter, to make the advertising work for the distinctive white soap. Bothered by the generic "White Soap" name, he sought something more memorable. His inspiration came during a Sunday church reading of Psalms 45:8: "All thy garments smell of myrrh and aloes and cassia out of the ivory palaces whereby they have made thee glad." The word "ivory" stood out in his mind, and on 18 July 1879, the product that would become P&G's first major national brand was trademarked "Ivory."

Procter's passion for the brand succeeded in swaying P&G's board in 1882 to allocate what was then a massive media budget of $11,000 to advertise Ivory nationally. The first Ivory ad appeared in a religious weekly, the *Independent,* on 21 December 1882. It was unusual in that it targeted consumers at a time when most ads targeted dealers or retailers. It read, "The Ivory is a Laundry Soap, with all the fine qualities of a choice Toilet Soap, and it is 99 and 44/100% pure."

The purity claim resulted from an independent chemical analysis commissioned by Procter, who was always searching for an edge to make Ivory stand out from other soaps on the market. By the chemist's reading, Ivory was purer than the three leading castile soaps on the market, with only 0.56 percent impurities. Procter was the first of generations of P&G managers who would use technical attributes as selling propositions, and he worked that phrase into Ivory advertising and packaging. He also recognized that the floating quality of Ivory would let consumers find bars of soap in the wash water.

Procter was convinced that the new national magazines coming on the scene in the late 1800s—*Good Housekeeping, Harper's Monthly,* and *Ladies' Home Journal*—would be the best advertising vehicles for Ivory. He sought consumer feedback from the outset. The brand's first ad in 1882 invited readers to share their experiences with new uses for the product, and their responses were compiled into a booklet titled "Poetical Selections." Another ad in the 1880s appealed to consumers to write the company about unusual uses for the product, and those were compiled into another booklet, "Unusual Uses of Ivory Soap."

P&G was an early adopter of other premiums and promotions. Although rival Schultz Soap Company in Zanesville, Ohio, was the first to offer such inducements, P&G was not far behind. Ivory's first premium offer was a miniature facsimile of a cake of Ivory Soap that could be attached to a watch chain.

Harley Procter continued to be one of P&G's traveling salesman as well as a one-man in-house advertising agency until 1900, when the company contracted with the Procter & Collier Company, run by Cincinnati, Ohio, printer Allen C. Collier, who handled advertising as a sideline. The Ivory baby became the brand's icon, with improved illustrations offering a large improvement over the original, which looked more like a wrinkled old man than a baby. Over time, Ivory ads became increasingly sophisticated color productions, with illustrations from some of the best-known illustrators of the time. P&G was paying $1,000 for illustrations, and Ivory's ad budget had skyrocketed to $300,000 by 1897.

What started as a cake of soap accidentally puffed with air became a megabrand for P&G. During the 20th century, P&G extended the Ivory brand with Ivory Flakes, later dubbed Ivory Snow. Ivory's longtime advertising agency, Blackman Advertising,

A 1937 ad for Ivory soap included the famous "99 44/100% pure"
slogan.
Courtesy of The Procter & Gamble Company.

was reorganized in 1937 as Compton Advertising and began to
move the brand into radio, producing such shows as *Life Can Be
Beautiful* (1938), *Against the Storm* (1939), *Brave Tomorrow*
(1943), and *I Love a Mystery* (1943). In the 1950s the company
extended the brand into a light-duty dishwashing detergent as
well, then into liquid hand soaps in the 1980s and moisturizing
body washes in 1996 with the introduction of Ivory Moisture
Care.

Compton Advertising remained the principal agency for Ivory
until 1982, when it was taken over by Saatchi & Saatchi. The
Compton name ultimately disappeared, but Ivory remained with
its successor until P&G switched responsibility for Ivory products
to Grey Advertising, later Grey Global Group, in 1997, as sales of
the former flagship brand continued to slip throughout the 1990s.
Ivory would go on to become a lower priority than other P&G
brands, such as Olay in skincare; Tide, Cheer, and Gain in laundry
detergent; and Dawn in dish care in the 1990s.

JACK NEFF

Further Reading

Decker, Charles L., *Winning with the P&G 99: 99 Principles and
    Practices of Procter & Gamble's Success,* New York: Pocket
    Books, 1998
Lief, Alfred, *It Floats: The Story of Procter & Gamble,* New
    York: Rinehart, 1958
Procter & Gamble: The House That Ivory Built, Lincolnwood,
    Illinois: NTC Business Books, 1988
Schisgall, Oscar, *Eyes on Tomorrow: The Evolution of Procter &
    Gamble,* New York: Ferguson, 1981
Swasy, Alecia, *Soap Opera: The Inside Story of Procter &
    Gamble,* New York: Times Books, 1993

J

Jack Tinker & Partners. *See under* Tinker

Japan

Japan is the world's second-largest advertising market, with ad spending of $39.7 billion in 2000. It is also home to the world's foremost agency brand (based on 2000 worldwide gross income) and fourth-largest ad organization, Dentsu. Tokyo rates as the number-two city worldwide in terms of advertising billings, after New York.

Origins

Japan's advertising industry has a long history, reaching back centuries. The closest thing in Japan to the type of agency that developed in Europe in the 17th century—which dealt in such matters as employment, real estate, leases, travel, and art brokerage—was probably the *kuchiireya,* a word that literally means someone who "puts in a word" for another. According to the dictionary, *kuchiireya* is one who recommends the services of others, passes on messages, makes recommendations or introductions, or arranges for the employment of domestic staff. The *kuchiireya* conducts these activities as a business.

People in this line of work came to be known as *keian,* named after the doctor Yamato Keian, who acted as a go-between for marriages among royalty during the Keian (1648–52) and Shoo (1652–55) periods. Yamato Keian is thought to have established his business in 1652; he was banished in 1665 for embezzling money from dowries. The business of managing information for the purpose of introducing people also came to be known as *keian.*

The first modern advertising company in Japan appeared in 1873 as a purveyor of imported goods. In a notice in a Tokyo daily newspaper the company announced that its orders department would henceforth accept advertising commissions. It did not focus on advertising alone but also operated as a trading company.

The first Japanese company to specialize solely in advertising was Kukido-kumi, established in 1880. Although documents of the company no longer exist, it was apparently a pioneer in newspaper advertising. The oldest advertising company still in existence, Nihon Kokokusha, was established in 1884 by Eto Naozumi and was known as Kohodo before World War II.

Among today's leading advertising organizations, Hakuhodo is one of the oldest. It was established in 1895 and sold advertising space in educational publications; while it grew to become the top agency in Japan in the 1920s, a downturn in the book publishing market, a key area for the agency, allowed rival Dentsu to make inroads on its position. Dentsu opened in 1901 as a news wire service, Telegraphic Service Company, providing war reports to newspapers in exchange for advertising space, which was sold by its sibling company Japan Advertising. In 1907 the two merged to form Denpo-Tsushin Sha, which was shortened to Dentsu. Forced by the government to give up its news reporting business in 1936, the company began to focus solely on advertising.

In 1944 another agency emerged, Daiko, which was formed by the merger of 14 advertising agencies that were facing closure due to World War II; it was initially known as Kinki Advertising Company until it changed its name to Daiko in 1960. Another top agency, Asatsu-DK, was created in 1956; in 1999 it merged with rival Dai-Ichi Kikaku, which opened in 1951, and added the shop's DK initials to its name.

The Industry Today

Dentsu was the leading agency in 2000, with gross income of $2 billion. Others in the top ten, according to figures from *Advertising Age,* were Hakuhodo, with gross income of $925 million;

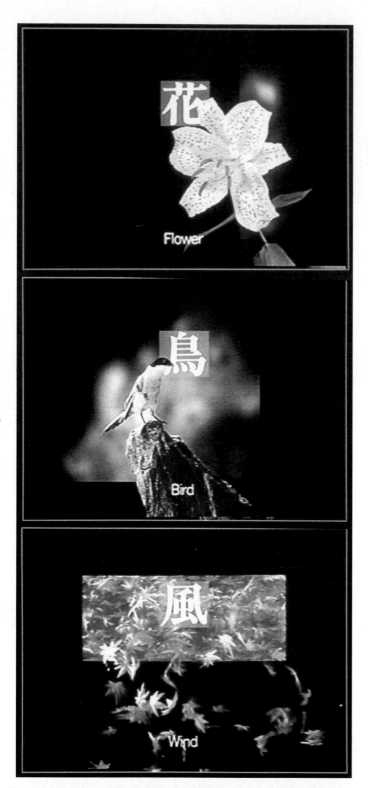

In a 1990 commercial for Gekkeikan Sake, Dentsu—the largest ad agency in Japan—appealed to consumers' senses with images from nature. *Courtesy of Gekkeikan Sake Company, Ltd.*

Asatsu-DK, $342 million; Daiko Advertising, $226 million; Tokyu Agency, $202 million; McCann-Erickson Japan, $139 mil-

lion; I&S Corporation, $118 million; Yomiko Advertising, $111 million; Asahi Advertising, $98 million; and Nikkeisha, $80.7 million.

The nation's top advertiser (1999 figures) was Toyota Motors, which spent $740 million. Honda Motors was next, with ad spending of $453 million, followed by Kao Soap, $449 million; Suntory, $408 million; and Nissan Motors, $368 million. While automotive companies dominate the list of top spenders, the country's top ad category in 2000 was cosmetics and toiletries, with $3.3 billion in spending, followed by food, $3.2 billion; information and telecommunications, $2.9 billion; beverages and tobacco, $2.9 billion; and transportation and leisure, $2.5 billion.

The country's leading advertising group, the Japan Advertising Agency Association, has only 130 member companies. If a non-member wishes to carry out a transaction with the mass media, it must do so through a member agency, which takes half of the commission. This practice accounts for the concentration of power in a relatively small number of top-ranking agencies. In addition, advertising agencies in Japan, unlike in many other countries, work on the accounts of more than one company in an industry. Thus, large Japanese agencies often handle a number of competitors.

All advertising in the media is done through agencies, and payment is made within one month after the ad is printed or aired. The advertiser pays the advertising agency by bank draft, but the agency must maintain a certain amount of liquidity because of the short grace period before payment is due to the media. This practice is another reason large agencies tend to become even bigger.

The advertising media in Japan are roughly divided into two categories: mass media and house media. Mass media include television, newspapers, magazines, and radio, while house media include outdoor (i.e., billboard), direct mail, publication inserts, mass transit advertising, cinema advertising, and events sponsorships. Zenith Media predicted that in 2001 television would draw 45.3 percent of the country's advertising media spending; newspapers, 27.1 percent; outdoor, 13 percent; magazines, 9.9 percent; and radio, 4.7 percent. Internet ad spending remained low, drawing $517.5 million in 2000, while the country's Internet penetration reached 30.5 percent.

Day-to-Day Business

As in most developed countries, the process of advertising in Japan begins with a marketer's development of an advertising strategy. In surveys of advertisers the task most frequently cited as the beginning of the process is setting the advertising goals, followed by determining the campaign period and developing the creative concept. The majority of advertisers said they do not initially give particular consideration to marketing data; many also said that budgets were not among the earliest concerns.

Once an advertising agency in Japan receives instructions from an advertiser, it proceeds with its planning. The major roles of the account executive include planning the marketing and advertising, overseeing creation of the ads, and buying space and time in the media. The emphasis is on planning, however. After receiving directions from the client, the creative staff of an agency gets one to five weeks before making its first presentation; it is rare, however, that the creative staff is given a month or longer for its work. The process of drawing up the draft of an advertisement involves free discussion among the creative personnel. At the same time, the account executive remains involved in the process to ensure that none of the advertiser's wishes are overlooked.

In the United States agencies often conduct what is called pretesting before they present the draft of an advertisement to the client. Such testing is seldom done in Japan; in one survey, for example, only 9 percent of the respondents indicated that they undertook any kind of advance testing. As a consequence advertising in Japan is sometimes less attuned to consumers' wishes than advertising produced in markets where pretesting is routine.

TOSHIO YAMAKI

Further Reading

"Top 10 Global Ad Markets," *Ad Age Global*, April 2001

"World's Top Ad Organizations," *Advertising Age*, 23 April 2001

Yamaki, Toshio, "Theoretical and Practical Approach to Creative Work," *Advertising Science* (1984)

Yamaki, Toshio, "Managerial Environment on Advertising Agency, 1926–1989," *Bulletin of Japan Advertising Agency Association* (1989)

Jingles. *See* Music and Jingles

John Smith's Bitter

Principal Agencies
Boase Massimi Pollit
GGT Advertising
TBWA Advertising

John Smith's Bitter, brewed in Tadcaster, Yorkshire, since 1847, is one of Northern England's most famous ales and Britain's number-one bitter brand; customers in the United Kingdom consume more than 1 million pints every day. It is also enjoyed in other parts of the world, including Australia, Africa, and the Arab Gulf region. John Smith's has annual retail sales in excess of $640 million (£450 million). Its principal impact in advertising has been via its TV campaigns, which have produced some of the U.K.'s best-known ads. More Brits are aware of John Smith's TV advertising than any other beer brand. It has remained the U.K.'s best-selling canned bitter since its launch in 1979. John Smith's Extra Smooth, introduced in 1995, sold more than 100 million pints in its first year and at the start of the 21st century had sales of more than $360 million (£250) per annum. With an annual marketing budget of $14 million (£10 million), company growth continues at more than 20 percent annually.

John Smith was just 24 years old when he purchased a run-down brew house and started a brewing heritage that has spanned more than 150 years. He quickly realized that Tadcaster's abundant supply of hard water, necessary for the brewing process, offered the area the potential to become one of the country's most prominent brewing centers. Smith was known for his energy, versatility, and gift for recognizing the needs of a changing world. He was skilled at choosing the right man for the job and creating good working conditions. Smith's foremost concerns were the need for quality ingredients and careful brewing techniques. By the time he died, the company was extremely successful and on the verge of expansion. Over the years numerous other breweries were acquired until, in 1970, John Smith's was taken over by Courage, Ltd., which subsequently became Scottish Courage, Ltd., after Scottish and Newcastle PLC purchased it from Fosters Brewing Group in 1995.

The agency that handled John Smith's advertising in 2001 was TBWA. The account had been handled by GGT Advertising, which, through a series of mergers in the late 1990s, became part of the new TBWA agency. TBWA handled John Smith's TV, radio, print, and poster campaigns, while Eleven, formerly Carlson, produced point-of-purchase marketing materials, direct-mail campaigns, and events.

TBWA is concerned only with John Smith's consumer advertising. The agency is particularly well known for its poster campaigns and caused a furor in the press with its "*fcuk*" campaign for French Connection. John Smith's first TV advertisements, which ran in 1971, had a typically Yorkshire feel and featured Yorkshire men who were unwilling to travel to distant football matches if it meant giving up their pint of John Smith's. Later, in 1979, came the first of four key campaigns featuring one of British advertising's most famous characters: the aging, flat-capped

Arkwright. These continued until 1988 and won numerous advertising awards before the actor who portrayed Arkwright, Gordon Rollings, passed away.

The "Great Stuff" ads, three years later, showed John Smith's to be the most remembered brand. While lager advertising became increasingly flashy and aggressive, John Smith's broke the mold with a "Back to Basics" campaign. It featured a beautifully lighted pint standing on its own, the implication being that the product spoke for itself.

John Smith's greatest advertising coup was the much-publicized addition of the widget for the launch of its Draught in 1993. A widget is a metal spiral built into the beverage can that ensures that the beer pours and behaves like draught bitter. Although the technology was invented by Guinness, John Smith's capitalized on it with an ad campaign that led it to be associated almost exclusively with the John Smith brand name. The popular campaign not only drove take-home sales even higher but also brought the word *widget* into everyday use in Britain. The commercials, which debuted in 1992, featured the then-relatively-unknown comedian Jack Dee. Each spot ended with the tag line, "When you've got a widget—you don't need gimmicks." The gimmicks, which included dancing ladybirds and penguins, provided the comic touch and complemented Dee's trademark deadpan delivery. The implication was that bitter drinkers shared Jack's no-nonsense attitude toward his favorite beverage. Agency Boase Massimi Pollit created the ads, and Mandy Fletcher, well known for the popular and critically acclaimed *Blackadder* TV comedy series, directed them. Special effects used in the ads were featured on the BBC program, *How Do They Do That?*

Extra Smooth, another product innovation, used a unique dispenser tap and increased nitrogen to replicate the taste of cask ale. It was introduced in pubs in 1995. Extra Smooth is also less temperature specific and so can be served cold, like lager. John Smith's Draught was given a new package design and a new name, John Smith's Extra Smooth, to establish a link with its sister product.

The Jack Dee ads came to an end in 1997, but the no-nonsense tag line was retained. A new series of ads launched in 1998 incorporated a cardboard cutout, No-Nonsense Man, which appeared in more than 20,000 pubs, clubs, and shops and quickly became part of the popular culture. More than 60 percent of people surveyed were aware of the campaign.

In addition to its award-winning TV ads, John Smith's has also benefited from high-profile sports sponsorships, including the Great Britain, England, and Wales Rugby League Teams. It also sponsors comedian Al Murray.

John Smith's marketing is product-led so there has never been any need to reinvent the brand. The challenge has been to take it from its traditional northern heartland to drinkers of all ages in all regions while remaining true to the original product.

HEATHER JONES

Further Reading

Stewart, Catherine, *Superbrands: An Insight into 50 of the World's Superbrands,* edited by Marcel Knobil, vol. 1, Horsham, West Sussex: Special Event Books, 1995, and vol. 2, London: Creative and Commercial Communications, 1996; see especially vol. 2

Johnson & Johnson

Principal Agencies
J. Walter Thompson Company
Young & Rubicam, Inc.
Sullivan, Stauffer, Colwell & Bayles
Saatchi & Saatchi Advertising

A household name for more than a century, Johnson & Johnson (J&J) got its start selling medicinal plasters. The company was incorporated in New Brunswick, New Jersey, on 28 October 1887, with $100,000 in capital stock. Robert Wood Johnson owned 40 percent, and his brothers, James Wood Johnson and Edward Mead Johnson, each held 30 percent. (Edward left J&J to found what would become Mead Johnson & Company, a nutritional supplement marketer, in 1897.) Robert died in 1910 and was succeeded as J&J president by James. Then in 1932 Robert's son, also named Robert Wood Johnson (but widely known as

"the General" following his service in World War II), took over the company from his uncle.

In 1924 J&J introduced its baby powder to relieve skin irritation caused by the company's plasters. That same year J&J launched its first overseas base, creating an affiliate in the United Kingdom. By 2001 the company had operations in more than 175 countries. J&J went public in 1944 and has never had an unprofitable year.

To advertise J&J's growing product lines, Robert Wood Johnson, Jr., turned to an acquaintance, J. Walter Thompson. Over the years, the two became good friends. Thompson handled the J&J account personally. Johnson was closely involved—he approved ads himself and was free with his advice to Thompson. His "Dear Walter" letters pulled few punches. In one, Johnson wrote, "I return the sketch and hardly see how you can make an advertisement out of it. It needs to have a very black background in order to throw out the white letters." That ad was killed. The relationship flourished, even if Thompson frequently had to remind himself of his cardinal rule: "Never get on stage in front of your client. No advertising can stand even the suspicion that you, not he, could have been responsible for its success."

Johnson did not trust ad agencies. In his opinion, copywriters were too enamored with what he called "their personal phraseology" and ignored the most basic ingredient of any ad: company name. To focus his agencies and marketers, he sent them display cards, printed in gold letters, which offered his formula for success:

Dramatics • Simplicity • Continuity
Brand Name Dominates
Brief and Legible Copy
Corporation Signature Strong

Johnson had strong ideas about the way he wanted his company represented. "We must create a format of advertising," he wrote. "The agency must collaborate, polish it, and above all, get out of the way so that they are not a liability instead of the asset that they should and can be."

Johnson would order entire campaigns killed if he found something he disliked. One ad for a new Red Cross Improved Bandage raised his ire, and he was quick to let the offending ad executive know: "When a mistake is made it is unfortunate. When we make the same mistake a second time it is serious. When we make the same mistake a third time we are guilty of incompetence, poor management, and lack of competitive strength. When we make the same mistake fifteen or twenty times it is reprehensible."

Although some of Johnson's techniques were criticized, J&J had some inarguable successes, including the campaign for Modess sanitary napkins. In the late 1940s Johnson grew concerned about the poor sales of Modess and often attended the advertising strategy meetings. It was he who suggested tying the ad campaigns to high fashion. To create a campaign radically different than those normally shown in women's magazines of the day, the ads, from Young & Rubicam, Inc. (Y&R), featured designs by some of the most famous couturiers of the time, including Christian Dior and Balenciaga, and used exclusively in the Modess ads. Well-known photographers shot glamorous cover girls such as Susie Parker and Dorian Leigh in exotic settings. J&J had determined that women were skittish about reading about sanitary napkins, so the tag line—"Modess . . . because"—carefully avoided using those words. By 1962 J&J was spending $2 million for color magazine ads featuring Modess. A 1929 Modess ad in the *Ladies' Home Journal* featured a young woman chastising her mother for the latter's old-fashioned ways—and taking six paragraphs of copy to do it. A 1963 ad for the same product in the same magazine contained only ten words of copy, including the "Modess . . . because" line.

Following World War II, J&J's sales climbed steadily—by 1957 they were three times greater than in 1945, according to *Advertising Age*. By 1957 J&J was the 44th-largest national advertiser, with annual ad expenditures of nearly $17 million, of which $8.6

MOTHER
DON'T BE QUAINT

MILLIONS of daughters are teasing mothers back to youth—slamming doors on the quaint ways of the nineties. One by one the foolish old drudgeries and discomforts pass. Living becomes easier, more pleasant—*sensibly modern*.

An example of this modern trend is Modess. Modess has three vital superiorities—it is really comfortable, can be disposed without danger of clogging and is an effective deodorant.

Its comfort is almost unbelievable, the first time you try it. Modess is graciously soft, yielding, conforming. The filler is not in stiff layers but is a fluffy mass like cotton—an entirely new substance invented by Johnson & Johnson, world's leading makers of surgical dressings.

The sides are smoothly rounded and the specially softened Johnson & Johnson gauze is cushioned with a film of downy cotton.

The deodorizing efficiency of Modess has been proved by laboratory tests to be higher than that of other napkins.

We are sure that you will be delighted to have discovered in Modess a napkin without fault—infinitely more comfortable, safer, more deodorizing and truly disposable. Since it costs no more, why not try it? It may be bought at most good stores.

MODERNIZING MOTHER . . . *Episode Number One*

SO INFINITELY FINER

Before adopting the succinct "Modess . . . because" campaign, Johnson & Johnson employed a more old-fashioned approach. The 1929 "Modernizing Mother" campaign used several paragraphs of copy to describe the benefits of the new sanitary napkin.
Courtesy of Johnson & Johnson.

was in measured media. The largest chunk, $3.8 million, was in magazines, while network television advertising accounted for $2.6 million. J&J advertised its baby products on the *Gary Moore Show* and *Our Miss Brooks*. J&J's "extended autonomy" system of decentralization was well in place. The company's affiliated businesses accounted for about $2 million of total measured-media spending.

By 1962 J&J was spending $21 million on advertising, including $1.7 million on newspapers, $2.5 million on magazines, and $5.7 million on network television. That year, with Y&R managing the account, J&J's Micrin oral antiseptics wrested about 15 percent of the market share from Warner-Lambert's industry-dominating Listerine. That battle was waged at a hefty price. J&J spent $15 million on advertising and promotions and failed to make a dime in profit off Micrin.

Executive ire at the Micrin expenditures, along with agency conflicts, spurred J&J to realign its ad agencies the following year, the same year Johnson retired. Y&R lost upward of $3 million in billings, though it remained J&J's primary agency with $8 million in billings and continued as the agency of record for all network television advertising. Sullivan, Stauffer, Colwell & Bayles (SSC&B) picked up about $4 million in billings, of which Micrin accounted for about 74 percent; N.W. Ayer & Son, which had about $750,000 in J&J billings, was dropped; and Norman, Craig & Kummel was assigned a new test product, the antacid Bi-Phase. J&J said officially that the changes were prompted by the need for a broadened agency base, but client-agency difficulties had been simmering for some time. Ayer had asked to be relieved of the J&J business because of conflicts with its Sterling Drug, Inc., and Smith Kline accounts. Disagreements with Y&R over Micrin were exacerbated by changes J&J had made to its marketing operations the year before.

By 1975 the company was spending $55.5 million in advertising, $24.8 million of that on network television. The almost $4 million spent to advertise diapers was nearly double the previous year's total; the ads, from SSC&B, featured actress Juliet Mills from the *Nanny and the Professor* series. Much of J&J's 1975 advertising sought to persuade consumers to view "baby" products—baby lotion, powder, and oil— as "all-family" products.

With Cadwell/Compton managing the account, J&J spent $8 million on the introduction of its o.b. tampons in 1976. The company vowed it would make o.b. the most heavily advertised tampon on radio and television, and the $8 million represented about half the amount spent in the entire category, which was dominated by Tampax. Television commercials promoting the o.b. tampon featured a young woman who grew up on "lots of love and Johnson & Johnson."

The mid-1970s saw a round of pain-reliever wars, with Tylenol, marketed by J&J's McNeil Laboratories division, and Bristol-Myers's Datril going head to head in comparison ads. Starting in March 1976 Datril ads (from Ted Bates & Company) claimed that it delivered more and faster pain relief than Tylenol. J&J complained to the three TV networks and the National Advertising Division of the Council of Better Business Bureaus, charging that the ads were not truthful.

In 1950, 26 years after Johnson & Johnson introduced its baby powder to the market, the advertising philosophy of company President Robert Wood Johnson, Jr., could still be seen in the product's advertisements: brevity, simplicity, and a strong focus on the brand name.
Courtesy of Johnson & Johnson.

In 1982 J&J faced one of the worst nightmares of any consumer products company, particularly one that had built its reputation around warm, comfortable images. In Chicago, Illinois, bottles of Tylenol capsules were found to have been laced with cyanide, and seven people died. Although the Federal Bureau of

Investigation declared it a terrorist incident, it seemed as though the tragedy might spell the end for Tylenol.

Led by Chairman-Chief Executive Officer James Burke, who took over the reins of the company in 1976, J&J began a public relations blitz. In fact, the company set the gold standard for crisis management. Previously, J&J officials had not been known as particularly media friendly, but Burke launched himself into a series of interviews and television spots to explain what J&J was doing to control the situation.

Tylenol was immediately taken off store shelves. The company published full-page ads explaining the chain of events and offering consumers an exchange of unaffected Tylenol tablets for the tainted capsules. J&J offered a $100,000 reward for information identifying the perpetrator. Overall, the company spent $100 million on the incident. It was money well spent: three months after the crisis, sales returned to 80 percent of pre-crisis levels. In the eyes of many observers, Burke's forthrightness and willingness to take responsibility saved the Tylenol brand.

Burke was succeeded in 1989 by Ralph Larsen, who made aggressiveness a key to the company's growth. In the 1990s J&J engaged in several high-profile slugfests with competitors in the area of over-the-counter medications. In 1995 Johnson & Johnson-Merck Consumer Pharmaceuticals Company, a joint venture between J&J and Merck & Company, launched Pepcid AC, the first in a new class of over-the-counter treatments for heartburn. Compton Partners, of New York City, a unit of Saatchi & Saatchi, was given the Pepcid account. That year, SmithKline Beecham, maker of rival product Tagamet HB, sued J&J for misleading advertising. J&J filed a countersuit. A ruling from the U.S. District Court for the Southern District of New York agreed with SmithKline's charge that Pepcid commercials contained a number of significantly false or misleading statements and required the withdrawal of 9 of 11 Pepcid commercials. The company was also ordered to halt its claims that "eight of ten doctors and pharmacists would recommend Pepcid AC more often than Tagamet HB," pending further scientific study. SmithKline was ordered to modify claims in its promotional materials about the number of prescriptions written for Tagamet.

Competition in the over-the-counter painkiller segment was heating up at the same time. By 1996 Tylenol had 30 percent of the $2.7 billion market, and J&J was spending $212 million through Saatchi & Saatchi's Healthcare Connection on its Tylenol account. J&J went on the offensive in 1995, engaging in very public mudslinging with Advil, an American Home Products (AHP) brand. J&J had run ads questioning the safety of ibuprofen, the key ingredient in Advil. AHP responded with ads pointing out the alcohol-interaction warning on Tylenol labels and suggesting that Advil was perhaps a safer product. The advertising wars moved to national newspapers after all four major television networks removed certain Advil and Tylenol ads, citing worries about consumer confusion. Tylenol ads appeared in 50 major publications, with a toll-free telephone number for consumers with questions. Advil's campaign featured a full-page ad in the *New York Times* describing a case of liver failure in a Tylenol user.

In 1998 J&J spent $816.5 million in advertising in the United States. Network television spots accounted for the greatest expenditure, $420.5 million. Next was magazine advertising, at $117 million. By brand, the most advertising dollars went to Tylenol remedies ($213.4 million), followed by Neutrogena personal care products ($73.4 million), and Motrin pain remedies ($58.7 million).

In 2000 J&J began to shift some ad dollars from direct-to-consumer prescription advertising to professional advertising. During the first quarter of the year J&J's magazine advertising dropped 54 percent. Magazine ads for Nicotrol NS (a smoking cessation aid), for example, had cost the company $1.9 million in 1999, compared with less than $100,000 in 2000. At the same time J&J more than doubled its advertising spending on the TV campaign for the oral contraceptive Ortho Tri-Cyclen and was exploring the feasibility of Internet marketing. That same year, for the series premiere of the ABC medical drama *Gideon's Crossing*, J&J purchased an exclusive presenting sponsorship. J&J received 60-second spots at the beginning and end of the episode, which was shown without other commercials.

J&J opted not to become an official $30 million sponsor of the 2002 Winter Olympics in Salt Lake City, Utah. Although scandals surrounding the machinations of various competing venues contributed to the decision, the company cited a lack of agreement among its brands as the primary reason. But J&J's absence from this high-profile event was not regarded as much of a setback for the company that had survived the Tylenol incident.

DEREK DATTNER AND AMY I.S. DATTNER

See also color plate in this volume

Further Reading

Brichacek, Andrea, "Big Pharma Spend Trends," *Pharmaceutical Executive* (September 2000)

"Court Orders SmithKline, J&J to Change Ads," *Supermarket News* (23 October 1995)

Foster, Lawrence G., *Robert Wood Johnson: The Gentleman Rebel,* State College, Pennsylvania: Lillian Press, 1999

"Four Agencies Affected in Big J&J Realignment," *Advertising Age* (18 July 1963)

Giges, Nancy, "J&J Sticks to 'False' Charge As Datril Airs Revised Spots," *Advertising Age* (28 June 1976)

"J&J Spending Heavily to Back O.B. Expansion," *Advertising Age* (12 April 1976)

Linsenmeyer, Adrienc, "No Band-Aid Solution," *Financial World* (21 January 1992)

Murray, Eileen, "Lessons from the Tylenol Tragedy on Surviving a Corporate Crisis," *Medical Marketing and Media* (February 1992)

O'Reilly, Brian, "J&J Is on a Roll," *Fortune* (26 December 1994)

Wilke, Michael, and Mark Gleason, "Painkiller Slugfest Could Be Expanding," *Advertising Age* (25 March 1996)

S.C. Johnson & Son, Inc.

Principal Agencies
Needham, Louis & Brorby, Inc.
Foote, Cone & Belding
Benton and Bowles, Inc.
Ogilvy & Mather
Leo Burnett Company
Needham, Harper & Steers
J. Walter Thompson Company
DDB Needham Worldwide
True North Communications

In 1886 Samuel Curtis Johnson, a carpenter in Racine, Wisconsin, bought the parquet flooring business of the Racine Hardware Company. His customers turned out to be as interested in taking care of the floors as they were in buying the flooring. Consequently, in 1888 Johnson introduced Johnson's Prepared Wax, and a powerhouse product line was born. From those modest beginnings, a marketing giant evolved.

Two hallmarks of S.C. Johnson & Son over its 115-year history have been its determination to remain a private, family-owned organization and its growth via line extensions and expansion into new product categories (the 2001 edition of the *Standard Directory of Advertisers* listed 80 separate trade names for Johnson products). In its fifth generation of family ownership and management at the beginning of the 21st century, the company has deep roots in Racine, a city of some 80,000 on Lake Michigan between Milwaukee, Wisconsin, and Chicago, Illinois, which has always been the corporate headquarters. Long noted for its liberal employment benefits, the company gave employees paid vacations beginning in 1900, started a profit-sharing program in 1917, established a 40-hour workweek in 1926, and developed a pension plan in 1934 during the depths of the Great Depression. Johnson began its international expansion in 1914, establishing a subsidiary in Britain. Operations followed in Australia in 1917 and Canada in 1920.

After the death of Samuel Curtis Johnson in 1919, his son, Herbert F. Johnson, took the reins and presided over a period of company growth. Annual sales had reached $5 million when he died unexpectedly in 1928. He left no will, precipitating a family struggle for control of the company that pitted the third-generation siblings against each other. The dispute took a decade to settle, and in 1938, Herbert's son, Herbert, Jr., who had become president and later chairman, got 60 percent of the company, while his sister, Henrietta Louis, received 40 percent.

The "Fibber McGee" Years

In the early years, wax was Johnson's primary offering. As late as the mid-1930s, the company's product line was limited to waxes, silver and furniture polishes, household cleaners, paints, varnishes, and enamels. And although the company had advertised since the 1880s, it did not become a major player in the ad world until April 1935, when its flagship brand, Johnson Wax, began sponsoring what would become one of radio's most popular programs, *Fibber McGee and Molly*. The comedy, which ran on NBC, became so closely linked with Johnson's Wax that in his 1970 book *The Great Radio Comedians,* Jim Harmon wrote, "Is there anyone over 30 in the United States who does not . . . think of Johnson's Wax when someone mentions 'Fibber McGee & Molly'"?

Through its ad agency, Needham, Louis & Brorby, Inc. (NLB), of Chicago, Johnson sponsored the show until 1950, a 15-year stretch that spanned virtually the entire period known as the "golden age" of radio. Announcer Harlow Wilcox, who was almost as well known as the show's stars, invariably delivered the commercials, which were often humorous and so well integrated into the story line that the words "Johnson's Wax" were likely to pop up almost anytime, giving the sponsor plenty of bang for its bucks. (Fibber himself—actor Jim Jordan—was reunited with his old sponsor in 1972 when he came out of retirement to appear in a print campaign for the company's Glo-Coat floor wax.)

Even with its sponsorship of *Fibber,* S.C. Johnson was not among the major advertisers of the day. In 1937 the company spent $463,700 in radio advertising and $117,900 in magazine ads, according to the *Standard Advertising Register.* These numbers paled in comparison with Lever Brothers, which spent $2.4 million in radio and $1.5 million in magazine ads that year, and Procter & Gamble Company (P&G), whose figures for the two media were $5 million and $2.3 million, respectively.

In the late 1930s Johnson made news far afield from the worlds of marketing and advertising—in architecture. The company commissioned the legendary Frank Lloyd Wright to design its new administration center in Racine. This modernistic and widely heralded structure housed a massive, vaulted-ceilinged space called the "Great Workroom." (In 1950 a second Wright building, the Research Tower, was opened on the Johnson campus, and in 1976 the two buildings were placed on the National Register of Historic Places.)

In 1950, the same year the company ended its sponsorship of *Fibber McGee and Molly,* it became a television advertiser for the first time, with *Saturday Night Revue.* Soon after, it also became a sponsor of *Robert Montgomery Presents* and *The Red Skelton Show.* (In 1961, as part of the company's 75th anniversary celebration, one of the Skelton TV shows originated from the Great Workroom at Johnson headquarters.)

Pride liquid furniture polish was introduced in 1951, heralded with spreads from NLB in publications including *Better Homes & Gardens, American Home, Ladies' Home Journal, Family Circle, Woman's Day,* and newspaper Sunday supplements. NLB, which had been on board since 1929, remained the sole domestic Johnson advertising agency until the early 1950s, when it was joined by another Chicago-based shop, Foote, Cone & Belding (FCB). FCB initially handled fabric finishes and auto polishes, with NLB retaining the lion's share of the company products.

JOHN RAKOWSKI
Known from Manitowish River
to Big Crooked Lake as a
fishing guide's guide!

New! Keeps mosquitoes away
5 full hours!

*Bomb
or Liquid*

OFF! Insect Repellent gives you positive protection from mosquitoes, flies, gnats, ticks, chiggers—all kinds of biting insects. OFF! chases these pests away <u>before</u> they bite. Lets you enjoy *more hours* of fun outdoors. So cover all the areas you want to protect with OFF! If you miss a spot, it could be a bug's next meal. Put OFF! in your tackle box now! It's a product of Johnson's Wax research.

THE ONE REPELLENT THAT <u>FEELS</u> <u>CLEAN</u>...CONTAINS NO OIL!

The 1958 launch of Off! insect repellent introduced a second S.C. Johnson & Son brand to the insecticide market, joining Raid, which had made its debut two years earlier.
Courtesy of SC Johnson—a family company for over a century.

It was also during the 1950s that S.C. Johnson made a major leap into new product areas. The company entered the insecticide field in 1956 with the introduction of Raid House & Garden Bug Killer, which vaulted to first place in sales among aerosol bug killers by year's end. Raid's introduction was quickly followed by that of Off! insect repellent. Other new products included Klear, a self-polishing floor wax, and Pledge, a pressurized furniture polish.

In 1957 S.C. Johnson was the 60th-largest U.S. advertiser, according to *Advertising Age,* with an estimated $12.5 million in spending. The company spent approximately 90 percent of this on TV advertising, including some $200,000 per week on the *Steve Allen Show.* In 1955 Benton and Bowles, Inc., of New York City, joined NLB and FCB on the Johnson agency roster, handling several wax products. FCB's growing share of the company's advertising pie by this time included Klear and Raid.

In the early 1960s the company entered the shoe polish and lawn-and-garden business and expanded its international operations, establishing Johnson-Kentoku in Osaka, Japan, a venture with Kentoku Ltd., a Japanese wax manufacturer. The international division built a plant near Amsterdam in The Netherlands, its largest outside the United States, to serve the European Common Market. By 1963 the company had 21 subsidiaries and 13 manufacturing plants overseas. A chemical division also was established in the early 1960s to market diphenolic acid, used in the manufacture of printing inks, paints, and varnishes. Later in the decade, this division introduced an acrylic polymer used in ink and a resin for the paint industry.

In 1961 the company, which was number one in sales in three categories—floor, furniture, and auto waxes—placed 51st in *Advertising Age*'s annual ranking of leading national advertisers, with estimated expenditures of $19 million. Again, the lion's share of these expenditures was in TV, including sponsorships of *Gunsmoke, The Garry Moore Show,* and *The Red Skelton Show.* The company continued its healthy growth through the 1960s and by 1966 had estimated sales of $150 million (a private company, Johnson does not release figures). Its estimated advertising expenditures of $26.5 million ranked it 50th among U.S. companies, according to *Advertising Age.* In 1966 Samuel C. Johnson became president and chief executive officer (CEO), the fourth member of the family to head the company. He succeeded his father, Herbert F. Johnson, Jr., who had been chairman since 1958 and president for 30 years before that.

"Kills Bugs Dead"

Among the company's most successful brand franchises was the Raid line of insecticides, introduced in the 1950s and made famous by the long-running campaign from FCB with its "kills bugs dead" theme. To make death, even the death of bugs, seem both palatable and desirable, the agency turned to a staff artist named Don Pegler, who created an unceasing flow of cartoon insects that invariably met their demise in devilishly funny ways when confronted with the deadly Raid mists. As a body of work, whether in print or television, the Pegler Raid bugs are among the finest examples of cartoon art in advertising. The Raid brand was

soon extended to other areas of pest control. One of the most memorable ad campaigns was the series of commercials created for Raid Mouse Killer, which featured an animated character, "Mac the Mouse." The spots, from FCB, had Mac eating grain pellets impregnated with the poison, which resulted in his departure to "that big piece of cheese in the sky." During these years, the company altered its TV strategy, switching from program sponsorships to a "scatter plan" and spreading its commercials over more than 100 daytime and prime-time programs on all three major networks.

By 1970 Johnson had risen to 46th in *Advertising Age*'s ranking of national advertisers, with expenditures estimated at $35 million. At the beginning of the new decade, the company was believed to have more than 50 percent of the $45 million furniture polish market, about 50 percent of the $80 million insecticide and repellent market, and 15 percent–18 percent of the $50 million-plus car wax market, according to *Advertising Age.* In 1970 the company acquired Johnson Reels of Mankato, Minnesota, a marketer of fishing reels and electric trolling motors, and also diversified into new product areas with Edge shaving gel, Crazylegs moisturizing shaving gel for women, and Rain Barrel fabric softener.

Ogilvy & Mather (O&M) became Johnson's newest major ad agency in 1973, getting accounts from other shops on the roster. Terence S. Malone, vice president of marketing in the United States, told *Advertising Age* that the addition of O&M was triggered by the need for increased advertising services resulting from the company's many new products. The agency churn continued in 1973, when Johnson severed its 44-year relationship with the Needham shop (by then known as Needham, Harper & Steers). Another Chicago agency, the Leo Burnett Company, was added, and products formerly handled by Needham were spread among the remaining agencies.

In 1977 the company entered the personal care field, launching its biggest-ever product introduction—for Agree, a cream rinse and hair conditioner. Johnson spent $14 million on the launch, $7 million on a TV and magazine campaign, and $7 million on a sampling program; Needham, which had been rehired, was the agency. The investment bore fruit as Agree rose to the number-one spot in the hair conditioner category within six months of its national debut.

More agency shuffling took place in 1978. The J. Walter Thompson Company (JWT), which had been a Johnson agency abroad, was added to handle the domestic business of Pledge furniture polish, Edge shaving gel, and Step Saver floor wax through its Chicago office. Benton and Bowles and Ogilvy & Mather ended their domestic relations with the company because of account conflicts in new-product areas and low billings. As the decade ended, Samuel C. Johnson, who had been CEO, was named chairman.

As the 1980s began, the company was the 83rd-largest national advertiser in *Advertising Age*'s rankings, with estimated expenditures of $51.4 million, a 28 percent increase over 1979. The Raid line of products, which controlled an estimated 45 percent of the insecticide category, accounted for $5.8 million, or more than 11 percent of the company's total ad expenditure for

1980. Agree shampoo's share of the market had fallen from 18 percent to an all-time low of 3 percent, at least partly because of strong competition from Procter & Gamble's Pert and Gillette Company's Silkience. Johnson revised its ad campaign for Agree, breaking a campaign with an "Escape the greasies" theme.

In 1983 Johnson again ended its relationship with Needham after a dispute over the company's policy of prohibiting agencies from handling other clients that had brands competing with any Johnson division. Needham's Agree and Enhance hair care and Glade air fresheners accounts went to JWT, and Soft Sense skin lotion went to Foote, Cone & Belding (FCB), also in Chicago.

In the mid-1980s, the company entered the over-the-counter (OTC) drug market through its Rydelle Laboratories subsidiary, which in 1985 introduced Fiberall laxative wafers, an extension of its Fiberall laxative powder. (Rydelle sold the Fiberall bulk laxative line to Ciba-Geigy Corporation in 1988.) Rydelle also acquired Cooper Dermatological Laboratories for further development of its skin care activities and set up a joint venture with Japan's Lyon Corporation to market oral care products in the United States and Canada.

Ad Consolidation

In 1989 Johnson consolidated virtually all of its U.S. consumer product advertising—about $90 million in spending—at longtime agency FCB. Losing out in the consolidation were J. Walter Thompson USA and Lotas, Minard, Patton, McIver of New York City.

As the 1990s began, Johnson ranked 66th in U.S. ad spending at $158.1 million, with almost half of that figure in TV advertising. After trying unsuccessfully to divest its Personal Care Products Division, the company turned its attention to promotional campaigns for its established household products and its insecticide and personal care lines.

Edge gel remained one of the company's strongest brands, maintaining its number-one spot in the highly competitive shaving cream market with a 27 percent share in 1991. Among Johnson's other leading products, Raid held about one-third of the household insecticide category, and Glade held about the same proportion of the air freshener category.

Early in 1993 the company further diversified with the purchase of Drackett Company from Bristol-Myers Squibb. This added to the Johnson stable Drano, the number-one brand in drain cleaners, and Windex, which accounted for about 40 percent of the window cleaner market. For a third time, Needham—now called DDB Needham Worldwide—was brought aboard, this time to handle both Drano and Windex. Also in 1993, the company sold the Agree and Halsa hair care lines to Dep Corporation.

In January 1996 Johnson combined its more than $300 million in worldwide ad spending with True North Communications, the Chicago-based parent of FCB. The move gave the company a single agency for all its worldwide brands and eliminated 27 other agencies, among them Needham (dropped for the third time), JWT, BBDO Worldwide, and Japan's Dentsu.

This was the last campaign created for S.C. Johnson & Son's Edge Shave Gel by the J. Walter Thompson Company before Johnson consolidated its consumer products accounts at Foote, Cone & Belding in 1989. *Courtesy of SC Johnson—a family company for over a century.*

In 1997 Johnson acquired DowBrands, the consumer products division of Dow Chemical Company. A few months later, the company sold three Dow products—Spray 'N Wash, Spray 'N Starch, and Glass Plus—to Reckitt & Colman to satisfy federal antitrust concerns. In March 1999 the company sold its skin care business, including Aveeno, Oentrax, and Rhuli, to Johnson & Johnson.

At the brink of the 21st century, S.C. Johnson had worldwide sales estimated at $4.2 billion. It was 79th among national advertisers in 1999, according to *Advertising Age*, with U.S. ad spending estimated at $358.4 million, a 1.1 percent drop from the previous year. As it had for years, TV continued to dominate, accounting for 94 percent of the company's media expenditures and 56 percent of all Johnson ad spending.

Glade air fresheners accounted for the largest single ad spending figure ($34.7 million), followed by Windex glass cleaners ($26.6 million); Pledge Grab It sweeper ($23.7 million); Drano drain cleaners ($17.4 million); Ziploc plastic bags ($17.3 million); Shower Shine cleaner ($15.1 million); AllerCare cleaning products ($14.7 million); Off! insect repellents ($12.1 million); and Raid insecticides ($11.4 million).

S.C. Johnson & Son has come a long way from the company known primarily for its waxes, polishes, and household cleansers, but it has never strayed from its corporate base in Racine nor from its familial leadership. In October 2000 H. Fisk Johnson was named chairman, representing the fifth generation of the family to head the company. His father, Samuel C. Johnson, was named chairman emeritus after retiring from the board on which he had served for 40 years.

ROBERT GOLDSBOROUGH

See also color plate in this volume

Further Reading

Barboza, David, "At Johnson Wax, a Family Passes On Its Heirloom; Father Divides a Business to Keep the Children United," *New York Times* (22 August 1999)

Gleason, Mark, and Laurel Wentz, "The Big Squeeze: S.C. Johnson Is Consolidating $300 Mil Ad Spend at True North; Reckitt's $230 Mil Goes to McCann," *Advertising Age* (15 January 1996)

Johnson, Samuel Curtis, *The Essence of a Family Enterprise: Doing Business the Johnson Way,* Indianapolis, Indiana: Curtis, 1988

Duane Jones Company, Inc.

Founded by Duane Dodge Jones in 1942; closed in 1951 during account piracy lawsuit; attempt to restart agency in 1955 was unsuccessful.

Major Clients

B.T. Babbitt (Bab-O cleanser)
G.F. Heublein & Bro., Inc.
Hudson Pulp & Paper Corporation
Manhattan Soap Company
Mennen Company (toiletries)
C.F. Mueller Company (macaroni)
Joseph Tetley & Company, Inc. (Tetley tea)

Duane Jones, a prominent advertising executive, opened his own agency in 1942 to service consumer goods marketers. The agency reached $15 million–$20 million in billings at its peak and was famous for box-top premiums. Duane Jones is best known, however, for winning a groundbreaking account piracy lawsuit against executives of the agency who left with its biggest clients and most of its employees.

Born in Fort Collins, Colorado, in 1897, Jones started his advertising career in 1923 in the Los Angeles, California, office of Lord & Thomas (forerunner of Foote, Cone & Belding). This followed a two-year stint publishing a trade paper, *Service Station News,* he had created. He was named vice president at Lord & Thomas in 1928, and in 1930 the agency moved him to New York City. Jones took a position as a vice president at Maxon, Inc., in 1932 and then briefly at Benton and Bowles in 1934. From there he moved to Blackett-Sample-Hummert (later Dancer, Fitzgerald, Sample) as executive vice president until 1940, when he rejoined Maxon, Inc., as a partner. He left Maxon to form his own agency in 1942.

Jones was a strong believer in hard-sell advertising with measurable sales results. Disdainful of corporate advertising designed to create goodwill, he once said, "The best goodwill is the kind you can ring up on the cash register." He started his agency with a staff of 15 and three clients billing a total of $12 million: B.T. Babbitt's Bab-O cleanser, Mueller's macaroni, and Tetley tea. To announce the opening of his firm, Jones took out newspaper page ads in which he stated his belief that awards should be given to ads that sold the most goods rather than those with the prettiest copy. He challenged manufacturers to let him make their cash registers sing by hiring him to advertise their goods in their worst markets.

Jones acquired the moniker "Box Top King" because he was almost single-handedly responsible for making premiums a permanent part of every package goods advertiser's toolkit. His most successful offer was the Blarney Stone Charm. Jones obtained several tons of stone from the same Irish quarry that produced the original Blarney Stone. He had the stone chipped and formed into all sorts of charms and jewelry. These trinkets were offered to consumers for a quarter and a box top from grocery products sold by the agency's clients. Millions of these premiums were distributed in connection with various campaigns, and his agency's reputation was made. Jones wrote a book called *Ads, Women & Boxtops* (1955).

After the Duane Jones Company lost a few accounts in 1950, 1951 saw the advent of the most famous lawsuit in advertising history. At the instigation of Frank G. Burke, Jr., vice president of client Manhattan Soap Company, several of the agency's top executives issued an ultimatum to Jones on 3 July 1951: sell the agency to them or they would leave. Jones refused, characterizing the offer as "coming to me with a .45 revolver and saying, 'Sell this to us at our price.'" The nine executives resigned as directors but temporarily remained employees of Duane Jones. They incorporated as Scheideler, Beck & Werner, Inc., on 23 August and eventually left the Jones agency. The exact date of each resignation was controversial and critically important to the case. The ex-employees opened their new agency on 10 September 1951

The January 1954 verdict in the Duane Jones account piracy case had repercussions throughout the U.S. advertising industry. *Advertising Age* ran the story on page 1.
Reprinted with permission from the 11 January 1954 issue of Advertising Age. *Copyright, Crain Communications, Inc., 1954.*

with 79 Duane Jones employees and billings of approximately $5 million from Jones clients Manhattan Soap, Hudson Pulp & Paper, Borden, and Heublein.

Jones resigned his few remaining accounts and in January 1952 filed a $4.5 million lawsuit against his former executives for conspiracy to ruin his agency. He charged the nine with soliciting and obtaining clients of Duane Jones Company while still officers of the agency with fiduciary responsibilities. Countercharges were filed, claiming that Jones was frequently intoxicated and that he "grossly neglected" the business. The defense also claimed that account changes were a common practice in the advertising industry.

After 30 months, a jury trial victory for Jones, and two appeals, the New York State Court of Appeals awarded Jones $300,000 plus court costs. The court concluded that the defendants had unfairly solicited Jones agency accounts while still employees. Jones felt vindicated and later said that the case

decided "whether you can take a drunk out, get him inebriated, and then pick his pocket." Milton Pollack, Jones's trial counsel, interpreted the significance of the case in a *Printers' Ink* article:

> The Duane Jones case marks out the line of permissible business practice—where the obligation of loyalty ends and when self-interest may be served . . . The Duane Jones case has received and deserves widespread attention. The basis for the case and the principles of the law and business conduct involved apply to every form of enterprise. The obligation of loyalty lasts until the end of an employee, partner, director, or officer relationship. After the effective end, personal interest need no longer be subordinated to such loyalty. Until that break-off of connection, a man may not fairly or legally serve two masters.

The Duane Jones case changed the rules for breakaway agencies. Prior to the 1950s, executives felt free to take accounts with them when starting a new agency without fear of legal repercussions. (Ted Bates left Benton and Bowles with Colgate-Palmolive and Continental Baking in 1940 and had no problems.) After Duane Jones, breakaways did not cease to happen, but departing employees were careful to avoid using agency time or resources and to abstain from soliciting or informing clients during the planning stages. There have not been many account piracy suits since this one, as they are difficult to prove, and agency principals usually determine that suing is not worthwhile. Significantly, in a situation where a lawsuit did take place, *WPP v. Lord, Einstein, O'Neill & Partners* (1988), WPP decided to concentrate on the betrayal of fiduciary responsibilities rather than the account piracy angle.

As for Jones himself, he unsuccessfully attempted to restart his agency in 1955. He died of a heart attack at a hospital near his Connecticut home in June 1961. Scheideler, Beck & Werner, Inc., closed in 1956 when the Manhattan Soap Company (the client that started all the trouble) was acquired and its account moved to another agency.

MARSHA C. APPEL

Further Reading

Danzig, Fred, "Lessons from Duane Jones," *Advertising Age* (28 March 1988)
"Duane Dodge Jones," *Broadcasting and Telecasting* (29 January 1951)
"High N.Y. Court Unanimously Awards Duane Jones $300,000 Damages in 'Account Piracy' Suit," *Advertising Age* (11 January 1954)
O'Gara, J., "Precedent-Setting Duane Jones Case Ruled on Account Shift Conspiracy," *Advertising Age* (10 March 1975)
Tolk, Bernard, "Duane Jones Wins Final Verdict," *Printers' Ink* (15 January 1954)

J. Stirling Getchell, Inc. *See under* **Getchell**

J. Walter Thompson Company. *See under* **Thompson**

K

Kellogg Company

Principal Agencies
N.W. Ayer & Son, Inc.
Kenyon & Eckhardt, Inc.
J. Walter Thompson Company
Leo Burnett Company, Inc.
Martin Agency

Kellogg Company, a global leader in the ready-to-eat cereal category, also markets other breakfast foods, such as Pop-Tarts and Eggo Waffles, and cereal-based snack foods such as Rice Krispie Treats. John Harvey Kellogg, a physician, invented wheat flakes in 1894 as a nutritious food for his health spa clients in Battle Creek, Michigan. The flaked cereal brand was born in 1906, when the Battle Creek Toasted Corn Flake Company was formed. But substantially the same product was first advertised under the brand name Sanitas in 1903. (Named for the Battle Creek Sanitorium, run by Dr. Kellogg, the Sanitas brand was created to market flaked cereal to former patients.) The Sanitas Nut Food Company became Kellogg Food Company in 1908. The company was incorporated in 1925.

Neither the brand nor the company was very successful until, in 1899, Kellogg invited his younger brother, William Keith Kellogg, into the business. The younger Kellogg had a natural instinct for marketing and advertising, writing his own ads and trying new ways to reach both consumers and the grocery trade. In 1903 he became the first to use house-to-house sampling.

"Push" Marketing

Kellogg spent $90,000 on advertising in 1906, including $4,000 for a page ad in the July issue of the *Ladies' Home Journal* pioneering the use of color in advertising. The *Journal* ad showed Kellogg's understanding of "push" marketing (marketing designed to get retailers to stock a product in anticipation of consumer demand). The ad included a coupon for customers to take to their grocers to sign and return requesting Corn Flakes. Con-sumers who successfully enlisted new stores received "a season's worth" of Corn Flakes for free.

Sales in 1906 soared from 33 to 2,900 cases a day. In the first six months of 1907, Kellogg's advertising budget reached $300,000. After the stock market crash of 1929, when many other advertisers were cutting back, Kellogg doubled its advertising budget.

By 1940 Kellogg's total advertising expenditures had passed $2.3 million, with approximately $1.5 million in print and $860,000 in network radio, including children's shows such as *Don Winslow of the Navy, Buck Rogers,* and *Superman.* Around that time, Battle Creek's daily newspaper, the *Enquirer and News,* reported that "much of the initial success of the company was the result of a decision at the outset to advertise extensively and intensively."

Kellogg was an innovator in packaging and consumer and trade promotion as well. He introduced the first wax-paper liner to preserve product freshness and the first in-pack premium in 1910, a "flip book" titled *The Jungleland Funny Moving Pictures Book.* Among his many trade promotions, he provided grocers with free samples of Corn Flakes to give away to customers who winked at them. Trade ads announced the upcoming "Wink Day."

In 1912 Kellogg owned the largest outdoor sign in the world: a 106-foot-wide by 50-foot-high electric sign in Times Square in New York City. The company also commissioned an animated electric sign in Chicago, Illinois, during the same period.

Rivals Emerge

The success of Kellogg's Corn Flakes spawned scores of imitators. Some 108 different brands of corn flakes were being produced by 40 different companies in Battle Creek by 1911. To differentiate Kellogg's Corn Flakes, Will Kellogg put his name on every box, supported by an advertising campaign that said, "None genuine without this signature—W.K. Kellogg." That signature remained the company logo into the next century.

Additional products quickly followed the success of Corn Flakes: Kellogg's Shredded Wheat and Krumbles cereal in 1912, All-Bran in 1919, Rice Krispies in 1928, Corn Pops in 1950, Frosted Flakes in 1952, Honey Smacks in 1953, and Product 19 and Pop-Tarts in 1963.

Kellogg appointed its first advertising agencies, N.W. Ayer & Son and Kenyon & Eckhardt (K&E), in the 1930s, adding the J. Walter Thompson Company (JWT) to the roster in 1938 and the Leo Burnett Company in 1949. K&E lost the Corn Flakes business to Burnett in 1951 and the rest of the account—Bran Flakes, Pep, Raisin Bran, and Rice Krispies—in July 1952. Burnett won the account by redesigning Kellogg packaging. Kellogg's business relationships with JWT and Burnett were still in place at the beginning of the 21st century, marking Kellogg as one of the most loyal of clients.

Kellogg's best-known contributions to advertising in the cereal category were memorable slogans, jingles, and characters from Burnett to support its family of brands. Perhaps the most memorable was the jingle:

Good morning, good morning,
The best to you each morning.
K-E-double L-O-double good,
Kellogg's best to you.

Kellogg used scores of other slogans for its flagship brand over the years. Among the more notable were: "What breakfast was meant to be," "Wins its favor through its flavor," "The original and best," "The best way to start the day," "The nation's breakfast," and "It's gonna be a great day."

"Sweetheart" of Corn

Will Kellogg commissioned the first advertising "character" for Corn Flakes in 1907. The character originated in a rejected ad for a farm equipment manufacturer: a country maid holding a sheaf of wheat, drawn by a staff artist at the Ketterlinus Lithograph Company in Philadelphia, Pennsylvania. Kellogg changed the image to one of a woman holding a shock of corn and dubbed her "The Sweetheart of the Corn."

The use of cartoon characters such as Snap, Crackle, and Pop (1941), which were later animated for television advertising, became a hallmark of Kellogg's advertising. Snap, Crackle, and Pop were the first and continue to be the longest-lasting cartoon spokes-characters in Kellogg ad history. In Sweden they are known as Piff, Paff, and Puff; Germans know them as Knisper, Knasper, and Knusper; and Mexicans call them Pim, Pam, and Pum.

Most of Kellogg's characters were created by Chicago-based Burnett, which is often referred to in the advertising industry as the "critter" agency because of its talent in creating characters such as the Jolly Green Giant, Charlie the Tuna, and the Pillsbury Doughboy. Burnett and Kellogg have created Tony the Tiger for Frosted Flakes (1952), Sugar Pops Pete (1958), Milton the Toaster for Pop Tarts (1971), Toucan Sam for Froot Loops (1963),

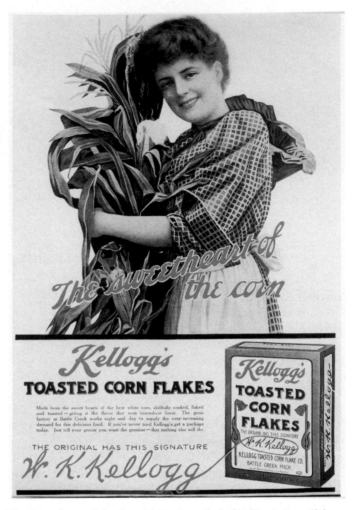

The "Sweetheart of the Corn," historic symbol of Kellogg's Corn Flakes, was depicted in a 1907 advertisement.
Kellogg's® logo, The sweetheart of the corn®, Kellogg's Corn Flakes®, and the W.K. Kellogg® signature logo are registered trademarks of Kellogg Company. All rights reserved. Used with permission.

Dig'Em the Frog for Sugar Smacks (1972), Cornelius the Rooster for Corn Flakes (1957), and many others.

Broadcast Advertising

Kellogg is also a major broadcast advertiser, using spot and network television since the early 1950s, sponsoring Jimmy Durante's *All Star Review, Space Cadet, Mark Trail,* and *Howdy Doody,* its first national buy. In the late 1950s Kellogg bought, financed, and produced one of the earliest syndicated television programs, *Wild Bill Hickock,* starring Guy Madison and Andy Devine. Both stars appeared in commercials in the show for Sugar Pops. The earlier Kellogg-sponsored radio show *Superman* moved into television, sponsored by Sugar Frosted Flakes. Other sponsorships during television's golden age included Arthur Godfrey's show, *Dennis the Menace, Captain Kangaroo,* and *The Beverly Hillbillies.*

Kellogg was the early and undisputed leader in ready-to-eat cereal in both U.S. and global markets. But the 1990s saw new challenges to its leadership. Kellogg's share of domestic cereal sales fell from 41 percent in 1988 to 32 percent in 1998. Along the way, the company sold subsidiaries Mrs. Smith's Pies to J.M. Smucker Company in 1994 and Lender's Bagel Bakery to Aurora Foods, Inc., in 1999.

To generate greater interest and increased brand loyalty, Kellogg created a cereal theme park in Battle Creek in 1998. Cereal City USA covers eight acres, with exhibits such as a working cereal production line, a film on cereal advertising history, and a ten-foot-tall Toucan Sam.

In 1999, troubled by the decline in sales of all cereals as the traditional sit-down breakfast lost favor and by an eroding market share, Kellogg took major steps to halt these trends. Early in 2000 heir-apparent Carlos Gutierrez replaced Chief Executive Officer Arnold Langbo.

Agency Shifts

The company added a new agency, the Martin Agency, of Richmond, Virginia, to its roster in 1999. It also shifted assignments, moving Honey Nut Crunch and a new product assignment from JWT to Burnett.

As consumers' tastes for a traditional breakfast waned, Kellogg made the transition into other products and other appeals. In 1999 it launched a new line of cholesterol-lowering foods under the Ensemble brand, which included 21 products ranging from cereal to bread to frozen lasagna. That initiative, which was handled by Y&R Advertising (the advertising subsidiary of Young & Rubicam) under the tag line, "Life your way," was unsuccessful.

The Martin Agency began its first work for Kellogg on a line of seven "nutraceuticals," fortified cereals advertised as "K-sentials." But by the end of November 1999, as reported by *Advertising Age*, the company decided that K-sentials multibrand advertising was no longer essential and stopped it in favor of more brand-specific advertising. Spending for all Kellogg brands was projected at more than $400 million for 1999. In 2000 the company made plans to spend its advertising budget on its largest single brands, including Froot Loops and Corn Pops. All this activity came as rival General Mills for the first time passed Kellogg in sales.

Advertising strategy at the start of the 21st century positioned Kellogg brands as adjuncts to a healthy lifestyle, a return to the company's wellness origins a century ago. An umbrella campaign was launched in 1999 with the tag line: "With Kellogg's, a healthier life is within your reach. So tomorrow morning, help yourself."

WAYNE HILINSKI

See also color plate in this volume

Further Reading

Butler, Mary, Frances Thornton, and Martin Ashley, *The Best to You Each Morning: W.K. Kellogg and Kellogg Company*, Battle Creek, Michigan: Heritage Society, 1995

Candey, Dana, and Reed Abelson, "Under Pressure, Kellogg Speeds a Shift at the Top," *New York Times* (6 January 1999)

Candey, Dana, and Reed Abelson, "Can Kellogg Break Out of the Box?" *New York Time* (24 January 1999)

Massie, Larry B., and Peter J. Schmitt, *Battle Creek, the Place behind the Products: An Illustrated History*, Woodland Hills, California: Windsor, 1984

Powell, Horace B., *The Original Has This Signature: W.K. Kellogg*, Englewood Cliffs, New Jersey: Prentice-Hall, 1956

Kenyon & Eckhardt, Inc.

Founded by Otis Kenyon and Henry Eckhardt through the purchase of Ray D. Lillibridge Company, 1929; purchased Coleman, Prentis & Varley, international advertising network, 1971; resigned Ford to take on Chrysler in what was then the largest account shift in history, 1979; purchased by Lorimar, 1983; merged with Bozell & Jacobs to form Bozell Worldwide under holding company Bozell Jacobs Kenyon & Eckhardt (BJK&E), 1986; BJK&E bought by True North Communications and dissolved, ending K&E as an advertising brand, 1997.

Major Clients
Chrysler Corporation
Ford Motor Company
Kellogg Company
Pepsi-Cola Company
Piels Bros. (beer)
RCA Victor
Shell Oil Company

The history of Kenyon & Eckhardt, Inc. (K&E), extends back to 1896 and the Ray D. Lillibridge Company, a small technical agency whose only claim to fame is that in 1918 it hired a 38-year-old engineer named Otis Kenyon. Kenyon had worked with the Railroad Test Commission and came to Lillibridge to work on the Canadian Pacific Railroad account. He had an engineer's faith in numbers and believed that the key to advertising lay in research. Eight years later Kenyon found a bright young fellow 14

Between pictures, say,

Pepsi, please"

WHETHER you're at your
favorite neighborhood theatre
. . . or a drive-in . . . you'll agree
today's modern people are feature
attractions. Their trim, slender
figures are the happy result of the
modern trend toward lighter,
less-filling food and drink.

Pepsi-Cola heartily supports this
sensible diet plan. For today's Pepsi,
reduced in calories, is never heavy,
never too sweet. It's the modern, the
light refreshment. Say "Pepsi, please"!

The *Light*
refreshment

Kenyon & Eckhardt helped position Pepsi-Cola as the choice of young moderns with this 1958 campaign.
Pepsi-Cola Company.

years his junior with a similar penchant for facts. Henry Eckhardt joined Lillibridge in 1926 and within two years was running the copy department. He was a literate man who had begun his career as a journalist and possessed a reformer's zeal for professional ethics. In October 1929, when Lillibridge decided to retire, the two men bought him out and formed Kenyon & Eckhardt.

To many advertisers in those days, Kenyon's mania for research was just another complication in a basically simple business. The client who prided himself on knowing his customers and felt advertising was in his bones had no wish to see his instincts second-guessed by a mathematician. So Kenyon closeted his research operation, developing a separate company with offices apart from K&E's New York City headquarters at 247 Park Avenue. The new owners were eager to break out of the industrial ghetto and move into consumer advertising. Their first opportunity came with the Axton Fisher Tobacco Company and its Spud Smoking Tobacco, which K&E built into a credible brand in the 1930s. In the 1930s one agency success led to another. Kellogg Company, a small Battle Creek, Michigan, breakfast food marketer, became a client in 1934 with its Kaffee Hag Coffee, followed soon by All-Bran and Gro-Pup Dog Food. By the end of the decade K&E had won Charles B. Knox Gelatine Company; Bosco Company; Abercrombie & Fitch Company; Munsingwear, Inc.; John B. Stetson Company; and Quaker State Oil Refining Company.

As the agency expanded, a second generation of management appeared on the horizon. First was Thomas D'Arcy Brophy, who joined in 1931 to bring in new business but whose career was almost ended two years later when he was severely burned in an auto accident. He returned to K&E in the fall of 1935 and in 1937 became president and chief executive officer, succeeding Eckhardt, who took the new position of chairman. (Brophy died in another car accident in 1967.)

Brophy had hired Edwin Cox as copy chief in 1933. His most famous headline was "A hog can cross the country without changing trains—but you can't!" for the Chesapeake & Ohio Lines railroad. After Brophy's accident, it was Cox who suggested that Dwight Mills be brought in to handle new business. When Brophy returned, the three men became heirs apparent, responsible for the growth that moved K&E to the top tier of New York City agencies by 1941.

The future came more quickly than expected for K&E's founding generation. In July 1942 Eckhardt died unexpectedly at age 48. Kenyon, the elder partner who had been content to run his research office and serve as treasurer, assumed the post of chairman, which he held until his death seven years later in 1949.

But real authority fell to Brophy, who would succeed Kenyon as chairman and finally close his career in 1957 after helping found both the United Service Organizations (USO) and the Advertising Council. Under his stewardship, the Kellogg accounts expanded to Bran Flakes and Pep, and by 1947 Raisin Bran, Rice Krispies, and the coveted Kellogg flagship, Corn Flakes. The list of other packaged goods grew as well: Wesson Oil & Snowdrift Sales Company, Morton Salt, Borden Company, Pepperidge Farm, and Bristol-Myers Resistab.

As its accounts multiplied, so did K&E's involvement in network radio. In 1944 the agency opened offices in Chicago, Illinois, and Hollywood, California. It needed someone with a solid radio background to command a growing broadcast department. That year Brophy hired one of the biggest radio men around, William Lewis. This college dropout and failed advertising man (he had been at the J. Walter Thompson Company before joining CBS in 1935) was already something of a broadcasting legend. As head of programming for CBS, he sent Edward R. Murrow to London in February 1937 and put Orson Welles and Norman Corwin on the air the following year. Lewis gave CBS a prestige and substance no other network could touch. Corwin later remarked that Lewis "made creative people feel cherished and gave them freedom. He praised good work, and above all he saw they got credit for it."

Corwin was not the only man impressed by Lewis's intelligence and charisma. Another was Henry Ford II. During World War II, the Ford Motor Company was so sloppily managed that the government seriously considered seizing it to keep B-24 bomber production going. In 1943 Washington ordered Henry Ford II out of the U.S. Navy and back to Detroit, where his failing grandfather still clung to power. The situation was ominous. Unable to wield decisive power, Henry Ford II went to the media in a public-relations effort to temper the storm of terrible publicity. At CBS he met Lewis and discussed Ford's situation with him. The two men came to respect each other.

After the war, with Lewis now at K&E, Ford tried to lure him to the car company as head of corporate communications. But Lewis was happy in New York. Regardless, he had a better idea. If Lewis would not come to Ford, perhaps Ford might come to Lewis, and to K&E. In March 1948 it did. While the Ford Division remained at Thompson, K&E won all Ford corporate business ("Ford has a better idea") and, soon after, Ford's Lincoln-Mercury Division and the Lincoln-Mercury dealer account.

The Ford account came just in time for television. In June 1948 Ed Sullivan went on a three-station CBS network with a variety program called *Toast of the Town*. Despite his lamppost deportment, Sullivan was no stranger to broadcasting. He had introduced Jack Benny to America on a similar variety show on radio in the 1930s. Lewis was looking for an opportunity to take Lincoln-Mercury into television. That and perhaps a lingering loyalty to CBS was all he needed to snap up the program after Emerson Radio pulled out in 1949. Sullivan not only became synonymous with Lincoln-Mercury in the 1950s, but the star appeared at hundreds of Ford corporate events and, during a trip to Paris, France, arranged for every Lincoln-Mercury dealer in America to get a personally addressed and signed postcard. With Ford money to spend, K&E wrote more than its share of television history. In 1949 *The Ford Theater* presented live dramas once a month. Ten years later, Ingrid Bergman made her television debut on *Ford Startime* (in *The Turn of the Screw*) with John Frankenheimer directing. Then Lewis dreamed up a once-in-a-lifetime concoction that the industry would dub television's first "spectacular." Airing on 15 June 1953, *The Ford 50th Anniversary Show* was a two-hour, $500,000 compendium of show business that the National Broadcasting Company (NBC) and CBS carried simultaneously.

Come Celebrate
Chrysler's 60th Anniversary.

For 60 days...if you buy a Dodge Aries K
or Plymouth Reliant K...you can have
automatic transmission at no extra cost.

From May 1st through June 30th, join us in celebrating
the Chrysler comeback, and the cars that made it happen.

Thanks, America.
We wouldn't be 60 without you.

The New Chrysler Corporation

Five years after the largest ad agency shift in history, a rejuvenated Chrysler Corporation celebrated its 60th anniversary with a campaign from the agency that made it possible—Kenyon & Eckhardt. *The reproduction of a 1984 Chrysler Corporation ad is used with permission from DaimlerChrysler Corporation.*

Yet for all the dazzle, the heart of it came down to a couple of stools, a dark stage, and a fast shuffle beat as Mary Martin and Ethel Merman ripped into a medley of songs that so electrified the nation Decca Records rushed it into LP release, thus making it the first commercially issued television sound track. In March 1954, K&E won the Radio Corporation of America (RCA) account and helped launch the first color television sets into the American market, in 1955. Agency billings reached $68 million in 1955 and $81 million in 1956, putting it briefly ahead of Ted Bates Company, Inc., Leo Burnett Company, and Foote, Cone & Belding.

Still, it was not an easy decade for the agency. Burnett had begun to pry apart K&E's grip on Kellogg, and in July 1951 it won the Corn Flakes account. Then during the "black spring" of 1952, the last of the Kellogg business went to Burnett one week after National Distillers and Piels Bros. left the agency. Losses came to nearly one-fourth of the agency's total billings. In desperation

K&E took on several new vice presidents who brought large "vest pocket" accounts with them. Salvation came just before Christmas 1955 with the Pepsi-Cola account, two months after the agency had lost a competition with McCann-Erickson, Inc., for the Coca-Cola account. For K&E the victory meant profit, stability, and seventh-place standing among U.S. agencies. For Pepsi, it meant a repositioning from a budget beverage to an upscale refreshment through the famous "Be Sociable" and "Pepsi, Please" campaigns, as well as a chance to hire several K&E executives away before it dropped the agency in May 1960. Growth slowed after 1956, yet by 1961 billings stood at around $90 million.

After Lewis became president of K&E in October 1951 and later chairman in 1960, he continued to oversee the Ford and Lincoln-Mercury business. (Lincoln left K&E in 1955, then returned in 1958.) After Lewis's retirement in 1967 to run the American Cancer Society, the Ford mantle passed to Leo-Arthur Kelmenson, a man of formidable credentials in both show business and advertising. His uncle, Ben Kelmenson, was president of Warner Bros., and he had come up through Lennen & Newell, Inc., as custodian of the dancing Old Gold cigarette packs on *Ted Mack's Amateur Hour* and *The Herb Shriner Show*. He arrived at K&E as a senior vice president in March 1967 from Norman, Craig & Kummel. The next year he became president and chief executive officer and began the process of taking K&E international. In 1971 K&E purchased the international advertising agency network of Coleman, Prentis & Varley (CPV). CPV added nearly $80 million in worldwide billings to K&E's domestic revenue, which totaled almost $100 million, and gave K&E offices in the Caribbean, Brazil, and Argentina, as well as Paris, France; Milan, Italy; Barcelona, Spain; Cologne, Germany; and Brussels, Belgium. But Kelmenson's association with Lee Iacocca, the Ford wunderkind, dwarfed all that. Iacocca had built the Mustang and lent his face to simultaneous covers of *Time* and *Newsweek*. Over the next decade the two men became more than business associates. They developed the kind of closeness Bill Lewis and Henry Ford II had had 25 years before, a relationship that preempted corporate protocols and made anything possible. In July 1978 Henry Ford II fired a frustrated Iacocca, who promptly accepted the top job at the moribund Chrysler Corporation, where he went to work on 15 November.

Chrysler lost $205 million that year, and Washington began to wonder whether America might be better off without a "Big Three." "The company had 250,000 cars rusting in Detroit," Kelmenson once said. "They were useless composites of old technology. But [it] could not start making new cars until those units were sold." Iacocca had to do something. If he could not change the product overnight, he decided, he could certainly change the advertising. Starting in early December, Iacocca and Kelmenson met frequently and secretly, perhaps 15 or 20 times. They rendezvoused in New York one week, Las Vegas another, and Los Angeles after that, avoiding restaurants and public places where they might be spotted by industry eyes. There were no preliminaries or presentations; they got right to the point.

When Iacocca called a press conference on 1 March 1979, Wall Street did not know what to expect. Iacocca disclosed that he had fired Young & Rubicam, Ross Roy, and Batten Barton Durstine & Osborn and moved all $120 million in consolidated Chrysler spending to K&E. According to *Advertising Age,* the move lifted the agency's overall billings to $328 million.

The shock wave quickly hit Detroit, where K&E dispatched a hand-delivered note to Ford telling him K&E was resigning his $75 million account. Rarely had so much seemed to ride on the sheer strength of relationship. It was the largest account shift in U.S. history to date. Most of K&E's middle and upper management knew nothing about it until the hour it happened.

That night at the restaurant "21," a stranger came over from another table. "You don't know me," he said to Kelmenson, "but I wanted to congratulate you on your great success today." Kelmenson got up, smiled, and for the first time shook the hand of Charles Peebler, chairman of Bozell & Jacobs (B&J).

After Chrysler stabilized its financial position with loan guarantees, and the advertising came together, Kelmenson began to think about the way agencies used to produce programming for their clients. He believed the agency could preempt the industry by getting an entrée into television production that K&E could then bring to clients. If Chrysler and other major advertisers could fund their own shows, he reasoned, they could not only have some impact on the quality, but they also could profit from their distribution overseas.

Kelmenson did not exactly find a partner. But he found Lorimar, then the producer of *The Waltons, Dallas,* and *Knots Landing.* The two companies had complementary objectives: K&E wanted to get the best programming for it clients; Lorimar wanted a good investment. And K&E, then the 23rd-largest agency (billing $434 million), looked like one. In 1983 Lorimar acquired the agency for $21 million, and Kelmenson became a member of the Lorimar board.

Lorimar's stock went from $20 to $31 in six months, and by 1985 it had a reserve of $58 million for more shopping. Lorimar Chairman Merv Adelson talked the party line about being a "communications company," as companies did. But Lorimar wanted to be rich, like its own J.R. Ewing of *Dallas.* And Adelson's partner, Lee Rich, a former Benton and Bowles executive who had worked with Sheldon Leonard to secure *The Dick Van Dyke Show* for Procter & Gamble Company, knew that the added diversity of owning a couple of big agencies could help smooth the boom-and-bust cycle of television production.

So in 1985 Lorimar put together the 14th-biggest agency in the United States. It acquired B&J for $41 million. At the time B&J billed $808 million; K&E, $412 million. B&J was eager to jump-start an aggressive growth strategy and felt it had to merge with something. When the agency decided K&E was a logical partner, it sold itself to Lorimar to do so.

Kelmenson, who knew nothing about any of this until the deal was done, threatened to leave K&E, taking Chrysler with him. An emergency meeting between Peebler and Kelmenson was arranged in July 1985. The two men came to an understanding. Against the expectation of many observers, they decided to try a six-month trial marriage. The deal closed in January 1986, and the two agencies became Bozell Worldwide under a parent company called Bozell Jacobs Kenyon & Eckhardt (BJK&E). BJK&E was acquired by True North Communications in 1997, and BJK&E was dissolved as a holding company, thus ending the K&E brand as a presence in advertising. Bozell continued to function as an independent worldwide operation until September 1999, when it was formally merged into FCB. Kelmenson became chairman of FCB Worldwide. The merger brought the huge Chrysler account briefly to FCB, before it was moved to BBDO, a unit of Omnicom, in 2000. The following year, 2001, True North was acquired by the Interpublic Group of Companies.

JOHN MCDONOUGH

See also Bozell Group; True North Communications, Inc.

Further Reading

"A Better Idea?" *Time* (12 March 1979)
"How Five Agencies Ran for the Bull," *Business Week* (14 April 1986)
Iacocca, Lee, and William Novak, *Iacocca: An Autobiography,* New York: Bantam, 1984; London: Sidgwick and Jackson, 1985
"K&E Lands Pepsi," *Advertising Age* (19 December 1955)
Kanner, Bernice, "Hollywood Squares," *New York Magazine* (16 May 1988)
"Lorimar Scores on TV," *Business Week* (22 October 1984)

Ketchum, MacLeod & Grove, Inc.

(Ketchum Communications)

Started by George Ketchum as a public relations firm, Ketchum Publicity, in Pittsburgh, Pennsylvania, 1919; created its first advertising effort, 1922; changed name to Ketchum-MacLeod Advertising, 1923; became Ketchum, MacLeod & Grove when Robert Grove joined, 1923; opened an office in New York City, 1956; bought the West Coast's Botsford, Constantine & McCarty to create Botsford-Ketchum, Inc., 1969; Ketchum Communications sold to Omnicom Group, 1996; Ketchum advertising unit disbanded, 1999.

Major Clients
Aluminum Company of America
American Honda Motor Company
Ciba Pharmaceutical Products
Gulf Oil Corporation
H.J. Heinz Company
Japan Air Lines Company
Jones & Laughlin Steel Corporation
Pittsburgh Brewing Company
Westinghouse Electric Corporation (consumer appliances)

Ketchum, MacLeod & Grove (KM&G) had its formal opening in 1923, after Robert Grove joined the Pittsburgh, Pennsylvania, agency started in 1919 by George Ketchum, the man largely responsible for its enormous growth over a period of 50 years. Ketchum started out in public relations, calling his shop Ketchum Publicity, which he formed with his brother Carleton and Norman MacLeod. In 1922, however, the agency created its first advertising effort and a year later changed its name to Ketchum-MacLeod Advertising. The implied direction of the shop had one major, almost immediate effect: Carleton Ketchum left to run his own fund-raising organization and was joined by MacLeod, whose name nevertheless would remain on the ad agency's door for many decades to come. It was then that Grove came aboard; he had met all three founders while the four were students at the University of Pittsburgh and was serving as assistant to the president of Tennessee Iron & Chemical Company. The agency's billings for 1923 were $100,000.

One of Ketchum's first moves was to hire a treasurer, another Pitt graduate, said to be "tight with a buck." That kind of discipline was necessary to thrive in Pittsburgh's heavy-industry business community; in these early days, agency survival depended on a large number of accounts requiring minimal advertising created by only a few employees. Ketchum had about seven in those days. During the Depression years, staff salaries were cut, and the principals went without pay until times improved. But the agency not only stayed in business, its billings improved every single year except one. Clients were diverse, though largely industrial, ranging from Jones & Laughlin Steel to Westinghouse Electric's consumer appliances to a local baker of bread.

The agency expanded steadily, and in the immediate post–World War II years maintained a staff of more than 200. In 1953 the agency's billings were $16 million, generated by 53 accounts—illustrating the diversity of its business, which included not only advertising but also merchandising, point-of-purchase promotions, sales and technical literature, and public relations (PR). In fact, in 1955 Ketchum's PR department consisted of 40 people and was one of the largest such operations in the United States. This was a period of unusual growth for the shop; its business doubled from 1950 to 1955, the year Robert Grove retired after 33 years with the agency. KM&G also was noted for its formal research and training programs. In 1953 it employed 24 men and women just out of college as account assistants. The PR

Ketchum, McLeod & Grove's "She's all you expect Japan to be" campaign, created in 1969 for Japan Airlines, promoted the gracious hospitality of the carrier's flight attendants.
Courtesy of Japan Airlines.

department maintained a 200-page directory of publications to ensure the worth of its mailings.

In 1956 KM&G's growth necessitated the opening of a New York City office, run by another Pitt graduate, Robert Lytle. The office expanded to new space just one year later. Total agency billings were $27 million in 1958. As the decade was ending, George Ketchum reported on a new trend he was seeing at his agency, with industrial marketers, which normally advertised only to other businesses or retailers, striving to reach the ultimate consumer with more consumer-oriented advertising. Late in 1959 the agency resigned the Jones & Laughlin business because of the increasing importance of another client, the Aluminum Company of America. Westinghouse also greatly expanded its accounts at Ketchum in 1960, giving the shop 15 additional divisions. And client Gulf Oil was the reason Ketchum opened a Houston, Texas, office that same year. New accounts in 1961 included Pittsburgh Brewing Company and Ciba Pharmaceutical Products.

At the same time, new management was being groomed; in 1962 Executive Vice President Edward T. Parrack succeeded Ketchum as president, only the second individual to hold that title. Ketchum remained chief executive officer (CEO) and became

Aluminum Fun Furniture designed for
the Alcoa Collection by Jay Doblin.
Photographed by Lester
Bookbinder.

FORECAST: *There's a world of aluminum
in the wonderful world of tomorrow . . .*
where you will match your moods
with furnishings of many-humored
aluminum . . . light, strong aluminum that shapes
to fun for patio, gameroom or pool . . . and takes
to color, design and texture as readily as mint to julep.
Aluminum Company of America, Pittsburgh.

ALCOA ALUMINUM

A 1960 ad from Ketchum, McLeod & Grove for the Aluminum Company of America focused on the versatility of aluminum.
Permission to reprint provided by Alcoa.

chairman of the board, a position vacant since Grove's retirement. New accounts in the early 1960s included ACF Industries, Air Express Company, McGraw-Hill Publishing, and the U.S. Army Recruiting Service. Closer to home the agency signed up Pennsylvania's Department of Commerce, West Virginia's industrial and travel development departments, and, on the consumer side, H.J. Heinz Company's beans, vinegars, sauces, and mustards.

When Parrack reported that billings had grown 22 percent to more than $45 million in 1963, he said that KM&G's business was 60 percent consumer and 40 percent industrial, a complete reversal of the proportions ten years earlier. The agency had recorded annual gains for 26 consecutive years; he attributed this success to the shop's "stability of employment" and its "total communications facility to formulate any kind of message to help the client sell" its goods and services.

In 1965 the agency's New York City office was billing $15 million of the total $60 million and had more than 100 employees. W. Stanley Redpath was named vice chairman of the board that year; Parrack had succeeded Ketchum as CEO. In 1967 Ketchum stepped down, and Redpath, who ran the New York City office, became chairman. Ketchum remained on the agency's board, however.

A key event for the future occurred in 1969, when KM&G bought Botsford, Constantine & McCarty, a Portland, Oregon, agency formed in 1918 by David Botsford, Sr., and Charles Constantine. It had acquired the McCarty Company of Los Angeles, California, in 1964. Billing $22 million in 1969 and serving major client Japan Air Lines, the agency became known as Botsford-Ketchum, Inc., and gained fame in the arenas of food and food service, among others, with its largest office based in San Francisco, California. The move also gave the agency new offices overseas, in Japan and England.

In 1970 KM&G elected its third president, as William Genge succeeded Parrack, with the latter moving to chairman of the board. Redpath succeeded George Ketchum as chairman of the executive committee, with Ketchum stepping back once again to director.

International operations expanded soon after, with KM&G buying an 85 percent interest in David Williams & Partners, London, England, and a "substantial" interest in Durana Werburg, Frankfort, West Germany, in 1970. International billings were more than $24 million in 1972. In 1973 Botsford-Ketchum grew in Japan via an affiliation with Tokyo PR Service, the same year Ketchum retired from the agency he had founded. He died in September 1975, and Robert Grove passed away in 1976. The year Ketchum died billings stood at $152 million.

In the 1980s and 1990s Botsford-Ketchum became an equal part of KM&G. The overall agency became Ketchum Communications, Inc., in 1982, with units Ketchum Advertising, Ketchum Directory Services, and, of course, PR operations. But Ketchum Advertising itself, following a high of around $120 million in billings in the late 1980s, went into a decline, although it serviced the highly visible Acura luxury car account from American Honda Motor Company. Ketchum Communications was sold to giant agency conglomerate the Omnicom Group in 1996. To illustrate its continuing decline, billings for the advertising unit were $79 million in 1999, compared with $145 million for the Yellow Pages unit; the advertising unit was shut down over time, and the flagship office was sold in 1999 to Earle Palmer Brown Companies (EPB), an agency started in Baltimore, Maryland. EPB changed the Pittsburgh shop's name to Egan/St. James, marking the end of the road for what had for seven decades been the city's largest ad agency. Under Omnicom, however, the PR unit thrived and under the single name of Ketchum was the sixth-largest public relations practice in 2000, a development that seemed fitting given the agency's beginnings.

LARRY EDWARDS

Kimberly-Clark Corporation

Principal Agencies
Charles F.W. Nichols Agency
Lord & Thomas
Foote, Cone & Belding
Kelly, Nason, Inc.
Ogilvy & Mather Worldwide, Inc.
Campbell Mithun Esty

A paper company founded in Neenah, Wisconsin, Kimberly-Clark Company has had a long history of dealing with sensitive subjects and breaking new ground in advertising. Over the years, its slow and carefully planned product diversification, doggedness when products fail, and far-reaching marketing efforts have yielded results. Although it is best known for consumer products such as Kleenex tissues, the company also makes products for commercial and professional health care uses, such as newsprint and hospital hand soap.

Four businessmen—John A. Kimberly, Havilah Babcock, Charles B. Clark, and Frank C. Shattuck—founded the company in 1872, naming it Kimberly, Clark and Company. The name was tinkered with once more before the designation Kimberly-Clark Corporation was adopted in 1906.

Despite the company's long history, much of the credit for Kimberly-Clark's position in the 21st-century marketplace goes to Darwin E. Smith, the company's chief executive officer from 1971

KOTEX

How War Nurses Found a New Use for Cellucotton

NECESSITY being the mother of invention, our war nurses in France first discovered a new use for Cellucotton, which has led to Kotex—a universal product at a universal price.

5¢ Each
12 for 60¢

"Cellucotton," they wrote, "is doing such wonderful work as a sanitary absorbent, that nurses are making sanitary pads from it for their own uses."

Thus when war ended, our laboratory developed the nurses' idea. For over two years experiments went on in preparing and also in marketing the new sanitary pads known as KOTEX—named from "cotton-like texture"—with the result that Kotex are now offered at a price every woman can afford in stores and shops that cater to women.

Kotex are more absorbent, cool, of lasting softness, cheap enough to throw away.

If KOTEX are not yet on sale in your neighborhood, write us for the names of nearest stores and shops that have them. Or send us sixty-five cents and we will mail you one box of a dozen Kotex in plain wrapper, charges prepaid.

CELLUCOTTON PRODUCTS CO.
208 South La Salle Street, Chicago, Illinois

INEXPENSIVE. COMFORTABLE. HYGIENIC and SAFE — KOTEX

This 1921 print ad celebrated the wartime medical experiences that led to the development of Kotex sanitary pads.
Copyright Kimberly-Clark Corporation. Used with permission.

Company, a Philadelphia, Pennsylvania, company that was started in 1879. At first, the acquisition was considered a masterful stroke, but integration problems surfaced, preventing any synergies from being realized for several years.

Consolidation of the ad agency lineup, however, came fairly quickly. Combined, the two companies spent $175 million on U.S. advertising in 1995. A year later, Scott agency J. Walter Thompson Company, New York City, joined Ogilvy & Mather Worldwide and Foote, Cone & Belding (FCB), Chicago, Illinois, as global shops. That ended relationships Scott had with McCann-Erickson Worldwide and Bozell Worldwide, both of New York City.

Kotex: Breaking Taboos

Throughout its history, Kimberly-Clark not only invented products that addressed vital, rarely talked about needs but also broke the taboo of talking about them. The company accidentally invented the category of feminine-hygiene protection; sanitary napkins were a by-product of World War I. A cotton shortage

Now a *new* way to
Remove Cold Cream

FOR years stage stars have known this secret of clear, radiant complexions. It is part of their stock-in-trade. Who ever saw an actress whose skin had infections, blackheads, pimples? Yet actresses *make-up* several times a day. Their skin is constantly exposed to hard use—yet remains charming.

Now you, too, may know this secret of famous stage beauties. It is simply the use of Kleenex in removing cold cream and cosmetics each night. This soft velvety absorbent is made of Cellucotton.

Kleenex is less expensive, *safer*, than towels or so-called clean cloths. Skin infections are often due to them.

Kleenex, at all drug and department stores, costs but 25c. A box contains about 200 sheets (size 6 by 7 in.) and lasts about a month. Use it once, throw it away. It's cheaper, better, safer. Beauty experts advise its use.

Today get a box of Kleenex and find out why it's so popular.

CELLUCOTTON PRODUCTS CO., 166 West Jackson Boulevard, Chicago

KLEENEX
The Sanitary Cold Cream Remover

In 1924 Kimberly-Clark's Cellucotton Products Company introduced a new product, a disposable sheet for removing cold cream. The product's name—Kleenex—has since come to be synonymous with the facial tissue category.
Copyright Kimberly-Clark Corporation. Used with permission.

to 1991. During his tenure, Smith restructured the company and entered new consumer businesses. He also had a knack for raiding competitors' marketing and research staffs and pushed the idea of spending extensively on advertising.

Kimberly-Clark cemented its status as a Goliath in the paper industry in 1995 with its $6.8 million acquisition of Scott Paper

Is your washroom breeding

Bolsheviks?

Employees lose respect for a company that fails to provide decent facilities for their comfort

TRY wiping your hands six days a week on harsh, cheap paper towels or awkward, unsanitary roller towels—and maybe you, too, would grumble.

Towel service is just one of those small, but important courtesies—such as proper air and lighting—that help build up the goodwill of your employees.

That's why you'll find clothlike Scot-Tissue Towels in the washrooms of large, well-run organizations such as R.C.A. Victor Co., Inc., National Lead Co. and Campbell Soup Co.

ScotTissue Towels are made of "thirsty fibre". . . an amazing cellulose product that drinks up moisture 12 times as fast as ordinary paper towels. They feel soft and pliant as a linen towel. Yet they're so strong and tough in texture they won't crumble or go to pieces . . . even when they're wet.

And they cost less, too—because one is enough to dry the hands—instead of three or four.

Write for free trial carton. Scott Paper Company, Chester, Pennsylvania.

ScotTissue Towels - *really* dry!

A 1930 ad from the J. Walter Thompson Company for ScotTissue Towels played on fears of employee disaffection, a prevalent concern at the time.
Copyright Kimberly-Clark Corporation. Used with permission.

during the war forced Kimberly-Clark to produce bandages for soldiers from a wood fiber called "cellucotton," invented by a company consultant named Ernest Mahler. Soon nurses in France began using them as sanitary napkins. After the war, in 1920, Kimberly-Clark began selling the product, called Kotex, but marketed it under a subsidiary—Cellucotton Products Company—because of the subject matter.

The first ad for Kotex, from the Charles F.W. Nichols Agency, Chicago, showed a nurse attending wounded soldiers who faced the viewer, but it was pulled before its first publication in the *Ladies' Home Journal*. "It was decided that men should not be featured in so intimate a discussion of feminine hygiene," Wallace Meyer, the ad's copywriter, later wrote. In the altered ad, which appeared shortly thereafter, three women surrounded a soldier sitting in a wheelchair, with his back to the viewer. The ad copy read, "Simplify the laundress problem. Kotex are good enough to form a habit, cheap enough to throw away and easy to dispose of. They complete the toilet essentials of the modern woman." Another ad featured a drawing of a sophisticated woman, with the headline "In the wardrobe of her royal daintiness."

To counter any embarrassment a woman might have about asking for Kotex at her local drugstore, the company picked up on the idea of a Wisconsin druggist and began wrapping Kotex packages in plain wrappers. The company also advised merchants to stack Kotex on a counter along with a box for the money. Debate continues about who actually created these first early ads for Kotex. Both the Charles F.W. Nichols Agency and Lord & Thomas took credit for the campaign.

By 1932, with the account firmly in Albert Lasker's hands at Lord & Thomas, Kimberly-Clark and its marketing had grown more daring, showing pictures of women in tight-fitting gowns to demonstrate that Kotex was invisible under clothing. A World War II-era ad encouraged women to join the nursing corps and to make sure to bring their Kotex with them. Other ads over the years showed mothers and daughters sharing knowledge about the product and descriptions of new product innovations. By 1965 Kotex controlled 62 percent of the U.S. feminine hygiene market and was spending $4 million annually on advertising.

That same year, Kotex tampons reached national distribution, and in 1966 Kimberly-Clark launched its biggest marketing push for a feminine hygiene product. To tout its Soft Impressions feminine hygiene product, Kimberly-Clark ran color spreads from FCB in 45 magazines. By the mid-1970s, Kotex was losing market share to newer entrants from competitors. It went back to the drawing board to develop new products and in June 1974 hired Kelly, Nason, Inc., of New York City to handle its account, severing its 50-year relationship with FCB.

By the turn of the century Kotex, still viewed as an older brand, was changing its advertising to attract younger consumers. "If a period is supposed to come at the end of a sentence, how come Mother Nature puts it wherever she wants, like, say, right in the middle of your beach vacation?" asked a fall 2000 commercial by Ogilvy & Mather, Chicago. Seen on the screen was black type dancing on a white background, and then punctuated by a bright red period. The tag line: "Kotex fits. Period!"

Huggies leak-resistant disposable diapers, introduced by Kimberly-Clark in 1978 with a strong ad effort, became a best-selling baby-care product. *Copyright Kimberly-Clark Corporation. Used with permission.*

Kleenex: "Swell Hankies"

Following up on its successful introduction of Kotex, Kimberly-Clark gave the world its first facial tissue, Kleenex, in 1924. It was introduced as a disposable, sanitary cold cream towel for women who were beginning to wear more makeup. After receiving letters that "Kleenex makes swell hankies," the company in 1930 began marketing Kleenex as a throwaway substitute for handkerchiefs; the pop-up tissue dispenser also made its debut. Ad copy from Lord & Thomas read, "Colds make handkerchiefs a menace but there's safety in Kleenex" and "World's worst job ended by Kleenex. No more handkerchief washing." Sales soared. Other marketing campaigns included contests for ways to use Kleenex. The first television ad aired in 1956, with a cartoon character crooning, "Soft, strong, pops up, too." That same year, Kleenex became a cosponsor of television's *Perry Como Show* on Saturday nights. A 1960s ad demonstrated Kleenex's durability, showing trumpeter Harry James's inability to blow through a Kleenex.

The popular product also played a role in Kimberly-Clark's cross-promotion efforts, which stepped up in the 1960s as the marketer moved to diversify its product lineup while also

This step may be as big as his first.

Introducing Pull-Ups® disposable training pants from Huggies:

Toilet training may be as important as your child's first step. That's why we created Pull-Ups training pants. They go on like underwear, and protect like a diaper. And that's what makes them unique. They look and feel like "big kid" pants, yet offer the protection your child needs.

Pull-Ups have tear-away side seams for easy removal, in case of messy accidents.

Pull-Ups training pants have a super absorbent pad that soaks up wetness, and a special moisture-proof layer to help protect against leakage. Even overnight. New Pull-Ups disposable training pants. When your son or daughter is ready for this big step, Pull-Ups can help.

For children 19-59 pounds. Available in limited areas.

Go on like underwear. Protect like a diaper.

In 1989 Kimberly-Clark introduced an extension of the Huggies line, Pull-Ups disposable training pants. Later campaigns for Pull-Ups revolved around the slogan, "I'm a big kid now."
Copyright Kimberly-Clark Corporation. Used with permission.

advertising the company as well as its brands. In a 1966 issue of the *Ladies' Home Journal,* a Kimberly-Clark corporate ad from FCB offered premiums such as dispensers for Kleenex and paper towels, a feminine hygiene kit for Kotex napkins for mothers of young girls, and a bath towel linked to its Delsey toilet tissue. (The company had tried to market a Kleenex brand of toilet tissue in the mid-1960s, but it was found not to be different enough from Delsey.)

By the mid-1960s, the biggest proportion of Kimberly-Clark's advertising budget, between $4 million and $5 million, was devoted to Kleenex. Product extensions included man-size tissues, juniors, purse packs, and the introduction of tortoiseshell foil boxes. But by the late 1970s, sales had stagnated, a fact Kimberly-Clark linked to its increasing use of recycled wood pulp in its tissues, which made them cheaper but less soft. The company brought back the softer texture and sales rebounded.

Among the more memorable campaigns in the 1980s was one from FCB, with the tag line, "Kleenex says bless you." One marketing stumble was Avert, a germ-killing extension of the Kleenex line introduced in 1985. The product was expensive—four times the price of Kleenex—and it actually did nothing to help the con-

sumer who bought tissues to avoid a cold. "Intellectually, it's a good idea," James D. Bernd, president of the company's household products sector, told the *Wall Street Journal* in 1987. "But the consumer said, 'No way. I'm not going to pay that price for something I have to use so my friend doesn't get my cold.'"

Kimberly-Clark went after the fast-growing, super-premium facial tissue segment with the introduction in 1993 of Kleenex Ultra, an oil-free, three-layer tissue. An early 1995 campaign from FCB used balloons to illustrate that sore noses need to be treated gingerly, highlighting the product's softness. By April 1995, 52-week sales of Ultra had topped $92 million, pushing Kleenex's total share of the $1.1 billion facial tissue category to 43.2 percent, according to Information Resources, Inc.

In March 1999 the J. Walter Thompson Company (JWT) won the estimated $100 million global ad account for Kleenex facial tissue and Cottonelle toilet tissue. FCB and its forerunner, Lord & Thomas, had been the agency for Kleenex for two long periods—since its introduction in 1924 until 1974 and again from 1983. JWT's first campaign for Kleenex used the tag line, "Thank goodness for Kleenex," replacing the long-running "Share the love, not the germs" effort from FCB. The TV spots included one showing a little boy with a runny nose running to hug his dad before he leaves for work. Kleenex comes to the rescue of the father who wants to embrace his son but stay dry in the process.

Another paper product whose marketing became cutting edge only in the 1960s was toilet tissue. Rival Procter & Gamble Company provided the segment's real excitement in 1964 when its character Mr. Whipple burst onto television, squeezing Charmin. Twenty years later, in 1984, Kimberly-Clark ended its production of Kleenex Boutique toilet tissue to focus on paper products with larger market share; despite its continued marketing of Delsey, the move was largely viewed as Kimberly-Clark's withdrawal from the market. Six years later, Kleenex-brand tissue was back, introduced with a $25 million campaign by FCB, but sales struggled.

Such spending paled in comparison to the dollars put behind a reformulated rippled-texture Kleenex Cottonelle toilet paper, which combined the Kleenex brand with Scott Paper's Cottonelle, in 1998. Kimberly-Clark's promotional tab for the new product was $100 million, more than double what it spent on the brand the previous year. The effort included 10 million free samples hung on doorknobs and an ad campaign from Ogilvy & Mather, Chicago, that carried the tag line, "Your fresh approach to toilet paper." The pitch drew on Kimberly-Clark's history of straightforwardness. Ad copy claimed Cottonelle left users "feeling cleaner than the leading brand" and called it "toilet paper," not bathroom tissue. It was the biggest marketing push in the category to date.

Disposable Diapers

What all mothers were talking about in the 1960s was the disposable diaper, and Procter & Gamble Company (P&G), which introduced its Pampers brand in 1961, had a seven-year lead over its competition. Kimberly-Clark was undeterred, however, and despite some stumbles vowed to capture significant market share.

Kimbies made its debut in 1968, and with every new city in which the brand was introduced, the marketing campaign included daytime and prime-time television spots on all three broadcast networks, coupons in newspaper ads, and extensive sampling to consumers, hospitals, and clinics. Within a year, Kimbies had gained 20 percent of the market in areas where it was available. Then Kimberly-Clark began to rest on its laurels and, in shifting its focus away from Kimbies, lost consumer interest. By the mid-1970s, sales of Kimbies were sliding, and there was talk of the company exiting the disposable diaper business completely. However, Smith remained committed and in 1978 introduced Huggies, a diaper with a new shape, better absorbency, and strong marketing support. Sales took off.

An improved Huggies Ultratrim was launched in 1992, months before P&G introduced "ultra" versions of its Pampers and Luvs brands. The redesigned diaper was more absorbent, but the design was 50 percent thinner than regular Huggies, a product attribute touted in ads by Ogilvy & Mather.

Product extensions soon began to appear. Pull-Ups toilet-training pants for toddlers were launched in 1989, to be followed by Huggies, Huggies Overnites, Pull-Ups Goodnights, and Little Swimmers swim diapers. Baby wipes under the Huggies name were introduced in 1990. By 1998 the successful marketing of product extensions tied to the Huggies brand enabled Kimberly-Clark to take the lead in the diaper stakes, with a market share topping 40 percent.

Depends: Another Groundbreaker

Incontinence products for adults also broke new ground. Depends undergarments entered the market in 1980, and a few years later, ads featuring actress June Allyson told viewers to "get back into life." The ad campaign was the first national advertising for adult incontinence products, and it was almost seven years before two of the three networks accepted spots for such products during prime time, after plenty of arm-twisting by Kimberly-Clark.

A product specifically for women, called Poise, followed, and in 1998 the line was extended to include Depends "protective underwear," disposable adult underpants that looked like regular underwear, right down to the elastic waistband. Ads from Campbell Mithun Esty touting the similarity to underwear were effective; Kimberly-Clark was unable to keep up with demand for the product.

MARY ELLEN PODMOLIK

Further Reading

Charlier, Marj, "Kimberly Clark Enlivens Market for Toilet Paper," *Wall Street Journal* (23 July 1990)
Edwards, Larry, "New Kimberly-Clark President Plans Diaper, Towel, Hygiene Share Growth," *Advertising Age* (19 February 1973)
Fox, Stephen R., *The Mirror Makers: A History of American Advertising and Its Creators*, New York: Morrow, 1984
Garfield, Bob, "Finally, a Feminine Hygiene Ad Gets Straight to the Point," *Advertising Age* (30 October 2000)
Mitchell, Cynthia, "Paper Tiger: How Kimberly Clark Wraps Its Bottom Line in Disposable Huggies," *Wall Street Journal* (23 July 1987)
Parker Pope, Tara, "The Tricky Business of Rolling Out a New Toilet Paper," *Wall Street Journal* (12 January 1998)

Kirshenbaum Bond & Partners

Founded by Richard Kirshenbaum and Jonathan Bond as Kirshenbaum & Bond, 1987; renamed Kirshenbaum Bond & Partners, 1995.

Major Clients

Blimpie International
Citibank AAdvantage Card
International House of Pancakes
Kenneth Cole New York
Mother's Cookies
Schiefflin & Somerset (Hennessy Cognac, Grand Marnier, Moët & Chandon Champagne, and Dom Perignon Champagne)
Snapple Beverage Corporation
Target Stores

Jonathan Bond, an account executive, and Richard Kirshenbaum, a copywriter, were bored with their jobs when they met in 1985. To relieve their frustration they started a freelance business and pitched an up-and-coming shoe designer, Kenneth Cole. They won the account with an all-type ad that read, "Imelda Marcos bought 2,700 pairs of shoes. She could've at least had the courtesy to buy a pair of ours." The Kenneth Cole campaign won a Clio Award, but the two ad men remained anonymous because they were still employed by larger agencies. Ironically, one day Kirshenbaum's boss at the J. Walter Thompson Company asked him why he could not create work like the Kenneth Cole ads. Kirshenbaum responded, "I did that. And I quit." Soon after, Bond left Sacks & Rosen.

With no financial backers and only one account, Kirshenbaum, 26, and Bond, 29, pooled their limited resources to sublet space in a friend's real estate firm on New York City's Madison Avenue in May 1987. Kirshenbaum & Bond (K&B) was born. The partners were determined to make it big and knew they had to create ads that made people talk. Their first opportunity came when the owners of Positano Restaurant asked them to create ads in exchange for free meals. They created an ad that looked as if it had been riddled with bullets: "An authentic Italian restaurant where no one's been shot. Yet." A credit line appeared in the corner: "Advertising Agency: Kirshenbaum & Bond."

Other clients soon followed. Like Positano and Kenneth Cole, these early clients had small budgets and needed ads that got people's attention, even if it meant creating a bit of controversy. The agency hired Donna Rice, a woman who gained notoriety through her association with one-time presidential candidate Gary Hart, to sell No Excuses jeans with the line, "I make no excuses; I only wear them." They risked offending customers with the message, "Dress British, think Yiddish," for Saint Laurie, a discount clothing store. And they introduced a new advertising medium by stenciling a message for Bamboo Lingerie on New York City sidewalks: "From here, it looks like you could use some new underwear." Kirshenbaum and Bond became known as the "ad brats."

In 1991 the brats grew up. K&B moved to New York City's trendy SoHo neighborhood, hired Nigel Carr from Chiat/Day to set up a brand-planning operation, and named Bill Oberlander a partner in the agency. Their new accounts, Coach handbags, Moët & Chandon Champagne, and Hennessy Cognac, also reflected this new sophistication. However, the agency maintained its philosophy of creating ads that got people talking. An ad for Moët & Chandon ran in the *New York Times* the day after the Gulf War ended. "Please tear this page into many small pieces and toss high into the air in celebration of peace," it read. Media across the country covered the confetti ad, and the *New York Times* ran it again for free.

In 1992, a mere five years after it opened, K&B was named one of *Adweek*'s ten hottest agencies. Recognizing the power of public relations, the agency established K&B Public Relations in 1993. The following year it added an in-house direct marketing operation.

By 1995 K&B had 175 employees and $200 million in billings. To ensure that every client had a managing partner overseeing its business, a new layer of management was put into place. Rosemarie Ryan, who had worked at K&B from 1991 to 1994, rejoined the agency as president. The three managing partners, Steve Klein, Oberlander, and Carr, assumed additional duties and reported to Bond, who was named chief executive officer, and Kirshenbaum, whose title was changed to chief creative officer/founder. To reflect the new structure, the agency was renamed Kirshenbaum Bond & Partners (KB&P).

The restructuring continued into 1996 and included a major renovation of the agency headquarters. That year KB&P won two Account Planning Group (APG) Account Planning Awards for its Citibank AAdvantage and Snapple campaigns. Ironically, the Snapple "100% natural" campaign became a victim of its own success. Quaker Oats Company bought the Snapple brand and

Dan Quayle

"Don't forget to vot."
—Kenneth Cole

In making fun of Vice President Dan Quayle's public misspelling of the word *potato*—and in omitting any mention of the product being advertised, namely shoes—this ad for Kenneth Cole from Kirshenbaum Bond & Partners typified the agency's "under-the-radar" approach to advertising.
Courtesy of Kenneth Cole Productions.

dumped KB&P. However, the year ended on a positive note, with KB&P winning the Target Stores account.

In 1997 the Art Directors Club presented a ten-year retrospective of KB&P's work, and the agency founders wrote *Under the Radar*, a book of insights on how to break through consumers' resistance to advertising. That same year, Klein started an interactive division and Carr opened KB&P/West in San Francisco, California, with Mother's Cookies as the first account.

KB&P has continued to win major clients on both coasts. In 2000 KB&P had gross income of $41 million on billings of $451.2 million, an increase of 10 percent over the previous year; also in 2000 the agency acquired the accounts of Bioré skin-care products and the Home Shopping Network, each worth an estimated $30 million in billings.

BONNIE DREWNIANY

Further Reading

Bond, Jonathan, and Richard Kirshenbaum, *Under the Radar: Talking to Today's Cynical Consumer*, New York: Wiley, 1998

Kanner, Bernice, "Brats No More: Kirshenbaum & Bond Grows Up," *New York Magazine* (20 July 1992)

Taylor, John, "The Ad Brats: Kirshenbaum & Bond Have No Shame," *New York Magazine* (13 November 1989)

Kodak. *See* Eastman Kodak Company

Kowloon-Canton Railway Corporation

(KCRC)

Principal Agencies
Ogilvy & Mather Advertising
Leo Burnett Company, Inc.
J. Walter Thompson Company

The Kowloon-Canton Railway Corporation (KCRC) is a transport operator owned by the Hong Kong government. The East Rail Division operates passenger trains that opened in 1910 with a 34-kilometer track running from the Kowloon town center to the Hong Kong–China border at Lo Wu. Trains were initially steam-powered; diesels were introduced in the 1950s, and full electrification was completed in 1983. The total number of passenger trips in 2000 was 288 million, of which 84 million passenger trips crossed the border. In 2000 the average daily ridership of the East Rail was 788,000 passenger trips. The intercity through-train services provided a link with the southern and northern cities of China as far as Shanghai and Beijing.

The Light Rail system was established in 1988 to provide passenger transport in the northwest part of the New Territories area, north of Kowloon. In 2000 the Light Rail on average carried 322,700 passenger trips a day. The Hong Kong government endorsed the building of the West Rail, a 30-kilometer domestic railway linking West Kowloon with Tuen Mun, in 1998; it was expected to be completed in 2003.

Prior to 1982, when it was part of the government structure, KCRC did not advertise. The first campaign for East Rail was launched in 1983 to announce the completion of electrification. The reduction in traveling time and increase in train frequency significantly improved the link between the New Territories and the urban area. The advertising message was "KCR makes the New Territories an integral part of Hong Kong." The campaign attempted to change the perception of the New Territories as being a remote location and to encourage people to move into the new towns being developed there. The East Rail campaign in the late 1980s promoted the convenience and efficiency of travel using slice-of-life ads. Owing to rapid population growth in the new towns, the service standard of the East Rail fell below a satisfactory level. Passengers complained about dirt, delays, and the poor design of the congested platforms. People living along the railway objected to the noise. With full passenger loads during rush hours in the early 1990s, KCRC ceased television campaigns for domestic travel on the East Rail. Instead the company used print and promotional campaigns to attract off-peak travel by publicizing trips to local attractions that were accessible along the rail.

As China opened its doors, there was a dramatic growth in travel to its mainland. Travelers were primarily businesspeople and those with family ties in China. KCRC had to compete with road and sea transport through other border points; the high cross-border passenger flow did not provide a comfortable environment. The company launched two campaigns, in 1996 and in 1997, featuring the unique benefits of its 340 trips to China each day and its offering of peace-of-mind travel for cross-border trips. The first campaign compared a frequent train schedule with that of a less-frequent one. The metaphors of a comb with few teeth and a tennis racket with a loose string were used. The second campaign featured passengers thinking about what would happen when they arrived at their destinations. These two campaigns emphasized the reliable service of KCR, which provided "an enlightening journey" for passengers, hence establishing an emotional bonding with customers. KCRC considered these narrowly focused campaigns to be effective; the growth in passenger trips was higher than that of the overall market of cross-border passenger trips carried by all public transport operators.

KCRC also ran corporate campaigns. The first one, named the "Choo-choo Train," was launched in 1991. It featured a group of children in the countryside pretending to be a train. The campaign appealed to emotions, attempting to make the train journey a memorable and dreamlike experience. It was an innovative campaign shot in Beijing and using mainland children as models. The TV commercial was supported by print advertisements. In the print ads, the company admitted its shortcomings and promised that service would be improved with new trains and the introduction of its performance pledge system. (The performance pledge system established and regularly monitored objective performance and safety indicators such as punctuality, availability of ticketing equipment, and injuries per million passengers.) The campaign's down-to-earth tone gave the company a personal and friendly touch. The commercial won awards for best music and best TV commercial in the corporate/utilities category at the 1991 Asian Advertising Awards.

The second corporate campaign, titled "The Way Ahead," was launched in 1998. The key message was that "KCRC extends the new service era by building the West Rail." It was an imaginative spot that featured a new train running across the territory using high-tech digital graphics. Unlike previous campaigns, this corporate campaign did not have the human touch. The company considered it well received, however.

KCRC had great concern about the portrayal of passenger image in the advertising campaign. Its major concern was minimizing the possible negative impact on the audiences. KCRC was extremely cautious in handling images of the passengers, avoiding the use of negative stereotypes. The railway acknowledged that as a public utility company, its weaknesses could not be concealed; it chose to focus on improved service and to redirect audience attention to its strengths.

KCRC ran advertising campaigns mainly in print media and on television, using the English, Chinese, and cable TV channels. It also sponsored a financial news program on cable TV during "The Way Ahead" campaign. The primary advertising effort focused on the local market, but occasionally KCRC conducted regional campaigns in mainland China, mainly promotions for the intercity services during trade shows periods.

KARA CHAN

See also color plate in this volume

Kraft Foods, Inc.

Principal Agencies
J. Walter Thompson Company
Needham, Louis & Brorby, Inc. (later Needham, Harper & Steers Advertising, Inc.)
Foote, Cone & Belding (later FCB Worldwide)
Ogilvy & Mather
Young & Rubicam
Leo Burnett Company

Throughout the history of Kraft Foods, Inc., advertising has played an important role in defining the company and its products, establishing its relationship with consumers, and driving its business success. Kraft has used advertising to create one of the most powerful brand portfolios in the food industry. It has also used advertising successfully to create brand value for consumers by determining their wants and needs more effectively than its competitors.

Kraft Foods, Inc., is the largest U.S.-based packaged food company. Its brand portfolio consists of more than 70 major brands, including Kraft natural and processed cheese products; Kraft box dinners and salad dressings; Maxwell House coffees; Post cereals; Oscar Mayer processed meats; Philadelphia Brand cream cheese; Kool-Aid drink mixes; Tombstone pizza; Minute Rice; Miracle Whip salad dressing; and Jell-O gelatin, pudding, and ready-to-eat snacks. Today's Kraft Foods is a result of the joining together of a number of major food companies over the years and, most notably, the acquisition by the Philip Morris Companies of Kraft, Inc., and General Foods Corporation. The advertising milestones of General Foods and Kraft—both pre- and post-acquisition—paralleled each other as these businesses developed.

A Tradition of Innovation

James L. Kraft began his cheese business in 1903 in Chicago, Illinois. Observing tremendous waste in the way that cheese was sold and recognizing the inconsistent quality of the cheese that was available to consumers, he developed a method of blending and heating a variety of natural cheeses to produce a more consistent, high-quality product. This revolutionary process was patented in 1916, the first of many patents obtained by the company. Beginning with cheese in tins marketed under the Elkhorn brand, by 1920 the company had begun producing process cheese in loaves under the Kraft brand. Since then, the company has expanded its product line through a combination of product innovations and mergers and acquisitions.

In 1930 the National Dairy Products Corporation (NDPC) acquired the Kraft-Phenix Cheese Corporation (as the company was called after Kraft's merger with Phenix Cheese Company in 1928). Kraft was an independent operating company of NDPC until it was assimilated into the parent organization, which was renamed Kraftco Corporation in 1969. The company was renamed Kraft, Inc., in 1976.

In 1988 Philip Morris Companies, Inc., acquired Kraft, Inc., and in January 1989 Kraft was merged with General Foods (which Philip Morris had acquired in 1985) to form Kraft General Foods. In January 1995 Kraft General Foods was reorganized into product-based business divisions and was renamed Kraft Foods, Inc.

J.L. Kraft was personally responsible for the early advertising efforts of his company. Kraft stressed quality and value, encouraging consumer confidence in the product. The company also introduced and trademarked the Johnny Appetite character, which was used for in-store displays and in Kraft print advertising in local markets.

In 1919 Kraft established its own advertising department. Harry Phelps was hired as the first advertising manager, and a short time later John Platt became his assistant. Phelps continued to manage Kraft's advertising through 1929. Although he then left Kraft and held jobs at three advertising agencies—Williams and Cunnyngham, Brennan-Eley Company, and Brennan-Phelps—he continued to work on the Kraft account. John Platt would later oversee Kraft's radio and television advertising until his retirement in 1962.

Early Ad Campaigns

Kraft was the first company in the cheese industry to launch a national advertising campaign. Print advertisements appeared in national women's magazines in 1919. The $40,000 campaign was conceived and created in-house by Phelps on the same desk that J.L. Kraft used to conduct business. The advertisement—"A Lone Asian Traveler," which depicted a shepherd from antiquity—featured Kraft's Elkhorn brand cheese in eight varieties. Kraft began experimenting with color advertising in 1919 and ran its first national color ad in 1921 in the *American Weekly*, a Hearst Sunday supplement. Kraft used hand-colored advertisements until the late 1940s, when the company began using color photography. In 1924, working with the General Outdoor Advertising Company, Kraft began advertising on billboards. By 1929 the company's annual advertising budget was more than $1 million.

The merger of Kraft and Phenix in 1928 led to significant changes in Kraft advertising. On 1 January 1930, the J. Walter Thompson Company (JWT) became the advertising agency for the newly formed corporation. This change reflected the demands of the international sphere in which Kraft-Phenix was operating (not dissatisfaction with the advertisements created under Phelps).

JWT was well known to Kraft-Phenix management. Phenix had been using the agency since 1922 to execute advertising campaigns for its Philadelphia Brand cream cheese, and JWT had been responsible for Kraft's advertising in England since 1927.

Kraft-Phenix's home economics department, the forerunner of today's Kraft Kitchens, was one of the company's greatest advertising assets. Established in 1924 to create educational materials for American consumers, the department provided recipes demonstrating new ways to incorporate cheese into meals. Through the years, Kraft has offered recipes through print advertisements, commercials, in-store displays, direct-mail campaigns, and promotions. Even as advertising media have changed, much of the focus of Kraft's advertising is still recipe based.

Although Kraft executives had originally been skeptical of radio's effectiveness as an ad medium, the company's radio advertising soon began to complement its print efforts and quickly became an integral part of the advertising mix. Kraft-Phenix first took to the airwaves in 1929, when it became one of the sponsors of the *Forecast Radio School of Cooking* program. It remained a sponsor of the program through the 1931 season.

The program featured recipes using the sponsor's products. Consumers could enroll in the school and obtain recipe cards from shows that aired during that week. In addition Kraft-Phenix sent its own recipe brochures to consumers who requested them. Commercials featuring recipes created in the Kraft Kitchens were also broadcast during the program. The show was presented three mornings a week over National Broadcasting Company (NBC) stations to homes in the eastern and midwestern sections of the United States.

Kraft-Phenix expanded its radio reach to the West Coast later in 1929 by becoming a sponsor of the *Woman's Magazine Hour*, which followed a format similar to that of the *Forecast Radio School of Cooking*. In 1931 Kraft also sponsored the *Hiram and Henry* show, which aired on more than 10 stations in the southeastern United States. This comedy program failed to meet the company's expectations, however, and was discontinued after the first year.

In 1930 Kraft-Phenix was acquired by NDPC. On 15 March 1931, NDPC inaugurated its radio programs with Sunday evening broadcasts on the NBC radio network. Advertisements for Kraft-Phenix products and other NDPC subsidiaries were broadcast throughout the programs, which covered famous trials in history and featured the noted attorneys Clarence Darrow and Dudley Field Malone. During the summer of 1931, the program format was changed to light and semi-classical music, and the program was expanded to Tuesday evenings and broadcast over 27 NBC stations across the United States.

The 1930s and 1940s

During the 1930s Kraft-Phenix began to bring its products directly to consumers through exhibitions and world's fairs. The 1933 Century of Progress Exhibition in Chicago, Illinois, served as the stage from which Kraft launched its Miracle Whip salad dressing; visitors to the Agricultural and Foods Building could watch the product being made in a glass-enclosed, air-conditioned room. The consumer response was dramatic—within a short time demand for Miracle Whip was so great that stores could not keep it on their shelves. In the second year of the exhibition, Kraft demonstrated production of its Philadelphia Brand cream cheese.

At the San Diego California Pacific International Exposition in 1935, Kraft featured displays of cheese and salad dressing

International packaged-foods giant Kraft Foods, Inc., started out in 1903 as a small wholesale cheese business owned by James L. Kraft. By 1925, when this ad was created, Kraft was a widely recognized brand.
KRAFT is a registered trademark of Kraft Foods Holdings, Inc.

production. Kraft products were also offered for sale. The New York World's Fair (1939–40) featured a similar exhibit and a lunch counter.

Encouraged by its initial sales results for Miracle Whip salad dressing in the eastern United States, Kraft decided to drive sales even higher by offering consumers a "double-your-money-back" guarantee. To launch this offer, Kraft worked with JWT to develop a radio program for the company. The agency suggested a musical variety program hosted by Paul Whiteman and his orchestra, with Deems Taylor as master of ceremonies. Kraft and JWT wanted the program to be something special. They decided that the program would be extended to two hours and that Al Jolson would appear as a special guest star. The premiere broadcast was on 26 June 1933 to the New York City metropolitan area, with a one-hour feed to audiences in New England. Rather than cut off Jolson in the middle of his finale, "Sonny Boy," Kraft bought an additional 15 minutes of airtime from NBC—as the program was being broadcast!

The *Kraft Musical Revue,* as the program was initially called, was an overwhelming success, as was Miracle Whip. The Association of National Advertisers ranked the program as one of radio's four most popular shows within two months of its initial airdate. The *Revue* aired on 53 NBC stations every week, and JWT signed Jolson to the program for the following season, which began on 3 August 1933.

One of the program's best features was its unobtrusive, soft-sell commercials. Initially, the commercials employed just about every available gimmick. When it soon became apparent that this approach was not going to work, JWT devised a more conversational and straightforward commercial style for announcer Ken Carpenter. The change was remarkable, and the commercials were extremely effective advertisements, first for Miracle Whip and later for Philadelphia Brand cream cheese and Kraft cheese spreads in reusable Swankyswig glass containers.

In the January 1934 issue of Kraft's employee newspaper *Cheesekraft,* John Platt, Kraft's advertising manager, observed that radio had become a primary ad medium for the company, joining print and in-store displays in promoting Kraft products. Platt noted, however, that Kraft's success in radio had been built upon a solid foundation of print advertising during the previous 15 years. Therefore, while radio would continue to be the choice for advertising newer, lesser-known Kraft brands, the more prominent brands would also be advertised in magazines. Thus, in the fall of 1933 the company placed magazine advertisements featuring trays of cheese to encourage consumers to purchase a greater variety and quantity of cheeses. Kraft began offering retailers serving trays for cheese known as Kraftrays for consumer purchase during the early summer of 1934.

The popularity of the *Kraft Musical Revue* continued despite Jolson's frequent absences due to film commitments. He left the program during 1934 and then returned as host from 1947 to 1949. JWT filled the void with various guest hosts. The program underwent a series of name changes during the 1934 season. It was referred to as the *Kraft All-Star Revue, Paul Whiteman's Musical Hall,* and finally *Kraft Music Hall.*

At this time, radio producers were increasingly interested in casting big stars, and Kraft and JWT decided in 1935 to move production from New York City to Hollywood in order to have better access to current stars. Whiteman elected to remain in the East and served as the program's host until Bing Crosby took over in January 1936. A friend of Whiteman's, having toured with him in the late 1920s, Crosby was a radio veteran.

The hour-long variety show format of *Kraft Music Hall* suited Crosby's many talents. (The program was cut to a half-hour in 1942.) Guest stars included Henry Fonda, Bob Hope, Mary Martin, and Jimmy Stewart, along with regular performers Bob Burns, Victor Borge, and orchestra leader John Scott Trotter. Each program featured a segment showcasing a variety of musical formats, including opera, jazz, and classical. JWT continued to write, produce, direct, and book talent for the program.

Crosby hosted *Kraft Music Hall* through July 1946. Subsequent hosts of the program were Eddy Duchin, Edward Everett Horton, Eddie Foy, Al Jolson, and Oscar Levant. The show went off the air on NBC after the 1949 summer season. It was reprised briefly on the CBS radio network in 1955 with Rudy Vallee—and later Mitch Miller—as master of ceremonies.

In addition to *Kraft Music Hall,* Kraft sponsored the many other radio shows, most of which were summer replacement programs for the *Music Hall: The Great Gildersleeve* (1941–54); *Summerfield Band Concert* (1947); *The Adventures of Archie Andrews* (1949); *Marriage for Two* (1949–50); *The Falcon* (1950–51); *Queen for a Day* (1951–52); *The Bobby Benson Show* (1951–52); *The Edgar Bergen Show* (1954); and *Kraft Five Star Newscast* (1955–57). In Canada Kraft sponsored *Le Cafe-Concert Kraft* (1941–50), a program similar to the *Music Hall.*

The most notable of these shows was NBC's *The Great Gildersleeve,* produced by Needham, Louis & Brorby, Inc., Chicago. It was also broadcast to Canadian audiences in 1949 over the Dominion network. This comedy featured Harold Perry and later Willard Waterman in the title role and initially aired on Sunday and later on Wednesday evenings. The program, set in the fictitious village of Summerfield, featured a cast that seemed to be as familiar as the neighbors down the street. The main character, Throckmorton P. Gildersleeve, originated in 1939 as a supporting character on the *Johnson Wax Program with Fibber McGee and Molly,* also produced by Needham, Louis & Brorby. The comic possibilities of Gildersleeve seemed so rich that the agency decided to create a separate show around him. It is said to have been the first spin-off in network broadcasting history.

The principal product advertised on these programs was Parkay margarine, which was introduced in 1940. Other products advertised on the program, such as Kraft Macaroni and Cheese Dinner, were handled by JWT.

In 1978, Kraft sponsored radio specials as part of its 75th anniversary. During that same year, it sponsored the *Ossie Davis/Ruby Dee Story Hour* series, and in the 1980s Kraft sponsored various radio specials.

In a 1938 speech to the Chicago Federated Advertising Club, Kraft advertising manager Platt reviewed the company's philosophy of radio advertising, insisting that entertainment and advertising must be kept separate and distinct. (For this reason, Kraft insisted that an announcer, not cast members, read its commercials.) According to Platt, quality entertainment led listeners up to the commercials, dropped them into the commercials, and took them back to the show. To be effective, Kraft commercials were single-product-focused, short, and to the point. Although this formula evolved through time (with cast members frequently joining the announcer), its basic principles remained intact.

Foray into TV

Kraft began television advertising on an experimental basis in 1947. The decision to move to television was based in part on the belief of the company's executives that the new visual medium would give it a competitive advantage in advertising food products. The first one-hour live drama series on television, the *Kraft Television Theatre,* premiered on 7 May 1947 with an episode entitled "Double Door," broadcast on NBC station WNBT to the New York City area, which at the time had reportedly fewer than 8,000 television sets. The series was produced and directed by JWT. Kraft decided to air the program on Wednesday evenings so that it would not compete with *Kraft Music Hall* on radio. Not surprisingly, however, as television's popularity grew, Kraft's presence on radio began to wane. To test the effectiveness of the new medium, a less well known Kraft product, Mac Laren's Cheese, was advertised on the early TV programs. This premium-priced cheese had received little Kraft advertising support prior to these commercials. Although critics' reactions to the early programs were mixed, the cheese flew off store shelves. The experiment had worked, and Kraft began advertising one of its more popular products—Kraft Mayonnaise—on television in 1947, supplementing a national print and radio campaign for the brand.

Kraft Television Theatre was well suited to early television. The year-long weekly broadcasts featured competent performers in adaptations of stage plays, novels, and occasional original works. The quickly expanding NBC television network soon provided Kraft with a nationwide audience. For more than a year, beginning in October 1953, the program was presented live on both the NBC and ABC networks, appearing on the latter network on Thursday evenings. Success and critical acclaim for the show increased as it matured. The teleplay "Patterns," written by Rod Serling, won an Emmy Award in 1955. The 1956 broadcast of "A Night to Remember," a reenactment of the *Titanic*'s last hours, was highly praised by the critics and the public.

In Kraft's television commercials during these programs, the product was the star. All of these commercials were recipe based and developed in the Kraft Kitchens in Chicago. To ensure accuracy, Kraft sent the studio still photographs depicting the steps of the recipe. With voice-over by Ed Herlihy, the ads became known as "hands commercials" because they showed only the hands of the demonstrator. This style of presentation, Kraft's ad executives reasoned, would help the homemaker to imagine herself preparing the recipe in her kitchen. Herlihy served as the voice of Kraft for more than 40 years.

Kraft was one of the first commercial sponsors to recognize the potential of television. This 1953 ad was created for distribution to local media to promote the *Kraft Television Theatre,* which offered original TV programming.
Reprinted Courtesy of Kraft Foods Holdings, Inc.

A commercial featuring a clam dip made with Philadelphia Brand cream cheese and a recipe booklet offer exemplifies the effectiveness of the "hands" approach. Two days after the commercial aired, grocery stores sold out of canned clams, and the response to the recipe booklet offer was 500 percent greater than anticipated.

Kraft was the first advertiser to air food commercials in color. The company, working with JWT, began experimenting with broadcasting color commercials in 1953, despite the scarcity of color television sets at the time. In 1956 Kraft began broadcasting the entire *Kraft Television Theatre* show in color every Wednesday night. The lessons and experience gained from working on these commercials proved invaluable as color TV gained wide acceptance.

NDPC's Kraft and Sealtest units (which became separate divisions in 1957) also sponsored children's TV programming in the 1950s. From 1951 to 1956, Sealtest sponsored CBS's *Big Top,* which originated from Philadelphia, Pennsylvania. As its name implied, the live, hour-long Saturday afternoon program featured circus acts. The divisions' products were advertised by actors throughout the performance. Sealtest withdrew its sponsorship in December 1956 and became a sponsor of NBC's *Shirley Temple's Storybook* anthology series in 1958.

Kraft also sponsored *Tom Corbett, Space Cadet* from January through June 1955 on NBC. This program depicted a world of interplanetary peace, devoid of violence and killing. Kraft advertised its confection products—Kraft caramels and marshmallows—on this Saturday afternoon series. In addition Kraft sponsored another program intended for a more select audience. Broadcast from Davenport, Iowa, *The Kraft Dairy Farm Hour* aired in 1954. In 1957 Kraft began telecasting 10 separate live commercials on NBC on Thursday afternoons between noon and 3:15 p.m.

In April 1958 Talent Associates, Ltd., took over production responsibility for *Kraft Television Theatre* from JWT. By that time, 650 episodes had been produced from 18,845 submitted scripts featuring nearly 4,000 actors and actresses, who put in 26,000 hours of rehearsal time and used 5,236 sets. As a result of the change in producers, the program's title was changed to *Kraft Theatre*. The format and title of the series were changed again when *Kraft Mystery Theatre* began airing in June 1958. The final episode of the series aired on 1 October 1958.

The demise of *Kraft Television Theatre* did not signal a decision to stop sponsoring quality television programming. On 8 October 1958, Kraft filled the Wednesday evening time slot with two half-hour programs: Milton Berle starring in a revival of the *Kraft Music Hall* and *Bat Masterson*, a western starring Gene Barry. Berle's tenure as host of the *Kraft Music Hall* lasted until 13 May 1959. The following week English comedian Dave King began serving as host for the summer replacement series, *Kraft Music Hall Presents the Dave King Show*. This show, along with *Bat Masterson*, aired until 23 September 1959. Perry Como hosted the weekly *Kraft Music Hall* during the 1959 through 1963 television seasons. Broadcast on NBC and the Canadian Broadcasting Company (CBC), this hour-long musical variety program featured Como and guests engaging in comedy skits, singing, and dancing. Commercials for Kraft now departed from the "hands" theme. Taped commercials with voice-over by Herlihy occasionally also featured the program's host. In addition, this program was produced by Roncom Productions instead of a Kraft advertising agency.

In 1960 Kraft sponsored two half-hour shows, *Happy* and *Tate*, produced by Roncom as summer replacements for the *Kraft Music Hall*. *Kraft Mystery Theatre*, an hour-long dramatic anthology, aired as a 16-week summer replacement series from 1961 through 1963. It was hosted by Frank Gallop—Como's announcer on *Kraft Music Hall*.

Beginning in the fall of 1963 *Perry Como's Kraft Music Hall* was broadcast as a series of seven specials, interspersed with other Kraft-sponsored programming. The Como program continued in this format through the 1966–67 season. Kraft ensured continuity in its media presence by sponsoring dramatic anthologies, westerns, and musical variety programs during the time slot. Initially, *Kraft Suspense Theatre*—an anthology drama series—was broadcast year-round between 1963 and 1965. This series, featuring well-known actors, was produced by Revue Productions and Roncom Productions.

Kraft elected to go with an all-music variety series for the 1965–66 season. *Kraft Music Hall Presents the Andy Williams Show* was interspersed with the seven Como specials. John Davidson hosted the *Kraft Summer Music Hall* during the summer of 1966. The dramatic one-hour western *The Road West*, starring Barry Sullivan, aired during the 1966–67 season.

Kraft Music Hall did not have a permanent host from 1967 through the 1970 regular season. All episodes were independent, variety-themed productions. Beginning in 1968, the *Country Music Awards* were broadcast as part of the series. Kraft sponsored this program through 1987, and from 1969 through 1987, the company was a co-sponsor of *America's Junior Miss Program*. *Kraft Music Hall* continued during the summers from 1969 through 1971. These programs featured English performers Tony Sandler and Ralph Young as hosts in 1969 and Des O'Connor as host in 1970 and 1971.

By the fall of 1971, Kraft no longer sponsored a weekly TV program. Instead, the company sponsored five or six annual specials, in addition to a dedicated schedule of advertising in network prime time, daytime, and children's programming. This change allowed Kraft to provide a broad advertising base with greater flexibility for the growth of its products. These specials attracted a large audience, not only because of the quality of the broadcast but also because of the Kraft recipes. Consumers looked to Kraft to provide meal solutions, and this advertising met that need. These commercials created a high level of consumer awareness for Kraft products. To further enhance consumer interest, in 1975 Kraft began placing recipes in advertising inserts in *TV Guide* magazine during the weeks that the specials aired. Kraft sponsorship of specials and this *TV Guide* tie-in continued until late 1987. The recipe strategy was also a constant presence in the major homemaking magazines targeted to women, and it continues to be a presence today.

In 1978 Kraft undertook what was then the most extensive marketing campaign in the company's history. This campaign recognized the 75th anniversary of J.L. Kraft's founding of the company. Foote, Cone, & Belding created the "family reunion" theme to celebrate 75 years of bringing good food and families together. The campaign had its own theme music and featured three television specials, including the *Kraft 75th Anniversary Special*. A radio special, consumer promotions, and sweepstakes were also part of the campaign.

Since 1968 Kraft has supplemented its prime-time television advertising with daytime spot advertising. The use of spot television advertising was increased to provide for maximum flexibility in local markets, to give exposure to a particular product, and to expand into specific geographic areas.

Spotlight on Brands

Since the 1980s, Kraft has told separate stories for each of its brands in 30-second commercials. Some of Kraft's more memorable campaigns include the Parkay margarine talking container (Needham, Harper, & Steers); "Annie," the young spokeswoman for Kraft Macaroni and Cheese Dinner (Foote, Cone & Belding); and the 10-year series of commercials for Miracle Whip Salad Dressing (JWT), featuring consumers lamenting that they have run out of the product.

One of the longest-running campaigns for a Kraft brand featured Bill Cosby. He became the spokesman for General Foods' Jell-O brand pudding and gelatin in 1974, long before General Foods and Kraft were merged in 1989. By 2002 he had appeared in more than 80 commercials for the brand, all from Young & Rubicam.

In 1992 Kraft returned to network television sponsorship after a five-year hiatus. *The Secret,* starring Kirk Douglas, debuted as the first *Kraft Premier Movie.* Premier movies provided a showcase environment for Kraft brand advertising. These quality, wholesome family programs have been broadcast each year except 1996. Also in 1992, Kraft became one of the major sponsors of the *Essence* Awards program. The awards are presented annually to African-Americans of note by *Essence* magazine.

Kraft's advertising efforts were not confined to network television. Cable television provided additional opportunities to reach consumers, and Kraft entered the cable arena in 1980. It was a charter advertiser on CBS Cable, a fine arts channel, where it re-ran episodes of *Kraft Music Hall.* In 1981 it sponsored the first cable mini-series, *Robert Louis Stevenson's Kidnapped,* on WTBS, with commercials from JWT. The company also placed commercials on MTV, the Cable News Network, and the Satellite News Channel.

In the 1990s Kraft and its agencies continued to explore ways to maximize the potential of television. In 1994 Kraft determined that strategic alliances among brands would lead to synergies in advertising, marketing, sales, and promotions, and the company accordingly created the Kids Marketing Task Force, which united 25 individual Kraft brands into the Kraft "Kids Brands."

In March 1996 Kraft and the cable network Nickelodeon formed an exclusive alliance for an integrated advertising, promotional, and marketing campaign centered on the network's Nick in the Afternoon programming. A special 1996 back-to-school event linking the network's programming and the Kraft "Kids Brands" was the most successful children's promotion in the history of Kraft Foods. In February 1998 a landmark alliance was formed between Kraft Foods, Tele-Communications, Inc. (TCI), and Grey Advertising to develop proprietary advertising and marketing programs. Using TCI's digital network, the coalition hoped to create micro-advertising applications to reach consumers on a house-by-house basis.

The success of the Kraft "Kids Brands" provided the model for an unprecedented initiative to tell consumers about Kraft products in an entirely new way. In August 1998 Kraft unveiled its Kraft Foods Equity (KFE) campaign to consumers. Created by JWT, this campaign was Kraft's first integrated marketing program that consistently leveraged all of the company's brands. KFE employed broad-based marketing strategies, including documentary-style print and television advertisements featuring consumers and their families; charitable giving; toll-free numbers; consumer promotions; direct mail campaigns; and Internet programming.

Kraft has also been a pioneer in the use of the Internet to reach consumers, through the Kraft Interactive Kitchen Web site launched in September 1996. Its genesis was the Kraft Kitchens, originally established in 1924. The Web site addresses a wide range of meal preparation needs and contains a cookbook featuring more than 600 recipes created by the Kraft Kitchens.

KFE's message was directed at mothers, Kraft's primary consumers, suggesting that Kraft wanted to help women connect with their families through food. The company used a variety of marketing programs, including the Kraft Kitchens, to demonstrate its understanding of consumers' needs and its desire to help make family mealtime an enjoyable and rewarding experience. KFE did not supplant brand advertising; it complemented such efforts.

Award-winning Creative Work

Kraft advertising campaigns have been recognized for their quality, execution, and effectiveness by advertising associations, publications, and organizations. Recent awards have included the Easter Seals 1995 Grand EDI Award for the Kraft Singles Moonbeams commercial (JWT); the David Ogilvy Award, presented by the Advertising Research Foundation, to Post cereals in 1997 (Grey Advertising), Miracle Whip (JWT) and Kraft salad dressings (Leo Burnett Company) in 1998, and Velveeta (Burnett), DiGiorno Rising Crust Pizza (FCB), and Shake 'n Bake (Ogilvy & Mather) in 1999; and the American Marketing Association's Effie Awards for Post Waffle Crisp and Post Honeycomb cereals ads (Grey Advertising), DiGiorno Rising Crust Pizza (FCB), Altoids mints (Burnett), Tang (Ogilvy & Mather), and Good Seasons salad dressings (JWT) in 1997, and Miracle Whip salad dressing (JWT) and Tang (Ogilvy & Mather) in 1998. The magazine advertising for Altoids mints (Burnett) won the 1998 grand prize Kelly Award for General Advertising Excellence from the Magazine Publishers of America. Throughout Kraft's history, its ads have both reflected and shaped the popular culture of the nation—by bringing some of the best-known brand names into consumers' homes and making them a part of their everyday lives.

As of 2000 Kraft's billing in the United States stood at $800 million, divided among four main agencies: JWT, Burnett, Ogilvy & Mather, and Young & Rubicam. The company was reported to be planning a consolidation of media-buying activity with a single agency, although creative work was expected to continue to be shared by the four agencies.

MICHAEL R. BULLINGTON

Kraft natural and process cheese products, Kraft box dinners and salad dressings, Maxwell House coffees, Post cereals, Oscar Mayer processed meats, Philadelphia Brand cream cheese, Kool-Aid drink mixes, Tombstone pizza, Minute Rice, Miracle Whip salad dressing, Jell-O gelatins, puddings and ready-to-eat snacks, DiGiorno Rising Crust Pizza, Altoids mints, Tang, Good Seasons salad dressings, Shake 'n Bake, and Kraft Interactive Kitchens are registered trademarks of Kraft Foods Holdings, Inc. The information contained in this article is from corporate records housed in the Kraft Foods, Inc., Archives Department.

See also color plate in this volume

L

Labatt Brewing Company

Principal Agencies
J. Walter Thompson Company
Ammirati Puris Lintas

The Labatt Brewing Company is one of two major Canadian breweries competing for domination of the Canadian marketplace. The Canadian beer market represents $11 billion (Canadian) in annual sales, with Labatt and its major rival, Molson, accounting for 91 percent of sales. Microbreweries, regional breweries, and imports share the remaining 9 percent. Labatt has five breweries across the country. Labatt Blue is Canada's best-selling brand and holds approximately 12 percent of the market. In addition, Labatt has a portfolio of leading Canadian brands designed to appeal to a wide range of tastes, including John Labatt Classic, Labatt Genuine Draft, Labatt Wildcat, Labatt Ice, Labatt "50," and Kokanee. Labatt also brews Budweiser and Bud Light under license from Anheuser-Busch, and Carlsberg and Carlsberg Light under license from Carlsberg of Copenhagen. Budweiser is the third-best-selling beer in the country, making Canada one of the largest markets for Anheuser-Busch outside the United States.

150 Years of Tradition

Originally named John Labatt's Brewery, the company was founded in 1847 in the town of London, Ontario, by John Kinder Labatt, who had a passion for the brewing industry, as well as business knowledge. Labatt's first brewery produced about 1,000 bottles of beer a year. The biggest problem facing early brewers was getting the product to market. Labatt quickly realized that the Great Western Railway, completed in the late 1850s, was the company's ticket to expansion. Shipping beer by rail allowed the local brewery to expand nationally.

John Labatt, Jr., took over the family business when his father died in 1866. The brewery continued to be committed to quality and innovation. To promote the quality of its products, Labatt devoted its marketing efforts to international expositions and fairs. These efforts soon reaped rewards; in 1876 Labatt won the silver medal at the Dominion of Canada Exposition in Ottawa, Ontario, for its India Pale Ale. For the next 35 years India Pale Ale claimed prizes at worldwide competitions and was the first of many Labatt beers to gain international recognition. Demand for the brewer's products grew in both Canada and the United States. Although Labatt faced significant challenges during U.S. Prohibition—the period of time (1919–33) when laws were enacted forbidding the manufacture and sale of alcohol—the brewery survived as one of only 15 in Canada. Since the advertising of alcoholic beverages was severely restricted during this period, Labatt looked for other ways to build ties with its markets. It supported community service programs such as the Labatt's Highway Courtesy Program as well as a number of social causes, allowing the brewer to strengthen its ties with the public and maintain healthy product sales.

In 1934 John S. Labatt, a descendant of the founder, was kidnapped for three days by the criminals Michael Francis "Three Fingered Abe" McCardell, Albert Pegram, and Russell Knowles. Although he was released unharmed, the experience made him a virtual recluse. As a consequence, Hugh MacKenzie emerged as an important figure in the company's history— first as comptroller, then as sales manager, and later as general manager. MacKenzie was a savvy businessman, leading Labatt out of the Depression, through World War II, and into a period of rapid expansion. During this period, Labatt bolstered sales through sponsorship of popular radio shows in the province of Quebec, Canada, and in Buffalo, New York. The company also founded its own advertising department and produced its first color magazine ads.

During World War II Labatt developed a campaign promoting tourism in Canada as a means of bringing in U.S. currency. U.S. currency was important to Canada as the country struggled to buy war supplies. In 1945 Labatt became publicly traded. Throughout the 1950s the company acquired a number of breweries and developed nationally. The 1950s also marked the introduction of two classic Canadian beers brewed by Labatt—its Fiftieth Anniversary Ale, later named "50," and its pilsner lager, Blue.

Early in its history Labatt's advertising consisted of little more than posters for local bars. Bar advertising was important since

Labatt used its association with the Toronto Blue Jays baseball team to advertise its Blue brand beer, as seen in this 1983 ad from a game program.
© *1983 Labatt Brewing Company Limited.*

home consumption of beer was not widespread in Canada in the late 19th century. Early newspaper ads touted the wholesome properties of Labatt's beer. During the 1920s and 1930s provincial liquor laws prevented companies from advertising specific brands. Labatt's communication strategy at this time focused on its community involvement; its ads highlighted ways in which it supported causes that helped the national welfare, such as its disaster relief efforts for flood victims. Labatt's commitment to Canadian welfare would continue into the 21st century, providing funding and assistance for a wide range of environmental and charitable initiatives.

During the 1950s and 1960s Labatt's advertising shifted; ads began to focus on the product itself and its taste profile. Only when the brewer hired the J. Walter Thompson Company and started advertising on television in the late 1960s did it begin associating its product with the lifestyle images of its target audience. In 1981 Labatt aired the first TV commercial advocating responsible use of its products. In 2000 Labatt marketed and advertised its products around the world. Its relationships with brewers such as Belgium-based Interbrew and Mexico's Fomento

Económico Mexicano, S.A. de C.V. (FEMSA), allowed the company to tap into international markets.

Throughout its history, Labatt has been a constant innovator in terms of both its products and its advertising. It was the first Canadian brewer to introduce a light beer and the first to form an international licensing agreement with a major U.S. brewery. Labatt also revolutionized beer packaging with the introduction of the first twist-off cap on a refillable bottle, and it created a whole new brewing technology with the introduction of its trademarked Ice Brewing process.

Blue—Number One in Canada

Labatt Blue was originally branded Pilsener Lager. People began calling it "Blue" because of the color of the label and Labatt's support of the Canadian Football League's (CFL) Winnipeg franchise, the Blue Bombers. During the 1960s and 1970s Labatt concentrated on developing its Blue brand nationally and turned to television to build its market share. In 1979 Blue became Canada's top beer brand.

Blue has been the focus of some of the company's most successful marketing campaigns. Labatt's use of memorable music became a hallmark of its advertising strategy in the 1960s. Many Canadians were humming the tune "When You're Smiling," the song Labatt used as a theme for Blue commercials. The music, combined with the Labatt Blue Balloon, became the symbol of a "free spirit" that was the measure of the time. Labatt's use of music as a strategic advertising tool moved beyond commercials, however. The company went on to sponsor music events and national concert tours, "Brought to you by Labatt Blue." At the start of the 21st century Labatt was one of Canada's most prolific advertisers.

Despite its long experience, Labatt has made some mistakes. Throughout the 1980s and 1990s, it tried a variety of positioning strategies for its flagship brand, Labatt Blue; these constant changes were a factor in the brand's muddled image. Research in the late 1990s revealed that the beer had lost its appeal to younger drinkers. Men age 19 to 24, the prime target market for Blue, saw it as an outdated brand, and some viewed it as "my Dad's beer." Such associations could have meant disaster for the brand. After extensive research, the marketer uncovered one key theme that appealed to its young target audience: young males associated beer with good times and spontaneity. It was this crucial insight that helped Labatt reposition the brand using its new theme "Out of the Blue," a tag line that captured the audience's desire for spontaneity, while uniquely associating such fun with the brand name. Blue's market share rose from about 10 percent to more than 12 percent over the course of 1998.

Integrated marketing communications was another means of building the brand equity of Labatt Blue. The advertising strategy integrated four important communication components: television advertising, music, sports sponsorship, and on-line loyalty marketing. The use of sports to promote its core brands began in the 1950s and would continue into the 21st century. Labatt owns 90 percent of the Toronto Blue Jays baseball team and 100 percent of the Argonauts football team. In 1997 it formed a partnership (effective for the 1998–99 broadcast season) with the National Hockey League and sponsored Saturday night televised games. It also sponsored the Toronto Raptors and the Vancouver Grizzlies of the National Basketball Association. Labatt has also been the sponsor of National Football League telecasts in Canada since 1986.

Labatt's sponsorship efforts have ranged from support for the Olympic Games in Calgary, Alberta, in 1988 to support of such grassroots sports activities as local slo-pitch tournaments and curling and fishing derbies.

Through its Web site, interactive kiosks in bars, and a magazine sent to members of the programs, Labatt promotes the Labatt Most Valuable Patron program, a database-driven, direct-marketing program used to reward its best customers and to inform them of special events and promotions. Labatt sees direct marketing as a valuable tool through which it can develop better profiles of its key customers and their preferences.

PEGGY CUNNINGHAM

Further Reading

Boisseau, Peter, "The Suds Stud," *Canadian Business* 70, no. 8 (July 1997)

Bosworth, David, and Laura Pratt, "Retrospective: Labatt Celebrates 150 Years," *Strategy: The Canadian Marketing Report* (23 June 1997)

Dingwall, James, George Clements, and Alan Middleton, editors, *Canadian Advertising Success Stories: Cassies,* Toronto: Canadian Congress of Advertising, 1994

Menzies, David, "Game On," *Marketing* 103, no. 38 (October 1998)

150: Good Things Brewing for 150 Years, Labatt, Toronto: *Marketing* Magazine, 1997

Lambert Pharmaceutical

Principal Agencies
Lambert & Feasley, Inc.
J. Walter Thompson Company

Lambert Pharmaceutical's Listerine (initially its sole product) started out as a remedy in search of a disease: in order for its product to succeed as a mouthwash, the St. Louis, Missouri–based company first had to invent halitosis, or bad breath. Next, it had to convince the American public of the dire consequences of this condition. It was a classic example of "constructive discontent"—a fabricated problem devised to sell a product.

At the end of the 19th century the English surgeon Joseph Lister developed a surgical antiseptic that was so toxic it could only be used with great care lest it damage surrounding tissue. An American named Jordan Wheat Lambert synthesized a less powerful version of the antiseptic and journeyed to England to ask Lister if he could use the already-famous name for the product. Lister was flattered and gave his approval. Lambert added the *-ine* suffix (indicating a liquid) to make it sound scientific.

Listerine was used not only for minor surgical procedures but also for all kinds of cleaning. Soon it came to be used as a floor cleanser, an aftershave, a nasal douche, a treatment for gonorrhea, even a scalp treatment for dandruff and baldness.

Inevitably it was discovered that Listerine was also good at killing germs in the mouth. In 1895 it was marketed to the dental profession, and in 1914 it became one of the first prescription products to be sold over the counter. (It still carried the American Dental Association's seal of approval in the 21st century.) But as yet there was no hint of its use as a mouth deodorant.

In the early 1900s Jordan and his wife died, leaving Lambert Pharmacal to their four sons. One son, Gerard, proved to be a business genius. In 1921 he summoned the two copywriters working on Listerine, Milton Fuessle and Gordon Seagrove, from Chicago, Illinois, to discuss their work. Although the human mouth had been recognized as a haven for germs, no one had yet focused on breath odor as a symptom of disease. As the three men were discussing the possibility that bad breath could be used as an "advertising hook," Lambert called for the company chemist. He wrote an account of the meeting in his book *All Out of Step:*

> When [the chemist] came into our room, I asked him if Listerine was good for bad breath. He excused himself for a moment and came back with a big book of newspaper clippings. He sat in a chair and I stood looking over his shoulder. He thumbed through the immense book.
>
> "Here it is, Gerard. It says in this clipping from the British *Lancet* that in cases of halitosis . . ." I interrupted, "What is halitosis?" "Oh," he said, "that is the medical term for bad breath."

Lambert took up the idea of halitosis and made it the central focus of his advertising. He made a pledge to increase his advertising each month by the same percentage as the increase of sales, and he claimed that he would stop only when sales leveled off.

Often a bridesmaid but never a bride

EDNA'S case was really a pathetic one. Like every woman, her primary ambition was to marry. Most of the girls of her set were married—or about to be. Yet not one possessed more grace or charm or loveliness than she.

And as her birthdays crept gradually toward that tragic thirty-mark, marriage seemed farther from her life than ever.

She was often a bridesmaid but never a bride.

* * *

That's the insidious thing about halitosis (unpleasant breath). You, yourself, rarely know when you have it. And even your closest friends won't tell you.

Sometimes, of course, halitosis comes from some deep-seated organic disorder that requires professional advice. But usually—and fortunately—halitosis is only a local condition that yields to the regular use of Listerine as a mouth wash and gargle. It is an interesting thing that this well-known antiseptic that has been in use for years for surgical dressings, possesses these unusual properties as a breath deodorant.

It halts food fermentation in the mouth and leaves the breath sweet, fresh and clean. Not by substituting some other odor but by really removing the old one. The Listerine odor itself quickly disappears. So the systematic use of Listerine puts you on the safe and polite side.

Your druggist will supply you with Listerine. He sells lots of it. It has dozens of different uses as a safe antiseptic and has been trusted as such for a half a century. Read the interesting little booklet that comes with every bottle.
—*Lambert Pharmacal Company, Saint Louis, U.S.A.*

For HALITOSIS use LISTERINE

Listerine made "Often a bridesmaid but never a bride" one of the most famous advertising headlines of its time and introduced the word *halitosis* into the popular vocabulary with this 1924 ad.
LISTERINE is a registered trademark of Warner-Lambert Company.

For as long as he owned the company, they never did. During the 1920s earnings rose from $115,000 to more than $8 million. By the time of the stock market crash in 1929, Listerine was one of the largest buyers of magazine and newspaper space, spending more than $5 million—almost the exact amount of yearly profits. In all that time, the product's price, package, and formula remained completely unchanged.

Once he found that the halitosis claim was four times as effective as all others, Lambert focused on it exclusively. All other claims were relinquished. The germ-free mouth belonged to Listerine. The company set up a house advertising agency called Lambert & Feasley, Inc., whose primary responsibility would be the marketing of Listerine, although it would serve other noncompeting advertisers in the years ahead. Its billings would rise to nearly $20 million during its peak years in the 1960s.

Lambert made it a point never to retouch any of the photographic images that made up the halitosis campaign. His usual targets were young adults of marriageable age. One ad featured Edna, whose "case was really a pathetic one. Like every woman, her primary ambition was to marry." We see her kneeling before her bureau clutching the wedding garments that would never be worn. The headline announced the price of halitosis: "Often a bridesmaid but never a bride."

The standard Listerine ad showed one or the other young eligibles having to deal with the problem that "Even your best friend won't tell you" about: "Could I be happy with him in spite of *that*?" "Don't fool yourself, it [halitosis] ruins romance," or the simple "Halitosis makes *you unpopular*." The copy style—called "whisper copy" in the 1920s—was always the same, a mimic of *True Story* magazine advice to the lovelorn.

It is hard to fairly assess Gerard Lambert's influence. Although it appears simple, his approach was a combination of staking a claim on a body part, knowing how to use constructive discontent (shame) as a selling tool, realizing the power of research, and hammering home a sales message. In retrospect, Lambert may have succeeded too well. By depicting the mouth as a cauldron of antisocial germs that could be tamed only by strong medicine, Lambert left open the possibility that competing claims could be staked out. In the 1960s rival Procter & Gamble Company's Scope did just that. Scope positioned itself as the feels good, tastes great, smells terrific, mouthwash that—in the spirit of the times—"had it all."

After a series of mergers in the 1950s, Lambert Pharmaceutical joined with Warner-Hudnut, Inc., to become Warner-Lambert Company in 1955, and Listerine was joined by a number of sibling brands in the new company's line-up, including Bromo-Seltzer, Schick, Anahist, and many others. Lambert & Feasley continued to play a role in Listerine advertising, but the mergers brought two major advertising agencies into the corporate marketing structure: Batten Barton Durstine & Osborn for Bromo-Seltzer and Ted Bates & Company for Anahist. By 1970 the main part of the Listerine product line, which included lozenges, cold tablets, antiseptics, and other brand extensions, was being handled by the J. Walter Thompson Company, which continued to handle the line at the turn of the millennium. (Lambert & Feasley continued to function at the parent company's Morris Plains, New Jersey, headquarters.)

Meanwhile, Warner-Lambert was left with Lambert's legacy of "medicine breath." Although it tried to battle back with a new generation of Cool Mint Listerine (blue) and Freshburst Listerine (green), the tough-guy claims of the amber-bottle parent remained etched deeply in the minds of consumers. The heritage of "Tastes bad, but it's good for you," "Kills germs that cause bad breath," and "The taste you hate, twice a day" continues. Amazingly, 99 percent of all mouthwash users have tried original Listerine. That is the problem: if Listerine excelled in convincing consumers that mouthwash must taste bad to work well, what could a good-tasting Listerine do?

JAMES B. TWITCHELL

Further Reading

Lambert, Gerard B., *All Out of Step: A Personal Chronicle*, New York: Doubleday, 1956

Lambert, Gerard B., "How I Sold Listerine," in *The Amazing Advertising Business*, New York: Simon and Schuster, 1957

Vinikas, Vincent, *Soft Soap, Hard Sell: American Hygiene in an Age of Advertisement*, Ames: Iowa State University Press, 1992

Watkins, Julian, *The 100 Greatest Advertisements: Who Wrote Them and What They Did*, New York: Moore, 1949; 2nd revised edition, New York: Dover, 1959

Lasker, Albert D. 1880–1952

U.S. Advertising Executive

Albert Lasker is widely regarded as a key figure in the development of the modern advertising agency. He ruled Lord & Thomas for more than 30 years, insisted on a major role in its clients' marketing decisions, and, along with Stanley Resor of the J. Walter Thompson Company and Ray Rubicam of Young & Rubicam, Inc., dominated U.S. advertising in the pre–World War II period.

Albert Davis Lasker was born on 1 May 1880 in Freiberg, Germany, while his parents were traveling. His father, Morris, was a

German native who had immigrated to the United States and settled in Galveston, Texas, in 1856. His mother, Nettie, was a U.S.
citizen of German descent. When Lasker was six weeks old, his
parents returned with him to Galveston, where he lived for the
next 18 years.

Lasker's academic record was undistinguished, largely because
he put so much energy into his own particular interests. In 1892
he started his own newspaper, the *Galveston Free Press,* serving as
the paper's chief editor and sales representative. The ads he sold
netted him a weekly profit of about $15 from the beginning.
Grades seemed insignificant to this young entrepreneur, who went
on to edit one of the country's first high school magazines. Graduating at 16, he joined the *Galveston Morning News,* and later the
New Orleans (Louisiana) *Times-Democrat* and the *Dallas* (Texas)
News, all before he turned 18. His ambition was to become a
Texas newspaper publisher and editor.

On the advice of his father, however, he went in 1898 to Chicago, Illinois, where the senior Lasker had used his influence with
Daniel Lord to secure him a position at Lord & Thomas (L&T),
one of the top-three advertising agencies at the time, with billings
of $800,000. Lasker went to work for the company for $10 a
week. He would probably have left the agency had he not lost
$500 to a gambler, a sum that he persuaded Ambrose Thomas to
cover for him. This obliged him to remain at Lord & Thomas,
where he moved from office boy to salesman. He began closely
scrutinizing the work the agency was doing for its clients and saw
opportunities for improvement. He persuaded the Wilson Ear
Drum Company to boost its agency commission to 15 percent on
the condition that he improve the effectiveness of its advertisements. After a year, Wilson's spending through L&T had grown
nearly sevenfold. On the strength of this success, Lasker married
Flora Warner in 1902. They had three children before her death in
1936.

In 1904 Lord retired and sold his share of the agency to
Lasker, who went about putting his stamp on the company.
Impressed with copywriter John Kennedy's notions of advertising
as salesmanship—or, as Kennedy called it, "salesmanship in
print"—he hired Kennedy and made his theories of copywriting a
fundamental aspect of L&T's advertising. The agency was a pioneer in what became known as "reason why" advertising, which
required each ad to present the consumer with a clear benefit that
would stand as a compellingly rational, irrefutable incentive to
buy the product. By 1905 Lasker oversaw all the copy that came
out of L&T. Kennedy left the shop the next year.

When Thomas died suddenly in 1906 Lasker acquired a portion of his share of the agency (the remainder went to another
partner, Charles R. Erwin, who later became a partner in the
Erwin, Wasey & Company agency). In 1912 Lasker acquired the
remaining share of L&T and became sole owner of the agency—
with billings of $6 million—a position he maintained for the next
30 years.

In 1908 Lasker hired Claude C. Hopkins, who had been working on a theory similar to Kennedy's "salesmanship in print."
Hopkins attracted Lasker's attention with ads for Liquozone and
for Schlitz beer, work the younger Lasker admired. Hopkins

Albert D. Lasker.
Courtesy of FCB New York.

worked writing copy with Lasker, who seldom wrote any himself
but instead served as editor. Hopkins rose to become the agency's
chief "reason-why" theoretician and served as president at the
agency twice. Among his achievements, Hopkins created the
"Shot from guns" slogan for Quaker Oats Company's Puffed
Wheat cereal, a name he suggested for the marketer's Wheat Ber-
ries brand.

One early success for Lasker and Hopkins was their campaign
for B.P. Johnson & Company's Palmolive soap, which landed at
L&T in 1911. They positioned the soap—the first green-colored
toilet soap—to appeal to women with such headlines as "Soap
from trees—nature's gift to beauty," playing on the brand's name,
which reflected the fact that it was made from both palm and
olive oils. The "beauty" strategy ignited sales of the brand, which
was propelled to the number-one rank of toilet soaps within a few
years. L&T rode to the top position among U.S. agencies on
accounts such as that before World War I by employing Lasker's
motto: "Make it [the advertising] sing."

Lasker also became active in Republican politics. As assistant
chairman of the Republican National Committee under Will
Hayes in 1920, he was a supporter of Hiram Johnson, a fierce isolationist and opponent of Woodrow Wilson's League of Nations.
With Harding's election, Lasker was appointed head of the United
States Shipping Board in 1921 and became a regular member of
the president's weekly "poker cabinet," which included many of
the Harding men who would later face indictments in the Teapot
Dome scandal. Lasker had been told by friends at Standard Oil

that U.S. Interior Secretary Albert Fall was giving out certain oil leases under suspicious circumstances, and he warned Harding of possible corruption in his administration. But the president disregarded his advice. Lasker escaped the Harding years with his reputation not only intact but enhanced by his effective reform of the Shipping Board, where he liquidated the derelict fleet left over from World War I and built a new merchant marine service for the nation.

After Harding's death in August 1923 Lasker returned to Chicago, where Hopkins had been running L&T while Lasker was in Washington, D.C. Hopkins had made changes Lasker did not approve of, such as creating an art department, and the two men found it difficult to accommodate each other. In 1924 Hopkins resigned. Lasker presided over a period of lively growth in the 1920s, through such accounts as RCA Corporation, American Tobacco Company, and Kimberly-Clark Corporation, for which Lasker helped boost Kotex and Kleenex. The agency became an early supporter of network radio, putting Pepsodent toothpaste (a sibling product to the disinfectant Liquozone) behind *Amos 'n' Andy,* a show that became the medium's first great runaway hit.

L&T's most important account came with the 1923 win of American Tobacco's Lucky Strike brand, which by the end of the decade accounted for 58 percent of the shop's total billings and occupied a great part of Lasker's time for the next decade. George Washington Hill ran American Tobacco after 1925, and the working relationship between him and Lasker—both strong personalities—resulted in some friction. But the distance between Hill in New York City and Lasker in Chicago eased some of the stress of the relationship.

Lasker's first effort for Lucky Strike was designed to get women to smoke. He initially enlisted female singers from the Metropolitan Opera to provide testimonials, followed by female stars of the then-novel moving pictures. The effort proved enormously successful, and women smokers came out of the closet to indulge in cigarettes in public. Lucky Strike sales, as well as the sales of all cigarettes, experienced remarkable growth.

After the death of his wife, Lasker's drive for success seemed to diminish. He would brook no second-guessing from his clients, and he resigned the business of several, including Quaker Oats and RCA, when they sought to evaluate the effectiveness of L&T's work through outside research, which he distrusted. He traveled widely, which took him away from the agency. He married and then divorced actress Doris Kenyon within a year. And in 1939 he married Mary Woodard Reinhardt.

In July 1938 Lasker stepped down as president of L&T, though he remained sole owner. He moved to New York City and became interested in psychiatry, medicine, and art, building one of the better private collections of French art in the United States. The generation of his peers on the client side was also retiring, and he took a dim view of many of their successors. With his son

Edward expressing no interest in an advertising career, Lasker finally decided in 1942 to sell the agency to the heads of its three principal offices: Emerson Foote in New York City, Fairfax Cone in Chicago, and Don Belding in Los Angeles, California. Lasker's agency ceased to exist under the Lord & Thomas name on 30 December 1942, reopening in January 1943 as Foote, Cone & Belding (FCB).

Lasker's politics turned more liberal, and he retreated completely from advertising. He became a strong interventionist before World War II, supported Wendell L. Willkie in 1940 for U.S. president, and voted for Franklin D. Roosevelt in 1944. After the war he became a Truman Democrat, though never registered as a party member. He was among the most prominent members of the American Cancer Society after the death of his brother Harry in the 1930s. He was also a strong advocate of birth control, ranking as one of Planned Parenthood's largest contributors in the 1940s. Lasker himself underwent surgery for cancer in 1950, but the doctors succeeded only in prolonging his life for a short time. He died on 30 May 1952.

EDD APPLEGATE AND JOHN McDONOUGH

Biography

Born 1 May 1880, Freiberg, Germany; grew up in Galveston, Texas; started *Galveston Free Press* 1892; joined Chicago's Lord & Thomas as an office boy, 1898; became part owner in 1904 and sole owner in 1912; became active in Republican politics; headed publicity operation of President Warren Harding's election campaign; served as assistant chairman of the Republican National Committee, 1920; appointed head of the U.S. Shipping Board, 1921; returned to L&T after Harding's death, taking over running of the agency, 1923; L&T regained its position as largest U.S. ad agency, 1930; stepped down as president of L&T, July 1938, while remaining sole owner; sold L&T to heads of its three principal offices, creating Foote, Cone & Belding, 1942; withdrew from advertising and became active in liberal politics; died 30 May 1952.

Further Reading

Applegate, Edd, *Personalities and Products: A Historical Perspective on Advertising in America,* Westport, Connecticut: Greenwood, 1998

Cone, Fairfax M., *With All Its Faults: A Candid Account of Forty Years in Advertising,* Boston: Little Brown, 1969

Fox, Stephen, *The Mirror Makers: A History of American Advertising and Its Creators,* New York: Morrow, 1984

Gunther, John, *Taken at the Flood: The Story of Albert D. Lasker,* New York: Harper, and London: Hamilton, 1960

Hopkins, Claude C., *My Life in Advertising,* New York and London: Harper Brothers, 1927; 11th edition, 1936

Lawrence, Mary Wells 1928–

U.S. Advertising Executive

At one time the world's highest-paid female advertising executive, Mary Wells Lawrence early on forged a reputation for glamour, elegance, excellent copywriting skills, and a keen business sense. Mary Wells Lawrence was born in Youngstown, Ohio, in 1928 and named Mary Georgene Berg. She was the only child of Waldemar Berg, a furniture salesman, and Violet Berg, a sportswear and millinery buyer for McKelvey's department store. Because she was shy as a child, her parents sent her to drama and acting classes, which led to her performing by the age of five with the Youngstown Playhouse, a regional theater. At 17, she moved to New York City for a year to study acting with the Neighborhood Playhouse School.

But Wells never pursued an acting career. Instead she attended the Carnegie Institute of Technology in Pittsburgh, Pennsylvania, for two years. While there, she met Burt Wells, an industrial design student (who later became an art director for Ogilvy & Mather in New York City); the couple married on 28 December 1949 and moved to Youngstown, Ohio, where Wells landed a job as a copywriter at McKelvey's department store.

In 1952 the couple moved to New York City, and Wells worked for several department stores before getting a job at Macy's as fashion advertising manager. In 1953 she took a position as writer and copy group head at McCann-Erickson, Inc., working on retail-oriented accounts including the International Silver Company and zipper marketer Talon, Inc.

Three years later Wells moved to the Lennen & Newell agency, tempted, she later told *Advertising Age,* by a "lavish" salary offer to join a new, 20-person "brain trust." However, the agency soon underwent a change in management; as a result, the brain trust was dismantled and its members let go with a generous payout. Wells decided to use the money for a trip to Europe while she decided whether to remain in advertising.

She returned from Europe with a renewed commitment to the advertising industry and in 1957 accepted a job as a copywriter at Doyle Dane Bernbach (DDB). There, Wells became known for her work for General Mills casserole meals and cosmetics marketer Max Factor & Company. Wells subsequently rose to become a vice president and associate copy chief at DDB, with a salary of $40,000. Of her seven years with DDB, Wells later said that agency principal Bill Bernbach told her, "You're not much of a writer but your thinking is pretty good," while principal Ned Doyle told her, "You're not much of a thinker, but your writing's pretty good."

Although her job at DDB was professionally challenging and rewarding, Wells later told *Advertising Age* that she sought a position in which she could "run something of my own." That opportunity turned out to be a position with Jack Tinker & Partners, a unit of the Interpublic Group of Companies that by the early 1960s was undergoing a change from a consultant role providing strategy and ad campaigns to other Interpublic agencies to more of a stand-alone, traditional agency. In 1964 Tinker lured Wells away from DDB with a salary of $60,000 per year and more creative freedom. There she worked with creative partners Dick Rich and Stewart Greene to develop for Miles Laboratories' Alka-Seltzer ad campaigns that have become well known, including the "No matter what shape your stomach's in" campaign that created a distinctive personality for the antacid product. The work won a Clio Award in 1964, and the TV jingle itself found a place on the hits charts of *Billboard* magazine.

Tinker's next client was Braniff International, an airline company. Again with creative partners Rich and Greene, Wells devised the "The end of the plain plane" campaign, which was introduced at the same time that the airline unveiled a new look for its planes and new uniforms for its employees.

In 1966, with these two major advertising successes to her credit, Tinker raised Wells's salary to $80,000, a very large sum for women executives at the time, but also demanded that she sign a long-term contract. Although she was by then divorced from her first husband and had custody of their two preschool-age daughters, Wells balked at signing the contract. Instead she resigned from the agency, and in April 1966 she opened her own shop with longtime creative partners Rich and Greene, who also resigned from Tinker.

The new agency, Wells, Rich, Greene, Inc. (WRG), signed Braniff International and Miles Laboratories almost immediately as its first clients. In all, 11 people from Tinker joined WRG. Although there were published comments at the time that the new agency was stealing employees from other agencies, *Newsweek* remarked that such defections were "an ancient tribal rite of advertising."

The fledgling agency, however, soon resigned the $7 million Braniff account to avoid potential charges of conflict of interest: on 25 November 1967, Mary Wells and Harding Lawrence, Braniff's president and future chairman, were married, and Mary Wells became Mary Wells Lawrence.

Even without Braniff, by the end of 1967 WRG was billing $30 million, with clients that included Philip Morris Inc.'s Benson & Hedges 100's cigarettes, Personna razor blades, and Burma Shave men's toiletries product lines, as well as West End Brewing Company's Utica Club Beer and V. La Rosa & Sons, Inc.'s La Rosa spaghetti.

The following fall, with the stock market doing well, Lawrence on 21 October 1968 took the agency public. But by 1974 both the market and Lawrence had changed direction, and she announced she intended to return the agency to private ownership.

As founder, chairman, chief executive officer, and president of WRG, Lawrence was one of the most powerful women in the advertising industry. Lawrence was "advertising's most widely publicized symbol of glamour-success-wealth-brains-and-beauty," *Advertising Age* said in 1969, when, at age 40, she became the

Mary Wells Lawrence.
Courtesy of Mary Lawrence.

youngest person ever inducted into the Copywriters' Hall of Fame. By 1976 she was earning more than $300,000 a year, making her one of the highest-paid U.S. women executives. That year WRG had billings of $187 million, making it the 15th-largest ad agency in the United States. Its client roster included Procter & Gamble Company, Trans World Airlines, Miles Laboratories, Philip Morris, Inc., Bic Pen Corporation, Ralston Purina Company, Midas, Inc., White-Westinghouse Electric Company, and Sun Oil Company. Under her direction, WRG created now-famous advertising slogans, including, "I love New York," to encourage New York tourism; "Quality is job 1" for the Ford Motor Company; and "Try it, you'll like it" and "I can't believe I ate the whole thing" for Alka-Seltzer.

Lawrence retired in 1990 at age 62, selling the agency to BDDP, a Paris, France-based international advertising network in 1991. In 1998 Wells BDDP ceased operations. In 1999 Mary Wells Lawrence was named to the Advertising Hall of Fame by the American Advertising Federation, which called her "the force behind one of the most creative shops in the history of advertising." Her memoir entitled *A Big Life (in Advertising)* was published by Alfred A. Knopf in 2002.

LAURIE FREEMAN

Biography

Born Mary Georgene Berg in Youngstown Ohio, 1928; became the fashion advertising manager for Macy's department store, New York City, 1952; named copy group head, McCann-Erickson, Inc., 1953; named copywriter, Doyle Dane Bernbach, 1957; hired as copy chief, Jack Tinker & Partners, 1964; founded Wells, Rich, Greene (WRG), 1966; took agency public, 1968; returned agency to private control through a bonds-for-stock exchange, 1974; retired and sold WRG to BDDP International, Paris, France, 1990.

Selected Publication

A Big Life (in Advertising), 2002

Further Reading

"Biography of Mary Wells," *Current Biography* (January 1967)

Braniff International: Mary Wells Lawrence <www.braniffinternational.org/people/Mary_Wells.htm>

Danzig, Fred, "After 10 Years, Wells, Rich, Greene Says It's Time to Get Its Act Together," *Advertising Age* (3 May 1976)

Donath, Bob, "WRG's Private Bid Seen Good for Shop, Not Stockholders," *Advertising Age* (9 September 1974)

Donath, Bob, "Private Bid: Can Mary Pull It Off?" *Advertising Age* (14 October 1974)

"Gone Public Lately? Scorecard Tells How Doyle, Others Fared on Stock," *Advertising Age* (19 June 1972)

Grant, Don, "If It Isn't Terribly Well Done, I'm a Little Miserable," *Advertising Age* (5 April 1971)

Lazarus, George, "All's Still Well for Ad Pioneer Mary Wells," *Chicago Tribune* (22 March 2000)

"Mary Tells Copy Club: 'You Ain't Felt Nothing Yet,'" *Advertising Age* (2 June 1969)

"Mary Wells Lawrence Looks at Consumers in the Year 2000," *Advertising Age* (1 August 1977)

"Moss Named Head of WRG; O'Reilly, Burns Are Promoted," *Advertising Age* (25 October 1971)

Norwich, William, "Artifacts from a Capital of the Art of Entertaining," *The New York Times* (17 May 2001)

Lazarus, Rochelle (Shelly) 1947–

U.S. Advertising Executive

Dubbed the "Queen of Madison Avenue" by the U.K. advertising industry trade publication *Campaign,* Rochelle (Shelly) Lazarus, who became chairman of Ogilvy & Mather Worldwide in 1997, has been at that agency for some 30 years. The length of her tenure at Ogilvy is unusual in an industry in which executives tend to move from one agency to another. Lazarus began her career in advertising in the early 1970s, at a time when female ad executives were a rarity.

Lazarus was born in New York City in 1947. She attended Smith College and graduated with a bachelor's degree in 1968. That year, looking for a job in order to help put her fiancé through medical school, she found that career options for women were limited; the choices seemed to be to learn typing and be a secretary or to become a teacher. It was suggested that with a graduate degree she might find a job in which she would not have to type. And so she enrolled at Columbia University, where she was one of four women in a class of 275. She graduated in 1970 with a master's degree in business.

Lazarus found her life transformed by two events while in graduate school. First, she took an internship at General Foods Corporation, where she worked in the Maxwell House division on the introduction of Maxim. Second, she found a required marketing course enjoyable. As part of that course, she attended a one-day advertising conference and found herself fascinated. "I had never thought about advertising as something that was thoughtful and strategic," she said in an interview with the *Sunday Post.* "It went on for five hours, but I could have stayed for another five hours."

After graduating from Columbia, Lazarus joined hair-care products marketer Clairol, Inc., as an assistant product manager. In 1971 she was approached by a recruiter for advertising agency Ogilvy & Mather, Inc., which was looking to add an account executive to its hair-care products team. Lazarus later quipped that two years at Clairol had made her a "hair expert," but even then she said she planned to spend only two years in advertising before moving on. But Lazarus had joined the agency at a time when founder David Ogilvy was still an active presence in the company, and she has credited Ogilvy's dedication to big ideas and creativity as a guiding influence on her own career and business philosophies. She chose to stay.

Lazarus has noted that early in her career, when she was often the only woman present at business meetings, she was always asked what other women would think of new ideas and campaigns. In this way, being female was advantageous to her career, but there were challenges as well. By the 1980s Lazarus was finding it difficult to balance her career commitments with her role as a mother of three children. Once, when asked to attend an all-day strategy meeting for American Express Company (AmEx), for which she was the newly appointed management supervisor, she told the client that she would be unavailable until midday because she wanted to attend her son's school sports day. The AmEx executive was shocked that she would miss any portion of this all-day meeting, but Lazarus pointed out to him that while in a week's time he would not be able to remember who had been at the meeting, her son would never forget it if she did not make it to the sports day. "It was 'bet your job' time . . . but it wasn't really. At another company I might have been fired . . . but this wasn't the way my company worked. Over the years I have made it my business to be at anything that is important to my kids, and I have told my clients that," she said in the *Post* interview.

As an account manager, Lazarus handled Ogilvy's high-profile accounts, including AmEx, Lever Bros. Company, and American Telephone & Telegraph Company, earning a reputation as a business strategist who worked hard to build relationships with senior clients. It was a skill that helped Lazarus to win and retain clients throughout her career.

One of her earliest victories came in 1992 when she helped regain the then-$60 million AmEx account after the financial-services marketer had moved its business to Chiat/Day, an Ogilvy rival, following a review. Lazarus, who by then had spent six years as group account director on the AmEx business, was in charge of the team sent to retake the account. She leveraged her relationships with Lou Gerstner, then AmEx's chief executive officer (CEO), and his marketing chief, Abby Kohnstamm, as well as utilizing new research and creative work by Ogilvy. With that win firmly under her belt, Lazarus was rewarded with a promotion in 1989 to president of O&M Direct U.S., Ogilvy's direct marketing division. In 1991 she moved to president of Ogilvy's New York City office.

The relationships that Lazarus had built over the years with Gerstner and Kohnstamm paid off again in 1994, when those executives moved to IBM Corporation and handed Ogilvy the $500 million IBM global advertising business; IBM's choice of Ogilvy represented the single biggest account switch in advertising history at that time. The move helped propel Lazarus in 1995 to the position of president and chief operating officer of Ogilvy & Mather Worldwide. She subsequently succeeded Charlotte Beers as CEO of Ogilvy & Mather Worldwide in 1996, and in 1997 she became chairman.

As chairman of Ogilvy & Mather Worldwide, Lazarus has been a steadfast advocate of the agency's concept of "brand stewardship," introduced by Beers in 1992, in which the agency sets out to build a brand over its lifetime, and its newer incarnation, "360 degree branding," introduced by Lazarus, a strategy designed to help the agency to uncover the emotional subtleties that consumers perceive as characterizing attributes of a brand. Lazarus has served on Ogilvy & Mather Worldwide's board as well as on its executive committee since 1991. In 2000 Lazarus served as the chairman of the American Association of Advertis-

Rochelle (Shelly) Lazarus.
Used by permission of Ogilvy & Mather.

ship. Since 1998 she has been listed among the top-ten women in *Fortune* magazine's annual ranking of the "50 Most Powerful Women in American Business." She has served on the board of directors of a number of industry, business, and academic institutions, including the board of the General Electric Company, Teacher's Insurance & Annuity Association-College Retirement Equities Fund, and the World Wildlife Fund. She is the chairman of the board of trustees for her alma mater, Smith College, and also is a member of the Council on Foreign Relations and the Business Council.

LAURIE FREEMAN

Biography

Born in New York City, 1 September 1947; B.A. in psychology/government, Smith College, 1968; M.B.A., Columbia University, 1970; joined Bristol-Myers Company's Clairol, Inc., division as an assistant product manager, 1970; moved to Ogilvy & Mather Worldwide, New York City, as account executive, 1971; named president of Ogilvy's direct marketing business, 1989; named president of Ogilvy's New York City office, 1991; named president of Ogilvy & Mather North America, 1994; named president and chief operating officer, Ogilvy & Mather Worldwide, 1995; added title chief executive officer, 1996; promoted to chairman, 1997.

Further Reading

Delaney, Tom, "Ogilvy's World," *The Delaney Report* (29 November 1999)
Estrich, Susan R., "The Trouble with Hilary," *Harper's Bazaar* (August 2000)
Freeman, Laurie, "Interactive Internet Fundamentally Changes Definition," *Marketing News* (6 December 1999)
"Madison Avenue's Queen Bee," *Sunday Business Post,* Dublin, Ireland (2 July 2000)
Marshall, Caroline, "The Kings of Madison Avenue: Shelly Lazarus—After 28 Years, O & M's Leader Is Steeped in Its Culture; Caroline Marshall Meets Shelly Lazarus," *Campaign* (21 April 2001)
Neff, Thomas J., James M. Citrin, and Paul B. Brown, *Lessons from the Top: The Search for America's Best Business Leaders,* New York: Currency/Doubleday, 1999; London: Penguin, 2000

ing Agencies. Ogilvy & Mather Worldwide, a unit of the WPP Group, had U.S. gross income of $3.97 billion in 2000.

Lazarus has been recognized for her leadership role by the Advertising Women of New York, which named her its "Advertising Woman of the Year" in 1994. She also was a recipient of the Women in Communications' Matrix Award and was named "Business Woman of the Year" by the New York City Partner-

Leagas Delaney Partnership, Ltd.

Opened by Tim Delaney and Ron Leagas in London, England, 1980; acquired by Abbott Mead Vickers (AMV), 1986; established Leagas Delaney Group, Ltd., as a buyout vehicle and bought all group companies from AMV, 1998; established French office as subsidiary shop and opened German subsidiary, 1999.

Major Clients
Ferraro
Goodyear
Harrods
Hyundai

Intercontinental Hotels & Resorts
Patek Philippe
Salomon (ski/extreme sports brand)
Virgin Mobile USA

The Leagas Delaney Partnership, Ltd., grew out of the aspirations of Tim Delaney, formerly managing director of BBDO, Ltd., in London, England, and Ron Leagas, formerly managing director of Saatchi & Saatchi Advertising, also in London. Both men wanted to start their own ad agency, and in August 1980 they brought their ambitions to fruition by creating London-based Leagas Delaney, immediately attracting clients, including Bass, ICI, Amex, and United Biscuits.

The early 1980s saw the agency put its creative stamp on the U.K. advertising industry. Leagas Delaney experienced rapid initial growth, developing a reputation for producing award-winning campaigns, such as its work for the family vacation packages company Pontins, which won a gold Lion at the Cannes (France) International Advertising Festival. By the end of its first year, the agency had $50 million in billings; two years later, the shop claimed 12 clients and billings of $100 million.

In 1986 the company was acquired by the London-based agency Abbott Mead Vickers (AMV). It was the first acquisition for AMV, which had only just gone public, and it was not without turmoil. Leagas left the shop and was succeeded as managing director by Bruce Haines, formerly the client services director at AMV.

Although the departure of Leagas proved difficult, Delaney insisted on maintaining the agency's original name—in essence, protecting the brand's reputation. Leagas Delaney continued to operate within the Abbott Mead Vickers Group for a number of years and greatly expanded its business base and reputation. By 1989 the company had returned to form and had added Harrods, Porsche, and Timberland to its growing client list.

Leagas Delaney's major international expansion followed in 1992, when it won the account of German sportswear marketer Adidas. In March 1986 Leagas Delaney opened in San Francisco, California, becoming the first British agency in 30 years to set up shop in the United States without attaching itself to an existing agency.

The result was positive and encouraged Leagas Delaney executives to consider expansion opportunities closer to home. The company identified client demand for single-center creative shops that could then roll out campaigns across national borders. Using its links with Adidas's local marketing offices, Leagas Delaney embarked on a European expansion program, opening offices in Paris, France, and Rome, Italy, in October 1997 and in Hamburg, Germany, in 2000.

At the same time, the agency was undergoing corporate restructuring. In April 1998 Leagas Delaney Group, Ltd., was established by KPMG (a business services network) to enable management to buy back the agency. It acquired full ownership from AMV that same year.

Nine months later, the agency converted its Paris office to a subsidiary and hired a team of French managers to run it. It also

Leagas Delaney created this humorous 1991 print ad for one of its premier clients, the world-famous London, England, retailer Harrods.

established a subsidiary in Düsseldorf, Germany, which moved to Hamburg in June 2000. In November 1999 Leagas Delaney established its own in-house Web site design team as a wholly owned company, the Digital Partners, Ltd. By the end of 2000, Leagas Delaney had developed six "shops" with combined billings of $526 million.

In May 1999 Leagas Delaney beat out three other contenders for a $15 million campaign that aimed to take Barclays, the second-largest U.K. bank, and brush some of the dust from its 300-year heritage. Barclays wanted to change its fussy image and trumpet its growing prominence in international business. Leagas Delaney devised a cinema, TV, and print campaign around the tag line, "A big world needs a big bank," and brought in heavyweight actors—Sir Anthony Hopkins, Tim Roth, and Nick Moran—for three brand-focused ads directed by Tony Scott (*Top Gun*).

Also attracting much attention was the agency's $75 million, in-country television campaign for Italy's largest advertiser, Telecom Italia. The campaign enlisted actor Marlon Brando, director

Woody Allen, and even former South African President Nelson Mandela. Tony Scott directed the Brando spot, while Allen directed himself, and Spike Lee directed the Mandela commercial. The campaign ran in Italy in 2000 and 2001.

In November 2000 Envoy Communications Group, in Toronto, Canada—which specializes in design, marketing, and technology—made a bid valued at about $85.5 million for Leagas Delaney. The deal was never completed. The following month Leagas Delaney was dropped as the lead agency for the British Broadcasting Corporation, ending a five-year relationship. In December 2001 the agency announced the departure of Haines from the chairmanship but did not announce a successor. Shortly afterward, major client Adidas ended its relationship with the agency. Martin Sorrell's WPP Group was rumored to be in takeover talks for Leagas Delaney, but WPP denied that a deal was in the works.

Advertising Age ranked Leagas Delaney number 18 among international agencies, based on number of markets and clients serviced on an international basis. For 2000, Leagas Delaney had gross income of $23 million, up 4.5 percent over the previous year, on billings of $156 million.

SEAN KELLY

Further Reading

Cozens, Claire, "WPP denies Leagas takeover plans," MediaGuardian (25 February 2002) <http://media. guardian.co.uk/advertising/story/0,7492,657989,00.html>

Garrett, Jade, "Ad guru to pocket millions in takeover windfall," MediaGuardian (7 November 2000) <http://media. guardian.co.uk/advertising/story/0,7492,393950,00.html>

Garrett, Jade, "Leagas Delaney exec blasts BBC," MediaGuardian (5 December 2000) <http:media.guardian.co.uk/broadcast/ story/0,7493,407081,00.html>

Sorkin, Andrew Ross, "Barclays Goes Big in Its Branding Campaign" *BusinessTimes* (7 June 2000)

Legal Issues

Advertising has generated a complicated body of law in the United States, forcing advertisers and advertising agencies to become increasingly dependent on legal counsel in all aspects of their business. Agencies rely on lawyers for review of their advertising campaigns at all stages of conception, production, and distribution; for compliance with both network and Federal Communications Commission (FCC) standards and practices for broadcast; for contract negotiations, talent agreements, and releases for use rights; and for guidance regarding sweepstakes, pricing, antitrust, and intellectual property concerns.

Lawyers often provide essential help to agencies that, while meeting the promotional needs of their clients, must nevertheless adhere to a complex body of governmental regulations. An agency may need legal assistance in administrative proceedings before the Federal Trade Commission (FTC), the Food and Drug Administration (FDA), the U.S. Postal Service, or any of the many other governmental bodies with jurisdiction over advertising and marketing. A law firm may also represent an agency before such self-regulatory bodies as the National Advertising Review Board and the National Advertising Division of the Council of Better Business Bureaus.

First Amendment Considerations

In the United States advertising was long considered the poor relation among various forms of speech and not generally protected by the First Amendment. In 1976 the Supreme Court changed course, however, and declared that even "purely commercial" speech should be afforded some constitutional protection, although the level of protection is lower than that for other types of speech. Four years later the Court devised a four-part test, known as the Central Hudson test after the case in which it was created, for determining when commercial speech may be regulated without violating the First Amendment. The four parts are:

1. the speech must concern a lawful product or service;
2. the speech must not be false or misleading;
3. the government must have a substantial interest in regulating the speech;
4. the regulation must be narrowly tailored and must actually serve the governmental interest at stake.

The Court's decision has significantly restricted the scope of government regulation of the content of advertisements. Still, courts have upheld government limits on advertising by members of professions that are regulated by the states, such as lawyers. In other cases courts have upheld regulations involving products or services that were illegal or heavily regulated, including alcohol, lotteries, and gambling.

Yet, generally speaking, it has become increasingly difficult to ban advertising in the United States. In June 1999 the U.S. Supreme Court unanimously invalidated a federal ban on radio and television ads for legal casino gambling (*Greater New Orleans Broadcasting Association, Inc.* v. *United States*). Though narrowly stated, the Court's rationale, according to the *Wall Street Journal,* seemed to be "if you can buy it, you can advertise it," an implication that may or may not extend to alcohol and tobacco.

The Federal Trade Commission

Although numerous state and federal agencies play a role in advertising regulation, the FTC is the largest such unit charged with oversight of advertising nationwide. Its congressional mandate is to prevent "unfair or deceptive" practices, "unfair methods of competition," and "false" and "deceptive" advertisements. In examining advertisements alleged to be unfair or deceptive, the commission looks to the overall impression of the ad on a "reasonable" consumer.

For an ad to be considered deceptive, the disputed representation (or omission) must be material; that is, it must be something that will influence the consumer's purchasing decision. One classic case involved three one-minute television commercials created in 1959 by the agency Ted Bates & Company, Inc., for Colgate-Palmolive Company's Rapid Shave shaving cream. The commercials claimed that Rapid Shave's moisturizing action worked so quickly it could soften even sandpaper in the 60 seconds it took to air the commercial; the agency did not use real sandpaper in the demonstration, however, but rather a Plexiglas mock-up of sandpaper. The U.S. Supreme Court in 1965 agreed with the FTC that the commercial had misrepresented the moisturizing capability of the shaving cream (which actually did soften real sandpaper, but in 80 minutes rather than one) and that the misrepresentation was both material and deceptive.

An ad can also deceive through innuendo or implication, by using technical or foreign language, or by omission of a material fact. One court found an ad offering new cars for "$49 over factory invoice" inherently misleading as the invoice price changed continually depending on a number of factors, making the term *invoice price* essentially meaningless to consumers.

Even the inclusion of qualifying language or a disclaimer may not protect an ad from being deemed misleading. The court in the above case rejected proposed disclaimers to clarify what a factory invoice was, including one that explained that the actual dealer cost was lower than the invoice price. Similarly the inclusion of "fine print" will not save a deceptive ad. If a false statement is more noticeable than the qualification, the statement is still considered false. While disclaimers or explanatory language do not protect an ad that is inherently deceptive, an agency may find it useful to clarify a claim that falls in the gray area.

It is not necessary to prove that anyone was actually deceived by an ad for it to be deemed deceptive. If the FTC finds that an ad has a "tendency to deceive," taking into account the relative susceptibility of the audience, the ad is considered unlawful.

"Puffery"—hyperbolic statements, exaggerations, or unprovable opinion—is a gray area but generally is allowed by the FTC and the courts, which assume that a reasonable consumer would know such statements are not meant as reliable fact. Calling a product "stupendous" or "best tasting" may be puffery; calling it "the cheapest in town" or "less irritating than Brand X" probably is not. The use of such statements can be risky for the advertiser as there is no clear line between what is permissible exaggeration and what is deceptive or a false statement of provable fact.

Finally, if an advertisement makes a claim about a product, that claim must be capable of substantiation. The proof of the claim must have a reasonable basis and not be contrived or based on distorted facts or statistics. Where the claim involves a matter of human safety, to back it up there must be "substantial scientific test data."

Agencies' Legal Duties

In addition to abiding by the rules of regulatory agencies, advertisers must be aware of the general legal issues that affect them. For instance, an advertising agency undertakes certain legal duties that arise from its contracts with its clients. To avoid problems, contracts should be in writing and should clearly spell out the rights and duties of both parties, including terms of compensation.

Contract law also plays an important role within the agency and can prevent "account piracy" when an employee leaves. Many agencies include a restrictive covenant in the employment contract of new employees, so that employees agree not to work for or contact the agency's clients for a specified period of time after they leave the agency. Such agreements will generally be upheld in court as valid contract provisions as long as the time period is "reasonable," usually no more than two years.

Because advertising agencies act on behalf of their clients, they take on additional legal duties based on that relationship that are not dependent on the provisions of their contracts. Among the duties to clients imposed by law is the duty of loyalty, the duty to preserve a client's trade secrets, the duty to avoid conflicts of interest, and accountability regarding client funds. In recent years, an expanding notion of civil law has opened the possibility that the ad agency may be legally accountable to its client for what might be called "advertising malpractice." In 1999 the retail shoe chain Just for Feet sued Saatchi & Saatchi over a commercial the agency prepared for that year's Super Bowl telecast. The commercial showed white hunters pursuing a barefoot black Kenyan. Widely panned as racist and inappropriate, the commercial seriously embarrassed the advertiser, which complained that it had been browbeaten by the agency into accepting the ad. Just for Feet sued the agency for $10 million for breach of contract and professional negligence.

Advertisers and agencies must take care to follow copyright and trademark laws and the federal and state statutes regarding unfair competition. They should also be aware of the body of law, known as "common law," that has developed through judicial decisions. Common law causes of action that affect advertisers include actions for defamation and product disparagement. Issues regarding invasion of privacy and its flipside, the right of publicity, are two areas of common law that most directly affect advertisers because they concern a person's right to control the use of his or her name or image.

"Appropriation" (sometimes called "misappropriation"), for example, is a common law cause of action for the unauthorized use of a person's name or image for commercial purposes. An individual has the legal right, based on a right to privacy, to control how his or her name or image is used and to prevent others from using it for their own purposes. One of the earliest appropriation cases involved an Albany, New York, resident named Abigail Roberson. In 1902 Roberson's picture appeared without her permission on posters advertising Franklin Mills Flour, along with a caption that said, "Flour of the family." Though the courts rejected her argument that her right of privacy had been violated, the case generated such a public outcry that the New York state legislature passed a statute providing civil and criminal penalties for the unauthorized commercial use of an individual's name or likeness. By the end of the 20th century, almost every U.S. state recognized a right to privacy, either through statute or as part of its common law.

An individual's right of publicity was first recognized in the United States in the 1950s. It is similar to appropriation but usually applies to celebrities or others whose names or images have commercial value. The right of publicity prevents the unauthorized commercial use of an individual's name, likeness, or other recognizable aspects of his or her personality or identity.

In the United States the right of publicity is protected either by state common law or statutory law. About half of the states have explicitly recognized this right, and in other states it may be indirectly protected through unfair competition laws. There is no federal right of publicity, although the federal Lanham Act governing trademark and unfair competition may apply where an advertiser's use of a person's name or image confuses or misleads the public as to the person's affiliation with or endorsement of a product.

Celebrities' Rights

Celebrities' rights have greatly expanded since the 1970s, growing to include much more than merely name and image. Depending on the jurisdiction, a person's publicity rights may extend to the use of his or her voice, signature, distinctive appearance, gestures, or mannerisms. Thus, such celebrities as Woody Allen and Jacqueline Kennedy Onassis have won lawsuits against advertisers that used look-alike models in commercials.

"Sound-alikes" can also bring legal problems. In 1988 singer Bette Midler filed suit in U.S. District Court in San Francisco, California, when the Detroit, Michigan, office of Young & Rubicam, Inc., hired one of her backup singers to imitate Midler's voice in singing her hit song "Do You Want to Dance?" in a Ford Motor Company commercial for its Lincoln-Mercury division. The agency had asked Midler to perform for the commercial, but she declined. The agency had the required copyright permissions for the song itself, but a jury nonetheless awarded Midler $400,000 in damages. Singer Tom Waits won a similar judgment against Frito-Lay for using a sound-alike to imitate his distinctive gravelly voice in a Doritos radio commercial from agency Tracy-Locke in Dallas, Texas. His damage award amounted to more than $2 million and included punitive damages because the commercial was created a mere three months after the Midler case had been decided.

Some observers believe that the right of publicity has been extended too far. In 1983 a federal court sided with comedian Johnny Carson in his attempt to prevent a marketer of portable

A 1955 newspaper ad identified a legal problem with Helene Curtis Industries' use of the brand name Nay, requiring a name change after the deodorant went to market.
Reprinted Courtesy of Unilever United States, Inc.

toilets from calling its product "Here's Johnny" and promoting it as "the world's foremost commodian." Although the phrase "Here's Johnny!" was spoken not by Carson, but by his sidekick, Ed McMahon, the court ruled that the phrase had become a part of Carson's identity and, therefore, he should be permitted to control its use. In 1993 a different federal court upheld a suit filed by Vanna White, the co-host and "letter-turner" of the television game show *Wheel of Fortune,* against Samsung over a TV spot from David Deutsch Associates, Inc., that featured a robot dressed and coiffed to resemble White on a set similar to that of *Wheel.* The court held that the advertisement had used White's "identity" even though her image was not in the ad.

Because the right of publicity is seen as a property right, courts in more than a dozen states now recognize a "post mortem" right of publicity. In these states, a celebrity's heirs must consent to any use of the deceased's name or image in an advertisement. There is still wide disagreement on this issue, however, as other courts have ruled that a person's name and image may be used freely after his or her death. Some courts have ruled that a celebrity's right of publicity continues after death only if he or she had exploited that right while alive.

Unlike the United States, the United Kingdom does not recognize a right of publicity or even a distinct cause of action for appropriation. That country's intellectual property laws and business tort law may offer some of the same protections to celebrities, however. Other countries, such as Argentina, Brazil, Canada, France, and Italy, recognize some measure of publicity rights, often through a combination of common law business torts and intellectual property laws.

Advertising Specialists

A number of U.S. law firms specialize in advertising law. Three of the biggest are Davis & Gilbert, LLP; Frankfurt, Garbus, Klein & Selz, P.C.; and Hall Dickler Kent Friedman & Wood, LLP. Davis & Gilbert, New York City, was founded in 1906, and is best known for representing companies involved in advertising, public relations, marketing, and promotion. The firm's work includes copy review and network clearance as well as counseling and representation regarding matters of trademark and copyright infringement, unfair competition and Lanham Act claims, and compliance with governmental regulations. Its clients include huge ad holding companies such as the Omnicom Group and WPP Group as well as some smaller independent agencies.

Frankfurt, Garbus, Klein & Selz, New York City, was founded in 1977. The firm represents numerous advertising agencies in every aspect of the industry, including the purchase and sale of agencies and the negotiation of talent and production agreements. The firm has expertise in right of publicity and privacy cases, having represented defendants in the Vanna White, Jacqueline Onassis, and Woody Allen cases described above, as well as in intellectual property issues and in merchandising, franchising, and sponsorship deals.

Hall Dickler Kent Friedman & Wood, New York City, has represented the advertising industry for more than 50 years and currently counsels more than 100 advertising and sales promotion agencies and many major corporations on advertising matters. The firm is active in international issues as the founder and U.S. member of the Global Advertising Lawyers Alliance, a worldwide consortium of lawyers and law firms specializing in advertising,

promotion, and marketing law. Hall Dickler is also the American representative to the European Advertising Lawyers' Association (EALA), an organization founded in 1989 to help advertisers make sure their international advertising campaigns comply with all applicable laws. Other countries represented in EALA are the United Kingdom, France, Germany, Finland, Sweden, Switzerland, Greece, Ireland, Italy, and The Netherlands.

Other American law firms with significant specialties in advertising work include Arent Fox Kintner Plotkin & Kahn, PLLC, Washington, D.C.; Loeb & Loeb, LLP, New York City; the Lustigman Firm, P.C., New York City; and Sidley & Austin, Chicago, Illinois. In Canada, Heenan Blaikie specializes in advertising and marketing law with offices in Toronto and Montreal. Law firms specializing in advertising and marketing law worldwide include Castrillo & Asociados in Buenos Aires, Argentina; Clayton Utz in Sydney and throughout Australia; Lawrence Graham in London, England; Vaisse Lardin et Associes in Paris, France; Redeker Schon Dahs & Sellner in Bonn and throughout Germany; Kojima Law Offices in Tokyo, Japan; and Skrine & Company in Kuala Lumpur, Malaysia.

KATHLEEN K. OLSON

See also color plate in this volume

Further Reading

Cirino, Paul, "Advertisers, Celebrities, and Publicity Rights in New York and California," *New York Law School Law Review* 39 (1994)

Jones, John Philip, editor, *International Advertising: Realities and Myths,* Thousand Oaks, California: Sage, 2000

Kent, Felix H., and Elhanan C. Stone, editors, *Legal and Business Aspects of the Advertising Industry,* New York: Practising Law Institute, 1982

McCarthy, J. Thomas, *The Rights of Publicity and Privacy,* New York: Boardman, 1987– (updated regularly)

Moore, Roy L., Ronald T. Farrar, and Erik L. Collins, *Advertising and Public Relations Law,* Mahwah, New Jersey: Erlbaum, 1998

Plevan, Kenneth A., and Miriam L. Siroky, *Advertising Compliance Handbook,* New York: Skadden Arps Slate Meagher and Flom, 1987; 2nd edition, New York: Practising Law Institute, 1991

Preston, Ivan L., *The Tangled Web They Weave: Truth, Falsity, and Advertisers,* Madison: University of Wisconsin Press, 1994

Lennen & Newell, Inc.

Predecessor agency Lennen & Mitchell, Inc., founded by Philip W. Lennen and J.T.H. Mitchell, 1924; renamed Lennen & Newell when H.W. Newell joined agency, 1952; acquired Geyer-Oswald, 1970; declared bankruptcy, 1972, leading to lawsuits and reexamination of the principle of agency sole liability.

Major Clients
Colgate-Palmolive Company (Lustre-Crème Shampoo)
National Distillers
Stokely-Van Camp

Lennen & Mitchell, Inc. (L&M), was founded in 1924 when Philip W. Lennen joined J.T.H. Mitchell (of the J.T.H. Mitchell agency, which had been in existence since 1916). It was renamed Lennen & Newell, Inc. (L&N), with the arrival of Herman W. ("Hike") Newell in 1952. Adolph Toigo ran the agency as sole owner from 1954 until its sudden business failure in 1972. During its heyday, the agency was the 13th-largest U.S. agency, had 600 employees, and billed $140 million. Its bankruptcy and subsequent lawsuits by media trying to recoup media dollars from L&N's clients shook the foundations of the sole liability principle and resulted in a permanent change in the client-agency-media financial system.

Lennen and Mitchell founded L&M in New York City in 1924 with a single account paying a $1,000 monthly retainer. Lennen had begun his career as a copywriter. Before starting L&M, he had been ad manager of the Royal Tailors, a Chicago, Illinois, mail-order clothier, and vice president at Erwin, Wasey & Company in Chicago. After Mitchell died in 1930, Lennen was almost a one-man show for several years, involved with every client and responsible for most of the ideas. In the late 1930s he charged Ray Vir Den, who was later named president, with modernizing the organization. By 1945 employees had health and life insurance and a pension plan, all paid for by the company. There was employee participation in management, and key employees could purchase dividend-paying agency stock.

L&M considered itself a "big idea" shop. A classic house ad written by Lennen, entitled "Find the man," proclaimed that "the best advertising . . . is not to be accomplished by mass production methods. People do that, not departments, plans boards, account groups, committees, commissions or bureaus." He meant that smart advertisers would look for an agency with people who could consistently generate powerful and creative advertising. Old Gold cigarettes benefited from the classic "Not a cough in a carload" and "Treat instead of a treatment" slogans.

Another L&M "big idea" made history in the silverware business. Lennen's field research for client International Silver Company revealed that the universally accepted practice of marketing six-piece silver settings was not meeting consumer needs. His "Pieces of Eight" campaign was a great success; eight-piece place settings were easier to sell than six and brought in more revenue, thus transforming the entire industry.

The agency was a pioneer first in radio advertising and then in television. Its *Hall of Fame* show for client Lehn & Fink brought actors John Barrymore, Joan Crawford, and Clark Gable and musician Jascha Heifetz to radio for the first time. In 1948 the agency published a report about television that told clients to "Get in or get left" but also warned that the payoff could be years away.

As of 1952 Phil Lennen was in poor health owing to several heart attacks. He was interested in merging with Geyer, Newell & Ganger (GN&G), a prominent agency formed in 1911 in Dayton, Ohio, that had moved to New York City in 1935. By 1950 it billed $18.5 million compared to $16 million for L&M that same year. Bertram B. Geyer, its founder and largest stockholder, opposed the deal. However, under the condition that L&M president Vir Den be ousted, Geyer Executive Vice President Herman W. ("Hike") Newell elected to join Phil Lennen. He brought several major accounts, 20 employees, and a former colleague named Adolph Toigo with him. The agency was renamed Lennen & Newell. (GN&G continued as Geyer Advertising until 1958, when it merged with Morey, Humm, & Warwick.)

Within three years, both Lennen and Newell were dead. Control of the agency and most of the stock passed to "Dolph" Toigo. Toigo was born in Benld, Illinois, in 1896. He played football at the University of Chicago, and he got his start in advertising in the research department of the John H. Dunham Company. After a stint at Benton and Bowles, he joined Geyer, Cornell & Newell (a predecessor of Geyer, Newell & Ganger) in 1941, where he met Newell. Toigo moved to William Esty & Company, Inc., in 1943 and remained there until Newell summoned him to L&N in 1952. His research skills came into play at Esty when pitching the Bromo-Seltzer account. Bromo had been marketed as a headache remedy, but Toigo discovered that at least 30 percent of purchasers were using it for stomach upset. The pitch he made based on this information won the account. When he left Esty in 1952 he was chairman of the plans board and supervisor of Esty's Colgate-Palmolive Company business.

Toigo's reign at L&N lasted 17 years. A considerable portion of the agency's impressive growth from 1954 through the 1960s was owing to an acquisition binge. Among the acquired shops were: Buchanan & Company and C.L. Miller Company, both of New York City (1958); Lawrence Fertig & Company, New York City (1961); L.C. Cole, San Francisco, California (1964); Richardson & Hance, San Francisco (1967); Wyatt, Dunagan & Williams, Dallas, Texas (1968); Ackerman Associates, Oklahoma City, Oklahoma (1969); and Dawson, Turner & Jenkins, Portland, Oregon (1969). At the same time, Toigo was expanding overseas through joint ventures. By 1969 L&N had 34 offices outside the United States, in addition to domestic offices in Dallas; San Francisco and Los Angeles, California; Seattle and Tacoma,

The bankruptcy declaration of Lennen & Newell (L&N) made headlines in trade and business publications in February 1972. Because L&N had delayed its media payments, its creditors sought payment from the agency's clients, thus challenging the principle of sole liability.
Reprinted with permission from the 7 February 1972 issue of Advertising Age. *Copyright, Crain Communications, Inc., 1972.*

Washington; Portland, Oregon; Anchorage, Alaska; and Honolulu, Hawaii.

In addition to a roster of blue-chip clients, L&N ran Hubert Humphrey's presidential campaign in 1968. It did notable work for American Airlines, National Distillers's Old Crow and Windsor Canadian liquors, Mazola oil, and Niagara starches. It introduced Vel detergent for Colgate and also handled its Lustre-Crème Shampoo. It launched cigarette brands Kent, Old Gold, Newport, and True. By 1969 its billings were $140 million, it had 600 employees, and it was the 13th-largest agency in the United States.

On 2 February 1972 L&N shocked the advertising world by filing for bankruptcy. The Chapter 11 petition listed liabilities of almost $11 million and assets of $6 million. Of the more than 500 creditors, the largest were the television networks CBS ($812,395), NBC ($498,931), and ABC ($460,145). Despite attempts to reorganize, client defections forced the agency to close

in April 1972. Several factors combined to cause the worst financial disaster in advertising agency history.

The beginning of the end started when L&N acquired Hike Newell's old agency in 1970, then named Geyer-Oswald. Its claimed billings of $30 million were greatly exaggerated, and L&N received $4 million less in operating revenue than expected from the acquisition. Other acquisitions had been unprofitable as well. Lennen & Newell lost 75 percent of its billings in 1971, reshuffled management, and sold several offices. Another factor was the one-man rule of Adolph Toigo, who had elevated his son, Oliver, to president in 1969. Observers claimed that he had ignored many of the generally accepted rules of agency financial management. In short, a combination of agency management problems, ill-advised foreign and domestic expansion, and poor financial controls were responsible for the downfall of L&N.

The repercussions changed the financial nature of client and agency relationships with suppliers forever. The accepted principle of sole liability meant that once an advertiser paid its agency for media time, the media must look only to the agency for payment. Historically, this often meant that an agency suffered if its client's business failed, as the agency was still responsible for paying media. In the unusual case of L&N, client payments to the agency were used to keep the agency afloat, delaying agency payments to media in what was called a "slow pay" problem. After the agency's demise, CBS sued L&N client Stokely-Van Camp to recoup more than $400,000 in media bills. The litigation dragged on for six years and resulted in a reaffirmation of the sole liability concept. The judge upheld Stokely's defense because CBS had failed to tell Stokely about the agency's financial woes and slow payment practices, yet it had continued to extend credit to the agency under those circumstances. CBS also had neglected to inform advertisers that it would hold them liable. However, the case prompted a long-term debate over sole liability that was finally resolved with a "sequential liability" compromise in 1991. Under "sequential liability," a medium could look to the agency for payment if the agency had been paid by the advertiser, but would be limited to seeking payment directly from the advertiser if the agency had not yet been paid.

MARSHA APPEL

Further Reading

Donath, Bob, "Judge Backs Sole Liability Concept, Rules in Favor of Stokely vs. CBS," *Advertising Age* (10 October 1977)

Grant, Don, "Merger of Geyer into L&N Recalls Frustrated Talks of 18 Years Ago," *Advertising Age* (2 March 1970)

MacGregor, James, "Lennen & Newell Files Chapter 11 Petition; Big Ad Agency Lost 75% of Billings in 1971," *Wall Street Journal* (3 February 1972)

MacGregor, James, "How Lennen & Newell, Guided by One Man, Fell from a Top Agency to a Chapter 11 Case," *Wall Street Journal* (7 February 1972)

"The Story of Lennen & Mitchell," *Advertising Agency and Advertising and Selling* 42 (August 1949)

Leo Burnett Company, Inc. *See under* Burnett

Lever Brothers Company/Unilever

Principal Agencies

Lintas (house agency)
J. Walter Thompson Company
Ruthrauff & Ryan
Lord & Thomas
Foote, Cone & Belding
Batten Barton Durstine & Osborn
Ogilvy, Benson & Mather, Inc. (later Ogilvy & Mather, Inc.)
SSC&B: Lintas Worldwide

Lever Brothers Company is a U.S.-based subsidiary of Unilever, Inc., a huge Anglo-Dutch conglomerate with headquarters both in London, England, and Rotterdam, The Netherlands. Unilever employed nearly 270,000 people in the late 1990s, held approximately 300 subsidiary companies, and marketed more than 1,000 brands in over 150 countries. Among Unilever's most recognized brands are the detergents Wisk, Surf, All, Rinso, Silver Dust, Breeze, and Drive; Snuggle fabric softener; Birdseye vegetables, Lipton tea, Wishbone salad dressing, Mrs. Butterworth syrup, Imperial margarine, Promise margarine, Good Luck margarine, and other foods; and many soaps and other personal hygiene products, including Dove, Lifebuoy, Lux, and Swan soaps, Rave shampoo, and Aim and Close-up toothpastes. Since its inception, the company has been not only a major force in the marketplace but one of the most significant and innovative advertisers worldwide.

Ad Pioneer

Lever Brothers was founded in London in 1885 by William Hesketh Lever, who gained early business experience in a wholesale grocery enterprise established by his father. Lever was a visionary businessman and humanitarian. He studied emerging trends in the advertising field, and he applied what he learned to fight a "soap war" against other soap manufacturers, first in England in the 1880s and 1890s and then in the United States. He launched an extensive advertising campaign to market his initial offering, Sunlight Soap, as the first packaged, branded laundry soap. Among the brands competing with Sunlight Soap were Pears' Soap, produced by A.F. Pears Company, Enoch Morgan's Sons' Sapolio, Kirk's White Russian Laundry Soap, and later, American Family Soap, marketed by James S. Kirk & Company. Another prominent competitor was Ivory, the creation of Harley Procter, founder of Procter & Gamble Company (P&G), which has been a continual rival of Lever Brothers and Unilever.

In the late 19th century, the growth of the soap industry was greatly stimulated by increasingly mechanized manufacturing processes, decreased labor costs, and more efficient use of raw materials. In this era, soap manufacturers (and others) also began to discover that they could introduce products, create consumer demand, and develop consumer loyalty to particular brands through the use of advertising. The soap manufacturers are collectively considered pioneers in the development of modern advertising, and Lever Brothers was one of the companies at the forefront of this trend.

William Lever purchased two original works of art in the late 1880s. The first piece, entitled "The New Frock," depicted a little girl holding a pretty garment; the other portrayed a woman showing off a dress to other women. Much to the chagrin of the two artists who created the works, Lever had the pieces reproduced in newspaper advertisements with the accompanying headline, "Sunlight Soap—As good as new." His innovative, though controversial, use of art produced for noncommercial purposes inspired many other advertisers to follow suit.

In 1888 Lever established Port Sunlight, an innovative planned community near London, for his employees. It served as an avenue for the company founder's extensive charitable giving and became a cornerstone of the paternalistic corporate culture and imaginative employee policies that for many decades were important factors in the success of Lever Brothers and Unilever.

Many now-common characteristics of advertising—including national (rather than regional) campaigns, slogans, jingles, and artistic illustrations—became popular in the 1890s, and once again the soap manufacturers led the way. At that time, Lever Brothers and other soap advertisers began using one-quarter and one-half page advertisements in publications, rather than the customary one- or two-column advertisements. An 1890 Lever advertisement with the headline, "A cheery old soul," questioned: "Why does a woman look older sooner than a man?" The copy read, "It is possible for a woman with increasing years to continue to do laundry work. Thousands who would have been laid aside under the old system of washing have proved what Sunlight Soap can do in reducing labour." However, Pears' Soap's "Good morning. Have you used Pears' Soap?" and Ivory's classic "It floats" and "99 44/100% pure" were the most popular campaign themes of the time period.

Early Agency Relationships

In 1899 Lever established an internal department to handle all advertising for the company's brands in Europe, Asia, and the Middle East. The house agency was called Lintas, which was a contraction of Lever International Advertising Services. Although Lintas was global in scope, it did not emerge as an American presence until the 1980s. Lever U.S. preferred to use American agencies for U.S. marketing.

In the first decade of the 20th century, soap manufacturers advertised extensively in the United States, taking advantage of the approximately 3,500 magazines and thousands of newspapers published across the nation. Lever Brothers and its rivals both stimulated and profited from the growing tendency of American consumers to equate personal and household cleanliness with elevated social status and the prevention of illness. A 1902 *Harper's Weekly* advertisement for what became one of Lever Brothers most successful brands, Lifebuoy, boasted that the product's "germ-destroying agent" dealt with any "taint of typhoid, cholera, or diphtheria floating in the air or concealed in the clothing of the individual." A 1904 advertisement in *Outlook* magazine proclaimed that "microbes kill about 15 million human beings a year" and that "exhaustive experiments by some of the world's greatest scientists proved that Lifebuoy soap destroys the microbes of disease."

Not all Lever Brothers soap advertising during those years appealed quite so directly to consumers' concerns about disease. A 1902 campaign for Lux cleansing solution simply used an artistic rendering of a well-dressed woman seated in one of the first automobiles with a large box of the product tied to the front of the car and a headline stating "Foremost" at the bottom of the advertisement. In the same year Lever Brothers began an association with the J. Walter Thompson (JWT) advertising agency that lasted into 2002.

In the early part of the 20th century, the public began to question the value of advertising, believing that soap and other products might cost less if their manufacturers did not spend so much money on ads. William Lever was widely criticized in newspapers in England. One particularly malicious attack against him by the Northcliffe newspapers led to a 1906 judicial settlement that required the newspaper company to pay substantial damages to Lever Brothers.

To lessen the expense of competitive advertising, Lever Brothers sought mergers with other soap manufacturers. One of the company's key acquisition was Pears' Soap, and some of the most successful Lever Brothers advertisements in the United States during the early part of the century supported this brand. Perhaps the most popular and memorable Pears' campaign was conducted in 1912 and featured magazine advertisements picturing a baby reaching out of a washing tub for Pears' Soap. The headline read, "Who will be the next president? He won't be happy till he gets it!"

William Lever was an early advocate of "persuasive advertising," the type of ad that suggests to the potential consumer that there are other reasons to buy a product besides its inherent functional benefits. In the early 20th century, studies from the field of psychology concluded that emotional appeals were more effective than rational arguments for reaching advertising audiences, who were essentially unable to reason well. Buoyed by such psychological findings, Lever and many other soap companies began to focus their ads on image rather than product and on beauty and romance rather than cleanliness and medicinal value. Thus, a 1919 Lever advertisement for Vim cleanser and polisher not only depicted a happy housewife accomplishing her polishing tasks with ease but also declared that Vim "brightens the home and the age." Another 1919 Lever campaign, for Sunlight Soap, featured two illustrations. The first showed an attractive, well-dressed mother reminding her equally attractive daughter to pick up Sunlight Soap at the grocer's on the way home from school, as airplanes filled the sky above the two characters. The second illustration depicted another mother asking her daughter to buy Sunlight Soap after school. In this picture, however, the year was supposed to be 1969, and the mother was sending her daughter to the "Academy of Futurist Philosophy" in a passenger airplane. The ad's headline declared, "Education endorses the worth of Sunlight Soap."

Lever Brothers, assisted by JWT, was involved in early efforts to sell personal care and household products to male, as well as female, consumers. A JWT-created campaign for Lux gave women, men, and children the opportunity to participate in a $12,000 contest in which the contestants submitted letters that described how and where they used Lux. In later ads, Lever Brothers used excerpts from the letters to demonstrate the many ways Lux was used by all kinds of people all over the world.

A successful 1929 campaign for Lux Toilet Soap exemplified the growing emphasis in Lever Brothers advertisements on image-oriented advertising and reflected the fact that Americans were highly beauty-conscious at that time. "Blondes, brunettes, redheads," the ad proclaimed. "Such widely varying types . . . yet all screen stars alike have the vital appeal of smooth skin." Sixteen female film stars were pictured; each offered testimony about the beautifying effects of the brand. They were among the "9 out of 10 screen stars" who "keep their skin lovely" with Lux.

Survival in the 1930s

From its beginning Lever Brothers grew by using the principles of vertical integration. By the 1920s William Lever owned plantations and conducted trade and invested in oil milling and transport in Africa, and Lever Brothers had business operations in the United Kingdom, Europe, Asia, Australia, and the United States. Between the end of World War I and his death in 1925, William Lever entered into the food business, buying fish, canned food, meat, and ice cream enterprises. Thomas J. Lipton, Inc., also became associated with Lever Brothers during the 1920s. Lipton remains a full subsidiary of Unilever, marketing many brands of tea, soup, and other food products. In 1929 Lever Brothers merged with a longtime competitor, the successful Dutch company, Margarine Union, which had a lengthy history of developing and marketing margarine, as well as other food and soap

Lever Brothers' ads for Lifebuoy soap introduced "B.O."—for body odor—into the vernacular.
Courtesy of Unilever HPC.

products, in the United Kingdom and throughout Europe. The new conglomerate was named Unilever, and its general strategic planning was conducted through a committee comprised of the chairmen of the two parent companies and a vice chairman. (Unilever continued to use this management structure into the 1990s.)

The stock market crash of 1929 and the severe economic slump that followed made it difficult for companies to sell consumer products during the 1930s. Although both Unilever and its subsidiary, Lever Brothers, were hurt by the economic downturn, Lever Brothers was the tenth largest magazine advertiser in 1930, more than doubling its 1929 advertising expenditures. Throughout the 1930s Lever Brothers was consistently among the top ten companies in the United States in terms of dollars spent on advertising across all media. Lever Brothers was one of the top radio advertisers during the period, as were its key competitors, P&G and Colgate-Palmolive-Peet. Lever Brothers sponsored two programs produced by Ruthrauff & Ryan: *Big Sister* (Rinso) and *Laugh with Ken Murray* (Lifebuoy). Lever Brothers also built considerable brand awareness in the 1930s through its long-running *Lux Radio Theater,* which was produced by JWT. "Lux Presents Hollywood" became a familiar phrase to radio

listeners as the brand positioned itself as the favorite soap of leading movie stars. By 1939 Lever Brothers was the third-largest radio advertiser, after P&G and General Foods, billing nearly $3.4 million in broadcast advertising alone.

Drug and toiletry products were the products most often sold through radio advertising. Market research in 1935 indicated that only 2 of 5 people brushed their teeth, and advertisers of toothpaste and tooth powders quickly seized the opportunity to make dental hygiene a fast-growing product category. Pepsodent (founded in 1916 and acquired by Lever Brothers in 1944) was the leading toothpaste brand of the period, owing much of its success to advertising on the popular *Amos 'n' Andy* radio program (1929–38) and *The Pepsodent Show Starring Bob Hope* (1938–48), both produced by the advertising agency Lord & Thomas and its successor, Foote, Cone & Belding.

In the 1930s—a period of rising consumer and governmental concerns over false claims in advertising and unfair competition—Lever Brothers' newspaper advertisements for Rinso and Lifebuoy were notably straightforward. In the early 1930s, the ads used a comic strip format. By 1935, Lever had added creative jingles and light, humorous drawings. In 1939 a print-based campaign for

Rinso "for the tub-washer and dishpan" offered a "double your money back" guarantee to consumers if they did not find "every claim we make" for the brand—including "more suds," "dazzling white washes," and "special new suds buster"—was true.

During World War II, Unilever was cut off from many of its businesses elsewhere in Europe and Asia. In 1943 the company acquired the rights to sell frozen food in the United Kingdom under the already well-established Birdseye name. Both the parent company and Lever Brothers continued to be leading advertisers of consumer products in the 1940s, using all available media. In 1943 Lever Brothers ranked fifth in total U.S. expenditures on magazine, newspaper, and radio advertising. It ranked second in purchasing of advertising time on the three major U.S. radio networks—CBS, NBC, and Mutual. Among the programs Lever was associated with as full-time sponsor were: *Grand Central Station* (Rinso), *My Friend Irma* (Pepsodent, Ennds), *Big Town* (Lifebuoy), *Grand Marquee* (Rayve Shampoo), and *Songs by Sinatra*. A particularly effective campaign for Lifebuoy bar soap used a comic strip format, print cartoons, and humor to warn consumers about the dangers of "B.O." (body odor). One 1944 ad featured a cartoon depicting a trapeze artist refusing to catch his flying partner, with the cut line, "So long Junior. I warned you if you didn't use Lifebuoy, I'd drop you from the act." Text below the cartoon read:

> "I warned you" said the man on the flying trapeze. But in real life others don't tell you when you have "B.O."—they merely avoid you. And *anyone* can offend because *everyone* perspires, summer and winter. So do as careful millions do. Guard against offending by using Lifebuoy in your daily bath—the only soap especially made to STOP "B.O."

The Move to Television

After World War II television began to emerge as a viable advertising medium, and Lever Brothers was one of the first major television advertisers, signing with CBS for four half-hour shows in 1945. The company continued to advertise heavily on radio as well. JWT encouraged Lever Brothers to continue its sponsorship of the popular *Lux Radio Theatre* program throughout the 1940s. From 1950 to 1957 the agency also produced for Lever Brothers the *Lux Video Theatre*, a well-liked television program on CBS, and later NBC, which was written by a number of noted authors, including William Faulkner, and hosted by Ronald Reagan. Lever Brothers continued to sponsor the successful *Bob Hope Radio Show,* although it replaced Pepsodent ads with ads for Swan Soap in 1949.

At the end of the 1940s, sales of Lever Brothers' and other laundry soaps dropped considerably as synthetic detergents were developed and sold in the United States and elsewhere. Unilever countered by moving into new product categories and investing heavily in research facilities in Europe, North America, and other parts of the world.

In the early 1950s, Lever Brothers used testimonial print and radio ads featuring *South Pacific* star Mary Martin singing "I'm Gonna Wash that Man Right Out of My Hair" to introduce Rave

Home Permanent shampoo. They also joined other advertisers in a mass exodus from radio to television.

In the early 1950s Lever Brothers was enjoying modest success in the detergent market with its products Surf, Rinso Blue, and Breeze, although sales of these products trailed behind those for the market leader, P&G's Tide detergent. In 1954 Lever tried to capture more of the market from Tide by introducing Wisk Liquid Detergent, a heavy-duty washing product. Launched by the ad agency Batten Barton Durstine & Osborn, Inc. (BBDO), with a $12 million campaign, Wisk has since become one of Lever Brothers' most successful brands. (By the time Wisk was introduced, another Lever Brothers brand, Lux Liquid detergent, had already been established as the leading light-duty soap of its type.) Also in 1954 Lever Brothers sought to revitalize its presence in the bath soap market by offering Lux bar soap in pastel colors and reintroducing Lifebuoy as a year-round bath soap. The latter campaign broke from the established message that people were most in need of the deodorant soap during the hot summer months. Good Luck was the third leading margarine brand in 1954, and Pepsodent had a 10 percent share of the toothpaste market. Lever Brothers was the eighth largest U.S. advertiser that year.

In 1955, W.H. Burkhart was named president of Lever Brothers, and J.J. Babb was promoted to chairman of the board. The company successfully launched Dove bar soap around that time, emphasizing that the soap's "1/4 cleansing cream formula has made baths luxurious." An account long held by Ogilvy, Benson & Mather, Inc., Dove became a consistent seller and one of the company's greatest success stories. Through the creative efforts of another of its advertising agencies, Foote, Cone & Belding, Lever Brothers implemented another of its most successful and unforgettable advertising campaigns in the mid-1950s. The slogan and jingle, "You'll wonder where the yellow went, when you brush your teeth with Pepsodent," solidified that brand's place as a product category leader at the time.

Challenges

Lever Brothers faced a series of legal challenges in the 1950s. In 1951 and 1952 the Federal Trade Commission (FTC) brought an antitrust suit against Lever Brothers and its two main rivals, Colgate-Palmolive-Peet and P&G, accusing the three companies of price fixing. The litigation lasted until 1954, when the suit was dropped. After Unilever acquired Monsanto Chemical Company's All detergent line and trademark in 1957, the U.S. government unsuccessfully tried to get Lever Brothers to drop All, which has since become another consistent performer for the company. Soon the company again found itself in trouble with the FTC, which challenged the veracity of a Pepsodent toothpaste campaign that stated that the product removed tobacco stains from the teeth of all smokers. The claim was eventually modified. Earlier in the decade, Lever Brothers had to defend itself against a Procter & Gamble suit that charged that Lever Brothers had introduced Swan Soap as an "imitation" of Ivory.

Lever Brothers scored another advertising first in 1963 when, at the urging of the New York chapter of the Congress of Racial

Equality, it aired a television commercial for Wisk that featured an African-American child and a white child playing together. Lever Brothers remained one of the most significant advertisers in the United States in the mid-1960s (ranking sixth in expenditures in 1964), although the company had fallen well behind its primary competitor in the personal and household products categories, Procter & Gamble, in this respect. Lever Brothers' expenditures on advertising then declined each remaining year of the decade. Sales of Rinso, Silver Dust, and Breeze, three of Lever Brothers' long-time brands in the detergent market, experienced declining sales. The latter two brands were noted for their in-pack premiums (e.g. towels and dishware) at the time.

Lever Brothers tried to stimulate sales by spending heavily on the promotion of Phase III, a deodorant soap bar, and by introducing a powdered form of its modestly successful Cold Water All brand and Soft-Spread Imperial, a new version of its premium margarine Imperial. The company also launched Drive, a detergent with enzymes, and Twice as Nice, a "shampoo and conditioner in one," which was supported by an Ogilvy & Mather campaign using the theme "the difference that makes a difference" and offering a money-back guarantee. These brands were heavily advertised on such popular network TV programs as *The Lucy Show*, *Mission Impossible*, *The Art Linkletter Show*, and *Let's Make a Deal*.

Drive, in particular, met with initial success (fourth in market share in the detergent category in 1969), as it was backed by a J. Walter Thompson campaign that called Drive "the hungry detergent" that "eats what other detergents leave behind." Animated characters symbolizing the enzymes in the detergent gobbled up every tough stain in sight. However, the brand was pulled from the market a few years later, a victim of growing public concern over the detrimental effects on the environment of enzyme-containing products.

Another setback for Lever Brothers occurred in 1968 when the FTC declared a television ad for 3B All to be a "rigged commercial," forcing the company to take it off the air. The commercial depicted a man in a giant washing machine talking about the cleansing power of the brand while water rose up and receded, revealing his clean clothes.

By 1969 Lever Brothers sales had dropped in half compared to sales in the mid-1960s, and its earnings declined 20 percent. In the same year, however, the veteran BBDO copywriter Jim Jordan created what became a classic advertising campaign for Wisk laundry detergent: the "ring around the collar" theme. The campaign, which pointed to Wisk's capacity to deal with the worst laundry problems, was consistently rated by consumers as one of the most irritating advertising campaigns ever, but it was memorable and was used to sell the product for 22 years.

Diversification

The 1970s proved to be a modestly successful period for Lever Brothers, although its growth and profits were sufficiently stagnant to motivate Unilever to become more involved with its U.S. subsidiary. For Unilever, the 1970s were a period of further

You don't need a collar to need Wisk.

WISK GETS RING AROUND THE COLLAR AND YOUR WHOLE WASH CLEAN.

In 1985, almost two decades after the introduction of the "Ring around the Collar" campaign, the catchy slogan was still being used to sell Wisk detergent.
Courtesy of Unilever HPC.

expansion and diversification, as the company moved into such fields as packaging, chemicals, and market research. Backed by considerable advertising, All, Wisk, Dove bath soap (the leading "complexion" bar in the United States), and Mrs. Butterworth, a pancake syrup in a distinctive bottle shaped like the old-fashioned matron herself, consistently did well in their product categories. Wisk became the best-selling brand in the history of Lever Brothers. Caress, "the body bar with 101 delicate drops of bath oil inside to soften your skin," secured and maintained a modest market share. The new bar soap known as Shield, as well as Lux, Surf, and other brands, enjoyed limited success. Among U.S. companies, Lever Brothers' advertising expenditures for the decade ranked between 12th and 25th.

Targeting Procter & Gamble's Crest and Colgate-Palmolive's Gleam, which together controlled 73 percent of the "therapeutic" toothpaste market, Lever Brothers introduced Aim, declaring that the new toothpaste's patented "stanous fluoride" gave it the edge over its competitors. By 1974 Aim had gained an 11 percent market share on the strength of the Ogilvy & Mather campaigns, which featured programs to enlist the support of dentists, claims that Aim was the first "really different" product to compete with

Crest and Gleam, a "soap opera" approach in commercials, and such advertising themes as, "If it tastes better, they'll brush longer," and "The new Crest should be better than the old Crest, but there's no reason to expect it to be better than Aim." A mint-flavored version of another successful Lever Brother's toothpaste brand, Close-Up, was also introduced, and Pepsodent topped the toothbrush category.

Lever Brothers launched a successful campaign for Promise, a margarine product that promised to help lower cholesterol, in a BBDO campaign that featured "slice of life" commercials. Signal was introduced in 1977 and quickly became the third-best-selling mouthwash. Advertising for Signal featured its effectiveness in fighting strong mouth odors—"even onions, even garlic." Unilever acquired Glamorene as a subsidiary in 1975, adding Drain Power and a line of carpet cleaners to the company's offerings, and Lawry's Foods in 1979, which was later merged with Lipton. Lipton dominated the tea bag and ice tea markets and was very strong in other product categories. Tea sales were helped by the ongoing "Lipton tea lover" campaign, which featured TV football announcer and former Dallas Cowboys star Don Meredith as a spokesman.

Despite a degree of success in the previous decade, Lever Brothers instituted changes at the beginning of the 1980s. Michael Angus replaced the retiring chief executive officer, Thomas Carroll. Angus was credited with leading the company to greater prominence by rejuvenating stagnant brands through aggressive marketing, buying and selling subsidiaries, and restructuring. He essentially abandoned a Lever Brothers experiment with in-house media buying that had lasted a number of years.

Several advertising campaigns were particularly successful during the 1980s. Sales of Signal mouthwash improved as a result of a BBDO campaign, "Kiss me. I got Signal." Sunlight dishwashing liquid, also handled by BBDO, was successfully launched with initial ad campaigns that focused on the "real lemon juice" that gave the detergent its "extra cleansing power," demonstrated in the commercial to clean away baked-on foods that another "leading brand" could not effectively remove. One especially memorable 1988 campaign for Sunlight used a pop-art approach, humorously parodying common commercial themes and formats used to advertise dishwashing products in the past. McCann-Erickson, which had taken over the Promise account, positioned the margarine as a healthful brand through a "Get Heart Smart" campaign. A powdered version of Wisk was introduced in 1987, backed by a JWT "Tsk, Tsk, Tsk. Wisk, Wisk, Wisk" campaign, which included summer-long fireworks exhibitions. Ogilvy & Mather produced a favorably received campaign for Surf detergent, showing highly active families who "smelled bad" and required Surf to handle their problem. A Foote, Cone & Belding campaign declaring that the Wishbone salad dressing line "gives salads their fondest wish" proved successful.

Sales of Aim toothpaste had grown stagnant by the mid-1980s, although a pump-dispensed version of the brand had been introduced in 1985. A 1986 campaign for Aim created by SSC&B: Lintas Worldwide was built around the theme, "We're aiming at zero cavities." Containing a new ingredient recently approved by the Food and Drug Administration, Extra Strength Aim was introduced through BBDO's comparative advertising spots ("Sorry Colgate. Looks like your 20 years of maximum fluoride protection is going right down the tubes" and "No matter how hard you try, you can't squeeze as much cavity-fighting fluoride out of Crest as you can out of this"). P&G unsuccessfully tried to have the campaign stopped by complaining to the National Advertising Division of the Council of Better Business Bureaus.

Lever Brothers also found success with Snuggle fabric softener liquid and sheets. The company created a new product category in the United States with the introduction of Impulse, a body spray, in 1984. (Body sprays were already common in Europe.) Decaffeinated tea was added to the Lipton line in the mid-1980s, promoted through the SSC&B campaign, "Lipton Tea, you've made decaffeinated just for me."

Concentration on Consumer Goods

Lever Brothers and Unilever expanded rapidly in the 1980s, acquiring around 80 companies between 1984 and 1988, while at the same time Lever Brothers sold most of its service and supplementary businesses in order to concentrate on its consumer goods lines. Among the product lines brought to Lever Brothers during this period were Shedd's Country Crock margarine spreads, Chesebrough-Pond's personal care products, and the Gold Bond line of ice cream. Acquisition of Faberge/Elizabeth Arden and Calvin Klein fragrances businesses enabled the company to make inroads into the prestige personal care products market with its higher profit margins.

In 1986 Angus became chairman of Unilever. Instituting a new centralized management structure, he gave oversight responsibilities in product development and manufacturing areas to global product management teams, rather than relying on local managers who tended to operate in a more costly and less accountable manner. Aggressive promotional spending by Unilever in the United States prevented rival P&G from making competitive inroads overseas.

Unilever acquired more than 100 companies between 1992 and 1997, including Helene Curtis Industries, which added such hair care brands as Suave, Finesse, and Salon Selectives to the company's personal care product holdings. The purchase of the Isaly Klondike Company gave Lever Brothers Klondike ice cream products, and the company bought Popsicle Industries from Empire of Carolina. The acquisition of Breyer's and Sealtest from Kraft General Foods made Unilever the world's largest maker of ice cream and the leading advertiser of ice cream outside the United States. Gorton's frozen foods and Ragú spaghetti sauces were also added to the Lever Brothers food products line. The 1996 purchase of Diversey greatly expanded the company's segment of the industrial cleaning area: at the end of the 1990s Diversey Lever was a $1.8 billion professional cleaning service for hospitals, restaurants, schools, and other institutions in 100 countries.

Unilever continued to be a heavy advertiser. The company ranked between 12th and 18th in advertising expenditures in the

United States from 1990 through 1998. In a 1990 effort to attract the increasing number of consumers interested in environmental issues, Lever Brothers pursued a "green" strategy, emphasizing the use of recycled plastic in Wisk, Surf, and Snuggle containers. In a campaign from JWT that some criticized for its blatant environmental appeal, Wisk Power Scoop claimed to be "concentrated, so there's less waste." Lever 2000, a new bar soap introduced into the competitive but sluggish U.S. market in the early 1990s, provided Lever Brothers with its most significant advertising success story of the decade. Based on research indicating consumers were unhappy with bar soaps available to them, Lever 2000 was marketed as a superior, futuristic product for the entire family, which combined moisturizing, deodorizing, and antibacterial ingredients in one soap. It was launched with a distinctive package, $25 million in initial promotional expenditures, and a well-coordinated JWT campaign. The campaign featured print advertisements in popular magazines, which used the "presenting some of the 2,000 body parts you can clean with new Lever 2000" theme, along with images of naked body parts of people of various ages and explanations of the ways in which Lever 2000 would address consumers' skin needs. Lever 2000 quickly became the second-best-selling soap in its product category and spawned imitations from competitors.

Unilever has been a leader in creating and testing interactive World Wide Web sites for brands and companies. In 1995 Unilever established an award-winning Web site for the Ragú brand, the first food-product Web site. In the same year, Unilever signed historic agreements with America Online and Microsoft for the purpose of developing the company's interactive marketing more fully. Unilever later formed an alliance with Netgrocer, the first on-line supermarket.

Unilever underwent another major corporate reorganization in 1996 in order to simplify the responsibilities and roles of executives and to add flexibility to top decision-making. A seven-member executive committee was given responsibility for overall strategy, while the chairmen of Unilever PLC and Unilever NV functioned in the role of chief executive officer. The reorganized company came to focus on promoting key product categories and brands that had been successful across markets and marketing in geographic regions where there was considerable promise for a competitive advantage.

Reorganization was in part an attempt to address market needs more quickly. In 1995 Unilever launched a new laundry pretreatment product under the Wisk name, in response to a Procter & Gamble introduction of a similar product under the Tide name. However, Shout, marketed by the much smaller S.C. Johnson & Son, proved to be a better product that was marketed more successfully than either the Lever Brothers or the P&G brands. Pointing to this example and other similar cases, a 10 per-

cent erosion in Unilever's share of the packaged goods market, and the failure of both Unilever and P&G to develop new product categories, business analysts began to question whether such gigantic global organizations could effectively compete with smaller, more agile regional companies. Industry observers also noted that although both Unilever and P&G had used many advertising agencies through the years, both companies had been extremely loyal to a small group of core agencies, and these observers asked whether such long-term affiliations with agencies inhibited the development of fresh advertising campaigns.

Despite these questions about whether Unilever had become encumbered by its sheer size—in the year 2000 the company continued to expand, acquiring Ben & Jerry's ice cream and Bestfoods—there was no doubt that it was one of the great business success stories of the 20th century. Its accomplishments are a testimony to its innovative use of advertising and other forms of promotion.

J.D. KEELER

See also Lintas: Worldwide; *and color plate in this volume*

Further Reading

Aoki, Hidehisa, and Mahon T. Tavakoli, "Lever Brothers Company: Lever 2000," in *New Product Success Stories: Lessons from Leading Innovators,* edited by Robert J. Thomas, New York: Wiley, 1995

Freeman, Laurie, "Wisk Rings in New Ad Generation," *Advertising Age* (18 September 1989)

Giges, Nancy, "Lever Hopes to Clean Up with Sunlight," *Advertising Age* (30 November 1981)

Griffiths, John, "'Give My Regards to Uncle Billy:' The Rites and Rituals of Company Life at Lever Brothers, c. 1900–c. 1990," *Business History* 37, no. 4 (October 1995)

Neff, Jack, "P&G and Unilever's Giant Headaches," *Advertising Age* (24 May 1999)

Norris, James D., "Any Fool Can Make Soap," in *Advertising and the Transformation of American Society, 1865–1920,* by Norris, New York: Greenwood, 1990

Power, Christopher, "Everyone Is Bellying Up to This Bar," *Business Week* (27 January 1992)

Turner, E.S., *The Shocking History of Advertising!* London: Joseph, 1952; New York: Dutton, 1953; revised edition, London: Penguin, 1965

"A 20-Year Look at Lever's Advertising Spending and Brand Shares," *Advertising Age* (26 May 1975)

Wilson, C.H., "Management and Policy in Large-Scale Enterprise: Lever Brothers and Unilever, 1918–1938," in *Essays in British Business History,* edited by Barry Supple, Oxford and New York: Clarendon, 1977

Levi Strauss & Company

Principal Agencies
Lord & Thomas (later Foote, Cone & Belding)
TBWA Chiat/Day

Levi Strauss & Company is the largest brand-name apparel manufacturer in the world with sales of $6.9 billion in 1997. The company markets products under the Levi's, Dockers, and Slates brands in 30,000 retail outlets in more than 60 countries. Levi's, the company's most valuable trademark, is registered in more than 200 countries. Traditionally, Levi Strauss has used clever marketing and powerful creative execution to launch its key brands and line extensions. The company's 68-year relationship with Foote, Cone & Belding (and its predecessor, Lord & Thomas) resulted in ad campaigns that helped shape several generations, using striking imagery and music to reach target consumers. Singing the "501 blues" or knowing the "501 reasons" to wear button-fly jeans helped propel Levi's jeans from just a product to a cultural icon.

In 1853 Levi Strauss, an immigrant from Bavaria, founded a dry goods business in San Francisco, California. Strauss built a successful business over the next 20 years. In 1872 Strauss received a letter from Jacob Davis, a Nevada tailor who was purchasing bolts of cloth from him. Davis described how he placed metal rivets at the points of strain on the pants he made. Davis did not have the money to patent the process; he asked Strauss to pay for the paperwork and to become his partner. The patent for riveted pants was granted in 1873. Strauss became the company's first president, a position that he held until 1902. From that simple innovation in clothing grew one of the world's best-known products. In fact, Levi Strauss & Company manufactured the only garment created in the 19th century that would still be worn at the beginning of the 21st century. Levi's brand advertising started in the 1800s with flyers. Billboards and other print advertising followed.

In 1967 Levi Strauss began airing its first television commercials, produced by Foote, Cone & Belding (FCB). In one of the ads a prospector ceremoniously buries an old pair of Levi jeans. The ads featured humor that conveyed the real value behind the brand. In 1969 FCB produced three groundbreaking television spots that used rotoscope—a film technique in which live-action shots are hand painted, creating a surreal appearance. In 1977 "Farmer," a spot produced by FCB, won first place at the American Advertising Federation awards and was named one of *Advertising Age*'s "100 Best of the Year" in television advertising. In 1978 the International Broadcasting Awards named FCB's "Having a fit" best in television and "Jogger" best in radio. In Japan Levi Strauss introduced the "Heroes" campaign, featuring U.S. film stars James Dean, John Wayne, and Marilyn Monroe.

The 1980s brought competition from designer-label jeans such as Calvin Klein and Guess. It was a time when the company had to diversify into more niche markets to maintain its overall share. In 1980 FCB's "Working man" and "Engine" highlighted U.S. traditions. Tag lines such as "We still build the Levi's jeans that helped build America" or "Go ahead, chase a dream in Levi's jeans" were winners. "Working man" was honored by *Advertising Age*'s annual TV awards and the International Broadcasting Awards. In 1984 Levi Strauss launched the well-known "Levi's 501 blues" campaign. With FCB at the helm, Levi Strauss would create its largest advertising effort to that date. The campaign featured actor Bruce Willis and singer Bobby McFerrin. One of the spots, "Bluesman," received a Clio Award, and ten other efforts from the campaign were finalists. In 1986 a radio spot from the "501 blues" campaign won a Clio for the best song category. Fourteen other ads from the "501 blues" campaign were finalists. In 1989 the "501 blues" campaign evolved into the "501 USA" TV campaign. The spots were shot in locations around the United States and showed people wearing 501 jeans in settings that ranged from gritty and urban to rural.

The 1990s marked a new phase for Levi Strauss. Its 501 "Button fly report," by film director Spike Lee, showed children doing what they do wearing their 501 jeans. One of Lee's TV commercials, "Max drummer," won *Advertising Age*'s best of 1990. Several important campaigns were launched in 1992. "No one does color like dockers" highlighted the fashion appeal of the brand. Levi's Loose—a line of loose-fitting jeans—was launched with a TV campaign tagged "A loose interpretation of the original." Fashion photographer Herb Ritts directed the spots, which helped make Levi's Loose successful. In 1992 Levi Strauss launched its "Women in motion" campaign, using abstract illustrations of women inspired by the work of the French artist Henri Matisse to demonstrate the fit of its jeans. A new 501 campaign, "Got to be real," was introduced as well. Filmed by "501 blues" director Leslie Dektor, the campaign featured young people sharing their feelings about wearing Levi jeans. In 1995 Levi Strauss introduced the Docker "Nice pants" campaign. Levi Europe's "Drugstore" TV ad won advertising awards in Berlin, Germany; London, England; Cannes, France; and Milan, Italy. European consumers ranked Levi's "Taxi" as the best commercial of the decade. In 1996 Levi's introduced Slates dress pants with an advertising campaign tagged, "These are those pants." In less than a year Slates became a category leader.

In the late 1990s changing demographics and increased competition from J.C. Penney Company's Arizona brand and VF's Lee and Wrangler brands posed a serious challenge to Levi Strauss. Its partnership with TBWA Chiat/Day resulted in several notable campaigns. "Who's worn Levi's jeans?" was introduced in May 1998. The outdoor campaign connected fashion designers as part of a larger repositioning to solidify the brand and to target younger consumers. Other efforts included a new "hard jeans"

A promotional sunscreen from the 1950s carried 60 years of Levi's trademarks: the back pocket Arcuate Stitching Design (1873), the Two Horse Brand leather patch (1886), and the Red Tab Device (1936).
Courtesy of Levi Strauss & Co. Archives.

campaign that featured a series of unscripted commercials with young consumers, a first-ever catalog, and an on-line store.

CLIFF SHALUTA

Further Reading

Bounds, Wendy, "Levi Strauss's New Ad Campaign Simply Says Its Rivals Wore Them," *Wall Street Journal* (5 May 1998)

Goldish, Meish, *Levi Strauss: Blue Jean Tycoon*, Vero Beach, Florida: Rourke, 1993

Johnson, Greg, "Jeans War: Survival of the Fittest; A Tight Denim Market Listens to What Younger Customers Want," *Los Angeles Times* (3 December 1998)

Ono, Yumiko, "TBWA Chiat/Day's Offbeat Style Helps It Win Levi's Jeans Account," *Wall Street Journal* (27 January 1998)

Van Steenwyk, Elizabeth, *Levi Strauss: The Blue Jeans Man*, New York: Walker, 1988

Liggett & Myers Tobacco Company

Principal Agencies
Foley Agency
Frank Seaman Agency
Newell-Emmett Company, Inc. (later Cunningham & Walsh)
Dancer, Fitzgerald, Sample, Inc.
McCann-Erickson, Inc.
J. Walter Thompson Company
Norman, Craig & Kummel

Once one of the "Big Three" in the cigarette industry, Liggett & Myers Tobacco Company all but disappeared in the last years of the 20th century. Its once-leading cigarette brands were sold to industry giant Philip Morris Companies, and the Liggett Group remained active only in the generic cigarette market. The company has the distinction of having been the first to break ranks with the industry in the tobacco wars of the 1980s and 1990s.

Beginnings

John Edmund Liggett was familiar with tobacco all his life, entering his grandfather's retail tobacco business as a teenager in the 1840s; George Myers became Liggett's partner in 1873 when he bought out Henry Dausman's share of Liggett and Dausman Tobacco, which was renamed Liggett & Myers Tobacco Manufacturing Company of St. Louis (Missouri). The company began producing cigarettes in the 1890s, creating such small, now long-forgotten brands as Sweet Moments, Good Form, and Long Voyage, but until the early 20th century Liggett & Myers was best known for its chewing, or plug, tobacco. Its first moderately successful brand of plug, the eponymous L&M, was introduced in 1876; by 1885 Liggett & Myers was the largest producer of chewing tobacco in the world.

The company's size and success made it a target for takeover by James Duke's American Tobacco Company in the late 1890s. Young James "Buck" Duke had gone into the tobacco business with his father, Washington Duke, after the Civil War and built the family business into a virtual empire by pioneering the mass production of cheap, ready-made cigarettes in the 1880s. "Buck" Duke did not forget the continuing popularity of chewing and loose smoking tobacco among U.S. consumers, however, and moved to establish himself in those branches of the business as well. Duke embarked on an all-out price war in the plug field that lasted much of the 1890s; his appropriately named Battle Ax brand underpriced and outsold the competition and brought most of the industry to heel. However, Liggett & Myers refused to sell. It was brought into Duke's grasp only through the machinations of Thomas Fortune Ryan, who had negotiated with Liggett & Myers to protect it from the trust but found an $11 million deal with Duke too lucrative to pass up. As a result, Liggett & Myers unwillingly became part of the Continental Tobacco Company, one of the many subsidiaries of Duke's American Tobacco Company, in 1899.

Liggett & Myers again became independent in 1911, when the U.S. Supreme Court ordered the tobacco trust dissolved. Liggett & Myers was one of four companies that shared in the division of American Tobacco's assets. Although it received one-third of the plug market and just one-fifth each of the smoking tobacco and cigarette markets, Liggett & Myers shed its reputation as a great plug manufacturer and became known primarily as a producer of cigarettes. It also made Velvet, a sturdy, if unlikely, challenger, to the national leader in the smoking tobacco field, Prince Albert, produced by the R.J. Reynolds Tobacco Company (RJR).

Turn-of the-Century Favorites

Velvet smoking tobacco was presented to the public through the character of "Velvet Joe," a weathered old man with a corncob pipe and a beat-up hat, who offered homespun advice on how to get smoking tobacco satisfaction "reg'larly": specify Velvet and "stick to specifications!" Joe remained a staple in Velvet's advertising for decades after the Foley agency, which had created him in the early 20th century, was replaced in 1925 by the Newell-Emmett Company. With humble Joe as a spokesman, Velvet stood in stark contrast to the more upscale, aristocratic image projected by RJR's Prince Albert tobacco. For that matter, Joe was largely out of keeping with the more elite image projected in advertising for Liggett's most popular cigarette brands, Fatima and, later, Chesterfield.

Fatima, along with Piedmont, Favorite, Oasis, and other brands, came to Liggett when the tobacco trust was disbanded.

Liggett & Myers capitalized on Americans' fascination with Eastern exoticism in advertisements for its Fatima cigarettes, as seen in this 1914 example.

Each of these brands had its own, usually regional, niche. Piedmont, for example, was popular throughout the south Atlantic states, while Fatima claimed a large following in the East and mid-Atlantic. Indeed, from 1910 to 1920 Fatima was the best-selling cigarette in the United States, despite the regionalism of the brand's appeal.

Fatima's popularity was part of the Turkish fad of the early 20th century. The first Turkish cigarettes to appear in the United States (in the 1870s) were hand-rolled for the so-called carriage trade. A generalized enchantment among Americans at the end of the 19th century with the mysteries and luxuries of the "romantic East" (evident in everything from fashion to art and music) prompted more smokers to demand cigarettes of sweet, mild, aromatic Turkish leaf tobacco. Liggett & Myers's Fatima actually blended Turkish and Bright domestic tobacco, but the product was marketed to project an Oriental pedigree. Its label, featuring a veiled woman flanked by a Maltese cross and the crescent and star, evoked Eastern exoticism.

Ads for Fatima accomplished the neat trick of being both tony and accessible. From 1917 to 1919, the Frank Seaman Agency created advertising that was clearly aimed at an educated, prosperous audience, the type of consumers who read such publications as *Town and Country,* one of the many new national magazines in which Fatima ads ran. These cigarettes—and the men who smoked them—were "Distinctively individual." Ads claimed that Fatima cigarettes were always appropriate after an elegant meal or a fashionable evening on the town. Men of taste and attainment found their work and leisure hours made more pleasurable by Fatima. Yet the paper-and-tinfoil cup in which Fatima cigarettes were packaged was simple and affordable, allowing Liggett to sell a package of 20 for 15 cents. This price may have placed Fatima beyond the reach of people buying the "nickel for ten" Piedmont cigarettes, but the brand showed up as a bargain when compared to more expensive brands such as the all-Turkish Pall Mall. Furthermore, like its 5 cent and 10 cent competitors, Liggett offered premiums to purchasers of Fatima, a strategy intended to attract smokers of all classes rather than just the sophisticates represented in the print ads.

Two developments pushed Fatima to the sidelines toward the end of the decade. First, the Turkish fad fell victim to politics as the alliances of World War I made the East seem less mysterious than treacherous to Americans. Second, and more importantly, Camel cigarettes came on the market in 1913. In Camel, RJR created a distinctive and flavorful blend that subordinated both domestic Bright and Turkish tobacco to the Kentucky Burley variety. Helped along by a brilliant advertising campaign authored by N.W. Ayer & Son, Camel was a runaway success. Coming out of nowhere in the cigarette market (RJR had received no brands in the 1911 trust settlement), RJR passed Liggett in market share in 1916. By 1925 Camels had 40 percent of the market, and RJR led the industry. Although Fatima continued to be part of the Liggett product line until the mid-1960s, its customer base aged and declined over the years.

Rise of Chesterfield

Liggett & Myers turned to Chesterfield, an almost new brand, to meet Reynolds's challenge. Liggett first introduced Chesterfield in 1912 as a straight Virginia-Bright blend and packaged it in a pricey box. When Camel appeared a year later, Chesterfield was going nowhere, and Liggett withdrew the offering. In 1915 Chesterfield was revamped and relaunched. The new cigarette followed Camel's lead and blended Burley, Bright, and Turkish varieties of tobacco. Liggett tweaked the proportion of Burley in Chesterfield to make it less sweet than Camels, but Camels had clearly set the standard for taste in the industry.

Liggett created a distinctive package for the "new" brand, however, that was easily distinguished from the packaging for both the original Chesterfield and the upstart Camel. Working again with the Seaman agency, Liggett presented Chesterfield in a

When the so-called tobacco trust was disbanded in 1911, Liggett & Myers took over Allen & Ginter, which, according to this 1915 ad, boasted that it had been manufacturing Richmond Straight Cut cigarettes since "our flag had only 37 stars."

white paper-and-foil cup, the Chesterfield name printed in fine gold lettering lending an air of dignity to the package. The package, which remained virtually unchanged for decades, became an important means of identifying the brand, and appeared in all print advertising for the brand produced from the mid-1920s onward.

RJR and Camel took the industry by storm in the 1920s, but Liggett & Myers was secure as one of the leading tobacco companies in the United States. In 1920 Newell-Emmett Company, Inc., took over Liggett & Myers's advertising, retaining the account until 1949. The agency created a simple but winning slogan for Liggett's new flagship brand: "It satisfies." And apparently it did. Chesterfield was a strong second behind Camel in 1925, with 25 percent of the market.

In 1926 Newell-Emmett and Liggett decided to see if Chesterfield would appeal to women and deliver that as-yet-untapped market to the company and its coffers. That women—and respectable women at that—had smoked since cigarettes were first available was an open secret in U.S. society. There had always been a few small producers that had catered to the female market and created "feminine" cigarettes, which were smaller, slimmer, and often scented, but until the early 1920s advertising did not directly address the female market. Liggett &

Along with World War I came a decline in the glorification of Eastern cultures and an increase in the import duty on Turkish tobaccos, resulting in new popularity for domestic tobacco such as that used in Piedmont cigarettes, promoted in this 1918 ad.

Myers was the first of the Big Three to market cigarettes to women. In fact, the company's appeal to women was indirect: the posters and magazine ads for Chesterfield that carried the "Blow some my way" tag line created by Newell-Emmett never showed a woman smoking or even holding a Chesterfield cigarette. The message of the ads was nonetheless clear—and highly suggestive. The initial ads which showed a couple in the moonlight and the woman asking her date to "Blow some [smoke] my way," linked women, sex, and cigarettes in a way that other cigarette ads, many of them also peopled with women, had not, suggesting for the first time that women smoked, and that they might want to smoke Liggett's product. Liggett was not so daring, however, and discontinued the somewhat controversial campaign. American Tobacco proved the big winner in the female market and thereby in the overall market. Its "Reach for a Lucky" campaign, inaugurated in 1928, spoke directly to women and catapulted Lucky Strike to brand dominance and American Tobacco to industry dominance by 1931. Camel and RJR slipped into second position, and Liggett was relegated to the number-three spot, where it remained throughout most of the 1930s and 1940s.

Liggett's advertising in those decades was marked more by consistency than by innovation. The company did take advantage of the relatively new medium of radio to put its name and product before the public. Like its competitors, Liggett & Myers sponsored a variety of radio programs, including most famously the *Glenn Miller Moonlight Serenade* series beginning in December 1939. Also in 1939 the agency created *Chesterfield Time,* which featured Fred Waring and ran from 1939 to 1944, when that program was replaced by the better-remembered *Chesterfield Supper Club,* which ran five evenings a week on NBC with Perry Como and Jo Stafford on alternating programs. It was Stafford who made "Smoke Dreams" (" . . . while a Chesterfield burns") one of the most famous advertising tunes of the postwar period. (The song had no relation to "Smoke Rings," the Glen Gray theme used on the early *Camel Caravan,* or the 1937 Nacio Herb Brown song "Smoke Dreams," which was introduced in the movie *After the Thin Man.*)

Although its range of advertising media expanded, Liggett's message changed less dramatically. The dignified white Chesterfield package remained the same; Newell-Emmett varied the images and fine print, but stuck to the tried-and-true slogan,

"They satisfy," in its Chesterfield advertising. In the 1930s, Liggett & Myers turned again to the women's market, now successfully breached by American Tobacco. Showing women in various settings puffing contentedly on Chesterfields, billboards and magazine advertisements announced that millions of women had found a "new smoking pleasure." In the 1940s the press to establish brand loyalty among female smokers continued, and Newell-Emmett briefly tested a "girl of the month" campaign that featured fresh, beautiful young women demonstrating that, whether canoeing or at home indoors, Chesterfield was always appropriate and satisfying.

World War II created millions of new smokers as the U.S. government made cigarettes part of every soldier's "kit," and sales soared when these men returned home from Europe and the Pacific after 1945. Loyal customers knew that Chesterfields were the "satisfying smoke," but Newell-Emmett created a fresh campaign to teach new customers the "ABCs" of smoking: "Always Buy Chesterfield," the brand that is "Always milder, Better tasting, [and] Cooler smoking."

Toward the end of 1949 Newell-Emmett, founded by C.D. Newell in 1918, was dissolved and reconstituted in 1950 under its senior management as Cunningham & Walsh (C&W). The agency's relationship with Liggett & Myers continued, as the company began shifting Chesterfield ads into television while still maintaining a strong position in radio. *Chesterfield Supper Club* became a radio-TV simulcast as cameras were moved into the radio studio. Also on radio, Chesterfield sponsored both *The Bing Crosby Show* and *The Bob Hope Show* simultaneously from 1950 to 1952. During this period, the Korean War was under way, and C&W created a campaign with a military theme, "Sound off for Chesterfields."

In 1950 for its Fatima brand C&W also picked up *Dragnet,* a new radio program produced by NBC that would become one of the most famous police dramas of the era. Fatima and later Chesterfield continued to sponsor the show when it moved to television early in 1952.

The 1950s: New Advertising Challenges

In the early 1950s, health claims about cigarettes began to trouble the public and the industry's bottom line. Cigarette marketers for years had tacitly acknowledged minor risks associated with smoking, such as coughing and throat irritation, in various advertising slogans and campaigns. When P. Lorillard's Old Gold brand debuted in the 1920s, it promised "Not a cough in a carload." The "toasting" process for the tobacco in Lucky Strikes allegedly offered "Your throat protection—against irritation—against cough." Every tobacco marketer acknowledged possible problems—in its competitors' products. In December 1953, however, two physicians, Ernst Wynder and Evarts Graham, published a scientific study in the journal *Cancer Research* that linked smoking to cancer. This report induced a measure of panic in the tobacco industry, and a 10 percent per capita decline in cigarette

consumption over the next three years indicated that the public was worried as well.

Liggett & Myers joined the rest of the cigarette industry in expanding its line of filtered cigarettes. L&M brand filtered cigarettes appeared early in 1953, launched by C&W. After the report was issued that December, L&M received more support from the company and enjoyed a favorable reception from the public. In 1954, the new L&M brand surged ahead of Lorillard's Kent, although it remained a distant second to Brown & Williamson's well-established Viceroy brand, available since 1936. Filtered cigarettes accounted for one of every ten sales industry-wide. Ironically, *Reader's Digest* reported in 1957 that, with the exception of Kent and its "Micronite" filter, the filtered brands actually delivered more tar and nicotine than did unfiltered brands. In a comparison of Liggett's filtered and unfiltered leaders, L&M delivered 18 percent more tar and 29 percent more nicotine than Chesterfield.

These findings did not prevent Liggett from making some exaggerated claims for L&M and its other products. The cancer scare of the early 1950s ebbed, but it transformed the context in which cigarettes were advertised, making it necessary for companies to invent fresh approaches to address the problem of the smoking public's confidence and comfort. Cunningham & Walsh understood the challenge and changed the face of Liggett & Myers advertising in the 1950s, creating brashly reassuring ads offering purportedly "scientific evidence" that smoking L&M and Chesterfield cigarettes was safe. In 1953 L&M was touted as "Just what the doctor ordered." In 1954 actresses Barbara Stanwyck and Rosalind Russell appeared in ads to sing the praises of L&M's alpha cellulose filter. Chesterfield smokers were often reminded that independent scientific organizations had concluded that Chesterfields left throat, sinus, and "accessory organs" unharmed. Moreover "modern science," in the form of the new AccuRay packer, could "increase your smoking pleasure" and deliver the "measurably smoother . . . cooler [smoke that is] best for you."

In the wake of the Wynder/Graham study, such advertising aroused the attention and ire of the Federal Trade Commission (FTC). In 1955 the FTC laid out guidelines for the tobacco industry that disallowed ads (such as that for L&M) that implied in any way that the medical profession approved of smoking or endorsed any given brand; broad claims about the beneficial effects of smoking on one's nerves, throat, or energy level were similarly disallowed. The FTC had little enforcement power, however, and had in any event left the door wide open for companies to describe their filtered cigarettes and leave the public to draw its own conclusions as to their health effects. In 1955 the FTC was prepared to object to fraudulent claims, but it had no hard evidence that cigarettes (filtered or unfiltered) were unquestionably harmful. The cigarette companies, including Liggett, continued in the public's good graces, as the 1950s were a decade of peak earnings. In 1956 Liggett & Myers dropped C&W and split its account, with Chesterfield going to McCann-Erickson, Inc., and L&M to Dancer, Fitzgerald, Sample, Inc.

Difficult Times

The 1960s proved a difficult decade for the whole of the tobacco industry. Just when it seemed that filter brands such as L&M, Viceroy, and Winston would be the salvation of the industry, U.S. Surgeon General Luther Terry issued a damning report in 1964, specifically linking cigarette smoking with disease, especially lung cancer. On the basis of this new report, the FTC moved again to restrict cigarette advertising and to mandate strong health warnings on cigarette packaging. Liggett & Myers and the rest of the industry, acting through the Tobacco Institute and the Tobacco Industry Research Committee (which had been formed shortly after the 1953 scare by the leading tobacco marketers' and growers' associations), joined the Advertising Federation of America and the National Association of Broadcasters to lobby Congress for an "end run" around the FTC. The industry triumphed when the watered-down Cigarette Labeling and Advertising Act of 1965 became law. The act required mild health warnings on packaging but blocked state and local actions against the industry and prevented federal agencies from taking action to regulate tobacco advertising.

The industry again avoided stringent federal oversight when tobacco marketers determined to withdraw voluntarily all radio and television advertising by January 1971. With this move, the industry avoided both regulation and the pressure of antismoking ads that would be aired under the Federal Communication Commission's Fairness Doctrine, which guaranteed that opposing viewpoints receive airtime. The industry's multimillion-dollar advertising campaigns shifted away from broadcast media (which had accounted for 80 percent of the industry's advertising spending) and back to print and outdoor advertising.

By the time the voluntary ban on broadcast advertisements went into effect in 1971, Liggett had slipped badly in terms of market share and had begun to distance itself from the tobacco business. Between 1960 and 1969 Liggett fell from third position (behind RJR and American Tobacco) and 10.7 percent of the market to sixth position and less than 7 percent of the market. In 1968 nontobacco products represented 36 percent of the company's overall sales, and the Liggett & Myers Tobacco Company was rechristened Liggett & Myers, Inc. In 1973 the company again changed identities, becoming the Liggett Group.

At no point was Liggett resigned to its troubled fate. In 1961 the company dropped Dancer, Fitzgerald, Sample and McCann-Erickson and consolidated $27 million in combined Chesterfield ($10 million) and L&M ($17 million) spending at the J. Walter Thompson Company (JWT). In 1963 JWT oversaw the launch of Liggett's Lark, a cigarette brand with a charcoal filter on which the company had spent years and millions of dollars on research and development. Lark did well overseas, but it could not compete in the United States with Brown and Williamson's Viceroy or RJR's Winston, launched in 1954 and soon the sales behemoth of the filter market.

Following the lead of Philip Morris and its Virginia Slims brand, Liggett introduced its own brand marketed to women, Eve, in 1970. The brand enjoyed moderate success in the niche market of women's cigarettes, but it never approached the sales figures garnered by Virginia Slims. In 1973 Liggett dropped JWT and again split its business, returning to Cunningham & Walsh and adding Norman, Craig & Kummel (NC&K). The muted ads for Eve by NC&K had none of the sass and brass of Virginia Slims' "You've come a long way, baby." In 1977 Liggett introduced Decade (so named presumably because it was ten years in development) to the low-tar market, which was already dominated by Philip Morris's Merit brand.

Liggett's troubles with the timing of its new product lines were exacerbated by troubles with advertising. The company turned in 1981 to the only sector of the market not yet dominated by any of its rivals, the generic market, which, by definition, eschews advertising. As a result, in the 1980s and 1990s Liggett's premium brands suffered from indifference and lack of attention. New ads for Chesterfield in 1992 were hailed as part of the first revival of the brand in 20 years. The repackaging of Eve and Lark in that same year made news in the advertising media, as their campaigns of the past two decades had not done. However, Liggett did not launch another media campaign for four years, when the new, longer Eve was introduced with the sly query, "Who says length doesn't matter?" Publicis-Bloom handled the advertising for Eve.

In 1999 Eve remained the only premium brand produced by Liggett, rival Philip Morris having bought out Liggett's Chesterfield, L&M, and Lark brands for $300 million in 1998. Liggett retained less than 2 percent of the domestic cigarette market and had become a pariah among its industry peers after breaking ranks in 1996 to settle a class-action suit against the tobacco companies. That action opened the floodgates, making the entire industry extremely vulnerable to further litigation, expensive settlements, and governmental regulation.

NANCY BOWMAN

Further Reading

"Durham: The Town Tobacco Built," *Durham News Observer* (11 August 1996)

Hilts, Philip J., *Smoke Screen: The Truth behind the Tobacco Industry Cover-Up*, Reading, Massachusetts: Addison Wesley, 1996

Kluger, Richard, *Ashes to Ashes: America's Hundred-Year Cigarette War, the Public Health, and the Unabashed Triumph of Philip Morris*, New York: Knopf, 1996

Lewine, Harris, *Good-Bye to All That*, New York: McGraw Hill, 1970

Miles, Robert H., and Kim S. Cameron, *Coffin Nails and Corporate Strategies*, Englewood Cliffs, New Jersey: Prentice Hall, 1982

Petrone, Gerard S., *Tobacco Advertising: The Great Seduction*, Atglen, Pennsylvania: Schiffer, 1996

Sobel, Robert, *They Satisfy: The Cigarette in American Life*, New York: Anchor/Doubleday, 1978

Lintas: Worldwide

(Lowe Lintas & Partners Worldwide)

Founded as house agency for London, England, soap maker Lever Brothers, 1899; became independent in 1930 after a merger creating Unilever, though still owned by Unilever; entered U.S. market in 1962 through partnership with Sullivan, Stauffer, Colwell & Bayles, Inc., which acquired a 49 percent stake in Lintas in 1970; became part of the Interpublic Group of Companies, 1979; merged with Campbell-Ewald to become Lintas: Worldwide, 1987; merged with Ammirati & Puris to become Ammirati Puris/Lintas, 1994; merged with the Lowe Group of Interpublic to become Lowe Lintas & Partners Worldwide, 1999.

Major Clients

Johnson & Johnson
Lever Brothers

Founded in England in 1899, Lintas was set up originally as a house advertising agency for Lever Brothers, which was then little more than a London soap manufacturer. The name Lintas refers to no individual but is instead an acronym for Lever International Advertising Services. For years it operated as a department within the Lever corporate structure, producing advertising for Lever brands, which included Sunlight, one of the earliest packaged laundry soaps. As would befit a London-based company during the era of the later British Empire, Lever was an aggressive international marketer that sold its products throughout Europe, Australia, India, and parts of the Middle East and Africa—wherever the empire led. Consequently, Lintas followed the activities of its parent company and developed an advertising operation accustomed to working on a global scale with a colonial view of nations and cultures.

One of the earliest Lever products introduced to the world was Lifebuoy soap, developed in 1894 and predating Lintas. The original formula contained a substantial amount of carbolic acid, which gave it the aroma of a hospital ward and opened the way for its initial positioning as a disinfectant soap. Whenever a disease or epidemic swept a region of the world in which Lever had distribution, Lintas would sweep the area with advertising for Lifebuoy, emphasizing its clinical benefits.

Lintas remained largely an international advertising operation working entirely outside the U.S. market. Lever Brothers chose established American agencies to build its brands in the United States. In 1924 it assigned its new Rinso wash soap to Ruthrauff & Ryan (R&R), which would remain a principal agency for more than 20 years. Other products briefly went to the Barton, Durstine & Osborn (BDO) agency. By the 1930s R&R and the J. Walter Thompson Company (JWT) had become the main Lever agencies in the United States.

In 1930 Lever merged with Margarine Union, a company based in The Netherlands. The result of the combined operations was a new global giant, Unilever PLC and Unilever NV, although in the United States Lever Brothers remained the trade name of record, a subsidiary of the Unilever parent company. As for Lintas, it was spun off as an independent agency based in London. Though it continued to be owned by Unilever and carried a substantial volume of Unilever business, Lintas was free to seek other noncompeting business as any agency would. Lintas confined its growth activities over the next three decades primarily to European clientele and companies marketing in Europe such as Johnson & Johnson. This accounted for about 20 percent of its billings by 1960, the balance being Unilever. With offices in 26 countries encompassing 49 languages by then, Lintas claimed to be Europe's largest advertising agency. Yet within the United States few people were aware that it existed.

During the rise of network radio and television in the United States, the stateside Lever Brothers, a unit of Unilever, relied on a group of U.S. ad agencies. JWT produced the long-running *Lux Radio Theater* for Lux soap, while R&R handled the *Lifebuoy Program with Al Jolson* as well as shows sponsored by Rinso and Spry. Batten Barton Durstine & Osborn (BBDO) joined the roster to produce the *Burns and Allen Show* for Swan soap in the early 1940s, during which time Lever acquired the Pepsodent Company (1944) along with its brilliant marketing chief Charles Luckman, who would one day head Lever Brothers. Lintas did not play a role in Lever's U.S. marketing during this period.

After World War II Lintas decided it could no longer ignore the world's largest advertising market. But it was not until the 1960s that it was able to find a suitable partner. The agency of Sullivan, Stauffer, Colwell & Bayles (SSC&B) was formed in 1946 when Raymond Sullivan, Donald Stauffer, and Heagan Bayles became dissatisfied over stock allocations to senior executives within the family-run R&R agency. They joined with Robert Colwell of JWT, the other major Lever agency, to launch SSC&B, which became one of the fastest-growing postwar U.S. agencies. Shortly after setting up shop it began to siphon off key Lever accounts, including the flagship Lifebuoy brand.

It was not until 1962 that the beginnings of a cooperative relationship between SSC&B and Lintas were put into place. That year, in a little-noticed gesture, several Lintas executives arrived at SSC&B's Lexington Avenue, New York City, offices for the stated purpose of learning U.S. advertising methods. Soon the flow of executive "trainees" swelled to more than 300, and in June 1967 Lintas and SSC&B announced the formation of a joint venture to be called SSC&B-Lintas International headquartered in London. The agreement made each agency's services available to the other and provided Lintas with a U.S. presence for the first time in its history.

Although its name was little known in the United States, Lintas had global billings of approximately $96 million by 1970 (about 80 percent of which were still linked to Unilever), making it

"Just for the Taste of It," developed for Diet Coke and seen in this 1990 ad, remained one of the most successful campaigns produced by SSC&B-Lintas.
Courtesy of The Coca-Cola Company.

among the largest European agencies. SSC&B's U.S. billings for 1970 were reported at around $122 million, which included not only Lever Brothers' spending but also that of Lipton, another Unilever subsidiary. It also made SSC&B the stronger of the two partners. In February of that year what had been achieved between Lintas and SSC&B by agreement in 1967 was solidified with equity. SSC&B bought a 49 percent stake of SSC&B-Lintas International, the London-based joint venture formed three years earlier, with 51 percent remaining with Lintas owner Unilever. The deal created the world's seventh-largest advertising agency.

SSC&B reportedly planned to acquire the remaining 51 percent in the future; however, throughout the 1970s an unexpected reversal of fortunes occurred. By 1977 Lintas was contributing billings of more than $550 million, while SSC&B's stateside business had grown only by about 34 percent, giving the U.S. office billings of $163 million. For Lintas, which expected to benefit from SSC&B's new-business growth among clients with international needs, this was a disappointment. SSC&B was also losing Lever Brothers business to McCann-Erickson, a unit of the Interpublic Group of Companies. There were rumors that Lintas was looking for a way out of a relationship that was not performing. A later story in the German trade paper *Der Kontackter* suggested that Unilever was so dissatisfied with SSC&B, it quietly communicated its feeling to Philip Geier, chairman of Interpublic.

As the number of mergers and acquisitions increased throughout the 1970s, Interpublic emerged as the most important buyer. Late in the decade Geier, perhaps at Unilever's suggestion, began to consider ways in which the international Lintas network might fit into the Interpublic structure. It would be a complex joint ownership arrangement, and negotiations with SSC&B went on for nearly a year. Finally in September 1979 Interpublic formally acquired SSC&B, whose most valuable asset by then was its 49 percent share of SSC&B-Lintas International. The other 51 percent remained with Unilever until 1982 when Interpublic finally acquired 100 percent equity, cutting forever all Lintas ownership ties to its founding parent. The name was changed in 1981 from SSC&B-Lintas International to SSC&B: Lintas Worldwide.

SSC&B: Lintas Worldwide became the third major group within the Interpublic family, which also included McCann-Erickson Worldwide, Marschalk, and Campbell-Ewald. SSC&B continued as the U.S. operating unit of SSC&B: Lintas Worldwide. What distinguished the Lintas unit from the beginning was its far-ranging international network of agency relationships. The Interpublic merger started off well and hit its stride in 1982 with one of the most successful new-product launches of the decade—the introduction of Diet Coke with the SSC&B: Lintas Worldwide campaign "Just for the taste of it." It was a major stripe for SSC&B: Lintas Worldwide, and one that helped make Lintas a name to be reckoned with in the U.S.

But through the early 1980s, nearly three-quarters of SSC&B: Lintas Worldwide's billings still came from abroad. In 1986 domestic billings stood at $460 million, versus $1.65 billion outside the U.S., a ratio that had been more or less consistent since the 1981 merger. The Lintas global heritage continued to overshadow that of SSC&B, a fact formally recognized in October 1987 when Interpublic merged the agency with sibling shop Campbell-Ewald and dropped the SSC&B initials from the name, retiring to oblivion the last vestige of that agency. So was born Lintas: Worldwide, a $2.8 billion unit of Interpublic that included two divisions. All overseas operations reported to Lintas: International, while Lintas: USA oversaw Campbell-Ewald, which continued as Lintas: Campbell Ewald, based in Warren, Michigan, near Detroit; all this was accomplished without a single account conflict. In the first year after the merger, Lintas: Worldwide brought in $250 million in new business, including MasterCard International, Inc., IBM Corporation's personal computer, and Princess Cruises.

Then over the first four years of the 1990s a string of reversals hit the Lintas: New York operation, as business seemed to flood out the door. From a high of $750 million, billings slid more than 50 percent to $350 million by 1994. Diet Coke left the agency, along with IBM and MasterCard.

The MasterCard business had been lost to Ammirati & Puris, a New York City agency that had developed a much admired creative reputation since its founding in 1973. Particularly enduring was its theme for the German car BMW, "The ultimate driving machine." With the fortunes of Lintas: New York in disarray, Geier saw Ammirati as a desirable merger prospect, especially after Lintas lost IBM, clearing the air of any possible conflict with Ammirati's Compaq Computer business. Moreover, Ammirati was on a roll, having just acquired Burger King Corporation. After four months of negotiations the purchase was completed in July 1994. Interpublic acquired Ammirati for approximately $50 million with the intent of merging it with Lintas: Worldwide. The name of the new $850 million agency would be Ammirati Puris/Lintas. Martin Puris would serve as president. After a minor shakeout of clients, the agency became simply Ammirati Puris Lintas Worldwide (APL) in February 1996, with Ralph Ammirati as chairman.

The Lintas name would survive yet one more reshuffling within the Interpublic organization before the end of the century. Five years after the APL deal, management decided that personnel problems and lower-than-expected growth numbers required a realignment. By 1999 Interpublic's four agency groups had evolved into McCann-Erickson Worldwide, the Lowe Group (originally Britain's Lowe Howard-Spink & Bell Agency), Draft Worldwide, and APL. Because Lowe and APL each had substantial international billings, executives felt that the two could work more efficiently together. So on 29 October 1999, Interpublic folded APL into the Lowe Group dropping Ammirati and Puris from the name, and the new agency group emerged as Lowe Lintas & Partners Worldwide with three U.S. offices and 94 others around the world, according to a 2000 *Advertising Age* Agency Report. Puris resigned and Frank Lowe stepped up to the posts of chairman and chief executive officer, and the agency that began in 1899 as an acronym for Lever International Advertising Services moved into the new century.

JOHN MCDONOUGH

See also Ammirati Puris Lintas

Further Reading

Bernstein, Peter W., "Here Come the Super Agencies," *Fortune* (27 August 1979)

Dougherty, Philip H., "SSC&B, Campbell Join Forces," *New York Times* (14 September 1987)

Enrico, Dottie, "For Lintas and Weithas, May Was a Banner Month," *Adweek* (16 May 1988)

Fahey, Alison, and Jean Halliday, "The Lintas Name Becomes a Burden," *Adweek* (13 March 1995)

Konrad, Walecia, "The Quiet Combination Rocking Madison Avenue," *Business Week* (16 January 1989)

Liquor. *See* Beverages, Alcoholic

Literature, Representations of Advertising in. *See* Motion Pictures, Television, and Literature, Representations of Advertising in

---

Logo

A logo is a symbol of a brand, corporation, or organization that provides instantaneous recognition for the entity it symbolizes. It represents not only the product or entity but also the values that each embodies. An organization's logo is one of its most valuable intangible assets. Businesses and other organizations use logos as a way to attract consumer attention to themselves, their products, services, or ideas.

Logos derived from relevant, simple ideas remain the best way to get consumers' attention. The principle behind the logo is as old as civilization itself and is embodied in such symbols as the Christian cross and the Jewish star. Logos operate on the idea that people are easily conditioned to respond to events and images in their everyday activities, a response mechanism that was first described by Pavlovian psychology. The logo functions as a stimulus to consumer purchasing behavior.

Today's organizations often change rapidly owing to the effects of evolving technology, sociocultural forces such as deregulation, globalization, and privatization, and other factors. Corporate identities often cannot keep pace with such changes. A logo, which is designed to reflect the values and ideals of an organization, thus becomes the physical manifestation of that organization. An appropriate, enduring logo therefore is vital in determining the public's perception of an organization. At the same time, however, logos must lend themselves to subtle changes—while retaining their essential aspects—that reflect changes in style and design trends in order to remain "contemporary."

Logos, like advertising, work most effectively if they originate in a strong central idea. The idea should be based on an organization's values as well as what it offers to its customers. One example is the apple logo—a long-standing symbol of knowledge—used by Apple Computer. With its logo the company suggests that it has taken a bite out of the knowledge of new technology. This symbol, among other things, helped the company define what it stood for in the marketplace. Apple's founder, Steve Jobs, believed that computers would become an integral part of everyday life, so his company's name and symbol needed to be things that people could identify with. Apple's logo remains strong and fresh because it is based on a simple, unique idea coupled with a style that makes it instantly recognizable.

Most logos are visual by nature. But there are rare examples of alternate corporate identifications. In 1926 when the NBC network was established as a subsidiary of the of RCA, the company faced the problem of creating a nonvisual logo for a radio network. Because the General Electric Corporation owned 30 percent of the new network, the notes G-E-C on the diatonic scale struck on chimes in sequence were used as a unique audio logo. The "NBC Chimes" have gone through many incarnations since, but have remained the fundamental NBC identifier.

Virtues of Flexibility

In addition to a good central concept and a unique style of execution, flexibility is another essential component of an ideal corporate logo. Having a logo that is flexible enough to incorporate diverse ideas is useful if an organization has, or plans to have, a wide range of product lines. For example, a strong central theme alongside its logo has eased the way for the Virgin Group to explore new areas ranging from financial services to cinemas as well as to diversify its business practices. (The Virgin logo is a simple, oblique, underlined, casually written version of the word "Virgin" that strongly conveys the exuberance of the company, but at the same time is flexible enough to be used for various products or services.) A strong and flexible logo can also enhance the competitiveness of an organization in cases where a brand name alone proves insufficient. Penton Media's name and its "swoosh-like" logo are seen by the corporation as reflections of the broadening scope of its strategic focus, which is offering a full array of business-to-business media.

What Can Go Wrong

Although a well-designed logo is an important asset, a poorly designed one can have negative implications, detracting from the company's image rather than enhancing it. An example is Best Western's former logo, an old-fashioned gold crown, which was adopted and used from the inception of the hotel chain. Research showed that the logo reinforced consumers' image of the hotel chain as an out-of-date economy lodging. The replacement logo, in blue, yellow, and red, emphasized the name "Best Western" and included a stylish and contemporary looking crown over the name. The new logo was designed to convey a more positive image of style and quality and to appeal to the chain's new target markets, such as the Young Travelers Club.

Creating a good logo can be challenging. Close communication between the designer and the marketer is necessary to yield the desired result. Logo designers must create designs that accurately reflect the company's goals and values. It is difficult to design a logo without the organization's objectives in mind. Nike's "swoosh" logo and its "Just do it" slogan not only convey the company's message of athletes eager to participate in their chosen sport, it also allows the marketer to extend the positive feelings engendered in consumers to nonsports-related aspects of their lives. A logo can also represent an image or lifestyle to which the consumer can relate instantly. Harley-Davidson, The Gap, Snapple Beverage Corporation, and others have shown that the image projected by a company can inspire some consumers to pay more or drive farther for a product that may not necessarily be superior to the others in the market.

Attractiveness itself is not enough to make a logo a success. Some corporate logos represent extremely elegant design work that is not connected to the organization or its products. Sometimes, however, a logo that is previously unrelated to the product may create a personality for a product that does not have one. For

Companies often rework their logos to redefine their corporate identities or reflect a more up-to-date look. Motorola redesigned its trademark type eight times between 1928 and 1996.
Reproduced with Permission from Motorola, Inc. © 2001, Motorola, Inc.

example, Apple Computer's logo, an apple with a bite taken out of it, previously unrelated to the product category (personal computers), created an image of "user-friendliness" of the product, which was not usually associated with personal computers at the time. Similarly, Yahoo's logo (Yahoo!) suggests the personality of the company—excitement and fun—that is thought to be appealing to its target audience. Such a strategy can prove to be an effective tool in the marketplace. Conversely, it can be a big risk.

Moreover, product category norms also influence logo design. Designers must keep in mind what the logos of similar products or organizations in the market look like while giving a new logo its own unique personality to differentiate itself from the competition.

Delicate Balance

Trends in fashion and contemporary culture also are important considerations in logo design, conveying the fact that a company is changing with its environment or merely to break the "boredom barrier." However a design must carefully avoid suggesting a marketer takes a frivolous attitude toward basic values, and traditional values embodied in a logo that has been used for years should not be discarded completely. One example is the rock logo used by Prudential Insurance Company of America, which has changed dramatically over the years to reflect contemporary design while continuing to embody the idea of solidity and stead-fastness.

After the logo has been designed, the next step is to devise an appropriate strategy for its use. Since sports are an important part of the lives of many consumers, companies believe a good way to gain exposure is to use people's favorite athletes as human bill-boards. That approach has proven sound, as the positive emo-tions that are associated with a favorite sports personality also become associated with the logo. A marketer often chooses to use professional athletes—such as racecar drivers and their pit crews—or other highly visible people as a canvas against which to display its corporate and brand logos. A single racecar driver's jumpsuit could be emblazoned with more than two dozen logos.

Conference sponsorships are also very popular as a means for companies to promote their brands via logos. To leverage their logos' sales-enhancing properties, companies such as Mercedes-Benz and Nike have invested millions in sponsoring conferences and sports. Judging from the high rate of growth of such sponsor-ships, it is clear that such investments bear dividends.

Another important aspect in the deployment of a logo strategy is the feasibility of the proposed idea. A company has to generate and evaluate several alternatives that can be used to produce the same desired outcome. For example, in the late 1990s Pizza Hut executives sought a way to project an image of their newly revised logo onto the Moon with lasers. After extensive research, they found that it would be more economically feasible to embla-zon it on the side of a Russian spaceship, where it was seen by about 500 million newspaper readers and TV viewers around the world.

Why Redesign?

Occasionally a marketer finds it appropriate or necessary to intro-duce a new logo or update an existing one. This may be done when a company is going public for the first time, planning a glo-bal expansion, or embarking on a totally new business direction.

Companies sometimes revamp their logo for other reasons, such as a change in management. Others update and revamp their logos to illustrate that their corporate culture is evolving and their business practices are becoming more sharply focused. Such changes should be evaluated cautiously. When replacing a tried-and-true logo in the wake of internal change, a company must weigh the consequences of the change on suppliers, investment analysts, employees, and consumers.

As corporations change or face major upheavals in the 21st century, the best way to preserve their identity in consumers' eyes may be through their logos. Marketers such as Coca-Cola Com-pany, BMW, and Nestlé have maintained their original logos, which are by now recognized globally, while PepsiCo and RCA Corporation have evolved as fashions changed.

Top 20

In 1999 Sunil Erevelles and colleagues conducted a study of logos and the qualities that contribute to their effectiveness. The sub-jects were executives from 17 different countries. In the first phase of the study, the participants were asked to recall 20 logos (not brands) in a free-recall task. In phase two, the top 20 most com-monly recalled logos were physically displayed and the partici-pants were asked to rate them on four dimensions: memorability, simplicity, uniqueness, and appropriateness for the product cate-gory. The scores on all four dimensions were then added together, and the logos were ranked (see Table 1). It probably is not a coin-cidence that the most highly rated logos also represent some of the most valuable brands in the world.

SUNIL EREVELLES

Table 1. Top 20 Logos.

Rank	Company
1	Coca-Cola
2	McDonald's
3	Mercedes-Benz
4	Nike
5	Microsoft
6	Levi's
7	Sony
8	Adidas
9	General Electric
10	Intel
11	Marlboro
12	Pepsi-Cola
13	Budweiser
14	Ford
15	Nescafé
16	Yahoo!
17	Apple Computer
18	BMW
19	Virgin
20	Polo (Ralph Lauren)

Further Reading

Blankenhorn, Dana, "Penton Gets New Name, Logo, Agency," *Advertising Age's Business Marketing* 83, no. 5 (May 1998)

Faust, William H., and Arthur Eilertson, "You've Got a Logo, You Need a Brand," *ABA Banking Journal* 86, no. 10 (October 1994)

Hightower, Jim, "The Ultimate Logo Opportunity," *Across the Board* 35, no. 4 (April 1998)

MacDonald, Julie, "Best Western Aims to Attract 111 Million Guests with New Logo," *Hotel and Motel Management* (22 November 1993)

Mendell, Mel, "Does Your Company Really Need a New Logo?" *World Trade* 12, no. 3 (September 1998)

Nicholas, Ruth, "The Logo Motive," *Marketing Week* (4 December 1997)

Southgate, Paul, "Why Logo Louts Spell Danger," *Marketing Technique, Packaging, and Design* (30 September 1993)

Venable, Yvette Anne, "New Logo Preserves Brand Equity," *Business Marketing* 78, no. 8 (August 1993)

"What's in a Logo," *Business Bulletins* 19, no. 7 (July 1994)

Williams, Hugh Aldersey, "You Are Your Logo," *Management Today* 8, no. 1 (January 1998)

Zuber, Amy, "Pizza Hut Logo Launch Fuels Chain's Re-Imaging Strategy," *Nation's Restaurant News* (11 October 1999)

Lord & Thomas

Founded in Chicago, Illinois, by Daniel Lord and Ambrose Thomas, 1881; Albert Lasker joined agency, 1898, and began buying up agency following Thomas's death in 1906; Lasker became sole owner of Lord & Thomas (L&T) by 1910; L&T merged with Thomas Logan, Inc., and briefly added Logan to its name, 1926; resumed operations as L&T, 1928; Lasker relinquished presidency, 1938, and in December 1942 gave agency to the heads of its three main offices, who were represented in its new name, Foote, Cone & Belding.

Major Clients

American Tobacco Company
Goodyear Tire & Rubber Company
Kimberly-Clark Corporation
Quaker Oats Company
Van Camp Packing Company

The name of Daniel Lord first appeared in advertising in 1871, two years before he opened Sharp & Lord, a Chicago, Illinois, advertising agency. Born in 1844, Lord had come to Chicago in 1870 from a life as a farmer on Long Island in New York. He worked first as collector for the Chicago Street Railway Company, but he soon moved into advertising, selling ads for a Presbyterian newspaper, *The Interior*. Among Lord's partners in his early agency ventures was Carter Harrison, who would later come to dominate Chicago politics. After Sharp & Lord, there would be two more predecessor agencies (Chandler, Lord & Company and Lord & Brewster & Company) before Lord joined with Ambrose Thomas to form Lord & Thomas (L&T) in 1881. Beginning as a space broker for newspapers and magazines, L&T evolved slowly into an agent for advertisers. By the turn of the 19th century, L&T was handling billings of approximately $900,000 and was the third-largest agency in the United States. Total advertising handled through all agencies then was about $12 million, according to an estimate by *Advertising Age*. Lord retired in 1904, and Thomas died in 1906. Lord, before he died in May 1930, would live to see the agency he had founded grow rich and powerful.

That work would fall to Albert Lasker, who arrived in Chicago at age 18 in 1898 from Galveston, Texas, to take a job with L&T.

He began buying up the company in 1906 after the death of Thomas, according to his biographer John Gunther. When he bought out the L&T interests of Charles R. Erwin (who later joined with Lou Wasey to found Erwin, Wasey & Company) in 1912, he became the sole owner of an agency with billings of $6 million. Ownership was a formality, however. Lasker had dominated the agency almost from the day he started.

Pre-Lasker advertising in the United States was a simple declarative statement of availability. It took demand for granted and rarely felt the need to persuade or motivate. This was because production capacity limited growth of the early consumer economy in the United States. Advertising, with the exception of that which ran in a few national magazines, was local and mostly retail. Lasker may not have fully appreciated this in 1904; he was too busy selling advertising to look beyond the job at hand. But pioneering copywriter John E. Kennedy had figured it out and shared his view of advertising with Lasker. "Salesmanship in print," as he called it, was driven by a reason why the consumer should make the purchase. The notion was not new; patent medicines had been using this technique for years. Lasker promptly hired Kennedy at $28,000 a year, although L&T had never paid a copywriter more than $1,600 per year. Lasker embraced the "reason why" principle as an ideology, recruited and trained a staff of nine young apostles in its formulas, and created an updated copy department, the first of its kind.

Kennedy left L&T in 1906 to form Ethridge-Kennedy Company, never to make such a splash again. But under Lasker's care, Kennedy's ideas would become the first creative "philosophy" to sweep the industry. What Lasker needed most now was a disciple to preach his gospel, make it work, and acquire converts. What he got was Claude Hopkins, a man who lived by the clock, measured each day by his productivity, and never argued with his boss. Although Hopkins's salary eventually rose to $185,000 a year, he regarded extravagance as immoral. The two men shared a common faith in systems of order.

In the first 20 years of the 20th century, advertising grew side by side with the march of science into daily life through electricity, the telephone, radio, recording, and transportation. The more that intellectuals contemplated the wonders of the Machine Age, the more they found in its specificity and predictability a system for understanding people. Charles Darwin's theory of natural

Keep that schoolgirl complexion

A fine, fresh and blooming skin, radiant with health and free from blemishes, isn't the attribute of early youth alone. Every woman can keep her schoolgirl complexion long after youth has flown.

Proper care is the secret—care which keeps the skin in perfect health. This means the scientific cleansing which makes each tiny pore and skin cell active. You must use soap and water freely—you must use it every day.

Begin this treatment today

Wash your face gently with the mild, creamy lather of Palmolive, massaging it softly into the skin. Rinse thoroughly and it will carry away all the dangerous accumulations which so often cause skin infection.

Then apply a touch of cold cream, smoothing it into the skin. You will be delighted at the way your complexion looks and feels, at its smoothness, fine texture and fresh color. This special face washing formula is thorough. It will not cause irritation.

Volume and efficiency permit us to sell Palmolive for

10c

Remember blackheads come from pores filling up with dirt—that pimples follow when this dirt carries infection.

Daily cleansing is your protection against skin troubles. Powder and rouge are harmless when applied to a clean skin.

Discovered 3,000 years ago

The use of Palm and Olive oil as cleansers is as old as history. Ancient Egypt discovered their value 3,000 years ago.

These oils are combined in Palmolive soap because modern science can discover no finer, milder ingredients. They are cosmetic oils, soothing and healing. They impart these virtues to Palmolive soap.

And best of all the price of Palmolive puts it, though so great a luxury, within the reach of all.

Only 10 cents

Although money can't command finer, milder, more beneficial cosmetic soap, modern manufacturing science has reduced the price to 10 cents a cake. The enormous demand keeps the Palmolive factories working day and night. It permits the purchase of the costly ingredients in gigantic volume.

Thus while women prefer Palmolive for their facial soap, it is also the popular family soap of America. The toilet luxury all may enjoy at the price of ordinary soap.

THE PALMOLIVE COMPANY
Milwaukee, U. S. A.
The Palmolive Company of Canada, Limited
Toronto, Ont.
Manufacturers of a complete line of toilet articles.
Copyright 1921—The Palmolive Co. 128:

Try Cleopatra's way to complexion beauty

She used cosmetics of every kind to enhance her charm, but cleansing with Palm and Olive oils came first. The same rule, applied today, will keep your complexion fresh, youthful and free from blemishes.

Use the same Palm and Olive oils, mild and soothing. They are scientifically combined for the use of modern women in Palmolive—the beautifying cleanser.

Lord & Thomas's "Keep that Schoolgirl Complexion" campaign, shown here in an ad from 1921, took Palmolive from an obscure toilet soap to one of the great brands of the 20th century.
Courtesy of Colgate-Palmolive Company.

selection was every businessperson's favorite metaphor because it allowed the individual free will but applied "scientific principles" to the group. Thus, it conveniently rescued economics from the reach of moral judgment. What trickled down to Hopkins and Lasker was the certainty that selling was a science and that effective selling was a matter of scientific principle.

L&T began to codify a series of advertising techniques that included coupons, sampling, copy testing, demonstrations, and above all the "preemptive claim." This was the idea that an ordinary product attribute, common to all, could be made to seem exclusive by claiming it first and then claiming it more often than anyone else. A perfect example was Hopkins's claim to the "preemptive claim" itself. L&T copy favored short sentences, tight, well-reasoned persuasion, and a clear serif typeface (Cheltenham bold). The agency believed that pictures wasted space. "We are a copy agency," Lasker decreed. It won L&T such early blue chip clients as Sunkist, Van Camp, Quaker Oats, and Goodyear. In Hopkins's first decade with L&T, billings tripled to $18 million, briefly making it the country's number-one agency.

By the end of World War I, vast production capacity built for war made possible a consumer-driven economy in which advertising would play a pivotal role. In 1923 L&T published its philosophy in a book called *Scientific Advertising,* written by Hopkins, who said that everything in advertising was either right or wrong. "Advertising has reached the status of a science," he wrote. "It is based on fixed principles." In the late 1920s L&T distilled its text into a series of 50 house ads that continue to make useful reading. Their empiricism not only defined L&T as an agency but set forth a policy of hard-selling advertising that would influence much of the profession for generations. Forty years later the uncommon irreverence of David Ogilvy's *Confessions of an Advertising Man* could not conceal its debt to Hopkins and was no less seductive in its prescriptive precision.

The more successful L&T became, however, the more it clung to a single advertising voice. Humor was outlawed, as was style, literary flair, and anything that might distract from Hopkins's armor-piercing copy strategies. "Ads are not written to interest, please or amuse the hoi polloi," he wrote. Spending is "a serious subject." As others pressed into new frontiers of market research, L&T preferred to put its trust in the inspired copy theme and its proven instincts.

In 1926 L&T ventured into its only merger when it combined with Thomas Logan, Inc. The merger briefly turned L&T into Lord & Thomas and Logan. When Logan died two years later, his name was removed from the agency and it became Lord & Thomas again. Lasker never considered adding his name to the banner.

The 1920s were inspired years for L&T. It built product categories that had barely existed before the war and helped make them a part of middle-class life. Some of these product categories signaled fundamental changes in U.S. mores. L&T made Kotex respectable to women of the era. It took Palmolive from an obscure toilet soap to one of the great brands of the century with a simple promise: "Keep that school girl complexion." Despite his success with Palmolive, Lasker would never forgive himself for

falling short of "The skin you love to touch," the line his archrival, J. Walter Thompson Company (JWT), devised for Woodbury soap. Lasker enviously credited JWT with being the shop that "put sex into advertising."

In the 1920s L&T not only made Pepsodent the country's leading toothpaste, Lasker became a major stockholder as well. When he learned that the formula contained a mild detergent called sodium alkyl sulphate, he asked Hopkins to coin a name, which he arbitrarily decided should contain three vowels and two consonants. The result was *Irium,* among the first in a line of "secret ingredients" the industry would invent for years to come. It was a classic refinement of Hopkins's preemptive claim. Another resulted from an early meeting with Frigidaire. L&T asked what made its refrigerators economical. A condenser, the company explained, with a single moving part. Lasker turned to a subordinate. "Name it," he said, "and make it the basis of the campaign." It became the "Motor Miser."

Lasker was not the only brilliant eccentric in advertising. Some were his clients, and none more so than George Washington Hill of the American Tobacco Company, which became an L&T client in 1925. Though it sold many products and brands, the one it chose to advertise heavily was Lucky Strike cigarettes. By 1930 L&T had built it into the country's number-one cigarette. Hill focused his interest on advertising. To those who objected to advertising, he reportedly remarked that "advertising is like rape. Relax and enjoy it." L&T created many Lucky Strike ads to his specifications. One pictured a ravaged Sabine woman being carried off by a Roman warrior. Yet Lucky Strike was the brand that liberated U.S. women from the taboos against smoking.

The agency, at Hill's insistence, built campaigns on remarkable claims. One advertised Lucky Strike as a cough cure because "it's toasted," a step in the refining process relatively common to all tobaccos. When it claimed that Lucky Strike could help women control their weight, it was too much for the Federal Trade Commission to accept. The ad campaign urged women to "Reach for a Lucky instead of a sweet." By 1929 American Tobacco not only represented nearly a third of L&T's $40 million in billings, it was the largest single account in advertising. By 1931 it had swelled to $20 million.

To accommodate an account of such influence was not always easy for L&T. One of the more curious affairs occurred in 1932 when Lasker was in New York City for a meeting with American Tobacco. The client company was then battling a stockholder suit over some excessively large bonuses Hill and other board members had voted for themselves. After the meeting, which had nothing to do with the case, Lasker was approached by Paul Hahn, Hill's assistant, who asked if L&T could accommodate a loan of $250,000 to tide several American Tobacco officers over a brief stock market squeeze. Lasker agreed without asking questions. Hahn insisted on offering L&T stock in a company called National Cellulose Corporation as collateral. A few days later a man stopped by L&T in Chicago, picked up the check, and left the stock. But the loan was never repaid. When Lasker examined the collateral more closely he was dumbstruck to find that it made L&T majority owner of a major competitor of Kimberly-Clark

Shall They Suffer

As you did from film on teeth?

PEPSODENT is largely for the coming generation. It brings to adults whiter teeth, new protection. But to children it means a new dental era.

Your teeth, perhaps, have always been film-coated, save right after dental cleaning. The luster has been dimmed by film. Film has caused decay, no doubt, despite your daily brushing.

Now dental authorities urge you to fight film. Above all, have your children fight it daily in this scientific way.

How troubles come

Modern science traces most tooth troubles to a film—to that viscous film you feel. It clings to teeth, enters crevices and stays.

The ordinary tooth paste does not end it. Much is left intact. Night and day that clinging film threatens damage to the teeth.

That is why well-brushed teeth discolor and decay. That is why tooth troubles have been constantly increasing.

Makes teeth dingy

Film absorbs stains, making the teeth look dingy. Film is the basis of tartar. It holds food substance which ferments and forms acid. It holds the acid in contact with the teeth to cause decay.

Germs breed by millions in it. Pyorrhea, and many other serious troubles, are chiefly caused by those germs and by tartar.

Dental science has for years been seeking a way to daily combat that film. It is the teeth's great enemy.

Two ways now found

Two effective film combatants have been found. Able authorities have subjected them to many careful tests. Dental science now approves them, and leading dentists, here and abroad, urge their daily use.

A new-day tooth paste has been perfected, complying with modern requirements. It is called Pepsodent. And these two film-combating methods are embodied in it.

Also starch deposits

Starch deposits also attack teeth. In fermenting they form acids.

Nature puts a starch digestant in the saliva. It puts alkalis there to neutralize the acids.

Pepsodent multiplies that starch digestant, also the alkalinity. Thus Nature's teeth-protecting forces are multiplied.

Thus twice a day, in all these ways, Pepsodent combats the enemies of teeth.

Millions of people now use Pepsodent, largely by dental advice. Anyone who once employs it can see and feel its need.

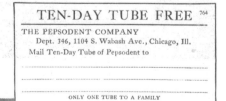

Watch the added beauty

Send the coupon for a ten-day test. Note how clean the teeth feel after using. Mark the absence of the viscous film. See how teeth whiten as the film-coats disappear.

The lasting benefits appear more slowly. But all who love clean, glistening teeth will see effects at once. And the book we send explains the reasons for them.

The glistening teeth you see everywhere now are largely due to Pepsodent. Learn how you can attain them. Cut out the coupon now.

Pepsodent
PAT. OFF.
REG. U.S.
The New-Day Dentifrice

The scientific film combatant, approved by modern authorities and now advised by leading dentists everywhere. Each use brings five desired effects. All druggists supply the large tubes.

During the 1920s Lord & Thomas invoked "modern science" to sell Pepsodent.
The PEPSODENT print advertisement was reproduced courtesy of Chesebrough-Pond's USA Company, Unilever PLC and Unilever N.V., copyright owners.

Corporation, one of his most valued clients. Both companies made feminine-hygiene products. Then the plot took another turn. The man who picked up the check and left the stock was not with American Tobacco but was a business partner of the judge hearing the American Tobacco stockholder case. L&T in effect had underwritten a bribe to a federal judge to ensure that the American Tobacco case would be decided in favor of the company's officers, which it was. Indictments later resulted, but none touched L&T.

Although Hill was a demanding client, Lasker made sure that L&T guarded its independence as a company. In June 1938 one of his oldest clients, Quaker Oats, submitted agency copy to an outside consultant. Townsend & Townsend was a copy evaluation company that claimed to score an ad's selling power based on "a fixed relationship between sales results and 27 basic selling elements." It sounded like something Claude Hopkins, who died in 1932, might have devised. Lasker, however, would have none of it. Without hesitation, the agency resigned Quaker, ending a relationship that had started in 1908.

Although L&T had adapted to change well, it had a blind spot: research. Early in the century L&T had been considered a research innovator when it set up a "record of results department." But as the field expanded, Lasker came to resent its second-guessing of the copywriter. Its rituals, protocols, and intrusiveness made him impatient. Frigidaire once set a $40,000 research document before him. He brushed it aside and said that a stenographer could tell him the same thing "quicker and cheaper." To prove it he called a stenographer. She not only did it quicker and cheaper but used only one sheet of paper. He loved subverting what he considered pretense, and he usually had the intelligence to do it without spilling his own blood. But Lasker suffered a common malady of the mighty: anything that challenged his judgment pinched a raw nerve. The appearance of the Townsend system was especially intolerable because it seemed scientific. There was rich irony in the fact that the agency that had done so much to advance the notion of advertising as a science should find itself beaned by its own boomerang.

Although L&T was slow to embrace advances in research, it became an early pioneer in radio. Lasker quickly retooled the old reason-why formulas for the air. In 1928 L&T and Pepsodent effectively baptized network radio with its first hit, *Amos 'n' Andy*. It was a landmark in broadcasting history. It drove radio sales to a critical mass, threw network expansion into high gear, and launched the stampede of advertisers to radio. A decade later when Amos's wife, Ruby, was to give birth, L&T helped engineer radio's first national promotional contest by inviting listeners to give the baby a name. The winner collected $5,000 in prize money.

In 1928 L&T took American Tobacco into radio with *The Lucky Strike Dance Orchestra*, initially featuring B.A Rolfe and then, after 1931, Arthur Pryor. In choosing this musical format for the cigarette brand, L&T was following the lead of Lennen & Mitchell, which two years earlier had debuted a musical program featuring the Paul Whiteman Orchestra under the sponsorship of P. Lorillard Company's Old Gold brand. In April 1935 Lucky

Strike introduced *Your Hit Parade*, which continued the pop song format but with the added element of a weekly ranking in popularity. The L&T radio department was responsible for tracking and tabulating sheet music and record sales and performance frequencies of current songs according to various formulas it devised. Secrecy was vital in order to build suspense for the number-one song, which concluded every program. (The program would move into television in 1950—produced by Batten Barton Durstine & Osborn—and run until June 1958, still in the format created by L&T decades before.)

Between 1927 and 1931 L&T is said to have controlled 30 percent of all radio ad dollars. It pioneered many of the basic broadcast formats: comedy, variety, soap operas, and police shows. In the fall of 1931 L&T was looking for a radio property for American Tobacco Company's Creamo cigars. It took on a young baritone, dubbed him the Creamo Singer, and put him on CBS. He was Bing Crosby. In 1938 the agency dropped *Amos 'n' Andy* on behalf of Pepsodent and replaced the show with a comedian fresh from Broadway, Bob Hope. In August 1942 the agency put another new singer, Frank Sinatra, on the air in a weekly program, *Songs by Sinatra*. The American Tobacco account went on to survive the reorganization of L&T and continued with it until 1948, by which time the agency was doing business as Foote, Cone & Belding.

The radio department at L&T wielded formidable power. Acting for its clients, L&T had control over the talent, content, and production of its clients' radio shows, carefully crafting programming environments for their selling messages. In the 1930s Lasker sat unchallenged atop his private empire, defending its role, relishing its intrigues, and confident that fate would do nothing untoward without his explicit consent. From his 18th-floor office in Chicago's Palmolive Building, his web of relationships spread from Chicago to Hollywood, California, and even to Congress. That began to change in the late 1930s. He left Chicago and moved to New York City. Shortly after the Quaker Oats affair in 1938, he gave up the presidency of L&T, though not ownership. Don Francisco was brought from the agency's Los Angeles, California, office in 1938 to New York City, where he assumed the presidency, clearing the way for Don Belding to take over the Los Angeles job.

Lasker began to express a cynicism toward advertising and his role in it. His politics became more socially conscious. He even submitted to psychoanalysis, a process that surely accelerated his separation from his profession. Lasker also recognized that the visionaries who had founded and built the mass-market industries of the 20th century on which L&T had thrived were either retiring or institutionalizing their empires. He watched companies created by brilliant despots such as himself become corporations. He watched his time pass.

In December 1942 Lasker made a shocking decision that would bring the history of L&T to an end. For a variety of legal and tax reasons, he virtually gave the agency away to the managers of its three main offices: Emerson Foote in New York City, Fairfax Cone in Chicago, and Belding in Los Angeles. (Don Francisco, whom Lasker loved as a son, would have been a founding partner, but with America now at war he had left the agency several months before to work for Nelson Rockefeller's Office of Inter-American Affairs.) He gave them the agency but not the name, snuffing out the Lord & Thomas brand. When he handed the agency over to its new partners on 29 December 1942, he said, "I will recommend my clients remain." It was an appreciated gesture and probably one that assured the continuity of the company, as it became Foote, Cone & Belding (FCB). In creating FCB, he decreed its partners, its name, its executive structure, its financing, and its client roster. On 4 January 1943, employees returned after the long holiday weekend to find the same offices, furniture, accounts, and colleagues. Nothing had changed but the name. Lasker lived for another decade but never became actively involved in advertising again.

JOHN MCDONOUGH

See also color plate in this volume

Further Reading

"The American Tobacco Company," *Fortune* (December 1936)

Bernstein, Sid, "Incredible Mark on Advertising Left by Lasker . . . ," *Advertising Age* (9 June 1952)

Cone, Fairfax M., *With All Its Faults: A Candid Account of Forty Years in Advertising*, Boston: Little Brown, 1969

"Daniel M. Lord, Pioneer Agent, Passes Away" *Advertising Age* (31 May 1930)

"End of Lord and Thomas Stirs Entire Advertising World," *Advertising Age* (4 January 1943)

Fox, Stephen, *The Mirror Makers: A History of American Advertising and Its Creators,* New York: Morrow, 1984

Gunther, John, *Taken at the Flood: The Story of Albert D. Lasker,* New York: Harper, and London: Hamish Hamilton, 1960

Lasker, Albert, "Freedom of Advertising and a Free Press," *Vital Speeches of the Day* (8 October 1934)

Lasker, Albert, "The Lasker Story As He Told It," *Advertising Publications* (1963)

Lord, Geller, Federico, Einstein, Inc.

Founded in 1967; purchased by J. Walter Thompson Company (JWT) in 1974 but continued as an autonomous unit until 1987, when JWT became part of Martin Sorrell's agency holding company, WPP Group (WPP); became independent again in 1988 when Richard Lord formed a new agency; was merged into another WPP agency in 1990 and disappeared.

Major Clients
Anne Klein II
Dean Witter Reynolds, Inc.
IBM Corporation
The New Yorker
Saab
Schieffelin & Somerset (Hennessy Cognac)
Steinway & Sons
Tiffany & Company

After earning a bachelor of arts degree at Hunter College in New York City under the G.I. Bill of Rights, Richard J. Lord rose through the ranks of advertising as a copywriter at Young & Rubicam (Y&R) and Cunningham & Walsh. He became a copy supervisor at Benton and Bowles (B&B) and by the 1960s was creative director at Warwick & Legler (W&L). In July 1967 Lord, then 41 years old, joined with art director Gene Federico (who had served at Grey; Doyle, Dane, Bernbach; B&B; and W&L) and John Southard (whose resume included B&B, Lennen & Newell, McCann-Erickson, and Chalmers-Johnstone) to open the agency

first known as Lord, Southard, Federico. In March 1968 Southard sold his interest and was soon replaced on the nameplate by account manager Norman Geller. In 1972 Nadeen Peterson joined as creative director/partner, and the agency became Lord, Geller, Federico, Peterson, Inc., until Peterson left in March 1974, when the agency reverted to the name Lord, Geller, Federico & Partners. Copy supervisor Arthur Einstein, whom Lord had first hired at B&B, was with the agency from the start, although his name was not added to the logo until 1978.

Billings rose steadily during the early years, reaching $9.6 million in 1973, as the agency handled small but prestige accounts (such as Steinway, Hennessy Cognac, Tiffany, *The New Yorker,* and Movado) and acquired a reputation for creative elegance and quality. Wishing to remain small and accessible, Lord, Geller reportedly hired no secretaries in the early years, requiring all employees to answer their own phones.

Seeking greater opportunities and believing that he needed the resources of a major agency behind him, Lord actively courted support from J. Walter Thompson Company (JWT), which had never before acquired a U.S. agency. In April 1974 JWT bought Lord, Geller for $325,000, a sum industry observers considered a bargain for an agency reportedly billing close to $10 million annually (although some sources estimate that the agency's billings at the time were closer to $5 million per year). Under the acquisition, the agency retained full autonomy and reported directly to JWT top management.

In 1978 IBM was seeking to replace Ally & Gargano, and the agency then known as Lord, Geller, Federico, Einstein (LGFE) found itself on a list of 25 firms invited to compete for the account. After a long process, LGFE won the account and was summoned to Boca Raton, Florida, for a secret meeting where the agency learned that it would create the campaign to launch the IBM personal computer. Creative work began in January 1980. At that time, leading computer companies routinely used celebrity spokespersons in their ads—Apple used Dick Cavett; Commodore, William Shatner; Texas Instruments, Bill Cosby. At LGFE, the creative staff came up with the idea of using a silent "spokesperson." After considering the celebrated mime Marcel Marceau, the agency decided to use the famous Charlie Chaplin character of the "little tramp." The campaign, which was dominated by clean, stark black-and-white images reminiscent of the silent film era, broke in print media and on TV in September 1980 and was widely praised. Agency billings soared to $207 million by 1984.

As the agency tried to balance its huge IBM billings by seeking other large accounts, its efforts were stymied by conflicts of interest between potential new accounts and the clients of the larger JWT agency. LGFE's efforts to attract the Jaguar business, for example, were blocked by JWT's relationship with Ford. By 1988, of the agency's total billings of $222 million, $150 million were with IBM. Around that time, Lord and his partners began thinking about a buyback from JWT in order to regain the agency's independence and also to protect employees after their own retirement, but these plans were derailed by a major crisis that would bring down the agency.

In June 1987 JWT agreed to be acquired for $566 million by the WPP Group, a British holding company headed by financier Martin Sorrell. Lord and Sorrell had a cordial meeting prior to the merger, but in the months afterward Lord came to see that his options and independence were more constricted than ever. LGFE already handled advertising for videotape when the agency had an opportunity to compete for the consolidated videotape and film business; however, that opportunity was blocked by Sorrell, who cited JWT's larger Kodak account. About the same time, Sorrell formed a network of European agencies called Conquest Europe with a view toward winning the Alfa Romeo account. He wanted to affiliate Conquest Europe with the prestigious name of LGFE, even though the European network would be run by JWT managers out of Milan, Italy. Lord flatly rejected the idea. Although JWT had lost the Ford business in Europe and no conflict of interest was involved, Lord suspected that the goal of Sorrell's plan was "to trick Ford." Sorrell went ahead, issuing a press release that indicated affiliation between Conquest Europe and LGFE. Lord was furious.

Lord proceeded with his efforts to buy the agency back from WPP. Highly placed friends at Y&R indicated that that agency would be willing to finance a deal if reasonable terms could be reached. However, Sorrell was unwilling to consider a sale at any price. Relations between LGFE and WPP soured further when LGFE was invited to compete for the $100 million Saturn account of General Motors (GM). Lord subsequently testified that he informed Sorrell, who approved the pitch despite JWT's Ford business; Sorrell, however, has denied that he knew anything about LGFE's efforts to court GM. In any case, when executives at Ford

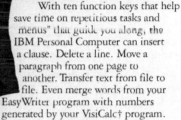

How to move a paragraph.

For memos or manuscripts, sales reports or book reports, a person could use the IBM Personal Computer.

Because, with the EasyWriter* software program, creating, revising and storing text is just that. Easy.

With ten function keys that help save time on repetitive tasks and menus" that guide you along, the IBM Personal Computer can insert a clause. Delete a line. Move a paragraph from one page to another. Transfer text from file to file. Even merge words from your EasyWriter program with numbers generated by your VisiCalc† program.

And when you're done, a copy of the finished product can be printed out at 80 characters a second.

So if you do any kind of writing, try it on the IBM Personal Computer at your nearest authorized dealer. You'll see that the performance, quality and price are really something to write home about.

IBM

The IBM Personal Computer
A tool for modern times

For more information on where to buy the IBM Personal Computer, call 800-447-4700. In Illinois, 800-322-4400. In Alaska or Hawaii, 800-447-0890.   * EasyWriter is a trademark of Information Unlimited Software, Inc.   † VisiCalc is a trademark of VisiCorp

Lord, Geller, Federico, Einstein's billings soared in the early 1980s, largely on the strength of its ads for IBM featuring the Charlie Chaplin "Little Tramp" character.
IBM Corporation.

heard about LGFE's approach to Saturn, they complained, and in February 1988 Sorrell insisted that Lord cut off all contact with GM immediately. The last minute withdrawal was a major embarrassment to an agency that put a high value on its independence.

Finally on 18 March 1988, with discussions between WPP and LGFE concerning future executive contracts at an impasse, Lord and five senior LGFE executives abruptly quit their own agency, unwilling to be controlled by Sorrell. Among the principals, only Geller, who was 67 years old, and Federico, 70, remained at the agency. Lord and his partners immediately set up a new agency called Lord Einstein O'Neill & Partners (LEO&P), with Y&R taking a 49 percent stake in the firm. According to *Fortune*, 50 of the approximately 330 LGFE employees—from vice presidents to mail room staff—defected to the new agency. Other accounts, however, put the number as low as 28.

Sorrell turned to the New York State Supreme Court, arguing that Lord and his partners had engaged in a conspiracy to sabotage LGFE in a manner that "breached their fiduciary duties and the loyalty that they owed the plaintiffs." The conspiracy issue took on new dimensions when detectives hired by WPP discovered several uncirculated memos written by one of the defecting partners referring to "clients we would probably want to take." Lord called the charges "absurd" and insisted he had never approached any LGFE clients about leaving. The court issued an injunction against any other LGFE employees moving to the new Lord Einstein agency, and it blocked Lord and Einstein personally, but not necessarily the new agency, from working with any former LGFE clients. (At that time only WNBC-TV and *The New Yorker* had moved their accounts.) In April Saab (never an LGFE client) awarded its $35 million account to the new agency, becoming its cornerstone business. Beyond the legal issues, the walkout and its effects, whether intended or unintended, stirred a lively ethical debate within the ad industry, especially in view of the behind-the-scenes role played by Y&R in financing the breakaway and the part that the financial consultant Dean Witter, an LGFE client, assumed by advising its own agency on the intricacies of a buyout.

The big question was what IBM would do. After assigning a single project to LEO&P, it pulled its entire account from LGFE and split it between Lintas and Wells, Rich, Greene. Eight days later LGFE, already having lost Dean Witter, Fuji, and the *Wall Street Journal*, laid off a third of its staff.

The matter lingered in the courts for 17 months until a settlement was finally reached in October 1988 in which Lord Einstein O'Neill & Partners paid WPP $7 million, far less than Sorrell had originally demanded. Each party had its own reasons for ending the matter: WPP, which had just bought Ogilvy & Mather at a premium price, wanted to concentrate on larger matters, and LEO&P and Y&R also wished to move forward. No public statements were made beyond the amount of the settlement.

In July 1990 the curtain finally rang down on a gutted Lord, Geller, Federico, Einstein when it was announced that WPP would be merging it with a sister agency within the WPP network, Brouillard Communications. The move was prompted by the loss of the business of Schieffelin & Somerset, maker of Hennessy Cognac, which had been a Lord, Geller client since 1969. The move effectively ended the life of LGFE. "Seldom do agencies as successful as [Lord, Geller] blow up in such a spectacular . . . and acrimonious fashion," *Advertising Age* editorialized.

Lord Einstein O'Neill & Partners fared somewhat better in the short run, reaching billings of $78 million in 1989. However, its fortunes reversed sharply when Saab took its $25 million account away from the agency in January 1990. New business made up the loss, but Y&R had other plans for the agency. Later that year the LEO&P name disappeared into the Dentsu Y&R partnership, whose U.S. operations became Lord Dentsu. By 2000 that firm had evolved into an integrated marketing communications unit called the Lord Group, with Richard Lord, then 74, still in place as chairman.

JOHN MCDONOUGH

Further Reading

Kanner, Bernice, "On Madison Avenue: Their Way," *New York Magazine* (24 October 1988)

LaFayette, Jon, "Conspiracy/Agency Breakaway," *Advertising Age* (4 April 1988)

"Lord, Geller Federico & Partners," *Madison Avenue* (November 1971)

Morrow, David J., "Madison Avenue's Bloodiest Brawl," *Fortune* (24 September 1988)

O'Leary, Nancy, "Tactics Questioned in the LEO&P to Freedom," *Adweek* (28 March 1988)

Selinger, Iris Cohen, "Curtain Rings Down on LGFE, Sorrell's Only Public Failure," *Adweek* (9 July 1990)

Winski, Joseph M., "Breakaway: How It Happened, Parts 1 and 2," *Advertising Age* 13 March and 20 March 1989)

Lorillard Tobacco Company

Principal Agencies

Lennen & Mitchell, Inc. (later Lennen & Newell, Inc.)
Young & Rubicam, Inc.
J. Walter Thompson Company
Foote, Cone & Belding, Inc.

Grey Advertising, Inc.
Benton and Bowles, Inc.
D'Arcy-McManus & Masius Worldwide, Inc.
Dancer, Fitzgerald, Sample, Inc.
Bozell, New York

Some historians credit the Lorillard brothers, Pierre and George, with creating the earliest known advertising campaign in 1789. It publicized goods sold by the family's tobacco shop, established by their father in colonial New York City in 1760. The brothers started their advertising campaign by printing broadsides touting their chewing tobacco, snuff, and "segars," and mailing them to every postmaster in the United States; post offices at that time were usually in general stores, the center of community life. The advertisement featured an American Indian smoking a long clay pipe as he leaned against a hogshead marked "Best Virginia." The names of the snuffs and "chaws" popular at the time are strangers to the market of the 21st century: common kitefoot, hogtail, pigtail, ladies twist, and Maccuba snuff.

The Lorillards' father was killed by Hessian soldiers during the British army's occupation of New York City, and the family eventually moved to the comparative wilds along the Bronx River, where they built a home and a snuff mill in 1792. The mill continued to operate until well after the U.S. Civil War. In the 1950s the P. Lorillard Company financed the restoration of the snuff mill, which would become a historic landmark.

The Tobacco Trust

Lorillard was among many small tobacco companies that flourished into the late 1800s, when Washington Duke built a factory on two acres near the railroad in Durham, North Carolina, in 1874. The company would eventually be named W. Duke Sons and Company, and in 1881 it began large-scale manufacturing of cigarettes that would make it the biggest cigarette producer in the country. Along the way the company bought up many of the country's smaller cigarette producers, including Lorillard.

The Dukes eventually pushed for a merger of all large-scale tobacco manufacturers, believing it would be a practical way of reducing selling and advertising costs as well as improving overall organization. The most important competitors at the time were Allen and Ginter Company, of Richmond, Virginia; F.S. Kinney Company and the Goodwin Company, both of New York City; and William S. Kimball and Company, of Rochester, New York.

After discussing the merger, and following a period of excessive spending on advertising (Duke spent an unheard-of $800,000 in billboard and newspaper advertising in 1889), an agreement for a merger was reached. In 1890 the five principal companies united to form the American Tobacco Company, which became known as the "tobacco trust" because of its nearly complete monopoly. But antitrust sentiment was rapidly growing in the United States at the turn of the century, and in 1911 the United States Supreme Court dissolved the American Tobacco Company. With that decision, four new tobacco companies emerged: a new American Tobacco Company, Liggett & Myers, R.J. Reynolds, and P. Lorillard & Company.

Birth of Old Gold

Lorillard's initial products included cigars and snuff. Striving to create a niche in the cigarette market, Lorillard in 1919 unsuccess-

Tobacco & Snuff of the best quality & flavor,
At the Manufactory, No. 4. Chatham street, near the Gaol
By Peter and George Lorillard,
Where may be had as follows :

Cut tobacco,	Prig or carrot do.
Common kitefoot do.	Maccuba snuff,
Common smoaking do.	Rappee do.
Segars do.	Strasburgh do.
Ladies twist do.	Common rappee do.
Pigtail do. in small rolls,	Scented rappee do. of different kinds,
Plug do.	
Hogtail do.	Scotch do.

The above Tobacco and Snuff will be sold reasonable, and warranted as good as any on the continent. If not found to prove good, any part of it may be returned, if not damaged.

N. B. Proper allowance will be made to those that purchase a quantity.   May 27—1m.

This 1789 notice is the earliest known advertisement of the oldest U.S. tobacco company, Lorillard.
Courtesy of the Rare Book, Manuscript, and Special Collections Library, Duke University.

fully targeted women with its Helmar and Murad brands. Undaunted, in 1926 the company introduced what would become one of its most important brands, Old Gold cigarettes, with expensive ad campaigns. The exuberant flappers of artist John Held, Jr., and the slogan "Not a cough in a carload" from agency Lennen & Mitchell helped the brand capture 7 percent of the market by 1930.

The Federal Trade Commission (FTC) issued a complaint about the slogan in 1943 and a cease-and-desist order in 1950—one of many that the federal agency issued to most of the major cigarette manufacturers that year. That ruling had a far-reaching effect on R.J. Reynolds's Camel as well as Lorillard's Old Gold brands. In a separate order against Lorillard, the FTC called for a halt to any ads that implied that Old Gold, or the smoke from Old Gold, contained "less nicotine, or less tars and resins, or is less irritating to the throat than the cigarettes or the smoke of any other leading brands."

Lorillard denied the use of any intentionally false or misleading advertising and claimed that the FTC's order was unjustified. It also said the advertising issue involved had been discontinued "long ago." Indeed, the J. Walter Thompson Company assumed the Old Gold account from Lennen & Mitchell in 1941 and soon changed the brand's dominant copy theme to read, "Something new has been added."

During the 1930s Lennen & Mitchell built the Old Gold brand on radio in much the same way other tobacco companies did, by advertising in music programming targeted toward young people and often teenagers. *The Old Gold Hour* was launched on CBS in 1929 and built around the popular Paul Whiteman Orchestra but evolved into more of a variety show by the mid-1930s with a procession of hosts and bands as styles changed. In 1938 and 1939 it was known as *Melody and Madness* and featured the swing music of Artie Shaw. In 1941 it switched to Benny Goodman in a program called *What's New* and later to shows built around the swing bands of Bob Crosby and Woody Herman. From 1945 to 1947 Old Gold sponsored *The Frank Sinatra Show* when the singer was at the height of his fame as an idol of teenage girls. On television Old Gold became know for its dancing cigarette packages (women wearing white boots and Old Gold packages), which tapped in time to an Old Gold jingle. All these shows ran on CBS and were handled by Lennen & Mitchell.

"Taking the Fear Out of Smoking"

In 1952 Lorillard's longtime agency Lennen & Mitchell was reorganized as Lennen & Newell (L&N) when H.W. Newell came to the agency from Geyer, Newell & Ganger, bringing with him Embassy Cigarettes, a small Lorillard brand, and consolidating all Lorillard advertising in one shop. But Lorillard was about to launch a new ad campaign, one that would spearhead the approach that came to be known as "fear advertising." Two studies released in 1950 revealed—for the first time—a strong correlation between cigarette smoking and lung cancer. By 1952 Lorillard, one of the smaller cigarette manufacturers with 6 percent of the market, introduced Kent, with a "Micronite" filter made from the filter material used in atomic energy plants. Ads from Young & Rubicam (Y&R) claimed that the new cigarette, named after then-Lorillard President H.A. Kent, greatly reduced tar and nicotine. With other companies quickly introducing their own filter bands, Lorillard began running Kent advertisements that read, "Sensitive smokers get real health protection with new Kent" and "Kent takes more nicotine and tars than any other leading cigarette—the difference in protection is priceless." In addition to its advertising claims, Lorillard ran TV commercials showing the dark residue deposited by tobacco smoke on Kent's filter—from which the smoker's lungs were presumably spared.

The new brands responded aggressively, and as in earlier years, the cigarette companies sought to gain business by scaring smokers about their competitors' brands. Viceroy advertised "double-barreled protection"; Philip Morris & Company said its brand "takes the fear out of smoking." Kent even ran afoul of the American Medical Association (AMA), when in 1954 Kent advertising used test findings from the *Journal of the American Medical Association* to bolster Kent's filter claims. The ads stated, "The American Medical Association voluntarily conducted in their own lab, a series of independent tests of filters and filter cigarettes. As

reported in the *Journal of the American Medical Association,* these tests proved that of all the filter cigarettes tested, one type was the most effective for removing tars and nicotine. This type filter is used by Kent . . . and only Kent!" The AMA condemned the Kent ads as "reprehensible and misleading," saying they "strongly imply that the AMA and the medical profession recommend to the smoking public the use of a specific filtered cigarette."

Meanwhile, the continued avalanche of advertising featuring doctors, filters, and tar measurements soon drew the attention of the FTC, which issued a draft set of cigarette advertising guidelines in the fall of 1954; it adopted these guidelines in the fall of 1955, blocking the use of all scientifically unsubstantiated tar and nicotine claims as well as any references to body parts and doctors.

New Campaigns

Amid the controversy over Kent and other filter brands, Lorillard in 1953 began advertising king-size Old Gold side by side with the standard brand; in 1957 it added a filtered variety. In 1958 it introduced Old Gold Straights with reduced tar and nicotine levels. With a launch campaign from L&N running in newspapers in more than 140 markets and extensively on radio and TV, Lorillard aimed the ads at what it called the "hard core of 22 million smokers who prefer their tobacco straight."

Lorillard typically broke its new campaigns in leading newspapers, making a big splash. For example, in 1957, with Y&R at the helm, it used a page in the *New York Times* to launch Newport menthol-cooled filter cigarettes in a crushproof box. That year it also tried a different promotional tack when, as part of a stepped-up ad campaign, it launched "Summer smoke," a fashion promotion aimed at style-conscious women. The promotion, created by the Chernow Advertising Agency in cooperation with Y&R, featured "filtered-light" chiffon summer fashions designed by couturier David Crystal. Stores that purchased the fashions featured ads and dresses in windows and store displays, print ads, and fashion shows built around the "Summer smoke" theme. Sample packages of "filtered-right" Kent were distributed.

Y&R eventually lost the Kent and Newport brands in 1957 when Lorillard moved all cigarette brands to L&N, which had handled Old Gold off and on for 30 years; Y&R originally introduced Kent and Newport. The decision to once again place all Lorillard brands at a single agency was attributed to company president Lewis Gruber, who thought too much was made of the advantages of having competing agencies. Gruber made some sharp advertising and marketing changes; expenditures for 1957 reached a high of $20 million as he repackaged brands and changed merchandising techniques.

Meanwhile, Kent caught a lucky break with an ad campaign in July, when it ran ads in 60 newspapers in 16 markets just as the August issue of *Reader's Digest* came out with a positive evaluation of Kent in its second article on filter cigarettes. The Kent ads claimed that tests had proved Kent was superior because of its new filter. The *Reader's Digest* article supported Kent with lab tests of its own. Charges that Lorillard and Y&R had designed the ads to allude to the article were denied.

Kent continued to play on the *Reader's Digest* article by running an ad in New York City and Los Angeles, California, newspapers claiming the brand was first in sales among filter-tip brands in those cities. However, the company declined to confirm its claim with factual data. (Owing to an FTC ruling in 1956, comparative sales figures could be used in advertising if the advertiser was prepared to justify its claims before the commission.)

At this time Kent had received the lion's share of Lorillard's $20 million advertising support; a year earlier the largest part of the Lorillard budget, estimated at $14.8 million, had been concentrated on Old Gold. In the last half of 1957, Kent was given the full treatment in newspapers, magazines, outdoor, radio, and television.

The "Tar Derby"

The tar and nicotine controversy was building again, thanks to new studies and cigarette ratings reports in *Consumer Reports* and *Reader's Digest* that spurred congressional hearings on filter cigarette ad claims. Filter brands were advertised heavily (without mentioning health), and their share of the market grew from 10 percent in 1954 to 35 percent in 1957. The public did not know how well the filters performed because FTC guides prohibited tar and nicotine claims that lacked "sound scientific data." In fact, studies showed Lorillard's Kent brand yielded six times more tar in 1952 than in 1950, due to a change from its original filter.

This finding was bad news for the tobacco business. Filter cigarettes had been so greatly modified to enhance flavor that their tar and nicotine yield was generally no better than that of nonfilter cigarettes.

Despite FTC guidelines, vigorous advertising of tar and nicotine content returned, new filter brands were introduced, existing filters were improved (in particular Kent's), and the tar and nicotine content of nonfilter cigarettes was greatly reduced. Earlier the FTC had declared that feat to be technically impossible. The FTC's "sound scientific data" provision provided a loophole for cigarette advertising. There was so much noncommercial data on the subject in technical journals and the popular media that the loopholes in the commission's policy became larger and larger. References to tar and nicotine in ads now relied upon competent third-party data usually reported in *Reader's Digest*. The FTC appeared to believe that there were no problems with companies using tests designed to favor their own brands.

The high-tar brands of the past—Camel, Lucky Strike, and Chesterfield—disappeared from the U.S. markets to be replaced by filter versions and nonfilter versions with much lower tar and nicotine. The climax of the "Tar Derby" came in fall 1959 when all six of the cigarette manufacturers introduced new lower-tar brands; all were in the process of mounting major ad campaigns when the FTC intervened. The FTC declared that all claims about tar and nicotine levels would be regarded as implied claims of positive health effects. Also, it said that epidemiological evidence of these health effects would be required.

Such evidence did not exist, and a means of providing it was not developed for several years. Shortly thereafter, the tag line of

Like other marketers of the early 20th century, Lorillard used premiums such as trade cards to promote sales.

Kent ads was changed from "Significantly less tars and nicotine than any other filter brand" to "Designed with your taste in mind." Lorillard then reintroduced the unfiltered king-size version of Old Gold and announced its advertising theme: "Tender to your taste."

The 1960s

Despite the new cheerier, less-threatening ad messages, Lorillard faced serious challenges in the mid-1960s. It was ranked number 30 among the largest national advertisers, spending an estimated $36.9 million on advertising in 1964. With cigarette sales down as a result of a report from the U.S. Surgeon General's office, Lorillard pushed hard to establish a strong position in the filter-tip and regular cigar market, introducing Omega as a companion to Madison and Between the Acts. Another new entry was Erik.

On network TV Lorillard's dollars were spread across the three broadcast networks, with CBS and NBC getting the lion's share. Lorillard had a penchant for personality shows such as those featuring Jack Paar, Dick Van Dyke, and Ed Sullivan. Magazines, which garnered about $6 million in color ads in 1964 from Lorillard, were the marketer's second choice of media.

During the first quarter of 1964, Lorillard sought to recapture some lost ground with a hard-hitting campaign claiming: "No medical evidence or scientific endorsement has proved any other cigarette to be superior to Kent." Most competitors thought this was Kent's way of striking back at Liggett & Myers's Lark, which had profited from favorable comments by a member of the Surgeon General's research team. In 1965 Lorillard, with agency L&N, launched a new modified ad push for Kent. The word "Micronite" was banished from the copy, and the tag line "Kent satisfies best" was exchanged for "Light up a Kent and you've got a good thing going."

In 1964 tobacco marketers voluntarily agreed to implement what came to be known as the Cigarette Advertising Code in an effort to minimize the FTC's ad restrictions. Drawn up by an industry committee, the code banned advertising and marketing directed mainly at those consumers under 21 years of age and ended advertising and promotion in school and college publications. While violators could be fined up to $100,000, no fines were ever levied. Because the code was voluntary, Lorillard refused to participate, earning a reputation as a maverick in the process. At the same time, Lorillard tried to appease government critics for its decision on the ad code by passing up an option to renew its contract in 1967 with the *Ed Sullivan Show*. It had run a Kent commercial in close proximity to a teenaged singing act, raising an outcry in Washington, D.C.

Similarly, Lorillard instituted a major marketing change in 1968 when it chose not to renew its sponsorship of CBS's broadcasts of National Football League games. The marketer said that the games were too youth-oriented, but maintained that the company did not drop any television advertising because of political pressures. Earlier, Senators Warren G. Magnuson and Robert F. Kennedy had criticized the advertising of cigarettes during professional football and other sports broadcasts.

The new role played by advertising at the company was announced in spring 1966 in an address to stockholders by Lorillard Chairman Manuel Yellen. Yellen said that advertising is one of the key factors in the growth of the industry, because of the intensity of competition for consumer interest. Subsequently, when stockholders heard in 1967 that Lorillard ad spending for the previous year was "high," they asked if the company should not be more cautious. Yellen replied, "Not if we can help it," adding that the company attracted more viewers, listeners, and readers for its ad dollar in 1966 than it had for eight or nine years previously.

In 1966 Lorillard spent $36.4 million in ads for its products, with Kent the most heavily advertised at $15.5 million. Almost half of the Kent money went to network television. Runner-up media included magazines, spot TV, and spot radio. Kent was still on the Sullivan show and drawing mountains of criticism for those commercials. Ads ran following the Beatles' performances on the show as well as in conjunction with other children's favor-

ites. When Lorillard moved Kent out of the popular show, it used the airtime instead for its Muriel cigars.

Lorillard's number-two cigarette brand in terms of spending was Newport, its chief menthol entry. Measured media spending for Newport in 1965 exceeded $10.5 million, with network TV the chief beneficiary. Next in line was Old Gold, recording $4 million in measured media, followed by Spring with $1.5 million. Lorillard launched its True brand in September 1966 in ten major U.S. markets, supporting the launch with buys in print, radio, and on NBC-TV's *Rowan and Martin's Laugh-In*. The tag line for the new brand: "Shouldn't your brand be True?"

At the same time, the company remained the leader in the little-cigar field with its Madison, Between the Acts, and Omega brands, the last of which was introduced in 1964. Lorillard supported Madison with about $200,000 in media spending—mostly in magazines—with Between the Acts garnering less than $150,000. Omega was advertised in spot and network TV as well as magazines with a budget of $200,000.

In 1967 Lorillard increased overall ad spending to $41.5 million in order to launch new brands. During this time, Lorillard's agencies included Foote, Cone & Belding (FCB) for True and Danville filter; Grey Advertising for Kent, Old Gold, Spring 100, and York Imperial 100; L&N for Newport, cigars, pipe, and chewing tobaccos as well as its Tabby cat food; and John C. Dowd, Inc., for Three Little Kittens.

Also, in September 1967 Lorillard introduced New Century in the New York City metropolitan area, calling it "the most heavily advertised cigarette in the nation's largest market" during a 13-week period. The saturation campaign included 28 newspaper pages, more than 200 local and network TV spots, and approximately 8,000 posters. The advertising, which pushed the product's taste, also contained the line, "It's what you are, not who you are that counts."

In 1968 the company increased ad spending 8 percent to $44.9 million, but Lorillard was trailing the other tobacco marketers in product diversification; non-tobacco products accounted for only 5 percent of its business. That year, Vince Cullers Advertising in Chicago, Illinois, joined the agency lineup to place advertising for all Lorillard products in black media in the United States.

In 1968 Lorillard was bought by Loews Theaters, Inc., and renamed Lorillard Corporation. With the purchase, ad decisions were made by the holding company, and Grey Advertising stood to lose the $14 million Kent campaign, which it had handled since 1966. By the second half of the year, FCB had taken over Kent, and Newport had moved to L&N. Reportedly, Grey retained about $7 million in billings for Old Gold filters and straights, Spring 100s, Erik cigars, and Omega little cigars. In 1970 True shifted from FCB to L&N. Benton and Bowles, which had released its first new Kent campaign, "What a good time for a Kent," in February 1969, resigned as the media shop for the brand.

In 1969 Lorillard also increased its targeting of women with Max, an all-white, super-long cigarette for female smokers. An introductory ad from agency FCB used the tag line, "Say hello to Max." A magazine ad for the brand depicted a model addressing the smoke, saying, "Hello long, lean, and delicious."

The 1970s

Cigarette marketers reacted to Congress's 1970 ban on all tobacco advertising on television and radio— which became effective in January— by moving their TV ad dollars to print and outdoor advertising. Lorillard started 1971 by introducing Maverick, its first new full-flavor cigarette since Old Gold; L&N's campaign made up for the lack of broadcast support by making heavy use of free samples. Also, as part of its venture in alternative forms of advertising, early in the 1970s Lorillard tried advertising in paperback books. Lorillard ads for Kent and True started appearing in 30 million books per month; deals were signed with about half of the paperback publishers.

Lorillard soon made another ad agency shift, appointing two shops, de Garmo, Inc., and Masius, Wynne-Williams, Inc., to handle four of its five brands that had been housed at L&N, after that shop folded in January 1972. An estimated $12 million had been spent advertising those five brands the previous year. De Garmo picked up True cigarettes, while Masius took on Maverick, along with Beechnut and Big Red chewing tobaccos. Both agencies were relatively young and regarded the accounts as important steps on their way to expansion. For de Garmo, it was the first major piece of business to come through the doors in nearly a year.

At the end of the decade Lorillard launched new ads for a reformulated Kent, which now offered reduced tar levels. The low-tar and low-nicotine emphasis continued to be a flashpoint for tobacco marketers into the 1980s owing to increasing pressure by health groups to restrict the areas where smoking was allowed. Every marketer, Lorillard included, advertised and compared tar and nicotine contents.

In the period from 1973 to the 1980s, Lorillard's brands continued to spend significant amounts on advertising. Kent spending grew from $15.6 million in 1973 to nearly $40 million in 1979. Golden Lights, introduced in 1978, spent $26 million and $27 million in its first two years. Newport started with spending of $3 million and by the end of the 1970s had reached $10 million.

The 1980s

In mid-1980 Lorillard began a market-research-based campaign aimed at showing that its Triumph brand tasted better than Winston Lights, Marlboro Lights, and Merit, all of which were R.J. Reynolds brands. Following a lawsuit that Lorillard lost, the company was required to tone down its message.

A year later Lorillard's share of the market had dropped by half a percentage point, from 9.7 percent to 9.2 percent. That year the company revived an old cigarette trademark, Maverick, and tested it as a women's cigarette. It also was one of the four major marketers to use free-sample trial of a brand; for Lorillard that brand was Triumph 100s.

Cut off from the medium of television, cigarette marketers tried different strategies. Lorillard's included testing a new nonmenthol brand, Newport Red. This marked a departure from the company's practice in recent years of sticking to low tars in its new-brand introductions and also a departure in that the nonmenthol brand followed, rather than preceded, its menthol counterpart.

As an alternative to TV, many manufacturers began sponsoring events. In 1982 Lorillard was running its "Kent Sports Business" newspaper column to promote that brand. Meanwhile, the company switched its True account from D'Arcy-MacManus & Masius to Dancer, Fitzgerald, Sample when Heublein, a D'Arcy client, acquired tobacco rival R.J. Reynolds. Among the Lorillard brands, only Newport had shown much growth in recent years.

Lorillard entered 1983 looking for a hot new brand. It had tested three, Heritage, Maverick, and Bistro, in the previous 18 months but without success. Another brand, Rebel, was being tested at the time but only in four markets. Thus, the company pinned its hopes on Satin, named for its satinlike filter. Ads for Satin presented a silky, smooth feminine image.

Antismoking Legislation

Like most of the tobacco companies, Lorillard spent the majority of the 1990s fighting tobacco legislation. In 1998 it tested a nonmenthol version of its Newport brand. Lorillard chose Avrett, Free & Ginsberg, New York City, to handle the account. The tag line was, "A star is born." Ads broke just as cigarette marketers jockeyed for position, waiting for what were expected to be stronger restrictions on tobacco marketing.

The industry spent more than $200 million in 1998 on outdoor ads, money likely to be redirected to other media as a result of the ban. Lorillard was the second-largest tobacco company to produce an antismoking advertising campaign. The first Lorillard spot was from Bozell, New York, and was set in a dark, dangerous-looking parlor. Its tag line was, "Tobacco is wacko if you're a teen."

In 1997 attorneys general from 46 states signed a pact with the major tobacco companies further restricting marketing options. No outdoor cigarette advertising was permitted; no human models or cartoons were allowed; and image advertising was restricted to print media that did not have a significant percentage of youthful readers. Sponsorships of sporting events or the arts were prohibited, and the terms "light" and "low tar" were essentially banned. Also, Internet advertising on any Web site that could be accessed from the United States was prohibited, a provision that drove the majority of cigarette advertising overseas. In the wake of the agreement restricting tobacco advertising, Lorillard's advertising and marketing philosophy underwent a radical change; its ads of the 21st century bear little resemblance to those from just a few decades earlier.

ALAN SALOMON

See also color plate in this volume

Further Reading

Fox, Stephen R., *The Mirror Makers: A History of American Advertising and Its Creators*, New York: Morrow, 1984
Ries, Al, and Jack Trout, *Positioning: The Battle for Your Mind*, New York: McGraw-Hill Book, 1981

Lowe, Frank 1941–

British Advertising Executive and Agency Founder

Frank Lowe's goal from the start was to bring an innovative, creative edge and quality to advertising, and his methods worked. Lowe's rapid rise began with the establishment of his first ad agency in 1981. By the turn of the 20th century he was in charge of a worldwide agency with annual billings of more than $12 billion and offices in more than 80 countries.

In 1960, at age 18, Lowe started his advertising career in the mailroom of the J. Walter Thompson Company's office in London, England. He worked his way through several agencies on both sides of the Atlantic, including Lintas and Benton and Bowles, Inc., before joining Collett Dickenson Pearce in London in 1970. Two years later he was the agency's managing director and remained there until 1981, when he ventured out on his own, starting, with Geoff Howard-Spink, the London agency Lowe Howard-Spink.

In a 1990 interview, the *Wall Street Journal* described the notoriously publicity-shy Lowe as a "47-year-old in blue jeans and a Rod Stewart hairdo who chain-smoked small cigars throughout the two-hour interview." Lowe is considered charismatic and flamboyant, and his agency's creative efforts have reflected those traits. Early on Lowe earned a reputation for producing solid, yet offbeat, spunky advertising for a top-notch client roster that has included the Coca-Cola Company, General Motors Corporation (GM), Heineken, Saab, and Sun Microsystems.

Lowe's first acquisition in the United States came when his agency bought a 30 percent interest in the Marschalk Company, Inc., New York City. But the world really started to take notice of Lowe in September 1987, when his agency, the renamed Lowe Howard-Spink & Bell PLC, agreed to spend $24.8 million to buy another New York City agency, Laurence, Charles, Free & Lawson, Inc. The acquired agency's accounts included American Brands, Inc., and McDonald's Corporation.

The U.S. operating name of Lowe & Partners was created in June 1990 from the combination of Lowe Marschalk and Lowe Tucker Metcalf (the latter having been formed by Frank Lowe and Bill Tucker from Scali McCabe). The name change coincided with Lowe's ambitious plans for his agency in the United States. One of his goals was to double the business, which at that time was billing $300 million annually. Another was to make it the best agency in the United States.

Lowe saw 1973 as a turning point in American advertising. Up to that time, American ads had been groundbreaking. All this changed, he observed, with the advent of the Arab oil embargo; American ads were now toned down so they would not threaten client relationships. "Advertising was invented here," he said of the United States in the 1990 *Wall Street Journal* interview cited above. "But somehow, it's lost its nerve."

With the change to Lowe & Partners in 1990, Lowe set about to turn the U.S. operation into a creative powerhouse. Both in London and the United States he became known for watching not just the bottom line but also the entire creative process. For a time he was approving every commercial script churned out by the London operation. He was said to have a need to be hands-on and admitted he could be volatile at times because, in his words, "there's a kind of conspiracy of mediocrity."

Later in 1990 the Interpublic Group of Companies, already a minority shareholder in Lowe & Partners, acquired the remaining 64.6 percent of the British agency group. The price tag for the remaining share was $160 million. The deal gave Interpublic a third independent ad network and, unlike McCann-Erickson and Lintas, Lowe was known for its offbeat work. As part of the deal, Lowe joined the board of Interpublic.

Lowe continued to focus on expanding his network. Lowe & Partners/SMS, New York, was formed in November 1993 after Lowe & Partners' acquisition of Scali, McCabe, Sloves from WPP Group. But 1993 is perhaps best remembered by Lowe as the year that the New York agency won the Coca-Cola Company's $70 million Diet Coke account away from Lintas, New York, Lowe's sibling agency at Interpublic. The win was considered a testament to Lowe's efforts to refocus the U.S. unit.

Nevertheless, what followed was a dry spell. Attempts to win accounts from companies such as Burger King, Digital Equipment Corporation, and America West Airlines were unsuccessful. The agency also lost the coveted Prudential Insurance Company of America business to Fallon McElligott, a $60 million account that it had snatched away from Backer Spielvogel Bates in 1990.

In 1994 Lowe again assumed a more active role at the U.S. operation, installing himself full time at Lowe & Partners/SMS to scrutinize the management ranks and the major account groups. By the end of that year he had realigned top management. The losing streak ended in 1995 when the agency was awarded Sony Electronics' $60 million U.S. advertising account.

Meanwhile, Lowe continued building the agency network. In 1996 he acquired William Douglas McAdams, New York City, and a share of Goldberg Moser O'Neill, San Francisco, California. He also acquired Roche Macaulay & Partners, Toronto, Canada, and launched agencies in Hong Kong and Denmark, while entering the South African market with Lowe Bull Calvert Pace and joining the GGK Occidental network in Austria and eight Eastern European markets. In addition, Lowe Direct, a direct marketing organization, was formed in London. The rapid global growth prompted the agency to split operations into four regions worldwide, overseen by a new worldwide board headed by Lowe himself.

In 1998 Interpublic named Lowe chairman-chief executive officer of Octagon, its new sports marketing arm. A year later the Lowe Group again expanded its U.S. operation by venturing into the Northeast, becoming partners with Mullen, a Boston, Massachusetts, agency.

Frank Lowe.
Courtesy of the Lowe Group. Photography: Lichfield.

Mercedes-Benz loss was offset when Lowe Lintas & Partners took on the $150 million GM (General Motors) Trucks account.

Ammirati Puris was an ailing agency at the time of the merger; the future of the huge Unilever business was in serious doubt, and many clients, including Johnson & Johnson, GM, Burger King, Dell Computer, and United Parcel Service, Inc., were deeply dissatisfied with their account service. Though the combined billings volume of the two companies came to $6.5 billion, about $1.23 billion would soon be lost. In the United States between November 1999 and February 2000, Lowe Lintas saw $910 million in losses, only half of which were replaced quickly. Net loss continued at a lower rate in 2001, but the critical relationship with Unilever was preserved and on its way to repair after new business wins from the food giant in January 2001.

MARY ELLEN PODMOLIK

Biography
Born 8 August 1941; educated at Westminster School, England; began career in advertising at J. Walter Thompson Company, London, 1960; worked at several U.S. and British agencies before joining Collett Dickenson Pearce, London, 1970; started his own agency, Lowe Howard-Spink, in September 1981 and soon afterward formed the Lowe Group; joined board of the Interpublic Group of Companies after Interpublic acquired Lowe Group, 1990; named Agency Executive of the Year, 1994, by *Adweek* and won Chairman's Award at 1998 British Television Advertising Awards; named visiting professor in communications, University College, London, 2000.

Further Reading
Goldman, Kevin, "Sony Ends Lowe's New-Business Drought," *Wall Street Journal* (31 March 1995)
Lipman, Joanne, "Lowe Chief Discusses Game Plan for U.S.," *Wall Street Journal* (19 July 1990)
Marcom, John, Jr., "U.K. Agency Lowe Howard-Spink to Buy U.S. Firm," *Wall Street Journal* (15 September 1987)
Wells, Melanie, "Lowe: Interpublic's New Power Brand," *Advertising Age* (11 October 1993)

But Lowe & Partners/SMS faced serious problems in its flagship New York City office with the loss of its key Mercedes-Benz business, valued at $125 million in February 1999. Philip Geier, chairman of the parent Interpublic, charged that Martin Sloves, the former chairman of SMS, had secretly worked to switch the auto account to Omnicom's Merkley Newman Harty while at the same time serving as a consultant for Interpublic at $650,000 a year. The matter went into arbitration, which a year later found for Sloves, who collected $1.3 million in damages.

In October 1999 Interpublic merged Ammirati Puris Lintas and Lowe & Partners Worldwide, creating Lowe Lintas & Partners Worldwide, with offices in more than 80 countries. Lowe was named chairman and chief executive officer. And soon the

Lowe Lintas & Partners Worldwide. *See* Lintas: Worldwide

Luce, Henry R. 1898–1967

U.S. Publisher

One of the most influential figures in 20th-century American publishing, Henry Robinson Luce created a media empire that produced *Time, Fortune,* and *Life,* among other influential magazines. One of four children of American missionaries, Luce was born in Tengchow, China, on 3 April 1898. At age 15 he went to Connecticut to attend the Hotchkiss School. There he edited the *Hotchkiss Literary Monthly,* and for the school newspaper he sold automobile advertising for $2 per page. Auto marketers Dodge and Pierce Arrow were among his clients. He attended Yale University, his father's alma mater, where he edited the *Yale Daily News.* But his first foray into journalism was the summer before he attended Yale, when he clerked in the business office of the Springfield, Massachusetts–based *Republican.*

Luce graduated as a Phi Beta Kappa from Yale in 1920 and did short stints as a reporter for the *Chicago Daily News* and the *Baltimore Sun.* He soon linked up with a former Yale classmate, Briton Hadden, and the two founded Time, Inc. Using subscriber lists bought from other publications, they began selling readers on the idea of a national digest that grouped news into various categories and on 3 March 1923 introduced *Time* magazine.

Luce believed that good advertising copy would boost sales of his news magazine, so he increased revenue by selling an abundance of ad space. Ads on atheism and evolution filled its pages. With ads representing various industries, *Time* began showing a profit four years after it was launched.

When *Time* was launched Luce was its business manager and Hadden its editor. Upon Hadden's death in 1929, Luce became editor-in-chief. He held the post until assuming the role of editorial chairman of Time, Inc., in 1964.

Advent of *Fortune*

Business news–focused *Fortune* was launched in February 1930, four months after the stock market crash in 1929. Despite the state of the economy, *Fortune* sold most of its ad space the year before the first issue hit newsstands. An oversized monthly printed on heavy paper, *Fortune* featured cardboard covers displaying industrial scenes depicted by artists such as Jacob Lawrence. The covers soon became collector's items. In 1930 *Fortune* had a circulation of 30,000; by the end of the decade that figure had more than quadrupled. By 1934 *Fortune* was in the black.

The magazine, though, was running into ethical complications as it ran stories about companies from which it accepted advertising. But Luce maintained that his editorial policy was not influenced by his advertisers. For example, Matson Line complained because an article had questioned the quality of some of the company's ships. Luce refused to retract statements made in the article, so the company canceled its advertising contract. "We ought to lose an account every month," responded Luce, who believed *Fortune*'s articles should be hard-hitting and should not shy away

from the truth. Contrary to many business publications, *Fortune* was relatively liberal in its editorial temper, accepted the fundamentals of the New Deal, and viewed both business and government with a tough-minded skepticism.

Luce created the radio program *The March of Time* as a way to tell Americans about current news events in dramatized form. Marking its first broadcast on CBS radio in March 1931, the show reenacted the news for nearly 9 million listeners. In one episode of the program, actors played Jews treated harshly in the German pogrom. The broadcast helped to increase awareness among Americans that the lives of German Jews were truly in danger.

"The March of Time" newsreel series was an offshoot of the radio program. The series, which eventually evolved to appear 13 times a year in more than 6,000 theaters across the country, won an Academy Award in 1936. The popularity of this "pictured" news prompted Luce to move forward with his idea for a picture magazine.

Life, which debuted 23 November 1936, had departments covering theater and the arts, as well as sports and sciences. Lively photos of subjects from Shirley Temple to the Amazon River—and even the birth of a baby—reeled in readers. Advertisers also

Henry R. Luce.
Reprinted Courtesy of Time Pix.

supported the magazine and often submitted colorful ads that competed with the allure of the editorial photographs.

By 1941 *Life*, with an average of 134 pages a month, had a subscription renewal rate greater than 80 percent. Luce had underestimated how successful *Life* would be, and as a result, many of his advertisers were paying relatively low rates thanks to long-term contracts signed before the magazine was launched.

Bulging with ads and a circulation of more than 4 million, the weekly had grown to an average of 156 pages a month by 1942. For soldiers, sailors, airmen, and their families back home who awaited their return, *Life*'s ads held "a promise for a better tomorrow," according to Luce biographer Robert E. Herzstein. He writes in *Henry R. Luce: A Political Portrait of the Man Who Created the American Century*, "World War II turned [Luce] into the great phenomenon of the publishing industry." During the second half of the 20th century, Time, Inc., launched several other magazines, including *Sports Illustrated, People, InStyle*, and *Money.*

SHEREE R. CURRY LEVY

Biography

Born in Tengchow, Shantung province, China, to American missionaries, 3 April 1898; graduated Phi Beta Kappa from Yale University, 1920; launched *Time,* 1923; *Fortune,* 1930; *Life,* 1936; *Sports Illustrated,* 1954; served as editor-in-chief of all Time, Inc., publications, 1929–1964; died in Phoenix, Arizona, 28 February 1967.

Selected Publication
The Ideas of Henry Luce, edited by John Knox Jessup, 1969

Further Reading

Baughman, James L., *Henry R. Luce and the Rise of the American News Media,* Boston: Twayne, 1987

Cort, David, *The Sin of Henry R. Luce: An Anatomy of Journalism,* Secaucus, New Jersey: Stuart, 1974

Elson, Robert T., *Time, Inc.: The Intimate History of a Publishing Enterprise,* 3 vols., edited by Duncan Norton-Taylor, New York: Atheneum, 1968–86; see especially vol. 1

Herzstein, Robert Edwin, *Henry R. Luce: A Political Portrait of the Man Who Created the American Century,* New York: Scribner, and Don Mills, Ontario: Macmillan Canada, 1994

Kobler, John, *Henry Luce: His Time, Life, and Fortune,* Garden City, New York: Doubleday, and London: MacDonald, 1968

Martin, Ralph G., *Henry and Clare: An Intimate Portrait of the Luces,* New York: Putnam, 1991

Neils, Patricia, *China Images in the Life and Times of Henry Luce,* Savage, Maryland: Rowman and Littlefield, 1990

Swanberg, W.A., *Luce and His Empire,* New York: Scribner, 1972

Lürzer, Conrad. *See under* Conrad

Luxury Goods

Purveyors of luxury goods have traditionally used various types of media and promotions but have focused on print ads in glossy magazines, exclusive events, and FM radio spots in subtle campaigns that emphasize exclusiveness, quality, and the idea that the consumer is "worth" the goods advertised. In the 1980s and 1990s events geared toward cultivating connoisseurship among new audiences proliferated at venues such as wineries, restaurants, museums, performances, and sports events. Throughout the 20th century, the luxury goods market remained one of the fastest growing of all product categories.

The wealthy appreciate smart advertising, so-called frequency programs (as in frequent flier and frequent diner), and, ironically enough, bargains. Whether promoting a $3,000 bottle of cognac or a $50,000 trip around the world, subtlety is the key. The end of the 20th century brought dramatic changes—in both the definition of luxury and its target audiences—forcing luxury marketers to change their tried-and-true methods.

"You're Worth It"

In the United States, the marketing of luxury goods began in earnest in the 1950s, when the country was celebrating peace and prosperity. Luxury goods marketers understood the difference between the old rich and the new in a country that prided itself on social mobility. A steady stream of newly wealthy people were becoming first-time luxury buyers. While they wanted to appear at ease with their new station, they also needed discreet guidance—thus, the requirement for subtlety and precision targeting on the part of advertisers. Martex was one of the first U.S. luxury goods marketers, confounding the textile industry by introducing

THE MOST

BEAUTIFUL TOWEL

EVER WOVEN...

MARTEX

Patrician

For the connoisseur who seeks superlative quality, particularly in highly personal possessions, Martex weaves the *Patrician*. It is an incredibly handsome terry, master-loomed of finest combed Egyptian cotton. Lavishly looped—sumptuous in size, too (the bath size, about 86, is 30″ x 52″). *Patrician* towel ensembles and matching bath rugs are designed in white and uniquely lovely pastels, clear and muted. For beauty of color, texture and quality, the *Patrician* has no peer. In your home and as a gift, it is an enduring expression of inspired taste. Write Martex, 65 Worth St., N. Y. 13, for the name of the store nearest you. Your inquiry will receive prompt attention.

In 1956 Martex revolutionized the towel industry by positioning and pricing its Patrician line of towels as a luxury item. *WestPoint Stevens.*

a luxurious Patrician towel. It followed with a posh, 14-piece Patrician gift set labeled as an "exclusive" in its ads. The words "limited edition" and "registered" were used in its *Wall Street Journal* advertising. It also created the "Towel Girl," an image that became the hallmark of Martex. Once the symbol was established, the company's advertising agency, Ellington & Company, reduced the size of its ads, placing more half-page and two-thirds-page ads instead of the customary spread.

Still, there were those children of the Depression who needed to be convinced that they deserved to own upscale goods. Pinch Scotch, in an effort to differentiate itself from other Scotch whiskeys, hammered home the theme that times had changed and that, more than ever before, people were pampering themselves and their families with "an inch of Pinch." Pinch was not just an ordinary scotch, the ads suggested—and one should pamper oneself by drinking it. The Pinch ads ran in leading business publications targeted toward upscale males. In the ads, the product's name was communicated strongly. Two different ads, "Wealthy" and "Worldly," with different copy each pictured a decanter of Pinch with a scotch glass. The copy read, respectively: "Wealthy: Look at it this way. Your daughter has never spent a nickel in her life.

$5, yes. $50, yes. $500, easy. But never once a nickel. Why are you still drinking ordinary scotch?" And "Worldly: Look at it this way. Your wife feels that the tan she gets in Greece is more even and long-lasting than the tan she used to get in Atlantic City. And you're still drinking ordinary scotch?"

Trying to reinforce the notion that the good life was no longer sinful, Manning's Continental coffee advertised that if its coffee was not worth an extra dime, the consumer should forget about it. A direct-mail campaign coincided with radio spots that emphasized specifics about the coffee. "We don't care what you do with your coffee, but don't pour cream and sugar into ours," read one pitch. Copy also stated that Manning's was made to taste "like we like it—straight black. Straight-forward. Real coffee." The commercial closed with "a quality taste requires a taste for quality," an appeal to the consumer's vanity.

Advertisers in the 1950s also tried to change traditional notions of what luxury was. Towle Manufacturing, which marketed sterling silver, used ad campaigns to alter some ingrained attitudes about silver. It also tried to change some attitudes about food. Young brides were no longer selecting sterling; they foresaw themselves as having to do their own housework. Investments in sterling instead went to work-saving appliances that led to a casual lifestyle. The new Towle campaign, created by the company's agency, C.J. LaRoche & Company, showed that sterling not only fit easily into the informal life but also would bring elegance and beauty to the meal, be it barbecue, buffet, or banquet. Ads showed mundane foods such as rice, baked beans, and spaghetti prepared in gourmet ways. Headlines declared: "Beans become cassoulet with Towle's new sterling pattern"; "Rice becomes Risotto Milanese"; "Spaghetti becomes a Roman holiday." The ads ran during the traditionally popular wedding months of May and June in *Holiday, House Beautiful, House & Garden, Living for Young Homemakers,* and *Seventeen.* Ads appeared in *Bride's, Bride & Home,* and *Modern Bride* over the summer months.

Advertisements for mink coats followed much the same line— that luxury items were not simply for the older, patrician person but for "on the move" everyday career girls, too. In 1970 the young married woman and the single career woman were targets of the Scandinavian Mink Association's fall and winter ad campaign for Saga mink. The all-print program aimed itself primarily at families with annual incomes of more than $15,000 per household and also at the younger woman who could be expected to move into the upscale market. Ads for Saga mink emphasized not only its luxury and fashion elements but also its practicality and youthful appearance. Ads were headlined, "Mink is Friday night and Saturday morning." Another was, "Life is too short and winters are too long to go without mink." To reach its target market, agency J. Walter Thompson Company selected general-consumer women's service and fashion magazines.

Subtlety and Sophistication

General Foods Corporation aimed its Gourmet Food copy at connoisseurs of food. Tossing aside the big-photo, small-text tradition in food advertising in favor of large text perked up by a few small sketches, General Foods launched a new line of fancy foods, including preserves, canapés, flaming desserts, and sauces. But it marketed the line without the tried-and-true formula of featuring a mouth-watering close-up of food ready for serving. Instead, the campaign in 1957 chatted in a light, humorous, and slightly sophisticated manner about "the finest foods from the four corners of the earth." Sketches illustrated not only the products but also things associated with them. This was to become a major characteristic of luxury advertising—advertising the image, not the product directly.

General Foods introduced the new line with a pair of teaser ads that pictured the gourmet line's white-and-gold packaging against nautical and culinary backgrounds. Ads for the main campaign ran in *Gourmet, Holiday, Sunset, The New Yorker,* and *Telefood,* and each featured one of the nine food categories that made up the line.

One of the most successful ways marketers create an upscale audience is by hosting "exclusive" events. Chrysler Corporation's events in 1958 succeeded in boosting sales of its Imperial by 300 percent. Chrysler and its agency, Young & Rubicam, realizing

This 1970 Saga campaign positioned the mink coat as an everyday necessity.
Saga Furs of Scandinavia.

that there was a certain class of car buyer who would never set foot in an automobile showroom, threw an "Imperial Ball in New York." Invitees were the cream of society. There was no sales pitch save for an Imperial automobile in the hall. Chrysler executives said they would be happy if guests only noticed the car. It was the same principle that advertisers such as Sprite would use in the 1990s to reach young people by "sponsoring" rock concerts and arranging dance parties featuring top name rap acts. Prior to the ball, Chrysler pushed the snob-appeal theme in upscale magazines and full-page ads in newspapers.

The next year Chrysler hosted golf exhibitions in Florida. The company invited nearly 7,000 upscale consumers to exhibitions by the game's top professionals. Clearly, the message was that Chrysler wanted the Imperial name to be associated only with those who could afford it.

Philippe Charriol, a Frenchman who left Cartier, Inc., to put his name on his own Swiss watch brand in 1983, knew well the principles of luxury marketing. While in Toronto, Canada, to promote his watches in the 1980s, Charriol booked a suite at the King Edward Hotel, where he met with potential buyers throughout the day. Then he hosted a champagne reception and dinner at Langdon Hall near Cambridge, Ontario. Representatives from the media were ferried to the event in a fleet of limousines, bad

Through the years, luxury goods advertisers such as DeBeers have targeted high-income consumers through niche publications, as seen in this ad from the 5 February 2001 issue of *Fortune* magazine.
DeBeers.

weather having stymied plans for helicopter transport. This was the sort of event the media loved; the next week, stories appeared in the *Toronto Star, Toronto Sun,* CTV's *By Design, L'Express, Les Affaires, Village Post, The Globe & Mail,* and *Lifestyle.* Sales took off, increasing on average 100 percent a year. Of course, Charriol understood other things about luxury marketing, including the importance of a memorable design. He chose the Celtic twist to represent his watch.

While it did host events, Parker Pen Company used nontraditional methods to promote its $50 pen in the 1960s. Parker did not use national media support in breaking the pen promotion. Instead the company supplied participating stores with various in-store and out-of-store displays. Stores also were able to participate in a co-op plan consisting mostly of newspaper ads and some local spot TV.

Magazines and FM: Two Preferred Markets

In the late 1950s and early 1960s, the Chrysler Imperial's advertising emphasized its own success story, subtly associating itself with the nation's most successful people. Chrysler print ads advised the "executive officers of America's 500 leading corporations" that they would receive an invitation to take a demonstration ride in a new Imperial. Chrysler created an atmosphere of mystery and intrigue, placing ads in *The New Yorker, Fortune, Sports Illustrated, Time,* and *Newsweek,* plus approximately 60 newspapers, including the *Wall Street Journal,* to alert the executives to expect an important event.

Cadillac had more money to spend than the other luxury car marketers and therefore did more advertising than the Imperial or Ford Motor Company's Lincoln Continental, which primarily used newspapers for ads created by Kenyon & Eckhardt. In addition to newspapers, Cadillac ad agency MacManus, John & Adams used spot radio. Chrysler's Imperial was the only model advertised on TV.

But magazines were the principal medium for all three automakers. It was in the print media that Cadillac marketing executives said they "zeroed in" on the Cadillac prospect. Luxury car companies were selective users of magazines for a selected audience. Ads aimed at women had the message, "Cadillac ladies say it better than we can" and "Ladies twist Cadillac around their little fingers." *Diplomat, Town & Country, Park Avenue Social Review,* and *Palm Beach Life & Social Spectator* all carried the Cadillac message. The Chrysler Imperial was advertised in more general-interest magazines.

In the mid-1960s FM radio became a new medium for reaching the wealthier consumer. FM listeners were demonstrated to be better prospects for the luxury market than other target groups and offered advertisers a compelling reason for selecting FM over other communications media. It was noted that selecting FM would give advertisers the opportunity to double their chances of reaching the luxury consumer, especially luxury car owners, within the audience available. In eight years, sales of FM radios increased 25 times, to more than 5 million sold in 1963.

The New Affluence

Luxury products in the 1980s and into the 1990s were purchased by investment-minded consumers who were highly educated and attentive to their buying decisions. They had money to burn, but not indiscriminately. Image did not mean as much to these newly affluent consumers as to their predecessors.

Tourneau, Inc., the luxury watchmaker, claimed that the company's $20 million radio and newspaper campaign during this time was not an attempt to gain market share from a competitor but rather an attempt to expand the entire market. The campaign was a blatant appeal to the idea that "when you wear a watch, you are somebody." The ads, from agency Lois/EJL, drove home the fact that more than a car or wardrobe, a watch affirms that "you've arrived." While in the past, luxury marketers could get away with relatively small advertising budgets, the situation started to change at this time. Cartier International, for example, increased its ad budget 35 percent in 1996. Media fragmentation made it possible to target wealthy investors and intermediaries more efficiently, thanks to the creation of specialized cable TV channels such as CNBC, MSNBC, and the Golf Network, as well as investment magazines and Web sites. Business and new-economy magazines became prime outlets for luxury advertising, as marketers targeted Wall Streeters and the new breed of dot-com millionaire. Luxury advertisers in *Fortune* magazine included Giorgio Armani and DeBeers Consolidated Mines. Marketing strategies designed to reach the wealthy continued to rely in large part on the traditional social events and entertainment outings, however; advertisers believed those types of affairs solidified personal relationships.

By the late 1990s a different type of upper-class was emerging, thanks in large part to the technology boom that produced so many instant millionaires. By 1999 about 30 percent of the world's 7 million millionaires lived in North America. In its 1999 ranking of the richest Americans, *Forbes* listed 267 people with a net worth of more than $1 billion, compared with only 13 in 1982. These new-money rich tended to value experience over traditional luxury goods. What separated the new money from the old was the newcomer's seemingly endless appetite for information; the new rich demanded unique experiences tailored to them and wanted to participate, be it in cooking classes in Provence, France, or wine classes at their local wine seller. However, the economic downturn that ushered in the 21st century hit the new rich hardest, leaving upscale marketers facing a new set of challenges.

ALAN SALOMON

Further Reading

Attracting the Affluent: The First Guide to America's Changing Ultimate Market, Naperville, Illinois: Financial Sourcebooks, 1991

Freeman, Laurie, "Marketing the Good Life to a New Breed of Wealth," *Advertising Age* (15 May 2000)

Stanley, Thomas J., *Marketing to the Affluent,* Homewood, Illinois: Dow Jones-Irwin, 1988

M

MacLaren McCann Canada, Inc.

Started in Toronto by Jack MacLaren in 1935, from the branch office of Detroit, Michigan–based Campbell-Ewald that he had opened in Toronto in 1922; acquired the Norris-Patterson Agency in 1942; purchased Goodis, Goldberg, Soren, 1975; acquired by LintasWorldwide (Interpublic Group of Companies) in 1988 and became MacLaren:Lintas; assumed control of McCann-Erickson, Toronto, and renamed MacLaren McCann, Toronto, 1995.

Major Clients
Bacardi-Martini
Black and Decker
Delta Faucet
Durex
General Motors Corporation
Good Humor-Breyers
Laura Secord
LEGO
Lever Pond's
Lipton
Lucent Technologies
McNeil
Molson Breweries
National Sea Products
Nestlé
Rogers Communications
Royal Bank of Canada

John Aiken ("Jack") MacLaren (1891–1955) was the acknowledged "dean of Canadian advertising." He came to the business from an early career in journalism. In 1922 he was hired by Henry Ewald to join a three-man branch office of Campbell-Ewald (based in Detroit, Michigan), which was opened to service the Canadian General Motors Corporation (GM) business. The agency continued to work for GM into the 21st century, making that relationship one of the longest lasting in advertising history. In the 1950s GM accounted for half of the agency's billings.

MacLaren's first new business success, which came almost immediately, was winning the General Electric account. Many others followed, and by 1930, he was president of the office. The year before, the legendary Conn Smythe, owner of the Toronto Maple Leafs, granted sole rights to broadcast hockey games from the soon-to-be-built Maple Leaf Gardens to MacLaren in perpetuity. The deal, made over a handshake on a golf course, is regarded as the most significant in Canadian radio history. *Hockey Night in Canada*, sponsored by MacLaren client GM and later Imperial Oil, began broadcasting in 1931 and quickly became a Canadian institution.

In the 1930s MacLaren was ready to run his own agency, and the president of Campbell-Ewald sold it to him outright in 1935, even guaranteeing a bank loan. On a Friday afternoon in January 1935, he called all the employees together and fired them, adding quickly that they should all come to work on Monday—at MacLaren Advertising. The agency soon established itself as a leader in Canadian advertising, being the first agency to have a radio department, research department, direct mail and sales promotion department, as well as a poster and store display division. As the business grew, Jack MacLaren established branches in Montreal, Quebec, and London, England.

In 1942, at the second annual awards dinner of the Association of Canadian Advertisers, Jack MacLaren was awarded the organization's Silver Medal for his distinguished service to advertising. Later that year, MacLaren acquired the Norris-Patterson agency, which was absorbed into Maclaren's business structure.

By 1954 MacLaren was Toronto's largest advertising agency and one of the top 50 companies in North America. Branch offices were opened in Vancouver, British Columbia; Winnipeg, Manitoba; and Ottawa, Ontario, soon after. Because of its early success in radio broadcast production, MacLaren was poised to be a major force in the early development of television in Canada. By 1955 the agency and its clients dominated the medium, with agency staff writing and producing some 85 percent of network programming, including *General Motors Presents, Cross Canada Hit Parade,* and of course *Hockey Night in Canada.* By 1960 MacLaren was Canada's largest agency.

After Jack MacLaren's death in 1955, leadership of the agency was passed to Einar Rechnitzer, a longtime employee who had

IMPALA 2000

FEEL GOOD AGAIN

Nearly eight decades after the relationship began, MacLaren McCann continued to create advertisements for General Motors of Canada, such as this 2000 Chevrolet Impala ad.
Courtesy of General Motors of Canada Ltd.

headed the GM business. When Rechnitzer retired in 1964, George Sinclair succeeded him. Sinclair had started in 1940 as a copywriter and became copy chief in 1950. Under his management, the agency established offices beyond Canada, acquiring agencies in London, England, and Paris, France, and opening offices in Nassau, Bahamas. At home MacLaren also expanded, opening an office in Quebec City and a public relations subsidiary, Carlton Cowan, in Toronto. In 1979 MacLaren opened a creative boutique called the Gloucester Group, which was later folded into the parent company.

MacLaren was closely tied to the Liberal Party of Canada, creating political campaign advertising for many years, until the Liberals lost power in 1979, causing massive layoffs and a complete restructuring of the agency. The restructuring spawned a new period of creative growth. Under Creative Director Bill Durnan, the agency broke the mold in several product categories, beginning in 1982 with a hard rock-and-roll campaign for Molson called "Dancin' in the Streets." To strengthen the agency's creative efforts, he hired two men from Canadian agency Carder Gray— Michael McLaughlin, an art director, and Stephen Creet, a writer. McLaughlin and Creet were among the best and brightest in Canadian advertising.

In 1984 the agency broke the pattern in detergent advertising with its campaign for Unilever's Sunlight detergent. Instead of a Tide "clean clothes" strategy, Sunlight adopted a lifestyle campaign, which recognized that for some people in the target audience, the whiteness of their laundry was not the most important issue in their life. "It's part of the family" and "We know you

have better things to do" were key themes that drove the Sunlight business in the 1980s.

Its ads for Molson continued to break the pattern for beer advertising, with the 1985 campaign "What beer's all about" and the 1992 "I am Canadian" campaign, which flaunted Canadian national pride. The account went into review, however, and the agency lost the business in 1999.

In 1988 MacLaren was sold to Lintas Worldwide and renamed MacLaren:Lintas. Many of Canada's largest agencies were being bought by U.S. companies at that time—Hayhurst Advertising by Saatchi & Saatchi, Foster Advertising by McCann-Erickson, and Ronalds-Reynolds by Foote, Cone & Belding.

The year 1990 saw the return of the Buick and Pontiac brands to the agency. In response to new ideas in client service, the agency became the first in Canada to separate its media department into an independent unit.

Named "Canadian Agency of the Year" by *Marketing* magazine in 1988, 1995, 1996 and 1999, MacLaren has been a perennial award winner for its creative work, particularly for Molson. The fourth-largest agency in Canada, at the turn of the 21st century it had offices in Toronto, Vancouver, and Calgary and a French-language agency, Marketel, in Montreal.

WAYNE HILINSKI

Further Reading
Marketing (29 November 1999, "Agency of the Year" issue)
Scotland, Randy, *The Creative Edge: Inside the Ad Wars*, New York: Viking, 1994

Magazine Advertising

A magazine is a periodical publication, usually paperbound and/ or accessed on-line, that typically contains written pieces (such as stories, essays, editorials, news reports, advice columns, poems, or reviews); visual features (such as photos, cartoons, or illustrations); and advertisements. Most readers either subscribe to magazines, purchase them over the counter, or download a digital copy. Magazines and other forms of media are important to marketers and advertisers because they are channels of communication that can effectively and efficiently carry advertising messages to target audiences and accomplish marketing goals.

Early History

The beginnings of the magazine business in the United States are difficult to determine. *Advertising Age* claims that an advertisement appeared in a Philadelphia, Pennsylvania, magazine called the *Weekly Mercury* as early as 1719. Other sources identify the birth date of the industry as 16 February 1741, when Benjamin Franklin published his first periodical, although publisher Andrew Bradford launched his *American Magazine* three days before Franklin's *General Magazine and Historical Chronicle*.

The growth of magazines in the 19th century was bolstered by a number of interrelated economic, technological, and cultural developments. Capitalism was on the rise. The industrial revolution made mass-produced goods available at affordable prices. Increasingly, manufacturers emphasized branding. The number and types of retail stores, products, and services proliferated in an increasingly competitive environment, and new markets were created. Mass communication technologies were invented and refined. As the middle class grew in size and prosperity, Western societies became more materialistic. The rising middle class was also thirsty for information and entertainment, and consumers turned to magazines for news, entertainment, and other features that would enrich their diversifying lifestyles. Advertising and magazines soon found respectability and glamour. The earliest magazines published in the United States were local journals that focused mainly on political opinions and issues.

Circulation and Ad Revenues

By the end of the 20th century, competition among magazines for advertising dollars was intense, as more than 12,000 magazine titles were published annually in the United States. A magazine's survival typically depends on its ability to attract both readers and advertisers. *Consumer Reports,* a magazine dedicated to assessing the safety and efficacy of products, is an exception. Its editors do not accept advertising because they think that advertising revenues would create a conflict of interest, dilute the magazine's commitment to reporting impartially the results of product tests, and undermine the magazine's integrity in the eyes of readers and executives. Another noted magazine that eschewed ads from its founding in 1921 until the mid-1950s was *Reader's Digest*. The

top 15 magazines in the United States in 1998 (based on circulation figures from the second half of 1998, according to *Advertising Age*) are listed in Table 1. Circulation numbers do not always transfer into advertising revenue, however, as demonstrated by a comparison between Table 1 and Table 2, which shows the top ten U.S. magazines in advertising revenue generated in 1998 (according to *Mediaweek*).

Types of Magazines

The fact that advertisers are more interested in targeting those readers who are likely to buy their products than they are in advertising to readers in general helps to explain why Tables 1 and 2 are not identical. Advertisers may be more attracted to magazines with lesser circulation numbers when those periodicals appeal to a

Table 1. Top 15 U.S. magazines in circulation, 1998.

Magazine	Circulation
Modern Maturity	20,534,357
Reader's Digest	13,767,575
TV Guide	12,579,912
National Geographic	8,612,102
Better Homes & Gardens	7,613,249
Family Circle	5,004,902
Good Housekeeping	4,584,879
Ladies' Home Journal	4,575,996
Woman's Day	4,242,097
McCall's	4,202,809
Time	4,060,074
People Weekly	3,635,146
Playboy	3,336,213
Sports Illustrated	3,264,345
Newsweek	3,135,281

Table 2. Top ten U.S. magazines in advertising revenue generated, 1998.

Magazine	Ad Revenues
People Weekly	$626.6 million
Time	$561.7 million
Sports Illustrated	$554.9 million
Parade	$517.1 million
TV Guide	$435.5 million
Better Homes & Gardens	$410.1 million
Newsweek	$400.0 million
Business Week	$361.6 million
PC Magazine	$314.2 million
USA Weekend	$274.5 million

particular population of consumers that advertisers wish to target. For example, different magazines reach different geographic areas, offering advertisers varying access to multinational, pan-regional, national, regional, state, and local readerships.

In addition to attending to geographic classifications, advertisers select magazines according to the types of readers that those periodicals serve. Consumer magazines—for example, *National Geographic, People, Time*—are purchased by individuals for pleasure and personal edification. Some consumer magazines target gender—*Maxim, GQ, Men's Journal,* and *Men's Health* target a male audience, while *Elle, Cosmopolitan, Ladies' Home Journal, Better Homes & Gardens, Working Woman, Redbook,* and *Sports Illustrated Women* appeal to a female readership. Still another category of consumer magazines consists of publications that target readers interested in particular lifestyles or hobbies (e.g., *Field & Stream, Popular Photography, Car & Driver, Rolling Stone, Soldier of Fortune, Fine Gardening, Down Beat, Popular Mechanics*). Some consumer magazines serve a specific ethnic group—for example, *Ebony,* which addresses an African-American audience; others are aimed at age-defined market segments, such as teenage girls (*Seventeen*), senior citizens (*Modern Maturity*), or children (*Sesame Street*).

Business magazines (trade papers, industrial magazines, and professional journals) serve executives, managers, business students, and others involved in particular industries or business sectors. Every industry has at least one trade paper, often published by its trade association, which is aimed at manufacturers, wholesalers, distributors, financial service providers, and the like. Examples include *Chain Store Age, Discount Store News,* and *Progressive Grocer.* Industrial magazines, such as *InfoWorld,* which serves computer and computer-related manufacturers and major users, provide information of interest to manufacturers and industry groups. Professional journals are of interest to well-defined groups of professionals, such as accountants, architects, advertisers, doctors, engineers, lawyers, and purchasing agents. *Architectural Digest, Sales & Marketing, National Law Review, American Family Physician, Electric Engineering Times,* and *Travel Weekly* are examples of professional magazines. Farm magazines, such as *Farm Journal, Successful Farming,* and *Progressive Farmer,* reach broad categories of farmers. Niche magazines—for example, *Peanut Farmer* and *Pig American*—serve smaller, specialized segments of the farm population.

Magazines service advertisers at every level of the distribution chain, from suppliers through consumers. Industrial marketers use trade magazines to influence manufacturers and other business firms; those same marketers also place advertisements in consumer magazines to convey a positive corporate image and otherwise communicate to the general public. Manufacturers use trade magazines to develop channels of distribution, and they advertise in consumer magazines to build brand recognition and image, increase sales, and indicate retail locations. Business-to-business marketers also use trade publications to promote their products and services to buyers and members of buying centers, whereas wholesalers and distributors purchase ads in the same types of magazines to attract both suppliers and retailers. Retail-

Dennis Wheeler, who designed some of the great poster ads of the 1960s, created this 1963 poster for *Life* magazine. *Courtesy of Time.*

ers send messages to selected audiences by placing advertisements in consumer magazines suggesting store image and highlighting featured products and/or services. Retailers, however, are more likely to use newspapers and radio than magazines to inform audiences about special events, demonstrations or shows, and sales.

Media Selection and Strategy

Before placing ads in any media, advertisers establish a set of media objectives (i.e., they determine the target audience, geographical coverage, campaign duration, and the timing of selling aperture) and then develop a media strategy that enables the advertiser to reach its media objectives. Such plans are systematically created through both qualitative and quantitative evaluations of the target audience's demographics, that audience's geographic location, and its lifestyles. Also profiled are the audience's information search patterns, media usage habits, general viewing patterns, and such characteristics of particular media as competitive practices, size and nature of the audience delivered (e.g., reach, frequency, gross rating points, share, rating points, etc.), media costs, and cost evaluations (e.g., cost per thousand, cost per rating point, quantity discounts, etc.). Advertisers also assess a medium's editorial policies and established standards and practices policy (the code stipulating advertising practices in the medium), that medium's inquiry-pulling ability (the history of coupon redemption attributed to a magazine), and the reputation and image of the vehicle.

Through such analysis, an advertiser determines the media mix for its impending campaign; that is, the advertiser decides which traditional and nontraditional media will be used to reach the audience and assesses the relative importance of each medium to the campaign. The media mix is thus a central part of the media plan, generally a written document, which outlines media objectives and media strategy. The plan also contains the media schedule, which identifies the specific vehicles that will be used to reach target audiences, when each advertisement will run, the size of each advertisement, whether the ads will be color or black-and-white, the cost of each advertisement, and the total estimated media expenditure.

Magazines offer a number of special features to advertisers, such as split run, gatefold, spread and center spread, full position, insert capability and bleed. In a split run, an advertiser places two or more print advertisements, equal in size, for the same product, in the same position and same issue of a magazine, and then the magazines containing the various versions are distributed in equal numbers within the same geographic area. Thus, a split-run test provides the advertiser with a "real-world" test of the relative effectiveness of different versions of copy, offers, or other specific variables in the ad.

A "spread" is an advertisement designed to occupy two full facing pages as a single unit of space. The center spread consists of two full facing pages of a publication with a continuous gutter in the center. A gatefold is a four-page sheet, creased and folded approximately halfway along its width so as to bind one end and open, like a gate, to double page size, avoiding the loss of space in the gutter of a two-page spread. Spreads and gatefolds allow advertisers to place products in a panoramic setting, develop complex messages that present several appeals, and/or dramatize one or more features of the product.

Bleed is a characteristic of a printing in which the inked impression of an advertisement or illustration extends beyond the trimmed edges of the page, thereby eliminating margins. Many advertisers are willing to pay extra for bleed because it allows a brand to be set in a desirable panoramic setting.

Full—or preferred—position refers to the placement of an advertisement either following and next to reading matter or at the top of a column next to reading matter. Advertisers pay a premium for full position ads in hopes of increasing exposure and readership.

These special features, although important, are not the advertiser's main concern when it decides to buy space in a magazine. Media planners are most concerned that a magazine will carry its message effectively and efficiently to their primary or key target audience. Therefore, advertisers become highly involved in evaluating the fit between the magazine's editorial content and its audience. To entice advertisers, each magazine publishes a "publisher's editorial profile"—a brief overview describing the type of magazine, profiles of its readership, its key contents, and any special sections—in advertising directories. For example, PC Magazine published the following editorial profile in Standard Rate and Data Service's *SRDS: Business Publication Advertising Source* on 30 June 1999:

> *PC Magazine* is a computer and business magazine that delivers authoritative, lab-based comparative reviews for Internet, PC software, networking and peripheral products both in print and online. It's written for buyers who are the key specifiers of technology brands and products to be purchased for their companies. It contains extensive product reviews based on benchmark lab testing in PC Labs, and also includes productivity solutions sections and opinion/analysis columns.

When selecting and rejecting magazines, media planners must place a great deal of trust in the accuracy of such publisher's editorial profiles. Therefore, advertisers and publishers cooperate to create these profiles. In a process known as "comparability" both parties work together to define, in each of the markets served by the magazine, the terminology used for the product-market served and report audience profiles and the coverage of the markets and audience. Comparability is completed market-by-market on a voluntary basis in open meetings.

Whereas media planners use publisher's editorial profiles for media selection decisions, publishers use them to verify circulation and establish advertising rates. Once the target reader is profiled, the description provides quantitative information about the magazine's "qualified circulation" (the number of issues, paid or unpaid, sent to qualified recipients in the market or field served within the past 36 months). A qualified recipient must receive every issue of the magazine, subject to normal removals and editions.

Audits play a role in verifying circulation, the main basis for establishing the advertising rates charged by magazines. The "unit audit" report attests to the number of units, plants, or establishments a publication is serving. An audit also typically provides a "breakdown," which delineates the types of businesses or industry a magazine reaches, the functions or titles of recipients, and/or their demographic characteristics or geographic locations.

Media surveys are sometimes used in measuring the extent of penetration of a particular medium into one or several markets. However, advertisers generally trust independent auditors to assess magazine circulation. The Audit Bureau of Circulations (ABC), for example, is an independent nonprofit organization of advertisers, agencies, and publishers that provides verified audits of the circulation of business publications, general magazines, and newspapers. Audits of magazine circulation also can be obtained from other firms, such as Business Publications Audit and Verified Audit Circulation. Not all circulation figures are audited. "Non-qualified distribution" is a circulation estimate that does not conform to the criteria used in audited circulation reports. To alert media planners when circulation figures have not been verified, publishers often provide such data in a form known within the industry as a "statement."

Media planners find information describing magazines in magazine directories. *The Standard Periodicals Directory* provides comprehensive directory information on U.S. and Canadian periodicals according to such subject areas as art, automotive, machinery, romance, lifestyles, and salesmanship. Magazines are indexed alphabetically and are classified as association, business, consumer, or scholarly publications. Each magazine's editorial content is explained in terms of the magazine's scope, purpose, and content. Standard Rate and Data Service (SRDS) publishes complete directories for both business publications and consumer magazines in the United States and Canada, which include audited and non-audited circulation statistics, guarantee statements, information about editorial content, guidelines concerning advertising costs, and details on split runs and other magazine capabilities.

Benn's Media Directory, a U.K. publication, identifies magazines, periodicals, and newspapers worldwide. Its data on some countries are sketchy and incomplete, indicating the challenges facing a media planner in international advertising.

In addition to basic circulation figures, media planers are concerned with duplication, that part of the total circulation or audience of a medium that is also served or reached by a second advertising medium. Duplication is considered desirable if frequency (i.e., a household's repeated exposure to the same advertisement) is more important to the media planner than reaching the maximum number of targeted consumers. (Conversely, if reach is most important, duplication is less desirable.)

In determining the role that magazines will play in a company's media strategy and media mix, advertisers consider the unique advantages and disadvantages of each medium. If marketers wish to influence a large or broadly defined audience, they advertise in general interest magazines, such as *Parade, Time, People,* or *TV Guide.* Today, advertisers benefit from the increasing number of successful niche periodicals, such as *Fitness Swimming* and *Fast Company,* which permit advertisers to reach narrowly defined target audiences. These special interest magazines cut the waste niche marketers negatively associate with advertising in more general magazines when they wish to reach only a select readership.

Effectiveness as an Ad Medium

Audiences are highly receptive to magazine advertisements, viewing them as informative, relevant, authoritative, credible, and trustworthy. Because people select the magazines they wish to read and choose which parts of them to read, magazine ads have an advantage over TV commercials, which are unsolicited and disrupt entertainment. Moreover, readers often develop personal relationships with particular magazines because those periodicals convey desirable lifestyles, values, or concepts. Captivating pictures and stories also enhance audience receptivity to magazines. Salespersons representing successful magazines of high market standing encounter little rebuttal from a media buyer when claiming their magazine adds prestige to brands and/or solidifies brand image. Obviously, an advertisement for an exclusive brand of business suits would be better received if placed in *Forbes* than in *The National Inquirer.*

Magazines also offer the advantage of comparatively long life spans. Whereas each radio or television spot provides a single opportunity to reach the consumer, and newspaper ads are typically seen only on the day the paper is published, a reader is likely to peruse magazine advertisements repeatedly, thereby increasing the effective frequency of such ads. For example, a reader of *TV Guide* may consult it several times during the week. Moreover, magazines have a "pass-along" advantage. Several different people—family members, friends, customers, patients, and others—can read the same magazine, increasing the reach of an advertisement.

Researchers have found that magazine readers are generally reflective when they read, processing information and contemplating the cues and images contained in the art and copy of magazine advertisements more slowly and carefully than they might treat ads in other media. Advertisers are also drawn to magazines by the superior visual quality of the media and its ability to handle the latest computer-based digital designs and desktop publishing software. Compared to newsprint, the high-quality paper used in magazines provides texture, contrast, and superior color reproduction.

Advertisers also appreciate that they can use magazines to offer coupons and explain rebates. Moreover, ads in magazines can convey the required legal "fine print" that companies must publish when offering special financing or lease programs. In a magazine mailed in an envelope or wrapper, advertisers can include free-standing inserts (FSI) or other loose supplements.

Drawbacks for Advertisers

As an advertising medium, magazines have limitations as well as advantages. One such limitation is the need for a long lead time. Advertisers must submit advertising materials well in advance of the publication date, sometimes as much as two months prior to publication. This problem is less pronounced today than it was in the past; improvements in desktop publishing and satellite transmission have allowed advertisers to submit advertisements and collateral material to some periodicals days, or even hours, before press time. Advertisers may also be hampered by a publication's editorial policy, which can limit what can be said or shown in a magazine. *Modern Maturity,* for example, discourages advertisers from showing elderly people suffering from pain or discomfort. Some magazines also have policies that limit advertisers from placing their advertisements in certain positions, for example, the front of the magazine.

Another drawback for advertisers is that readers often do not open a magazine as soon as it is delivered. Two or more weeks may transpire before a given issue is read. This delay poses negative consequences for advertisers attempting to influence immediate action and caring less about the long-term effects of their ads. The desire for fast results drives advertisers to select newspapers, radio, or other promotional tools offering more immediate, although more temporary, effects on purchasing decisions.

Still another disadvantage of magazines, especially general interest magazines, is the high cost of their advertisements relative to those in other media. Special interest magazines can be cost effective, however, and appeal to advertisers seeking a tightly defined target audience. Because most magazines receive limited attention from retailers and fail to enjoy a broad pattern of distribution, many (especially those for specialized audiences) are difficult to locate and purchase over the counter, another drawback for advertisers.

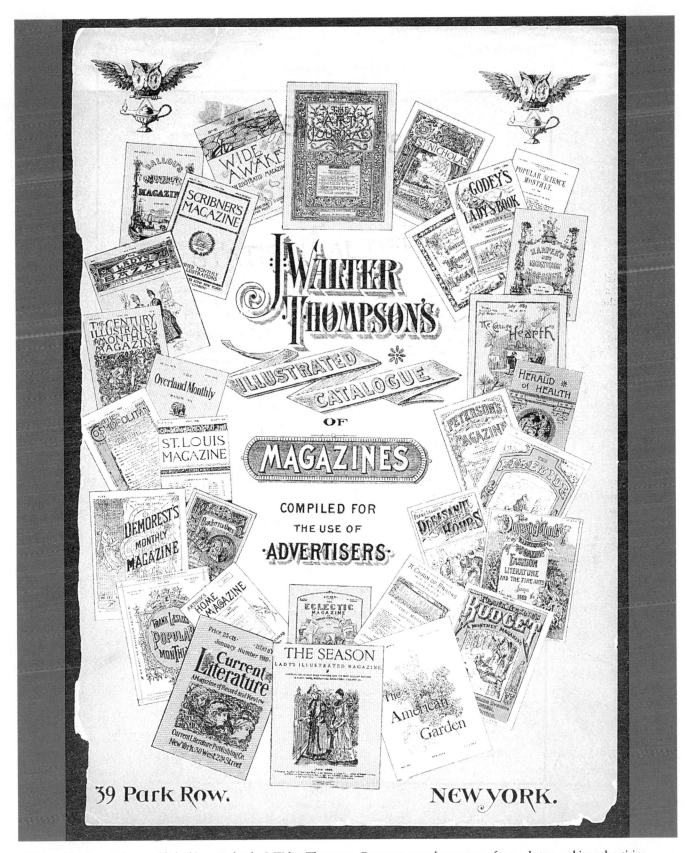

This catalog of magazines, published in 1887 by the J. Walter Thompson Company, served as a source for marketers seeking advertising venues for their products.
Courtesy of J. Walter Thompson Company.

Financial Considerations

Advertisers developing media plans go beyond evaluating audiences and relative merits of a medium. They also examine cost efficiency. Cost per thousand (CPM) is the most commonly used technique to assess cost efficiency. CPM is found by dividing the cost of a vehicle, or entire media plan, by the number of thousands in the circulation. Effective CPM, a more rigorous test, uses only the number in thousands of the advertiser's primary audience who read the magazine rather than the larger general circulation.

Publishers inform advertisers about the cost of an advertisement in several ways, such as through SRDS publications, in special promotions, by using sales representatives and advertising agents, and by publishing rate cards, which give space rates, information on technical and mechanical requirements, and closing dates. SRDS directories summarize rate cards.

Publishers attract advertisers by offering discounts. Quantity or time discounts are percentage reductions in price given to advertisers according to the frequency or regularity with which they insert advertisements in the same publication. Cash discounts, usually two percent of net cost or future space, are returned to advertisers for timely payment of invoices. Group discounts lower rates for advertisers placing advertisements in several magazines owned by one publisher.

Advertisers may elect to pay premium rates for bleed, color, inserts, gate-folds, and other special features, including special or preferred positions. Preferred positions are choice locations that command higher prices. Higher rates are charged for the back cover ("cover four," the most expensive one-page position), the inside front cover (IFC, or "cover two"), and the inside back cover (IBC, or "cover three"). If advertisers decline to order a premium or preferred position, or if the desired position is not available, they are offered a "run-of-paper" (ROP) position. ROP indicates that an advertisement is placed anywhere within the magazine at the convenience of the publisher. Today, final rates are often negotiated.

Future Outlook

Digital technology, e-commerce, and on-line access to magazines will undoubtedly affect the future of the medium, as will the demand for truly multinational media. Technological advances that will spawn a host of new products and services are also likely to have an influence on magazine publishing. Readers today have become "human scanners" able to quickly and superficially peruse printed material; they are less likely than readers of earlier generations to look beyond pictures and display type. Therefore, contemporary magazine advertisers must rely more on visual cues and headlines than on lengthy copy to persuade modern audiences.

In the future, advertisers will demand clearer audience profiles and readership results, particularly if the cost of magazine advertising rises. The number of new magazines introduced into the market declined in the late 1990s, and this trend is expected to continue, particularly in the lifestyle markets. Publishers are making every effort to strengthen the competitive position of their current magazines, but marketers are seeking ways to build their customer bases without relying as heavily as in the past on such mass advertising vehicles.

In the international arena, countries with emerging economies are likely to offer advertisers a broader range of technically advanced trade and consumer magazines in both general and special-interest formats. There is a positive correlation between the developmental stage of a country's economy and the diversity of that nation's consumer magazines. Pan-regional magazines, especially those tied to ethnic and religious groups, and airline magazines offer especially attractive audiences to international advertisers. In addition, *Newsweek, Reader's Digest, The Economist, Time,* and many others have international editions.

As products proliferate and the competitive pressures facing advertisers mount, publishers should expect to encounter greater demands from advertisers for free publicity and favorable product reviews. Conflicts of interest are likely to remain an important issue in magazine advertising, as business practices increasingly come under the microscope, and publishers and advertisers seek independent goals.

ALLEN E. SMITH

See also Trade Publication

Further Reading

Bovee, Courtland L., and Willaim F. Arens, *Contemporary Advertising,* Homewood, Illinois: Richard D. Irwin, 1982

Burnkrant, Robert E. (1976), "A Motivational Model of Information Processing Intensity," *Journal of Consumer Research,* 3, 2

Jones, John Philip, *The Advertising Business: Operations, Creativity, Media Planning, Integrated Communications,* Thousand Oaks, California: SAGE Publications, 1999

Krugman, Dean M., Leonard N. Reid, S. Watson Dunn and Arnold M. Barban, *Advertising: Its Role in Modern Marketing,* Forth Worth: Dryden, 1961; 8th edition, 1994

Lamb, Charles W., Jr., Joseph F. Hair, Jr., and Carl McDaniel, *Principles of Marketing,* Cincinnati, Ohio: South-Western Publishing Company, 2nd edition, 1994

McGann, Anthony F. and J. Thomas Russell, *Advertising Media,* Homewood, Illinois: Irwin, 1988

O'Guinn, Thomas C., Chris T. Allen and Richard J. Sememik, *Advertising,* Cincinnati: South-Western Publishing Company, 1998, 2nd edition, 2000

Parente, Donald, *Advertising Campaign Strategy: A Guide to Marketing Communications Plans,* Fort Worth: Dryden Press, 2nd edition, 2000

Russell, J. Thomas and W. Ronald Lane, *Kleppner's Advertising Procedure,* Upper Saddle River, New Jersey: Prentice Hall, 1988, 14th edition, 1999

The Standard Periodical Directory, Deborah Striplin, Editorial Director, New York, 23rd edition, 2000

Standard Rate and Data Service, *SRDS: Business Publication Advertising Source,* Des Plaines, Illinois: Standard Rate and Data Service, 2000

Standard Rate and Data Service, *SRDS: Consumer Magazine Advertising Source,* Standard Rate and Data Service, Des Plaines, Illinois: Standard Rate and Data Service, 2000

Vakratsas, Demetrios and Tim Ambler, How Advertising Works: What Do We Really Know?" *Journal of Marketing,* 63 no. 1 (1999)

Wells, William, John Burnett and Sandra Moriarty, *Advertising Principles and Practices,* Upper Saddle river, New Jersey: Prentice Hall, 1989, 5th edition, 2000

Market Research

The American Marketing Association (AMA) defines market research as "the function that links the consumer, customer, and public to the marketer through information—information used to identify and define marketing opportunities and problems; generate, refine, and evaluate marketing actions; monitor marketing performance; and improve the understanding of marketing as a process."

Market research is a multistep process involving: (1) specifying the information required to address the issues; (2) designing the method for collecting information and managing and implementing the data collection process; (3) analyzing the results; and (4) communicating the findings and their implications. When the data under consideration belong to an individual client company, the research is deemed *proprietary.* When several clients sponsor the research and the data are owned by the research company, the research is *syndicated.* As the AMA definition indicates, there are myriad applications of market research.

Types of Market Research

Product market research focuses on products and services (the content and subjects of the advertising) and on the consumers of these marketed products and services (the target audiences for advertising). This research is essential to advertising strategy development, providing information about a product and brand attributes, benefits and purchase/use, brand/product perceptions, as well as the brand's competitive strengths and weaknesses. Examples of product market research are: (a) brand equity research, which assesses the added value consumers associate with a brand; (b) consumer research, which profiles the demographics, behaviors, and sometimes the psychographics of various target consumer options; and (c) market geography research, which examines the market by the current and potential purchase or consumption levels of products/services within defined geographic markets.

Clustering is a geodemographic market segmentation method commonly used in market research. It is based on the theory that people with similar lifestyles tend to live near one another. Clusters are often used in direct mail, media planning, site analysis, and product positioning. Marketers use clusters to identify and profile target markets, measuring whether geographic zip codes perform at above average or below average rates for their products and services. By identifying the neighborhood types where existing customers live, marketers can predict the types of neighborhoods where prospective customers are located. It is estimated that U.S. marketers spend $300 million annually on clustering techniques.

In the United States, PRIZM (potential rating index by zip markets) is the most commonly used clustering system. The system was developed in 1974 by the founder of Claritas Corporation, Jonathan Robbin, who created a program to extract data from the census to create lifestyle clusters. By the 1990s, it described every U.S. neighborhood in one of the 62 clusters with distinct lifestyle types. Built with 1990 census data, current-year demographics, and data from millions of consumer-purchase records, PRIZM clustered social groups from the affluent executives of "Blue Blood Estates" to the remote rural families of "Blue Highways."

Advertising effectiveness research encompasses research aimed at assessing the effectiveness of the advertising message, tracking the impact of a total communications campaign (which increasingly involves more than just mass advertising), as well as research to document audience delivery. Included under this broad topic are both message ("copy") research and audience ("media") research.

Copy/message research deals with consumer retention and perception and ultimately with the behavioral response to an advertising message. When research is conducted on "prefinished" ads and commercials (i.e., well-rendered mockups), it is called a "pretest." Pretesting research systems include the services provided by companies such as McCollum-Spielman, Mapes & Ross, ASI, and Research System Corporation. Some of these companies pretest ads by buying channel time from cable operators (the split cable method) to air the commercials to a selected audience and obtain their responses; others pretest ads in theater settings. When the research on individual ads is conducted after the advertising has aired, it is called a "post test." Many of the same companies also conduct "day after" tests of finished, aired ads and commercials.

In contrast with the testing of single ad executions, ad tracking research continuously monitors the growth or decline over time in

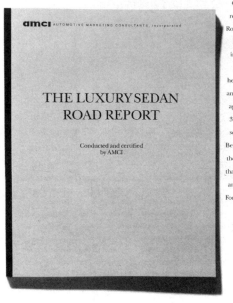

Finally, proof in advertising.

amci AUTOMOTIVE MARKETING CONSULTANTS, Incorporated

THE LUXURY SEDAN ROAD REPORT

Conducted and certified
by AMCI

Car companies make lots
of claims about their cars.
"It's faster." "It's bigger."
"It's sexier." At Nissan; we
don't just make claims about
the *Nissan Altima*— we offer
proof. The proof is free.
Call 1-800-NISSAN-3, to
receive the Luxury Sedan
Road Report. It contains the
surprising results of an
independent study which
shows the *Altima* going
head-to-head in emergency
and performance road tests
against cars like the BMW
325i, the Acura Legend L
sedan, and the Mercedes-
Benz 190E 2.3. Think of it as
the study that demonstrates
that luxury and affordability
are not mutually exclusive.
For your FREE Luxury Sedan
Road Report call:

1-800-NISSAN-3
ext. 332

The New Nissan
Altima

It's time to expect
more from a car."

In 1993, to document claims for the Altima, Nissan featured in its ads the cover of an independent report that compared leading luxury sedans. *Copyright, Nissan (1992). Altima is a registered trademark of Nissan. Courtesy Automotive Marketing Consultants, Inc. (AMCI).*

consumer responses to the total advertising/communications campaign. Measures include consumer awareness, image and attribute associations, intentions, and actual purchase of a brand.

Audience and media research is concerned with media usage behavior and advertising exposure of a target audience. This type of research allows the advertising planner to estimate the size of the audience delivery for an advertising campaign and to select the most efficient media mix for reaching the target audience.

Media model research attempts to predict the effects of advertising by media selection through the use of probability theories. The parameters of media models are reach and frequency distribution of audience exposure to an advertising schedule. The introduction of media model research largely came from European researchers such as J.M. Agostini, Pierre Hofmans, and Richard Metheringham in the 1960s. Many media models have been incorporated into media planning software currently used by the advertising industry.

In addition, many advertisers are interested in optimizing spending levels for their brands. They examine the relationship of advertising expenditures to consequent sales or traffic (or some

other specified goal) and apply statistical analysis to determine the budget levels they should use to achieve these goals. This type of research is called advertising budget research.

Industry Pioneers

Walter Dill Scott, a German-born psychologist at Northwestern University in Evanston, Illinois, was one of the first to apply experimental techniques to advertising. He placed emphasis on the voluntary actions of consumers and the cumulative effects of advertising, and produced two seminal books, *The Theory of Advertising* in 1903 and *Psychology of Advertising* in 1908. These laid the theoretical foundation for the "reason-why" approach to advertising.

The J. Walter Thompson Company (JWT) was the first advertising agency to establish a formal research department, after Stanley Resor purchased the agency in 1916. JWT also published *Population and Its Distribution,* the first book in which census bureau demographic and economic data were related to advertising planning. In 1920 John B. Watson, a psychologist, joined the agency and promoted behavioral theory applications to advertising practices. JWT applied motivational studies to advertising, initiated the use of scientific and medical findings as a basis for copy, and established the Consumer Panel, composed of families whose buying habits were analyzed and the analysis supplied to clients. John Caples of Batten Barton Durstine & Osborn (BBDO) published *Tested Advertising Methods* in 1932, which summarized research into the "pulling power" of print advertising headlines—that is, their ability to attract readers' attention to the ads.

Scientific market research emerged in force after the Great Depression in 1929, when consumer sales declined and advertising was faced with corporate budget cuts. Advertising practitioners attempted to use research to improve advertising effectiveness and to regain advertising's credibility. Pioneer researchers during this period and the World War II era included Daniel Starch, George Horace Gallup, and Arthur C. Nielsen.

Starch, recognized as one of the founding fathers of advertising research, was a psychology professor at Harvard University in Cambridge, Massachusetts, when he became interested in advertising and its impact. In 1923, at the age of 40, he began to study advertising effectiveness for commercial clients. His book *Principles of Advertising,* published in 1923, is considered one of the seminal works of the industry. In 1927 Starch and other market researchers founded the Market Research Council. The Starch readership report greatly influenced the measurement of print ad readership throughout the industry. In 1966 Starch published *Measuring Advertising Readership and Results.* The Starch print-ad database consists of 25,000 ads in more than 400 magazine issues, with raw readership scores—the percentage of readers who saw the ad and read the copy and ranked the ad not only against other ads in the issue but also against other ads in its product category over the past two years. Database users are thus able to judge the performance of the ad over time and against the competition.

*"Good morning,
Madam, the
J. Walter Thompson Company
would like to know if you are happily married."*

This 1934 Perry Barlow cartoon took a humorous look at market research.

Gallup is well known for his scientific sampling applications to polling. His use of sampling and of new advertising measurement techniques transformed advertising research by adding scientific rigor to large-scale surveys. In the area of media research and audience research, Gallup measured newspaper and magazine editorial and advertising content by actual reading (i.e., readers read the real ad in real publications and respond to it). Gallup obtained information on radio audience size and composition, pioneering the use of "telephone coincidental" and "diary" methods of research, the first based on random telephone calls to homes, the second on written records kept by listeners. In 1937 he founded the Audience Research Institute to measure the size and composition of movie audiences and to study what audiences "want to see."

To examine the effectiveness of advertising messages, Gallup developed the Impact method, requiring that respondents "play back" the sales message. He also created an activation measure of advertising's sales effect, asking respondents to show how advertising had contributed to actual purchases.

Gallup was hired by Young & Rubicam as research director in 1932. There he established the first independent ad agency copytesting department in 1938. In 1948 Claude Robinson and Gallup cofounded Gallup and Robinson, an advertising pretesting firm. By 1958 Gallup had established the Gallup Organization, which conducted marketing and survey research across the spectrum of communications applications. David Ogilvy, founder of Ogilvy & Mather Advertising, worked as the associate director of Gallup's Audience Research Institute early in his career. Ogilvy was strongly influenced by Gallup's scientific research methods; his advertising efforts drew heavily on what he learned from consumer research.

Nielsen founded A.C. Nielsen Company in 1923 at the age of 26. Nielsen Media Research, the TV ratings company serving the United States and Canada, shares a common heritage with the A.C. Nielsen Company. The companies split in 1996 as part of a general restructuring.

Market research development after World War II was strongly influenced by motivational psychology and behaviorism. In the mid-1960s psychologist Ernest Dichter, considered the founder of motivational research, advocated that a product's image is an inherent feature of that product. Since advertising plays an important role in creating a product or brand image, Dichter's theory led to a proliferation of image measurement in advertising research.

Role of Trade Associations

Apart from the importance of theory in advertising research development, trade associations have been a driving force in the expansion of research applications to advertising. The Association of National Advertisers (ANA) comprises some 300 major manufacturers and service companies that are clients of agencies belonging to the American Association of Advertising Agencies. In 1961 the ANA sponsored a report prepared by Russell Colley titled, *Defining Advertising Goals for Measured Advertising*

Results (DAGMAR). The report proposed a model that required a defined target audience, used intended communication effects in setting advertising goals, and evaluated advertising effectiveness with measurable communication task goals. The DAGMAR model was closely related to the AIDA (Awareness-Interest-Desire-Action) "hierarchical" effects model, which breaks the effects of advertising into several stages (e.g., awareness of the product after ad exposure, interest in the product, desire to buy the product, and finally, purchase of the product). The AIDA model is still reflected in the types of advertising "impact" measures regularly employed by many advertisers. By emphasizing benchmark measures and measurable communication goals, DAGMAR contributed greatly to the increased use of research in both advertising planning and advertising evaluation.

The American Association of Advertising Agencies (AAAA), often referred to as the "Four A's," is the national trade organization of most of the largest 650 advertising agencies in the United States. It has emphasized the necessity of research in advertising in its Services Standards for its members. Member agencies are committed to work with client marketing staffs to enhance advertising effects through research. In addition, ANA and AAAA cosponsor research on advertising industry issues such as the impact of advertising "clutter."

The Advertising Research Foundation (ARF) was founded in 1936 by the ANA and the Four A's. It continued as a nonprofit corporate membership association, and its stated mission was to improve the practice of advertising, marketing, and media research in pursuit of more effective marketing and advertising communications. Some of the key research initiatives undertaken through the ARF included: (1) the Copy Research Validity Project, which analyzed the validity of measures of copy testing; (2) the development of the Gold Standard for measuring magazine readership; and (3) a study of the effects of interviewing attempts on survey results. The ARF regularly issues research-based guidelines to advertisers, agencies, and research suppliers. It also publishes the *Journal of Advertising Research,* the leading journal of advertising research in the industry.

The American Marketing Association (AMA) was an outgrowth of several groups including both educators and business practitioners. Created in 1937 for "the advancement of science in marketing," the AMA has emphasized the study, research, planning, dissemination, and use of marketing knowledge to improve marketing methods and management. It publishes several research journals including *Marketing Research* and the *Journal of Marketing Research.*

The research departments of many advertising agencies have also designed and sponsored their own marketing research. A sample of agency-initiated proprietary research would include the Life Style studies of DDB Needham and the FCB Grid of Foote, Cone & Belding, which differentiate product categories by decision-making process and consumer involvement; the BBDO Techsetter Web site, a now defunct site that used the World Wide Web to collect and disseminate information on consumer attitudes; and Young & Rubicam's Brand Assets, a tool for evaluation of brand equity.

Account Planning

The introduction of account planning in the 1970s in the United Kingdom revolutionized the research departments of many advertising agencies. Under an account planning system, the research department of an ad agency acts as the voice of the consumer and takes an active part in the development of advertising.

The concept of account planning was introduced in 1965 by Stanley Pollitt, a media director at Boase Massimi Pollitt, of London, England. It was not until the 1980s, however, that account planning gained a strong foothold in the United States, when Chiat/Day adopted the account planning approach and achieved competitive successes in winning accounts.

Single-Source Data

Despite the emphasis on intermediate communication effects (e.g., awareness and attitude change) by many in market research, there are many managers who assess advertising performance primarily through increased sales. The use of scanners at supermarket cash registers has made possible research that combines data on exposure to cable TV advertising with data on store purchases. This is called "single-source" data research, in which a group of consumers participates in a panel where both their TV viewing behavior and purchases are monitored.

Usage of Market Research by Leading Advertisers

According to the 1998 survey of leading advertisers' usage of market research by ARF, the actual implementation of market research studies has moved largely to outside research agencies. Packaged goods brands have continued to spend more on market research than most nonpackaged goods (including consumer durable goods). The average external market research budget as a percent of sales is .77 percent for packaged goods and .35 percent for non-packaged goods. In a 1999 ARF survey of 141 research companies, 70 percent of the research conducted by research companies was quantitative in nature.

Media Audience Research

There are two commonly used methods to tap readership of magazines. Mediamark Research, Inc. (MRI), and Simmons Market Research Bureau (since 1994) measure readership by the "most recent reading method." Readers are given a list of more than 200 magazines and interviewed face to face. They also fill out an extensive product purchase/use questionnaire. A second method, called "through the book," is used by Starch and previously was used by Simmons. Readers are shown the pages of magazines and asked if they have read the content or advertisements of that magazine. Under a new joint venture, Simmons will mail an Audits & Surveys questionnaire to a database compiled from a magazine's circulation list. MRI will be the syndicated provider of product information, and A&S/Simmons Magazine Metrics will attempt to provide audience information for more than 600 magazines.

Scarborough Research in New York City measures 75 local markets via combined telephone and mail surveys among adults ages 18 and up using detailed demographics, lifestyle, leisure, and reported media use, as well as an array of retail, products, and services usage. In 1996 the Gallup Organization began offering competing syndicated local newspaper and radio/TV research in the top 15 markets and in other selected U.S. markets, using rigorous sampling methodologies combined with high-quality data collection procedures. Arbitron, Inc., also in New York City, specializes in local radio audience research and has provided rating services since 1949.

U.S. Ratings Research

Nielsen Media Research, Inc., is the leading provider of television audience measurement in the United States and Canada. Nielsen provides audience estimates for all national TV programs using a national People Meter panel and also estimates local audiences for each of the U.S. television markets using diary methods, in addition to the electronic metering of TV viewership in 47 markets. Nielsen provides competitive advertising intelligence information through Nielsen Monitor-Plus, and since 1988 has been providing Internet usage and advertising information through Nielsen//NetRatings.

Nielsen Media Research had previously measured viewership in the 1960s and 1970s via a combination of TV set meters and diaries. Beginning with the 1973 television season, Nielsen Media Research introduced a new "Audimeter" technology for its nationwide rating service. The Audimeter automatically records and stores minute-by-minute tuning records for channel, time of day, and duration of tuning. Introduction of the Audimeter resulted in faster service and made possible the introduction of a daily national ratings report.

The Nielsen People Meter, which at the end of the 20th century was in approximately 5,000 U.S. households, provides daily household and persons-viewing estimates based on a single sample of households. Each household member pushes an assigned button to indicate they are in the viewing audience. The People Meters have received criticism regarding alleged bias against multiple TV set households and the impact of fatigue stemming from continually requiring the viewers to identify themselves.

Future Development

New market research techniques will continue to develop with the advances in both data collection technology and advertising theory. For instance, collecting and disseminating research results through the Internet is gradually becoming a common practice in the industry. Dissatisfaction with current methodology will also drive changes in market research. Nielsen, for example, remains under pressure from advertisers and agencies alike to abolish misleading "sweep" periods from TV ratings and to substitute for them 13-week averages. Similarly, magazine audience research is under pressure by advertisers and agencies to reform and standardize readership measurement.

LOUISA HA

Further Reading

Blankenship, Albert B., and George E. Breen, *State of the Art Marketing Research,* Lincolnwood, Illinois: NTC Business Books, 1993; 2nd edition, by Blankenship, Breen, and Alan F. Dutka, 1998

Davis, Joel J., *Advertising Research: Theory and Practice,* Upper Saddle River, New Jersey: Prentice Hall, 1997

Dunn, Theodore F., et al., compilers, *Understanding Copy Pretesting,* New York, Advertising Research Foundation, 1994

Ferber, Robert, editor, *Handbook of Marketing Research,* New York: McGraw Hill, 1974

Ha, Louisa, "Media Models and Advertising Effects: Conceptualization and Theoretical Implications," *Journal of Current Issues and Research in Advertising* 17, no. 2 (1995)

Leckenby, John D., and Joseph T. Plummer, "Advertising Stimulus Measurement and Assessment Research: A Review of Advertising Testing Methods," *Current Issues and Research in Advertising* 5, no. 2 (1983)

Michman, Ronald D., *Lifestyle Market Segmentation,* New York: Praeger, 1991

Spaeth, Jim, and Rob Duboff, *Market Research Matters,* New York: Advertising Research Foundation, 2000.

Starch, Daniel, *Measuring Advertising Readership and Results,* NewYork: McGraw Hill, 1966

Sumner, Paul, *Readership Research and Computers,* New York: Newsweek International, 1985

Marschalk Company

Founded as Marschalk & Pratt by Harry C. Marschalk, 1923; merged with McCann-Erickson, 1954; became McCann-Marschalk, 1960; name changed to Marschalk Company, 1965; became Lowe Marschalk, 1986; changed to Lowe & Partners, 1990.

Major Clients
Coca-Cola Company
Gillette Company
Heublein, Inc.
International Nickel Company, Inc.
National Lead Company (Dutch Boy paints)
Revlon, Inc.

Marschalk & Pratt Company broke new ground when McCann-Erickson acquired the New York City agency in 1954 but continued to operate it intact as a division of McCann-Erickson that handled competing accounts. This marked the first time an advertising agency had run a specialized agency as a division and the first time an agency division had been operated in the same city as the parent company.

Marschalk & Pratt was founded by Harry C. Marschalk in 1923. Marschalk served as president until the merger with McCann-Erickson, when he became chairman of the division. At that time, S.L. Meulendyke, who had been an executive vice president, became the agency's president. Marschalk & Pratt, which then billed about $6 million, brought its specialized knowledge of industrial and business advertising to the union, while McCann-Erickson's central research and TV and radio departments benefited Marschalk. "There are some advertisers who elect to work with a small agency rather than a large one—which is their privilege. We put a smaller agency in our organization simply to be of service to them," McCann-Erickson President Marion Harper, Jr., said of the merger with Marschalk & Pratt.

The agency operated under its original name until 1960, when it became McCann-Marschalk with the creation of Interpublic, Inc., which in 1964 became the Interpublic Group of Companies. Stuart Watson served as chairman of the new McCann-Marschalk, and Meulendyke was vice chairman. William E. McKeachie assumed the presidency, and Marschalk acted as honorary chairman until he retired in 1964. McCann-Marschalk specialized in meeting the needs of growth companies and had six U.S. offices and four offices abroad. Agency billings grew from about $20 million in 1957 to more than $56 million in 1965.

In 1965 the Interpublic Group made it a separate agency under the name Marschalk Company, with offices in New York City; Atlanta, Georgia; Chicago, Illinois; and Cleveland and Columbus, Ohio. F. William Free became president, and Watson continued as chairman and chief executive officer. The name change was spurred by Interpublic's desire to emphasize the separateness and competitiveness of its affiliates.

As a result of Interpublic's merger of agency Fletcher Richards with Marschalk in 1967, Marschalk picked up $5 million in Heublein, Inc., billings. Watson, who had left Marschalk as its chairman, was Heublein's president at the time. The agency merger was seen as a way for Interpublic to economize; a similar change occurred the following year, when Johnstone, Inc., another Interpublic agency, became a division of Marschalk.

The late 1960s was a time of executive turmoil and account losses for the agency. In August 1969 John G. Avrett became the fourth person to be named Marschalk president within 18

Used 50 times, served 1500 cups, and the nickel stainless steel has never been polished.

Its rich elegance needs so little care. The best coffeemakers, holloware, cookware, storm doors, garden furniture and many other products are nickel stainless steel. Nickel in the steel adds extra corrosion resistance. Nickel's contribution is quality.

NICKEL STAINLESS STEEL QUALITY

International Nickel
New York, N.Y. 10005

Marschalk Company's advertisements for client International Nickel sought to raise consumer awareness of nickel's contribution to the durability of many household products.

months. He succeeded Paul Caravatt, chairman and chief executive officer, who had added the title of president in December 1968 after Richard Bowman was quietly reassigned to a senior vice president position at Interpublic. Bowman had held the presidency since February 1968, replacing Free, who left to form his own agency. The leadership changes occurred at the same time that the agency lost several accounts, which totaled $5 million in billings. These losses included International Nickel Company, which had been at Marschalk for 40 years.

In 1970 Willard C. Mackey, Jr., succeeded Caravatt as chairman and also later became president. For the previous two years, Mackey had been international director of marketing for Coca-Cola, a major Marschalk client, but before that he had worked for both McCann-Erickson and Marschalk. Mackey was responsible for several internal changes at Marschalk, including the creation of a new key management position, general manager (filled by Robert James, who became chairman and president in 1976); an organizational switch from a creative director to creative teams; and the addition of a management advisory committee.

During the 1970s Marschalk did significant work for Mutual of New York, including a life insurance campaign that was among the first to candidly discuss death, as well as for Gillette and its Foamy and Trac II shaving creams and Earth Born shampoos. But the agency also lost the accounts of Coca-Cola's Fresca, Tab, and Hi-C beverages, while Dutch Boy paints left after 43 years with Marschalk. By the mid-1970s, the agency was reduced to offices in Cleveland and New York City.

Michael S. Lesser was chairman and Andrew J. Langer was president in 1981 when Marschalk became a division of Marschalk Campbell-Ewald Worldwide, a subsidiary of Interpublic Group of Companies. In 1983 Marschalk Company acquired Houston, Texas–based Metzdorf Advertising, which gave the agency a presence in the Midwest and West Coast markets. That year, Marschalk's creative work also got attention for its Alex the dog TV spots for Stroh's beer.

In 1985 Interpublic created Lowe Marschalk Worldwide, based in the United Kingdom, to replace U.S.-based Marschalk Campbell-Ewald Worldwide. Marschalk Company, with 1985 billings of $300 million, was the largest agency in the new group. By 1987 the agency's offices in Cleveland; Houston, Texas; New York City; and San Francisco, California, sported a different name—Lowe Marschalk, Inc.—but top management remained the same. In 1990 the Marschalk name disappeared as the agency became Lowe & Partners, Inc., continuing with Langer as chief executive officer and Richard Villante as president, while maintaining many of the agency's long-standing accounts, among them Braun and Coca-Cola Foods.

NANCY DIETZ

Further Reading

Fox, Martin, *The Print Casebooks*, 6 vols., Washington, D.C.: RC, 1975; 5th edition, 1982; see especially vol. 1

"Marschalk Agency Is a Division of McCann," *Advertising Age* (13 December 1954)

Mayer, Martin, *Madison Avenue, U.S.A.*, New York: Harper, 1958

Mars, Inc.

Principal Agencies
Grant Advertising
Ted Bates & Company
Leo Burnett Company
Knox Reeves Advertising
Needham, Louis & Brorby
Ogilvy & Mather
D'Arcy Masius Benton & Bowles
Grey Advertising (later Grey Worldwide)
BBDO Worldwide

Mars, Inc., McLean, Virginia, is the largest candy producer in the world, with overall sales, including its Uncle Ben's rice products and pet foods, of $15.6 billion in 1999. By the end of the 20th century, the family-owned and -operated company marketed the number-one candy in the United States—M&M's—and was the 46th-largest advertiser, according to *Advertising Age*.

The company was founded in 1922 as the Mar-O-Bar Company by Frank C. Mars in a small kitchen in Minneapolis, Minnesota, according to Joël Glenn Brenner in her book, *The Emperors of Chocolate*. Mars made several failed attempts to enter the candy business before his venture in the Twin Cities (Minneapolis/St. Paul) in the early 1920s, where he finally found success with a creation he called Victorian Butter Creams. In 1924 he introduced the Milky Way bar, which had sales of nearly $800,000 in its first year. Spurred by the demand for Milky Way, in 1927 the company, by then called Mars, Inc., began building a production facility on the west side of Chicago, Illinois, just north of suburban Oak Park, and by 1929 was producing 20 million candy bars a year.

Line Expansions

Mars soon added more candy bars to its line, including Snickers in 1930 and 3 Musketeers, three pieces of chocolate-covered nougat in strawberry, chocolate, and vanilla, in 1932. The company, which reached $25 million in sales that year, was also investing in advertising. Frank Mars started advertising his small efforts in 1921, putting $300 mostly into point-of-sale materials. He later expanded into outdoor advertising, and in 1929 began advertising in national magazines, including *Collier's* and *Saturday Evening Post*.

The company was experiencing internal turmoil, however. Forrest Mars, Frank Mars's son from his first marriage, had joined the company after graduating from Yale University in 1928. But increasingly he was at odds with his father, contentiously questioning his decisions and his plans for the company's future. In 1932 Frank Mars asked Forrest to leave, giving him $50,000 and the foreign rights to Milky Way, according to *The Emperors of Chocolate*.

Forrest Mars moved to Europe, eventually settling in Slough, a small town in southern England. He set up a small kitchen where he created the Mars bar; by 1939 he had turned Mars, Ltd., into England's third-largest candy manufacturer. He also had bought a small company, Chappel Brothers, which canned meat by-products for dogs at a time when most pet owners were feeding their pets table scraps. Mars renamed the company Petfoods, Ltd., and promoted the product as more nutritious than its rivals; within a few years the company dominated the pet food market in Europe and became the base for Mars's pet food business, which by the end of the 20th century accounted for almost half the company's total sales.

With the start of World War II, Mars returned to the United States with an idea for a new candy product that would form the base for his U.S. operation. Although his father had died in 1934, control of Mars, Inc., had passed on to Frank's second wife and their daughter. Forrest instead approached William Murrie, president of the Hershey Chocolate Company in Hershey, Pennsylvania, with his idea, suggesting that Murrie's son, R. Bruce Murrie, join him in the venture. Rather than being viewed as a rival, Hershey at the time was supplying Mars, Inc., with the chocolate covering for its products. Murrie agreed, and in 1940 Mars and R. Bruce Murrie formed M&M (for Mars and Murrie), Ltd., based in Newark, New Jersey. During the war, Hershey kept the company supplied with chocolate; because M&M's product did not melt in tropical climates as other chocolate candy did, M&M's biggest buyer through the war years was the U.S. Air Force, closely followed by the U.S. Army, which distributed the candy to troops in North Africa and the Pacific Theater. But Mars and Murrie did not get along, and in 1949 Murrie quit, selling his share of the company to Mars for $1 million.

"Melts in Your Mouth"

In 1950 Mars, concerned with the slow sales of M&M's, hired Chicago-based Ted Bates & Company to determine why the candy was not more popular. The agency soon found that while children loved the brightly colored candies, their parents were not familiar with the product. Rosser Reeves, Bates's legendary ad executive, was known for his hard-sell, reason-why, product-driven creative campaigns. At his first meeting with M&M President John McNamara, Reeves discovered that the advertising idea was inherent in the product itself: M&M's was the only candy in America that had chocolate surrounded by a hard, sugar shell. From this simple observation came the now-classic slogan, "Melts in your mouth, not in your hand."

In 1954 Bates introduced the cartoon characters Mr. Plain and Mr. Peanut, representing Peanut M&M's, which had been introduced that year, and then launched an animated spot that showed M&M's characters jumping into a chocolate pool before rinsing off in showers that coated them with their shells. The ad ran on children's television programs such as *The Howdy Doody Show* and *The Mickey Mouse Club*. By 1956 sales hit $40 million, and M&M's had become the number-one candy in the United States.

Before becoming famous as the candy that "melts in your mouth, not in your hand," M&M's was known as the "all-weather" candy. The marketer, M&M, Ltd., kept the U. S. armed forces supplied with the confection during World War II.
Reproduction of the ad 1943 M&M's® "The all-weather candy-coated chocolate" made available courtesy of Mars, Incorporated. All Rights reserved. M&M's® is a trademark of Mars, Incorporated.

By this time Forrest Mars had rejoined Mars, Inc. When his father's second wife died in 1945, she left Forrest half her stock in the company, as had been stipulated in Frank Mars's will. The company had continued its growth following the death of Frank Mars. In 1939 it hired Grant Advertising, of Chicago, and advertised Milky Way through sponsorship of the radio program *Dr. I.Q.* in Atlanta, Georgia; the show was picked up by NBC and became so popular nationally that Mars introduced a Dr. I.Q. candy bar in 1941. It dropped the candy bar in 1946 and the show sponsorship in 1947, and in December 1949 Grant resigned the account. The association had been profitable for Mars: its sales grew from $9 million in 1937 to $47 million in 1949.

In the 1950s Mars, Inc., now with the Chicago-based Leo Burnett Company, became a sponsor on Art Linkletter's *People Are Funny* on the CBS radio network as well as on several children's TV shows, including *Super Circus, Buffalo Bill Jr.,* and *Howdy Doody.* In 1956 Burnett resigned the $2 million account, and Mars hired Knox Reeves Advertising, of Minneapolis. While Mars continued to invest in TV sponsorships, it also advertised in newspapers, magazines, and comic books. One ad that ran in the comic section of 140 newspapers in February 1958 as part of a Valentine's Day promotion for Forever Yours, a dark chocolate version of Milky Way, was a cartoon strip drawn by "Peanuts" creator Charles M. Schulz.

In November 1959 Mars moved its then-$3 million account to Needham, Louis & Brorby, also based in Chicago, which introduced "Mooky," the animated cow, to create an image for Mars products. The company also ceased national TV advertising after failing to see any return on its sponsorships of *Disneyland* and *Broken Arrow* in the 1959–60 season and turned to local spot TV and outdoor advertising. In 1961 Mars estimated it was spending 50 percent of its ad budget on spot TV, 48 percent on outdoor advertising, and the remaining 2 percent on subway cards in New York City.

Corporate Consolidation

Meanwhile Mars began pushing the Mars, Inc., board to expand and automate candy production. The work was completed in 1959 and made Mars, Inc., the largest producer of chocolate-covered candy bars. At the same time, Mars continued to push for more control over his father's company, and as the power struggle escalated, the company's sales began to fall, and candy quality suffered. In 1964 Mars succeeded in convincing his half-sister to sell him her share of the company; in exchange he agreed to change the name of the umbrella corporation from Food Manufacturers, Inc., which was his company, to Mars, Inc. With the consolidation, which gave Forrest Mars total control, Mars, Inc., owned the original Mars, Inc.; M&M, Ltd.; Uncle Ben's rice, developed from a rice mill that Forrest Mars had acquired in 1942; the fourth-largest candy company in Europe; and the largest pet-food marketer in the world.

Following the consolidation, Forrest Mars concentrated on expanding the company to produce its own chocolate. In 1965 he notified Hershey that Mars would phase out its use of Hershey's chocolate coating and then began overhauling his production facilities to accommodate chocolate production. In 1966 the company divided the $8 million advertising budget for its confectionary division almost evenly between Ted Bates & Company, Chicago, and Ogilvy & Mather, Chicago, after pulling 3

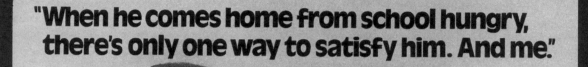

"When he comes home from school hungry,
there's only one way to satisfy him. And me."

When my kids come home from football practice, or band or just knocking
around, I know it's time for SNICKERS.®
    Because a   SNICKERS Bar does more than satisfy my family's
                    hunger between meals. It also satisfies my desire to
                    give them something good.
                        SNICKERS has no preservatives.
                    That's important to me. It's packed with
                    fresh peanuts, peanut butter nougat, caramel
                    and milk chocolate. And like many good foods,
                    each SNICKERS is freshness dated.
                        So when they come home hungry, I give them
                    something they love. And I like. SNICKERS.

**Packed with peanuts,
SNICKERS® really satisfies.™**

© Mars Inc. 1984

Two continuing themes in Mars's advertising have been natural ingredients and family values, both of which were emphasized in
this 1984 ad for Snickers.

*Reproduction of the ad 1984 SNICKERS® "When he comes home from school hungry, there's only one way to satisfy him. And
me." made available courtesy of Mars, Incorporated. All Rights reserved. SNICKERS® is a trademark of Mars, Incorporated.*

Musketeers, Mars bar, Milky Way, Snickers, and Forever Yours from Needham, Harper & Steers (formerly Needham, Louis & Brorby) in December 1965. In 1968 the division, now named M&M/Mars, consolidated its account at Bates. Earlier, in 1966, Mars, Inc., had expanded its pet-food empire with the purchase of Kal Kan in the United States.

In 1970 Mars began to feel pressure from Hershey, which launched its first advertising campaign in response to falling market share. Prior to that time the company had followed the philosophy of its late founder, Milton S. Hershey, who claimed that a good product, well distributed, would sell itself. In 1972, despite early success with its campaigns, Hershey canceled its entire ad budget in the face of spiraling sugar and cocoa prices. Mars, Inc., responded to Hershey's retreat by aggressively expanding its advertising, and in the fall of 1973 it surpassed its rival, emerging as the top U.S. candy maker for the first time.

Meanwhile, Forrest Mars retired in 1972, turning the company over to his children, Forrest, Jr., John, and Jacqueline. In 1980 the elder Mars came out of retirement to found Ethel M Chocolates, a line of fine, liqueur-filled chocolates named after his mother, setting up a factory in Las Vegas, Nevada; by 1999 the company had $150 million in annual sales with 70 stores in the western United States, according to *The Emperors of Chocolate*. He died on 1 July 1999 in Miami, Florida, leaving an estate estimated at $4 billion.

Mars, Inc., continued its aggressive advertising effort, adding D'Arcy-MacManus & Masius to its agency list in 1976 and launching its memorable "A Snickers really satisfies" campaign. It also introduced Starburst Fruit Chews and Twix bars that year. At the same time, a commercial that showed a glass of milk turning into a Milky Way bar drew a Federal Trade Commission consent order; Mars agreed not to misrepresent the nutritional value of its products.

Industry Obstacles

The candy industry as a whole was facing obstacles. Per capita candy consumption in the United States had declined sharply, from 20.3 pounds in 1968 to 15.4 pounds in 1980. The probable reason was that the number of children between the ages of 5 and 13 had dropped from 36.7 million (17.9 percent of the population) in 1970 to 31.2 million (13.7 percent) in 1980. Moreover, sales of M&M's suffered in the mid-1970s when government studies linked two red food dyes with cancer, and Mars, Inc., ceased to produce red M&M's—despite the fact that the food colorings implicated in the studies were not used in the candy.

Mars, however, continued its aggressive advertising, increasing ad spending for M&M/Mars to $36.1 million in 1980, a 46.4 percent increase over 1979 spending (which, in turn, represented a 51 percent increase over expenditures in 1978). By 1979 Mars held 36 percent of the chocolate bar market in the United States, leading Hershey, which had 29 percent. It continued its advertising push until 1983, when it had 41 percent of the U.S. chocolate candy bar market versus Hershey's 28.5 percent. In 1980 Mars took another aggressive step and increased the size of its candy

bars by 20 percent–30 percent, while holding its wholesale prices steady. It announced the move in newspaper ads around the country. As a result, sales of some Mars products increased by as much as 60 percent.

Still, the company was at the beginning of a period of stagnant growth. By 1984 its share of the candy bar market stood at 37 percent; Hershey was only slightly behind, with 36 percent, thanks in large part to new-product launches. Mars, on the other hand, had not embarked on any national launches since Starburst and Twix.

In 1982 Mars missed out on a major promotions opportunity. The producers of Steven Spielberg's film *E.T. the Extra-Terrestrial* contacted Mars about using M&M's in the movie as the candy that cements a friendship between a young boy and a lonely alien. Upon learning of Mars's lack of interest in the proposal, the producers turned to Hershey and made a deal to feature its Reese's Pieces. Hershey, with a $1 million investment in promoting the film, saw sales of Reese's Pieces jump 70 percent the month after the film's release. Two months later, more than 800 movie theaters had started to carry Reese's Pieces.

By the mid-1980s Mars, Inc., was taking a more aggressive approach. In 1986 it launched Kudos, a chocolate-covered granola bar, with a $4.5 million media campaign. Within a year, the product had captured 20 percent of the highly competitive $387 million granola bar category in the United States. It also reformulated the U.S. version of Milky Way, making it less sweet (and more like its European version) and backed the move with an $8 million campaign from Bates, which had in the meantime become Backer Spielvogel Bates. It bought DoveBar International, an ice cream specialties marketer, in August 1986 and assigned the $10 million account for Dove Bar and Rondos to Grey Advertising of New York City. It also fired Leo Burnett USA over a conflict with an account the agency had in the rice market, even though Burnett handled no Uncle Ben's business for Mars; more than $30 million in assignments were moved to Backer Spielvogel Bates and D'Arcy Masius Benton & Bowles (DMB&B). Mars also began to use cable TV as a medium for its advertising. Of the top-ten cable advertisers in 1986, Mars was number six, spending $8.2 million, and the only candy company on the list.

Despite Mars's efforts, in 1988 Hershey finally overtook it, becoming the foremost U.S. candy marketer and securing 39 percent of the U.S. candy market with its purchase of Cadbury Schweppes's U.S. operations, including its Peter Paul Almond Joy and Mounds and Cadbury's chocolate bars. In response Mars mounted an aggressive marketing and product push through the early 1990s. It signed a multiyear marketing agreement with the Walt Disney Company, including a $24 million tie-in with Disney's video release of the animated film *Bambi*. It launched a number of line extensions, including Peanut Butter Snickers and new flavors for Kudos, Twix, Starburst, and Skittles; expanded its seasonal candy offerings; introduced Bounty, a chocolate-covered coconut bar popular in Europe, to the U.S. market to compete with Mounds and Almond Joy; and in January 1990 reintroduced Forever Yours as Milky Way Dark. In 1991 it launched Dove chocolate bars via Grey and in April 1992 introduced the Milky

For all who crave candy... here's a real delight for you!

Twenty minutes from Chicago on the Chicago, Milwaukee and St. Paul Railroad is the station of Mars. Within sight of the station itself is a building which looks like a spacious home in the Mediterranean type of architecture you so frequently see in the sunniest parts of our country. This is the home of a community of candy makers—the home of "Milky Way". - - - Closer inspection reveals that it is more like an immense solarium, for all the space from the red tile roof to the white foundation is glass. Fresh air and sunlight are essential ingredients of "Milky Way". - - - White tile and gleaming glass, the sheen of mirror-polished pans and kettles, the snowy caps and aprons of the candy makers—what an unusual setting for the making of a candy bar! - - - Small wonder that "Milky Way" tastes so good, is so pure and wholesome—that the news of its goodness has been carried to the far corners of the country by those who like it so well.

This craving for good candy—how natural it is! It knows no age or occupation. It knows no time or place. And it is not to be denied. Energetic people—people who are active mentally or physically—are most frequently beset by this craving for good candy—for candy, pure candy, is the quick producer of energy. When you feel this natural candy hunger, get a "Milky Way". Wherever there is a store that sells good candy, there you can get "Milky Way" *fresh*. And you'll say that nothing has ever tasted so good or satisfied your candy hunger so completely as this mouth-melting, pure "Milky Way".

MARS, INC.
2019-2059 N. Oak Park Avenue, Chicago, Ill.

Milky Way

"When you crave"   "good candy"

A 1929 ad for Milky Way promoted the candy bar as the choice to satisfy the "natural" craving for candy. The copy claimed that "Candy, pure candy, is the quick producer of energy."
Reproduction of the ad 1929 MILKY WAY® "For all who crave candy...here's a real delight for you" made available courtesy of Mars, Incorporated. All Rights reserved. MILKY WAY® is a trademark of Mars, Incorporated.

Way II, with 25 percent fewer calories and less fat than Milky Way. It also began emphasizing the Mars name on its products and launched an umbrella campaign with the theme "Making life a little sweeter—Mars" (DMB&B).

Brand Building

In the 1990s Mars expanded internationally, including building production plants in Russia and China, and moved to a more standardized advertising and sales promotion approach. It reduced the number of different brand names it used worldwide to lower its production costs and heighten brand identification among consumers, giving each of its chief products a single name in all markets as well as consistent packaging worldwide. For example, Marathon, the European version of Snickers, was renamed Snickers. In addition, it moved to make its advertising pitches consistent around the globe.

In 1995 the annual American Customer Satisfaction Index, a survey of 30,000 consumers about 3,900 goods and services, ranked Mars second, with a score of 89 out of a possible 100;

only the Dole Food Company, Inc., ranked higher, scoring 90. The survey covered consumers' perceptions of service, quality, and value. Others scoring above the average of 73.7 included Hershey (88), Nestlé (86), and Cadbury Schweppes (85).

In the 1990s Mars used consumer promotions heavily to boost sales, encouraging people to buy brands at a lower price or with a special deal. Typical consumer promotions used sampling, coupons, premiums, rebates, contests and sweepstakes, bonus packs, and price-off incentives. In one unusual contest handled by BBDO Worldwide, consumers were invited to choose the next new M&M color; blue was the winner.

BBDO, which won the account in 1995 after Mars dropped Bates, also stirred new interest in Mars products with a series of commercials for Snickers, using the theme that Snickers was the one candy bar to have available if "you're not going anywhere for a while." The agency also revived the use of M&M's candy spokes-characters, named Red, Yellow, and Blue to coincide with their shell colors, telling hungry consumers that M&M's were the "Candy of the new millennium, MM means 2000." In addition, the first female M&M appeared, Green, a flirtatious character that apparently played off the urban myth that green M&M's have aphrodisiac properties. The popular characters were also featured on their own Internet Web site.

By the end of the 20th century Mars, Inc., was the leader in the global candy market. Its overall worldwide sales in 1999, covering M&M/Mars, Kal Kan Foods, and Uncle Ben's, totaled $15.6 billion; U.S. ad spending reached $589.8 million, including $203.3 million for its major candy brands. Agencies for its M&M/Mars division, based in Hackettstown, New Jersey, were DMB&B, St. Louis, Missouri (Mars, Milky Way, Skittles); Grey Worldwide, New York City (Dove chocolate, Starburst, Twix); BBDO Worldwide, New York City (M&M's, Kudos, Snickers); and UniWorld Group, New York City (3 Musketeers), with MediaVest, New York City, handling media buying. In fall 2001 Mars, Inc., organized all of its U.S. divisions under one umbrella group called Masterfoods USA.

TOMMY V. SMITH

Further Reading

Applegate, Edd, editor, *The Ad Men and Women: A Biographical Dictionary of Advertising*, Westport, Connecticut: Greenwood, 1994

Berkman, Harold, and Christopher Gilson, *Advertising Concepts and Strategies*, New York: Random House, 1980; 2nd edition, 1987

Brenner, Joël Glenn, *The Emperors of Chocolate*, New York: Random House, 1999

"Cable TV Ad Spending," *Advertising Age* (1 December 1986)

Cohen, Dorothy, *Advertising*, New York: Wiley, 1972

Curme, Emmett, "Mars Ad Budget Grew from $300 in '21 to $3,000,000; Puts Half in Spot TV," *Advertising Age* (22 May 1961)

Evans, Joel, and Barry Berman, *Marketing*, New York and London: Macmillan, 1982; 7th edition, Upper Saddle River, New Jersey: Prentice Hall, 1997

Fox, Stephen, *The Mirror Makers: A History of American Advertising and Its Creators*, New York: Morrow, 1984

Higgins, Denis, *The Art of Writing Advertising: Conversations with William Bernbach, Leo Burnett, George Gribbin, David Ogilvy, Rosser Reeves*, Lincolnwood, Illinois: NTC Business Books/ Contemporary, 1965

Meyers, William, *The Image-Makers: Power and Persuasion on Madison Avenue*, New York: Times, 1984

"Profiles of Top 100 Advertisers (100 Leading National Advertisers)," *Advertising Age* (28 September 1998)

Reeves, Rosser, *Reality in Advertising*, New York: Bates, 1960

Schudson, Michael, *Advertising, the Uneasy Persuasion: Its Dubious Impact on American Society*, New York: Basic Books, 1984

Sivulka, Juliann, *Soap, Sex, and Cigarettes: A Cultural History of American Advertising*, Belmont, California: Wadsworth, 1998

Solomon, Michael, and Elnora Stuart, *Marketing: Real People, Real Choices*, Upper Saddle River, New Jersey, and London: Prentice Hall, 1997

Vanden Bergh, Bruce, and Helen Katz, *Advertising Principles: Choice, Challenge, Change*, Lincolnwood, Illinois: NTC Business Books, 1999

Marsteller, Inc.

Founded by William A. Marsteller as Marsteller, Gebhardt and Reed, Inc., through the purchase of Gebhardt & Brockson, Inc., 1951; sibling public relations company Burson-Marsteller formed, 1953; ad agency merged with Rickard & Company to become Marsteller, Rickard, Gebhardt & Reed, Inc., 1955; became Marsteller, Inc., 1966; acquired by Young & Rubicam, 1979.

Major Clients

Ad Council ("Keep America Beautiful" campaign)
Clark Equipment Company
Dannon Milk Products
Renault
Rockwell Industries

A lone American Indian paddles a canoe down a river. As he lands his craft, he sees what modern civilization has done. As he takes in the pollution of the water, a single tear rolls down his cheek. Simple, powerful, and visual, the "Crying Indian" campaign became perhaps the most widely known television advertisement in the United States in the realm of "cause marketing." The Marsteller agency's place in advertising history was assured.

The Marsteller agency was born in the post–World War II era of the early 1950s. Its significant contributions to advertising include its creativity in cause, or issues, marketing and its melding of the public relations (PR) and advertising fields. Previously, public relations companies and ad agencies had kept themselves strictly segregated; at Marsteller, the two worked side by side, becoming a single entity.

Marsteller, Inc., created the tag line "Millions of satisfied owners are our best testimonial" for a 1979 campaign that used testimonials to promote the Renault Le Car to Americans.
Renault North American Center.

Marsteller's antecedents are found in the Commercial Art Engraving Company of Chicago, which set up an ad placement division in 1921. In 1926 the name of the division was changed to the Commercial Advertising Agency, and it was operated as a completely separate company until 1937, when the two companies were reconsolidated as the Commercial Advertising Agency. After the retirement of company founder Maurice Blink, the company name was changed to Gebhardt & Brockson, Inc., in 1942.

Mergers

William A. Marsteller bought out the company in 1951 and shortly thereafter acquired the Pittsburgh, Pennsylvania, office of McCarty Company; McCarty's manager, Rodney Reed, became a principal of the new agency, which was renamed Marsteller, Gebhardt and Reed, Inc. In 1955 it merged with Rickard & Company of New York City, which at one time had been the premier business-to-business ad agency in the United States, to become

Marsteller, Rickard, Gebhardt & Reed. Marsteller turned the Rickard office into his agency's New York City headquarters, and within five years, it had become the agency's largest branch office. In 1960 William Marsteller moved to New York City from Chicago to oversee that office. During that period, Marsteller also took the unusual step of creating a PR agency, Burson-Marsteller, to work closely with the ad agency.

Marsteller, who had started his career working for a daily newspaper while he was still in high school during the Depression, got his advertising start in the field of industrial marketing (later known as business-to-business marketing). During World War II Marsteller, who was medically exempt from active service, worked for the Edward Valve Company, East Chicago, Indiana, which was part of the defense industry. As others around him were drafted, Marsteller took charge of various areas of the operation: advertising, employee motivation, labor negotiations, some sales, and entertaining government expediters. This variety of experience would serve him well.

After the war, the company was merged into what became Rockwell Manufacturing Company. Marsteller was placed in charge of developing the company's first corporate advertising program, as well as its first corporate PR effort. As a result, he was named vice president; ultimately, he was placed in charge of marketing. During his tenure at Rockwell, Marsteller helped begin development of a market research department, then a fairly new concept in the industrial field.

Eventually, he decided to branch out from what was essentially the Rockwell family business, determining to form a market research consultancy specializing in technical and scientific products and services for industrial companies. Richard Christian, with whom he had worked at Rockwell, joined him in this venture. They decided to go into advertising as well, and set about buying out Gebhardt & Brockson, a local Chicago ad agency.

In 1952 Rockwell Chairman W.F. ("Al") Rockwell, Jr., bought a helicopter for business use—quite unusual in those days—and asked the fledgling company to publicize it. Marsteller and Christian, recognizing that this was more a public relations affair than an advertising proposition, contacted several people in the PR field. Harold Burson, who owned a small business, responded first, and a new partnership was formed. As it turned out, there were several delays in the acquisition of the helicopter, so Burson worked with Marsteller for about a year on other projects. This serendipitous delay was crucial to the company; before long, Marsteller and Burson formed a business partnership. The ad agency and a PR agency were working together—and doing quite well. Burson-Marsteller, created 1 March 1953, was the first company to successfully combine public relations and advertising services and was among the forerunners of modern business-to-business marketing shops.

The large ad agencies had retreated from the public relations field in the 1960s, reentering in the late 1970s. Burson-Marsteller's example was crucial, legitimizing the idea of the two disciplines working together. By the end of the 20th century, nine of the top ten PR agencies were owned by ad agencies.

"le"

This 2-letter French word may well be the most successful (if not the only) 2-letter marketing strategy in the annals of advertising. This simple, yet eloquent "le" has put Renault's "Le Car" happily in the U.S. car-buying public's consciousness. It positions; it defines; and for the media-inundated consumer, provides an easy, memorable handle. Usually it takes many more letters and many more words to do all this.

Happily our little "le" has put across the fact that we are the car company of France. You can't blame us for sighing "Vive le 'le'!"

RENAULT

"et"

Another 2-letter French word. We believe this one laconically sums up our business philosophy yet is as eloquent as our "le" in indicating how we organise for future growth.

For that simple "et" expresses the agreements we've recently signed with three great U.S. corporations. That "et" in effect proclaims our growth policy of co-operation for mutual benefit; it says that we will work together to achieve our independent goals.

Finally, that little "et" says we're not a "take-over" company, but rather, a "work-with" company. And so we sigh " 'Et'. Bien."

RENAULT

Marsteller's successful U.S. campaigns for Renault included this "bilingual" 1979 Renault Le Car ad.
Renault North American Center.

An Anomaly among Agencies

In the 1960s and 1970s the agency clung to a culture and structure that made it an anomaly among major agencies. The atmosphere was extremely conservative, with strict dress codes in an era when most agencies were relaxing such traditions. Even more unusual, Marsteller maintained no separate creative department outside of a staff of art directors and a small number of creative directors. While advertising was undergoing its "creative revolution," Marsteller was a "copy-contact" agency, in which account executives prepared copy while at the same time providing their accounts with regular client services. The philosophy was that the person closest to the client in day-to-day contact was in the best position to understand its marketing needs and prepare the advertising. It was an approach well suited to the agency's business-to-business specialty.

From 1966 through 1978, the agency was known as Marsteller, Inc. In the 1960s it worked to develop a presence in Europe, starting or buying several small offices. The agency grew to become a leader in business-to-business advertising. For several years, it was the primary agency for the *Wall Street Journal* and McGraw-Hill Company. In the early 1970s the agency moved to expand to consumer business. Business-to-business marketing was a fairly limited field at that time. In order to grow, the agency had to become more generalized.

In August 1968 Marsteller acquired Zlowe Company, a small, New York City–based ad agency. Its principal account, for which it had gained a lot of attention, was Dannon Milk Products, the marketer of Dannon Yogurt. Zlowe had introduced Dannon to the United States. Marsteller's TV spot, featuring a 100-year-old Russian who attributed his longevity to eating yogurt, became one of its better-known campaigns and was named by *Advertising Age* as one of the top 100 advertising campaigns of the 20th century. In fact, of the 50 best commercials cited by the Museum of Television, Marsteller created two: the "Crying Indian" commercial for the Ad Council's "Keep America Beautiful" campaign and the Dannon Yogurt spot featuring the 100-year-old Russian.

Marsteller acquired Schwab & Beatty, a small direct-mail advertising company, in the early 1970s as the agency continued its quest for diversification into the consumer retail field. The agency achieved this goal, with about half its business coming from consumer advertising and half from business-to-business.

In 1979 Young & Rubicam (Y&R) acquired Marsteller, Inc. In 1985 Y&R and the European agency network Eurocom entered into a joint venture, Havas Conseil Marsteller, which, in 1989, became HDM with the addition of Japanese advertising agency giant Dentsu. The effort—and Marsteller's advertising entity—folded in 1990 when Eurocom bought out Y&R's and Dentsu's shares of European agencies in the partnership. Burson-Marsteller continues as a unit of the WPP Group (acquired in WPP's purchase of Y&R) and, as of 2000, was the third-largest public relations company in the United States.

BARBARA KNOLL

Further Reading

Cummings, Bart, *The Benevolent Dictators: Interviews with Advertising Greats,* Chicago: Crain Books, 1984

Earle, Richard, *The Art of Cause Marketing,* Lincolnwood, Illinois: NTC Business Books, 2000

Kanner, Bernice, *The 100 Best TV Commercials—And Why They Worked,* New York: Times Business, 1999

Marsteller, William A., *Creative Management: A Euphemism for Common Sense,* Chicago: Crain Books, 1981

Mass Communications Theory

The American Association of Advertising Agencies has estimated that 1,600 advertising messages are aimed at the U.S. consumer in an average day. According to Nielsen Media Research, the average American watches over four hours of television per day; further, according to the American Academy of Pediatrics, the average American child watches 20,000 commercials a year. With the proliferation of advertising media in the form of cable television networks, satellite broadcasts, and the Internet, these numbers probably underestimate the actual reach and frequency of advertising messages.

But is mass communication—and especially advertising—really the all-powerful influence many claim it to be? Opponents of this view point to the fact that people are apparently able to ignore certain messages with ease. Thus, one could argue, despite the constant ad theme that "thin is beautiful," an increasing proportion of Americans are overweight; however, just because physical changes are not visible does not mean that advertisers have not changed the way people think about their bodies.

Over the years, many theories have been proposed to account for the extent of media influence and its mode of operation. The Canadian media authority Marshall McLuhan, author of *The Medium Is the Message* (1967) and one of the most popular and influential mass communication theorists, argued that innovations in technology would unquestionably lead to cultural change. He proposed that cultural change does not necessarily stem from changes of content within a medium but from changes in the medium itself. Thus, in the tribal age, people listened to stories passed on from their elders, while in the print age, reading became the primary tool for gathering information. The electronic age was ushered in with the invention of the telegraph in 1837. Today, television, film, radio, and computers are changing the nature of social interaction around the globe. McLuhan's popular mantra "the medium is the message" implies that once people create a new medium, the new medium in turn creates a new type of person. But the question remains: just how powerful is any medium at influencing the attitudes and/or behaviors of consumers?

Historical Overview

In the early days of mass communication theory, it was believed that the media were all-powerful, while the audience consisted of nothing more than persuadable "sheep" awaiting instruction from their shepherd. Metaphorically speaking, mass communication was perceived as a "hypodermic needle" that could effortlessly and effectively inject ideas into the mind of the viewer. The belief that Nazi propaganda successfully injected anti-Semitism into the German thought process enhanced the credibility of the hypodermic-needle metaphor. The United States quickly followed in the 1940s with patriotic propaganda films of its own. By this time, however, social scientists were already questioning whether mass communication functioned in this predictable way. Further attempts to influence human behavior cast reasonable doubt on the metaphor of the hypodermic needle.

The decades that followed witnessed increasing academic debate and a proliferation of new theories. Some 60 years later the true power of mass communication and its mechanism of action remain an enigma. Whether consumers are really sheeplike creatures waiting to receive instructions on how to live their lives is questionable; the audience may ignore the message of the media at will. Or perhaps the media have significant influence in some situations and less or none in others. Mass communication theorists have been grappling with such issues for years without reaching any firm conclusions.

Elihu Katz and Paul F. Lazarsfeld, in their 1955 book, *Personal Influence: The Part Played by People in the Flow of Mass Communications,* proposed a two-step flow hypothesis. They suggested that mass communication alone is not all-powerful and that media alone are not always able to exert direct influence. Rather, they posited, interpersonal interaction is crucial to the success of persuasive messages. According to this view, information flows from the mass media to opinion leaders, who then facilitate communication through discussion with others. These opinion leaders are the key to mass media influence, the "gatekeepers." They may be respected members of a community, or they may be individuals who have positions in the media structure itself. If the media wanted to promote the concept that the thinner one is, the more attractive one is, public acceptance of this concept would not come about via media messages alone. Opinion leaders would have to endorse this notion, and individuals would also have to accept it. If the media promoted the concept, but the opinion leaders rejected it, it would likely never make its way into the public consciousness.

"Cultivation theory" is another theoretical framework for explaining the effects of mass communication. This approach, initially proposed in 1969 by George Gerbner, professor and dean of the University of Pennsylvania's Annenberg School for Communication from 1964 to 1989, suggested that the media do not change individual attitudes but rather social expectations. Concerned with the effect of media content and with the totality of the pattern communicated through this content, cultivation theory claims that the media provide a common experience and therefore a shared worldview. The proponents of cultivation theory claim this effect is problematic because the world of the media does not necessarily reflect the world of reality. If, for example, television presents a world that is more violent and untrustworthy than the real world, heavy TV viewers will see the world as frightening and dangerous. Cultivation theorists suggest that the media do indeed have a persuasive impact on people's perception of the world and, in turn, on the very fabric of society.

In their 1992 article "The Elastic Body Image," Philip Myers and Frank Biocca reported that the women portrayed in ads and seen in the media were continuing to become thinner. A cultivation theorist would propose that since the media constantly portray women as slimmer and slimmer, most television viewers would be "cultivated" to believe that the average woman is far thinner than is actually the case in the real world, thereby causing many females to actively strive to be thinner.

While cultivation theory assumes that viewers are passive receivers of information, accepting everything they see on television as reality, the uses-and-gratification model proposes that the audience takes a more active and goal-directed role. This approach, formulated in 1972 by Karl Erik Rosengren, assumes that viewers select and use mass media to satisfy their own personal needs and desires. In other words, it is not the media that "use" the audience, but rather the audience that "uses" the media to gratify its own needs. According to this theory, a television viewer may be in search of information about the ideal body type and may therefore choose to watch soap operas. These programs may very well influence the viewer's perception of the world but not in such a blanket manner as is proposed by cultivation theory.

The uses-and-gratification model claims that the decision to watch soap operas—or any other kind of program—is a conscious choice made by the viewer. For example, the viewer's notion of what the opposite sex finds attractive may be heavily influenced by what he or she happens to choose to see on television. On the other hand, if a viewer believes that he or she knows what body type the opposite sex finds attractive and regards the images on

Marshall McLuhan, a Canadian educator and media expert, was an influential theorist of mass communications.
Courtesy of University Archives, Toronto University.

the TV screen as nothing more than a generic portrayal of reality, the effect on this viewer's conception of the ideal body image will be minimal.

The agenda-setting model, initially tested in 1972 by Donald L. Shaw and Maxwell McCombs, currently at the University of North Carolina at Chapel Hill, claims that while the media do not tell people what to think, they do influence what people think about. The news media, for example, have to be selective in what they decide to present as news to the public. The TV network must decide which story should lead the newscast and how much time should be spent on each story. For example, NBC may decide to air as its top story a piece about advertising's continual portrayal of abnormally thin women. It can be predicted that viewers of the story will be influenced to think about their own body weight. However, some viewers of the newscast may be prompted to think of their own need to lose weight, while others may see the newscast as a confirmation that they should be happy with their bodies as they are. If the news manager had rejected the story, the viewers likely would not have thought about their own body images at that specific time. Could the media influence people to think about their bodies? Yes. But could the media tell the public how to think? No, according to the agenda-setting model. The agenda-setting model claims that the media can establish certain issues as salient in the mind of the public, but the public will make its own decisions about how to think about the issue.

Implications for Advertising

Although more than half a century of mass communication research has provided different theoretical frameworks for explaining the effects of mass communication, a host of questions remains unanswered, particularly from the perspective of an advertiser; nonetheless, these theories can be of extreme utility given an understanding of their limitations. The magic-bullet theory, claiming that TV viewers will believe every message shot in their direction, obviously underestimates viewers. If the magic-bullet theory were true, and viewers were like sheep following every command of their electronic shepherd, advertising would be a much more predictable and uniformly successful enterprise.

Katz and Lazarsfeld's two-step flow hypothesis proposes that information flows from the mass media to opinion leaders, who then facilitate communication through discussion with peers. But this hypothesis fails to explain what happens once people begin to discuss the issues made salient via the opinion leaders. Drawing again upon the body-type example introduced above, such discussion could lead to some individuals deciding to lose weight; it could also lead to individuals feeling more insecure about their bodies, but not enough to make them diet. Some people might discuss the issue but decide not to change their current lifestyles. This model will not offer much to advertisers seeking to directly influence consumers. At best, the advertisers could hope to influence the gatekeepers, who would then influence consumers to discuss their products. However, such discussion would not necessarily lead to a decision to purchase the product at a particular time.

Again, cultivation theory proposed that the media do not necessarily change individual attitudes, but rather social expectations. Even if this theory is taken as accurate, it still does not explain much about what effect a change in social expectations would have on the viewers. If viewers perceive the average female to be thinner than the average female actually is, the question of what effect this would have on the viewer still remains. Once again, it might influence some viewers to start losing weight. It might influence some viewers to feel more insecure about their bodies, or it might have no effect. The cultivation model offers little help to advertisers looking for ways to increase their immediate sales.

Claiming that viewers are more active in their viewing than they were portrayed to be in previous theories, the uses-and-gratification model proposes that viewers are not used by the media, but use the media based on their own needs and desires. Although this model does claim that the effect of the media will vary based on why the viewer is watching, critics may argue that it does not necessarily lend much practical advice to advertisers that wish to use the media to influence viewers to buy products. At best the model lets advertisers know that viewer motives will dictate how they will be affected by a particular advertisement. For the theory to be useful, advertisers must be quite familiar with it as well as American viewers' needs and motivations.

The agenda-setting model also gives viewers more credit, claiming that the media can influence what the viewers think about, but not how to think about it. In other terms, advertisers might be able to influence what viewers think about, but they have little control over how they think about it. However, it does increase the salience of a product or idea that can be built on by the advertisers.

Mass communication theories attempt to explain the effect of mass media on the viewing public. Although the theories presented here give explanations on how viewers as a group may be affected by the media, advertisers may find a number of persuasion theories—in addition to media effects models—quite useful in explaining the effects of advertising on their viewers.

JASON SIEGEL, EUSEBIO ALVARO, AND MICHAEL BURGOON

Further Reading

Bagdikian, Ben, *The Media Monopoly,* Boston: Beacon Press, 1983; 6th edition, 2000

Barnouw, Erik, et al., editors, *International Encyclopedia of Communications,* 4 vols., Oxford and New York: Oxford University Press, 1989

Bretl, D.J., and J. Cantor, "The Portrayal of Men and Woman in U.S. Television Commercials: A Recent Content Analysis and Trends over 15 Years," *Sex Roles* 18 (1988)

Bryant, Jennings, and Dolf Zillmann, *Media Effects: Advances in Theory and Research,* Hillsdale, New Jersey: Erlbaum, 1994

Crano, William D., and Michael Burgoon, editors, *Mass Media and Drug Prevention: Classic and Contemporary Theories and Research,* Mahwah, New Jersey: Lawrence Erlbaum, 2002

Eagly, Alice Hendrickson, and Shelly Chaiken, *The Psychology of Attitudes,* Fort Worth, Texas: Harcourt Brace Jovanovich College, 1993

Frank, Ronald Edward, and Marshall Greenberg, *The Public's Use of Television: Who Watches and Why,* Beverly Hills, California: Sage, 1980

Garner, D.M., et al., "Cultural Expectations of Thinness in Women," *Psychological Reports* 47 (1980)

Huston, Aletha C., et al., *Big World, Small Screen: The Role of Television in American Society,* Lincoln: University of Nebraska Press, 1992

Katz, Elihu, and Paul F. Lazarsfeld, *Personal Influence: The Part Played by People in the Flow of Mass Communications,* Glencoe, Illinois: Free Press of Glencoe, 1955

McLuhan, Marshall, and Bruce Powers, *The Global Village: Transformations in World Life and Media in the 21st Century,* New York: Oxford University Press, 1989

Myers, Philip N., Jr., and Frank A. Biocca, "The Elastic Body Image: The Effect of Television Advertising and Programming on Body Imaging Distortions in Young Woman," *Journal of Communication* 42, no. 3 (Summer 1992)

Schramm, Wilbur Lang, editor, *Mass Communications*, Urbana: University of Illinois Press, 1949; 2nd edition, 1960

Smith, Joel, *Understanding the Media: A Sociology of Mass Communication*, Cresskill, New Jersey: Hampton Press, 1995

Maxon, Inc.

Founded in Detroit, Michigan, by Lou Maxon, 1927; split into two separate agencies, Clyne & Maxon, Inc., New York City, and Maxon, Inc., Detroit, 1965; Clyne & Maxon, Inc., acquired by Batten Barton Durstine & Osborn, 1966; Maxon, Inc., acquired by Geyer, Morey & Ballard, Inc., 1966; Clyne Maxon-BBDO merger reversed, 1967; merged with Dusenberry Ruriani Kornhauser, Inc., to form Clyne Dusenberry, Inc., 1974.

Major Clients
Ford Motor Company
General Electric Company
Gillette Safety Razor Company, Inc.
H.J. Heinz Company
Lincoln National Life Insurance Company
Packard Motor Car Company

Maxon, Inc., the Detroit, Michigan, advertising agency that came to be known as "the Gillette agency," was largely built and maintained on the strength of a personal relationship that began when the shop first opened in the late 1920s. Lou Russell Maxon established Maxon, Inc., in Detroit in 1927. Among the agency's first successes was a direct-mail campaign in 1928 for the Valet Company, a marketer of razors and razor blades, which tapped Maxon for its double-edge razor blade account the following year.

In 1931 Valet was acquired by the Gillette Safety Razor Company, and Maxon became Gillette's agency until 1933, when the marketer switched its account to Ruthrauff & Ryan. Craig Smith, who had handled the Gillette business as account executive at Maxon, followed the account to the new agency; four years later, Smith joined Gillette as advertising manager and returned the account to Maxon. The move created an agency-client relationship that would become one of the more durable bonds in advertising. Another longtime client relationship started in 1928 when Maxon won the H.J. Heinz Company account, business that the agency would retain for 36 years.

The agency's early growth was also fueled by the General Electric Company's home appliance and radio divisions, Lincoln National Life Insurance Company, and the Reo Motor Car Company. Over the next ten years, Maxon established offices in Chicago, Illinois, serving Edison Electric Appliance Company, Inc., and Montgomery Ward & Company's export division; in Cleveland, Ohio, handling Pittsburgh Plate Glass Company; and in New York City, where it served a number of foreign import clients, including Mitsubishi of Japan before World War II.

Despite its other work, Maxon came to be known as the Gillette agency. When Maxon regained the Gillette account in 1937, the marketer's share of the razor blade market was about 18 percent, and it was sponsoring a network radio variety show, *Community Sing*, with Wendall Hall, the Happiness Boys, and a young comic named Milton Berle. Lou Maxon however, had different ideas about where to reach Gillette users who, he believed, were men driven by ambition and a sense of competition. For example, he promoted the company's new low-priced Thin Blade with comic-strip-style ads in newspapers and magazines showing how the product helped build successful careers.

But his main focus was on sports; Maxon believed that Gillette and sports had a natural affinity through their common appeal to men. He backed his belief by using a quarter of the ad budget to sponsor the 1939 World Series. When Gillette Tech Razor reached sales of 2.5 million units that fall, the commitment to sports was sealed. Gillette sponsored football games and the Kentucky Derby. In June 1941 the agency added sponsorship of prize fighting and launched the *Gillette Cavalcade of Sports,* which started on radio and moved to television during its 25-year run on NBC.

Out of Maxon's relationship with Gillette would come advertising that produced such durable tag lines as "Look sharp, feel sharp, be sharp," and the accompanying Gillette icon, Sharpie the parrot, introduced in 1951. Gillette's percentage of the market during its peak time with Maxon reached 50 percent by the mid-1960s.

By the mid-1930s, Maxon's New York City office had grown to the point where it was virtually as large as the Detroit home office. In 1936, in order to bring the two halves of Maxon to parity, executive authority was divided between the two main offices. Lou Maxon assumed the title of chairman in the Detroit office where he had been president, while T.K. Quinn became president based in the New York City office. This arrangement continued until 1943, when Quinn left, and Maxon became president as well, while remaining in Detroit.

The client list shrank in the 1940s, but Maxon retained some notable marketers. It handled Lincoln and Mercury for Ford during the period when Edsel Ford was head of the company, and Maxon is credited with setting up the Ford Dealer Advertising

Fund. (It has been suggested that nepotism was a factor in the acquisition of the client: the Lincoln and Mercury business came to the agency when Harry Wismer, the husband of Edsel Ford's niece, joined Maxon in 1941.) The agency also had Packard Motor Car Company from 1951 to 1954. Maxon ranked number 22 among U.S. agencies in 1944 with $10 million in billings; within a decade, it had tripled those billings. Growth in billings slowed, then plateaued in the mid- to upper 20s rank range after 1955. Billings rebounded in the 1960s, growing from $31 million in 1960 to $54 million in 1965. About 40 percent of the agency's billings at that time were from Gillette.

But the 1960s also brought major changes. In January 1962 C. Terence Clyne, formerly with the Biow Company, Inc. (1946–54), and McCann-Erickson, Inc. (1954–61), joined Maxon's New York City office as an executive vice president. In the summer of 1963, Lou Maxon suffered a heart attack and withdrew from active involvement in the agency, though he continued to hold a 12.5 percent stake in the company. (He died 19 May 1971.) Meanwhile, Craig Smith, who had established Maxon's relationship with Gillette, retired from the marketer in 1964. Clyne replaced Lou Maxon as chairman and in May 1964 became president and chief executive officer as well. At the time, serious merger talks were under way with Post-Keyes-Gardner, Inc., which had opened on 1 March 1963 in Chicago. But client conflicts ultimately derailed the talks.

Meanwhile, Maxon's two main offices were approaching a parting of the ways. In an effort to bring greater autonomy to each, in April 1965 the New York City office had been renamed Clyne & Maxon, Inc., with about $50 million in billings, while the much smaller Detroit office remained Maxon, Inc., with $11 million in billings. Each had its own management structure, with the Detroit office wholly owned by its employees and run by George Eversham, executive vice president, and Hunter Hardee, senior vice president. One reason the two agencies apparently held on to the Maxon name was Gillette, which was believed to be committed to dealing with both agencies as long as the Maxon name was in use. In November 1965 Gillette moved about $8 million in billings from Clyne Maxon, Inc. (the ampersand had been dropped from the agency's name), to Doyle Dane Bernbach, leaving about $22 million, including Techmatic and toiletries advertising, at the agency.

A month earlier, however, in October, Clyne Maxon announced that it was being acquired by Batten Barton Durstine & Osborn (BBDO), effective 1 January 1966. The deal was done, then undone in 1967 when the agency separated from BBDO. Gillette, however, along with about a dozen key Maxon executives, remained at BBDO. Meanwhile, six months after the original Clyne Maxon-BBDO merger in 1966, Maxon, Inc., was bought by Geyer, Morey & Ballard, Inc., and merged into its operation, eliminating one branch of the Maxon name.

Clyne Maxon continued in somewhat reduced circumstances, ending the decade with billings of less than $30 million. On 6 December 1971, it affiliated with Chalk, Nissen & Hanft and built new business with American Home Products' Whitehall Laboratories (Anacin sinus tablets). On 1 April 1974, Clyne Maxon merged with another American Home Products agency, Dusenberry Ruriani Kornhauser, Inc. The result was Clyne Dusenberry, Inc., which brought an end to the Maxon name in U.S. advertising.

JOHN MCDONOUGH

Further Reading

"BBDO, Clyne Maxon Consolidation Is Set," *Advertising Age* (18 October 1965)

"Geyer Absorbs Maxon Agency," *Advertising Age* (27 June 1966)

"Gillette Moves Razors, Blades to Doyle Dane," *Advertising Age* (29 November 1965)

"$2,000,000 Heinz Soup Business Is Switched to DDB," *Advertising Age* (24 June 1963)

Maytag Corporation

Principal Agencies
Cramer-Krasselt Company
McCann-Erickson, Inc.
Leo Burnett Company, Inc.

The first Maytag washing machine was introduced to consumers by Frederick Louis Maytag in 1907 as a means of keeping his agricultural implement company profitable during its slow season. For nearly a century since then, Maytag has managed to survive both as a brand name and as a corporate entity through its adver-

tising. Among its campaigns was "The lonely Maytag repairman," which began in 1967 and became the longest-running live-character campaign on network television. Maytag became synonymous with dependability and with premium, top-of-the-line products, and the term *Maytag effect* was coined by social scientists to describe consumers' expectations that high-priced products are better than their lower-priced counterparts. Independent observers such as *Consumer Reports,* however, have indicated that although Maytag products on average fare well, in terms of quality and reliability they are not uniformly the best. The National Advertising Division of the Council of Better Business

Bureaus has even challenged some of Maytag's advertising claims about the dependability of its leading competitor, the Kenmore appliance line sold by Sears, Roebuck & Company. Nevertheless, the success of Maytag's advertising campaigns, created since 1955 by the Leo Burnett Company, cemented the concept of dependability with consumers, much as Volvo automobiles came to be associated with safety and Coca-Cola with refreshment.

Making Wash Day a Joy

The Pastime Washer, Maytag's first, looked and worked much like a large butter churn. It consisted of a cypress wood tub on legs with an agitator in the lid that moved when the operator turned a metal handle. Clothing was forced through the water and soap and against the corrugated sides. The company's earliest advertising, which began in 1911, concentrated on the ease of operation and employed the slogan, "So simple, a child could do it." Frederick Maytag later claimed that he had learned an important lesson from an early farm implement called Success. In spite of its name, the cornhusker often broke down, and farmers frequently called on Maytag to travel to their fields to fix it. Maytag determined from that point on that his products would be dependable. "In all business, there is a factor which cannot be compensated for in dollars and cents," he later wrote. "[It] is represented only by the spirit of love which the true craftsman holds for his job and the things he is trying to accomplish." The simply designed and solidly built Pastime was the first Maytag washer to fill that bill.

Maytag improved on his design and introduced the Hired Girl, the first electric washing machine, in 1911, and, beginning in 1914, a version powered by a gasoline engine for rural customers who did not have access to electricity. Maytag's national magazine ads showed a contented housewife putting clothing into her wooden washer with the headline "This wonderful power washer makes wash day a joy." The gasoline version was used in U.S. Army training camps during World War I, and one 1918 ad showed soldiers using a Maytag gasoline machine in a camp setting with the copy "Simple yet sturdy, convenient, easy to operate, washes with the thoroughness and deftness of human hands." Maytag's advertising budget went from a few ads in magazines such as the *Saturday Evening Post* and *Country Gentleman* at the beginning of the 1910s to $100,000 a year by 1918. The Milwaukee, Wisconsin-based advertising agency Cramer-Krasselt produced the newspaper and magazine ads, which used simple line drawings to illustrate the copy.

Personal experience convinced thousands of soldiers to buy Maytags for their wives after the war, and the firm abandoned its farm implement line forever. It introduced the Cabinet Washer in 1919, tagged as "the baby grand of electric washers." The Gyrofoam, the first washer to clean with water action only—without the use of friction—debuted in 1922. Instead of a peg-studded pillar attached to the lid, the new washer featured a finned agitator that was attached to the bottom of the tub and that turned from side to side. By 1924 one of every five washers in the United States was a Maytag, and sales of the new machine pushed Maytag from

the 38th-largest U.S. washing machine company into first place. In 1925 Maytag began running monthly ads in *House and Garden* magazine, and the following year the company erected a $70,000 electric sign at the corner of 49th Street and Broadway in New York City, helping to illuminate Times Square. By the time a 1928 ad appeared noting that "Commander Byrd chooses Maytags for South Pole expedition," the company had produced more than 1 million washing machines, owned 43 percent of the American market, and had an overall advertising budget exceeding $1 million.

Massive advertising helped, but in-house literature, which was published in English, German, French, Spanish, Italian, and Polish, and a good word-of-mouth reputation created a considerable share of Maytag's market during the 1920s. In addition, university extension services provided detailed information on household machinery, thus educating consumers at no cost to the manufacturers. The Maytag company also loaned washers to every domestic science department in high schools with 300 or more students. The conventional wisdom was that washing machines had become such an established feature of home life in the United States and Canada during the 1920s that representatives of the leading commercial laundries—the American Laundry Machinery Company and the Laundry Owners Association—felt that they had to run an aggressive national ad campaign to convince women that doing their laundry at home took them away from important activities such as golf, the theater, and reading to their children.

The conventional wisdom changed in 1929, however. Anna E. Richardson of the American Home Economics Association wrote that modern manufacturing had made it "impossible for the homemaker to have command of all the information demanded to buy intelligently." Instead, wives had become cogs in the corporate process of production for the home. This view, in tandem with the Great Depression, forced washing machine companies to develop new advertising strategies. One ad campaign held that rural women should "let your corn stalks buy a Maytag," a reference to a short-lived paper industry based on corn stalks that developed during the Depression. Another campaign capitalized on women's resentment that limited family resources often went to acquire automobiles for city dwellers or new field and barn equipment for farmers rather than household devices. A 1930 Maytag ad showed a man in an apron and carrying a full load of laundry with the headline, "Change places with your husband next washday." A 1935 ad argued that Maytag could give women more time to spend on other activities, echoing the ads of the American Laundry Machinery Company in the 1920s. Toward the end of the Depression, Maytag ads held that consumers should not wait to replace their aging home machinery, especially as electricity became more commonplace in rural areas. The company used a picture and the name "Master Washer" to advertise its first all-white washing machine, introduced in 1939. At about the same time Maytag switched to the McCann-Erickson agency and ran color print ads in seven women's magazines, including the *Ladies' Home Journal*, *McCall's*, *Better Homes & Gardens*, and *Good Housekeeping*.

Although Maytag repairman Gordon Jump got the job only in 1989, the Lonely Repairman icon has symbolized the dependability of Maytag products since Jesse White originated the role in 1967. *Courtesy of Maytag Corp.*

The Maytag Corporation, headquartered in Newton, Iowa, was a pioneer in broadcast advertising. Frederick Maytag sponsored his first broadcast, a vocal ensemble known as the Maytag Troubadours, on clear-channel radio station WHO in nearby Des Moines in 1924. In 1927 he tested a 30-minute musical every Tuesday through Saturday at 9 P.M. on the Chicago, Illinois, station WHT and sponsored another program called *Household Talks* in the afternoon. In 1928 the largest independent radio network at the time broadcast *The Maytag Happiness Hour,* a 30-minute program featuring the Maytag Orchestra (which sounded suspiciously like the house band of the Edgewater Beach Hotel in Chicago), a cast of soap opera actors, and vocalists who included a group known as the Maytag Ramblers. Six stations—KDKA in Pittsburgh, Pennsylvania; WHT in Chicago; WCCO in Minneapolis, Minnesota; WBAP in Fort Worth, Texas; WHO in Des Moines; and KEX in Portland, Oregon—comprised the network, and four more were added before the end of the year. The earliest programs were recorded live on phonograph records and shipped to the various stations, where they were played simultaneously, giving the impression of a much more expensive live network hookup. Every show ended with the theme song "Let a Smile Be Your Umbrella and a Maytag Your Washer." On Monday eve-

nings beginning in 1930, the company also sponsored the *Maytag Radio Program* on the National Broadcasting Company (NBC) network. Not long before his death in 1937, Frederick Maytag sponsored University of Iowa football broadcasts with announcer Ronald "Dutch" Reagan. During the 1930s and 1940s several Hollywood movies included Maytag washer placements, among them the 1939 film *Blondie Meets the Boss* with Penny Singleton and Arthur Lake.

World War II and After

During World War II the company made military components and munitions, but it kept its dealer network intact through newspaper and magazine advertisements that encouraged consumers to have their washers repaired by Maytag dealers to keep them in good working order until the war ended. "Maytagisms" became a part of popular culture during the war years. Military pilots who washed out in training were said to have "been through the Maytag," and small observation or training planes were frequently known as Maytags. "That's what I've been waiting for," read one postwar ad as an attractive woman watched a new washing machine being carried into her house. In 1946 the company began marketing and advertising a line of ranges and refrigerators made by other companies under the Maytag name. It introduced the first automatic washers in 1949, added a line of dryers in 1953, and began offering Maytag Supermatics, top-of-the-line washer-and-dryer combinations in soft greens, yellows, and pinks. Halo of Heat dryers, produced by Maytag beginning in 1953, were giveaway items on popular television game shows such as *It Could Be You,* hosted by Bill Leyden.

During the 1950s full-line appliance makers such as General Electric, Whirlpool, and Frigidaire began to challenge Maytag's dominance in the washing machine and dryer markets. In 1955, when President Frederick Maytag II learned that McCann-Erickson had signed on with rival Westinghouse, the company hired the Leo Burnett Company to handle its advertising. Burnett's research indicted that Maytag appliances were longer lasting and required fewer repairs than did other brands. Falling back on the theme first advocated by Frederick Maytag, Burnett wrote ads based on letters from customers complimenting Maytag on the durability of its machines. "We're a 3-generation Maytag family," one ad claimed, showing a grandmother, mother, and daughter gathered, smiling, around their washing machine. A 1961 ad noted, "Married in 1932, got Maytag in 1933." Maytag began television advertising on NBC's *Today* show in 1954. To promote the broadcasts, the company set up television sets in branch and distributors' offices and at sales meetings. The much-maligned J. Fred Muggs, the primate companion of host Dave Garroway, joined in on the live ads, and Maytag gave away thousands of J. Fred Muggs puppets as a promotion. Resuming its dependence on print advertising in 1956, the company returned to television in 1961 with a campaign that featured its print-oriented theme of unsolicited testimony claiming that Maytag was "the best you can buy."

Lonely George

The idea for a campaign using a fictional Maytag repairman (with the name Lonely George or Ol' Lonely) most likely came from a distributor in Quebec, Canada, who received a letter from a customer in 1966 commenting that she had never needed a repairman. The concept was simple. George and his basset hound, Newton (named for Maytag's hometown), never had any work because the appliances were made so well that they were maintenance-free. The campaign was doubly effective because it capitalized on the previous "best you can buy" strategy but with a more entertaining presentation.

The Lonely George ads were memorable but difficult to produce because the punch line was so predictable. For years the repairman never left his office. In one 1988 commercial he spent an entire 30-second spot snoozing, feet up on his desk, as "Silent Night" played in the background. One of Burnett's tactics was to replace the original repairman, character actor Jesse White, with situation comedy actor Gordon Jump in 1989. Another was to create dramatic plots—such as having the repairman rescue Maytag owners trapped in giant detergent bubbles or terrorized by runaway machines—which occurred only in the repairman's dreams. But through the end of the 20th century the repairman remained in his office, playing solitaire and lamenting his fate in life.

In the early 1990s Maytag found itself facing a costly advertising problem. Its acquisition of the Hoover brand in 1989 included Hoover Europe, a well-established line of washers, dryers, refrigerators, dishwashers, and other appliances sold primarily in the United Kingdom and Australia but also in continental Europe. In 1992 Hoover Europe advertised two free transatlantic airline tickets to anyone buying a Hoover product in the United Kingdom for as little as $165. More than 220,000 people responded to the offer, which was almost too good to be true and which led to a financial nightmare and a near public-relations disaster when the company delayed getting tickets to claimants. Years of litigation followed, along with the firing of three top Hoover Europe executives. Maytag was forced to take a $30 million charge in 1993 to cover the costs of the ill-fated promotion, one of the most expensive advertising campaigns in its corporate history.

The secret of the Maytag repairman's durability was a much-discussed topic among advertisers. "Familiarity breeds boredom and annoyance which could lead to unfavorable behavior on the part of the consumer," warned Stephen A. Greyser, a marketing professor at the Harvard Business School, in the *Wall Street Journal* in 1993. Linda Eggerss, Maytag's marketing manager, warned in 1995, "We know that he boosts awareness and sales. But it's difficult to quantify because he's been around so long." John Thomas, director of advertising, told the *Minneapolis Star Tribune* in 1977, "Great advertising creates an image in the consumer's mind of what the company stands for." And he added, "That's what Ol' Lonely really is." According to *USA Today*, Maytag received hundreds of unsolicited letters and e-mail messages from repairman fans every year, and Total Research, which tracks consumer perceptions of product quality, ranked Maytag as one of the world's top brands. As Maytag struggled for corporate survival during the 1980s and early 1990s, Ol' Lonely became solidly established in American popular culture. When starting pitchers made it to the seventh inning in 12 consecutive games in the 1980s, a *Boston Globe* sportswriter wrote that "the Red Sox bullpen is filled with Maytag repairmen." During the 1988 presidential primary campaign, U.S. Senator Bob Dole said of opponent Vice President George Bush, "He's like the Maytag repairman—waiting for years and nobody calls." Seven Canadian jet fighter technicians became known as "the Maytag repairman" during the 1991 Persian Gulf War because the planes they serviced never broke down. And *Chicago Sun-Times* columnist Irv Kupcinet wrote of a local election in 1995, "The Chicago Board of Election Commissioners had so few complaints that its staff resembled the Maytag repairman."

RICHARD JUNGER

Further Reading

Funk, A.B., *Fred L. Maytag: A Biography*, Cedar Rapids, Iowa: Torch, 1936

"Gordon Jumps to It; Maytag's Lonely Guy Still Draws WKRP Fans," *Toronto Sun* (17 May 1996)

Hoover, Robert, *An American Quality Legend: How Maytag Saved Our Moms, Vexed the Competition, and Presaged America's Quality Revolution*, New York: McGraw-Hill, 1993

"Loneliness in a Long-Running Pitch," *New York Times* (15 May 1992)

"Maytag Corporation," in *Encyclopedia of Consumer Brands*, edited by Janice Jorgensen, Detroit, Michigan, and London: St. James, 1994

"Rare Breed Still Works on Madison Ave.," *USA Today* (29 December 1995)

"Repetitive Ads Keep Viewer Recall Going," *Wall Street Journal* (7 April 1993)

Spirit of Maytag: 100 Years of Dependability, 1893–1993, Newton, Iowa: Maytag, 1993

McCaffrey and McCall, Inc.

Founded as LaRoche, McCaffrey & McCall, 1966; became McCaffrey and McCall, 1972; acquired by Saatchi & Saatchi, 1983; became a subsidiary of Bates Worldwide, 1995; name changed to Bates Midwest, 1996.

Major Clients

Exxon Corporation
Mercedes-Benz of North America, Inc.
Pfizer, Inc.
Hiram Walker & Sons Ltd.

James J. McCaffrey and David B. McCall left Ogilvy, Benson & Mather in 1962 to become part owners with Chester J. LaRoche in his ad agency, C.J. LaRoche & Company. The LaRoche agency had been founded in 1942 when Chet LaRoche, who had built the reputation of Young & Rubicam, Inc. (Y&R), as a major force in network radio and been president of the company since 1934, had a falling out with Raymond Rubicam. LaRoche was a founder of the War Advertising Council in 1942, and Rubicam felt that because of this additional responsibility, his loyalties were divided. LaRoche left Y&R that year and formed his own agency, which would become a successful mid-size shop. In 1963 McCaffrey became chairman and chief executive officer (CEO), and McCall became president of C.J. LaRoche & Company.

Soon after their arrival at C.J. LaRoche, the two attracted attention in the industry by sending a blind questionnaire to 300 advertising and business executives to ascertain what image the agency projected. Later in their careers the men would also achieve notoriety by speaking out about the industry's need to respond to the public's and the government's negative views of advertising, the "silliness" of advertising awards, the "sin" of advertisers' expecting agencies to create new work on speculation, the lack of minority hiring in the industry, and the proper use of research in advertising.

The C.J. LaRoche agency became LaRoche, McCaffrey & McCall on 1 January 1966, with billings of $28 million for that year, up from $12 million in 1962, when McCaffrey and McCall had joined the company. That growth occurred despite McCaffrey's philosophy, "We resign accounts we cannot be happy with." This theme would be echoed in 1969, when the company went public and released its new business philosophy: "Accept as clients only relatively large, successful businesses, or businesses that have, in the opinion of the company management, a rapid growth potential." In 1962 the agency had 11 clients, with approximately $11 million in billings; in 1968 it had 18 clients and more than $42 million in billings.

In addition to speaking their minds, the pair also ran an agency that earned praise from its clients. In 1966 Hartford Insurance Group named LaRoche, McCaffrey & McCall as its agency after 14 years with the Marschalk Company, saying, "[LaRoche,

McCaffrey & McCall] bowled us over with its interest and involvement." One Hartford executive also cited enthusiastic endorsements of the agency by its other clients.

In 1975 McCall echoed his partner's earlier pronouncements, telling a gathering of ad agency personnel, "We believe most new business isn't worth having and that we must represent great companies to be a great agency." By then the agency had 15 clients and billings of $72 million.

In 1972, after LaRoche retired, the agency dropped the LaRoche name. Also that year the agency joined with Charles Barker & Sons of London, England, to form Barker McCaffrey McCall, but the partnership was dissolved within a year, after McCaffrey and McCall decided they did not need an international operation. In 1973 McCaffrey retired, and McCall assumed the roles of chairman and CEO. In 1975 Don Durgin became president of the agency after having served as an executive vice president for several months.

1965 Rolls-Royce Silver Cloud III — about $17,000 and so easy to drive your wife will love it (see 3 below)

How to buy a Rolls-Royce

Myth has it that Rolls-Royce is very aloof about who can buy a Rolls-Royce or Bentley car—and that if you are lucky enough to buy one of these cars, it will be taken away from you if you don't take proper care of it.

Nonsense. Rolls-Royce is as anxious to sell its products as any manufacturer is. It's easy to buy a Rolls-Royce, and more fun to own and drive one than you'd ever imagine.

Here's how we suggest you go about buying one:

1. Call your dealer (see listing) and ask him to bring a Rolls-Royce to your home or office. Or, if you prefer, stop by his showroom.

Kick the tires. Take a good look at the outside of the car. Inspect the trunk—carpeting, fitted toolbox, tire pump. Notice the chrome-plated tail pipe.

Next, get inside the car and look around. Familiarize yourself with the dashboard—rear window defroster switch, adjustable shock absorber switch, low-fuel warning light, built-in picnic

tables—and all the other standard equipment on a Rolls-Royce.

2. Take a test drive. Start by heading straight for the heaviest traffic you can find—to get rid of any old-fashioned ideas that a Rolls-Royce is hard to handle.

Maneuverability and your view of the road are incredibly good.

Acceleration is unbelievably smooth. Everything *works* beautifully.

Next, head for the open highway and a full-throttle acceleration test—0 to 60 mph in 10.5 seconds or less in most tests.

Automatic transmission, power assisted steering and braking make driving anywhere a pleasure.

3. Let your wife take the wheel. Many women tend to shy away from driving a Rolls-Royce—until they get in it, drive it around a bit, discover that it's a *family car*—and give their husbands an ultimatum to buy one by such and such a date —*or else.*

SUGGESTION: Invite your wife out for lunch or dinner while you're testing your Rolls-Royce. That's one of the best ways

to discover what it would actually feel like to own a Rolls-Royce of your own—an important thing to know before you get around to laying any money out.

4. Thoroughly investigate all the details of buying and owning a Rolls-Royce.

Prices start around $17,000 ($300 less for a Bentley—same car, different grille) not including local taxes. You can often get immediate delivery on a Rolls-Royce Silver Cloud III. Custom models take longer.

Air conditioning and a host of other accessories are available at extra cost.

Check into parts and service. Investigate the possibilities of a *used* Rolls-Royce or Bentley—and don't shy away from the ones five or ten years old.

Our sole objective is to sell you a Rolls-Royce that interests you.

For more information, please write to: Rolls-Royce Inc., Room 466, 45 Rockefeller Plaza, New York 20, N. Y.

◀ **See where to buy a Rolls-Royce on opposite page**

This 1964 Rolls-Royce ad was part of a successful campaign created by C.J. LaRoche & Company's James McCaffrey and David McCall, who went on to start their own agency.
Reproduced with permission from Rolls-Royce & Bentley Motor Cars, Limited.

The next decade included many significant changes for the agency. In 1976 it lost the Rolls-Royce Motor Car account, which it had held for 12 years. It acquired the $10 million Avis Rent-A-Car System corporate account in 1982 (amid some controversy concerning the use of David Mahoney, chief of Avis's parent company, Norton Simon, Inc., as spokesperson in the campaign), while Avis's national franchisees moved their $6 million campaign to Bozell & Jacobs. Then, in 1983, London-based Saatchi & Saatchi acquired McCaffrey and McCall in its quest to gain a strong creative presence in the United States. McCaffrey and McCall continued to operate independently, however. Major accounts in the 1980s included Hiram Walker & Sons and Mercedes-Benz of North America.

A noteworthy executive shift occurred in 1986 when Robert H. Cherins became president and chief operating officer while McCall continued as chairman, CEO, and creative director. Cherins is believed to be the first direct-marketing executive to be named president of a general ad agency; he had started McCaffrey and McCall's direct-marketing division in 1981. The promotion was an indication of the agency's commitment to providing direct-marketing services. Of the agency's 20 general advertising clients, 17 also used the direct-marketing division.

In 1988 McCall left the agency to join a political and corporate communications company, and in 1993 he formed his own communications, consulting, and advertising agency. He also was the creator of the television program *Schoolhouse Rock*. He was killed in a car accident in 1999 while on a relief mission in Albania.

McCaffrey and McCall became a subsidiary of Bates Worldwide in 1995. In 1996 its name was changed to Bates Midwest, based in Indianapolis, Indiana.

NANCY DIETZ

Further Reading

Alter, Stewart, "Direct Approach Suits McCaffrey Just Fine," *Advertising Age* (4 August 1986)
Bernstein, Henry R., "Be Choosy in Taking New Accounts, McCall Urges," *Advertising Age* (26 May 1975)
"Hartford Insurance Picks LaRoche; Likes Its Client Involvement," *Advertising Age* (19 December 1966)

McCann-Erickson Worldwide Advertising

Created in 1930 by the $15 million merger of the Erickson Company and the H.K. McCann Company; by 1936 had offices in Canada, England, France, Germany, Argentina, and Brazil; in major agency switch, won domestic business of Coca-Cola from D'Arcy Advertising, 1955; restructured into four divisions reporting to a single company, Interpublic, Inc. (later renamed the Interpublic Group of Companies), 1960; established McCann-Erickson WorldGroup as an umbrella management company overseeing McCann-Erickson Worldwide Advertising, 1997.

Major Clients

California Packing Corporation
Chesebrough Manufacturing Company
Chrysler Corporation
Coca-Cola Company
Ford Motor Company
R.J. Reynolds Tobacco Company
Standard Oil Company
Texas Instruments

The McCann-Erickson WorldGroup was established in September 1997 by the Interpublic Group of Companies as an umbrella management company encompassing McCann-Erickson Worldwide Advertising, itself a network of advertising agencies that includes McCann-Erickson Worldwide and a diverse portfolio of marketing communications companies.

Under the leadership of James R. Heekin, chairman-chief executive officer (CEO), McCann-Erickson Worldwide posted worldwide gross income of $2.6 billion in 2000, according to *Advertising Age*. The McCann-Erickson WorldGroup is headquartered in New York City and employs about 12,000 in offices worldwide. In 2001 it was comprised of the following agencies and marketing communications companies: McCann Erickson Advertising; Amster Yard; Anderson & Lembke; Jay Advertising; Torre Lazur McCann Healthcare Worldwide; McCann-Relationship Marketing Worldwide; FutureBrand; Momentum Worldwide, and digital marketing agency Zentropy Partners.

The original agency of McCann-Erickson WorldGroup is McCann-Erickson Worldwide Advertising, itself a large and geographically diverse global advertising agency network, with operations in 131 countries as well as majority- or wholly owned agencies in 67 countries. McCann-Erickson, with billings in 2000 of more than $17.4 billion, is ranked by industry analysts as a top-five agency in almost every market in which it operates, as well as a pan-regional leader in all regions of the world. The agency, named "Agency of the Year" in 2000 by an unprecedented four industry publications, is considered one of the most experienced in multinational advertising.

Origins

McCann-Erickson Worldwide Advertising was established in the early part of the 20th century by two advertising executives who found common ground as partners in the nascent advertising industry. Alfred W. Erickson, known as Eric, started the Erickson Company in 1902, with McCutcheon's Department Store as his first client. Harrison King ("H.K.") McCann was an advertising manager of the Standard Oil Company before the U.S. government forced the breakup of the Standard Oil monopoly. "H.K." seized the opportunity in 1912 to open his own advertising agency, with the remade Standard Oil as his first client. McCann's initial accounts, according to company records, represented about $500,000 in advertising contracts, including the Standard Oil Companies of New Jersey, New York, Louisiana, and California (Esso), and the Chesebrough Manufacturing Company. Some of these earliest accounts, such as Esso, Chesebrough (Vaseline), and California Packing Corporation (Del Monte), remained with McCann-Erickson well into the 1990s.

McCann and Erickson shared a common background: each had been a client advertising manager just before starting his own agency and each had launched his agency with a former employer as an initial client. According to Stewart Alter's history of McCann-Erickson, *Truth Well Told*, McCann said in later interviews that the idea of a merger appealed to him as "our companies had no competing accounts and both companies had excellent reputations."

On 2 October 1930 a newspaper advertisement announced the merger of "two groups of longtime friends, who, in standards of service and of agency practice, have thought as one for many years." The $15 million merger of the H.K. McCann Company and the Erickson Company into McCann-Erickson, Inc., was at the time the ad industry's largest. McCann became president, Erickson chairman. The new agency's chief competitors included N.W. Ayer & Son, Inc.; the J. Walter Thompson Company (JWT); Batten Barton Durstine & Osborn; Lord & Thomas; Erwin, Wasey & Company; and the Campbell-Ewald Company.

Several years after the McCann-Erickson merger, Standard Oil asked the agency to provide its South American affiliates with advertising assistance, and McCann responded by opening offices in Argentina and Brazil. Indeed, Standard Oil is credited by the agency with helping it launch what grew into a vast McCann-Erickson international network. McCann also opened agencies in Europe initially to service Standard Oil, but those offices went on to win new business. "We felt that we should follow the flags of our clients," said McCann, according to *Truth Well Told*.

By 1936, the year Erickson died, the *Standard Directory of Advertising Agencies* entry for McCann-Erickson, Inc., listed 17 offices in the United States, Canada, England, France, Germany, Argentina, and Brazil. Clients that year included well-known corporations such as the Bon Ami Company; the Borg-Warner Corporation; Chesebrough; the Ford Motor Company; Fanny Farmer Candy Shops, Inc.; Mack Trucks, Inc.; and the National Biscuit Company (Nabisco).

In the early 1930s, when radio emerged as a strong advertising medium, Dorothy Barstow emerged as one of McCann-Erickson's early radio producers. (She later married McCann in 1939.) Barstow was the force behind *Real Folks,* the radio show launched in 1929 for Chesebrough as an advertising vehicle for its Vaseline Hair Tonic, as well as *Death Valley Days,* sponsored by Pacific Coast Borax Company's 20 Mule Team Borax and featuring a young Ronald Reagan. With her first husband, Josef Bonime, Barstow helped change the course of American musical history by launching the career of bandleader Benny Goodman on the *Let's Dance* program for Nabisco, thus striking the spark that ignited the swing era around the world. Other prominent shows produced by the agency were *Inner Sanctum Mysteries* for Bromo Seltzer (1946–50) and *Grand Central Station* for Pillsbury (1944–51).

But radio was only one ad medium expanding in the 1930s. On-screen advertising in movies began in that decade, with McCann-Erickson's animated campaign "Quick, Henry, the Flit" for Stanco, Inc.'s Flit insecticide, another early advertiser. Outdoor advertising—in particular billboards for Standard Oil—also earned McCann renown; many of its outdoor ads were included among the "100 Best" in the Annual Exhibition of Outdoor Advertising Art shows conducted in the 1930s and 1940s.

In mid-1932 McCann-Erickson for the first time established a separate outdoor advertising department. The following year, a sales promotion department was established. Six years later, a young mailroom employee, Marion J. Harper, Jr., was transferred to the research department, where he made his reputation producing a research study that identified 30 factors common to the best-rated ads. Harper shared the research with the agency's creative department as a "guideline on how ads could attract more attention and readership."

One strength the agency seemed to exhibit early on was the ability to build an account into an entire area of expertise and develop that expertise into new business. This ability was seen in McCann's handling of agriculture accounts, tourism, and public utility companies, as the company built out from areas of expertise to attract new businesses.

The agency's most significant account win in the 1930s was the Ford dealer advertising business. Within a six-month period, the agency added 27 of Ford's 32 branch territories across the United States, which involved setting up a network of interlinked offices. The Ford account grew to $2.7 million in billings by 1939, or 12 percent of the agency's U.S. total of $21.7 million.

By 1937 the agency had 827 employees. Two years later, despite losses in its overseas agencies, it posted $483,000 in operating profits.

Between 1940 and 1944, McCann opened agencies in Atlanta, Georgia; Dallas, Texas; Minneapolis, Minnesota; and Boston, Massachusetts. At the same time, World War II caused tremendous upheaval in the agency's European operations. McCann-Erickson, London, England, operated continuously throughout the war, although McCann-Erickson, Paris, France, was liquidated after France was invaded in 1940. The office in Frankfurt, Germany, closed in 1941; it was revived in 1946 by Max Pauli,

McCann-Erickson began to work on Del Monte in 1917 and continued with the brand into the 21st century, making theirs one of the longest-lasting client-agency relationships in the industry. This 1918 ad featured the familiar Del Monte shield and an illustration by Norman Rockwell.
Reproduced with permission of Del Monte Foods.

who resumed directing the office after serving time in a German prisoner of war camp. Prewar clients such as Esso, Opel, and Reemstma cigarettes returned, and new clients were added, including Agfa A.G. Over the decade, McCann's billings in Europe grew from an insignificant amount to $3.5 million.

While growth in Europe was stalled by the war, the agency's Latin American network continued to move forward. McCann opened agencies in seven Latin American countries between 1942 and 1946—Puerto Rico (1942), Cuba and Colombia (1944), Chile and Venezuela (1945), and Uruguay and Peru (1946). The Latin American region's nine agencies were billing $5.5 million by 1949, $2 million more than the operations in Europe. Total worldwide billings that year were $60 million, 17 percent of which came from outside the United States.

Other international firsts during the 1940s included the agency's first advertising campaign in China (in 1946 for Schenley Reserve Whiskey); campaigns from local offices appeared in South Africa and the Philippines in 1947.

Harper's Influence

The research study Harper had undertaken led to "The McCann-Erickson Continuing Study of Reader Interest in Magazine Advertising." This study was overwhelmingly accepted by McCann offices both in the United States and overseas, and by 1942 Harper had been named head of copy research. His abiding interest in research and how it might contribute to more effective advertising led to the hiring of noted researchers—including Hanz Zeisel and Herta Herzog—and made McCann a leader in developing new research methods and applying them to the advertising business.

In 1946 Harper was named vice president-research director of McCann, succeeding Louis Weld, who had established McCann's annual estimates of advertising spending, a project that in 1950 was taken over by Robert "Bob" Coen, senior vice president-director of forecasting. Coen predicted that worldwide advertising spending in 2000 would reach $494 billion. Since 1950 the annual forecast has grown from estimates of radio, magazine, and newspaper spending to encompass the Internet, Yellow Pages directories, outdoor advertising, and direct mail, as well as network, spot, cable, and syndicated television.

At the time that Harper took over the daily running of McCann as president in 1948 at age 32—"H.K." McCann moved up to chairman—the agency had billings of $54 million and was ranked fifth among all agencies. JWT was more than twice its size, with $115 million in total billings. One of Harper's ambitions was to make McCann into an agency that would overtake JWT, which by then was the industry leader in the United States and abroad. By 1960 McCann was approaching its rival: only JWT and McCann billed more than $350 million.

McCann is said to have predicted that Harper would make an exciting agency president, and an early signal that this would prove true came in 1954, when McCann-Erickson decided to buy Marschalk & Pratt as part of a consolidation strategy. But instead of folding the Cleveland, Ohio, agency into McCann, Harper

decided that it would be wise to keep Marschalk as a separate agency, with its own name and client list. Harper believed Marschalk could handle small clients on a more profitable basis than the larger McCann agency and possibly—and most controversially—could even handle some competitive accounts, as the agencies would operate under different names and in different offices.

McCann's emphasis on coordination of global marketing strategies reaped tremendous rewards for the agency in the 1950s, when it parlayed an overseas relationship with the Coca-Cola Company into a domestic one. In October 1955 McCann-Erickson was appointed agency of record for Coca-Cola's $15 million account, which had been with the D'Arcy Advertising Company, Inc., for almost 50 years. Coca-Cola's decision to make the switch came from its "desire to integrate further international and domestic advertising," according to *Advertising Age*. McCann-Erickson already handled Coca-Cola Export Corporation advertising in Latin America. The account move was shocking insofar as many D'Arcy executives had ties with Coca-Cola, including seats on the board of the company, investments in bottling plants, and stock equity. As the incumbent agency, D'Arcy was thought to be too well entrenched to be removed.

Coca-Cola, which was faced with increasing challenges to its top market position from the Pepsi-Cola Company, already had a long and rich advertising history when it shifted its business to McCann. The company's catchphrase "Delicious and refreshing" dated to 1889 and "The pause that refreshes" to 1939.

Coca-Cola was interested in McCann research showing that consumers wanted "refreshment" and the suggestion that the soft-drink marketer think of itself as being in the refreshment and not merely the soft-drink business. An early TV commercial produced by McCann in 1958 positioned Coke as a "Lunch time treat." Another spot featured the singing McGuire Sisters pausing to enjoy a Coke. The theme was "Be really refreshed, pause for Coca-Cola."

Harper's promise of a dedicated team within the agency assigned only to the Coca-Cola business was, according to McCann, another reason why the agency won the account. Initially, 121 people were assigned to "the Coca-Cola Group," covering all functions within the agency from account management to media and copywriting. The agency also promised it could integrate Coca-Cola's international advertising efforts with its domestic campaigns.

In February 1958 Harper again stunned the ad industry when McCann resigned the $26 million Chrysler automotive account to take on the smaller, $24 million Buick account from General Motors Corporation (GM). GM had been with the Kudner Agency since 1935. According to *Truth Well Told*, Harper's explanation for switching clients had more to do with the fact that McCann already had GM's Opel account in Europe, and it was becoming harder to avoid conflicts while handling GM business overseas and Chrysler's accounts in the United States.

By 1956 the McCann agency had spread out into 24 offices in 15 countries and employed 1,300 people outside the United States. McCann quickly adopted television, helping produce programs such as *Garroway at Large* for Congoleum-Nairn, *Studio*

One for Westinghouse, *Treasury Men in Action* for Chrysler, and *The Show Goes On* for the American Safety Razor Corporation and Columbia Records. By 1957, 85 percent, or $106 million, of McCann's client money targeted for broadcast was placed in television, representing 48 clients in eight McCann offices in the United States.

Harper also oversaw much of McCann's international growth. Global advertising opportunities were a top priority, one that Harper expounded on by continuous office openings and acquisitions. By 1956 nine of the agency's top-20 international clients used McCann both in the United States and overseas.

Birth of Interpublic

In 1960 Harper made his vision of "the agency of the future" into reality, restructuring McCann into four operating units, each reporting to a new holding company that would eventually be known as the Interpublic Group of Companies. Each of the four units, McCann-Erickson Advertising (U.S.), McCann-Erickson Corporation (International), McCann-Marschalk, and Communications Affiliates (a collection of diversified communications agencies) was to be run independently but be interconnected.

McCann-Erickson Advertising, then with $170 million in billings, was positioned as a "pure" advertising agency, concerning itself with creative advertising functions. Named to head the agency as chairman was Robert E. Healy who had joined McCann in 1952. Healy would become vice chairman and eventually chairman of McCann's parent, the Interpublic Group of Companies. The reorganization of the company effectively split the McCann agency into two, with U.S. and international divisions both reporting to Harper in dual roles at McCann and the new parent company, Interpublic.

Over the next five years, international growth overshadowed the domestic side of McCann. Interpublic made 38 acquisitions and opened new agencies in Africa, Australia, and the Far East. In 1960 international business represented 30 percent of the agency's total. By 1969 the international agency billed $257.8 million versus $553.3 million for the U.S. agency. By 2001 international business accounted for two-thirds of the company's total volume.

Geographic expansion and global account strategy grew together. As the agency increased its presence in a particular part of the world, it would strive to win a consolidated, multicountry assignment from its clients. In 1968, for example, the Gillette Company assigned McCann to handle its account in Spain and Brazil. By that time, the agency already was handling the marketer's products in 27 countries, including Japan, the Philippines, France, and Italy.

One of the most noted campaigns in the 1960s was McCann's campaign for Standard Oil, featuring the newly minted Esso tiger and the slogan "Put a tiger in your tank." The campaign was first launched in 1964 in the United States and quickly expanded internationally. In 1965 *Advertising Age* noted that the Esso tiger was "a success in 23 countries and over five continents." The following year, the Sales and Marketing Executives Association gave Standard Oil a special award in international marketing for taking the Esso tiger around the world and making it an international symbol.

The agency credited its ability to train its executives to operate on a global stage as crucial to furthering its clients' advertising strategies. Interpublic continued its rapid expansion, buying agencies that would become part of McCann-Erickson proper as well as adding full-service agencies that would compete with McCann internationally. Between 1958 and mid-1965, Interpublic made 38 acquisitions; McCann-Erickson's international expansion was a key part of that growth. Agencies were added in Mexico, Central America, the Caribbean, Sweden, Spain, and New York City as part of this rapid acquisition cycle. In 1961 McCann itself signed a joint venture with Hakuhodo, then Japan's number-two advertising agency.

At a 1968 meeting in Madrid, Spain, top McCann-Erickson executives announced that the agency had enjoyed an excellent business year worldwide, gaining $10 million in new business outside the United States and Canada. Among the new international clients were Unilever, Johnson & Johnson, Bayer, and W.R. Grace.

Ever interwoven with the fortunes of its parent company, McCann-Erickson rode out the rocky events of 1967, when Interpublic's $9 million bank debt threatened to pull the agency into insolvency. The board of Interpublic ousted Harper on 9 November 1967 and named Healy as CEO, then chairman, in February 1968 when Harper left the company. Healy put in place a restructuring program, arranged for $10.2 million in revolving credit, and, with the help of clients willing to advance media commissions, restored the company's cash flow. By 1968 the agency had regained its financial footing; billings in 1969 were $719.1 million.

In 1971 *Advertising Age* reported that McCann Erickson finally had achieved its goal of supplanting JWT as the leader in international billings. From 1967 to 1972, international billings increased 114 percent. But in the fall of 1973, Interpublic Chairman Paul Foley announced that McCann-Erickson would once again be reunited as a single worldwide agency with its own consolidated management. It was recognition that clients increasingly were thinking of their advertising strategies on a global basis and wanted their advertising agencies to adopt the same business strategy.

Under Foley's leadership, McCann produced some of its most memorable advertising for Coca-Cola. In late 1963 Coca-Cola and McCann launched the "Things go better with Coke" campaign, designed from the outset with the idea that whenever an ad for Coca-Cola appeared, it would bear a strong "family resemblance" to every other advertisement for Coca-Cola. The strategy was to give the soft drink a familiar image and sound no matter where it appeared. By 1969, with the launch of the "It's the real thing" campaign, this approach had been refined to one of integrated marketing across all media advertising and promotional materials, including vending machines and delivery uniforms and vehicles. In 1971 McCann created another memorable TV commercial for Coca-Cola as part of the "It's the real thing" campaign. Young people of all nationalities and races were gathered on an Italian hilltop to sing, "I'd Like to Teach the World to

McCann-Erickson's 2000 campaign for DuPont featured a new slogan, "The miracles of science," as part of an initiative to reshape the company's image.
Reprinted courtesy of DuPont.

Sing." The song was written by William Backer, who later formed the Backer & Spielvogel advertising agency. As later recorded by the New Seekers, it became a top-40 hit. In 1979 McCann again scored creatively for Coca-Cola with the "Have a Coke and a smile" commercial featuring football star "Mean" Joe Greene and a young fan. In the commercial, an injured Greene, limping back to the locker room during a game, encounters a boy who sympathetically offers his hero his Coke. In appreciation, Greene takes off his jersey and tosses it to the startled youth. The spot, ranked as one of the best-recalled commercials in history, was the recipient of many awards. The concept was so successful that McCann offices in other countries made similar commercials featuring local sports stars.

On 1 January 1981 Willard C. Mackey was given the task of reintegrating McCann-Erickson as a combined U.S. and international agency. In that role, he became the fourth worldwide CEO of McCann. Mackey and his team added several networkwide accounts in the early 1980s, including the $20 million Texas Instruments account and the $100 million R.J. Reynolds Tobacco Company account. Goodyear in 1984 consolidated all its overseas advertising with the agency. By the end of 1988, when John J. Dooner, Jr., was named president of McCann-Erickson North America, the McCann-Erickson, New York, agency had grown to $675 million in billings from $290 million in 1984.

In the early 1980s it was McCann's domestic network that took off while international billings remained relatively flat. That cycle would switch in the latter part of the decade, as international billings again took over the rapid-growth slot and the U.S. economy slowed. By 1985 McCann's U.S. billings had grown to $834 million; international billings were flat at $1.47 billion, accounting for just less than two-thirds of McCann's total billings.

Still, with $2.2 billion in worldwide combined billings in 1984, McCann had dropped to number seven among leading global agencies. Acquisition sprees by other agencies kept McCann out of the top ten domestically as well.

The mid-1980s were a time of frenzied merger and acquisition activity among advertising agencies, although McCann stayed out of much of the fray. Robert L. James, who had been tapped as president-CEO in 1985, gathered company executives in 1987 in a worldwide agency meeting in which he mapped out the company's strategy for the next five years; it called for an internal growth plan, heavy on global advertising and multinational accounts. The meeting was capped by a videotaped message from U.S. President Ronald Reagan.

In the period between 1986 and 1991, McCann nearly doubled its worldwide billings from $2.8 billion in 1986 to more than $5.4 billion in 1991. Even in the tough business climate of 1992, McCann's worldwide billings rose another 14.8 percent to $6.2 billion. By 1993 McCann achieved its goal to place among the top five agencies worldwide as ranked by Advertising Age and Adweek. The agency pulled in $6.7 billion in billings; only Dentsu, the Japanese advertising conglomerate, was larger.

By the mid-1990s McCann, which had given rise to Interpublic, was again credited as being the growth engine for the holding company, accounting for more than half of its size and more of its profits than any of the several other agencies the holding company had acquired. In July 1995 John J. Dooner, Jr., was named CEO of McCann-Erickson Worldwide, which two years later renamed itself McCann Erickson WorldGroup. In March 2000 Dooner was named chairman-CEO of Interpublic effective 1 January 2001. He succeeded Philip Geier.

In late March 2001 the Interpublic Group announced a plan to acquire True North Communications in a deal estimated to be worth $2.1 billion. The acquisition enabled Interpublic to surpass the WPP Group as the world's largest advertising organization and made siblings of McCann and True North's Bozell Group and FCB Worldwide.

LAURIE FREEMAN

Further Reading

Alter, Stewart, *Truth Well Told: McCann-Erickson and the Pioneering of Global Advertising*, New York: McCann-Erickson Worldwide, 1994

Grant, Don, "Kummel Is Named McCann President As Agency Revamps," *Advertising Age* (10 September 1973)

"Half a Century in Ad Business 46 Heading Own Shop—McCann Found It 'Never Boring,'" *Advertising Age* (22 December 1958)

Link, Luther J., "Creativity, Research Are Keys to Effective Marketing in Japan," *Advertising Age* (30 August 1971)

"Marschalk Agency Is a Division of McCann," *Advertising Age* (13 December 1954)

"M'Cann Sheds Chrysler to Take Buick Account," *Advertising Age* (17 February 1958)

"McCann Adds $20,000,000 in Overseas Billings," *Advertising Age* (9 December 1968)

"McCann-Erickson Replaces D'Arcy on $15,000,000 Coca-Cola Account," *Advertising Age* (17 October 1955)

McCann Erickson WorldGroup <www.mccann.com>

McDonald's Corporation

Principal Agencies
D'Arcy Advertising Company
Needham, Harper & Steers Advertising, Inc.
Leo Burnett USA
DDB Needham Worldwide

McDonald's Corporation, operator of the world's largest fast-food chain, has a presence in more than 100 countries. Eighty-five percent of McDonald's 20,000 restaurants around the world are operated by nearly 4,500 franchises and affiliates. From its beginning, McDonald's has had an aggressive marketing philosophy, and the company boasts that its ads have been among the most identifiable over the years. In addition, McDonald's has put a major emphasis on philanthropic work, mainly through the McDonald Charities, including the Ronald McDonald Houses.

It was actually the milkshake—not the hamburger—that set off the chain of events leading ultimately to today's McDonald's. The first McDonald's Restaurant was opened in Pasadena, California, in 1937 by two brothers, Maurice ("Mac") and Richard ("Dick") McDonald. Although the establishment sold hamburgers, it otherwise bore little relation to the giant franchise it would one day become. The true founder of the McDonald's chain, Ray Kroc, was originally a purveyor of the Multimixer automatic milkshake mixer. In 1954 he went to see the McDonald brothers at their drive-in restaurant in San Bernadino, California, where, he had heard, they had eight of his mixing machines in constant use—obviously indicating a large business volume. He negotiated an agreement with the brothers that would allow him to open his own McDonald's. Kroc's first establishment opened in 1955 in the Chicago, Illinois, suburb of Des Plaines. In July of that year, he added his second store in Fresno, California. Total annual sales for the company were initially only $193,772, but by the time of his death in 1984, Kroc had expanded the chain to almost 8,000 outlets worldwide and had made the "Golden Arches" an internationally recognized symbol of American enterprise.

Creating the Prototype

Kroc created in his early venture the prototype of the stripped-down fast-food operation that the McDonald's Corporation would later use throughout the world. Only after Kroc had shown the initiative to re-create and run the chain himself did the McDonalds agree to Kroc's expansion idea. At the end of 1956 McDonald's 14 restaurants reported sales of $1.2 million, and they had served some 50 million hamburgers. During 1958, the 100-millionth burger was sold.

By 1959 McDonald's had begun billboard advertising. In 1960—the year the chain sold its 400-millionth hamburger—Kroc opened Hamburger University in the basement of a restaurant in Elk Grove Village, Illinois (another Chicago suburb). This site became the main training facility for new franchisees and store managers. Also in 1960, McDonald's touted its "All-American menu—a hamburger, fries, and a shake" as an ad campaign theme.

In 1961, with more than 200 McDonald's restaurants licensed, Kroc bought out the McDonald brothers for $2.7 million. That same year, the slogan "Look for the Golden Arches" gave sales a big boost. This was McDonald's first jingle and first national advertising campaign. In 1962 the ad campaign theme became "Go for goodness at McDonald's," and McDonald's replaced "Speedee," the hamburger-man symbol, with the Golden Arches logo. A national McDonald's ad appeared in *Life* magazine on 5 October 1962. The first McDonald's TV commercial appeared in 1963. Also in 1963, the company served its billionth hamburger to Art Linkletter on his national TV show and introduced the Ronald McDonald character. (In 1999 *Advertising Age* placed Ronald second on the all-time list of top-ten advertising icons.)

In 1965 McDonald's retained D'Arcy Advertising and began advertising on network television. That same year, McDonald's also became a public company, selling its shares over the counter for $22.50. On 5 July 1966 the company became listed on the New York Stock Exchange. Also in 1966, the first McDonald's restaurant with seating opened in Huntsville, Alabama.

Between 1965 and 1967 D'Arcy introduced several ad campaign themes: "McDonald's—Where quality starts fresh everyday" in 1965; "McDonald's—The closest thing to home" in 1966; and "McDonald's is your kind of place" in 1967. In 1966 Ronald McDonald made his national television debut in Macy's Thanksgiving Day Parade, appearing with the world's largest drum.

McDonald's success in the 1960s was largely due to the company's aggressive marketing and its flexible response to customer demand. In 1963 the Filet-O-Fish sandwich, billed as "The fish that catches people," was introduced in McDonald's restaurants. In 1968 the Big Mac and the hot apple pie joined the menu. In 1969 McDonald's sold its five-billionth hamburger.

Entering the 1970s

By 1969 Ronald McDonald was "speaking" more than 25 languages, and he was recognized by 96 percent of all American children—a major accomplishment for any advertising icon. In 1970 McDonald's moved its $5 million account to Needham, Harper & Steers, Inc., which launched the highly successful "You deserve a break today" ad campaign in 1971. It was a campaign generated largely on the basis of research that showed that many families chose McDonald's because of the convenience it afforded housewives and parents. McDonald's sales reached $587 million, earned from almost 1,600 restaurants in all 50 states and four other countries. In 1999 *Advertising Age* listed the "You deserve a break today" campaign fifth on its list of the 100 top ad campaigns of the 20th century, while the jingle ranked first on the magazine's list of best jingles.

The first McDonald's playland opened in Chula Vista, California, in 1971, and "McDonaldland" soon became the setting of a new series of commercials aimed at children and their parents. The company pioneered breakfast fast-food with the introduction of the Egg McMuffin in 1973 when market research indicated that customers would welcome a quick breakfast. Four years later, the company added a full breakfast line to the menu.

In 1974 McDonald's acted on Kroc's philosophy of "giving something back" to the community by opening the first Ronald McDonald House in Philadelphia, Pennsylvania. Such facilities have since been established across the United States, providing a welcome "home away from home" for the families of children undergoing treatment in nearby hospitals.

In 1974 the ad campaign theme, "McDonald's sure is good to have around," proved to be a modest success. A year later, the "Two all beef patties special sauce lettuce cheese pickles onions on a sesame seed bun" promotion introduced McDonald's most famous advertising jingle for the Big Mac. This rather long, but quite catchy piece echoed time and again in the ears of the millions who heard it on the radio and on television.

"We do it all for you," introduced in April 1975, was another blockbuster ad campaign from McDonald's. In that same year, McDonald's made a crucial marketing decision when it opened its first drive-through location. By 1996 drive-through sales accounted for half of McDonald's income in the United States.

In 1977 McDonald's president and chief executive officer (CEO), Fred Turner, was named chairman of the board, succeeding Ray Kroc, who was named senior chairman. Meanwhile, Keith Reinhard, the creative director who had guided the McDonald's campaigns, became president of the Needham ad agency in Chicago.

International Expansion

McDonald's made a big international push in the last three decades of the 20th century. Once most major European and Asian nations had been graced with the Golden Arches, the next goal of the company was to increase the number of restaurants in each of those nations and to open new sites in other countries. In 1976 the company's 4,000th outlet opened, in Montreal, Quebec; the new ad campaign was, "You, you're the one." In 1978 the giant fast-food chain chose the ad campaign theme "Nobody can do it like McDonald's can."

The 1980s proved to be a fast-paced decade for McDonald's. The efficiency of the restaurants' service, combined with an expanded menu, continued to draw customers. The fast-food chain—already entrenched in the suburbs—began to focus on urban centers, introducing new architectural structures, such as a floating McDonald's on the Mississippi River in St. Louis, Missouri, which opened in 1980. The early 1980s became known as the era of the "burger wars," as McDonald's and other fast-food chains launched aggressive advertising campaigns and slashed prices. Although competitors used advertisements to challenge McDonald's, its sales and market share continued to grow.

Despite many experts' claims that the fast-food industry in the 1980s was saturated, McDonald's continued to expand. Innovative promotions—such as the "When the U.S. wins, you win" giveaways during the 1980 Olympic Games (created by Needham)—proved to be a huge success. McDonald's celebrated its 25th anniversary in 1980, and that same year, Birdie, the "early bird," joined the cast of McDonaldland characters. The first tollway McDonald's opened (in DeKalb, Illinois) in 1981; and the first railroad station McDonald's opened in Philadelphia in 1983.

Then, after 11 years at Needham, McDonald's stunned the ad industry by moving its $75 million account to Leo Burnett USA in 1981. The move was a shock because it undermined the industry's often stated faith in the power of outstanding creative people. It was widely believed that Needham had done superior work. Burnett, on the other hand, had pursued a different strategy. Realizing that McDonald's was expanding rapidly into other countries, the agency won small pieces of the McDonald's business outside the United States. Using these outpost positions to show what Burnett could do, the agency pursued a strategy of what its CEO, Jack Kopp, called "strategic encirclement," and that strategy finally paid off.

In 1981 Burnett revived McDonald's most successful campaign: "You deserve a break today." In 1982 the American Marketing Association Achievement Award, the marketing profession's highest honor, was presented to McDonald's Corporation for excellence in marketing programs. "Together, McDonald's and you" was the new ad campaign theme in 1983. In June 1984 a more response-evoking ad theme was introduced: "It's a good time for the great taste of McDonald's."

Kroc's Influence

On 14 January 1984 Ray Kroc died, just as McDonald's broke $10 billion in sales. "McBlimp," the world's largest airship, appeared in skies over New York City in 1985, introducing the latest form of McDonald's advertising. The company sold its 70-billionth hamburger in 1988.

In 1989 Kroc was posthumously elected to the Advertising Hall of Fame in recognition of his special contributions to the advertising industry and the community at large. In 1999 *Advertising Age* placed Kroc at number 26 on its list of the top 100 advertising people of the century. Kroc fundamentally altered the eating habits of Americans and the world. "As he successfully advertised and championed quality/value for McDonald's burgers-fries-shakes, he raised fast-food standards," *Advertising Age* noted.

In 1990 *Life* magazine named Ray Kroc one of the 100 most important Americans of the 20th century. In that year the ad campaign theme, "Food, folks, and fun," was introduced. Although Needham had lost the McDonald's account in 1981, Reinhard never solicited a competing fast-food account to replace the business. Rather, he committed himself to winning back the McDonald's account. Substantial pieces of the business did return

Studies have shown that McDonald's Corporation's Ronald McDonald spokes-character, featured on a Happy Meal box in this 1992 advertisement from the "What You Want Is What You Get" campaign, is second only to Santa Claus in recognition by youngsters in the United States.
Courtesy of McDonald's Corporation.

for example, 7,030 restaurants in 89 countries produced sales of $14 billion. In addition, formerly communist nations in Eastern Europe began welcoming McDonald's restaurants, with sites opening in Moscow, Russia, in 1990 and in Warsaw, Poland in 1992. McDonald's also began operations in Beijing, China, in 1990. By 1996 McDonald's had developed a two-pronged strategy to reach children between the ages of two and seven years and the "tweens," spending $20 million on an ad campaign with five TV spots, a Happy Meal promotion, and a McWorld "Ninja-Zord" quiz.

McDonald's did experience some high-profile marketing stumbles in the mid-1990s. The most notable slip occurred in 1996, when the company spent $200 million to introduce the Arch Deluxe in a campaign aimed at adults. The series of ads featured Ronald McDonald looking and acting adult, grooving to disco, shooting pool, and wearing a business suit. The Arch Deluxe sandwich promotion failed to reverse stagnant domestic sales, however, and the venture risked the franchise's favorable positioning with kids.

In 1996 McDonald's boasted nearly 20,000 restaurants in 101 countries and signed a ten-year contract with the Walt Disney Company, making it McDonald's primary promotion partner in the restaurant business. Also in 1996, Burnett won a Reggie Award from the Promotion Marketing Association for McDonald's "Mighty Morphin Power Rangers" movie promotion, which was, in turn, supplemented by additional McDonald's super-hero promotions that summer, which linked the fast-food chain with 20th Century-Fox, Saban Entertainment, and their agency partners. In addition to the failed Arch Deluxe, McDonald's introduced the Crispy Chicken Deluxe, the Fish Filet Deluxe, and the Grilled Chicken Deluxe in 1996, and the restaurants added bagel sandwiches to the menu in 1999.

Marketing Changes

In 1997 McDonald's embarked on an ambitious plan to transform itself into a more nimble local competitor. In July the company reorganized into five geographic divisions, each with its own management team, to move the process of decision-making closer to the company's U.S. restaurants. Funds from McDonald's nearly $600 million annual advertising budget were funneled from national to local coffers. Whereas some 75 cents of every ad dollar had been earmarked for network TV campaigns in 1996, that figure dropped to about 50 cents in 1999. The chain also doubled the number of weeks it devoted to local marketing. Some observers suggested that the local emphasis on advertising would help McDonald's; others thought that the brand name would be eroded if it were not supported by heavy national advertising.

Also in 1997 McDonald's switched ad agencies in an effort to revive faltering markets, giving lead status on its account back to DDB Needham Worldwide, Chicago, after 15 years at Leo Burnett USA, Chicago. However, the latter continued to handle McDonald's advertising aimed at children. The change was widely considered a major personal victory for Reinhard, who had persisted in his attempts to win back the business since 1981.

to what was then DDB Needham Worldwide in 1990, with more to come later in the decade.

Burnett negotiated with the cable TV sports channel ESPN for Burnett's clients—including McDonald's—to spend $6 million advertising on ESPN's Sunday National Football League Package. In 1991 Burnett also offered a season-long added-value commitment that included billboards and other enhancements. The ad campaign theme, introduced in 1992, was "What you want is what you get at McDonald's today."

In 1993 McDonald's switched its "tweens" advertising account, targeting youths 8 to 13 years of age, from DDB Needham Worldwide to Leo Burnett USA. The latter began promoting the after-4 P.M. menu and special price programs. In line with a larger advertising trend of targeting the lucrative market of (now middle-aged) baby boomers, McDonald's launched campaigns in the 1990s aimed at more mature consumers. In 1995 the chain introduced the "Have you had your break today?" tag line.

McDonald's international operations were playing an increasingly important role in the company's financial fortunes. In 1995,

The campaign "My McDonald's" was introduced in 1997; "Did somebody say McDonald's?" followed in 1998. Company insiders, Wall Street analysts, and franchise owners noted that these changes, along with the increased emphasis on local marketing, made the fast-food giant a stronger player in the highly competitive $100 billion U.S. fast-food market.

McDonald's began supporting the Olympics at the 1968 Winter Games. The chain was a worldwide sponsor for the 1998 Winter Games in Nagano, Japan, and the 2000 Summer Games in Sydney, Australia.

By 1999 McDonald's began focusing on "can't miss" promotions aimed at children and families. Promotions included a campaign highlighting the chain's signature Big Mac sandwich and a Teenie Beanie Babies effort, a tie-in with Walt Disney. The latter was MacDonald's third offer of the plush toys; this promotion, while targeted at children, proved popular with all ages and became an annual occurrence. McDonald's also continued to be a major presence around the world at the end of the 20th century: when the Russian economy worsened during 1998 and 1999, McDonald's remained one of the last fast-food choices surviving in Moscow.

During the 1990s McDonald's served 30 million customers each day (18 million daily in the United States). The restaurant chain had become one of the world's great entrepreneurial organizations. Four out of every five restaurants worldwide were run by a franchisee or affiliate partner of the company. In addition, McDonald's was second only to Coca-Cola in terms of worldwide brand name recognition. (Coca-Cola is the only soft drink supplier for the fast-food giant.)

SAMMY R. DANNA

See also color plate in this volume

Four Decades of McDonald's Advertising Themes
1960: "All American menu—A hamburger, fries, and a shake"
1961: "Look for the Golden Arches"
1962: "Go for goodness at McDonald's"
1965: "McDonald's—Where quality starts fresh everyday"
1966: "McDonald's—the closest thing to home"
1967: "McDonald's is your kind of place"
1971: "You deserve a break today"
1974: "McDonald's sure is good to have around"
1975: "We do it all for you"
1976: "You, you're the one"
1979: "Nobody can do it like McDonald's can"
1981: "You deserve a break today"
"Nobody makes your day like McDonald's can"
1983: "Together, McDonald's and you"
1984: "It's a good time for the great taste of McDonald's"
1989: "Good time, great taste"
1990: "Food, folks, and fun"
1992: "What you want is what you get at McDonald's today"
1995: "Have you had your break today?"
1997: "My McDonald's"
1998: "Did somebody say McDonald's?"

Further Reading
Derdak, Thomas, and John Simley, editors, *International Directory of Company Histories,* vol. 7, edited by Paula Kepos, Detroit, Michigan, and London: St. James, 1993

Kroc, Ray, and Robert Anderson, *Grinding It Out: The Making of McDonald's,* Chicago: Regnery, 1977

Love, John F., *McDonald's: Behind the Arches,* New York: Bantam, 1986; London: Bantam, 1989; revised edition, New York: Bantam, 1995

McDonald, Ronald L., *The Complete Hamburger: The History of America's Favorite Sandwich,* Secaucus, New Jersey: Carol, 1997

Sivulka, Juliann, *Soap, Sex, and Cigarettes: A Cultural History of American Advertising,* Belmont, California: Wadsworth, 1998

Smart, Barry, editor, *Resisting McDonaldization,* London: Sage, 1999

Toerpe, Kathleen D., "Small Fry, Big Spender: McDonald's and the Rise of a Children's Consumer Culture, 1955–1985," PhD. diss., Loyola University of Chicago, 1994

Media

In advertising the term *media* refers to communication vehicles such as newspapers, magazines, radio, television, billboards, direct mail, and the Internet. Advertisers use media to convey commercial messages to their target audiences, and the media depend to different degrees on advertising revenues to cover the cost of their operations. In 2001 U.S. advertising expenditure in media was estimated at $233.7 billon, of which television accounted for 22.5 percent, direct mail 19.8 percent, newspapers 19.3 percent, radio 7.7 percent, Yellow Pages 5.8 percent, magazines 4.7 percent, and the Internet 1.8 percent, with other media accounting for the remainder.

The media are usually classified into either mass or niche media. Newspapers, magazines, television, and radio are considered mass media because they deliver messages to a widespread, anonymous audience. There were 1,483 daily U.S. newspapers in 2000, with total circulation of 47.2 million on weekdays and 59.9

million on Sundays. In September 2001 the five largest U.S. newspapers were *USA Today,* the *Wall Street Journal,* the *New York Times,* the *Los Angeles Times,* and the *Washington Post.* There were 3,188 consumer and farm magazines, with paid circulation of 399 million. In the beginning of 2000, there were 1,248 commercial television stations and 10,220 commercial radio stations in the United States. The wide coverage of the mass media makes them ideal vehicles for advertisers who need to reach a large audience.

Advertising media such as cable television and direct mail are often viewed as "niche" media because they reach a narrowly defined audience with unique demographic characteristics or special interests. With 54 or more cable channels available in 62.1 percent of U.S. wired cable subscriber households in 2000, for example, audiences can tune in to CNN for continuous coverage of events around the world, to Home & Garden TV for information on home improvement, or to Cartoon Network for children's programming. Direct mail, the second largest advertising medium in the United States in 2001, offers more flexibility in terms of precision targeting and content customization. Direct mail can be used to reach almost every consumer with personalized messages.

The Internet has emerged as a medium for marketing and advertising since 1994. The Internet is different from conventional advertising media in several respects. First, it can serve as not only a communications channel but also a transaction and distribution channel. Consumers can get information and make purchases and payments all through the Internet. No other medium can accomplish these marketing functions instantly, without resorting to other means. Second, the Internet is by nature interactive. Users can initiate a shopping process by visiting a Web site and then clicking on hyper-linked text for more information. It is a two-way communication, with the Internet serving as a provider of customized content that meets an individual's needs. Third, it has the capacity for multimedia content. It can carry not only text and graphics but also audio and video content. The multimedia nature of the Internet is suitable for high-impact advertising. The Internet has become an integral part of the media mix for many advertisers, and new forms of advertising have filled the World Wide Web landscape, including animated banner ads, sponsor logos, interstitials, "advertorials," "advertainment," and 3-D visualization.

Audience Measurement

Audience size is the currency of advertising media. For national television ratings in the United States, Nielsen Media Research uses a sample of more than 5,000 households containing more than 13,000 people. Nielsen technicians install metering equipment called People Meters on TV sets, VCRs, cable boxes, and even satellite dishes in each sample home. The meters automatically keep track of times when the sets are turned on and what they are tuned to. Each member of a sample household is required to push a button when he or she begins and stops watching television. Information from the meters is combined with set-tuning records to generate Nielsen TV ratings. A rating point represents 1,022,000 households, or 1 percent of the estimated 102.2 million TV homes in the United States.

To measure audiences for local television stations, Nielsen gathers information from diaries in which a sample of TV viewers record their viewing behavior during a measurement week. The diary measurement is conducted in all 210 TV markets in the United States four times a year, during "sweeps" months—February, May, July, and November. According to Nielsen, in 1999 an average home watched television for seven hours and 24 minutes per day. The Arbitron Company measures radio audiences in more than 260 markets by collecting more than 1 million diaries to compile estimates of listening behavior. Research indicated that in 1999 an adult in the United States spent an average of two hours and 48 minutes daily listening to radio.

Readership in print media is measured by surveys or estimated by circulation. The Audit Bureau of Circulations provides data on more than 1,500 daily and weekly newspapers and 1,000 periodicals in the United States and Canada. In addition, Mediamark Research, Inc., and Simmons Market Research Bureau use what is called a "recent reading method" for measuring magazine readership. A sample of respondents is shown individual cards with magazine logotypes and asked if they have read the magazines within the past month and where they did so. Demographics and product usage also are collected from the respondents to generate an audience profile for each magazine. A similar method, asking what was read the day before, is sometimes used to measure the readership of a newspaper. On average, a single copy of a newspaper in 2000 was read by 1.88 or more people.

Billboard advertising audiences are measured through driver surveys. A sample of drivers is asked about the routes traveled as shown on a map, and a transparent overlay is then placed on the top of each driver's map to reveal billboard structures that were passed. The number of passengers in a vehicle is estimated by a vehicle load factor, 1.35 adults per vehicle.

Internet audiences are often measured through surveys and tracking. There are two common tracking methods—Web-centric and user-centric. The Web-centric method uses log files on a Web server to calculate the number of people who have visited the site. This method tends to underestimate the actual number of visitors because of a network practice called "caching," by which Internet service providers store copies of popular Web pages on their own servers for quick access. The user-centric method requires the installation of proprietary metering software on a computer in a sample household or office. The software automatically tracks the computer usage and Web sites that are visited on a continuous basis. The information is combined with the user's demographics to generate audience profiles for various Web sites. Telephone surveys also are used to assess the number of Internet users. For instance, a survey conducted in 2001 by the UCLA Center for Communication Policy found that 72.3 percent of Americans had online access, up from 66.9 percent in 2000.

Media Costs

Advertising rates are more stable for print media than broadcast media largely because print media can adjust the number of advertising pages on an issue-to-issue basis, while broadcast media have a fixed amount of daily programming hours. Thus, demand by advertisers has a stronger impact on the rates for broadcast time. Newspaper space is usually sold according to rate cards; buyers of large volumes get discounted rates. Magazine space is sold similarly. Advertising rates for radio and television are normally determined through negotiation and often vary by the time of day. A 30-second spot on network television costs the most in prime time (8:00 P.M. to 11:00 P.M. in the Eastern U.S. time zone) and the least during daytime (10:00 A.M. to 4:00 P.M.). According to Optimum Media, in the third quarter of 1999, a 30-second commercial on U.S. network television cost $190,000 in prime time but $21,960 in daytime.

Advertisers use CPM (cost per thousand impressions) and CPP (cost per rating point) to compare media costs. CPM is used for both print and electronic media, while CPP is more popular for electronic media. CPM is calculated by multiplying the unit cost of a media vehicle by 1,000 and dividing the result by the audience size of the vehicle. The unit cost of a media vehicle is the cost for a single ad placement in that vehicle. For example, if a 30-second commercial in a TV program costs $5,000 and the program has an audience of 250,000, then CPM for the commercial will be $20. CPP is calculated by dividing the unit cost of the media vehicle by the rating of the vehicle. If a 30-second commercial in a TV program costs $5,000 and the program has a rating of 10 in the market, CPP for the commercial will be $500. CPP can also be used to compare newspaper or magazine costs if the audience is described as a percentage.

Media Planning and Buying

"Media planning" is the process of selecting time and space in various media for advertising in order to accomplish marketing objectives. Media planners often use three terms in describing a planning process: objectives, strategy, and tactics. A media objective states what the planner wishes to accomplish. It is usually specified in terms of the target audience, reach, and frequency. The target audience is often defined by demographics, product usage and psychographics. Reach refers to the unduplicated proportion of an audience that is exposed to a media schedule (not necessarily to the advertising message) at least once during a designated time period (usually four weeks). Frequency refers to the number of times within a given period of time an audience is exposed to a media schedule. A frequency of 3.0, for example, means that the target audience is exposed to a media schedule three times during a given period of time. Of course, not all audience members are exposed exactly three times; some may be exposed more than three times and some less. A frequency distribution shows how many audience members are exposed at each level of frequency. With a frequency distribution, a media planner can determine effective frequency and effective reach. Effective frequency is defined as the level of frequency that is necessary to achieve the desired communication goals. Effective reach is the reach at the level of effective fre-

quency. Gross rating points (GRPs) are the product of reach and frequency, representing the total gross delivery of a media schedule to the target audience.

A media strategy specifies the means for achieving the media objectives. A strategic decision is how to allocate the media budget geographically; that is, deciding in which markets to advertise and how much to spend in each of these markets. In making these decisions, the media planner is guided by past sales and market shares of a brand in different markets as well as future expectations. Category and brand development indices are often used for these purposes. A defensive media strategy allocates more money in a market where sales are high, whereas an offensive strategy allocates more money in a market where sales are low but there is potential to grow. Media class strategy refers to the allocation of the budget to different media classes. Budget allocation in media classes focuses on matching media audiences with the target audience in addition to creative considerations. For instance, television may be the best media class if both audio and video are present in a commercial, while magazines may be more effective if detailed copy is required. The third strategic decision involves advertising scheduling over a campaign period. "Continuity" refers to advertising on a regular and constant basis throughout the campaign period. "Flighting" means advertising intermittently, a period of advertising followed by a period of no advertising at all. "Pulsing" is a combination of both continuity and flighting, periodically building high levels of advertising on the top of lower yet continuous levels of advertising. The seasonality of sales often guides scheduling of advertising.

Media tactics consist primarily of the activities of selecting media vehicles in the most cost-effective manner to ensure the successful execution of media strategies. Among the criteria for selecting media vehicles are target audience delivery, cost efficiency, the editorial environment, advertising clutter, reproduction quality, and ad positions with the vehicle. Media planning software is often used along with media cost data and audience information to select and compare media vehicles. Contingency plans are often created to meet unexpected changes in the marketplace.

Media plans are implemented through media buyers. Media buyers are professionals who are knowledgeable in estimating media costs and skillful in negotiating rates. Different media vehicles have different rate cards and discount policies. Some may offer added values such as combination rates, merchandising, and event marketing. Faced with such a complicated media environment, media buyers need creative ways of calculating and comparing media costs. Many media vehicles are flexible in terms of pricing, and a savvy negotiator can purchase the same space or time at a much lower price than others even when all contract terms are equal. Media buyers also monitor the implementation of a media plan to assure its value is fully realized.

HAIRONG LI

Further Reading

Barban, Arnold M., Steven M. Cristol, and Frank J. Kopec, *Essentials of Media Planning: A Marketing Viewpoint,*

Chicago: Crain, 1976; 3rd edition, Lincolnwood, Illinois: NTC, 1993

Jugenheimer, Donald W., Arnold M. Barban, and Peter B. Turk, *Advertising Media: Strategy and Tactics,* Dubuque, Iowa: Brown and Benchmark, 1992

Karten, Tammy, editor, *Marketer's Guide to Media,* New York: ASM, 2001

Katz, Helen, *The Media Handbook,* Lincolnwood, Illinois: NTC, 1995

Rossiter, John R., and Peter J. Danaher, *Advanced Media Planning,* Norwell, Massachusetts: Kluwer, 1998

Sissors, Jack Z., and E. Reynold Petray, *Advertising Media Planning,* Chicago: Crain, 1976; 5th edition, by Sissors and Lincoln Bumba, Lincolnwood, Illinois: NTC, 1996

Media Agency

In 1975 the list of independent media-buying companies in the *Standard Directory of Advertising Agencies,* the comprehensive listing of U.S. agencies, filled barely six pages. By the end of the century, the names filled more than 40 pages, and the list did not even include the giant, semi-independent media-buying companies spun off from the largest agencies that functioned as units within the major advertising holding companies. The rise of the independent media-buying business, operating outside the structure of the traditional ad agency media department, and the divestiture of those departments from the agency system were two of the more unexpected advertising trends to emerge in the later years of the 20th century.

Traditionally, the media-buying function was among the most basic duties of the full-service ad agency. Indeed, the first modern agencies of the late 19th century grew out of the space buyer's function, as buyers and sellers of magazine and newspaper space began to offer copy and layout services to clients and, later, research and marketing expertise. As the independent structure of the ad agency evolved, the media department developed for the purpose of planning the most efficient ways possible of delivering the clients' advertising messages. This meant determining the target audience, analyzing audience and readership data provided by various media, allocating spending between broadcast and print, negotiating the best rates, contracting the purchases, and paying the bills. Because agency income was based on commissions from media purchases, the media department became the financial heart of every agency, a labor-intensive numbers factory of data and dollars whose costs were absorbed by the agency as part of the general overhead of doing business and never passed on to the client.

A number of smaller advertising agencies served local clients whose spending never approached the levels necessary to support network broadcast buys. These agencies, which might only provide creative or account services, as well as advertisers that did not use agencies at all, had no media departments. They relied on independent media-buying companies to fill that vital function, particularly when it came to placing radio and television spots. During the 1950s and 1960s when such companies were beginning to spring up, they had a reputation as the "back alley rogues" of the business, according to *Advertising Age,* doing business informally and sometimes off the books entirely in the manner of an underground economy. "Time banking" was a common device in which a time buyer might give a local station something of value (e.g., free products or premiums) in return for a multiple of that value in the form of a time credit. The buyer could then charge back the amount of the credit to a client at full retail (without disclosing the credit) and pocket the entire payment. Although it was technically legal, it did not encourage independent media judgment.

In the late 1960s, the major ad agencies were beginning to feel challenged by independent media buyers. Some independents confined themselves to specialties. Democratic Associates, for example, worked only on political campaigns. But by the early 1970s some were beginning to bill substantial amounts: Clifford A. Botway, Inc., $42 million; Independent Media Services, Inc. (IMS), $49 million; and National Outdoor Advertising Bureau, Inc., $70 million. Several big agencies commissioned studies on the impact of the independents. For a time, the Ted Bates Company considered spinning off its own media department as an independent but decided that it made no sense to do so. The first major agency operation to compete in the independent arena was the Interpublic Group of Companies, which set up Communication Counselors Network, Inc., in 11 cities.

In 1969, the same year Botway and IMS were founded, Walter Staab, the vice president at Bates who had written the agency's independent media study, joined with Robert Frank of CBS and Stanley Moger of Storer Broadcasting, Inc., to form SFM Media, one of several early independents to operate according to agency-level business standards. It did no barter or time banking, disclosed all billings, and targeted blue-chip clients. When Herb Maneloveg, vice president of media at Batten Barton Durstine & Osborn (BBDO), agreed to become SFM president, he not only brought credibility to SFM but also to the entire independent media movement, which, according to *Advertising Age* in 1970, was "radically changing the media buying scene."

While the range of independent media service companies grew over the next 20 years, the basic structure did not fundamentally change. Clients were still being served by their agency media departments or by independents, as they chose. By the late 1980s, however, the agency structure was changing though mergers, acquisitions, and the creation of huge holding companies that oversaw many of the world's leading agency brands. Media departments that once had competed against each other were now becoming siblings within large advertising organizations. The media provider landscape was also changing, as Fox became the first viable fourth TV broadcast network since the demise of the DuMont Television Network in 1955. The UPN and WB networks would soon follow, along with many more options via cable television. Beyond that was the less understood, less tested power of the Internet. Advertisers and agencies increasingly faced new-media alternatives that seemed to require knowledge more specialized than a traditional "below-the-line" media department could provide.

As clients surveyed the shifting relationships between once independent agencies, they also began looking at fresh options in media buying. At the same time, senior media executives within agencies were also rethinking old ways. One concern that began to receive particular attention was the relationship of the media department to its parent agency. Under the traditional system, media was bundled into the package of agency services. If an agency lost an account because of poor creative work, the media department would automatically lose, too, even though it may have been doing superior work. A good media department was entirely dependent upon the fortunes of the agency for its clients and could not build its own independent client base.

This had been one of the problems at N.W. Ayer & Sons in the 1980s. Coming off a series of very good years in the 1970s, the momentum slowed in the 1980s, costing the agency such dependable clients as DeBeers Consolidated Mines, despite the high evaluations it accorded the Ayer media operation. In 1993 a business plan was developed that called for a more independent relationship between department and agency. The idea was to "unbundle" media from the menu of agency services and set it free. The following year, a unit called the Media Edge was created within N.W. Ayer. When Ayer was acquired by the MacManus Group in 1996, a major client conflict loomed between Ayer's AT&T Corporation account and the SBC Communications account at MacManus subsidiary D'Arcy Masius Benton & Bowles (DMB&B). Executives at Media Edge suggested that the unit be sold to another company in order to keep AT&T's media account; AT&T at the time wanted to continue working with Media Edge Managing Director Beth Gordon. As a result, Media Edge was sold for $3.5 million to Young & Rubicam (Y&R), where the media shop grew as a revenue center serving both Y&R clients and its own.

As the original Media Edge business plan was being written in 1993, Irwin Gotlieb of DMB&B was organizing the spin-off of TeleVest from DMB&B to become MediaVest. Over the next five years the trend to "unbundle" media operations reached a critical mass. The Leo Burnett Company launched Starcom as its media unit in 1998. In 2000, with the merger of DMB&B and Burnett, the two media companies were combined to become Starcom MediaVest Worldwide, the media holding company within the Bcom3 Group, although each unit remained separately branded and either competed or cooperated depending on the need. It promptly picked up $2.9 billion in consolidated media planning business for General Motors Corporation (GM), while the creative assignments remained within the existing GM agency lineup (which included Burnett and DMB&B, plus Interpublic's Campbell-Ewald).

In 1997 the WPP Group began the process of melding the media departments of its J. Walter Thompson Company (acquired in 1987) and Ogilvy & Mather (acquired in 1989). Their combined resources became the basis of MindShare, which first established operations in Europe, Asia, and Latin America. By the time MindShare opened an office in New York City in April 2000, it had become the largest media specialist company both in the United States and the world, billing $6.546 million and $17 million, respectively.

At the beginning of 2001, nine of the top ten media buying organizations in the United States were unbundled spin-offs of major agencies. In order of U.S. billings, these were (1) Mindshare, a unit of WPP; (2) OMD Media from Omnicom (the media arm for DDB, BBDO, and TBWA); (3) Initiative Media from Ammirati Puris Lintas Worldwide, a unit of Interpublic; (4) Universal McCann from McCann-Erickson Worldwide, also an Interpublic unit; (5) Starcom Worldwide, with roots in Leo Burnett and a unit of Bcom3; (6) TN Media from True North Communications; (7) MediaVest from DMB&B, which was merged with Starcom in 2000); (8) Media Edge from Y&R; and (10) Optimedia, part of Publicis. Only the ninth-ranked Zenith Media Services was not a spin-off; it was owned jointly by Cordiant Communications Group and Publicis Group. SFM Media, which had no agency roots in its history, ranked 11th after being acquired by Havas and merged with Media Planning Group to become SFM Media/MPG in 2000.

The increasing consolidation at the advertising holding company level, however, is likely to narrow the field of major media agencies still further. Since 2000, True North has become part of the Interpublic Group of Companies, which in 2001 formed Magna Global, an aggregate negotiation arm across all the Interpublic media buying operations, designed to amass negotiating clout in dealing with the huge media conglomerates. And in 2002 Bcom3 announced its intention to be acquired by Publicis, a move expected to bring further consolidation to the field of media agencies.

Among the major advertising holding companies at the turn of the 21st century, Interpublic ranked a strong number one, a position that would become even more secure with its acquisition of TN Media in 2001. Not even WPP's acquisition of Y&R in 2000 pulled it ahead of Interpublic, although no one was likely to challenge their top-ranked positions for some time. Other leading holding companies included Bcom3, Grey Advertising, Publicis, Cordiant, and Aegis, parent of Carat and the only company without advertising agency holdings.

By the end of the 20th century, the media function had substantially separated itself from the top-tier agency lineup, as the parent ad organizations expanded the size and scope of their media shops through acquisitions, consolidations, and in some cases spin-offs into such specialties as Internet buying. While some media company billings continued to come from work done directly with advertisers without the involvement of an ad agency—the billings came to $27.3 billion in 1999, according to *Advertising Age*—the biggest area of growth was in the billings that media companies handled for agencies. Those billings grew to $28.5 billion in 1999. As for agencies, they continued to place media through their own media departments. In 1999 agency media department billings totaled $32.1 billion.

Early in the history of advertising, a separate independent media sector developed outside the traditional agency structure to serve the other side of the media equation—the sellers of broadcast time and publication space. The media representative, or rep, became the sales agent for many local media outlets outside major urban centers, companies that were too small to support a national sales staff but still seeking national advertiser business. Media reps would prove useful to major ad agencies wishing to reach only certain geographical areas through spot advertising (buying time or space on selected local stations and newspapers in desired markets). Media reps saw to it that the major New York City and Chicago, Illinois, ad agencies were aware of their local station and publication clients around the country and of how they could deliver desired audiences. The first media rep firm in the United States was the E. Katz Special Advertising Agency, of New York City, established in 1888 by Emmanuel Katz, who two years before had started a company with William Randolph Hearst to sell *San Francisco Examiner* newspaper advertising in the East. The company expanded into radio in the 1930s, representing ten stations. A number of other rep firms followed and worked closely with agency media departments and more recently with media specialist companies. They have remained a large presence in the advertising business. But as sellers, they remained outside the modern purchasing networks.

JOHN MCDONOUGH

Further Reading

Cuneo, Alice Z., "Tradition-Bound Major Shops Shudder at Idea of Unbundling," *Advertising Age* (25 July 1994)

Endicott, R. Craig, "Media Specialists Shine," *Advertising Age* (24 April 2000)

Kelly, Keith J., "Sell-offs Could Unbundle Media Ziff, Viacom Packages May Be Split Up," *Advertising Age* (27 June 1994)

Mandese, Joe, "Unbundling Media Unit to Compete with Indies," *Advertising Age* (12 September 1994)

Rothenberg, Randall, "Unbundling in Entertainment Doesn't Threaten TV Revenues," *Advertising Age* (24 July 2000)

Wentz, Laurel, "Media Players Bulk Up to Stay Competitive," *Advertising Age* (13 July 2001)

Mediamark Research, Inc.

As of 2001 Mediamark Research, Inc. (MRI), was one of the largest magazine readership research and demographic/psychographic modeling companies in the United States. Its traditional competitor has been the Simmons Market Research Bureau. Although the two companies address many of the same questions, they use different methodologies and thus frequently come up with widely divergent results, pointing up the inexactness of reducing consumer behavior to a science. Both companies are widely respected, however, a fact that led one advertising executive in 1985 to point out the dilemma of never knowing for sure which one was right.

MRI is based in New York City and is a leading U.S. syndicated magazine research company. It is a wholly owned subsidiary of United Business Media and claims to be the only national multimedia audience research service to be accredited by the Media Rating Council, Inc., the organization whose mandate is to maintain industry confidence and credibility in audience research.

Mediamark was founded in January 1979 as Magazine Research, Inc., by Timothy Joyce, Philip Wenig, and Alain Tessier. Joyce, a graduate of the University of Cambridge, was a founder of the British Market Research Bureau's Target Group Index. The British Market Research Bureau, at that time a subsidiary of the J. Walter Thompson Company, later became a subsidiary of the British holding company the WPP Group.

MRI moved around a good deal in its early period. The company originally set up operations in Wenig's New York City apartment, then moved to a borrowed office on 23rd Street, and then into the San Carlos Hotel on 50th Street. By the end of 1979 MRI moved to two floors of a narrow corner building at 44th Street and Madison Avenue.

Joyce was the principal force behind MRI in the beginning, designing and defending its product and ultimately making it work. In 1981 the company added the measurement of advertised goods and services usage to the survey, and Magazine Research, Inc., became Mediamark Research, Inc. MRI's basic service menu was in place and the company became the U.S. research subsidiary of Mills & Allen International, a London, England-based financial and media services company.

In August 1985 MRI acquired Nabscan National Scanning Services, which had been founded in 1975 by the Newspaper

Courtesy of Mediamark Research Inc.

Advertising Bureau. Nabscan was an early entrant into the field of product movement tracking through the use of Universal Product Code (UPC) emblems and checkout scanners located in 900 supermarkets by 1985. Nabscan's principal competitor at the time was A.C. Nielsen Company's ScanTrak, which had equipment in 150 supermarkets. The acquisition of Nabscan boosted MRI revenue more than 23 percent to $9.5 million and enabled it to speed tracking study results commissioned by advertiser and supermarket clients from four to six weeks to seven to 10 days.

MRI collects and analyzes data on consumer demographics and tracks product and brand usage as well as exposure to all forms of advertising media, linking its data over the years to the Prizm, Acorn, Vision, and Clusterplus geodemographic models as well as the VALS psychographic index of values and lifestyle types. Major clients for MRI data include magazines, television, and other media; some 450 advertising agencies (including 89 of the top 100, according to MRI); and manufacturers and marketers, which use MRI date to help guide product launches, line extensions, and brand repositionings.

Since 1979 the company has also continuously studied the adult consumer population (all persons 18 and older) of the United States, surveying the demographics, product usage, and media exposure in the contiguous 48 states. The 13,000 respondents MRI polls (the numbers have varied over the years) are selected on a strict area probability basis. "A computer list of approximately 90 million households is merged with other sources necessary to construct a properly stratified sample," according to company literature. It divides its sample into three sections: metropolitan areas; nonmetropolitan counties; and ten major U.S. markets—New York City; Los Angeles, California; Chicago, Illinois; Philadelphia, Pennsylvania; San Francisco, California; Boston, Massachusetts; Detroit, Michigan; Washington, D.C.; Cleveland, Ohio; and Dallas-Fort Worth, Texas.

Each of the sample sections contains a number of designated household "clusters," selected according to various methods. In rural areas, clusters are defined by the random selection of a single household address and consist of that dwelling and several that follow in geographical sequence. In metro and suburban areas, each specific address is listed. MRI representatives interview (when possible) one adult in each household between the initial and final address in the cluster, including any unlisted or newly constructed homes that are in the sample. "Each listed household is predesignated with the sex of the prospective respondent," MRI explains in its basic literature. "If the household does not have any adult member of the predesignated sex, then the available respondent is selected. This is done in such a way that men and women constitute, in effect, separate samples of randomly selected individuals."

The completed MRI sample consists of more than 25,000 respondents, the company says, and each year the pool is completely redrawn, with 13,000 new respondents entering the survey every six months. About 2,400 new clusters are selected yearly from a constantly updated master list. Two six-month waves of fieldwork are done each year involving about 13,000 people. These include a combination of face-to-face interviews, which focus on demographics and media usage, and questionnaires, which are left behind and cover personal and household usage of some 500 product categories and services and 6,000 brands.

Since 1979 Mediamark Research, Inc., based in New York City, has conducted continuous studies of consumer behavior.
Courtesy of Mediamark Research, Inc.

Many techniques are used to gather data. Typically, however, households are notified by mail in advance that they will be contacted by an MRI interviewer. As many as six attempts are made to contact hard-to-reach subjects. Specialists contact non-English-speaking consumers. Each interview runs about an hour, and respondents are given $20 for their time, which includes a questionnaire to be returned by mail. Other special tools and reports include business-to-business, Upper Deck (affluent market), teen market, and the Cable Report.

Timothy Joyce died in 1997. In June 2000 Kathleen D. Love replaced David C. Bender as president and chief operating officer after Bender left MRI to join sister company Audits & Surveys Worldwide, Inc.

NANCY ENGELHARDT AND JOHN McDONOUGH

Further Reading

Abrahamson, David, editor, *The American Magazine: Research Perspectives and Prospects*, Ames: Iowa State University Press, 1995

Gunter, Barrie, *Media Research Methods: Measuring Audiences, Reactions, and Impact*, London and Thousand Oaks, California: Sage, 2000

Hay, James, Lawrence Grossberg, and Ellen Wartella, editors, *The Audience and Its Landscape*, Boulder, Colorado: Westview, 1996

Lazer, William, *Handbook of Demographics for Marketing and Advertising: Sources and Trends on the U.S. Consumer*, Lexington, Massachusetts: Lexington Books, 1987

Moores, Shaun, *Interpreting Audiences: The Ethnography of Media Consumption*, London and Thousand Oaks, California: Sage, 1993

Medicine Show

The North American medicine show was an itinerant form of marketing that flourished in American small towns and rural areas in the 19th century by combining entertainment with the sale of pills and potions of dubious medicinal value. The entrepreneurs who made and sold these quack remedies developed an impressive arsenal of promotional techniques.

Derided as hucksters, grifters, or pitchmen, these "con men" could trace their roots back to the mountebanks who worked the market fairs in Europe during the Middle Ages. Today their counterparts promote patent medicines, psychic hot lines, and therapeutic devices through TV commercials and infomercials. Although traveling medicine shows first showed up in America as early as the 1700s, it was in the last five decades of the 19th century that they enjoyed the greatest popularity. The Pure Food and Drug Act of 1906 sounded their death knell, and by 1920 few survived. The last big splash was the success of "The Hadacol Caravan," which toured with big-name entertainers to promote Dudley J. LeBlanc's tonic (composed of B vitamins, honey, and alcohol) across the South and Southwest in 1950 and 1951.

After the Civil War, makers of patent medicines, who were already advertising extensively, regarded touring shows as living billboards. First among the major manufacturers who capitalized on the strategy, John A. Hamlin mounted his own touring company in the 1870s to sell Hamlin's Wizard Oil: "The great medical conqueror." The performers wore frock coats, silk hats, and spats and dropped in to sing with church choirs. At the other end of the scale were "low pitch men," who sold samples out of a satchel mounted on a tripod.

There were three broad themes among the traveling shows. First were those who capitalized upon the public's image of Quak-ers as gentle and honest folk; they dressed in fawn-colored clothing, wore wide-brimmed, low-crowned hats and called each other "thee," "thou," and "brother." So-called Oriental healers were popular because the Far East symbolized mystery and exotic wisdom. Using names such as "Lotus Blossom," some pretenders claimed to have escaped from China or Tibet. But the greatest crowd-pleasers were the "Indian" medicine men, because Wild West shows had idealized Native Americans as "noble savages" who understood nature's secrets.

Based upon practical psychology, the strategies of these "pitch doctors" varied to suit the clientele. Never far from one of its key sources of performers, the circus, a medicine show usually was preceded by some sort of spectacle to gather a crowd. Major shows were heralded by a parade down Main Street, with a band, if one was available. A huckster working solo on the frontier might hire an open cab and in it seat a boy whose head he had wrapped in a red bandanna. Then he would drive around town, standing up and waving a huge butcher knife while announcing loudly, "Hurry down to the park corner, where you can see the biggest free show on earth. The great decapitation act, which has mystified millions. It's free for everybody. Hurry, hurry, or you'll be too late."

Because minor discomfort focused the audience's attention, and thereby increased sales, an outdoor site was better than a hall, and a street corner where loiterers could be drawn in was ideal. The opening entertainment might consist of slapstick comedy, a balladeer accompanied by a banjo player, or Indians chanting and dancing in front of a teepee. When the "doctor" appeared, he was likely to address the audience as "my friends" and state his objectives: first, to win their good will by sharing the latest medical

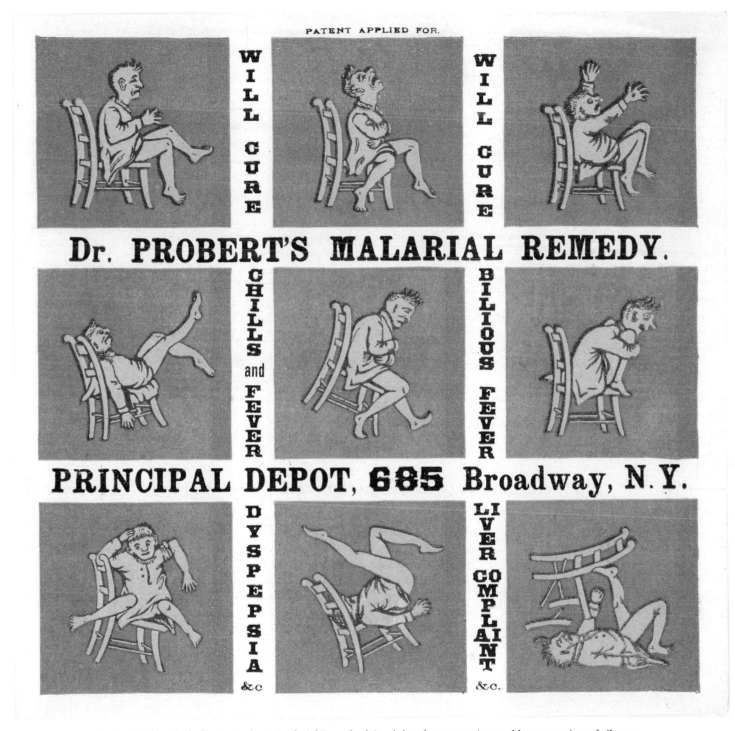

This 1881 broadside for Dr. Probert's Malarial Remedy claimed that the preparation could cure a variety of ailments.

marvel with them; and then to accomplish the surest kind of advertising in the form of satisfied customers.

Savvy practitioners paid attention to technical details: good lighting was important, and the position of the platform had to enable the speaker to get close to his audience. The experienced spieler carefully watched the changing expressions of the crowd in order to know when to make the sale. A stereotyped message was the general rule: "Tell it to them until the telephone and telegraph lines know it by heart. Then you'll start doing business." But the more successful spielers were able to vary their approach and even ad lib when needed.

As licensing and regulations became stricter near the turn of the century, more sophisticated grifters teamed up with an "examiner," a medical doctor who could present bona fide credentials despite having a drinking problem or some other disability that prevented him from carrying on a settled practice. The M.D. not only conferred an air of legitimacy but also brought in more money. Every package of medicine sold would have a ticket attached that entitled the holder to a so-called full, complete, and scientific examination performed by a qualified physician. The diagnosis varied to fit the patient, but its tenor was always the same: more "medicine" was needed. If the examiner discovered some malady he could treat, he would quote a large fee (usually an odd amount, laboriously calculated). A combination of fear and pride often inspired the patient to come up with the money.

The most famous and highly regarded of the touring shows was sent out by the Kickapoo Indian Medicine Company, organized in 1881 by two men, John Healey and Charles Bigelow, who had no connection to the Indian tribe. In their heyday the "Kicks" annually sent out more than 70 carnival companies, most of which included an Indian "brave" and maybe even a woman with a papoose. But the man selling the remedies was always an "Indian agent," dressed in buckskin. These remedies included a cough syrup (made of rum and molasses), a "worm expeller," and their best-seller, a concoction called "Kickapoo Indian Sagwa." Advertised as a cure for digestive problems and rheumatism, Sagwa (the word was made up) was supposed to be concocted by elders of the Kickapoo tribe, with a secret ingredient that defied laboratory analysis. Their ads included an endorsement from Buffalo Bill Cody, who claimed that Sagwa once saved his life and added, "An Indian would as soon be without his horse, gun, or blanket as without Sagwa." The company's advertising magazines also used a fabricated symbol of Indian healing, the princess "Little Bright Eye," whose sayings accompanied idealized illustrations of "Life and Scenes" among the Kickapoos at home in the West. The tours ended in 1914, but imitators persisted as late as the 1930s. Cartoonist Al Capp memorialized the brand in his popular comic strip "Li'l Abner" with allusions to "Kickapoo Joy Juice."

JERRY B. LINCECUM

Further Reading

Calhoun, Mary, *Medicine Show: Conning People and Making Them Like It,* New York: Harper and Row, 1976

Holbrook, Stewart, *The Golden Age of Quackery,* New York: Macmillan, 1959

McNamara, Brooks, *Step Right Up,* Garden City, New York: Doubleday, 1976; revised edition, Jackson: University Press of Mississippi, 1995

Stratton, Owen Tully, *Medicine Man,* Norman: University of Oklahoma Press, 1989

Young, James Harvey, *The Medical Messiahs: A Social History of Health Quackery in Twentieth-Century America,* Princeton, New Jersey: Princeton University Press, 1967

Merchandising. *See* Promotions and Merchandising

Merger

Advertising agencies are the control centers of the advertising business, and as with any control center, they must constantly change and adjust to the evolving business environment. The emergence of the global economy in the 1980s and 1990s created a sense of urgency among many corporations to develop a global approach to their marketing and advertising strategies. Some marketers turned to international advertising agencies to promote their products in several countries at one time. The perceived need for global "mega-agencies" to represent marketers on a worldwide basis led many agencies to combine forces with others so that they could better serve their clients.

In the late 1800s, when full-service advertising agencies first came into being, they were small and geographically limited. Today, however, many advertising agencies handle billings in the billions of dollars and have hundreds of employees, scores of large clients, and offices around the world.

History of Mergers in Advertising

Agencies have merged or sold out to other agencies since the beginning of the advertising business. In fact, some of the most important agencies came into being as the result of mergers. When the George Batten Company (founded in 1891) and Barton, Durstine & Osborn (formed in 1919) merged in 1928, the result was Batten Barton Durstine & Osborn (BBDO), which became a dominant agency. However, such combinations typically involved a larger agency acquiring a smaller agency for the purpose of gaining a client, a strategic location, desired personnel, or a means of increasing billings. Among the larger agencies there was general stability.

In the late 1950s there was a steep increase in merger and acquisition activity, prompted in part by sagging profits and in part by the rising importance—and rising costs—of television advertising. According to *Advertising Age,* 120 agencies made such moves in 1958, compared to only 50 in 1955. Prominent among them were the mergers of Paris & Peart into Gardner Advertising; of Silverstein-Goldstein into North Advertising (which later merged with Grey); of Buchanan & Company into Lennen & Newell; and of five different agencies to form Reach, McClinton. Most of the acquired agencies lost their identities, as when Stromberger, LaVene, McKinzie, of Los Angeles, California, was bought by the larger Fuller & Smith & Ross. But when two of the biggest agencies of the 1940s merged in 1959, their names were simply joined to create Erwin, Wasey, Ruthrauff & Ryan. In a few cases the larger agency permitted the acquired agency to continue operating as a separate profit center under its own name. This was the case when McCann-Erickson purchased Marschalk & Pratt in 1954. McCann Erickson would ultimately pull ahead of the J. Walter Thompson Company in the 1960s on the strength and volume of its mergers.

In 1960, a year in which 128 agencies were involved in mergers, McCann-Erickson established the Interpublic Group of Companies, the first agency holding company, whose sole purpose was to buy and merge other agencies. Meanwhile, as near equals came together in greater numbers, mergers grew in size. In 1963 Keyes, Madden & Jones merged with Post, Morr & Gardner to form Post-Keyes-Gardner, which became a hot Chicago, Illinois, shop in the 1970s on the basis of large Brown & Williamson tobacco billings. And in 1964 the second biggest advertising merger in history up to that time joined Needham, Louis & Brorby with Doherty, Clifford, Steers & Shenfield to form the powerful national agency of Needham, Harper & Steers Advertising, Inc.

Because all agencies were privately held, the mergers and acquisitions to that point had been by mutual consent. But when Papert, Koenig, Lois, Inc., went public in 1962, the basis was laid for the unwelcome mega-mergers of the 1980s, as agency equity became a product of the free market and thus vulnerable to any investor willing to pay the price. Other agencies—including Foote, Cone & Belding; Doyle Dane Bernbach, Inc.; and Ogilvy & Mather—soon went public. The primary incentive was to permit senior executives to exchange their share of ownership for cash without giving up control of their agencies. Few ever considered that the practice would expose their companies to hostile takeovers.

Emergence of Global Agencies

Global mega-agencies are advertising and public relations firms that operate on a worldwide basis through a portfolio of institutions with local, regional, and international scope. They emerged in the 1990s as a response to the global marketing activities and needs of multinational enterprises. One of the first agencies to act

The Sony Jumbotron in New York City's Times Square announced the November 1985 merger of D'Arcy-MacManus & Masius and Benton and Bowles to form D'Arcy Masius Benton & Bowles, or DMB&B.

on the trend of global marketing needs was Saatchi & Saatchi Compton Worldwide. The move by Saatchi & Saatchi to consolidate, restructure, and strengthen its offices in the western United States, with regional headquarters in San Francisco, California, was a globally minded measure aimed at positioning itself for Pacific Rim business.

In the 1986 *Advertising Age* roundtable "How major clients view mergers," a group of advertising professionals evaluated the advantages and disadvantages of mega-mergers. Arguments for such mergers included the suggestions that they may help advertising agencies solve financial problems and improve creative work. Mergers sometimes involve the acquisition of foreign offices, hence making it easier for clients to conduct marketing activities in other countries. And mergers may add additional and peripheral services such as public relations or research offices, which can provide greater convenience for the variety of promotional strategies many clients desire.

The largest agencies benefited from the increasing volume of global advertising. From 1976 to 1989 the market share of multinational agencies rose from 14 percent to 30 percent of billings worldwide, as companies aligned their brand advertising with the same agencies across North America, Europe, and Asia. By 1992 the top ten agency networks had a combined share of more than 48 percent of the global spending on advertising. The largest agency network was Interpublic, which included McCann-Erickson, Campbell-Ewald, and three other agencies. The second largest network was the Ogilvy Group, whose four main agencies had 1992 worldwide billings of nearly $4 billion.

In general, the top ten multinational advertising agencies fared well in the 1990s. In 1995, for example, Dentsu Worldwide had a gross income of $1.93 billion; McCann-Erickson Worldwide Advertising, $1.15 billion; J. Walter Thompson Company, $1.01 billion; Hakuhodo Worldwide, $958.6 million; BBDO Worldwide, Inc., $857.5 million; Leo Burnett Company, Inc., $803.9 million; DDB Needham Worldwide, $785.7 million; Grey Worldwide, $777.3 million; Ogilvy & Mather Worldwide, Inc., $714.1 million; and Foote, Cone & Belding Worldwide, $679 million.

The Effects of Mergers

Despite the merger mania that began in the late 1980s, which created even larger advertising conglomerates than in previous decades, the mergers and acquisitions did not always lead to better company performance or improved profit margins. Saatchi & Saatchi, for example, announced that profits in 1989 were significantly lower than in 1988. Because of a reorganization, the agency reported a post-tax loss of $24 million in 1989 against a profit of $139 million in 1988. After its acquisition spree Saatchi & Saatchi lost the Colgate-Palmolive Company account, with billings estimated at $110 million, and Procter & Gamble Company later announced that it would pull $85 million worth of accounts from the agency.

On the other hand, when advertising agencies merged across international borders, they sometimes acquired operational strength in individual countries. For example, before its merger with Publicis of France in 1988, Foote, Cone & Belding Communications lacked any European presence and was strong only in the United States, Latin America, and Asia. Publicis had a strong European network, with offices in several European capitals, but no U.S. presence.

The merger trend has taken on many faces. It has, for example, extended to agencies targeting specific ethnic markets. Thus, Sosa, Bromley, Aguilar & Associates merged in late 1994 with Noble & Associados to create the largest Hispanic advertising firm in the United States. The new agency, renamed Sosa, Aguilar, Noble & Associates, had capitalized billings of $106 million and 125 employees. The rise of advertising on the Internet created another reason for mergers. In the United States, for example, CKS Group merged with US Web at the end of 1998 to create US Web/CKS.

As the century drew to a close, three huge mergers narrowed the field of independent shops still further. First, the Leo Burnett Company merged with D'Arcy, Masius, Benton & Bowles to create the Bcom3 Group, itself acquired by the Publicis Group in 2002. Then the venerable Young & Rubicam was acquired by the WPP Group, and True North Communications, which already held Foote, Cone & Belding and Bozell & Jacobs, became part of Interpublic, making it the largest advertising organization in the world.

KENNETH C.C. YANG

Further Reading

Blackwell, Roger D., Riad Ajami, and Kristina Stephan, "Winning the Global Advertising Race: Planning Globally, Acting Locally," in *Globalization of Consumer Markets: Structures and Strategies,* edited by Salah S. Hassan and Erdener Kaynak, New York: International Business Press, 1994

"Bowtie versus Calculator," *Economist* (6 May 1989)

Graves, D. Lucas, "Trading Spaces," *Brandweek* (16 November 1998)

Jaffe, Andrew, "The Blowup between FCB and Publicis Illustrates the Perils of Equal Partnership," *Adweek* (Eastern Edition) (15 May 1995)

Koepp, Stephen, "The Not-So Jolly Advertising Giants," *Time* (17 November 1986)

Krajewski, Steve, "Sosa-Noble Merger," *Adweek* (Southwest Edition) (30 January 1995)

"The Saatchi Brothers Retreat," *Economist* (9 December 1989)

Thorson, Esther, *Advertising Age: The Principles of Advertising at Work,* Lincolnwood, Illinois: NTC Business Books, 1989

Wells, William, John Burnett, and Sandra Moriarty, *Advertising: Principles and Practice,* London: Prentice-Hall International, and Englewood Cliffs, New Jersey: Prentice Hall, 1989; 5th edition, Upper Saddle River, New Jersey: Prentice Hall, 2000

Mexico

At the turn of the 21st century, Mexico was the 13th-largest ad market in the world. Total advertising spending in 2001 was projected to reach $6.1 billion, up from $5 billion in 2000, and the country was on the verge of rapid growth in this area. At the same time, it was the second-largest user of the Internet among Latin American countries, trailing only Brazil.

Economic Climate

Mexico, with a population of more than 100 million, has a free-market economy with a mixture of both modern and traditional industries and agriculture. Increasingly, the economy has been dominated by the private sector; its main industries are food and beverages, tobacco products, chemicals, iron and steel, petroleum, mining, textiles, clothing, motor vehicles, durable consumer products, and tourism.

The country has an abundance of farmland, and Mexican farmers and ranchers spend millions of dollars a year on farm equipment, fertilizers, and pesticides; the commercial centers contain large retail operations and offer many opportunities for companies producing consumer goods and services. The Mexico City metropolitan area accounts for 40 percent of the country's total consumption of consumer products.

In Mexico more than in most countries, disposable income is strongly linked to gross domestic product. When Mexicans have extra cash, the impact on sales is immediately apparent. Thus, as the standard of living rises, Mexican consumers are expected to increase the amount they spend on nonessential goods such as cosmetics and alcoholic beverages.

The Ad Industry

Advertising in Mexico is regulated by two government agencies: the Secretariat de Salubridad, which has the authority to change both advertising copy and visual materials, and Godernacion, which has final approval on whether a TV commercial will be broadcast. The ad industry is divided into two groups: agencies that offer advertising services only, and those that offer integrated marketing communications, including advertising, public relations, market information, artistic work, and modeling. By the late 1990s there were approximately 100 advertising agencies, although only 54 were members of the Mexican Association of Advertising Agencies. As of 2000 the leading agencies in Mexico (by billings) included McCann-Erickson Mexico, with billings of $285.7 million; BBDO Mexico, $204.4 million; Young & Rubicam, $199.4 million; FCB Mexico, $161.3 million; and Panamer/Graficoncepto (Ogilvy & Mather), $131.6 million.

As the Mexican economy has expanded, the amount spent on advertising has increased dramatically. Top advertisers in the country in 1999, according to *Advertising Age Global*, were: Comercial Mexicana, spending $176 million; Radiomovil Dipsa, $113.8 million; Gigante, $109.2 million; Procter & Gamble Company, $107.5 million; Colgate-Palmolive Company, $101.5 million; Telmex, $98.2 million; Wal-Mart Stores, $82.4 million; Coca-Cola Company, $75.8 million; General Motors Corporation, $64.4 million; and Nestlé, $56.8 million.

Media Structure

The largest media organization in Mexico is Grupo Televisa, S.A., the leading entertainment conglomerate in the Spanish speaking world. In 2000 the company produced more than 10,000 hours of programming and owned more than 250 TV stations and four networks; 17 radio stations; a majority stake in the cable venture Cablevision and in Innova, which operated the Sky direct-to-home satellite system; and more than 30 Spanish-language magazines. Televisa is majority-owned by the family of its chairman and chief executive officer, Emilio Azcarraga Jean, through the holding company Televicentro. Televisa held an estimated 70 percent of the country's $1.8 million TV ad market in 2000, according to *Advertising Age Global*.

Televisa's closest competitor is TV Azteca S.A. de C.V., a relative newcomer to the Mexican market. With less than a decade of experience at the turn of the century, TV Azteca owned more than 250 Mexican TV stations and operated two TV networks, which it bought in 1993.

While television is popular, the radio audience for Mexican advertising is substantial, since many people who cannot afford a

FORD DE MEXICO EXPORTA

Desde hace 3 años, el herramental especializado que Ford de México ha venido exportando a diversos países, es de vital importancia para el ensamble de sus vehículos Ford. Consiste desde prensas pequeñas para armar costados, pisos, frentes, hasta la "Prensa Principal" con la que se ensambla todo el vehículo. Más de 20 plantas de Ensamble Ford en diversos países del mundo arman sus vehículos con este herramental diseñado y fabricado por los técnicos de Ford de México.

Ford
MOTOR COMPANY, S.A.
Y LA UNICA RED DE DISTRIBUIDORES EN 115 CIUDADES DE LA REPUBLICA

Así contribuye Ford de México a lograr y mantener la Calidad Universal Ford

CALIDAD UNIVERSAL FORD

Ford of Mexico's corporate ads have emphasized its contributions to the automaker's global operations as a supplier of parts to production facilities around the world.
Courtesy of Ford Motor Company.

TV set do own a radio. There are 900 radio stations in Mexico, and all are commercially supported. The content of radio advertising is determined by considering what is suitable for the "appropriate stream," or audience. News and stereo FM stations air commercials aimed at what is known as "class A," that is, the more affluent consumer sector, while the commercial messages of soap operas or local music stations are addressed to "class B" or "class C" consumers, stratified by income.

The Directorate General of Radio, Television and Cinematography (RTC) is responsible for granting concessions for radio stations and television channels in Mexico, which was the first Latin American country to have television. The government requires all radio and television stations to allot a designated amount of airtime daily for news and government-sponsored announcements. In addition, all radio and TV stations are required to render one-eighth of their airtime to the government, which the RTC is responsible for programming. The agency is also in charge of Radio Mexico Internacional, a short-wave radio service, and *La Hora Nacional,* an official government bulletin carried on Sunday evenings by all radio stations in the country.

Despite the model's eye-catching garb, footwear was actually the product being sold in this 2000 ad from Grupo Andrea, a Mexican shoe marketer.

A 1999 print ad for Televisa, the giant Mexican media company, emphasized its ability to reach targeted consumers throughout the country.

In the 1970s the government created a holding corporation to oversee competition among commercial stations. The broadcasting facilities for commercial and government television channels were consolidated into a single production and broadcasting center. The government controls the programming of its own provincial television stations and controls that of the privately owned network affiliates as well. Independent (local, non-network) stations are not government controlled.

Other Ad Media

The fastest-growing advertising medium in Mexico is the Internet. The country had 1.7 million Internet accounts by the end of 2000 (compared to 1.5 million the previous year), representing approximately 3.4 million users (2 million in 1999). Access to the Internet was expected to remain relatively low, however—at about 10 percent of the population—owing to the country's lack of a developed telecommunications infrastructure as well as poverty in rural areas.

Newspapers are one of the most accessible media for advertisers in Mexico. Mexico City has 15 daily newspapers; more than 320 papers are published throughout the rest of the country. Many papers feature color ads, and government notices are often published in several of the larger, more popular papers. Trade and industry magazines offer large circulation bases to commercial enterprises throughout Mexico. There are approximately 200 trade magazines, many of them specialized business publications, plus 155 non-trade, mostly consumer-oriented magazines in circulation, of which only two are printed in English.

Almost all newspapers in Mexico are published in Spanish, and although most are privately owned, they operate under government regulation. Mexico City has benefited from one of the most open publishing climates in Latin America and has become a leading center for Spanish-language books and magazines. The major Spanish-language newspapers include *El Economista, El Financiero, Excelsior, El Universal, Uno Mas Uno,* and *El Dia.* The oldest existing newspapers, which are still among the leaders, are *El Universal* (established in 1916), *Excelsior* (1917), and *La Prensa* (1928). At least one Spanish-language daily newspaper is published in every state capital in Mexico. Monterrey's *El Norte,* which is widely recognized as the best regional daily, is available in cities throughout the north.

Outdoor boards are another popular ad medium in Mexico. The use of billboards has expanded rapidly in major cities, and by the late 1990s at least 100 agencies offered this medium to their clients. Some 60 companies produce different types of billboards, ranging from traditional paper to electronically controlled displays.

Direct mail is a relatively new industry in Mexico, and it works especially well in this comparatively "uncluttered" market. Direct marketing companies find that in Mexico—unlike in the United States—most people actually read whatever is sent to them in the mail. The Mexican Association of Direct Marketing has grown dramatically. One major concern about the use of direct mail in Mexico, however, is the reliability of the country's postal system, which has a history of inefficiency.

Analysts expect the Mexican advertising market to grow rapidly in the 21st century. This projection is based partly on the advent of innovative forms of advertising made possible by technological advances—in particular the Internet. But the demand for ad agency services is also predicted to increase as a consequence of the North American Free Trade Agreement. New manufacturing industries are expected to develop in Mexico, and the number of retail stores will also increase. Strategic alliances between U.S. and Mexican companies in various areas of the economy are also expected to contribute to growth.

MELVIN PRINCE

Further Reading

Berkowitz, Ron, *Mexico and the Economy,* New York: Random House, 1995

Castañeda, Jorge G., *The Mexican Shock: Its Meaning for the United States,* New York: New Press, 1995

Czinkota, Michael, Ilkka Ronkainen, and Pietra Rivoli, *International Business,* Chicago: Dryden, 1989; 5th edition, by Czinkota, Ronkainen, and Michael Moffett, Fort Worth, Texas: Dryden, 1999

Engholm, Christopher, *Doing Business in Mexico,* Paramus, New Jersey: Prentice Hall, 1997

"Global Marketers: Top 10 by Country," *Ad Age Global,* November 2000

Gregory, Gary D., and James M. Munch, "Cultural Values in International Advertising: An Examination of Familial Norms and Roles in Mexico," *Psychology and Marketing* 14, no. 2 (March 1997)

Hoover's Online UK, www.hoovers.com/uk

"Key Battlegrounds: Argentina, Brazil and Mexico Still Dominate Internet Market," *Ad Age Global,* March 2001

Morrison, Terri, *Dun and Bradstreet's Guide to Doing Business around the World,* Englewood Cliffs, New Jersey: Prentice Hall, 1997

Sutter, Mary, "Key Battlegrounds: Mexico," *Ad Age Global,* March 2001

Sutter, Mary, "Televisa Heir Plays Down Family Drama," *Advertising Age International,* 19 September 1997

Teichman, Judith, *Privatization and Political Change in Mexico,* Pittsburgh, Pennsylvania: University of Pittsburgh Press, 1995

"Top Agencies in 124 Countries," *Advertising Age,* 23 April 2001

"Top 10 Global Ad Markets," *Ad Age Global,* April 2001

Ueltschy, Linda C., and John K. Ryans, Jr., "Employing Standardized Promotion Strategies in Mexico: The Impact of Language and Cultural Differences," *International Executive* 39, no. 4 (July/August 1997)

Usunier, Jean-Claude, *International Marketing: A Cultural Approach,* New York and London: Prentice Hall, 1993; 3rd edition, as *Marketing across Cultures,* Harlow, Essex: Financial Times/Prentice Hall, 1998; New York: Prentice Hall, 1998

Michael Conrad & Leo Burnett. *See under* Conrad

Microsoft Corporation

Principal Agencies

Keye/Donna/Pearlstein

Ogilvy & Mather

Wieden & Kennedy, Inc.

Anderson & Lembke (later McCann-Erickson/A&L)

William H. (Bill) Gates dropped out of Harvard University in 1974 to form Microsoft Corporation with partner Paul Allen. In 1977 the Tandy Corporation hired the new company to develop software for its personal computer (PC), the TRS-80. Microsoft's future was secured when the IBM Corporation selected the company's MS-DOS (Microsoft disk operating system) software for its PCs in 1981. Microsoft's growth was so rapid that by 1982 the company had formed a European subsidiary in anticipation of a global market. By 1983, 40 percent of all personal computers were shipped with Microsoft software, and Gates appeared as a 27-year-old computer wunderkind in the pages of magazines such as *Business Week* and *Inc.* The company's disk operating system became the industry standard, as its Windows environment, which was modeled after Apple Computer's interface, did later. Microsoft software for word processing, spreadsheets, and database programs soon followed. The company entered the end-user market through retail stores and dealers and quickly adapted its own programs and developed new ones for the home market. As the power of computers increased, Microsoft sustained its product lines with new releases of existing software; it also created new products, in the process achieving virtual monopolies with DOS and Windows.

By 1991 more than 80 percent of the world's PCs operated on MS-DOS. The Internet grew explosively in 1993 and 1994, but Microsoft did not at first make a commitment to it. By 1995, however, Gates decided to throw the weight of his company's resources into support of the new medium, characterizing it in a memo as the next great opportunity—an "Internet tidal wave." The company launched Microsoft Network (MSN), a proprietary on-line service that at first dabbled in a concept of TV-styled Internet "shows," such as travel adventure show *Mungo Park*; *Underwire,* a woman's program on love, sex, marriage, and fitness; and *15 Seconds of Fame,* a contest show of "funniest" stories from viewers hosted by Charles Fleischer, the actor who was the voice of Roger Rabbit. The company also pursued an increasing number of investments and acquisitions. Whereas its early acquisitions were small software developers, alliances with such companies as NBC, Black Entertainment Television, Dreamworks SKG, MTel subsidiary SkyTel, cable giant Comcast Corporation, Web TV, Tandem, and Apple Computer pointed the company toward multimedia and the convergence of computers, television, and telephony. Microsoft increased the number of its acquisitions and investments to 13 in 1995 and to 20 in each of the following two years. In 1998 Microsoft invested in 17 companies and acquired six. Development of Explorer, the company's Internet browser, continued, and Microsoft expanded into the role of content provider, issuing the *Encarta* CD-Rom encyclopedia and travel site MSN Expedia. Microsoft entered into an alliance with NBC to provide on-line news content through Microsoft network (MSN), which became MSNBC. Thus Microsoft made the transition from a software company and major advertiser to a media company that itself solicited advertising for its on-line properties.

The company's meteoric rise and the dominance of MS-DOS and the Windows interface for personal computers worldwide prompted an investigation by the U.S. Federal Trade Commission (FTC) beginning in 1990. The commission investigated allegations that Microsoft had inserted hidden codes into early copies of its Windows 3.1 software for the purpose of making a rival operating system appear to be incompatible. The rival operating system, OS/2, was originally a joint development of both Microsoft and IBM; however, the partnership unraveled after Microsoft proceeded to develop and release Windows NT. In addition, there were claims that Microsoft had used "lockout contracts" that required manufacturers to pay for a copy of MS-DOS on every computer shipped, whether or not it was actually installed, a practice that effectively locked competing disk operating systems out of the market. The FTC deadlocked twice on whether to issue an administrative complaint against Microsoft. The Antitrust Division of the Department of Justice then reviewed the allegations against Microsoft and in 1993 began its own investigation.

In 1995 the antitrust charges were settled through a consent decree worked out between Microsoft and the Justice Department. The arrangement limited licensing agreements to less than one year, enjoined Microsoft from pressuring personal computer vendors to pay for more MS-DOS systems than they actually sold, and prohibited Microsoft from refusing to sell its software to computer manufacturers that also offered competing software. Microsoft felt sufficiently vindicated and held a lavish, high-profile kickoff of its Windows 95 product. Nonetheless, evidence of Microsoft's practice of "preannouncing" products that were not yet ready for the market as a means of heading off competitors, producing what was known as "vaporware," convinced a judge to throw out the settlement between the government and the company.

In 1997 the company again became the subject of antitrust hearings, this time because of plans to bundle its Explorer browser with its Windows 98 platform. The Justice Department and a group of state attorneys general filed an antitrust suit and began hearings with the manufacturers of personal computers and Intel Corporation, the largest maker of the chips used in personal computers, seeking evidence of anticompetitive market practices by Microsoft. The negative publicity generated by the lawsuit affected the company's advertising and publicity campaigns.

"The Perfect Business Tool"

In 1983 Keye/Donna/Pearlstein of Beverly Hills, California, became Microsoft's first major agency. Like many business-to-business marketers in the computer industry, Microsoft relied heavily on public relations and promotions such as Microsoft University, a program that invited key dealers and customers to preview new products. Keye/Donna/Pearlstein adopted a strategy of print advertising in selected computer and business publications, since at the time less than 10 percent of the public were prospects for the company's software. With the debut of Microsoft Word in 1984, 100,000 subscribers to *PC World* magazine received a sample disk for the new program, a promotion that cost an estimated $350,000. This kind of mass sampling of computer software was an innovation, and it required that the agency overcome production problems in binding the disk into the magazine. A total of $1 million—more than double the cost of developing the software itself—was spent promoting Microsoft Word in its first year in ads in the *Wall Street Journal, Byte, Infoworld,* and other publications. Head advertising executive Jean Richardson, who had been recruited from Apple Computer to become vice president of corporate communications in 1985, had the packaging for the software redesigned and a new logo developed. Richardson's arrival marked the beginning of a new marketing sensibility that included a substantial increase in the print advertising budget. In 1985 the company introduced Microsoft Windows and Excel spreadsheet software. A two-pronged campaign in 1987 for Microsoft Works, which combined word processing with spreadsheet, database, and communications functions, relied upon a national print campaign and a two-week, in-store promotion called "Work Days," supported by extensive local radio spots and newspaper ads. The Work Days ads used an image of a Swiss army–style knife with the headline, "Introducing the perfect business tool for a less than perfect world." An updated version of a Word print campaign measured its abilities against competing products with the line, "Numbers speak louder than words."

The heavy reliance on print in trade and business publications, buttressed by heavy marketing at trade shows such as Comdex, initially served Microsoft well. But the move to the use of personal computers by a broader segment of consumers prompted

the development of mass media campaigns. In the fall of 1987, Keye/Donna/Pearlstein resigned the Microsoft account, which had grown to $8 million, citing frustration with the marketer over its inability to develop a sustained corporate theme, something that was attributed to the company's decentralized management system. Despite the lack of a brand strategy, however, Microsoft had sustained unparalleled growth, going from $69 million in sales in 1983 to $345.9 million in 1987 and surpassing Lotus Development Corporation as the leading independent seller of software in the United States. The company made an initial public offering in 1986.

Brand Strategy

In 1988 Ogilvy & Mather, Los Angeles, California, won the Microsoft account, focusing its initial pitch on the importance of adopting a brand strategy. Microsoft's advertising budget was increased substantially, to approximately $14 million to $20 million per year, reflecting both a commitment to a branding strategy and the anticipated release of a number of new products. By the end of the year the first branding ad, "Making it all make sense," was released in an eight-page insert promoting Microsoft's technological milestones and a full range of its products. Senior Vice President of Marketing Scott Oki established an approval process for branding campaigns, although individual product managers continued to have input into the advertising for their own products. By the late 1980s the company had expanded its global reach, with subsidiaries in India, Japan, South Korea, and China, and had become the world's leading marketer of software for the personal computer. In 1990 print campaigns were launched for two new products, Microsoft Windows 3.0 and Microsoft Office, the latter a bundled software package for business users. That same year the FTC, eyeing the dominance of the company in the personal computer software market, began a series of antitrust hearings into Microsoft's practices. By 1991 Ogilvy's yearly budget for media promotions was $17 million to $19 million, with print advertising predominating. Spending in electronic media was increased in recognition of the growth of personal computers in the home, and in 1992 Ogilvy crafted the first television campaign for Microsoft targeted at the home computer market. The $8 million broadcast and cable network television campaign promoted an enhanced version of Windows (3.1) and Windows-based software applications to broader audiences. Microsoft expanded in Europe as well, establishing subsidiaries in Eastern Europe and Moscow in 1992 and 1993, respectively.

In 1993 Microsoft released MS-DOS 6.0, as well as a new operating system, Windows NT, aimed at the business market. Microsoft dominated the spring Comdex show with its marketing blitz and its "Making it easier" tag line. As Microsoft pursued the home market, it considered creating a new brand that would be friendlier and more approachable than the company's business-oriented products. But the cost of establishing a new brand and the asset of the cult of personality that had been built up around Gates by the media as the "unassuming billionaire" made the extension of the company's products under the name Microsoft

Home a logical choice. The Microsoft Home line consisted of home office software, games, and *Encarta,* a CD-ROM encyclopedia. Microsoft Home was supported by a direct-response TV campaign crafted by Ogilvy & Mather Direct/West, Los Angeles.

The increasing association of the brand with founder Gates was inescapable. Gates served as the chief marketer and spokesman in high-profile events. Yet with few exceptions, Ogilvy and its successor, Wieden & Kennedy, Inc., avoided making Gates the center of advertising campaigns for Microsoft, owing to the uneasy truce between the Justice Department and the company and a generally negative perception of Gates among others in the industry.

In 1993 Ogilvy introduced a new Microsoft Office logo for use by third-party software vendors that had integrated their offerings with Office. These third-party software vendors filled in holes in Microsoft Office, and the logo let them benefit from the cachet of the "Microsoft Office Compatible" logo. In 1994 Ogilvy's Los Angeles office abruptly resigned the Microsoft account, which by then had grown to $50 million, when the agency's New York City office won IBM's global account, valued at $500 million.

Ascendancy

In June 1994 Wieden & Kennedy of Portland, Oregon, whose widely praised work for Nike had invoked the mystique of sports, won the Microsoft account, with responsibility for both global image and consumer campaigns. The image campaign was introduced six months later with the ad "Anthem," which suggested that Microsoft's operating system and market strength made it the ideal provider of products that consumers could use to express themselves. "The stuff we make is powerful. It makes you powerful," the ad suggested before the tag line, "Where do you want to go today?"

Over eight months Microsoft spent $100 million on the campaign, which featured a montage of images of international locales, faces representing 50 nationalities, and software products to convey the sense of "discovery" and "spontaneity" that the software allowed. The campaign was the largest in history for any software, and it marked the beginning of a dialogue with consumers by a company that had previously only been willing to use TV advertising intermittently. In March 1995 the global branding strategy encompassed six countries (Australia, Canada, France, Germany, the United Kingdom, and the United States) that accounted for 74 percent of the company's revenue.

Despite the Justice Department's investigations, 1995 was the year in which Microsoft's ascendance was perhaps most publicly celebrated. Gates published a book, *The Road Ahead,* which quickly became a best-seller. In August 1995 the long-awaited and much-hyped launch of Windows 95 took place as part of a $200 million global campaign, an unprecedented amount spent on software advertising. An additional $500 million was spent by retailers and by hardware and software allies, anticipating that the product would become the new standard. Even IBM, whose rival OS/2 system was battling Microsoft's offerings, offered Windows 95 on its personal computers. The launch included promotional

In the early 1990s, print campaigns promoting Windows 3.0 software targeted the rapidly growing personal computer market with ads that sought to ensure Microsoft's preeminence in personal computing. *Windows is a trademark of Microsoft Corporation. © 1991 Microsoft Corporation. All rights reserved. Reprinted with permission from Microsoft Corporation.*

events, something that was not traditional for the software industry, and mass-market ad campaigns in 20 countries and a dozen languages. The colors of the Windows 95 logo bathed the Empire State Building in New York City, a 300-foot sign was erected on the CN Tower in Toronto, a four-story Windows 95 box sailed into Australia's Sydney Harbor, a decorated submarine in Poland took patrons to the bottom of the Baltic Sea, and copies of software were thrown to passersby from a decorated bus in Johannesburg, South Africa. A 60-second TV commercial featured the Rolling Stones hit "Start Me Up," lending a hip image to both the product and the industry that had produced it. The song, associated with the rock 'n' roll baby boomer generation, began at the moment a computer mouse selected the "start" icon on the Windows logo. (Although the 30 seconds of the tune cost Microsoft millions and the publicity stated that it was the first time the Rolling Stones had allowed one of their post-1972 songs to be used for commercial purposes, "Start Me Up" actually had already been used for a Volkswagen ad campaign in Germany earlier that

Multitasking was the theme of this 1995 ad introducing Microsoft's Windows 95 software.
Windows and the Windows logo are registered trademarks and Where do you want to go today? and the Windows Start logo are trademarks of Microsoft Corporation. © 1995 Microsoft Corporation. Reprinted with permission from Microsoft Corporation.

summer, and a Snickers commercial had used the Rolling Stones song "Satisfaction" in 1990.) The 60-second ads included images of people from all walks of life using the software and employed tinted monochromatic scenes with superimposed rolling titles such as "Start exploring," "Start discovering," "Start learning," "Start managing," "Start organizing," and "Start creating" and ending with the tag line "Start Windows 95."

The marketing tactic behind the Windows 95 launch was to use a mix of traditional strategies—a combination of television, print, and cooperative ads—along with public relations and publicity stunts. These elements were combined to build a media blitz and global hype. On 24 August computer stores around the world opened at midnight for customers eager to buy the product. Within a year 40 million copies of Windows 95 had been sold, and a $4 million to $5 million anniversary campaign was implemented in the business and computer press.

In the fall of 1996 Wieden & Kennedy took on new Microsoft assignments, including media buying for business software applications and the Windows NT operating system, with a combined estimated budget of $200 million. For the Microsoft branding

campaign Wieden devised a symbol—the Hand—to function as an icon for Microsoft much as the "swoosh" had done for Nike. In late 1996 Microsoft ads began to feature the Hand as an icon for Web links on the Internet, which put the focus on the brand image rather than any particular product. The Hand symbolized interconnectivity, human agency, and the future, along with Microsoft's ability to deliver these elements. The symbol anticipated the realignment of Microsoft to focus on the Internet as a key part of its business.

In the fall of 1997 Microsoft spent an estimated $10 million on a print and Internet campaign pushing Explorer 4.0. The Explorer product was central to the restaging of the company around the Internet. From the inception of Explorer, Microsoft set out to unseat Netscape, then the dominant browser (developed by the inventor of the first modern browser, Marc Andreessen) by offering the product for free. Netscape countered by offering its product as a "free trial." Both programs were provided for free by most Internet service providers. Explorer was also a part of the Microsoft operating system software package, although it was not yet built into its operating system. This turn to the Internet also meant that the company saw advertising on the Internet as an important strategy. Microsoft's Internet-based advertising was handled by the San Francisco, California, agency Anderson & Lembke. The agency produced ads for the Internet for consumer magazines such as *Time* and *Sports Illustrated*, and for computer and business publications. All carried the theme, "The Web the way you want it."

In a January 1998 interview, Michael Prieve, creative director of Anderson & Lembke, said that Microsoft had to be persuaded to abandon its "nerd scientist" ideas on marketing and coaxed into a consumer-oriented, sophisticated, and persuasive approach. As if to counter its traditional image, the corporation's premier nerd was shown in a 1998 spot with a "Why I love my PC" list. In the commercial Gates cited playing games with his daughter, staying in touch with his lawyers, and writing to the Justice Department to explain why Internet Explorer was a good product. Other ads featured employees, a further attempt to soften the image of the company. Despite increased spending for television and a commitment to Internet-based advertising, Microsoft reported that print would remain its principal medium for the 1999 fiscal year. Print spending was estimated at $174 million and broadcast spending at $130 million. The global budget for Microsoft's advertising for 1999 was estimated at $400 million, divided primarily between Wieden & Kennedy and Anderson & Lembke.

Two-Agency Approval

In 1994 Anderson & Lembke was designated as Microsoft's product advertising shop, with a $50 million budget; Wieden & Kennedy continued to handle branding and consumer work. Microsoft's two-agency approach was intended to allow the flexibility product managers demanded while also permitting the development of a unified image in the consumer market. The following year Anderson & Lembke boosted its Microsoft billings to nearly $85 million when the account for Bob, Microsoft's computer interface, was shifted from Wieden & Kennedy. The change reflected the practice at Microsoft of allowing marketing division managers to choose agencies from an approved list. The company's product managers often preferred a product-oriented advertising style, which they felt was more successful for the business market, despite the push from headquarters for the unified corporate and consumer image provided by Wieden & Kennedy.

The fortunes of Anderson & Lembke, which operated as Microsoft's "second" agency, waxed and waned. In February 1996 the agency resigned a $15 million to $20 million business-to-business direct marketing account. Hans Ullmark, Anderson & Lembke's president and chief executive officer, said that the agency had labored to keep up with growth on the Microsoft account and had received a "wake-up call" from a Microsoft division, leading to a new agency management team. By the fall of 1996, however, Anderson & Lembke had lost a large portion of its Microsoft business—including media buying for business software applications and the up-and-coming Windows NT operating system—to Wieden & Kennedy. Following the reassignment, Anderson & Lembke's principal relationship with Microsoft was

its role as the company's agency of record for interactive products and for new media buying.

The agency's fortunes began a turnaround after Bob Herbold, Microsoft's new executive vice president and chief operating officer, brought an increasingly intense style of research and testing into the relationship with the company's agencies. Herbold, who went to Microsoft after 25 years at the Procter & Gamble Company, publicly supported both Wieden & Kennedy's and Anderson & Lembke's work. The company saw different strengths in the two agencies. By March 1998, following the realignment of several of its product groups, Microsoft had moved the print and on-line advertising duties for its consumer software and hardware brands from Wieden & Kennedy to Anderson & Lembke. In the summer of 1998, as part of the consolidation of its far-flung interactive group marketing, Microsoft also shifted its MSN account and the Microsoft Investor Web site to Anderson & Lembke. The shop's assignment was redefined, with an increased emphasis on Internet-based advertising. Microsoft spent approximately $41 million on Internet ads in the year ending 30 June 1998, approximately 7 percent of all Internet advertising. Microsoft executives predicted that, although Microsoft had turned to television to build its brand with mass markets, its Internet advertising would soon match or exceed its TV budget.

Anderson & Lembke also undertook several campaigns in 1998 to soften the image of Microsoft and to counter the charges of the antitrust suit brought by the Justice Department. One print campaign was aimed at software industry workers and computer resellers, using humorous understatement such as, "Apparently there are those who do not subscribe to an all-Microsoft approach." Another ran in five urban newspapers and promoted the idea that the marketplace should determine what innovations consumers wanted: "At Microsoft, the freedom to innovate for our customers is more than a goal, it is a principle worth standing up for."

Another campaign launched late in 1998 used a 30-second spot evoking nostalgic images of software innovators of the 1970s. The ad emphasized that the high-tech industry owed its rapid advancement to the contributions of such people and obliquely suggested that the velocity of change in technology would prevent the development of a monopoly. It concluded with a final voice-over: "So what else is impossible? We salute the imagination that drives the developer."

When it came time to consider the roll-out of its Windows Millennium product in 1999, Microsoft told Wieden & Kennedy that the company wanted to move to "a unified advertising strategy with a single agency." McCann-Erickson in San Francisco joined its sister company and Microsoft's long-time agency for various product lines, Anderson Lembke of San Francisco (both owned by the Interpublic Group of Companies), to make a bid for the campaign. The joint effort paid off, and the two agencies merged to form McCann-Erickson/A&L.

The growth of new product lines such as Windows Millennium proceeded against a background of Microsoft's legal woes. Microsoft's antitrust case came to a head when appellate court judge Thomas Penfield Jackson ruled that it was a monopoly in 1997 and ordered Microsoft to unbundle Explorer from Windows and ordered the company split. Microsoft argued that it had not been given a hearing on other possible remedies and asked the appeals court to clarify its earlier ruling to provide guidance over unbundling. Following the election of a more pro-business Republican president, George W. Bush, in 2000, Judge Jackson's handling of the antitrust case was criticized by the nation's second-highest court, which ordered a new judge to hear subsequent motions and vacated the order to split the company. However, the appeals court upheld that the company had violated the Sherman Antitrust Act, although in November 2001 the Justice Department recommended a settlement with Microsoft. The settlement required Microsoft to let software developers create competing products that interoperate with the Windows operating system, along with other provisions. It did not force Microsoft to unbundle software such as Explorer from Windows, even in the upcoming Windows XP release. Nine U.S. states, however, refused to go along with the settlement and pursued a separate trial. Windows XP's roll-out was delayed by the events of 11 September 2001, and given the sensitive timing of a roll-out a month later, the ad tag lines were altered from "Prepare to fly" to "Yes you can." The ads by McCann-Erickson featured digitally composited images of people soaring through the skies and over hills. On-screen text suggested people "soar," "mix," "edit," "e-mail," and "share." Windows XP was released with Explorer bundled into its operating system.

L. CLARE BRATTEN

Further Reading

Cox, Anna Marie, "Microsoft Is Trying to Make You Forget about Its Nerdy CEO through a Multimillion-Dollar Sleight of Hand," *Mother Jones* 23, no. 1 (January 1998)

Goldstein, Alan, "June Debut of Microsoft's Windows 98 Will Be Subdued," *Dallas Morning News* (16 April 1998)

Horton, Cleveland, "Microsoft to Boost Spending," *Advertising Age* (28 September 1987)

Horton, Cleveland, "Software Publisher Tries Brand Strategy," *Advertising Age* (5 December 1988)

Johnson, Bradley, "Windows 95 Opens with Omnimedia Blast," *Advertising Age* (28 August 1995)

Johnson, Bradley, "Microsoft Web Ad Spending to Explode," *Advertising Age* (11 August 1997)

Johnson, Bradley, "Microsoft to Refocus Its Advertising," *Advertising Age* (1 June 1998)

Johnson, Bradley, and Jo McIntyre, "Wieden Wins the Nike of Software," *Advertising Age* (4 July 1994)

"Justice Department Charges Microsoft with Violating 1995 Court Order, Seeks $1 Million per Day Penalties," *Antitrust Report* 24, no. 5 (September/October 1997)

Kelly, Jane Irene, "Microsoft Says Thank You," *Adweek* (Western Edition) (23 November 1998)

Mermigas, Diane, "Bill Gates Mines Internet Gold," *Advertising Age* (1 April 1996)

Parloff, Roger, "What Was Microsoft Thinking?" *The American Lawyer* (March 1998)

Schlender, Brent, "What Bill Gates Really Wants," *Fortune* (16 January 1995)

Sigel, Efrem, "The Selling of Software," *Datamation* (15 April 1984)

"27 States Back Federal Antitrust Action against Microsoft," *Antitrust Report* 25, no. 2 (March/April 1998)

"Ultimate League Table Wieden and Kennedy, the Advertising Agency Based in Portland, Oregon, That Came Up with 'Where Do You Want to Go Today?'" *Creative Review* (2 January 1998)

Middle East

The Middle East is to a large extent considered to be a homogeneous market. It is primarily Muslim and for the most part shares a common language, Arabic (the main exceptions being Israel, Iran, and Turkey). The Middle East occupies a large geographical area and extends from the shores of the Atlantic Ocean in the west to the Persian Gulf in the east. (Israel is discussed in a separate essay in this encyclopedia.)

In the 1990s advertising in the Middle East was characterized by a heightened attention to the presentation of detail; at the same time, new standards of technical excellence were gradually being adopted. The principle that the package should be as good as what is inside it, often taken for granted in the West, was still relatively new in this part of the world.

The Middle East and the North African countries were largely unaffected by the international economic events of 1998. Nonetheless, economic growth in the region was slowed by a drop in oil prices, the uncertain status of the Arab-Israeli peace process, and possibly the situation in Iraq. Growth in gross domestic product (GDP) varied from a high of 6.3 percent in Morocco, which had experienced a drought the previous year, to a low of 1.7 percent in Iran. Algeria, Egypt, and Tunisia all achieved a growth rate of approximately 5 percent, and Jordan, Lebanon, the West Bank and Gaza, and Yemen had rates of growth ranging from 2 percent to 4 percent in 1999 according to the World Economic and Social Survey.

While the region saw overall improvement on the economic front in the 1990s, the logistics for executing economic and social development plans were not in place. According to the World Bank, problems included high unemployment rates, widespread poverty, environment-related issues such as water scarcity, and large gaps between rural and urban areas in terms of income, infrastructure, and human services.

Oil and the Economy

The behavior of oil prices in international markets was a major factor affecting economic growth, especially in western Asia, in the late 20th century. In oil-producing countries — mainly in the Persian Gulf region—oil was the main export product and the source of government profits, which ultimately controlled most investment and employment markets. On the other hand, oil-importing countries suffered from lower export rates and drops in workers' remittances from oil-exporting countries.

The region's volatile political situation had a detrimental effect on investment and the flow of trade. With the exception of Kuwait, most oil-exporting countries suffered declines in their account balances. They then tried to make up for the deficits by drawing upon their international reserves and foreign assets. Meanwhile, in 1998 the oil-importing countries benefited from lower oil prices and improved their balances.

In some oil-exporting countries, domestic demand declined when investment expenditures were cut, and multiplier effects led to a deceleration of growth. A solid example is Iran, where austerity measures led to a slump of 10 percent in the construction sector of its economy. In other countries, almost nonexistent external demand limited the manufacturing sector, such as petrochemicals and aluminum. With the decline in employment rates, domestic demand slowed as well. The result was deceleration in growth even in countries such as Bahrain and the United Arab Emirates (UAE) with mixed economies.

Outlook for Advertising

At the turn of the 20th century advertising agencies were optimistic about the future of the industry in the region, and businesses were increasingly realizing the need to maximize the value of each and every advertising dollar. This was good news for private agencies, whose survival depended on the demand for high-quality, professional services. The advertising industry in the Middle East was dominated by major public-sector and private agencies such as AL Ahram, AL Akhbar, and Tarek Nour in Egypt; Tahama, Impact/BBDO, and Promo Seven in Saudi Arabia; Intermarkets and Publi-Graphics in the UAE; and Americana in Kuwait. Their dominance owed less to the quality of their services than to large-scale financing, which enabled them to offer clients attractive payment schedules and ease of access to the major media. Neverthe-

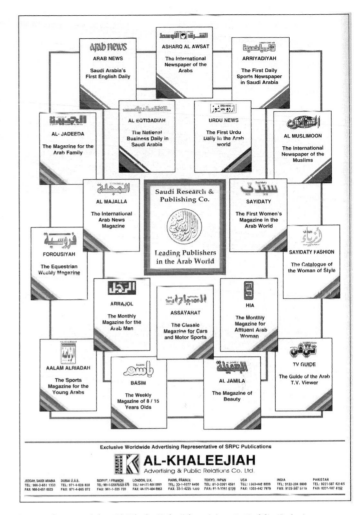

A 1998 house ad for Al-Khaleejiah Advertising & Public Relations, a Jeddah, Saudi Arabia–based company, showed the wide range of publications it represented for SRPC (Saudi Research & Publishing Company), one of the largest publishing houses in the Middle East.

less, notable improvements in quality were seen in the 1990s. The future of the advertising industry in the Middle East will depend largely on the success of efforts to train and educate advertising professionals, as there has been a serious shortage of qualified people. Some efforts were made in Egypt and Lebanon to introduce national styles of advertising, but many commercials still reflected a predominantly Western style. Western ideas, treatments, and music prevailed in print and broadcast advertisements throughout the region.

Advertising research and audience analysis developed well in the 1990s, but more effort in these areas was still needed. There was also a need for trained market researchers and for advertising practitioners who understand how to make use of the data generated by such research. Governments needed to understand that good advertising in the region could proceed efficiently only if it had access to an adequate base. The Pan Arab Research Center was considered to be an effective regional organization in this respect.

The Saudi Research & Publishing Company bestows the Sword Press Award annually to the best advertisements that appear in its publications.

National Media

The Egyptian media played a leading role in the Middle East in the 1990s. Egypt hosted the region's largest news agency, and the major papers, widely read throughout the region, were important in forming regional opinions. Both radio services and television programs were very popular and conveyed the Egyptian dialect of Arabic throughout the region. Egypt's dominance was a result of historical, geographic, and demographic factors. Egypt published 14 daily newspapers, both state-run and opposition, and 35 public and private weeklies, for a daily newspaper circulation of 2.6 million. The country had one state-owned news agency and 27 publishing houses. Besides its own satellite broadcasting network, NileSat, which broadcast over six specialized stations across the globe, there were eight Egyptian state-owned TV channels that covered different parts of Egypt. Egypt also had seven public radio stations. By comparison, Egypt's longtime rival for media dominance, Lebanon, published 14 daily newspapers and 28 weeklies, for a daily newspaper circulation of 330,000, and had nine television channels and 18 radio stations, both private and public, in the late 1990s.

The main news source in the Islamic republic of Iran was the official Khabargozari-ye Jomhuri-ye Eslami (Islamic Republic News Agency, or IRNA). Iran had 17 daily newspapers, at least five of which had national circulation. The revival of advertising in Iran started in 1989 with the liberalized economic policies of former president Akbar Hashemi Rafsanjani. Under the Islamic fundamentalist regimes, advertising was considered antireligious, vulgar, and symbolic of a capitalist economy. The state-owned television network with its five channels posed a major challenge for advertising agencies in Iran. There were more than 1,000 advertising agencies in Iran, and more than 80 percent of advertising spending went to television, with the rest going to newspapers.

Saudi Arabia hosted 17 daily newspapers and 15 weeklies, two news agencies, and 10 publication houses in the 1990s. Daily newspaper circulation was 1.06 million. The two television stations were state run. Despite a ban on satellite television receivers, a visitor to any urban center in the monarchy could spot thousands of dishes on rooftops, although there was no official estimate of the number.

In the late 1990s Jordan produced five daily newspapers and 26 weeklies, for a daily newspaper circulation of 250,000. The

Impact/BBDO's campaign for Ikea in the Middle East used startling images to highlight the quality and usefulness of the Swedish home-furnishings company's products.

country had one state-run news agency, two publication houses, and two public television channels, one of which was broadcast throughout the region.

The most important news sources in Turkey in the 1990s were Anadol Ajansi (AA) and Akdeniz Ajansi (AKAJANS). There were more than 340 daily newspapers, but the overwhelming majority were local papers with very low circulation. The most dominant daily was *Cumhuriyet;* other influential papers included *Milliyet, Gunes,* and *Tercuman.* Families or individuals owned most publications. A number of radio and television stations were run by Turkiye Radio and Televizyon Kurumu (TRT).

The local press in the United Arab Emirates was strong and quite independent in the late 20th century. There were 18 dailies, 16 weeklies, one wire service, and three publication houses. Daily newspaper circulation was 300,000. Public television transmission began in 1969 and later expanded to eight channels. The Space Network of Dubai started in 1992 and covered all Arab countries and parts of Asia, nearly one-third of the world's population.

Kuwait had nine daily newspapers and 11 weeklies for a daily newspaper circulation of 655,000 in the late 1990s, as well as one state-run news agency and six publication houses. The airwaves were all public, with four local TV stations and two radio stations. Kuwait's satellite television channel began transmission in 1992 and was seen in the Middle East, southern Europe, and East Asia.

In the late 1990s, Bahrain had three daily newspapers and seven weeklies, for a daily newspaper circulation of 70,000. It was served by a local news agency, seven publication houses, and four international TV channels. Qatar hosted four daily newspapers and six weeklies, with a daily newspaper circulation of 80,000. It also had one national news agency, five publication houses, and two local TV channels. Oman had five daily newspapers and six weeklies, with a daily newspaper circulation of 63,000. The sultanate had one state-run news agency, six publication houses, and one state-run television station.

In addition to local print and broadcast media, the region hosted a number of regional media in the 1990s. These included

Egyptian, Jordanian, Lebanese, Syrian, UAE, and Qatari satellite television networks; regional networks such as ART and MBC; 14 weekly and 34 monthly regional newspapers; *Al Hayat* newspaper published in London, England; and MBC and Monte Carlo radio stations. These media reached all the Arabic-speaking countries in the Middle East.

Dominance of Pan-Arab Ad Media

At the 1999 advertising awards ceremony in Cairo, Egypt, pan-Arab media in the region received a standing ovation for a their performance in the advertising market in the Middle East. These media increased their consolidated advertising revenues by 10 percent from $511,521 in 1998 to $563,679 in 1999. This increase followed an even larger increase the previous year, when revenues jumped 73 percent over 1997. Pan-Arab media attracted close to one of every five advertising dollars generated in 1998 by all Arab media combined.

The pan-Arab market dominated the Saudi and principal Gulf advertising markets and exerted increasing pressure on local television in these markets. The reason, apparently, was the unwillingness of local advertisers to invest a sufficient amount to reach consumers in the main Gulf markets. As a result, pan-Arab satellite television slowly increased its market share at the expense of the local press. In 1999 television garnered 78 percent of the advertising revenue generated by the pan-Arab media, while magazines attracted 18 percent, and newspapers and radio drew a total of 4 percent. By comparison, in 1995, for example, television's share of advertising revenue was 31 percent, and newspapers and magazines garnered 47 percent and 18 percent, respectively.

Such trends could have far-reaching ramifications. In 1998 pan-Arab media shared 25 percent of the combined Arab media markets compared to just 20 percent four years previously. Total advertising expenditures in the pan-Arab, Gulf Cooperation Council (GCC), and Levant markets registered a 6 percent increase to $2.04 billion in 1999, but in 1998, expenditures had increased by 21 percent to $1.93 billion compared to the previous year. Forty-six percent of the 1997–98 increase was generated by pan-Arab satellite television. The media in Egypt accounted for another 24 percent of the increase, with the rest of the media in the region combined accounting for the remaining 30 percent.

Per-Country Ad Spending

Second only to the pan-Arab media in advertising expenditures in 1999 was Egypt. Ad expenditures jumped 5 percent over the year before to reach $392 million. Newspapers received the most, for a 54 percent share, an increase of one percentage point from 1998. Television, the main Egyptian entertainment medium, collected 38 percent, a decline of one percentage point from 1998. Magazines received only 8 percent, and radio, which is mostly non-commercial, less than 1 percent, or $765,000 in advertising expenditures.

Among the Arab-speaking markets in the region, Saudi Arabia ranked third in advertising expenditure in 1999 after pan-Arab media and Egypt. Total advertising expenditure in the kingdom continued a slow decline from $350 million in 1998 to $328 million in 1999. The highest monthly expenditures coincided with the Muslim holy fasting month of Ramadan, when people watch an immense amount of television after sunset and usually indulge in spending sprees for food, services, and other preparations for the Bairam feast. In terms of local advertising expenditures, newspapers held a 70 percent market share in 1999, amounting to $229 million. Magazines, outdoor advertising, and television followed with the sums of $56 million, $24 million, and $19 million, respectively.

Lebanon ranked fourth in advertising spending. In 1999 its spending rose by 10 percent over the previous year, to $229 million. The increase was due mainly to increased television and newspaper advertising, with a slight increase in outdoor advertising as well. Television's share was 51 percent, and newspapers received 26 percent of advertising expenditures. Magazine advertising expenditures, on the other hand, decreased 2 percent compared to the previous year, for a 9 percent share; radio and outdoor advertising claimed 8 percent and 6 percent, respectively.

The United Arab Emirates ranked second in advertising expenditures within the GCC markets in 1999 and fifth in Arabic-speaking markets. Expenditures decreased 5 percent from $194 million in 1998 to $184 million in 1999. Driven by the historically strong local newspapers, newspapers' advertising share was 56 percent with a value of $103 million, followed by television, the only media that increased its market share, and magazines at 18 percent each. Less than 9 percent of expenditures went to radio, outdoor advertising, cinema, and video, which was higher than the combined market share of similar media in any other GCC market. Video advertising dropped from $609,000 in 1998 to $238,000 in 1999 as satellite viewing rose. Local brands including Emirates Airlines and the Dubai Shopping Festival topped the list of the 20 most advertised brands in all media. Expenditures for local brands totaled $14.8 million.

Kuwait maintained sixth position in the local Arab advertising market with $170 million in expenditures in 1999, a drop of $2 million from the previous year. Newspapers dominated the market with a 66 percent share, followed by magazines with 21 percent, and TV with only 6 percent of advertising expenditures. The rest, including radio, outdoor ads, and video, accounted for 7 percent.

Bahrain ranked seventh among Arab advertising markets with $37 million in expenditures in 1999, a 9 percent increase from 1998. Television and newspaper advertising traded places in one year, as television took the lead with a 45 percent market share in 1999, versus 30 percent in 1998. Newspapers dropped from a 49 percent to a 38 percent share. Magazines' market share decreased from 20 percent to 16 percent and radio's share remained at 1 percent.

Advertising revenues in Qatar stood at $36 million in 1999, a 1 percent increase over 1998 and a strong 24 percent increase over 1997. Compared to many other Arab markets, the advertising scene in Qatar was unique: newspapers were historically, and remained, the dominant media, with a 94 percent market share.

The remaining 6 percent was divided among television, with ad expenditures of $26,000, and magazines and video with expenditures of $2,000.

Jordan's advertising expenditures decreased to $32.7 million in 1999, a 2 percent decline from the previous year's level. In Arab markets, it lagged behind all Gulf countries except Oman. Most advertising spending went to newspapers, which retained a 65 percent share, four percentage points less than in 1998. Television's share, on the other hand, rose three percentage points from 28 percent in 1998 to 31 percent in 1999. Magazines and radio shared the remaining 4 percent of advertising expenditures.

The Middle Eastern print and electronic-media environments underwent major changes in the last decade of the 20th century. For example, the number of TV stations increased substantially in both the private and the government sectors. Satellite dishes became common in all countries in the Arab world, and the Internet brought the countries of the region closer together. The advertising industry took full advantage of new technology in the region.

HUSSEIN YOUSSRY AMIN AND HANZADA FIKRI

See also Israel

Further Reading

Amin, Hussein Y., "An Overview of Problems Affecting the Advertising Industry in Egypt," *Proceedings of the International Association for Mass Communication Research (IAMCR) Conference*, Bled, Yugoslavia, 1990

Amin, Hussein Y., "Egypt and the Arab World in the Satellite Age," in *New Patterns in Global Television: Peripheral Vision*, edited by John Sinclair, Elizabeth Jacka, and Stuart Cunningham, Oxford and New York: Oxford University Press, 1996

Amin, Hussein Y., "Satellite Revolution in the Arab World: A Quest for Regulations," Paper presented at the FUTURETENSE Congress of the International Advertising Association (IAA) and the Pan Arab Research Center (PARC), Dubai, March 20-22, 1999

Drost, Harry, *The World's News Media: A Comprehensive Reference Guide*, Harlow, Essex: Longman Group UK, 1991

Middle East (videocassette), New York: London International Advertising Awards, 1993

World Economic and Social Survey, 1999: Trends and Policies in the World Economy, New York: United Nations, 1999

Miles Laboratories, Inc.

Principal Agencies

Wade Advertising Agency

Jack Tinker & Partners

J. Walter Thompson Company

Doyle Dane Bernbach, Inc.

Wells, Rich, Greene, Inc.

McCann-Erickson

What started as a humble midwestern company hawking a home remedy ultimately developed into one of the largest pharmaceutical companies in the United States. Largely through aggressive advertising and promotional efforts, Miles Laboratories created some of the most memorable brands of the 20th century: Alka-Seltzer, Bactine, One-A-Day vitamins, and Flintstones vitamins.

Certainly the talents of key executives—Herbert Thompson, Oliver Capelle, and Charles Tennant, among them—played a role in the success of Miles Laboratories, which was acquired by Bayer AG in 1978. But the company's heavy, strategic use of advertising—beginning with calendars and almanacs and moving into radio and television—was a pivotal factor in the success of its products.

Early "Advertorial"

Miles Laboratories dates to the early 1880s, when Franklin L. Miles, a country doctor in Elkhart, Indiana, began bottling Restorative Nervine, a remedy of his own devising that had proved useful in treating a number of chronic illnesses. Miles was 38 years old when he and two partners founded the Dr. Miles Medical Company, which was to become Miles Laboratories, Inc., in 1884. One of Miles's first products was Miles Nervine, essentially the same as Restorative Nervine, one of the first mass-marketed home remedies. It claimed to alleviate all sorts of ailments, including "nervousness or nervous exhaustion, sleeplessness, hysteria, headache, neuralgia, backache, pain, epilepsy, spasms, fits, and St. Vitus' dance." In other words, it was a sedative.

The introduction of Miles's calming cocktail also led to the publication, starting in 1884, of *Medical News*, a journal designed primarily to market the remedy. It was an early example of an "advertorial." Miles also got the word out through calendars and almanacs, spending $200,000 on these materials in 1893.

Although Miles died in 1929 while still active in the company, which was being run in Elkhart by his son, Charles Foster Miles, he lived to see the company enter the modern era of pharmaceutical research. As the Great Depression swept across the United States in the 1930s, Miles was known as a modestly successful company but hardly a pharmaceuticals giant. Its first annual report, a 14-page document published in 1929, disclosed sales of $1.6 million and profits of $140,000. A slump in profits was attributed to increased production, selling, and advertising expenses (the company advertised Nervine on a Fort Wayne, Indiana, radio station in 1929 and again in 1931). Promotional programs accounted for 53 percent of sales as the company produced 2.5 million laxative and Aspri-Mint samples along with 18 million "Little Books," 18.5 million almanacs, and 5 million calendars.

The Development of Alka-Seltzer

Sales climbed to $1.7 million in 1930. The annual report for the year cites slashed advertising budgets in the face of the ongoing Depression. In 1932 Miles, then nearly a half-century old, was at a turning point. The company outlook was bleak save for a spectacular new product, which was to become Alka-Seltzer. The brainchild of A.H. ("Hub") Beardsley, Alka-Seltzer consisted of a powdered laxative called Pura-Laxa to which was added an effervescent.

Alka-Seltzer, the company's best-known and most-advertised product through the years, succeeded because it worked and was superbly promoted. Marketing of the product began in the spring of 1931 in Elkhart and six other cities. Newspaper ads, so successful in advertising older Miles lines, invited readers to try a free drink of the product at their local drugstore.

A paper shortage during World War II forced Miles to cut back on calendars and almanacs, limiting their distribution to druggists in the country's ten largest cities. Radio soon became the primary medium for Alka-Seltzer ads. Alka-Seltzer spots were first heard on the Chicago, Illinois, station WLS in January 1932. Before World War II, Miles spent $4 million to $5 million annually on advertising, most of it on Alka-Seltzer. The effort was spurred on by Charles Beardsley, known as a marketing genius among his colleagues. Until his death in 1936, Beardsley was an advocate of strong advertising budgets. He liked to say that he measured the success of commercials with a trip to the company's loading dock, where he could see the tangible result.

Through the 1930s the company continued its emphasis on excess systemic acid, using the slogan, "Be wise—alkalize with Alka-Seltzer." But perhaps most significant was Alka-Seltzer's sponsorship of WLS's *Saturday Night Barn Dance*. Alka-Seltzer was first advertised on the program in 1933. Sales climbed, and at the end of its contract with WLS, Miles renewed its sponsorship and the show expanded to Detroit, Michigan, and Pittsburgh, Pennsylvania. In September 1933 *Barn Dance* went national on 200 of the National Broadcasting Company's (NBC's) Blue Network stations. Few programs in advertising history have contributed so much to a single product's success. Alka-Seltzer subsequently sponsored *Barn Dance*'s summer replacements, *Quiz Kids,* and pianist Alec Templeton's show. Alka-Seltzer continued its sponsorship of *Quiz Kids* even after the show got its own regular time slot.

Miles's knack for getting spots on highly rated shows continued into World War II and beyond. *One Man's Family* was an example of a popular show that it sponsored. Alka-Seltzer spots, as well as those for other Miles products, were heard on many network radio shows. Even *News of the World* was sponsored by Miles products.

Rhymes were popular early on in the history of Alka-Seltzer. "When your tablets get down to four, that's the time to buy some more" was used until 1954. "An extra package in the grip can become handy on a trip" and "An extra package in the car can act just like a spare; you may not need to use it, but it's wise to have it there" are other examples of Miles's efforts.

"The Stipulation"

In 1939, in the midst of Alka-Seltzer's push into radio, the first of many bombshells that wounded egos, shattered convictions, and changed the course of the product's advertising and promotions exploded over corporate headquarters. Known internally as "The Stipulation," it was an agreement between Miles and the Federal Trade Commission (FTC). The FTC had accused Miles of using "false, misleading, and deceptive" advertising claims that systemic acidity caused various bodily disturbances and that Alka-Seltzer could relieve such symptoms. Walter Ames Compton, a physician and Miles executive, struck a compromise with the FTC, agreeing to drop the claims involving systemic acidity from Alka-Seltzer advertising and to submit all future ad copy and claims for FTC review and approval. In spite of the controversy, sales did not suffer. (But even into the 1980s, the company's own medical department was a stern monitor of promotional copy. It did not like the word *stop* in ad copy, since that implied complete relief; neither was *treatment* considered suitable. It also insisted that *suffer* be eliminated and that *misery* and *distress* be used with caution. *Soothe,* however, was approved.)

New Products, New Ads

Miles, though, was not dependent on Alka-Seltzer for profits. The company's first vitamin preparation, trademarked One-A-Day, arrived in distributors' warehouses in October 1940. Miles immediately moved One-A-Day into national radio, promoting and advertising it aggressively via the Wade Advertising Agency. Spending was estimated at $4 million to $5 million.

Commercials bore the tag line, "Look for the big one on the package." It worked well and, with some modifications, lasted a long time. Grandparents, adults, and children were all promotional targets, and as with early Alka-Seltzer ads, verse was incorporated:

The One-A-Day vitamin twins are we,
B Complex and A & D
And we're the ones, we must confess,
Who give you more, yet cost you less.

Such concepts as "tissue starvation" also were introduced into ad copy, as Miles embarked on an instructional campaign to teach the public about vitamins. Early on, the product struggled for product awareness among consumers, and during those grim times volume declined. Success came slowly with the new B-complex tablets introduced in 1942 and the One-A-Day multivitamins in 1943.

In 1949 the company unveiled a "First-aid" theme for Alka-Seltzer. In 1952 the slogan, "Feel better while you're getting better," was first heard and lasted for nine years, along with "Alka-Seltzer—for that feel-better feeling." "Triple comfort relief" stressed stomach symptoms in 1955 as did "Action in the glass" and the more famous, "Relief is just a swallow away," which would emerge in 1957 and run for several years. Wade Advertising—which won the Miles account in 1917 and retained the account until 1964, when it moved to Jack Tinker & Partners—was responsible for all these efforts.

Perhaps most significantly, Wade created Speedy Alka-Seltzer, a cartoon character who went on to represent the product for ten years until he gave way to advertising's creative revolution of the 1960s. Speedy, originally albeit briefly called "Sparky," was conceived in 1951 and won many awards. Walter Compton, a Miles vice president, spearheaded a drive to put Speedy into print and promote him heavily to the drug trade. A four-page booklet, "Miles Ahead," went to 58,000 drug retailers to introduce the character in 1952. On radio, actor Richard Beals became the voice of Speedy.

Speedy fully blossomed when Miles moved him to TV in 1954. He had an immediate impact, becoming so popular that ad gurus at both Miles and Wade began to worry about overkill. While his appearances were carefully monitored, Speedy showed up in more than 100 spots for Miles. The "spokestablet" was resurrected in 1976 for the U.S. Bicentennial, and emerged again briefly before the 1980 Olympic Games. But when the United States pulled out of the Summer Games, Speedy returned home with the American athletes.

Television Sponsorships

The 1950s ushered in the era of television as a prime advertising medium for Miles. In 1951 and 1952 Miles's Alka-Seltzer sponsored *One Man's Family*, *Garry Moore*, and *Ernie Ford* along with news broadcasts. After a brief hiatus, Miles in 1954 returned to network TV, spending approximately $700,000 that year. The company continued to increase its use of network and spot TV each year thereafter, at the expense of its radio budgets. By the end of the 1950s, Miles's network radio spending had dropped to less than $6 million as the company moved support behind local spot buys. The theory was that local spots reached listeners for a lower cost-per-thousand than the same commercials placed in network shows. Its last network radio sponsorship was on *CBS News* in late 1958.

In the late 1950s, Miles, then the nation's 47th-largest advertiser with total spending estimated at $15.1 million, sponsored several TV shows, including *Wednesday Night Fights*, *The Rifleman*, *Bonanza*, *Laramie*, *The Andy Williams Show*, *Hawaiian Eye*, *The Tonight Show* with Jack Paar, *Combat*, *The Naked City*,

Spokes-character Speedy, featured in this 1955 ad, made his debut in ads for Miles Laboratories' Alka-Seltzer in 1951.
© 1969 Miles Laboratories, Inc., and used with permission of Bayer Corporation. Permission also granted by Warner Bros. Consumer Products.

Hootenanny, and *The Flintstones*. By 1959 the company was devoting $21.5 million to advertising.

Miles's ad spending in 1960 jumped 10 percent from the previous year to $23.5 million, making it the 39th-largest U.S. advertiser. In 1960 Miles dropped all radio spots and went entirely to TV, allotting nearly 72 percent of its ad budget to that medium. In the early 1960s, in rankings among all network TV advertisers, Miles rose from number 20 to number 15. At its peak in the 1960s, the Miles Products division sponsored 13 evening and ten daytime TV network shows.

At about the same time, Miles began to develop a new product: children's vitamins. In 1968 the J. Walter Thompson Company (JWT) suggested that Miles manufacture the vitamin tablets in the shape of the well-known Flintstones cartoon characters. The idea proved wildly successful, and JWT began to work for Miles in 1969. Another product, Bactine, continued through the late 1960s as the leading first-aid antiseptic in sales, market share, and ad spending.

Agency Switches

In 1964 Miles removed Alka-Seltzer from Wade, appointing Jack Tinker & Partners, a creative think-tank of the Interpublic Group of Companies' top talents, to find new approaches for Alka-Seltzer, by now a mature product. Over the next few years, Miles would move its new Bactine skin cream and One-A-Day vitamins and the remaining products of its consumer division, which billed more than $10 million annually, from Wade to Tinker, ending a 50-year relationship.

The impact on Wade was disastrous, and two years later Wade announced it was closing its doors. Several Wade executives, including Albert Wade II, a former Wade chairman, joined Tinker to work on Miles.

Miles executives said they made the move without a review to avoid a flood of speculative presentations for the business from other agencies. Tinker immediately dropped Speedy in favor of a new creative approach. The new commercials, featuring lines such as "No matter what shape your stomach's in," won many awards, including a Clio. *Advertising Age* selected the "Stomach's Montage" as one of the best spots of 1964.

After nearly five years at Tinker, Miles turned to Doyle Dane Bernbach (DDB), but that association was short-lived (though the agency continued to handle the company's S.O.S soap pad account). Some observers believed that the agency lost the account because its advertising was not product-oriented enough at a time when Miles's profits were slipping. Another reason for the move was said to be that DDB's ads for the new Alka-Seltzer Plus line extension had cannibalized sales of Alka-Seltzer.

By the late 1960s, advertising for Alka-Seltzer consisted almost exclusively of TV commercials, with a number of different spots being used in rotation. The potpourri of 30-second and 60-second messages consisted of usually humorous vignettes of everyday situations calling for effervescent soothing. Commercials featured a man and his stomach discussing their problems with a psychiatrist, as well as a "Diagram man," which used a human as an illustration.

Disputes over Advertising

In December 1970 Miles moved its account again, after only 16 months, this time to Wells, Rich, Greene (WRG), reuniting with Mary Wells Lawrence. There was internal turmoil over WRG's new ads for Alka-Seltzer, and after six months on the account, the agency's new campaign for the brand was not yet on the air.

WRG's new Alka-Seltzer campaign had been scheduled to break in mid-May 1971, but it was delayed because company attorneys were concerned that the ads were too bold in the face of tightening governmental restrictions.

Battle lines were drawn between Lawrence, president of WRG, and Miles Chairman Walter Compton. Compton backed the attorneys, and the campaign was axed.

WRG kept the account until 1983, when it again was shifted—this time to McCann-Erickson. WRG is remembered for such copy lines as "Try it, you'll like it" and "I can't believe I ate the whole thing." *Newsweek* selected the latter as one of the ten best quotes of the decade. Among the creative hot shop's most successful and best remembered efforts for the brand was one tagged "Plop, plop, fizz, fizz."

Advertising expenditures by Miles in the early 1970s remained near the $48 million mark, although the company opened a new marketing front in 1970 through the acquisition of Worthington Foods, Inc., which marketed a line of vegetarian products via Hammeroff & Associates. But during the early 1970s, Alka-Seltzer, the vitamin lines, and several other proprietary lines, which accounted for a little less than half of Miles's sales, still received more than 80 percent of the ad budget. Miles spent approximately $35.4 million—or 75 percent of its total ad budget—in television.

Through the mid-1970s, Miles's ad budget crept up slightly, reaching $49 million in 1976. The increase was primarily a result of the heavy promotional effort behind the national introduction of an Alka-2 line extension, formulated without aspirin. In addition to network and spot TV spending, more than $3 million was spent on consumer promotions for the chewable antacid tablet, including heavy couponing and sampling. Media spending for most of Miles's other consumer products remained at the same levels, with the exception of its Morningstar Farms line of food products; its spending dropped 35 percent.

The mid-1970s also saw the national relaunch of Alka-Seltzer Cold Medicine, with a new formula, packaging, and a somewhat revised name. Advertising for the remedy, from WRG, positioned it as more clearly for the relief of major cold symptoms and trumpeted its lemony flavor and effervescence. It received $15.5 million of the $22.8 million in measured media Miles spent behind its Alka-Seltzer brand.

In a 1976 effort to reach new users, Miles began an intensive promotional campaign on 280 college campuses across the country to create an awareness of Alka-Seltzer among students to build product trial and dosage among young adults. Student representatives at each college were responsible for the execution of the multifaceted effort, which included posters, sampling, and contests. That same year, Miles moved Alka-2 from JWT to WRG, its agency for Alka-Seltzer and Alka-Seltzer Plus. JWT continued on the vitamin line.

In 1979 Miles revived DDB's earlier "Honeymooners" TV commercial while WRG was working on interim advertising for Alka-2. At the time, Miles was unhappy with WRG's interim ads, none of which made it to the air. DDB recovered the account after barely a year's absence.

Acquisition by Bayer

West Germany's Bayer AG acquired Miles in 1979. Bayer, which in 1967 began acquiring companies to bolster its North American presence, in 1994 purchased Sterling Winthrop's North American OTC drug business for $1 billion, including all trademark rights in Canada and the United States related to the Bayer name and Bayer cross logo.

Everything from subway cards to high-exposure television kept Alka-Seltzer in the public eye over the years. Miles's advertising succeeded because it remained simple, direct, and attuned to the everyday speech of ordinary people. It never tried to be fancy; it kept a light, humorous tone and discussed common ailments in everyday terms. The visuals had the same simple charm.

In April 1995 the German parent company changed the name Miles Canada, Inc., to Bayer, Inc., seeking the operating advantages of a single company name worldwide. Miles, Inc., became the Bayer Corporation at the same time. The company began a name-change campaign in March in more than 35 newspapers, magazines, and business publications targeted at business and opinion leaders and consumers. The folksy campaign theme: "After all these years, it's time you called us by our first name, Bayer." By the end of the century, Alka-Seltzer, with ad spending of $47.8 million, was handled by BBDO Worldwide, New York City, while One-A-Day, with ad spending of $35.2 million, was with Euro RSCG Tatham, Chicago.

ALAN SALOMON

See also Alka-Seltzer; *and color plate in this volume*

Further Reading

Bayer Group <www.bayer.com>

Careless, James Maurice Stockford, and Piet J. Koene, "History of Bayer," in *Canada: A Celebration of Our Heritage*, by Careless, Mississauga, Ontario: Heritage, 1994

Cray, William C., *Miles, 1884–1984: A Centennial History*, Upper Saddle River, New Jersey: Prentice-Hall, 1984

Verg, Erik, Gottfried Plumpe, and Heinz Schultheis, *Meilensteine*, Leverkusen, Germany: Bayer, 1988; as *Milestones: The Bayer Story, 1863–1988*, Leverkusen, Germany: Bayer, 1988

Military Advertising

Throughout modern history, advertising has been used to help gain support for military mobilization. In the United States, advertising has often been the main method for recruiting military personnel and has been instrumental in promoting a positive image of the armed forces, especially following the Vietnam War, when the U.S. military's image was at an all-time low.

Modern military advertising, in the form of national campaigns initiated and funded by the government, emerged for the first time during World War I as Great Britain and the United States, in particular, sought to draw public support for the war. To buttress the cause and image of their militaries, each country established new government agencies to work with its military branches. In 1917 Britain created the Ministry of Information and the Enemy Propaganda Department. That same year in the United States, President Woodrow Wilson established the Committee on Public Information (CPI).

These government agencies were created primarily to organize and influence public opinion in favor of the war, not only to boost morale and encourage enlistment but also to persuade businesses and civilians of the need to put resources behind the war effort. Both governments worked to control press reports of the war and distributed films, leaflets, and posters to draw citizens' support. The British campaign helped counter public objections to a conscription bill that had passed in May 1916, calling for compulsory enlistment for all men age 18 to 41. In an attempt to persuade the reluctant, isolationist United States to enter the war, Britain also began a propaganda campaign featuring battle footage depicting "German atrocities" committed against the British.

The U.S. Campaign

Because the war in Europe did not directly affect most Americans, the U.S. government faced the difficult task of persuading its citizens to support the war effort. However, in the interest of President Wilson's plea to "make the world safe for democracy," the CPI began urging enlistment in the army and navy while asking those not eligible for service to buy Liberty Bonds, join the war production effort, and be wary of spies and traitors. N.W. Ayer & Son developed the ad campaigns for the first three Liberty Loan drives. The CPI published 75 million pamphlets, 6,000 press releases, and 14,000 drawings in support of the war effort; it also posted an official daily bulletin about the progress of the war in every U.S. military camp and post office. People were inundated with news stories about atrocities committed by German soldiers, who were referred to as "Hun barbarians" and depicted in propaganda posters as almost inhuman.

As part of this campaign, artist James Montgomery Flagg, a well-known magazine illustrator, joined the U.S. Division of Pictorial Publicity and created the most famous recruitment poster of the period and perhaps of all time: "I Want You for U.S. Army," depicting Uncle Sam pointing a finger at every able-bodied American male. In a more subtle approach, a Navy Publicity Bureau poster by artist Howard Chandler Christy featured the "Christy Girl," a fetching young woman in a sailor suit, coyly wishing she were a man so she could join the navy.

While there were still some who opposed U.S. entry into the war, the campaign succeeded beyond its goal of driving patriotic nationalism. In May 1917, rather than wait for recruiting efforts to muster a volunteer force, the U.S. Congress passed the Selective Service Act, creating a draft that registered 24 million men and supplied 60 percent of the nearly 5 million American men who served during World War I. The effective propaganda campaign succeeded in establishing virtually total acceptance of the draft, the nation's support for its soldiers, and a common sense of purpose behind the country's involvement in the war. Further contributing to the patriotic fervor were a number of popular songs of the day, including George M. Cohan's 1917 hit song "Over There," which won Cohan the Congressional Medal of Honor in 1936.

Following the war, military forces in the United States and Europe returned to their normal peacetime dimensions. But by the mid-1930s, German Chancellor Adolph Hitler had started rebuilding his armed forces, recruiting millions of men for the military and children for his Hitler Youth Corps. At the same time, he launched a massive propaganda campaign, headed by his propaganda minister, Josef Goebbels, to persuade Germans of their superiority.

Preparing for World War II

In 1939, as Europe faced a second world war, Britain again called for a national draft. However, it faced much greater resistance than it had some 20 years earlier; its efforts to build support for World War I had backfired in the long run, as the British public discovered its government had misrepresented conditions on the front lines and fabricated accounts of the enemy.

The United States also faced resistance from many of its citizens, who saw little reason to get involved in another foreign war. However, in 1940, with Hitler's aggressive expansion unchecked and the threat of a war in the Pacific, Congress passed the Selective Service and Training Act, establishing the country's first peacetime draft. With that the U.S. Army began a recruiting effort that would for the first time include the efforts of a major ad agency—Ayer. Public sentiment toward the war underwent an about-face on 7 December 1941 with Japan's surprise attack on U.S. forces stationed at Pearl Harbor in Hawaii.

In 1942 President Franklin D. Roosevelt organized the War Advertising Council with the American Association of Advertising Agencies and the Association of National Advertisers. The council mustered $350 million in free public service messages promoting the purchase of war bonds, the need to keep sensitive information from the country's enemies, and the importance of women to the war effort at home. It was to promote the latter that the famous "Rosie the Riveter" icon was created. The Ad Council, as it was later known, was so successful that President Roosevelt asked it to continue administering public service messages after the war. It would prove essential to future military advertising campaigns.

Print, radio, and feature films were used to promote the war effort both at home and at the front. In 1942 movie director Frank Capra joined the U.S. Army Signal Corps, where he produced an Oscar-winning, seven-film documentary series, *Why We Fight,* to convince Americans of the threat posed by the Axis powers and encourage the country to enter World War II. While the U.S. government intervened much less in the nation's media than it had during World War I, the U.S. War Department's own publications and training literature promoted patriotism and presented distorted images of the enemy. In all, the Ad Council estimated that the U.S. advertising industry donated approximately $1 billion to the war effort in work done and space contributed.

Once again, some of the country's foremost artists and illustrators designed posters to recruit soldiers and inspire patriotism. Motivated by a speech by President Roosevelt in which he enumerated the "Four Freedoms"—freedom of speech, freedom to worship, freedom from want, and freedom from fear—illustrator Norman Rockwell created his "Four Freedoms" paintings, which were turned into posters. Flagg's iconic "I want you" poster from World War I was reprinted, directing men to "enlist now." Posters also stressed the fear of domination by the Axis powers by exaggerating the closeness of the enemy; one poster read, "Warning! Our homes are in danger now!" Others attempted to show that crimes against humanity occurring overseas could happen in the United States unless the country took action. Another popular theme included warnings against actions that might compromise national security. One poster showing an innocent-looking housewife bore the headline, "Wanted! For murder. Her careless talk costs lives."

U.S. propaganda efforts promoted the idea that American soldiers were the "good guys" fighting "with God on their side." The American campaign extolled freedom at the cost of soldiers fighting overseas. Japanese soldiers were urged to die for their emperor in the cause of ridding the world of American domination.

As World War II ended, soldiers returned home to be restored to civilian life, though both Britain and the United States reserved the right to continue to draft troops. In the early 1950s, however, Britain gave up the draft in favor of voluntary enlistment and a smaller military, while the United States would keep the draft for another 20 years. In 1952, with the war in Korea still under way, Congress passed legislation to freeze funds destined for recruitment advertising, then planned at about $1 million, on the grounds that a national media campaign to recruit men for general service was unnecessary when recruits were already available through the draft. Congress also sought to reduce the number of service people working in the recruiting field in local communities.

Over the next several years, however, budgets were cautiously restored, particularly to encourage reenlistment and for recruitment of specialists and women, mostly in medical posts. But the U.S. government would show a general weariness toward advertising for the military, with apprehension by some legislators that it was a waste of taxpayer money.

In terms of recruitment efforts, the U.S. Army continued to work with ad agencies after the war, though the relationships

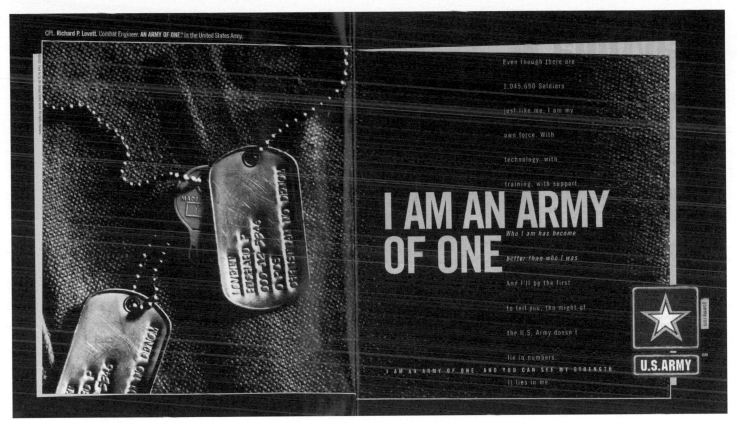

CPL. Richard P. Lovett. Combat Engineer. AN ARMY OF ONE." In the United States Army.

Even though there are 1,045,690 Soldiers just like me, I am my own force. With technology, with training, with support

I AM AN ARMY OF ONE

Who I am has become better than who I was. And I'll be the first to tell you, the might of the U.S. Army doesn't lie in numbers. I AM AN ARMY OF ONE. AND YOU CAN SEE MY STRENGTH. It lies in me

U.S. ARMY

The U.S. Army's 2001 ad campaign addressed prospective recruits' sense of individualism and desire to meet challenges.
Army materials courtesy of the U.S. Government.

were often fleeting. (The U.S. Navy used no paid advertising for recruitment until the 1960s.) As the war ended, Ayer, which also handled National Guard advertising, was spending $1 million on behalf of army recruiting at the end of 1945. The amount dipped in 1946, then partially recovered in 1947, to approximately $850,000. As America's postwar occupation responsibilities grew, however, recruitment needs mounted rapidly. In 1948 army billings and fees grew to $4.5 million, making army advertising a major piece of business for any ad agency. After losing the National Guard to Gardner Advertising, Inc., in 1947, Ayer saw the U.S. Army account follow in 1948. But army selection procedures were indecisive, and once the business was given to Gardner, the account soon became inactive, and each of the army's six units (the First Army, the Second Army, and so on) became affiliated with a separate agency. Within a year Gardner resigned the business, along with the National Guard, and the now fragmented account passed to Grant Advertising, Inc., with Gardner continuing through the end of 1949.

According to the *Standard Directory of Advertising Agencies* (1950), the army worked briefly with J. Walter Thompson Company (JWT) at midcentury, while National Guard recruiting was shared by Cecil & Presbrey, Inc., and Fletcher Richard, Inc., which handled radio spots. In 1952 the consolidated army and air force recruiting business switched to Dancer, Fitzgerald, Sample (DFS). The air force went to Ruthrauff & Ryan in 1954, but the

army remained at DFS for several years before going in-house, and then back to Ayer in the 1960s. The navy began using paid advertising in the 1960s with MacManus, John & Adams.

The Vietnam Years

In the early 1960s, the United States found itself increasingly involved in the ongoing military conflict in Vietnam, which the government portrayed to the public as a necessary effort to stop the spread of communism. In 1964 Congress authorized President Lyndon Johnson to commit U.S. military forces to fighting communist aggression in Vietnam. However, the government did not launch a specific ad campaign to gain public support for its military actions in Southeast Asia. But as U.S. involvement deepened and progress stalled, public outrage over the war grew to major proportions.

The draft had come under grave criticism because of exemptions that enabled college students and others in privileged groups to avoid military service. As the protests grew louder in the face of official support for the war effort, what American GIs did hear was the voice of North Vietnamese radio propaganda by a Vietnamese woman named Trinh Thi Ngo, or "Hanoi Hannah" as she was called by U.S. soldiers. Between popular songs, Ngo urged U.S. servicemen to quit the war effort while citing the names of recently killed or captured Americans and reading U.S.

magazine articles that informed them of antiwar demonstrations at home.

Faced with the declining morale of the country, the U.S. government attempted to raise support for the war in 1967 with a public relations campaign that claimed progress toward an eventual victory. However, the damage done to the military's image could not be undone. Americans had not learned enough about the Chinese and Soviet presence or the atrocities inflicted on the South Vietnamese to fully justify U.S. involvement. In 1971 a Yale political activist launched an antiwar campaign called "Unsell" with the aid of some within the advertising industry. Maxwell Dane joined Jim McCaffrey and David McCall of McCaffrey & McCall, which won a Clio award in 1972 for a television commercial produced for the antiwar campaign.

U.S. military recruitment efforts were stepped up sharply in the beginning of the 1970s, first to offset a decision to decrease draft calls and then to replace the draft, which was stopped in 1973. With the military now competing with business for manpower, many top Pentagon officials feared the armed services would attract a lower echelon of people at a time when the military's public image was at an all-time low. This concern led to larger advertising budgets to back campaigns boosting the military's image as well as its enrollment. Despite dramatic cuts in government spending through the mid-1970s, military ad budgets had been growing steadily since the mid-1960s; for example, the army, which consistently had the largest recruiting ad budget of the military's five main branches—army, navy, air force, marines, and coast guard—grew from less than $2 million in the mid-1960s to $35 million in 1974. Recruiting at the time made up 75 percent of the government's total advertising expenditures. Advertising dollars were allocated generally in national and local recruiting efforts distributing informational materials to targeted youth through direct mail and schools as well as magazine and outdoor advertising. JWT handled the marines; D'Arcy-MacManus & Masius, the air force; Grey Advertising and Ted Bates & Company, Inc., the navy; and Ayer, the army.

Declining Recruitment

Despite large advertising budgets, those responsible for military advertising were encouraged to cut costs at every opportunity. As a result, the branches often competed to be chosen for public service campaigns by the Ad Council, which gave them free creative services from volunteer professional advertising agencies and donated broadcast time, charging them only for production and distribution costs. At the same time, each military branch did annual agency reviews for its recruiting campaign contracts. Congress, citing high costs and disappointing results in earlier tests, had denied the military unrestricted use of radio and TV spots through the early 1970s. But a lack of quality recruits that finally approached an emergency level led to widespread use of radio with some television spots by all branches by 1977.

Recruitment endeavors were further hindered by advertising budget cuts in the late 1970s when congressional critics attacked the usefulness of recruitment advertising efforts. The five major

military branches were pushed to accept a new corporate-type joint advertising campaign to cut costs. Campaigns were designed to provide a better general understanding of the services while paving the way for continued individual recruiting efforts. The initial slogan, "A chance to serve, a chance to learn," was soon replaced with a new theme, "Armed Forces. It's a great place to start." The effort, developed by Grey, continued to serve an important role in overall military recruiting efforts for years, particularly by targeting parents and other role models to encourage enlistment.

Testimonial ads in magazine spreads told the stories of those who had enlisted and were happy with their choice and included reply cards to request more information or toll-free numbers. In late December 1976, the Marine Corps targeted youth unhappy with low-prestige job options in the private sector with a TV campaign from JWT based on the theme "The few. The proud. The Marines." The army and navy were on radio at the same time, with "Join the people who've joined the army" and "It's not just a job, it's an adventure," respectively, from N.W. Ayer ABH and Ted Bates. But even with increased incentives such as higher pay and a high U.S. unemployment level in the late 1970s, the military was forced to take on less qualified recruits just to meet recruitment quotas.

With the 1980s and the election of Republican Ronald Reagan as president, more government money was allocated to defense spending, including military recruitment efforts. Under the Reagan administration, the armed services expanded their incentives to recruits, offering increased pay and enlistment bonuses, a more technologically advanced military, and increased higher education aid designed to draw more talented high school graduates and keep those already enlisted.

"Be All That You Can Be"

Along with this, the military turned to television for the bulk of its advertising spending, seeing it as the most efficient vehicle for reaching teens. In 1981 the most memorable slogan of the modern military, "Be all that you can be," was created for the army by Ayer. The theme would be used until 2000, with the addition of the line, "Get an edge on life," in 1988. The army's advertising budget for 1988 was $86 million. Other recruiting efforts targeted the advantages of individual services. The navy's long-term slogan, "Live the adventure," and 1989 theme, "You and the Navy: Full speed ahead," promoted travel opportunities via BBDO, of New York City. The marines' "Swords" campaign, created in 1984 by JWT, glorified the prestige of being a marine while quieting fears that military advertising was sidestepping the importance of "duty, honor, and country," the U.S. military mantra, in favor of luring new recruits with glittering incentives. The joint services campaign also grew considerably during this period, creating an image of unity and an air of general opportunity, via a $10 million to $12 million campaign from Grey with the theme "Opportunity is waiting for you" in 1989.

The final decade of the 20th century brought some of the biggest changes and challenges to the military as the various services worked to redefine the role of the military for the post–Cold War era, the end of the arms race, and the new threats of terrorism that required different military tactics. Despite the smaller forces required in the 1990s, nations in the business of selling their military, such as the United States and Great Britain, still could not find enough qualified recruits to meet demand by the late 1990s. One major challenge facing recruiters was teens' lack of interest in enlisting—owing in part to decreased military advertising during the downsizing of the 1990s that gave youth little exposure to positive military images. In addition, a higher percentage of high school students was able to choose college rather than the military for educational advancement.

Entering the 21st century, the military went after fresh, integrated, and smart campaigns backed by new market research that had showed current military "brand names" to be incompatible with what modern youth wanted. The army finally replaced "Be all that you can be" in January 2001 with a new campaign from Leo Burnett Worldwide, of Chicago, Illinois. The year before, Burnett had replaced Young & Rubicam, which had spent 12 years handling the army's $110 million annual account. Burnett, working with Cartel Creativo, a San Antonio, Texas, agency specializing in the Hispanic market, and Images USA, an Atlanta, Georgia, agency focused on the African-American audience, launched a campaign with the new theme "An army of one." It was an appeal to the individualism and challenges America's youth were seeking. The new advertising emphasized the personal and trade skills young people would learn in the military that would carry over into any endeavor, and directed those interested in learning more to go to a Web site, www.goarmy.com.

The navy and the air force also hired new agencies in 2000. The navy hired Warren, Michigan-based Campbell-Ewald for its $30 million account; the agency introduced the theme, "Accelerate your life," replacing, "Let the journey begin." The air force, ending a 14-year relationship with Bozell Kamstra, awarded its $40 million account to GSD&M, of Austin, Texas, but planned to retain its theme, "No one comes close." The U.S. joint services advertising operation also launched a new campaign appealing to parents, mainly via magazine ads, as well as offering a Web site (www.todaysmilitary.com) with an overview of each service branch and links to individual sites for additional information. Similarly, in the United Kingdom, military executives were working to redefine their image in an attempt to make the military seem less tough and more approachable.

MEGAN CASSADA

See also color plate in this volume

Further Reading

"Ad Cuts May Force Services into Increased Broadcast Use," *Advertising Age* (15 December 1975)

"Advertising Council Supports Women Volunteer Drive," *Advertising Age* (19 November 1951)

"Armed Forces to Get Together for Test of Direct Mail Effort," *Advertising Age* (15 September 1975)

Attarian, John, "Rethinking the Vietnam War," *World and I* 15, no. 7 (July 2000)

Bacevich, Andrew J., "Who Will Serve," *The Wilson Quarterly* 22, no. 3 (Summer 1998)

Daniloff, Nicholas, "As the Kremlin Whips Up Hatred of Americans," *U.S. News and World Report* (27 August 1984)

"Defense Dept. Seeks $8,000,000 for '74 Military Campaign," *Advertising Age* (11 June 1973)

"Defense Officials Needling Senators for More Ad Money," *Advertising Age* (28 April 1952)

"Defense Officials Take Step toward Paid Advertising," *Advertising Age* (17 December 1951)

Hall, Mitchell, "Unsell the War: Vietnam and Antiwar Advertising," *The Historian* 58, no. 1 (Autumn 1995)

"Hope Renewed for Advocates of Paid Ads for Military," *Advertising Age* (26 November 1973)

"Joint Service Recruit Ads Set for Test by Pentagon," *Advertising Age* (19 July 1976)

McKenna, Kristine, "An Exhibit of Vietnam War Posters Recalls One of Printed Propaganda's Final Flourishes," *Los Angeles Times* (4 February 1996)

"Military Eyes Radio; Senate Sets Budgets," *Advertising Age* (26 July 1976)

"Not All That It Can Be; Low Morale May Be at Root of U.S. Military Recruiting Woes," *Sarasota Herald Tribune* (14 January 2000)

Powers of Persuasion: Poster Art from World War II <www.nara.gov/exhall/powers/powers.html>

"Radio Days: During the War in Vietnam, Trihn Thi Ngo Was Hanoi Hannah," *People Weekly* (24 April 1995)

"Sad State of Affairs—Navy Account Goes Begging," *Advertising Age* (7 May 1973)

Thomas, Davis M., "Operation Dire Straits; Here's Why the Military Is Failing to Attract the Right Recruits," *The Washington Post* (16 January 2000)

Wooden, Ruth, "WWII Spawned the Ad Council," *Advertising Age* (29 March 1999)

Miller Brewing Company

Principal Agencies
Roche, Williams & Cunnyngham, Inc.
H.C. Mulberger, Inc. (later Mathisson & Associates, Inc.)
McCann-Erickson, Inc.
Backer Spielvogel Bates
Leo Burnett USA
Fallon McElligott
Ogilvy & Mather Worldwide

The Miller Brewing Company began in 1855 when German immigrant Frederick Miller bought Plank-Road Brewery in Milwaukee, Wisconsin, for $8,000. Within 20 years it had 4,130 competitors in the United States. The number eventually decreased amid consolidation that paved the way for behemoths such as Anheuser-Busch, Pabst Brewing Company, and crosstown rival Joseph Schlitz Brewing Company. Although the number of breweries dwindled during Prohibition (1913 to 1933), Miller survived the 18th Amendment by producing soft drinks, malt syrup, and nonalcoholic products for home brewing. It spent World War II providing U.S. troops with Miller High Life, having discontinued its other brands. Sports, spending, and segmentation tell the story of how the small-time midwestern brewer came close to being the number-one U.S. brewer by the late 1970s but then embarked on a two-decade-long slide. The company ended the 20th century as the number-two brewer in the United States.

The brewery remained in family hands for its first 111 years. In fact, at the dawn of the 20th century, the face of Miller High Life's girl-in-the-moon logo was the founder's preteen granddaughter, who struck the pose that would adorn High Life bottles on and off for the next century.

Miller's first major ad agency was Roche, Williams & Cunnyngham, Inc., of Milwaukee, Wisconsin. In the late 1930s it switched to H.C. Mulberger, Inc., also of Milwaukee, which became Mathisson & Associates, Inc., in the 1940s and would continue with the brand until the 1960s. Miller High Life was consistently promoted as the "champagne of bottled beer."

In 1966 Miller's descendants sold most of their stock to W.R. Grace & Company for approximately $36 million. Grace, a chemical company, held a controlling interest until 1969, when it rejected a $120 million offer from PepsiCo in favor of another worth $7 million more from the Philip Morris Companies. That check, along with another $100 million paid to a Catholic foundation that owned the remaining shares of Miller, turned the brewery into a division of the cigarette company in 1970. Thirty years later, that $227 million investment would be worth more than $540 million in annual sales.

When Philip Morris took control, Miller had just 4 percent of domestic market share. Then came a plan for Miller to corner the market on sports advertising, a first among brewers. With Philip Morris's packaged-goods money, Miller had a public, multinational checkbook to fund its efforts. The brewer was 115 years old, and things were getting ready to pick up. About that same time McCann-Erickson, Inc. (M-E), resigned its $1 million G. Heileman Brewing Old Style business, clearing the way for Miller. Meanwhile, Miller snapped up just about every major sporting event on network TV, including *Monday Night Football,* the college football game of the week, the World Series, the 1980 Moscow Olympics, and the Indianapolis 500.

Then came the brewer's 1975 launch of the nation's first palatable low-calorie beer. Lite, a trademark obtained when Philip Morris bought Chicago's MeisterBrau brewery in 1972, helped Miller attain a 23 percent share, but before that, it had to convince consumers that "low-calorie" did not mean "cut with water." Although the category would account for 43 percent of domestic beer consumption by the end of 2000, Miller risked the beer's relegation to the status of "a woman's drink" if it was not established correctly.

Unable to use active professional athletes in ads for alcoholic beverages, M-E signed 40-ish former stars such as retired New

This early 1980s campaign positioned Miller High Life as the beer of choice among blue-collar workers.
Courtesy of Miller Brewing Company.

York Jet and Super Bowl veteran Matt Snell for a manly campaign that showed athletes in a locker room talking up the brand. In one mid-1970s spot from M-E, National Football League great Bubba Smith ripped the top off a Lite can.

With M-E's "Tastes great, less filling" stable of ads, health-conscious consumers were reassured that they need not feel guilty about loading up on low-alcohol brews that happened to taste good. Miller increased its ad spending as never before—spending twice the per-barrel industry average. Not only did the company see its market share almost triple, but profits rose fivefold, from $6 million to $29 million. The tag line endured for 17 years.

Heavy spending in sports was married to the then-novel idea of segmenting the market. By pegging different brands and marketing campaigns to different groups of consumers, Miller leap-frogged from the country's number-seven brewer in 1970 to a strong number two in 1977. By 1978 Miller had come within 10 million barrels of catching Anheuser-Busch, narrowing what had been a 21 million-barrel gap six years earlier. It was the closest the two would ever get. By 1985 Miller lagged by 27 million barrels, 57 million by 2000.

With Miller High Life, the brewer changed the face of beer advertising by building ads that celebrated the working man. No longer was the beer touted as "the champagne of bottled beers," as it had been since 1906; now it was "Miller time"—and time to make stars of welders, farmers, and factory workers heading to the bar after a hard day on the job. "If you've got the time, we've got the beer" turned around Miller's sales. Backer Spielvogel Bates's "Miller time" theme, started at McCann in 1971, would end the 20th century as a Miller Lite tag.

Anheuser-Busch—frozen out of network sports but motivated by Miller's success—answered the challenge with huge increases in advertising spending and the 1982 launch of Bud Light. Within a decade the two brewers' combined ad spending totaled more than half a billion dollars annually, and Bud Light was on its way to passing Lite in volume, which it did in 1994. Bud Light was marketed to consumers who had already embraced the merits of low-calorie beer.

Miller tried to get its swagger—and market share—back in 1996 when it moved the Lite account from Leo Burnett USA to Fallon McElligott, of Minneapolis, Minnesota. Sales volume continued to be anemic under "Dick, the Creative Superstar" and other ill-fated Fallon campaigns; however, sales increased shortly before Fallon was dismissed in 1999 when the agency revived the venerable "Miller time" tag for Lite. The brand continued to sag under Fallon's replacement, Ogilvy & Mather Worldwide. By the end of 2000 Lite was selling just 16.2 million barrels—18 percent below its all-time high and about 50 percent of Bud Light's 2000 volume. In fact, 2000 was the year Miller's flagship was supplanted by Coors's leading seller, Coors Light, as the country's number-three brew overall.

Lite's decline—and that of the brewer as well—stemmed partly from an attempt by Philip Morris in the 1980s to increase its profit margins on Lite and a decision to allow Miller's valuable exclusivity contracts in sports to lapse. When Miller pulled back, Anheuser-Busch, which had long been blocked from network

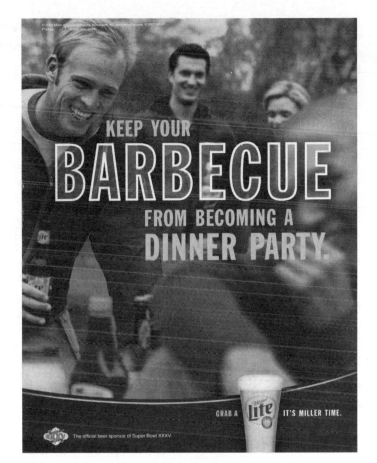

KEEP YOUR BARBECUE FROM BECOMING A DINNER PARTY.

GRAB A Lite IT'S MILLER TIME.

The official beer sponsor of Super Bowl XXXV.

Miller revived its popular "It's Miller time" slogan in this 2000 campaign. *Courtesy of Miller Brewing Company.*

sports, found an entrée into the category, and big-ticket sporting events have been its territory ever since.

After it launched Miller Genuine Draft in 1986, Miller began to use advertising from Backer & Spielvogel, Inc., of New York City, that touted the brand's cold-filtering process, a technique long used by the Coors Brewing Company but not mentioned in Coors's advertising. The men from Golden, Colorado, who had said they doubted the value of advertising, watched as the Miller brand sold more beer in its first year than any other brew in history.

Miller's share rose fairly consistently, from 4 percent in the early 1970s to a peak of 23.1 percent in 1994, but the company ended the 20th century with market share stagnant at 21 percent, its lowest since 1986. Whereas in 1978 Miller had come close to overtaking Anheuser-Busch, the gap between the two had widened to a gulf by 2000. Though Miller was in no immediate danger of losing its second-place showing to Coors, the distant number-three brewer was narrowing Miller's lead.

HILLARY CHURA

See also color plate in this volume

Further Reading

Baum, Dan, *Citizen Coors: An American Dynasty*, New York: Morrow, 2000

Hernon, Peter, and Terry Ganey, *Under the Influence: The Unauthorized Story of the Anheuser-Busch Dynasty,* New York: Simon and Schuster, 1991

Krebs, Peter J., *Redhook: Beer Pioneer,* New York: Four Walls Eight Windows, 1998

Van Munching, Philip, *Beer Blast: The Inside Story of the Brewing Industry's Bizarre Battles for Your Money,* New York: Times Business, 1997

Zyman, Sergio, *The End of Marketing As We Know It,* New York: HarperBusiness, and London: HarperCollins, 1990

Minorities: Employment in the Advertising Industry

Although at the outset of the 21st century the ad industry employed African-Americans, Hispanics, and Asians in various positions, from the entry level to the top executive ranks, statistics confirmed that diversity had not yet truly arrived in U.S. advertising agencies. Both agencies and marketers had yet to develop an inclusive environment for minority professionals at every level.

According to the 1999 report "Job Patterns for Minorities and Women in Private Industry" by the U.S. Equal Employment Opportunity Commission (EEOC), of those employed by advertising agencies with more than 100 employees (the only ones required to report), 84.4 percent were white, 7.1 percent black, 4.5 percent Hispanic, and 3.7 percent Asian/Pacific islander. About 56.5 percent of the white employees were women. Of those labeled as officials and managers, 92.1 percent were white, 2.7 percent were black, 2.3 percent were Hispanic, and 2.8 percent were Asian/Pacific islander. Among those employees categorized as professionals, 85.4 percent were white, 5.3 percent were black, 4.1 percent were Hispanic, and 5.0 percent were Asian/Pacific islander. Of those employees considered office and clerical workers, 69 percent were white (52.9 percent of them white females), 17.7 percent were black (13.4 percent female), 8.1 percent were Hispanic (5.6 percent female), and 4.9 percent were Asian/Pacific islander (2.2 percent female). Thus, for the most part, the advertising business remained the predominantly white, male business it had been since well before 1900.

The first ethnic inroads into the industry were made by Jews and Italians who worked on the creative side of the agency structure, though their influence was not fully felt until the 1950s. Stephen Fox wrote in *The Mirror Makers* (1976): "From the 1920s through the 1950s, the major agencies . . . were all known as WASP preserves, with some Jews in the creative departments, but hardly any in management." The great exception was Albert Lasker, a Jew who was among the most influential of the early advertising figures.

Lawrence Valenstein founded Grey Art Studio in 1918, changing the name to Grey Advertising in 1925. He built his business primarily on Jewish retail clients. Grey eventually developed into a general marketing agency after winning the *Good Housekeeping* magazine and Mennen accounts.

As the marketing industry matured throughout the period from the 1940s to the 1960s, it was the Jewish and Italian creative people and copywriters who were able to break down the initial barriers of racism, opening the way for other ethnic groups. Doyle Dane Bernbach was born out of Grey in 1949. Describing the atmosphere at the time, Fox wrote: "Advertising humor, ca. 1960, at the height of Marion Harper's adventures with Interpublic: a rumor that Grey Advertising would merge with BBDO [Batten Barton Durstine & Osborn] to form the Interfaith Group."

Nonetheless, the agencies were not quick to fill their ranks with minorities. African-American men who first achieved success at major agencies included Roy Eaton, the first black hired (in 1955) by Young & Rubicam. Other aspiring African-Americans opted to strike out on their own. Thomas J. Burrell began his advertising career in the mailroom of Wade Advertising in Chicago, Illinois, in 1960. He worked as a copywriter for the Leo Burnett Company, also in Chicago, for three years before moving to Foote, Cone & Belding in London, England, and then to a copy supervisor post at Needham, Harper & Steers. In 1971 at the age of 32, he opened his own shop to concentrate on marketing to black consumers. Other black marketing leaders who focused their business on marketing to black consumers include Byron Lewis, who founded UniWorld Group in New York City; Don Coleman, founder of Don Coleman Advertising in Southfield, Michigan; and Frank Mingo and Caroline Jones, who started their agency Mingo-Jones in 1977 in New York City.

In 1970 Georg Olden, an African-American art director, challenged his dismissal from McCann-Erickson, which insisted that declining business had necessitated staff reductions. He took his complaint to the EEOC. The commission ruled against Olden in 1972, but it noted that of the 410 people employed at McCann's New York City headquarters, there were only 22 black people and seven individuals with Spanish surnames—at a time when 22 percent of the city's population was black and 12 percent Hispanic. At the time, Young & Rubicam employed 1,471 people, of whom 150 were black and 48 had Spanish surnames. Doyle Dane Bernbach employed 1,032 people, including 150 who were black and 58 with Spanish surnames. The J. Walter Thompson Company and BBDO declined to release their information.

THE AD INDUSTRY'S
'DIRTY LITTLE SECRET'

After a brief hiring flurry 20 years ago, blacks have again become invisible men in the agency workplace. What went wrong?

By Joseph M. Winski

"I propose that the agencies in New York set this minority group employment minimum goal for the end of 1972: 13% in the clerical area and 13% in the professional areas."
—Jock Elliott Jr., chairman of Ogilvy & Mather and the American Association of Advertising Agencies' special committee on equal employment opportunities, October 1969.

If it weren't so terribly *unfunny*, the plight of black people in the ad business might make a nifty good news/bad news joke, says Lowell Thompson, a black freelance art director from Chicago.

The good news is black people have escaped the massive firings that have occurred in the agency business.

The bad news is there weren't any blacks to fire in the first place.

Mr. Thompson isn't laughing. Nor are others who've watched the agency business gradually slip from a professed leadership role in recruiting blacks to a position that can be charitably characterized as quiet indifference.

The agency industry's record on minority hiring is a "dirty little secret," says Jo Muse, chairman of Muse Cordero Chen, a multicultural Los Angeles agency.

Many industries can, of course, be accused of failing to give blacks adequate opportunities, but few have been as remiss as the the ad business. Indeed, two decades after it was to be reached, Jock Elliott's goal of 13% minority employment at ad agencies remains elusive.

According to U.S. Bureau of Labor Statistics, blacks, who constitute 10.1% of the total work force, account for 5.2% of ad agency employment at all levels, a figure heavily weighted with clerical and secretarial employees. (The figure for all minorities is of course somewhat higher.)

While management figures for ad agencies alone weren't available, blacks constitute just 2.1% of all marketing, advertising and public relations managers, the bureau said. That's the lowest percentage of blacks in 18 management categories and 336th lowest of 351 occupations monitored by the bureau. And clients are generally thought to have better minority hiring records than agencies, so even 2.1% may be high.

Some industry followers estimate the figure for black managers at mainstream agencies at as low as 1% of the total.

Things are no better in the creative department. In an unpublished article aptly titled "The Invisible Man in the Gray Flannel Suit," Mr. Thompson counts about 60 blacks among the 6,500 creatives he estimates are employed by the 25 largest U.S. agencies.

Photographs in this newspaper underscore the point. Of the 658 people (exclud-

1969: Black adman William Sharp writes a book that attests to the difficulty of getting a job in the business.

ing celebrities and spouses whose jobs aren't identified) shown so far this year on *Advertising Age's* "Photo Review" page—a weekly snapshot of sorts of the leaders and strivers in media, advertising and marketing—six were black.

Only two blacks (not counting a shot of the U.S. Olympic basketball team) have been pictured so far this year on AA's first three pages: Whoopi Goldberg and Spike Lee.

A 1985 AA report on the 100 "best and brightest young people" in the nation's ad agencies featured only one black, and she worked at UniWorld Group, a black-owned agency.

The Four A's doesn't compile figures on black employment of member agencies.

"My feeling is that we don't do a very good job of recruiting and keeping blacks," concedes John O'Toole, Four A's chairman.

Individual agencies are reluctant to say how many black employees they have. Of the 25 largest U.S. agency "brands," only five would give AA any figures *(see chart on Page 38)*.

Most of the others said it was company policy not to disclose such numbers. Among those that nonetheless claimed good minority-hiring records were J. Walter Thompson USA and Young & Rubicam; both said they have federal contracts requiring them to employ minorities and to file hiring records with Washington but that the government won't let them make the numbers public.

The situation is fraught with irony: An

1992: Black adman Lowell Thompson writes a proposed ad that attests to the difficulty of getting a job in the business.

Percentage of managers and professionals who are black:

Public officials and administrators	11.3%
Actors and directors	10.5%
Accountants and auditors	7.6%
Salespeople	6.6%
All executives and managers	5.7%
College and university teachers	4.8%
Editors and reporters	4.5%
Financial managers	4.0%
Engineers	3.6%
Doctors	3.2%
Lawyers	2.6%
Marketing, advertising and public relations managers	**2.1%**
Architects	2.1%
Airline pilots and navigators	1.5%
Percentage of blacks in total work force	**10.1%**

Source: U.S. Bureau of Labor Statistics, January 1992

industry that eagerly does pro bono advertising for racial equality, as well as numerous other causes, turns out to employ few blacks itself.

"How in the world can your publication call on the advertising community to stop riots by creating advertising [AA, May 4] when they won't hire any black people? It's outrageous," says a black creative who now runs his own agency. He asked not to be named because, he says, his activism has caused him to be labeled an unemployable "troublemaker" at mainstream agencies.

There's historical irony as well, because in the wake of the civil rights movement of the 1960s, the agency business swung its doors open wide to black people.

It wasn't pure altruism: Both the New York Urban League and the New York City Commission on Human Rights singled out the agency business—then highly visible in its so-called "golden age" of creativity—for criticism. The commission even held public hearings on agency hiring practices.

Activists picketed Benton & Bowles in the early 1960s for alleged discrimination in hiring. A few years later, there were protests at the Clio presentation against an award given to Wells Rich Greene, which activists charged hired blacks only for menial jobs like serving coffee.

Blacks in advertising formed the Group for Advertising Progress to press for more hiring of blacks and Puerto Ricans. With the Four A's, GAP created what it called the Basic Advertising Course, taught by prominent agency figures, for minorities in New York and Chicago.

In time, blacks began to break into the once WASP-dominated business in considerable numbers, as Italians and Jews had done a decade earlier. Some agencies boasted publicly of their progress in hiring minorities.

"We had a lot of stirring, and we had a lot of hope," recalls Doug Alligood, one of the founders of GAP who worked at BBDO in New York and today is the agency's VP-special markets.

The industry was brought up short when William Sharp, then a group supervisor at JWT in Chicago, told the Four A's at its annual meeting in 1969: "You white advertising folks are a lot happier about the progress of integration than us black advertising folks."

His speech—which Mr. Sharp, who now owns Sharp Advertising in Atlanta, says he could give essentially unchanged today—proved prophetic.

The nation's attention drifted from civil rights to Vietnam and Watergate, the economy staggered, and agency board rooms, like the country at large, grew increasingly silent on minorities.

By the 1980s, "a kind of racial forgetfulness" had set in, says Phil Gant, exec VP-chief creative officer at BBDO, Chicago, probably the highest-ranking black creative at a major agency.

"The industry, as a whole, seems to me to have regressed," he says. "The country to me has regressed."

Hard economic times, which have caused agencies to slash payrolls, have hardly helped.

"What happened to all the black people who came into the business when I did?" asks Mr. Thompson, the Chicago art director, who can easily name 35 black advertising people who were prominent or promising two decades ago.

A handful, such as Messrs. Gant and Alligood, have succeeded in the general agency business. A far greater number, says Don Richards, Leo Burnett Co. senior VP-director of resource development and another of the successes from the 1960s, "just dropped out."

"I think quite frankly . . . we were more interested in getting the numbers and less in the problem that would arise as people tried to move up," Mr. Richards says. "The system wasn't ready to propel people upward. It hadn't thought it through."

Some blacks left to start their own agen-

(Continued on Page 38)

"The Ad Industry's 'Dirty Little Secret,'" published in *Advertising Age* in 1992, revealed that the number of African-Americans employed by ad agencies in the United States fell far short of goals set in the late 1960s by an industry committee on equal employment opportunities. *Reprinted with permission from the 15 June 1992 issue of* Advertising Age. *Copyright 1992, Crain Communications, Inc.*

In 1971, with his partner Emmett McBain, Thomas J. Burrell became the first African-American to own a major advertising agency.
©2001 *Powell Photography, Inc. Credit Photo By Victor Powell.*

U.S. Bureau of Labor Statistics reported that African-Americans comprised 6.9 percent of all executives and managers.

It seems somewhat ironic that at the outset of the 21st century, in an era when multicultural marketing had become an increasingly significant component of many marketers' ad budgets, many corporations continued to face accusations of racism or sexism. Notable among those corporations cited in lawsuits was Texaco. In 1994 the company faced a class-action suit in which the plaintiffs were awarded $176.1 million and an 11 percent salary increase. Altruism aside, public revelations of intolerance had the capacity to become public relations nightmares for marketers. As the U.S. population became increasingly diverse, the industry recognized that its recruitment and retention policies had the potential to affect the bottom line: profits.

With advertisers becoming more aware of the growing ethnic consumer market, the major agencies and their holding companies developed an interest in establishing ethnic agencies of their own or forging links with existing ethnic agencies. As of early 2001, those that had acquired stakes in ethnic shops included Young & Rubicam (in New York City), with its own Hispanic agency Bravo Group (New York City) and with a 49 percent interest in Asian specialist shop Kang & Lee (New York City); Publicis Group (Paris, France), with a 49 percent stake in Burrell Communications Group; and True North Communications (New York City), with a 49 percent stake in African-American agency Don Coleman Advertising, Hispanic agency Siboney USA (New York City and Miami, Florida), and Asian agency Imada Wong (Los Angeles, California), as well as a 40 percent share in African-American specialist Stedman Graham & Partners (New York City).

NANCY COLTUN WEBSTER

See also Women: Careers in Advertising

The situation did not change radically during the next decade. In 1992 *Advertising Age* took note of the hiring discrepancy in the industry. In an article titled "The Ad Industry's 'Dirty Little Secret,'" the publication revealed that only 5.2 percent of those working in U.S. agencies were African-American.

Major marketers and agencies have been slow to develop a pool of high-ranking minority executives, leading to recruitment and retention problems among the lower ranks as young employees sometimes become discouraged at the relative scarcity of role models. In 1987 A. Barry Rand was named president of the domestic marketing group for Xerox Corporation. At the time, Korn Ferry International reported that after a survey of the 1,000 largest companies, it had found four black senior executives immediately below the chief executive level—one executive more than was reported in 1979.

Rand remained the highest-ranking African-American corporate executive in the United States until 1997, when Kenneth I. Chenault was named president-chief operating officer, the number-two executive post, at American Express Company. That year the

Further Reading

"The Ad Industry's Dirty Little Secret," *Advertising Age* (15 June 1992)

Baker Woods, Gail, "Is Madison Avenue Missing the Mark on Minority Hiring, Marketing?" *Black Issues in Higher Education* (1995)

Egerton, Judith, "Area Ad Agencies' Favorite Color Is White," *Courier-Journal Louisville* (2 March 1993)

Fox, Stephen R., *The Mirror Makers: A History of American Advertising and Its Creators,* New York: Morrow, 1984

Graves, Earl G., "How to Succeed in Business without Being White," *Black Enterprise* (1 March 1997)

Golphin, Vincent F.A., "Roy Eaton: Award-Winning Pianist Draws Energy and Inspiration from Challenges," *About Time Magazine* (1998)

Hicks, Jonathon P., "Black Attains Milepost Job with Xerox," *New York Times* (28 May 1987)

Job Patterns for Minorities and Women in Private Industry, Washington, D.C.: U.S. Equal Employment Opportunity Commission, 1999

Mitchell, Jacqueline, "Breaking Down Corporate Barriers," *The Network Journal* (30 April 1997)

Powell, Jacquelyn, "Protective Coloration: Many Blacks Say They Must Hide Heritage on the Job," *Washington Post* (3 March 1997)

Smith, Eric L., "Playing the Corporate Race Card: Texaco Scandal Shows Glass Ceiling Remains Uncomfortably Low in Corporate America," *Black Enterprise* (1 January 1997)

"Texaco Hit with Discrimination Lawsuit," *The Record* (30 March 1994)

Minorities: Representations in Advertising

Since the earliest days of advertising, images of people from various cultural and racial groups have been used to sell goods and services. In the United States, as advertisers and marketers have sought to expand their consumer base, the groups portrayed in ads have included the Irish, Italians, African-Americans, Latinos, Asians, and Native Americans. Some ethnically derived advertising characters have become ubiquitous, attaining the status of cultural icons.

The influx of immigrants into America in the late 1800s was one of the factors that played a pivotal role in increasing the racial and ethnic diversity of characters seen in advertisements. In fact, advertising was itself used to attract immigrants from other countries. According to Juliann Sivulka, author of *Soap, Sex, and Cigarettes: A Cultural History of American Advertising*, "Agents for railroads and western states ran newspaper ads, circulated posters, and handed out pamphlets in front of churches and other gathering places in European towns and cities." At the same time, the low cost of travel via steamship and the establishment of laws that legalized and even encouraged immigration made it easier for Europeans to come to America.

By 1910 the majority of the population in such major American cities as Boston, Massachusetts; Chicago, Illinois; Cleveland, Ohio; Detroit, Michigan; and New York City were immigrants. The heritage of Irish, Italian, and other immigrant communities was infused throughout advertising copy and layout, and the increased consumer base stimulated the production of more consumer goods and services. Later, as their improving economic status made them more attractive to advertisers and they came to be identified as constituting viable markets, African-Americans, Latinos, and Asian-Americans also appeared prominently in U.S. advertising. Some critics have also observed that advertising was used as a mechanism for keeping these groups "in their place," while at the same time reinforcing the privileged position of white Anglo-Saxon Protestants.

The use in advertising of images of African-Americans, Asians, Latinos, and American Indians was more noticeable and figured more prominently than representations of other groups, such as Irish- and Italian-Americans. The appearance of various minority groups in advertisements came at different intervals in history and generally increased with their numbers and rising socioeconomic status. During the early years, these groups were often maligned in ads. Some of the most offensive (by today's standards) of these early advertisements featured images of African-Americans with physical characteristics derived from the repertoire of minstrelsy—bright red, thick, saucer lips and bulging eyes. Asian-Americans were pictured with long, black shiny braids swallowing live rats while joyfully washing other people's clothes.

Nonetheless, there were also instances of these groups being represented in a positive light in advertising. Often these ads acknowledged outstanding individuals or celebrated distinctive cultures and heritages. The Metropolitan Life Insurance Company was one of the first companies to realize the potential of the Asian-American consumer market. In ads from agency L3, the company used a variety of tag lines and headlines in a campaign that emphasized the theme of family. One ad, in which an adult is seen holding a young baby, asked the question, "You protect your child, but who protects you?" Another ad featured a baby apparently taking its first steps. Reebok featured tennis star Michael Chang in an ad campaign and saw sales soar among Asian-Americans. Some groups remained conspicuously absent from advertising for many years because of such factors as age, religion, or sexual orientation. Still, the presence of minority groups in advertising became much more noticeable in the 1980s and 1990s than at any prior time in the century.

Historically, African-Americans have commanded the largest and most dominant presence of any minority group in advertising. Advertising archivists have noted that the images of African-Americans depicted in advertising, although often affectionate, were at the same time condescending and patronizing and appealed primarily to the stereotypes embraced by white audiences. From the early to mid-20th century, blacks were most often shown in subservient roles, embodied in such well-known brand symbols as Uncle Ben, Rastus, the Cream of Wheat chef, and an apron-clad plantation mammy named Aunt Jemima—all images with roots going back to slavery.

These images slowly dissipated owing to the Civil Rights movement of the late 1950s and early 1960s, which demanded more positive images of blacks and other minority groups in advertising as well as in other public representations. Another significant factor was the dawn of segmented marketing in the 1970s, which led to increased recognition of racial and ethnic minorities as viable markets. The rise of social consciousness during the 1970s also

A late-19th-century ad for rat poison exemplifies the stereotypic depiction of Asians that was common at the time.

dent of Creative Focus, a firm that specializes in the psychological assessment of advertising, has noted that Kodak's Instamatic advertisement directly addressed multi-ethnic alienation from a white Santa Claus.

Representation of African-Americans

The appearance of African-Americans in advertising begins in advertisements for the sale of slaves and the capture of runaway slaves. The first advertisement featuring representations of blacks appeared as early as 1827 in the first black newspaper, *Freedom's Journal,* and was for the Higher School for Colored Children of Both Sexes. Until the era of the civil rights movement in the 1960s, blacks were depicted by white advertisers in a manner that exemplified the racial divide in the United States. Prior to the 1960s blacks in print ads in general circulation publications were depicted in service roles such as maids, butlers, train porters, and cooks. These portrayals reflected the context in which white Americans most often encountered them. They were also depicted in stereotypical representations that often distorted their physical features and placed them in situations that made them appear ignorant.

Many of the changes that occurred in the appearance and portrayal of African-Americans in advertising were directly related to the protests, sit-ins, and marches staged during the civil rights era. It was during this period that organizations such as the National Association for the Advancement of Colored People (NAACP), the Congress of Racial Equality (CORE), and People United to Serve Humanity (PUSH) began to demand that more blacks be featured more prominently in advertising and that the portrayals be more positive. The efforts of these groups became evident when New York Telephone ran the first ad featuring an African-American to appear in a general circulation publication—the *New York Herald Tribune*—on 7 May 1963. The ad, from Batten Barton Durstine & Osborn (BBDO), showed a well-dressed model about to enter a sidewalk telephone booth; the headline read, "A man of action knows—you get action when you telephone." The Kerner Commission, appointed to examine the causes of the urban riots of the summer of 1967, concluded that blacks and whites in the United States constituted virtually separate societies and were becoming increasingly alienated from each other. The commission recommended, among other measures, that "Negro reporters and performers should appear more frequently . . . in news broadcasts, on weather shows, in documentaries, and in advertisements." Following this recommendation, black models portraying various occupations could be seen in advertising touting the virtues of products ranging from hair spray to cigarettes.

Surveys conducted during the 1990s showed that African-Americans were depicted in a little more than 11 percent of the advertisements in general circulation advertising; they represented 12.6 percent of the population at that time. Despite this near parity in numbers, however, blacks were more often shown in minor, background roles in ads rather than in major, prominent roles.

According to Brian Wright O'Connor, writing in *Black Enterprise,* African-American–owned advertising agencies accounted for less than 1 percent of the business by volume as late as 1995. These

saw the dawn of the women's movement, and this led to the denouncement of demeaning portrayals of women in ads. These historical events were instrumental in the rise of affirmative images of minority groups in advertising.

An early success in multicultural advertising was a 1949 ad campaign by Doyle Dane Bernbach for Henry S. Levy & Sons of New York City. In these ads Chinese-Americans, African-Americans, and Native Americans declared, "You don't have to be Jewish to love Levy's real Jewish Rye." As Carol Nathanson-Moog notes in her essay "The Psychological Power of Ethnic Images in Advertising," the Levy's ad "sold a perception of openness and mutual respect for differences." Coca-Cola Company and McDonald's Corporation first began advertising to Latinos in Spanish in the 1960s. However, the value of multiethnic advertising was not fully appreciated until the 1970s.

One of the most dramatic advertisements to emphasize the ideal of multiculturalism came early in the 1970s. In 1972 Eastman Kodak Company and J. Walter Thompson Company (JWT) advertised Kodak's Pocket Instamatic camera in *Ebony* magazine with an image of a black Santa Claus. Nathanson-Moog, presi-

agencies also employed fewer than 350 of the 150,000 blacks employed by advertising agencies. Overall, black opportunity and achievement have remained relatively low in American life, with the exceptions of the entertainment and sports fields. A few African-American icons in these fields—among them, Michael Jordan, Tiger Woods, Bill Cosby, Vanessa Williams, Halle Berry—have become among the most sought-after for commercial endorsements.

Latino Images

Realistic depictions of Latinos did not appear in mainstream American advertising with any consistency until the 1960s. The Chiquita Banana trade character (created by BBDO) was introduced in 1944 to put a personal face on the multinational United Fruit Company (UFC). She might have disappeared if it had not been for the popular song "I'm Chiquita Banana" written for her that same year by Garth Montgomery and Len MacKenzie. By the end of World War II Chiquita's song had become a genuine hit. In addition to its being heard in radio commercials, the song was performed by Carmen Miranda, among others, and played by dance bands, radio disc jockeys, and on jukeboxes. To further promote bananas, beginning in 1947 the UFC placed Chiquita stickers on each bunch of bananas it sold.

Probably no Latino advertising figure made more of an indelible impression on mainstream, middle-class America than the corn-chip–snatching Frito Bandito. Emerging in the 1960s, this mustached, cartoon figure was clad in an oversized sombrero and armed with a six-gun and a sinister smile. Created as a parody of the Alfonso Bedoya "Gold Hat" character in the classic John Houston film *Treasure of the Sierra Madre*, the Bandito made a habit of stealing Fritos corn chips from unsuspecting victims. The Frito Bandito became a well-known advertising caricature and boosted sales for the Frito-Lay Corporation. Nevertheless, civil rights organizations and activists objected to the campaign (from Foote, Cone & Belding). They argued that the image of Mexicans as "mustached thieves" perpetuated historical stereotypes. In 1970, after protests, threatened boycotts, and the refusal of some television stations to air the offensive cartoon character, Frito-Lay withdrew the campaign.

A little more than ten years later, a band of hard-riding, nefarious-looking Mexican bandits appeared in an ad for Arrid deodorant. In this ad an obese, sombrero-wearing, mustached figure calls his followers to a screeching stop, reaches into his saddlebag for a small can of Arrid spray deodorant, lifts up his arms and sprays. A voice over says, "If it works for him, it will work for you." Needless to say, the campaign was not well received by the Latino community.

A commercial by Liggett & Myers for L&M cigarettes featured Paco, a lazy Latino who never "feenished" anything, not even the revolution he is supposed to be fighting. Latinos did not embrace this depiction either. A spokesperson for the company defended the commercial, saying, "Paco is a warm, sympathetic, and lovable character with whom most of us can identify because he has a little of all of us in him, that is, our tendency to procrastinate at times."

The gay market was the target of this 2000 Miller Lite ad that appeared in *The Advocate* magazine.
Courtesy of Miller Brewing Company.

In 1998 a Spanish-speaking Chihuahua (the breed is named after a state in Mexico) made its debut in a $60 million campaign from TBWA/Chiat/Day for the fast-food restaurant chain Taco Bell. In the ads, the dog peers out of the television screen and seductively says, "Yo quiero Taco Bell" (I want Taco Bell). Although the campaign was a huge hit in terms of recognition, ratings, and money, some Latinos found it offensive. Groups called for a nationwide boycott of Taco Bell until "Dinky" was taken off the air. Mexican-American critics, in particular, were vehement in saying that it was insulting to have a dog representing their country on national television. "It's like saying all Mexicans are dogs," some protesters said. But many dismissed the protest as an excess of "political correctness."

Based on the proportionality criterion, Latinos were considerably underrepresented in U.S. advertising, appearing in 4.7 percent of all advertising—a figure considerably lower than the 9 percent of the U.S. population the group constituted in 1999. Latinos appeared in more advertisements with a business setting than in any other.

Latinos were featured in 5.8 percent of all television commercials and constituted 1.5 percent of the speaking characters in network television advertisements. When appearing in TV ads they were most often shown in background roles as part of a group and appeared most frequently in ads for food products, entertainment, alcoholic beverages, and furniture. Latinos have been documented as the most underrepresented of the three major ethnic/racial groups (the others being blacks and Asian-Americans) in magazine advertising. Latinos occupy a middle ground in terms of their representation in advertising. They appear in ads less frequently than blacks but more often than Asian-Americans and American Indians. Historically, they have been pictured in mainstream advertising hosting dinner parties, washing dishes, or drinking coffee. During the late 1980s the Winn-Dixie supermarket chain promoted holidays and dishes native to the individual Latin countries using the theme, "Winn-Dixie tiene el sabor de mi pais" (Winn-Dixie has the flavor of my country). Nike made history in 1993 by running the first Spanish-language commercial ever broadcast in prime time on a major American network. One explanation given for the comparatively low rate of representation is that Latinos are not always easily identifiable as such and therefore do not convey the strong multicultural message an advertiser may be striving to present. Nonetheless, advertisers have gradually increased their references to Latino cultures in an attempt to distinguish and position their products.

Roles for Asian-Americans

Asian images are used in advertising, but not as frequently as those of African-Americans or Latinos. In the 1990s some agencies and marketers were trying to find a way to integrate Asian-American culture into their messages without being patronizing, condescending, or otherwise offensive. An Asian stereotype was emerging that was the antithesis of that of blacks and Latinos. It was an image that combined high achievement with academic excellence and good grooming to create the notion of the Asian as extremely competitive in all areas of American life.

One of the first appearances of Asians in advertising came through the popularity of the Yellow Kid comic strip character, created by R.F. Outcault for the *New York World* in 1895. The strip became very popular, both for the *World* and for William Randolph Hearst's *New York Journal,* where Outcault took his talents in 1896. Outcault recognized the commercial potential of his character and, beginning in 1896, licensed the Kid's use on a variety of products, including candy, cookies, and two competing brands of chewing gum (one was called Grove's Yellow Kid Chewing Gum). Other names given to products represented by Asians included: Rough on Rats Vermin Exterminator, Chinese Rat Destroyer Poison, Laugh at Mice Vermin Exterminator.

In a Yankelovich Partners survey of 1,600 Asian-Americans consumers in 1992, 72 percent said brand names were a strong influence on purchasing decisions, compared with 34 percent of all Americans. Thirty-nine percent said that seeing Asians in ads was a strong influence to purchase. During 1992–93 Charles Taylor, Barbara Stern, and Ju Yung Lee conducted a content analysis of more than 1,300 prime-time television advertisements assessed the frequency and nature of Asian-American representation. The study found that Asian male and female models are over-represented in terms of proportion of the population. The group was over-represented in ads for technical products, with more than 75 percent of appearances falling into this product category. In another study researchers randomly selected sample issues of the largest magazines available. They found that, using the proportionality criterion, Asian-Americans were slightly over-represented in these print ads. Members of the group were present in 4 percent of the advertisements in the sample, a figure higher than the 3.3 percent of the population they represented. Furthermore, representation of Asian-Americans was highly skewed toward the business press and technical publications, as opposed to women's and general interest magazines. In fact, Asian-American models were portrayed in business settings in 81.2 percent of the ads in which they appeared and were rarely portrayed in outdoor, home, or social settings.

Ninety-three percent of Asian-Americans lived in metropolitan areas such as New York City; Los Angeles, California; San Francisco, California; and Chicago, Illinois, in 2000. The returns on advertising dollars spent on Asian media averaged 60 percent higher than those in the general print and broadcast vehicles. Phone companies spent the most targeting Asian-Americans (Asian-American consumers spend between $750 million and $1 billion annually on long-distance telephone service), followed by insurance companies and banks. Eliot Kang, president of Amko Advertising, estimated in 1994 that 40 U.S. companies have targeted Asian-Americans, with budgets of about $1 million or more each. Advertising with Asian-American themes was frequently seen in California, where the Asian population was significantly larger than in other states. In the year 2000, the U.S. Asian-American population was 12 million, which represented 4 percent of the total 275 million population.

The number of Asian-Americans in the U.S. population was predicted to grow steadily in the first two decades of the 21st century. Asian-Americans had a median income of $44,460 annually in 1997, 19 percent more than the national average. Additionally, the rate of Asian immigration outpaced that of any other group. By the end of the 20th century, Asian-Americans were more prevalent in advertising than at any other time in history. They were seen in a variety of roles advertising a wide selection of products.

How American Indians Are Seen

Native Americans, of all prominent ethnic minorities, have least often been featured in advertising. As was the case with other minority groups, the brands named after this group—Savage, Noble Savage—implied stereotypes that were less than flattering, and illustrations featuring American Indians often reflected negatively on the group's heritage. When companies adopted images of American Indians as trademarks, they were attempting to appeal to idealized notions of the group as depicted in novels of the Old West. Indian figures were also used by businesses in the same way as buffaloes and eagles, as a symbol of a primeval

Sally Wetzler drives a Stanza Wagon
for the same reasons other people do.
It's great for families, it carries a lot of
stuff, and it's easy to get in and out of.

Meet Sally Wetzler, a very nice woman in Richmond, Virginia, who has some very nice things to say about her Stanza® Wagon.

"I've been driving my Stanza for almost two years now, and it's by far the best car I've ever owned.

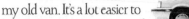

"It's more economical than my old van. It's a lot easier to handle. But most important, the two sliding doors make it totally accessible. I really feel as if Nissan® designed it for me."

Actually, it was designed for Sally Wetzler. And for everybody else who drives a family wagon.

For example, to make it easier to get in and out of, the Stanza Wagon has sliding rear doors on both sides.

Because families need to carry a lot more than themselves, the Nissan Stanza Wagon not only has fold-down seats so you can really load it up, it also has a low cargo floor so you can load it up easily.

And since most folks like to see where they're going, the engineers at Nissan raised the roof and the driver's seat. For a better view of the road.

It all comes down to Human Engineering. Which simply means thinking about what a car is supposed to do for people. All kinds of people. And then making sure it does it.

Built for the Human Race.

Nissan has been one of only a few advertisers to feature disabled people in its advertising, as seen in this 1988 ad.
Copyright, Nissan (1988). Nissan and the Nissan logo are registered trademarks of Nissan.

America and an unwritten assurance that the product in question was made there.

The use of native Americans as trademarks peaked from the 1880s through the early 20th century, after the Indian resistance in the west had been suppressed. Some of the most prominent of these trademarks included those for Hiawatha canned corn, Wampum canned food, Bow-Spring dental rubber, Cherokee coal, American baking powder, and Totem Pole canned and packaged foods.

Powhatan, the symbol of the American Tobacco Company, was the chief of the confederacy of Algonquian tribes when the first English settlers landed at Jamestown. According to legend, had his daughter Pocahontas not interfered, he would have killed Captain John Smith. Pocahontas was captured in 1613 in a raid by the settlers and held hostage at Jamestown. In 1614 she married John Rolphe, who discovered a method for curing tobacco. It was probably this connection that inspired American Tobacco to adopt Powhatan as its trademark.

Red Cloud Chewing Tobacco was the trademark used for Ingraham, Corbin and May of Chicago, Illinois. Red Cloud was a chief of the Bad Face band of the Oglala tribe, who in 1866 com-

manded both Sioux and Cheyenne warriors in attacks on U.S. soldiers around Fort Kearny, in what is now Nebraska. In 1868 he signed a treaty that provided for the Sioux reservation that covered all of South Dakota, west of the Missouri River.

William Wright mixed the first batch of Calumet Baking Powder in 1889 in a rented room in Chicago that doubled as a laboratory and bedroom. The name Calumet (a common place-name in the Chicago area) was first used by the French as a name for the peace pipe offered to Jacques Marquette when he explored the shore of Lake Michigan in 1675. The Calumet Baking Powder brand became a part of General Foods in 1928.

National Shawmut Bank of Boston, Massachusetts, has used an Indian as its symbol since 1854. A young Boston artist named Adelbert Aner, Jr., sculpted a bust of the Shawmut Indian in 1910. According to the bank, the image is that of Offatinewat, the Mushauruomeog chief who signed a treaty with Miles Standish in 1621.

R.R. Donnelly & Sons chose an Indian for a trademark because its Lakeside Press in Chicago stood not far from the site of the 1812 Fort Dearborn Massacre, in which settlers were forced from the region by American Indians. The company has been in the printing business since 1864; J.C. Leyendecker designed the company's first mark in 1897. Theodore Haploid revised it in 1926, with a slightly less horrific warrior. Rockwell Kent drew an Art Deco version in 1930, and Joseph Carter returned to a simplified, traditional mark in 1953.

One of the most widely known native American brand characters is that of the food and agricultural cooperative Land O'Lakes, Inc. The Minnesota Cooperative Creameries Association began conducting business in 1921 in Arden Hill, Minnesota, as a central shipping agent for a group of small farmer-owned dairy cooperatives. The association's business centered largely on the sale of butter produced by the cooperatives, and after three years it decided to add a single brand name to the packages. Farmers in the member cooperatives were asked to send in suggestions for a name, and Land O'Lakes was chosen. No one remembers how the image of the Indian maiden came to be, but by the end of 1924 she appeared on the butter cartons with the new brand name. Other products using female native Americans for their logos included Winona Fabric Gloves and Wayagamack Wood Pulp.

The logo of the gun manufacturer Savage Arms is a fearsome Indian warrior who looks as if he just jumped from the pages of a classic Western novel. The company chose the stereotypical image to echo the name of its founder, Arthur Savage. Savage started his gun business in Utica, New York, in 1894, after spending most of his 35 years in the West Indies and Australia. The warrior symbol was introduced in 1906 and has been modified over the years to look less and less like a "savage."

Trademarks using the native American legacy have run the gamut from excessively offensive to tasteful. In 1991 a controversy arose within the Indian community when a new malt liquor dubbed Crazy Horse was introduced. The namesake for the product was the legendary Lakota chief. Community representatives objected, noting that the chief abhorred alcohol, blaming it as a substance that contributed to the downfall of his people.

In 1996 native Americans were angered to learn that Anheuser-Busch was using images of beer-guzzling American Indians to sell Budweiser beer in Britain. The Budweiser ad, dubbed "Pale Rider," was created by London-based Omnicom Group's DDB Needham Worldwide unit. The advertisement followed a truck driver for a company called Chieftain Cement who finds himself in a dimly lit bar patronized by a crowd of American Indians. The bartender, a silver-haired Indian, is shocked by the man's ghostly pale face, which is covered with cement dust. So the driver dunks his head in a barrel of water, washing the dust away and revealing that he, too, is an Indian. The camera zooms in as he gulps down a bottle of Budweiser. The campaign became Budweiser's most popular ever in Britain. Nonetheless, Indian advocacy groups in the United States saw the ads as insensitive to the alcoholism issue.

Other Groups

Unlike the groups mentioned previously, the gay community was not stereotyped by advertisers but was basically neglected because some advertisers feared a backlash from other consumers. The economic power of this market has been recognized by Madison Avenue, however, and it has become more commonplace to see advertisements featuring same-sex couples. According to surveys conducted in 1994, the average gay male household had an annual income of between $50,000 and $60,000—an average considerably higher than for mainstream consumer households. Homosexual consumers tend to travel, dine out, and go to the theater more often than their heterosexual counterparts and to read and drink more.

According to reporter Brett Chase, Miller Lite, through its ad placement in gay magazines, has been the "beer of choice" for lesbians for more than ten years. American Express, Virgin Atlantic Airways, Ikea, Honda, and Toyota are a few of the companies that are recognizing the buying power of this market. Overlooked Opinions, a Chicago-based research organization, has concluded that gay consumers support companies that support them and substantiates this assumption with data showing that 79.3 percent of gay men and lesbians make purchases based on advertising in gay media. Advertising in gay-oriented publications varies in approach, ranging from ads that depict people of no particular sexual orientation to a jewelry ad with an inset picture of two men.

Advertisers did not acknowledge the 43 million people in the United States with disabilities in any significant way until the mid-1980s and early 1990s. Until this period, images of disabled people were relegated to public service announcements and charity telethons. In 1984 Foote, Cone & Belding developed advertising for Levi Strauss & Company's 501 jeans that included a man in a wheelchair. In the spot, young people were dancing, jogging, and playing double Dutch, while a young man happily popped his wheelchair to a blues tune. Another company that has consciously used disabled people in its ads is Nissan, which featured Sally Wetzler, a disabled certified public accountant, in its national advertising campaign for its Stanza wagon. In the 1990s it became increasingly common to see physically challenged people in magazine, television, and newspaper advertising. McDonald's has successfully introduced people with disabilities into its advertising campaigns. A case in point, is the "Silent Persuasion" advertisement, which shows a deaf boy trying to persuade a girl to quit studying and go to lunch with him. Communication takes place in the commercial through sign language and the words are subtitled on the screen.

With the exception of a handful of aging celebrity spokespersons—Parker Fennelly (Pepperidge Farm), Margaret Hamilton (Maxwell House), Ella Fitzgerald (Memorex tape), John Houseman (Smith-Barney)—senior citizens were also noticeably absent from advertising until the last decades of the 20th century. Advertising has traditionally promoted a youthful ideal, and it has consciously selected young models. McDonald's brought the issue of senior citizens in advertising to the fore with an ad that showed an elderly gentleman working at a McDonald's. The advertisement depicted old and young people working together and enjoying it.

There was a rationale and a precedent for ignoring seniors. Older consumers have been exposed to a lifetime of advertising and tend to be less persuadable than younger consumers. Many have developed strong brand loyalties and are less likely than their younger counterparts to be influenced by ads. Traditionally, the elderly have also had smaller incomes. Toward the end of the 20th century, however, the financial stability of the senior citizen market made it increasingly attractive to advertisers. According to U.S. government statistics, in the period from 1984 to 1999 the median net worth of households headed by seniors increased by approximately 70 percent. At the same time, the number of elderly citizens was also increasing. In the United States, as in other industrial countries, the over-65 population was growing faster than any other age group—from about 9 percent of the population in developed nations in 1960 to a projected 25 percent in 2030. Moreover, since World War II, the average global life expectancy has risen from about age 45 to age 65, a larger increase in the past 50 years than over the previous 5,000. At the outset of the 21st century, throughout the developed world, life expectancy was 75 years.

Older Americans 2000: Key Indicators of Well-Being, a report published by the Federal Interagency Forum on Aging Related Statistics, suggested that marketers who have shied away from the mature market would do well to reconsider this strategy. Many advertisers have heeded this message and are aware that this observation is not limited to American interests but has worldwide implications. The "Gray" movement, a 1970s initiative to protect the rights of senior citizens and gain them increased respect, played a pivotal role in increasing advertisers' awareness of this significant consumer block.

The use of multicultural groups in advertising has occasionally given rise to global controversy, as evidenced by the experience of the Ford Motor Company in 1996. The company had to apologize for deliberately superimposing the faces of white individuals on photos of its black and South Asian workers used in a marketing campaign in Europe. The deception was discovered when several black, Indian, and Pakistani workers in Britain, who had posed for a photograph along with their white counterparts, saw an altered version of the photo in a company brochure. In reporting the incident, the *Wall Street Journal* noted that the act of removing dark-skinned people from an advertisement to reflect the makeup of a target market highlighted the dilemma faced by multinational companies that advertise in different markets around the world.

Over the years, images of minority group members have been used to advertise myriad products all over the world. In the postmodern era many found these depictions to be pejorative and designed more for the consumption of the majority in various countries than for the groups pictured in the ads. However, over the years, advertising agencies, marketers, consumers, civil rights organizations, and many activists have sought to eliminate the negative images that have appeared in advertising. Their efforts have proved effective, and there are also many more images of diverse groups in advertising worldwide. At the end of the 20th century, these groups, including people of color, those with same-sex preferences, the elderly, and those who are physically challenged, were being portrayed more often and more positively than at any time. Some negative advertising involving these groups still exists, but positive advertising portrayals of all people, regardless of age, race, gender, sexual preference, or physical ability, are becoming the norm.

MARILYN KERN-FOXWORTH

See also African-Americans: Representations in Advertising

Further Reading

Biagi, Shirley, and Marilyn Kern-Foxworth, *Facing Difference: Race, Gender, and Mass Media,* Thousand Oaks, California: Pine Forge, 1997

Bowen, Lawrence, and Jill Schmid, "Minority Presence and Portrayal in Mainstream Magazine Advertising: An Update," *Journalism and Mass Communication Quarterly* 74, no. 1 (Spring 1997)

Dates, Jannette L., and William Barlow, editors, *Split Image: African Americans in the Mass Media,* Washington, D.C.: Howard University Press, 1990; 2nd edition, 1993

Ellis, William, and Eddie T. Arnold, "A History of African-American Owned Advertising Agencies: American Advertising Foundation's Salute to African-American Advertising Agencies" <www.aaf.org/aaf/afamhistory.html>

Kern-Foxworth, Marilyn, "Aunt Jemima, the Frito Bandito, and Crazy Horse: Selling Stereotypes American Style," in *Mass Politics: The Politics of Popular Culture,* edited by Daniel M. Shea, New York: St. Martin's/Worth, 1999

Martinez, Thomas M., "How Advertisers Promote Racism," *Civil Rights Digest* (Fall 1969)

Moog, Carol, *"Are They Selling Her Lips?" Advertising and Identity,* New York: Morrow, 1990

Morgan, Hal, *Symbols of America,* New York: Viking, 1986

Sivulka, Juliann, *Soap, Sex, and Cigarettes: A Cultural History of American Advertising,* Belmont, California: Wadsworth, 1998

Sturgis, Ingrid, "Black Images in Advertising," *Emerge* (September 1993)

Synder, Rita, and James Freeman, "Magazine Readership Profiles and Depictions of African Americans in Magazine Advertisements," *Howard Journal of Communication* 6 (October 1995)

Taylor, Charles, Ju Yung Lee, and Barbara Stern, "Portrayals of African, Hispanic, and Asian Americans in Magazine Advertising," *American Behavioral Scientist* 38, no. 4 (February 1995)

Taylor, Charles R., and Barbara B. Stern, "Asian Americans: Television Advertising and the 'Model Minority' Stereotype," *Journal of Advertising* 26, no. 2 (1997)

Westerman, Marty, "Death of the Frito Bandito," *American Demographics* 11 (28 March 1989)

Woods, Gail Baker, *Advertising and Marketing to the New Majority,* Belmont, California: Wadsworth, 1995

Minorities: Targets of Advertising

The term *minorities* refers, in its strictest sense, to groups that are numerically smaller than the majority. Historically, *minority* in the United States has included African-Americans, Hispanics, Asians, Jews, and American Indians, all culturally or racially distinctive groups that represented a comparatively small percentage of the population. Minority can be a misleading label, however, as a minority population may exceed the majority population in some locations. In the United States at the turn of the 21st century, minority populations were increasing at a faster rate than the general population.

Minorities have often been seen as a problem for the media, making it necessary for them to change business methods and appeal to groups of people with different cultural perspectives. The differences in language, culture, religion, and lifestyle can be seen as a threat to predominate cultural values. Traditionally, in an effort to appeal to mass audiences, advertisers sought to focus on matters of common concern that transcended ethnic issues, since it was assumed that minorities aspired to the lifestyle of the majority. When the minority was depicted in advertisements, those depictions were often stereotypical. From a historical perspective, advertising in the United States has occasionally spoken to the central market using depictions of minority groups epitomized in such trade characters as the Frito Bandito, Aunt Jemima, and Chiquita Banana, each of which is a composite of stereotypical characteristics. The images were modified only after advertisers received complaints from representatives of the various ethnic groups in question.

Targeting African-American Consumers

In the United States, the realization that African-Americans constituted a separate market with money and the willingness to spend it dates back as early as 1916, when a Rock Hill, South Carolina, gas company sponsored a cooking school for black servants and ended up selling 12 stoves. In the summer of 1922, the Fuller Brush Company enlisted four black schoolteachers to sell $2,083 worth of brushes to their Tulsa, Oklahoma, community. A 1931 survey estimated the buying power of the African-American market to be more than $1.5 billion.

By the mid-1930s it had become evident that there was indeed a separate African-American market, with differences in brand preferences and consumption patterns. To tap into this minority market, advertisers needed to display concern for the black consumer, use black spokespeople to sell products, and tailor messages to meet the needs of the market. It was not until well after the end of World War II, however, that this market received any national interest.

In 1952 *Sponsor*, a media magazine, began publishing an annual black issue designed to bring the Negro market to the forefront. In its sixth annual black issue, *Sponsor* reported that, regardless of advertisers' awareness of minority groups among the mass audience, most national advertisers tended to use general mass media rather than minority-oriented media to reach this particular market segment. They reasoned that the general media reached everyone. However, advertisers did not account for differences in consumption patterns and emerging demographics of the minority market.

In the decade following World War II, the median income of black Americans increased more than 350 percent. They made up the second-largest (18 million) and fastest-growing market segment in the United States by the mid-1950s and accounted for an estimated $16 billion in buying power. The trend in black population shifts during this time was from the rural South to northern urban areas, where the influx of many other minorities also tended to concentrate.

These trends signaled burgeoning opportunities for astute advertisers. There were large unified groups, with more buying power, more sophisticated consumption patterns, more economic and social stability, and more education and know-how emerging in the marketplace. While more companies began examining the sales potential of the market, many still believed that attracting the black consumer did not require a specialized approach. Public opinion research supported the belief of many marketers that by simply reading and listening, black consumers were exposed to the general media's messages.

Others believed that messages sent via general media often went unnoticed by black consumers because this was not "their" media, and even racially sensitive general media gave little, if any, representation of minority life. Virtually everything produced for the general mass media was designed and targeted for the white consumer. It should be no surprise that African-Americans found it difficult to identify with most advertisements. Ads that touted "lovelier, whiter hands with ABC soap" or promoted contests where winners receive a week's stay at a sunny, southern (segregated) resort were unintentionally insulting and distasteful.

"Desegregation" of Advertising

As early as 1961, it was suggested that advertisers use cartoons, animals, and sun-tanned rather than pale-skinned models to help "desegregate" advertisements. It was believed that such measures would circumvent the need to create two different, expensive advertisements. Others insisted that if advertisements depicted a naturally integrated environment—for example, a service station where blacks and whites were working together—both audiences would be receptive.

Research showed that the purchase and consumption patterns of African-Americans differed greatly from those of their white counterparts in the same income brackets. For example, black consumers spent more for clothes, cosmetics and toiletries, groceries, frozen vegetables, and soft drinks. In addition, they were found to be more brand-conscious and were willing to pay higher prices for certain items. Yet stereotypes often held marketers back from reaching minority audiences. Biases and faulty logic tainted

Colon Cancer among African-American men and women is on the rise.

Here's something you can do about it.

While colon cancer rates are dropping among most Americans, colon cancer among African-Americans is rising. The National Cancer Institute contends that a third of all cancer deaths may be diet-related.

By switching to a high-fiber, low in fat diet, you may lower your risk of colon cancer. A great way to add essential fiber to your diet regularly is to start each day with *Kellogg's* ® whole-grain or bran cereals.* Add skim milk, whole-grain toast and fruit and you've got a breakfast that's not only delicious, but good for your health.

* *Kellogg's* Bran Flakes and *Kellogg's* Raisin Bran are just two high-fiber favorites from *Kellogg's.*

Kellogg's

A NUTRITION TRADITION.™

In 1990, when statistics showed that colon cancer was on the increase among African-Americans, the Kellogg Company used its ads to encourage blacks to switch to high-fiber, low-fat Kellogg cereals.
© *1990 Kellogg Company.*

research before it was even conducted. The assumption that African-Americans did not have dandruff, for example, discouraged any attempt to market medicated hair-care products to them.

The minority-oriented media have traditionally been the most effective outlets for reaching their communities. In the late 1950s nearly 200 black newspapers had an estimated combined circulation of 3 million. *Ebony, Jet,* and *Tan* magazines were the most successful of the three dozen black magazines published in the United States during this same period, with combined circulation reaching nearly 1 million households.

Whereas African-Americans have typically comprised approximately 11 percent of the population, advertising dollars targeted toward them have only amounted to about 2 percent of the national total. Although researchers have shown that ethnic-oriented media have been an essential ingredient in reaching minority markets, many advertisers have chosen to ignore this finding. Those few minority members who held powerful positions in large corporations tended to believe that business had an obligation to the minority community to adopt special programs in education, public relations, promotions, and employment opportunities, and to use minority-oriented media to strengthen and broaden marketing appeals.

Until the U.S. Civil Rights movement of the 1960s, Madison Avenue media planners largely ignored the country's black population. However, progress in civil rights and rapid political, economic, social, and educational advancements made advertisers acutely aware of this market, and some—in particular, advertisers of alcohol, cigarettes, and soft drinks—successfully utilized a variety of media to reach this audience.

While some advertisers employed certain techniques (integrated TV commercials) or token approaches (use of black models) in an attempt to reach the market, simply casting minority models in TV ads did not lure the black consumer. A total approach of black-appeal media—radio and magazines coupled with promotion, merchandising, public relations, and employment practices—had to be included in the marketing mix in order to capture this consumer. Some companies launched minority-appeal campaigns in efforts to ward off national boycotts. But the use of black-oriented media had to be designed with a measure of sincerity to elevate the company in the eyes of the black consumer.

Many African-Americans did not believe that ad messages via general media were targeted to them, even if a black model or actor was featured in the ad. Advertisers could not assume that blacks shared the same program preferences as whites. Variety shows and situation comedies were watched by considerably fewer blacks than whites; yet blacks watched more westerns. Thus, advertisers could not calculate the black audience based solely on rating points.

Pressure placed on large advertisers by various civil rights groups such as the Mayor's Committee on Job Advancement in New York City, the National Association for the Advancement of Colored People (NAACP), the Congress of Racial Equality (CORE), the Urban League, and Black Women on the March began to turn the tide toward integrating advertising. Integration efforts by CORE were carefully executed. The group targeted blue-chip advertisers, which were considered the industry leaders with the most influence and biggest budgets. CORE fought vigorously for integrated advertising and by the end of 1963 had struck agreements with 15 advertisers and with another 50 by the end of 1964.

Television became integrated in the 1963 season. Alert advertisers were aware of the milestone: Gillette aired a national network campaign featuring black models; advertisers indicated an interest in sponsoring pilot programs designed to appeal to black audiences; black newscasters joined the ABC network; Pharmaco cosmetics cast all black commercials; and the nation's first black-appeal TV station was launched in Washington, D.C.

By the mid-1960s, advertisers were aware that black consumers were important to their sales and that they sought representation in advertising pages; they also believed this audience could be reached via general media outlets. As whites moved to suburbia, blacks and other minorities rapidly became the urban dwellers. By 1966 almost half of the black population's $27.6 billion effective buying income was concentrated in just 25 U.S. counties. Urban blacks and other minorities represented a great marketing potential because most were concentrated in a "market segment" of less than a few square miles.

Targeting "Ethnic" Markets

The recording industry was one of the earliest to appreciate the value of producing distinct lines for different minority groups. The 1921 Columbia Records catalog included not only products for several different language markets (including French, Spanish, Russian, Polish, Croatian, Serbian, Greek, and Italian) but also a separate "race" category of jazz and blues marketed to black Americans. Companies such as McDonald's and Coca-Cola began advertising to the Hispanic community in Spanish in the late 1960s. However, the full value of ethnic target marketing was not appreciated until the 1970s, when companies discovered that blacks were spending more than $250 million a year on consumer goods. Corporations such as Philip Morris and Quaker Oats gradually won praise and customers by running ads that depicted minorities in positive and nonstereotypical roles. Hispanics, who spent $180 billion annually in 2000, have also been fervently pur-

sued. Spending on Hispanic media more than tripled from its mid-1980s level, to $224 million. Each ethnic group has its own product preferences and consumption patterns.

Over a 20-year period beginning in 1980, the U.S. Hispanic community increased 53 percent and the African-American population increased 15 percent. At the outset of the 21st century, the total income of African-Americans in the United States was estimated at $276 billion; Hispanics at $134 billion; and Asians at $35 billion. Still, the general media failed to reflect this; *Esquire* magazine, for example, had 25.5 percent African-American readership, but only 2.4 percent black representation in its advertisements. Waves of immigrants from Asia, Latin America, and Africa added to an already growing minority population and were radically reshaping the buying habits of the "typical" American consumer. Ethnic-minority shoppers, mostly African-Americans, Hispanics, and Asians, spent an estimated $600 billion on everything from cosmetics to clothes to automobiles in 1997, an 18 percent increase since 1990. By the year 2000, minorities accounted for 30 percent of the U.S. economy.

Arab, Asian, Hispanic, Russian, Eastern European, African, and Caribbean immigrants are best reached via their native languages and have the potential purchasing power of about $400 billion. As with black consumers in the 1960s, many new immigrants are geographically clustered, which makes them easier to reach. One of the best ways to reach minority groups tends to be working through community groups and promotional efforts.

Both to profit and to avoid mistakes, more and more companies recruit ad agencies that specialize in ethnic marketing. Time Advertising, a San Francisco, California–based agency owned by Chinese-Americans, produced spots for AT&T. Burrell Communications, an African-American agency in Chicago, Illinois, handled McDonald's and Coca-Cola, among other accounts. Many of the big Madison Avenue firms either acquired or started their own ethnic-oriented divisions, such as Young & Rubicam's Bravo Group, a Hispanic-market specialist. Foote, Cone & Belding, Leo Burnett Company, and Grey Advertising Agency also had Hispanic departments.

In their quest for ethnic consumers, advertisers by 2000 were depending less on traditional forms of mass marketing, such as network television and general-circulation magazines, and more on specialized media, such as cable TV and ethnic- or subject-oriented magazines. Ethnic spending power was estimated at $500 billion annually in 2000. The major ethnic communities in the United States are comprised of Hispanic (Latin America, Mexico, Puerto Rico, Cuba), Asian (predominantly China, Korea, and Japan), Indian (India and Pakistan), Middle Eastern, and European (primarily Eastern Europe and Russia) people. The African-American community is a separate category. There were 22 million Hispanic-American households in the United States in the 1990s, at which time they surpassed the general-market growth rate four-to-one. In addition, about 7 million Asian-Americans represented close to $225 billion in purchasing power at the start of the 21st century.

If there is one distinctive element of the ethnic market, it is brand loyalty. Ethnic consumers tend to be much more brand

In this 1999 Spanish-language print ad, Sears targeted the Miami, Florida, Hispanic community.
The 1999 "Todo para ti" Sears advertisement is reprinted by arrangement with Sears, Roebuck and Co. and is protected under copyright. No duplication is permitted.

loyal than white Americans. The 1990 Simmons Study of Media and Markets revealed that more than 88 percent of black consumers surveyed expressed a preference for reading black-oriented publications, whereas black readership of general audience publications is usually below 30 percent. National marketers continue to spend a disproportionately small share of their promotional dollars in black-oriented media sources, disregarding the fact that black consumers are more responsive to advertising in their own media. It has been suggested that white marketers have not really understood the motivations of African-Americans as consumers.

The face of America has changed. The 1990 U.S. Census documented that 25 percent of the U.S. population was African-American, Hispanic, or Asian-American. For companies trying to sell their products and services, there is business in diversity. While *micromarketing* is the new buzzword, it does not go far enough in acknowledging the role that culture plays in the purchase decision process.

A large number of minorities who live in the poorer neighborhoods of big cities worry about their children's safety and schools. Companies such as Colgate-Palmolive and PepsiCo build brand loyalty by sponsoring community school clean-up and literacy programs in those neighborhoods.

Minorities are underrepresented in nationally circulated magazine advertisements. A late 1990s study revealed that while African-Americans comprise 12 percent of the U.S. population and 11.3 percent of the readership of all magazines, they represented only 3.2 percent of people shown in advertisements. Many believe, however, that advertising not only has no obligation but also no business trying to depict diversity.

TARA ANNE MICHELS

Further Reading

Astor, Gerald, *Minorities and the Media,* New York: Ford Foundation, 1974

Malick, Ibrahim Sajid, "New Americans: The Overlooked $400 Billion Market," *Marketing News* (15 July 1996)

McCarroll, Thomas, "It's a Mass Market No More," *Time* (1993)

New York Department of Consumer Affairs, *Invisible People: The Depiction of Minorities in Magazine Ads and Catalogs,* New York: New York Department of Consumer Affairs, 1991

O'Barr, William, *Culture and the Ad: Exploring Otherness in the World of Advertising,* Boulder, Colorado: Westview, 1994

Reese, Shelly, "A World of Differences," *Marketing Tools* (August 1997)

Schreiber, Alfred, "Defining the 'New America,'" *Advertising Age* (3 August 1998)

Thomas, Erwin, and Brown H. Carpenter, editors, *Handbook on Mass Media in the United States: The Industry and Its Audiences,* Westport, Connecticut: Greenwood, 1994

Wilson, Clint, and Félix Gutiérrez, *Minorities and Media: Diversity and the End of Mass Communication,* Beverly Hills, California: Sage, 1985; 2nd edition, as *Race, Multiculturalism, and the Media: From Mass to Class Communication,* Thousand Oaks, California: Sage, 1995

Modem Media Poppe Tyson

(Modem Media)

Poppe Tyson originated as O.S. Industrial Advertising, product of the merger of de Garmo, Inc., and O.S. Tyson & Company, Inc., 1974; merged agency renamed Poppe Tyson by 1976; Modem Media founded, 1987; Poppe Tyson acquired by Bozell, Jacobs, Kenyon & Eckhardt, 1992; majority interest in Modem Media acquired by True North, 1996; Poppe Tyson acquired by True North with purchase of Bozell, 1997; Poppe Tyson folded into Modem Media by True North, agency renamed Modem Media Poppe Tyson, 1998; went public, 1999; renamed Modem Media, 2000.

Major Clients

AT&T Corporation
Citibank
Delta Air Lines
General Electric Company
John Hancock Mutual Life Insurance Company
Netscape
Silicon Graphics
Union Carbide

The 1998 merger of Modem Media and Poppe Tyson created a partnership that united two pioneers in Internet advertising. Poppe Tyson helped invent the Internet banner ad and took part in the design of what would become the Netscape Web browser. Modem Media's work for its early clients, the AT&T Corporation and Coors Brewing Company's Zima beverage, made it a leader among digital marketing companies.

Poppe Tyson's roots predate the Internet. The agency was founded as O.S. Industrial Advertising when two New York City–based agencies, the Complan division of de Garmo, Inc., and the industrial agency O.S. Tyson & Company, Inc., merged in 1974. Fred Poppe was named president and chief executive officer (CEO), and Irwin Tyson was appointed executive vice president; by 1976 the agency was doing business under the Poppe Tyson name. The shop opened its doors with $7 million in billings and clients that included Otis Elevator, Oxy Metal Industries, and Union Carbide.

Poppe Tyson grew to become one of the biggest U.S. business-to-business ad agencies, taking on additional technology accounts. In 1988 it had billings of more than $65 million. In the late 1980s Fred Poppe resigned, and the company went through a series of ownership changes that ended with the shop at Bozell, Jacobs, Kenyon & Eckhardt in 1992.

During this period, Poppe became one of the first ad agencies to embrace the Internet. The agency had been doing work for Silicon Graphics, a manufacturer of 3-D computer graphics workstations. Jim Clark, Silicon Graphics founder and chairman and a visionary in the areas of interactive TV and the Internet, left the company in 1994 and went on to cofound Mosaic Communications Corporation, which marketed the first Internet browser. Clark enlisted Poppe to help design the interface for Netscape.

The Web design work gave the agency a jump start in the industry. Poppe created its own Web site in 1994 to solicit more work, making it one of the first agencies to do so. Within 90 days, Intel Corporation, Hewlett-Packard Company, and others had hired Poppe for Internet branding projects. Poppe's Mountain View, California, office staff swelled to about 190 and its New York City staff to more than 300. U.S. Vice President Al Gore hired the shop to design the Web site for the White House. As one of the first agencies to do Web design work, Poppe saw its revenue increase from $10.5 million in 1995 to $35 million in 1997.

Perhaps its greatest claim to fame came in 1995, when Mosaic, by then renamed Netscape after its chief product, decided to sell ads on the browser. Poppe helped negotiate the first ad sale and created one of the first banner ads, a simple ad sold to the AT&T Corporation for $40,000 a quarter. This event led Poppe into the ad sales business, representing Netscape and other clients, among them Excite. But the plan backfired as Poppe's sales forces competed against each Web site's internal sales teams.

To remedy the situation, in November 1995 the agency quietly spun off DoubleClick, an independent, wholly owned subsidiary, to provide sales representation for clients selling ad space on their sites in an ad network (a business that represents various Web sites for ad sales). DoubleClick started in Poppe Tyson's Mountain View office. Later headquartered in New York City, DoubleClick came to be considered the leader in the ad management business and evolved to serve and manage on-line ads as well as handle e-mail ad campaigns and other on-line media. DoubleClick had a market capitalization of $1.93 billion in 2000.

Poppe was not as successful. Revenue before the company's 1998 merger with Modem fell sharply, to about $22 million. This was a period of management turmoil and disagreement over how much emphasis the agency should put on Internet work. The company planned to go public in the fall of 1996 but shelved those plans in December of that year, citing poor market conditions. Exactly a year later, True North picked up Poppe when it bought its parent, Bozell Worldwide.

Modem Media, on the other hand, was founded expressly to be a digital marketing company (hence its name, which founder Gerald M. O'Connell admitted would quickly become outdated). O'Connell founded the shop with Douglas Ahlers in 1987 in Westport, Connecticut. For its first client, the General Electric Company (GE), Modem Media began building the GEnie on-line mall. Its work for GE gained attention, and its client roster soon grew to include the J.C. Penney Company; Hammacher, Schlemmer & Company; and Godiva Chocolates. Early forms of digital media efforts by Modem took the form of CD-ROMs, fax on demand, and interactive voice response.

Modem began working with AT&T in the early 1990s. In 1993, as the Internet began showing glimmers of marketing potential, Modem started aiming its focus there. A Modem team developed some of the first Internet marketing programs for AT&T as well as for the Coors Brewing Company's Zima beverage. The AT&T campaign was integrated into the launch of HotWired, the on-line unit of *Wired* magazine. It featured a tour of art museums whose collections were available on-line.

In 1996 Modem Media sold a majority interest to True North Communications (TN) and became part of TN Technologies, a holding company unit for TN's interactive properties. After months of rumors, in June 1998 TN merged Modem with the interactive components of Poppe Tyson. Poppe's traditional agency services were merged into True North's other assets. In 1998 the combined agency won a CASIE Award for a John Hancock Mutual Life Insurance Company campaign.

Modem went public in early 1999 as Modem Media.Poppe Tyson, and in 2000 the company dropped the venerable Poppe Tyson name. Through acquisition of companies in Germany, France, and Japan, it has offices in New York City; San Francisco, California; Norwalk, Connecticut (company headquarters); Toronto, Canada; London, England; Paris, France; Munich, Germany; Hong Kong; Tokyo, Japan; and São Paulo, Brazil. Its client roster includes global brands such as Citibank, General Motors Corporation, Delta Air Lines, General Electric Company, IBM Corporation, and J.C. Penney Company.

Modem has received numerous industry awards for its interactive marketing campaigns, Web sites, banner advertisements, and CD-ROMs, including the Zima.com campaign and Web site, the AT&T Olympic Games Connection Web site, the AT&T "Intermercial" campaign, the AT&T Worldnet CD-ROM, and iVillage.com's "About Work." But like many companies in Internet professional services, Modem has suffered some reverses as well. It lost one of its biggest clients in 1999 when it parted company with AT&T.

PATRICIA RIEDMAN

Further Reading

"De Garmo, Tyson Form New Agency," *Advertising Age* (1 July 1974)

Modernity

The development of the advertising industry in the 20th century and its increasing importance as a cultural force can perhaps best be understood in the context of modernity. While the more familiar term *modernism* describes an artistic movement and style, *modernity* refers to a particular organization of society based on industrialization, urbanization, mass production, and consumption. The ideological foundations of modernity are rooted in the Enlightenment and the French Revolution, movements characterized by a faith in progress and the belief that the world could and would be transformed by human thought and behavior based on rationalism.

Fundamental to the concept of modernity is the idea that human beings are rational creatures who always, and primarily, use cognition as a survival tool and are thus capable of creating great civilizations through scientific development and technological advances. Indeed, concepts such as progress, freedom, individuality, and democracy are central to the notion of the modern.

The history of advertising goes hand in hand with these fundamental assumptions. Products and services are attractive not only because they represent innovations that can improve people's lives but also because their production and consumption promote a society's economic and ideological system. Consumption, in turn, becomes a practice that converges with modern ideological propositions, namely exerting an individual's right of choice as a statement of his or her freedom and individuality.

In contemporary societies advertising functions as a public narrative; it describes people's relationships with each other, with products and services, and with their concepts of society in general. Advertising frames consumer culture, emphasizing consumption as a way of successfully establishing, or reinventing, one's individual identity. During the first quarter of the 20th century, being "modern" was one of advertising's most common themes; acquiring a "modern identity" was the mandate of the era, and consumption, the way of accomplishing it.

Advertising and the Modern Self

As the 1900s began, an expanding middle class, eager to climb the social ladder, was desperately looking for models of social distinction. In this sense, characters such as the Gibson Girl and Gibson Man, the debonair creations of artist Charles Dana Gibson, served as ideals of youth, beauty, competence, and elegance for Americans on the threshold of the 20th century. The concept of being modern meant a transformation of the self but was primarily manifested in a transformation of the way one looked and behaved. Being modern meant that one rejected old forms of individual and social identities and practices.

This is particularly clear in an ad for Lux soap published in the *Ladies' Home Journal* in March 1918. At the top of the ad are illustrations of two blouses. On the right is "the sheer blouse of today. Washed the modern way—the Lux way—pure suds and no rubbing." At the left, "the [shirt]waist of years ago. Rub-rub-rub

fabrics had to be strong to stand being washed with cake soap." The ad puts forward the notion that the modern way is essentially equal to the brand name. But more important—more than a simple contrast between the products used to wash each blouse—this ad is constructed around the contrast between Puritan values and modern fashion. The Puritan (or Victorian) fashions, covering the entire body, seem to trap the wearer. The modern fashion, on the other hand, is less rigid and controlling, with a long V-neck that ends in a casual knot. The ad for Lux can be interpreted as a lesson on cultural appropriateness.

Advertising was a socializing force in the new consumer culture. It not only suggested what to wear but also how to care for those fashionable new goods in modern ways. The message is clear: if one is to dress as a modern person, one's domestic practices must be transformed as well. The Lux ad copy contrasted the old washing practice (rubbing) with the modern (dipping the garment up and down), giving a lesson on how to wash clothes in a simpler, modern, and more refined way. Modernity, then, has to do not only with progress, refinement, and sophistication but also with making life simpler.

Advertising promoted the consumption of "new" products, which, in turn, led to new ways of organizing and performing daily routines. The transformation of domestic practices, such as washing clothes with a new product, also had an economic impact. With sufficient demand created through consumption, that demand promoted the development of mass production, thus boosting the economy. Advertising not only promoted the consumption of products as a way of reinventing or improving one's life, it also became an integral part of the expansion of capitalistic economies.

Given a belief in science and rational behavior, early 20th century advertising offered solutions to personal problems as well as methods for improving self-esteem and personal power. The need for social acceptance, along with modern concerns about health, turned advertising into an informal public education device as it guided consumers through new hygiene practices inherent in modern life. Lifebuoy soap promised a solution to the problem of "B.O." (body odor). Listerine invented its own problem ("halitosis") and then offered itself as the solution. Ivory soap warned female consumers against the dangers of cosmetics and encouraged them to wash their faces. Pepsodent and other toothpastes reinforced the idea of brushing one's teeth as a habit. As advertising promoted the use of these products, their consumption began generating new domestic rituals.

In a print ad for Edna Wallace Hopper's beauty method published in *Vogue* in 1929, the copy reads, "Changing one's face—it's easy if you follow the method of Edna Wallace Hopper." Cosmetic advertisements from this period encouraged women to create beauty by using myriad different products. Beauty was no longer a natural condition—now it was a state that could be achieved, managed, and changed by both buying cosmetic products and practicing new rituals of embellishment. Using the rational narratives of modernity as models, advertisements were constructed around feature-benefit relationships—that is, features of the product that promised benefits to the user. Thus, Ivory soap could promise perfect skin and a wonderful complexion because of its purity.

Development of Advertising as a Discipline

One of the main propositions of modernity is in the establishment of boundaries and groupings, separating things and people into categories. Professions, too, need to have an identity and a place in society. At the turn of the century, however, the advertising profession did not have a clear profile. From the crier in ancient Greece to contemporary advertising practitioners, Western history has recorded ambivalence toward the "profession" of advertising. With its use of artistic techniques as well as sales persuasion, advertising was cast as a hybrid occupation often stigmatized for its commercial and manipulative practices and highly criticized for being a decadent form of art.

The quest for professionalism in advertising began in the early 1900s, as concerns over ethical codes, licensing, and certification requirements surfaced. However, one can argue that achieving professional respect would also help overcome the characterization of the advertising practitioner as both merchant and artist. Turning advertising into a discipline could only be achieved, in modern terms, by transforming it into a science, and in that way finally overcoming the split personality of the advertising practitioner as both artist and merchant.

Advertising as an industry is best thought of as a group of institutions—agencies, marketing research firms, particular clients, media—and the power relationships that exist among those institutions and between them and consumers. This complex system of relationships is committed to developing a particular kind of knowledge about the market that eventually will be translated into a specific advertisement. However, this "knowledge" has a somewhat transient existence since it is limited to the segment, the category, or, even more restrictively, to the brand. Without a systematic body of knowledge such as other professions had developed, early 20th century advertisers turned to marketing, the social sciences, and statistics in order to develop theories, methodologies, and measuring instruments needed to construct that knowledge for their business.

So the core question for practitioners was, "How does advertising work?" The construction, over time, of a set of principles to answer this question has been sensitive to trends in communications as well as social and behavioral science theories and methodologies. The development of new concepts about the consumer was key to advertising practitioners' claims that they could minimize uncertainty while managing the marketplace and the consumer.

This need for control, typical of rationalization processes and fundamental to modernity, resulted in an orderly profile of consumers and their decision-making processes. Traditional advertising based its view of consumers on one of the pillars of modernity: namely, the belief in a rational, autonomous human being. At the same time, it embraced the scientific method as a

With its marked contrast between contemporary fashions and Victorian-era clothing, this 1918 print ad for Lux soap can be interpreted as a selling message as well as a lesson on cultural appropriateness. *Courtesy of Unilever HPC.*

modern and legitimate way of understanding and explaining consumer behavior. In other words, advertising practitioners believed that utilizing objective scientific inquiry and controlled laboratory settings while establishing predictable categories of consumers and the existence of manageable markets would successfully articulate the creative approach, the media, and the message to be employed in any ad.

Bill Bernbach's Revolution

The 1960s brought challenges to these assumptions. The struggle between the positivism of the scientific approach and the intuitive creative direction was the focus of the efforts generally attributed to one of the most important advertising contributors of the 20th century, William Bernbach. He promoted a sort of "anti-advertising" that had, as one of its objectives, the desire to legitimize the roles of intuition and creativity as valid forms of advertising insight.

Bernbach's work and management style reflected an open, intuitive approach to the creation of advertising that depended less on marketing research and more on the creative process. Some of his statements became proverbial:

- "Rules are what the artist breaks; the memorable never emerged from a formula."
- "Research inevitably leads to conformity."
- "I warn you against believing that advertising is a science."

While the legendary advertising man David Ogilvy put forth rules prescribing what should be done when creating advertising, Bernbach's "creative revolution" served as a new, vital alternative to that process. In that sense, modern concerns over control and predictability in the advertising process generated a reaction that launched Bernbach's postmodern era.

Bernbach saw the need to overcome power relationships among different players in the advertising industry. His efforts essentially set the standards by which advertising agencies would be judged. The importance of creative leadership in agency management and of the creative work produced continued to be the defining parameters of excellence into the 21st century. If the 1960s introduced a revolution against the practice of scientific market and advertising research, it was carried out from a Romantic perspective of the advertiser as an artist, uniquely possessing the ability to elaborate an imaginative truth. According to Bob Levenson in his 1987 book *Bill Bernbach's Book,* Bernbach referred to this idea as follows:

> There are a lot of great technicians in advertising. And unfortunately they talk the best game. They know all the rules. They can tell you that [pictures of] people in an ad will get you greater readership. They can tell you that a sentence should be this short or that it should be long. They can tell you that the body copy should be broken up for easier and more inviting reading. They can give you fact after fact after fact. They are scientists of advertising. But there's one little rub. Advertising is fundamentally persuasion and persuasion happens to be not a science, but an art.

Bernbach, indeed, introduced a postmodern turn in the management and creative process in advertising; however, in the last two decades of the 20th century, a new schism appeared, this time among advertising academicians. Many scholars began to advocate the inclusion of interpretive theories and methodologies in marketing and advertising research. The shift from positivistic and quantitative methods to interpretive and qualitative research approaches can be seen as the need to create, in late modernity, a new center of legitimacy for the knowledge produced by marketing and advertising academicians. In this sense, postmodern consumer research represents an effort to reinvent the consumer and the market from a perspective antithetical to the prevailing concept of autonomous, rational individual behavior and beyond the positivism and behaviorism of traditional marketing and advertising research. A postmodern consumer, a "de-centered subject" whose identity is created and negotiated through consumption choices, took the place of the rational individual depicted by modernity and characterized by traditional decision-making models drawn from behaviorism and theories of reasoned action.

Postmodern consumer research is not only the incorporation of nontraditional research methods and theories but also a way of giving voice to consumers, treating them as individuals and viewing their consumption experiences in the context of their attitudes and values. Thus, while traditional advertising research dealt almost exclusively with so-called rational and quantified processes, the symbolic and social side of consumption, often hard to quantify yet operative in consumer choice, became a legitimate focus of study. Moreover, giving voice to consumers raised ethical issues regarding the relationship between researchers and consumers, who were now seen as participants, as subjects, and not as objects of the research process.

Apple Computer's "1984": Toward Postmodernity

Apple's "1984" TV spot was both a clever way of introducing Macintosh products as viable alternatives to rival personal computers and an insightful metaphor describing the relationship of advertising, capitalism, and modernity. The commercial, which launched the Apple Macintosh as a rival to IBM Corporation's personal computer empire, builds on the imagery of George Orwell's novella of the same name, which portrayed masses of people dominated and manipulated by a totalitarian regime.

For the viewer, the commercial's dark tone and imagery—row upon row of faceless, almost robotically similar workers—was evocative of life in Stalinist Russia or any other oppressive regime. The "woman as heroine" in the commercial represents the personal empowerment and liberation that come with Apple's signature "thinking differently." The heroine serves as an approachable symbol for those entering the marketplace and wanting to feel empowered by the "Apple experience." While "1984" was regarded as revolutionary in the realm of advertising, the models it drew upon for its imagery had many antecedents and are worth noting.

By equating the exercise of rationality, free will, and individuality—all pillars of modernity—with the purchase of an Apple computer as a source of empowerment and liberation, the commercial legitimizes the logic of capitalism: the spot is not focused on the product but on how consumption and possession define people as individuals. Consumption understood as an experience was accepted as a source of empowerment and legitimacy for individuality, converging, in this sense, with the main tenets of modernity. Therefore, following the thematic message of the commercial, not living the "Apple experience" was a form of alienation from the creative lifestyle one desired. Experience and individuality continued to be major and minor thematic components of Apple campaigns. Even the introduction of vivid colors for the product line represented a paradigm-shattering concept for an industry that was overinstitutionalized. And with the introduction of a new tag line in 1997, Apple's message was clearly epitomized in that slogan/command: "Think different!"

Changing One's Face—It's Easy

If you follow the method of Edna Wallace Hopper

Edna Wallace Hopper
as she looks today

"WOMEN should change their faces every week," declares Miss Edna Wallace Hopper, the noted actress who at sixty looks like a girl of sixteen. "A woman simply cannot make the most of her appearance if she wears the same face all the time. There is no need of it. A woman can always change her face by changing her hair. Re-arranging one's hair is delightfully simple if one first dampens the hair with Wave and Sheen."

Wave and Sheen — This liquid makes the hair as easy to work with as clay. With it, you can mould a coiffure to suit your tastes—curl, wave, or fluff your hair as you please—and when your hair dries, it will stay as you put it. Its use will make your hair as soft as down and give your hairdress that appearance of naturalness so desired. Wave and Sheen makes it possible for you to "change your face" by making it easy for you to change your coiffure. Wave and Sheen not only leaves your hair as you want it but it gives the hair a wonderful new vibrant luster that you may never have dreamed your hair possessed.

ANOTHER possibility, if you use the methods of Miss Hopper, is the seeming exchange of an old complexion for a new complexion . . . by the bi-weekly use of Facial Youth, the new penetrative liquid cleanser. The pores of the face fill up with impurities which cream or soap simply cannot remove. This clogging causes dull or muddy complexions, eruptions, blemishes. Facial Youth penetrates, dissolves the clogged accumulations, keeps the pores open and functioning normally — making possible that cellular health on which the beauty of your complexion depends. It helps to release the natural beauty that comes from within. Use Facial Youth daily for the next month and the happy message that your mirror will flash you will seem too good to be true.

Facial Youth

Both Edna Wallace Hopper's Wave and Sheen and Edna Wallace Hopper's Facial Youth can be secured at all leading toilet counters.

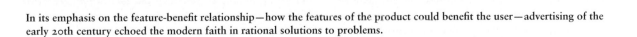

In its emphasis on the feature-benefit relationship—how the features of the product could benefit the user—advertising of the early 20th century echoed the modern faith in rational solutions to problems.

The Apple experience gained acceptance in accordance with the premises of modernism. First, cognition, basic for rationality, was emphasized. Second, the inducement to be different ultimately served not only an individual interest in terms of authentic liberation from an oppressive "regime" but also the relationship between consumption and capitalism. Third, human agency in search of freedom, originality, and empowerment was accomplished only through a consumption experience where technology as liberator played a fundamental role. For modernity, some of the means of empowerment were increased emphasis on rational process and technological achievement.

At the same time, the notions of liberation and the possibility of being different, perhaps creative, lost their original, modern political dimension and were represented by the consumption experience. This revolution in thought and personal values took place in the private space of consumption; it became an individual revolution. Paradoxically, one can argue that "1984" was both a modern and a postmodern commercial. On one hand, it appropriated the themes of modernity; on the other, it proposed the Apple experience as a lifestyle. Linda Scott, writing in the *Journal of Popular Culture* in 1991, referred to Macintosh and its ethos:

> Macintosh is young, wears blue jeans, and lives in an '80s version of the '60s counterculture. He/she is both creative and committed, believing strongly that his/her work ultimately matters. But Macintosh is impatient, uncomfortable, and contemptuous of everything that is conventional or hierarchical.

While modern identity tended to be fixed as a continuum, postmodern identity is a permanent discontinuity. Modern identity was related to one's profession or function in the public sphere or in the family as well as in political and national associations; postmodern identity is centered on looks, image, and consumption. The Apple computer commercial can be interpreted as a call to be different by identifying with a set of values that define a lifestyle.

Identity was marketed as a lifestyle and was divorced from the social and public implications that it had in earlier—modern—times. Advertising during the 19th and 20th centuries educated consumers on how to become modern. It encouraged its audience to live with and enjoy the widely accessible new products and services—and thus succeed both as citizens and as consumers. Advertising mapped out new cultural meanings for products and services. But the need for increasing product and segment differentiation led to the fragmentation of modern forms of collective identities into discrete, highly stylized lifestyles. When identity came to be defined by consumption, existing standards of community and political participation established by modernity failed as defining characteristics.

The development of advertising as an industry and as a profession was not only fundamental to the economic development of capitalist society, but it also promoted the ideological propositions of the modern paradigm. Advertising transformed forever the private and the public spaces in which people live. Advertising not only guided individuals through the challenges imposed by new forms of social and economic organizations but also gave a new dimension to the individual's participation in society. But as this consumer culture grew, it offered people new ways of identifying themselves beyond traditional modern identities such as nationality or citizenship and, in turn, enabled advertising to move beyond the science of modernity to the emotional components of human existence. Thus, advertising became the way in which the economic aspirations of society were articulated, as well as the language through which societies dreamed and desired.

VANESSA FONSECA AND NEAL M. BURNS

Further Reading

Bernbach, Bill, *Bill Bernbach Said . . .*, New York: DDB Needham Worldwide, 1989

Ewen, Stuart, and Elizabeth Ewen, *Channels of Desire: Mass Images and the Shaping of American Consciousness,* New York: McGraw-Hill, 1982

Frank, Thomas, "Advertising As Cultural Criticism: Bill Bernbach versus Mass Society," in *Consumer Society Reader,* edited by Juliet B. Schor and Douglas B. Holt, New York: New Press, 2000

Jameson, Fredric, *Postmodernism; or, The Cultural Logic of Late Capitalism,* Durham, North Carolina: Duke University Press, and London: Verso, 1991

Jhally, Sut, *The Codes of Advertising: Fetishism and the Political Economy of Meaning in the Consumer Society,* New York: St. Martin's Press, and London: Pinter, 1987

Kellner, Douglas, *Media Culture: Cultural Studies, Identity, and Politics between the Modern and the Postmodern,* London and New York: Routledge, 1995

Lears, T.J. Jackson, *Fables of Abundance: A Cultural History of Advertising in America,* New York: Basic Books, 1994

Levenson, Bob, *Bill Bernbach's Book: A History of the Advertising That Changed the History of Advertising,* New York: Villard Books, 1987

Lury, Celia, and Alan Warde, "Investments in the Imaginary Consumer: Conjectures Regarding Power, Knowledge, and Advertising," in *Buy This Book: Studies in Advertising and Consumption,* edited by Mica Nava et al., London and New York: Routledge, 1997

Marchand, Roland, *Advertising the American Dream: Making Way for Modernity, 1920–1940,* Berkeley: University of California Press, 1985

Marcuse, Herbert, *One-Dimensional Man: Studies in the Ideology of Advanced Industrial Society,* Boston: Beacon Press, and London: Routledge and Kegan Paul, 1964

Norris, James D., *Advertising and the Transformation of American Society, 1865–1920,* New York: Greenwood Press, 1990

Presbrey, Frank, *The History and Development of Advertising,* Garden City, New York: Doubleday, 1929; reprint, New York: Greenwood Press, 1968

Scott, Linda, "For the Rest of Us. A Reader-Oriented Interpretation of Apple's '1984' Commercial," *Journal of Popular Culture*, Vol. 25:1, Summer 1991 (1991)

Slater, Don, *Consumer Culture and Modernity*, Cambridge: Polity Press, and Cambridge, Massachusetts: Blackwell, 1997

Vankratsas, D., and Tim Amber, "How Does Advertising Work?" *Journal of Marketing* 63 (1999)

Mojo Partners

Founded by Alan Morris and Allan Johnston in Sydney, Australia, 1974; merged with Monahan Dayman Adams to become Mojo MDA, 1986; Mojo MDA acquired Allen & Dorward in San Francisco, California, 1986; opened offices in Auckland, New Zealand, 1987, and London, England, and New York City, 1988; acquired by Chiat/Day to become Chiat/Day/Mojo, 1989; sold to True North Communications, 1993; 40 percent share sold to Australian executives Graeme Wills and Nicholas Davie, 1996; remaining 60 percent acquired by Publicis to form Mojo Partners, 1997.

Major Clients
Club Med
GE Petrol
Kraft Foods
Nestlé
Rémy (alcoholic beverages)
Sydney Sun-Herald
Toyota Motor Corporation
Whirlpool Corporation

In 1974 two freelance copywriters, frustrated with the culture and the restrictions of Australian advertising agencies and tired of working in isolation, teamed up to make advertising more Australian, more memorable, and more fun. At that time the "advertising culture" was English in its orientation. People portrayed in ads spoke grammatically correct English, rather than using the more colorful expressions of ordinary Australians. Their agency, Mojo Partners, grew from a small office in Darlinghurst, an inner-city suburb of Sydney, into one of the country's advertising legends.

Alan Morris (Mo) and Allan Johnston (Jo) were part of a hardcore "larrikin," or maverick, influence in Australian advertising. Together with their contemporaries John Singleton and Jim Walpole, they "Australianized" the industry, drawing upon self-revealing images and introducing Australian language, characters, and humor into the ads they created. Mojo's ads became part of the vernacular, and jingles such as "Come on, Aussie, come on" (for Australian Cricket) and "You oughta be congratulated" (for Meadow Lea Margarine) were anthems for a national style of advertising. In 1998 the agency's work was described in Austra-

lia's leading ad industry publication *Ad News*: "iconic ads and jingles that people actually love, remember for years, and even enjoy singing along to."

The Mojo strategy was to forge an emotional bond with the customer by appealing to the heart, not the head. Its most memorable advertising packaged the product promise in the chorus of a jingle, such as "How do you feel? Like a Tooheys or two" (for Tooheys beer). Another international campaign, this one for the Australian Tourist Commission, featured actor Paul Hogan welcoming travelers and offering to throw "another shrimp on the barbie."

Mojo's advertising was popular with the Australian public and advertisers alike, as evidenced by the dramatic increase in billings for the agency. Its first job in 1974, freelance work for Grey Advertising, was paid for in secondhand office furniture from Grey. By 1979, however, the partners were recruiting staff and building an agency.

The success of Mojo attracted the attention of the country's largest advertising agency, Monahan Dayman Adams (MDA). With a blue-chip client list that included Qantas, Australia Post, and Westpac, MDA merged with Mojo in 1986 to become Mojo MDA. The clash of agency cultures soon became obvious to Morris and Johnston, who felt they had re-created the kind of advertising environment from which they had fled in the 1970s. Advertising industry figure John Singleton likened the merger to "the Beatles merging with the Post Office."

The year after the merger the new firm moved its offices to Cremourne, Australia, and shifted its positioning to that of a serious business organization, sacrificing some of the larrikin quality on which it had been built. Soon afterward it opened international offices in San Francisco, California; Auckland, New Zealand; London, England; and New York City. In July 1989 Chiat/Day acquired 100 percent of Mojo MDA to form Chiat/Day/Mojo. Once again, it was an uneasy partnership. The Mojo culture did not fit easily into the Chiat/Day mold. In 1991 Morris left the agency to join John Singleton Advertising. Johnson remained with Mojo until 1994 when he rejoined Jim Walpole as a consultant.

Chiat/Day/Mojo was wholly acquired by True North Communications in January 1993. Three years later Australian executives Graeme Wills and Nicholas Davie negotiated a 40 percent management stake with the remaining Mojo Partners shares sold to

Undaunted by the devil's heat of a remote outback sheepstation, with hundreds of miles to his next post, the sheepshearer is ever on the move: a rugged, free-spirited folk hero, long celebrated in Australian lore.

QANTAS
The Airline of Australia

Down Under. It's down home to us.

This award-winning 1989 campaign for Qantas Airways was created by Sydney, Australia–based Mojo Partners.
Qantas Airways, Ltd.

France-based multinational Publicis as part of the failed joint venture between True North Communications and Publicis in 1997. Wills and Davie set about reengineering an agency that had suffered from a series of difficult mergers, a succession of international partners, an unsuccessful stock market listing, a controversial split from its original founders, and significant client and staff losses. The new management team disbanded departments and profit centers to encourage multidisciplinary solutions and a client-focused organization. The reengineering, which took three years, represented not just a change in the organizational structure but also a shift in thinking to embrace a new way of doing business.

The resulting Mojo Group comprised 15 business groups. These included Mojo Partners (advertising agency), Publicis Consultants (strategic communication), Echo and APB Campaigns (direct marketing), Optimedia (media strategy and buying), Service Partners (call center and database management), Publicis Digital (new technology ad agency), Cato (graphic design), Smarts (street and sales promotion), Publicis International (global resources), Welfare (health care agency), Locum Brand Communications (medical production), Shop Publicis (retail and fashion research), Drum (public relations), and Publicis Zip (virtual studio). Clients readily embraced the new Mojo Partners, and billings from existing clients and new business increased significantly. In three years its revenue grew 44.8 percent.

The early jingles of Morris and Johnson struck a chord with the Australian public. The new Mojo Partners has orchestrated a different way of connecting with consumers, using multidisciplinary communication strategies, the strength of an international group, and the unique Australian quality of the Mojo brand.

GAYLE KERR

Further Reading

"The Final Act in Mojo's Reincarnation," *Australian Financial Review* (13 July 1999)

"Jo's Fingers Are Hurtin' Again," in *The Legends of Advertising: Ad News, 1928–1998*, edited by Edward Charles, Surry Hills, New South Wales: Yaffa, 1998

"Mojo Restructure Bears Fruit," *B and T Weekly* (10 September 1999)

"Proof of Mojo's Restructuring Success Is in the Pudding," *Australian Financial Review* (7 September 1999)

Molson, Inc.

Principal Agencies
MacLaren McCann
Cockfield, Brown & Company

Molson, Inc., one of Canada's oldest businesses, competes with Labatt Breweries for dominance of the Canadian beer marketplace. At the beginning of the 21st century Molson was Canada's largest brewery, a major competitor throughout North America, and a respected player in the international market.

Molson was founded in 1786 in Montreal, Quebec, by John Molson shortly after he emigrated from England. The start-up brewery was no small operation. It produced 4,230 gallons of beer annually, equivalent to about 53,000 of today's bottles. Molson, who was not shy about his accomplishments, reportedly proclaimed, "My beer has been universally well-liked beyond my most sanguine expectations."

Not only was Molson an extraordinarily successful entrepreneur, he also had a well-developed sense of social responsibility. He was the driving force in a group of private citizens who founded Montreal's first public hospital, Montreal General Hospital, and he worked to establish the city's first permanent theater, the Theatre Royal. Molson's social programs today spring from these traditional roots. The company supports worthy endeavors such as AIDS research, and many of its marketing efforts are conducted in association with arts venues and rock concerts.

Molson has also long been renowned for its marketing innovations. In 1807 the brewer ran its first advertisement in the magazine *Canadian Courant*. The mid 1800s saw the company making changes to its packaging and branding to help promote the direct retail sales initiatives begun in 1859. Anheuser-Busch was not the only brewer known for its "horse power": Molson's beer was being delivered in four-wheeled brewery drays drawn by matched chestnut horses at the close of the 19th century. Until 1930 Molson developed its advertising and promotional material in-house. That year an advertising agency was engaged for the first time.

Molson is perhaps best known for its association with professional hockey, which began in 1957 when the brewery purchased the Montreal Canadiens and the arena they played in, the Montreal Forum. At this time Molson also became a cosponsor of *Hockey Night in Canada*. By then the company was dividing its advertising between Cockfield, Brown & Company (representing the Montreal brewery) and MacLaren (Toronto brewery).

Even after more than 200 years of brewing history, Molson finds competing in the Canadian beer market difficult. Demographics are not on the side of beer marketers. Baby boomers,

Quintessentially Canadian scenes began to dominate Molson's advertising in the 1980s, as shown in this 1982 print ad.

once the prime target market, have grown increasingly health and weight conscious. In 1979, when beer consumption reached its peak in Canada, the average Canadian consumed 85 liters of beer per year. By the start of the 21st century, consumption had fallen to 65 liters. Beer marketers were fighting for their share of a shrinking pie and could only gain at the expense of their competitors. Meanwhile, competition increased. Whereas in the early 1980s there were only eight beer companies in Canada, by the year 2000 there were 60. Microbreweries accounted for approximately 5 percent of beer sales. With the advent of free trade between Canada, the United States, and Mexico, more imports than ever before were making their mark in the Canadian arena.

Beer is sold largely on image. Blind taste tests have shown that one brand tastes much like another. Beer drinkers tend to identify with the product, however, and what they drink reflects their self-image. Because self-image often has a regional basis, a campaign that works well in Atlantic Canada may be a flop in the west.

In the 1980s and 1990s the ads for major beer brands began to look much alike. Most pictured a party setting with fashionably attired young people dancing to loud music, beer bottle clutched in hand. That is, the ads looked alike until 1994, when Molson

launched its long-running radio, TV, and print "I am Canadian" campaign for its flagship brand, Molson Canadian. The images in the visual media showed quintessentially Canadian scenes. The TV ads consisted of a montage cut in quick succession—for example, a bungee jumper with a Canadian flag painted on his face, Canadian hockey hero Paul Henderson and a winning goal, and a toothy beaver. The campaign also featured hard-edged music, outdoor imagery, and the manic energy of extreme sports. The common thread linking the ads was their spirit of self-expression and their celebration of what it meant to be a young Canadian at the turn of a new century. While the campaign enabled the target audience (beer drinkers ages 19 to 34) to belong to a cohesive group and express their Canadian identity, it also allowed viewers to interpret what "I am Canadian" means to them. Research indicated that as a result of the campaign, the target audience had highly positive associations with Molson Canadian beer. However, Canada's regionalism had, to some degree, limited the campaign's success. In the province of Quebec, for example, where separatist sentiments run high, the "I am Canadian" campaign was not aired.

Molson was so pleased with the campaign, which was created by MacLaren McCann of Toronto, that the company moved its Export brand to the agency. "I am Canadian" won a Cassie (Canadian Advertising Success Stories) Gold Award in 1997. These awards are given not for the creative merits of the ads, but for campaigns that result in significant increases in sales. Winning awards does not guarantee that all is well in the advertising business, however; in May 1999 Molson fired MacLaren McCann, ending a 40-year relationship with the agency. The "I am Canadian" campaign was relaunched by Bensimon Byrne D'Arcy, Toronto, which created the famous "Rant" ad.

In 1995, to support the campaign and foster closer relationships with consumers, Molson launched a Web site, www.iam.ca, that allowed visitor to chat with other beer drinkers, post messages, check out concert listings, join hockey and baseball pools, learn about Molson-sponsored events, and read an electronic magazine. One area allowed browsers to obtain a demographic and social profile (i.e., age, gender, hobbies and interests, etc.) of other recent, frequent visitors to the site. In another section, Molson sought feedback on the effectiveness of its ads. The site registers some 7,000 visits a day. To keep it fresh and interesting, Molson radically redesigned it several times since its inception. In July 1998, however, the site crashed, wiping out the entire user database. This was no small loss. Molson had spent $400,000 to create the site and $150,000 annually to maintain and update it. Users demonstrated their loyalty to the company and the site by returning and reentering their personal information.

In addition to its Web page, Molson sponsors a "Youth Posse," a team of 35 young adults from across the country who visit bars and other pop music venues in search of new bands so that Molson can be on the leading edge of emerging trends in music. Information gathered by the team is used to implement Molson's grassroots marketing efforts.

PEGGY CUNNINGHAM

Further Reading

Cunningham, Peggy, "Beer Wars," in *Principles of Marketing,* 4th Canadian edition, Scarborough, Ontario: Prentice Hall Canada, 1998

Latimer, Joanne, "Canada's Leading Creative Agencies: MacLaren McCann: Better Creative, Better Results," *Strategy: The Canadian Marketing Report* (8 June 1998)

Stone, Kyle, "Promotion Commotion," *Globe and Mail Report on Business Magazine* (December 1997)

Wright, Diane, "Technology and Communications Tools for Marketers: Molson Site Crash Yields Valuable Lessons," *Strategy: The Canadian Marketing Report* (14 September 1998)

Motion Pictures

In the 100 year history of motion pictures, the companies that make and distribute this unique form of mass entertainment have used the tools of advertising to attract patrons—"getting butts into seats," in the vulgar parlance of an industry that sprang from the rough-and-tumble immigrant culture of New York City. In 1902 the first true movie theater was opened in downtown Los Angeles, California, by former cowboy Thomas Talley, promising "an hour's amusement and genuine fun for 10 cents admission." "Nickelodeons," named after their five-cent price tag, opened around the country, attracting lower-middle-class patrons with posters and banners. By 1913 Hollywood, California, had emerged as the U.S. movie capital, and during the studio era (1920–60) and beyond, the movie business exported American culture around the globe at 24 frames per second.

Selling a movie is unlike other kinds of consumer marketing. Movies are a form of popular entertainment that, at times, rise to the level of art. Moviegoing is an experience, not a tangible product people can touch and feel. Each movie is unique. Each is in the spotlight briefly. There are no movie brands, per se, although from the 1930s into the 1950s the films of Warner Bros., Metro-Goldwyn-Mayer (MGM), 20th Century Fox, and other studios all had distinctive visual and audio characteristics. No one buys a ticket because a film is from a particular studio, with the possible exception of movies from the family-oriented Walt Disney Company. The closest thing to brands are the star actors and a handful of directors who possess the power to "open" a film—attracting audiences on the first weekend of release—by virtue of their names.

Days of Trailers and Lobby Cards

Movie marketers must select the right elements to sell a film—the visual icon, copy lines, and the right mix of media—and succeed quickly. If a movie does not find its audience fast, it faces quick banishment to sub-run houses, although nearly every film now achieves renewed life in ancillary markets such as home video and television.

Movie marketing was not always this way. In fact, the word *marketing* was not part of movie industry lingo until the 1960s and 1970s. In the years before the popularity of television dramatically decreased movie attendance, Hollywood film studios sold their pictures through advertising and publicity created by the bluntly named "exploitation" departments. During the studio era, these departments maintained large staffs that tightly controlled the flow of information about upcoming pictures and their stars.

"Previews of coming attractions"—short films featuring highlights of upcoming motion pictures—have been around as long as the movies. These previews, or "trailers" in movie industry terminology, are still one of the most effective ways to reach potential movie audiences, as they are seen by the most likely target group—existing movie audiences.

Point-of-purchase materials have long been the studios' most fundamental advertising tools. In the early days, studio publicity departments sent "lobby cards" to theater owners; these were sets of 11-by-14-inch advertising materials consisting primarily of reproductions of movie stills. Theaters would mount the cards on easels behind the box office or inside the lobby to tweak patrons' curiosity about upcoming releases. Over time, lobby cards grew more sophisticated, with the studios often producing them in color even though the motion pictures were black and white. At times, effects became more elaborate. For the 1927 film *The Jazz Singer,* promoters installed stills of the first talking picture's cast around microphones. Supporting this was a revolving drum containing recordings of pieces of *The Jazz Singer* dialogue. Sound would go on as each card popped up—the first talking lobby card.

Although much of the day-to-day movie advertising and artwork was ground out in-house in the studio advertising departments, from the 1930s into the 1960s when the studio system was at its peak, all the major motion picture companies retained advertising agencies, most of them based in New York City, where Hollywood financial decisions were typically made. Some employed major diversified shops. MGM had a long relationship with Donahue & Coe, Columbia Pictures with the Biow Company, and RKO with Lord & Thomas and its successor Foote,

Aleksandr Rodchenko's startling 1924 poster *Film Eye*, a classic work of realist art, was an advertisement for a series of films by the Polish-born filmmaker Dziga Vertov.
RODCHENKO, Aleksandr. Kino Glaz {Film Eye}. 1924. Lithograph, printed in color, 36 1/2 x 27 1/2" (92.5 x 70 cm). The Museum of Modern Art, New York. Gift of Jay Leyda. Photograph © 2001 The Museum of Modern Art, New York.

Cone & Belding before going in-house in the 1950s. Hollywood studios were not troubled by what might have been seen as conflict of interest in other industries; agencies sometimes handled more than one studio client simultaneously. Thus Donahue & Coe worked with both MGM and United Artists, while Buchanan & Company handled Paramount and Monogram at the same time without difficulties. Other studios chose agencies more specialized in the entertainment business. Warner Bros. used the Blain-Thompson Company for more than 30 years.

Movie posters did not speak, but they were—and remain—a mainstay for the selling of motion pictures. In the early days, studios maintained small staffs to supervise production of advertising art, often hiring talented freelance artists to create handsome graphics to promote pictures. MGM, for example, hired Al Hirschfeld, the future caricaturist of Broadway stars, and book illustrator John Held, Jr., to create "one-sheets" (single-sheet posters, typically 27-by-41 inches), which theaters placed in display cases. In the 1940s famed graphic illustrator Norman Rock-

well worked for the movie industry. The pop artist Peter Max did too, creating the key art for the Beatles' 1968 animated fantasy *Yellow Submarine*. In the early 1990s, when frenzy around the *Batman* film franchise was at its peak, vandals stole elaborate posters of the Caped Crusader from Los Angeles–area bus shelters. The crimes became a news event that helped promote the film, although Warner Bros. had not necessarily planned it that way.

Publicity stunts have at times been used to market movies. For example, to promote the 1947 film *The Egg and I*, press agent Jim Moran sat on an ostrich egg for 19 days, 4 hours, and 32 minutes—until it hatched. During the egg's gestation, a costumed Moran charged visitors 50 cents each to watch him; reportedly 1,500 people paid to see this event, and it generated much media attention. Three decades later, another press agent, Marty Weiser, staged a special premiere for horses at a Los Angeles area drive-in movie theater to promote Mel Brooks's 1974 comedy *Blazing Saddles*. More than 250 horses filled the car spaces and munched free oats at a "horsepitality bar."

Growing Sophistication

Twenty years later, movie marketing seemed much more serious and professional. Following an influx of executives from Madison Avenue and packaged-goods companies, movie marketers have come to employ a full arsenal of sophisticated techniques to figure out what audiences want and how to reach them. This process involves extensive market research, advertising in an array of outlets, and targeted promotional efforts aimed at ethnic segments. Licensing and merchandising, staples since the studio era, have become big business, with studios locking up major fast-food and soft-drink partners to help share the financial burdens associated with "event" films. Studios still use the tried-and-true pre-release publicity blitz, making use especially of TV programs that specialize in "puff" pieces about entertainment.

As Americans moved to the suburbs and TV became more popular in the 1950s, the movie industry faced dark times. But the business fought back with technical improvements such as 3-D, Cinemascope, and stereo sound that rekindled interest, although movie attendance would never again reach the levels of the pre-TV heyday (despite rising box office returns from higher ticket prices). The movie business has adapted to the public's changing habits, now embracing the medium that almost killed it.

Veteran movie executives point to the second release of the film *Billy Jack* as a key event in motion picture advertising history. That contemporary Western melodrama played in a handful of drive-ins and adult theaters in its first unsuccessful release in 1971. The movie's director and star, Tom Laughlin, sued the distributor for allegedly mishandling the picture. Two years later, *Billy Jack* received a second chance. This time, promoters played it on numerous screens in key cities and supported it with saturation television advertising, an unheard of practice at the time, when, typically, 65 percent–70 percent of all film promotional budgets went to newspapers. Instead, 80 percent of the promotional expenditures for *Billy Jack* went to television. The picture

Chiquita Banana
stars in Spot Movie Ads for United Fruit Company

Colorful, captivating Chiquita Banana dramatizes selling stories of irresistible appeal on the screens of movie theatres in key markets. Sponsors: United Fruit Company. Agency: Batten, Barton, Durstine & Osborn, Inc. There's drama and color in these 80-second Spot Movies. They sell with sight, sound and demonstration.

IS YOUR ADVERTISING AGENCY CONSIDERING SPOT MOVIES IN THEATRES FOR YOUR PRODUCT?

Before you allocate another dollar for media, why not ask Movie Advertising Bureau to show you these Chiquita films. Make sure your agency sees them. They're a revelation of the power of the medium — a preview of the hard-hitting job Spot Movie ads can do for your own product. You'll see how this medium sharpens brand remembrance, puts color to work, dramatizes sales points, wins fixed attention.

Your scheduling can be easy and exact, thanks to the Bureau's Continuing Study, which gives data on movie theatres throughout the U.S. From the 11,250 available theatres, you can select as few or as many as you need.

Call or write Movie Advertising Bureau's nearest office for a 16 PAGE STORY of the Bureau's exclusive CONTINUING STUDY OF THEATRES for Movie Advertising.

MOVIE ADVERTISING BUREAU
EASTERN OFFICE: 70 East 45th Street, New York 17, N. Y. • Phone MUrray Hill 6-3717
MID-WEST OFFICE: 333 North Michigan Avenue, Chicago 1, Ill. • Phone ANDover 3022

Member Companies:
UNITED FILM SERVICE, INC.: KANSAS CITY • CHICAGO • CLEVELAND
MOTION PICTURE ADV. SERVICE CO., INC.: NEW ORLEANS • NEW YORK • BIRMINGHAM • ATLANTA • MEMPHIS
Representatives throughout the 48 States

Spot Movie advertising (40, 60 and 80-second films in theatres) is used by such other representative companies as these:

Ford Motor Company	**Ward Baking Company**
Agency—J. Walter Thompson Company	*Agency—J. Walter Thompson Company*
Chevrolet Division of General Motors Corp.	**American Chicle Company**
Agency—Campbell-Ewald Company, Inc.	*Agency—Badger and Browning & Hersey, Inc.*
Sinclair Refining Company	**National Biscuit Company**
Agency—Hixson-O'Donnell Advertising, Inc.	*Agency—McCann-Erickson, Inc.*
Dr. Pepper Company	**Rit Products Corporation (Best Foods)**
Agency—Tracy-Locke Company, Inc.	*Agency—Earle Ludgin & Company*

PLUS 48,000 LOCAL MERCHANTS

Throughout the 1940s and 1950s, movie houses in the United States were an important venue for advertising, and a host of products were featured in short advertising films. This ad from the Movie Advertising Bureau dates from 1948.
Chiquita Brands International, Inc.

grossed a then-whopping $32.5 million, and it changed marketing thinking in Hollywood.

Another watershed in motion picture marketing came with the release of *Star Wars* in 1977, an event that revolutionized the financial possibilities of movies. The huge success of this film, followed by the spectacular grosses of *E.T. the Extra-terrestrial, Raiders of the Lost Ark,* and sequels to *Star Wars,* pushed the film business to a new level of economic expectation. Increasingly, Hollywood marketing turned its attention to the creation of the mega-hit, rich with the potential for generating licensing incomes from toys, clothes, and premiums. In the decades that followed, marketing expenditures rose dramatically as the major studios and production companies increasingly bet their fortunes on a smaller number of huge productions intended to gross enormous sums.

In this high-stakes environment, Hollywood's attention shifted to each picture's performance on the opening weekend of its release. In the weeks preceding an opening, studios bombard the airwaves with commercial images. And because the summer months and the Christmas holidays tend to produce the largest potential audiences, studios fight to market their biggest films during the most crowded release periods of the year; at the same time, they look for an opening weekend with minimal competition. This all-or-nothing strategy of the major studios has made it difficult for small pictures to get produced, a situation that has opened the field to independent productions, some of which became surprise hits. This in turn has become an incentive for the major studios to acquire or set up subsidiaries that specialize in marketing lower-budget independent and foreign-language pictures to smaller audiences.

According to the Motion Picture Association of America the average per-picture marketing cost in 2000 was $27.3 million—or close to half of the average production budget. By way of comparison, in the pre-TV era, advertising and publicity budgets were rarely more than 10 percent of a movie's production budget.

Advertising clutter poses great challenges for movie studios. Studios and the creative agencies that work for them routinely churn out advertising images with a certain sameness or trailers that reveal too much—by-products, some say, of the risk-averse mind-set of studio executives trying to survive in a volatile industry. The ad makers must also deal with Hollywood idiosyncrasies associated with credits, star billing, and countless approvals.

In spite of these pitfalls, there have been some memorable movie ad campaigns throughout the years, particularly in a remarkable stretch of breakthrough moviemaking in the 1960s and 1970s. "Pray for Rosemary's baby," would-be audiences were advised, in an artful teaser campaign dreamed up by former Young & Rubicam Creative Director Stephen Frankfurt for Roman Polanski's 1968 thriller about the devil's spawn. Ads for *Bonnie and Clyde,* a seminal film with antihero leads and a gritty depiction of violence, trumpeted, "They're young. . . . They're in love. . . . And they kill people." Francis Ford Coppola's 1979 surreal evocation of Vietnam, *Apocalypse Now,* did not use cliché war movie images to sell itself; instead, the posters and print ads featured a stark, all-red graphic showing a smoking horizon. The copy line, "Just when you thought it was safe to go back into the water," lives in the collective memory from the 1978 release of *Jaws 2.*

In the 1990s, as movie marketers struggled to break through ad clutter, yet another new medium appeared: the Internet. Many credit the World Wide Web with the seemingly out-of-nowhere success of *The Blair Witch Project,* a super-low-budget independent film that became one of 1999's box office standouts. Its distributor, Artisan Entertainment, set up a clever Web site well before the film's release that allowed its target audience (youth) to feel as if they had discovered the quirky little film on their own—an example of "guerrilla marketing" at its best. Many believe this emerging medium will offer unprecedented opportunities for direct marketing of films.

JENNIFER PENDLETON

Further Reading

Elley, Derek, editor, *Variety Movie Guide,* London: Hamyln, 2000

Fuhrman, Candice Jacobson, *Publicity Stunt! Great Staged Events That Made the News,* San Francisco: Chronicle Books, 1989

Great Movie Graphics, Rockport, Massachusetts: Rockport, 1995

Handel, Leo A., *Hollywood Looks at Its Audience Research,* Urbana: University of Illinois Press, 1950

Karney, Robyn, editor, *Cinema Year by Year, 1894–2000,* London and New York: Dorling Kindersley, 2000

Malcolm, Vance, *The Movie Ad Book,* Minneapolis, Minnesota: Control Data, 1981

Miller, Frank, *MGM Posters: The Golden Years,* Atlanta, Georgia: Turner, 1994

Sweeney, Russell C., *Coming Next Week: A Pictorial History of Film Advertising,* South Brunswick, New Jersey: Barnes, and New York: Castle Books, 1973

Motion Pictures, Television, and Literature, Representations of Advertising in

It is perhaps because the business of advertising—as opposed to the advertising itself—is by nature discreet and prefers to function out of public view that fiction writers and filmmakers have portrayed it less frequently than they have law, medicine, law enforcement, and other more open, public professions. Partly for this reason, the popular stereotypes of the business are based on a relatively small quantity of work.

Advertising as a dramatic and literary genre is a subcategory of a larger genre portraying "big business," a topic that has frequently fascinated fiction writers. Until the Great Depression, businessmen were seen in a variety of contexts and story lines. Because they were played as both heroes and villains, no clear mass media stereotype emerged, save for the one that developed within the literature of the left and that critiqued business from a populist, progressive, or Marxist perspective. Depending on the state of the economy, the image of the businessman ranged from greedy plutocrat to benevolent builder. With the coming of the Great Depression, however, journalism and social science writing that sought to expose the methods of big business and hold it accountable for the national economic crisis of the period greatly influenced business fiction. Increasingly, the rich businessman was fashioned in the robber baron image of a ruthless and greedy predator, accumulating vast wealth in antisocial (at best) or criminal (at worst) ways.

Advertising, to the extent it was portrayed, became an agent of the robber baron, manufacturing falsehoods to deceive a gullible public into buying useless products. It was more vulnerable than most to such easy stereotyping because, unlike most of the clients it served, agencies produced no tangible products by which they could be judged, maintained no factories, and had only an indirect relationship with the public. Advertising was a semiconcealed business of ideas and relationships whose trustworthiness, in the public mind, was dubious.

Literature

It was perhaps the secretive nature of the business that prompted James Joyce to chose advertising as the profession for Leopold Bloom, protagonist of his novel *Ulysses* (1922), one of the most discussed and influential works of 20th century English literature. Although Joyce's Bloom was an advertising salesman, the time and location of the book—Dublin, Ireland, in 1904—place it well before the beginning of what is regarded as modern advertising. Moreover, little of Bloom's professional life is portrayed by Joyce.

One prominent novelist of the 1930s had actually worked at a major agency and used his agency experiences in his novels. John P. Marquand had spent a brief period as a copywriter at the J. Walter Thompson Company in New York City in the 1920s, and his novel *H.M. Pulham Esquire* took place against the background of a similar agency. Young Pulham is a Boston, Massachusetts-bred aristocrat back from World War I and eager to break away from his family and build a life in New York. He joins a large New York agency and falls in love with a copywriter but ultimately returns to Boston and the proper marriage his family expects. Although the novel is, like much of Marquand's work, a study in class relationships and an affirmation of tradition, the agency background is well sketched and without hostility. In fact, the fictional agency president, J.T. Bullard, is widely considered to have been based on Thompson's chairman, Stanley Resor. The character is drawn as somewhat scholarly, with a professorial air but overlaid with the confidence that comes with business success. The novel was filmed quite faithfully by MGM in 1941 with Robert Young, Hedy Lamarr, Douglas Wood (who played the Bullard role), and Van Heflin (as a cynical ad executive).

After World War II, as millions of young men went to college on the GI bill and went on to become part of the corporate culture that had earlier been so vilified for its greed, a fundamental shift occurred in writing about the business world. Fiction increasingly abandoned the mogul and examined critically the extent to which the individual white collar worker compromised his integrity and personal life for the company in pursuit of middle- or top management success. Other postwar novels that drew on the advertising world for it backgrounds and characters included *Please Send Me, Absolutely Free* by Arkady Leokum (1946), *Aurora Dawn* by former Fred Allen writer Herman Wouk (1947), *The Glorification of Al Toolum* by Robert Alan Arthur (1953), *The Last Angry Man* by Gerald Green (1956), *The Detroiters* by Harold Livingston (1956), *A Twist of Lemon* by Edward Stephens (1958), *The Adman* by Shepherd Mead (1958), and *The Insiders* by James Kelley (1958). To a large extent, fiction followed journalism and social science, which probed a culture of conformity and preoccupation with image over substance in American life and business. Among the widely read books that described these phenomena were *White Collar* and *The Power Elite* by C. Wright Mills, *The Lonely Crowd* by David Riesman, Nathan Glazer, and Reuel Denney, and *The Organization Man* by *Fortune* magazine writer William H. Whyte.

Film

In the 1930s and 1940s director Frank Capra made a series of films that examined the power of the mass media to mold public opinion for the purpose of selling, although Capra was more concerned with the selling of political power than with the marketing of merchandise. In films such as *Mr. Smith Goes to Washington* (1939) and *Meet John Doe* (1941), actor Edward Arnold transformed the standard robber baron he portrayed in *You Can't Take It With You* (1938) into the quintessential media magnate, covertly pulling the strings of his newspaper and radio station empire in the cause of political corruption (as Jim Taylor in *Mr. Smith Goes to Washington*) and advancing his own right-wing political ambitions (as publisher D.B. Norton in *Meet John Doe*).

After the war Capra returned to politics with *State of the Union* (1948), this time, however, to critique the way in which the presidential marketing process and the mass media force a decent man (a businessman roughly based on a prominent Republican of the time, Wendell Willkie) to surrender to special interests precisely the qualities that make him an attractive candidate. The corrupting power of the selling process at the hands of mass communication can be seen in movies as far back as the 1920s (*The Power of the Press*, 1928), and also drove more modern political dramas such as *The Best Man* (1964) and *The Candidate* (1972); satires such as George S. Kaufman's *The Senator Was Indiscreet* (1947); and in a roundabout way John Ford's *The Last Hurrah* (1958), which suggested that in the modern campaign the media will replace the handshake and the people will end up electing fools. What Ford had foreseen in the 1950s became something of a *fait accompli* 28 years later in Sidney Lumet's *Power,* the one film that looks directly into the role of the amoral political advertising consultant in packaging a candidate for television.

The role of the advertising agency rarely figured in prewar films. To the general public they were shadowy institutions that kept a low profile. Comedian Fred Allen, whose radio shows were produced at various times by Young & Rubicam, the J. Walter Thompson Company, and Newell-Emmett, was the first to use the agency as a point of comic caricature. As principal writer of his own material, he reacted to the frustration of having his jokes reviewed and cut in the agency bureaucracy. In a radio sketch with actor Maurice Evans, Allen imagined Shakespeare trying to interest an ad agency (called "Batten, Foote, Ruthrauff & Rubicam," a composite of several prominent agency names) in *Hamlet* and having to deal with the judgments, jargon, and artificial cordiality that, in his view, characterized agency culture: "Well I'll tell ya, Shakespeare, I need a serial program. It's for a new soap powder called Doesn't [a takeoff on Procter & Gamble's Duz]. All the other soap powders do something. 'Doesn't' doesn't do a thing." Allen projected a comic image of the ad agency that millions accepted as more or less the real thing, in part because it was virtually the only image being projected by anyone. A decade later satirist Stan Freberg, himself deeply influenced by Allen, took the stereotype to new heights, often playing on it in the many commercials he created for the agencies he scorned. In a 1958 radio sketch he played an upstanding suburban werewolf who went to the office every morning and turned into "an advertising man," the monster of his upside-down horror sketch. Bob Newhart, a popular standup comic who emerged in the early 1960s, built a famous monologue on the promise of what a Madison Avenue ad agency might do to market Abraham Lincoln in an age of "image makers."

In motion pictures, perhaps the most indicting film was one starring a young Lucille Ball, *Beauty for the Asking* (1939), in which the development of an advertising campaign was played out in the larger context of the cosmetics business and efforts to market a harmful product. Advertising was portrayed as an unethical process concerned only with selling and never pausing to assess the products it pushes. It was perhaps no coincidence that the film was made a year after Congress passed the first legislation regulating the cosmetics industry.

The first motion picture centering entirely on the politics and protocols of the modern agency was *The Hucksters* (1948), based on the novel by Frederic Wakeman. By the late 1930s Wakeman found his way to the Lord & Thomas (L&T) agency, where he worked on the Lucky Strike campaign and moonlighted as a part-time novelist. He left Foote, Cone & Belding (successor agency to L&T) in 1943 to serve in the U.S. Navy. After the war he published his first novel, *Shore Leave,* which later became the basis for a play and a 1957 movie. When *The Hucksters* was published in 1946, the character of Evan Llewellyn Evans, chairman of Beautee Soap, was widely viewed as a fictionalized version of George Washington Hill, the real-life chairman of American Tobacco, maker of Lucky Strike. MGM immediately optioned the book and released its movie version in 1947, starring Clark Gable and Sidney Greenstreet.

In *The Hucksters* the Kimberly advertising agency is portrayed as a business generating rich material rewards but totally without a will, culture, or moral vision of its own; an enterprise where success or failure depends on the ad man's ability to anticipate, align himself with, and become the alter ego of the culture and mind-set of the agency's largest client. As such it became one of the first postwar novels and films to touch on the extent to which the individual must surrender intellectual honesty to rise within a corporate environment.

Evans was an oppressive corporate dictator who ruled by fear and whom no one dared challenge. Adolphe Menjou played the agency president who had learned to live with fear to become rich. With *The Hucksters,* the image of the tyrannical client and the brow-beaten agency executive became the standard matrix through which the public would view the advertising industry for years to come. Not even the presence of Victor Norman (played by Clark Gable) as a relatively principled, self-possessed account executive willing to challenge Evans balanced the systemic nature of the oppressive agency-client relationship portrayed in the picture, and that reflects even today a certain moderated degree of truth (if only because the client employs the agency).

Norman's differences with Evans, however, produced several trenchant debates in the film on the nature and purpose of advertising (hard-sell versus soft-sell) and on brand building that are still highly relevant and to the point. (Evans: "There's absolutely no difference in soaps, none! The difference is in advertising.") As a film, it emerged not only as a strong protest against tasteless and infantile advertising but also against the degree to which ad agencies held a virtual stranglehold over broadcasting and the programming content of network radio. This was a fact of network business life at the time, a structure that would not change until the 1950s and early 1960s, when that control passed to the networks. Nevertheless, more than a half century after it was made, it remains the best primer on advertising in American film. At least one major agency today, DDB, uses portions of the film in its business presentation tape.

If *The Hucksters* seemed to take up the theme of individual freedom versus materialism almost by accident, another novelist, Sloan Wilson, did it very much by intent. In *The Man in the Gray Flannel Suit,* which became a film in 1957, Wilson offers two heroes, both surprisingly decent: a principled broadcasting tycoon (Frederic March) whose empire has come at the expense of time with his family, and Tom Rath (Gregory Peck), a young executive who must decide how much he wants from his career and what it is worth in terms of his personal life. Although, contrary to what is generally believed, the story does not deal with advertising at all but public relations, the title became synonymous with the Madison Avenue advertising man. A few years later the same studio (20th Century Fox) produced *Madison Avenue* (1962), based on the Jeremy Kirk novel, *The Build-Up Boys*. Here the amoral Machiavellian intrigues of agency life are the dramatic business. Although earlier films such as *Executive Suite* (1954), *Woman's World* (1956), and *Patterns* (1957) had probed the insider cut-throat politics of upper management, advertising proved an especially fertile arena with its surface slickness overlaying a ruthlessly competitive jungle typically ruled by a charming egomaniac with a smile on his face and a knife up his sleeve. Norman Corwin's screenplay paints one of the most cynical and seedy portraits of an ad agency on film.

Another cynical look at advertising, although one taken from the television network perspective and laced with keen satire and elements of farce, was Paddy Chayefsky's original screenplay *Network*, directed by Sidney Lumet; both men had launched their careers creating dramas in the early days of television under the scrutiny of ad agencies. Although the subject of the film is the extent to which a network (and thus advertisers and agencies) will corrupt its news department to gain ratings, the larger theme is the power of advertising money to corrupt everything, even a revolutionary Marxist black feminist (played by Beatrice Straight) who ends up negotiating over gross rating points and residual payments for the sale of her story as a series. By the time *Network* was made in the late 1970s, control over programming had shifted from ad agencies to broadcasters. But if Wakeman had blamed ad agencies for broadcasting's ills in *The Hucksters*, Chayefsky found no remedy in the moral authority of the networks, which he viewed as equally corrupt. The most telling scene is when an errant news anchor (played by Peter Finch) is called to the inner sanctum of the ultimate chief executive officer (actor Ned Beatty), who warns that he is meddling with "primal forces" of the universe.

Elia Kazan made two films dealing with the media power of advertising. The first was a collaboration with Budd Schulberg called *A Face in the Crowd* (1957), a social protest film that touched on the more sinister elements of *Meet John Doe*. Andy Griffith played Lonesome Rhodes, a Southern drifter propelled to national fame through a combination of luck, calculation, and charisma who attempts to channel his newfound power into the political arena. Along his way to media stardom, an advertising agency links its client's product to Rhodes's public persona in order to reform the image of an ordinary vitamin pill called Vitajax into a powerful aphrodisiac. A montage of commercials provides a satiric look at television ad styles of the day. When Rhodes escapes the control of his managers at the agency, an overstressed account executive pleads with him to cooperate lest he lose his job. The scene ends when the ad man has a heart attack. These

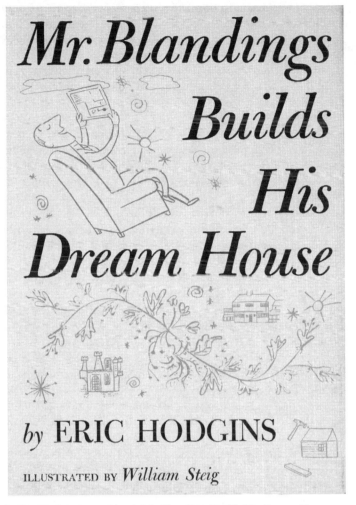

In Eric Hodgins's 1946 book *Mr. Blandings Builds His Dream House*—made into a motion picture in 1948—the title character is an advertising executive who must come up with a slogan for a product in order to keep his job.
Dust Jacket from MR. BLANDINGS BUILDS HIS DREAM HOUSE by Eric Hodgins. Illustrated by William Steig (New York: Simon & Schuster, 1946). Courtesy of Simon & Schuster. Illustrations © William Steig.

details support the larger theme—the dangers of advertising if deployed in the advancement of a demagogue.

This same theme was at the center of an obscure 1947 comedy called *The Senator Was Indiscreet*, which starred William Powell as an inept but harmless senator who wants to be president. The party chairman dismisses the effort. But the public relations man behind the senator is more serious. "I was in the advertising business once," he says, "so believe me, if you can sell the American public the idea that one cigarette is different from another or that one toothpaste is better than another, you can sell them anything, even Mel Ashton." It was the only film ever directed by the playwright George S. Kaufman.

Kazan also chose advertising as the venue in which to set his indictment of soul-destroying materialism, *The Arrangement*, which became a best-selling novel in 1967 and a film two years later. Kirk Douglas plays an advertising executive who attempts suicide at the beginning of the film, a consequence of having sold out himself and his talents in a wasted advertising career that made him rich but left him empty. The scenes in which Douglas makes his insidiously exaggerated ad presentation selling the Zephyr Cigarette campaign (a "clean" cigarette) without ever using the word *cancer* ("the big C," he calls it) symbolize everything that Kazan sees as morally corrupt in his hero's life of advertising.

The notion of advertising as a corrupting moral environment as a well as a high-pressure, demanding profession probably influenced J.P. Miller to make the hero of his drama about alcoholism, *Days of Wine and Roses,* an ad executive. Originally written for the CBS television series *Playhouse 90* (and broadcast 2 October 1958 starring Cliff Robertson and Piper Laurie), it became an Oscar-winning movie in 1962 starring Jack Lemmon and Lee Remick. Its popularity further strengthened the public's association of advertising with cynical and unsavory behavior.

Other postwar films, mostly comedies, used advertising as a relatively nondescript field in which to plant a hero and occasionally permit screenwriters to make wry observations on the petty hypocrisies and superficialities of agency life. Advertising became a minor subplot in Eric Hodgins's novel *Mr. Blandings Builds His Dream House,* in which the hero (Cary Grant in the 1948 film) must come up with a slogan by the end of the picture to keep his job. In a denouement portraying the creative process in advertising as a totally chance process, the family's housekeeper innocently drops the winning line at dinner: "If you ain't eatin' Wham, you ain't eatin' ham." Grant's character instantly recognizes a campaign when he hears it and all is saved. Grant returned to advertising 11 years later in the lead role in *North by Northwest,* in which screenwriter Ernest Lehman defined the ad not as a lie but as "the expedient exaggeration."

Two films of the period specifically treated closely related ad topics: market research and outdoor advertising. In *Magic Town* (1947), writer Robert Riskin and director William Wellman created a Frank Capra-esque fable about an opinion researcher (James Stewart) who stumbles upon a small town that is a perfect microcosm of national public opinion on every issue. When word of the town's unique power leaks out, everybody tries to cash in, the power vanishes, and the town nearly disintegrates. A more insightful comedy was *It Should Happen to You* (1954), written by Garson Kanin and directed by George Cukor. When Gladys Glover (Judy Holliday) decides to become somebody by buying a billboard in Columbus Circle and posting her name on it, she begins a buzz. Soon one board leads to another and all of New York is talking about her. She becomes a celebrity, a brand, but an empty one without meaning. In one scene, while surrounded in a department store by autograph seekers, a passerby asks her boyfriend (Jack Lemmon) who is causing all the excitement. "Nobody," he says, "Believe me, nobody." Without bitterness, the movie comments on the power of advertising to create something out of nothing. It is the one classic film on outdoor advertising.

The something-out-of-nothing theme was taken to hysterical extremes in *Lover Come Back* (1962), the second in the cycle of three Doris Day/Rock Hudson comedies. It satirizes a range of

behavior that audiences found easy to assume existed in the agency business, with two competing ad executives fighting to win the VIP account, which is actually a nonexistent brand for which Hudson has fabricated a campaign as a ruse to lure an attractive model to bed. It also attests to the power of advertising. When the inept agency owner (Tony Randall) discovers the campaign and (unaware of the nonexistence of the VIP) orders it launched, a sudden national demand materializes for a product that must then be invented.

In more recent years films have portrayed the conflicts between the heavy demands of advertising careers and raising children. In *Kramer vs. Kramer* (1979), Dustin Hoffman plays a recently divorced man expected to care for his son while attending to the long hours of his job as an art director and creative director at a large New York City agency. This same premise served actress Diane Keaton in *Baby Boom* (1987) as a savvy, driven, dressed-for-success career woman, also in a New York City agency. When an unexpected baby turns up in her life and career, her workaholic singleness of purpose comes into conflict with the team discipline of the agency. Both films were more focused on satirizing the yuppie have-it-all phenomenon than on advertising, which served a background function and was played with reasonable accuracy, including a bold job interview in *Kramer vs. Kramer.* It was as if advertising had been worked over sufficiently in previous movies to reduce the usual points of parody to cliché to be avoided.

Two all-out satires of advertising agencies include *Putney Swope* (1969), which was released during the height of the black power phase of the American civil rights movement, and *Crazy People* (1990). Written and directed by Robert Downey, *Putney Swope* showed what might happen if a Black Panther–like radical took over a large white Manhattan agency and placed black identity politics in competition with the prospect of material success. Swope's black revolutionary in a white agency is an interesting comic premise, but the results are more absurd that witty, and the film made no serious comments on advertising that had not been made better already. Nevertheless, its sheer outrageousness earned it a small cult following. *Crazy People,* written by Mitch Markowitz, took a more inventive approach and imagined advertising taking a satirically honest approach. When an ad man suffering from burn-out (Dudley Moore) decides to create truthful ads for an airline client—"Most of our passengers get there alive"—he is shipped off to a mental institution that is considerably more lucid and humane than the agency he left. When the ads are mistakenly run, however, business booms and Moore is rehired. The film pits every ad person's dream of honesty against the reality of advertising and a typically dictatorial but amusing agency president (J.T. Walsh). The ultimate joke is when Moore has the inmates at the mental institution start writing the ads.

The 21st century was not long under way before advertising became the topic of a major commercial film. In Paramount's 2000 romantic fable *What Women Want,* the issue is the sexist values of the traditional "man's man" versus those of the educated career woman played out in the context of a Chicago ad agency called Sloane Curtis. The man's man view is represented by a senior creative officer (played by Mel Gibson) who sees no paradox in using images of male sexual fantasies to sell products to women. He is soon confronted with a woman creative director (Helen Hunt) recruited from another agency to fill a job he expected to receive. When an electrical mishap presumably rewires his thinking, his smug arrogance is replaced by an ability to read women's thoughts verbatim, giving him an empathy for women's attitudes that is quickly reflected in his creative work. In a way, it is a throwback to *Magic Town*. Both stories offer fantasy as a premise for achieving profound insight into consumer behavior and then withdraw it, leaving the characters wiser—and reformed—for their experience. *What Women Want* situates its fictional agency in a fashionably hip, restored office building, offers facts and figures on the buying power of women consumers, and portrays the process of developing creative strategy and execution for a real product, Nike ("No games, just sports"). Alan Alda plays a reasonably intelligent agency president seeking to modernize his agency's reputation.

Theater and TV

The Broadway stage has given relatively little attention to advertising as subject matter, one exception being *Will Success Spoil Rock Hunter?* (1957), written by George Axelrod and adapted for the screen by Frank Tashlin in 1957. The story concerns a hapless advertising man (Tony Randall) who nearly loses but then saves the agency's key lipstick account by lining up a big Hollywood star (Jayne Mansfield) as an endorser. The film breaks the "fourth wall" at the halfway mark when Randall addresses remarks about advertising directly to the audience.

Among the best-remembered ad agencies on a television show is McMann and Tate, which provided the professional background for Darrin Stephens in the series *Bewitched* (1964–72). The agency and its head, Larry Tate, seemed constantly at the mercy of Stephens's wife Samantha (Elizabeth Montgomery), a witch. The action of the stories tended toward farce, generally revolved around the home, and seldom commented seriously on advertising.

By far the most probing and realistic portrayals of advertising were seen between 1987 and 1991 on the ABC drama series *thirtysomething*, whose larger goal was yet another reflection of the cultural preoccupation with yuppies. Nevertheless, advertising played a major role in the stories, all of whose characters nurtured creative ambitions. During the show's first two seasons, Michael Steadman (played by Ken Olin) and Elliot Weston (Timothy Busfield) headed their own agency more or less as equal partners, although Steadman was the dominant personality and more cool-headed than Weston. Their efforts to win and keep small clients exerted constant financial pressure on them and their families. Although minor ethical issues occasionally became story elements, both characters were played as decent men eager to do their best creative work. Their agency encounters frequent crises and finally, facing bankruptcy, folds in 1989. Steadman, after much soul searching, decides to put aside his entrepreneurial desires and join the Miles Drentell agency, which is housed in a fashionably hip warehouse full of fishbowl offices, spiral staircases, and bare brick walls (then stylish among real-life hot creative shops, especially in San Francisco, California). The series possessed a keen eye for the detail of such alternative "new age" agencies and the way in which they used office style to separate themselves from more traditional shops.

More interesting than the decor was the mercurial character of Miles Drentell (David Clennon) himself, who exuded a strange charisma that was both compelling and creepy. Well tailored, with a dignified beard and a penetrating, disciplined mind, he ruled with a far more subtle brand of fear than the bombastic Evan Llewellyn Evans had employed 50 years before in *The Hucksters*. Drentell preferred soft-spoken mind games and psychodrama that both attracted and repelled Steadman, who by the last season had withstood the constant psychic stress to become a kind of heir apparent. The intrigues became especially intense when Steadman tried to engineer a palace coup under Drentell's nose by undermining a client relationship and taking the business to reestablish his own agency. Weston had joined the Drentell firm by then but was in a subordinate position and never knew whether he could trust his former partner. Occasional and convincing debates over marketing strategies lent a further authenticity and verisimilitude to the agency landscape. By the 1990s *thirtysomething* was bringing the public the most nuanced and sophisticated fictional advertising agency it had ever seen. Implicit in the continuing story was the early postwar anxiety of the price of material success, but it was woven so tightly into the fabric of the drama that the stories could transcend such old questions and explore other, unique workplace tensions. Similarly, the ethics and purpose of advertising were of little concern in the ongoing story. Advertising no longer needed to justify itself or make excuses for its means. It was now an accepted part of American life. The young, hip, TV-literate audience to which *thirtysomething* was targeted was on to all its tricks. Except for the egomania of Drentell that pervaded the lives of all who worked for him, general agency protocols and rituals were played with a maturity and an eye for detail that have yet to be surpassed in popular fiction.

What has been consistently lacking in popular portrayals of advertising in literature, films, and television, however, has been a sense of the profession's role and importance in a capitalist economy. By ignoring the larger context in which advertising functions, filmmakers and novelists, including those who have themselves worked in the business, have found advertising an easy and tempting target for ridicule and, it could be argued, have done it a disservice.

JOHN McDONOUGH

Further Reading

Leokum, Arkady, *Please Send Me, Absolutely Free . . . : A Novel*, New York and London: Harper and Brothers, 1946

Packard, Vance, *The Hidden Persuaders*, New York: McKay, and London: Longmans, 1957; revised edition, New York: Pocket, 1980; London: Penguin, 1981

Pohl, Frederik, and C.M. Kornbluth, *The Space Merchants*, New York: Ballantine, 1953; London: Heinemann, 1955

Wakeman, Frederic, *The Hucksters*, New York: Rinehart, 1946

Motorola, Inc.

Principal Agencies
Albert Kircher Company
Gourtain-Cobb Advertising
Leo Burnett Company, Inc.
FCB Worldwide
McCann-Erickson Worldwide

Historically, Motorola's advertising programs have been characterized by adherence to two overriding principles: a focus on brand and an effort to target advertising vehicles to suit specific audiences. This emphasis on basics served Motorola well as the company went through radical shifts in product and market orientations.

Motorola's advertising maintained a consumer orientation during its early years, when its Chicago, Illinois, factory turned out auto and home radios and other "entertainment" products. The company evolved toward a business-to-business mode from the 1940s through the 1980s as specialty communications devices and semiconductors became its dominant wares. Since then it has returned to a consumer orientation as its pagers and cellular products have been embraced by mass markets.

Paul Galvin and his brother Joseph opened the Galvin Manufacturing Corporation in 1928 with the introduction of the "battery eliminator," a product that allowed battery-operated radios to be powered by household current. In 1930 the Galvin brothers manufactured the first affordable radio for installation in automobiles. This series of products was named "Motorola"—a combination of "motor" and "ola" (as in Victrola), representing a synthesis of music and motion.

Building Brand Recognition

Building a reputation of quality around this brand name and developing targeted advertising programs were among Paul Galvin's first initiatives. The Galvin brothers traveled the country establishing and training a network of dealers to provide expert installations for customers. The original dealer network was expanded in 1934 to include hundreds of B.F. Goodrich stores and garages. Offering installations by expertly trained personnel helped the company build brand recognition as a quality product among consumers, and fair pricing and service support spurred the growth of a loyal distributor network. Early marketing was dealer-focused and included store displays, product brochures, uniforms, and premiums—all supporting the brand. Dealers were able to participate in co-operative advertising programs as early as 1932 so they could promote the brand along with their dealerships in local newspapers.

Dealer advertising programs were supported by an innovative national roadside campaign developed by Victor Irvine, the company's first advertising manager. Signs touting Motorola's "world famous car radio" were spaced at frequent intervals along popu-

lar routes, encouraging motorists to visit local dealers—reaching potential auto radio customers in their cars.

The original logo depicted the word "Motorola" in an Art Deco–style script with the "T" crossed by a lightning bolt—a symbol frequently associated with radio waves—and was the core component of store displays, signage, and print advertising. The term "Vita-tone" appeared in early advertising to describe Motorola's sound quality.

In 1936 the Galvin Manufacturing Corporation expanded into the home radio market. With this move came a new emphasis in consumer print advertising and use of endorsements by celebrities, many of whom had become known to the American public through their presence on the radio. Ads produced by the Albert Kircher Company of Chicago featured small photos of a particular model of radio against a large picture of a famous star, declaring the model to be "My favorite personal radio." Early celebrity shots included actresses Betty Grable and Rita Hayworth, as well as bandleader Lawrence Welk. The late 1930s and 1940s saw a variety of print campaigns running in popular magazines such as *Collier's, Better Homes & Gardens,* and the *Saturday Evening Post,* as the company switched to Gourfain-Cobb Advertising, of Chicago.

During World War II the Galvin Manufacturing Company stopped production of its entertainment lines to focus on making two-way radios. These innovative devices were both technologically sound and very portable and were considered essential by the military. While consumers could not buy radios for their homes during this time, a special print advertising campaign was orchestrated to maintain a positive brand name in the public eye. Approximately 20 print pieces were created, featuring colorful artist renderings of soldiers using the "Handie Talkie," a two-way AM radio. Headlines and copy positioned the company as an ally in the war effort: "When Motorola Radio comes home from the war. . . " and "Motorola Radio Handie-Talkie coordinating our march to victory."

In 1947, as an indication of the success achieved by the company's brand of radios, Paul Galvin changed the name of the company to Motorola, Inc. At this time the company committed itself to developing new technologies and followed this pledge with the introduction of a variety of communications devices for specialty markets. Products included two-way radio systems that were used primarily by police and fire departments. Aggressive marketing and advertising programs were used to establish "the Dispatcher Line" within the public safety and industrial markets, including print ads in industry journals and active participation in trade shows and public safety conferences.

Pitching the Pager

In 1955 Motorola developed a small radio receiver, known as a pager. Targeted advertising programs involved pitching this device to hospital executives as a replacement for public address systems.

These pitches were produced as short films depicting the uses and benefits of the product. As a sort of infomercial precursor to Power Point sales presentations, this approach proved very effective in establishing the product in this new market.

That same year Motorola also updated its logo, hiring award-winning graphic artist Morton Goldsholl for the job; Goldsholl also created the sparkling 7-Up logo and the floral apostrophe used on the striped wrappers of Brach Candies. The mark, consisting of the name Motorola set in a modern typeface alongside a stylized M, was chosen to signify strength. While the insignia has undergone a few minor changes since 1955 (a circle was added around the stylized M logo in 1967), it continued to serve as a symbol of strength and quality and remained a very important element of the company's advertising into the 21st century.

During the late 1940s and early 1950s, while expanding automotive and radio communications product lines—supplying Ford Motor Company, Chrysler Corporation, American Motors Corporation, and other manufacturers with radios for factory installation—Motorola reentered the home electronics market via its Golden View television in 1947. This was the first TV set available for less than $200. Early advertising for the set, which was composed of a seven-inch screen embedded in wood cabinetry, emphasized price and shared family experiences and proclaimed, "Now, everyone can afford this new entertainment for the entire family." Promotional campaigns were built around America's increasing appetite for this new type of entertainment. Again, outdoor advertising and radio spots were used. Motorola also sponsored one of the first network television programs to reinforce brand recognition. Broadcast through an American Broadcasting Corporation (ABC) affiliate and hosted by Paul Galvin's son Robert, the one-hour weekly drama used the melody to "Happy Birthday" with the line "Motorola to you" to continue to build brand recognition and loyalty.

As the economy boomed in the 1950s, households were acquiring second and third radios and developing a greater demand for televisions. In response Motorola manufactured a wide variety of models. The corresponding print and early television advertising depicted this variety (portables, different colors, and combinations such as units that included radios and clocks or turntables) and emphasized consumer choice. These spots, created by the Leo Burnett Company, were referred to as the "More to Enjoy" campaign, which ran from 1956 to 1959.

For Motorola the 1950s also heralded a new focus on engineering. A clear goal for the company was to become a manufacturing leader in transistors and semiconductors. With this new identity as a "technology" company, Motorola established itself in a variety of original equipment manufacturer, or OEM, markets. Corresponding business-to-business advertising was developed to reach automotive and other types of manufacturers. This emphasis on technical innovation became part and parcel of consumer advertising and brand building. In 1959 the company introduced the "all transistor" shirt pocket radio, and in 1967 Motorola introduced the Quasar color television. Using this latest technology, print and commercial spots created by the Clinton E. Frank, Inc., agency, of Chicago, featured pictures of the model's

In this 1944 ad, Motorola highlighted its contributions to the war effort and assured customers it would resume production of home entertainment equipment as soon as the war was won.
Courtesy of Motorola Archives © 2000 Motorola, Inc.

"works in a drawer" miniature circuitry. The successful branding efforts of this product were demonstrated when Matsushita chose to retain the Quasar name after purchasing Motorola's television business in 1974.

Global Expansion

During the 1960s and 1970s, as the company increased its manufacturing operations (divested of home electronics products, the focus was on communications devices and microprocessors), the new thrust in advertising became internationalization. With a presence as an employer in countries such as Australia, France, Malaysia, South Korea, Singapore, the United Kingdom, and Germany, Motorola also wanted to be known as a supplier in these same consumer markets. Corporate communications materials were developed in every language where the company had a plant, and advertising offices were established in local markets to tailor programs to meet local custom and buying trends. (As an example, ads in many Asian and Latin American countries tried to

With minimal copy, this 1994 ad for the latest Motorola cellular phone emphasized the phone's up-to-date technology and the company's experience in the telecommunications business.
Courtesy of Motorola Archives © 2000 Motorola, Inc.

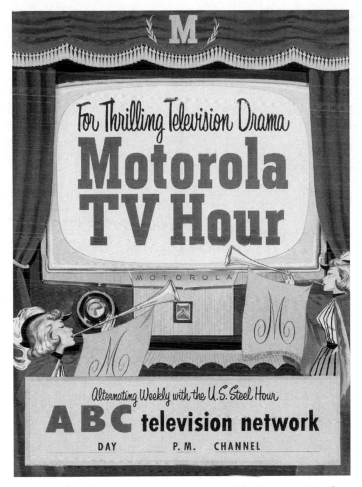

Commercials on the *Motorola TV Hour*, a biweekly drama program that debuted in 1953, promoted the company's research efforts and products. *Courtesy of Motorola Archives © 2000 Motorola, Inc.*

emphasize the company's history because these cultures strongly considered this factor when forming impressions.) While major inroads were made, many foreign markets still presented considerable hurdles for entry. For example, Motorola was not allowed to sell its pagers in the Japanese market.

In 1981 Young & Rubicam developed a series of 20 ads, "Meeting Japan's challenge." These ads, which appeared in general consumer publications such as *Life* and business publications such as the *Wall Street Journal*, set out to portray Motorola as a champion of quality and a pioneer in challenging protected markets in Japan and elsewhere. Much of the copy was technical and specific to actions Motorola was taking to ensure quality manufacturing. The headlines often challenged other companies to step forward on quality issues as well—for example, "Has Japanese innovation replaced good old Yankee ingenuity?" Significant

efforts to improve the quality of its products, collaborations with government on trade policy, and related advertising to the business community helped Motorola earn the first Malcolm Baldrige Quality Award in 1988.

Motorola has apparently come full-circle in its advertising emphasis. While using cutting-edge technology, consumer markets for cellular and messaging products are again significant complements to company sales to OEMs, phone companies, and the public safety industry. In 1990 cellular phones were a 2 billion dollar-a-year business; they represented 20 percent of company sales and were available in all major markets throughout the world. Instrumental in this growth was a series of ten advertisements aimed at educating consumers about cellular, "Making cellular work for you."

After educational campaigns ran their course, the company typically focused on more creative advertising. In 1989 a major campaign featured a color poster in the style of Andy Warhol, with four different head shots of a woman using a cellular phone. The caption simply stated, "Perfecting the art of communication."

During the 1990s Motorola also returned to using celebrity spokespersons for commercial spots and print ads aimed at specific audiences. Professional golfer Lee Trevino was an early cell phone spokesman (1991) selected because of his appeal to golf-loving businessmen. Lending the Motorola logo and company sponsorship to major cultural and sporting events has also become a major aspect of the company's advertising strategy. Motorola sponsored America's Cup yacht racing teams (1991–95) and has linked its name to the PGA Tour's Western Open (1994–98), Lance Armstrong and the U.S. Tour de France bicycle racing team (1991–96), and, beginning in 1998, the National Football League. At century's end the company employed several agencies, including FCB Worldwide for corporate advertising and McCann-Erickson Worldwide for the radio products group.

DEBORAH HAWKINS

Further Reading

Burstyn, H.P., "It's AT&T vs. Motorola in Burgeoning Mobile Phone Market," *Electronic Business* (November 1980)

Galvin, Robert W., *The Idea of Ideas*, Schaumburg, Illinois: Motorola University Press, 1991

Morone, Joseph G., *Winning in High-Tech Markets: The Role of General Management: How Motorola, Corning, and General Electric Have Built Global Leadership through Technology*, Boston: Harvard Business School Press, 1993

Motorola Museum of Electronics, *Motorola: A Journey through Time and Technology*, Schaumburg, Illinois: Motorola, 1994

Petrakis, Harry Mark, *The Founder's Touch: The Life of Paul Galvin of Motorola*, New York: McGraw-Hill, 1965

MTV, Influence of

Since MTV was first introduced in 1980, it has had a significant impact on advertising. Not only are commercials aired during its programs, but the videos themselves can be viewed as advertisements for CDs, tapes, and other music-related products. Music videos came about as a result of a recession that occurred in the music industry during the early 1980s. Initially, the incentive to develop music television was advertiser led. Just as other TV networks are in the business of selling audiences to the advertisers of automobiles, laundry detergents, and antacids, MTV was developed largely to deliver consumers between the ages of 12 and 34 (the median age of the MTV audience is 23) to the producers of tapes, records, and videos.

MTV became an effective advertising medium because it uses music, visual elements, popular culture icons, and the socializing effect of television to drive its selling message. As noted, its primary goal was—and remains—to promote the artist or band performing in the video clip, thereby influencing consumers to purchase CDs as well as other band-related products. But more often than not, the video clip sells a great deal more than just music. Lifestyles, fashions, cosmetics, cars, and other products are promoted in the process of showcasing hip, contemporary pop music. And at the same time, social and consumer behaviors are molded by the medium. Advertisers have therefore looked to MTV for ideas on how to better communicate with the youth market and have adopted the styles and techniques of MTV to deliver their message. MTV has been especially successful at targeting the 12-to-34-year-old audience; an estimated 218 million people per month in this age group watch MTV, more than 80 percent of them outside the United States.

Music, Mood, and Marketing

Research suggests that music can evoke a number of emotions—from pride and passion to rage and fear. Consumers exposed to different kinds of music can become either relaxed or excited, perhaps because music tempo affects humans at a subconscious level. Music and images interact in complex ways, and music can make an image either more or less effective or memorable. It has been shown, for example, that when background music in a commercial is both attention-getting and message-incongruent (i.e., the style of the music is at odds with the images being shown), listener attention can be diverted from the message, with negative effects on recall. It has also been demonstrated that the consumer's level of involvement or interest, along with the presence or absence of music in an advertisement, affects how brand attitudes are formed. Thus, in studies where levels of consumer involvement were low, music had a facilitative effect on brand attitude; where involvement levels were high, music had a distracting effect.

Predicting consumers' moods in marketing situations, such as how they feel while viewing or listening to a group of ads, enables market researchers to better understand how consumers will react to the ads themselves. Research in psychology suggests that mood can influence both attitudes and recall. Music, films, and music videos have been shown to affect listeners' and viewers' feelings. In the context of MTV, moods evoked by events in the video—such as Michael Jackson's transformation into a werewolf in *Thriller*—can influence consumer responses to the images displayed in that context. Specifically, mood associations generated by the video may attach themselves to the products displayed, particularly when this is the consumer's first exposure to the product. Otherwise, preexisting judgments of and feelings toward the product counteract the video's influence. Furthermore, the visual imagery of music television often is highly ambiguous, a characteristic that serves to heighten arousal and attention.

Consumer research conducted in the 1990s suggested that studies examining the effects of advertising must consider the social and cultural context in which that advertising takes place. In many ways MTV represents a subculture of its own, and music videos show fans the T-shirts and other trappings they need to project the appropriate image and thereby attain membership in the rock subculture.

A steady trend in advertising has been to show the product as an integral part of overarching social purposes and processes. Music video clips can be extremely influential in this regard. Consumption activities that occur within the clips are part of the image that viewers associate with the performer. If teenagers are influenced by or rely upon pop/rock music icons for the latest fashions trends, then they may perceive these products as important for peer acceptance.

Shaping the Consumer Culture

Researchers who study music videos have commented on the close similarities in visual style, background music, and format of MTV videos and commercials, noting that it is sometimes difficult to distinguish the two. Consider, for instance, the animation in a video by the group Tool as compared with the animation of the MTV logo in an ad for the network. While the tone of the songs and the ads differs (i.e., one somber, the other bouncy), both use similar visual techniques to gain attention. Similarly, it has been asserted that all the components of a music video assist in the marketing of the video. The performance motivates the viewer to buy that particular song. Graphics appear at the beginning and at the end of the video clip, stating the name of the group, song, and album, motivating the viewer to remember it. The performance thus sells not just the song but the video itself. As Basil G. Englis pointed out in 1991, the "enormous popularity of music television has the potential to influence consumers via its power to shape consumer culture through its influence on commercial structure and positioning." It is no wonder then that MTV has become an attractive medium for advertisers, especially those trying to reach teenage consumers.

01 Hey everybody! Want to grow? About 15% of your height is added during your teen years and milk can help make the most of it. That's why it's #1. Milk rocks!   > Carson

MTV personality Carson Daly was featured in this 2000 "milk mustache" ad. MTV's programming has both influenced and been influenced by advertising.
Courtesy of Carson Daly and Bozell Worldwide, Inc.

The phenomenon of synaesthesia has been suggested by some authorities as an approach that can help researchers better understand the effects of music television. Synaesthesia is the process whereby sensory impressions are carried over from one sense to another—for instance, when one pictures sounds in the "mind's eye." Thus the visual imagery in the video attempts to tap into visual associations that exist prior to the production of the video itself, an internal sign system already existing in the audience.

Research shows that the tempo of popular music is clearly represented in the visual rhythm of music video clips. A variety of techniques are used, including camera movement, editing, special effects during production, postproduction computer effects, and the performer's actions in the video clip. The fast cutting that is a feature of many videos reflects the tempo of the sound track. A similar technique was evident in a number of popular TV commercials of the 1990s, particularly those for sporting goods such as exercise machines. Lyrics can, of course, play a key role in establishing the mood of a video clip, given their role in constructing meaning.

It has been suggested that music videos make use of three kinds of visual "hooks" to encourage viewer interest. Regular close-ups of the performer's face are one kind of visual hook. An example cited by Andrew Goodwin, in his book *Dancing in the Distraction Factory*, is Peter Gabriel's *Shock the Monkey* video, which continually provides close-ups of Gabriel's face; moreover, each time the camera returns to him, he looks different, thus creating continuing visual interest.

A second kind of hook involves placing attractive models throughout the videos to encourage viewers to keep watching: examples of this technique include Robert Palmer's *Addicted to Love* and *Simply Irresistible*, as well as David Lee Roth's *California Girls*. The sexual content of music videos is often used to encourage repeat viewing. The use of erotic imagery can also generate a "media event" to aid in promotion, for example, the airing of Madonna's *Justify My Love*.

The third hook relies on the association of a musical motif with a visual image. In the music video *Rock the Casbah* by the Clash, an armadillo appears every time the minor chord piano pattern is repeated. The image of the armadillo—on the album cover, for example—may aid in recognition when a consumer is in a music store. In some ways, then, the connection between image and music is a branding technique.

Various studies have examined how television exposure influences consumers' perceptions of the world. Advertisers have started utilizing popular culture, relying upon the knowledge of TV viewers—especially heavy viewers—as "readers" of television, to promote their products. Intertextuality is the process by which this occurs. Intertextuality has been defined as the use of recognizable textual references that allow the viewer to read the text in relationship to other texts. For example, in featuring actor Michael J. Fox in the diet Pepsi campaign, the soft drink company relied on his popular appeal and familiarity as a star of the long-running sitcom *Family Ties*.

Advertisers seek to select celebrities who not only generate interest in the product among members of the target market but whose popular culture profile will be readily associated with the brand. In this way music videos can play an influential role in the social development of their teenage audience by preparing them to become educated consumers.

BRETT MARTIN

Further Reading

Allen, Robert, "Audience-Oriented Criticism and Television," in *Channels of Discourse, Reassembled: Television and Contemporary Criticism,* edited by Allen, 2nd edition, Chapel Hill, University of North Carolina Press, and London: Routledge, 1992

Andersen, Robin, *Consumer Culture and TV Programming,* Boulder, Colorado: Westview, 1995

Aufderheide, P., "Music Videos: The Look of the Sound," *Journal of Communication* (Winter 1986)

Bryant, J., R.A. Carveth, and D. Brown, "Television Viewing and Anxiety: An Experimental Examination," *Journal of Communication* 31 (Winter 1981)

Englis, Basil G., "Music Television and Its Influences on Consumers, Consumer Culture, and the Transmission of Consumption Messages," *Advances in Consumer Research* 18 (1991)

Englis, Basil G., Michael R. Solomon, and Richard D. Ashmore, "Beauty before the Eyes of Beholders: The Cultural Encoding of Beauty Types in Magazine Advertising and Music Television," *Journal of Advertising* 23, no. 2 (June 1994)

Englis, Basil G., Michael R. Solomon, and Anna Olofsson, "Consumption Imagery in Music Television: A Bi-Cultural Perspective," *Journal of Advertising* 22, no. 4 (December 1993)

Fowles, Jib, *Advertising and Popular Culture,* Thousand Oaks, California: Sage, 1996

Gardner, Meryl P., "Mood States and Consumer Behavior: A Critical Review," *Journal of Consumer Research* 12, no. 3 (December 1985)

Gerbner, G., and L. Gross, "Living with Television: The Violence Profile," *Journal of Communication* 26, no. 2 (Spring 1976)

Goodwin, Andrew, *Dancing in the Distraction Factory: Music Television and Popular Culture,* Minneapolis: University of Minnesota Press, 1992; London: Routledge, 1993

Gunter, Barrie, and Michael Svennevig, *Behind and in Front of the Screen: Television's Involvement with Family Life,* London: Libbey, 1987

Harrison, Kristen, and Joanne Cantor, "The Relationship between Media Consumption and Eating Disorders," *Journal of Communication* 47, no. 1 (1997)

Kinder, M., "Music Video and the Spectator: Television, Ideology, and Dream," *Film Quarterly* 38 (Fall 1984)

Myers, P.N., and F.A. Biocca, "The Elastic Body Images: The Effect of Television Advertising and Programming on Body Image Distortions in Young Women," *Journal of Communication* 42, no. 3 (1992)

O'Guinn, Thomas C., and L.J. Shrum, "The Role of Television in the Construction of Consumer Reality," *Journal of Consumer Research* 23, no. 4 (March 1997)

Park, C.W., and S. Mark Young, "Consumer Response to Television Commercials: The Impact of Involvement and Background Music on Brand Attitude Formation," *Journal of Marketing Research* 23, no. 1 (February 1986)

Postman, Neil, *Amusing Ourselves to Death: Public Discourse in the Age of Show Business,* New York: Viking, 1985; London: Heinemann, 1986

Scott, Linda M., "Understanding Jingles and Needledrop: A Rhetorical Approach to Music in Advertising," *Journal of Consumer Research* 17, no. 2 (September 1990)

Signorielli, Nancy, "Television's Mean and Dangerous World: A Continuation of the Cultural Indicators Perspective," in *Cultivation Analysis: New Directions in Media Effects Research,* edited by Signorielli and Michael Morgan, Newbury Park, California: Sage, 1990

Wernick, Andrew, *Promotional Culture: Advertising, Ideology, and Symbolic Expression,* Newbury Park, California, and London: Sage, 1991

White, M., "Ideological Analysis and Television," in *Channels of Discourse, Reassembled: Television and Contemporary Criticism,* 2nd edition, edited by Robert C. Allen, Chapel Hill: University of North Carolina Press, and London: Routledge, 1992

Multinational Campaign

Exactly when the first ad crossed a national border is an object of much speculation and little documentation. What is known, however, is that some of the first agencies in the business of international advertising—the J. Walter Thompson Company (JWT) and H.K. McCann Company, for instance—were still in the ad industry in some form or another at the onset of the 21st century.

In 1899 JWT opened an office in London, England, its first outside the United States. In the early 1900s Helen Lansdowne Resor, wife of Stanley Resor (who purchased JWT in 1916 and became president of the agency in 1917), created ads for Pond's for use in Japan and other overseas markets.

Although World War I temporarily interrupted these early moves across borders, the practice resumed with the end of hostilities. In August 1927 the H.K. McCann Company announced it would handle advertising for the Standard Oil Company (New Jersey) in several European countries, including Belgium, France,

Germany, Poland, Sweden, and Switzerland. Other clients followed. In 1928 Squibb's Lentheric Perfumes assigned its French and German advertising to McCann, which became McCann-Erickson in 1930.

Despite the stock market crash of 1929 and the ensuing Great Depression, international advertising efforts continued. McCann in 1929 began promoting the cooperation of its various international offices as a benefit to advertisers. In 1930 it ran a test campaign for Mistol (a brand of nose drops) in England, France, Germany, Italy, and Spain and placed ads for Nujol (a treatment for constipation) in medical publications in three European countries.

On 8 April 1938, a group of 13 publishers and advertisers, including Packard Motors Export Corporation and *Export Trade & Shipper* magazine, created the Export Advertising Association (EAA) to coordinate and foster international advertising. By its first anniversary, the group had 67 members.

World War II slowed multinational campaign development. Some multinational advertisers, including Standard Oil's Esso, the Coca-Cola Company, and American Home Products, shifted their focus to Latin America. But advertisers soon began to wrestle with the new issues that came about as a consequence of crossing borders—standardization of rates, for example, and the need to lower customs duties.

Translation in advertisements became an issue. One Caribbean newspaper ad translated the English ad for Packard, "Ask the man who owns one," as "Try to find a man who owns one." A fountain pen producer's ad promising "Avoidance of embarrassment" from leaks and blotches, came out in Spanish as "Avoid pregnancy," leading one retailer to try to buy an entire railroad carload of the product.

With the end of the war, munitions factories began retooling to produce consumer goods, and the postwar boom was under way. Former soldiers who were now becoming captains of industry were quick to grasp the advantages of foreign markets as well as the threat of foreign competition. In a speech to the EAA in 1949, National Export Advertising Service President Paul Kruming said, "Much has been said of the importance of advertising and sales promotion in the current seller's market here at home. Among us, it is generally conceded that the task is doubly difficult abroad for from now on, the competition from England, Germany, Japan, and other nations will be more intense. Therein lies the challenge."

By the 1950s the U.S. government's Marshall Plan, launched in 1948 to help finance the rebuilding of Western Europe after the war, had sent foreign investment into high gear. In 1953 the EAA was renamed the International Advertising Association, which began an advertising industry movement encouraging self-regulation. *The International Advertising Code of Ethics and Standards,* published in 1956, continued in use into the 21st century.

By the end of the 1950s, the concept of creating a European Common Market was gaining momentum. In the 1960s McCann-Erickson developed the idea of "one-sight, one-sound," a plan to create a homogenous worldwide campaign for the Coca-Cola Company. Under this concept, each Coke ad would look and sound similar to all others around the world.

The confluence of consumerism and jet travel helped push the multinational agency trend. In 1969, the Leo Burnett Company purchased the London Press Exchange, a network of agencies in 25 countries. With it, Burnett instantly became a global enterprise. The multinational company and agency hit their stride in the 1970s as marketers around the world stretched beyond their own borders. Advertising was transformed as the international campaign grew up.

The one-sight, one-sound global campaign was now being tailored to meet local niches. A cost-efficient common strategy began to be used instead, emphasizing the commonalities between consumers. For instance, Lintas created multinational ads for Unilever's Impulse perfumed body spray. A boy-meets-girl premise was the foundation of the creative aspect, but each country's ads were produced locally, incorporating local social mores and customs for courtship.

While many multinational companies had been based in the United States, marketers in other countries, such as France, began to think across borders as well. French brands such as Dior, Chanel, and Lacoste began to carry worldwide weight.

The 1980s were the decade of the global village, according to Harvard Business School Professor Ted Levitt and *Megatrends* author John Naisbett. This was reflected in ad spending. In 1980 non-U.S. ad expenditures among U.S. companies matched U.S. expenditures for the first time. The development of satellite and cable TV networks such as CNN International and MTV further advanced the notion that marketers could sell the same product in the same way everywhere.

Meanwhile, agencies adjusted to the times by following the example of their clients and entering into large mergers. BBDO International, Doyle Dane Bernbach Group, and Needham Harper Worldwide joined in 1986 to form Omnicom; Ted Bates Worldwide merged with Saatchi & Saatchi. These new giant holding companies were poised to give the Interpublic Group of Companies (parent of McCann-Erickson Worldwide and Lintas Worldwide) a run for its money in the global advertising scene. The Berlin Wall fell in 1989, opening new markets in Eastern Europe that had previously been contained behind the Iron Curtain.

During the 1990s consolidation was the key. Politics led business, with the 1989 North American Free Trade Act, the dissolution of remaining barriers among the countries of the European Economic Community, and trade agreements between Japan and Korea highlighting the era. At the same time, many of the world's largest advertisers began to consolidate their global advertising accounts, a move that led to huge account shifts, such as the $800 million global Citibank account's move to Young & Rubicam in 1997.

JULIANNE HILL

See also International Advertising Association

Further Reading

Baudot, Barbara Sundberg, *International Advertising Handbook: A User's Guide to Rules and Regulations,* Lexington, Massachusetts: Lexington Books, 1989

Levitt, Theodore, *The Marketing Imagination,* New York: Free Press, and London: Collier Macmillan, 1983; new, expanded edition, 1986

Naisbitt, John, *Megatrends: Ten New Directions Transforming Our Lives,* New York: Warner Books, 1982; updated edition, 1984

Murdoch, Rupert 1931–

International Media Magnate

Rupert Murdoch signaled his intentions to revolutionize global media when he agreed to give up his country for his kingdom in 1985. He swapped his Australian birthright for U.S. citizenship to satisfy ownership regulations when his News Corporation acquired Twentieth Century Fox Film Corporation. He used the studio as the cornerstone upon which to build Fox Broadcasting and launch the fourth-largest U.S. broadcast network in 1986 at a time when industry experts warned that there would not be enough viewers and advertising dollars to support it. His gentlemanly demeanor fronts a shrewd business mind, as evidenced by his ever-growing media empire based on the newspapers, television stations, and satellite distribution services owned by his Australia-based News Corporation.

Keith Rupert Murdoch was born on 11 March 1931, in Melbourne, Australia, the second of four children, and the only son of Keith and Elisabeth Murdoch. After studying at Worcester College in Oxford, England, Murdoch took his first job as an editor on Lord Beaverbrook's *London Daily Express,* where he developed a penchant for the sensational and racy headlines and photographs that have since characterized many of his own newspapers. Murdoch returned to Australia following the 1952 death of his father, Sir Keith Murdoch, a famed Australian war correspondent and publisher, to take over the family business. He operated the *Sunday Mail* and the *News,* both of Adelaide, Australia, upon which he constructed a substantial newspaper and magazine empire in Australia, the United States, the United Kingdom, and Hong Kong.

In 1981 his company, News Corporation, acquired the *Times* and the *Sunday Times* in the United Kingdom. Murdoch bought his way into the U.S. media market with the *New York Post, New York Magazine, New West,* the *Village Voice,* and the *Chicago Sun Times.* The need to pay off heavy debt prompted Murdoch to sell many of his U.S. publications, although he sold and then repurchased the *New York Post.*

But it was television—broadcast, cable, and satellite—in which Murdoch has had his most formidable impact. In 1985 Murdoch acquired Twentieth Century Fox Film Corporation and the independent television station group from John Kluge's Metromedia to create Fox, Inc. Launched with 79 affiliated TV stations and 80 percent coverage of U.S. homes, Murdoch soon moved to a full week of prime-time programming as Fox built viewer and advertiser support with series such as *The Simpsons, America's Most Wanted, Married With Children,* and *The X-Files.* The network gradually added children's and sports programming divisions. By 2000 Murdoch had successfully launched cable channels for news and children's fare, as well as amassing a larger regional sports cable network and gobbling up pricey professional sports rights. He bought the Los Angeles (California) Dodgers Major League Baseball team in 1999, in the city that Murdoch has called home for more than 13 years.

In 1994 Murdoch's Fox network startled the industry by outbidding CBS for broadcast rights to the National Football League's National Football Conference games over the next four years. The price was $1.6 billion. The repercussions were swift and included a virtual domino effect of network affiliation switches that left the "Big Three" TV broadcast networks, especially CBS, scrambling to find new outlets in major markets.

News Corporation mirrored its stunning 1994 acquisition of eight New World CBS-affiliated TV stations by winning an aggressive bidding to acquire ten major-market TV stations from Chris-Craft Industries for $5.4 billion in cash and stock. The deal enabled Murdoch to take advantage of new conditional regulations allowing broadcasters to own and operate two TV stations in larger markets. It also promised to give him a hand in determining the future of UPN Network, an independent television network controlled by Viacom.

At the same time Murdoch became an international satellite force, building on Sky Television, his four-channel satellite service, which merged with rival British Satellite Broadcasting in 1990 to form British Sky Broadcasting. In 1993 he purchased Star TV, a pan-Asian television service based in Hong Kong, as part of his plan to build a global network. Two years later he aligned with MCI Communications Corporation, a major provider of long-distance telecommunications services in the United States.

His crowning achievement, however, promised to be the "roll up" of all of News Corporation's satellite operations in a new publicly traded subsidiary called Sky Global. The spin-off, which Murdoch described as "a company-transforming event," was expected in the first half of 2001. At the end of that year, however, his grand plans were upset by another maverick, Charlie Ergen, whose rival EchoStar Communcations, snatched up Hughes Electronics' DirecTV with a competing bid. In early 2002, regulatory approval was still pending for the deal, which would create a dominant U.S. satellite service provider. Although Murdoch graciously bowed out of the picture, many industry observers believed he would return to the scene if the DirecTV-Echostar deal fell through. Many also believe he eventually would seek to acquire the combined U.S. satellite firm in order to complete his global satellite game plan. The company also was in the process of acquiring the 49.5 percent interest in Fox Family it did not own from partner Haim Saban. That done, Fox quickly turned around and sold its Fox Family operation to the Walt Disney Company for $5.2 billion in late 2001.

In 2000, at age 69, Murdoch was successfully treated for prostate cancer. Years earlier he had begun involving his children in the family business in what was portrayed in the press as a rivalry for power. Lachlan, his oldest son, was named deputy chief executive officer of News Corporation and heir apparent after successfully overseeing the company's print operations, mostly in Australia, New Zealand, and the United States. James Murdoch,

Rupert Murdoch.

Post and the airwaves of Turner's Cable News Network. Although he has been accused of using his daily newspapers in New York City and London to try to shift public sentiment in his favor and against his adversaries, Murdoch, by and large, has dueled with his wits and wisdom.

After cable giant John Malone became a close and influential adviser, Murdoch began catapulting his News Corporation into Internet ventures and developing closer ties to powerful companies such as Gemstar TV Guide, a leader in navigational tools for interactive television.

DIANE MERMIGAS

Biography

Born in Melbourne, Australia, 11 March 1931; attended Worcester College, Oxford; took over family-owned newspapers the *Sunday Mail* and the *News,* Adelaide, Australia, 1954; his News Corporation acquired the *Times* and the *Sunday Times* in the United Kingdom, 1981; began buying U.S. publications, including the *New York Post* and *New York Magazine,* in the 1980s; became a U.S. citizen to satisfy media ownership regulations when his News Corporation acquired Twentieth Century Fox Film Corporation to create Fox, Inc., 1985; launched the fourth-largest U.S. TV broadcast network, 1986.

Further Reading

Bates, James, "Watch the Money: Like It or Not, Rupert Murdoch Is Touching the Lives of Everyone in Southern California; How Can Anyone Predict Where He'll Strike Next?" *Los Angeles Times* (31 January 1999)

Lippman, John, Leslie Chang, and Robert Frank, "Meet Wendi Deng: The Boss' Wife Has Influence at News Corp.," *Wall Street Journal* (1 November 2000)

Malone Increases Stake in News Corp. and Satellite Operations," *Satellite Week* (2 October 2000)

"News Corp.'s China Campaign Rumored to Be Headed by Deng," *Asia Pulse* (3 November 2000)

Roberts, Johnnie, "The Man behind Rupert's Roll: Media Titan Rupert Murdoch Has Much to Savor," *Newsweek* (12 July 1999)

Shawcross, William, *Rupert Murdoch: Ringmaster of the Information Circus,* London: Chatto and Windus, 1992; as *Murdoch,* New York: Simon and Schuster, 1993

who had advanced News Corporation's Internet and new media efforts, was assigned to expand the company's Asian businesses. However, Murdoch looked to confidant and News Corporation Chief Executive Officer Peter Chernin not only to mentor his sons but also to oversee the daily operations of his sprawling global media empire.

Still, there never yet has been a moment when Murdoch did not completely rule every corner of his kingdom, outmaneuvering his peers in deals for media properties. Murdoch is one of the global media's most strategic players, and his ideology has, at times, led to open clashes with his peers, most notably Ted Turner. Their running feud has spilled onto the pages of Murdoch's *New York*

Museums and Archives

Both as artifacts of the advertising industry's history and as cultural symbols, advertising memorabilia have been collected and archived throughout the world. From the general collection of advertising at the American Advertising Museum in Portland, Oregon, to the specific collection of Coca-Cola memorabilia housed at the World of Coca-Cola in Atlanta, Georgia, the history of advertising has been exhaustively documented and exhibited. Because advertising reflects the times in which it is created, these museums

A poster for the American Advertising Museum by David M. Davis mingles images of some of the memorable icons in advertising history. *Illustrator: David M. Davis. Courtesy of the American Advertising Museum. Characters are trademarks of their respective subsidiary owners.*

and archives offer advertising scholars and practitioners, as well as the general public, rich examples of past advertising campaigns, which, in turn, provide insights into popular culture.

One of the most notable collections of advertising historiography is located at Duke University's John W. Hartman Center in Durham, North Carolina, which is home to the J. Walter Thompson Company Archives, along with an extensive collection of advertising and marketing materials from other agencies. Among other interesting items, this collection includes advertisement tear sheets and proofs created by the J. Walter Thompson Company (JWT) from 1875 through the 1990s, internal company memoranda and publications, and tapes and transcripts of oral interviews with the agency's staff between 1963 and 1979.

The American Advertising Museum in Portland is dedicated solely to the advertising industry. Established in 1986, this museum includes extensive advertising exhibits and archives; it also sponsors traveling exhibits throughout the United States.

Many advertising collections are available on-line to anyone with Internet access, including display ads for Eastman Kodak, outdoor advertisements for Levi's, and radio advertisements from Australia. Additionally, a number of archives have established databases of their material that can be searched on-line. It is possible, for example, to obtain a listing of the commercials aired during a specific nightly news broadcast, dating as far back as

1968, by searching on-line the Vanderbilt University Television News Archive in Nashville, Tennessee. The University of Texas, in partnership with Gannett Outdoor Advertising, has established a Web-based index of the advertisements in its collection, as has Duke University. Another on-line resource is the Ad Council's Web-based archive, which features such historical campaigns as the World War II admonition "Loose lips sink ships" and the campaign to prevent drunk driving.

When searching for information about ads for a particular product, it is often best to turn to the source of those ads. Some of the museums and archives that have been established are highly specialized and are the product of the corporate entity they represent. For example, the Butterick Company maintains an archive in New York City that includes marketing material for the sewing industry. The Museum of Beverage Containers and Advertising in Millersville, Tennessee, houses more than 36,000 items dealing specifically with beverage containers. Atlanta's World of Coca-Cola, with Coca-Cola memorabilia dating back to the inception of the company in 1886, is the world's largest collection of beverage paraphernalia. The Henry Ford Museum and Archive in Dearborn, Michigan, is rich with historical advertisements and information about Ford automobiles.

Whether one is searching for a specific product advertisement or an entire campaign, a vast array of resources is available. The following is a selection of the advertising museums and archives accessible to the public that highlight more than a hundred years of advertising history. (Addresses for the museums and archives discussed below are listed alphabetically at the end of the essay.)

Museums

American Advertising Museum, Portland, Oregon

The collection of the American Advertising Museum is one of the most comprehensive, containing artifacts collected from advertising agencies, advertisers, various media, private collections, and other museums. Founded in 1986, with a mission of preserving, interpreting, and exhibiting U.S. advertising from all media, the museum focuses on award-winning creative work. The main facility, including a library and archive, is located in Portland, Oregon; however, the museum also has a national outreach program that lends videos and sponsors traveling exhibits. The archive contains print ads and radio and TV spots; it includes materials dating from 1700 to the present. Highlights of the museum include a 15-foot neon Greyhound sign, a 20-foot tall Jantzen swimwear diving girl, a 6-foot-tall Bob's Big Boy statue, and an original set of the Claymation California Raisins.

Museum of Broadcast Communications, Chicago, Illinois

The Museum of Broadcast Communications (MBC) opened in 1987. In addition to general television and radio exhibits, it maintains the A.C. Nielsen, Jr., Research Center and Archives, and the G.D. Crain, Jr., Advertising Center. The archives contain more than 13,000 historic television commercials, including such popular ads as the "Mikey" spot for Life cereal. The advertising center features the One-Minute Miracle exhibit, which describes the influence of commercials, and the Four Steps exhibit, which shows how a commercial is created. Two small theaters present Mobius winners and other award-winning television spots from around the world.

Museum of Television and Radio, New York City and Beverley Hills, California

The Museum of Television and Radio opened in New York City in 1991; in March 1996 the museum opened in Beverly Hills with facilities similar to those in New York. In addition to radio and television scripts and tapes, the collection contains more than 10,000 commercials from the 1920s to the present. The facilities of the museum include 96 television and radio consoles, four screening theaters, a radio listening room, a radio broadcast studio, and satellite up and down links. Of special interest is the video production *The Super Bowl: Super Showcase for Commercials,* which features more than 50 Super Bowl television advertising spots and is narrated by Joe Namath.

Strong Museum, Rochester, New York

The Strong Museum contains a collection of advertising materials representing U.S. advertising from 1840 to the present. The collection of more than 50,000 objects includes trade cards, handbills, posters, labels, business cards, and display pieces. The archive functions as a reference collection for individual campaigns and as a resource for assessing broad social and cultural trends that relate to advertising.

Museum of Beverage Containers and Advertising, Millersville, Tennessee

This museum's collection includes more than 36,000 items. Displays are also available at the museum Web site.

American Museum of the Moving Image, Astoria, New York

The collection is primarily devoted to materials related to television and motion pictures, including film posters and advertising memorabilia related to those media.

GreatAbiliTOYS! Museum of Advertising Icons, Coral Gables, Florida

This collection features more than 700 advertising icons dating back to 1939. The museum features trademark figures used in advertising and promotions for consumer goods, including Mr. Bubble, Charlie Tuna, Speedy Alka-Seltzer, and Tony the Tiger.

World of Coca-Cola, Atlanta, Georgia

The history of the Coca-Cola Company from the beginning of the corporation in 1886 to the present is presented through hundreds of artifacts, exhibits, and videos. More than 1,000 pieces of marketing and advertising memorabilia are exhibited at the World of Coca-Cola. In addition to a collection of bottles used around the world, specific advertisements and coupons are also on display.

Musée de la Publicité, Paris, France

The collection, established in 1978, contains 40,000 French and other posters dating from the mid-18th century to 1949. Additionally, more than 45,0000 contemporary posters have been donated by advertising agencies, advertisers, and graphic designers. The collection also contains contemporary advertisements and publicity films. The museum's information center was created in 1980 and deals primarily with the history, creation, and techniques of posters. The center holds examples of the works as well as monographs on advertising artists, advertising agencies, printers, and publishers.

Archives

John W. Hartman Center for Sales, Advertising, and Marketing History, Duke University, Durham, North Carolina

The John W. Hartman Center for Sales, Advertising, and Marketing History was created in 1992 as a part of the Duke University Special Collections Library. It is the home of the corporate archives of D'Arcy Masius Benton & Bowles and the J. Walter Thompson Company. The center also holds the archives of the Outdoor Advertising Association of America and the Mobius Advertising Awards Collection (10,000 television and radio commercials from the 1980s through the early 1990s).

J. Walter Thompson Collection, Duke University, Durham, North Carolina

The most complete and informative corporate record of the advertising industry, this collection contains more than 1 million advertising documents covering the period from 1875 to the 1990s. The collection includes Thompson advertisement tear sheets and proofs (arranged by client) from 1875 to the 1990s, advertisement tear sheets from competitor agencies from 1916 to the 1990s, personnel files, company publications, notes from staff meetings and memoranda, and the minutes from board meetings. Access to JWT Archives is through the Hartman Center.

Wisconsin Center for Film and Theater Research, Madison, Wisconsin

The Wisconsin Historical Society, located on the campus of the University of Wisconsin in Madison, was founded in 1846 and is home to the Wisconsin Center for Film and Theater Research. The center maintains more than 300 manuscripts, in addition to paper records, motion pictures, television shows, still photographs, promotional graphics, and several thousand sound recordings. Publicity materials housed at the center include photographs, posters, press books, playbills, clippings, scrapbooks,

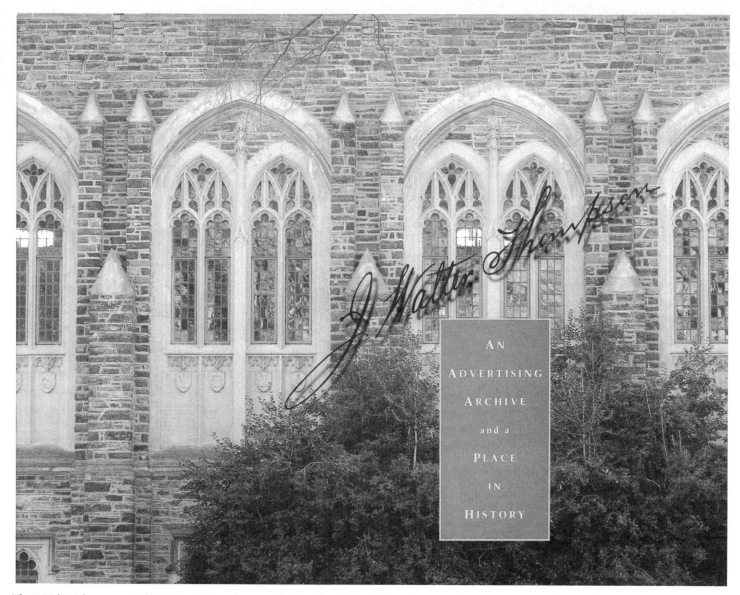

The J. Walter Thompson Archive is the largest of many collections housed at Duke University's John W. Hartman Center for Sales, Advertising, and Marketing History.
Les Todd/Duke University Photography.

graphics, and ephemera. Promotional stills and graphics from more than 40,000 domestic and foreign motion pictures titles from the 1890s to the present are contained at the center.

Television News Archive, Nashville, Tennessee

Since 1968 the Television News Archive has recorded, indexed, and preserved network television newscasts; it is the world's most accessible, extensive, and complete archive of television news. Television commercials that ran during the evening news broadcasts from 1968 to the present are catalogued and identified by product. News stories in which advertising itself was the subject (e.g., stories about political advertisements or Super Bowl ads) are also cataloged. The archive's Web site includes a searchable database.

D'Arcy Collection of the Communications Library, Urbana, Illinois

This collection comprises nearly 2 million original advertisements published between 1890 and 1970. Donated by the D'Arcy-Mac-Manus & Masius agency (which later became D'Arcy Masius Benton & Bowles) in 1983, the collection contains advertisements that appeared in newspapers, magazines, and trade journals as well as brochures, signs, and programs. Included in the collection are ads for consumer products, as well as ads from public service organizations and governmental bodies (e.g., American Red Cross, NATO, and New York City's Lincoln Center). An index of the advertisements in the Communications Library can be found on the library's Web site.

Smithsonian Institution, Washington, D.C.

The National Museum of American History Archive Center contains two important advertising archives: the Warsaw Collection of Business Americana and the N.W. Ayer Collection. The former holds materials dating back to the 18th century and includes 2 million items related to business advertising, such as trade cards, posters, and correspondence. In-depth studies of modern ad campaigns such as those created for Pepsi-Cola, Marlboro, Alka-Seltzer, Federal Express, Campbell's soup, and Nike are also included in the collection. The N.W. Ayer Collection includes more than 600,000 proof sheets from campaigns the Ayer agency created between 1889 and the 1970s.

Henry Ford Museum and Greenfield Village, Dearborn, Michigan

The collection contains Ford Motor Company records regarding public relations and advertising, as well as the personal papers of many individuals associated with Henry Ford or the Ford Company. Nearly 400,000 photographs and 400 oral histories are included in the collection. An index and examples of Ford advertising are available on the Web site.

Butterick Archives, New York City

Holdings include records of advertising and marketing related to fashions in the apparel and home sewing industries. The archive contains more than 600 linear feet of patterns, books, and advertisements.

History of Advertising Trust Archive, Raveningham, England

The History of Advertising Trust Archive (HAT Archive) contains some 2 million items related to advertising, marketing, media, public relations, and related topics. HAT holds material ranging from the archive of R.F. White, the United Kingdom's first ad agency (ca. 1800), to the latest television commercials.

American Association of Advertising Agencies (AAAA), New York City

The AAAA, or "Four A's," holds a vast clip file on all present members. It also has a collection of clippings on past members no longer in business.

Internet-based Sources

Radio Advertising Archive <http://www.rab.co.uk>

Since 1994 this on-line collection has contained award-winning radio advertising from the United Kingdom, the United States, South Africa, Australia, and New Zealand.

University of Texas Out-of-Home Archive <http:// advertising.utexas.edu/research/gannettarchive/outdoor. html>

This on-line database of outdoor advertising from 1992 to 1995 was compiled by preeminent outdoor advertiser Gannett Outdoor Advertising and the Advertising Department at the University of Texas at Austin. It serves as a resource for students, faculty, and other interested parties. Advertisements featured in the database include those for Bacardi rum, BMW automobiles, and clothing from The Gap and Levi Strauss & Company.

Ad*Access <http://scriptorium.lib.duke.edu/adaccess>

This database contains more than 7,000 advertisements printed in U.S. and Canadian newspapers and magazines during the first half of the 20th century. The collection is divided into five categories: beauty and hygiene, radio, television, transportation, and World War II. The images in Ad*Access are part of the "Competitive Advertisements Collection" of the J. Walter Thompson Company Archives and are sorted by product type.

The Emergence of Advertising in America, 1850–1920 <http://scriptorium.lib.duke.edu/eaa/>

This digital library was funded in part by the Library of Congress and Ameritech and consists of 8,500 images relating to the history of advertising. Included in this collection are Eastman Kodak ads, posters and insert cards for tobacco products, and advertisements for bicycles, patent medicines, and food.

Ad Council <http://www.adcouncil.org>

Historical public service advertising campaigns produced by the Ad Council are available from the organization's Web site. Materials include posters from World War II, as well as campaigns for forest fire prevention, antipollution initiatives, crime prevention, and drunk driving prevention.

NANCY ENGELHARDT

Addresses: Museums

American Advertising Museum
5035 SE 24th Ave.
Portland, Oregon 97202
U.S.A.
503-226-0000
<http://www.admuseum.org>

American Museum of the Moving Image
35 Avenue at 36 Street
Astoria, New York 11106
U.S.A.
718-784-4520
<http://www.ammi.org>

CreatAbiliTOYS! Museum of Advertising Icons
1550 Madruga Ave., Suite 504
Coral Gables, Florida 33146
U.S.A.
305-663-7374
<http://www.toymuseum.com>

Musée de la Publicité
Palais de Louvre
107 rue de Rivoli
75001 Paris
France
33-1-44-55-57-50
<http://www.ucad.fr/pub>

Museum of Beverage Containers and Advertising
1055 Ridgecrest Drive
Millersville, Tennessee 37072
U.S.A.
800-826-4929
<http://www.gono.com/vir-mus>

Museum of Broadcast Communications
Chicago Cultural Center
Michigan Avenue at Washington Street
Chicago, Illinois 60602
U.S.A.
312-629-6000
<http://www.mbcnet.org>

Museum of Television and Radio
25 W. 52nd Street
New York, New York 10019
U.S.A.
212-621-6600
and
Museum of Television and Radio
465 North Beverly Drive
Beverly Hills, California 90210
U.S.A.
310-786-1000

Strong Museum
One Manhattan Square
Rochester, New York 14607
U.S.A.
716-263-2700
<http://www.strongmuseum.org>

World of Coca-Cola
55 Martin Luther King Drive
Atlanta, Georgia
U.S.A.
404-676-5151
<http://www.coca-cola.com>

Addresses: Archives

American Association of Advertising Agencies (AAAA)
405 Lexington Avenue, 18th Floor
New York, New York 10174
U.S.A.
212-682-2500
<http://www.aaaa.org>

Butterick Archives
161 Avenue of Americas
New York, New York 10013
U.S.A.
212-620-2790

D'Arcy Collection of the Communications Library
University of Illinois at Urbana-Champaign
810 S. Wright Street
Urbana, Illinois 61801
U.S.A.
217-333-2216
<http://www.uiuc.edu/providers/comm/DArcy>

Henry Ford Museum and Greenfield Village
Ford Archives
20900 Oakwood Boulevard
Dearborn, Michigan 48124
U.S.A.
313-271-1620
<http://www.hfmgv.org>

History of Advertising Trust Archive
HAT House
12 Raveningham Centre
Raveningham Norwich NR14 6NU
England
44 (0) 1508-548623
<http://www.lib.uea.ac.uk/hatwelc/welcome.htm>

J. Walter Thompson Company Archive
John W. Hartman Center for Sales, Advertising, and Marketing
    History (address below)
<http://scriptorium.lib.duke.edu/hartman/jwt/archives.html>

John W. Hartman Center for Sales, Advertising, and Marketing
    History
Duke University
Box 90185
Durham, North Carolina 27708-0185
U.S.A.
919-660-5827
<http://scriptorium.lib.duke.edu/Hartman>

Smithsonian Institution
National Museum of American History

Archive Center
12th and Constitution Avenue, N.W.
Washington, D.C. 20560
U.S.A.
202-357-3270
<http://www.sil.si.edu>

Television News Archive
Vanderbilt University
110 21st Avenue South, Suite 704
Nashville, Tennessee 37203
U.S.A.
615-322-2927
<http://tvnews.vanderbilt.edu/>

Wisconsin Center for Film and Theater Research
816 State Street
Madison, Wisconsin 53706
U.S.A.
608-264-6466
<www.shsw.wisc.edu/wcftr>

Further Reading

Applegate, Edd, *Personalities and Products: A Historical Perspective on Advertising in America,* Westport, Connecticut: Greenwood Press, 1998

Dotz, Warren, Jim Morton, and John William Lund, *What a Character! 20th-Century American Advertising Icons,* San Francisco: Chronicle Books, 1996

Guide to Manuscript Collections in the National Museum of History and Technology, Washington, D.C.: Smithsonian Institution Press, 1978

Lears, T.J. Jackson, *Fables of Abundance: A Cultural History of Advertising in America,* New York: Basic Books, 1994

Morgan, Hal, *Symbols of America,* New York: Viking, 1986

Presbrey, Frank, *The History and Development of Advertising— With More Than Three Hundred and Fifty Illustrations,* New York: Doubleday, 1929; reprint, New York: Greenwood Press, 1968

Sivulka, Juliann, *Soap, Sex, and Cigarettes: A Cultural History of American Advertising,* Belmont, California: Wadsworth, 1998

Watkins, Julian Lewis, *The 100 Greatest Advertisements: Who Wrote Them and What They Did,* New York: Moore, 1949; 2nd revised edition, New York: Dover, 1959

Music and Jingles

From the earliest days of advertising, music and song have been used to promote goods and services. In the United States, vocal advertising messages can be traced as far back as the era of the Yankee peddlers.

One of the earliest American musical commercials, dating from 1830, was written not by a member of the advertising profession but by a Midwest land developer. It urged pioneer families to settle in Illinois, and like much of the later, more sophisticated advertising, it promised consumers a clear benefit:

Move your family westward,
Bring all your girls and boys,
And rise to wealth and honor
In the state of Illinois.

Another early jingle promoted Lydia Pinkham's Vegetable Compound, a medicinal product (which, like other remedies of its kind, was largely alcohol) for female complaints:

Sing, oh, sing of Lydia Pinkham and her love for the
    human race,
How she makes her vegetable compound and the papers
    they publish her face.

Widow Brown, she had no children though she loved them
    very dear.
So she took some vegetable compound and she has them
    twice a year.

Some songs that praised products were not written specifically for advertising purposes but rather were popular tunes that referred to brands or products in their lyrics. One still-remembered example is the 1905 Gus Edwards-Vincent Bryan song, "In My Merry Oldsmobile." Another early example was this 1915 song that linked romance and beer:

Come, come, come and make eyes with me under the
    Anheuser Busch.
Come, come, come drink some Budweiser with me under
    the Anheuser Busch.
Hear the Old German Band! *Ach du lieber Augustin*
Let me hold your hand, do, do, do.
Come and have a stein or two under the Anheuser Busch.

As early as 1930 vaudeville singer Harry Frankel opened and closed his radio program with the theme song "Singing Sam, the Barbasol Man":

Barbasol, Barbasol, No brush, no lather, no rub-in.
Just wet your whiskers and begin.
Barbasol, Barbasol, get it, try it, buy it, use it—Barbasol.

The 1961 version remained close to the original lyrics:

Barbasol, Barbasol,
No brush, no lather, no rub-in.
Wet your razor then begin,
Barbasol, Barbasol,
Soothing, smoothing, cooling Barbasol.

The original Barbasol jingle prompted objections from Burma-Shave—which, since the mid-1920s, had been employing roadside rhymes and radio jingles—claiming it was too similar to two of its own verses:

Shave the modern way
No brush
No lather
No rub-in
Big tube 35 cents drug stores
Burma-Shave

and

Shaving brush
All wet
And hairy,
I've passed you up
For sanitary
Burma-Shave.

Leonard Odell, president of Burma-Vita Company (now a division of Philip Morris Companies, Inc.) was not overly concerned about the similarity, however, because he had a virtually never-ending supply of fresh verses. Every year, beginning in the mid-1920s, Burma-Shave held a national competition seeking new jingle ideas from the general public, paying $100 for each verse accepted. The verses appeared on a series of five roadside signs, each bearing a line of the jingle, spaced several yards apart to pique viewer curiosity and build interest (a final, sixth sign always read, "Burma Shave"). Some of the more memorable boy-girl jingles were:

Said Juliet,
To Romeo,
If you
Won't shave,
Go homeo

and

To get
Away from

Hairy apes
Ladies jump
From fire escapes.

The roadside rhymes translated easily to radio and then to television, quoted by celebrities who mentioned them during their programs, including *Amos 'n' Andy*, Jimmy Durante, and Bob Hope. The Burma-Shave campaign became part of the culture. Commenting on a writer's lack of literary talent, the popular radio character Fibber McGee (of *Fibber McGee and Molly*) once scoffed, "I've read better poetry than that on Burma-Shave signs with the last two posts missing." In 1941 Bob Hope featured a 15-minute skit about the ads in one of his radio shows, and Fred Allen created a skit called "The Murder of the Burma-Shave Poet" for the *Texaco Hour*.

Early Days of the Singing Commercial

The full-fledged singing commercial has been traced to shortly before World War II when disc jockeys aired customized musical commercials between records. Some historians claim that the first singing commercial—a ditty promoting Interwoven socks, sung by the Happiness Boys (Billy Jones and Ernie Hare)—was broadcast on WEAF in New York City in 1923, but radio was so localized at that time that it is impossible to verify this assertion. Many early commercials were based on popular folk songs; an example is the Camel jingle sung to the tune of "Eatin' Goober Peas":

Rich, rich, mild, mild, Camel cigarettes.
Rich, rich, rich with flavor, Camel cigarettes.

Likewise, an early Pabst Blue Ribbon beer jingle was sung to the tune of "Ten Little Indians":

What'll you have? Pabst Blue Ribbon.
What'll you have? Pabst Blue Ribbon.
What'll you have? Pabst Blue Ribbon.
Pabst Blue Ribbon beer.

Just as the Camel jingle emphasized product benefits, so did the 1937 Wheaties commercial, one of the longest-running jingles on record (31 years). It was not based on a folk tune; instead, the announcer loudly intoned, "Jack Armstrong, the All-American boy," while a live, on-air male quartet sang:

Have you tried Wheaties? They're whole wheat with all of
   the bran.
So just try Wheaties. For wheat is the best food of man.
They're crispy, they're crunchy the whole year through.
Jack Armstrong never tires of Wheaties and never will you.

Another enduring jingle was the one for Robert Hall, which ran for some 30 years prior to the demise of the 367-unit national retail chain in 1977. The Robert Hall jingle was created by Jack

Pepsi wrote itself into advertising history in 1939 with this early jingle.
Pepsi-Cola Company.

Wilcher and Frank Sawdon in just 15 minutes. Sawdon, owner of the ad agency that had the account, and Wilcher, the agency's creative director, joined forces. Sawdon wrote the first two lines of the memorable jingle:

When the values go up, up, up,
And the prices go down, down, down.

Wilcher then added music and more lyrics. Over its history the music of the jingle was arranged for all kinds of musical genres, from choral to folk song to rock 'n' roll to soul. Artists who performed it included Pearl Bailey, Les Paul and Mary Ford, and Arthur Fiedler and the Boston Pops. Wilcher also created Chiclets and Dentyne gum commercials and a popular jingle for Adam Hats that ran for 25 years.

Perhaps the most famous early jingle campaign was that of Pepsi-Cola Company. In 1939 the company was looking for a major ad agency. Among the contenders was the eminent Lord & Thomas (L&T) agency. In preparing its presentation, L&T commissioned two songwriters, Alan Kent and Austin Croom Johnson, to develop a musical theme that could be used on radio. In March 1938 Johnson had adapted and arranged a swing version of an old English folk ballad called "Do Ye Ken John Peel," which was recorded for Decca Records by Bob Crosby and his orchestra. In July 1939 Johnson turned to this melody once again, and he and Kent created the words that would soon become famous:

Pepsi-Cola hits the spot,
Two full glasses, that's a lot.

Twice as much for a nickel too.
Pepsi-Cola is the drink for you.

When Walter Mack, president of Pepsi, heard the jingle during the L&T presentation, he was excited by its potential, but his conviction that a client should always know more about advertising than its agency prompted Mack to pass over L&T in favor of Newell-Emmett Company, Inc. (which later became Cunningham & Walsh), a shop he felt he could control more easily. According to a 1955 account in *Advertising Age*, however, he kept the jingle L&T had commissioned, told Newell-Emmett to "clear away the spinach" (meaning the 45 seconds of announcer copy that went with it) and run it on as many local stations as possible in 15-second time slots, where brevity would buy frequency. It broke in September 1939 on WOR, New York City, between news bulletins of Hitler's invasion of Poland. Soon everybody was humming it. Mack imagined the jingle on jukeboxes as well as radios, so band leader and trumpet virtuoso Bunny Berigan was brought in to record a full big-band version with the Pepsi lyrics sung by Fredda Gibson, who would become famous in the 1950s as pop singer Georgia Gibbs. Among other stars hired to do the Pepsi jingle was Billie Holiday.

By the time television arrived, the singing commercial, or jingle, was about to become extinct. The television medium revived it, however, and gave it a new voice. As early as 1957 composers had begun to complain that the use of their music for jingles diminished their reputations. In the spring of 1957 Roy Gilbert, who had written "You Belong to My Heart" and the 1948 Academy Award–winning song "Zip-a-de-doo-dah" and other hits, sued Hills Bros. Coffee, Inc., the advertising agency N.W. Ayer &

Son, the music publisher George Simon, Inc., and others. He claimed he had been "irreparably and irrevocably harmed" with "future performance revenues impaired" by the use of the "Muskrat Ramble" (to which he had contributed the lyrics), without his consent, in radio and TV commercials. The application of his music to an advertising message, he claimed, damaged his reputation as a musician/songwriter by "reducing him in the eyes of the music profession and public to the level of a jingle writer."

Raiding the Top 40

The Beatles were equally irate over the commercial use of their early hits, including "Revolution" (used by Nike in 1987), "Day Tripper" (Volkswagen Beetle, 1998), and "Getting Better" (Philips TV, 2000). They were powerless to prevent advertisers from co-opting their music, however, because the singer Michael Jackson, with Sony Music, owned the rights to the songs. Despite rejecting a $5 million offer from Volkswagen to celebrate a special edition of a new model—the White Beetle—and mark the 30th anniversary of the Beatles's "White Album," the surviving members of the group could not prevent the use of "Day Tripper." Paul McCartney charged that Jackson was cheapening Beatles songs, but Jackson was adamant. Although Volkswagen went forward, it risked the ire of fans. "It could backfire," said Bill Heckle of Cavern City Tours in Liverpool, England. "Fans will regard it as distasteful, and if they know the band isn't happy, it could well have an adverse effect."

Another composer who rejected all commercial use requests was Irving Berlin, who controlled most of his work through Irving Berlin Music, Inc. Only after his death at 102 in 1990 did his estate relent in selected cases.

Even the reuse of an old jingle, as opposed to an old song, can backfire, as did the 1998 Isuzu spot, which featured a 1970 Slinky jingle, along with retro images of people with dated hairdos and clothing. The spot was pulled in response to consumer complaints.

Not all artists refuse commercial offers. In fact, some willingly sell the rights to their music, as the Rolling Stones did in 1995 when they accepted $8 million from Microsoft for the rights to "Start It Up." Other artists who have licensed their hit songs have included the Beach Boys, who sold the rights to their 1960s hit "California Girls" to Clairol for its Herbal Essence shampoo in 1976, and Carly Simon, whose "Anticipation" became part of a long-running campaign for Heinz ketchup.

There is always a risk when an advertiser rewrites the lyrics to someone's favorite tune. In the spring of 1999, when Nortel Networks borrowed the Beatles's song "Come Together," delivering it spoken rather than sung during an ad showing a teleconference, one line was changed because of unresolved trademark issues. Easily detectable by any Beatles fan, the change could have offended some and may have had an adverse effect on the impact of the message. At the close of the music the catchphrase "How the world shares ideas" appears. The campaign concept, created by Nortel Networks and Temerlin McClain of Irving, Texas, was designed to link the Nortel name with the promise of global communication. Although it may have successfully targeted baby boomers through the Beatles' music, it is not clear that it successfully translated into sales. More successful was the 1999 campaign by Mercedes-Benz using Janis Joplin's late 1960s song about the car (including the lyrics, "Lord, won't you buy me a Mercedes-Benz? / My friends all drive Porsches, I must make amends.").

In the mid-1980s Lincoln-Mercury turned to 1960s hits such as Marvin Gaye's "Ain't No Mountain High Enough" and the Beatles's "Help!" to target an audience ten years younger than its current one: 35-year-olds rather than 45-year-olds. The music was accompanied by images of grown-up baby boomers driving modern Lincoln-Mercury cars, an attempt to link viewers to memories of their adolescence. The result was an increase in market share from 5.5 percent to 6.5 percent. Gaye's 1968 hit "I Heard It through the Grapevine," reintroduced in 1986 by the California Raisin Advisory Board and paired with hip clay-animation raisins, resulted in a notable increase in sales, which had hitherto been flat.

The list of pop tunes that have been used as jingles is a long one, with hit songs touting everything from cars in Nissan's 1996 commercial (by TBWA Chiat/Day) set to Van Halen's "You Really Got Me" to soft drinks with Coca-Cola's 1999 use of the Platters's 1950s classic "Only You." An especially effective use of retro music was Nike's 1999 spot (by Wieden & Kennedy) with Joe Cocker's 1970s hit "You Are So Beautiful" as the musical backdrop for painful images of athletic injuries. The visuals, featuring Olympic skier Picabo Street's surgically scarred knee, a marathon runner's battered feet, and a rodeo cowboy's kicked and blinded eye, served as a tribute to the pain and commitment of true athletic grit. A brief list (see Table 1) of old hits in commercials from 1990 to 2000 exemplifies the persuasive power of music to create a mood, connect to a product, and target an existing or new market.

This is nothing new. In 1954 WNEW aired commercials in which the song lyrics were reworked to mention General Motors ("Sunny Side of the Street") and Ronson lighters ("Milwaukee Polka" sung by Patti Page), among others. One particular song, "Me Gotta Have You," recorded by 1950s pop singer Julius LaRosa, mentioned so many names (Burma Shave, Adler shoes, Toni home permanents, Halo shampoo, Swift bologna, and Smith Bros. cough drops), however, that it offended WNEW owner-manager Richard D. Buckley, who decided to ban such songs from his station.

Ironically, some jingles became hit songs. Among the more recognizable ones are Chock Full O' Nuts' "Heavenly Feeling," "Chevrolet Mambo," "A Western Jingle for Nescafe" (recorded by Bernie Knee), Rainier Brewing Company's "Rainier Waltz," the "Mission Bell" wine song, and the classic "Chiquita Banana" song. This trend, in fact, has continued over the decades. Several mid-1960s jingles that became instant hits included Alka-Seltzer's humorous "No Matter What Shape Your Stomach's In," Pepsi-Cola's "Music to Watch Girls By," and "I'd Like to Teach the World to Sing."

Table 1.   Songs in Commercials, 1990–2000.

Year	Advertiser	Music—Artist (Year recorded)
2000	Gap, Inc.	"America" from "West Side Story"—Leonard Bernstein (1961)
		"Jump, Jive an' Wail"—Louis Prima (1956)
	Pert	"One (Is the Loneliest Number)"—Harry Nilsson (1968)
	Ramada	"What a Day for a Daydream"—Lovin' Spoonful (ca. 1966)
	Hyundai Sonata	"I Wanna Be Free"—Monkees (1966)
	Wisk	"Mr. Lonely"—Bobby Vinton (1963)
	Prestone	"Hit Me with Your Best Shot"—Pat Benatar (1980)
	Old Navy	"Can You Dig It?"—Monkees (1968)
	Baby Magic	"This Magic Moment"—The Drifters (1960)
1999	Mirage Resorts Bellagio Casino	"Con Te Partiró"—Andrea Bocelli (1999)
	Nike	"You Are So Beautiful"—Joe Cocker (1970)
1997	Nabisco/Chips Ahoy	"Sing, Sing, Sing"—Benny Goodman (1937)
1996	AT&T	"Georgia on My Mind"—Ray Charles (1960)
	Toyota	"Hot, Hot, Hot"—Buster Poindexter (1988)
1995	Chevrolet	"Like a Rock"—Bob Seger (1986)
1990	Earthlink	"Unchained Melody"—Righteous Brothers (1965)
	United Air Lines	"Rhapsody in Blue"—Paul Whiteman Orchestra (1924)

Your Hit Parade of Jingles

Some artists seem to have a natural ability to create jingles that become hits. Roger Nichols has written catchy tunes that became instant favorites (some examples are cited below). "We've Only Just Begun," with lyrics by Paul Williams, was originally commissioned in 1969 by the ad agency Batten Barton Durstine & Osborn for its San Francisco, California, client Crocker National Bank. A year later the song topped the charts when recorded by the Carpenters. The same thing happened to the 1971 Coca-Cola jingle "I'd Like to Teach the World to Sing." Unlike most jingle writers who sell their music for a flat fee, Nichols, along with Williams and A&M Records (owned by trumpeter/bandleader Herb Alpert) held the publishing and recording rights, while Crocker Bank retained the advertising rights, allowing it to reuse the jingle in future campaigns.

For the J. Walter Thompson Company's Kodak account, Nichols wrote "Times of Your Life" (lyrics by Bill Lane) for a TV spot featuring singer Paul Anka, with ground-breaking two-minute radio spots sung by Peggy Lee, Barry Manilow, Anne Murray, and other artists. It was so successful that Anka recorded it for national distribution and it became a top-ten song, greatly increasing Kodak's exposure at no additional cost to the company.

Nichols's songs have crossed the boundary between art and commerce in the other direction as well. In a 1976 ABC-TV fall promotion his lyrics to "Let Me Be the One" (first sung by the Carpenters) were adapted to produce "Let Us Be the One." Some of Nichols's other well-known hits of the time included: "I Won't Last a Day without You" and "Rainy Days and Mondays" (again a collaboration with Paul Williams). Another prolific jingle/songwriter was Barry Manilow, whose unforgettable jingle hits have included "You Deserve a Break Today" (McDonald's), "We're the Pepsi People Feelin' Free" (Pepsi-Cola), "Most Original Soft Drink" (Dr Pepper), "Get a Bucket of Chicken" (Kentucky Fried Chicken) and "Like a Good Neighbor, State Farm Is There" (State Farm Insurance).

Decades before Manilow and Nichols began writing pop tunes and jingle hits, another talented musician, Raymond Scott, had paved the way. Scott penned the original Lucky Strike jingle, "Be Happy, Go Lucky," while he was head of the Jingle Workshop. No stranger to commercial success, he had earlier composed the title song for the popular 1950s TV show *Your Hit Parade*.

Besides having been targeted through music, audiences have also been approached through language. In the mid-1950s Roy Eaton, a multilingual novice copywriter and classically trained musician, easily created jingles using commonly known foreign phrases to make the products sound more authentic. His Chef Boy-Ar-Dee pizza jingle was written to the classic Italian tune "La Tarantella":

> *Oh! che pizza molte bene,* What a tasty pizza pie.
> Boy-Ar-Dee's the chef that treats you
> To that real Italian style.
> Boy-Ar-Dee Italian pizza pie by Chef Boy-Ar-Dee . . . Chef
>   Boy-Ar-Dee . . .
> Chef Boy-Ar-Dee.

His Kent cigarette song was such a hit that Eaton and his wife later rewrote the lyrics and Aladdin Records released the tune. The original jingle lyrics were:

> Smoke Kent . . . Smoke Kent . . . Smoke Kent with the
>   Micronite filter.

It is the mild, mild cigarette. It's got the freshest, cleanest taste yet,
It is the mild Kent cigarette. Smoke Kent with the Micronite filter.

The first Chiquita Banana jingle (1944) represents an even earlier attempt to infuse an exotic element into the American commercial jingle. Written by Len MacKenzie (music) and Garth Montgomery (lyrics) in what the sheet music described as a "calypso rhythm," it was an integral part of a campaign to teach consumers how to properly store and ripen bananas:

I'm Chiquita Banana, and I've come to say
Bananas have to ripen in a certain way.
When they are fleck'd with brown and have a golden hue,
Bananas taste the best, and are the best for you.
You can put them in a salad.
You can put them in a pie—aye.
Any way you want to eat them
It's impossible to beat them.
But bananas like the climate of the very, very tropical equator.
So you should never put bananas
In the refrigerator.
No, no, no, no!

Over the years the jingle appeared in several different versions. In 1997, for example, the company sponsored a competition for health-conscious lyrics. The winning entry came from a California schoolteacher. Yet another version was introduced in 1999 as part of a new TV campaign for the company's 100th anniversary. It, too, emphasized health benefits:

I'm Chiquita Banana, and I've come to say
I offer good nutrition in a simple way.
When you eat a Chiquita you've done your part
To give every single day a healthy start.
Underneath the crescent yellow
You'll find vitamins and great taste.
With no fat, you just can't beat them.
You'll feel better when you eat 'em. . . .

Finding Value in Oldies

To reach a specific age group, many advertisers in the 1990s seized upon classic rock hits, such as Sunkist's use of the Beach Boys' "Good Vibrations," Nike's use of the Beatles's "Revolution," and Chevrolet's adaptation of Bob Seger's "Like a Rock." Other advertisers that have tried this approach include Mercedes-Benz ("What the World Needs Now" and Joplin's "Mercedes-Benz"), Nissan ("You Really Got Me"), Dr Pepper ("Son of a Preacher Man"), Burger King ("Get Ready," "Urgent," "Ain't Nothin' Like the Real Thing," "Good Morning Sunshine"), Ford ("I Can't Explain"), and AT&T ("Rocket Man" and "Girls Just Wanna Have Fun").

Other advertisers have reached back even further in time, sometimes choosing music that predates the target audience rather than tunes that evoke their youth. To reach baby boomers, some advertisers have chosen performers (such as Robert Goulet for ESPN and Mercedes-Benz, and Mel Torme for Mountain Dew) whose careers peaked as the boomers were reaching puberty. In so doing, these advertisers run the risk of appearing dated. Their hope, however, is to evoke nostalgia for the era before computers, downsizing, 60-hour workweeks, and widespread job insecurity. People, they imagine, are looking to a time when life was simpler and more enjoyable. Advertisers are discovering that familiar images such as Elsie the cow on milk cartons and the reappearance on restaurant menus of pot roast and mashed potatoes evoke the 1950s and 1960s, a time for which many adults at the end of the 20th century felt a nostalgic longing.

In the 1990s Converse sought to target a young market by reviving the 1970s, using Peter Max artwork and Stevie Wonder's "Higher Ground." but The Red Hot Chili Peppers had reintroduced that music in the late 1980s, so it was still familiar to the audience. On the other hand, Wide Leg took a gamble when it used David Cassidy singing "I Think I Love You." Young people found it funny and were amused by the novelty of it; it caught their attention because it stood out.

One advertiser has managed to use retro music successfully to reach a most unlikely audience: 75 million teenagers. Gap, Inc., has been able to appeal to this traditionally hard-to-reach group by depicting "cool" people their age wearing Gap clothes and dancing to music of vastly different genres—swing, go-go, and country. Moving to Madonna's mid-1980s song "Dress You Up," they wore Gap vests, not three-piece-business suits. Teenagers across America sported Gap vests as a direct result of the spot.

Other advertisers have ventured outside the venue of hit songs to woo the youth market. The Jack in the Box fast-food chain assembled its own teen band, dubbed the Meaty Cheese Boys, to mimic teen idols such as 'N Sync and Back Street Boys. Reaching out to the teeny bopper audience, the burger band sings lyrics such as:

Girl you know there's one thing that I love.
It's not you I'm thinkin' of.
I want the ultimate cheeseburger.
Cheese meat. Cheese, cheese meat. And that's it.
Baby you know it's hot and juicy
'Cause Jack won't make it till you order it.

Writer/director Dick Sittig of Jack in the Box's in-house Santa Monica, California, agency, Kowloon Wholesale Seafood Company, focused on reaching Jack in the Box's core audience: 16-year-old boys. The idea worked with remarkable success: 18 consecutive quarters of per-store sales increases. The imitation music video produced real results.

The use of obscure songs and little-known groups started in the mid-1990s, the idea being to sound fresh and original. In 1996 Mitsubishi Motors commissioned Republica, a British pop band with modest sales but excellent reviews, to promote vehicles with

This 1946 advertisement featured the music for Chiquita's popular jingle.
Courtesy Chiquita Brands International, Inc.

the song "Ready to Go." Then in 1998, Gap, Inc., turned to the barely known American duo Crystal Method for its futuristic, electronic sound and its song "Busy Child." A rock music radio station in Chicago, Illinois, received so many calls it finally placed the song on its playlist, proving that positive public reaction can greatly affect the future of any song or group, known or unknown. In 1998 when Gap featured khaki-clad models jitter-bugging to 1950s trumpeter/bandleader Louis Prima's "Jump, Jive an' Wail," record sales of a group that had recently covered the song (the Brian Setzer Orchestra) increased dramatically. Like-wise, when Mirage Resorts' Bellagio Casino adopted Andrea Bocelli's version of "Con Te Partiró" by Quarrantotta, record sales doubled and tripled in some areas.

Some musical groups have been launched on the strength of the advertising exposure of the their music. In 1998 Nike's "Bitter Sweet Symphony" spot played during the Super Bowl, giving glo-bal recognition to the unknown group The Verve. When Swatch adopted the song "Breathe" by British singer Midge Ure, his sales soared. The same reaction took place when Volkswagen intro-duced the Da Da Da Trio, a dormant German band, unheard of for a decade, resulting in more than 50,000 album sales.

Even early commercial music writers recognized the impor-tance of what some call "stopability"—the ability of the jingle to completely arrest viewers' and listeners' attention. Irv Olian, who penned the Jay's Potato Chips jingle "I Can't Stop Eating 'Em, Can't Stop Eating 'Em, Can't Stop Eating 'Em" and Edelweiss' "What a Man Won't Do for an Edelweiss Brew," (a predecessor of the Klondike campaign, "What Would You Do for a Klondike Bar?") has said:

> I look for the "interrupting" idea, the sound, the phrase, the melody that possesses the ability to break into a per-son's train of thought and command attention. The impor-tant thing I always keep in mind is the gimmick. It must have a twist, something the kids will pick up, ape, chant, or sing. If they do that, I know we're in.

The same thought was expressed by Jaleh Bisharat, vice president of marketing for Amazon.com, about the company's catchy Christmas jingle campaign based on the "12 Days of Christmas" carol, showcasing the ease of online holiday shopping: "We don't want anyone to be turning on the TV and not be humming our tune." Using Christmas carols is not a new idea, either. In 1997 Staples chose a popular Christmas song for its back-to-school commercial, bringing back "The Most Wonderful Time of the Year."

Pepsi found stopability by using the chubby-cheeked little girl Hallie Eisenberg in its 1999 and 2000 commercials. She has been seen lip-syncing to such different celebrity voices as Joe Pesci, Aretha Franklin, Marlon Brando (as Don Corleone), and rhythm-and-blues singer Isaac Hayes (as an unknown disc jockey).

Advertisers trying to reach teens have had to steadily increase the "coolness" factor. Some have stopped using jingles and have come up with new music-based solutions. Levi's, whose sales fig-ures dropped markedly after 1986, replaced the jingle and forged

a connection with SFX, a concert producer. This association granted Levi's a unique opportunity: to reach 10 million difficult-to-catch consumers by sponsoring a "pre-show" at more than 1,000 main shows a year. Trying to reclaim its former cool image, Levi's also sponsored Grammy-winner Lauryn Hill's first world tour, Lilith Fair, and the MTV Music Video Awards. In addition, Levi's products were showcased in the MGM film "Mod Squad." This approach is a break from the traditional single-artist spon-sorship of the past. Likewise, Nabisco reached an older market by creating a promotional concert for Air Crisps. Fans responded by attending the reunion concert of the 1980s band the B-52s.

Other musical promotions include the Kellogg Company's 1998 tie-in with the American Heart Association on cereal boxes with healthy tips. It allowed consumers to send in for CDs by John Tesh, Clint Black, and Trisha Yearwood, among others, for less than $5.

Rick Lyon of Lyon Music has suggested that "audiences today are too intelligent and sophisticated [for jingles]"—they can spot a jingle and ignore it. Therefore newer jingles should just be music that does not promote or mention the product. Instead of ham-mering home product features, jingles now create impact by "bor-rowing interest" or applying the music's value to the product.

Pop music has been recognized for years as a conduit of time, an emotional trigger that transports listeners back to a specific period in their lives. It is no surprise that advertisers choose to license songs and benefit from the "hit" syndrome, which com-bines the sounds of the times, the memory of the artist, and the power of the album with the effects of other media from movies to videos. A case in point is Nissan's 1997 Altima spot with Johnny Cash singing a *Laverne & Shirley* theme song, accompa-nying himself on guitar as he strolls past the Nissan assembly line—a performer with a 50-year-long career, singing a 1970s tune from a 1950s-based TV show.

Advertisers will continue to look for unique ways to use music—both old and new—and performers and groups—both well known and as-yet-undiscovered—to sell their products. Even songs with no commercial value may allow musicians to "paint" on a new canvas, while creating a new sound for a prod-uct. In 1999 Gap, Inc., hired LL Cool J., Luscious Jackson, and other musical artists and, rather than having them perform known hits, gave them 30 seconds of unrestricted musical expres-sion. Likewise, Nike and Calvin Klein have sought out experi-mental and alternative groups such as Faust, Tortoise, and Flying Saucer Attack, capturing the specific characteristics that make them noncommercial.

Tunes such as the funky melody used in a 1999 Volkswagen Jetta commercial and those created in specialized jingle-writing shops are developed specifically for their "stopping" power. Jingle writer Mark Barasch, who has integrated the sounds of cannons and even whales to add interest to his work, has said, "In life, we get to use five senses, but in film or TV we can only use two: sight and sound. Sound is half the message in commercials."

Despite the continual search for new sounds, many advertisers have chosen to revive or modify jingles from earlier campaigns, such as Campbell's "Mm, Mm, Good" becoming "Mm, Mm, Better" and McDonald's "You Deserve a Break Today," becoming "Have You Had Your Break Today?" Two other advertisers reached back to the 1950s at the turn of the 20th century: Chock Full O' Nuts revived its "Heavenly Coffee" and Chevrolet reintroduced "See the USA in Your Chevrolet."

For years, advertisers have integrated sound effects to help their jingles get noticed. During the 1950s Rinso detergent used the whistle of a bobwhite, which matched the rhythm of its slogan ("Rinso white, Rinso bright"). Also from the 1950s: "Use Ajax (BOOM, BOOM) the foaming cleanser" and "Winston tastes good like a (CLAP, CLAP) cigarette should." Other memorable examples include the "Snap! Crackle! Pop!" of Rice Krispies (1960s); the trolley bell of "Rice-a-Roni, the San Francisco Treat" (1970s); the talking Parkay margarine container ("Butter.") from the 1980s; and from the 1990s, Little Caesars' "Pizza, Pizza" and the croaking of the Budweiser frogs.

Ownership Issues

Jingles and music for commercials are either commissioned or produced as work for hire. Music directly commissioned by an advertiser through its agency remains the property of the advertiser and can be used indefinitely and in any manner, subject to specific accommodations to the composers and/or performers that may be spelled out in special contract terms. In many cases the copyright may be jointly held in some use circumstances. In commissioning a composer of noted reputation such as Stephen Sondheim or Marvin Hamlish to write a commercial jingle, the advertiser may have to offer special concessions on copyright and royalty issues, given the composer's prestige and reputation.

In the great majority of cases, however, the music is bought from the writer on a work-for-hire basis, usually from a "music house," that is an outside supplier specializing in the writing and production of advertising music. Such companies usually maintain a staff of writers and arrangers but may subcontract to fulfill specialized needs.

In the case of widely known pre-existing music and songs, a use license must be negotiated with the copyright holder, which would be the publisher, the record company, and often, but not always, the composer or composers. Songwriters typically sell their work outright to a publisher or record company for a lump sum up front, which is considered an advance on royalties. Not until that advance has been recouped by the publisher does the composer receive additional money. Only the most successful songwriters profit from an ad license: Jule Styne, Harold Arlen, Hamlish, Bob Dylan, and so forth. In most cases the composer of a routine rock hit would not even be able to veto its use as a jingle. It would be licensed at the discretion of the publisher. The license would specify the details of the rights granted: the composition, the product, the type of use (radio, in-store, television, premium offer, etc.), synchronization rights for video and film, the territory of use (local, regional, national), the media, time period of use (often with options for renewal), specific dates in some cases, and perhaps the number of repeat performances permitted. The licensor of a pop hit, depending on its value to the licensee,

can assert contractual control over performers, arrangements, session producer, and even the studio. Most licenses are granted for the length of a campaign. When the advertiser wants not only a song but an original performance of that song, additional licenses must be made with the performers.

In rare cases, a piece of music may become a long-term theme of identification. Phillip Morris Companies used Ferde Grofe's "Grand Canyon Suite" for 30 years, for example, while for more than a decade United Airlines has extended its use of George Gershwin's "Rhapsody in Blue" from television commercials to the music played on the telephone as callers wait to make reservations. United and its agency Leo Burnett USA had a long history of music use prior to "Rhapsody in Blue," some borrowed (John Denver's "Leaving on a Jet Plane") but much original and enduring: "Fly the Friendly Skies" (1965) and "Mother Country" by Bonnie Koloc (1973).

Certainly in the United States advertising jingles and music have become an integral part of daily life. Singer-composer Barry Manilow routinely does a medley of his jingles in his performances, and film composer Elmer Bernstein rarely performs a concert without including his "Theme from the Magnificent Seven," which subsequently became the music of Marlboro cigarettes. Even after tobacco advertising was banned from U.S. television in 1970, the Bernstein music continued to be used in Europe and other world markets where TV ads for tobacco products were still legal. In the late 1960s bandleader Lester Lanin recorded a popular album for Epic Records, "Lester Lanin Plays Madison Avenue," a compendium of ad jingles for such products as Mr. Clean, Newport cigarettes, Robert Hall, Ipana, Wildroot, Halo shampoo, Chiquita, Brylcreem, Lestoil, TWA, and many more.

MARGO BERMAN

Further Reading

"Agency Head Irv Olian Turns Out Jingles While Driving, Doesn't Get Paid for It," *Advertising Age* (25 January 1964)

Bechtos, Ramona, "Tunesmiths, Admen Can Commingle—When There's Green Stuff In a Jingle," *Advertising Age* (29 May 1961)

Cuneo, Alice Z., "Amazon Unleashes $50 Million for the Holidays: 60's-Theme Ads Urge Shoppers to Flee the Mall," *Advertising Age* (15 November 1999)

Ebenkamp, Becky, "Boomerang Branding: Marketers Have Turned to Advertising and Cultural Icons and Jingles of the Past to Reach Baby Boomers," *Brandweek* 38, no. 42 (November 1997)

"For Ad Jingle Fans This Little Book'll Do Ya," *Advertising Age* (11 October 1976)

Friedman, Wayne, "Levi's Uses Music to Heat Up 'Coolness' Factor: Long-Term Sponsor Deal with SFX Links Jeans Brand with New Bands," *Advertising Age* (8 March 1999)

Garfield, Bob, "Nortel's Beatles Rap Misses a Selling Point," *Advertising Age* (12 April 1999)

Garfield, Bob, "Gap Secretes Sweet Smell of Ad Success," *Advertising Age* (16 August 1999)

Garfield, Bob, "With Jack, Faux Video, Parody Spot's a Winner," *Advertising Age* (30 August 1999)

Garfield, Bob, "Nike 'So Beautiful' Everything Hoped For," *Advertising Age* (8 November 1999)

"Gilbert in Jangle over 'Muskrat Ramble' as Jingle," *Advertising Age* (13 February 1967)

Halliday, Jean, "Isuzu Pulls Commercial That Parodied Slinky Ads," *Advertising Age* (18 May 1998)

Janis, Pam, "Robert Hall: Three Decades of Ads from One Tune," *Advertising Age* (29 August 1977)

"Jingles Have Long History, Stracke Says," *Advertising Age* (13 February 1967)

"Kent Jingle No Musical Insult," *Advertising Age* (17 June 1957)

Leland, John, "Advertisements for Themselves," *New York Times Magazine* (11 March 2001)

McDonough, John, and Allen Ross, "Jingle Jangle: Who Makes $inging Commercials and Why," *High Fidelity* 26, no. 11 (November 1976)

McLaren, Carrie, "Licensed to Sell," *Emigré Magazine* 49 (Winter 1999)

Norback, Peter, and Craig Norback, editors, *Great Songs of Madison Avenue,* New York: Quadrangle, 1976

Reilly, Patrick M., "TV Commercials Turn Obscure Songs into Radio Hits," *Wall Street Journal* (8 October 1999)

Rowsome, Frank, Jr., *Verse by the Side of the Road,* Brattleboro, Vermont: Greene, 1965

Sherrid, Pamela, "Emotional Shorthand: Popular Songs for Advertising Jingles," *Forbes* 136 (4 November 1985)

"Station Bans Popular Songs Incorporating 'Commercial Plugs,'" *Advertising Age* (14 June 1954)

"Versatile Adman, Roy Eaton," *Advertising Age* (17 June 1957)

Wells, Melanie, "Ads That Carry a Tune Top Charts," *USA Today* (24 May 1999)

Wingis, Chuck, "Songwriter Nichols Bemoans 'Budget' Jingles," *Advertising Age* (13 September 1976)

Wroe, Martin, "Will Beatles Plug Beetle?" *Minneapolis Star Tribune* (20 February 1998)

N

Nabisco, Inc.

Principal Agencies
McCann-Erickson, Inc.
Kenyon & Eckhardt, Inc.
Ted Bates & Company
William Esty and Company, Inc.
Ogilvy & Mather
Foote, Cone & Belding Communications (later FCB Worldwide)

An international marketer of crackers, snacks, and other premium food products, Nabisco has been feeding consumers for more than a century. Its U.S. operating companies make and market many of the best-known brands in the supermarket, including Oreo, Fig Newton, Chips Ahoy!, and SnackWell's cookies; Ritz and Premium crackers; and Triscuit wafers.

First "Cracker"

Nabisco's heritage dates back to 1792, when Pearson's Bakery was established in Massachusetts to bake pilot bread, or ship's biscuits, which sailors took on long journeys because they kept for some time without spoiling. A few years later, in 1801, the Josiah Bent Bakery invented the first biscuit that was not described as pilot bread. It called the product "crackers" for the crunchy sound it made when chewed.

In 1889 William Moore united several eastern U.S. bakeries—Pearson's, Bent, and six others—to form the first bakery consortium, the New York Biscuit Company. At virtually the same time Adolphus Green united approximately 40 midwestern bakeries to form the American Biscuit & Manufacturing Company. In 1898 Moore and Green merged their groups to form the National Biscuit Company (NBC). Green became president of the new company headquartered in Chicago, Illinois, in the first modern skyscraper.

To make NBC crackers stand out from those sold in bulk in grocery store cracker barrels, Green created Uneeda Biscuits, the first high-quality soda cracker sold in a moisture-proof cardboard package. NBC's advertising efforts began early and in earnest. Green launched a national advertising teaser campaign, the first of its kind on this scale, to make the public aware of Uneeda Biscuits.

The following year, 1899, the NBC board of directors approved Green's request for an advertising budget that would reach the staggering sum of $7 million over the next decade. The first year's appropriation was hailed as the largest commitment to advertising ever made; advertising efforts included streetcar and trolley car placards, store displays, and magazine and newspaper ads.

In 1900 NBC patented the moisture-proof inner package (In-Er-Seal) already used for Uneeda and several other products. The company adopted as its symbol the colophon, a cross with two bars and an oval; a 15th century Venetian printers' symbol representing the triumph of the moral and spiritual over the evil and material, the colophon stood for NBC's commitment to giving consumers the freshest, highest-quality biscuit products possible. The company continued to use the symbol more than a century later.

Green coined the name Nabisco in 1901 by condensing the company's full name. It first appeared on the company's new Sugar Wafers product but would not come into widespread use until 40 years later. Barnum's Animals Crackers appeared for the first time at the end of 1902. Two companies had previously sold animal-shaped cookies to groceries in wooden boxes, barrels, and cans, but Nabisco was the first to "cage" them in take-home packages shaped like circus wagons with a string attached so the boxes could be hung from the Christmas tree.

The company moved its headquarters to New York City in 1906, building a large bakery complex there. NBC's offerings had expanded to include Premium Saltine crackers and Fig Newtons. The flat, crispy Premium soda cracker had been best known west of the Rockies; it took first prize at the St. Joseph, Missouri, county fair in 1876. "Millions prefer this fresher, flakier cracker," said an early ad slogan.

Cookies and "Cakes"

Fig Newtons were introduced in 1891. They were advertised as Fig Newton "cakes," not cookies, from the start. That concept was resurrected more than 100 years later when Nabisco agency

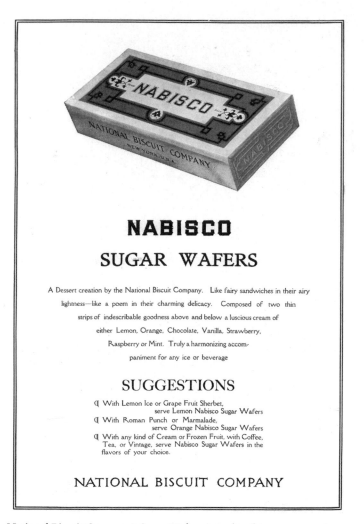

National Biscuit Company's Sugar Wafers, introduced in 1901, was the first product to feature the Nabisco brand name.
Courtesy of Kraft Foods Holdings, Inc.

FCB Worldwide created TV spots with the theme, "Not a cookie. It's fruit and cake."

The Oreo creme sandwich cookie was introduced in 1912 and has been among America's favorite cookies ever since. There are several stories about how Oreo got its name; one tale points to French and Greek origins for the word, while another says it took the *re* from the word *creme* and "sandwiched" it between the two "O's" in chocolate. Early advertising showed the cookie being twisted apart to reveal the tasty creme center; studies in the 1990s showed that twisting and dunking were the most popular ways to consume the treat.

Mallomars debuted in November 1913. The marshmallow cookie covered in pure dark chocolate was available only from October to mid-March. In the early 21st century 70 percent of Mallomars sales were in the New York metropolitan area.

When the United States entered World War I in 1917, NBC produced 800,000 servings a day of bread rations, similar to hardtack biscuits, to sustain the troops. In 1928 NBC acquired the Shredded Wheat Company, founded in 1901, and with it the

Triscuit wafer. Triscuit had been developed in 1895 as an easy-to-digest food in the style of Shredded Wheat cereal, which its inventors had introduced three years earlier. Initially Triscuit's developers dreamed of selling thousands of shredding machines to bakeries, kitchens, and hotels, but their products proved more popular than their mode of preparation. A 1903 magazine ad showed Niagara Falls, where Triscuit was made, and touted the novelty, "baked by electricity." Print advertising from 1906 called the shredded wheat wafer "The toast of the town"; another ad, from 1907, urged consumers to "Choose the wafer that's full of chews."

Radio and TV Sponsorship

NBC's biscuit division hired McCann-Erickson, Inc., of New York City, to handle its cookies and crackers business in 1934. (The Federal Advertising Agency was assigned its shredded wheat products.) Almost immediately McCann-Erickson moved to get Nabisco into radio. The format decided upon was a three-hour program of dance music to be called *Let's Dance* and broadcast live every Saturday night from coast to coast starting at 10:30 eastern time. The music director at McCann was Josef Bonime, whose wife headed the agency's radio department. Between the two they set out to find three bands to fill the show's time. Bonime chose a sweet-sounding band led by Kel Murray, a Latin group under Xavier Cugat, and, to appeal to the college-age audience, a jazz-oriented big band that could play what was called "hot" music. It was the latter that would make history. Bonime hired a then-unknown clarinet virtuoso named Benny Goodman, who would use the Nabisco program to introduce swing to America and the world.

McCann promoted the program heavily with point-of-purchase materials in grocery stores. It aired from December 1934 through March 1935 before the agency canceled it. According to legend, Goodman was heard too late in the East to make a deep impression. But the show found a large and enthusiastic audience on the West Coast where it was heard three hours earlier, and this became the basis on which Goodman and swing would soon sweep the country. Bonime had chosen Carl Maria von Weber's "Invitation to the Dance" as the program's theme and commissioned a swing version for Goodman to play. When the show ended, Goodman continued using the tune ("Let's Dance") as his own theme for the next 50 years, making it one of the most famous signature tunes in all of American music. *Let's Dance* would be NBC's most famous foray into radio. Following the show's demise, the company concentrated its budget largely in magazine and store displays. In 1936 NBC launched Ritz Crackers, which within three years became the largest-selling cracker in the world, according to the company.

By 1941 the National Biscuit Company decided to leave its acronym NBC to the growing National Broadcasting Company and began using Nabisco as the company name. In 1945 then-new Nabisco President George H. Coppers began a 12-year modernization program for the company. His philosophy, "You have to spend money to make money," continued to be reflected in the ever-increasing ad budgets of the 1950s when Nabisco began a heavy television schedule. In 1953 Nabisco planned to spend more than $7.5 million—a new high—on cracker and cookie advertising, principally for Premium Saltines, Ritz, Nabisco Grahams, pretzels, Oreos, and Fig Newtons. The company had long held to the theory that if it pushed its leading brands, they would help the others.

That same year Nabisco expanded its broadcast TV advertising beyond sponsorship of certain shows and began a new spot-buying strategy to reach large, diversified audiences. In 1954 Nabisco spent $9.1 million on total domestic advertising, $6.1 million of that in measured media, according to *Advertising Age*. The company became a sponsor of *The Adventures of Rin Tin Tin* on the ABC network via its agency, Kenyon & Eckhardt, Inc.; it remained a sponsor for the next five years.

By 1957 Nabisco's domestic advertising expenditures were up to $21 million, $12.8 million in measured media, according to *Advertising Age*. The following year saw the biggest promotion for a single cracker product in the company's history: a fall ad drive for Premium Saltine crackers in print, newspaper supplements, and co-sponsorships of the prime-time *Wagon Train* series, the *Concentration* game show, and other daytime programming through McCann-Erickson.

Nabisco enjoyed its finest year to date in 1959, according to *Advertising Age*. Although it sharply decreased its magazine and spot TV spending, it intensified its network TV efforts. Sponsorship or co-sponsorship of 12 network TV series, including *Howdy Doody* and other children's shows, soap operas, game shows, and *Wagon Train* and *Rawhide*, enabled Nabisco to reach youngsters on Saturday, homemakers in the daytime, and families in the evenings.

For the second year in a row, in 1960 Nabisco trimmed its spot TV spending and invested more heavily in network TV. In 1960 the company spent $10.3 million in network TV, up from $7.6 million in 1959; Nabisco spent $1.3 million in spot TV in 1960, down from $2.1 million the previous year. The number of network TV shows it sponsored or co-sponsored stood at 18. The company also added more than $1 million to its magazine budget. Two years later, record sales pushed Nabisco past the half-billion-dollar mark for the first time. The company's domestic advertising spending rose to $33 million. By 1963 Nabisco was sponsoring or co-sponsoring 23 daytime and prime-time TV shows and three children's shows.

Nabisco introduced Chips Ahoy! cookies in 1963, which it marketed as the first commercially produced chocolate chip cookie with a homemade taste. The company reached another milestone in 1964 when it set a sales record of $607.5 million. Its network TV sponsorship and co-sponsorship rose to 35 daytime and prime-time programs and three children's shows.

McCann-Erickson created an innovative Nabisco cookie campaign for the September 1964 issue of *McCall's* magazine. Children moved cardboard pieces provided on a perforated card insert around the Chewza Cookie color game-board spread. When they landed on certain squares the children were directed to take Nabisco cookies as prizes.

A flavor so tempting you just can't stop eating them. That's what's made Ritz America's greatest cracker sensation... put them in millions of homes from coast to coast... started thousands of families clamoring for them every day in the week. All in the space of one short year.

In some mysterious way Ritz actually improve the flavor of everything you serve them with. They're magical with cheese, salads and spreads. And the way they go with drinks makes them the perfect party cracker. Ask your grocer for Ritz in the 1-pound or ½-pound package today. Let your whole family enjoy them tonight.

 A Product of NATIONAL BISCUIT COMPANY
makers of **Uneeda Biscuit** *and hundreds of other favorite varieties*

Introduced in 1934, Ritz quickly became "America's most popular cracker."
Courtesy of Kraft Foods Holdings, Inc.

If NABISCO puts all these luscious chocolate chips into one bag of <u>new</u> CHIPS AHOY cookies...

and there are about 40 cookies in one bag; and we call new CHIPS AHOY cookies the 16-chip cookie...

how many chips are there on this page?

If you hate arithmetic, just buy a bagful and enjoy

About 640 chips altogether.
Baked into crunchy cookies.
Put into reclosable bags,
to keep them fresh.

© NABISCO 1966

Originally called Chipits, then renamed Nabisco Chocolate Chip cookies, these cookies became a market leader after the name was changed to Chips Ahoy! in 1963.
Courtesy of Kraft Foods Holdings, Inc.

Sales hit a new high for the seventh consecutive year in 1965 when Nabisco budgeted $38.3 million for domestic and international advertising. Although it had been rumored that Nabisco and the Coca Cola Company might merge, talks were called off by November of that year. Merger plans announced by Nabisco and Colgate-Palmolive in February 1967 also proved short-lived.

Cutbacks, Change, and Resurgence

In 1968 Nabisco cut its agency roster from four to three. McCann-Erickson, which had handled the entire biscuit division for 34 years, lost $1.8 million in billings in the shuffle but remained the dominant agency. Ted Bates & Company gained $4 million–$5 million in cookie and snacks accounts and the Shredded Wheat and Spoon Size Shredded Wheat business. William Esty and Company, Inc., also gained about $3 million through Oreos and the snack cracker line. The big loser proved to be Kenyon & Eckhardt, which lost $4 million in Nabisco spending. Nabisco's 1968 ad expenditures climbed to $43 billion, including overseas advertising.

For the first time in a decade company sales failed to break records in 1969. An eight-week production strike against Nabisco closed most major U.S. production facilities in September and October and significantly affected operations. Nabisco's total ad budget dropped 19 percent compared with the previous year, to $35 million. But a strong comeback by the biscuit division in 1970 mitigated the strike's effects.

Nabisco ended its 38-year relationship with McCann-Erickson in November 1972, moving its $6 million-plus in U.S. ad spending to Ogilvy & Mather, Inc. Ogilvy was awarded Premium Saltines, Ritz crackers, Fig Newtons, Chips Ahoy!, and Lorna Doone shortbread.

In 1973 Nabisco's total ad expenditures were $69 million; $32.2 million of that went to network TV buys and $11.2 million to national spot TV. The company's prime-time schedule included NBC's Walt Disney series and ABC's *Monday Night Football*.

Nabisco tried cross-couponing, adding multiproduct coupons to packaging, in early 1974 and was so pleased with the results that it increased cross-couponing and included it in a 40th birthday "sale-a-bration" for Ritz Crackers in 1976. That year Nabisco's biscuit division launched a testing system that divided the United States into 100 "cells," each representing about 1 percent of the total market. Every product sold by the division—from Nabisco's large franchise brands to new entries—was subjected to analysis in small-market area tests. In general, Nabisco found that its cookie and cracker categories were underpromoted and responsive to advertising and merchandising. The company expanded its ad spending and discovered that by doubling or tripling advertising for mature brands, such as Ritz, it could significantly boost the whole product category. The national campaign, "Everything tastes great when it sits on a Ritz," was developed from such testing.

Ad spending jumped to an estimated $80.7 million total in 1975. Total sales that year increased to $1.97 billion, another new company record. Double Stuff Oreos, boasting a double dollop of creme filling, were also introduced. Swiss Cheese brand snack crackers debuted in February 1976 with a campaign from Esty that bore the slogan, "Tastes so much like Swiss cheese they even have holes." Nabisco claimed that it proved to be the fastest-selling new snack cracker ever introduced. By 1976 Nabisco's biscuit division had captured 40 percent of the overall U.S. cracker and cookie market. Total company sales tallied $2.03 billion, with biscuit sales representing about 60 percent of total revenue.

That same year Esty gained $6 million in biscuit-division spending formerly handled by Ogilvy & Mather. Parkson Advertising, in New York City, began buying TV time for Triscuit and occasionally for other brands. With the 1977–78 TV season, Parkson became the agency of record for network TV purchases for Nabisco and its major operating divisions.

In 1985 R.J. Reynolds Industries bought Nabisco brands and renamed itself RJR/Nabisco (later RJR Nabisco). The conglomerate split itself into a tobacco company and a food company in March 1999.

In 1988 Foote, Cone & Belding Communications, Inc. (later FCB Worldwide), won the Nabisco cookies account from Esty. When the SnackWell's line debuted four years later, the agency's New York City–based FCB/Leber Katz Partners unit played up Nabisco's inability to keep SnackWell's products, in particular the fat-free Devil's Food Cookies, on the shelves: demand so exceeded supply that it took nearly two years for Nabisco to catch up. In fact, the marketer temporarily cut advertising to avoid alienating consumers who could not find their favorite SnackWell's products on store shelves. TV spots featured a beleaguered SnackWell's employee who was tracked relentlessly by a group of hungry women hounding "The Cookie Man" for more treats. The campaign was recognized by the American Marketing Association as the most effective advertising of 1994.

In 1994 Nabisco invested $107 million pitching its cookies and crackers. By 1997 Nabisco claimed it had captured 55 percent of the U.S. cracker business, with Ritz the top-selling cracker nationwide. But the company's ad expenditures had decreased to $72 million as its earnings dropped owing to increased competition in the marketplace. Savings from plant closings and other cutbacks were earmarked to be pumped back into advertising.

In 1997 Nabisco issued the "1,000 Chips Challenge" promotion via FCB, offering consumers scholarships and prizes for the most creative way to confirm there were at least 1,000 chocolate chips in every 18-ounce bag of Chips Ahoy! cookies. FCB had already introduced the animated "1,000 Chips Delicious" TV campaign in 1993; it continued into the 21st century.

Nabisco put itself into an unusual position for a food company when, again via FCB, it warned consumers "Don't eat the winning Oreo" for a 1999 contest. Nabisco imprinted the winning information right on the cookies. The grand prize was a new Volkswagen Beetle—filled with cookies. Another way the company kept the 88 year-old Oreo brand growing and fresh

At Nabisco,® our devotion to making wholesome great-tasting snacks is never ending.

If you're looking for wholesome snacks
that taste great, look no further. Look for Nabisco.
You'll find that many of our snacks are low
in saturated fat with absolutely no cholesterol.
And with the nutritional label on every package,
you'll know exactly what you're eating in each serving.
Make delicious Nabisco cookies and crackers
part of your balanced diet.

© 1990 NABISCO BRANDS, INC.

In this 1990 corporate ad, Nabisco capitalized on the American public's growing interest in health and fitness by emphasizing the low fat content of its products and calling attention to nutritional information on package labels.
Courtesy of Kraft Foods Holdings, Inc.

with consumers was the limited edition Oreo Magic Dunkers, launched in April 2000. These cookies created swirls of blue milk when dunked. A humorous TV campaign from FCB showed "Cow Outrage" over kids who turned their milk blue. In 2001 FCB continued to run "The Only Oreo" campaign, which began in 1997; it also promoted the dunking method of consumption.

Having been separated from one tobacco partner, Nabisco prepared for the new millennium by linking with another. In June 2000 the world's largest tobacco company, Philip Morris Companies, Inc., parent of Kraft Foods, announced it would purchase Nabisco Holdings Corporation, the company that had spun off from the former RJR food group. Nabisco Holdings was 80.6 percent owned by Nabisco Group of Parsippany, New Jersey.

Kraft and Nabisco together produced revenue of $34.9 billion in 1999; the combined food company was expected to be second in the world only to Nestlé of Switzerland.

CHRISTINE BUNISH

Further Reading

Cahn, William, *Out of the Cracker Barrel: The Nabisco Story, from Animal Crackers to Zuzus,* New York: Simon and Schuster, 1969

Haugh, Louis J., "Nabisco Finding New Ad Muscle via 'Cell' System," *Advertising Age* (13 June 1977)

Nabisco <www/nabisco.com>

O'Gara, James V., "200 Nabisco Products Backed by $7,500,000," *Advertising Age* (9 March 1953)

Nast, Condé 1873–1942

U.S. Publisher

Condé Nast was born in New York City on 26 March 1873 to William and Esther Nast. When Nast was three, his father moved to Europe to look for work, and his mother and the four Nast children went to St. Louis, Missouri, to live with relatives. With financial support from a wealthy aunt, the wife of William A. Gamble of the Procter & Gamble Company, Nast attended Georgetown University. In his first year he became the first student president of the Yard, the university's athletic association, where he learned about scheduling and controlling finances, as well as about raising money.

While at Georgetown, Nast developed a friendship with Robert J. Collier, whose father owned *Collier's Weekly,* a journal offered as a premium to book buyers, and the Collier's book business. The two worked together on various projects, including the university's newspaper, the *Journal.* After graduation in 1894, Nast remained at Georgetown to study law while Collier moved back to New York City to work for his father.

Nast returned to St. Louis in 1895 to study law at Washington University, but quickly found he was more interested in a small, failing printing plant his family had invested in. He left school to develop marketing angles to improve the plant's business.

Hearing of his friend's new interest, Collier invited Nast to move to New York City and work for *Collier's Weekly* for $12 a week. In 1900 Nast became advertising manager of the magazine; when he left ten years later, he had played a key role in boosting circulation from 19,159 to 567,073.

According to the biography *The Man Who Was Vogue,* Nast was called "Figure Jim" because he produced materials crammed with statistics and facts. He wrote a successful pitch letter that read:

> I am the Advertising Manager of *Collier's,* but I don't expect you to give me any business. Most manufacturers don't believe in weeklies; and it has only taken three month's canvassing to prove to my perfect satisfaction that the few who do won't use *Collier's.* However, I accept the situation. I don't want to argue with you. I merely want your residence address. We want to send *Collier's* to you regularly. Certain things are going to happen; things that you have neither the time nor inclination to inquire into. . . .

The letter got *Collier's* the attention it sorely needed. The magazine was redesigned in 1904 and targeted primarily at men. Nast believed that top writers and artists attracted readers, so the work of figures such as Upton Sinclair and Frederic Remington appeared on a regular basis. Color was added to make the publication even more dramatic. Nast also introduced the "special number," an issued devoted to a particular topic or individual. For example, in February 1904, *Collier's* published the "Gibson Number." The issue had 20 drawings, as well as a spread of exclusive drawings created by Charles Dana Gibson, a popular illustrator of the time who was famous for his "Gibson Girls."

Nast was promoted to business manager of the magazine in 1905 and by 1907 was earning $40,000 per year, a hefty sum for that day. When he resigned Collier told him no one would pay

Condé Nast.
Courtesy of Condé Nast Archive.

him that much money again. During his tenure there, Nast had taken *Collier's* from last place to first among magazines that carried advertising.

A few years before leaving *Collier's*, Nast had also become vice president of the Home Pattern Company, a manufacturer and distributor of women's dress patterns (owned by the *Ladies' Home Journal*). Patterns had become a big business because they gave women access to fashions once available only to the wealthy, and one of Nast's goals was to find ways to sell advertising in the company's catalogs. That presented a challenge, as pattern books were mostly given away free in department stores and often discarded by customers.

Through his pattern business Nast became acquainted with a small society journal called *Vogue*. Although there were at least ten major women's magazines covering fashion in the early 1900s, only *Vogue* was targeted at the elite. In 1905 Nast began negotiations to buy the publication from its owner, Arthur B. Turnure, but before they could reach an agreement, Turnure died, and the magazine was inherited by his sister-in-law, Marie Harrison, who had been editor of *Vogue*.

After four years of negotiations Nast purchased *Vogue* in 1909, when he was 36 years old. When he bought it the publication had a slipping circulation of only 14,000 and annual advertising revenue of $100,000. However, *Vogue*'s readership included some of the most prominent members of New York society, an audience Nast wanted. It proved to be his ticket to life as part of the exclusive and aristocratic New York society.

Nast quickly made his mark on *Vogue*, cutting the frequency from weekly to biweekly and raising the issue price from ten cents to fifteen cents. The first new department he added was called "Sale and Exchange," a place for personal messages from reader to reader. *Vogue* became the source for society news, including weddings and parties. In addition to pictures of every social event, the publication also started tackling bigger issues. For example, a new department was added featuring socialites helping the less fortunate.

The magazine averaged 100 pages an issue in 1911, compared with 30 when it was a weekly. Advertisers included Armour Toilet Soap, J.M. Gidding & Company (women's apparel), Athena Underwear, and Plexo Cream. *Vogue* competed with publications such as the *Ladies' Home Journal, Harper's Bazar* (which subsequently changed its spelling), and the *Woman's Home Companion.*

Nast's strategy was to charge top dollar for the "privilege" of advertising in *Vogue.* In a 1933 interview quoted in *The Man Who Was Vogue,* he stated that the magazine served to eliminate "waste circulation" for those advertising quality goods. "I determined to bait the editorial pages in such a way as to lift out of all the millions of Americans just the 100,000 cultivated people who can buy these quality goods." Nonetheless, Nast kept dress patterns a part of *Vogue,* knowing that not all women with taste could afford Paris couture. He maintained that good taste was not an exclusive attribute of people with money but could also be exercised by those who aspired to wealth. Nast was aided in his efforts at *Vogue* by its editor, Edna Chase, who had an unerring eye for styles and consumer tastes despite many rapid changes over the years.

With *Vogue* flourishing Nast bought an interest in *House & Garden* and *Travel.* Together with his old friend, Robert Collier, he purchased *The Housekeeper*—in order to get the subscription list for *House & Garden. Travel* was sold, making *House & Garden* the second publication in Nast's portfolio. He revamped it from a men's publication into an authority women could turn to for help in decorating their homes. (*The Housekeeper* was shuttered in 1912.)

In 1913 Nast bought *Dress,* a magazine he saw as a rival to *Vogue,* from Doubleday. He also snapped up *Vanity Fair* and combined the two in a publication called *Dress and Vanity Fair,* which debuted in September 1913. The magazine had articles on fashion, art, music, theater, and international news considered too specialized for *Vogue.* Part of the magazine's eventual success was thanks to Frank Crowninshield, who became editor and friend to Nast. He accepted the title of editor only after Nast agreed to drop *Dress* from the title. To further distinguish *Vanity Fair,* Crowninshield commissioned articles from up-and-coming authors such as Dorothy Parker, e.e. cummings, and Clive Bell. Well-known writers such as F. Scott Fitzgerald were also contributors. By the end of 1915 *Vanity Fair* carried more lines of advertising than any other U.S. monthly, according to *Printers' Ink* magazine.

Taking the advice of experts, Nast invested in Wall Street. In 1927 Goldman, Sachs & Company and Shearson, Hammill & Company bought a substantial common stock interest in Condé Nast Publications; Nast retained a controlling majority. It proved to be a stellar year, with the stock almost doubling. But on 29 October 1929 the market crashed and many fortunes were lost; Condé Nast stock dropped from $93 per share to $4.50, and Nast lost controlling interest in stock that was virtually worthless.

In an effort to rebuild, Nast borrowed to invest in better printing plants. He worked feverishly to bring the magic back. In 1930, however, Sidney J. Weinberg, a senior partner of Goldman,

Sachs & Company, was named director of Condé Nast Publications, meaning that control of the company passed into the hands of bankers.

Efforts continued to revive the publications. During those years Condé Nast publications helped launch the careers of editor Carmel Snow, photographer Horst P. Horst, and artist Claire Avery. Other new titles emerged, such as *Glamour of Hollywood*. While the publication was different from the classy publications Condé Nast was known for, the publication that would later be known simply as *Glamour* hit the mark with a growing cadre of career women. The company also ventured, with mixed success, into international publishing.

While his company was recovering, Nast in 1941 was suffering from high blood pressure and needed an oxygen tank. He suffered his first heart attack in December 1941 and died after his second on 19 September 1942.

FAYE BROOKMAN

Biography

Born in New York City, 26 March 1873; joined *Collier's Weekly*, becoming advertising manager in 1900; became vice president of Home Pattern Company, 1904; bought *Vogue*, 1909; bought *Dress* and *Vanity Fair*, which he merged in what would be the new *Vanity Fair*, 1913; Goldman, Sachs & Company and Shearson, Hammill & Company bought a substantial common stock interest in Condé Nast Publications, Inc., 1927; lost control of his company to his bank partners, 1930; died in New York City, 19 September 1942.

Further Reading

Chase, Edna Woolman, and Ilka Chase, *Always in Vogue*, New York: Doubleday, and London: Gollancz, 1954
Seebohm, Caroline, *The Man Who Was Vogue: The Life and Times of Condé Nast*, New York: Viking Press, and London: Weidenfeld and Nicolson, 1982

National Biscuit Company. *See* Nabisco, Inc.

Needham, Harper & Steers Advertising, Inc.

(DDB Needham Worldwide)

Formed by merger of Chicago, Illinois, agency Needham, Louis & Brorby, Inc., and Doherty, Clifford, Steers & Shenfield, 1964; went public, 1972; bought itself back, 1978; merged with Doyle Dane Bernbach (DDB) to become DDB Needham Worldwide and, along with Batten Barton Durstine & Osborn, formed the holding company Omnicom, 1986; Needham name dropped, 1999.

Major Clients

American Honda Motor Company
Anheuser-Busch, Inc.
Household Finance Corporation
S.C. Johnson & Son, Inc. (Johnson's Wax)
Kraft Foods
McDonald's Corporation
State Farm Insurance Companies
Xerox Corporation

The agency that had been Needham, Harper & Steers (NH&S) and later Needham Harper Worldwide prior to its 1986 merger with Doyle Dane Bernbach (DDB) began life in Chicago, Illinois, on 2 January 1925 as the Maurice H. Needham Company. Maurice Needham was born in suburban Hinsdale, Illinois, graduated from the Louis Institute (now the Illinois Institute of Technology) in 1910, and began his career with Nichols & Finn, a Chicago agency. In 1921 he took a partnership in another Chicago agency, Husband & Thomas, and five years later went into business for himself with $1,500 of his own money and three small clients billing about $270,000.

In 1929 he took on two partners, and the agency became Needham, Louis & Brorby (NL&B). Melvin Brorby had joined Needham in 1925 as a copywriter and became a partner with the name change. John J. Louis joined in 1929 from the Charles Daniel Frey Agency and brought with him an asset that would give the agency its defining early client: his wife was the sister of H.F. Johnson, chairman of S.C. Johnson & Son in Racine, Wisconsin, which soon named NL&B its agency.

Nepotism has seldom been so richly rewarded. It was Louis's wife who, late in 1934, first heard a local Chicago radio show called *Smackout* on WMAQ and suggested her husband listen.

The duplicators for those who appreciate the virtues of simplicity.

When you push a few buttons on a Xerox high-speed duplicator, a miracle occurs.

A multitude of complicated jobs are converted instantly into simple ones.

For example, you can get a Xerox duplicator that copies on both sides of a piece of paper, automatically.

That reduces, automatically. Collates, automatically.

Feeds and cycles up to 200 originals, automatically.

And even makes two-sided 8-1/2″ x 11″ copies from unburst computer printouts, automatically.

But of all the virtues of simplicity, the greatest is this:

It increaseth productivity.

Since Xerox duplicators are so easy to use, people can spend more time using them, and less time figuring out how. Anyone who can master the technology of pushing buttons can operate one of our duplicators.

So if you appreciate the virtues of simplicity, look into the virtues of a Xerox 9200 or 9400 duplicator.

We'll even arrange a simple demonstration at your convenience.

Just in case you don't accept miracles on faith alone.

XEROX® 9200® and 9400 are trademarks of XEROX CORPORATION.

This 1979 ad for Xerox high-speed duplicators was from the "Monk" campaign. Produced by Needham, Harper & Steers Advertising, the campaign has been cited as one of the most memorable campaigns ever created for office products.
XEROX® is a registered trademark of Xerox Corporation.

On 16 April 1935, the show's stars, Jim and Marian Jordan, went on the air with a revised version of their show, now called *The Johnson's Wax Program with Fibber McGee and Molly*, for the launch of Johnson's Glo-Coat brand. NL&B would produce the show for the next 15 years. It was a measure of the loyalty of both S.C. Johnson & Son and the agency that they stuck with the show even when Marian Jordan's alcoholism prevented her from making any appearances from 1937 to 1939. It was on this program that NL&B became one of the first agencies to use the "integrated commercial," in which an ad message presented at the midpoint in the show by announcer Harlow Wilcox was woven into the story line.

As NL&B pushed into network radio, its reputation and billings began to rise. In 1939 it opened a Hollywood office when Johnson's production moved to Los Angeles, California. By 1941 the agency had won Kraft Foods and, in seeking a radio property for its new client, hit on another broadcast innovation, *The Great Gildersleeve*. Created for Kraft from a character developed on the Fibber McGee program, Throckmorton P. Gildersleeve, the show was the basis of the first spin-off series in the history of network broadcasting, setting the precedent for countless series to follow.

State Farm Insurance became another major client in the years before World War II. But even with two successful network series on the air, billings were still only around $2.5 million. During the war Needham and his partners decided they wanted to be a big agency and aggressively pursued growth from within. Swift, Morton Salt, and Pepsodent tooth powder were added to the roster. By 1945 NL&B was billing an estimated $8 million and broke into the still exclusive $10-million-and-up club in 1946, the same year a young copywriter named Paul Harper joined the agency.

Agencies were highly secretive about their billings in those days, something Needham saw no need for. In 1951 NL&B became the first major agency to fully disclose all operating numbers to employees and the trade. Billings were $15 million. The numbers continued to grow well into the 1950s, as a second generation of management began taking over from the founders. Louis retired in 1957, and Needham relinquished the presidency to Harper in 1960 and became chairman. By 1956 NL&B had become the second- or third-largest agency in Chicago. It hit a series of bumps that year, as accounts departed (Quaker, Ken-L Ration, Hotpoint, Wilson Company) and people left "in droves," according to *Advertising Age*. Some felt its survival was in question. But by 1959 the agency had made the turnaround, hitting $38 million that year.

In January 1964 Needham retired as chairman and left active participation in the agency he had founded. He died in June 1966. Louis died in February 1959, while Brorby lingered on in semi-retirement into the 1970s.

Meanwhile, Harper moved to strengthen the agency's New York profile by merger. In 1944 Francis Doherty, Arthur Cobb, and Lawrence Shenfield had spun off from 44th-ranked Pedlar & Ryan (P&R), which would fold in 1952, to form Doherty, Cobb & Shenfield (DC&S). Cobb soon left and was replaced on

"The Night Belongs to Michelob," a campaign created by Needham, Harper & Steers, ran in both print and television for several years beginning in the mid-1980s; this print ad appeared in 1986.

the nameplate after his death in 1952 by Donald Clifford, another P&R vice president. Also making the shift was P&R media director William Steers, a 1930 Dartmouth graduate, whose name was added to the logo in 1952 (Doherty, Clifford, Steers & Shenfield, or DCS&S). Steers became president in 1956.

DCS&S took many prominent Bristol-Myers brands away from P&R, including Ipana, Vitalis, and Mum, and would bill about $29 million by the time Harper began talks in June 1964 with Steers, now DCS&S chairman. The merger, signed 31 December 1964, was the second biggest in advertising history at the time. Needham, Harper & Steers began life as the 10th-ranked U.S. agency, billing $90 million.

After several immediate client losses in New York, including Bristol-Myers, Harper relocated to the Manhattan office. But NH&S continued its relationships with Johnson's Wax, Kraft (Parkay, Manor House), and State Farm; the latter became the first account Keith Reinhard worked on when he joined in 1964, shortly before the merger. Steers would retire in 1970, and Reinhard would eventually become president of the Chicago office. New business would include Xerox (1968), for which the agency produced the celebrated "It's a Miracle" commercial (1975), a classic of fractured history in which a medieval scribe miraculously produces several hundred copies of a document using a Xerox machine. Other highly praised campaigns NH&S produced during the 1970s and 1980s included "The Night Belongs to Michelob" for Anheuser-Busch and "We Make it Simple" for Honda.

The agency lost the S.C. Johnson account in 1974 after a 43-year relationship. This split was reportedly over disappointing sales from the company's Step Saver brand, which NH&S launched in 1973. The relationship resumed in 1977, then ended again early in 1983 after NH&S took on Clorox Pre-Wash. Johnson regarded the product as competitive with its Shout, which, although handled by Foote, Cone & Belding, was part of the company's household products division. NH&S handled Glade, which was part of that group.

Seeking expansion in Europe, in November 1966 NH&S partnered with the Benson Group in London, England, to form Benson-Needham Europe and acquired majority interest in agencies in Frankfurt, Germany; Paris, France; and Madrid, Spain, in 1967. Univas/Havas joined the combine in 1970. In the 1980s the agency would expand into public relations with the acquisition of Porter Novelli, and later into direct marketing through the DR Group.

In 1970 Reinhard, now a senior vice president and creative director, led the new-business team that won the $5 million McDonald's Corporation account from D'Arcy MacManus. According to Yolanda Brugulletta, then an NH&S research director, the data from focus groups suggested that the convenience of McDonald's gave customers a feeling of relief. Reinhard and his team translated this insight into "You deserve a break today," a campaign that drove NH&S's growth and reputation for the next decade.

The industry, not to mention Reinhard, was jolted when, in October 1981, McDonald's moved the bulk of the account, now worth $53 million, to the Leo Burnett Company. Widely circulated public relations photos of a grinning Jack Kopp, chief executive officer at Burnett, chomping on a Big Mac seemed to rub Needham's nose in its loss. The move also had a chilling effect on every creative director's basic article of faith, that winning creative work cannot lose.

Ignoring conventional practice, Reinhard never sought other fast-food business. Instead, he began the work of winning back McDonald's. Nine years later, after the agency had merged with DDB and Reinhard had become CEO of the combined agencies, DDB Needham recovered $55 million of the McDonald's business, though Burnett still held on to $245 million. Reinhard's strategy was to nibble away at Burnett's hold on the business by picking off various parts of McDonald's overseas business and demonstrating the agency's value through the quality of its work. Finally, in 1997, the bulk of the remainder followed, for a total account gain of approximately $300 million. The business victory for DDB Needham, however, seemed less fascinating to many than the victory for Reinhard, who downplayed publicity that viewed it as a personal triumph.

In April 1972, two years after winning McDonald's for the first time and with billings at $50 million, NH&S joined the trend of agencies going public. Six years later, however, it reversed course and returned to private ownership.

The agency had been an object of merger interest since the late 1970s. One interested party was DDB, which had briefly opened a Chicago office in October 1958. It was not successful, but the experience taught DDB management that if it wanted a Chicago presence, it would do better finding a Chicago partner with roots of its own.

One such agency was NH&S, named "Agency of the Year" in 1977 by Advertising Age. In the late 1970s Harper reportedly had several serious meetings with William Bernbach with a view toward a package in which each would gain strength in the other's city. But nothing materialized.

Several years later, things had changed. Bernbach's death in 1982 led to a slow atrophy of the Bernbach spirit, still honored but increasingly ignored in the face of short-term growth pressures. DDB veterans left the agency: Julian Koenig, Phyllis Robinson, Gene Case, and later Marv Honig and Bob Levenson.

The man most alarmed by this drift had never worked at DDB or even lived in New York. Nine hundred miles to the west, Reinhard sat in his Chicago office and felt he was watching the agency that had inspired him turn into just another big advertising factory. "My idea," he told Advertising Age in 1999, "was to get together with DDB for reasons of creative passion and bring Bernbach's ideas to life again." But having succeeded the retiring Harper as CEO in 1984, Reinhard had interests of his own to serve as well. Harper had put together a global network for Needham on relatively little money; this led Reinhard in 1984 to drop "Steers" and rename the company Needham Harper Worldwide. The name change, though, did not change the reality: the agency ranked only 16th in the world in income.

To Reinhard, however, the move was symbolic; he had staked out a position. "It's going to be very tough to bootstrap our way from 16 into the top tier," he told the executive committee. "We're going to need a partner. Any suggestions?" It was a rhetorical question. Reinhard had already worked out the structure he envisioned for a future DDB Needham Worldwide. It was more than an alliance of geographic muscle. "I sorted out all the strengths," he said in the 1999 Advertising Age interview. "We would take this from this culture and that from that culture. Here are the compatibilities and here are the conflicts in terms of clients and executives."

In the summer of 1985, with Needham ranked 20th in world billing compared to 11th for DDB, Reinhard approached DDB top executives Niel Austrian, Barry Loughran, and John Bernbach in New York City to discuss merger and other options. But he was at a disadvantage as a would-be partner because at that moment DDB lacked an incentive to merge. By September talks were considered dead.

In April 1986 that suddenly changed. Saatchi & Saatchi was hungry and targeting DDB for a takeover. It made a bid on the 24th, and DDB, which had been talking to Needham and BBDO since 1 March, rejected it. At the same meeting the three agencies approved the now legendary "big bang" deal that joined Needham, DDB, and BBDO. DDB and Needham were merged into a single agency with Reinhard at the helm, while BBDO functioned independently, all under the Omnicom umbrella. At the time of the merger, Needham billings stood at $847 million. The Needham name survived in the agency trademark until 1999, when it was finally dropped.

JOHN MCDONOUGH

See also DDB Worldwide, Inc.; Omnicom Group

Further Reading
"Maurice Needham Retirement from NL&B Ends 54-Year Career," *Advertising Age* (27 January 1964)
McDonough, John, "A Half Century of Unprecedented Creativity," *Advertising Age* (15 November 1999)
"Needham, Louis, and Brorby Hits Big Time Billings," *Advertising Age* (26 November 1951)
"NH&S on Way with Judicious Mix of Young Turks," *Advertising Age* (3 February 1969)
"NL&B Merger with DCS&S Is Confirmed," *Advertising Age* (14 December 1964)

Negative Advertising

Negative advertising is advertising that attacks or criticizes the sponsor's competitors or their brands, products, or services by emphasizing attributes that are similar to but weaker than those of the sponsor. Negative advertising is a method of direct comparison designed to draw the audience's attention to an opponent's weakness through an aggressive and one-sided assault. While positive advertising focuses on the sponsoring party's attributes and strengths, negative advertising focuses on exposure of the competitors' failings.

There are two forms of comparative advertising: direct comparative advertising, which contains a specific brand-directed message, and implied comparative advertising, which contains implicit messages that do not mention competitors' names or products. Most negative advertising is in the former category and differs from objective comparative advertising in that it is one-sided, a feature that may generate a perception of unfairness.

In the 1930s Plymouth ads advised prospective car buyers, "Look at all three, before you make a decision." This was one of the first major comparative advertising campaigns in the United States. Even though the slogan was a fairly general statement, it implied that drawbacks existed in the competition—widely understood by implication to be Chevrolet and Ford—that would become obvious to an informed shopper.

In 1971 the Federal Trade Commission (FTC) advocated the use of comparative advertising in national print and broadcast media to provide more information to consumers as well as to offer increased effectiveness for advertisers. The prevalence of comparative advertising increased from 15 percent in the mid-1960s to 80 percent in 1990, and the practice became more persuasive.

As the business climate has become increasingly competitive, however, comparative advertising has grown more direct and negative. Implied definition of the competitive brand ("leading brand" or "Brand X") has been replaced by explicit definition, which names a specific brand that has similar attributes to the advertiser's product or service. There have been several famous cases of negative ad campaigns, such as the battle between AT&T and MCI, the attack by Visa on American Express (which featured stores, restaurants, resorts, and other businesses that would not accept the American Express card), and the heated competition between the soft-drink giants Pepsi-Cola and Coca-Cola.

In the 1970s the negative comparison tactic shifted from a focus on quality attributes to an emphasis on price, environmental and social issues, and the value of the brand. In addition, the use of negative advertising was extended from so-called low-involvement food and household products to high-involvement services and personal products. The practice of negative advertising was accepted and used by a majority of advertising agencies, particularly the larger ones. Of the predominant advertising media, television and magazines carried the highest percentage of negative advertising.

Pro and Con

The arguments against negative advertising focus primarily on the risks of reducing the effectiveness of the ad message or misleading the public and the possibility of reactions—rebuttal advertising, punitive action by the National Advertising Review Board, or a lawsuit. The acceptability of negative advertising also varies from one country to another. For instance, Wendy's "Where's the beef?" campaign, attacking McDonald's, was banned in some European countries in 1994. Five major Tokyo TV stations refused to broadcast Pepsi's negative ads against Coke in 1991. Issues of local taste and accepted practices need to be considered by any advertiser planning to launch a negative campaign.

Both beneficial and detrimental effects often result from negative advertising. One of the benefits of negative advertising is the attention gained. Negative advertising provides information on differences not found in the other types of advertising, and it is more likely to be remembered. Negative advertising is also more efficient than other kinds of advertising in getting consumers to share a specific perspective. The presentation of the negative comparative message also increases consumers' interest in and awareness of the product, which, in turn, increases their intention to purchase.

In the evaluation stage of the decision-making process, consumers draw comparisons between competing products based on information from a variety of sources—personal experience, word of mouth, and comparative advertising. Advertisers take advantage of this opportunity, using negative ads to provide information about the brand and to help new or unknown products reduce market-entry barriers. In the mature stage of the product life cycle, advertisers use negative advertising to build competitive advantage. By attacking and assaulting competitors, advertisers seek to create a negative image of them and to shift favor to the promoted brand.

Not all negative advertising works as intended, however. The attack format may decrease the credibility of the sponsoring company. Moreover, some people view negative advertising as unethical and therefore reject the ad message. Still another concern is that the frequent use of negative advertising may overwhelm the target audience with too much information, resulting in a loss of interest. And there is always the possibility that the competitor may respond with a negative ad of its own, leading to a negative cycle that can increase consumer confusion and decrease the effectiveness of the advertising investment.

The inclusion of the competitor's name or brand also may be a source of confusion and can distort the focus of the ad. For example, many viewers were confused by an advertising campaign for the Jack in the Box fast-food chain, in which McDonald's and Burger King were compared with Jack in the Box. The attention of the audience was diverted from the core message, which was intended to be the superiority of Jack in the Box.

Another major concern when using negative advertising is the risk of provoking a lawsuit. The competing brand may sue, claiming misleading messages or false statements. In one such action, Jartran was forced to pay $40 million in damages for attacking U-Haul with misleading messages. In another, as-yet-undecided case, GTE sued AT&T for ads that attacked the reliability of GTE's long-distance network.

Guidelines for constructing negative ads are set forth by the Lanham Act, common law, state unfair-competition laws, and the Federal Trade Commission Act. When a company attacked by a negative campaign can prove a negative statement false, or can prove material and meaningful deception, it is likely that the plaintiff will win a court case.

Going Negative in Politics

Negative advertising has been widely used in political campaigns and became a particularly important force in U.S. politics in the late 20th century. Negative advertising can be used to expose a candidate's undesirable or shameful personal characteristics, such as a history of poor health, adultery, or substance abuse—or similar failings on the part of family members—as well as to criticize a candidate's public record or position on issues. Negative political advertising has been considered more effective than negative product advertising because the U.S. political system does not adhere to the same standards of truthfulness as product advertising. However, many people perceive a negative campaign as unethical because the message often includes personal attacks. Negative ads may, therefore, have the effect of lowering voting rates and creating a public distaste for politics in general.

In sum, negative advertising can be a successful tactic for drawing attention to a product or brand and reacting to competitors, but it often produces only a temporary increase in market share. It is important, therefore, for an advertiser to balance negative advertising with advertising that focuses on positive attributes. The keys to the effective use of negative advertising are: (1) limiting the amount of negative content (to guard against loss of credibility and audience interest) and (2) avoiding messages that can be proven false (to prevent lawsuits).

LINDA WANG

Further Reading

Gronhaug, Kjell, "Positive and Negative Advertising Appeals Revisited," *Marketing and Research Today* 6, no. 2 (1978)

Koprowski, Gene, "Theories of Negativity," *Brandweek* (20 February 1995)

Pinkleton, Bruce, "The Effects of Negative Comparative Political Advertising on Candidate Evaluations and Advertising Evaluations: An Exploration," *Journal of Advertising* 26, no. 4 (1997)

Thomas, Barry, "Comparative Advertising: What Have We Learned in Two Decades?" *Journal of Advertising Research* 23, no. 2 (1993)

Nestlé S.A.

Principal Agencies
Lord & Thomas
Cecil & Presbrey
Dancer, Fitzgerald, Sample
McCann-Erickson

William Esty and Company, Inc.
J. Walter Thompson Company
Leo Burnett Company
Jordan, McGrath, Case & Taylor, Inc.
Messner Vetere Berger McNamee Schmetterer/Euro RSCG

Nestlé S.A. is the world's largest food company, with more than 500 factories and a total workforce of more than 230,000. It is also one of the world's most international companies; only 2 per cent of its sales are made in its home country, Switzerland.

Nestlé's roots go back to two companies: the Anglo-Swiss Condensed Milk Company and the Nestlé Company. Two American brothers founded the Anglo-Swiss Condensed Milk Company in Switzerland in 1866; separately, Henri Nestlé started the Nestlé Company in 1867 to produce and sell the infant formula he invented.

Nestlé's factory, built in Vevey, his hometown, was next door to a chocolate factory. Two foremen at the adjoining factories decided to mix Nestlé's condensed milk with the chocolate paste, creating a better-tasting milk chocolate. The new chocolate was a success, and in 1896 Nestlé moved into chocolates.

In an early advertisement for Nestlé condensed milk, a poster from the late 1800s by Th.-A. Steilen pictures a cherub-faced girl sitting in a chair, sipping milk from a bowl. Three cats beg for some of the milk. The background is simple and the text is short, with only the product name and a simple tag line, "Richest in cream."

Another advertisement from the turn of the century was designed by Alphonse Mucha in the ornate French Art Nouveau style, which was garnering international attention. The ad shows a mother in flowing gown with flowing hair feeding Nestlé's Milk Food to a fat, healthy baby in a rocking crib. The background has an intricate pattern, and the simple text "Nestlé's food for infants" is printed in an Art Nouveau–style font.

In 1905 the Nestlé Company and Anglo-Swiss Condensed Milk Company merged to become the Nestlé and Anglo-Swiss Condensed Milk Company. During World War I, the company shifted production from war-torn areas to keep up with demand. Then in the 1920s, the company added several products: malted milk, powdered beverages, and powdered buttermilk for babies. The U.S. stock market crash and worldwide depression that ushered in the 1930s did not significantly affect the company.

By 1936 the company had changed its name to the Nestlé and Anglo-Swiss Condensed Milk Company Ltd. to reflect that it had become a holding company. Nestlé introduced its first non-milk product in 1938. A Brazilian coffee industry representative is said to have asked Nestlé to invent a use for Brazil's large coffee surplus. After eight years of research, Nescafé instant coffee was born. Nestlé was unable to produce enough Nescafé to distribute it widely, so it was introduced to the world market quietly, without fanfare. Nescafé was especially popular in the United States, as was Nestea, a powdered tea introduced by Nestlé in the early 1940s.

Lord & Thomas was the company's agency in the United States in the 1930s. With the outbreak of World War II, the company split in two, one part headquartered in Switzerland and another in Stamford, Connecticut. Nestlé produced Nescafé and powdered milk for the U.S. military throughout the war. The U.S.-based company hired the Leon Livingston Agency, a small ad agency in San Francisco, California.

Decaf, the first instant decaffeinated coffee marketed by Nestlé, was introduced via this 1956 advertisement.

With the end of World War II, U.S. advertising reflected the country's new optimism. A 1951 in-store promotion in Liggett Drugstore in New York City caught the spirit of the times: five tons of Nestlé's bars were set up in a mountainous pile in the store with signs heralding the "world's largest display of chocolate."

Now—Satisfy Your
"COFFEE HUNGER"
with NESCAFÉ®

—tastier coffee made the modern way!

Good company, blazing logs and delicious Nescafé Coffee . . . nothing could be pleasanter! Or easier for the hostess! For Nescafé has deep-down 100% coffee goodness that truly satisfies "coffee hunger." Here's how simple it is to make it:

Recipe for Company Coffee

In your prettiest coffee server, put one teaspoonful of Nescafé (more or less, depending on strength desired) and a coffee cupful of boiling water for each cup of coffee. Cover, let coffee steep for a moment. Result—extra aroma, delicious flavor! *Tastier* coffee that wins compliments all around!

© 1956 The Nestlé Company, Inc.

When you're hungry for tastier coffee, try Nescafé

Nescafé, featured in this ad from 1956, became one of Nestlé's most profitable products.

Market research in the early 1950s showed that short blocks of copy drew in the reader, a finding that led to the use of comic strips in advertising. In keeping with this trend, Nestlé began a campaign for its cookie mix and semi-sweet chocolate morsels with a four-page, color comic strip insert in 1952 in *American Girl*, the magazine published by the Girl Scouts of America. These ads, the first ever allowed in the publication, were organized by Cecil & Presbrey, which won work for Nestlé in 1950.

By 1955 the Nestlé Company, the U.S.-based subsidiary of Nestlé, was spending $9.5 million annually on U.S. advertising, according to an *Advertising Age* estimate. Through the mid-1950s to 1959, Nestlé generally was one of the top-60 companies in U.S. advertising spending as ranked by *Advertising Age*. Nestlé's marketing in the 1950s focused on Nescafé, Decaf, Nestea, Nestlé chocolate morsels, and new product introductions.

By the mid-1950s, Nescafé, once the leader in instant coffee, had fallen to a distant second behind General Foods' Maxwell House, which had roughly 40 percent of the market compared with Nescafé's 12 percent to 14 percent. Because Nescafé was one of Nestlé's most profitable products, the company focused on regaining that market share. In 1956 Nestlé placed an ad in the 18 March issue of *Life* magazine. It was a six-page, color insert tracking the evolution of coffee, from its discovery to the introduction of Nescafé. Believed to be the largest magazine ad ever placed in the coffee industry, it cost Nestlé $250,000. The ad featured seven specially commissioned paintings by Robert Riggs and carried a copywriter's byline for Roger Purdon, then with Bryan Houston, Inc.

When Nestlé introduced its first instant decaffeinated coffee, Decaf, in 1956, it again had its sights on a General Foods competing brand, Sanka. The Decaf advertising budget was spent primarily for TV spots that first pitched that Decaf "lets you sleep" and then shifted to the pitch that Decaf "never gets on your nerves."

In 1957 Nestlé announced a diversification of its TV sponsorship to six shows, worked out by Nestlé's three agencies: Bryan Houston, Inc.; Dancer, Fitzgerald, Sample, Inc. (DFS); and McCann-Erickson. And by 1958 Nestlé had moved its coffee emphasis to TV commercials, spending roughly $1.7 million on TV spot ads in 1958, mostly on Nescafé and Decaf coffees.

Unlike its struggle in instant coffee, Nestlé's Nestea instant tea was a market leader, competing strongly against Standard Brand's Instant Tea Leaf and Lipton's Instant tea. In the mid-1950s DFS managed the Nestea account with a small budget spent mostly in magazine advertising. In 1957 Nestlé spent only $83,592 on Nestea advertising, but in 1958 the brand got a major marketing push. Its magazine budget increased 65 percent with ads running in *Ladies' Home Journal, McCall's, Good Housekeeping, Woman's Day,* and *Family Circle,* on TV with sponsorships of the *Gale Storm Show* and the *Garry Moore Show,* and on radio.

The Nestea magazine ads were visually clean and realistic, featuring a photograph of a Nestea jar and a glass of tea with ice cubes, a slice of lemon and a sprig of mint. Tag lines included "Now—100% pure tea that dissolves instantly—even in cold tap water!" and "Nestea is the largest selling instant tea!" By 1959 Nestlé had moved most of its TV budget to spot commercials, and Nestea's overall TV budget increased to almost $420,000, according to *Advertising Age.*

Other categories with sizable ad spending included Nestlé's Quik, its chocolate line, and new products. Nestlé advertised Quik mostly on television and Nestlé Chocolate Morsels mostly in recipe-based magazine ads.

In April 1959 Nestlé took several accounts away from DFS owing to increasing conflicts between Nestlé's new products and other clients DFS represented. Nestlé gave Decaf and Nestea to McCann-Erickson. Nestlé also moved its Nescafé account from Bryan Houston to the William Esty Company.

In the early 1960s Nestlé moved some accounts away from McCann-Erickson, mostly to Leo Burnett Company, Chicago, Illinois. As with its previous agency dispute, the switch was due to a disagreement between Nestlé and McCann-Erickson regarding the agency's ability to work for competitors. But McCann-Erickson International received the Nestlé milk products and Maggi soups accounts in Central America.

Throughout the 1960s Nestlé's U.S. advertising budget increased from roughly $12 million in the early 1960s to $19 million by 1969, but that increase did not keep pace with overall U.S. advertising spending. By 1969 the company dropped to 91st in U.S. advertising spending. Nestlé's largest advertising budget continued to be spent on coffee, especially Nescafé. But there was a break in Nescafé advertising in the early 1960s as McCann-Erickson took over the account and developed Nescafé's new theme: "Minute brew Nescafé."

In 1967 Nestlé Canada ran a contest promoting Nescafé with three Ford Motor Company Mustangs as the top prizes and the tag line, "The first instant coffee with fresh ground flavor." Meanwhile Nestlé continued Decaf's TV sponsorship with the tag line, "Wakeup flavor! But no caffeine."

Then with the international launches of Nestlé's freeze-dried instant coffee brands, the company's coffee marketing focus shifted. In 1964 Nestlé began marketing Nescafé Gold and Nescafé Filtre freeze-dried instant coffees in Europe and Taster's Choice in Canada in 1966. These launches intensified the instant-coffee market competition, and in 1966 General Foods sued Nestlé for alleged infringements on patented freeze-drying techniques. Taster's Choice overtook Nescafé as the company's most promoted brand by 1969. Nestlé introduced Taster's Choice in the United States with almost $5 million in TV spots and $1 million in print and radio ads.

But as Nestlé shifted its focus in coffee marketing in the 1960s, Nestea remained the solid marketing winner in instant teas. In 1961 a white "Miss Nestea" donned a sari and adopted "far-eastern hand gestures" in print and TV ads to promote the "100% pure" tea. By 1962 Nestea had the largest market share in the instant-tea business, 38 percent, compared with Lipton's 24 percent. Nestea's success was due in part to the introduction of a large three-ounce jar. Nestea's ad budget was doubled in the summer of 1962 with promotion on five TV shows and color ads in *Good Housekeeping, Reader's Digest, Family Week,* and *Parade.*

During the summer of 1964 Nestea ran special offers in magazine ads with the tag line, "1/3 more free!" By 1967 Nestlé had such confidence in Nestea that it extended the brand by launching Nestea instant hot tea using Sunday supplement ads and spot TV.

Advertising attention also grew for Nestlé's Quik chocolate and strawberry drink mixes in the 1960s. Quik campaigns centered on cute characters to attract children, including Farfel, a hound-dog puppet used in the early 1960s. Farfel and his puppeteer sang the jingle, "N-E-S-T-L-E-S, Nestlé's makes the very best chocolate." Nestlé ran ads on children's TV shows publicizing its offer of a foot-tall stuffed Farfel that could be purchased with two dollars and the serial code from one Quik tin. By the end of the 1960s, Farfel was retired and Nestlé introduced Little Hans the Chocolate Maker, a redhead with a mustache and lederhosen. Farfel was reintroduced briefly in 1992 in a TV commercial developed by the WPP Group's J. Walter Thompson Company (JWT).

In other advertising campaigns in the 1960s, Nestlé publicized new products ranging from five-cent candy bars to baby foods in Australia. In 1961 McCann-Erickson developed newspaper ads featuring three candy bars together with "5 cents" as the very large headline to promote Nestlé's new, smaller bars. Also in 1961 Nestlé expanded the Keen instant soft drink line to five fruit flavors and promoted Keen in children's daytime TV shows and women's magazines.

Where do they get all that energy?

Copyright 1963, The Nestlé Company, Inc.

from Nestlé's® QUIK® and milk

Mix it with cold milk for the most delicious chocolaty refresher—the most sensible summer drink. **Nestlé's Makes The Very Best Chocolate.**

Nestlé's most famous slogan, "Nestlé's makes the very best chocolate," was used to market Nestlé's Quik in this 1963 ad.

In 1963 Nestlé tested its new baby foods line in Australia, trying to break Heinz's dominance in that market. Print ads showed smiling babies and pitched the benefits of Nestlé's glass jars, the major difference between Nestlé's and Heinz's product. The campaign, developed by the Pritchard, Wood, Inc., agency, included ads in women's magazines, newspapers, daytime TV, direct mail, and sampling.

Nestlé continued to grow in the 1970s through the purchase of other companies and increasing its advertising. Advertising expenditure estimates varied throughout the 1970s, depending in part upon which Nestlé companies, subsidiaries, and partial-ownership companies were included in the accounting. But generally, Nestlé advertising increased from around $28 million in the early 1970s to more that $50 million in the late 1970s, all the while remaining within the ranks of the top-80 U.S. advertisers. The majority of Nestlé's spending was in TV, which ranged from cosponsorship of *Lassie* reruns with Kellogg in 1976 to buying ad time on the new *Saturday Night Live* comedy program in 1975.

Nestlé continued to heavily advertise its coffee, especially Taster's Choice. A decaffeinated version of Taster's Choice was added in 1971. Nestlé's other decaffeinated brand, Decaf, was not freeze-dried and had only a 1 percent market share. Burnett ran the Taster's Choice Decaffeinated ad campaign, which included prime-time TV spots, fringe TV, radio, newspapers, and magazines ads.

Also in 1971 Nestlé introduced another version of Nescafé with chunkier crystals that more closely resembled ground coffee. Magazine ads announced the change with the tag line, "We're making Nescafé more like you make fresh ground coffee." The ads from Burnett ran in Sunday supplements.

Nestlé further diversified its instant coffee offerings in 1973 when it premiered Nescafé Gold Cup freeze-dried coffee, attempting to attract ground-roast users skeptical about the taste of instant coffee. "You've never tasted a freeze-dried coffee with this kind of dark, rich flavor," a TV commercial for Gold Cup announced. The spot began with the sound of beating drums, a jungle scene, flashes of lightning, and a frightened monkey's face, and then described the blending of beans from Africa and South America for Gold Cup.

A severe frost in Brazil in 1975 damaged that country's coffee crop, sending world coffee prices soaring in 1976 and 1977. Prices rose so significantly that consumers threatened to boycott coffee altogether. In reaction, Nestlé's advertising for Nescafé, by Burnett, emphasized cost savings in color spreads in 95 newspapers in 89 cities. Nestlé also ran price comparison TV spots for Taster's Choice.

Despite the challenging climate for coffee products, Nestlé rolled out yet another instant brand, Sunrise, in 1976. Sunrise's tag line, "Mellowed with chicory," emphasized its mild flavor and set up the brand to go after the expanding instant coffee business, spending $95,600 on the product launch.

Nestlé's Quik continued with its cute character campaigns, developing one of the best in 1973 when it debuted the Nestlé's Quik Bunny. In commercials the bunny slurped down Quik and said, "You caaaan't . . . drink it sloooow." The bunny proved so popular that it remained the character representing Quik through the turn of the millennium, though its tag line changed to "Chocolate milk? Think Quik" in the 1990s.

Nestea remained dominant in the instant tea market in the 1970s, increasing its 50 percent market share. Nestlé took advantage of the brand's success by adding Nestlé Instant ice tea mixes and flavored iced tea mixes, and by distributing canned and bottled Nestea iced tea via soft-drink distributors beginning in 1971. In 1972 Nestlé began its largest regional TV ad campaign with region-specific spots; a Northeast commercial, for example, featured a reenactment of the Boston Tea Party. And in 1975 Nestlé began to air an ad touting the results of 165 taste tests that showed people preferred the taste of Nestea instant tea to the leading Lipton tea bag. But perhaps the most well-known Nestea campaign was the "Take the Nestea Plunge" campaign, which ran from the mid-1970s through the 1980s in both TV and magazine ads. The ad featured people taking a sip of the prepared ice tea drink and then plunging into a refreshing swimming pool.

Nestlé's new-product launches in the 1970s were mostly in the chocolate category, which also was handled by Burnett. In 1971 Nestlé produced the ten-cent ChocoLite puffed chocolate bar with honey chips and promoted it in newspaper and TV ads. The newspaper ads featured the word "ChocoLite" in puffy, bubble lettering and a coupon for one free bar. Nestlé introduced another chocolate bar line in 1976—a 12-cent bar in animal shapes—with ad support in Sunday supplements. The Nestlé's Crunch bar was featured in 30-second TV commercials that included alternating shots of young moviegoers enjoying Crunch bars and shots of chocolate being made. Ads for Nestlé's "minis" line of candies ran in newspapers.

Despite Nestlé's many marketing successes in the 1970s, the decade ended in difficulty as the company faced an international boycott for its methods in marketing infant formula to mothers in underdeveloped nations. U.S. activists began the boycott in 1977, accusing Nestlé of distributing free samples of infant formula in underdeveloped nations; when mothers used formula instead of breastfeeding their babies, their bodies stopped producing breast milk. Once the free samples stopped, these very poor mothers either were unable to feed their babies or, because of the cost of the formula, fed them very diluted formula, the activists said.

In 1981 Helmut Maucher became the new managing director of Nestlé and addressed the boycott directly by working with the World Health Organization to develop rules for marketing infant formula in the developing world, though accusations against Nestlé lingered into the early 1990s.

Nestlé's expansion continued in the 1980s, and its advertising budget swelled as the company supported its newly acquired and created brands. By the mid-1980s, its advertising budget was $187 million, according to the *Standard Directory of Advertisers*.

Its acquisitions and new lines ranged from frozen food to chocolates. In 1981 Nestlé introduced the Lean Cuisine reduced-calorie frozen-food line from Stouffer's, which it had recently purchased. In 1988 it bought the leading British chocolate producer, Rowntree, as well as an Italian pasta maker, Buitoni.

Nestlé also invested in coffee: in 1985 it bought Hills Brothers, Inc., a large U.S. ground-coffee marketer. Other changes in Nestlé's coffee line included moving the Taster's Choice account from Della Femina, McNamee WCRS to McCann in 1989.

Nestlé bought Carnation, a U.S. marketer of milk, pet, and culinary products, in 1984. With this purchase, Nestlé entered the U.S. infant formula market in 1988, a move that once again brought criticism of the company's marketing. Carnation introduced two infant formulas to the U.S. market: Good Nature and Good Start H.A. Breaking with industry practice, the company marketed the formulas directly to mothers via TV commercials and magazine ads. The Good Start H.A. label had "hypoallergenic" printed in bold type on the front. The formula was predigested, but the company's hypoallergenic claim lured mothers of milk-allergic babies. Some of these babies had allergic reactions, and a number of leading pediatricians said the company's claims were misleading. In response, Carnation retained Ogilvy & Mather to help smooth its dealings with the Food and Drug Administration and removed "hypoallergenic" from the front of the Good Start label, but the claim remained in the fine print on the back of the can and in medical journal ads.

In the 1990s Nestlé introduced several banner campaigns, including Butterfinger ads using cartoon characters from *The Simpsons* television series and the Taster's Choice serial commercials, which resembled a soap opera. Nestlé increased its non-U.S. advertising expenditures, and *Advertising Age* ranked it one of the top-ten spenders outside the United States. Nestlé attempted to reorganize its advertising to make its brands globally recognizable.

In 1990 Nestlé and ad agency Jordan, McGrath, Case & Taylor, Inc., developed *The Simpsons* Butterfinger campaign with the tag line, "Nobody better lay a finger on my Butterfinger." The campaign later moved to the San Francisco office of J. Walter Thompson USA and included three contests. In 1993 Nestlé ran a $50,000 grand prize contest based on the theft of the Bart Simpson character's Butterfinger, played out in TV spots. In 1998 Nestlé held *Simpsons* trivia contests on the new Butterfinger Web site and set up a "Simpsons family reunion," awarding prizes to look-alikes, sound-alikes, and fans.

Another Nestlé 1990s marketing triumph, which became part of British and U.S. pop culture, was the Sharon and Tony soap opera ad campaign. McCann-Erickson developed the Sharon and Tony commercials for a British audience to sell Gold Blend coffee in 1987. The commercials, with a running soap opera–like story line of a flirtation between neighbors in an apartment building, were a hit in the United Kingdom, and McCann-Erickson revamped the TV ads to run in the United States to reposition Taster's Choice as a sexier product.

Also in the 1990s Nestlé began co-marketing with other big names such as the Walt Disney Company and the Coca-Cola Company. In 1992 Nestlé invested heavily in promotions for Euro Disneyland after signing a ten-year promotional rights contract for the park. Nestlé also formed a joint venture with Coca-Cola called the Coca-Cola Nestlé Refreshment Company, to help market Nestea's bottled ice teas in traditional cola markets and via vending machines. The original "Nestea plunge" idea was revamped by McCann-Erickson; it developed TV commercials with the tag lines "Taste the plunge" and "Plunge in."

Lean Cuisine enjoyed another of Nestlé's successful 1990s marketing campaigns. In 1994 Nestlé changed agencies for the account, hiring Messner, Vetere, Berger, McNamee, Schmetterer/Euro RSCG, which designed the "It's not just lean, it's cuisine" campaign. Lean Cuisine continued to use the tag line throughout the 1990s; by 1999 the line had expanded to include more than 100 entrées. The majority of Lean Cuisine's ad budget was spent on TV commercials with the remainder spent on print ads in such magazines as *People, Health, Self,* and *Good Housekeeping.*

In 1998 Nestlé launched its biggest multi-brand marketing push in the United Kingdom in conjunction with Turner Broadcasting System's pan-European Cartoon Network. The campaign featured ten of Nestlé's brands as part of the Nestlé birthday club, which tied into a weekly cartoon dedicated to a selected birthday girl or boy.

After the U.K. marketing push, Nestlé made plans in 1999 to bring a favorite British candy line to the United States. The move came as part of Nestlé's desire to build Willy Wonka—named after characters from the 1964 book *Charlie and the Chocolate Factory* by Roald Dahl and its 1971 movie adaptation *Willy Wonka and the Chocolate Factory*– into its signature children's brand worldwide. Nestlé planned to back the launch of Exploder, a chocolate bar with sizzling crunchies, and Oompas fruit chews by a national TV campaign developed by Dailey & Associates, West Hollywood, California. The ads ran during Saturday morning network kids' shows and on Nickelodeon with the tag line, "What will he think of next?"

Nestlé's attention to the Willy Wonka brand reflected its focus on the globalization of its brands at the end of the 1990s. Other efforts included changing the name of Quik to NesQuik, as well as planning a relaunch, scheduled for April 2001, of the Nescafé brand via McCann-Erickson Worldwide, New York, with an estimated budget of $60 million.

As Nestlé entered the 21st century, its total advertising budget was estimated at $192 million. The company invested part of its TV budget in the production of content for family viewing via McCann-Erickson. Nestlé also promoted products through Internet advertising on Web sites such as SnowballCollege.com, a site aimed at consumers in their late teens and early 20s.

Nestlé bought Perrier Group in the early 1990s to move into the bottled water market and began ad campaigns by Publicis Conseil SA to refocus Perrier's image from that of a stodgy consumer to a younger, more active one. Nestlé also planned the launch of a new bottled water line in Europe via Publicis, Paris, France. By late 2000 Nestlé was one of the few dominant companies in nonflavored bottled water.

Nestlé also purchased the PowerBar brand of protein-rich snack bars sold as a healthy alternative to candy bars and moved the account from Wieden & Kennedy, Portland, Oregon, to Publicis, Dallas, Texas. And in 2001 Nestlé bought Ralston-Purina, making it the largest marketer of pet foods.

JENNIFER WHITSON

Further Reading

Cope, Nigel, "Corporate Profile: Nestlé—Sweet Dreams Are Made of This," *The Independent* (13 December 2000)

Cracking the Code: Monitoring the International Code of Marketing of Breast-Milk Substitutes, London: Interagency Group on Breastfeeding Monitoring, 1997

Heer, Jean, *Reflets du monde, 1866–1966: Presence de Nestlé*, Lausanne, Switzerland: Imprimeries Réunies, 1966; 2nd edition, as *Nestlé: 125 ans de 1866 á 1991*, Vevey,

Switzerland: Nestlé, 1991; as *World Events, 1866–1966: The First Hundred Years of Nestlé*, Lausanne, Switzerland: Imprimeries Réunies, 1966; 2nd edition, as *Nestlé: 125 Years, 1866–1991*, translated by F.J. Benson and Constance Devanthéry-Lewis, Vevey, Switzerland: Nestlé, 1991

Nestlé, *This is Your Company*, New York: s.n., 1946

Riggs, Thomas, editor, *Encyclopedia of Major Marketing Campaigns*, Detroit, Michigan, and London: Gale Group, 1999

Netherlands, The

Despite its relatively small size and population, The Netherlands has developed a reputation as a European advertising center, serving as the European base for numerous advertising agencies in the United States and Japan. The work coming out of Amsterdam, Amstelveen, and Rotterdam has earned respect for its creativity and humor.

The Dutch advertising industry was established in the early 1880s with the founding of the first advertising agencies, including De la Mar, Ltd., which set up shop in 1880. The industry experienced its greatest periods of growth during the 1950s, 1960s, and 1970s, with many of the country's top agencies having originated during the last of those three decades.

In 2000 The Netherlands (population: 15.8 million) ranked as the sixth-largest advertising market in Europe, behind Germany, the United Kingdom, France, Italy, and Spain. Ad spending in the country in 2000 was more than $4 billion, representing a gain of about 17 percent over the previous year. That represented a significant improvement over recent growth; in 1999 ad spending increased only about 4 percent over 1998.

Agencies and Advertisers

According to the Dutch government's Central Bureau for Statistics, there were more than 1,300 advertising agencies in The Netherlands at the turn of the 21st century, and about 20 of those had an annual income of $5 million or more. The 115 agencies that are members of the Dutch Association of Communication Agencies account for 75 percent of ad industry billings.

The top Netherlands-based ad agencies are those affiliated with or owned by global agency powerhouses. In 2000 these included Lowe Lintas & Partners, with gross income of $58.3 million on billings of $388.9 million; TBWA Netherlands, $56.9 million on billings of $379.6 million; BBDO Nederland, $55.4 million on billings of $369.1 million; Publicis, $47.8 million on billings of $318.7 million; and PMS&vW/Y&R, $46.6 million on billings of $564.6 million.

Other major agencies in Holland include AppNet; Asatsu Europe; Bates Not Just Film; Borremans & Ruseler (Draft Worldwide); Carlson Marketing Group; Creative Direct Response International; DMB&B; Euro RSCG Netherlands; FCB/BK&P; Grey Worldwide; HLPB Hettinga, De Boers (Testa); KKBR Conquest; Lowe Lintas & Partners Worldwide; Ogilvy & Mather; PPGH (JWT); Rapp Collins Netherlands; Saatchi & Saatchi; TBWA/H Europe (TBWA/Hakuhodo); TMP Worldwide; and Wieden & Kennedy, Amsterdam. Only two of the top 25 agencies are independent.

Most of the country's agencies, especially the larger, full-service shops, are based in the highly populated western cities of Amsterdam, its suburb of Amstelveen, and Rotterdam. Amsterdam is ranked as the ninth-largest advertising market in Europe on a city-by-city basis, generating $3.7 billion in total billings. When viewed singly, however, none of the ad agencies based in The Netherlands ranks among Europe's top 100.

In the local market, some of the top advertisers ranked on the basis of spending are the packaged-goods companies Unilever, Nestlé, and the Procter & Gamble Company; financial services companies RVD Holding Den Haag, ING Groep, and KPN Holding Den Haag; brewery Heineken; publisher VNU; and retail chain Ahold. The Netherlands is headquarters to many large, global advertisers, among them Unilever, VNU, Heineken, the electronics marketer Philips Electronics, and the Dutch national airline, KLM. It has been estimated that between 25 percent and 30 percent of Dutch ad agency assignments are executed outside Holland.

Food is the most important advertising sector, generating $300 million in ad spending in 1999, followed by retail and financial services. As for media, newspapers accounted for 49.3 percent of ad spending in 1999, according to Zenith Media Worldwide, followed by magazines with 22.9 percent and television with 17.2 percent; radio and outdoor advertising account for the remainder. The country's major broadcasters, each with more than 10 percent market share, are Nederland 1, Nederland 2, RTL 4, and SBS 6.

SERIOUS WHISKY   RIDICULOUS PRICE

Results DDB's 1990s campaign for Mansion House Scotch whisky won international recognition and solidified Results' position as one of The Netherlands' most respected ad agencies.

Industry Practices

Historically, the mid-1950s and early 1960s were turbulent times for the advertising industry in The Netherlands. The business was governed by a set of rules, the Code of Advertising, which had been established in 1948 through collaboration among advertisers, agencies, and newspapers. It decreed that 15 percent was the standard agency commission and set up a powerful Council of Advertising that recognized agencies, settled disagreements, and imposed penalties on organizations that violated tenets of the code. The code also set up rules regarding the publication and calculation of circulation figures, disallowed rebates, and required adherence to the prices set forth in a publication's rate card. The council had the ability to impose fines, and its rulings were accepted by civil court judges. All these regulations were intended to create stability in the industry.

In the 1950s, however, advertisers wanted to abolish some of the rules, namely those regarding the commission percentage, so that they could negotiate advertising rates. Advertising spending was on the rise, U.S. subsidiary companies were setting up manufacturing plants in the country (220 foreign subsidiaries were based in The Netherlands at the time, with 42 percent from the United States), and retailing was undergoing a growth period with 200 self-service stores in operation. There were 600 major advertisers, led by the Dutch company Unilever and its competitor Procter & Gamble Company, and 76 recognized ad agencies.

By the mid-1950s commission rates had become a contentious issue and had created significant bad feeling among newspapers, advertisers, and advertising agencies. The controversy continued through the early 1960s—a similar dilemma had occurred in the United States a few years earlier—when The Netherlands Advertisers Association withdrew from The Netherlands Rules of Advertising. By the mid-1960s all the parties came to the realization that they had to work together for the good of the industry.

Although codes of advertising governing the advertising business in The Netherlands have evolved over the years, the country maintains a strict set of regulations similar to the one it had adopted in 1948. These rules, collectively called The Netherlands Advertising Code, have provided the foundation for industry self-regulation since 1974. The code outlines the current standards for advertising, while the Advertising Code Committee enforces those standards. The Netherlands Advertising Tripartite, founded in

1977, is the group of advertisers, communications agencies, and media—including their respective associations—that oversees the code and dictates changes.

By 1961 the country's association of communications agencies estimated the advertising market at $158 million, or about 2 percent of the gross national income, with per capita spending on advertising at slightly more than $14. Newspapers accounted for about one-third of the market, followed by direct advertising with 23 percent, and business and professional publication advertising at 13.5 percent. A new development was radio advertising. Although there was no commercial radio, the pirate station Radio Veronica accepted advertising and took over a significant share of the ad spending market. The success of Radio Veronica—amid much controversy and government threats of closure—foreshadowed developments to come in the emerging television market.

By the mid-1960s spillover of commercial television from Germany and Belgium exposed Dutch audiences—40 percent of whom could pick up foreign channels—to the concept of TV advertising. Meanwhile, by 1964 a pirate television station operated by Reclame Exploitate Maatschappij (Advertising Operating Company) had moved its base of operations from a position near Cork, Ireland, to an artificial island in the North Sea off the coast of The Netherlands. Called TV North Sea and run by a British company, the station reportedly generated more than $1 million in advertising revenue before being seized by the Royal Dutch Navy. The Dutch government had passed special legislation against commercial broadcasting targeted specifically at the pirate station.

The programming of TV North Sea whetted viewers' appetites for more entertaining fare; the Dutch domestic TV schedule tended to be serious and often religious or political, with the two television and two radio stations controlled by the country's dominant political parties, some of which had religious affiliation. Finally, as a result of pressure from viewers and advertisers, the Dutch House of Commons (Tweede Kamer) passed a bill authorizing commercial radio and television by the end of 1965. The bill stipulated the creation of a council for radio and television advertising and a code for advertisers specifically dealing with broadcast advertising. Initially, a 15-minute-per-day period was set aside before and after newscasts for commercials; radio was allowed 24 minutes per day of advertising.

The advent of commercial television and radio expanded the opportunities for advertising and enhanced the position of advertising agencies. Some of the leading agencies in the mid-1960s included Smit's, Prad, De la Mar, LPE Nederland, and Van Maanen, all independent Dutch shops. By 1968 television accounted for 14 percent of measured media in The Netherlands, and by 1989 more than 85 percent of homes had television sets. Other important media outlets were newspapers, women's magazines (which reached two-thirds of adult females), trade publications (which numbered 1,200), and direct mail, which accounted for a third of Dutch advertisers' budgets.

The Netherlands' reputation as a global advertising hub had begun as early as the 1960s, when the establishment of the European Common Market in 1961 encouraged Dutch agencies to expand their international client bases. Two of the leading Dutch agencies of the era, Prad and Smit's, each organized separate international units in the early 1960s. The interest of global agencies in The Netherlands also traces its roots to the 1960s. In 1965, for example, Ted Bates & Company acquired local agency N.V. Reclame-Adviesbureau Noordervliet and formed Ted Bates-Nederland.

By the 1970s much of the turbulence of the 1950s and 1960s had subsided, but other challenges arose. Newspapers were suffering because ad dollars had moved away from print and toward commercial television and radio; several newspapers had merged or shut down in 1970 and 1971. In 1972 the Dutch government authorized $9.6 million in funds to subsidize the industry for two years.

Meanwhile, with several new agencies starting up during the decade, competition was growing. This development not only raised the stakes in the battle for clients but also decreased agency profit margins. The number of agencies had grown from 114 to 150 between 1969 and 1972, while employees in the industry had decreased from 3,600 to 3,400 during the same period, suggesting that more competition had resulted in financial difficulties and layoffs.

Meanwhile, the Dutch public did not strongly support advertising. Although they tended to be brand-conscious, liked luxury goods, and embraced items that made their lives easier, they did not accept high-pressure tactics and preferred messages that treated them as cost-conscious consumers. Surveys at the time showed that only 18 percent of the 13 million Dutch people thought advertising was important. Consumer groups were on the rise and started to attack advertising, a trend that the government, still somewhat wary itself, did not oppose.

Innovation: The First Personalized Ad

In 1975 the Dutch market was the location for an advertising first. The November issue of the Dutch edition of *Reader's Digest* (*Het Beste Uit Reader's Digest*) carried a three-page back-cover gatefold and a facing page in which General Motors Corporation, represented by McCann-Erickson (Nederland), introduced its new Opel line, marking what is thought to be the first attempt at a personalized ad. The inside cover featured a letter to the subscriber, with five references by name scattered throughout the text, while the outside cover was a coupon imprinted with the subscriber's name and address. The issue was mailed to 350,000 subscribers. Other advertisers, such as Nederlands Boekenclub (Dutch Book Club), tried the same technique in *Reader's Digest* within the year.

The 1980s witnessed a continued expansion of the advertising industry, with leading agencies such as Kuiper & Schouten and Campaign Company (now affiliated with Lowe Lintas & Partners Worldwide and TBWA Worldwide, respectively) founded during this decade. In addition, many U.S. agencies set up their European subsidiaries in The Netherlands during the 1980s. By the middle of the decade, it was estimated that 25 percent of the Dutch advertising market was held by U.S. agencies.

During the 1990s ad expenditures grew at the fastest pace in Dutch history, with much of the increase attributed to new commercial radio and television stations such as SBS 6, Fox, and RTL 4 and 5. Advertiser demand was on the rise at the same time as available airtime was expanding. Meanwhile, more business was coming into the country from abroad, as multinational advertisers increasingly chose Netherlands-based shops as their lead agencies for global campaigns. The country's agencies gained a reputation for coming up with effective campaign concepts. All sectors of advertising experienced growth, including press, radio and television, door-to-door advertising, and direct mail. The last was the largest sector with more than $1 billion in sales, according to the Dutch Central Bureau for Statistics.

The Netherlands' reputation as a creative hub—with both small and large agencies known for their innovative work—was solidified in the early 1990s. Many observers credit commercials director Paul Meijer, known for his storytelling strengths, for this trend. He put Holland on the map, they say, with his work for Mazda, KLM, Sony, and others for the Dutch agency PMS&vW/ Y&R. Today, agencies including KesselsKramer, Wieden & Kennedy, TBWA/Campaign Company, DDB Needham Worldwide, and many others carry on the country's creative tradition.

By the 1990s The Netherlands was becoming known for its technological sophistication, especially in graphics and video. The Dutch government had pioneered the standardization of digital data within Europe. Several ad agencies allied themselves with new technology companies in the late 1990s, including Benjamens, Van Doorn-Euro RSCG, which announced a merger with two interactive technology companies, Webnet and Cyberlab. The merged entity became known as Euro RSCG Interactive.

Despite the various links between Dutch and global agencies at the start of the 21st century, many smaller, independent shops exist and are sought after by international accounts, largely because of the respect that their creative work has earned. Agency 180, founded in 1998 by former Wieden & Kennedy executives to service Adidas-Solomon, and Strawberry Frogs, another small house founded in the late 1990s, are examples. These agencies, which have an international outlook, selected the Amsterdam area as their base of operations because they say it is a "more European" city than London, England, not to mention less expensive. It has a preponderance of interactive agencies, a lively advertising community, and a large pool of creative talent. This talent comprises not only Dutch creative professionals but many transplanted from other countries. (Several of the latter head up agencies in The Netherlands.)

From a business point of view, Amsterdam is one of Europe's main industry hubs, with companies from Tommy Hilfiger to Nike having their European headquarters there. As of 2000 The Netherlands counted more than 1,600 U.S. companies doing business there, in part because the country is known for its fluency in multiple languages, its tolerance for other cultures, and its ability to work with companies based in the countries around it. At the same time, Dutch companies have long had a great deal of international business, mainly because their domestic market is so small.

Ironically, some of The Netherlands' smaller creative agencies with worldwide reputations are not considered Dutch by the locals. Despite their high profiles among international clients, they do not get mentioned in the trade press or win trade awards. In fact, there is a definite schism, with a portion of agencies specializing in international clients and the remainder focusing almost exclusively on work for the Dutch market.

Advertising targeted at local consumers is often based on intuition and experience rather than research, which is one reason the country's reputation for creativity has flourished. Media are relatively inexpensive, the country has a rich art heritage, and the culture is forward-thinking, tolerant, and liberal, all of which contributes to the industry's willingness to experiment, often coming up with risqué or crazily humorous campaigns. Humor, often broad and specifically Dutch, tends to work in advertising, as does storytelling, while the hard sell does not.

Members of the creative community in Amsterdam tend to move frequently from agency to agency and have become a tight-knit group. Many observers believe that this atmosphere has helped make The Netherlands a place where creativity thrives, a situation that is evident in nearly all the country's advertising agencies, large and small.

KAREN RAUGUST

Further Reading

"Bow of Commercial Broadcasting Stirs Rumpus among Dutch," *Advertising Age* (27 December 1965)

Cowen, Matthew, "The Dutch Capital Moves Closer to Centre Stage," *Campaign* (8 September 2000)

"Dutch Advertiser Group Withdraws from Code Set Up," *Advertising Age* (26 November 1962)

"Dutch Agencies Facing Competition, Inflation," *Advertising Age* (24 September 1973)

"Dutch 'RD' Subscribers Get Personalized Ad from GM," *Advertising Age* (17 November 1975)

"European Media Map 2000," *Advertising Age International* (June 2000)

Horkan, Kay, "'Pirate' TV Venture Defies Dutch Government, Plans Telecasts," *Advertising Age* (8 June 1964)

"Netherlands," *Advertising Age* (4 June 1956)

Newspapers

The function performed by newspapers has changed little over the centuries. Their task is to report news events as well as to inform readers about products and services available to them—that is, to advertise. These tasks continue to make newspapers an important element in society. From the daily newspapers published in Europe's major cities to the weekly newspaper distributed in small towns across North America, newspapers play a major role in people's lives.

Classifications

Newspapers may be classified by size and format, frequency of issue, content, and market audience.

Size and Format

Newspapers are normally printed in one of two sizes: broadsheet, or standard size (approximately 22 by 13 inches), and the smaller tabloid size (approximately 10 by 13 inches). Most newspapers use the standard-size page, which is usually divided into six columns.

Frequency

A daily newspaper is one that comes out four or more times per week. A newspaper that comes out less often during the week is considered a weekly. Still other newspapers are distributed less often, and some are only distributed on an as-needed basis. These less frequent papers typically do not report the news but instead meet special needs, such as information about special events that would be of interest to tourists or similar groups.

Content

The content of newspapers is quite varied. A newspaper may contain little or no "hard" news. Such newspapers are often called "shoppers" and contain mostly ads and perhaps general news stories. Some papers concentrate on local community news, and still others contain a mixture of general and local news. Major metropolitan papers concentrate on "hard" news while their suburban competitors tend to favor "soft" news such as the engagements, marriages, and birthdays of their readers. Some newspapers tailor their content to specialized markets. For example, the *Wall Street Journal* concentrates on the business and finance markets, while *USA Today* designs its paper for the reader on the go, both at home and around the world.

Market Audience

Most newspapers serve a market based on geography. The common element among readers of most newspapers is that they live and work in the immediate geographic area served by that paper. Other demographic market variables also may affect a newspaper. For example, a newspaper may serve the student body of a university, or it may be printed in a foreign language to serve a market audience in its area. The market audience will vary in size from the few hundred readers of many small weekly papers to such newspapers as the *New York Times* and *Los Angeles Times,* which have more than 1 million readers daily each, and the *Wall Street Journal* and *U.S.A. Today,* whose readership is national, although advertising is sold on a sectional basis.

Advertising Advantages

Geographic selectivity, editorial support, secondary readership, and flexibility are all viewed as advantages of newspapers as an ad medium.

Geographic Selectivity

Most papers serve a defined geographic region, either a city, county, a group of related counties, or a state. For many businesses, newspapers offer a way to reach a well-defined market without waste circulation.

Editorial Support

Unlike newspaper advertisements, which get editorial support, a direct-mail advertisement presents more challenges because it does the job alone. In the process of reading a newspaper article, a person sees several ads. Such readers may be directed to ads as a result of their interest. An advertisement for a fishing lure placed in the sports section, for example, takes advantage of the special interest of those who are reading that particular section. Editorial support also comes at times just by having an ad in a particular paper. Financial ads have more clout with some readers because they appear in the *Wall Street Journal* or *Barron's*. Editorial support takes many forms and is a major advantage that newspapers have.

Secondary Readership

Secondary or pass-along readers enhance a newspaper's advertising value. One newspaper in a house of four people might result in four readers. Newspapers found in public places such as libraries, restaurants, and medical offices also promote multiple readership. Such multiple readers enhance the value of the advertisements in the newspaper.

Flexibility

Magazines often require several weeks lead time for placement of an advertisement. Newspapers, on the other hand, generally allow an advertiser to place an ad, change it, or delete it with minimum lead time. Such flexibility makes newspaper advertising popular with retailers and others that require quick reaction to changing market conditions.

An award-winning newspaper advertisement from Hampdel/Stefanides used current events—and a
newspaper clipping—to promote the Smith & Wollensky Restaurant Group.
The Smith & Wollensky Restaurant Group, Inc.

Advertising Disadvantages

Poor quality product, lack of permanence, and limited demographic orientation are disadvantages of newspapers as an advertising medium. From an advertising perspective, these very same disadvantages represent potential advantages for magazines.

Poor Quality Product

If an advertiser wishes to place an ad in an environment with much advertising clutter, then the typical newspaper is the place. Newspapers are full of advertisements competing for attention. Many ads are missed owing to the distractions within the pages of a newspaper, which make it difficult to impress a reader. And because of mechanical limitations and paper quality, the typical newspaper cannot provide the advertiser with as finely detailed a printed picture as is found in most magazines. Illustrations with fine detail or subtle changes in gray tones are generally difficult, if not impossible, to see in a newspaper.

Lack of Permanence

Moreover, newspapers lack permanence. If the advertiser wants long life for the impact of the advertisement, then magazines are the media vehicle of choice. The award-winning advertisement in the daily paper on Tuesday is on the kitchen floor for the puppy on Wednesday. Advertisements in weekly newspapers as well as those ads in the features sections of the typical Sunday newspaper tend to have a longer life, perhaps up to one week. Since most people have little interest in yesterday's news, there will be little interest in the advertisements that accompany them.

Limited Demographic Orientation

The strong suit for magazines is demographic orientation. One or more magazines exist for every demographic niche. Newspapers, on the other hand, tend to favor an orientation toward "geographics." An advertiser that wants to target a demographic group by using newspapers will encounter waste circulation, as the ad will typically reach numerous individuals not normally found within the target market. Waste exposures and wasted dollars are the result.

Preferred Positions

Newspaper advertisements bought at the lowest possible cost are purchased at a run-of-paper (ROP) rate. The ROP rate allows the newspaper to place the advertisement anywhere in the newspaper, whether the location is good or bad. For the standard newspaper page, an advertisement located above the fold is preferred, as is an ad at the front or back of the section. Placing an advertisement in the appropriate section brings the ad and the interested reader together. Advertisements featuring women's products usually do better in the women's section; auto products have better success when advertised in the auto section.

Generally any advertisement placed next to editorial copy is preferred over an ad located next to another ad; the more editorial copy around the advertisement the better. In some cases, preferred positions are obtained by paying a premium rate. In other cases, the advertiser need only request such positions in order to obtain them. All purchase orders for advertisements should include a placement request even if the newspaper does not offer a rate differential.

Audience Measurement

According to the Vienna, Virginia-based Newspaper Association of America, more than 56 million newspapers are sold every day in the United States, with an average of 2.33 readers per copy, which means that 112 million adults read a newspaper on a daily basis. To look at the data in a different way, almost six out of ten adults—or 58 percent—read a newspaper every day. And more than six out of ten adults (63.7 percent) read a newspaper every Sunday.

A good source of audience measurement is the Audit Bureau of Circulations, founded in 1932. The Audit Bureau, located in Schaumburg, Illinois, provides an established methodology for determining circulation of newspapers by county. Periodic reports verify the circulation counts for the newspaper. The Audit Bureau also provides demographic data to assist advertisers in understanding the audience being tapped by the ad placements in the particular paper. Though the Audit Bureau does not audit all newspapers, the majority of large-market newspapers are participants in the audit process.

Costs

More promotional dollars are spent in newspaper advertising than almost any other medium. In 2000, $49 billion was spent on newspaper advertising in the United States compared with $12.4 billion spent on magazines during the same period. Of the major media, only television exceeded the advertising volume of newspaper advertising—by less than $1 billion. As for other media, direct mail had an advertising volume of $44.5 billion, and radio's advertising volume amounted to $19.3 billion.

The lowest advertising rate in a newspaper, the ROP rate, would typically be quoted in terms of the cost for one column inch (one column wide by one inch deep) with possible discounts based on volume purchases. Other discounts might result from running the same advertisement in companion newspapers (newspapers owned by the same company) or in morning and afternoon papers serving the same market.

A unique cost feature of newspapers is the dual rate structure, which often finds national advertisers paying more for the same column-inch ad than a local advertiser would pay. The local or retail rate typically does not have a commission structure and is low in cost. On the other hand, the national or general rate usually includes a commission and may be quoted at a rate that is up to double that of the local rate. Some newspapers offer national advertisers a rate that reduces the national rate as more column inches are purchased. Such discounts bring the two rates closer together.

Using an emotional appeal, this 1998 ad for the *St. Louis Post-Dispatch* highlighted the selfless actions of members of the paper's readership community.
St. Louis Post-Dispatch.

Special costs may be incurred if the advertiser chooses to use freestanding inserts (FSIs). FSIs are printed separately and then inserted in the newspaper for delivery. Particularly popular in Sunday editions, FSIs typically stand out since they are printed with strong colors on better-quality paper than the newspaper. The main drawback to FSIs is their clutter; many Sunday newspapers have numerous FSIs, competing for the readers' attention.

Uses

The advertiser can use the newspaper in several ways. One option is to use classified advertising, or want ads. A second option is to use display advertising. Most newspapers use Standard Advertising Units (SAU) to provide uniform ad size. The SAU system, established in 1984, provides more than 50 standardized advertising sizes for the standard newspaper page. A third choice is the use of Sunday magazines, such as *Parade* and *USA Weekend*. The comics are yet another option. Advertisers may also choose to use special sections or issues such as back-to-school or graduation sections as they attempt to reach their target markets.

Another alternative for advertisers is the "advertorial"—an advertisement presented in a news format. It is analogous to the infomercial on television. To the untrained eye, the ad is news and therefore carries the credibility of a news story. Although this type of advertising can be effective, it raises ethical considerations on the part of the advertiser. Many newspapers allow this format and most label it as advertising. Often, however, the small print indicating that it is an advertisement is not detected by the reader.

WILLIAM H. BOLEN

See also Audit Bureau of Circulations

Further Reading

"Newspaper Advertising" (annual section), *Advertising Age* (30 April 2001)

Newspaper Association of America <www.naa.org>

SRDS Newspaper Advertising Source (1995–)

Sampson, Henry, *A History of Advertising from the Earliest Times,* London: Chatto and Windus, 1874; reprint, Detroit, Michigan: Gale, 1974

Wells, William, John Burnett, and Sandra Moriarty, *Advertising: Principles and Practice,* London: Prentice-Hall International, and Englewood Cliffs, New Jersey: Prentice Hall, 1989; 5th edition, Upper Saddle River, New Jersey: Prentice Hall, 2000

New Zealand. *See* Australia and New Zealand

Nielsen Corporation. *See* ACNielsen Corporation

Nike, Inc.

Principal Agencies
John Brown & Partners
William Cain, Inc.
Chiat/Day
Muse, Cordero and Chen
Wieden & Kennedy, Inc.

Nike's primary products include athletic footwear, apparel, and equipment. Acquisitions have included Cole-Hahn shoes, Bauer skates, and Sports Specialties. Until December 1981 the company was officially known as Blue Ribbon Sports. (The Nike trademark, however, was established in 1971.) Legend has it that the name "Blue Ribbon" was created in 1962, when Phil Knight, a recent graduate of the MBA program at Stanford University, was meeting with Onitsuka (Shoe) Company, Ltd., executives in Kobe, Japan, and he impulsively told them that he owned a company called Blue Ribbon Sports. In fact, there was no such business. Upon Knight's return to Portland, Oregon, however, he started the company, initially managing all sales and marketing (including advertising) himself.

By the following year, Blue Ribbon did exist, but primarily as a handshake deal between Knight and Bill Bowerman, formerly Knight's track coach at the University of Oregon. Bowerman agreed to invest $500 to help Knight launch a business importing running shoes from Japan at lower prices than the West German imports then dominating the market. By 1964 Blue Ribbon Sports was operational, and Knight was selling track shoes out of the trunk of a car.

Other than letters written to track coaches, Blue Ribbon's first official advertising was a printed "handout" designed by Knight; the headline read, "Best news in flats: Japan challenges European track shoe domination." The handout's copy reported that "Bill Bowerman calls it 'one helluva fine shoe'" and explained that low Japanese labor costs made it possible for the company to offer the shoes at the modest price of $6.95. The flier concluded with Knight's home address in Portland and a phone number to call for further information.

From these simple efforts, Nike's advertising would blossom under the watchful eye of Knight and company executives, who frequently challenged the concept of traditional footwear advertising. In 1977, for example, John Brown & Partners of Seattle, Washington, created a memorable print ad entitled, "There is no finish line," which concluded with the tag line, "Beating the competition is relatively easy. Beating yourself is a never-ending commitment." Despite the company's use of such creative campaigns, however, Knight was not convinced of the power of advertising. During his first meeting with advertising executive Dan Wieden in 1980, Knight reportedly introduced himself saying, "I'm Phil Knight and I hate advertising."

Knight may have hated advertising, but he loved athletes. At Nike's first marketing meeting, a Knight voice-over intoned, "We've seen sports change a lot, but our attitude at Nike remains the same. We understand the athlete, those who battle the odds and battle the system. Those who crave the bell lap, the last inning, or the final seconds of the season." It is because of Knight's philosophy that athletes have always taken center stage in Nike's advertising. In the late 1970s posters by Art Director Denny Strickland at Brown featured such basketball players as George Gervin ("The Iceman Cometh"). Another poster created by Brown, which was featured in a Smithsonian Institution exhibit of American advertising, depicted 22 basketball players who were members of Nike's Pro Club dressed up as "The Supreme Court."

Although it parted ways with Brown in 1979, Nike continued to seek dynamic representations of the athletes the company had signed to wear and endorse its shoes. Advertising for Nike was managed in-house by Peter Moore until 1982, when Moore called on Wieden, then a copywriter for William Cain, Inc., to create ads for the company.

Wieden and David Kennedy, both working in the creative department at Cain, started Wieden & Kennedy on 1 April 1982 in Portland. Over the next 20 years, Wieden worked with the staff to create and produce some of the most lauded television commercials ever. In 1984 Nike signed Michael Jordan, then a rookie with the Chicago Bulls basketball team and captain of the U.S. Olympic team, to a five-year contract for a reported $2.5 million. The "Air Jordan" campaign solidified Nike's position as the leading athletic shoe and launched Jordan as one of the most

WE HAVEN'T FORGOTTEN WHY THEY'RE CALLED SWEATS.

This 1983 Nike advertisement from Chiat/Day defined a new fitness ethic and helped make Nike a leader in sports apparel.
Reprinted courtesy of Nike, Inc. Photographer: Dennis Manarky. Agency: Chiat/Day.

successful product endorsers in advertising history. When *Entertainment Weekly* magazine listed the 50 greatest commercials of all time, Nike was one of only three companies with two spots on the list. The 1989 "Spike and Mike" spot with Jordan and film director Spike Lee ranked 16th, and the "HIV positive" commercial of 1995, which featured marathon runner Ric Muñoz, ranked 45th. The Muñoz commercial was the first TV spot ever to use an HIV-positive person as a role model. Both commercials were produced by Wieden & Kennedy, which also created the Nike "Just do it" campaign in 1988. That campaign was ranked fourth by *Advertising Age* in its list of the 20th century's greatest advertising.

Similarly, advertising reporter Bernice Kanner included two of Wieden & Kennedy's efforts for Nike in her 1999 book *The 100 Best TV Commercials*. The first, the "Bo knows" spot from 1989, featured the versatile athlete Bo Jackson playing a variety of sports while other athletes and, finally, musician Bo Diddley acknowledged Jackson's knowledge and ability in all things athletic. The commercial ends with Diddley saying, "Bo, you don't know Diddley!" The second spot that made Kanner's list was the 1996 commercial "Good vs. Evil," which featured soccer greats from around the world, including Eric Cantona of France, Jorge Campos of Mexico, and the Brazilian superstar Ronaldo. With "Good vs. Evil," in particular, Nike once again challenged established conventions in advertising. The commercial featured apocalyptic imagery of an ancient soccer stadium in which Nike players faced off against the forces of evil. The spot was rife with scenes of violence (both on the field and in the stands), and the menacing tone caused it to be banned from Scandinavian TV.

Nike (and Wieden & Kennedy) have often dared to try approaches never before attempted in advertising. In 1987 Nike became the first company to license music by the Beatles ("Revolution") for use in advertising; it was the first advertiser to show an elderly person realistically participating in a sport (running) in an ad, and the first to produce ads featuring a handicapped athlete (wheelchair racer Craig Blanchette).

Nike, which won numerous advertising awards in the 1980s and 1990s, was also one of the first companies to celebrate women in sports, with a 1995 commercial entitled "If You Let Me Play." That ad featured young girls talking about the benefits society reaps when females participate in sports, such as higher academic performance by girls in school, fewer teenage pregnancies, and a reduction in male violence targeted at women.

Nike rang out the second millennium with an ad called "The Morning After," which ran during the last months of 1999 and poked fun at the growing "Y2K" hysteria. The ad followed a hung-over jogger who went for a run on 1 January 2000 while every possible thing that could go wrong did so, all around him. At the time it aired, the commercial was criticized by some who thought Nike was being irresponsible in feeding off the fear of the impending Y2K disaster. When the world did not end, Nike picked up an Emmy Award for "The Morning After" a few months later.

In September 2000 Nike debuted a new ad campaign during the opening ceremonies of the Summer Olympic Games in Sydney, Australia. The campaign featured three ads, each asking the question "Why Sport?" and having the ad provide the answer in an unexpected way. One showed Tour de France champion Lance Armstrong using his powerful lungs to provide mouth-to-mouth resuscitation to a downed circus elephant, while another showed a skateboarder using his board skills to outmaneuver a Roman gladiator, bent on dicing the boarder into pieces.

But the ad that started the campaign, aired just prior to the lighting of the Olympic flame, created a firestorm of controversy for Nike. The 60-second ad, featuring U.S. Olympic 1,500-meter runner Suzy Hamilton, was called "Horror" and was intended to be a parody or spoof of so-called teen "slasher" movies, in which an isolated young woman meets an untimely and grisly ending. However, in the Nike ad, Hamilton uses her athletic abilities to outrun the chainsaw-wielding attacker, who eventually doubles over from exhaustion and gives up the chase. The tagline: "Why sport? You'll live longer." Many understood the message, but more than 300 viewers called NBC to voice their outrage, and the network quickly pulled the ad, as did ESPN. The ad did continue to air on a half-dozen other networks during the two weeks of the Olympics, including MTV, UPN, Fox, and WB, and received only a handful of viewer comments; a possible explanation for the lower number of complaints is that these networks broadcast programming appealing to younger audiences, who make up a majority of those who enjoy the slasher genre. Nike quickly learned that when and where an ad airs is as important as the content of the ad itself.

Other campaigns of the new millennium (post-2000) included "Just," a revisiting of the celebrated "Just Do It"; "Freestyle," which featured basketball players bouncing a ball and scuffing their feet to a frenetic and pounding rhythm; and "Move," a campaign that celebrated the shared movements and emotions of various sports. On the technology side, Nike introduced "whatever.NIKE.com," which featured commercials that began on TV but could be finished on the Internet, and "Play," the first TV ad to be streamed on ESPN.com.

RICK BURTON

Further Reading

Jacobs, A.J., and Ken Tucker, "The Pauses That Refreshed: The 50 Greatest Commercials of All Time!" *Entertainment Weekly* (28 March 1997)

Kanner, Bernice, *The 100 Best TV Commercials—And Why They Worked,* New York: Times Business, 1999

Katz, Donald, *Just Do It: The Nike Spirit in the Corporate World,* Holbrook, Massachusetts: Adams, 1994

Strasser, J.B., and Laurie Becklund, *Swoosh: The Unauthorized Story of Nike, and the Men Who Played There,* San Diego, California: Harcourt Brace Jovanovich, 1991

Nissan Motor Company

Principal Agencies
Parker Advertising
William Esty and Company, Inc.
Chiat/Day, Inc.

The history of Japanese automakers in the United States has been as much a battle of cultures as one of market share. The conservative, practical approach the Japanese take toward their cars and trucks contrasts starkly with the expressions of style and personal freedom Americans attach to vehicle ownership.

Asian automakers with long sales tenures in the United States have been able to adjust to this fundamental cultural divide. Though grudgingly at first, they modified their existing product lines or designed new vehicles to suit American tastes. But the desire of the home office in Tokyo, Japan, to curb the un-Japanese elements that made its U.S. sales arms a success—risk-taking and relative autonomy—often loomed in the background.

In an industry distinguished by names that have existed for the better part of a century, the Nissan Motor Company had a relatively late start. The company was founded 1 June 1934, commencing with the takeover of the automobile manufacturing division of Tobata Casting Company, Ltd., by Jidosha-Seizo Kabushiki-Kaisha (Automobile Manufacturing Company, Ltd.). Its automobile make, Datsun, had been manufactured by a variety of predecessors since 1914. The "sun" was added after one company failed and its successor decided to market the car as the "son of Dat." *Dat* means "fast hare" in Japanese, and the "son of Dat" referred to a smaller, sportier version of a preceding model. The spelling was briefly "Datson" but was changed owing to its similarity to a Japanese phrase meaning "to lose money."

Like most Japanese automakers, Nissan stayed close to its homeland during its first three decades of existence. The economic depression of the 1930s, paired with Japan's military buildup leading into World War II, meant vehicle production was often diverted for military contracts. The primitive state of Japanese roads also impaired domestic vehicle sales. Japanese domestic vehicle production in fact did not surpass 100,000 units until 1956. After that threshold was reached, the major automakers began eyeing export markets.

Nissan made the decision to sell its vehicles in the United States because of the confluence of two events in early 1958: a strong showing by its vehicles at the Australian Mobil Gas Trial, a grueling 10,000-mile endurance event, and the favorable reception for its models at the Los Angeles (California) Imported Motor Car Show.

Nissan had entered the U.S. market when most Americans still thought of Japan as a source of cheaply made goods. Looking to fill a niche as the provider of the "second vehicle" to American households, it would first have to overcome engineering problems with its initial sedan. Despite stepping up its compression ratio to wring more acceleration from its 37-horsepower engine, Nissan's vehicle still lacked the power to keep pace on U.S. highways. Its poorly insulated engine compartment guaranteed a toasty environment for driver and passenger, and its small battery meant owners in colder climates struggled to start it on winter mornings. In its first year in the United States a total of 83 Datsuns were sold, well behind the initial sales target of 500 vehicles a month. The following year, 1959, sales reached only 1,300.

But Nissan did have things going for its Datsun line. Aside from the sedan, it also offered a compact pickup truck—a first for the U.S. market. The truck appealed to the tastes of the early Datsun buyer: a moderate-income blue-collar worker, often with some connection, real or sentimental, to an agrarian lifestyle. Many early buyers were also former military personnel who had been to Japan, were familiar with the ruggedness of its roads, and correctly assumed the trucks were durable. The relatively strong initial sales gave the company the required forward momentum until other models could be introduced.

Ironically, there was another eager buyer for the pickups: Japanese gardeners in Los Angeles. They had been introduced to the product by Yutaka Katayama, a 25-year Nissan veteran who had come up through the advertising ranks and moved to America as vice president of Nissan's western U.S. division in 1960, when the automaker formally incorporated on American shores. Western U.S. division sales were routinely double those in the eastern states during the first years of operations.

Never hesitating to plunge headfirst into his work, Katayama had sold Datsun pickups by going door to door in the Japanese neighborhoods of Los Angeles. There was no one around to curb his decidedly un-Japanese brashness: Takashi Ishihara, who had been named U.S. division president and would lead Nissan a decade later, remained in Tokyo.

Though Katayama considered selling his company's product in the United States a fantastic opportunity, he had been a perennial bridesmaid in the subtle yet bruising office politics that define Japanese corporations. He simply did not fit in. Born to a wealthy family in a country where little wealth then existed, a converted Christian in a nation where there were virtually none, an unabashed lover of fast cars and gaming tables, Katayama was all but an outcast among the Japanese. Although Katayama had convinced his superiors in Tokyo to enter Datsun in the Australian Mobil Gas Trial, thus paving the way for sales in the United States, they considered his American assignment to be little more than banishment.

Katayama was perfect for the job. Shunning Japanese formality, he embraced the open casualness of American culture. He was willing to deliver vehicles himself to meet and talk with customers. Not only did Katayama love the social interaction, he also was able to discern what American consumers desired in an import car. But the knowledge he had gathered during his decades at Nissan told him it would be a tremendous struggle to get his superiors to make the necessary changes to their products. He predicted that it would take a decade before he could sell a vehicle that would truly appeal to the American market. His estimate was pessimistic but accurate.

Meanwhile, Nissan's United States division went ahead with its fledgling advertising campaigns, first managed by the Standard Advertising News Agency of Tokyo. But in 1961 it hired little-known Los Angeles agency Parker Advertising, mainly because its young founder, John Parker, seemed bright, was willing to do anything to snag an automobile account, and had hit it off with Katayama. According to author David Halberstam, Parker's initial annual budgets were microscopic, perhaps $50,000 a year.

The monetary limitations did not deter Parker. He shot the first U.S. Datsun commercial in 1962 to advertise the Patrol, a four-wheel-drive vehicle that had been introduced that model year. Parker's crew included himself and a police photographer friend who owned a movie camera. They spent a few days shooting a Patrol driving through some of the canyons in the foothills of Los Angeles. A year later Parker convinced cowboy star Roy Rogers

Introducing Datsun's 1932 EPA mileage champ.

Long before the EPA (Environmental Protection Agency) began rating gas mileage figures, Nissan Motor Co., Ltd. was making fuel-efficient cars and trucks.

Not surprising when you consider that there has never been one,

single, solitary oil well in Japan.

Which means that owners of 1977 Datsun cars and trucks will be getting a whole lot more than just economy, durability and value.

They'll be getting the benefits of nearly half a century of research

and development and nit-picking technological refinements.

All in an effort to assure the world that as the needs of drivers change, Nissan and Datsun will be at the forefront with innovative, responsible solutions.

WE'RE NISSAN
The strength behind Datsun's future.

A 1977 corporate ad for Nissan Motor Company focused on the company's long history of producing fuel-efficient automobiles. *Copyright, Nissan (1977). Datsun is a registered trademark of Nissan.*

to act as spokesman for the Patrol. Rogers's fee for his commercial work: one Patrol and two pickup trucks. Though the Patrol sold just 2,616 units in America, it was part of the Datsun product line for eight years and was its longest-lived U.S. model of the 1960s.

As Katayama engaged his superiors in a battle for modifications, the rest of the U.S. Datsun line was mostly comprised of a series of underpowered, awkward-looking sedans. Datsun enjoyed more success with its Fair Lady 1500 and 1600 series of convertible sports cars. They boasted larger engines and were more in line with American tastes. In early print campaigns, the convertibles were put in drawings suggesting they were in racing competitions, accompanied by the line "World's most exciting sports car buy." More than 42,000 Fair Lady cars were sold in the United States during the 1960s.

Although Nissan's U.S. operations had turned profitable by 1964 and Datsun was among the top-ten import car makes by 1965, U.S. sales were still below 20,000 a year and represented barely 2 percent of the import market share. Katayama, who by then had been named president of the U.S. division, was certain his unit would go no further without a larger engine and sportier design for its sedans.

Katayama finally got his wish in 1968 when the 510 sedan reached American shores. The car was a first for a Japanese sedan, boasting an overhead cam 1,600-cc engine generating 96 horsepower, four-wheel independent suspension, and a decidedly sporty look. Priced at around $1,800, it was not much more expensive than Nissan's first U.S sedan had been a decade ago and cost less than half of its nearest competitor, the BMW 1600. Katayama personally created the television spot for the 510, which portrayed a beautiful woman driving the sedan in the rain through the hills of California's picturesque Big Sur peninsula, the car's windshield wipers clicking to the strains of Vivaldi. There was no voice-over. Known inside Nissan as the "baroque" commercial, it foreshadowed television spots that would appear two decades later.

According to a Datsun advertising executive, the 510 itself was a revolution, "a Yuppie car before the Yuppies had been properly identified." Datsun's 1968 sales were more than triple what they had been three years before. Some 300,000 510s were sold over the next five years.

Datsun had a second hit just a year later with its redesigned Fair Lady sports car, now a grand touring coupe with a 2,400-cc, 150-horsepower engine. Emboldened by the success of the 510 and disgusted that Nissan had kept the old model name, Katayama and his staff tore off the Fair Lady badging as the cars arrived in port. They then sold it as the 240Z, Nissan's internal designation for the vehicle. The 240Z sold nearly 120,000 units in four years. Datsun's 1970 U.S. vehicle sales topped 150,000; they had multiplied nearly nine-fold in just five years.

As Datsun became more popular, its advertising spending ballooned, approaching $45 million by the late 1970s, or nearly 1,000 times Parker's original budget. The campaigns also became more sophisticated, edging away from the regional fare of its earlier years. In 1971 Datsun cosponsored the Glen Campbell Los Angeles Open race, garnering the company its first major exposure on network television.

The year 1973 proved critical to Nissan. Its $2 million "Own a Datsun Original" campaign—a tie-in between its 1200 subcompact sedan and artists such as Peter Max and Salvador Dali—was its first major placement of commercials on network television, and gave an increasingly urbane sheen to its vehicles. But far more significant to the 1200 and its marketer was the Arab oil embargo imposed on the United States after the war that October with Israel.

The oil crunch depressed U.S. car production by more than a quarter. Buyers scrambled to find more economical models. The first-ever mileage tests conducted by the Department of Transportation concluded that the 1200 was the most fuel-efficient model in the country, at 33 miles per gallon. Katayama sent out a camera crew to shoot the 1200 crossing the country; it reached 40 miles per gallon during the filming. The resulting commercial and slogan—"Datsun saves"—were synonymous with the brand for the rest of the decade. By 1975 Datsun was the leading U.S. auto importer.

Ironically, Katayama was the victim of his own success: Nissan's U.S. operations had become so big that Tokyo could no longer ignore its importance. With no political capital within the corporation, Katayama was "retired" and unceremoniously returned to Japan.

Nissan dropped Parker Advertising in 1977 primarily because its lucrative, informal contract had always rankled Nissan's Tokyo executives. After a lengthy search the carmaker went with William Esty and Company, Inc., New York City, satisfying what John Parker believed was Nissan's urge to go with a bigger agency. *Advertising Age* called it "the biggest switch in Madison Avenue memory." The Parker agency closed shortly after Nissan's move.

Esty's early campaigns focused on the engineering of Datsun cars rather than the vehicles themselves, making it difficult to establish a brand identity during the 1980s and 1990s. Not long after the switch to Esty, Nissan decided to replace the Datsun name in the United States with Nissan, even though 90 percent of American buyers did not recognize the Nissan name. As a result, most ad campaigns in the first half of the 1980s included both the Datsun and Nissan names. Though the campaign worked well with the Nissan Sentra, a new economy car that premiered in 1982 to strong sales, the changeover caused problems. Despite spending nearly $250 million by 1986 to promote the new Nissan brand, as much as 20 percent of the dealer network still sold Nissans as Datsuns, and many newspapers continued to list dealerships under "d" in directories.

Moreover, the changeover could not have happened at a worse time. By the early 1980s Japanese automakers had truly broken out of the economy-car class in the United States and had gained obvious advantages in engineering and quality over their American counterparts. Consumers were willing to pay premiums over sticker prices for the best-established makes such as Toyota and Honda. Struggling to remake itself in the image envisioned by its parent company in Tokyo, Nissan missed the opportunity to become a premium automaker, even though its products were just

HORSEPOWER: 222
MILES PER GALLON: 28
CARS LIKE IT: 0

THE NEW 2000 MAXIMA. *The numbers don't lie. But what's most impressive is that these performance gains were achieved on a powerplant already hailed as "simply the best V6 engine."* *What these numbers don't reveal are the hedonistic comforts of the new Maxima's interior—including a new, available, custom-tuned, 7-speaker Bose* audio system with CD player and an even more generous bounty of rich Seton* leather trim. Add to this a re-engineered steering system so responsive it feels connected to your synapses. A re-tuned suspension that provides a taut, yet silken ride. Even a reinforced body structure that helps silence the entire cabin. Tally it all up and you'll net out to the 2000 Maxima. And nothing else. Inquiries? Phone: 800-335-1426. Click: nissandriven.com. The new 2000 Maxima.* **CARS LIKE IT: 0.**

©1999 Nissan North America, Inc. Nissan, the Nissan Logo, Maxima and DRIVEN are trademarks owned by or licensed to Nissan. Bose* is a registered trademark of the Bose Corporation. 2000 EPA mileage figures shown. Actual mileage may vary with driving conditions. Use for comparison only. *Ward's Auto World, 1999. 17" wheel late availability.

NISSAN
DRIVEN.

A 1999 ad for the Nissan Maxima cleverly implied comparison without naming a single rival marque.
Copyright, Nissan (1999). Maxima is a registered trademark of Nissan.

as good as its competitors. While vehicle sales topped 500,000 a year by the mid-1980s, Nissan was relegated to the second-tier of import automakers, a market that quickly became crowded with such makes as Mitsubishi, Daihatsu, Isuzu, Suzuki, and Hyundai entering the U.S. market.

Despite more than quadrupling its ad budget over the previous decade, Nissan's U.S. market share dropped to 4.8 percent in 1986, down from 5.2 percent in 1985. Nissan dropped Esty in 1987 in favor of Chiat/Day, Inc., Los Angeles.

Chiat/Day's premier "Built for the human race" campaign was heavily criticized. Early commercials were shot with shaky cameras and centered on actors playing Nissan engineers who all but patted themselves on the back. The vehicles themselves were given relatively short shrift. When 1988 vehicle sales were down more than 15 percent from 1987, the campaign was retooled.

In November 1989 Nissan introduced Infiniti, a luxury marque to compete with Toyota's Lexus division. Hill, Holliday, Connors, Cosmopulos, Inc., in Marina del Rey, California, won Infiniti's $60 million account. The first Infiniti commercials focused on Zen-like nature shots with an abundance of trees and rocks. The cars were conspicuous by their absence. Lexus, mean-

while, built a following much the way the 510 had two decades before, by imitating European automakers in style and design and keeping prices relatively low. By the first quarter of 1990 Lexus sales were nearly triple that of Infiniti's. The "rocks and trees" ad campaign was revamped.

By the early 1990s it had become obvious Nissan would not escape its second-tier status in the United States quickly. Honda and Toyota had captured huge segments of the market with their popular Accord and Camry sedans, while Nissan's sportier lineup lacked a solid sales leader. The situation was exacerbated further by a steep recession in the United States, whose effects lasted well into the mid-1990s, and a strong yen that made Japanese vehicles more expensive. Without the "premium" label attached to its models, Nissan had little hope of keeping its ground.

By the mid-1990s Nissan's marketing campaigns were characterized by nostalgia. In 1996 Nissan took another stab at regaining its lost market share with the massive "Enjoy the Ride" campaign. The anchor was an elderly, somewhat mystical Japanese man and his dog. Known as "Mr. K," the figure was meant to elicit the long-departed Katayama and the success he created during his reign. However, the campaign centered more on image building than on sales growth. One celebrated commercial featured Barbie and G.I. Joe lookalike dolls tooling around in a toy roadster to promote the 300ZX, a model that was selling just a few hundred units a month and was just months from being phased out. Although Chiat/Day won several awards for the campaign, dealers grumbled that the spot was not selling cars, and it, too, was eventually changed.

In 1997, not long after the 300ZX was phased out, Nissan began selling fully restored 240Zs for nearly $25,000, or about seven times their original sticker price. Two years later, reeling under a debt load of more than $20 billion, Nissan took a nearly unprecedented step, selling a 36 percent stake in its global operations to French automaker Renault SA. Although subsequent cost-cutting made Nissan far more profitable, it remained to be seen whether it could re-create the past successes it enjoyed in the United States.

RON SHINKMAN

Further Reading

Halberstam, David, *The Reckoning*, New York: Morrow, 1986; London: Bloomsbury, 1987

Rae, John Bell, *Nissan/Datsun: A History of Nissan Motor Corporation in U.S.A., 1960–1980*, New York: McGraw-Hill, 1982

Nokia Corporation

Principal Agencies
Sek Grey Oy
Richards Group
Peak/Biety

Finnish mining engineer Fredrik Idestam founded Nokia in 1865 as a wood-pulp mill in southern Finland. The company evolved through several industries, including paper, chemicals, and rubber, before settling into the telecommunications market in the second half of the 20th century. In the 1960s Nokia's electronics department began researching radio transmission; through the next 30 years, Nokia established itself as a global leader in digital communications technology.

Before 1992 the Nokia name was used primarily for corporate marketing, with only a few consumer-marketing applications stemming from its involvement in the home electronics business. In 1992, however, Nokia underwent far-reaching change: the company named Jorma Ollila president and chief executive officer and simultaneously decided to divest its noncore operations, such as its cable and television businesses, in a move to focus on the telecommunications market. The company divided into two main operating groups, one focused on networks and the other on mobile phones.

At the same time, Nokia undertook an active management of its brand, including agreeing on "Connecting people" as an overall corporate slogan and hiring Sek Grey Oy, Helsinki, Finland, as its ad agency of record for the European region. The company spent more than two years on intensive brand-building aimed at making Nokia mobile phones a global brand by focusing on the products' advanced technology, ease of use, and durability.

While the company's brand was gaining strength in Europe and Asia, Nokia made a strong commitment in the United States to promote its brand by embracing large advertising campaigns, promotional marketing, product placements in several movies and television programs, and event marketing programs. By the mid-1990s Nokia began pumping more money into its U.S. ad budget as the cellular phone shifted from primarily a business tool to a mass-market consumer device.

In 1996 Nokia launched a print ad campaign incorporating the tag line, "Everything. Everywhere." The campaign was developed by Sek Grey Oy and ran in publications that covered Europe, including the *Financial Times, Harvard Business Review, National Geographic, Newsweek, Time,* and the *Wall Street Journal Europe.* The company won the European Advertising Achievement Award, presented by the European Association of Advertising Agencies, for its cross-border ad campaigns and long-standing brand building.

In 1996 Nokia's advertising efforts in the Asia-Pacific region earned it the Advertiser of the Year award as well as an award for the most creative use of media by *Media* magazine. The company's advertising efforts in the region aimed to set Nokia apart from other mobile-phone marketers by focusing less on the technical features of the products and more on their emotional benefits. Nokia won the same award in 1998.

In the United States, Nokia became the sponsor of the Sugar Bowl college football event and leveraged its sponsorship through promotions. Before the 1997 Sugar Bowl, for example, Nokia sponsored a national promotion that culminated in a halftime contest that gave three people a chance to win $1 million by throwing a football at a designated button on a 15-foot inflatable cellular phone.

By 1998 the Nokia brand had gained worldwide acceptance, and the company launched several important marketing campaigns aimed at bolstering its brand strength. The company started off the year by running a corporate spot during the

National Football League's Super Bowl XXXII. The Richards Group, located in Dallas, Texas, created the commercial, which starred the comedian Drew Carey.

Later that year Nokia launched massive ad campaigns in several of its markets. In Japan, for example, the company launched a nationwide advertising campaign in line with the market launch of a new mobile phone with a voice-recognition function called YO-BE-BA. The campaign, which included TV, newspaper, magazine, station poster, and train car ads, was the largest ad campaign run in Japan since Nokia's 1994 entrance into the market.

Nokia also launched an ad campaign in Canada aimed at linking its unique features with individual lifestyles and characteristics. By November 1998 Nokia ranked 87th on *Advertising Age International*'s list of the top 100 global marketers ranked by ad spending outside the United States. According to ACNielsen Company, Nokia spent $41 million on Asian advertising between January and August 1998, compared with $45 million for all of 1997.

Meanwhile, in the United States, Nokia embarked on one of its most successful ad campaigns. The company joined with AT&T Wireless to promote AT&T Wireless's flat-rate Digital One Rate wireless service plan. Nokia's 6160 series phones were featured exclusively in the ads, which were created by AT&T Wireless agency Foote, Cone & Belding, New York City. In the ads, a Nokia phone was depicted in red, white, and blue. The campaign was highly successful and led to strong demand for both AT&T Wireless's service plan and the Nokia phones featured in the ads.

Nokia continued its marketing efforts in 1999 when it launched a marketing push in the United States estimated at between $20 million and $25 million. The campaign included TV and print advertising, product placement, and national promotions, and it represented Nokia's largest-ever marketing effort. The TV commercials and print ads, created by the Richards Group, emphasized the depth and breadth of Nokia's mobile-phone product line. TV spots began during the 1999 Emmy Awards show, at which all winners and presenters were given the company's sleek, chrome-colored 8800 series phone. Nokia also placed freestanding inserts in Sunday newspapers to publicize the show.

In 2000 Nokia made an effort to reach the Latin American market by launching ads featuring the Colombian singer Shakira. The campaign, created by Peak/Biety, a Tampa, Florida, agency, aimed to raise brand awareness and preference among Latin American teens and young adults.

In Europe the company launched a pan-European print and TV campaign developed by Sek Grey Oy to promote its 7110

model, one of the first wireless application protocol–, or WAP-, based phones to be launched in Europe. Spots ran on CNN International, Eurosport, and BBC World, and ads ran in *Time* and *Newsweek,* among others, with the tag line, "The world at your fingertips."

Nokia's products have themselves become an advertising medium. The company formed partnerships to allow companies to send localized advertisements to wireless subscribers on their handsets. Nokia is a founding member of the Wireless Advertising Industry Association.

Nokia has relied heavily on relationships and sponsorships to promote its brand. The company has forged partnerships with Big Brothers Big Sisters of America, the nonprofit arts organization Gen Art, and the Guggenheim Museum. It also has sponsored a variety of TV programming, including the Teen Choice Awards, Grammy Awards, Emmy Awards, and CNN International's year-long *Voices of the Millennium* series in 1999, broadcast to an audience of 125 million households in Africa, the Asia-Pacific region, Europe, and the Middle East. The company also has sponsored a variety of sporting events, including the Sugar Bowl, the U.S. Youth Soccer Organization, the Indianapolis 500 auto race, and the International Ski Federation Snowboard World Cup. Nokia was ranked the fifth-most-valuable brand by the international consultancy group Interbrand in its 2000 survey of world brands, behind Coca-Cola, Microsoft Windows, IBM, and Intel. In 2000 Nokia was the top ad spender in the mobile phone category in the United States, according to figures from Competitive Media Reporting (CMR). Nokia spent $48.7 million in 2000, up from $37.9 million in 1999. CMR estimated that Nokia held a 36 percent share of the U.S. market in 2000, versus a 40 percent share the year earlier.

KRISTEN BECKMAN

See also color plate in this volume

Further Reading

Elkin, Tobi, "Nokia Unleashes Biggest-Ever Blitz," *Advertising Age* (6 September 1999)

Madden, Normandy, "2 Mobile Phone Marketers Break into Top 100 Ad Ranks," *Advertising Age International* (9 November 1998)

Siler, Charles, "Nokia Dials Up Winning Tactic for Electronics," *Advertising Age* (20 February 1995)

Snyder, Beth, "Nokia: Matt Wisk," *Advertising Age* (28 June 1999)

Trout, Jack, and Steve Rivkin, *Differentiate or Die: Survival in Our Era of Killer Competition,* New York: Wiley, 2000

Nordic Countries

As business becomes increasingly international, more and more marketers view Scandinavia, or the Nordic region, as a single northern European market. The Nordic region consists of four countries—Sweden, Finland, Norway, and Denmark—with a combined population of 25 million. While they may be considered one market, these countries differ in many ways, including in the history and development of their advertising industries.

Sweden

Of the four, Sweden has always been a leader in the advertising industry. Sweden spends more on advertising than its neighbors, and Swedish advertising has been awarded the most international prizes, including the Grand Prix at the International Advertising Festival in Cannes, France, awarded to Paradiset DDB in 1997 and 2001 for its work for the apparel merchandiser Diesel.

The Swedish advertising industry began more than a century ago when Sofia Gumaelius opened the advertising agency Gumaelius in Stockholm in 1877. The agency was successful, and even then internationalization was important; when she died in 1915 the agency had offices in Malmö and Gothenburg, Sweden; Oslo, Norway; and London, England.

Advertising continued to grow in Sweden through the first half of the century. After World War II, three agencies dominated: Telegrambyrån, Ervaco, and Stig Arbman Annonsbyrå. In 1950 *Resumé*, the first advertising trade magazine in Sweden, was launched.

But it was in the 1960s that the modern advertising industry really started in Sweden, thanks largely to the influence of Leon Nordin, a copywriter and later creative director at Stig Arbman Annonsbyrå. The agency dominated the Swedish ad industry in the 1960s and early 1970s, serving as a training ground for most of the country's major advertising professionals, who worked together at the shop for many years.

Nordin instituted changes in the way the agency operated, and began pushing for industrywide reforms as well. He focused intently on clients and on involving top management in advertising decisions. He created an ad for the country's biggest newspaper, *Dagens Nyheter,* in the early 1960s, demanding that advertising agencies be paid for their creative work, instead of being paid under the system that was then in place whereby agencies were paid using a formula based on ad placement rather than on creation (the provision system). The ad created quite a stir, and his idea soon became the new standard. In addition, in 1961 the Golden Egg advertising competition was held for the first time; it remains the most important local advertising competition in Sweden.

Abolishment of the provision system and the introduction of the Golden Egg changed the structure and the position of the advertising industry. People began leaving big, full-service agencies such as Ervaco and Gumaelius to start small, creative shops.

Stig Arbman Annonsbyrå continued to dominate the Swedish advertising landscape until 1972, when creative team Ove Pihl and Lars Falk left the agency to start their own shop, Falk & Pihl. One year later, copywriter Jan Cederquist and art director Lars Hall also left Arbman to start Hall & Cederquist. The agency soon became the best in Sweden while Arbman continued to lose ground.

In the 1980s, the style of the ads themselves changed. The amount of text was reduced, while graphics and the look of the ads became more important. Hall & Cederquist continued as one of the top agencies, although it gained some fierce competition in 1980, when Hans Brindfors and Leon Nordin started Hans Brindfors Annonsbyrå with the goal of becoming the premier creative agency for big clients. For many years these two agencies dominated the Swedish ad industry, each with a different style. Hans Brindfors Annonsbyrå became the most successful agency in the 1980s, handling clients such as Ikea, SAS, and Pripps. The agency grew, with almost 200 employees and several offices abroad during its peak.

In the mid-1980s Hall & Cederquist and Brindfors got competition from a new rival, Rönnberg & Company. It was established by well-known copywriters and art directors who wanted to concentrate on creativity, and soon large companies such as H&M (fashion), Statoil (gasoline), and *Expressen* (then Sweden's largest newspaper) joined its client ranks. The secret behind Rönnberg's success was a formula used by most successful advertising agencies in the Nordic region: small size, democratic organizational structure, a great deal of flexibility, creative ideas, and brave clients.

In 1986 another new agency opened that would become a Nordic powerhouse by the turn of the century. The agency, Forsman & Bodenfors, won its first Gold award in the 1990 Golden Egg competition. Within a few years, the agency began dominating the Swedish and Nordic ad industries, winning awards in Sweden and internationally for such clients as Volvo, Ikea, Arla, Libero & Libresse, and Göteborgs-Posten. The agency also is remarkable for being situated not in Stockholm, the center of the ad industry, but in the southwestern city of Gothenburg.

Meanwhile, Paradiset was established in 1990, and the agency's provocative, ironic, and challenging work soon began to draw the interest of marketers. Paradiset, which joined with DDB Needham in 1993, also began winning awards, including the 1997 Grand Prix at the Cannes festival (for its work for Diesel), an award no other Nordic agency had won before. At the 2001 Cannes festival, Paradiset DDB and Diesel were awarded their second Grand Prix, this time in the Press & Poster category.

While the Swedish advertising industry has been the dominant force in Nordic advertising, the other three countries also have a long history in advertising, with some shops dating back to the 1800s. At the start of the 21st century, along with the local shops, many of the multinational agencies were also represented.

Forsman & Bodenfors created quirky ads for Ikea, the Sweden-based worldwide marketer of home furnishings.

Denmark

Denmark's advertising industry dates to the 1860s, when the first agencies opened for business. Of the early shops, only Weber & Sørensen, founded in 1879, was still active at the beginning of the 21st century. Modern Danish advertising, however, was born in the 1920s and 1930s. One of the largest and most influential agencies was Amussen, founded in 1934 by Wahl Amussen. The agency was later bought by Bates and came to be known as Bates Copenhagen. The second big agency in the early years was Harlang & Toksvig, also founded in 1934, by Frantz Harlang and Frithjof Toksvig. In 1975 it was bought by Ogilvy & Mather.

In Denmark, one local agency, Wibroe, Duckert & Partners, continues to dominate the ad industry as it has for decades. It was established in the 1970s by Peter Wibroe and John Duckert. Wibroe, for many years the most famous person in the Danish ad industry, left the agency, although Duckert remained, and the agency is still privately owned. As in the rest of the region, most of the international networks were represented in Denmark at the end of the 20th century. By 2001 the country's leading shops were Grey København; Bates A/S; DDB Needham; Wibroe, Duckert & Partners; and a new shop named Robert/Boisen & Like-minded.

Norway

In Norway the first advertising agencies were actually news agencies. It was not until the mid-1930s that the first "modern" advertising agencies were established. Among the early big agencies were Myres, Thau, Forenede, and Høydahl-Ohme. Following World War II, the advertising business started to grow again, but there were changes. For example, Myres was the first Norwegian advertising agency to recruit copywriters; previously, copy had been written by project/account managers.

By the end of the 1960s, a new trend was under way as international networks began moving into the country and buying local shops. For example, Myres became Myres-Lintas and later BBDO Myres; Trea & STB became STB and later Ogilvy & Mather; and Alfsen & Becker became Alfsen, then Becker & Bates, and eventually simply Bates.

By 2001 the Leo Burnett Company was the leading agency; it moved into the country in 1989, buying a small creative shop, Nordskar & Thorkildsen, which had opened in Oslo in 1981. Its main competitor was JBR McCann, with New Deal DDB/Norway, Dinamo Norge, and Bates among the other top agencies in Norway.

Finland

In Finland, four ad agencies dominated the market at the beginning of the 21st century. The best known was Hasan and Partners, founded by Ami Hasan, who earned a reputation as a controversial figure; the other three were Paltemaa Huttunen Santala TBWA, Sek & Grey, and Taivas.

Finland's first ad agency, Suomen Ilmoituskeskus OY (later called ILMO), opened in 1923, and was followed by Suomen Reklaamitoimisto, Liiketaloudellinen Neuvontatoimisto, and Erwin, Wasey & Company, Ltd. Under the leadership of W.K. Latvala, Erwin, Wasey became the country's biggest agency until World War II. In the postwar period and into the 1960s, two major agencies emerged to dominate the Finnish advertising scene: Oy Mainos Taucher Reklam and Oy Sek, which later became Sek & Grey.

Trends in Common

Finland holds a special place in Nordic advertising history: it has had TV commercials for more than 40 years. The other countries of the region have had commercials on TV for only about ten years; before that, commercials were shown only in movie theaters. In Sweden commercials were introduced in 1987, but the big break came in 1990 when TV4 started broadcasting to all of Sweden. This profoundly changed the advertising industry. Before, agencies such as Hall & Cederquist and Brindfors mostly worked in print, but thanks to TV4, broadcast commercials became the new trend.

With the advent of television, good directors and production companies also started to appear, for example Leo Film in Norway and Moland Film Denmark. In Sweden, director Roy Andersson made a name for himself in the 1980s, while in the mid-1990s, Swedish directors such as Jhoan Camitz at Modfilm started to get international recognition. Traktor, a collective of directors and producers, was among the best-known production companies in the region. In 1997 Traktor moved from Stockholm to Santa Monica, California, and in 2001 worked with top Swedish and international agencies.

By the end of the 1990s, the Internet began to draw the attention of the Nordic advertising community. Many agencies started their own Web shops and began to talk about the importance of integrated communication.

At the same time, many Nordic agencies, especially those that are members of international networks, began adopting a full-service concept, uniting many specialists under one roof. For example, by 2001 Burnett in Stockholm had six different specialist agencies in one place, as did Ogilvy. On a national level, the Swedish communications groups A-Com and Audumbla both consisted of many different agencies.

But even as the multinationals moved in and agencies embraced full-service strategies, other shops maintained a more intimate, creative atmosphere. And the founders of many of the large shops that joined the multinationals were branching out on their own. Hans Brindfors, who sold his agency to Lowe in 1992, went on to start a new design agency, Brindfors Enterprise. Hall & Cederquist was bought by Young & Rubicam in 1989, but the founders went on to work in new agencies. Even Bo Rönnberg, who sold his agency to McCann in the early 1990s, later left the agency. In 2000 he started Collaborate, a new ad agency, as a part of the A-Com Group. In January 2001

Paradiset DDB created this humorous campaign for Swedish paper *Sport Bladet*, showing great events in world history—in this case, the fall of the Berlin Wall—being overshadowed by milestones in sports.
Courtesy of Aftonbladet.

Joakim Jonason left Paradiset DDB to start a new multicultural agency in London called Cave Anholt Jonason, which only existed for six months. Joakim Jonason later became the creative director at the London-based advertising agency Euro RSCG

Wnek Gosper. He remains the most awarded advertising professional in the Nordic countries.

PIA GRAHN BRIKELL

Norman, Craig & Kummel, Inc.

Established in New York City by former employees of William H. Weintraub & Company, 1955; renamed NCK Organization, 1961; merged with Foote, Cone & Belding Communications and ceased to exist under its own name, 1983.

Major Clients
Chanel, Inc.
Colgate-Palmolive Company
Hertz Corporation
Maiden Form Brassiere Company
Revlon, Inc.

Norman, Craig & Kummel, Inc. (NCK), was launched in June 1955, after the buyout of New York City–based William H. Weintraub & Company. In January 1955 William Weintraub, Sr., had sold his controlling interest in the company to four agency executives: Elkin Kaufman, Norman B. Norman, Eugene Kummel, and B. David Kaplan. Kaufman, president of the restructured agency, resigned in June, and Norman, who had been executive vice president, succeeded him. With the hiring of Walter Craig as vice president in charge of radio and television later that year, the agency was renamed Norman, Craig & Kummel.

Norman was a 1934 Columbia University social psychology graduate who entered advertising as an unpaid research assistant with the Biow Company, Inc., in New York City, immediately after graduation. He soon moved to William H. Weintraub & Company as an account executive, where he worked until joining the U.S. Navy in 1942. In 1948 he returned to Weintraub as executive vice president; he was responsible for the Revlon, Maiden Form, and Ronson accounts when he and the others bought the agency in 1955.

NCK arrived on Madison Avenue in the mid-1950s, when the United States was experiencing rapid economic expansion. Big-name ad agencies such as Ted Bates & Company, Inc., and Ogilvy, Benson & Mather, Inc., were developing new schools of creative thought and building up their workforces to accommodate the changing times. Norman, competitive by nature, knew his agency needed a sound staff and an original sales approach to compete with the bigger agencies, and he was responsible for luring Craig, a broadcasting expert, away from his job as advertising manager of Pharmaceuticals, Inc., to head up the new agency's radio and television efforts. Norman also was responsible for formulating NCK's sales approach. Bates had its "unique selling proposition" and Ogilvy its "brand image"; Norman called his agency's strategy "Empathy." The theory consisted of six canons or tenets; when put together, the first letters of each tenet spelled P E O-P-L-E: Put people in the sell; Excitingly different look and sound; Open the way through the heart—not the head; Put in an important reason why; Living visuals people will talk about; Eliminate any nonpreemptive selling proposition. Empathy simply meant putting the product into people's lives. This approach led to the agency's success with such notable campaigns as Maiden Form's "I Dreamed . . . ," Hertz's "Let Hertz Put You in the Driver's Seat," Ajax's "Stronger than Dirt" (the White Knight), and Chanel's "Every Woman Alive Loves Chanel No. 5."

One of the earliest examples of this philosophy was the agency's quiz show, *The $64,000 Question*, launched in 1955, which was brought to NCK by independent TV producer Louis G. Cowan. It was the only time in the history of broadcasting that an agency bought a program with its own money. Craig was put in charge of the show. The agency developed the show with the idea, new at the time, that a single sponsor would be featured during the program. Craig, after much effort, convinced Revlon, Inc., a client since 1948, to be the show's sole sponsor. It was a boon to Revlon, which often went over its one-minute time slot to get more exposure on the air.

The show premiered on 7 June 1955 and within four weeks reached the number-one position in the ratings. It raised Revlon's sales and profits and significantly increased consumer awareness of Revlon's products, pushing the company far out in front of its competitors. The show was such a success that it was widely copied. But despite the program's popularity, after only 13 weeks Revlon owner Charles Revson fired NCK, the marketer's agency of seven years. Norman attributed the firing to his dispute with Revlon's vice president over agency commission, a charge that Revlon denied. Revlon then hired Batten Barton Durstine & Osborn (BBDO).

The move spurred a bitter rivalry between NCK and BBDO that extended from the entertainment stage to the political arena. NCK's contempt for BBDO was evidenced in 1956 when the shop accepted the account of the U.S. Democratic National Committee. At that time many big agencies were unwilling to take the Democrats' account for fear of alienating the Republican businessmen who headed many client companies. NCK, however, went after the multimillion-dollar account with great fervor to go head-to-head with BBDO, which handled the Republican National Committee account. The agency got its wish in 1956. Two of the agency's principals, Kummel (then vice president and secretary) and Craig, were directly in charge of the campaign of presidential candidate Adlai Stevenson. At the convention, they added touches that were totally new in the annals of American politics. For example, they helped the convention manager in Chicago, Illinois, hire singers, performers, and a color guard. Craig took over most of the work of planning the candidate's arrival and departure—what routes he should follow, what signs the crowd should carry, and what cheers the audience should utter. He also wrote and directed a "quiz" that ran on the platform during the convention. The "quiz" involved two former contestants of *The $64,000 Question* and TV quizmaster Hal March, who questioned them about national problems.

NCK also provided the introduction to the keynote speech of the convention, with a script written by the agency prior to the convention. For the first time in history, the campaign of the Democrats appeared more a political show than a simple exercise in advertising. Hollywood and Broadway were well represented. The convention's entertainment director was Dore Shary, head of MGM. Another well-known party official, Lynn Nichols, was responsible for supervising demonstrations both inside and outside the convention hall. Despite the efforts of NCK, however, Dwight D. Eisenhower—and BBDO—won the election.

Meanwhile, in devising campaigns for its cosmetics and lingerie accounts, NCK switched gears in its "Empathy" approach, incorporating sexy imagery and themes into its ads for such clients as Maiden Form, Colgate-Palmolive Company's Veto deodorant, Sportsman cologne, and Chanel No. 5. Sex, the agency believed, sold cosmetics and lingerie products. In its 1956 ad for Veto deodorant, the agency stretched its philosophy as far as the law would allow. The ad pictured a girl stretched out on a leopard-skin rug; a man's shoulder intruded into the image, hinting at a sexual encounter.

NCK's suggestive Maiden Form ads, which began appearing in 1949, also stretched the boundaries of what was acceptable at that time. Mary Filius, a former Weintraub copywriter, and S.A. Halpern, Weintraub's former creative director, were in charge of the ads. They used as the marketing premise the notion that women are basically exhibitionists and can laugh at their own weaknesses. The ads, which bore the tag line, "I dreamed . . . in my Maidenform bra," featured half-clad female models alongside fully dressed men in environments such as financial offices or architects' drafting rooms. The campaign infuriated feminists. In response to the criticism, NCK shifted to images of women on their own at work in high-level jobs. But these, too, aroused the ire of the female audience. In 1956 the Leo Burnett Company conducted a poll among housewives; respondents, asked to rate three fashion advertisements, gave the Maiden Form ad the lowest rating. The negative feedback delighted Kay Daly, NCK's fashion director, who said, "Housewives *should* think those ads are shocking. That's the point." Despite the controversy, the Maiden

Form ads had an astounding effect on women and society. The "I dreamed" idea served to pioneer the mention of unmentionables in advertising. In addition, after the campaign began, women abandoned the old-fashioned word *brassiere* for the hipper term *bra*.

NCK resigned the $1.5 million account in 1971 after 23 years. It was believed the shop gave up the account because Maiden Form's ad budget had remained flat for too long.

The sexy selling approach not only worked to transfix women, NCK was also able to use it successfully to attract teenage girls to Chanel No. 5—long considered a woman's fragrance. NCK put Chanel No. 5 in teens' lives for the first time in 1956. The ads abandoned the image of the perfume's classic bottle in favor of sexy models in their teens and copy that referred to growing up and falling in love. The agency placed monthly ads in *Seventeen* with a tag line that read, "If the exciting things of growing up are happening to you, you're ready for Chanel." One showed a boy and girl in slickers walking obliviously in the rain. The copy under the illustration said: "When you'd rather be we then me . . . you're ready for Chanel." The campaign quickly established the fragrance among this age group.

NCK used a similar approach in its fragrance ads featuring men, but the ads for brands such as Sportsman cologne and Veto deodorant depicted men as sexual in a different manner. The ads featured men as rough and tough. "Empathy is more difficult when it's a man," Norman once remarked. "Let's face it. It's easy to make a girl sexy, but a man—the only way is roughness. Men have to fight, that's how they win dames."

The choice of photographers and models was crucial for these image-based ads. The agency was the first to use photographer Richard Avedon, who shot racy photos for *Harper's Bazaar,* to shoot its print ads, hiring him to photograph many of its Maiden-form ads. Daly also hired Dan Wynn, a magazine photographer who shot the Sportsman campaign, and Todd Webb, photographer for the Chanel No. 5 ads.

Because packaged goods and automotive services could not be advertised in the same way as fragrances and lingerie, NCK took a different approach to the "Empathy" principle with its clients Ajax and Hertz. Norman once cited NCK's Hertz campaign of 1959 as the best example of "Empathy." The ads featured a vivid TV demonstration of a man dropping into the driver's seat of a car from the sky. The tag line, "Let Hertz put you in the driver's seat," became one of the most widely recognized ad slogans. Hertz became the number-one car rental business following the campaign. When the number-two rental company Avis inched its way up in the rankings with its "We try harder" campaign, NCK lost the Hertz account.

NCK's empathy-driven campaign for Colgate-Palmolive's Ajax cleanser—featuring a knight on horseback and the tag line "Give me something stronger than dirt"—was also a runaway success. Until the "White Knight" campaign, Procter & Gamble's Tide, Dash, and Cheer had been the best-sellers in the household cleanser category. The Ajax campaign featured an armored knight on a white horse holding a spear with an Ajax banner. A brilliant flash of light—like a comic-book zap—represented

I dreamed I went whistle-stopping *in my* ***maidenform bra***

I'm a sure winner because I'm on the right track! My platform: a vote for me is a vote for Maidenform. No wonder I'm the people's choice for the figure of the year! The dream of a bra: new Maidenform Pre-Lude*—the bra with the contour-band that gives you an entirely new kind of under-and-up up-lift to make the most of every curve you own. *In white embroidered broadcloth. A, B and C cups, 2.00. Prices slightly higher in Canada.* *REG. U. S. PAT. OFF.　©MAIDEN FORM BRASSIERE CO., INC., N. Y. 16

This attention-getting 1956 Maidenform ad was part of a long-running campaign from Norman, Craig & Kummel, Inc. *Maidenform, Inc. All Rights Reserved.*

Ajax's cleaning power. The campaign shook Procter & Gamble, which spent a great deal of money trying to unhorse the "White Knight." The campaign ran from 1962 to 1967 and helped Ajax win a significant share of the $12 million detergent market.

NCK's empathy approach was not limited to its U.S. ad campaigns. The agency also used it to promote products overseas. To promote Ajax-with-Ammoniasol window cleaner in England it developed "The Great Window Race" TV commercial, which featured three window washers racing down the side of an office building on scaffolds as the announcer, in the best sportscaster tradition, described the action. For Ajax dishwashing liquid, British TV viewers were treated to crackling bolts of lightning hitting a kitchen sink, each blinding flash producing sparkling clean dishes as the housewife, husband, and children look on approvingly. Another British TV commercial, for Green Ajax "with Hex-ammonia," featured a woman walking on her walls ("Green Ajax gets the floor too clean to walk on"). In Germany, Ajax kitchen cleaner was flown into use by a neighbor, à la Peter Pan, and, as the commercial ended, was being flown along a residential street by the airborne housewife.

Norman initiated NCK's overseas growth in 1960 to assist clients looking to expand abroad. Until 1970 Norman followed one rule of thumb when expanding overseas: he bought into an ongoing operation. NCK initially bought large minority shares with arrangements for continued growth toward full ownership. The agency believed a strong, successful U.S. agency working as a partner with an equally strong national agency that shared the same philosophy would provide better service to an international advertiser than an American agency with no local ties.

Norman stuck to his international expansion principles until 1972, when NCK moved into Mexico and built Arellano, NCK Publicidad S.A. de C.V. from the ground up. The agency was awarded Colgate-Palmolive's $1.7 million assignment in 1972, boosting the shop to the top of the Mexican agency ranks. By 1982 NCK had gained more than 50 accounts worldwide, including Colgate in Mexico, Cadbury-Schweppes in The Netherlands, and Hertz in Austria.

In 1961 the parent company of NCK was named the NCK Organization. By 1982 the NCK Organization had 1,184 employees in 32 offices worldwide. It reported gross income of $69.8 million and worldwide billings of $433.4 million. By 1983 the company had become the fourth-largest European agency network. That year the NCK Organization merged with Foote, Cone & Belding Communications, and the NCK name disappeared.

Norman retired in 1979 but continued to serve as honorary chairman of the board until the agency closed its doors in 1983. He died in 1991. Kummel left in 1964 to join the Interpublic Group of Companies. He retired as chairman of McCann-Erickson Worldwide in 1987. Craig left the agency in 1968 to join Harisen Rubersohn McCann Erickson in Sydney, Australia. He died in 1972. In his obituary, *Advertising Age* noted that Craig had once referred to himself as "the guy that picked 'The $64,000 Question,' and lost the account."

SARA TEASDALE MONTGOMERY

Further Reading

Day, Barry, *100 Great Advertisements*, London: Times Newspapers, 1978

Fox, Stephen R., *The Mirror Makers: A History of American Advertising and Its Creators*, New York: Morrow, 1984

Mayer, Martin, *Madison Avenue, U.S.A.*, New York: Harper, 1958

Packard, Vance Oakley, *The Hidden Persuaders*, New York: McKay, and London: Longman, 1957; 2nd edition, London: Penguin, 1981

Tobias, Andrew P., *Fire and Ice: The Story of Charles Revson, the Man Who Built the Revlon Empire*, New York: Morrow, 1976

N.W. Ayer & Son, Inc. *See under* Ayer

O

Ogilvy, David 1911–1999

British-U.S. Advertising Executive

David Ogilvy was one of a handful of leaders who founded U.S. advertising agencies that set the standards for the business after World War II. At his death in 1999 he was the last survivor of a group that had included Raymond Rubicam, Leo Burnett, William Bernbach, and Ted Bates.

Born David Mackenzie Ogilvy in West Horsley, England, on 23 June 1911, he was educated at Fettes College in Edinburgh, Scotland, and at Christ Church College, Oxford, England, though he did not graduate from Christ Church. After college he spent a year as a sous-chef in a Paris, France, kitchen in the early 1930s and another year selling Aga Cooker stoves door to door in Great Britain. His experience with Aga Cookers initiated him into the art of professional persuasion. He took to it with such vigor that in 1935 he committed his accumulated wisdom on selling to a terse pamphlet called *The Theory and Practice of Selling the Aga Cooker*. Thirty years later *Fortune* magazine called it "perhaps the liveliest and most engaging sales manual ever written."

It was this pamphlet, along with an exercise in nepotism, that brought Ogilvy into one of London's oldest and most distinguished advertising agencies, Mather & Crowther. The firm had a considerable history, dating back to 1850. When Ogilvy was hired in 1936, his older brother Francis was general manager.

In 1938 Ogilvy persuaded the agency to stake him to a one-year sabbatical in New York City to learn about U.S. advertising. He extended his stay to work for George Gallup as associate director of the Audience Research Institute in Princeton, New Jersey. Gallup was a major influence on Ogilvy's thinking. On 9 February 1939 readers of London's *World's Press News* received Ogilvy's first public pronouncements on advertising. Asked to name his "All-American Agency Team," Ogilvy submitted his assessments of 13 leaders in U.S. advertising. It was a list that showed both perception and, in the case of Rosser Reeves (who, at that time, was still a virtually unknown copywriter at Blackett-Sample-Hummert), considerable prescience. The list also cited Frank and Anne Hummert, Claude Hopkins, John Caples, George Gallup, A.C. Nielsen, Ray Rubicam, Roy Durstine, Don Francisco, Gordon Seagrove, J. Stirling Getchell, and William Esty.

Prescience, however, had an ally in Ogilvy's interest in Reeves's sister-in-law, Melinda Street, an 18-year-old student at the Julliard School of Music in New York City. Ogilvy returned to the United States to marry her just as World War II was breaking out in Europe. (Divorced in 1957, the couple had one son, David Fairfield.) The war postponed Ogilvy's advertising ambitions. After three years with Gallup, he joined British intelligence in 1942 and later worked in the British embassy in Washington, D.C. After the war he became a farmer, briefly and somewhat mysteriously, in Lancaster County, Pennsylvania.

In 1948 Ogilvy went to his brother at Mather & Crowther, this time with a plan to launch a "British agency" in the United States. Mather & Crowther and S.H. Benson Ltd., another London shop, invested $45,000 with the proviso that Ogilvy, who had been out of advertising for nearly ten years at this point, hire someone who knew how to run an agency. Reeves, Ogilvy's first choice, declined, preferring to stay at Ted Bates, Inc. Instead, the J. Walter Thompson Company's Anderson Hewitt, whom Ogilvy had met briefly in 1941 at J. Stirling Getchell, Inc., was chosen for the job.

The agency opened in September 1948 under the name Hewitt, Ogilvy, Benson & Mather. It was built on clearly defined principles reflecting the view of its founder. Ogilvy stated these principles early in his career and rarely amended them. He believed that the function of advertising is to sell and that it is possible to determine empirically which techniques are most likely to produce sales. While still in London in 1936 he insisted that "every advertisement must tell a whole sales story . . . every word of the copy must count," adding that "permanent success has rarely been built by frivolity, and people do not buy from clowns." Fifty-six years later, in a speech to the Association of National Advertisers in the United States, he sounded the same theme: "If you focus your advertising budget on entertaining the consumer, you may not sell as much of your product as you like. People don't buy a

David Ogilvy.
David Ogilvy, Ogilvy & Mather Worldwide.

new detergent because the manufacturer told a joke on television last night. They buy it because it promised a benefit."

Ogilvy was one of the central figures in advertising's "creative revolution." Among the campaigns that established his reputation were his "man in the eye patch" ads for Hathaway shirts, his "Commander Whitehead" campaign for Schweppes, and a print ad for Rolls-Royce that carried the headline, "At 60 miles an hour the loudest noise in this new Rolls-Royce comes from the electric clock."

Ogilvy's readiness with a bon mot made him one of advertising's most-quoted figures. From his pronouncement, "The consumer is not a moron. She is your wife. Don't insult her intelligence," to "Unless your campaign contains a Big Idea, it will pass like a ship in the night," Ogilvyisms, as they came to be called, peppered Ogilvy's writings.

His 1963 book *Confessions of an Advertising Man* made Ogilvy's influence palpable not only within the trade but also with the public at large, which delighted in his iconoclasm and irreverence. During a decade in which consumerism was emerging as a force in the marketplace, he seemed to be on the side of the public, asserting that much advertising was stupid, an opinion people found refreshing coming from an insider.

Ogilvy believed that research could identify the elements that go into successful advertising and that it was the agency's duty to know and understand such data and not to go blindly against them. This was a point of view that was easy to sell to clients.

He liked to quantify effective design. For a time he even had a point system. A new ad would start with a possible 100 points. Nine points would be deducted if the brand was not "visible at a glance"; another six if a drawing was used; four if the type was reversed out of a dark background—until the hapless art director might be left with a total of zero points. He believed that testing could justify his system.

Ogilvy saw himself with the same clarity he brought to his client's products. He once referred to his *Confessions* as "unrelieved egotism"; it was one Ogilvy opinion neither his friends nor his enemies had cause to challenge. He knew that frankness often implied more than it said. In the 1960s his official agency biography read: "David Ogilvy is a copywriter at Ogilvy & Mather. He is also chairman of the board." The real message in this understated and seemingly backward description was that this was a man who regarded his work as more important than his titles. Many clients wanted just such a person doing their advertising.

Ogilvy merged his agency with his original backer, Mather & Crowther, in 1964 and served as chairman until 1965, when he dropped that title in favor of the title creative director. The next year he changed the agency's name to Ogilvy & Mather and formed a holding company, Ogilvy & Mather International (OMI), with himself as chairman. Later that year he took the company public at $22 a share. In 1973 Ogilvy gave up day-to-day management duties and moved to Bonnes, France, where he and his third wife, Herta Lans, moved into a chateau called Touffou. (He had married his second wife, Anne Cabot, in 1957 and was divorced from her in 1972; he married Lans in 1973.) Ogilvy remained in touch with business in such detail, however, that the post office serving Touffou was upgraded by the French postal authorities, winning a raise for the local postmaster. He retired as chairman of OMI in 1975 but continued to influence agency affairs that interested him and to represent the company to clients. He unsuccessfully fought a hostile takeover by Martin Sorrell's WPP Group in 1989. By the late 1990s his active involvement in agency business had ended. He died at home in Chateau Touffou on 21 July 1999 shortly after his 88th birthday.

JOHN MCDONOUGH

Biography

Born in West Horsley, England, 23 June 1911; attended Christ Church College, Oxford, 1929-31; founded Hewitt, Ogilvy, Benson & Mather, New York City, 1948; developed reputation for stylish, sophisticated creative work in 1950s; company renamed Ogilvy, Benson & Mather when Hewitt left, 1953; published the book *Confessions of an Advertising Man*, which became a best-seller, 1963; company name changed to Ogilvy & Mather (O&M), 1966; named Commander of the British Empire, 1967; retired as chairman of parent company, Ogilvy & Mather International, and moved to France, 1975; awarded membership in U.S. Avertising Hall of Fame, 1977; named chairman of WPP Group, 1988; takeover of O&M by Martin Sorrell, 1989; elected to France's Order of Arts and Letters, 1990; died 21 July 1999.

Selected Publications

Confessions of an Advertising Man, 1963
Ogilvy on Advertising, 1983

The Unpublished David Ogilvy, 1986
David Ogilvy: An Autobiography, 1997 (originally published as
   Blood, Brains, and Beer in 1978)

Further Reading
Winski, Joseph, "A Giant Bows to 'Jackasses': David Ogilvy
   Learns New Lessons," *Advertising Age* (22 May 1989)

Ogilvy & Mather Rightford

(Rightford, Searle-Tripp & Makin)

Founded in Cape Town, South Africa, as Rightford, Searle-Tripp & Makin from the Mortimer Tiley agency, 1976; acquired the Volkswagen account, doubling its business, 1979; bought Johannesburg, South Africa, agency Van Zijl & Schultze, Lund & Tredoux, an Ogilvy & Mather shop, and changed its name to Ogilvy & Mather Rightford, 1982.

Major Clients

Automobila Association
British American Tobacco
Lion Match
M-Net/MultiChoice (subscription TV service)
Motorola
Old Mutual (life insurance)
SA Tourism
South African Breweries
Volkswagen

For 13 years, from 1988 through 2000, Ogilvy & Mather Rightford (O&M Rightford) resided comfortably at the top of the ad agency heap in South Africa, with a share of the advertising market at times as high as 15 percent. For much of that time it accomplished the relatively rare feat of being the country's biggest as well as its most creative agency, being named *Advertising Age International*'s "Agency of the Year" in 1996.

That same year it also earned a tribute from Charlotte Beers, then chairman of Ogilvy & Mather Worldwide, who said in a videotape recorded to celebrate O&M Rightford's 20th anniversary that of the 272 O&M offices around the world, O&M South Africa was "the jewel in the crown." She added that the agency had disproportionate power in the network because it produced "absolutely brilliant advertising." In 2001 the 25-year-old O&M Rightford remained a potent force in its home market, with a reputation as a builder of brands.

Bob Rightford, the agency's client service director; Brian Searle-Tripp, art director; and Roger Makin, copywriter, met while working for a large Cape Town, South Africa, agency, De Villiers & Schonfeldt. In 1975 Rightford was offered an opportunity to acquire equity in a small, unprofitable agency, Mortimer Tiley. Rightford invited Searle-Tripp and Makin to join him, and 18 months later they bought control of the agency and renamed it Rightford, Searle-Tripp & Makin.

The client base was thin, but Rightford, who was known in the South African agency world as a rainmaker, quickly brought in Morkels, a furniture chain; All Gold, a canned-food brand; and some Rembrandt Tobacco business. The first major account for the newly named agency was match manufacturer Lion Match, with a budget of $500,000—a big account in 1976. Lion remained a client, albeit a much smaller account, into the 21st century.

But the agency's most important early milestone was its acquisition of the Volkswagen account in 1979, which more than doubled Rightford's business. Since then it has produced a series of advertisements that has helped keep Volkswagen among South Africa's leading automobile sellers. One of its most creative ideas came in 1984, when Volkswagen asked the agency to produce a campaign to move its inventory of the original Golf model off showroom floors before the launch of a new Golf. The agency came up with the idea to reposition the original model as a "Citi Golf" entry-level vehicle, painted in bright colors and supported by a campaign that appealed to the youth market. So successful was this effort that the life of the model was extended by more than ten years, and at the start of the 21st century it still accounted for 6 percent of all new-car sales in South Africa.

By 1982, when the agency was six years old, it had become Cape Town's biggest and most exciting ad agency, ranked number ten nationally. But Johannesburg, the country's main business and advertising center, beckoned. Without a strong presence in that city, the agency's prospects would always be limited. Rightford engineered a takeover of a bigger but somnolent agency, Van Zijl & Schultze, Lund & Tredoux, known as VZ. And as much as he craved the additional size, Rightford also coveted that agency's association with Ogilvy & Mather. Ogilvy & Mather was more than happy with the acquisition, because VZ was considered a drab, unimaginative shop, while Rightford, Searle-Tripp & Makin was well known as the leading creative shop at the time. With the acquisition—and a name change to Ogilvy &

A 1996 poster for ICI's Dulux Paints brand, created by Ogilvy & Mather Rightford, took an ordinary pedestrian crossing and transformed it into a statement about the expressive potential of Dulux's color range.

Mather Rightford—the agency rose to number seven in the 1983 agency rankings, and by 1988 it was number one.

O&M Rightford, in which O&M Worldwide holds a 40 percent equity stake, also played a significant role in building O&M's global network in Africa. The 1994 election of Nelson Mandela as South Africa's first democratic president provided an opportunity for advertising agency networks to expand across the African continent by using South Africa as a springboard, with its good communications and modern production infrastructure. This development coincided with a wave of democratization across the continent that encouraged the development of new, independent media. Global marketers such as Unilever, Procter & Gamble Company, Nestlé, and Coca-Cola Company raced to establish their brands, a development that, in turn, fostered the growth of the advertising industry. O&M moved quickly and within two years had built an African network with offices in 19 African countries. It served global clients as well as local marketers such as South African Breweries as it expanded into the African hinterland.

In 1994 O&M Rightford set up an advertising school, the Red and Yellow School, which turns out 60 graduates a year—copy-writers, designers, art directors, and account managers. The agency underwrites the school with a hefty subsidy. This, said Searle-Tripp, who at the turn of the century was running the school full time, is "the kind of thing an agency the size of Ogilvy should do."

In 1995 Chief Executive Officer Robyn Putter succeeded Rightford at the agency's helm and developed the brand-building and brand-stewardship philosophy that has been adopted by O&M affiliate agencies worldwide. Rightford served on the board of Ogilvy & Mather Worldwide from 1988 to 1994. Putter served as head of O&M Worldwide's international creative council for five years in the late 1980s. By 2001 O&M's group was a miniature version of its holding company, the WPP Group, comprising 16 companies offering a range of services, including promotional campaigns, direct marketing, medical advertising, retail advertising, and brand consultancy. The group had four advertising agencies; in 2000 its media agency was absorbed into Mindshare, the WPP media agency.

Total fee and commission revenue in 2000 was $27.5 million. In local currency (rand) terms, this was a 12 percent increase over

1999, but thanks to depreciation of the rand, it represented a decrease in terms of U.S. dollars. Media billings for the group were $161 million. The group had 138 clients in 2000, many of which had been with it for more than two decades. However, after 13 straight years at the top, O&M Rightford was toppled from its perch by FCB South Africa in 2000. (FCB enjoyed 28 percent growth, which took its revenue to $28 million and its billings to $172 million.)

TONY KOENDERMAN

Further Reading

AdFocus (annual review of South African advertising) (May 2001)

Ogilvy & Mather Worldwide, Inc.

Opened in New York City as Hewitt, Ogilvy, Benson & Mather, 1948; went public, 1966; acquired in a hostile takeover by the holding company WPP Group, 1989.

Major Clients

C.F. Hathaway Company
Lever Brothers
Merrill Lynch, Pierce, Fenner & Smith
Rolls-Royce, Inc.
Schweppes, Ltd.
Shell Oil Company

In 1948 British advertising executive David Ogilvy, 37, launched the U.S. branch of the venerable London, England, agency Mather & Crowther. Founded as Mather & Company by E.C. Mather in 1850, it was the second-oldest agency in Britain, though in the beginning it functioned as a contractor and space broker whose primary relationship was with newspapers and not advertisers. Its first offices were at 71 Fleet Street, the center of London's newspaper business. Mather was succeeded by his son, H.L. Mather, who in 1888 struck a partnership with E.O. Crowther, formerly of Cassell & Company, and a London book publisher. Mather & Crowther established new offices nearby at 10–12 New Bridge Street.

When Francis Ogilvy, David's older brother, joined M&C in 1929, the agency was billing the equivalent of about $3 million, after pioneering the creative role of the ad agency as well as techniques of co-op advertising. By the time Francis Ogilvy died in 1964 the agency had grown into a $37 million shop.

A "British" Agency in New York

In 1936 Francis hired his brother David, who worked for Mather & Crowther for several years prior to the outbreak of World War II. Resuming his advertising career in 1948, the younger Ogilvy went to his brother with a plan to launch a "British agency" in the United States, where he had spent 1938 and 1939 gathering research on the American advertising industry, before joining the Audience Research Institute in Princeton, New Jersey, as associate director from 1939 to 1942. Mather & Crowther and S.H. Benson, Ltd., another London shop, invested $45,000, with the proviso that Ogilvy, who had been away from the business for several years at this point, hire someone familiar with the running of an agency. His first choice, Rosser Reeves (to whose sister-in-law he was married), preferred to stay at Ted Bates, Inc., so instead he hired Anderson Hewitt, an account executive with the J. Walter Thompson Company whom Ogilvy had met briefly at J. Stirling Getchell, Inc., in 1941.

The new agency opened its doors in September 1948 under the name Hewitt, Ogilvy, Benson & Mather (HOB&M). New York City was not impressed by the arrival of this "British agency." Business was slow until February 1949, when Hewitt brought in the first big account, Sun Oil. With no track record or creative reputation, the advantage of HOB&M over its competition was Hewitt and, according to a later article in *Fortune* magazine, a willingness to kick back 40 percent of its commissions to the client. Even at that, the account was profitable.

After three years the agency was billing about $9 million, a substantial amount in 1951, but it had yet to acquire an account on which Ogilvy could put his defining imprint. All that changed that year, when the agency was asked to create ads for a small shirtmaker from Waterville, Maine. The C.F. Hathaway Company's budget was so tiny—only $30,000—that even HOB&M wondered if it would be worth it. When Hathaway promised never to change a word of the agency's copy, Ogilvy took the business.

Today the Hathaway man with his trademark eye patch implying a life of danger, sophistication, and high adventure remains one of the most famous of all ad icons and perhaps Ogilvy's greatest hit. The ads crackled with a literacy that flattered the readers' intelligence. Even those whose vocabulary was not up to such words as *ineffable* and *doyen* appreciated Hathaway's assumption that they might be.

About a year later, Ogilvy's London partners asked him to take on another small account, billing only $15,000. It was the Schweppes Company, a British maker of tonic (quinine) water and other mixer beverages. The company had the rather unorthodox notion of using its own advertising manager, Commander Edward Whitehead, in its ads.

Viewpoint, an Ogilvy & Mather house organ, addressed agency-specific topics and broader industry issues.
Used with permission by Ogilvy & Mather.

The distinguished-looking, bearded Whitehead exuded poise and well-tempered elegance—in many ways an Ogilvy alter ego. What began as a single introductory ad built around him grew into a television campaign that went on well into the 1960s. The commander's subtle appreciation of life's finer things, including beautiful women, delighted Americans and is said to have been a model for actor Sean Connery's portrayal of James Bond a decade later.

"Carriage-Trade" Image

But there was more to Hathaway and Schweppes than upscale intrigue. The product personalities created for these two small clients also reflected their creator and his agency. They had a refinement about them and thus required a refined environment in which to be seen. That was why Ogilvy saw fit to favor a certain magazine that would help define the agency as effectively as its clients. "In those days *The New Yorker* was incomparably more important in sophisticated circles than it would be 40 years later," recalled Joel Raphaelson, one of Ogilvy's closest associates for many years. "Even though the magazine had a small circulation, wherever it made any sense at all, [Ogilvy] saw to it that our clients ran in *The New Yorker*. Hathaway, Helena Rubinstein, Rolls-Royce, Schweppes all ran there. And more quickly than you might think, a very important group of readers became aware of [Ogilvy]."

It was hard not to become aware of Ogilvy in the early 1950s. He was a natural publicity hound, loaded with presence, glamour, and charm, and full of opinions that made outrageously good sense. He was also producing 90 percent of the work that was getting the agency noticed. He was in demand for interviews and speeches, and his remarks provoked talk. In 1952 he warned of the hazards of bigness and accused older agencies of "creative burnout," bait to which his brother-in-law, Rosser Reeves, could not resist rising. The result was a battle of press releases that was the talk of Madison Avenue for a week. The two men found much to argue about in a constant competition for attention. "At parties each liked to dominate the room," historian Stephen Fox wrote in *The Mirror Makers*. "If Reeves came in a loud dinner jacket, Ogilvy appeared in a kilt." He blanketed new business prospects with his new and improved 12-point "creative credo." Late in 1952 the agency picked up $6 million in Rinso business from Lever Brothers, its first real package-goods account.

Meanwhile, Hewitt, despite his title of chief executive officer (CEO), which made him Ogilvy's boss, was hardly getting noticed at all. Hewitt took a dim view of the agency's carriage-trade image and the British upper-class tone of some of his partner's pet accounts. The two clashed repeatedly, and in February 1953 Ogilvy resigned.

Francis Ogilvy and Bob Bevan, representing the London stockholders Mather & Crowther and S.H. Benson, flew to New York City to patch up the rift. Although they came to arbitrate, they quickly recognized that they would have to choose. Their choice was David Ogilvy. Eighteen months later, in September 1954, the agency moved to 589 Fifth Avenue and dropped Hewitt's name. The agency was now Ogilvy, Benson & Mather (OBM).

In October 1955 Ogilvy confessed to a change of mind: the quick-sale, hard-sell style was out, and advertising as a long-term investment in brand building was in. But for all his apparent dogmatism, such basic strategy questions posed a constant dilemma for him. He was more comfortable on the tactical level, where he could boil everything down to a list. In 1957 he startled the British Advertising Association by propounding a catechism of 39 "rules for ad writing" that, among other things, warned copywriters to get to the point and avoid sentences of more than 12 words. The speech was the hit of the association's convention—and Ogilvy, it must be said, followed most of his own rules.

For all the speeches, though, the agency faced serious problems without the professional marketing savvy of Hewitt, who left the agency with several key account people, along with the business of Sun Oil and Chase Bank. Left to its own devices, the agency fumbled and lost Franco-American and Rinso soon after, though Lever offered Dove soap, for which the agency would go on to write the well-remembered tag line "with 1/4 moisturizing cream," as a consolation prize.

Knowing where his weakness lay and recognizing that brilliant ads were not enough, Ogilvy went looking for the strength the agency needed to start growing again. He found it in a retired

Benton and Bowles vice president named Esty Stowell. According to *Fortune*, he told Stowell that the agency's media and research departments were in poor shape, and its account executives were "the most extraordinary collection of bums you ever saw." Ogilvy was to handle the creative work, while Stowell ran everything else. The deal was done in 1956.

While Ogilvy delighted in controversy, he understood that his clients did not, especially in their advertising. So the flap caused by the first campaign for Bristol-Myers's Ban deodorant surprised him. Because no network wished to show real people using a deodorant, Reva Korda, a young copywriter who would later become head of all OBM creative works, decided to represent the idea of anatomy with a montage of images of nude statues. In the voice-over a narrator with a British accent intoned, "In the mature male and the mature female. . . ." Although discreet, the ad was controversial and was withdrawn after several months.

Rolls-Royce and Mercedes-Benz

While OBM handled the routine maintenance of its bread-and-butter clients, which by now included Maxwell House coffee, Dove soap, Good Luck margarine, and Pepperidge Farm, another quintessential high-prestige, low-profit, David Ogilvy–style brand came knocking in December 1957. Despite its meager $50,000 budget, Rolls-Royce had a seductive appeal for Ogilvy, who ignored Stowell's warning that it would further typecast the agency as an elitist boutique.

It made no difference. Ogilvy decided that he was born to ride in a Rolls. Besides, big accounts, he was learning, were inclined to inhibit his better instincts, not to mention meddle in his copy. The little ones that came begging for his favor did not dare to interfere. On that simple premise, the third of his defining moments was at hand, though the cleverness that would forever attach to him was not his work at all.

The ingenious 1958 headline ("At 60 miles an hour the loudest noise in this new Rolls-Royce comes from the electric clock") was in fact lifted from an article in *The Motor*, a British auto magazine, proving another pair of Ogilvy truisms: that journalists are the best advertising writers and that the best ads imitate journalism. (Ogilvy fully credited his source in the ad, and the headline was in quotes.) The copy that followed was pure Ogilvy, enumerating 13 engineering advantages as if he were handing down his own rules of good advertising. The Rolls-Royce ads would seal Ogilvy's reputation and define his style.

The agency's later campaign for Mercedes-Benz took the emphasis on engineering detail even further. The car was in a tiny niche defined by elegance and luxury, words used endlessly in its advertising. At OBM these words were never used. Writer Bruce McCall produced lengthy essays on engineering and performance that many felt influenced U.S. awareness of what made good cars.

Shell Oil and American Express

By 1960 it was time to get down to serious growth. That year the agency lured away one of the most promising young executives at

A 1985 house ad announced the opening of Ogilvy & Mather's 201st office, in Edinburgh, Scotland, the city where ad executive David Ogilvy (pictured) began his career. The ad ran in Scotland's national newspaper, *The Scotsman*, on 29 May.
Used with permission by Ogilvy & Mather.

BBDO, Jock Elliott, a tough-minded former marine who had a remarkable ability to convert his most powerful bosses into dedicated mentors. His job was to manage the largest single account OBM had ever won, Shell Oil.

The Shell business made big news, less for its size than its conditions. The company wanted to substitute a negotiated annual fee based on a cost-plus formula for the traditional 15 percent commission system. The details were announced on 13 November before the Association of National Advertisers and were the talk of the trade. Ogilvy became a high-visibility advocate of fee arrangements. "It made sense to him," Elliott later said. "The client paid for what it got. I don't recall David being a great fee advocate before Shell. But after we got the account, we both made endless speeches about why we thought it was so good."

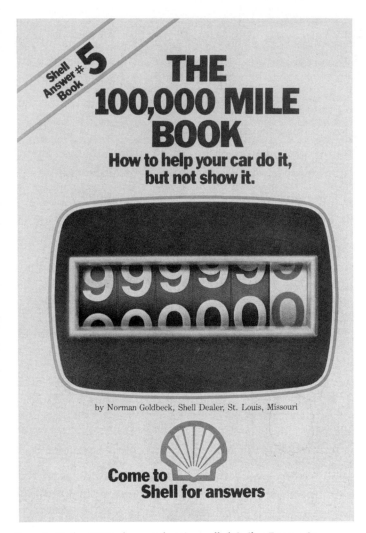

In 1960 Ogilvy & Mather—at that time called Ogilvy, Benson & Mather—acquired its largest account to date, Shell Oil Company. Among the work Ogilvy created for Shell was the "Come to Shell for Answers" campaign, which featured booklets such as this 1976 example offering advice for car owners.
Printed with permission granted by the Shell Oil Company.

The American Express account came to the agency in 1962 on a fee basis reportedly valued at $1.4 million. It grew rapidly as the agency produced some of its most famous work for the financial services company. In 1975 it launched a campaign for American Express credit cards in which a procession of people with famous names but not necessarily famous faces asked viewers, "Do you know me?" *Advertising Age* ranked the campaign 17th in its list of the 100 best ads of the 20th century. In a later campaign for American Express Travelers Checks, Ogilvy introduced actor Karl Malden as the enduring brand spokesman with his warning, "Don't leave home without them."

Ogilvy's public profile hit its peak with the publication in October 1963 of his book *Confessions of an Advertising Man*, which sold 1 million copies and was translated into 14 languages. In the 1960s and 1970s OBM spun off a series of house ads from the book that were quickly tacked onto many agency walls.

Going Public

Inside OBM, growth was bringing in mass merchandisers such as Sears, Roebuck & Company to balance Ogilvy's rarified *New Yorker* clients. Billings were approaching $80 million. And more and more, he and his management "partners" began to see advertising's future on a global basis. On 19 November 1964, OBM and its venerable London partner, Mather & Crowther, announced an "equal partnership" merger to form a single operating company, known simply as Ogilvy & Mather, a parent company joining OBM and M&C. The merger created a combined billing strength of $130 million and made Ogilvy a power all over Europe. With the stroke of a pen, Ogilvy's agency shot from 21st to eighth in the annual *Advertising Age* rankings. His one regret was that his brother Francis, who had brought him into Mather & Crowther in 1935 and originally proposed the merger, had died eight months earlier. Ogilvy & Mather was no longer a boutique in which Ogilvy turned out most of the award-winning gems.

"David was aware of the need to institutionalize the company," said Elliott, "and took steps to do so. He wanted to build a cadre of people who would be there. We used to have a list of 'crown princes.' 'Keep a close eye on the crown princes,' David would say, 'and make sure they are being brought along.'"

In December 1965 Ogilvy dropped his title of chairman to become creative director, and Stowell gave up the presidency. Elliott became chairman, a first among equals in an uneasy and ill-fated management triumvirate in which his principal rival was James Heekin, an ambitious president. In November 1969 this charged situation exploded when the board replaced Heekin with Andrew Kershaw, who had been president of Ogilvy & Mather (Canada), Ltd., in Toronto since 1960, and Heekin left the agency. In January 1966 all the offices officially adopted the common name Ogilvy & Mather, and Ogilvy & Mather International (OMI) was formed as the parent, with Ogilvy as titular chairman. Benson was dropped from the nameplate.

The 41 stockholders in Ogilvy & Mather had to decide whether or not to become rich—that is, to go public. Ogilvy owned 17 percent of the shares, valued at around $3.65 a share, or about three times earnings. But he had seen a handful of agencies such as Doyle Dane Bernbach; Foote, Cone & Belding; Grey Advertising; and Papert, Koenig, Lois sell publicly at four times that price-earnings ratio. He felt the time was right. Not all his colleagues saw it that way. Stowell, for one, was violently opposed.

But Ogilvy, whose annual salary was $100,122, wanted to be rich and felt he deserved to be. So on 24 March 1966, the agency filed a registration statement with the U.S. Securities and Exchange Commission for a sale of 32 percent of the shares. The media, as was customary, received a statement of the agency's need to finance improved client service, a fabrication none took too seriously. "Sheer greed," Elliott called it later. The sale opened on 21 April in both New York City and London (a first for an ad agency) at $22 per share. Of the possibility of a hostile takeover, Joel Raphaelson told *Advertising Age* in 1998, "In all the board's discussion, pro and con, the notion the company might be vulnerable

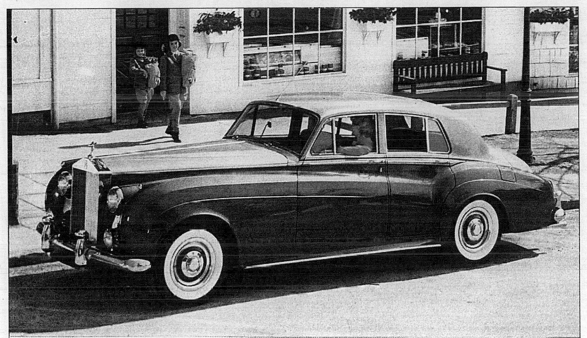

The Rolls-Royce Silver Cloud—$13,995

"At 60 miles an hour the loudest noise in this new Rolls-Royce comes from the electric clock"

What __makes__ Rolls-Royce the best car in the world? "There is really no magic about it—it is merely patient attention to detail," says an eminent Rolls-Royce engineer.

1. "At 60 miles an hour the loudest noise comes from the electric clock," reports the Technical Editor of THE MOTOR. Three mufflers tune out sound frequencies—acoustically.

2. Every Rolls-Royce engine is run for seven hours at full throttle before installation, and each car is test-driven for hundreds of miles over varying road surfaces.

3. The Rolls-Royce is designed as an *owner-driven* car. It is eighteen inches shorter than the largest domestic cars.

4. The car has power steering, power brakes and automatic gear-shift. It is very easy to drive and to park. No chauffeur required.

5. The finished car spends a week in the final test-shop, being fine-tuned. Here it is subjected to 98 separate ordeals. For example, the engineers use a *stethoscope* to listen for axle-whine.

6. The Rolls-Royce is guaranteed for *three years*. With a new network of dealers and parts-depots from Coast to Coast, service is no problem.

7. The Rolls-Royce radiator has never changed, except that when Sir Henry Royce died in 1933 the monogram RR was changed from red to black.

8. The coachwork is given five coats of primer paint, and hand rubbed between each coat, before *nine* coats of finishing paint go on.

9. By moving a switch on the steering column, you can adjust the shock-absorbers to suit road conditions.

10. A picnic table, veneered in French walnut, slides out from under the dash. Two more swing out behind the front seats.

11. You can get such optional extras as an Espresso coffee-making machine, a dictating machine, a bed, hot and cold water for washing, an electric razor or a telephone.

12. There are three separate systems of power brakes, two hydraulic and one mechanical. Damage to one will not affect the others. The Rolls-Royce is a very *safe* car—and also a very *lively* car. It cruises serenely at eighty-five. Top speed is in excess of 100 m.p.h.

13. The Bentley is made by Rolls-Royce. Except for the radiators, they are identical motor cars, manufactured by the same engineers in the same works. People who feel diffident about driving a Rolls-Royce can buy a Bentley.

PRICE. The Rolls-Royce illustrated in this advertisement—f.o.b. principal ports of entry—costs $13,995.

If you would like the rewarding experience of driving a Rolls-Royce or Bentley, write or telephone to one of the dealers listed on opposite page. Rolls-Royce Inc., 10 Rockefeller Plaza, New York 20, N. Y. CIrcle 5-1144.

With typical modesty—and only a bit of hyperbole—David Ogilvy, in his book *Ogilvy on Advertising*, described this example of his work as "the most famous of all automobile ads." The ad used the long copy that Ogilvy believed was more effective than short messages in persuading consumers to make a purchase. *Reproduced with permission from Rolls-Royce & Bentley Motor Cars Limited.*

to a hostile takeover was never mentioned once by anyone in the company or the trade press."

Going public stimulated the agency's appetite, and particularly Kershaw's, for international expansion. There was a small exchange of stock with Publicis in 1968. The next year Ogilvy began buying up agencies in Venezuela, Colombia, Brazil, and Argentina. In July 1971 it bought S.H. Benson, Ltd., one of its original backers in 1948. Ogilvy condemned agency megamergers as the work of "megalomaniacs." Yet he warned in September 1970 that agencies operating in only one country would "be washed up on the beach in a few years."

Ogilvy was buying American as well. In December 1970 it acquired Carson/Roberts, the largest agency on the West Coast where Ogilvy had been all but invisible. In 1976 it picked up Scali, McCabe, Sloves, one of the hottest creative shops of the decade. In 1975 Ogilvy opened an office in Chicago, Illinois, which became a $40 milllion shop almost overnight, largely on the basis of its Sears business. Ogilvy acquired Cone & Weber in Seattle, Washington, in March 1977.

Finally in 1979, with huge cash reserves and a reputation as the best-managed agency in the business, Ogilvy & Mather quietly went after the biggest prize of all, the J. Walter Thompson Company (JWT). The initiative came from Elliott, who began sending out some quiet feelers. Each agency was strong where the other was not, and there were minimal client conflicts and many clients in common. Elliott undertook quiet conversations on the matter, which was code named "Toto." In the end, JWT wanted to go ahead, but the Ogilvy board did not.

Thompson & Ogilvy never materialized. But Elliott was not the only one interested in JWT. A year or two later Ogilvy called Shelby H. Page, his treasurer, and said he was sending a young Englishman to his office who wanted to talk about JWT. Page talked to the man for an hour or so and was impressed with the detail of his questions. He gave him all the information he could. At the end of the talk, he thanked Page and went on his way. David Ogilvy had written in 1963 that "the British have always abhorred the whole idea of advertising." He would soon learn all that was changing. The young man's name was Martin Sorrell; he would one day build one of the world's largest advertising holding companies, the WPP Group.

Ogilvy's original community of "gentlemen" was being overwhelmed by success and size. He retired as chairman of OMI, the parent company, in 1975, and Elliott took over. But Ogilvy continued to influence what he wished to influence by the force of what was now his legend. "He was always my boss," Elliott said. "Even when I became chairman of OMI, I never once ever used the title CEO, even though I was the CEO. I thought it was wholly inappropriate with David still actively involved."

In 1979 Ogilvy brought Norman Barry from England to be creative chief. And Barry brought in Hal Riney to run the San Francisco, California, office. In 1982 Ogilvy was named *Advertising Age*'s "Agency of the Year." By 1985, with billings of $2.4 billion, OMI was involved in so many related businesses that it became the Ogilvy Group, overseeing a money-making machine in which advertising accounted for only 62 percent of revenue.

Triumph of WPP

Then in January 1989, 17 months after a failed takeover bid by Ted Bates, the company's stock price experienced unexplained "gyrations." The board took immediate defensive measures against an adversary it could not identify. Suspects included Sorrell's WPP Group, which was still $120 million in debt after buying JWT in 1987; Dentsu; VPI, a London communications company; and London media baron Robert Maxwell.

By the first week in May, however, all cards were on the table, and Sorrell had come out of the shadows. Clients sat on the sidelines as $500 million in possible client conflicts, including American Express, General Foods, and Unilever, teetered on the outcome. Wall Street estimated it would take $700 million to buy Ogilvy. Ken Roman, Ogilvy Group chairman, said "Not at any price."

At that point David Ogilvy, now 77, emerged from retirement in France. He said he felt very sad, and he dismissed Sorrell as an "accountant." In a moment of candidness rare even for him, he referred to Sorrell as "an odious little shit." Ogilvy's associates bit their lips and grinned, delighted that age still had its privileges. But not even Ogilvy's invective could stay the force of economic determinism. On 16 May the Ogilvy Group passed to WPP at $54 a share. A month later Ogilvy moved into offices at Worldwide Plaza, 309 West 49th Street, New York City.

If Sorrell came out of it with his image intact, so did Ogilvy, who accepted the title of WPP honorary chairman. "I didn't like it," said Elliott, the then-retired chairman, who ten years before had tried to bring Ogilvy and JWT together. "It wasn't that it was a bad thing. It was that we were used to doing things like that, not having them done to us." Chairman Shelly Lazarus, who also opposed the takeover, concurred.

After a respectable period, Roman moved on, to be replaced by Charlotte Beers, an Ogilvy first: never had a CEO been recruited directly from another agency (Tatham, Laird & Kudner, which shortly thereafter became Euro RSCG Tatham). It was feared that there might be a clash of philosophy and behavior with a woman some called "rude" and "insolent." But after a visit to Touffou, Ogilvy's chateau south of Paris, France, Beers came back with the founder's imprimatur.

"I think WPP thought we needed new leadership," Lazarus told *Advertising Age* in 1998. "It was tiring to the management that had just been through the whole [takeover] roller coaster. A company pre- and post-takeover is not necessarily better or worse. But it's different. That's the problem of keeping the same management."

Beers's legacy would be the demise of *Viewpoint,* perhaps the most erudite and substantive company magazine in the industry. But a larger, healthier Ogilvy came into being, along with a fresh phrase in the agency lexicon: brand stewardship. It was a semantic repackaging of the traditional gospel of long-term brand building.

In 1996 the pendulum swung back to home-grown leadership with the appointment of Lazarus as CEO. She will almost certainly be the last individual to occupy that office who could boast of significant contact with Ogilvy, who died in July 1999 at age 88. Ogilvy & Mather Worldwide had gross income of $1.54 billion in 2000, up 21.2 percent over 1999, on billings of $13.51 billion, up 21.8 percent over the year earlier.

JOHN McDONOUGH

Further Reading

"David Ogilvy Talks about How He Writes Copy," *Advertising Age* (15 March 1965)

"How and What Ogilvy Sold Shell," *Advertising Age* (12 December 1960)

Kershaw, Andrew, "Living with David Ogilvy," *Advertising Age* (25 June 1973)

"Mather & Crowther . . .Grew Large Under Francis Ogilvy," *Advertising Age* (8 June 1964)

McDonough, John, "Ogilvy & Mather at 50," *Advertising Age* (21 September 1998)

Ogilvy, David, "Image and the Brand," *Advertising Age* (14 November 1955)

Ogilvy, David, "How to Lead a Creative Organization," *Advertising Age* (22 October 1962)

Ogilvy, David, *Confessions of an Advertising Man*, New York: Atheneum, 1963; London: Longmans, 1964

Ogilvy, David, *Ogilvy on Advertising*, New York: Crown, and London: Pan, 1983

"The Ogilvy Shell Arrangement," *Advertising Age* (28 November 1960)

"Paeans over Fee Setup," *Advertising Age* (21 November 1960)

"Shell Setup IS Forward Step," *Advertising Age* (28 November 1960)

Viewpoint (December 1994) (final issue of Ogilvy and Mather company magazine)

Winski, Joseph, "A Giant Bows to 'Jackasses': David Ogilvy Learns New Lessons," *Advertising Age* (22 May 1989)

Ohrbach's

Principal Agencies

Grey Advertising Agency, Inc.
Doyle Dane Bernbach, Inc.

Ohrbach's, a bargain fashion store with branches in New York, New Jersey, and California, achieved a national reputation in the 1940s and 1950s for its low-priced, high-quality copies of French couture designs. On 4 October 1923 Nathan M. Ohrbach and Max Wiesen opened a store on New York City's 14th Street to sell irregular clothing, job lots, and manufacturers' overstocks. A sign announced, "Ohrbach's, a bonded word for savings . . . more for less or your money back." Crowds overwhelmed the store on opening day. Police were called to control the crowds and additional merchandise had to be rushed in to fill the empty racks. A Miracle Day Sale, a duplicate of the opening-day event, was held at the end of every month for the next three years.

The two owners disagreed about business policies, however, and in 1928 Wiesen sold his interest to Ohrbach, who quickly discontinued the special sales. Ohrbach explained:

> Promotion is like taking dope. You use one dose of it, and you have to have another, and another, and then another. A store advertises a sale of shoes that originally retailed at $24.50, for only $14.95. Actually, they are telling the customer: "We thought we could get you to pay $24.50 for these things and you wouldn't. So now we are trying to get you to buy them for $14.95."

Ohrbach instituted the policy of making every day a sale day and coined the slogan, "A business in millions . . . a profit in pennies." In 1928 he hired Grey Advertising Agency, Inc., to create ads promoting the store. Many of these early advertisements were one-panel cartoons depicting the adventures of a young lady called Melisse who always snared her man and asserted that "the girl in the Ohrbach dress" was irresistible in all situations.

Ohrbach's institutional advertisements were extremely effective. At the opening of its Los Angeles, California, store in 1948, thousands of customers were lured in by the radio and newspaper ads. Nine minutes after the doors were opened, they had to be closed, and the police were called in to keep order. By afternoon, radio announcements told listeners, "Please don't come to Ohrbach's today; come tomorrow, or next week."

Ohrbach grew unhappy with Grey and asked Bill Bernbach, Grey's vice president of copy and art, to start his own agency with Ohrbach's as its first client. On 1 June 1949, Bernbach formed an agency with Ned Doyle, a vice president and account executive at Grey, and Maxwell Dane, who was running a small agency at the time. Thus, Doyle Dane Bernbach, Inc. (DDB), was launched.

Bernbach designed the Ohrbach ads personally. With a small media budget, he created an image that caught the attention of Madison Avenue. Whimsical illustrations, ample white space, and short, often humorous copy characterized the advertisements. The most famous ad featured an image of a cat with a large hat and long cigarette holder saying, "I found out about Joan," followed by catty copy about how Joan dressed like a millionaire by shopping at Ohrbach's.

It's in,
but maybe
you shouldn't
be in it.

Some girls look sensational in hot pants. Front, back and sideways. So for these gorgeous girls Ohrbach's has an assortment of stylish hot pants and warm pants. All at Ohrbach's fabulously low prices.

But no one style is right for everybody. And a girl who

looks absolutely divine in one outfit can look positively dreadful in another.

That's why Ohrbach's has so many thousands of fashions to choose from. We know there's a right look for everyone, and when you come into our store we want to be sure

you'll find the one that's right for you.

And at a price you can afford. At Ohrbach's, we believe that it isn't right if it isn't right for you.

OHRBACH'S Where you always find the right fashion and the price that's right for *you*.

Charge it at Ohrbach's
New York, 34th St., Mon., Thurs., Fri. till 9. Newark, N.J. Market & Halsey, Wed., Fri. till 9.45 Westbury, L.I. at the Parkway Mon.—Fri. till 9.30 Paramus, N.J. Bergen Mall Mon.—Sat. till 9.30 Wayne, N.J. Willowbrook Mon.—Sat. till 9.30 Woodbridge, N.J. Woodbridge Center Mon.—Sat. till 9.30

In the 1960s, ads for Ohrbach's department store emphasized the retailer's large and varied selection of fashions with the tag line "a right look for everyone."

Stephen Fox in *The Mirror Makers* reports that in 1960 the Ohrbach's campaign was named one of the ten best of the previous decade in a poll of creative directors at 100 agencies. In his book *The Benevolent Dictators*, Bart Cummings quotes Bernbach: "Every time an Ohrbach ad ran, the bell rang. We won Best Retail Advertising awards—I would say for 15 years in a row. Ohrbach sometimes got so mad, he said, 'Here I've built this wonderful store, and all people remember me for is my advertising.'" The success of Ohrbach's attracted other accounts to DDB, including Henry Levy & Sons Bakery, Avis Rent a Car, and Volkswagen. As Bob Levenson wrote in his 1987 book about Bernbach, "There might not have been a Doyle Dane Bernbach had it not been for the Ohrbach's business."

Through smart advertising and merchandising, Ohrbach's was transformed from an unfashionable odd-lots store to a "high fashion at low prices" boutique. Ohrbach's assortment of designer fashions and line-for-line copies of French couture fashions attracted bargain-hunters of all economic backgrounds. Customers included movie stars Joan Crawford, Jane Russell, and Lauren Bacall and members of royalty. *Life* magazine devoted a cover story to Ohrbach's in its 26 January 1953 issue.

Ohrbach's moved its New York City headquarters to West 34th Street off Fifth Avenue on 26 August 1954. This new location brought Ohrbach's into direct competition with Macy's, Gimbels, Lord & Taylor, and B. Altman. Some 100,000 persons crowded into the store on opening day. Macy's ran an advertisement welcoming its new neighbor: "If you live through this, you are ready for Macy's."

In the early 1960s Ohrbach's had approximately $80 million in annual revenue. Ohrbach was an octogenarian, however, and his son was not interested in continuing the business. The chain was sold in 1962 to the Brenninkmeyers, a Dutch merchant family who shifted the business' direction. The store, once famous for its quality copies of designer apparel, sold lower-priced and poorer-quality merchandise in the 1970s and 1980s. The advertising, once known for its witty, unexpected approach, featured specific merchandise and prices. The Ohrbach's that Nathan M.

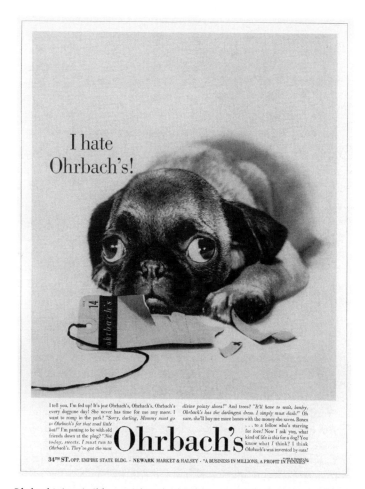

I hate
Ohrbach's!

I tell you, I'm fed up! It's just Ohrbach's, Ohrbach's, Ohrbach's every doggone day! She never has time for me any more. I want to romp in the park? "Sorry, darling, Mommy must go to Ohrbach's for that mad little hat!" I'm panting to be with old friends down at the plug? "Not today, sweets, I must run to Ohrbach's. They're got the most

divine pointy shoes!" And trees? "It'll have to wait, lamby, Ohrbach's has the darlingest dress. I simply must dash!" Oh sure, she'll buy me more bones with the money she saves. Bones . . . to a fellow who's starving for love! Now I ask you, what kind of life is *this* for a dog? You know what I think? I think Ohrbach's was invented by cats!

Ohrbach's

34TH ST. OPP. EMPIRE STATE BLDG. · NEWARK MARKET & HALSEY · "A BUSINESS IN MILLIONS, A PROFIT IN PENNIES"

Ohrbach's irresistible appeal to the fashion-conscious shopper was the premise of this playful 1958 ad.

Ohrbach and Bill Bernbach had made famous was gone. The store went out of business in 1987.

BONNIE DREWNIANY

Further Reading

Cummings, Bart, *The Benevolent Dictators: Interviews with Advertising Greats,* Chicago: Crain, 1984

Drew-Bear, Robert, *Mass Merchandising: Revolution and Evolution,* New York: Fairchild, 1970

Fox, Stephen R., *The Mirror Makers: A History of American Advertising and Its Creators,* New York: Morrow, 1984

Higgins, Denis, *The Art of Writing Advertising: Conversations with William Bernbach, Leo Burnett, George Gribbin, David Ogilvy, Rosser Reeves,* Lincolnwood, Illinois: NTC Business Books, 1965

Levenson, Bob, *Bill Bernbach's Book: A History of the Advertising That Changed the History of Advertising,* New York: Villard, 1987

Mahoney, Tom, *The Great Merchants: America's Foremost Retail Institutions and the People Who Made Them Great,* New York: Harper and Row, 1951; new edition, 1966

Oil Companies

Retail advertising in the oil industry—considered to include gasoline and lubricants sold directly to consumers—is dominated by two primary themes: the creation of market distinctions for what is essentially a commodity product; and the establishment of a positive corporate image. Many of the major oil companies maintain separate departments for corporate and product advertising and have, at times, employed different agencies for these purposes.

At its most basic level, gasoline fuel, as a refined oil product, is no different whether supplied by one retailer or another. Through the use of additives, some companies engineer distinctions into their refining process, but for the most part the products marketed under various brands are essentially the same. This lack of product distinction has prompted many retailers to seek other factors around which to anchor their ad campaigns. Over time, the challenge of creating a perception of "uniqueness" has been approached in a variety of ways.

In the early years of the industry, fuel was treated much like nails or other generic household commodities. In fact, hardware stores were common distribution points for gasoline during the early part of the 20th century. As roads were built in the United States, early advertising often played into the romantic notion of traveling by automobile. From the 1920s through the 1950s companies worked hard to create unique brand identities. Attention went into developing logos, introducing memorable jingles, and appealing to target markets through sponsorship of various entertainment venues.

In the 1960s and 1970s the emphasis on brand gave way to performance claims or advertising promotions, giveaways, and games. During the 1980s and early 1990s sponsorship of popular events such as the Olympic Games continued to be used to garner customer loyalty, while several campaigns tried to resurrect feelings of brand loyalty by using popular characters and symbols from the past.

Toward the turn of the 21st century, as consolidation of ownership became the trend, many aspects of product advertising came full circle. Gasoline was recognized as a low-margin item. A good deal of product-oriented advertising returned to positioning fuel as a commodity item and focusing on the other goods or services a retailer might provide, such as car washes, coffee, convenient payment systems, and traditional "TBA" marketing (industry shorthand for tires, batteries, and accessories).

Image has traditionally been an important aspect of advertising in the industry as well. Even before the Exxon *Valdez* oil spill disaster, a variety of events called into question the major companies' sense of environmental and social responsibility, business practices, and involvement in political issues such as boycotts and embargoes. The oil industry was born under public scrutiny, and because of its impact on consumers' pocketbooks and its influence on other energy-related industries, it seems destined to remain an industry people love to hate. As a consequence, oil companies spend a significant amount of their advertising dollars reminding customers of their better qualities.

History and Consolidation

In 1859 Edwin Drake, under the direction of several investors who formed the Pennsylvania Rock Oil Company, became the first person to successfully drill oil from the ground. Refined into kerosene, it initially was used as fuel for light, though other applications quickly followed. Drake's success led to an oil rush as dozens of small companies dug wells. While it was easy to entertain dreams of great profits, the challenges of underwriting the costs of digging, refining, and transporting liquid fuel did not entail riches for many of those involved.

Starting in 1865 John D. Rockefeller began to consolidate many small refining companies into the Standard Oil Company. In 1906 the company was sued for violation of the Sherman Antitrust Act, and in 1911 the conglomerate was ordered to dissolve: Standard Oil of New Jersey became Exxon; Standard Oil of New York eventually became Mobil; Standard Oil of California became Chevron; Standard Oil of Ohio became Sohio and then BP Amoco; Standard Oil of Indiana became Amoco; Continental Oil became Conoco; and Atlantic became Arco.

The breakup of the American oil industry created more than a number of individual gasoline marketers—it also produced one of America's most important ad agencies. Harrison McCann had joined the advertising department of Standard Oil early in the century and had risen to the upper ranks of management by 1911. When the company was broken apart, McCann was offered the opportunity to set up an independent agency to serve the various spin-offs, including Standard Oil of California, Indiana, Louisiana, Nebraska, New Jersey, Ohio, and Pennsylvania. This was the beginning of McCann-Erickson, the ad agency that continued to serve many of Standard Oil's incarnations throughout the 20th century.

Meanwhile, in the 1870s and 1880s the Royal Dutch Company (which would later become the Royal Dutch Petroleum Company and parent to Shell Oil) expanded into global exploration for fuel sources. In 1901, when Spindletop, Texas, proved to be an enormous source of oil, Sun Oil/Gulf Oil and Texaco were launched. A century later the U.S. retail gas market continued to be dominated by a handful of players: BP Amoco, Chevron, Exxon, Mobil, Phillips, Shell, and Texaco. Several of these companies merged or entered into joint ventures for production, and other smaller, regional enterprises were ripe for acquisition.

While the technology of refining advanced and additional uses for oil products were uncovered—including military applications during World War I—the oil industry boom did not begin in earnest until 1919. The U.S. Army launched a cross-country motor caravan to demonstrate the potential for motor transportation and to spark interest in creating a national highway system. The convoy started on 7 July 1919 from the White House lawn in Washington, D.C., and arrived in San Francisco, California, on 6 September. To a great extent, this event kicked off Americans' love affair with cars and their penchant for road trips.

Rise of the Service Station

By the end of the 1920s more than 23 million cars were registered in the United States, and the average miles traveled per car increased over the decade from 4,500 to 7,500 miles per year. In Daniel Yergin's monumental book on the industry, *The Prize: The Epic Quest for Oil, Money & Power* (1991), he wrote, "The transformation of America into an automotive culture was accompanied by a truly momentous development; the emergence and proliferation of a temple dedicated to the new fuel and the new way of life—the drive-in gasoline station." Before this, gasoline, bearing no brand name and often of questionable origin, was primarily sold by storekeepers or delivered house-to-house in wagons. By 1920 approximately 100,000 general retailers sold gasoline; by the end of the decade, that number had grown to 300,000, and most of these outlets were garages or retailers specializing in gasoline sales.

As service stations proliferated, so did the competition among them. Major distribution entities began to develop and use trademarks to assure brand identification. These trademarks—Texaco's star, Shell's scallop shell, Sinclair's brontosaurus, Standard of Indiana's red crown—began to represent something special to drivers. While consumer choices may have been made on the basis of service received from their neighborhood retailer, once on the road and far from home, motorists started looking for those familiar signs. In these early days, advertising and publicity, largely in the form of signage, was an essential aspect of the business.

Bruce Barton, a successful ad executive in the 1920s, encouraged key men in the oil industry to reflect on what he referred to as "the magic of gasoline." He went on to assert, "It is health. It is comfort. It is success." Consumers did not purchase gasoline; they purchased the freedom of the road or a particular image an oil company wanted to project.

In 1929 well-known painter and illustrator McClelland Barclay turned his talents to advertising, creating a series of posters (used as print ads) for Texaco. The series featured "beautiful people," wealthy, young sophisticates of the time enjoying sports, travel, and social outings. These pictures of the good life, alongside a description of Texaco's "Golden Motor Oil," were well received. This campaign was part of a larger strategy created by Harry Tipper, an Englishman who became Texaco's first advertising manager in 1909. He used print ads in national newspapers and magazines, along with road signs, emblems on uniforms, and station window displays, to promote the brand.

Some of his innovations revolved around advertising the chain's service perks. One of Texaco's most successful print campaigns from the 1930s, "All nite long, you're always welcome," showed a driver on a rainy night being greeted by a smiling, uniformed station attendant. Pictured just underneath the glowing Texaco star logo was a sign proclaiming, "Registered Rest Room—A Texaco Dealer Service." The company boosted its national image further by creating the Halvoline thermometer, a 21-story structure, and an exhibit at the 1933 World's Fair in Chicago, Illinois.

Phillips's early advertising capitalized on America's passion for the budding aviation industry. Charles Lindbergh's successful transatlantic flight and a promotional flight from Oakland, California, to Honolulu, Hawaii, piloted by a Hollywood stunt man were both powered by Phillips's aviation grade gasoline; subsequently, Phillips launched a complete aviation-oriented campaign. Posters and print ads featured attractive female aviators with the slogan, "Phill-up and fly."

In the summer of 1939 clean rest rooms and travel assistance became the focus of an innovative marketing and advertising program that featured Phillips's "Highway Hostesses." These "hostesses" were registered nurses who literally cruised their territory helping motorists and inspecting rest rooms to make sure they were clean. While the majority of drivers were men, Phillips understood that women greatly influenced families' gas purchasing decisions.

As World War II approached all the major oil companies were associated with prominent agencies: Atlantic with N.W. Ayer & Son; Cities Service with Lord & Thomas; Gulf with Young &

Big League Action!

Fire-Chief gasoline gives you big league action every
mile of your way. You get faster power at the start,
in traffic and up the hills. You can buy Fire-Chief
at *regular* gasoline prices too. So make your next tankful
Fire-Chief — at your Texaco Dealer.

He's the best friend your car ever had.

. . . and don't forget the best motor oil your money can buy.

THE TEXAS COMPANY
TEXACO DEALERS IN ALL 48 STATES
Texaco Products are also distributed in Canada and Latin America

TEXACO
FIRE-CHIEF
GASOLINE

TEXACO
T
REG. T.M.

Faithfully yours
50
for Fifty Years

TUNE IN: On television—the TEXACO STAR THEATER starring MILTON BERLE—every Tuesday night. See newspaper for time and station.

Texaco introduced Fire-Chief gasoline in 1948 and promoted it along with its Tuesday night TV program, *Texaco Star Theater*, in
this 1952 print advertisement.
Courtesy of Texaco, Inc.

Rubicam; Humble Oil with McCann-Erickson; Pure (later merged with Union 76) with the Leo Burnett Company; Shell with the J. Walter Thompson Company (JWT); Standard with McCann-Erickson; and Texaco with Newell-Emmett (later Cunningham & Walsh).

Creating Personality

Establishing a distinctive personality was a major focus of early industry advertising. While Texaco established itself as a friendly service-provider (using images of its star-capped, smiling attendants) and Phillips highlighted its Highway Hostesses, Shell used advertising creatively to demonstrate its humor and humanity. In 1938 and 1939 it launched a popular print campaign consisting of half-page magazine ads that combined humor with information about the new industry and the merits of using Golden Shell Oil. The ads told consumers that the oil was "fast-flowing," "tough-bodied," and "only 25 cents per quart." The ads, which often used slang, embodied an "everyman" quality. They were composed of a cartoon illustration and a dialogue that featured a Shell station attendant dispatching customer concerns in a down-to-earth, often tongue-in-cheek way. While the influence of ads (such as "Off the bridge, you landlubber") on sales was not tracked, anecdotal research indicated that they gave readers a positive impression of Shell as a good-humored and friendly company.

During World War II gasoline was a rationed item, and product advertising was lean, although it did not disappear altogether. Print pieces, including a series by Phillips that depicted Boeing's Flying Fortress (running on Phillips fuel), demonstrated support of U.S. war efforts. Following World War II demand was unleashed again. New investments were made in exploration and refining and, in 1948, imports of foreign oil exceeded exports for the first time.

As gas stations proliferated in the 1950s, price wars reigned. Many independents were forced out of the market, and most of the major companies reverted to promoting service to gain customers. Credit cards were introduced in the early 1950s, and in subsequent years the oil companies focused on slogans and jingles to reestablish brand loyalty.

Sponsoring Entertainment

The most innovative and important aspect of industry advertising during this time was the development of entertainment sponsorship, a concept launched for radio and adapted by the budding television broadcast industry. In the early 1930s Texaco sponsored *The Ed Wynn Show* on radio, in which Wynn's identity merged with that of the Texaco Fire-Chief, a character named for Fire-Chief gasoline. The company subsequently sponsored Jimmy Durante (1935–36) and Eddie Cantor (1936–38) before launching its long-running variety show, *The Texaco Star Theater,* which featured a succession of hosts including Fred Allen, Tony Martin, and Gordon McCrae. Angling for a more sophisticated audience than was attracted by the *Star Theater,* Texaco began sponsoring live broadcasts from New York City's Metropolitan Opera in 1940. At the turn of the 21st century, these broadcasts were still being aired on many radio networks.

Shell was also an active network advertiser with its *Shell Chateau* program with Al Jolson, credited with launching the career of Judy Garland. JWT was the producer. Pure Oil was long associated with the commentator H.V. Kaltenborn, and Gulf sponsored *Gulf Headliners* with Will Rogers (1933–35) and *The Gulf ScreenGuild Theater* (1939–42). However, no oil company was among the top 20 radio advertisers during the 1930s.

In 1948 Texaco, the only oil company with locations in all 48 states, and its agency Kudner Advertising decided to transfer its radio success to the new arena of television. Texaco chose quick-witted comic Milton Berle for the role of host. Sticking with the vaudevillian recipe for entertainment, the live broadcasts featured celebrities of the era performing song, dance, and comedy.

Subsequent advertising built on the themes Texaco had established in the 1940s and 1950s through its sponsored broadcasts. In 1962 advertising focused around the jingle, "You Can Trust Your Car to the Men Who Wear the Star." In 1974 the company gave this theme a twist when it hired comedian Bob Hope to wear the Texaco service station's "starred" uniform and featured him in countless spots.

One of the most memorable brand images came from Esso-U.K., a subsidiary of what is now Exxon: the Esso "tiger." This symbol was first used in Europe shortly after the end of World War II to give an identifiable face to the product. It first appeared as a brightly colored illustration of a tiger leaping forward. In following years the symbol took on the look of a cartoon superhero, and the company's catch phrase became, "Put a tiger in your tank." While the first incarnation of the symbol was not introduced in the U.S. market, eventually the tiger became synonymous with Esso/Humble Oil through the work of Humble's agency, McCann-Erickson. In 1972, when Exxon decided to standardize its name and update signage at 25,000 outlets by dropping the Humble Oil name, a key slogan of the supporting campaign referred to the tiger: "We're changing our name but not our stripes."

The late 1950s and early 1960s marked the beginning of the additive craze. In the mid-1950s, 13 of the top 14 gasoline marketers offered a premium gasoline, and advertising began to focus on performance claims. Sinclair's Power-X formula supposedly inhibited rust. Mobil introduced what it referred to as a "high-energy" gasoline. Consumers could choose among multiple grades, and different marketing approaches seemed to have different results. In the spring of 1955 Phillips, with its agency Lambert & Feasley, Inc., New York City, launched a major campaign that included exposure in farm and trade magazines, billboards, television, radio, and newspapers, aimed at introducing the company's new slogan, "It's performance that counts."

One of the most successful performance-oriented campaigns of this era was developed by Ogilvy & Mather for Shell after 1960, when the account shifted from a 30-year-relationship with JWT. Diverging from earlier ads that featured cartoon characters and sappy slogans, these ads created a new persona for Shell in the form of a lab-coat-wearing research chemist. In the ads, detailed chemical information was presented describing Shell's unique formulation. A variety of demonstration-style TV commercials followed, many depicting cars fueled by Shell with "Platformate" breaking through paper barriers that represented the limited mileage achieved by cars fueled with inferior products. These spots ran throughout the early 1960s.

Market Expansion

Market expansion also represented an important goal for major retailers. In 1953 Phillips began an aggressive initiative to put a retail outlet in every U.S. state. (At this time Texaco was the only company that could make this claim). It replaced its original orange-and-black shield emblem with a red-and-white version and introduced products such as "Trop-Artic" motor oil to appeal to diverse geographical markets. Phillips splashed the slogans "Go first class" and "Go Phillips 66" across billboards and newspaper ads in major markets. In March 1965 Phillips ran an eight-page color insert—the first of its kind—in *Life* magazine aimed at positioning the company as a global enterprise. More than 20 similar ads were placed in *Look*, *Reader's Digest*, and *Saturday Evening Post* within the year. During its final wave of expansion into West Coast states, which included establishing an outlet in Anchorage, Alaska, on the company's 50th anniversary, Phillips adopted a new advertising campaign, proclaiming its product "The gasoline that won the West." In addition to consumer-oriented national advertising, Phillips created a variety of sales aids—including giant fiberglass cowboys wearing white hats—for retail outlets under the guidance of JWT. While profitably serving a national market did not prove feasible (in 1972 Phillips pulled out of several northeastern markets), the advertising campaigns themselves were very successful.

Standard Oil of Indiana was also geared for expansion in 1960. While Standard—with a strong market presence in 15 Midwest states—had purchased in 1954 the American Oil Company (a regional chain in the northeastern and Gulf states), the newly combined company did not have a unified brand identity. In 1961 the company launched "The Big Step." This campaign from D'Arcy Advertising Company, Chicago, Illinois—one of the largest ever presented by the company—was aimed at creating a single brand identity as the company sought expansion into new geographical markets. While Standard and American Oil outlets continued to operate under their respective names in their own markets for several more years, they all sold "Amoco" branded gasoline. During this campaign the company ran numerous television commercials and print ads in major market dailies and business publications such as the *Wall Street Journal* explaining the "Big Step" and its benefits to consumers. In conjunction with this consolidation of brands Standard Oil established new outlets in West Coast states only to discover that, like Phillips, it could not compete profitably nationwide.

Prior to the "Big Step" campaign, and through Standard's merger with British Petroleum (BP) in 1998, a key area of the company's advertising focused on the customer's perception of quality. In 1954 the slogan, "You expect more from Stan-

Fresh-killed chicken.

A 1966 reality campaign from Mobil was designed to create awareness of the problem of reckless driving by teens.
Permission to reprint granted by Exxon Mobil Corporation.

dard . . . and you get it" (coined by D'Arcy in 1954) was so successful it remained even after the company name changed, becoming "You expect more from Amoco . . . and you get it." In 1956 Amoco launched the "Quality makes a difference" campaign, which touted the superior performance provided by its blended products.

American Oil ran a series of ads under the name "Final Filter," aimed at educating customers on the importance of filtering out impurities before the fuel goes into the gas tank. In the 1980s several campaigns featured entertainers and sports celebrities, such as basketball star Bill Russell and singer Charlie Pride, who told consumers that car performance was directly linked to gas quality. Using the tag line, "Your car knows," the ads implied that a vehicle would not be fooled into running as well with a lesser grade of gasoline. While not flashy, these messages apparently hit their mark. For years market research indicated that customers chose Amoco, especially when buying premium grades, over other brands because they believed it to be superior quality. They were even willing to pay more.

Games and Giveaways

In the late 1960s industry advertising started to revolve around games, retail promotions, and giveaways. In 1967 Humble tried to lure customers with Tigerino and Tigerama. Mobil Oil pitched Play Safe and Winning Line games, and Standard Oil of Indiana featured All Pro and Super Pro games. Most of these games became a strong feature of regional advertising. Standard kicked off its Super Pro game with page ads in major dailies, offering Ford Mustangs and cash prizes as giveaways. Mobil print ads featured instructions for playing Winning Line. Special promotions were pitched through mailings to credit card customers, tear-off coupons on products such as road maps, and premium offers redeemable with fill-ups. In 1969 Mobil—through agency Doyle Dane Bernbach, Inc. (DDB), New York City—made ironstone coffee mugs available as a premium, simultaneously featuring photos of these mugs in print ads under the caption, "Get mugged free at Mobil."

DDB was responsible for Mobil's innovative campaigns toward the end of the 1960s, creating ads that were neither product-oriented nor image-oriented in the traditional sense. Instead, they were public-service oriented. The agency's "We Want You to Live" campaign (1966) featured in-your-face photographs and captions about driving safety. In one, a photo of a wheelchair appeared under the headline "26,320 people will be traveling a little slower after this weekend." In another, a young auto fatality, head covered with a jacket, appears with the headline, "Fresh-killed chicken." These ads won many awards (including the Deutsch and Shea Award given by Rutgers University's Business School) and were recognized for fostering an image of responsible corporate citizenship.

DDB added its flair to Mobil's product advertising in 1972 when it used actor Ronnie Graham as a dirty old man and Bonnie & Clyde–era villain in TV, radio, and print spots pitching Mobil's new detergent gasoline. In these spots, Graham, dubbed "Mr. Dirt," took the wheel for a hapless driver, while the audience was reminded of the only sure way to combat his mischief: "Dirt has an enemy. Mobil detergent gasoline."

Games resurfaced in the early 1970s—Mobil's World Passport and Shell's Play Bingo for Cash were among the most popular—though the key theme of advertising switched to image advertising in reaction to the oil crisis and the negative impressions consumers held of the industry at the time.

Image Advertising

In 1972, prior to the energy crisis, Exxon spent approximately $34 million in U.S. advertising, mostly on product advertising.

In 1974, with the oil crisis well under way, expenditures dropped to $24 million and the focus switched from product to image. Network television advertising focused on news shows such as *Meet the Press* and National Football League games, and the spots themselves featured conservation themes. During this time the company spent more than $3 million in support of public television broadcasts such as *Theater in America* and *Great Performances*.

Once the shortage hit, every company made advertising cuts. In June 1973 *Advertising Age* reported that industry expenditures were to be cut by $40 million. Product advertising was practically eliminated, while themes promoting conservation and the search for new oil sources abounded. Mobil and Shell ads during 1974 featured location shots of drilling in the North Sea and the Gulf of Mexico. Phillips, Amoco, and Shell ran ads on how to conserve gas, and several oil companies ran ads featuring their other products. Phillips, for example, ran "performance" stories on how their plastics products were being used. It was obvious the public was in no mood to be pitched gasoline.

Coming out of this shortage period, Shell Oil, through agency Ogilvy & Mather, Houston, Texas, developed a new advertising approach that became the core of its public image for years to come. Historically, Shell had focused much of its advertising on product-specific themes. A major exception to this strategy was its corporate image campaign, "Come to Shell for Answers." Begun in 1976 the campaign was intended to bolster Shell's image by using a nameless spokesperson to represent responsibility and helpfulness. The campaign featured television commercials and print advertising. During the course of the campaign 32 "answer" booklets, featuring helpful tips on automotive maintenance and performance, were included as special inserts in national magazines. The "Answer Man" proved to be the most popular of the series, and the company continued to field requests for the booklets long after the campaign had ended. While the advice offered was simple enough, it was presented in a positive, human way that greatly improved perceptions of oil and gas producers as "people" with some useful answers.

Ogilvy & Mather helped relaunch the campaign in 1990 after the Exxon *Valdez* disaster. The first booklet in this phase of the campaign was entitled, "Simple Ways to Deal with Car Trouble on the Road." While somewhat successful, owing largely to residual popularity from the original campaign, the "Answer Man" did not seem to work in the 1990s, and the ads had a shorter run.

In 1988, after 25 years of related campaigns (many using the "You can trust your car" theme), Texaco launched a major initiative that turned its emphasis from selling service to creating a new image for the company. Its "Star of the American Road" campaign gave the company a marketing message that was considered more appealing to younger consumers, and it served to repair its status in the industry after several major problems. (For example, in 1985 the Pennzoil Company won a judgment against Texaco stemming from its takeover of Getty Oil.) The campaign was designed to have broad appeal by linking earlier advertising messages of trustworthiness and dependability to more contemporary concerns.

The campaign sought to raise patriotism as well as interest in Texaco's renovated convenience stores, called "StarMarts." Launched during the Winter Olympics, the campaign enjoyed a high-profile debut, with spots appearing on all major networks along with billboard ads and cable. In 1992 the campaign was infused with new money and the theme relaunched. During this time Texaco also sponsored a major Beach Boys tour and used a variety of endorsements from celebrity spokespersons, including race car driver Mario Andretti. Post-campaign research indicated the campaign succeeded in elevating consumer perceptions about the brand.

The *Valdez* Crisis

In March 1989 the entire oil industry was again viewed darkly as the Exxon *Valdez* oil tanker went aground near Prince William Sound, Alaska, creating an oil spill that caused unparalleled damage. Exxon's response to the disaster included a flurry of print ads aimed directly at introducing the company's corporate conscience to the consumer. Ads quoted Chairman L.J. Rawles's apology: "I want to tell you how sorry I am that this accident took place. We cannot, of course, undo what has been done. But I can assure you that since it has occurred, the accident has been receiving our full attention and will continue to do so." While funds were diverted to restore local businesses and concerns, consumers believed Exxon did too little too late and its market share had yet to return to preaccident levels by 2001. The reaction of the public to this accident did succeed in awakening the industry as a whole to the need to portray itself as a supporter of the environment.

The early 1990s were characterized by stiff competition. While there were more cars on the road, the automakers were required to make them more fuel-efficient. This put pressure on the oil companies to develop and market fuels that were environment-friendly, clean, and efficient. The necessary research and development costs meant margins were low and, facing a flat market, growth meant the major players had to find innovative ways to steal a little business from competitors. While federal law required all major oil companies to include detergent additives in their products, each company had its own formula and each company's patented chemistry became the focus of several series of "claim" ads.

In 1995 Chevron launched "Talking Cars," a $35 million campaign to introduce its version of clean fuel, Techtron. This was an unusually high budget for the San Francisco, California-based company. Like its competitors, Chevron made claims regarding the superior performance provided by the new formula. But the success of "Talking Cars," according to the San Francisco *Business Times*, owed more to the way the campaign brought "warmth and personality" to the company's image. Television commercials produced by Young & Rubicam, San Francisco, California, featured clay-animation cars as humanlike characters, each with a specific personality, that would hold forth about their individual challenges. In these spots, Wendy Wagon, Holly Hatchback, and Tyler Taxi, among others, touted the virtues of Techtron fuel within the context of their unique operating con-

cerns. These car characters helped American consumers connect personally with a product that typically does not convey much warmth or excitement.

The ads boosted short-term sales as families scurried to Chevron stations to purchase gas in pursuit of "Talking Car" toys, such as Peter Pick-Up and Wendy Wagon, and their accessories, which were in high demand throughout the promotion. The company also featured related games and puzzles on its Web site. The campaign was successful on several levels. In 1996 Chevron was awarded a Gold Clio for animation. Other oil companies responded with their own ad efforts. Exxon launched a major program in 1997 to promote its Phase V "clean" gasoline; Unocal used ads that directly questioned Chevron's pitch ("What do you want from your gas station: dancing cars or something a bit more useful?"); Amoco featured an animated cartoon engine asking its owners to fill it with Amoco Ultimate; and Shell ran colorful animated commercials featuring dancing credit cards.

Advertising in the last half of the 1990s continued to embrace the industry's two dominant themes: establishing an image and creating distinctions unrelated to the product. Regional retailers such as Clark strongly promoted items sold through their convenience stores, while expedited payment systems, such as Mobil's Speed Pass, remained another type of benefit commonly promoted in commercial spots.

As image advertising abounded, the line between advertising and public relations blurred. In 1997 Texaco, through BBDO Worldwide, launched "A World of Energy" campaign. This effort was intended to elevate general impressions of the brand by highlighting the company's role in the "global" energy market; the campaign used approximately half of the company's $60 million advertising budget for the year. As mergers and joint ventures Shell and Texaco, Exxon and Mobil, for example—were expected to continue in the industry, high spending on image advertising seemed likely to continue.

In March 2000 Ogilvy & Mather, of Chicago, Illinois, was named to handle advertising for the newly formed BP Amoco. Early commercial spots introduced a new logo for the company. In these spots, a green flower is formed out of the converging movements of separate petals. Besides emphasizing core BP values, such as innovation and environmental awareness, the new look of the logo also conveyed dynamism and change. The company was expected to hoist the new symbol over its 18,000-plus U.S. outlets, while continuing to take advantage of traditional loyalties by selling Amoco branded gasoline.

The U.S. oil industry, with ad expenditures of $291.9 million in 1999 (TV, print, and radio advertising, excluding local spending), ranked 34th out of 38 major categories in advertising spending. While not insignificant, ad expenditures for the category in relation to sales remained low.

DEBORAH HAWKINS

Further Reading
Akins, Linda, "A Decade of Changes," *Advertising Age* (26 January 1981)

Alter, Stewart, *Truth Well Told: McCann-Erickson and the Pioneering of Global Advertising,* New York: McCann-Erickson Worldwide, 1994

Boyd, Harper W., Jr., Vernon Fryburger, and Ralph Westfall, *Cases in Advertising Management,* New York: McGraw-Hill, 1964

"Cable Ad Spending Gains Momentum" *National Petroleum News* 86, no. 7 (June 1994)

Day, Barry, *100 Great Advertisements,* London: Times Newspapers, 1978

Finney, Robert, et al., *Phillips, the First 66 Years,* Bartlesville, Oklahoma: Phillips Petroleum, 1983

Goodrum, Charles A., and Helen Dalrymple, *Advertising in America: The First 200 Years,* New York: Abrams, 1990

Greyser, Stephen A., *Cases in Advertising and Communications Management,* Englewood Cliffs, New Jersey: Prentice-Hall, 1972; 2nd edition, 1981

McGovern, James, *The Oil Game,* New York: Viking Press, 1981

Pike, David, "BP Moves to Leave Its Brand on U.S. Market," *The Oil Daily* (22 March 2000)

Riggs, Thomas, editor, *Major Marketing Campaigns Annual: 1998,* Farmington, Michigan: Gale Research, 1999

"The Spirit of the Star: 1902–1992," *Texaco Today* (November 1992)

Wall, Bennett H., C. Gerald Carpenter, and Gene S. Yeager, *Growth in a Changing Environment: A History of Standard Oil Company (New Jersey), Exxon Corporation, 1950–1975,* New York: McGraw-Hill, 1988

Watkins, Julian Lewis, *The 100 Greatest Advertisements: Who Wrote Them and What They Did,* New York: Moore, 1949; 2nd revised edition, New York: Dover, 1959

Yergin, Daniel, *The Prize: The Epic Quest for Oil, Money, and Power,* New York and London: Simon and Schuster, 1991

Omnicom Group

Since its formation in 1986 the holding company Omnicom Group has matched consistent leadership with consistent growth. The marketing giant, which battled for first place among the world's ad organizations in the 1990s, has seen only three top executives in its history. Allen Rosenshine, chairman of Batten Barton Durstine & Osborn (BBDO), created the company in 1986 by joining together BBDO, Doyle Dane Bernbach (DDB), and Needham, Harper & Steers in an attempt to counter the expansion of Britain's Saatchi & Saatchi. Although the creation of Omnicom resulted in the loss of $117 million in billings among the three agencies because of client conflicts, the company has never looked back. The group reported worldwide billings of $45.5 billion in 1999.

After leading the company for three years, Rosenshine resigned as president and chief executive officer (CEO), and Bruce Crawford became chairman. He had been general manager of New York City's Metropolitan Opera since 1983; before that he had served as president of BBDO from 1975 to 1983. Crawford was chairman and CEO until 1996, when John Wren became CEO in addition to being Omnicom's president. Crawford continued as chairman.

In 1986 Omnicom consisted of BBDO Worldwide; DDB Needham Worldwide (created by the merger of Doyle Dane Bernbach and Needham, Harper & Steers); and Diversified Agency Services, whose member companies provided services in direct response, public relations, promotional marketing, and specialty communications. It also owned 7 general advertising agencies and 20 specialized agencies. Within ten years after its founding, the company had more than 19,000 employees and billings of $15.8 billion.

In the late 1990s the conglomerate expanded to include two more holdings. The Omnicom Media Group consisted of two global media services companies, Optimum Media Direction Worldwide and the PhD Network. London, England–based Optimum Media Direction, with offices in 35 countries, provided services in strategic media planning, media buying, merchandising, and promotional support as well as entertainment, event, and sports marketing. Another Omnicom company, Communicade, held minority interests in leading interactive agencies, which in 1998 accounted for about 1,500 employees and $180 million in revenue, about one-third of the interactive market that year. These agencies included Agency.com, Razorfish, Organic, Red Sky Interactive, and Headhunter.net.

At the turn of the 21st century, the Omnicom Group included three of the top ten global ad agency networks: BBDO Worldwide, New York City; DDB Worldwide, New York City; and TBWA Worldwide, New York City, which it added in 1994. It also owned four U.S.-based national ad agencies that acted independently: Goodby, Silverstein & Partners, San Francisco, California (whose clients included Nike and Hewlett-Packard Company); GSD&M, Austin, Texas; Martin/Williams Advertising, Minneapolis, Minnesota; and Merkley Newman Harty, New York City (whose clients included Mercedes-Benz). Diversified Agency Services consisted of more than 100 companies in 60 countries and generated more than one-third of Omnicom's revenues.

Late in 2000 the Omnicom Group (specifically BBDO World-wide) landed what was probably the largest account in the automotive industry: DaimlerChrysler's $1.8 billion global advertising account for its Dodge, Chrysler, and Jeep brands. A DaimlerChrysler executive noted that Omnicom's size had been a factor in the automaker's decision. The holding company announced plans to create a new agency, called PentaMark Worldwide, to handle the business.

Big has proved to be better for Omnicom, which has expanded its reach far beyond traditional advertising. The holding company reported gross income in 2000 of $6.9 billion, up 11.9 percent over 1999, on billings of $55.65 billion, up 13.5 percent over the year earlier.

NANCY DIETZ

Further Reading

Gardner, Herbert S., *The Advertising Agency Business,* Chicago: Crain Books, 1976; 3rd edition, Lincolnwood, Illinois: NTC Business Books, 1998

Oscar Mayer Foods Corporation

Principal Agencies

Mitchell-Faust Advertising Company
Sherman & Marquette, Inc.
J. Walter Thompson Company

The Oscar Mayer Foods Corporation has marketed a variety of meats since the late 1800s. The company is best known for its wieners and bologna, linked indelibly to ad jingles that became part of Americana during the last 30 years of the 20th century.

German immigrant Oscar F. Mayer and his brother Gottfried opened a meat market on the north side of Chicago, Illinois, in 1883, and the shop's reputation and sales quickly grew. But Oscar Mayer's expertise was not just in shaping meats in casings. He also had a flair for marketing, which included sponsoring polka bands in the city's German neighborhoods and the German exhibit at the 1893 Chicago World's Fair. As the popularity of their products grew, Oscar, Gottfried, and another brother, Max, decided in 1904 to identify their products with the Edelweiss brand to separate them from the competition, which largely sold products in bulk and without packaging. Thirteen years later, the company ran its first newspaper ads, replacing the Edelweiss trademark with "Approved Brand."

Over the years, the core products remained the same, but technological innovations meant big changes in marketing for Oscar Mayer. In 1924 packaged, sliced bacon made its debut. Five years later, workers at the Chicago plant began affixing by hand the signature yellow bands that still wrap the wieners in the 21st century.

To continue his company's mass marketing appeal, Oscar Mayer approved the first color newspaper ad ever run by a meat company in 1944. The *Chicago Tribune* carried the ad, which highlighted the invention of a new machine that would automatically wrap the yellow bands carrying the Oscar Mayer name. Early advertising agencies in the company's history included small local shops such as Howard H. Monk Advertising and M. Glen Miller & Company.

In 1936 the company introduced the Wienermobile, which continued as a fixture of American pop culture more than 60 years after its debut. The Wienermobile was the invention of Carl G. Mayer, nephew of the company founder, who thought a 13-foot-long hot dog on wheels would be the appropriate vehicle for Little Oscar, the company's first spokesman—a man dressed as a chef who attended events to promote wieners. The General Body Company, Chicago, built the first Wienermobile for $5,000. The most recent model has a flip-up "bunroof" for sunny days and a state-of-the-art stereo broadcasting system that plays different versions of the widely known "wiener" jingle. Another product tie-in, Wienerwhistles, began appearing in hot dog packages in 1958.

Television sponsorships were the company's next marketing vehicle, starting in the 1950s, by which time the company had hired a major advertising agency, Sherman & Marquette, Inc. By 1968 Oscar Mayer was sponsoring prime-time TV shows such as *Gentle Ben, Here's Lucy,* and *The Wonderful World of Disney.*

Oscar Mayer had been using two different ad agencies until 1959; on 28 August of that year, however, the company, now headquartered in Madison, Wisconsin, moved its account to the J. Walter Thompson Company (JWT). The agency's idea was to associate the brand with children, happiness, and goodness. In 1963 "I Wish I Were an Oscar Mayer Wiener" debuted on Houston, Texas, radio stations, and national play quickly followed. The catchy jingle was the winning entry in a competition conducted by the agency. (Oscar Mayer was consistently challenged by its principal competitor, Armour, for prime position as a children's food. Armour also used a childlike jingle, created by Young & Rubicam: "Armour . . . Armour hot dogs. What kind of kids eat Armour hot dogs?")

"Before putting it on the air, we exposed our new wiener song to the trade," said William B. Walrath, Jr., Oscar Mayer's general advertising manager, in 1963. "When they reacted favorably, we knew for sure we had a winner, but we had no way of knowing then how fantastic this thing would be—in sales and in fan mail."

One of Oscar Mayer's most memorable TV spots featured a curly-haired youngster with a fishing pole singing the now well-known jingle "The Bologna Song."
Courtesy of Andrew Lambros, Cyberweb, Inc. and www.andyworld.com.
OSCAR MAYER is a registered trademark of Kraft Foods Holdings, Inc.

Listeners to radio stations even began calling in to request what they thought was a pop tune, not an ad for hot dogs.

Use of the tune on radio quickly spread to television; the Vienna Symphony even arranged and produced a special version of the jingle for a 1968 commercial. And it proved to have staying power. The wiener jingle was reprised on television in 1998, and in 2000 the company used it in a promotional talent search contest. In 1974 JWT unveiled "The Bologna Song," the first line of which ("My bologna has a first name, it's O-S-C-A-R") became a part of American popular culture.

Product line extensions and promotions followed. In 1988 the company introduced a line called Lunchables: prepackaged, ready-to-eat lunch combinations of meat, cheese, and crackers that grew to 43 varieties by the beginning of the 21st century. Children continued to be the target market. Lunchables, the campaign explained, would let kids "make fun of lunch" by allowing them to put it together themselves. Single-serve packages of hot dogs, including condiments, chips, and dessert, appeared under the Lunchables brand in 1998.

In 1971 the family-owned company went public. Ten years later, General Foods Corporation acquired Oscar Mayer. Four years later, General Foods became part of the Philip Morris Companies. Philip Morris acquired Kraft, Inc., in 1988, and a year later combined Kraft and General Foods into one operating company under the name Kraft Foods, Inc. The changes did not affect Oscar Mayer's relationship with JWT; in fact, Kraft had worked with the agency since 1922.

Product and marketing efforts also have been aimed at adults, who previously had been thought of simply as the parents who bought hot dogs for their children. In the mid-1990s Oscar Mayer introduced the "Big & Juicy" hot dog, designed to appeal to grown-up palates. To introduce the oversized hot dogs, JWT looked to former heavyweight boxer George Foreman, someone with a larger-than-life personality himself, who successfully promoted the product. In 1996 and 1997 Oscar Mayer was the half-time sponsor of the National Football League's Super Bowl, which tied in with the company's yearlong talent search promotions featuring children.

By 2000 Oscar Mayer decided it was time to try new ideas and take the company beyond the Wienermobile (although the Wienermobile was not retired). Spurred by the introduction of packaged, sliced smoked ham, JWT came up with the tag line, "Oscar like you've never seen before." While it was a new message, the print advertising and packaging carried the signature yellow of Oscar Mayer.

MARY ELLEN PODMOLIK

Oscar Mayer, Lunchables, and Wienermobile are registered trademarks of Kraft Foods Holdings, Inc.

Further Reading

Pollack, Judann, "Ball Park, Oscar Mayer Brands Ready New Tactic," *Advertising Age* (30 August 1998)
Spethmann, Betsy, "Promotion Used to Be a Vehicle for a Quick Hit," *Brandweek* (3 March 1996)
Thompson, Stephanie, "Oscar Mayer Hams It Up for New Lunch Meat Line," *Advertising Age* (31 July 2000)

Outdoor Advertising

In the closing decades of the 20th century, the definition of what constitutes outdoor advertising—traditionally, billboards and signs—was changing. Innovations in technology were expanding the possibilities for outdoor displays, and advertisers were increasingly recognizing the diversity of media choices available to them as part of an integrated marketing communications program. In the United States alone, outdoor advertising was a $4.4-billion-a-year industry in the 1990s and provided advertising space on approximately 400,000 billboards, 68,000 buses and bus shelters, and 13,000 subway cars, as well as displays at park-

Arnold Communications' billboard campaign for Volkswagen, with its humorous reference to the occasional shortcomings of the classic Beetle, won the Outdoor Advertising Association of America's 1999 Best of Show Obie Award.
Courtesy of Volkswagen of America and Arnold Communications.

ing garages, shopping malls, airports, sports stadiums, and other venues.

The term *outdoor advertising* itself was also being replaced with the more inclusive terms *out-of-home advertising* or *outdoor media*. This newer conceptualization included all media that carry messages to consumers when they are away from their place of residence, including mobile billboards, building-sized images, and aerial advertising.

Outdoor advertising is a high-intensity medium that reaches most population segments at high-frequency levels. It can effectively create awareness and instant visibility, reinforce brand image, and provide reminders to consumers. And it does so for a relatively low cost, while generating retention levels comparable to those of other media. The advantages of geographic flexibility, repeat exposure, relative absence of competing advertisements, and compatibility with the lifestyle of an increasingly mobile audience must be balanced against the creative limitations inherent in presenting only fleeting impressions to a mobile audience, namely restricting copy to a few words or a single powerful graphic. Agencies that specialize in outdoor advertising have developed a rating system that measures the visibility of the message and takes into account such factors as length of the approach to the display, angle of the structure bearing the display and its position relative to other structures, and travel speed of those viewing the message.

Both the Greeks and Egyptians used outdoor advertising as early as 5,000 years ago. A merchant in ancient Babylonia is credited with being among the first to hang a sign above his place of business. It was during the Roman Empire that the use of signage began to address specific consumer needs. Because of both high illiteracy rates and large numbers of foreign travelers, signage typically displayed a wide variety of objects—the goat for the dairy, the knife for the cutler, the flask for the tavern—designed to attract attention and inform the consumer regardless of his or her native language or reading ability.

The importance of signage increased over the centuries. In Europe during the 1300s innkeepers and merchants were required by local officials to display signs so that consumers could readily identify their businesses. These signs became one of the earliest forms of business licenses.

In its earliest stages, the growth of the outdoor medium paralleled the development of mass media. With the invention of movable type by Johannes Gutenberg in the 15th century, the concept of mass communications changed dramatically, and advertising in the modern sense was born. The dividing line between ancient and modern outdoor advertising is marked by a number of technological innovations in the 1870s. The development of a web-fed printing press, paper-folding machines, and a new lithograph halftone process gave printing and lithography expanded commercial applications that included outdoor advertising. By the late 1800s, as the U.S. population became increasingly mobile and people no longer patronized the same local merchants as their parents had, outdoor advertising became an important medium for establishing brand identities.

Outdoor advertising has not been without its detractors. Among its critics was Lady Bird Johnson, the wife of President Lyndon B. Johnson, who tried to rid the interstate highways of billboard advertising by supporting passage of the Highway Beautification Act of 1965. Under the act, billboards on interstate and federal highways are restricted to commercial and industrial areas; size, lighting, and spacing are regulated by states and municipalities. Beyond the specific provisions of the act, states were left with the authority to enact further provisions to control signs, although these actions have met with mixed success. In 1977 a proposition to prohibit billboards in San Francisco, California, was rejected by voters, while in 1983 the U.S. Supreme Court declared a San Diego, California, antibillboard ordinance unconstitutional.

The first industry group in outdoor advertising, the International Billposters' Association of North America, was founded in 1872. It had little influence but paved the way for other groups, such as the Associated Billposters of the United States and Canada, a number of state billposter organizations, the Painted Outdoor Advertising Association (1909), and the National Outdoor Advertising Bureau (1915). The most active and significant organization operating at the beginning of the 21st century was the Outdoor Advertising Association of America (OAAA). While its goal is to promote the use of outdoor media, its code of industry principles stresses respect for the environment, maintenance of good working relationships with local communities, provision of an effective and attractive product, support for worthy public causes, and observation of the highest free-speech standards. The Obie Award, established by the OAAA in 1942 to recognize excellence in outdoor creative executions, is among the oldest awards in advertising. The recipients include agencies from around the world.

In the 1980s and 1990s the number and composition of outdoor media changed dramatically. Entertainment, travel, business and consumer services, restaurants, publishing, retail, and packaged-goods industries posted more than 300 percent growth in their use of outdoor media. Packaged-goods firms supplanted tobacco advertisers as the dominant product category in terms of revenue. During this same period the industry experienced significant consolidation. Nearly 100 mergers took place in the mid-1990s. By the turn of the century the largest U.S. outdoor companies included Outdoor Systems, Inc., Eller/Clear Channel Communications, Transportation Display, Inc., and Lamar Advertising Company, each with more than $300 million in annual gross revenues.

Outdoor advertising's share of the total advertising budget is predicted to grow significantly, supported by continued growth in regional marketing and the declining dominance of network television. In virtually every country where there is a visually oriented, commercial society moving by car, bus, train, and plane from one location to another, outdoor media will continue as a vital component of advertisers' marketing communications plans.

MICHAEL R. LUTHY

Further Reading

Bernstein, David, *Advertising Outdoors: Watch This Space!* London: Phaidon, 1997

Claus, Karen E., *The Sign User's Guide: A Marketing Aid*, Palo Alto, California: Institute of Signage Research, 1978; revised edition, Cincinnati, Ohio: ST, 1988

Kobliski, Kathy J., *Advertising without an Agency: A Comprehensive Guide to Radio, Television, Print, Direct Mail, and Outdoor Advertising for Small Business*, Central Point, Oregon: Oasis, 1998

Starr, Tama, and Edward Hayman, *Signs and Wonders: The Spectacular Marketing of America*, New York: Doubleday, 1998

Sutte, Donald T., *The Appraisal of Outdoor Advertising Signs*, Chicago: Appraisal Institute, 1994